AIA GUIDE TO NEW YORK CITY

New York Chapter
American Institute of Architects

AIA GUIDE TO NEW YORK CITY

Fourth Edition

Norval White & Elliot Willensky

THREE RIVERS PRESS • NEW YORK

Copyright © 2000 Norval White and the Estate of Elliot Willensky

Published by Three Rivers Press, New York, New York. Member of the Crown Publishing Group.

Random House, Inc. New York, Toronto, London, Sydney, Auckland
www.randomhouse.com

THREE RIVERS PRESS is a registered trademark and the Three Rivers Press colophon is a trademark of Random House, Inc.

Originally published, in a different form, by Macmillan Publishing Company in 1968 and 1978 and by Harcourt Brace Publishing in 1988.

Library of Congress Cataloging-in-Publication Data
AIA Guide to New York City.
Includes index.
1. Architecture–New York (N.Y.)–Guide-books.
2. New York (N.Y.)–Buildings, structures, etc.–Guide-books.
3. New York (N.Y.)–Description

White, Norval, 1926-
Willensky, Elliot, 1933-1990
New York Chapter, American Institute of Architects

Hardcover ISBN 0-8129-3106-8
Paperback ISBN 0-8129-3107-6

10 9 8 7 6 5 4 3 2

CONTENTS

THE BRONX

BROOKLYN

QUEENS

STATEN ISLAND

MAPS

USING THE GUIDE

The Guide is designed to serve a whole spectrum of readers, from the casual wanderer to the serious historian; from the provincial New Yorker who rarely, if ever, ventures west of the Hudson River, to the visitor who wants to see more than the well-touted monuments, musicals, and museums.

Some of you may explore familiar neighborhoods before venturing into unfamiliar places. Braver souls will immediately "go abroad" as tourists in other parts of the city, savoring new and exotic precincts. Some may wish to start at the Battery, working their way geographically or following the chronological development of the city.

For the less athletic, you may leave the Guide on your coffee table to leaf through the pages at your leisure, and enjoy excursions of the city in the mind, without ever stepping outside your door. And you will also be able to use the guide to show visitors from Paris, Tokyo, San Francisco, or even Hackensack how to view and relish not only New York's major monuments, landmarks, and historic districts but also the richness of its buildings and precincts in every borough.

Organization: The Guide, like the city, is divided into five boroughs. Manhattan, at whose southern tip the city began, is first. The outlying boroughs (The Bronx, Brooklyn, Queens, and Staten Island) follow in that order.

Each section is organized to illustrate the complexity and richness of a particular borough and, within that borough, its various sectors (Lower Manhattan, Northern Brooklyn, Northeastern Queens, etc.). The sectors, in turn, are divided into neighborhood areas, called precincts (Financial District, Greenpoint, Fresh Meadows, etc.).

Boroughs, sectors, and precincts are prefaced by a short historical introduction, a capsule description of the topography, and a history of physical development.

Entries: Each entry in the Guide is numbered—the numbers appear within brackets—and is identified by name in boldface type. (Sometimes there is also a former or original name or names.) This information is followed by the address and/or block location, the date of completion (or projected completion), and finally by the designer's name. When no other title follows a designer's name, it should be assumed that title is architect. Identification lines at the top of left-hand pages indicate the borough and sector being discussed. Right-hand pages show the precinct(s) being dealt with and the map page on which the entries appear.

Security: New York is a vast, busy, and complicated city, with much to see. But at certain times and in certain places, sightseers—gawkers, if you will—can inadvertently send out signals of distraction or vulnerability that are cues to those with less than lofty motives. Beware. Remember that there is safety in numbers. Don't walk in desolate areas. Don't tour at night. Do take a friend along—it's more fun that way.

Officially Designated Landmarks: Individual structures and natural-objects scenic landmarks, and historic districts, officially designated by the N.Y.C. Landmarks Preservation Commission (and confirmed by the Board of Estimate) are identified by a solid apple 🍎 . Designated interior landmarks are noted separately, also with a solid apple 🍎 . Entries lying within the boundaries of designated historic districts are noted with an open apple ⌖.

Style Symbols: Symbols printed in color signify that an entry is a notable example of a particular architectural style or stylistic group:

Colonial/Colonial Revival. Literally the architecture of New York as a colony, whether of The Netherlands or Great Britain. It doesn't necessarily imply either white clapboard or shutters and is best exemplified in Manhattan by St. Paul's Chapel (the only "Colonial" building remaining from before 1776) and by some of the Dutch Colonial farmhouses of southeastern Brooklyn. The Revival of the late 19th century provided overblown versions for a romanticized Colonial Revival.

Georgian/Federal/neo-Georgian/neo-Federal. The Federal style was the first—and therefore the "modern" (in its day)—architecture of our new republic, a modification of the contemporaneous Georgian architecture of London. Dignified and restrained, it emphasized geometric form and harmonious proportion and was executed in both wood and masonry. The neo-Federal and neo-Georgian are early 20th-century revivals of 18th- and 19th-century originals.

Greek Revival. The product of both political and aesthetic interests. The Greek Revolution made Greece independent of the Turks (the Ottoman Empire) in the 1820s. The newly won independence recalled, to fascinated American intellectuals, the patrician democracy of ancient Greece and its elegant architecture, created more than 400 years before the birth of Christ. In America, classical columns and orders were used mostly for decoration, often at entrance doorways in otherwise simply designed row houses. Whole buildings, however, sometimes were also recalled: Sailors' Snug Harbor in Staten Island and Federal Hall National Memorial on Wall Street are reincarnations of great Greek temples.

Gothic Revival/neo-Gothic/neo-Tudor/neo-Byzantine. In its purest form Gothic Revival refers to the literary and aesthetic movement of the 1830s and 1840s, coincidental with that in England. Interest in the presumed "goodness" of long-gone medieval times suggested that the emulation of its Gothic architecture would instill a similar goodness among the present wicked. The posture gained enough adherents to inspire a re-revival around 1900 and later, particularly for colleges, urban high schools, and major churches, in styles labeled neo-Gothic and neo-Tudor (with all its Scarsdale suburban-style stockbroker "half-timbering").

Italianate and/or Villa Style. Buildings with gently pitched (they seem flat) roofs crowning a boxy volume often with a frieze of tiny attic windows. In its more romantic version, the Villa Style, it utilizes a tall, usually asymmetrically placed tower. Litchfield Villa in Brooklyn's Prospect Park is the city's finest example.

The Picturesque: **Romanesque Revival/Stick** and/or **Shingle Style/Queen Anne**. The late nineteenth-century Romanesque Revival is a vigorous style more common in Chicago than in New York and is based on the bold arch-and-vault construction of the early medieval Romanesque. Architect H. H. Richardson was its greatest American exponent, but Brooklyn's Frank Freeman was not far behind. The wooden architecture that exploited the balloon frame's formal possibilities, and/or celebrated exposed timber as a structural-decorative exterior armature (The Stick and/or Shingle Styles), was often designed at the same time by the same architects in the 1870s through 1890s. Both are picturesque.

Renaissance Revival/Anglo-Italianate/Beaux Arts. Drawn from the architecture of 15th- through 17th-century Italy, France, and England. On this side of the Atlantic, Italian palazzi, French châteaux, and English clubs became the stylistic image for banking institutions, super town houses, clubs and government buildings, and even mercantile establishments (cf. the Federal Reserve Bank of New York and many of SoHo's cast-iron loft buildings). Proselytized through the Ecole des Beaux-Arts in Paris, the Beaux Arts style, from about 1890 to 1920, inflated classical allusions to truly supergrandiose proportions, as at Grand Central Terminal, the Custom House at Bowling Green, and the New York Public Library.

Roman Revival/Baroque Revival. Roman Revival was more pompous and posturing than Greek Revival. It brought back some of the histrionics of classical Rome, particularly through use of domes, columns, pediments, and sculpture of a grandiose nature. Baroque Revival echoed similar elaborations found in the quirkier and even more ornate Baroque era that followed the Renaissance.

Art Deco/Art Moderne. The largely French-inspired styles of the era between World Wars I and II, when cubistic structures were embellished by the use of florid ornament inspired by the Paris Exposition of 1925 (Art Deco) and later by sleek streamlined ornament that also influenced the Paris Exposition of 1937 (Art Moderne). Many polychromed works of Ely Jacques Kahn exemplify Art Deco; the corner-windowed "modernistic" apartment houses of the Grand Concourse in the Bronx and the Majestic Apartments at Central Park West and 72nd Street are Art Moderne.

Modern/Post Modern. The breakdown of Modern (or Modernist) into component styles is a new phenomenon, based on the concept that Modern as we know it today has its own internal history: beginning with the works of Louis Sullivan (the Condict Building on Bleecker Street) and Frank Lloyd Wright (best known here for his much later Guggenheim Museum); followed by Art Deco and Art Moderne (see above) and the Bauhaus and/or International Style as imported by Walter Gropius, Marcel Breuer, and Ludwig Mies van der Rohe (cf. the Seagram Building).

ACKNOWLEDGMENTS

Since 1966, when research on the first version of the Guide began, innumerable individuals have contributed information, ideas, comments, corrections, and considerable moral support. Previous editions and reprintings have recognized their contributions in the acknowledgments.

This Fourth Edition is a linear descendant of the original, self-published version feverishly prepared over a nine-month period for the 1967 convention of the American Institute of Architects in New York City. Because its approach profoundly influenced subsequent updatings of the Guide, it seems appropriate to credit once again those who helped the authors to set the first edition's tone: writers John Morris Dixon, Ann Douglass, Mina Hamilton, Roger Feinstein, Henry Hope Reed, Jr., Sophia Duckworth, and Richard Dattner.

As we have done in previous editions, we wish to recognize that legion of supporters who contributed anything from a correction of punctuation to a suggestion for a new entry. We, whose names begin with W and are usually listed last, therefore list these individuals in *reverse* alphabetical order:

John Zukowsky, Joseph Zito, Shirley Zavin, G. Young, Jean Wynn, William Wright, Jeremy Woodoff, Ira Wolfman, Jay Weiser, Stephen Weinstein, Maron Waxman, V. Frederick Vender, Ernest Ulmer, Marcel Turbiaux, Anthony Max Tung, Charles Tresnowske, Barbara M. Topf, Woodlief Thomas, Jr., Stephen F. Temmer, Adam Taylor, John Tauranac, Peter Switzer, Richard Sullivan, Diane Stuart, Lawrence Stelter, Robert B. Snyder, Susan Smpadian, Jerry Slaff, Robert Sink, John Victor Singler, Donald E. Simon, Stanley Shor, Jay Shockley, Gaynor Wynne Shay, Rebecca Shanor, Vincent F. Seyfried, Susan Sekey, Joseph Schuchman, Ms. P. Sanecki, Larry Samuels, Peter R. Samson, M. Sallstrand, James Rossant, Jane M. Ross, Richard Rosenthal, Halina Rosenthal, Brenda A. Rosen, Ellen Fletcher Rosebrock, Anthony Robins, Anne Richter, F. Rex, Phil Ressner, Thomas J. Reese, S.J., Thomas E. Range, Donald Presa, Don Plotts, Adolf Placzek, Marjorie Pearson, Mitchell J. Paluszek, Gary Ostkoff, Fred Ost, Georgia O'Dea/Helen Mills, Peter Obletz, Daniel Nydick, Gregory Nolan, Francis J. Murray, Louis Morhaim, Margaret and Truman Moore, Ava Moncrief, Joe Mitchell, Dorothy Miner, Joseph Merz, James D. Merritt, Joseph N. Merola, David Ment, Nancy McKeon, Priscilla McGuire, John Margolis, Jerry Maltz, Duncan Maginnis, Joseph Pell Lombardi, Nicholas Lobenthal, Martin H. Levinson, Walter E. Levi, Peggy Latimer, Lenore Latimer, Sarah Bradford Landau, Andrew Lachman, James Kraft, Rev. Arthur Kortheuer, Joseph E. Konkle, Gwen and Maury Kley, Adriana R. Kleiman, Steven V. Kaufman, Bernard Kabak, David Edmund Jones, Christopher Jones, William H. Johnson, Marjorie Johnson, Jeanne Jantosca, Jack Intrator, Judith S. Hull, Christina Huemer, Alice C. Hudson, Holly Huckins, Sidney Horenstein, Merrill Hesch, Dozier Hasty, Alex J. Hartill, Jay and Rosalie Harris, Gale Harris, Hannelore Hahn, Cecilia Haas, David Gurin, Christopher Gray, Christabel Gough, Dorothy Twining Globus, Vernon and Diana Gibberd, Michael George, Ann George, Deborah Shaw Gardner, David Garcia, Charles P. G. Fuller II, Paul Fritz, Peter Freiberg, Gloria Okun Freedgood, John Frazier, Elizabeth Foster, Christopher Forbes, Richard C. Fitzpatrick, Jr., Anne E. Finelli, Gary Eriksen, Martin Dubno, Erin Drake, Ethelyn Underwood (Mrs. George E.) Dowling, Andrew Dolkart, Jim Dillon, John Diele, Norman Dick, Harry Denker, Laurence G. Dengler, Fred Del Pozzo,

L. J. Davis, Philip I. Danzig, Dina Dahbany-Miraglia, Naomi Curtis, Arthur Cohen, Marion Cleaver, Carol Clark, Albert Cattan, Mrs. Robert C. Carey, Michael J. Byczek, Natalie Bunting, Esther Brumberg, R. Michael Brown, Hal Bromm, Joe Bresnan, Paul H. Bonner, Jr., Mary T. Bronham, Kevin Bone, Louis Blumengarten, Avis Berman, Daniel Beekman, Ann Bedell, L. A. Becker, Sherene Baugher, Ernestine Bassman, Peter J. Bartucca, Patti Auerbach, Michael Armstrong, R. Boulton Anderson, Andrew Alpern, Oliver Allen, William Alex, Emma Albert, Louella Adams.

And for this edition we salute our new publisher and its devoted editor, Philip Turner; our meticulous book designer, Hiram Ash; our accomplished computer production team at Foxprint; and particularly Teresa Fox. In addition to executing the layout of the book in Quark XPress, Teresa designed and produced the 143 new maps. The long index, an extraordinary job, was created by Shirley Kessel. Andrew Dolkart read the manuscript on behalf of the New York Chapter, AIA, and offered myriad comments, additions, and corrections. Joel Honig not only performed the function of copy editor, as he did on the Third Edition, but also added much detail from his extensive knowledge of the City. Staten Island has been surveyed afresh with the eyes and photographs of architectural historian James Sexton.

Of special regard to both authors has been Howard Morhaim, friend, source of endless encouragement, a contributor in so many ways, and yet again the perfect agent.

Norval White

GLOSSARY

A

air rights Rights to fill additional airspace with building volume under zoning laws. Nineteenth-century landmarks, for example, usually are of much less volume than current zoning permits; air rights are therefore the rights to the additional unbuilt volume transferred, say, to the new office building next door.

antefix Anthemion-ornamented finials that embellish the edge of a Greek temple above the entablature, covering the open ends of its roof tiles and forming a serrated silhouette.

anthemion A stylized honeysuckle ornament in Greek, Greek Revival, and neo-Grec architecture.

archaeology The study of artifacts and, in particular, buildings of a poorly documented ancient, lost, or even recent but ignored period.

architrave The "chief beam" of a Classical entablature, spanning directly above and between columns, and, in turn, supporting frieze and cornice.

archivolt The decorated band around an arch.

arcuated Composed of arches.

Art Deco A modern style first presented at the Paris Exposition Internationale des Arts Décoratifs of 1925 and rehonored in the late 1970s: a style of geometric ornament rather than form.

articulate To set off and/or emphasize by means of a joint, as a brick is articulated by deeply incised mortar, or a building's wing is articulated by the link that connects it with its parent.

Art Moderne A modern style: streamlined stucco and chromium, as if buildings traveled at the speed of automobiles. Inspired by the Paris International Exposition of 1937.

Art Nouveau When Samuel Bing opened his shop, "Art Nouveau," in Paris (1898), little did he know that the sinuous style that we have inherited would be so named: vegetative ornament that not only became the surface decoration of the then "modern" architecture but also contributed to form, particularly in Hector Guimard's Métro entrances.

ashlar Stone cut for a wall; either regular and in courses, or "random." It implies a rough and variegated stone (as in Manhattan schist or Fordham gneiss) as opposed to the smooth and monolithic sawn granite, limestone, or polished marble.

atrium A center courtyard within a house.

avant-garde The cultural front-runners—artists and architects ahead of the pack.

B

balustrade The assemblage of railing, balusters, and newels that leads you and your hand up and down the staircase.

Baroque The exuberant late Renaissance style supported by the Jesuits in their attempt to lure the flock back to Rome in the face of Luther's Reformation: extravagant architectural stagecraft for the Counter-Reformation.

battered A battered wall is one, the exterior face of which slopes away from its base, thick at its bottom, thinner at the top.

battlements The toothy parapet atop a castle or would-be castle: crenellations.

Beaux Arts Literally "fine arts," from the Parisian architectural school (École des Beaux-Arts) that served as fountainhead for formal American architectural education. The progeny of the school produced grand (sometimes pompous) public architecture: the Paris Opéra, the Chicago World's Fair of 1893, the New York Public Library, Grand Central Station, and so forth.

berm A linear mound of earth; sometimes a landscape device to shield something ugly from a passerby's view, as around a parking lot.

board and batten Flat boards with square trim covering their joints that gave "verticality" to the Gothic Revival wood cottage. Modern architects have used boards and battens on occasion more to be different than meaningful.

bollard A short, fat, round concrete masonry, metal pier, set freestanding into the street, that constrains wheeled traffic but allows pedestrians to pass.

boss A round, decorative, sometimes sculpted ornament, as at a Gothic or neo-Gothic intersection of vaulting ribs—here in stone.

brick Brick is made mostly of kiln-baked clay, but concrete brick also exists as well as the sun-dried adobe of America's southwest, Mexico, and other preindustrial countries. Once brick was mostly in standard sizes, hence standard brick. Other popular sizes now include:

standard The brick of early America, of New York's Georgian, Federal, and Greek Revival architecture, from the James Watson house to the Colony Club. It also sheathed most of New York's high-rise housing, from Park Avenue to the vast towers of the Housing Authority: $2\frac{1}{4}$" high × 8" wide.

Roman The only size the ancient Romans used and popular in late 19th-century American architecture, particularly with the Chicago School: 2" high × 12" wide.

jumbo Builders of the 1940s and 1950s found that masons could lay a larger, heavier brick at the same rate as standard brick (and the unions agreed), reducing the cost of a wall. The sizes were modestly different from "standard" visually, resulting in a distorted building scale. Only later, when very much bigger brick was produced, did economics and aesthetics conjoin once more (see double and imperial brick): $2\frac{3}{4}$" high × 8" wide.

double A first attempt at producing a brick aesthetic combined with the new masonry economy, particularly in the early work of Davis, Brody & Associates at Riverbend Houses. Here brick simulates the scale of tile: $5\frac{1}{2}$" high × 8" wide.

imperial The later upscaling of the "double" to a square face: 8" high × 8" wide.

Broadacre City A utopian vision of Frank Lloyd Wright where all dwell in single-family freestanding houses on generous lots; an antiurban idea served by automobile and television, where public transportation and face-to-face meetings are thought unnecessary.

broken pediments Pediments broken apart explosively as in Baroque and neo-Baroque architecture.

brownstone Brown sandstone from the Connecticut River Valley or the banks of the Hackensack River. Soft, porous, and perishable.

Brutalism The bold concrete architecture inspired by Le Corbusier's work and his followers. Also, New Brutalism.

butted glass Glass sheets, as in a shopfront, where there is no mullion and the glass, necessarily thicker, meets its neighbor with a joint filled with silicone (plastic). Great transparency results.

C

campanile The freestanding bell tower of an Italian church.

cantilever A stationary lever, the arm of which supports a load, as in a fishing pole.

Carpenter Gothic The jigsaw and lathe allowed carpenters to capture quickly and inexpensively an idea of Gothic in Gothic Revival American wood houses: ogees and finials decorated windows, porches, and cornices.

caryatid At the Erectheum on Athens' Acropolis, erect ladies serve as the columns of its porch (now replaced with concrete copies due to deterioration from pollution). Any such female figure used as architectural supports are caryatids.

casement A hinged window that opens out like a door.

cast iron Liquid iron poured into a shapely mold and thence cast. Fragile in comparison to wrought iron or steel, cast iron is good for compression but shatters if you bend it.

castle Now largely a romantic idea. Strictly speaking, a fortified royal residence.

catacomb A chambered cellar serving as a cemetery in, particularly, ancient Rome.

catenary The natural curve of a hanging string (or a cable, or a suspension bridge), supported at both ends. A discrete mathematical shape.

chamfer To dull, or cut off the edge of, say, a rectangular column.

château A French country castle, with or without fortifications.

Chicago School The early modern style of Louis Sullivan, John Wellborn Root, William Le Baron Jenney, and company: birthschool of the skyscraper.

clapboard Linear shingles that clad (clap) each other in courses. Used in Federal, Greek Revival, and other Victorian stylistic ventures.

classic Of a superior and/or eternal design.

Classical Of and/or relating to the Classical period of architecture and civilization, i.e., Greek and Roman.

Classical Revival A literal revival of Greek and Roman architecture, rather than the Renaissance arrangement of Classical detail in a new fashion.

clinker bricks Bricks overburned in the kiln and then used decoratively in counterpoint to the rest of the normal brick wall that they share.

close The lawn and landscape around an English cathedral or church, usually with other religious buildings defining its limits. Where a French or Italian cathedral would relate to street and plaza, the English one is served by its close.

Colonial The architecture of, particularly, America when it was a colony. (Strictly speaking before July 4, 1776.)
   In Manhattan only one extant building can claim the Colonial title, St. Paul's Chapel of 1766. Other Colonial build-

ings, now encompassed by an expanded New York, were rural outposts when built.

Colonial Revival A revival of the architecture of the Colonial and Federal periods at the turn of the nineteenth into the twentieth century.

colonnade A row of columns usually supporting a beam, architrave, or series of arches.

colonnettes Little columns for decorative purposes.

column The vertical sticklike support of a building or structure as opposed to the fatter "pier" or the archaic "pillar." Columns may range from matter-of-fact supports, such as a modern steel column, to those participating in ornate orders of Classical architecture: Doric, Ionic, and Corinthian.

Composite Mixed orders, where Doric and Ionic might share the same column.

concrete Particularly Portland cement concrete: a chemical coalescense of materials (sand, water, and an aggregate such as crushed stone) into an artificial stone. Reinforced with steel bars, it become the structure of buildings, roads, or bridges; plain, it fireproofs steel buildings by encasing the structure protectively.

concrete block If your society lacks clay, it may be rich in limestone, and from limestone we create Portland cement. Such cement + aggregate (sand and stones) becomes concrete and thence concrete block for those who need an alternate to brick (made from clay).

console bracket The enscrolled bracket that supports many a Renaissance and neo-Renaissance cornice. Also, cornice bracket. *See* modillion.

corbeled Bracketed out; in masonry, bricks are corbeled when each succeeding layer (course) projects slightly over the one below.

corbel table A series of corbeled bricks or stones supports a string of small decorative arches, frequently following the gabled end of an Italian Lombardian Romanesque church or its revival.

Corinthian The late Greek (Hellenistic) and early Roman order of architecture that produced acanthus-leaved capitals (as opposed to Ionic "ram's horns" and Doric austerity).

cornice The crown of a building, its edge against the sky, particularly part of a Classical order's entablature.

course A layer of masonry or wood brick, block, board, or stone.

crenellated Crowned with a cornice of solid teeth (merlons) that protect the warrior, interrupted by voids that allow him to shoot.

cresting The cast-iron filigreed crest atop a Victorian mansard roof.

crocket The teat on a Gothic finial.

cul-de-sac A dead-end street, alley, or road.

D

dentil The toothy blocks under the cornice of a Greek or Roman entablature, reminiscent of the wood joinery in earlier temples from which Greek architecture in marble was derived.

distyle With two columns, as in a temple.

distyle in antis Two columns flanked by two blank walls.

Doric The austere and elegant set of parts (called an "order") developed in the 6th and 5th centuries B.C. in Greek architecture (particularly Athenian, and of Athenian colonies).

dormer An upright window projecting from a sloping roof. It makes usable a sloping attic space as well as those myriad mansard roofs of Paris, the steep pitch of which provides normal rooms on the inside and a roofclad wall facing the street.

Dutch Colonial The simple house style of New Amsterdam and environs, including those deep-eaved, gambrel-roofed, rural farmhouses (see Brooklyn's various Wyckoff houses) and the stepped gables of town houses at the tip of Manhattan. The former are numerous; the latter have totally vanished. One needs to view Curaçao to see their equivalents built in the same 17th-century period.

E

Eastlake Charles Eastlake (1836-1906), architect, writer, and furniture designer, influenced late 19th-century New York with incised geometric decoration.

eclectic In architecture the borrowing of assorted styles and stylistic details for a single building.

Egyptian Of or relating to Egypt from approximately 3000 B.C. to its conquest by Alexander the Great, 332 B.C.

embrasure The splayed slot through which one might shoot at an approaching enemy. In medieval fortifications the opening without was small and that within, broad.

English basement The ground-floor of a row or town house, a few steps above the sidewalk.

entablature The set of roof parts in a Classical building that the columns support: i.e., architrave (or first beam over the columns), frieze and cornice or top-ending. The frieze is an opportunity for cartoon graphics, as in the animal frieze at the Parthenon (the Zoophorus) or that at Brooklyn's zoo (also animals).

entasis The slight swelling of a Classical column that reinforces the visual impression of strength. The best, (i.e., the Parthenon) is so subtle that one is aware of it only after conscious intellectual effort.

esplanade A linear walking part along the water's edge, like that at Brooklyn Heights or Battery Park City.

exedra A large semicircular alcove (annex) to a central space (particularly in Classical architecture).

F

face brick Brick with (at least) one side with a weather and visual finish. Common brick, on the other hand, is used as a backup and for internal invisible structural walls.

faience A fine pottery glaze adapted to architectural decor.

Federal The first "American" style of architecture, based on English Georgian.

festoon A pendant wreath; it also describes any exuberant decoration.

fillet The flat ribbon separating the flutes of an Ionic column.

finial The ultimate end of a Gothic pinnacle decorated with crockets, a finger in silhouette against the sky.

Flamboyant Used to describe the flamelike tracery of late French Gothic; later, to describe anything that is ostentatiously ornate.

French flats At first New York termed apartment houses French flats, for in Edith Wharton's words in *The Age of Innocence*, "that was how women with lovers lived in the wicked old societies in apartments with all the rooms on one floor."

frieze The bas-relief (or painting) in a band that decorates the top of a room or participates in a Classical entablature.

G

gable The triangular ending of a two-way pitched roof.

gambrel roof The double-pitched roofs employed by Dutch and later Victorian architects.

garland A collection of flowers, as in a wreath, or festoon.

General Grant The good general was a passive participant in this mid-Victorian eclectic melange—usually ornate wood houses with mansard roofs that otherwise might be termed "Charles Addams."

Georgian Of the Georges, those imported German kings of England who were in charge when the best of English urban design was around. Simple but elegant brick and limestone.

Gothic Revival The romantic revival of largely Gothic detail in the 1840s. Some felt (like John Ruskin) that the medieval period was filled with good people, and a revival of that architecture might make citizens of the 1840s equally good. Bad psychology, but it left some smashing architecture.

Gothick An English-style neo-Gothic building.

granite The hard, fine-textured igneous (solidified from a liquid state) stone of mixed quartz, mica, and other ingredients. Sedimentary stones (limestone, brownstone) erode, wear out; granite is forever.

Greek Revival The Greeks were revived for both archaeological and political honors (the 1820s revolution liberating them from Turkey). In the 1820s, 1830s, and 1840s American houses were decorated with Greek parts, and occasionally whole buildings took on Greek temple form: cf. New York's Federal Hall National Memorial.

H

hammer beam The bracketed wood structure of a Gothic or neo-Gothic hall: a kind of wood supercorbeling.

headers The short ends of bricks in a wall used as ties to connect (bond) two thicknesses (wythes) of brick.

hip roof A roof without a gable and with eaves all around.

hood molds Moldings crowning and enveloping the head (top) of a window, particularly in neo-Gothic architecture.

I

imbricated Bearing overlapping shingles or plates arranged as in the scales of a fish. Victorian roofs, both mansard and single-gabled, frequently were imbricated in several colors.

impost block A block that bears the load, as in those corbeled limestone blocks bearing the ribs or timbers of a Gothic or neo-Gothic vault.

incunabulum A precocious affair strictly speaking, a book printed from movable type before 1501, but implying equivalent childlike precocity in any activity, including architecture.

intaglio An incised pattern or decoration, or a printing block so incised that will create printed relief.

Ionic The elegant voluted order of Greek architecture. Its capitals are sometimes compared to ram's horns.

Italianate Of an Italian character, particularly in mid 19th-century villas copied from Italian prototypes.

J

jerkinhead roof A gabled roof with a chamfered, or sliced-off, plane at its ends.

jerry-built Shoddily, cheaply, or unsubstantially built.

L

light A windowpane or, technically, the compartment in which it fits.

limestone Sedimentary stone, mostly from ancient seabeds, the silted and pressed product of sand and seashells. Soft, workable, and subject to erosion in time.

M

machicolation The stepped-out cornice of a Gothic structure that allows the protected to pour boiling oil on an enemy attempting to scale the walls.

maisonette A British term for duplex apartments within an apartment house, like a "little house."

mansard The steep roofs developed by the French 17th-century architect François Mansart, co-opted by Victorian architects of the 19th century (particularly in Paris, where they squeezed in an extra illegal floor).

marble Pressed and heated (metamorphized) limestone, pressed for extra eons to a harder, finer texture. It can be polished to bring out its striations; in its purest form it is without veins, as in the Pentelic marble of the Parthenon or Carrara marble from Italy.

mastaba The battered (sloping-walled) tomb buildings of early Egyptian nobles subordinate to the pyramids that they surrounded (cf. Gizeh).

merlon The tooth of a crenellated wall; a solid between two voids (the warrior behind a merlon shoots between the merlons).

modillion The horizontal enscrolled bracket that supports many a Renaissance and neo-Renaissance cornice. *See also* console bracket.

mullion The vertical member supporting a glass wall, as in a storefront, or between repetitive windows.

muntin A small bar that divides a window's sash into panes: the little sticks that make up the framing of six-over-six double-hung sash and so forth.

N

nave The central space of a Christian church; the space for worshippers, as opposed to the space for clergy (chancel) or monastic brethren (transepts).

neo-Grec The late 19th-century style that brought back Greece for a second time (Greek Revival in the 1820s, 1830s, and 1840s was the first). Here it was a more decorative and less columnar affair.

neo-Renaissance A revival of Renaissance buildings and parts, in New York mostly those of England and Italy but with an occasional French example. (The New York County Lawyers' Association, the Metropolitan Club, and the Towers Nursing Home, respectively.)

New Brutalism A second coming, in the 1960s, of Brutalism (q.v.).

nosing The projecting edge of a step.

O

oculus An eyelike round window.

ogee The double-curved arch of both Moorish and French Flamboyant Gothic architecture. S-shaped.

ogival Having a pointed arch or vault, as in the nave of a Gothic church.

Order The base, columns, and entablature in Classical architecture: Doric, Ionic, Corinthian, Tuscan, or Composite orders.

oriel A small bay window that captures a view for its resident.

P

palazzo The super town house of Italian nobility (i.e., palace), later a description of any big, urbane building in an Italian town.

palimpsest A surface that has been reused for writing, symbols, or carving, only partly obliterating a previous message underneath.

Palladian Of and/or relating to the 16th-century Italian architect Andrea Palladio (Jefferson went bananas over him), particularly used in reference to the paired columns flanking an arch, as at the Basilica of Vicenza.

parapet The wall around a building's roof (literally a "breast guard").

parge To weatherproof a surface by coating it, as with stucco, but with a lighter cement wash—usually where unseen, below grade, or on the rear (unseen?) of a building.

pediment The triangular gable end of a Classical temple and part of that architecture's order; later used separately as a decorative part of Renaissance architecture.

pergola A trellised walkway, usually festooned with vines; with grapevines it would be termed an arbor.

Perma Stone Fake masonry simulating stonework or brick, composed of colored stucco with struck joints in a contrasting color to imply "mortar."

piazza The Italian word for plaza—and sometimes an American word for porch (particularly in the Midwest).

pilaster The flat remembrance of a column that articulates a wall, and frequently repeats the rhythm and parts of an adjacent colonnade. Usually decorative and nonstructural.

pillowed rustication Baroque architects gave stone the imagery of wormwood, marshmallows, and other fantasies. Here, in neo-Baroque, pillows take over.

pinnacle The tower atop a Gothic buttress.

plaza The English (and now American) version of the Italian piazza: an outdoor space contained by different buildings. New York has some annexed to private construction (cf. Seagram's Plaza), few publicly created ones: The Plaza at 59th Street and Fifth Avenue; the Police Plaza next to the Brooklyn Bridge; and the World Trade and World Financial Center Plazas—the last three all since 1960.

plinth The base that holds it all up, as at a column or a wall.

point block A British term for an apartment tower.

polychromy Of many colors, particularly in architecture.

Pompeian red The deep red of Pompeian frescoes.

Post Modern A catchall term for (1) the renewed interest of contemporary architects in the history of architecture, including, in their own work, allusions to a historical vocabulary; and (2) a permissive approach that allows many to claim that "anything goes," now that they are released from the constraints of "modern" and "functionalism," with their concomitant morality and lack of ornament.

Po Mo Short for Post Modern.

porte cochere The covered portal to a house or public building, meant originally for the horse and carriage but now just as useful for a stretch limo.

Q

Queen Anne Style Originally the pre-Georgian style of Queen Anne's reign (1702-1714); in 19th-century American architecture the style is that of a mixture of medieval and Classical parts: Tudor, Federal, and Greek Revival grown fat, bulbous, rich, and encrusted. Eclectic extravaganzas of delight.

quoins Cornerstones of a building that articulate that corner, frequently in a different material, as in the limestone quoins of a brick Georgian building (say "coins").

R

range Particularly in brick, where the natural baking process in a kiln produces (from the bricks stacked within) a range of color, some darker, some lighter, depending on the individual brick's placement in the kiln's stacks.

rectory The dwelling of a priest (whether Catholic or Episcopalian).

reentrant corner An interior corner.

Renaissance The rebirth or revival of the Classical Greek and Roman worlds, their humanism, individual creativity, and, in architecture, the adaptation of the Classical vocabulary to new building types, such as churches and palazzi.

reredos A background screen behind an altar and, occasionally, a major art object itself, like the reredos by Frank Freeman in Brooklyn Heights' Holy Trinity Church.

retardataire Laggard, behind the times, a Johnny-come-lately to the art or architecture of the moment—but mostly a pejorative for the avant-garde putting down the architecture of what went before and then hung on.

reveals The sides of a window or door opening that "reveal" the thickness of the encompassing walls.

rock-faced Rock made more rocky by artful sculpture; neat stones faced with hewn-rock forms.

Roman The imperial organizers of the Classical world who brought engineering to architecture, creating great public works—vaulted, domed baths and temples, arched aqueducts—all decorated and ordered with the parts developed by 5th-century B.C. Greece.

Romanesque The round-arched and round-vaulted sturdy early medieval architecture of Europe that was succeeded by the more elegant and sinuous Gothic. Its revived forms were highly popular in the late 19th century (e.g., Jay Street Firehouse, Brooklyn).

row house Houses that share common walls and form a row, or what the English term terraces. Town house is the elegant social promotion of the same physical place.

Ruskinian Relating to the ideas of the English writer, art critic, social theorist, and historian John Ruskin (1819-1900). *See* Gothic Revival.

rusticated Stones that have deeply incised joints to exaggerate their weight and scale. A Renaissance device.

S

sash The subframe carrying the pane(s) of glass in a window, as in one of two double-hung window sashes, or one of two halves of a casement window.

schist Laminations of rock, the product of hot geology, as a napoleon or baklava has layers of pastry. Manhattan island's skyscraper core is founded on Manhattan schist.

Second Empire The period of Napoleon III in France (1852-1870) that brought to reality Baron Haussmann's Paris with its concomitant mansard roofs and neo-Renaissance detail. In America this style was aped in the 1870s and 1880s.

serpentine Anything that is serpentlike in its undulating form. Stone called serpentine has such striations.

sgraffito The polite antecedent of graffiti, here enhancing architecture with an elegance of writing rather than defacing it, as in urban decay.

Shingle Style The romantic and picturesque style of the 1880s and 1890s that brought the freestanding architecture of America to a special apogee: the plastic forms resulting were clad in wood shingles. But the style's name extended to woodless buildings, based on the same picturesque forms.

soffit The underside of an architectural part, as the soffit of a balcony, commonly misused to describe the infill vertical panels to the ceiling above kitchen cabinets.

spandrel The space between the window head of one floor and the window sill of the floor above; opaque masonry or paneling that conceals the floor construction behind. In Renaissance architecture it was the triangular space between two adjacent arches.

star anchors Tension rods from front outer wall to back outer wall stabilized early 19th-century buildings, and the hand that held the outside face of a building inward was often a cast-iron star, a decorative end to an engineering need.

stele The memorial finial or slab set in the ground that remembers persons, places, or events. A tombstone is a stele, as are the Druidic remains of Stonehenge.

stepped gable The masonry end (usually) that covers a pitched roof's triangular profile, rising above it in rectilinear steps; a Dutch device that presented itself to the street (English gables ran parallel).

strapwork A 16th-century northern European decoration similar to leather or fretwork.

surround That framing material that surrounds an opening, window, door, or whatever.

swag A draping of cloth, frequently remembered in stone; also termed a festoon.

T

taxpayer A low (1- or 2-story) modest building where many stories might be permitted by zoning but where the owner, because of limited finances (particularly during the 1930s depression), wished only to have sufficient income to pay the expenses and taxes until better times arrived.

tempietto A little temple in Italian.

tenement A 19th-century, low-rise walk-up apartment house that covers most of its site; now a pejorative term.

terrace A group of row houses (English).

terra-cotta Literally "cooked earth" in Italian, terra-cotta is baked clay. A hard, red-brown material used for pottery, paving, shingles, statuary, and, in late 19th-century New York, for fireproofing steel (by encasing it in terra-cotta blockwork).

tesserae The tiny mosaic tiles (originally of marble) that created Roman floors. Nowadays they may be of glass.

tetrastyle Having four columns, usually in the Greek temple manner.

thermal granite Sawn slabs of granite, the surface of which has been treated under intense flames, producing a roughened texture, as at the CBS Building by Eero Saarinen.

torchère A simulated torch powered by gas or electricity.

torus A convex, half-round molding, in Classical architecture at the base of an Ionic column; also used in the Renaissance and neo-Renaissance.

town house Originally the secondary residence of the English country gentleman. Now not necessarily a house in town but one in an urban arrangement: i.e., row house. Town house is a classier term—to increase sales. Some of New York's 19th- and early 20th-century town houses are equivalent to the Italian palazzo.

Tuscan The Roman version of Doric with a simplified capital and, usually, no flutes.

tympanum Within an arched entry the semicircular space above the doors below, sculpted in high relief in Gothic and Romanesque architecture.

U

U.L.U.R.P. Uniform Land Use Review Process, wherein variations in the zoning laws, or large-scale development, are reviewed by the local Community Planning Board, before a final review by the City Planning Commission and Board of Estimate. A lengthy process.

V

verandah The airy porch imported from India, partially screened for outdoor living, not just rocking.

verdigris The green patina (oxide) on weathered copper, brass, or bronze. It is the handsome equivalent on copper of iron's rust, both resulting from oxidation.

vergeboard A board trimming the underedge of a gabled roof, sometimes called a bargeboard.

vernacular The ordinary architecture of a culture without benefit of architect, as in the stuccoed houses of the Mediterranean's rim (Greece, Capri, North Africa) or the verandahed farmhouses of 19th-century America.

viaduct An elevated roadway that is the trafficked equivalent of an aqueduct, supported on many columns or piers, as opposed to a bridge, which spans the space in question.

Victorian A loosely defined catchall word. The architecture of the Industrial Revolution was largely coincidental with the reign of Victoria (1837-1901), which spanned from carpenter Greek Revival to the steel-framed skyscraper.

villa A country house for a well-to-do city dweller's escape (Italian).

volutes The scroll-like cresting of, for example, an Ionic capital.

voussoir The wedge-shaped stones or radial backs of an arch, cut to fit its shape, whether circle, ellipse, or ogee.

W

water table The level of water underground (that may affect a building's foundations), or the deflecting molding that skims water away from a building like a skirt near the ground on the building's perimeter.

wrought iron More easily wrought and less brittle than cast iron, it now serves for railings and decoration. It was once used for structural beams and railroad rails, before the more refined steel was invented.

wythe A single plane of brick (usually 4 inches); part of a wall composed of two or more wythes bonded by metal tics or brick "headers." A cavity wall is composed of two wythes with an air space between (say "with").

Z

ziggurat The stepped or spiral pyramidal holy places of ancient Babylon.

zoning The legal constraint of building to protect one's neighbors and oneself from noxious uses, to preserve or ensure one's quota of light and air, and to control density of land use.

AIA GUIDE TO NEW YORK CITY

Manhattan

MANHATTAN

Borough of Manhattan/New York County

1

To most people, Manhattan is New York, the place to "go to business," the downtown of all downtowns. This is where the action is, where money is earned and, in large part, spent. To non-New Yorkers, Manhattan is known in excerpts from the whole: Fifth Avenue, Broadway, Greenwich Village, Wall Street, the caricatures of the chic, of bright lights, of the offbeat, of big business—excerpts symbolic of the public power and influence of Manhattan as the capital of banking, corporate headquartering, the theater, advertising, publishing, fashion, tourism, and, to a lesser degree, the United Nations. This passing parade of visitors mostly misses Manhattan's myriad local neighborhoods with handsome buildings and areas of visual delight. That there are distinguished architecture and urban design in Harlem, on the vast Upper West Side, or in the loft districts of Lower Manhattan will startle and, we hope, pleasantly surprise those visitors who have savored only the well-publicized monuments, musicals, and museums.

 Colonial

 Georgian/ Federal

 Greek Revival

 Gothic Revival

 Villa

 Romanesque Revival

 Renaissance Revival

 Roman Revival

 Art Deco/ Art Moderne

 Modern/ Post-Modern

Lower Manhattan skyline

Lower Manhattan

L

**FINANCIAL DISTRICT • WATER STREET CORRIDOR
SOUTH STREET SEAPORT • BROADWAY-NASSAU
BATTERY PARK CITY • TRIBECA/LOWER WEST SIDE
CIVIC CENTER • CHINATOWN/LITTLE ITALY
LOWER EAST SIDE • SOHO**

Manhattan's toe:

Manhattan's toe, that 1½-square-mile triangle pulsating south of Canal Street and contained by the confluence of the Hudson and East Rivers, is where Manhattan—all of New York for that matter—began. Here lay **Nieuw Amsterdam**, founded in 1625, the first permanent settlement of Europeans in this area, the first fortifications, the first business district, the first community.

Where once all of the settlement's activities—even farming— took place in the toe, population growth and urbanization divined that specialization would take command. For Manhattan's tip the specialties would become shipping and ware- housing, and the necessary backup of accounting, banking, and speculating that inevitably followed. And, of course government.

Until recently, few people had lived in Manhattan's toe— since the turn of the 19th into the 20th century. Public policy in the 1970s and onward changed all that, and conversion of older office buildings (pre-air conditioning), with small floors and many windows, has attracted a new luxury residential market.

Exploring the toe:

Routes for visiting the area's architecture have been turned into a series of walking tours that radiate outward from the Battery to create armatures for exploration. The walks take convenient path- ways; Lower Manhattan's development over time has taken more complex routes.

__Note__: For the Staten Island Ferry and the Ferry Terminal, see Water Street Corridor.

FINANCIAL DISTRICT

The Financial District's twisted streets, varying both in direction and width, occupy that part of Manhattan's tip originally laid out by early colonists, vividly recalling the irregular medieval street patterns of northern European settlements. It is this part of the toe, the original part, that became the foundation for the slender skyscrapers built between the turn of the century and the Great Depression of the 1930s. It is also the part abundantly served by the three subway systems whose stations dot the area.

Surrounding the district's early core on the waterside are a later series of concentric landfills. They support the successive waves of warehouses, countinghouses, and wharves that would serve the water-oriented enterprises that gave New York its early profits, power, and fame. In time these activities faded even as the core prospered, giving birth to the Financial District's canyons. Yet the twentieth century did not saturate the perime- ter of the toe until after World War II, when large-scale sky- scraper development bulldozed what had become outlying, seedy, low-scale areas, still abundant with architectural signifi- cance but marginal economically. The special visual character of these late 18th- and 19th-century commercial precincts is evi- dent today only in the South Street Seaport Historic District.

LOWER MANHATTAN KEY MAP

Walking Tour A—*Lower Manhattan's Medieval Street Plan: From Battery Park to the vicinity of Cass Gilbert's 90 West Street Building, near the World Trade Center. Start at Castle Clinton National Monument. (The IRT Seventh Avenue local (Nos. 1 and 9 trains) to South Ferry Station and BMT Broadway Line local (N and R trains) to Whitehall Street Station will deposit you at Battery Park. The IRT Lexington Avenue Line express (Nos. 4 and 5 trains) to Bowling Green Station leave you a short walk away.)*

Battery Park and its perimeter:

[F1] Battery Park.

The Battery signals the bottom of Manhattan to most New Yorkers, where tourists are borne by ferry to the **Statue of Liberty**, and "provincial" Staten Islanders start their homeward trek to that distant island which turns out to be, surprisingly, part of New York City. Battery was the namesake of a row of guns along the old shorefront line now approximated by State Street between Bowling Green and Whitehall. During the War of 1812, the status of the gunnery was elevated: **Castle Clinton**, erected on a pile of rock some 300 feet offshore, was known as **West Battery**; while **Castle Williams**, on Governors Island, became **East Battery**. The intervening years have seen landfill entirely envelop Castle Clinton (and its various transmogrifications), forming Battery Park, a flat and somewhat confused stretch of (originally) **Robert Moses** landscaping that provides greenery and summer delight to New Yorkers from nearby offices. A fresh, if sometimes pungent, breeze from the Upper Bay is an antidote for the doldrums or any bad mood aggravated by heat.

Nearby, **Verrazano** (the first explorer to actually enter the harbor while sailing the east coast) gazes out at the harbor, perhaps admiring his bridge. ([F3] 1909, **Ettore Ximenes**, sculptor.)

The buff, bland Coast Guard Building at the east edge of the park's bay front vies with the slated-for-demolition, eye-ease green, Staten Island Ferry Terminal as the city's most unfortunate structure in a prominent location. The Coast Guard site in earlier years was successively occupied by two richly conceived U.S. Government Barge Offices designed by Supervising Architects of the Treasury Department: **James G. Hill** (1880) and **James Knox Taylor** (1914).

F3

[F2] Castle Clinton National Monument/earlier New York Aquarium (1896-1941)/earlier Emigrant Landing Depot (1855-1890)/earlier Castle Garden (1824-1855)/originally West Battery (1808-1811, renamed Castle Clinton, 1815). **Lt. Col. Jonathan Williams** and **John McComb, Jr.** 🖼 Open to the public: 7-5 daily. 212-344-7220.

Until recently, one of the most vitally involved structures in the city's life and history. Built as West Battery for the War of 1812 to complement Castle Williams across the waters on Governors Island (it never fired a shot in anger), it was originally an island fortification some 300 feet offshore, connected to Manhattan by a combination causeway bridge. Twelve years after the war it was ceded to the city. As a civic monument it served for the reception of distinguished visitors at the very edge of the nation (**General Lafayette, Louis Kossuth, President Jackson, Prince Albert**). Remodeled as a concert hall and renamed Castle Garden, it enjoyed a moment of supreme glory in 1850 as the site of the much ballyhooed, **P. T. Barnum**-promoted American debut of the Swedish soprano **Jenny Lind**. Only five years later it was transformed into the Emigrant Landing Depot, run by N.Y. State, where some 7.7 million new Americans were processed, some into the Union army, others into the Lower East Side. Scandal led to its closure, and the processing of immigrants was transferred to federal control, at the

F2

Barge Office in 1890 and at Ellis Island in 1892. Not to be forgot-
ten, however its innards were juggled and its decor changed by
McKim, Mead & White, and it reentered the fray as the
Aquarium, the much beloved grotto of New Yorkers until 1941.

It was then apparently doomed by **Robert Moses**' call for its
demolition to build approaches for his ill-fated harbor bridge to
Brooklyn—today's Brooklyn-Battery Tunnel. A loud civic clam-
or and the reported intervention of **Eleanor Roosevelt** miraculously saved it though it languished inside a construction fence
for decades. In 1946 the ruin was belatedly dubbed a **National
Historic Monument**.

With its sea life displays removed to makeshift quarters at
the Bronx Zoo, and then permanently installed in new facilities
at Coney Island, the fort awaited a new purpose. Urged on by
the 1976 Bicentennial, the National Park Service schmaltzified
this once lusty place into a tame tourist attraction, a neat lawn
surrounded by a shingle roof within its rock-faced brownstone
shell. In 1986 it lost out to commerce, reduced to service as a
ticket office for the boats to National Park Service attractions in
the harbor.

The **Statue of Liberty** and **Ellis Island** [see The Other
Islands] are must-visit attractions only a short, privately operated boat ride away, sitting in the Upper Bay near the New Jersey
shore but in plain view of visitors to Battery Park.

*Miss Liberty: Perhaps three times the height of the Colossus of
Rhodes, which was one of the "Seven Wonders of the World,"
Liberty, until the 1986 centennial, was considered corny but corn
was a necessary ingredient here. Like an old shoe to New Yorkers,
she is always there and continues to wear well, particularly since
the restoration on the occasion of her birthday. Take the special
boat out to her, ascend the spiral stairway through her innards to
the crown, and you will look back on one of the romantic glories
of the world: the New York skyline. She, still doing her own thing,
is meanwhile saluting the rising sun of France.*

F4

[F4] **East Coast Memorial**, Battery Park. 1960. **Gehron &
Seltzer**, architects. Sculpture, 1963, **Albino Manca**.

Eight solid sawn-granite monoliths (steles) with the rolls of
those merchant mariners who died at sea off this coast in World
War II. An aggressive basalt eagle guards this mall of steles.

[F5] **Control House, Bowling Green Subway Station**,
Nos. 4 and 5 trains (old IRT Subway System), Battery
Park, State St., SW cor. Battery Place. 1904-1905. **Heins & La**

Farge. ☛ **Old IRT Bowling Green Subway Station**, Nos. 4 and 5 trains (old IRT Lexington Avenue Line), under Bowling Green. 1908. **Heins & La Farge**. Redesigned, 1974, **Transit Authority Architectural Staff**.

A Flemish Revival masonry station entry, companion piece to the same firm's cast-iron kiosks, which once dotted Manhattan's street corners along the route of the city's first subway system, the Interborough Rapid Transit Company (IRT). Only one cast-iron version exists, and it is a replica (Astor Place). The subway station itself is a total redesign in lipstick red wall tile (1975, NYC Transit Authority Architectural Staff).

From the park savor the wall of buildings that defines its space.

[F6] **Liberty Gateway**, Pier A, NYC Department of Docks & Ferries (once Fireboat House), off Battery Park, Battery Place SW cor. West St. 1884-1886. **George Sears Greene, Jr.**, engineer. Additions, 1900, 1904, 1919. ☛ Reconstruction master plan, 1991. **Beyer Blinder Belle**. Project architect, 1999. **Ehrenkrantz & Eckstut** with **Allenbrook, Benic, Czajka, Architects**.

Both the pier, built atop granite arches sunk to river bottom, and the pier building, its once ornate, Beaux Arts-ornamented tinplate siding restored (in 1999, after a brief encounter [1964-1999] in aluminum), are the oldest survivors of this kind of construction in Manhattan. The clock in the tower at the pier's tip was installed in 1919 as the nation's first World War I memorial. Recent work converted the pier to a visitors' center.

Walk out into the harbor for magnificent backviews to the Battery and Battery Park City.

F7a

A short diversion to the north along West Street, then back again:

[F7a] **21 West Street** (formerly offices, now apartments), SE cor. Morris St. 1931. [F7b] **Downtown Athletic Club**, 19 West St., bet. Morris St. and Battery Place. 1926. Both by **Starrett & Van Vleck**.

21 West bears a chromatic range of salt-glazed tile, from burnt oranges to brown. This is the material of which silos are frequently made: a natural glaze, resistant to urban "fallout," without the crassness of the popular white glazed brick of the 1950s and 1960s. The arcade with recessed ground floor sports corbeled arches, reminiscent of Moorish architecture. Corners are cantilevered—making corner windows a natural. An Art Deco delight.

The following three structures on the north side of Battery Place define the southern edge of the Financial District against Battery Park:

[F8] **Whitehall Building** (offices), 17 Battery Place, NE cor. West St. 1902. **Henry J. Hardenbergh**. Rear addition, 1910, **Clinton & Russell**.

F8

This colossal bulk offers the best views of the harbor from any of the Battery's older buildings.

[F9] **Brooklyn-Battery Tunnel Ventilation Building**, Battery Place bet. Washington and Greenwich Sts. N side. 1950. **Aymar Embury II**.

The windowless ventilator is one of three constipated Classico/Modern necessities for the tunnel, but was appropriated in the science-fiction movie, *Men in Black*, as a command center (underground, of course) to manage the aliens in our society. Appropriate.

[F10] **International Merchant Marine Company Building** (United States Lines)/originally Washington Building, 1

FINANCIAL DISTRICT

see pages 5–23

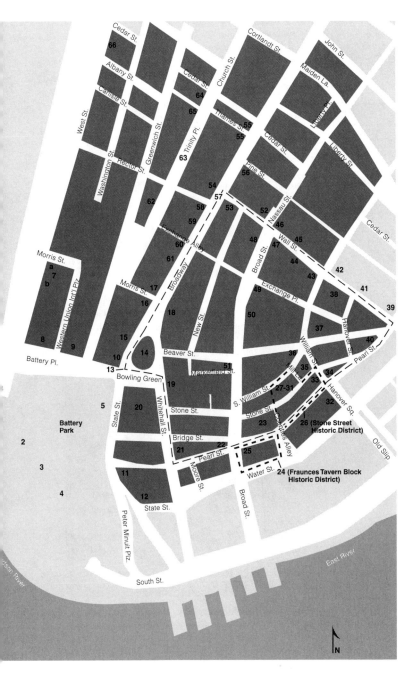

Broadway, NW cor. Battery Place at Bowling Green. 1882-1884.
Edward H. Kendall. Refaced in limestone, 1919-1921, **Walter B. Chambers**. ●

No. 1 Broadway, having come to see a second life in 1922, was again redone in the 1980s. Citibank occupies the ground floor space that once served as the U.S. Lines booking hall.

Along Battery Park's eastern boundary, State Street:
__Note:__ For the US. Custom House, the northernmost structure on State Street, see [F 20].

F11

F12

[F11] **17 State Street** (offices), on former site of Seamen's Church Institute, SE cor. Pearl St. 1987-1989. **Emery Roth & Sons**.

A sleek columnar mirror from the park, No. 17 replaced the Seamen's Church Institute hostel for mariners after only 16 years [see Necrology]. In 1819, **Herman Melville** was born in a house on this site. The understructure showing crossbracing and glazed elevator shafts is fun.

[F12] **Rectory of the Shrine of St. Elizabeth Ann Bayley Seton** (Roman Catholic)/originally James Watson House, 7 State St., bet. Pearl and Water Sts. NE side. 1793-1806. Attributed to **John McComb, Jr.** ● Restoration and additions, 1965, **Shanley & Sturges**.

A single survivor of the first great era of mansions, the façade is original. Federal both in the archaeological and political senses, it was built in the fifth year of **George Washington**'s presidency of the federal republic in a style that is separately considered Federal. Slender, elegant, freestanding Ionic columns and delicate late Georgian detailing.

Mother Seton, born on Staten Island, baptized Episcopalian, and converted to Roman Catholicism, was canonized as America's first saint in 1975.

Peter Stuyvesant's mansion, at 1 State Street, NW cor. Whitehall Street (ca. 1657), was renamed **Whitehall** by the first English governor and occupied a tiny peninsula projecting from the east end of the Battery at this point. **Robert Fulton** resided in a different building on the same site a century later.

Leave the Battery Park area and enter the space of Bowling Green, the widening of Lower Broadway in front of the Custom House.

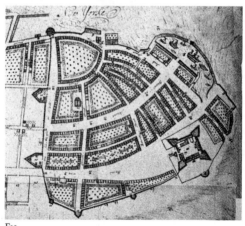

F13
Bowling Green:

[F13] **Street Plan of New Amsterdam and Colonial New York**, the full width of all street beds lying within an irregular curved triangle bounded by (and including the street beds of) Wall St. on the N; Broadway, Bowling Green, and Whitehall Streets on the W, and Pearl Street on the E. ●

With the demapping of a part of Stone Street for the construction of No. 85 Broad Street, the Landmarks Preservation Commission in 1983 designated as a landmark the old boundary lines of the streets that still mark the paths of the city's venerable Dutch and English colonial thoroughfares, many of which date from the 1600s. The officially designated irregular street pattern, in vivid contrast to later gridiron layouts, reflects the organic approach found in medieval European city building quite familiar to those who settled Manhattan in the 17th and early 18th centuries.

Naming of Streets: The early streets of New Amsterdam and New York were often named for their pioneering functions, rather than more abstract sources (numbers, plants, trees, heroes, et alia). Pearl Street was once the edge of the island where mother-of-pearl (oyster shells) littered the beach, Bridge street served the first bridge to span the old Dutch canal at Broad Street. Broad Street was broad as it was laid out to have the canal at its center and service roads on each side. Water Street was under water when the mother-of pearl defined Pearl Street. Wall Street, the most famous, was the site of the northern boundary of New Amsterdam, where a wall (palisades of sharpened logs) was erected against the English and the Indians. And so forth.

[F14] **Bowling Green**, foot of Broadway. Altered, various years. Restored, redesigned, reconstructed, 1978, **M. Paul Friedberg & Assocs.**, landscape architects.

F14

Adjacent to the Dutch cattle market, this oval open space became a "parade" and was leased in 1733 for the annual fee of one peppercorn as a quasi-public bowling ground (or green), for the "Beauty & Ornament of the Said Street as well as for the Recreation & delight of the Inhabitants." The fence remaining today was erected in 1771-1772 🍎 , although its decorative crowns were snapped off by exuberant patriots after the reading of the **Declaration of Independence** on July 9, 1776. The same patriots pulled down the gilded lead statue of **George III**, much of which was then reportedly melted down into bullets used against the redcoats.

The 1978 reconstruction removed an atrocious "1950s Modern" glassed-in, flat-topped subway entrance and relocated the 1896 **de Peyster** statue, thereby restoring the simplicity of this patch of green amid the district's sunless canyons.

Clockwise, enclosing Bowling Green, from the west (see above for No. 1 Broadway):

[F15] **Bowling Green Offices**, 5-11 Broadway, at Bowling Green. W side. 1895-1898. **W. & G. Audsley.** Altered, 1920, **Ludlow & Peabody.** 🍎

F15

"Eclectic" was invented for stylistic collections such as this (the architects described it as "Hellenic Renaissance"). The battered "Egyptian" pylons framing the entrance are bizarre imports. Above the 3rd floor, however, the spirit changes: strong glazed-brick piers with articulated spandrels have much the bold verticality of the Chicago School. Built by financier **Spencer Trask**, founder of Yaddo, the writers' colony in Saratoga Springs, N.Y.

[F16] Originally **Cunard Building** (offices), 25 Broadway, SW cor. Morris St. 1917-1921. **Benjamin Wistar Morris**, architect; **Carrère & Hastings**, consulting architects. Great Hall: ceiling sculpture, **C. Paul Jennewein**; ceiling paintings, **Ezra Winter**; iron gates, **Samuel Yellin.** 🍎 Interior 🍎 Conversion to post office, 1977, **Handren Assocs.**

F16

This "Renaissance" façade and its neighbors handsomely surround Bowling Green with a high order of group architecture. What matters most at No. 25, however, is its great booking hall, with its elaborately decorated groined and conical vaults. It was in this grand setting that passage on such liners as the *Queen Mary* and the two *Queen Elizabeths* was purchased. (The Classical container is home to a freestanding post office space frame that could have been considered appropriate there only in the 1970s. Luckily it permanently damages nothing of the walls or vaults.)

[F17] **29 Broadway** (offices), NW cor. Morris St. to Trinity Place. 1929-1931. **Sloan & Robertson.**

F17

F18

The tower's slim 31-story Broadway face widens to a broad Trinity Place backside, but what a wonderfully ornamented Art Deco experience it all is—except for the 6-story Broadway annex (where once was Schrafft's), which is just a timid refacing. Survey the tower's lobby.

[F18] **26 Broadway** (offices)/originally Standard Oil Building, NE cor. Beaver St. Expanded from 1884-1885 Standard Oil Building, 1920-1928. **Carrère & Hastings** and **Shreve, Lamb & Blake.** 👁

This curving façade reinforces the street's group architecture, working particularly well with its friend, No.25, across the green. Begun as The Standard Oil Building, built by the Standard Oil Trust Organization, the earlier structure on the site (1884-1886 **Ebenezer L. Roberts**) was only 10 stories tall. Enveloped and enlarged over the years, it served until **John D. Rockefeller**'s trust was broken up, in 1911. Then, one of the trust's five offspring, Standard Oil Company of New York, Socony (later called Socony-Vacuum, Socony-Mobil, and now Mobil), lived here until it removed to its new building on East 42nd Street in 1956.

The 480-foot-high pyramidal tower seems squared to the city's uptown gridiron, rather than to the loose geometry of lower Manhattan's street pattern. The designers were concerned with the tower as an element in the city's skyline, not as a local form.

[F19] **2 Broadway** (offices), bet. Stone and Beaver Sts. E side. 1958-1959. **Emery Roth & Sons**. Remodeled and reskinned, 1999. **Skidmore, Owings & Merrill**.

Another fashionable New York curtain wall reskinning, this time for this bulky replacement of the old Produce Exchange.

*The **Produce Exchange** (1882-1884. **George B. Post**) was one of the city's greatest architectural losses in the post-World War II years. That enormous red terra-cotta-and-brick Romanesque Revival construction is echoed today only in miniature by Post's extant Brooklyn Historical Society. The ruddy Exchange contrasted vividly with its newer, paler, limestone and granite neighbors until its demolition in 1957.*

F20

[F20] **Alexander Hamilton Custom House** (National Museum of the American Indian and Federal Bankruptcy Court)/originally U.S. Custom House, 1 Bowling Green, bet. State and Whitehall Sts. to Bridge St. 1899-1907.

Cass Gilbert. Sculptures, "Four Continents": E to W: Asia, America, Europe, Africa, **Daniel Chester French**; Adolph A. **Weinman**, associate. Cartouche at 7th-story attic, **Karl Bitter**. Rotunda ceiling paintings, 1936-1937, **Reginald Marsh**.  Partial interior  . Alterations for the National Museum of the American Indian, 1994. **Ehrenkrantz & Ekstut**. Museum open 10-5 daily. 212-283-2420.

Until the establishment of a federal income tax, in 1913, the primary means of financing the costs of national government was through the imposition of customs duties. New York being the busiest point of entry for foreign goods, this Custom House became the nation's largest collector of such funds. It's no accident that this structure is so grand, one of the city's most splendid Beaux Arts buildings, now reloved by modernists searching for fresh meaning in the history of architecture. The monumental sculptures by **French** (better known for his seated **Lincoln** at the memorial in Washington) are very much part of the architecture of the façade, their whiteness—and that of those at the attic by other sculptors—a rich counterpoint to the structure's gray granite, both in form and color.

No less grand is the interior, whose giant oval rotunda, embellished by **Reginald Marsh**'s WPA-commissioned murals, is both the crowning architectural space and the challenge for the structure's reuse. It has remained vacant except for temporary activities since the Customs Service vacated the Custom House in favor of the World Trade Center in 1973. Happily, the Museum of the American Indian has infilled much of these spaces since its installation.

The commanding site south of Bowling Green has been successively occupied by:

Nieuw Amsterdam's, and subsequently New York's, fortification, Fort Amsterdam (renamed Fort James, Fort Willem Hendrick, Fort James [again], Fort William, Fort William Henry, Fort Anne, and finally Fort George).

Government House, built in 1790 to be George Washington's executive mansion (except that the nation's capital removed to Philadelphia after one year); then used as the Governor's Mansion (until the state capital moved to Albany in 1797); briefly leased as John Avery's tavern; and then used as temporary Custom House until lost to a fire in 1815.

A row of fine town houses, minor mansions, later occupied by the world's leading shipping companies (and so dubbed Steamship Row).

Its current occupant, the U.S. Custom House building.

Walk south down the Custom House's left (western) flank, Whitehall Street, and turn left (west) on Pearl Street.

Pearl Street:

[F21] **Broad Financial Center** (offices), 33 Whitehall St., NE cor. Pearl St. to Bridge St. 1986. **Fox & Fowle**.

F21

BFC's developers wanted to link its name to Broad Street, a block away from the main entrance. The intervening, low, surrealist limestone Clearing House Association [see below] wanted to sell its air rights. A deal was struck whereby the pale blue, mirrored office tower bought the air rights, overhung its low neighbor, and obtained a tenuous tie to the desired street.

[F22] **New York Clearing House Association**, 100 Broad St., bet. Pearl and Bridge Sts. W side. 1962. **Rogers & Butler**.

F22

A funky little building whose occupant provides a vital financial service. It makes certain that banks observe a coherent system of clearing each other's checks.

F23

[F23] **85 Broad Street** (offices), bet. Pearl and S. William Sts, to Coenties Alley. 1983. **Skidmore, Owings & Merrill**.

The structure's enormous—and ungainly—bulk (close to a million square feet) results from the purchase and transfer of air rights from the Fraunces Tavern Block across the street, its tan cast-stone wall surfaces from an interpretation of the Zoning Law's mandate that they harmonize with the Historic District's protected façades. Harmony? Certainly not in scale, and the relationship of materials is a joke.

Although arcaded No. 85 excised part of ancient Stone Street's curving route, it pays homage to that thoroughfare's path via a curved elevator lobby and the introduction of vestigial curbs where Stone Street once intersected Broad. With eyes already directed to the ground, turn the Pearl Street corner and view evidence of the 17th century in two glassed-in displays below the sidewalk surface, discovered in an archaeological survey required of the developer by the Landmarks Preservation Commission.

Broad Street was in Dutch times de Heere Gracht [The Gentleman's Canal], a drainage and shipping canal that reached today's Exchange Place, where a ferry to Long Island docked. The canal was filled in 100 years before the Revolution, but its path remains in the street's extraordinary width—at least for this part of town. Manhattan's oldest streets cross Broad: Bridge Street was at the first bridge immediately adjacent to the waterfront at Pearl Street; Pearl should be "Mother of Pearl," in fact, for the glistening shells that once lined its shore—and its pavement; Stone Street was the first to be cobbled. The geometry of the space has not greatly changed, except that Broad's meeting with the shoreline is some 600 feet further into the harbor than at the time of the canal's fill, making Water, Front, and South Streets on landfill of a later date.

*The **Stadt Huys**, seat of Dutch colonial government, stood on the north side of Pearl St. (No. 71) between Broad Street and Coenties Alley. During preliminary explorations for foundations for an office building on this site, archaeologists turned up a number of colonial artifacts. Here, old shoreline was so close that tides at times lapped against the Stadt Huys steps.*

Proceed north along Pearl Street, as it curves parallel to today's East River shoreline; remember that Pearl Street once marked the edge of Nieuw Amsterdam and was earlier called the wal (embankment) by the Dutch and The Strand by the English.

[F24] **Fraunces Tavern Block Historic District**, bounded by Pearl, Broad, and Water Sts., and Coenties Slip. ❧ Block created on landfill, ca. 1689. Structures (including Fraunces Tavern), 1719-1883 with 20th-century additions, restorations, alterations, reconstructions, **Stephen B. Jacobs & Assocs.**, **Samuel S. Arlen & Frederick B. Fox, Jr.**, and others.

Faced with the rapid diminution of Lower Manhattan's stock of Federal style and other early buildings, a circumstance prominently decried in **Ada Louise Huxtable**'s 1964 book *Classic New York*, this block was singled out for historic designation. It is regrettable that no two sides of any street were included, denying future visitors a sense of the true scale and environment of contained space of that era. But to savor such space, visit the nearby South Street Seaport Historic District.

[F25] **Fraunces Tavern** (restaurant and museum), 54 Pearl St., SE cor. Broad St. 1904-1907. **William Mersereau**.

❧ ♂ Museum open to the public: Mo-Fr 10-4:45; Sa 12-4; closed Su. 212-425-1778.

The tavern of **Samuel Fraunces** occupied this plot and achieved great historic note in the Revolution: for ten days in 1783 it served as **Washington**'s last residence as general. On

F25

December 4 he bade farewell to his officers there and withdrew to his estate at Mount Vernon. He returned six years later and five blocks away to Broad Street's head, to take office as president of the United States at old City Hall, by then renamed Federal Hall.

The present building is a highly conjectural construction—not a restoration—based on "typical" buildings of "the period," parts of remaining walls, and a lot of guesswork. With enthusiasm more harmless when attached to genealogy than to wishful archaeology, today's tavern has been billed as the Real McCoy. Such charades enabled George Washington Slept Here architecture to strangle reality in much of suburban America.

[F26] **Stone Street Historic District**, bounded by Pearl St., Hanover Square, South William St., and Coenties Alley. ☙ Block totally rebuilt after the fire of 1835. 1835-1929.

Push-me-pull-you buildings had first presented façades to both Pearl and Stone Streets in Greek Revival brick and granite followed by the grand Italianate brownstone of the Hanover Bank (India House) today. They were joined over the next 94 years by:

[F27] New facades, **13-15 South William St.** and **57 Stone St.**, bet. Coenties Alley and Hanover Sq. **C.P.H. Gilbert.** No. 13, 1903. No. 15, 1908. ♺

F27

The stepped gables ape, at a larger scale, the houses of New Amsterdam, all of which have long since disappeared. The street-front gable allowed 17th century buildings to hoist goods to a storage attic, necessary in cellar-less Amsterdam, with its canals and high water table. Here it's just for fun.

[F28] New façade, **17 South William St.**, bet. Coenties Alley and Mill Lane. 1906. **Edward L. Tilton.** ♺

[F29] **Neo-Tudor Club**, 21-23 South William St., bet. Coenties Alley and Mill Lane. 1927-1928. **William Neil Smith.** ♺

Ornate, mock half-timbering here provided another cultural stage set for its original club members.

F29

[F30] **Chubb & Sons**, 54 Stone St., bet. Coenties Alley and Hanover Sq. 1919. **Arthur C. Jackson.** ♺

Steel and rivets append a modern cornice in scale with its neighbors.

[F31] **William H. McGee & Co.** (marine insurers), 9-11 South William St., bet. Coenties Alley and Mill Lane. 1929. **William Neil Smith.** ♺

Crisp limestone offices with some neo-Gothic gestures.

F31

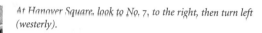

At Hanover Square, look to No. 7, to the right, then turn left (westerly).

F32

[F32] **7 Hanover Square** (offices), bet. Water and Pearl Sts. S side. 1982. **Norman Jaffe**, design architect. **Emery Roth & Sons**, architects.

Twenty-six stories of "Georgian" red brick and limestone-like lintels over 1,000+ windows, squatting atop an overscaled reinterpretation of **Frank Lloyd Wright**'s Midway Gardens. All of this is supposed to harmonize with the architecture of tiny, 3-story brownstone India House (whose air rights were trans-ferred), quietly minding its own business across narrow Pearl Street.

F33

[F33] **India House**/originally Hanover Bank, New York Cotton Exchange, and W. R. Grace & Company, 1 Hanover Sq., bet. Pearl and Stone Sts. 1851-1853. **Richard F. Carman**, carpenter.

A "Florentine palazzo," typical of many brownstone com-mercial buildings that once dotted this area, now replaced by newer and denser construction. Brownstone is so associated with the New York row house that we almost do a double take on seeing it clothing a Wall Street building; now a club, it har-bors a maritime museum. Handsome stripped-Corinthian columns. Carman, the carpenter (as he sometimes listed himself in the city directory), was later responsible for Carmansville, a village that stretched along Broadway from today's West 142nd to West 158th Streets.

[F34] **Hanover Square**, along Pearl St. bet. William and Hanover Sts. 1976.

Until the 1970s ancient Stone Street, with both curb lines intact, ran through this space. Now it is a pleasantly paved area that is a happy home to the seated bronze figure (1896, **George E. Bissel**) of **Abraham de Peyster**, a wealthy Dutch goldsmith; it had previously added to the clutter of Bowling Green.

Hanover Square was the original printing house square. At 81 Pearl, **William Bradford** established the first printing press in the colonies in 1693. The great fire of 1835 substantially destroyed all buildings in an area of which this square was the center: the area between Coenties Slip, Broad, Wall, and South Streets, excepting the row facing Broad, and those facing Wall between William and Broad.

F35

Five Corners: intersection of William, South William, Beaver Sts.

F36

[F35] **Banca Commerciale Italiana** (offices)/originally J.W. Seligman & Co. Building/later Lehman Brothers Building, 1 William St., SW cor. Hanover Sq. 1906-1907. **Francis H. Kimball & Julian C. Levi**. Alterations, 1929. **Harry R. Allen**.

Alteration and addition for Banca Commerciale Italiana, 1982-1986, **Gino Valle**, architect; **Jeremy P. Lang**, associate architect; **Fred L. Liebmann**, consulting architect.

A Renaissance Revival structure in stone, rusticated from sidewalk to cornice. Although regrettably divorced from its orig-inal windows, it is now happily married to a brilliant modernist addition that poetically harmonizes with many of its venerable architectural nuances.

[F36] **Delmonico's** (building and restaurant), 56 Beaver St., SW cor. South William St. 1891. **James Brown Lord**.
 Converted to condominiums, 1996. **Mark Kemeny**.

Occupying, like the Flatiron Building uptown, a valuable but awkward triangular space left between two converging streets. A distinguished restaurant for almost a century, this palatial head-quarters was designed by Lord at the height of Delmonico's prestige and popularity. Orange terra-cotta and brick; the porch columns were reputedly brought from Pompeii by the Delmonico brothers themselves for their previous location (burned down in the great fire of 1835).

Bear right (north) on William Street.

F37

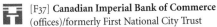 [F37] **Canadian Imperial Bank of Commerce** (offices)/formerly First National City Trust Company/originally the City Bank Farmers' Trust Company, 22 William St. (or 20 Exchange Pl.), bet. Beaver St., Exchange Place, and Hanover St. 1930-1931. **Cross & Cross.** ●⟋

A slender fifty-seven-story tower of limestone, from the awkward period of architectural history between buildings-as-columns and steel-cage construction: neo-Renaissance vs. Art Moderne.

Look up to see the Brobdingnagian coins—not quoins—that ring the building's limestone base.

Wall Street:

An area filled with history—and a host of historical plaques, markers, cornerstones, and notices of building erection, mostly in A.D. MCMXCVIII terms.

Wall Street*: The Dutch wall of 1653 (a palisade of wood palings) was built as protection against attack from English colonies to the north. The English took it down, but the name remains.*

Turn right (east) on Wall Street's south side to Pearl Street, make a U-turn, and return (west) on Wall Street's north side.

F38

[F38] **Regent Wall Street Hotel**/formerly First National City Bank/lower portion onetime U.S. Custom House (1863-1899)/originally Merchants' Exchange, 55 Wall St., bet. William and Hanover Sts, and Exchange Pl. 1836-1841. **Isaiah Rogers.** Converted to Custom House, 1863, **William A. Potter.** Remodeled and doubled in height, 1907-1910. **McKim, Mead & White.** ●⟋

Smoked granite. After the destruction of the first Merchants' Exchange in the great fire of 1835, **Rogers** erected on the same site a 3-story Greek Revival "temple" (the 12 Ionic columns are monolithic) with a central domed trading hall. Later used as the Custom House, it was remodeled in 1907 (after the Fed's

removal to Bowling Green) as the head office of the National City Bank: another tier of columns, this time Corinthian, was superimposed to double the cubic content.

To call it a grand hotel would belittle it. Its central space (dining and catering), the former main banking hall, is a facility unequaled in America.

The great hall of **McKim, Mead & White**'s First National City Bank has become the grand ballroom of the gourmand, and perhaps the gourmet.

F39

[F39] Originally **Seamen's Bank for Savings Headquarters** (offices), 74 Wall St., NW cor. Pearl St. 1926. **Benjamin Wistar Morris**.

Craggy ashlar with a tall round-arched opening into the banking room. A friendly, romantic addition to the cold Wall Street canyon.

[F40] **Beaver Building**/later New York Cocoa Exchange Building, 82-92 Beaver St./1 Wall St. Court, at Pearl St. (just south of Wall St.). 1903-1904. **Clinton & Russell**. 🖤

Glazed terra-cotta and brick above, neo-Renaissance cartouches below.

F40

[F41] **Morgan Bank Headquarters** (offices), 60 Wall St., bet. Pearl and William Sts. N side to Pine St. 1988. **Kevin Roche John Dinkeloo & Assocs**.

Planted on 1¼ acres is this massive 1.7 million-square-foot, 52-story tower, which not only reinterprets in contemporary terms the Classical column elements of base, shaft, and capital but almost literally replicates the column itself. The bold street-front arcade is meant to echo the forms of No. 55, across narrow Wall Street [F38]. The transfer of Citibank's air rights made possible the bulk on this side.

F41

[F42] **Bank of New York Building** (offices), 48 Wall St., NE cor. William St. 1928. **Benjamin Wistar Morris**. Conversion to condominiums, 1999. **Frank Williams & Associates**.

The banking room, particularly as seen through the large arched windows on both Wall and William Streets, is a special and serene space. Sadly you can enjoy the crowning Corinthian-columned temple and mounted bronze eagle only from afar (walk a bit down William Street). **Morris**' grandest New York

F42

effort was at the Cunard Building: again a magnificent interior behind a subdued façade.

Compare the coolness of this architecture with the same

architect's other, more romantic bank office building at the block's east end.

Buildings probably to be demolished for the proposed new Stock Exchange include the following [F 43] and [F 44]:

F43

[F43] **Apartments**/originally Atlantic Insurance Company, 45 Wall St., SW cor. William St. 1997. **Meltzer/Mendl Architects**.

A bland building grasps for distinction in its new residential posture with an elegant steel and glass marquee.

[F44] **Old Morgan Guaranty Building**, 37 Wall St. Bet. William and Broad Sts. ca. 1900.

A Beaux Arts façade of some pomp. In Paris it would be classed as *pompier* (or fireman) style, the dying extravagance of the late 19th century.

F44

[F45] **The Trump Building**/originally Bank of the Manhattan Company Building, 40 Wall St., bet. William and Broad Sts. 1929-1930. **H. Craig Severance**, architect. **Yasuo Matsui**, associate architect. **Shreve & Lamb**, consulting architects. ● Lobby and storefront alterations, 1997. **Der Scutt**.

A skyline bank building, now best observed from an upper floor of the composite bank to which it has moved its quarters: the Chase Manhattan on Chase Manhattan Plaza to the north. The pyramidal crown was the strong and simple symbol of the original bank. Chartered first as a water company (the Manhattan Company) and the city's first quasi-public utility, it sold its waterworks to the city in 1808. Always permitted by a clause in its charter to engage in banking, it continued solely as the Bank of the Manhattan Company, the latter, parent organization becoming incidental to its offshoot. (In the years following World War II this tower fell victim to a collision by a small airplane.)

F45

[F46] **Federal Hall National Memorial**/formerly U.S. Subtreasury Building (1862-1925)/originally U.S. Custom House (1842-1862), 28 Wall St., NE cor. Nassau St. 1833-1842. **Town & Davis**, architects. **Samuel Thompson**, builder, succeeded by **William Ross** and **John Frazee**. ●

F46

Interior ● . Open to the public: Mo-Fr 9-5; closed Sa & Su. 212-264-8711.

No, **George Washington** did not take his oath of office in front of this building but, rather, its predecessor, the former city hall, renamed Federal Hall. It had been remodeled by **Pierre L'Enfant** from the old shell, to which local government had been removed in 1701 from the Dutch Stadt Huys on Pearl Street. The current name, Federal Hall National Memorial, commemorates the earlier structure.

This Doric-columned temple and Staten Island's Sailors' Snug Harbor are the institutional stars of New York's Greek

Revival The Wall Street façade is a simplified Parthenon, without the sculptured frieze or pediment. Carved from marble quarried in Westchester County, it is raised on a high base to handle the change in grade from Pine to Wall. Inside the rectangular volume is a very non-Greek rotunda, the principal, and startling, space—rather like finding a cubical space in a helical conch shell.

The old Assay Office (1823, **Martin Thompson**) stood to the east until the building was demolished to make room for bigger things; its façade was rescued and is currently to be seen at the Metropolitan Museum's American Wing.

J(ohn) Q(uincy) A(dams) Ward's statue of Washington (1883) stands on the approximate spot where the man himself took the oath, in 1789.

Broad Street: South of Wall Street

[F47] **Morgan Guaranty Trust Company**/formerly J. P. Morgan & Company, 23 Wall St., SE cor. Broad St. 1913. **Trowbridge & Livingston.**

Interesting more for its history than its architecture: J. Pierpont Morgan epitomized Wall Street to capitalists, communists, radicals, and conservatives alike. And, of course, when Wall Street was to be bombed, this was considered its sensitive center of control: on September 16, 1920, an anarchist ignited a wagonload of explosives next to the Wall Street flank. 33 persons were killed, 400 injured. The scars remain visible in the stonework.

F48

[F48] **New York Stock Exchange**, 8 Broad St., bet. Wall St. and Exchange Pl. W side. 1901-1903. **George B. Post.**
 Pediment sculpture, **J.Q.A. Ward** and **Paul Bartlett.** Open to the public: Use 20 Broad St. entry. Addition, 1923, **Trowbridge & Livingston.**

One of the few great architectural spaces accessible to the public in this city. The original Roman temple façade by Post is a far cry from his Queen Anne style Brooklyn Historical Society 22 years before. The Columbian Exposition of 1893 had swept such earth-colored picturesque architecture under the rug. The rage for neo-Classical architecture and cities was compelling even to those who had been the Goths of architecture. The original mythological figures of the pediment became so deteriorated that their stone was replaced with sheet metal, secretively, so that the public would not know that any facet of the Stock Exchange was vulnerable.

The Trading Floor Center (1998, **Asymptote**) is a marvel of both technology in action, and the technological architecture surrounding the action.

F49

[F49] **The Exchange** (apartments), 25 Broad St., SE cor. Exchange Pl. 1899. **Robert Maynicke.** Revised, 1900. **Clinton & Russell.** Condominium conversion, 1998. **Costas Kondylis.**

Worthy of the best on Park Avenue, this stalwart housing for finance (once headquarters of the City Investing Company) now houses the apartments of Wallstreeters.

F50

[F50] **Bank of America International** (offices)/originally Lee-Higginson Bank, 37-41 Broad St., bet. Exchange Pl. and Beaver St. E side. 1929. **Cross & Cross. Frieze, Leo Friedlander,** sculptor.

This chaste convex bow that follows Broad Street's curve is a comforting gesture. Contrary to what usually transpires during a building boom, this 9-story structure replaced the 26-story Trust Company of America Building (1907, **Francis H. Kimball**).

F51

[F51] Wall Street Kitchen & Bar/originally American Bank Note Company Headquarters, 70 Broad St., bet. Marketfield and Beaver Sts. W side. 1908. **Kirby, Petit & Green.** Restoration of exterior, 1996. **Joseph Pell Lombardi.** Conversion to restaurant/bar, 1996. **Ingrid Hustvedt.**

Look up to see the true swelling of Classical columns: an elegant small palazzo now offering food and drink.

Back up Broad Street's hill—its wide part was the site of the Curb Exchange, meeting indoors on Trinity Place since 1921 as the American Stock Exchange. The Curb's brokers literally met on the curb, out of doors, between 1865 and 1921.

Take a left (west) back on Wall Street.

[F52] Bankers Trust Company Building (offices), 14 Wall St., NW cor. Nassau St. 1910-1912. **Trowbridge & Livingston.** Addition, 1931-1933. **Shreve, Lamb & Harmon.**

The stepped pyramid, later logo of the resident bank, tops one of the grand skyline finials of the city. When built, it was called the world's tallest structure (540 feet) on the smallest plot (94 × 97 feet). The pyramid is invisible from the sidewalk.

F52

Broadway, at the head of Wall Street.

[F53] Bank of New York/originally Irving Trust Company (offices), 1 Wall St., SE cor. Broadway. 1928-1932. **Ralph Walker** of **Voorhees, Gmelin & Walker.** Addition to S, 1965, **Smith, Smith, Haines, Lundberg & Waehler.**

Ralph Walker's experiments in the plastic molding of skyscraper form, both in massing and in detail, culminate in this shimmering limestone tower, a fitting companion of quality to Trinity Church across Broadway. Don't miss the lobby, which resonates to the same Art Deco melodies. Now, as for the annex, that's another matter.

[F54] Trinity Church (Episcopal), Broadway at the head of Wall St. W side. 1839-1846. **Richard Upjohn.** William Backhouse Astor Memorial Altar and Reredos, 1876-1877. **Frederick Clarke Withers.** All Saints Chapel, 1911-1913. **Thomas Nash.** Bishop William T. Manning Memorial Wing, 1965. **Adams & Woodbridge.** Churchyard. 1681.

Nestled in the canyons of Broadway and Trinity Place, Trinity's form is totally comprehensible to the pedestrian: on the axis of Wall Street the canyon walls read as surfaces, while Trinity sits importantly, a crisp brownstone, bedded in a green baize cemetery. The cemetery offers a green retreat for summer-tired office workers at noontime. Bronze doors designed by Richard Morris Hunt (donated in memory of John Jacob Astor III) were executed by Charles Niehaus, Karl Bitter, and J. Massey Rhind (left entrance, main entrance, and right entrance, respectively) from 1890 to 1896.

F54

Cemetery monuments of particular note include the pyramid of **Alexander Hamilton**, **Robert Fulton**'s bronze bas-relief, and that of **William Bradford.**

The attached chapel must not be confused with Trinity's "colonial" chapels, which were separate and remotely located church buildings serving this immense Episcopal parish. Typical of the latter is St. Paul's Chapel at Fulton and Broadway. The parish is an enormous landowner (Fulton to Christopher Streets; Broadway west to the river was its original grant from Queen Anne in 1705). Thus, the proselytizing of the faith through missionary activities could be financed comfortably (St. Augustine's and St. Christopher's Chapels on the Lower East Side are further examples).The original Trinity Church was founded in 1696, erected in 1698, enlarged and "beautified" in

F55

F56

1737, and burned to the ground in 1776. A second building, constructed in 1788-1790, was demolished in 1839.

[F55] **Trinity and U.S. Realty Buildings** (offices), 111 and 115 Broadway, straddling Thames St. W. side. 1904-1907. Both by **Francis H. Kimball** Renovated 1988-1989. **Swanke Hayden Connell**.

Rich buildings from top to bottom. their narrow ends at Broadway are broken Gothic forms with strongly scaled details. They have a great deal of personality vis-à-vis the passing pedestrian. Unlike the blank austerity of 1 Wall, the temple entrance of 100 Broadway, or the modern openness of Chase Manhattan's vast transparent lobby for bureaucrats en masse, these are buildings for individual people. Many feel possessive about them.

[F56] Onetime **Bank of Tokyo**/originally American Surety Company, 100 Broadway, SE cor. Pine St. 1895. **Bruce Price**. Alterations, 1921, **Herman Lee Meader**. 1975, **Kajima International**, designers. **Welton Becket Assocs.**, architects.

Kajima, through designer **Nobutaka Ashihara**, recycled **Price**'s "rusticated pillar" into modern and economic elegance. The Italians excelled at this in the 1950s (as at the Castello Sforzesco in Milan, converted to a museum); the Japanese now equal the Italians' best in New York. The ladies above, by sculptor **J. Massey Rhind**, are a stern Athenian octet. Tenancy in flux.

[F57] **Wall Street Subway Station**, IRT Lexington Avenue Line, under Broadway at Wall St. 1905. **Heins & La Farge**. Redesigned, 1979, **NYC Transit Authority Architectural Staff**.

A restrained **Heins & La Farge** design upgraded by the TA in full height, ultramarine blue glazed brick. (If you're feeling blue, don't venture here.) The restored, golden oak and bronze change booth on the downtown side is a minor bow to the past.

F58

[F58] **Empire Apartments**/originally Empire Building, 71 Broadway, SW cor. Rector St. to Trinity Pl. 1895-1898. **Francis Kimball** of **Kimball & Thompson**. An ornate wall, it forms a backdrop to Trinity Churchyard to the north. U.S. Steel managed its empire from here, 1901-1976. Now its resident Wallstreeters can savor the Trinity greensward to the north. The entrance is a triumphant Roman ensemble.

Financier Russell Sage was almost assassinated in 1891 in an older Empire Building that occupied this spot before replacement by this Empire Building. He quickly threw his male secretary at the bomber, muffling the intended damage to himself but almost killing his secretary. Sage withstood his assistant's law suit and died very rich. His widow later established the Russell Sage philanthropies, among them Forest Hills Gardens.

F59

[F59] Now **J. J. Kenny/Standard & Poors Building**, originally American Railway Express Company Building (offices), 65 Broadway, bet. Exchange Alley and Rector St. W side to Trinity Pl. 1914-1919. **Renwick Aspinwall & Tucker**. Altered, 1979, **Carl J. Petrilli**.

An H-plan results in a pair of slender 23-story wings, embracing (and arching over) light courts fore and aft. Note the asymmetric eagle on the lower arch and the symmetric one on the arch atop the building.

F60

[F60] **One Exchange Plaza** (offices), Broadway SW cor. Exchange Alley to Trinity Pl. 1982-1984. **Fox & Fowle**. [F61] **45 Broadway Atrium** (offices), bet. Exchange Alley and Morris St. W side to Trinity Pl. 1983. **Fox & Fowle**.

A pair of sleek, exquisitely detailed, brick and glass towers by the same developer (HRO International) and architects. They would never have been separate structures were it not for the exorbitant price asked by the tiny fast-food holdout between. Note the brickwork mural on the wall facing the Atrium's windows—to appease those whose view is north.

Take a right (west) down the narrow, repaved brick Exchange Alley to Trinity Place, and turn right (north).

F62

[F62] Originally **American Express Company** (warehouse), 46 Trinity Pl., bet. Exchange Alley and Rector St. W side. ca. 1880.

Note the terra-cotta seal (now weather-beaten and painted) with the company emblem in relief. A façade of brick arches redolent of pre-skyscraper New York.

[F63] **Trinity Place Bridge**, Trinity Parish, linking Trinity Churchyard and 74 Trinity Pl. Trinity Pl. bet. Rector and Thames Sts. 1987. **Lee Harris Pomeroy Assocs.**

As Trinity's congregation grew older and traffic on Trinity Place greater, the church felt a need to separate its aging parishioners commuting to their activity rooms across the street at No. 74 from the danger of cars, trucks, and bicycles. This 80-foot-long bridge is the answer.

F63

[F64] Originally NYU Graduate School of Business Administration: Originally **Nichols Hall, NYU Graduate School of Business Administration**, 100 Trinity Place bet. Thames and Cedar Sts. W side. 1959. **Skidmore, Owings & Merrill.**

[F65] Originally Charles E. Merrill Hall, NYU Graduate School of Business Administration/now **High School**, 90 Trinity Place, SW cor. Thames St. 1975. **Skidmore, Owings & Merrill.**

A pair, connected by an enclosed bridge high over Thames Street. Stylish in 1959, the northerly Nichols has, in retrospect, become a dull, white-speckled brick ancestor to the off-black Merrill monolith to the south, a classic background Modernist monument.

F64

Turn into Thames Street between the two NYU buildings, and walk west; zigzag left on Greenwich and right (west) again on Albany street to the last stops on the tour.

[F66] **90 West Street Building** (offices), bet. Albany and Cedar Sts. E side. 1907. **Cass Gilbert.**

Limestone and cast terra-cotta. Increasingly interesting and complex the higher you raise your eyes: designed for a view from the harbor or the eyries of an adjacent skyscraper, rather than the ordinary West Street pedestrian. A similar, but less successful, use of terra-cotta than **Gilbert**'s spectacular Woolworth Building.

In 1985 the upper-floor colonnades and mansard roof were brightly lighted, surprising many people who had never given this building any notice.

F66

The Hudson-Fulton Celebration 1609-1909, as part of the fall festivities, illuminated many of the city's prominent buildings and bridges—not with floodlights but with necklaces of bare electric bulbs, then a relatively new technique.

END of Tour A. The nearest subways are in the World Trade Center (Old IRT Seventh Avenue Line Cortland Street Station (Nos. 1 and 9 trains), old BMT Broadway Line (N and R trains), or the old IND Eighth Avenue Line, Chambers Street/World Trade Center Station (C and E trains).

WATER STREET CORRIDOR

Lower Manhattan's Street of Million-Square-Foot Towers.

Under **Mayor Robert F. Wagner**, City Planning Commission chairman **William F. R. Ballard** commissioned the Lower Manhattan Plan of 1966, prepared by **Wallace McHarg Associates** and **Whittlesey, Conklin & Rossant**. It promised a lively and handsome pedestrian world south of Canal Street, foot-eased by small and unnoxious electric buses and enlarged through landfill to the pierhead line. New residential communities surrounding riverside plazas—"windows on the waterfront"—would be provided. With some adjustments, detours, and compromises we have the World Trade Center, Battery Park City, and a new Lower Manhattan skyline of million-square-foot, flat-topped boxes that line the Water Street Corridor.

From the harbor and the Brooklyn Heights Promenade it is these towers, the ones along Water Street and others, that have come to encircle the Financial District's heart. They have muffled from view the constellation of tall, slender, 1920s and 1930s Art Deco office buildings and the flamboyant pinnacles of their earlier, shorter, neo-Classical cousins, the structures that made up the inspired—if unplanned— Lower Manhattan skyline that was once the world-renowned symbol of New York City.

Walking Tour B: A Water Street walk northward from the Staten Island Ferry Terminal to South Street Seaport, at Fulton and Water Streets. START in Peter Minuit Plaza in front of the ferry terminal. (No. 1 or 9 train to South Ferry, N or R train to Whitehall Street Station. Alternates: A short walk from the start are the 4 and 5 trains at the Bowling Green Station or the 2 and 3 trains at the Wall Street Station. When leaving the alternates, ask which way to the ferry terminal.)

Before embarking up Water Street, spend a moment in front of the ferry terminal:

Staten Island Ferry, foot of Whitehall and State Streets at Battery Park, not only ranks as a tourist mecca of great delight but also explains the overall arrangement of the water-bound city quickly, clearly, and with pleasure. You will experience, for free, one of the world's greatest (and shortest) water voyages, through the richly endowed harbor, past buoys, the West Bank Light House, Governors and Liberty Islands, and the U.S. Army Military Ocean Terminal (the old Bayonne naval base), to the community of St. George at Staten Island's northeastern shore. (If you decide to stay, turn to the Staten Island section of this guide. Otherwise, just travel the ferry route in reverse.) This is the low-income substitute for a glamorous arrival in New York by transatlantic liner, receiving first Liberty's salute and then the dramatic silhouette of Lower Manhattan's skyline. On a lucky day you will surge through the wake of freighters, container ships, tankers, tugs, sludge boats, pleasure craft, and the few extant liners used for cruises—and maybe even an occasional warship.

[W1] **Staten Island Ferry Terminal**, City of New York, South St. foot of Whitehall St. 1954. **Roberts & Schaefer**, consulting engineers.

The terminal continues to rank as the world's most banal portal to joy (a public rest room en route to Mecca). Kafka would have had the shivers, although regular users seem inured to its bile-colored shortcomings. A blight on the celebration of arrival and departure at a great city, soon, one hopes, to be remedied by **Schwartz Architects** with **Ron Evitts** and **TAMS**.

WATER STREET CORRIDOR AND SOUTH STREET SEAPORT

see pages 24–37

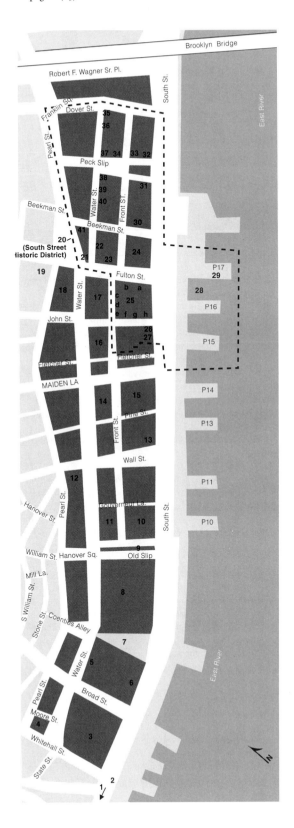

W2

Upstream from the ferry terminal is another, older ferry terminal:

W2

[W2] **Battery Maritime Building, NYC Department of Ports International Trade & Commerce**, originally Municipal Ferry Piers, NYC Department of Docks & Ferries, 11 South St., foot of Whitehall St. S side. 1906-1909. **Walker & Morris.** ●

The false front on these aging ferry slips presents a raised porch with 40-foot columns to Whitehall. Green paint over sheet metal and steel structural members simulates verdigris copper. The Governors Island ferry leaves from here. The only historical style that this inherits is the very idea of a colonnade; the columns, however, are original and relate to the material, sheet metal. Note particularly the Guastavino tile vaults under the porch roof.

Ferry service to most points in Brooklyn ended on March 15, 1938.

Find Water Street in the leaky open space that bears the Peter Minuit name, and proceed northeasterly. It's the wide street one full block inland from the river.

Water Street: curving version (towers cheek by jowl) of midtown's Avenue of the Americas (Sixth Avenue).

W3

[W3] **1 New York Plaza** (offices), Whitehall St. bet. South, Water and Broad Sts. 1969. **William Lescaze & Assocs.**, design architects. **Kahn & Jacobs**, architects. Plaza reconfiguration, 1990s.

A behemoth. Thousands of interior decorators' picture frames form an unhappy façade on this all too prominent, dark, brooding office tower. Some aggressive light standards have recently been added to guard the occupants.

[W4] **3 New York Plaza** (offices)/originally U.S. Army Building, 39 Whitehall St., bet. Water, Pearl, and Moore Sts. 1886. **S. D. Hatch**. Reconstructed and reclad, 1986, **Wechsler, Grasso & Menziuso**.

Concealed inches behind that slick green-and-white graph paper curtain wall is the masonry ghost of the building where hundreds of thousands of army inductees took their physical for World War II and Korea. Occupying an entire (small) city block, it rests on the original foundations of the 1861 Produce Exchange, by **Leopold Eidlitz**.

W4

[W5] **4 New York Plaza** (offices), Water St. bet. Broad St. and Vietnam Veterans Memorial Plaza (old Coenties Slip). S side. 1968. **Carson, Lundin & Shaw**.

[W6] **2 New York Plaza** (offices)/briefly American Express Plaza, 125 Broad St. NW cor. South St. 1970. **Kahn & Jacobs**.

Twenty-two-story No. 4, Manufacturers Hanover Trust's handsomely carved monolith of rich earth-toned salt-and-pepper speckled brick, is the earliest of the New York Plaza giants. Its careful choice of materials and details was meant to harmonize in quality, if not in scale, with the tiny Federal and Greek Revival survivors that were still its neighbors in the 1960s. Those survivors (except the Fraunces Tavern Block [see F24, p. 14]) and the color scheme rapidly gave way to non-ideas like the 40-story No. 2.

W5

Coenties Slip: As the landfill crept seaward, this "slip," a tiny artificial bay for wharfing ships, was created with a diagonal breakwater paralleling the present west boundary. Eventually the breakwater was absorbed, as land projected even beyond its former tip.

[W7] **New York Vietnam Veterans Memorial**, Vietnam Veterans Plaza/earlier Jeanette Plaza/originally Jeanette Park, on the bed of Coenties Slip bet. Water and South Sts. Jeanette Plaza, 1972, **M. Paul Friedberg & Assocs**. Memorial added, 1985. **William Britt Fellows**, **Peter Wormser**, architects. **Joseph Ferrandino**, writer.

A 70-foot-long, 14-foot-high rectangular prism surfaced in 12-inch-square glass blocks, lined with a granite shelf for visitors' offerings, and penetrated by two unadorned portals. The glass blocks, made luminescent by night, are etched with excerpts from speeches, news dispatches, and letters written home by those who were fighting in Nam. Chosen in a national competition, the winner is simple, thoughtful, carefully detailed, and neatly executed. But in sharp contrast to the emotionally powerful Vietnam Memorial in Washington (also a national competition winner), New York's fails to touch the heart.

W7

[W8] **55 Water Street** (offices), bet. Coenties and Old Slips. SE side to South St. 1972. **Emery Roth & Sons**, architects. Terrace over South St., **M. Paul Friedberg & Assocs**., landscape architects.

With 3.68 million square feet, it was the world's largest private office building when opened. But awkward. The deal for its bulk, arrived at through zoning modifications, also financed the redesigned Jeanette Plaza [see above]. A 1990s canopy swoops out and up, providing a new entrance identity for the taxiing executive.

Take the up-escalator between its south and north wings to visit its own elevated plaza.

W8

At Old Slip, turn right (southeasterly).

[W9] **New York City Landmarks Preservation Commission Offices**, originally 1st Precinct, NYC Police Department, 100 Old Slip, bet. Front and South Sts. N side. 1909-1911. **Hunt & Hunt**. 🖤✦

A rusticated Renaissance Revival palazzo, miniature in size, majestic in scale. It's considered the city's first modern police station.

W9

[W10] **1 Financial Square** (offices), Front St. bet. Old Slip and Gouverneur Lane to South St. 1987. **Edward Durell Stone Assocs**.

One million square feet. Trading on the transfer of development rights from two low-rise neighbors, a demolished fire station (whose functions are now enveloped within the skyscraper) and 100 Old Slip [see above], this 36-story high rise is built on the former site of the U.S. Assay Building [see Necrology].

W10

W11

W12

W13

Financial Square's stone-clad base is supposed to harmonize with the stonework of the old station house.

Back to Water Street.

[W11] **77 Water Street Building** (offices), bet. Old Slip and Gouverneur Lane. E side to Front St. 1970. **Emery Roth & Sons**, architects. Street, level and roof elements, **Corchia-de Harak Assocs.**, designers.

A simple, sleek, workmanlike building that simultaneously delivers class and economic success. Thanks to developer Mel Kaufman, the street-level pools and bridges and an old-fashioned "candy store" under the arcade add a bit of eccentric pedestrianism to the neighborhood.

[W12] **Barclay Bank Building and Park**, 75 Wall St., bet. Water and Pearl Sts. side. 1987. **Welton Becket Assocs**.

A deep, generous entrance arch through a flamed granite base offers a promise, but the flat detailing above doesn't deliver. The park provides the obligatory waterfall, but little to promote pedestrian serenity.

A peek at the foot of Wall Street:

[W13] **120 Wall Street** (offices), NW cor. South St. to Pine St. 1930. Office of **Ely Jacques Kahn**.

A powerful, symmetric, wedding cake silhouette. Very early for a large commercial building to brave a relatively inaccessible East River site. A Wall Street address and the nearby Second and Third Avenue elevated on Pearl Street, still operating in the 1930s, helped.

R.M.S. Queen Elizabeth Monument: *Bronze letters from the majestic British ocean liner that sank in Hong Kong waters on January 9, 1972, are preserved in the plaza south of Wall Street Plaza, as is a bronzed telegram from Kurt Waldheim when secretary-general of the United Nations. The adjoining sculpture is Disk and Slab (1973, Yuyu Yang).*

[W14] **Wall Street Plaza** (offices)/originally 88 Pine Street Building, bet. Water St., Maiden Lane and Front St. 1973. **I. M. Pei & Assocs**.

W14

A white, crisp elegance of aluminum and glass (no mullions; one of the earliest examples here of butted glass that fills whole structural bays). Water Street's classiest building.

W15

A detour of a short block to the right (east) along Maiden Lane will reveal:

[W15] **Continental Center** (offices), 180 Maiden Lane to Pine St., Front to South Sts. 1983. **Swanke Hayden Connell & Partners**.

One million square feet. A deceptively suave but actually tacky green monster with a greenhouse base, a project of the Rockefeller Center Development Corporation. (The resemblance to Rockefeller Center ends with the developer's name.)

[W16] Originally **National Westminster Bank USA** (offices), 175 Water St., bet. Fletcher St. and John St. S side to Front St. 1983. **Fox & Fowle**.

Half a million square feet. Mirrored glass cylinders (there are two) in the embrace of the brick-and-glass horizontal-strip-window jaws of the rest. Neither fox nor fowl.

(During excavation for this building the remains of a mid 1700s ship were found buried in the landfill. It had been scuttled to act as a cofferdam for late 18th-century earthmoving operations. The prow was successfully salvaged and removed to Mariners' Museum in Newport News, Va.)

W16

[W17] **1 Seaport Plaza** (offices), 199 Water St., to Front St. bet. John and Fulton Sts. 1983. **Swanke Hayden Connell & Partners**.

One million square feet. Developer **Jack Resnick & Sons'** "first contextual office building." Its main façades were designed to differ from one another, ostensibly to address the glitzier obligations of a Water Street frontage on the inland side, while granting low-scale Schermerhorn Row its due on Front Street. The height of 1 Seaport Plaza: 34 stories; the height of Schermerhorn Row: 4 stories plus. Contextual?

W18

[W18] **127 John Street Building** (offices), NW cor. Water St. to Fulton and Pearl Sts. 1969. **Emery Roth & Sons**. Lobby, plaza, street level, and mechanical floor elements, **Corchia-de Harak Assocs.**, designers.

A no-nonsense building with a happy nonsense-filled lobby and sidewalk. Outside, pipe and canvas structures play with light and shelter pedestrians. An adjacent electric display clock is a building in its own right. Developer **Mel Kaufman** is the person to thank.

The Edison Electric Illuminating Company's first large-scale, permanent commercial power and incandescent lighting system began operations on Monday, September 4, 1882, from a generating station located at 255-257 Pearl Street, between John and Fulton Streets. The area serviced included nearly a square mile, enclosed by Wall, Nassau, Spruce, and Ferry Streets, Peck Slip, and the East River. The generator ran until 1890, when it was partially destroyed by fire.

[W19] **Seaport Tower** (offices), 40 Fulton St. bet. Pearl and Cliff Sts. 1989. **Fox & Fowle**.

A slender articulated office tower that erased a 1-story McDonald's. A lively neighbor to many bland buildings surrounding.

END of Tour B. For refreshments, you couldn't be in a better place, at the gateway to South Street Seaport. And if you're in the mood for more touring, see the South Street section, below. Otherwise, the closest subways are along Fulton Street in a complex, interconnected Fulton Street/Broadway-Nassau Station: including A,C,J,M,Z,2,3,4,5 trains.

W19

SOUTH STREET SEAPORT

At the north end of boulevard-wide Water Street—at Fulton Street it reverts to its 50-foot width—lies the South Street Seaport area. The enclave of low-rise, small-scale structures—some dating to the 18th century, others new—owes its survival to a number of events: 1) the establishment of the South Street Seaport Museum, spearheaded by **Peter Stanford**, in 1967; 2) the subsequent banking of the area's air-rights development potential, later to be purchased by property owners to the south, where whopping office towers now stand; 3) the State of New York's purchase of the Schermerhorn Row block in 1974; 4) a series of official landmark designations; and 5) the establishment, in cooperation with the City's Public Development Corporation, of a "festival marketplace" by the Rouse Company.

Transfer of development rights over buildings that occupy less bulk than zoning allows became a favored technique in the superheated 1980s. At South Street, the area encompassed by the transfer spanned a number of blocks—normally it includes merely a number of lots.

Ships, Lower East Side, 1840s

The South Street air-rights banking strategy, supported by influential board members of the museum, worked hand in hand with real estate interests attempting to contain northward growth of the Financial District. By limiting supply in an era of great demand, they sought—and, in the end, achieved—higher land values in Manhattan's toe. After a tentative period marked by sporadic designations of individual structures in the South Street area, the Landmarks Preservation Commission acted decisively in 1977 and designated an (almost) all-embracing historic district. Entry to the Seaport area is best achieved by walking toward the East River on Fulton Street. (The nearest subway stop is the rabbit warren of interconnected Fulton Street/ Broadway-Nassau Stations of the A, C, J, M, Z, 2, 3, 4, 5 trains.)

Orientation: The thoroughfare called South Street is literally at the south flank of Manhattan Island, where the adjacent (and parallel) East River runs very roughly an east-west course (more pronounced above the Brooklyn Bridge). Logically, streets in this area that are perpendicular to perimeter South Street have (very roughly) east and west sides. For our purposes, and to tie this grid to the remainder, South Street will be considered running north and south, according to popular, but mildly inaccurate, convention.

Shop, shop, shop! Buy, buy, buy! Eat, eat, eat! As commendable as the preservation of the South Street Seaport area generally is, incessant invitations to spend are quite intrusive: tourist baubles, T-shirts, fast food, as well as tonier items and pricey meals. Built with enormous municipal, state, and federal subsidies, like its clones in Boston and Baltimore, this festival marketplace caters primarily to middle-class families, yuppies, and the Financial District singles set, imparting to the development a theme-park quality at odds with the true grit that the waterfront and the fish market once had.

[W20] **South Street Seaport Historic District**, an irregular L-shaped area including parts of both sides of South St. from the East River waters below Pier 15 (including Piers 15, 16, and 17); then on a line W to Front St. bet. the S frontage of John St./Burling Slip and Fletcher St., N on Front St. to Fulton St., W along Fulton to Water then Pearl Sts. and on to Dover St. 🍎

    Ada Louise Huxtable's *Classic New York* warned in 1964 of the rapid demise of the physical vestiges of the city's 18th- and 19th-century waterfront heritage, much of which was still visible on South Street, the wide thoroughfare along the sheltered, narrow (relative to the Hudson) East River. This area, radiating out from the intersection of Fulton and South Streets, became the city's last holdout against mass demolition; its survivors evoke that period of commercial development which was generated by the city's role as a great domestic and international port.

Manhattan ever widening: The mucky shore became hard-edged and then was pushed outward, the new profile delicately balancing the needs of ships with those of shippers. Wild hills were tamed, and the earth from early cellar holes—and, much later, from deeper skyscraper excavations—was carted to the island's edge. Early on, Pearl Street (after the mother-of-pearl shells with which it was paved) marked the East River shore. As water lots were filled, the names of newly created streets reflected their succession to the perimeter: first Water Street, then Front, and finally—at least for now—South Street.

W21

[W21] **Titanic Memorial Lighthouse**, in Titanic Memorial Park, Fulton St. bet. Pearl and Water Sts. N side. Installed, 1976, **Charles Evans Hughes III**. ☞

    Originally installed in 1913, by public subscription, atop the Seamen's Church Institute Building overlooking the East River at South Street and what was then Jeanette Park. Visible from the river, it signaled noon to ships in the harbor with the falling of a black ball, at a signal received from Washington. It was taken down upon its host's demolition in 1968 and stored on a pier by the Seaport Museum until reerected here.

South Street Seaport Museum Block:
Water to Front Streets, between Fulton and Beekman Streets.

🏛 [W22a] **207-211 Water Street** (warehouses), bet. Beekman and Fulton Sts. E side. 1835-1837. ☞

    Greek Revival granite piers support austere, but elegant, brick bearing walls, with granite lintels and slender muntined

W22a

W22b   W23

double-hung sash. They are adaptively reused storehouses: No. 207, the Museum Visitors' Center; No. 209, the Museum Books and Charts Store; No. 211 is Bowne & Co. Stationers, the Museum's 19th-century print shop, where old techniques and equipment are still employed, to visitors' delight.

[W22b] Originally **A. A. Thompson & Company** (metals warehouse), 213-215 Water St., bet. Beekman and Fulton Sts. E side. 1868. **Stephen D. Hatch**. ⟁ Restored, **Beyer Blinder Belle**, 1983.

No. 213-215, large-scaled and glassy, has been the Seaport Gallery, an exhibition space.

Cannon's Walk:
A passageway between 19 Fulton Street, W of Front to 206 Front Street, N of Fulton.

[W23] **The "Bogardus" Building**, 15-19 Fulton St., NW cor. Front St. 1977-1983. **Beyer Blinder Belle**. ⟁

Perhaps the result of the first building ever physically stolen. It was this site that was chosen for the reerection of ironmonger **James Bogardus'** demountable cast-iron façade (removed from the warehouse that stood at Washington and Murray Streets). Later purloined from the safekeeping of the Landmarks Preservation Commission, it was melted down by the perpetrators. With the façade elements gone, the architects attempted to suggest its color, texture, rhythms, and proportions, using similar—but not identical—iron and/or steel materials. This successful effort—the wire-glass wraparound canopy is a particularly welcome addition—is made even more impressive because this building needed to enclose an existing 3-story IND subway ventilation structure, which remained in operation during construction.

[W24] Originally **Fulton Market Building**, 11 Fulton St., bet. Front and South Sts. N side to Beekman St. 1983. Benjamin Thompson & Assocs. ⟁ Open to the public. Under renovation.

W24

Echoing the vivacious spirit of the original 1883 Fulton Market Building, which stood on this block until razed in 1948, is this articulate essay, inside and out, of marketplace architecture. Its exterior, wrapped with a massive suspended iron canopy redolent of its predecessors, is intricate without being fussy; its majestic interior is filled with activity day and night. A tribute to the Rouse Company, who commissioned it as their initial addition to the Seaport area, to their architects, and to the Landmarks Preservation Commission, who recognized its genuine appropriateness.

Streetscape: A particularly satisfying aspect of the Seaport Historic District is the use of substantial materials underfoot: Belgian block street pavement modulated by slabs of granite that evoke the horsedrawn era, with bluestone sidewalks and re-creations of varying lamppost designs of 19th-century Manhattan.

W25

All this is a result of Benjamin Thompson & Assocs.' working closely with operating and regulatory City agencies.

[W25] **The Schermerhorn Row block**, 2-18 Fulton St., 189-195 Front St., 159-171 John Sts., 91-92 South St. 1811-1849. Variously altered and expanded. [W25a] **Schermerhorn Row (east part)**, 2-12 Fulton St., SW cor. South St., and 92-93 South St., bet. Fulton and John Sts. W side. 1811. Altered and expanded. [W25b] **Schermerhorn Row (west part)**, 14-18 Fulton St., SE cor. Front St. 1812. 191 Front St., bet. Fulton and John Sts. E side. 1812. Variously altered and expanded. Both parts restored, 1983, **Jan Hird Pokorny**. Storefront consultants, **Cabrera-Barricklo**.

Peter Schermerhorn filled the land on these, his "water lots," to a point 600 feet out from the original shoreline and built his row in two stages a year apart. Served by these buildings, among many others, South Street was lined with ships, parked bowsprits in, oversailing the wheeled, hoofed, and pedestrian traffic below. (The bulkhead was at approximately the line of the west, or inner, row of columns supporting the highway viaduct.)

These were originally Georgian-Federal ware- and counting-houses, with high-pitched, loft-enclosing roofs, built as an investment by the Schermerhorn family. No storefronts at first: arched business entries of brownstone, quoined, and double-hung windows for light and air; only later did show windows appear at street level. Soon Greek Revival granite and cast-iron shopfronts brought a merchandising cast to serve the great crowds brought here, beginning in 1814, by the stream-powered Fulton Ferry from Brooklyn. **To eat and drink:** North Star Pub (South Street corner), Sloppy Louie's (South Street).

W25c

[W25c] **191 and 193 Front St.** (lofts), bet. Fulton and John Sts. E side. Before 1793[?]. Altered and expanded upward, 19th century. Restored, 1983, **Jan Hird Pokorny**.

The oldest on the block but not visibly so, since their fronts were drastically altered in the mid and late 19th century.

John Street between Front and South Streets widens to twice its normal dimension as a result of its earlier configuration as Burling Slip, an inlet for ships off the East River. In 1835 the slip was filled in.

W25d,e

[W25d] Originally **Josiah Macy & Son** (shipping and commission house), 189 Front St., bet. John and Fulton Sts. E side (also known as 159-165 John St.). [W25e] Originally Mackle, **Oakley & Jennison** (grocers), 181 Front St., NE cor. John St. (also known as 159-163 John St.). Both behind Schermerhorn Row. No. 181 expanded upward, 1917. Restored, 1983, **Jan Hird Pokorny**.

A pair of Greek Revival commercial structures built when Burling Slip was filled in, their façades offering the pattern on which easterly neighbor No. 165 was refaced.

South Street, 1830s

W25f

IIII [W25f] **Children's Center, South Street Seaport Museum**, 165 John St., N side bet. Front and South Sts., behind Schermerhorn Row. 1811. Rebuilt, late 1830s-1840s. 🍎 ♂ Restored, 1983, **Jan Hird Pokorny**.

Following its reconstruction, it assumed a Greek Revival façade like its western neighbor. But, unlike its neighbor, it was never increased in height, so the original fascia, cornice, and roof line are all there.

W25g

IIII [W25g] **The A. A. Low Building, South Street Seaport Museum**/originally A. A. Low & Brothers (counting-house)/later Baltimore Copper Paint Company, 167-171 John St. N side (behind Schermerhorn Row), bet. Front and South Sts. 1849. Altered. ♂ Restored, 1983 **Jan Hird Pokorny**.

The youngest of Schermerhorn Row block's treasures, built by traders whose China clippers parked across South Street. Merchant **Abiel Abbot Low** (father of sometime mayor and Columbia University president **Seth Low**) lived only a ferryboat ride away at No. 3 Pierrepont Place. Restored brownstone honors the original brownstone, revealed after years of stucco and paint were removed.

Note: The vacant lot in the Schermerhorn Row block, at the NW corner of South and John Streets, lost its group of 4-story brick, hip-roofed buildings from the block's heyday as recently as 1956 (in favor of a gas station, since demolished). There are plans to fill it in with an appropriate neighbor:

W26

▌ [W25h] **South Street Seaport Museum Exhibit of the Port of New York**, 207 Front St., NW cor. South St. 2001. **Beyer Blinder Belle**. ♂

A glassy foil to the brickwork of Schermerhorn Row, this airy pavilion provides access to the "Exhibit of the Port of New York," buried high and deep within the body of the Schermerhorn Row block.

IIII [W26] Originally **Hickson W. Field Building**/formerly Baker, Carver & Morrell (ship chandlery), 170-176 John St., bet. Front and South Sts. S side. 1840. 🍎 ♂ Expanded upward, 1981-1982. **Buttrick, White & Burtis**.

The last survivor of a commercial building type first imported from Boston by **Town & Davis** in 1829. The austere granite blocks and piers offer a dour face to the street. The Yankee Clipper restaurant within is a good tenant: in character.

To the south, along South Street:

[W27] Originally **Maximilian Morgenthau tobacco warehouse**, 84-85 South St., bet. Fletcher and John Sts. W side. 1902. **G. Curtis Gillespie**. ♂

Despite the brutal surgery on its base this is one of South Street's—and the city's—unique treasures: terra-cotta Art

Nouveau tobacco leaf motifs applied to a late Romanesque
Revival storehouse,

Across South Street and onto the piers:

[W28] **South Street Seaport Museum ships**, anchored along
Piers 15, 16, 17, East River. Piers ☾ open to the public.

    The great glories of the Museum are the ships moored at the
wharves and those, like the tall ships, which periodically tie up
for brief visits. Floating architecture is honored here by the
Wavertree and *Peking* (1885 and 1911. Steel bathtub square-
riggers: bathtubs to keep the water out rather than in); the old
humanoid *Ambrose Lightship* (1908: Its successor is an electronic
rig on stilts); the *Lettie G. Howard* (1893, a venerable oysterman
from Gloucester); the *Maj. Gen. William H. Hart* (1925. One of
the city's smaller ferryboats); and others. In addition there are
sometime excursions on the *Andrew Fletcher* and the 1885
schooner, *Pioneer*.

W27   W28

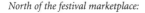 [W29] **Pier Pavilion, Pier 17**, East River, opp. Fulton
Street. 1984. **Benjamin Thompson & Assocs.**, design
architects. **The Eggers Group**, consulting architects. ☾

    The Rouse Company's other great Seaport contribution, a
pier large enough to moor a dirigible in. Conceived in a grand
manner to bring back some of the vernacular waterfront architecture that was once ubiquitous along South Street. Gigantic,
playful, adroitly detailed, and twinkling with lights well into the
night. An instant urban landmark. The 3-story high interior
space of the transept is remarkable.

W29

North of the festival marketplace:

[W30a] **142-144 Beekman Street** (lofts), NE cor. Front St. 1885.
George B. Post. ☾

    Built for a Schermerhorn descendant, **Ellen S. Auchmuty**.
Particularly note the whimsical terra-cotta maritime ornament:
decorative fish motifs, cockleshells, and starfish.

[W30b] **146-148 Beekman Street** (lofts), bet. Front and South
Sts. N side. 1885. **George B. Post**. ☾ [W30c] **150-152 Beekman
Street** (lofts), bet. Front and South Sts. N side. 1883. **David &
John Jardine**. ☾

W30a

    Colorful giant signs hawking wholesale seafood—FRESH,
SALT AND SMOKED FISH/OYSTERS AND CLAMS—that cross the
brick street façades, are what count here. An advertising strata-
gem growing increasingly rare. Hold that line!

[W31] Formerly **Meyer's Hotel**, 116-119 South St., SW cor. Peck
Slip. 1873. **John B. Snook**. ☾

    Its original use is unknown, but it became Meyer's Hotel in
1881. The building and its streetfront corner bar and restaurant
(Paris Café) make perfect backgrounds for Hollywood nostalgia.

W31

[W32] Originally **Jasper Ward House**; 45 Peck Slip, NW cor. South St. 1807. ♂ Restored, 1983, **Robert E. Meadows**.

Built on a water lot on landfill and impaired by time and unequal settlement. Thoughtful restoration, keeping the unevenness of decades, adds to the apparent integrity of this doughty survivor.

W33

[W33] **Consolidated Edison electrical substation**, 237-257 Front St., bet. Peck Slip and Dover St. E side to South St. 1975. **Edward Larrabee Barnes**, design architect. **Con Edison**, production architect. Mural, **Richard Haas**, artist. ♂

A reasonable attempt by the city's big electrical utility to be a harmonious neighbor to the Seaport, in the days before the historic district was enacted. (The Seaport's Restoration and Development Committee approved the design.) A mural on Peck Slip was a happy idea, but depicting the Brooklyn Bridge—with the real thing looming in the background—was a silly conceit.

W33

[W34] **Best Western Seaport** (hotel), Peck Slip, NW cor. Front St. 1840s. ♂

A much needed facility has recycled some local vernacular architecture.

[W35] **Bridge Café** (restaurant), 279 Water St., SE cor. Dover St. Building, 1794. ♂

The district's only extant wood-frame building, built for grocer **Peter Loring**, has remained a commercial structure for more than two hundred years. In 1888 it lost its peaked roof and was sheathed in novelty siding and other ornament of the era. Today, a good place for a drink and a repast. Maroon and black??

W34

[W36] Originally **Captain Joseph Rose House and shop**/onetime Sports' Man's Hall, 273 Water St., bet. Peck Slip and Dover St. E side. As early as 1773/no later than 1781. ♂ Reconstructed, 1998. **Oliver Lundquist**.

A phoenix from what was, 10 years ago, a ruin. Fires in 1904 and 1976 compromised this structure, the South Street District's oldest and Manhattan's third oldest (after the Morris-Jumel Mansion and St. Paul's Chapel). The reconstructed result is worthy of Williamsburg (Virginia, that is, where the squeaky clean modern reconstructions miss the lusty vitality of the original buildings). Rose was in the business of shipping Honduras mahogany to the New York market.

W35

A sign heralding **Kit Burns**'s "Sports' Man's Hall" was not included in the rebuilding.

W36

Christopher (Kit) Burns, tavern keeper at 273 in the 1860s, put on dog and rat fights to divert patrons. In "The Secrets of the Great City" (1868) Edward Winslow Martin declared that "It is simply sickening. Most of our readers havde witnessed a dog fight in the streets. Let them imagine the animals surrounded by a crowd of brutal wretches whose conduct stamps them as beneath the struggling beasts, and they will haved a fair idea of the scene at Kit Burns." Rentals now $4,000 a month? Kit would have been impressed.

W38

[W37] **21-23 Peck Slip** (lofts), NE cor. Water St. 1873. **Richard Morris Hunt**. ♂

Six wonderful stories of polychromed brick with carefully modulated windows and, on the Front Street façade, 45 neatly spaced star anchors tying in the timber floors to the masonry street wall. This structure was built for the trustees of Roosevelt Hospital, at the same time as Hunt's Roosevelt Building was under construction.

[W38] **251 Water Street** (tenement), SE cor. Peck Slip. 1888. **Carl F. Eisenach**. ♂

Even a tenement design was infused by South Street fervor: the tympanum over the ornately framed apartment entrance is a joyous explosion of terra-cotta sunflowers. At the 4th-story windows, terra-cotta keystones carry faces surveying the streetlife below.

W39

[W39] **247 Water Street**, bet. Peck Slip and Beekman St. E side. 1840s. ♂

The offices of **Frank Sciami**, the builder of the Seamen's Church Institute, were here and left it in elegance.

[W40] **Seamen's Church Institute**, 241 Water St., bet. Beekman St. and Peck Slip. E side. 1989-1991. **Polshek Partnership**. ♂

A stylish understatement that provides a textbook example of the best of modernist architecture, while complementing its 19th-century context.

W40

[W41] **Seaport Park** (apartments)/in part originally Volunteer Hospital/later Beekman Street Hospital, 117 Beekman St., bet. Water and Pearl Sts. S side. 1918. **Adolph Mertin**. Conversion and extension, 1981. **Rafael Viñoly Architects**. ♂

Long after ending its service as a hospital, the older part became part of a notorious nursing home scam and scandal. Converted, the combination of old and new is among the handsomest buildings in these parts.

W41

W40

BROADWAY-NASSAU

Lying between Wall Street and the southern tip of City Hall Park, from Church Street to South Street Seaport, is one of Lower Manhattan's least recognized—and therefore most intriguing—areas. Since it bestrides Fulton Street, under which lies the IND Eighth Avenue Line's Broadway-Nassau Station, this area has been dubbed after that station's name. It includes Chase Manhattan Plaza, the Nassau Street pedestrian mall, the Federal Reserve Bank of New York, and the old AT&T Building. But, more important, it includes many minor but delicious background buildings from the days of the earliest skyscrapers.

Entries begin at Pearl and Pine Streets, one block north of Wall. (The closest subway stop to the first entry is the Wall Street Station of the IRT Seventh Avenue Line express: Nos. 2 and 3 trains.)

[N1] **American International Building** (offices)/earlier 60 Wall Tower/originally Cities Service Building, 70 Pine St., NW cor. Pearl St. to Cedar St. 1931-1932. **Clinton & Russell** and **Holton & George**.

One of the Financial District's most slender towers, it sports Art Deco details everywhere—including its "Gothic" crown, unseen from the canyons in which the tower sits and therefore best appreciated as part of the skyline or from a neighboring eyrie. (To help passersby comprehend what they cannot fully see from the street, the architects provided 3-dimensional stone replicas of the building at the Pine and Cedar Street entrances.)

Double-decker elevators, serving two floors of the tower at a time, such as are found at the Citicorp Tower uptown, were first used here. They proved unpopular and were later changed.

N2

[N2] **56-58 Pine Street** (offices)/originally Wallace Building, bet. Pearl and William Sts. N side. 1893-1894. **Oswald Wirz.** 💀

Romanesque Revival in stone, brick, and terra-cotta. The incised decoration is in the spirit of **H.H. Richardson** and his peers.

[N3] **Down Town Association** (club), 60 Pine St., bet. Pearl and William Sts. N side. 1886-1887. **Charles C. Haight.** 💀 Addition, 1910-1911. **Warren & Wetmore**.

Anonymous and understated, this appropriately somber club serves many distinguished financial executives and lawyers, principally at lunchtime.

N4

[N4] **Banco Atlantico**, 62 William St., SE cor. Cedar St. 1896.

Neo-Romanesque brickwork supports a sturdy cornice.

N5

BROADWAY-NASSAU DISTRICT

see pages 38–44

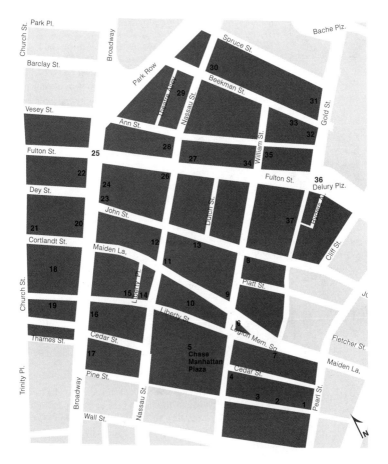

[N5] **Chase Manhattan Bank Tower** (offices) **and Plaza**, 1 Chase Manhattan Plaza, bet. Pine and Liberty Sts., from William to Nassau Sts. 1960. **Skidmore, Owings & Merrill**.

David Rockefeller and his fellow board members, in their 1950s act of faith in building this Gargantua, here cried "Excelsior," and the flagging spirit of the Financial District took courage. Architecturally less successful than the later and more sophisticated Marine Midland by the same firm, it provides, however, the first gratuitous plaza hereabouts. Many have appeared since: the Home Insurance Company, Marine Midland, Liberty Plaza, the World Trade Center, and so forth.

A sheer 800 feet of aluminum and glass rise from the paved plaza surface, which is accessible from both Nassau and Pine Streets. The topography unfortunately forces down the Liberty and William Street sides, detaching them from participation in the plaza's space.

A sunken circular courtyard is paved with undulating forms of granite blocks, crowned with sculpture, and caressed in summer by a fountain and pools: all by sculptor Isamu Noguchi. Goldfish were resident at first, but the urban fallout and sentimentalists' "coins in the fountain" destroyed even those resilient carp.

The plaza sculpture **Group of Four Trees** (1972. **Jean Dubuffet**), on the axis of Cedar Street, looks like papier-mâché but isn't: it gives out a temporary, expendable feeling.

N5

N6

[N6] **Louise Nevelson Plaza/Legion Memorial Square**, Maiden Lane, Liberty St., William St. 1978. Shadows and Flags, 1978, **Louise Nevelson**, sculptor.

A unique public space devoted to a single sculptor, and named after her. Sit down and measure her work against the rich rustications of the Federal Reserve Bank.

N7

[N7] **90-94 Maiden Lane** (lofts), bet. William and Pearl Sts. S side, at Louise Nevelson Plaza. 1815. Cast-iron front, 1870-1871, **Charles Wright**. 🍎

An unlikely spot for a carefully preserved cast-iron remnant owned over time by **Cornelius Van Schaick Roosevelt** and his son **James Alfred Roosevelt**. At only 4 stories in the Financial District's canyons, can it survive? Perhaps its unlikely and graciously installed new tenant, McDonald's, will be its savior: Has McDonald's been to Brooks Brothers?

N7

[N8] **100 William Street** (offices), bet. Platt and John Sts. E side. 1972-1973. **Davis, Brody & Assocs.**

Green schist (split from natural geological strata) slate. A diagonal gallery slashes the form with a 4-story, stepped, street volume: a humanist place, rich, natural, and elegant, creating a vista terminating at the plaza in front of the Home Insurance Group's offices.

[N9] **Plaza in front of Home Insurance Group** (offices), 59 Maiden Lane, NW cor. William St. Building, 1966, **Office of Alfred Easton Poor**. Redesigned, 1987, **Kohn Pedersen Fox Assocs.**

It's the plaza that counts here (although awkward and detailed with a heavy hand). Public space contained by buildings can benefit from being small; increasing the size would diminish rather than enhance its quality.

N10

[N10] **Federal Reserve Bank of New York**, 33 Liberty St., NE cor. Nassau St. to Maiden Lane. 1919-1924. Extension E to William St., 1935. All by **York & Sawyer**. Decorative ironwork, **Samuel Yellin**. 🍎 Open to the public by advance reservation.

A Florentine palazzo conserves within its dungeons more money than Fort Knox. This is a great neo-Renaissance building of rusticated Indiana limestone, Ohio sandstone, and elegant ironwork. A bank for banks, this is the great stabilizer and equalizer of their separately erratic activities. In the five levels below the street, the gold of many nations is stored—and moved, in the balance of trade, from nation to nation—without ever leaving the building.

The stony south wall, on Liberty Street, is a magnificent foil to the crystalline glass and aluminum of Chase Manhattan Bank Tower. We hope that the Federal Reserve will live forever. (Florence, not having the luxury of 15th-century elevators, couldn't imagine such large-scale grandeur.)

Nassau Street Pedestrian Mall: From Maiden Lane to Beekman Street, Nassau serves as a most active local shopping strip: medium- to modest-priced chain stores, discount houses, and small, specialized shops. Panty hose, radio equipment, dresses, shoes, all of the personal and portable items that a lunch-hour shopper would be most inclined to inspect and purchase. The ground-floor activity and clutter of show windows and signs keep the eye at street level. The form and detail of buildings above, no matter how tall, are rarely noticed, almost never observed. Closed to vehicles to fulfill its pedestrianism. Too bad it has no curbs any more or even some emblematic recognition of their earlier existence.

N11

[N11] **33 Maiden Lane** (office tower), NE cor. Nassau St. to John St. 1984-1986. **Philip Johnson/John Burgee**.

Occupies a site intended in the 1970s for an annex to the Federal Reserve Bank across Maiden Lane, a powerful **Kevin Roche** design. The substitute is a building suspended between a group of giant buff-brick crenellated tubes (which permitted the developer to offer 7 "corner" offices per floor).

N13

[N12] **63 Nassau Street** (lofts), bet. Maiden Lane and John St. W side. ca. 1860. **James Bogardus?**

A tattered façade distinguished by 3-story, fluted cast-iron columns sitting on bases, one bearing a relief portrait bust of **Benjamin Franklin**. Indefatigable **Margot Gayle**, founder of Friends of Cast Iron Architecture, rediscovered this out-of-the-way structure.

N12

[N13] **John Street United Methodist Church**, 44 John St., bet. Nassau and William Sts. 1841. Attributed to **William Hurry** and/or **Philip Embury**. ☛

Irish Wesleyans built their first church in America here in 1768: this, however, is the third building on the site. The congregation is, therefore, the oldest Methodist Society in America.

[N14] **Liberty Tower**/onetime Sinclair Oil Building, 55 Liberty St., NW cor. Nassau St. 1909-1910. **Henry Ives Cobb**. ☛ Restored and converted to apartments, 1981. **Joseph Pell Lombardi**.

Glorious terra-cotta (similar to Cass Gilbert's gothicized 90 West Street) over limestone as high as a person can reach.

N14

[N15] Originally **Chamber of Commerce of the State of New York**/now International Commercial Bank of China, 65 Liberty St., bet. Nassau St. and Broadway at NW cor. Liberty Place 1900-1901. **James B. Baker**. ☛ Restored and converted, 1990-1991. **Haines Lundberg Waehler**.

Rich, ornate Beaux Arts; a minor palace of imposing scale and rich detail. Rusticated, Ionic columns, mansard roof, oval porthole windows.

N15

[N16] **Marine Midland Bank Building** (offices), 140 Broadway, bet. Liberty and Cedar Sts. E side to Nassau St. 1967. **Skidmore, Owings & Merrill**.

A taut skin stretched over bare bones. The sleek and visually flush façade is in melodramatic contrast to the ornamented masonry environment surrounding it. The matteness of black spandrels breaks up the reflections of the neighbors into more random, mysterious parts. The plaza at Broadway had a major impact on the scale of this neighborhood until the plaza across

Broadway deprived it of its enclosing street walls.

Cube (1973. **Isamu Noguchi**) sits on the plaza's lap at Broadway, teetering 28 feet tall and vermilion, gored by a cylindrical punch.

[N17] **Equitable Building** (offices), 120 Broadway, bet. Pine and Cedar Sts. E side to Nassau St. 1913-1915. **Ernest R. Graham & Associates**. (of **Graham, Anderson, Probst & White**, successors to **D. H. Burnham & Co.**). ☛ Restoration, 1983-1990. **Ehrenkrantz, Eckstut & Whitelaw**.

N17

More famous for what it caused than what it is. An immense volume, it exploited the site as no building had before: 1.2 million square feet of floor area on a plot of just under an acre, or a floor area of almost 30 times the site's area. The hue and cry after Equitable's completion led to the adoption of the nation's first comprehensive zoning resolution, in 1916.

[N18] **1 Liberty Plaza** (offices)/briefly Merrill Lynch Plaza, Broadway, Liberty, Church and Cortlandt Sts. 1971-1974. Skidmore, Owings & Merrill. [N19] **Liberty Plaza** (park), Broadway, Cedar, Church, and Liberty Sts. 1974; SE corner holdout, 1980. **Skidmore Owings & Merrill**.

A gloomy, articulate, cadaverous extravaganza of steel: handsome and somber as the Renaissance of Florence. It replaced the great Singer Tower (1908-1970) by **Ernest Flagg**, an eclectic palace-tower and the tallest building ever demolished. Bollards and chains surround the low, depressed basement that seems designed, consciously, to crush the passer and enterer. A hovering hulk.

N20

Across Liberty Street to the south is a large, bleak, red granite treed plaza dedicated to the public, part of the zoning calculations that allowed the developers (U.S. Steel) to add bulk to their behemoth. The plaza links, in a chain, Marine Midland and Chase Manhattan Plazas to the east, and the World Trade Center to the west.

[N20] **Germania Building** (lofts), 175 Broadway, bet. Cortlandt and Dey Sts. W side. 1865.

A miraculous tiny holdover from the city's Reconstruction days: grand Corinthian columns and segmental arches. For how much longer?

[N21] **Century 21**/originally East River Savings Bank, 26 Cortlandt St., NE cor. Church St. to Dey St. 1931-1934. **Walker & Gillette**. Expanded upward.

Cool neo-Classical Art Deco with marvelous stainless steel winged eagles over both entrances, in the spirit of the Chrysler Building but nowhere near as daring.

[N22] Originally **American Telephone & Telegraph Company Building** (offices)/now 195 Broadway Building, bet. Dey and Fulton Sts. W side. Built in three sections: 1912-1923. All by **Welles Bosworth**. Addition to W, 1989, **Eli Attia**.

N22

The square-topped layer cake of New York: a deep-set façade of 8 Ionic colonnades (embracing 3 stories within each set) is stacked on a Doric order: handsome parts assembled into a bizarre and wonderful whole: more Classical columns than any façade in the world, the columns within the lobby extending that record. (All was surmounted by **Evelyn Beatrice Longman**'s *Genius of the Telegraph* until that colossal gilded sculpture was moved to the then new AT&T Building at 56th Street, and thence to New Jersey.)

[N23] **Corbin Building** (offices), 13 John St., NE cor. Broadway. ca. 1888-1889. **Francis H. Kimball**.

N23

Romanesque Revival arches with ornate voussoirs asserting strong individuality above a tawdry commercial corner.

[N24] **Girard Building** (lofts & store), 198 Broadway, bet. John and Fulton Sts. E side. 1902. **Walter H. Wickes**.

Assyrian Revival on a rampage (above the sleazy commercial chaos below).

Note: For St. Paul's Chapel and northward, see Civic Center/ Chinatown.

East on Fulton Street:

N24

[N25] **Fulton Street Subway Station**, Nos. 5 and 6 trains, under Broadway at Fulton St. 1905. **Heins & La Farge**. ☙ Restoration, 1987, **Lee Harris Pomeroy & Assocs**.

A straightforward restoration with exceptionally fine new lighting. Check the ceramic tile plaques of **Robert Fulton**'s steamboat, the *Clermont.*

[N26] Originally **Fulton Building** (offices), 87 Nassau St., SW cor. Fulton St. 1893. **De Lemos & Cordes**.

[N27] Originally **Keuffel & Esser Building** (offices), 127 Fulton St., bet. Nassau and William Sts. N side. 1893. **De Lemos & Cordes**.

Richly ornamented masonry façades from the architects who later brought you Siegel-Cooper and Macy's department stores.

N26

[N28] Originally **Bennett Building** (lofts), 93-99 Nassau St. and 139 Fulton St., with a 3rd façade on Ann St. 1872-1873. **Arthur D. Gilman**. Mansard roof removed and upper 4 floors added, 1890-1892. **James M. Farnsworth**. Ann Street extension, 1894. **James M. Farnsworth**. ☙

A glassy building with a deeply 3-dimensional and lavish cast-iron structural grid. For years its tacky Nassau Street stores diverted eyes from the splendor above. Now, a set of trendy mid-1980s store signs and a new tutti-frutti pastel paint job (including trompe l'oeil lot line extensions) remedy the situation markedly. The building's name, incidentally, is that of **James Gordon Bennett** (*New York Herald*), father and son, each of whom owned it.

N28

[N29] **Temple Court** (offices), 119-129 Nassau St., and 5 Beekman St. to Theater Alley. S part, 1881-1883, **Silliman & Farnsworth**. N part, 1890-1892, **Benjamin Silliman, Jr**. ☙

Two mighty, pointed steeples cap this purply red-painted brick office building whose name (lifted from its London counterpart) suggests that it originally catered to the city's legal profession, way before Foley Square. Within, a nine-story atrium, with cast-iron balustrades, all walled off at present, but rumor suggests a reopening.

N29

[N30] Originally **Morse Building** (lofts)/now 12 Beekman Street (apartments), NE cor. Nassau St. 1879. **Silliman & Farnsworth**. Converted, 1980, **Hurley & Farinella**.

A hearty red-brick many-arched loft structure, understated but powerful.

N30

▌[N31] **Wiggin Pavilion, New York University Downtown Hospital**/originally Beekman Downtown Hospital, 170 William St., bet. Beekman and Spruce Sts. E side to Gold St. 1971. **Skidmore, Owings & Merrill**.

A block of serious modernist architecture, a bit forbidding on the Gold Street side due to its high base, unintentionally giving a humane institution an inhumane posture.

▌[N32] **Staff Residence, New York Infirmary Beekman Downtown Hospital**, 69 Gold St., bet. Beekman and Ann Sts. W side, 1972. **The Gruzen Partnership**.

A vigorous work in reinforced concrete and brick masonry units responding to a simple set of programmatic requirements on a tiny site.

N31

N33

N36

N37

[N33] **Engine Company 6, NYC Fire Department**, Beekman St, bet. Gold and William Sts. S side. 1903. **Horgan & Slattery**

A Beaux Arts façade with an ornate cornice and swags enlivens this stripped modernist streetfrontage.

[N34] **ILX Systems**/formerly Aetna Insurance Company Building (offices), 151 William St., NW cor. Fulton St. 1939-1940. **Cross & Cross** and **Eggers & Higgins**.

Curious rounded limestone: a modernist evolution from the earlier 90 Church Street Federal Building, also (in part) by Cross & Cross. Cloaked in stripped-down neo-Classical, it seems to have left Art Deco behind but hasn't found an adequate replacement.

[N35] Originally **Royal Insurance Company Building** (offices)/later Royal Globe Insurance Company Building, 150 William St., bet. Fulton and Ann Sts. E side to Gold St. 1927. **Starrett & Van Vleck**.

A stately occupant of a full-block site. The gentle setbacks on all 4 façades terminate in a pedimented Classical temple at the roof.

[N36] **John J. DeLury, Sr. Plaza**, at NE intersection of Gold and Fulton Sts. 1985. **Bronson Binger**, architect; **Christopher Kusske, Elizabeth Hand**, landscape architects; **NYC Department of Parks & Recreation Capital Projects Division**.

A model public: sleek bollards and chains define, as on a 19th-century pier, pedestrian space. **DeLury** (1904-1980) was founder of the city's Uniformed Sanitationmen's Association and president for 40 years.

[N37] Originally **Excelsior Power Company** (powerhouse/now apartments), 33-48 Gold St., bet. Fulton and John Sts. W side. 1888. **William Milne Grinnell**. Converted, 1979. **Wechsler, Grasso & Menziuso**.

Coal-fired electrical generators once occupied this lusty Romanesque Revival brick monolith. Now, yuppies do.

BATTERY PARK CITY

Once upon a time, not too long ago, Lower Manhattan's Hudson River shoreline was crammed—like teeth in a comb—with piers, wharves, and ferry slips. But with the end of labor-intensive break-bulk cargo in favor of efficient containerization, and an increasing need to dispose of enormous volumes of earthen fill from excavations like that of the World Trade Center—and who knows from how many others?—a symbiotic opportunity arose to create a 92-acre add-on to Manhattan Island: Battery Park City.

The idea blossomed in the late 1960s under **Governor Nelson Rockefeller** (riparian rights make the river's landfill State-owned), when the State's Battery Park City Authority commissioned **Harrison & Abramovitz** to design a development isolated from Manhattan's existing urban fabric. (It would be prophetic of their later Albany Mall —named for Rockefeller—designed to be isolated from the urban fabric of the state capital.) After many enthusiastic announcements—but no demonstrated capacity to sell the necessary revenue bonds—BPCA finally began its first aboveground project, Gateway Plaza.

But the real beginning came in 1979, when a master plan by **Cooper, Eckstut Associates** proposed developing the area as an extension of Lower Manhattan, rather than as an isolated futuristic "project." The lines of existing east-west streets were to be integrated into the project, and new north-south avenues would be oriented to Manhattan's street grid north of Houston Street. A public waterfront esplanade and other public park space were envisioned. Not only were specific land uses proposed—a mix of commercial, residential, recreational, and arterial—but the visual character of the various developments was also defined in a set of design guidelines. The southern residential areas—guidelines by **Stanton Eckstut**—were to resemble such desirable Manhattan neighborhoods as Gramercy Park, Tudor City, and Riverside Drive. It is no accident that the South Residential Quadrant looks like "instant past."

The commercial area, the World Financial Center—developed according to guidelines by **Alexander Cooper**—is a totally private effort by Canadian developers **Olympia & York**. It lies immediately west of the World Trade Center complex, embracing the earlier Gateway Plaza towers and largely concealing them from Lower Manhattan streets. To the south and north are a string of high-density residential communities with structures allocated to different developer-architect teams. Each team was beholden to the design guidelines' tenets but still exercised its own design and economic initiatives, later reviewed and approved by the Authority.

As the financial center and the southerly residential complexes emerged, the fundamental wisdom of the master plan made itself evident.

[B1a] **The Esplanade**, entire W edge of site. 1983-1990. **Stanton Eckstut** of **Cooper, Eckstut Assocs.**, architects. **Hanna/Olin, Ltd.**, landscape consultants.

Seventy-five feet wide, 1.2 miles long, and admittedly derivative—but it works. The design vocabulary draws from the best of the city's existing park design, particularly the Carl Schurz Park promenade atop FDR Drive, the city's traditional "B-pole" park lampposts, and Victorian-replica cast-iron and wood benches used in (of all places) the Art Moderne 1939-1940 New York World's Fair.

Entries begin beyond Pier A in the northwestern corner of Battery Park and proceed uptown through Battery Park City:

BATTERY PARK CITY

see pages 45–52

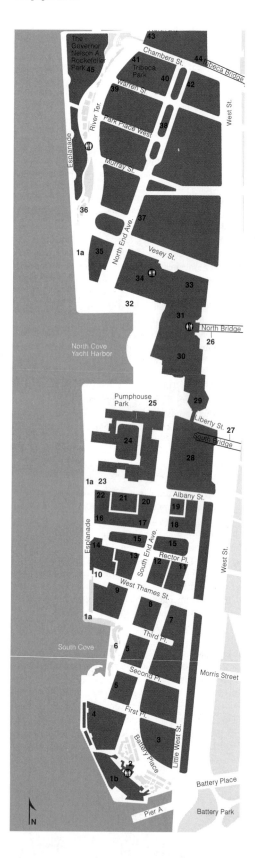

Battery Place residential neighborhood:
The southernmost area.

[B1b] **Robert F. Wagner, Jr. Park**, N of Pier A. 1989. **Olin Partnership**, **Machado & Silvetti**, and **Lynden Miller**.
    A series of interlinked gardens.

[B2] **Wagner Park Café and Viewing Platform**, in Robert F. Wagner Jr. Park, N of Pier A. 1996. **Machado and Silvetti**.
    A grand brick sculpture serving as viewing platform, café, and rest rooms. The stairs to the top are monumental: a stairway, not to heaven, but to a panorama of the harbor.

B2

[B3] **Ritz Carlton Downtown (hotel), Condominiums & Skyscraper Museum**, bet. Battery Place and 1st Place. 2001. **Polshek Partnership** and **Gary Edward Handel & Associates**.
    Another chic hotel for Wall Street's peripatetic fellow-travelling investors and out-of-town gurus: when the Internet breaks down (or doesn't live up) and face-to-face dealing is in order.

B3

[B4] **Museum of the Jewish Heritage**, Battery Place, W of 1st Place. 1996. **Kevin Roche, John Dinkleloo & Assocs.** Visitor center and security checkpoint, 1997. **Claire Weisz** and **Mark Yoes**. Museum open to the public. East Wing, 2002.
    The museum presents a linear exhibition of the timeline of Jewish history plus a memorial to the victims of the Holocaust.

B4

[B5] **River Watch and South Cove Plaza**, N and S of 2nd Place on Battery Place. 1999. Both by **Hardy Holzman Pfeiffer**.
    Low-rise housing facing the delights of South Cove Park.

[B6] **South Cove Park**, surrounding South Cove bet. 1st and 3rd Place. 1988. **Mary Miss**, artist. **Stanton Eckstut, The Ehrenkranz Group & Eckstut**, architects. **Susan Child, Child Assocs.**, landscape architects. **Howard Brandston Lighting Design, Inc.**, lighting.
    An effort to bring the changing character of the seasons, the tides, and the Hudson River itself into an artful interplay with the southern terminus of the Esplanade, the end of 1st Place, and the Museum of the Jewish Heritage complex.

B7

[B7] **Liberty View** (apartments), Battery Place bet. 3rd Place and W. Thames St. E side. 1990. **Ehrenkranz, Eckstut & Whitelaw** and **Costas Kondylis**. [B8] **Cove Club** (apartments), Battery Place SW. cor. W. Thames St. to South End Ave. 1990. **James Stewart Polshek & Partners**. [B9] **The Regatta Condominium**, 21 South End Ave., SW cor. W. Thames St. 1989. **Gruzen Samton Steinglass**.
    Developments, all within the original design guidelines, that added to the initial housing inventory of the south residential complex as the BPC Authority, developers, and architects reached agreements. Less constrained than the Rector Place grouping.

B8

[B10] **"Living Room,"** E of the Esplanade at foot of W. Thames St. 1988. **Richard Artschwager**, sculptor.
    Conran's furniture, sized for Paul Bunyan, fashioned in granite, cast iron, and redwood, and occupying a triangular "waiting area."

Rector Place residential neighborhood:
The first residential quarter built under the master plan and
Eckstut's residential design guidelines. To comment at length on any individual group is to forget what was intended by the design guidelines and what, in the end, really counts: the totality of the complex.

B9

B11

[B11] **Liberty Court** (apartments), 200 Rector Place, SW cor. West St. 1987. **Ulrich Franzen**. [B12] **The Soundings** (apartments), 280 Rector Place, SE cor. South End Ave. 1987. **Bond Ryder James**. [B13] **Battery Pointe** (apartments), 300 Rector Place, SW cor. South End Ave. 1987. **Bond Ryder James**. [B14] **Liberty Terrace** (apartments), 380 Rector Place, SE cor. The Esplanade. 1987. **Ulrich Franzen/The Vilkas Group**.

Like West End Avenue: no stars, but very good actors putting on a performance that is greater than the sum of its parts.

B14

[B15] **Rector Park**, within the Rector Place loop, W and E of South End Ave. 1986. **Innocenti-Webel** with **Vollmer Assocs.**, landscape architects. **Gateway**, 1987, **R. M. Fischer**, sculptor.

As befits the surrounding architecture, centrally placed Rector Park is veddy, veddy propuh, using the finest materials very carefully detailed. Meant to be looked at, not played in. The gateway at the west end is certainly witty, if not serene.

[B16] **Liberty House** (apartments), 377 Rector Place, NE cor. The Esplanade. 1986. **James Stewart Polshek & Partners**.

B15

[B17] **River Rose** (apartments), 333 Rector Place, NW cor. South End Ave. 1986. **Charles Moore** and **Rothzeid, Kaiserman, Thomson & Bee**.

The most mannered and exuberant of the Rector Park group.

[B18] **Parc Place** (apartments), 225 Rector Place, NE cor. South End Ave. 1986. **Gruzen Samton Steinglass**.

Understated with appropriate detailing.

[B19] **Hudson View East** (apartments), 250 South End Ave., SE cor. Albany St. 1987. **Mitchell-Giurgola**.

Bland of hue and spartan in detail; savor the subtle highlights of blue glazed brick and the robust wrought window grilles at street level.

B17

[B20] **Hudson View West** (apartments), 300 Albany St., SW cor. South End Ave. 1987. **Conklin & Rossant**.

Articulated brickwork atop a 2-story limestone and granite plinth.

[B21] **320-340 Albany Street** (town house apartments), bet. The Esplanade and South End Ave. S side. 1986. **Davis, Brody & Assocs**.

Six 5-story apartment buildings meant to echo the forms and organization of the city's brownstones. The tiers of connected rear balconies lined with black ships' railings reveal a more masterful command of the problem. Visible from the inner parking area.

B19

[B22] **Hudson Tower** (apartments), 350 Albany St., SE cor. The Esplanade. 1986. **Davis, Brody & Assocs**.

Above a limestone base, the brick body offers bay windows and cantilevered corner windows to capture the harbor view. A happy building.

[B23] "**Upper Room**," Albany Street Park, E of the Esplanade at foot of Albany St. **Ned Smyth**, sculptor.

No need to voyage up the Nile. Smyth's evocative, eclectic, open-to-the-sky forms offer a cartoon of both Egypt's dynasties and Rome's empire.

B20

Robots and tempiettos: *Alexander Gorlin's whimsical guard booths provide security, both literal and psychological, to the workers and residents. The robots (inspired by Japanese transformer-robot toys) can be moved about as needed. Gorlin describes them as "like urban soldiers clad in ceremonial helmets, they proudly serve their civic duty with expressive, gestural designs that communicate elements of imagination and wit"…Got it? Or they'll get you.*

B23

Gateway Plaza

B24

[B24] **Gateway Plaza** (apartments), 345, 355, 365, 375, 385, 395
South End Ave. 1982, 1983. **Jack Brown** and **Irving E. Gershon**,
associate architects. Interior plaza, **Abel, Bainnson & Assocs.**,
landscape architects.

    Sam Lefrak in Manhattan: 1,712 units divided among three
34-story lackluster towers and other containers; the scullery
maids of Battery Park City residences. Nevertheless, its central
green space (except for the enclosed pool) is serene.

[B25] **Pumphouse Park**, E of Esplanade, N of Gateway Plaza.
1986. **Synterra, Ltd.**, landscape architects.

    Two 66-inch-diameter river water intake and outfall tubes
for the World Trade Center were relocated to make possible the
Liberty Street vehicular entry between the twin Gatehouses.
These tubes, together with the required pumping apparatus, are
under this park.

Gorlin's robot

World Financial Center:

*The 7-million-square-foot commercial center, encompassed in a
group of towers sheathed in reflective glass and thermal granite.
The towers vary in height from 33 to 51 stories, and each has a different geometric termination—mastaba, dome, pyramid, stepped
pyramid. The overall design concept was developed by design
architect* **Cesar Pelli** *with* **Adamson & Associates** *as coordinating
architects. As bulky as the towers are, they begin, in Pelli's irregular placement (dictated by landfill configurations), to soften the
impact of the neighboring World Trade Center's raw, 110-story
prisms. After years of lonely exposure, the Trade Center's out-of-
scale twin towers have finally been shoehorned into a context with
Lower Manhattan.*

Gorlin's tempietto

[B26] **North Bridge** (200-foot clear span, 40 feet wide)
connecting U.S. Custom House to the Wintergarden.
[B27] **South Bridge** (220-foot clear span, 25 feet wide)
connecting Liberty St. to South Gatehouse. Both 1985. **Cesar
Pelli**, design architect. **Haines Lundberg Waehler**, architects.
Lev Zetlin & Assocs. and **Thornton Thomasetti**, structural
engineers.

    Pedestrian access from "Little Old New York" across the
great gulf formed by West Street. From the inside the bridges are
long narrow ballrooms; from the outside they resemble levitating Brobdingnagian interstate buses minus their tires. (The

B29

bridges are formed of Vierendeel trusses of great span to accommodate the uncertainties of a multibillion-dollar Westway that was destined never to come.)

These bridges are the least successful part of the project.

[B28] **1 World Financial Center/Dow Jones & Company Building and Oppenheimer & Company Tower**, West St. opp. Cedar St. W side. 1985. **Cesar Pelli**, design architect. **Adamson Assocs.**, architects.

Mastaba-topped, 40 stories high.

B31

[B29] **North and South Gatehouses**, West St. W side framing Liberty St. **Cesar Pelli**, design architect. **Adamson Assocs.**, architects. 1980s.

The marbled interiors of these bulky octagonal pavilions are spacious, lavishly clad, fussily detailed, and embarrassingly devoid of purpose.

[B30] **2 World Financial Center/Merrill Lynch World Headquarters**, South Tower, West St. bet. Liberty and Vesey Sts. W side. 1987. **Cesar Pelli**, design architect. **Haines Lundberg Waehler**, architects.

Dome-topped, the tallest tower at 51 floors.

B31

[B31] **The Wintergarden**, opp. North Bridge. 1988. **Cesar Pelli**, design architect. **Adamson Assocs.**, architects. **Lev Zetlin & Assocs.** and **Thornton Thomasetti**, structural engineers. **M. Paul Friedberg & Partners**, landscape architects.

It's hard to fathom why London's 19th-century Crystal Palace was framed in so gossamer a structure, while this is encased in so heavy a steel-pipe frame. Nevertheless, it's a welcome, sunny, barrel-vaulted, palm-filled interior public space measuring 130 × 230 feet, roughly the size of Grand Central's concourse. (The 90-foot-tall palms are Washingtonia robusta, specially chosen for heartiness from among the world's 2,780 species.)

B32, pylons

[B32] **World Financial Center Plaza**, W of 2 World Financial Center and the Wintergarden. 1988. **Siah Armajani** and **Scott Burton**, artists. **Cesar Pelli**, architect. **M. Paul Friedberg & Partners**, landscape architects.

Poised around the indented North Cove, the Plaza comprises the Terrace, the Court, Summer Park, and West Park. The New York City Police Memorial (**Susan B. Crawford**, 1997) contrasts water and polished granite, on which the names of officers lost in the line of duty are engraved.

B34

The Belvedere (1995. **Mitchell/Giurgola**) comprises a platform with a bosquet of trees and a belvedere. Stainless steel pylons (1995. **Martin Puryear**) provide welcome symbols to arriving ferryboaters.

Ferry service : Happily reinstituted, New York Waterways wafts you to Hoboken/Colgate, and to Jersey City. The ride is more important than getting there. New building. 2001. FTL Happold.

[B33] **3 World Financial Center: American Express Headquarters**, West St. SW cor. Vesey St. 1985. **Cesar Pelli**, design architect. **Adamson Assocs.**, architects.
  Pyramid-topped.

[B34] **4 World Financial Center: Merrill Lynch World Headquarters**, North Tower, Vesey St. SE cor. North End Ave. 1986. **Cesar Pelli**, design architect. **Haines Lundberg Waehler**, architects.
  Step pyramid-topped.

[B35] **5 World Financial Center: New York Mercantile Exchange**, Vesey St. bet. West St. and North End Ave. N side to Murray St. 1997. **Skidmore, Owings & Merrill**.
  No hat this time, but cool views of the Hudson reward its traders. **David Dunlap** (in the *New York Times*) described the trading floor: "…nothing about its gray-flannel façade betrays the sheer pandemonium within….clad in the eye-popping colors of a medieval pageant, shouting and gesturing wildly, they buy and sell futures and options in crude oil,…platinum, copper, silver and gold."

[B36] **Vesey Green**, along Vesey Street. 1995. **Barbara Stauffacher Solomon**, architect. **Nellie King Solomon**, artist. **Quennell Rothschild Assocs.**, Landscape Architects.

[B37] **Embassy Suites Hotel and Regal Cinemas**, North End Ave. at Vesey St. 2000. **Perkins Eastman**.
  Contiguous with the cluster of World Financial Towers, this will house visiting businessmen and supply their evening entertainment at the movies.

[B38] **North End Avenue mall**. 1989. **Weintraub & di Domenico**.
  The antecedents of this central green space are Boston's Back Bay, not our Park Avenue or upper Broadway.

[B39] **21 River Terrace**, SE cor. Warren St. St. 2001. **Gruzen Samton**.
  More than 300 apartments.

[B40] **The Hallmark, Brookdale Senior Living**, 455 North End Ave., bet. Warren and Chambers Sts. W side. 2000. **Lucien Lagrange** and **Schuman Lichtenstein Claman Efron**.
  Housing for the elderly.

[B41] **Tribeca Park**, 34 River Terrace, SE cor. Chambers St., 1999. **Robert A. M. Stern**, with **Costas Kondylis**.
  A three-dimensional collage of parts that simulates a group of buildings

[B42] **Tribeca Bridge Tower/P.S.-I.S. 89**, 450 North End Ave., bet. Warren and Chambers Sts. 1999. **Pasanella + Klein Stolzman + Berg** (school) with **Costas Kondylis** (apartments) and **Richard Cook**.
  A 151-unit apartment tower rises over a public school and retail space. With too many chefs (among the architects), it's not surprising that the whole is less than the sum of its parts. The school interiors (P+KS+B) are striking.

B41

B42

B43

B44

[B43] **Tribeca Pointe Tower**, 41 River Terrace, NE cor. Chambers St. (W of Stuyvesant High School). 1999. **Gruzen Samton**.

The base matches the Chambers Street grid across West Street, the tower that of Battery Park City to the south.

[B44] **Stuyvesant High School**, West St. NW cor. Chambers St. 1992. **Cooper Robertson & Partners** and **Gruzen Samton Steinglass**. Connecting **Tribeca Bridge**, 1993. **Skidmore, Owings & Merrill**.

A replacement for one of the city's special—admission by competitive test only—high schools, long on East 15th Street. Its multistory volume anticipated the new apartment buildings that now surround it: both urban and urbane, its umbilical cord to the older city across West Street is an overbearing bowstring trussed bridge: too much self-absorption in its own form.

[B45] **Gov. Nelson A. Rockefeller Park and Park House**, 1992. **Carr, Lynch, Hack & Sandell**, landscape architects. **Kiosk**, 1992. **Demetri Porphyrios**.

Seven acres echo **Olmsted & Vaux**'s Riverside Park, which adjoins the Hudson opposite the Upper West Side. Children's playground, handball, and volleyball courts supply active areas. For contemplation, a Greek temple pavilion.

B45, Kiosk

TRIBECA/LOWER WEST SIDE

Lower West Side:
A bit of history: After the Civil War, shipping shifted from the East River to the North (Hudson) River. Bowspritted South Street on Manhattan's southeast flank [see South Street Seaport] was abandoned for the longer, many-berthed piers of steam-powered shipping on this, the west flank. Later, Washington Market, a venue for produce, expanded from the market buildings and spread throughout the local streets, reusing the area's Federal and Greek Revival houses and warehouses as storage for fruits and vegetables.

Much later, truckers to the market and the still active piers brought street congestion that forced the building of the West Side (Miller) Elevated Highway atop West Street to accommodate through automobile traffic. The elevated highway was demolished in the early 1980s when "deferred maintenance" finally caused a partial collapse; its planned replacement, Westway, a multibillion-dollar underground superhighway (some called it boondoggle) yielded to the needs of the Hudson's striped bass population in a notable court ruling. A smaller west side highway is finally being put in place. After the produce market moved to new City-built facilities at Hunts Point in the Bronx, the Lower West Side (a term less and less used) became **Tribeca**.

See below for separate sections on the World Trade Center, the Greenwich Street Corridor, and the heart of Tribeca above Chambers Street; see the preceding section for Battery Park City.

The World Trade Center

[T1] **1 and 2 World Trade Center** (north and south towers), **4, 5, and 6 World Trade Center** (plaza structures), Church to West Sts., Liberty to Vesey Sts. WTC 1, 1973. WTC 2, 1972. WTC 4, 1977. WTC 5, 1972. WTC 6, 1974. **Minoru Yamasaki & Assocs.**, design architects. **Emery Roth & Sons**, architects. Plaza sculptures: Globe, **Fritz Koenig**. Ideogram, **James Rosati**. Unnamed granite, **Masayuki Nagare**.

Two shimmering 1,350-foot-tall, 110-story, stainless steel towers (which tourists simply call "The Twin Towers") are flanked by somber, brown, low buildings and a plaza larger than Piazza San Marco in Venice. When completed, these stolid, banal monoliths came to overshadow Lower Manhattan's cluster of filigreed towers, which had previously been the romantic evocation that symbolized the very concept of "skyline." The coming of the World Financial Center's shaped-top towers in Battery Park City softened the impact of the Trade Center's pair—at least for viewers in New Jersey.

T1

Ten million square feet of office space are here offered: 7 times the area of the Empire State Building, 4 times that of the Pan Am. The public agency that built them (Port Authority of New York & New Jersey) ran amok with both money and aesthetics.

A visit to the top, however, is a must: to the indoor-outdoor Observation Deck and its exhibition area in WTC 2 and/or to Windows on the World, the pricey but memorable restaurant atop WTC I ("If only you could eat the view!" Redesigned, 1996. **Hardy Holzman Pfeiffer**). The public accommodations at both are superb.

Below, in the enclosed WTC concourse, which drains the plaza of any meaningful activity (rush hour or noon is the time to see the crowds streaming through the concourse's corridors), are a profusion of eateries.

T2

Viaduct

[T2] **Marriott Hotel**/originally Vista International Hotel/ 3 World Trade Center, SW cor. WTC Plaza. 1981. **Skidmore, Owings & Merrill**.

With its elegant, horizontal-striped aluminum-and-glass curtain wall and its somewhat diagonal orientation, this handsome hotel looks out of place next to—but better than—its enormous WTC neighbors. The looming canopy is just one of those that have proliferated in the city's hotels in the 1990s.

WTC 1-6 connect to WTC 7 via a pair of 2nd-story pedestrian viaducts (one is cocooned against wind and rain by a Star Wars–style transparent cylindrical container) that throw much of the sidewalks along this part of Vesey Street into shadow. This is particularly regrettable since WTC 7's overshadowed, arcaded neighbor to the west is the old Barclay-Vesey Building.

[T3] **7 World Trade Center** (office tower), Vesey to Barclay Sts., Wahington St. to West Broadway. 1987. **Emery Roth & Sons**.

Contrasting with the 25-foot-tall, bright red Alexander Calder stabile, *Three Red Wings*, are the sheer 47-story walls of polished and flame-roughened red granite veneer that corset this 1980s addition to the original WTC project. Built atop complicated trusswork that spans the Center's original one-story utility and service ell, No.7 achieved fame not for its structural gymnastics or unrelenting form but for the unexpected cancellation, just a year before completion, of a 2 million square foot, $3 billion rental deal by expected tenant Drexel, Burnham, Lambert, Inc., as a result of tax law changes and an insider-trading scandal.

Greenwich Street Corridor

Charles Harvey's experimental cable elevated railway began operation astride Greenwich Street's eastern curb in 1870 and soon evolved into the Ninth Avenue Elevated Line. In the interim Greenwich Street remained a narrow, dark, noisy thoroughfare lined with 3-, 4-, and 5-story commercial and residential structures along its 2½-mile length, from the Battery to Gansevoort Street. Though the street's share of light improved when the el structure was taken down just before World War II, it retained its threadbare character at the southern end until the assemblage of the World Trade Center site, when the surplus stores of Radio Row were demolished to clear the required super-superblock for the WTC super-supertowers. Greenwich was wiped out entirely between Liberty and Barclay Streets, and as new projects were okayed by the authorities (after a 100-foot-high lid was zoned between Reade and Murray Streets), the narrow roadway north of WTC was widened to near-boulevard width.

[T4] **New York Telephone Company** (office building), also known as The Barclay-Vesey Building, 140 West St., bet. Barclay and Vesey Sts. to (now demapped) Washington St. 1923-1927. **McKenzie, Voorhees & Gmelin**.

Distinguished, and widely heralded, for the Guastavino-vaulted pedestrian arcades at its base, trade-offs for widening narrow Vesey Street. This Mayan-inspired Art Deco design by **Ralph Walker** proved a successful experiment in massing what was, in those years, a large urban form within the relatively new zoning "envelope" that emerged from the old Equitable Building's greed. Critic **Lewis Mumford** couldn't contain himself. A half century later, Roosevelt Island's Main Street used continuous arcades as the very armature of pedestrian procession. Why not elsewhere in New York to protect against inclement weather and to enrich the architectural form of the street? Why, indeed, not next door at 7 World Trade Center?

see pages 53–64

TRIBECA / LOWER WEST SIDE

T4

[T5] **101 Barclay Street** (offices), NW cor. Greenwich St. to Murray St. 1983. **Skidmore, Owings & Merrill**.

A Jordan almond, green graph-papered monolith. Actually two linked towers sandwiching what was once part of Washington Street, the building defines the path of the missing thoroughfare by creating a glaring white full-height atrium over the street's 60-foot width. At the far end the space is pierced by the half cylinder of 23-story-high elevator banks. (The experience is not unlike entering Cape Canaveral's Vertical Assembly Building and gazing up at a Saturn rocket ready for launch. The only thing missing is a cloud forming under the roof.)

T5

[T6] **75 Park Place** (offices), bet. Greenwich St. and West Broadway. N side to Murray St. 1987. **Emery Roth & Sons**.

A block-square silvery structure, somewhat squat in these parts at only 14 stories, but made debonair by thin blue stripes that alternate with the strip windows.

 [T7] **75 Murray Street Building**/originally Hopkins Store/now residential, bet. W Broadway and Greenwich St. N side. 1857-1858. **James Bogardus**. 🍎

Another grand **James Bogardus** façade, here remembering the Venetian Renaissance (those glassy buildings along the Grand Canal).

T7

[T8] **The College of Insurance**, 101 Murray St., bet. Greenwich and West Sts. N side. 1983. **Haines Lundberg Waehler**.

A clever, complicated, crystalline confection of pink precast panels. The designers of this complex of interlocking forms were evidently at the top of their class in descriptive geometry, but it was conceived as a freestanding building on its own grounds, not as a participant in its urban design context.

[T9] **Greenwich Court I and II** (apartments), 275 and 295 Greenwich St., bet. Murray and Chambers St. E side. 1987-1988. **Gruzen Samton Steinglass**.

A simple vocabulary of large red brick set in a red field, generous, rounded corners that ease the turning of odd-angled streets, with green-framed sliding sash that add depth to the façade. But labored.

T9

The city's oldest extant cast-iron building, an officially designated landmark warehouse built by ironmonger **James Bogardus** *in 1849, stood in the way of progress in the Washington Market area, at the northwest corner of Washington and Murray Streets (today a nonexistent intersection). In 1970 its cast-iron façade, and those of its neighbors, were disassembled; the parts, early examples of building prefabrication, were stored in a nearby vacant lot to be later re-erected at Borough of Manhattan Community College's new campus. In the dead of a 1974 night two-thirds of the cast-iron pieces were spirited away (Landmarks chair* **Beverly Moss Spatt** *shouted "Someone has stolen my building!") and sold to a junk yard by the scrapnappers. Three years later much of the remainder vanished, this time from a City storehouse ("Someone has stolen my building again!").*

[T10] **Public School 234**, Manhattan, Greenwich St., bet. Warren and Chambers Sts. W side. 1988. **Richard Dattner**.

A fanciful mix of eclectic architectural elements drawn in the architect's imagination from the daydreams of kids who study here: watchtowers, sentry boxes, walled courtyards, arches from Historic Williamsburg, and **Buck Rogers** classroom wings. Excellent.

T10

Holdout: *Ever since the inception of the Washington Market Urban Renewal Area project back in the 1950s, one lone structure has resisted the city, the developers, the lawyers, the courts, and the wrecking ball: 179 West Street (1845), just north of Warren. Dingy, ill-kempt, bedraggled, sporting a twisted fire escape and leaky downspouts, a victim of continuing uncertainty, it alone in this multiblocked area of the new reminds us of the old.*

[T11] **Dalton on Greenwich** (apartments), 303 Greenwich St., NE cor. Chambers St. 1987. **Beyer Blinder Belle**.

A muted design vocabulary and a subtle palette of grays echoes—but doesn't mimic—the same architects' "Bogardus" Building at South Street Seaport. But what worked for 4 stories at the Seaport doesn't work for 11 here. The flatness compromises the design.

T11

[T12] **311 Reade Street** (apartments), SE cor. Greenwich St. 1989. **Rothzeid, Kaiserman, Thomson & Bee**.

Hard on the heels of its 3 successful downtown neighbors came this simpler red brick development.

[T13] **Washington Market Park, NYC Department of Housing, Preservation & Development**, Greenwich St. bet. Chambers and Duane Sts. W side. 1983. **Weintraub & di Domenico**.

Memorializing in its name the former market area, a modern miracle, a spirited amalgam of the natural and the artificial, in the spirit of Olmsted & Vaux. Voluptuous landforms, a witty neo-Gothic enclosing fence, a gazebo—even a few relocated

T12

T14

granite Art Deco ornaments from the erstwhile West Side Highway entry ramps—combine to make this one of the city's best small parks.

[T14] **Borough of Manhattan Community College (CUNY)**, 199 Chambers St., NE cor. West St., along West St. to N. Moore St. Construction halted 1976; completed 1980. **CRS (Caudill Rowlett Scott Partnership)**.

A megastructure stretching north from Chambers Street over what were once more than five blocks (Reade, Duane, Jay, Harrison, Franklin, North Moore). A curiosity from that brief era when architects told us that megastructures would cure all urban ills.

T15

[T15] **Independence Plaza North** (housing complex), Greenwich St. bet. Duane and North Moore Sts. 1975. **Oppenheimer, Brady &Vogelstein** (**Barry Goldsmith**, project designer), and **John Pruyn**, associated architects.

Overpowering 40-story middle-income blockbusters of brick and striated concrete block. The design was intended to minimize them by plasticity, through cantilevers and steady increases in bulk at the top, and toothiness, by silhouetting balconies against the sky.

Verdict: they're still Brobdingnagians. To exacerbate their Brobdingnagianism (!), their shadow falls upon a flock of exquisite Federal houses:

T16

[T16] **Harrison Street Houses**, 25-41 Harrison St. SW cor. Greenwich St. Partly relocated and restored, 1975, **Oppenheimer, Brady & Vogelstein**. 🌿
[T16a] Originally **Jonas Wood House**, originally at 314 Washington St. 1804. 🌿 [T16b] **25 Harrison Street**. Originally 315 Washington Street (town house). 1819. **John MComb, Jr.** 🌿 [T16c] **27 Harrison Street**. Originally John McComb, Jr. House, originally at 317 Washington St. 1796. **John McComb, Jr.** 🌿 [T16d] Originally **Wilson Hunt House**, originally at 327 Washington St. 1828. 🌿
[T16e] Originally **Joseph Randolph House**, originally at 329 Washington St. 1828. 🌿 [T16f] Originally **William B. Nichols House**, originally at 331 Washington St. 1828. 🌿
[T16g] Originally **Sarah R. Lambert House**, 29 Harrison St. 1827. 🌿 [T16h] Originally **Jacob Ruckle House**, 31 Harrison St. (original site). 1827. 🌿 [T16i] Originally **Ebenezer Miller House**, 33 Harrison St. (original site). 1827. 🌿

These were originally elegant Federal houses, recycled (and rejected) as produce market buildings, 2 on Harrison Street and a group from a now extinct part of Washington Street. Their reincarnation included moving the Washington Street group 2 blocks to this enclave. They have been lovingly restored—perhaps too lovingly: the patina from the passage of time has been totally erased (cf. Williamsburg, Va.). Note that McComb, City Hall's co-architect, lived in one!

T17

[T17] **Shearson Lehman Plaza**: [T17a] **Faulkner Information Services Center**, 390 Greenwich St., SW cor. Hubert St. to West St. 1986. **Skidmore, Owings & Merrill**. [T17b] **Smith Barney**, member, Travellers Group, 388 Greenwich St. NW cor. N. Moore St. 1989. **Kohn Pedersen Fox**.

Modern Jeff and Post Modern Mutt. The newer 39-story, 1.5-million-square-foot tower occupies much of the original Shearson Garden, a larger parklet that briefly greened the construction site to be, and is remembered fondly by nearby Tribecans. The substitute hemidemisemi-parklet is much smaller. A Travellers umbrella logo can shade you while you wonder at this immense incursion onto the edges of SoHo.

Tribeca

The acronym for the **Triangle Below Canal** (say Try-beck-a) was developed in the mid 1970s when an imaginative realtor, sensing a displacement of manufacturing and warehousing and an influx of artists from places like SoHo, decided to give the area an ear-catching identity (better than Lower West Side) to promote momentum. It did.

[T18] **Tribeca Historic Districts** (Tribeca South, Tribeca East, Tribeca West, and Tribeca North), generally (but following their own distinctive courses) embraced by Broadway, Canal, Greenwich and Chambers Streets, with bumpouts at the north-western and northeastern corners, and indents where the Holland tunnel erupts, and on some parts of Leonard, Worth, Thomas and Duane Streets. 🍎

Land development by both Trinity Church and the Lispenard family provided grids in these precincts for industrial and commercial architecture that retain exemplary examples from the second half of the nineteenth century; buildings now converted to more gracious uses: up-scale housing, restaurants, and offices. Architects included **Samuel Warner**, **John B. Snook**, **James H. Giles**, **Henry Fernbach**, and **Isaac Duckworth**.

T19

Around these corners at Greenwich and Harrison are some of those immense granite slabs that served nineteenth century New York as both sidewalk and curb in a single piece. How about 4½ × 7 feet and almost a foot thick? Can you find some bigger? Tell us.

 [T19] Originally **Fleming Smith warehouse**, 451-453 Washington St., SE cor. Watts St. 1891-1892. **Stephen Decatur Hatch.** 🍎

T20

Fanciful Flemish. As much a surprise in Tribeca as it would be anywhere in the city: a golden-hued, gabled, and dormered fantasy with weathered copper details at its picturesquely silhou-etted roof. The ground floor has housed the Capsouto Frères bistro since 1980.

 [T20] **57 Laight Street**, SW cor. Collister St. 1893. **Horgan & Slattery.** ♂

Smooth Roman Brick and brownstone give this a special level of elegance missing in its more lusty neighbors. The cor-nice is spectacular.

T21

[T21] **135 Hudson St**. (warehouse), NW cor. Beach St. 1886-1887. **Kimball & Inhen.** ♂

A laid-back masonry warehouse, converted and now occupied by laid-back artists who appreciate true grit in architecture. As just a

T22a

sample of what to look for, note the cast-iron impost blocks at the top of the street-floor brick piers. And be on the lookout for more.

[T22a] **145 Hudson Street**/originally Hudson Square Building, bet. Hubert and Beach Sts. W side. 1929. **Renwick, Aspinwall & Guard**. Remodeled for residential lofts, 2000. **Joseph Pell Lombardi**. [22b] **5 Hubert Street** (new apartment building), bet. Hudson and Greenwich Sts. N side. 2000. **Joseph Pell Lombardi**. ○

Art Deco + Neo-Art Deco for the unexhausted lofters seeking an ambience redolent of an earlier Manhattan.

[T23] **Northmoore** (condominium apartments) 1) **Castree Building**, NW cor. North Moore and Hudson Sts. 1891. **Thomas R. Jackson**. 2) **Supporting buildings** along Hudson. 1890s. **Charles C. Haight**. ○

Why don't we build lofts anew? From scratch. With high ceilings and open plans.

T24

[T24] **53 North Moore Street** (lofts), bet. Hudson and Greenwich Sts. 1891. **Thomas R. Jackson**. ○

Roman Revival arches consort with a Classical cornice in this vigorous brick and terra-cotta warehouse.

[T25] **Holland Tunnel exit rotary**, Port Authority of New York & New Jersey/originally St. John's Park/later site of New York Central & Hudson River Railroad Freight Depot, Hudson to Varick Sts., Ericsson Place to Laight St.

A space occupied since 1927 by the exit roadways of the Holland Tunnel, this was once a square in a class with Washington Square and Gramercy Park: the houses surrounding it were grand Federal and Greek Revival places. Its owners, the Trinity Church Corporation, experiencing real estate decline, sold the great space to **Commodore Vanderbilt** for a railroad terminal (1869). Later the railroads moved uptown (passengers), and to the north and west (freight), and the railroad's abandonment made it a found-place for the car to penetrate New York's edge by tunnel.

T26

Until 1918 a handsome Georgian-Federal church, St. John's Chapel (1807. **John McComb, Jr.**) stood at the east side of the square (Varick Street) and gave the place its name. St. John's Lane, east of and parallel to Varick Street, memorializes the chapel. An *Evening Post* of 1847 lyrically describes St. John's Park as a "spot of eden loveliness . . . It seems as if retiring from the din and tumult of the noisy town to enjoy its own secret solitude." At this, amid the noise and tumult of belching autos, we heave a historical (and sometimes hysterical) sigh.

[T26] Originally **4th Precinct, NYC Police Department**/now 1st Precinct, 16 Ericsson Place (originally Beach St.), SW cor. Varick St. 1912. **Hoppin & Koen**. ○

A limestone Renaissance Revival palazzetto whose public interior in no way reflects the opulence of the exterior—except for the stable on the Varick Street side. The paddocks and other equine accoutrements have a quality that exceeds that provided for the officers.

T27

[T27] **The Ice House**/originally Merchants' Refrigerating Co., 27 N. Moore St., bet. Hudson and Varick Sts. 1905. **William H. Bickmire**. Renovations, 1998. **Joseph Pell Lombardi**. ○

Grand terra-cotta capitals top the small entrance façade on North Moore, and the larger one facing what was once St. John's Park (now the tunnel exit ramps). Would that the park were still there!

[T28] **AT&T Headquarters**/originally AT&T Long Lines Building, 32 Sixth Ave., bet. Walker and Lispenard Sts. to Church St. Originally 24 Walker Street Building. 1918. **McKenzie, Voorhees, & Gmelin**. Vast expansion, 1930-1932. **Voorhees, Gmelin & Walker**. ● Interior (lobby) ●

High Art Deco on an irregular site by one of its New York masters, architect **Ralph Walker**, responsible for New York Telephone's sprinkling of office towers during this period and for the nearby Western Union building as well. The lobbies, too, are worth a visit.

*On that long vacant site south of **Ralph Walker**'s old AT&T Longlines Building, an unlikely developer is building the "Tribeca Grand Hotel" (Avenue of the Americas/Sixth Avenue at White St). **The Hartz Mountain (birdseed-financed real estate) Architectural Staff** is doing the honors.*

[T29] **White Street**, W. Broadway to Church St. ♂
No. 2. 1808-1809. 🍎 A Federal house (**Gideon Tucker**), now merely a store propped up by a steel pipe-column, but a real building with a real use. The long-time liquor store has been usurped by a bar/restaurant called, not surprisingly, The Liquor Store.

T29

T29, Nos. 8-10

Nos. 8-10. 1869-1870. **Henry Fernbach**. Elaborated Tuscan columns. Watch for the neo-Renaissance trick of foreshortening each floor to increase the apparent height.

[T30] Originally **High Pressure Service Headquarters, NYC Fire Department**/later Department of Water Supply, Gas & Electricity, 226 W. Broadway, bet. Franklin and White Sts. W side. 1912. **Augustus D. Shepard, Jr.** ♂
This small gem is a sculpted, cream-glazed terra-cotta galaxy of Fire Department icons that remind one of society's need for water under pressure: hydrants, pipe couplings, valves, and the City's seal. Next door at 228 the eclectic façade rises over The Bubble Lounge.

T31

[T31] **218-224 West Broadway** (lofts), NW cor. Franklin St. to Varick St. 1881-1882. **George W. DaCunha**. ♂
The battered rusticated base distinguishes this bold, red brick behemoth, cousin to [T46 and T47] below, and other members of their family in the great late 19th-century masonry tradition.

[T32] **El Teddy's** (restaurant)/formerly Teddy's Restaurant, 219 W. Broadway, opp. Franklin St. E side. 1956. **Louis A. Bellini**. Redesigned, 1985, **Antonio Miralda**. Remodeled, 1989. **Christopher Chesmutt**. ♂

T32

T34

The earlier, pinkie-ring Teddy's (reputedly for the gravel-voiced set) reopened as El Internacional while the Statue of Liberty was briefly closed for repair, perhaps explaining artist **Miralda**'s 1¼-ton replica crown on its roof. The seeming apparition is particularly startling if you're walking up Franklin Street, as it pokes out from above the restaurant's painted, Dalmatian-patterned stone veneer wall (also the artist's idea). Whew!

[T33] **140 Franklin Street**, NW cor. Varick St. 1887. **Albert Wagner**. Altered to condominiums, 1999. **Sanba Inc.** ♂

Cream-colored Romanesque Revival. Built for the Walton Company, a manufacturer of wrapping papers. Wagner's more famous work was the Puck Building at Houston Street.

T35

[T34] **143 Franklin Street** (lofts), bet. Hudson and Varick Sts. 1897-1898. **Henry Anderson.** ♂

An eclectic melange of multicolored brick limestone, arched and banded. Urban Archaeology is an upscale distributor of lighting and bathroom fixtures that are recycled or merely copies.

[T35] **152 Franklin Street** (lofts), bet. Hudson and Varick Sts. N side. 1891. **John B. Snook & Sons.** ♂

Ruddy Romanesque Revival with a grand scale of piers and arches.

T36

[T36] **108 Hudson Street** (lofts), NE cor. Franklin St. 1902-1904. **George Howard Chamberlin**. Converted to residential, ca. 1980. ♂

Savor those rusticated marshmallow columns at the entrance portico of this marvelous Victorian Baroque heap.

[T37] Originally **Pierce Building** (lofts)/later Powell Building, 105 Hudson St., NW cor. Franklin St. 1892. **Carrère & Hastings**. Extension to N and upward, 1905, **Henri Fouchaux.** ♂

In the spirit of the Renaissance Revival triggered by Chicago's 1893 World Columbian Exposition. Actually a 7-story, 50-foot-wide corner building expanded 25 feet in width and 4 stories in height. Can you find the joints in this Renaissance Revival brick and terra-cotta façade?

T37

[T38] Originally **New York Mercantile Exchange**, 6 Harrison St., NW cor. Hudson St. 1884. **Thomas R. Jackson**. Converted to office condominium, 1987. **R. M. Kliment & Frances Halsband.** ♂

Romantic and picturesque in pressed brick and contrasting granite, with a prominent, incomparable tower. A hearty pile and a must-see work.

[T39] **175 West Broadway Building**, between Leonard and Worth Sts. E side. 1877. **Scott & Umbach.** ♠ ♂

Corbeled brick, polychromy, and the architects were from Newark?

T38

[T40] **39-41 Worth Street** (lofts), bet. W. Broadway and Church St. N side. 1860. **Samuel A. Warner**.

The first floor has been castrated by a banal "modernization."

[T41] **47 Worth Street** (lofts)/now New York Law School, Broad Student Center, bet. W. Broadway and Church St. N side. ca. 1860.

Recently restored to its Corinthian columned cast-iron grandeur.

T42

[T42] **Western Union Building**, 60 Hudson St., bet. Thomas and Worth Sts., E side to W. Broadway. 1928-1930. **Voorhees, Gmelin & Walker.** ♠ Interior (lobby) ♠

Nineteen shades of brick from brown to salmon form a subtly shaded palette. The lobby is luxuriant with the undulations of vaulting brickwork. From the same people who brought you AT&T Long Lines.

T41

[T43a] Originally **House of Relief, New York Hospital**/later U.S. Marine Hospital No. 70, 67 Hudson St., NW cor. Jay St. to Staple St. 1893. **Cady, Berg & See**. Converted to residential, 1985. New entry, 1999. **Audrey Matlock**. ♂ [T43b] Originally **Ambulance Annex**, 9 Jay St., NW cor. Staple St. 1907-1908. **Robertson & Potter**. ♂

T43a

The House of Relief was the Lower Manhattan emergency room of New York Hospital (then on West 15th Street near Fifth Avenue). The small structure to the west, which carries the hospital's NYH monogram, was later the ambulance quarters and is still attached across narrow Staple Street by an enclosed overhead bridge. Now a residential building.

Walk the 2-block-long, charming backwater that is Staple Street, named for the butter, eggs, cheese, and other staples shipped to the area.

[T44] **55 Hudson Street** (lofts), SW cor. Jay St. 1890. **McKim, Mead & White**. ♂ [T45] **165 Duane Street** (lofts), NW cor. Hudson St. overlooking Duane Park. 1881. **Stephen D. Hatch**. ♂

T44

A grand pair of 8- to 10-story bold, red brick monoliths, cousins to [T31] above, and to the old Federal Archives Building in the West Village.

Duane Park area:
Once the butter, eggs, and cheese market; such dealers are still to be found.

[T46] **Duane Park**, bet. Hudson, Duane, and Staple Sts. 1795. Reconstructed, 1940. Reconstructed once more, 1999. ♂

Annetje Jans' farm was near here (despite the WPA carvings on the flagpole base) after 1636. Family farmers included **Roeloff Jans**, whose widow married a Bogardus. The farm was later sold to **Governor Lovelace**, then the Duke of York confiscated it and gave it to Trinity Church. The city purchased it as a public park in 1797 for $5!

North (odd) side:

[T47] **171 Duane Street** (lofts), NW cor. Staple St. ca. 1859. ♂
Cast iron for an offbeat design.

T47

[T48] **173 Duane Street** (lofts), bet. Greenwich and Staple Sts. N side. 1880. **Babb & Cook.** ♂

A grand brick monolith. Note the naturalistic incised terra-cotta archivolts banding the great arches.

South (even) side:

T49

[T49] **Lovinger Cohn Associates**/formerly World Cheese Co., 172 Duane St., bet. Greenwich and Hudson Sts. S side, 1871-1872. **Jacob Weber**, designer. Remodeled 1994. **V. Polsinelli.** ♂

A modern elegance implanted behind the semielliptical cast-iron arches. **Brunelleschi** was handsomely remembered here but so was **Pierre Chareau**, whose Maison de Verre in Paris (1931) gave the world its first modernist monument in glass block. Note the curved triangles in the spandrels (the space between the arches).

T50

[T50] **168 Duane Street** (warehouse), W of Hudson St. opp. Duane Park. S side. 1886. **Stephen D. Hatch.** Converted to residential, 1986, **John T. Fifield Assocs.** ♂

Before commissioning his more flamboyant Washington Street warehouse [T19], developer **Fleming Smith** had Hatch do this one, perhaps as a trial run in the neo-Flemish style. After years as an eggpacking and cheese-making plant, it was converted into condos by **John D. Rockefeller**'s great-granddaughter, **Meile Rockefeller.**

T51

[T51] **36 Hudson Street** (lofts), NE cor. Duane St. 1891-1892. **Babcock & Morgan.** ♂

More Romanesque Revival. Vigorous.

[T52] **155 West Broadway** (lofts)/now New York City Supreme Court, NE cor. Thomas St. 1865. **Jardine, Hill & Murdock.** ♂

Two-faced and wonderful: noble Anglo-Italianate high style on wide West Broadway, brick-plain on industrial, narrow, side street Thomas.

[T53] **62 Thomas Street** (lofts), bet. W. Broadway and Church St. S side. 1864. ♂

A rare neo-Gothic cast-iron building once painted dark brown. We said (in 1988) that brown was a suitable medieval color. Is white less medieval? Note the polygonal columns.

[T54a] **The Odeon Restaurant**/originally The Tower Cafeteria, 145 W. Broadway, SE cor. Thomas St. 1888. **William Kuhles.** Cafeteria, ca. 1935. Altered into restaurant, 1980. **Lynn Wagenknecht, Brian McNaily, Keith McNally**, owner-designers. [T54b] **145-147 West Broadway** (lofts). 1869. John J. O'Neil. ♂

The only way to preserve even a vestige of New York's once ubiquitous streamlined, chrome, wood-paneled, and terrazzo self-service cafeterias is to gentrify them into popular, pricey, places like this. (An addition is the Bakelite mosaic of the Manhattan skyline recycled from the demolished Woolworth's flagship store at Fifth Avenue and 39th Street.) Included are the cafeterias' traditional blank checks (in historic times punched to indicate cost of purchases). They emerge from a semiautomatic check dispenser at the door: BONG!

The building that the Odeon occupies is an interesting work of cast iron that replicates a quoined stone wall.

CIVIC CENTER

The flavor of city life rests largely in the sharp juxtaposition of manifold activities—government, commerce, industry, housing, entertainment—with differing ethnic and economic groups. These precincts are a caricature of that thought.

Spreading out from City Hall, the neighborhood's center of gravity, are government offices (federal, state, and city), middle-income and public housing, commercial warehousing, the fringes of the financial district, Chinatown, and that ancient viaduct which made possible New York's consolidation with the City of Brooklyn: the Brooklyn Bridge.

These streets are some of New York's most venerable, but only a smattering of the structures that originally lined them remain. Slowly the blocks have been consolidated, and larger and larger single projects of all kinds are built or planned— housing projects, government structures, and a college campus.

Civic Center Walking Tour: From St. Paul's Chapel to Chambers Street and West Broadway, encompassing City Hall, the old newspaper publishing district, the Municipal Building and Foley Square, and the Other cast-iron district (as contrasted with SoHo). START at Broadway and Fulton Street (IRT Lexington Avenue express [Nos. 4 or 5 trains] to Fulton Street Station or any train to Fulton Street or Broadway-Nassau Stations [2, 3, 4, 5, A, C, J, M, N, R, or Z]).

[C1] **St. Paul's Chapel (Episcopal) and Churchyard,** Broadway bet. Fulton and Vesey Sts. W side to Church St. 1764-1766. Porch, 1767-1768. Maybe **Thomas McBean.** Tower and steeple, 1794-1796, **James Crommelin Lawrence.** 🍎

Manhattan's only extant pre-Revolutionary building. Although the city's present territory contains a dozen older structures, they were isolated farmhouses or country seats that bear no more relation to the city than do still-rural 18th-century houses in outlands surrounding today's metropolis. Unlike Fraunces Tavern, St. Paul's is as close to the original as any building requiring maintenance

CIVIC CENTER
see pages 65–78

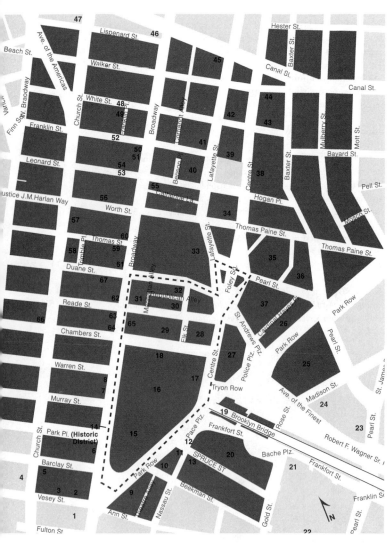

over 200 years could be. Stone from the site (Manhattan schist) forms walls that are quoined, columned, parapeted, pedimented, porched, and towered in Manhattan's favorite 18th- and 19th-century masonry, brownstone.

A gilt weathervane forms a finial to the finial of a tower crowning a "Choragic Monument of Lysicrates" (Hellenistic Greek monument for Renaissance and neo-Renaissance copycats).

The graveyard is a green oasis, dappled with sunlight, an umbrella of trees over somber gravestones. Ivy. Squirrels. Lovely.

It is rumored that **Pierre L'Enfant**, the soldier-architect who designed the Federal Hall, America's first capitol, and laid out the plan for Washington, D.C., designed the golden sunburst (gloire) over the high altar.

Governor Clinton's and **President Washington**'s pews are within.

[C2] **New York County Lawyers' Association**, 14 Vesey St., bet. Church St. and Broadway. 1929-1930. **Cass Gilbert.** 🖤

C2

Subdued white limestone in Gilbert's late, fainthearted years.

Built almost two decades after he completed the Woolworth Building nearby, it is the wimp of the neighborhood, but forming a neutral backdrop for some views of St. Paul's.

[C3] Originally **New York Evening Post Building** (offices)/later Garrison Building, 20 Vesey St., bet. Church St. and Broadway. 1906-1907. **Robert D. Kohn**. **Gutzon Borglum** and E**stelle Rumbold Kohn**, sculptors. 👁

The interest here is at the top. **Kohn**, his wife, **Estelle Rumbold Kohn**, and **Borglum** collaborated to create sculptured limestone and copper Art Nouveau.

C3

[C4] **Federal Office Building**, 90 Church St., bet. Vesey and Barclay Sts. W side to W. Broadway. 1935. **Cross & Cross** and **Pennington, Lewis & Mills, Inc**. **Lewis A. Simon**, Supervising Architect of the Treasury.

A boring limestone monolith that has trouble deciding between a heritage of stripped-down neo-Classical and a new breath of Art Deco.

[C5] **St. Peter's Church** (Roman Catholic), 22 Barclay St., SE cor. Church St. 1836-1840. **John R. Haggerty** and **Thomas Thomas**. 👁

C5

A granite Greek Revival temple with smooth Ionic columns. The wood-framed pediment and roof structure are sheathed in sheet metal molded to the appropriate profiles.

Columbia College (originally King's College) occupied the blocks between West Broadway, Barclay, Church, and Murray Streets. The river's edge was then 250 feet away, approximately at Greenwich Street, offering a view and sea breezes to the then-rural student and faculty bodies. In 1857 the college moved north, occupying the former buildings of the deaf and dumb asylum between 49th and 50th Streets, Madison and Park Avenues.

[C6] **Woolworth Building** (offices), 233 Broadway, bet. Park Place and Barclay St. W side. 1910-1913. **Cass Gilbert**. 👁 Partial interior 👁 Façade restored, 1977-1981. **Ehrenkrantz Group**.

Once much maligned for its eclectic Gothic detail and one-time charcoal Gothic crown, this sheer shaft is one of New York's most imposingly sited skyscrapers. Rising 792 feet without setback, it soars; only the Seagram and CBS Buildings have the combination of articulate architecture and massing to achieve similar drama. The lobby is clothed in Skyros veined marble. **Horace Walpole**, who built a Gothic "castle" at "Strawberry Hill" and wrote *The Castle of Otranto* (1765), could have set his action here.

C6

The lobby sculpture is amusing: **Woolworth** counting nickels; **Gilbert** holding a model of the building; **Gunwald Aus**, the structural engineer, measuring a girder; and others.

[C7] Originally **Postal Telegraph Building**/now annex to Home Life Insurance Building (below), 253 Broadway, bet. Murray and Warren Sts. W side. 1892-1894. **Harding & Gooch**. 👁

C8

[C8] Originally **Home Life Insurance Building** (offices), 256-257 Broadway, bet. Murray and Warren Sts. W side. 1892-1894. **Napoleon Le Brun & Son**. 👁

Home Life is a lordly midblock building, with a steep pyramidal top, that was among the world's tallest when it opened. **Pierre**, son of **Napoleon**, was the son-in-charge. 253 is a pallid brick annex to the vigorous 256.

Park Row:
The east boundary of City Hall Park, from south to north.

C9

[C9] Originally **Park Row Building** (offices)/also known as Park Row Syndicate Building, Ivins Syndicate Building, 15 Park Row, bet. Ann and Beekman Sts. E side. 1899. **R. H. Robertson.** 🍎

Twin towers for the romantic businessman—guarded by 4 caryatids on the 4th floor. From 1899 to 1908 it was the world's tallest building, at 386 feet.

C10

[C10] **Potter Building** (originally offices/now apartments), 38 Park Row, NE cor. Beekman St. 1882-1886. **Norris G. Starkweather.** 🍎 Converted to apartments, 1979-1981.

An elaborately ornate confection in cast and pressed terra-cotta, an early use in New York of a material that was to become the rage, producing repetitive elaboration economically. The invisibly used structural steel of this building is the first in New York to be fireproofed by terra-cotta.

Jack Finney's marvelous redolence, *Time and Again*, takes place in and around the burning of the first Potter Building. Within its pages you can conjure up the sensory flavors of 1882.

C11

[C11] **Pace University**/originally The New York Times Building, 41 Park Row, bet. Beekman and Spruce Sts. 1889. **George B. Post.** Expanded upward, 1905, **Robert Maynicke.** 🍎

Rusticated granite that would have been exemplary in any hands other than Post's (see the Long Island Historical Society in Brooklyn for vintage Post). The *Times* left here for what was to become Times Square.

[C12] **Benjamin Franklin statue**, Printing House Sq. at the intersection of Park Row, Nassau, and Spruce Sts. 1872. **Ernst Plassman**, sculptor.

C12

Here, where the *Times*, *Tribune*, *Herald*, *World*, and *Sun* were once published, is a square that commemorates old Newspaper Row and the many job printers who located hereabouts. A beneficent bronze Franklin holds a copy of his *Pennsylvania Gazette*.

[C13] Originally **American Tract Society Building** (offices), 150 Nassau St., SE cor. Spruce St. 1896. **R. H. Robertson.** 🍎

The fascination here is at the roof, where giant "Romanesque" arches provide a geometry of architecture separate from the rusticated granite below.

C13

[C14] **African Burial Ground and the Commons Historic District.** 🍎

The Commons served eclectically as pasture, parade ground, and place for celebrations and executions. It harbored at various times powder magazines, an almshouse, and a jail. What a venerable palimpsest for what became New York's first park (1780s), setting for the new City Hall (1802+), and, between Chambers and Duane Streets, a cemetery for both slaves and freed Africans!

[C15] **City Hall Park**/formerly The Common, bet. Broadway and Park Row/Centre St., from Vesey/Ann St. to Chambers St. ca. 1730. ⚙️

In the early 18th century the city itself extended barely to Fulton Street, when the eastern boundary of The Common was determined by the Boston (or Eastern) Post Road. On its northward trek it spawned other thoroughfares that linked the island's scattered villages and settlements.

Buildings, seemingly for random purposes at random locations, occupied pieces of this turf from time to time. One of special note was Vanderlyn's Rotunda (near the southwest corner of Chambers and Centre Streets), a mini-Pantheon for the display of panoramic views, such as that of Versailles, which, in a pre-photography, pre-electronic world simulated the experience of being there very nicely. The biggest guest building was

C15

C16

the Post Office by **Alfred Mullett**, much maligned at the time; in retrospect it was a rich building inspired by **Napoleon III**'s Paris. Mullett's more famous, and preserved, building is the Executive Office Building in Washington.

Assorted sculpture is also present: **Nathan Hale** (1893. **Frederick MacMonnies**, sculptor; **Stanford White**, architect of the base) is looking into the BMT for his tardy date. **Horace Greeley** (1890. **J. Q. A. Ward**) is grandly seated before the Surrogate's Court.

New events include the replacement of the 1871 Jacob Wrey Mould fountain exiled to Crotona Park, and a new fence cast from the one removed to a Bloomingburg, N.Y., cemetery.

[C16] **City Hall**, City Hall Park, bet. Broadway and Park Row. 1802-1812. **Joseph François Mangin** and **John McComb, Jr**. Altered, 1860, **Leopold Eidlitz**; 1898, **John Duncan**; 1903, **William Martin Aiken**; 1907, 1915, 1917, **Grosvenor Atterbury**; 1956, **Shreve, Lamb & Harmon**; 1998, **Cabrera Barricklo**. 🏛 ♂ Interior 🏛

A minipalace, crossing French Renaissance detail with Federal form, perhaps inevitable where the competition-winning scheme was the product of a Frenchman and the first native-born New York City architect. **Mangin** (who had worked in Paris with **Gabriel** on the Place de la Concorde) was the principal preliminary designer and theorist; **McComb** supervised construction and determined much of the detailing.

The central domed space leads past the offices of mayor and city councilmen, up twin spiral, self-supporting marble stairs to the Corinthian-columned rotunda serving as entry to both the City Council Chamber and the old Board of Estimate chambers. The Governor's Room, originally for his use when in New York City, is now a portrait gallery replete with portraits by **Sully**, **Inman**, **Jarvis**, **Trumbull**, and others.

Interiors have been restored and refurbished, and the exterior peeled off and reproduced in new Alabama limestone (piece by piece). The soft original Massachusetts marble had badly eroded by joint attacks of pollution and pigeons—the rear of the building had been built in brownstone to save money!

A bronze tablet in front of City Hall commemorates the commencement of construction of the first viable subway system in America: the IRT (Interborough Rapid Transit) in 1900.

Real and imaginary disturbances of the peace (or perhaps just of the Mayor's ego) have led to some governmental paranoia. The fence and gates that now surround the Park hinder access to the outside of the building, and visits within are problematical for any without specific business.

[C17] **City Hall Station**, IRT Lexington Avenue Line local, below City Hall Park. 1904. **Heins & La Farge**. 🏛 Not open to the public. ♂

Under City Hall Park, and sealed like King Tut's tomb, is the world's most beautiful (former) subway station at the south

edge of the loop that turns the Lexington Avenue IRT locals around from "Brooklyn Bridge" pointed south to "Brooklyn Bridge" pointed north. **Heins & La Farge** were the architects (1904). Serious citizens have proposed using these grand spaces for a new transit museum. If successful, they will return a glorious civic place to the public.

C18

[C18] Old **New York County Courthouse** ("Tweed" Courthouse)/now municipal offices, 52 Chambers St., bet. Broadway and Centre St. S side. 1861-1872, **John Kellum** and **Thomas Little.** Enlarged, 1877-1991. **Leopold Eidlitz.** ✿ Interior ✿ Restorations, 1990s. **John Waite.** ♂

A building both maligned and praised: maligned mostly because of the great scandal in its construction (the Tweed Ring

C19

apparently made off with $10 of the $14 million construction "cost"); praised because of a new understanding of, and interest in, Victorian architecture: perhaps a late Victorian version of an English Renaissance country house.

[C19] **Brooklyn Bridge**/originally New York & Brooklyn Bridge, Park Row, Manhattan, to Adams St., Brooklyn, 1867-1883. **John A. and Washington Roebling.** ✿

A saunter across the raised central boardwalk to Brooklyn Heights is one of the great dramatic strolls of New York. As a side tour from City Hall, it is a unique experience, viewing Brooklyn, Manhattan, their skylines, and the harbor through a filigree of cables.

The steel and cables have been repainted their original sprightly colors—beige and light brown—instead of the somber battleship gray that gloomed for a misguided generation.

C20

"Brooklyn Bridge, which is old, . . . is as strong and rugged as a gladiator, while George Washington Bridge, built yesterday, smiles like a young athlete. In this case the two large Gothic towers of stone are very handsome because they are American and not "Beaux-Arts." They are full of native sap . . ."

—**Charles Edouard Jeanneret** (**Le Corbusier**) *When the Cathedrals Were White,* 1947

[C20] **Pace University**, New Building, Nassau, Frankfort, Gold, and Spruce Sts. 1970. **Eggers & Higgins**. Expanded upward, 1984, **The Eggers Partnership**.

Limestone and bronze-anodized aluminum trying to look Modern. Benign.

C21

[C21] **New York City Department of Housing, Planning & Development (HPD)**/formerly Bache Plaza, 100 Gold St., SE cor. Frankfort St. 1969. **Gruzen & Partners**.

A delicate concrete cage reminiscent of Alvar Aalto. A pleasant and glassy understatement.

[C22] **Southbridge Towers** (housing complex), Gold, Frankfort, Water, and Fulton Sts. 1969. **Gruzen & Partners**.

The charm of this scheme is in the contained urban spaces surrounded by 6-story buildings—new at the time in publicly assisted housing. This is a Mitchell-Lama middle-income housing project.

[C23] **New York Telephone Company** (switching center), 375 Pearl St., SW cor. St. James Place to Avenue of the Finest. 1976. **Rose, Beaton & Rose**.

Through its height and proximity to the Brooklyn Bridge's Manhattan tower, this humorless, windowless, high-rise monster diminished much of the majesty of that great span.

C23

[C24] **Murry Bergtraum High School**, 411 Pearl St., S cor. Madison St. to Avenue of the Finest. 1976. **Gruzen & Partners**.

A sleek, purple-brown triangular "fort," complete with corner turrets, financed, through the Educational Construction Fund (a sometime experiment in school financing, now defunct), by the overwhelming telephone building next door. (The air rights of the school provide zoning credit for the telephone building; the latter, in return, pays off the bonds that built the school.)

C24

[C25] **NYC Police Headquarters**, bet. Park Row, Pearl St., and Avenue of the Finest. 1973. **Gruzen & Partners**, architects, **M. Paul Friedberg**, landscape architect.

One of New York's most urbane civic buildings since the City Hall of 1812, largely because of its elegant—but ill-maintained—plaza, stepped pedestrian passageways, and terraces that form an interlock for people in this otherwise car-infested area. An orange/brown brick cube of office space hovers over special police facilities below.

Five in One, a sculpture by **Bernard (Tony) Rosenthal** in self-weathering (consciously rusty) steel, looms over the Municipal Building end.

C25

[C26] **Metropolitan Correctional Center**, bet. Park Row, Duane and Pearl Sts. 1975. **Gruzen & Partners**.

An annex to **Cass Gilbert**'s U.S. Courthouse provides offices and a detention center. It forms a happy foil to the same firm's Police Headquarters and plaza adjacent.

C26

[C27] **Municipal Building**, Centre St., opp. Chambers St. E side. 1907-1914. **McKim, Mead & White** (**William M. Kendall and Burt Fenner**). Façade restoration, 1990. **Wank Adams Slavin**. 🍎

This is urbane architecture, boldly straddling a city street. In those days the ways of traffic were entwined with architecture (see **Warren & Wetmore**'s Grand Central Terminal of 1913). The "Choragic Monument" atop this composition is, in turn, surmounted by *Civic Fame* by **Adolph A. Weinman**. For Guastavino tile fans, move under the arcaded south wing (over the subway entrance); look up.

C27

[C28] **Surrogate's Court/Hall of Records**, 31 Chambers St., bet. Centre and Elk Sts. N side. 1899-1907. **John Rochester Thomas** and **Horgan & Slattery**. 🍎 ⚲
Interior 🍎

Civic monuments were designed to impress the citizen in those days—not merely humor him, as is most often the case today. Therefore, his records were kept in a place of splendor. Go in. The central hall, in a small way, is worthy of **Charles Garnier**'s earlier Paris Opera.

[C29] Originally **Emigrant Industrial Savings Bank Building**/now City of New York office building, 51 Chambers

C28

C30

C31

St., bet. Broadway and Elk St. N side to Reade St. 1908-1912. **Raymond F. Almirall.** 🍎 ♂ Interior. 🍎

The third facility of the Emigrant Bank to occupy this site. Organized in 1851 to serve the city's Irish Catholic immigrant population, the Emigrant was once America's wealthiest savings bank. The building, a mix of Beaux Arts and Art Nouveau, is now used by the City's bureaucracy. Note the ranks of copper oriels in the light courts and the spirited—if somewhat flat—sculptures that top each wing: the source of **Almirall**'s ornament was Vienna, not Dublin.

[C30] **NYC Department of City Planning**, 22 (formerly 14, 16, 18, 20, 22) Reade St., bet. Lafayette St. and Broadway. N side. No. 14, 1878. Nos. 16, 18, 20, 22, ca. 1858. Restored, 1987, **NYC Department of General Services Architectural Division.** ♂

After a quarter century next door, in the undistinguished Court Square Building—more familiarly known simply as 2 Lafayette Street (1927, **Buchman & Kahn**)—the Planning Department and its commissioners took up residence in this once-again distinguished row of 6-story, 19th-century business buildings. Though they're not designated landmarks, preservation certainly did prevail.

[C31] **Federal Offices**, 290 Broadway, NE corner Reade St. 1994. **Hellmuth, Obata & Kassabaum.**

The Post-Modernists have quietly arrived: quietly, as most of the spectacle is at the top, to be seen from afar, and the streetscape seems a pleasant reprise from the Rockefeller Center era of polished brass and granite.

[C32] **African Burial Ground Memorial**, SW cor. Duane and Elk Sts. 2001. **CR Studio Architects.** ♂

A timber platform floating above the surrounding sidewalk acts as base for a terra-cotta vessel of many panels allowing one to peer into a memorial space.

Foley Square
Big Tom's Square: *The chaotic irregular subdivided excuse for a public space, around which are gathered many of the Civic Center's noble structures, is—in the old New York tradition—named for* **Thomas F. ("Big Tom") Foley** *(1852-1925). He was an alderman, sheriff, saloonkeeper, Tammany Hall district leader, and political mentor of* **Governor Alfred E. Smith**. *The square, site of Big Tom's last saloon, was named for him by his successors on the Board of Aldermen in 1926, before construction had even begun.*

C33

Clockwise around the square from the west:

[C33] **Jacob K. Javits Federal Office Building and Court of International Trade** (Customs Court), 26 Federal Plaza, Foley Sq. bet. Duane and Worth Sts. W side. 1963-1969. **Alfred Easton Poor, Kahn & Jacobs, Eggers & Higgins**, associate architects. Western addition on Broadway 1975-1977, **Kahn & Jacobs, The Eggers Partnership, Poor & Swanke**. New plaza landscaping, 1997. **Martha Schwartz**.

The building: an ungainly checkerboard of granite and glass was built along Foley Square, later extended westward to Broadway with a continued heavy hand.

The tranquil work of **Martha Schwartz** has succeeded the vibrant sculpture of **Richard Serra**. Fortunately, the benches and sculpted mounds of grass are a happy event. Serenity replaces passion.

"Tilted Arc," 1981, **Richard Serra**, sculptor. Removed 1990s.

The sculpture: a prerusted 75-ton steel work rested on the building's Foley Square plaza, becoming the subject of contention when added as part of a federal .5% set-aside-for-art program.

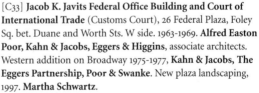

Opponents: "A symbol of artistic noblesse oblige."

Serra: "This newly created concave volume has a silent amplitude which amplifies your awareness of yourself and the sculptural field of the space."

A great work, but the philistines won this round.

[C34] Originally **NYC Department of Health Building** (offices)/now Health, Hospitals, and Sanitation Departments Building, 125 Worth St., bet. Lafayette and Center Sts. N side to Leonard St. 1935. **Charles B. Meyers**.

C35

The interest here, aside from the spandrel ornament and bas-reliefs on the boxy neo-Classical *cum* Art Deco cube, is in the finely crafted pairs of anthropomorphic bronze Art Deco torchères that flank the main entrances. Mmmmm, luscious!

[C35] **New York County Courthouse**/now New York State Supreme Court, 60 Centre St., bet. Pearl St., Hamill Place, and Worth St. in Foley Sq. E side. 1913-1927. **Guy Lowell**.
🍒 Interior 🍒

This Hexagon anticipated the Pentagon by 30 years. Lowell's scheme won a 1912 competition (but wasn't built until much later) in the spirit of both City Hall and the Municipal Building. The imposing Corinthian portico is handsome Roman archaeology but doesn't measure up to the vigorous planning of the building. A grand form to view from above.

C36

[C36] **U.S. Courthouse Annex**, behind New York County Courthouse, 500 Pearl St. bet. Worth St. and Park Row. 1995. **Kohn Pedersen Fox Associates**.

Concave and convex, recessed and bellied out: two mannerisms of the current crop of new Federal Buildings that separate them from the neo-Rockefeller Center crowd.

C37

[C37] **U.S. Courthouse**, 40 Centre St., SE cor. Pearl St., in Foley Sq. E side. 1933-1936. **Cass Gilbert** and **Cass Gilbert, Jr**. 🍒

Capped by another Gilbert gold pyramid in the manner of the New York Life Insurance Company Building. Dour granite.

The northern Civic Center:

[C38] **NYC Criminal Courts Building and Men's House of Detention**, 100 Centre St., bet. Leonard and White Sts. E side to Baxter St. 1939. **Harvey Wiley Corbett** and **Charles B. Meyers**. House of Detention redesigned, 1986, **The Gruzen Partnership**.

C38

The Tombs was named after its Egyptian Revival, long-gone, twice-over ancestor (across the street). This is a ziggurated construction overlaid with stylish detail of the 1930s: Art Moderne, as at the Paris Exposition of 1937. The redesign is largely within.

[C39] **Civil Courthouse, City of New York**, 111 Centre St., SW cor. White St. 1960. **William Lescaze** and **Matthew Del Gaudio**.

A sleek but dull cube fills the site facing an open plaza, under which the City concealed the area's air-conditioning equipment. Another monster court will soon fill this void. Bas-reliefs by **William Zorach**.

C40

[C40] **Family Court**, City of New York, 60 Lafayette St., bet. Leonard and Franklin Sts. 1975. **Haines, Lundberg & Waehler**.

Black, polished, and pretentious. A busy, somber, relentlessly competitive group of cubistic granite forms. What message does this building's architecture send to families with problems?

[C41] **Ahrens Building**, 70-76 Lafayette St., bet. Franklin and White Sts. W side. 1894-1896. **George H. Griebel**. ●✤
Smooth and stylish Romanesque Revival brick archwork.

C41

[C42] Originally **Engine Company No.31, NYC Fire Department**/now Downtown Community Television Center, 87 Lafayette St., NE cor. White St. 1895. **Napoleon LeBrun & Sons**. ●✤

This was a house for fire engines, disguised as a Loire Valley château; now happily reincarnated as a nonprofit TV center, it is still disguised as a Loire Valley château.

[C43] **White Street Correctional Facility**, NYC Department of Correction, bet. Centre and Baxter Sts. N side to Walker St. 1989. **Urbahn Assocs., Inc**. and **Litchfield-Grosfeld Assocs.**, joint venture.

High-rise maximum-security detention for 500 inmates, rising from a base of little shops, a community clock, and a bridge of sighs connecting to the Tombs. Tootsie Rolls?

C42

[C44] **Chung Pak Building** (housing, social welfare agencies, and shops), 125 Walker St., bet. Centre and Baxter Sts. 1991. **The Edelman Partnership**.

Housing for the elderly rises over a health clinic, child care, and shops. Vertical zoning for these very urban Chinatown residents.

Cast-Iron District 1 (South of Canal Street)

C44

Cast iron gave an inexpensive means of reproducing elaborate detail, previously possible only as carving in stone. More Corinthian, Ionic, Doric, Composite, Egyptian and Lord-knows-what-else columns were cast for New York façades of the 1850s and 1860s than Greece and Rome turned out in a millennium. The two great centers were between Broadway and West Broadway, Canal to Duane (here and in Tribeca described), and, to the north, Crosby Street to West Broadway, Canal to Houston Streets, now rechristened SoHo [a separate precinct, below].

These handsome loft spaces have been used by assorted commercialdom, principally for warehousing, sometimes for light manufacturing, often for studios by the neighborhood's many real or would-be artists, but more and more for those seeking the seemingly chic syle of loft living.

C45

[C45] **254-260 Canal Street** (lofts), SW cor. Lafayette St. 1857. Cast-iron façades attributed to **James Bogardus**. ●✤
Converted to offices, 1987, **Jack L. Gordon**.

One of the city's earliest surviving cast-iron façade buildings. If in fact the castings are by **Bogardus**, this would be the largest and most important of his extant works. Beautiful!

[C46] **415 Broadway** (shops and offices)/originally National City Bank of New York, bet. Canal and Lispenard Streets. 1927. **Walker & Gillette**. Remodeled, 1998. **Joseph Pell Lombardi**. ●ᶜ

Art Moderne. 1812 on the upper façade is the date of the bank's founding.

C47

[C47] Former **United States Post Office**, SW cor. Canal and Church Sts. 1937. **Alan Balch Mills**.

Art Moderne. The articulated inset bay-windows on Church Street are a wonderful mannerism (often used in late 19th-century architecture). They give the illusion of scanning the street north and south, and add plasticity to the building.

[C48] **White Street**, Church St. to Broadway. [C48a] **No. 36**. "Let There Be Neon." Formerly on West Broadway, a shop that elevates neon to an art form.

C48a   C48b

[C48b] **No. 46-50**. 1865. Formerly Woods Mercantile Building. ●ᶜ A set of buildings organized by its pediment. [C48c] **No. 52**. Tuscan columns, segmental arches. [C48d] **Nos. 54-56**. Italianate brownstone over the cast-iron ground floor. [C48e] **Nos. 55-57**. Condict Store (saddlery). 1861. **John Kellum & Son**. Another **Daniel D. Badger Architectural Iron Works** project, unhappily with a mutilated ground floor. ●ᶜ [C48f] **Nos. 60-66**. 1869. Crisp white piers and cornices.

C50

[C49] **Congregation Shaare Zedek** (Civic Center Synagogue), 49 White St., bet. Church St. and Broadway. S side. 1965-1967. **William N. Breger Assocs**.

Interrupting the street frontage, Shaare Zedek unrolls a ribbon of undulating marble tiles to reveal a garden behind: unhappily (due to modern security needs) barred from the passerby by wrought-iron fencing. Dated.

[C50] Originally **James S. White Building** (lofts), 361 Broadway, SW cor. Franklin St. 1881-1882. **W. Wheeler Smith**. ●ᶜ Renovations, 2000. **Joseph Pell Lombardi**.

A corner building with two intersecting late cast-iron façades. Catercorner, across the street at 362, are some resident stern-eyed Classical caryatids (breastplates attached) holding up the third floor.

C52

[C51] Originally **Thompson's Saloon**, 359 Broadway, between Franklin and Leonard Sts. W side. 1852. ●ᶜ

Brady's Gallery occupied the upper three floors. **Abraham Lincoln** came here to be photographed the morning after his famed Cooper Union speech, which many believe won him the presidency.

[C52] **Franklin Street**, bet. Church St. and Broadway. 1860s.

C53

More white, brown, and simulated (cast-iron) stone. Savor the Corinthian capitals, the glassy windows, the rich and variegated variations on a theme. Until recently a tired but elegant block, it is now blossoming with paint and washed windows. It is said that **Renwick and Co.** did No. 71 (not much glory for Renwick here). Nos. 86-88 make a rich stone and cast-iron set.

[C53] **Leonard Street**, bet. Church St. and Broadway. 1860s.
Limestone (white), brownstone, and cast iron. The game is to look to separate them: the iron tends to be more slender than the brittle stone. For cast iron at No. 85, see below; Nos. 87-89 (1860-1863) are similar but simpler, and of stone, matching **Bogardus'** cast iron. Nos. 80-82. 1860-1862. **James H. Giles**; Nos. 74-78 Leonard. 1860s. Grand Corinthian capitals; No. 73. 1863. **James F. Duckworth**; No. 71. 1860. **Samuel A. Warner**.

C54

[C54] Originally **Kitchen, Montross & Wilcox Store**, 85 Leonard St., bet. Church St. and Broadway. 1861. **James Bogardus**. 🌂
Sperm-candle style (a new classification for the cocktail-party preservationist) provides two-story columns emulating candles. The fire escapes mask much of the guts of this rare Bogardus remnant.

C55

[C55] Originally **New York Life Insurance Company Building**/now New York City Municipal Offices, 346 Broadway, bet. Catherine Lane and Leonard St. E side to Lafayette St. (originally Elm St.) also known as 108 Leonard St. E end, 1894-1899. **Stephen D. Hatch** with **McKim, Mead & White**. W end, **Stanford White** of McKim, Mead & White. 🌂 Various interior spaces. 🌂
N.Y. Life occupied the Broadway end of this long narrow block since 1870. **Hatch** was engaged to design an eastern addition but died (1894) before construction was completed. **MM&W** joined in the completion of the addition and went on to demolish the original Broadway structure and design its successor, with its distinguished Classical clock overlooking Broadway.
N.Y. Life vacated the building in 1928 for its uptown tower; No. 346 has been owned since 1967 by the City. Do look at the semicircular elevator bank and visit:

[C55a] **Clocktower Gallery**, 108 Leonard St., bet. Broadway and Lafayette St. Open to the public erratically, when special exhibits are on display. 212-233-1096.
A not-for-profit gallery of avant-garde art located in the grand, cubical, top-floor room of the N.Y. Life tower, operated by the Institute for Art & Urban Resources, which also operates, with MOMA (Museum of Modern Art), P.S. 1 in L.I.C.

C56

[C56] **65-85 Worth Street** (lofts), bet. Church St. and Broadway. N side. ca. 1865.
This handsome remnant row of neo-Renaissance whitestone buildings once faced a fabulous cast-iron row, replaced by [C57] below.

C57

[C57] **American Telephone & Telegraph Company Long Lines Building**, Church St. bet. Thomas and Worth Sts. E side. 1974. **John Carl Warnecke & Assocs**.
A giant electronic complex in the guise of a building. Pink, textured (flame-treated) Swedish granite sheathes a stylish leviathan that looms over the city with architectural eyebrows. The only bow to the neighboring humanity is a bleak plaza to the east. Ma Bell, why didn't you leave the air for people and place your electrons underground?

C59

[C58] **NYS Insurance Fund** (offices), 199 Church St., bet. Thomas and Duane Sts. E side to Trimble Place. 1955. **Lorimer Rich Assocs**.
A white glazed-brick monolith atop a polished red granite base. The funky flaring stainless-steel entrance canopy is a dated 1950s relic.

C60

[C59] **8 Thomas Street Building**/formerly David S. Brown Store, bet. Broadway and Church St. S side. 1875-1876. **J. Morgan Slade**. 🏛

An elaborate confection of Romanesque, Venetian Gothic, brick, sandstone, granite, and cast-iron parts, worthy of **John Ruskin**, whose polemics inspired such thoughts as this and the Jefferson Market Courthouse.

Lofts for sale: we'd love an apartment on almost any floor.

[C60] Originally **Metropolitan Life Insurance Company Home Office**, 319 Broadway, NW cor. Thomas St. 1869-1870. **David & John Jardine**. 🏛

More of the **Daniel D. Badger Architectural Iron Works "Good Works"** stands as a sentinel marking the entrance of Thomas Street; now seriously marred by grossly unsympathetic commercial alterations at the street. Very elaborate, this is a cast-iron gem of the first order. The New York Life Insurance Company began in rented rooms in this structure before graduating to [C55] above.

[C61] **Langdon Building** (lofts), 305 Broadway, NW cor. Duane St. 1892-1894. **William H. Hume**.

Handsome clustered Romanesque Revival colonnettes form piers with ornamented capitals that are equal to the natural incised bas-reliefs of **Louis Sullivan**.

C62

[C62] **East River Savings Institution Building**, 291 Broadway, NW cor. Reade St. 1910-1911. **Clinton & Russell**.

Corinthian pilasters hold up an impressive entablature; the frieze alternates windows and cartouches where the metopes and triglyphs were placed in Classical temples.

C63

[C63] **287 Broadway** (lofts), SW cor. Reade St. 1871-1872. **John B. Snook**. 🏛

A glassy mansarded, wrought-iron-crested, Ionic- and Corinthian-columned, cast-iron delight. Lovely!

[C64] **Broadway Chambers Building** (offices), 277 Broadway, NW cor. Chambers St. 1899-1900. **Cass Gilbert**. 🏛

Carefully stacked granite, brick, and limestone. Renaissance Revival. Look up. The top presents an arcade crowned with a cornice including the heads of ladies and lions. **Gilbert** was fascinated with architectural sculpture (his own image in the Woolworth Building included; not to mention his role in the Supreme Court pediment in Washington). A Nedick's hot dog

C64

stand once scarred the corner; note the carefully matched and replaced granite.

[C65] **280 Broadway** (municipal offices)/formerly Sun Building/originally A. T. Stewart Dry Goods Store, NE cor. Chambers St. 1845-1846. **John B. Snook** of **Joseph Trench & Co.** Additions: 1850-1851, 1852-1853, **Trench & Snook;** 1872, **Frederick Schmidt;** 1884, **Edward D.Harris.** 1921. ● Rehabilitation, 1999. **Beyer Blinder Belle.**

Here **Stewart** founded America's first great department store, later to occupy grand premises at Broadway between 9th and 10th Streets (known to recent generations as Wanamaker's, who bought out all of Stewart's enterprises). **Henry James** and **Anthony Trollope** both lavished words of wonder on these premises. Later the *Sun* was published here. The corner clock, long frozen, is now running again (frequently).

C66

[C66] Originally **Cary Building** (lofts), 105-107 Chambers St., NW cor. Church St. to Reade St. 1856-1857. **King & Kellum.** Cast-iron façade by **D. D. Badger's Architectural Ironworks.** ● Storefronts altered, 1985, **Grandesign Architects.**

C67

This Anglo-Italianate palazzo, despite its losses (and pleasant retail gains) at street level, reflects the talents of **John Kellum,** who went on to design some of the city's finest cast-iron structures, such as the now demolished, full-block A. T. Stewart Store. Construction of The Cary heralded the establishment of a commercial center north and west of City Hall in the mid 19th century. Once a midblock structure, it has boasted an inadvertent east façade ever since Church Street was widened for the IND subway in the late 1920s.

[C67] Formerly **Fire Engine Company No. 7**/Hook & Ladder Company No.1/now Hook & Ladder Company No. 1 and Fire Department Bureau of Fire Communication, 100 Duane St., bet. Church St. and Broadway. 1904-1905. **Trowbridge & Livingston.** ●

An Anglicized palazzo in banded brick and rusticated limestone; a stylish stable for fire engines.

Colonnaded block: Look carefully at the storefronts surrounding the block bounded by West Broadway and Reade, Duane, and Church Streets, and you'll discover along the ground floor a series of fluted Corinthian cast-iron columns carrying the masonry façades of the upper floors. Some are asphyxiated with modern materials or just hidden behind unwashed show windows, but they are there. What a wonderful contribution to the urbanity of this rediscovered district as they become revealed!

*END of Civic Center Tour. The nearest subways are along
Chambers Street: IRT Seventh Avenue Line at West Broadway,
and IND Eighth Avenue Line at Church Street.*

CHINATOWN/LITTLE ITALY

Chinatown

In most large American cities Chinese have formed enclaves that
are sought by tourists and relished by city dwellers with an
appetite for China's diverting cuisines. Since the 1840s New York's
Chinatown has traditionally been centered in the eight blocks
encircled by Canal, Worth, and Mulberry Streets and the
Bowery/Chatham Square. In the early 1970s Chinese began to
push out the enclave's historic boundaries, although Mott Street
below Canal remains Main Street, along whose flanks and side
streets are located the most popular places to dine and shop.
Chinese expansion is evident in every direction, dissipating the
Italianness of Little Italy and replacing with Chinese ideographs

L1

the Yiddish signs that were once ubiquitous along East Broadway
to the Forward Building and beyond. Except for Confucius Plaza
and the Manhattan Bridge, the area east of Chatham Square and
the Bowery is covered in the Lower East Side.

Park Row: Toward Chatham Square

[L1] **Chatham Towers** (apartments), 170 Park Row, bet.
Park Row and Worth St. N side. 1965. **Kelly & Gruzen.**
Sculpted concrete, this joins the ranks of distinguished
housing architecture: the Dakota, Butterfield House, 240 Central
Park South, and East Midtown Plaza are its peers from all eras.
All are participants in the city's life and streets, rather than towered islands, as in most public housing, or vulgar towers, as are
many of the arriviste condominiums sprouting about the East
and West Sides of Mid-Manhattan. As with all strong architectural statements, Chatham Towers rouses great admiration and
great criticism.

L2

[L2] **Chatham Green** (apartments), 185 Park Row, bet.
Pearl St. and St. James Place. S side to Madison St. 1961.
Kelly & Gruzen.

L4

L5

A great undulating wall: open-access galleries are served by vertical circulation towers. Barney Gruzen designed it after seeing **Alfonso Reidy**'s undulating slabs at Pedregulho in Rio de Janeiro.

East of St. James Place (formerly New Bowery)

[L3] **Governor Alfred E. Smith Houses**, NYC Housing Authority, bet. South, Madison, and Catherine Sts. and St. James and Robert F. Wagner, Sr., Places. 1952. **Eggers & Higgins**.

Al Smith lived a stone's throw away—this is his turf. These are typical of New York's public housing of the 1940s and 1950s: dull warehouses for people—expensive for the taxpayer, cheap for the poor and well maintained. For the school and recreation center on the northeast boundary of the site:

[L4] **Public School 126, Manhattan, The Jacob Riis School, and Alfred E. Smith Recreation Center** (within Governor Smith Houses site), 80 Catherine St., bet. Cherry and Monroe Sts. W side. 1966. **Percival Goodman**.

A neatly articulated school and community recreation center. Both are aging prematurely.

 [L5] **St. James Church** (Roman Catholic), 32 James St., bet. St. James Place and Madison St. E side. 1835-1837. Maybe **Minard Lafever**. 🍎

Beautifully restored brownstone Greek Revival Doric saved by the Ancient Order of Hibernians (Catholic Irish in America). Distyle (2 columns) in antis (between flanking blank walls). Compare it to Mariners' Temple below.

[L6] **First Shearith Israel Graveyard**, 55 St. James Place, bet. Oliver and James Sts. S side. 1656-1833. 🍎

The only man-made remnant of Manhattan's 17th century, this bears the remains of Sephardic Jews (of Spanish-Portuguese extraction) who emigrated from Brazil in the mid 1600s.

 [L7] **Mariners' Temple** (Baptist)/formerly Oliver Street Baptist Church, 12 Oliver St., NE cor. Henry St. 1844-1845. Perhaps **Isaac Lucas**. 🍎

A stone, Greek Revival Ionic temple. Black and Chinese communicants worship in a sailors' church that might well be a temple to Athena.

[L8] **St. Margaret's House**/originally Robert Dodge House, 2 Oliver St., bet. St. James Place and Henry St. E side. 1820. **James O'Donnell**. 3rd floor added, 1850.

A Federal house, its roof raised and flattened, now part of adjacent Mariners' Temple's work.

[L9] **Knickerbocker Village** (apartments), Catherine to Market Sts., Monroe to Cherry Sts. 1934. **Van Wart & Ackerman**.

A blockbuster, with 1,600 apartments on 3 acres (New York City public housing averages 80 to 100 units per acre). The central courtyards, reached through gated tunnels, seem a welcome relief by contrast with their dense and massive surroundings. This was the first major housing project even partially aided by public funds. It maintains its reasonably well-kept lower-middle-class air today.

L10

 [L10] **51 Market Street**/originally William Clark House, bet. Monroe and Madison Sts. W side. 1824. 🍎

Another Federal two-story gambrel-roof elevated to four floors. Its fanlit entranceway is Federal at its most superb.

L11

CHINATOWN / LITTLE ITALY
see pages 79–87

L12

L14

L16

L17

L18

L19

[L11] **The First Chinese Presbyterian Church**/onetime Sea and Land Church/originally Market Street Reformed Church, 61 Henry St., NW cor. Market St. 1817-1819. ☛

A Georgian-Federal body punched with Gothic Revival windows of dressed Manhattan schist, with brownstone surrounds (enframement) and trim.

[L12] **Confucius Plaza** (apartments) and Public School 124, Manhattan, The Yung Wing School, bet. the Bowery, Division St., Chatham Sq. and the Manhattan Bridge approaches. 1976. **Horowitz & Chun**.

A "dual use" construction of school and housing interlocked. The curved slab is arbitrary but a pleasant skyline form.

[L13] **Manhattan Bridge**, bet. Canal St. and the Bowery in Manhattan and Flatbush Ave. Ext. in Brooklyn. 1903-1910. **Leon Moisseiff**, engineer, **Henry Hornbostel**, architect (1903-1904), **Carrère & Hastings**, architects (1904-1910).

Perhaps the least inspiring design of any of the city's suspension bridges. A proposal for a new pedestrian walk by **Frank Gehry** gives hope.

[L14] **Manhattan Bridge Arch and Colonnade**, at entrance to bridge. 1910-1915. **Carrère & Hastings**. ☛ Under renovation.

A regal and monumental horseshoe-shaped colonnade that has somehow overcome all past attempts by highway engineers to remove it; now the Department of Transportation has restored it.

The heart of Chinatown:

[L15] **Republic National Bank**/originally Citizen's Savings Bank, 58 Bowery, SW cor. Canal St. 1924. **Clarence W. Brazer**.

The enormous bronzed dome across from the Manhattan Bridge arch and colonnade.

[L16] Originally **Edward Mooney House**/now Metro Communications Center, 18 Bowery, SW cor. Pell St. 1785-1789. Alterations, 1807. Restoration, 1971. ☛

Built after the Revolution but before Washington's inauguration. This is presumably Manhattan's oldest row house; it combined Georgian elements with the incoming Federal style.

[L17] **Republic National Bank**/originally Manhattan Savings Bank branch, 17 Chatham Sq., SW cor. Catherine St. 1977. **George W. Clark Assocs**.

A virtuoso mock-Chinese temple naively commissioned to serve as a branch bank for Chinatown. Like the former pagoda telephone booths, it's harmless, amusing kitsch.

Mott Street:

[L18] **Church of the Transfiguration** (Roman Catholic)/originally Zion English Lutheran Church, 25 Mott St., NW cor. Mosco St. 1801. ☛

Like Sea and Land [see L11], a Georgian church with Gothic (small-paned double-hung) windows; here they are composed with Gothic tracery. Dressed Manhattan schist makes neat building blocks, with brownstone detail. The octagonal tower, copper sheathed, is from the 1860s.

[L19] **67 Mott Street** (tenement), between Bayard and Canal Sts. W Side. 1890s.

Long before the ground floor became Chinatown shopping, this regal cornice crowned a simple tenement, one of thousands that garnished these "warehouses" for immigrants. Architecture was an essential to marketing space then, like a rose in your lapel.

[L20] **Chinese Merchant's Association**, 85 Mott St., SW cor. Canal St. 1958.

Grauman's Chinese Theater architecture. On this both Beijing and Taipei might agree.

L20

[L21] **Bank of East Asia**, SE cor. Canal and Mulberry Sts. 1980s.

A cool modernist building more in tune with the economics of Hong Kong and Shanghai than the gimcracks of Chinatown.

[L22] **5th Precinct, NYC Police Department**/originally 6th Precinct, 19-21 Elizabeth St., bet. Bayard and Canal Sts. W side. 1881. **Nathaniel D. Bush.**

A dignified Italianate station house. The department's house architect, **Bush**, was designing all of them during this period of rapid constabularial growth.

[L23] **Hong Kong Bank Building** (offices)/originally Golden Pacific National Bank Headquarters, 241 Canal St., NW cor. Centre St. 1983. Ornament and tiles, from Taiwan artisans.

L23

A red lacquer, polychromed, embellished, Pagoda style, Chinese confection. Not a building: an event.

*"**The Bloody Angle**": The unexpected sharp turn midway down blocklong Doyers Street was named for the tong (gang) wars fought there between 1880 and 1926 by the On Leong Tong and the Hip Sing Tong for control of local gambling and opium trafficking.*

Little Italy:
Canal to Houston Streets, Lafayette Street to the Bowery, is still, in large part, the most important old Italian center of New York—but now with old Italians, as the newest generation has made the move to suburbia. They return, however, for festivals and family festivities: marriages, funerals, feasts, and holy days. Meanwhile, the Chinese have rapidly moved north across the former cultural moat of Canal Street and partially share this turf.

L24a

[L24] **Most Precious Blood Church**, 113 Baxter St. bet. Canal and Hester Sts. E side. 1890s??

The façade of the church that harbors the shrine of Saint Gennaro. At its rear, opening on Mulberry, is a tacky brick suburban house that manages the festival of this gourmand saint each September.

L25

[L24a] **Paolucci's Restaurant**/originally Stephen van Rensselaer House, 149 Mulberry St., bet. Hester and Grand Sts. W side. 1816. ✏

A Federal 2-story, dormered brick house, a surprising remnant in these tenemented streets (but it was moved from the corner of Mulberry and Grand). The gambrel roof and dormer windows join with incised stone lintels as signals of its Federal ancestry (but the stucco overlay on its brick body is tragic).

L26

[L25] **Banca Stabile** (former bank), 189 Grand St., SW cor. Mulberry St. 1885.

A onetime Italian family bank totally bypassed by time. Tin ceilings, terrazzo floors, oscillating electric fans, bare-bulb incandescent fixtures. One of the brass teller's cages still offers steamship tickets (at least that's what the gilt lettering reads). And there are no signs reading "Early withdrawal may result in substantial penalties." The son of the last owner maintains the relic while conducting a real estate office from the premises, a personal landmark according to his neighbors.

[L26] **Ferrara's** (pastry and coffee shop), 195 Grand St., bet. Mulberry and Mott Sts. S side. Altered, 1980, **Sidney P. Gilbert & Assocs**.

L28

While the family has been making *dolci* since 1892, this is a new departure, a modern building in which to serve its devoted public. Very different, very flat, a flock of windows.

[L27] **Il Fornaio** (restaurant), 132A Mulberry St., bet. Hester and Grand Sts. E side. 1985. **Studio Morsa**, designers.

An evocation of an old-time Italian restaurant but with no sentimentality, only good design sense.

[L28] Originally **NYC Police Headquarters**/now Police Building Apartments, 240 Centre St., bet. Grand and Broome Sts., and Centre Market Place. 1905-1909. **Hoppin & Koen.** ✏ Converted to residential, 1988, **Ehrenkranz Group & Eckstut**.

In the manner of a French hôtel de ville (town hall), this is tightly arranged within the city's street system, not isolated palatially (as is City Hall or almost any state capitol). Ornate

Renaissance Revival architecture is laced with bits of Baroque. The shape of the building even follows that of the wedge-shaped plot it occupies.

[L29] **165-171 Grand Street**/originally Odd Fellows Hall, SE cor. Centre St. 1847-1848. **Trench & Snook**. Roof addition, 1881-1882. **John Buckingham**.

The grand Corinthian pilastered palace of the Odd Fellows, a high-rise in brownstone second only to the Cooper Union. Snook contributed many cast-iron buildings in the SoHo district to the west.

L30

[L30] **Bowery Savings Bank**, 130 Bowery, bet. Grand and Broome Sts. 1893-1895. **Stanford White** of McKim, Mead & White. Pediments sculptor, **Frederick MacMonnies**. 🍎 Interior 🍎 [L30a] **Grand St. Branch, Citibank**, 124 Bowery, NW cor. Grand St. 1902. **York & Sawyer**.

Roman pomp wraps around Renaissance luster on the Bowery, at the edge of Little Italy. They have served as architectural and economic anchors through the Bowery's years of hard times. The interior of the Bowery bank is one of the great spaces of New York. Go in.

The Feast of San Gennaro fills Mulberry Street from Columbus Park to Spring Street in the middle of September. Happily, autos are exiled. Arcaded with a filigree of electric lights, the street becomes a vast al fresco restaurant, interspersed with games of chance, for the benefit of this venerable Neapolitan saint. Fried pastries and sausages steam the air, and for one evening you may become part of the gregarious Italian public life (are those vendors really Italian? Greek? Jewish?).

L31

[L31] **Engine Company No. 55**, NYC Fire Department, 363 Broome St., bet. Mott and Elizabeth Sts. S side. 1898. **R. H. Robertson**. 🍎

Ornate, eclectic Renaissance Revival.

[L32] **375 Broome Street** (tenement), bet. Mott and Mulberry Sts. S side. ca. 1885.

Who is that figure peering out of the deep sheet metal cornice? **Jupiter**, **Michelangelo**, **Mazzini**, **Garibaldi**—or is it **Moses**? Note the terra-cotta stars of David (commonly found in turn-of-the-century architectural ornament with no Jewish connection).

L32

[L33] **Most Holy Crucifix Church** (Roman Catholic), 378 Broome St., bet. Mott and Mulberry Sts. N side. 1926. **Robert J. Reiley**.

A vest-pocket church, occupying just one lot in this crowded precinct. Everything is arrayed one above the other, as in the adjacent tenements.

[L34] **Storefront for Art and Architecture**, NE cor. Kenmare and Centre Sts. 1993. **Stephen Holl** and **Vito Accomci**.

A sliver of a slice in plan: the building is only five feet wide at its Centre Street end. The Storefront is, however, an offbeat and exciting venue for exhibitions.

L33

[L35] **Milan Laboratories**, 57 Spring St., bet. Mulberry and Lafayette Sts. N side.

The center for vinocultural chemistry, both for ingredients and equipment. Here one can outfit oneself to produce Chianti in the cellar. Apparatus and advice are available, as well as spices.

[L36] **Ceci-Cela Patisserie**, 55 Spring St., bet. Mulberry and Lafayette Sts. N side.

Next door to Milan labs, but equally important to the gourmand-gourmet. An elegant pastry shop.

L34

L38

[L37] Originally **14th Precinct, NYC Police Department**/later Police Department Storehouse/now offices, 205 Mulberry St., bet. Kenmare and Spring Sts. W side. ca. 1870. **Nathaniel D. Bush**.

An Italianate station house with mansard, somehow spared from both demolition and "modernization." The old "house of detention" is on the left.

L40

[L38] **St. Patrick's Old Cathedral** (Roman Catholic), 260-264 Mulberry St., bet. Prince and E. Houston Sts. E side. 1809-1815. **Joseph Mangin**. Restored after fire in 1868. **Henry Engelbert**. ●

The original Roman Catholic cathedral of New York; the present St. Patrick's uptown replaced it after a disastrous fire. Restored, this building was demoted to parish church status. The interior is a grand, murky brown "Gothicized" space, with cast-iron columns supporting a timber roof. The original (pre-fire) shell is in the Gothic-decorated Georgian tradition of Sea and Land or the Church of the Transfiguration, both in the Chinatown area.

[L39] **Old St. Patrick's Cathedral Rectory**, 263 Mulberry St., opp. church.

Very eclectic, very well maintained, very fine ironwork.

L41

[L40] **Saint Michael's Russian Catholic Church**/formerly St. Michael's Chapel/originally Saint Patrick's Chancery Office, 266 Mulberry St., bet. Prince and E. Houston Sts. 1858-1859. **James Renwick, Jr.** and **William Rodrigue**. ●

Neo-Gothic sandstone and painted brick, built in a shape and location as if on a tenement lot.

[L41] **Ciao Bella Ice Cream Factory, Store and Condominiums**, 282 Mott Street (factory), bet. Prince and E. Houston Sts. E side. ca. 1885.

The unusual softly rounded corners along window openings in this brick Romanesque Revival industrial building make for a very different sense of masonry.

[L42] **Old St. Patrick's Convent and Girls' School**/originally Roman Catholic Orphan Asylum, 32 Prince St., SW cor. Mott St. 1825-1826. ●

A Georgian-Federal building with a classy Federal entryway. Here the vocabulary of a Federal house was merely inflated to the program requirements of a parish school (originally an orphan asylum).

*Chuck Close: On the west lot-line wall of 26 Prince Street, between Mott and Elizabeth, is a portrait by painter **Chuck Close** done as a giant outdoor mural: a technicolor mosaic of squares arrayed like a halftone.*

L43

[L43] Originally **14th Ward Industrial School**/Astor Memorial School/now apartments, 256-258 Mott St., bet. Prince and E. Houston Sts. E side. 1888-1889. **Vaux & Radford.** ●⟋
Gothic Revival buttresses, colonnettes, and some Louis Sullivanesque terra-cotta ornament give this somber relic panache.

[L44] **21 Spring Street** (apartments), bet. Mott and Elizabeth Sts. N side. 1983. **Pasanella + Klein.**
A severe, dark red brick monolith embracing a midblock garden. Mundane, but sober and satisfying. For more Pasanella, see the Twin Parks area in the Bronx.

L45

[L45] Originally **Young Men's Institute, YMCA,** 222-224 Bowery, bet. Spring and Prince Sts. W side. 1885. **Bradford L. Gilbert.** Converted to commerce. ●⟋
A romantic red brick and Nova Scotia sandstone Queen Anne minor extravaganza intended to reform by its appearance alone. Library, gymnasium, and classrooms later became storage areas for merchandise and studios for artists. The Y moved out in 1932.
Fernand Léger painted here in 1940 and 1941; dental equipment was distributed from here through 1958; and then writers and artists shared studio and living quarters here: **William S. Burroughs**, **Mark Rothko**, and others.

L46

[L46] **Puck Building** (originally printing plant), 295-309 Lafayette St., bet. Jersey and E. Houston Sts. E side to Mulberry St. N part, 1885-1886. S addition, 1892-1893. Both by **Albert Wagner.** Relocated W front to accommodate widened Elm Place (now Lafayette St.), 1899, **Herman Wagner.** ●⟋ Rehabilitated, 1983-1984. Further restoration, 1995. **Beyer Blinder Belle.**
A colossal gold-leafed Puck holds forth from a 3rd-story perch at the corner of Mulberry and Houston (**Casper Buberl**, sculptor); a smaller version welcomes those who enter on Lafayette Street (**Henry Baerer**, sculptor). Built by the publishers and chromolithographer of the color cartoons that distinguished *Puck,* the nationally renowned satirical magazine published in both German- (1876-1896) and English-language (1877-1918) editions, between the publication's founding and its demise. After years of neglect as a marginal structure in the printing trades, the rich red-brick building has now been resurrected and sensitively restored.

Far more significant historically than architecturally, this area harbors the legions of tenement buildings that warehoused the wave of homeless, tempest-tost immigrants who arrived from the 1880s up to World War I.

Six-story masonry blocks covered 90 percent of the lots in question, offering no light and air except at the 90-foot-distant ends of these railroad flats and through minuscule sidewall air shafts. (Rooms strung end to end like railroad cars gave rise to the term "railroad flats.")

On a 25- by 100-foot lot, at 4 families per floor, 24 families (not including boarders, in-laws, and double-ups), living with bathtubs in the kitchen and toilets in the hall, were the standard. Post-1930s reaction against overcrowding has produced an unhappy overcompensation. The density per acre remains the same or greater, but the edges of the Lower East Side have become dominated by high-rise, freestanding structures (it seems the taller and further apart the better). Project dwellers are supposed to yearn for light and air, or at least the apparent virtues of light and air. In that cause they sacrifice the urbanity that exists, say, in Brooklyn Heights or Greenwich Village in the name of great sweeping lawns (that you can't touch or cavort upon).

If there is a significant building type in this precinct it is the synagogue. In the years before World War I, some 500 Jewish houses of worship and talmud torahs (religious schools) were built here. Few remain and fewer still are in use. A sampling follows, together with other landmarks of the community.

For our purposes the Lower East Side lies E of The Bowery, NE of the Manhattan Bridge and its approaches, and S of East Houston Street. The area N of Houston and E of The Bowery up to 14th Street is sometimes also referred to as part of the L.E.S. It is covered on pages 168-177.

South of Canal Street and Seward Park:

[E1] **Intermediate School 131**, Manhattan, The Dr. Sun Yat-Sen School, 100 Hester St., bet. Forsyth and Eldridge Sts. 1983. **Warner, Burns, Toan & Lundy**.
Curvilinear, extroverted, expansive—it burst forth and wiped out a block of Forsyth Street's pavement.

E1

[E2] **Hester-Allen Turnkey Housing**, NYC Housing Authority, 45 Allen St., NW cor. Hester St. 1973. **Edelman & Salzman**.
Simple, straightforward concrete and ribbed block housing with some thoughtful detailing at the ground plane.

[E3] **St. Barbara Greek Orthodox Church**/originally Congregation Kol Israel Anshe Poland (synagogue), 27 Forsyth St., S of Canal St. E side. ca. 1895.
A proud religious edifice seeing reuse as a church.

[E4] **Congregation K'hal Adath Jeshurun** (synagogue), 12-16 Eldridge St., bet. Forsyth and Canal Sts. E side. 1886-1887. **Herter Brothers**. ● Restoration, 1998. **Giorgio Cavaglieri**.
Eclectic: Flamboyant Moorish embellishment and a Gothic wheel window as well. This ornate façade, the finest of any of the Lower East Side synagogues, makes the tenements of Eldridge Street look even more squalid. Unfortunately, vandalism has taken its toll of the stained glass.

E3

The unfolding of the immigrant experience in the Lower East Side became the focus of an effort, beginning in 1984, to establish a historic/cultural enclave in which that experience could be commemorated and interpreted. The single block of Eldridge Street between

E4

Forsyth and Canal, filled as it is with Old Law tenements, the K'hal synagogue, and other remnants of 19th- and early-20th-century life, emerged as the center of the effort by the Lower East Side Historic Conservancy, a private not-for-profit group. The 20th century has added Chinese to the cultural/historical bouillabaisse.

[E5] Originally **Electrical Substation, Manhattan Railway Company**, 100 Division St., NW cor. Allen St. ca. 1892.

The elevated rapid transit ran above city streets because they offered a readily available and inexpensive right-of-way. When turns from one narrow thoroughfare into another were required, private land had to be purchased over which the viaduct would curve. When electrification came to the els these private sites also became the location for electrical substations, as is this one, skewed to clear the curve of the now-removed viaduct. This facility served the Second Avenue elevated, which clattered east out of Chatham Square along Division Street and turned northward into Allen Street (only 50 feet wide until 1932). Allen Street's perpetual darkness and noise made it an undesirable place—it was one of the city's most notorious red-light districts as a result.

[E6] Originally **Sender Jarmulovsky Bank Building**, 54-58 Canal St., SW cor. Orchard St. 1912. **Rouse & Goldstone**.

There are those who considered the domed, columned "temple" once atop this building's 12 stories a local architectural landmark. Sadly, it's been removed. But to those who know the saga of this bank, it is a historical landmark. Jarmulovsky's was established in 1873 (as the bronze lettering over the entrance still proclaims) as a local bank catering to the growing number of non-English-speaking immigrants being drawn to the area. As assets rose, largely from the working-class depositors' self-denial, rumors began to spread about insolvency. With the coming of World War I many wished to withdraw deposits to help relatives caught in Europe. Runs on this and other local banks soon developed, and then actual riots. For the Lower East Side, black Tuesday was August 4, 1914, when this and another bank were ordered closed as being "in an unsound and unsatisfactory condition." Thousands lost their savings; the Jarmulovskys received a suspended sentence.

E6

E7

[E7] Originally **Loew's Canal Street Theatre**, 31 Canal St., bet. Ludlow and Essex Sts. N side. ca. 1920.

LOWER EAST SIDE

see pages 88–97

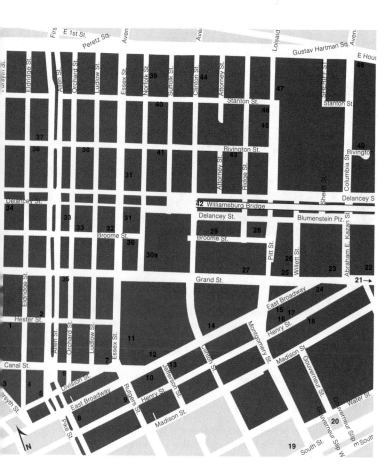

The lobby's ornate glazed terra-cotta and glass façade remains (as does the theater's brick box behind); the marquee is long gone.

[E8] **Sung Tak Buddhist Temple**/originally Congregation B'nai Israel Kalwarie (synagogue), 15 Pike St., bet. E. Broadway and Henry St. E side. 1903. ●

Rundbogenstil (German round-arched neo-Romanesque) in limestone, rounded sash echoing the framing arches. The Temple occupies most of the old sanctuary, with stores below and apartments above.

[E9] **St. Teresa's Roman Catholic Church**/originally First Presbyterian Church of New York, 16-18 Rutgers St., NW cor. Henry St. 1841.

An ashlar Gothic Revival church that served a rural congregation long before the great flux of immigration.

[E10] **Condominium Apartments**/originally Forward Building, 173-175 E. Broadway, bet. Rutgers and Jefferson Sts. S side. 1912. **George A. Boehm.** ● Conversion to condominiums. 1999. **Alfred Wen.**

Once the citadel of Yiddish thought and culture. Lettering in polychrome terra cotta on the roof parapet still reads FORWARD despite the relocation of New York's (and America's) foremost

E8

Yiddish-language newspaper to Harper & Row's old space at 49 East 33rd Street. The building's 12 stories housed not only the editorial offices of the newspaper but also the main headquarters of a distinguished social organization, the Arbiter Ring (Workmen's Circle), which relocated with the *Forward*, and those of many other Jewish social and benevolent organizations (*landsmanshaftn*) and burial societies.

Seward Park: A bit of green (3 acres) at the intersection of East Broadway and Canal and Essex Streets seems less rare today than it did before urban renewal, when tenements were cleared and towers were placed on lawns. The park was named for Lincoln's secretary of state, **William H. Seward** *(1801-1872).*

E9

[E11] **Recreation Building**, in Seward Park. 1939. **NYC Department of Parks & Recreation**.
A Greek temple updated in the style of the Paris Exposition of 1937. Limestone with an ultramarine blue terra-cotta frieze (and lots of calligraphic graffiti—added later).

[E12] **Seward Park Branch, New York Public Library**, 192 E. Broadway, opp. Jefferson St. W side. 1909. **Babb, Cook & Welch**.
A palazzo for book users (on the exterior at least). When built, the area was bulging with people and land was scarce, so the roof was planned as an outdoor reading area. Note the balusters and verdigris beginnings of a trellis.

E12

[E13] **David Sarnoff Building, Educational Alliance**, 197 E. Broadway SE cor. Jefferson St. 1889. **Brunner & Tryon**. Remodeled, 1969, **David Kenneth Specter**.
A Romanesque Revival settlement house with its spirit extended by the great new entrance arch.

E13

[E14] **Bialystoker Center Home for the Aged**, 228 E. Broadway, E of Clinton St. N side. 1930.
Surviving amid acres of adjacent post-World War II projects, this is an amusing Moorish Art Deco product of the Roaring Twenties. Two families vying for recognition are represented in two cornerstones, at the façade's far ends: Lutenberg (west), and Marcus (east). Shrubbery conceals the rivalry (both).

[E15] **Isaac Ludlum House**, 281 E. Broadway, just E of the SE cor. of Montgomery St. 1829.
A Henry Street settlement annex, backing up to the original Settlement headquarters below. A Federal house with intact dormers, but the entrance has seen better days. 279 next door may see an equal revival as a house in private hands.

E14

[E16] **Henry Street Settlement**/originally Nurses Settlement, 263 and 265 Henry St., bet. Montgomery and Gouverneur Sts. N side. 1827. 267 Henry St. 1834. New façade, ca. 1910. **Buchman and Fox**. Restorations, 1996. **J. Lawrence Jones Associates**.
Federal and Greek Revival town houses now happily preserved (in altered form) by a distinguished private social agency, founded by **Lillian Wald** (1867-1940), who is personally memorialized in the public housing bearing her name between East Houston and East 6th Streets on the river. No. 265 is the Federal star. Greek Revival No. 267 was "updated" to Colonial Revival around 1910.

E16

[E17] **Engine Company No. 15, NYC Fire Department**, 269 Henry St., bet. Montgomery and Gouverneur Sts. 1883. **Napoleon LeBrun & Sons**.
A virtuoso façade of brick over a cast-iron ground floor. Particularly enlivening are the pair of corbeled cornice brackets and marvelous, textured spandrels.

E17

E18

[E18] **St. Augustine's Episcopal Church/** originally All Saints' Free Church, 290 Henry St., bet. Montgomery and Jackson Sts. S side. 1827-1829. Attributed to **John Heath**. 📷

Georgian body with Gothic Revival windows. Compare Chinatown's Church of the Transfiguration (page 82) or the Sea and Land Church [L11] (page 80). Built with Manhattan schist and crisp white pediments.

[E19] **Land's End I** (apartments), 257 Clinton St., bet. Cherry and South Sts. W side. 1977. **Harold Edelman** of **The Edelman Partnership**.

One of a number of housing developments—this one a high rise with precast concrete balconies—that emerged from the Two Bridges Urban Renewal Project. (The two bridges, of course, are the Manhattan and the Williamsburg, between which the project area lay.)

[E20] Formerly **Gouverneur Hospital**, Franklin D. Roosevelt Drive bet. Gouverneur Slips E. and W. N side. 1901. Attributed to **McKim, Mead & White**. Converted to treatment center, 1997. **Thanhauser & Esterson**.

The tiers of curved, screened verandas that jut out toward the Drive are familiar to the thousands of motorists who pass this old City hospital every day. Surpassed medically by its modern replacement, though its architectural merits remain. On its way to condo-land.

E20

Banana boat piers: With the advent of containerization and its need for enormous backup space, Manhattan in the 1970s and 1980s lost its shorefront piers, docks, and wharves. The last active freight operations were those of the Netumar Line at Piers 35 and 36, East River, at Clinton Street. Until 1987, bananas were offloaded here, giving motorists on the elevated FDR Drive a last glimpse of one of the city's former glories. In writing of the demise in the New York Times, ***Sam Roberts*** *described it as "the ultimate banana split."*

[E21] **East River Houses**/Cooperative Village (International Ladies Garment Workers Union)/originally called Corlear's Hook Houses, N and S of Grand St., bet. Lewis and Jackson Sts. to Franklin D. Roosevelt Dr. 1956. **Herman Jessor**.

E21

Five thousand people dwell in these carven brick monoliths that excel their descendants at Co-op City in cost, architecture, and views.

[E22] **Hillman Housing,** 500, 530, and 550 Grand St., bet. Abraham Kazan Place and Lewis St. 1951. **Springsteen & Goldhammer.** [E23] **Amalgamated Dwellings,** 504-520 Grand St., NW cor. Abraham Kazan St. (formerly Columbia St.), to Broome St. 1930. **Springsteen & Goldhammer.**

E23

Two generations ago, the late **Abraham Kazan,** as president of the United Housing Foundation, explored the world of mass housing on behalf of the Amalgamated Clothing Workers, providing, in concert with his architects, these pioneer projects. Times have changed: his 15,500-unit Co-op City in the Bronx is not in the same class of avant-garde thinking as these antecedents.

The pre-Depression project, a hollow rectangular doughnut, was heavily influenced by the work of **Michel de Klerk** (1884-1923), founder of the Amsterdam school, and 1920s public housing, especially **Karl Ehn**'s Karl Marx Hof in Vienna. The parabolic arched opening from Broome Street offers a view into the fine central courtyard. The post-World War II section begins to reflect the tower on the lawn approach. It comes off poorly in comparison.

E24

[E24] **Ritual bathhouse** (mikveh)/formerly Young Men's Benevolent Association, 313 E. Broadway, W of Grand St. 1904.

This ornate façade clads a building now used for the ritual baths that Orthodox Jewish women are required to take prior to the marriage ceremony and monthly thereafter. According to the Scriptures the water must be unadulterated—when possible it is rainwater captured in cisterns.

E25, Abrons Center

[E25] **Louis Abrons Arts for Living Center, Henry Street Settlement and Neighborhood Playhouse,** 466 Grand St., bet. Pitt St. and Bialystoker Place (formerly Willett St.). N side. 1975. **Prentice & Chan Ohlhausen.** Gallery open 12-6 daily. 212-598-0400.

An urban exedra, these buildings make a civic space in this wasteland of amorphous streets. A high moment of architecture that brings a suggestion of urbane Manhattan (cf. Greenwich Village, Gramercy Park) to this Rego Park-styled area.

E25, Old Playhouse

[E26] **Bialystoker Synagogue**/originally Willett Street Methodist Episcopal Church, 7-13 Bialystoker Place (formerly Willett St.), bet. Grand and Broome Sts. W side. 1826. 🌑

Manhattan schist, brownstone, and whitestone. Shifting ethnic populations create changing uses for venerable buildings such as this. Originally a rural Protestant church, it now serves the dense Jewish population in this neighborhood.

[E27] **St. Mary's Roman Catholic Church,** 438 Grand St., W of Pitt St. N side. 1833. Enlarged, present façade added, 1871. **Patrick Charles Keely.**

The second-oldest Roman Catholic church structure in all of the city (old St. Patrick's was first: 1815)—the somber gray ashlar rear portion, that is. The amusing red brick front and its twin spires are by the prolific church architect.

E26

[E28] **7th Precinct Station House, NYC Police Department,** and Engine Company No. 17, Ladder Company No. 18, NYC Fire Department, 19½–25 Pitt St., NW cor. Broome St. 1975. **William F. Pedersen & Assocs.**

Articulated form, each function with its special shape and view, the antithesis of **Mies van der Rohe.** Specific, plastic, slotted, revealed—a unique building for unique uses. Note the use of clinker bricks to develop a subtle texture seen only up close.

E28

E30

[E29] Seward Park Extension (east part), NYC Housing Authority, 154-156 Broome St., E of Clinton St. N side. 1973. **William F. Pederson & Assocs**.

The sibling of [E30] (next entry) but minus a community facility annex. This slab's rich façade faces east to the river.

B'nai B'rith: *A plaque on the courtyard wall of the public housing calls attention to the birth at that site of B'nai B'rith, the nation's first national service agency, on October 13, 1843.*

[E30] Seward Park Extension (west part), NYC Housing Authority, 64-66 Essex St., bet. Grand and Broome Sts. E side. 1973. **William F. Pedersen & Assocs**.

One of two tall tan slabs whose design is concentrated on one rich, plastic, 3-dimensional, balconied façade, this one facing south. Adjacent is an outdoor court and a low recreation building.

[E30a] **Congregation Beth Hamedrash Hagodol**/originally Norfolk Street Baptist Church, 60-64 Norfolk St., bet. Grand and Broome Sts. E side. 1850. **William F. Pedersen & Assocs**. 🖌

E31

[E31] Essex Street Market, City of New York (originally NYC Department of Markets), Essex St. bet. Broome, Delancey, Rivington, and Stanton Sts. E side. 1940.

The Department of Markets no longer exists in the City's table of organization (a result no doubt of the preservatives in junk food), but this indoor market does, obligatorily upgraded to the New Essex Street Market. Art Moderne in red brick, industrial steel sash, and incised lettering that makes no reference to "New." Other markets of this LaGuardia-era genre include First Avenue and East 10th Street, Arthur Avenue in the Bronx, and Thirteenth Avenue and 40th Street in Brooklyn.

Between Delancey and East Houston Streets: *The marketplace: Ethnically the Lower East Side has changed markedly since the beginning of the century. From what was once an almost entirely Jewish community, a mixed settlement pattern has evolved: Chinese settling along East Broadway and environs, Hispanics moving in north of Delancey Street, and so on. But as these changes occur, one quality remains: that of the citywide marketplace, particularly on Sundays.*

The attraction which brings thousands back to this area to shop: bargains. Don't expect genteel salespeople or elegant displays—this is New York's most exciting bazaar.

[E32] Originally **Eastern Dispensary**/later Good Samaritan Dispensary, 75 Esscx St., NW cor. Broome St. ca. 1895.

Today, 4 stories of yarn; once the eastern outpost of a dispensary system for Lower Manhattan. Stately golden brown and salmon brick.

E32

[E33] **Lower East Side Tenement Museum**, 97 Orchard St., bet. Broome and Delancey Sts. 1863. Visitors center at 90 Orchard, NE cor. Broome St. Su 10-5; Tu-Fr 11-5; closed Sa & Mo. 212-431-0233.

A time capsule with living units that were sealed off from 1935 to 1988. Its lifetime graduates include more than 7,000, some of whom had lived in tight quarters: as many as 13 to an apartment. A **National Trust Historic Site**.

E33

[E34] **Seventh-Day Adventist Church of Union Square**/originally Congregation Poel Zedek Anshe lleya (synagogue), 128-130 Forsyth St., SE cor. Delancey St. ca. 1895.

This house of worship is reached by a symmetrical flight of steps on the Forsyth Street sidewalk, which had permitted retail establishments to occupy the ground floor on Delancey Street. The combination of worship (sacred) and business (profane) did well.

E34

[E35] Originally dry goods store, **319-321 Grand St.**, SW cor. Orchard St. ca. 1870.

Before and after the Civil War, Grand Street east of the Bowery was the city's center of women's fashions. Lord & Taylor, at Grand and Chrystie Streets, and Edward Ridley's, at Allen Street, were the two most popular dry goods stores.

E35

[E36] **University Settlement House**, 184 Eldridge St., SE cor. Rivington St. 1901. **Howells & Stokes**.

A neighborhood institution by a team of architects better known for their later accomplishments. **Howells**, son of author **William Dean Howells**, won the Chicago Tribune Tower competition with **Raymond Hood**. Stokes wrote the definitive work *The Iconography of Manhattan Island*.

E37

[E37] Originally **Congregation Adath Jeshurun of Jassy** (synagogue)/later First Warsaw Congregation, 58-60 Rivington St., bet. Eldridge and Allen Sts. N side. 1903.

A magnificent eclectic façade with bits and pieces from a variety of styles and influences. Damaged by vandalism, so its days may be numbered. Worth an extra trip anyway.

[E38] **Congregation Shaarai Shomoyim First Roumanian American Congregation** (synagogue)/ originally Allen Street Methodist Church, 83-93 Rivington St., bet. Orchard and Ludlow Sts. S side. ca. 1890.

Solid, stolid Romanesque Revival flattened by paint and soot.

E38

E39

E40

[E39] **Angel Orensanz Foundation**/originally Congregation Anshe Chesed (synagogue)/later Ohab Zedek/later Anshe Slonim, 172- 176 Norfolk St., bet. Stanton and E. Houston Sts. E side. 1849-1850. **Alexander Saeltzer**. 🖌

   With the exception of this distinguished house of worship—once in a state of painful disrepair—all Lower East Side Jewish congregations that occupied buildings built before 1850 had purchased and converted existing churches. This edifice, the city's oldest (and for a time its largest) synagogue (and its first Reform temple), was built by an established Jewish community whose members moved northward, together with their Christian neighbors, as the area became a refuge for Eastern European immigrants. Congregation Anshe Chesed is today on the Upper West Side. Spanish sculptor **Angel Orensanz** bought the fading building in 1986 for art shows and theatrical events. A small orthodox congregation still worships in the basement.

   [E40] **Intermediate School 25**, Manhattan, 145 Stanton St., bet. Norfolk and Suffolk Sts. S side. 1977. **David Todd & Assocs**.

   New Brutalist: a powerful combination of creamy white concrete horizontals with dark red, giant brick infill—all embraced by the strong forms of the stair towers at the corners.

Matzos and wine: Two important industries remain along Rivington Street in the heart of the Lower East Side, Shapiro's Wine Company (No. 126) and Streit's Matzoth Company (No. 150). Both prepare their products for sacramental purposes, although many in the community (and elsewhere) enjoy them throughout the year. Need one add that they are prepared under rabbinical supervision and are kosher?

E41

[E41] **Public School 160**, Manhattan, 107 Suffolk St., SW cor. Rivington St. ca. 1898. **C. B. J. Snyder**.

   What a lift this light-colored neo-Gothic/Renaissance confection must have had upon the impacted Lower East Side when it first opened! Even now, after so many decades of "deferred maintenance," its forms offer refreshing relief.

[E42] **Williamsburg Bridge**, from Delancey and Clinton Sts. in Manhattan to Washington Plaza in Brooklyn. 1903. **Leffert L. Buck**, chief engineer. Rehabilitation, 1993. **Beyer Blinder Belle**.

   To the former City of Williamsburgh, now part of Brooklyn. The unusual (straight) cables on the land side of the towers result from the fact that support is by truss and pier, rather than pendant cable as in the Brooklyn Bridge. The latter's landside cables hang in a catenary curve, in contrast.

E43

[E43] **Public School 142**, Manhattan, 100 Attorney St., SE cor. Rivington St. 1975. **Michael Radoslavitch**.

   A fashionable form in plan, a banjo, fails to come to life as architecture.

[E44] **Congregation Chasam Sofer** (synagogue)/originally Congregation Rodeph Sholom, 8-10 Clinton St., bet. Stanton and E. Houston Sts. E side. 1853.

   The second-oldest surviving synagogue in the city. Rodeph Sholom left these parts in 1886. Today its temple is on West 83rd Street.

E44

[E45] **Mision Guadalupana**/originally Our Lady of Sorrows Roman Catholic Church, 101 Pitt St. bet. Rivington and Stanton Sts. W side. ca. 1890. [E46] **School of Christian Doctrine**, 219 Stanton St., SW cor. Pitt St. ca. 1890. [E46a] **Rectory**/originally Capuchin Monastery, 213 Stanton St., bet. Ridge and Pitt Sts. S side. ca. 1890.

   A spectacular religious complex, once down at the heels and now resuscitated in Latino polychromy.

E45

[E47] **Hamilton Fish Park Play Center,** NYC Department of Parks, NYC Department of Parks & Recreation/originally Hamilton Fish Park Gymnasium and Public Baths, in Hamilton Fish Park, 130 Pitt St., bet. Stanton and E. Houston Sts. E side. 1898-1900. **Carrère & Hastings.** Restored, 1985, **John Ciardullo Assocs.** ✿ **Park,** 1898-1900, **Carrère & Hastings.** Park altered, 1903. Swimming pool added, 1936, **Aymar Embury II.**

The play center's design is a miniaturization of **Charles Girault**'s widely acclaimed Petit Palais in Paris, designed in 1895 for the Paris Exposition of 1900, an oompah Beaux Arts pavilion built to serve the recreation and bathing needs of immigrants drawn to this precinct even before the turn of the century. Though monumental in scale, it surely failed to be adequate in size. (Almost immediately after completion, C&H's formal park was totally in ruins "owing, it is said, to the radical defects of the original plan and to the strenuous nature of the youth of the neighborhood"; it was redone in 3 years.)

E47

[E48] **Junior High School 22,** Manhattan, The Gustave V. E. Straubenmuller School, and **Hamilton Fish Park Branch, New York Public Library,** 111 Columbia St., SE cor. Houston St. 1956. **Kelly & Gruzen.**

A square doughnut on stilts and an adjacent, earthbound library. Its modern materials wore poorly. Stylish in its time, it is now dated.

[E49] **DeWitt Reformed Church,** 280 Rivington St., NE cor. Columbia St. 1957. **Edgar Tafel.**

A simple brick box that contains a sanctuary faced in reused brick and a cross of tree trunks: rustic and humane charm amid overpowering housing.

E49

SOHO

SoHo (or South of Houston), as an acronym, is stretching it, recalling the "Greenwich Village" of London: Soho. These 20-odd blocks between Canal and Houston (How-stun) Streets, West Broadway and Broadway, contain the city's quintessential stock of cast-iron-fronted buildings, a high point in urban commercial architectural history. They are, largely, to be noticed not as individual monuments but as parties to whole streets and blocks that, together, make the most glorious urban commercial groupings that New York has ever seen. Mostly Italianate, some might be termed Palladian: they are surprising precursors of Modern exposed structural expression in another material—concrete—seen at Kips Bay Plaza and the American Bible Society.

Once these were called Hell's Hundred Acres because of the many fires in overcrowded, untended warehouses filled with flammables. Then given over in large part to artists' (and would-be artists') studios and housing, the once-empty streets and buildings became a lively, urbane place, much tended and loved, and hence no longer a potential lonely inferno. Huge lofts here give possibility of great space for large paintings or sculptures and equally great space for living. Initially rediscovered by artists, it has since been invaded by those with deep pockets. Prices for lofts have skyrocketed.

The richest single street is Greene, then Broome—but wander throughout. Not only the revived architecture but also shops, stores, galleries, and boutiques of elegance and delight abound.

Confusion: SoHo, being south of Houston, is also south of Manhattan's street grid established by the commissioners' plan of 1811. SoHo is arranged on a grid in which the long blocks stretch north-south, their axes exactly perpendicular to those above Houston Street. Similarly, in contrast to Manhattan's main grid, the wide streets in SoHo (except for Broadway, West Broadway, and the much later Sixth Avenue) run east-west, and are all called streets, none avenues. Not surprisingly, the direction and placement of house numbers vary from thoroughfare to thoroughfare. So watch carefully and make no rash assumptions about SoHo.

SoHo entries appropriately begin south of Houston Street along Broadway (below V Manhattan/Astor Place & Environs). They sequentially snake around, first south, then north, moving generally to the west. Feel free to break the sequence—we did.

[H1] **SoHo-Cast Iron Historic District**, irregular area E of W. Broadway's center line bet. center lines of W. Houston and Canal Sts. to Broadway, and E of Broadway bet. center lines of E. Houston and Howard Sts. on center line of Crosby St. 🍎

Within the 26 blocks of this Historic District are arrayed, according to the official designation report, "the largest concentration of full and partial cast-iron façades anywhere in the world." Their protection under law in 1973, after having been saved in the late 1960s from destruction for the ill-fated Lower Manhattan Expressway, was a great victory for preservation activists. Cast iron and other bountiful structures from the city's late 19th-century business boom abound on these streets. Remember, SoHo's festooned fire escapes and its bumpety Belgian block pavements are also part of this wonderfully gritty scene.

SoHo's north edge is bounded by the expressway-scaled Houston Street which, having been widened for the IND Sixth Avenue Subway, caused the body of SoHo to offer a ragged edge to

SOHO
see pages 98–111

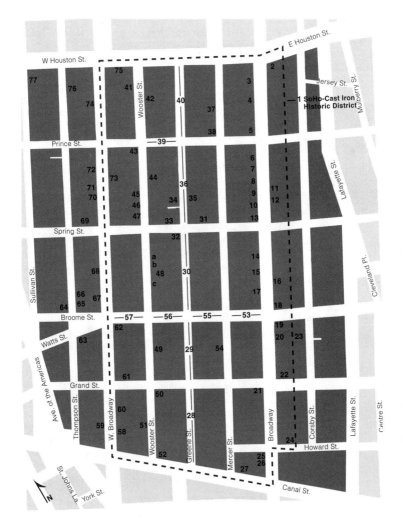

Greenwich Village on the north. Gas stations, lots, and unkempt buildings' sides are all that SoHo here reveals of its inner splendors. Later roadwork widened the asphalt pavement itself and inserted the slender traffic island down the middle. More recent projects such as the former University Village and NYU's sports center disguise the gash, but the little 2-story polychrome taxpayer between Wooster and West Broadway emphasizes it by its shallow depth.

Broadway: Between Houston and Prince Streets.

[H2] **600 Broadway** (loft building). E side. 1883-1884. **Samuel A. Warner**. ♂
Corinthian columns of descending height for each successively ascending floor. The ground-floor now sports an appropriately understated branch of the ubiquitous Pottery Barn, the Ralph Lauren of home furnishings.

[H3] **Museum of African Art**, 593 Broadway. W side. Building, 1860. Interiors, 1993. **Maya Lin** and **David Hotson**. Open: Su 12-6; Tu-Fr 10:30-5:30; Sa 12-8; closed Mo. 212-966-1313. ♂
Founded in 1984 as the Center for African Art, its successor Museum moved here in 1993.

H2

H4

H5

[H4] **New Museum of Contemporary Art**/originally Astor Building, 583 Broadway. W side. Building, 1896-1897. **Cleverdon & Putzel**. Expanded and remodeled, 1998. **Colin Cathcart** of **Kiss + Cathcart**. Open to the public: Su & We-Fr 12-6; Sa 12-8; closed Mo & Tu. 212-219-1355. ♂

With the Museum of Modern Art aging (intellectually, not physically), the Whitney becoming self-satisfied, and the Met encyclopedically trying to corner new art as well as all other, it was time for a new museum. Hence, The New Museum: serious avant-avant-garde exhibitions displayed in one of SoHo's most magnificent loft buildings. Expanded to four floors, The Museum dropped the The, added contemporary art, and upgraded its architecture through the hand of **Colin Cathcart**.

Outside, the carapace that shelters this hermit crab is magnificent: Corinthian columns and reentrant bay windows join to present a lush Classical ensemble.

[H5] **Guggenheim SoHo**/originally Rogers Peet Store, 575 Broadway, NW cor. Prince St. 1881-1882. **Thomas Stent**. Remodeled, 1996. **Arata Isozaki**. Open Su, Mo, We 11-6; Th-Sa 11-8; closed Tu. 212-423-3500. ♂

The multinational Museum (New York, Bilbao, and Venice so far) has reached out to this shifting cultural center in SoHo. In the Ruskinian manner, exuberant cast-iron Corinthian-Victorian columns support a stone and brick volume.

Broadway: Between Prince and Spring Streets.

[H6] **Singer Building**/earlier Paul Building/originally The Singer Manufacturing Company, 561 Broadway, bet. Prince and Spring Sts. Secondary façade on Prince St. S side. 1902-1904. **Ernest Flagg**. ♂

"The Little Singer Building," to distinguish it from the now demolished Singer Tower [see Necrology]. Curled steel, recessed glass, and textured terra-cotta—all avant-garde for their time. The façade foretells the curtain wall, that delicate metal-and-glass skin in which much of Manhattan of the 1950s and 1960s is clad—grossly it seems, when compared to this post-turn-of-the-century charmer. Its original name can still be seen cast in iron on the Prince Street store transom of this L-shaped structure.

H6

[H7] **Scholastic Books**, 557 Broadway, bet. Princc and Spring Sts. W side. 2001. **Aldo Rossi and Gensler Associates**.

A first foothold in New York for the Italian architect Aldo Rossi. A man who models solids, rather than sheathing his works with transparency, Rossi approaches architecture in a neo-traditional manner.

[H8] Originally **Charles Broadway Rouss Building** (lofts), 555 Broadway. 1889-1890. **Alfred Zucker**. Attic pediments added, 1900.

A tribute to a debt-ridden Virginian whose name mightily adorns this through-block behemoth. **Rouss**'s construction sign modestly stated, HE WHO BUILDS, OWNS, AND WILL OCCUPY THIS MARVEL OF BRICK, IRON, AND GRANITE, THIRTEEN YEARS AGO WALKED THESE STREETS PENNILESS AND $50,000 IN DEBT.

[H9] **547 Broadway** (lofts). W side. 1888. **O. P. Hatfield**.
Brick and stone, bearing tiers of intricate fire escapes bowing graciously over the sidewalks of Broadway.

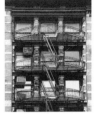

H9

[H10] **545 Broadway** (lofts). W side. 1885. Samuel A. Warner.
Freestanding cast-iron colonnettes.

[H11] **542 Broadway**, E side. 1864.
Composite Corinthian columns support, in their turn, draped caryatids.

[H12] **540 Broadway** (lofts). E side. 1867. **David & John Jardine**.
Others of its time were already employing cast iron, but this out-of-the-ordinary dour façade is very 2-dimensional: intaglioed sheets of marble.

H11

[H13] **537-541 Broadway** (lofts). W side. 1868-1869. **Charles Mettam**.
Corinthian-columned cast-iron with colossal windows.

Broadway: Between Spring and Broome Streets.

[H14] Originally **De Forest Building**, 513-517 Broadway (lofts). W side. 1884. **Lamb & Rich**.
Six stories of floriated, polychromed red brick and terra-cotta detail make a magnificent, rich, deeply modeled Queen Anne façade. O, were only there more of these to admire!

H12

*St. Nicholas Hotel: Nos. 521-523 Broadway represents the only remaining part of the much larger 1,000-bed hotel complex (built 1851-1853 and expanded by 1854. **John B. Snook** or **Griffith Thomas**?) which, together with Astor House, was among Broadway's most prominent hostelries in the 1850s and 1860s. During the Civil War the hotel became the headquarters of the War Department.*

[H15] Originally **Loubat Stores**, 503, 507, 511 Broadway. W side. 1878-1879. **John B. Snook**.
A generous composition of 3 warehouses with demure (and grave) cast-iron façades produced at the Cornell Iron Works.

H16

[H16] Originally **C. G. Gunther's Sons Store**, 502 Broadway. E side. 1860. **John Kellum & Son**.
Slender, 2-story arches exquisitely worked in stone, not cast iron. When new, smooth, and pristine white, the tall, graceful columns gave rise to the term "Sperm Candle Style," after those made of whale oil.

[H17] Originally **New Era Building** (lofts), 491 Broadway. W side. 1896-1897. **Buchman & Deisler**.

H17

H18

An Art Nouveau marvel: from the squat street-level Doric columns, fairly bulging from the weight of the masonry walls above, to the colossal multistory verdigris copper mansard, 6 floors up.

[H18] Originally **E. V. Haughwout & Co. Store**, 488-492 Broadway, NE cor. Broome St. 1856-1857. **John P. Gaynor**. Cast-iron facade by **Daniel D. Badger Architectural Iron Works**. Restored, 1995. **Joseph Pell Lombardi**. 🍎 ♂

Palladio would have been proud of this offspring in cast iron, ever a rich participant in the urban scene (now repainted in its original "turkish drab"). A proud and handsome, but not egocentric, building here proves that quality does not demand originality for its own sake. Built for **Eder V. Haughwout**, a merchant in china, cut glass, silverware, and chandeliers, it also housed the first practical safety elevator, installed by **Elisha Graves Otis**, founder of that ubiquitous elevator company.

The Corinthian columns that flank the arches are sometimes remembered as Serlian, after the drawings and writings of **Sebastiano Serlio** (1475-1554), later lifted by **Andrea Palladio** (1508-1580) and most elegantly displayed at the Basilica in Vicenza.

Broadway: Between Broome and Grand Streets.

[H19] Formerly **Mechanics & Traders Bank** (lofts), 486 Broadway, SE cor. Broome St. (also known as 437-441 Broome St.) 1885. **Lamb & Rich**. ♂

The Broome Street façade of this Romanesque and Moorish Revival bank building has long been tattooed with an appliqué of fire escapes.

H20

[H20] Originally **Roosevelt Building**. 478-482 Broadway. E side. 1873-1874. **Richard Morris Hunt**. ♂

Filigreed cast iron, with Composite columns on a huge scale, built for the trustees of Roosevelt Hospital. Note particularly the openwork brackets that carry the flat cornice and the curved cast-iron screens at the top of the 4th-floor windows. A very different style of Hunt (20+ years later) can be seen at the Metropolitan Museum's Fifth Avenue entrance. (One bay of the Roosevelt Building continues through the block to become No.40 Crosby Street, which carries an abbreviated form of façade. See H23 below.)

Next door, at 476, great Ionic columns foreshadow the Classical Revival after 1893, the direction that Hunt would follow in those years.

[H21] Originally **D. Devlin & Co. Store**, 459-461 Broadway, SW cor. Grand St. (also known as 115-119 Grand St.). 1860-1861. ♂

A late Italianate temple of commerce whose beautifully weathered stone surfaces are pierced with ranks of finely proportioned round-arched windows.

[H22] Originally **Mills & Gibb Building**, 462 Broadway, NE cor. Grand St. to Crosby St. 1879-1880. **John Correja.** ♂

This mammoth cast-iron commercial palace evokes memories of the French Renaissance. The ground floor has been mutilated by suffocation from polished red granite, a malady often reversible in cast-iron buildings. Let's hope. L'Ecole, the dining room of the French Culinary Institute, occupies the ground-floor space and offers trendy, pricey fare.

H21

H22

Detour: Crosby Street/Mercer Street
Twin streets in the sense that both reveal the rear of the large structures that line Broadway's originally prestigious flanks. In many respects, from their expanses of poorly maintained Belgian block street pavers to their abundance of fire escapes and loading docks, Mercer and Crosby continue to show a SoHo that predates gentrification.

🏛 [H23] Originally **Roosevelt Building** (lofts), 40 Crosby St., bet. Grand and Broome Sts. 1874. **Richard Morris Hunt.** ♂

The single-bay rear of 472-484 Broadway.

H23

Broadway: Between Grand and Howard Streets.
A neo-Georgian "suburban" bank building (originally Franklin National Bank) provided a tree-canopied plaza at the northwest corner of Broadway and Howard Streets (1967. **Eggers & Higgins**, *architects.* **Zion & Breen**, *landscape architects). The impulse to provide amenities was commendable, but the result strange and inappropriate in this virile cast-iron environment. Incidentally, the Georges never used the hexagon for building: that is a later, Greek Revival game.*

The boom in SoHo housing has provided the impetus for much more intense development of this site.

H24

[H24] **34 Howard Street** (lofts), bet. Broadway and Crosby St. N side. 1868. **Renwick & Sands.** ♂

Unusually distinguished (more in the sense of the unusual than that of pure excellence)—but no surprise since its architects were **James Renwick, Jr.** and his then partner, **Joseph Sands.**

Broadway: Between Howard and Canal Streets.

[H25] Originally **A. J. Dittenhoffer Warehouse**, 429 Broadway, SW cor. Howard St. 1870-1871. **Thomas R. Jackson.** ♂

Two dozen cadaverous arches spring from Corinthian columns facing Broadway in this lusty, glassy place.

H25

[H26] Originally **Le Boutillier Brothers Store**, 425 Broadway. W side. 1869. **Griffith Thomas.** ♂

A small neighbor to No. 429, with a broken pediment against the sky.

Canal Street:

🏛 [H27] Originally **Arnold Constable & Company** (dry goods store), 307-311 Canal St., NE cor. Mercer St. to Howard St. Corner, No. 309-311, 1856. No. 307, 1862. 5th-story addition, 1862. ♂

H27

H28, 28-30 Greene

Years of grime and Canal Street's déclassé retail history conceal the lyrical architecture of this once elegant block-long bazaar. Look this one over carefully. Here the wall dominates, with windows subordinate, in contrast to the cast iron of SoHo, where the columnar structure acts in concert with huge glass areas. Success and changing land-use fashions propelled the enterprise to a new location uptown in Ladies Mile.

Greene Street:

[H28] **Greene Street, bet. Canal and Grand Sts.** ♂ **Nos. 10-14** Greene St. 1869. **John B. Snook.** Tuscan columns and pilasters. **Nos. 15-17** Greene St. 1895. **John A. Warner.** Delicate Corinthian pilasters. **Nos. 16-18** Greene St. 1880. **Samuel A. Warner. Nos. 19-21** Greene St. 1872. **Henry Fernbach.** Bold Tuscan columns by the architect of Central Synagogue. **Nos. 20-26** Greene St. 1880. **Samuel A. Warner.** Two buildings in grand Corinthian. **Nos. 23-25** Greene St. 1873. **Isaac F. Duckworth.** Sparsely leaved Corinthian. **Nos. 28-30** Greene St. Blue-painted leafless Corinthian, with a Second Empire roof. **No. 31** Greene St. 1876. **George W. DaCunha.** Extraordinarily ornate. **No. 32** Greene St. 1873. **Charles Wright.** Leafless Corinthian. **No. 34** Greene St. 1873. **Charles Wright.** Tuscan. **Nos. 83-87** Grand St., SW cor. Greene St. 1872. **William Hume.** Serene Tuscan over elaborate Corinthian.

H29, 37-43 Greene

[H29] **Greene Street, bet. Grand and Broome Sts.** ♂ **No. 33** Greene St., NW cor. Grand St. 1873. **Benjamin W. Warner.** Composite columns above, Tuscan below. **Nos. 37-43** Greene St. 1884. **Richard Berger.** Green composite columns over a Corinthian base. **Lehmann Maupin Gallery** at **No. 39** (1996. **Rem Koolhaas**) The creator of *Delirious New York* comes to earth here for his first New York City architectural adventure. **No. 45** Greene St. 1882. **J. Morgan Slade.** Crisp white Composite columns.

[H30] **Greene Street, bet. Broome and Spring Sts.** ♂ **No. 60** Greene St. 1871. **Henry Fernbach.** Bold Corinthian. **No. 62** Greene St. 1872. **Henry Fernbach.** Bulky Composites. **No. 66** Greene St. 1873. **John B. Snook. No. 65** Greene St. 1873. **John B. Snook.** Bold Tuscan. **Nos. 67, 69, 71, 75, 77, 81** Greene St. 1873. **Henry Fernbach.** All bold Tuscan. **Nos. 72-76** Greene St. 1873. **Isaac F. Duckworth.** The creamy king of this block: a magnificently fashioned, projecting-pedimented porch of Corinthian columns and pilasters. **No. 75** Greene St. 1878. **Henry Fernbach. No. 80** Greene St (Helmut Lang). 1873. **Griffith Thomas.** Blue-painted Tuscan, its base supports simplicity and within are the elegant spaces of **Helmut Lang** (1998. **Gluckman Mayner**).

H30, 62 Greene   H30, 72-76 Greene

Spring Street:

[H31] **113, 115 Spring Street** (lofts), bet. Greene and Mercer Sts. N side. 1878. **Henry Fernbach**. ♂
Freestanding Tuscan columns enliven a pair of cast-iron fronts: strapwork fire escapes added later suggest woven basketry.

[H32] **132 A Spring Street** (taxpayer), SW cor. Greene St. 1879-1880. **Henry Fernbach**. Radically renovated, 1936. ♂
Moderne in red and black, matte-finished brick with subtle modeling and textures.

H31

[H33] **131-135 Spring Street** (lofts), bet. Greene and Wooster Sts. N side. 1891-1893. **Franklin Baylies**. ♂
Rose pressed brick, granite, and limestone. spruced up with pink-painted columns. Sounds awful. Looks great.

[H34] **SoHo Hotel**, 101-111 Greene St., bet. Spring and Prince Sts. 103-105. 1880s. **Henry Fernbach**. New buildings, 101 and 107-111, 2000. **Joseph Pell Lombardi**. ♂
Fernbach's pair are replicated at 101, but **Lombardi** turns to riveted steel at 107-111, contrasting with neighboring cast iron. The Soho Kitchen and Bar (**Tony Goldman**, developer and owner of SoHo K&B) stood where it was at 103. (Dark, romantic, popular: pizza, pasta, fish.)

H33

[H35] **Sidewalk subway map**: On the east sidewalk of Greene Street in front of the Rouss Annex is "Subway Map Floating on a New York Sidewalk" (1986) by artist **Françoise Schein**. It is an abstracted map of the interlocking subway systems of Manhattan. Set into a black-on-black matrix, the routes are of stainless steel bars with the individual stations represented by glass roundels of the type once used to illuminate below-the-street sidewalk vaults. Curiously, Schein and colleague **Petar Gevremov** reversed the design, so the systems are out of sync with Manhattan. That "uptown" is "downtown" on this map is at first difficult to comprehend, since the map shows no other geography: no street grid, no shorelines, no Central Park. Obscurantism.

H34

[H36] **Greene Street, bet. Spring and Prince Sts**. ♂
Nos. 93-99 Greene St. 1881. **Henry Fernbach**. Three buildings sporting Composite Ionic, now spruced up. **No. 96**

H36, 114-120 Greene

Greene St. 1879. **Henry Fernbach**. Tuscan. **No. 100** Greene St. 1881. **Charles Mettam**. "Corinthionic!" **No. 105** Greene St. 1879. **Henry Fernbach**. Modified Corinthian. **No. 112** Greene St. 1884. **Henry Fernbach**. Slender brown Ionica. **No. 113** Greene St. **Henry Fernbach**. Attenuated abstract colonettes and lintels of wrought iron. **Nos. 114-120** Greene St. 1882. **Henry Fernbach**. Two in Composite Ionic with stylized acanthus leaf antefixa atop the cornice. This one is very grand.

H37

Mercer Street:
Like Crosby Street on the other side of Broadway, a service thoroughfare.

[H37] Originally **Firemen's Hall**/later Hook & Ladder No. 20, N.Y.C. Fire Department, 155 Mercer St., bet. W. Houston and Prince Sts. 1854. **Field & Correja**. Altered. ○

When this was built, the city's fire laddies were volunteers. Most of the original ornate trim and moldings are gone, but some of its early form is visible in the quoins. Here noted for its use more than its present presence.

H38

[H38] **Hotel Mercer**, 99 Prince St., NW cor. Mercer St. 1887-1888. **William Schickel & Co.** Renovations, 1986-1994. **Harman Jablin**. Façade restoration, **Marc Markowitz**. ○

A masonry exception in this cast-iron precinct, it once housed John Jacob Astor's fur coat fabrications. Now such high style is partially replaced by a preppie J. Crew store.

[H39] **Prince Street, bet. Greene and Wooster Sts.** ○

No. 109 Prince St., NW cor. Greene St. (also known as 119 Greene St.). 1889. **J. Morgan Slade**. **Nos. 112-114** Prince St. 1890. **Richard Berger**. Altered, 1975, **Hanford Yang**. A City Walls, Inc. photo-realistic painted façade by **Richard Haas** extrapolates rich cast-iron architecture to the side wall. Note the trompe l'oeil cat at the "open" window.

H39, 109 Prince

[H40] **Greene Street, bet. Prince and Houston Sts.** ○
No. 121 Greene St. 1883. **Henry Fernbach**. A cream-colored and classy Corinthian. Savor the monolithic granite sidewalks, self-curbed, an old and disappearing local amenity. **No. 129** Greene St. 1881. **Detlef Lienau**. Lienau's only work in the district: brick with enormous windows. **Nos. 132-140** Greene St. 1885. **Alfred Zucker**. Three buildings wear a free-spirited Ionic façade (capitals turned sideways). **No. 135** Greene St. 1883. **Henry Fernbach**. A delicate Tuscan-ordered building. Originally **Anthony Arnoux House**, 139 Greene St. 1824-1825. A lonely but rare and elegant brick Federal holdout. **No. 142** Greene St. 1871. **Henry Fernbach**. Bulky Tuscan. **No. 148** Greene St. 1884. **William Worthen**. Magnificent brick with light and elegant ironwork.

H40, 121 Greene

H40, 139 Greene

[H41] **141-145 Wooster Street** (loft building), bet. W. Houston and Prince Sts. W side. 1897. **Louis Korn**. ○
Bland Renaissance Revival: a latecomer to SoHo, a building more comfortable around Washington Square East. (Chalk & Vermilion Gallery used to be here. 1987. **Smith-Miller & Hawkinson**.)

[H42] **Gagosian Gallery**, 136 Wooster St., bet. W. Houston and Prince Sts. E side. 1992. **Gluckman Mayner**. ○
A glazed garage door, when opened, displays monumental sculpture to the street. It is the experience, more than the building, that matters.

[H43] **130 Prince St.** (office buildings), SW cor. Wooster St. 1988. **Lee Manners & Assocs.**, designer, **Walter B. Melvin**, associate architect. ○

H42

A pair of structures: the corner one neo-Art Deco, the mid-block a former commercial bakery reconfigured. Impressive design.

[H44] **Comme des Garçons** (men's and women's boutique), 116 Wooster St., bet. Prince and Spring Sts. E side. 1984. **Rei Kawakubo**, designer. **Takao Kawasaki**, associate designer. **Howard Reitzes**, architectural consultant.

Like the world-renowned Japanese fashions that its designer designs, this boutique pursues a goal of total unity, or *ma*. Utilizing a delicious sparseness, it succeeds. (Building, 1908. **Frederick Fabel**.)

[H45] **Knoll International Design Center**, 105 Wooster St., bet. Prince and Spring Sts. W side. Lofts, 1892, **Charles Behrens**. Altered, 1982, **Paul Haigh**, designer.

Outside, the insertion of a series of half-cylindrical roll-down shutter covers adds a modern look that enriches the original Ohio sandstone and brick structure. Inside, witty games of changing scale are played with the neo-Classical ornament of the cast-iron columns. Superb.

H46

[H46] Originally **Engine Company No. 13, NYC Fire Department**/now Stephen Spruce (boutique), 99 Wooster St., bet. Prince and Spring Sts. W side. 1881. Napoleon LeBrun. Altered, 1987.

A cast-iron bottom supporting a masonry top. The piers carry shields that once contained the engine company's insignia. Now a "post punk" emporium.

[H47] **97 Wooster Street** (lofts), bet. Prince and Spring Sts. W side. 1897. **George F. Pelham**.

Powerful corbels, each with a stern face, support bold attached columns; incised ornament embellishes both a mid-height band and the cornice.

H47

[H48a] **84 Wooster Street** (warehouse), bet. Spring and Broome Sts., E side. 1896. **Albert Wagner**. [H48b] **80 Wooster Street** (warehouse). E side. 1894. **G. A. Schellenger**. [H48c] **64 Wooster Street** (warehouse), E side. 1899. **E. H. Kendall**.

Arches and cornices here creep into these cast-iron precincts: 7- and 8-story Renaissance Revival depositories, larger and more pretentious than their neighbors.

H48a

[H49] **42-46 Wooster Street** (lofts), bet. Broome and Grand Sts. E side. 1895. **F. S. Baldwin**. Reconfigured (together with 50 next door) with central atrium, 1999. **Bogdanow Partners**.

Brick Romanesque Revival, with rock-faced brownstone and cast iron in concert. Here the attempt is at grandeur, more than the spartan elegance of cast iron alone.

[H50] **28-30 Wooster Street**, SE cor. Grand St., also known as 71 Grand St. Wooster St. brick façade, 1879. Grand St. cast-iron façade, 1888. Both, **Mortimer C. Merritt**.

Two wonderful façades in different materials, at a different time, but by the same architect.

H49

[H51] **The Drawing Center**, 35 Wooster St., bet. Broome Grand Sts. W side. Gallery open: Tu, Th, Fr 10-6; We 10-8; Sa 11-6; closed Su & Mo. 212-219-2166.

The contents here, not the 1860s building, are the pearl in the oyster, although there are some lovely Corinthians. Inigo Jones's "complete architectural drawings" were once displayed here. You can't beat that.

[H52] **2 Wooster Street**, NE cor. Canal St. 1872. **W. H. Gaylor**.

All of a piece, the Corinthian capitals have mostly rusted away.

H50

H53

Canal Street becomes a casbah between the Avenue of the Americas (Sixth Avenue to everyone) and Centre Street. Here shops spill into the street; their wares—"bargains" real or apparent—abound: VCRs, Swatch watch knock-offs, 9-volt batteries, recycled clothes, plastic shapes, sheet metal—you name it. A great place for the browsing gadgeteer, do-it-yourselfer, or the serious bargain hunter familiar with his or her needs.

Broome Street: From Broadway to West Broadway.
Four blocks of SoHo at its most idiosyncratic. A mixture along the breadth of Broome Street of mostly cast-iron façades in varying states of disarray, decay, and delight. In Paris, these structures might line one of the great boulevards.

H54

[H53] **Broome Street**, bet. Broadway and Mercer St. ♂
No. 448 Broome Street. 1871-1872. **Vaux & Withers**.
    An imaginative 5-story cast-iron creation by **Calvert Vaux**, intricately ornamented.

[H54] **47-49 Mercer Street** (lofts), bet. Broome and Grand Sts. W side. 1873. **Joseph M. Dunn**.
    Crisp and lusty white cast iron. ♂

[H55] **Broome Street, bet. Mercer and Greene Sts.** ♂
    Originally **Hitchcock Silk Buildiing**, Nos. 453-455 Broome St. 1873. **Griffith Thomas**. Corinthian. **No. 461** Broome St. 1871. **Griffith Thomas**. Tuscan. **No. 467** Broome St. 1873. **Isaac F. Duckworth**. Tuscan encore.

The Gourmet Garage is harbored in the ground floor of 453-455 (SW cor. of Mercer St.): an economy version of Dean & Deluca.

H55, 467 Broome

H56, 469 Broome

[H56] **Broome Street, bet. Greene and Wooster Sts.** ♂
The Gunther Building, No. 469 Broome St., SW cor. Greene St. 1873. **Griffith Thomas**. Note the rich Corinthian foliage and the elegant curved and glazed corner. **Nos. 477-479** Broome St. 1885. **Elisha Sniffrn**. Corinthian. **Nos. 476-478** Broome St. 1873. **Griffith Thomas**. Green-painted Corinthian. **No. 480** Broome St. 1885. **Richard Berger**. Composite Ionic columns.

H57, 484 Broome

[H57] **Broome Street, bet. Wooster St. and West Broadway.** ♂
No. **484** Broome St., NW cor. Wooster St. 1890. **Alfred Zucker**.

Grand Romanesque (in scale) Revival brick and rock-face brownstone. Entwined serpents form corbel arch supports in sandstone.
In the 1970s and 1980s it was headquarters of the avant-garde
Kitchen performance space. Not in cast iron but still one of SoHo's
best. **Nos. 489-493** Broome St. 1873. **J. Morgan Slade**. Note the similarity to **Griffith Thomas'** Gunther Building [above]. **Nos. 492-
494** Broome St. 1892. **Alfred Zucker**. While it lost 3 floors in 1938, it
didn't lose the foliate ornament up the sides.

West Broadway:
*Practically every street in SoHo is a shopping street, but this is the
shopping street.*

*Note: In originally designating the SoHo Cast-Iron District, the
Landmarks Preservation Commission did not include the west
side of West Broadway.*

[H58] **307 West Broadway** (lofts), bet. Canal and Grand Sts. E
side. 1892. **Douglas Smyth**. ♂
   A powerful Ionic capital anchors the façade.

H59

[H59] **SoHo Grand Hotel**, 310 W. Broadway, bet. Canal and
Grand Sts. W. side. 1990s. **David Helpern**.
   More interesting for where it is than what it is. Hotels in
SoHo? Near Canal Street? The shifting geo-economics of hot
neighborhoods continues.

[H60] **357 West Broadway** (house), bet. Canal and
Grand Sts., E side. 1820s. ♂
Another rescued Federal house.

[H61] **Water Tower** (sculpture), 60 Grand St, nr. Grand
and W. Broadway. 1998. **Rachel Whiteread**. ♂
   Ice in space? The void of a water tower becomes a translucent solid: hovering water over SoHo. (Stand on the southwest
corner of Grand and West Broadway and look northeast.)

H60

[H62] **Kenn's Broome Street Bar** (restaurant), 363 West
Broadway, SE cor. Broome St. ca. 1825. ♂
   Another Federal house, advertised with elegant Victorian gilt
lettering, is home to a pleasant pseudovintage eating and drinking place. Plants. Ceiling fans. Stained glass.

Broome Street, West of SoHo:

H61

*Adorning the seemingly forgotten paved triangle between Broome,
Watts, and Thompson Streets is the outdoor display (1972-) the
detritus of rusted iron delights of welder-sculptor **Robert S. Bolles**
(known locally but inaccurately as **Bob Steel**). Non-maintenance
has allowed it to become junk in fact.*

[H63] **NEXT** (nightclub)/Thompson Street Brewery (and restau-
rant), The Manhattan Brewing Company/originally New York
Edison Company electrical substation, 40 Thompson St., SE cor.
Watts St. ca. 1920. Altered, 1984, **Lemberger Brody Assocs**.
   Sophisticated reuse of a humdrum utilities structure. The
projected copper vat through the upper wall is a bizarre gesture.

H62

[H64] **Tunnel Garage**, 520 Broome St., NW cor. Thompson St.
1922. **Hector C. Hamilton**.
   The allusion to the nearby Holland Tunnel and the very
graphic graphics applied to an austere, recessive round-
cornered structure are what make this early accommodation to
the motor car so special.

[H65] **54 Thompson Street** (lofts), NE cor. Broome St. ca. 1900
Converted, 1999.
   Some modest rock-faced granite and brick, embellished with
a private garden contained within an articulated sheet-steel wall
(Sculpture Garden Fence. 1995. **Architecture Research Office**).

H65

[H66] **Thompson Street Hotel**, 62 Thompson St., bet. Broome and Spring Sts. 2000. **The Stephen Jacobs Group**.

SoHo has become the latest "in" precinct for hotels—conversions and/or completely new buildings. Among the latest.

West Broadway: Between Broome and Spring Streets.

[H67] **380 West Broadway** (lofts). W side. ca. 1870.

Prosperous cast-iron front: a renovation done neatly but without pizzazz.

*Name change: Between 1870 and 1899 West Broadway assumed the name South Fifth Avenue (a name change later espoused—unsuccessfully—by **Robert Moses**), and during that period its house numbers ascended southward from Washington Square to Canal Street. The number 159, cast into the iron pilaster of today's 383 West Broadway, dates from that period.*

H68

[H68] **394 West Broadway**, W side. 1850s.

Somber gray and green Tuscan columns.

[H69] **Metropolitan Lumber & Mill Works**/originally Metropolitan Railway Company electrical substation, 175 Spring St., bet. West Broadway and Thompson Sts. N side. ca. 1885.

The Sixth Avenue elevated ran up West Broadway before it turned at West 3rd Street to find Sixth Avenue. This robust brick and stone structure served the el's electrical needs after steam propulsion became passé. The mural, in a somewhat different color scheme, dates from 1973, when commissioned by a former occupant, Gem Lumber Company.

H69

West Broadway: Between Spring and Prince Streets.

[H70] **420 West Broadway** (lofts). W side. ca. 1890.

Cut granite over black Tuscan stone: somber elegance housing art galleries.

[H71] **426 West Broadway** (lofts), W side. 1870s.

The exposed steel girders and decorated columns that embrace the façade give an engineering counterpoint to the brick and banded limestone above.

H70

[H72] **430-434 West Broadway** (mixed-use complex). W side. 1988. **Arpad Baksa & Assocs.**, architects. **Don-Linn Consultant Design Corp**.

Five levels of glitz that serve the merchandisers but is out of place on West Broadway.

H71

[H73] **429 and 431 West Broadway** (lofts), E side. 1872. **Robert Mook.** ♂

Two Corinthians free-standing at 431.

[H74] **468 West Broadway** (lofts), W side. 1890s.

Magnificent maroon arches, with black spandrels, metal strapwork and highlights.

H74

▮ [H75] **65-77 West Houston Street** (taxpayer), bet. West Broadway and Wooster St. S side. 1984. **Beyer Blinder Belle.** ♂

A horizontal sliver clad in colored tiles. It resembles a large Indian headband, 2 stories high.

Thompson Street: *South of West Houston Street.*

[H76] **Warehouse**, 138-144 Thompson St., bet. Prince and W. Houston Sts. E side. 1883. **Oscar Seale.**

Off the beaten track: tall brick arches worthy of a Roman aqueduct carry a "cornice" of small, windowed spaces.

H76

Sullivan Street: *South of West Houston Street.*

🏛 [H77] **St. Anthony of Padua Roman Catholic Church**, 155 Sullivan St. E side. ca. 1888. St. Anthony's Pious League, 151 Thompson St. W side. ca. 1880.

A hard neo-Romanesque church where rough rock-faced ashlar contrasts with cut limestone pediments and arches. It is the parish of the South Village's Italian community.

H77

The Villages

GREENWICH VILLAGE • WEST VILLAGE
SOUTH VILLAGE • ASTOR PLACE AND ENVIRONS
EAST VILLAGE

GREENWICH VILLAGE

 Colonial

 Georgian/ Federal

 Greek Revival

 Gothic Revival

 Villa

 Romanesque Revival

 Renaissance Revival

 Roman Revival

 Art Deco/ Art Moderne

 Modern/ Post-Modern

Nonconformist: In its street grids (they differ from each other as well as from those of the rest of Manhattan), in the life-styles it tolerates (or is it nurtures?), and in its remarkable variety of architecture, Greenwich Village is a concentration of contrasts in a city of contrasts. But in the Village's case, these contrasts have long been synonymous with its identity: bohemia. This is less apparent today than when both aspiring and successful artists and writers gravitated to this crooked-streeted, humanely scaled, out-of-the-way, low-rent enclave passed over by the city's growth northward. Actually, today's Village encompasses the long-fashionable side streets along lower Fifth Avenue as well as those irregular byways to the south and west that are featured in picture postcard views.

Since around 1900 the Village has been not only a proving ground for new ideas among its creative residents but also a symbol of the forbidden, the free life—the closest thing to Paris that we had in this country. With the opening up of Sixth and Seventh Avenues and the subways beneath them, the area became even more accessible. After the hiatus caused by the Depression and World War II, the Village once again attracted interest, this time from high-rise housing developers, from smaller entrepreneurs who created little studio apartments with minispaces inversely proportional to their high rents, and from tenants who left the "duller" (meaning the outer) parts of the city to taste forbidden fruit. Creators were swept out by observers (middle-class doctors, dentists, cloak and suiters, and other vicarious residents). The people of the visible Village changed—leaving West Village families, such as those written about by urbanist **Jane Jacobs**, and those of the South Village (the Italian community), to go about their own business, largely unnoticed. In the 1950s it was the beat generation; since then, after a bout with the drug culture (which has moved easterly) it has returned to beckon yet another younger generation with its special raffishness.

As its nostalgic glamour fades, however, it continues to fulfill a variety of seemingly conflicting roles: a genteel place to live, a fashionable step up the professional ladder, a spawning ground for movements such as feminism and gay liberation, a singles' haven, a place to raise a family—in short, a perplexing but certainly not colorless community.

Heritage: Always a village, the first one was an Algonquin community, Sapokanikan. The Dutch, upon their arrival in 1626, quickly kicked out the natives, taking over the fertile rolling farmland for their own profit and pleasure.

Growth was leisurely since the village was completely separated from the bustling community concentrated at the lower tip of the island; but its stature rose suddenly in the 1730s with the land purchases of socially prominent naval **Captain Peter Warren**. When Captain Warren bought a large parcel in 1731, he was the first of a long line of affluent individuals to settle in the Village. His mansion was soon followed by Richmond Hill (owned by **Aaron Burr**, among others) and the **Brevoort** homestead. Richmond Hill was the best known of these homes, which for nearly 100 years gave the Village an unsurpassed social status.

The city commissioners, having already contemplated the future growth of Manhattan, appointed **John Randel, Jr.**, who from 1808 to 1811 prepared maps and plans for the present grid-

Washington Arch

iron of Manhattan's streets. The Village escaped most of this layout, however, since it was simply too difficult to impose it over
the well-established pattern. The commissioners, though, had
their way with the hills, leveling them all by 1811 and taking with
them the grandeur of the old estates. These properties were then
easily divisible into small city lots, and by 1822 the community
was densely settled, many of the settlers "refugees" from a series
of "downtown" epidemics.

Sailors' Snug Harbor and Trinity Parish have both had leading roles in the Village's growth. The Harbor was founded in
1801, when **Captain Robert Richard Randall** deeded in perpetual lease 21 acres of land (around and north of Washington
Square), together with a modest cash grant, for the support of a
home for aged seamen. It was moved to Staten Island in 1833,
and since then has received its income from its leased Village
land. Prior to the 1920s, its property had been divided into small
lots, rented mainly for individual residences. Since then, land
values have skyrocketed, and the Harbor understandably sought
to increase its income from its holdings. In doing so, however, it
leased rather indiscriminately, permitting the demolition of
many historic and architectural treasures and their replacement
by mediocre works, to the detriment of the area.

Trinity Parish made great contributions to the development
of the West Village in the 19th century, encouraging respectful
care and beautification of its leased land. In 1822 it developed a
residential settlement around St. Luke's Church, which to this
day is a positive influence upon the neighborhood.

Residents: Perhaps as important as the architectural heritage
are the people the Village has attracted: the artists and writers,
entertainers, intellectuals, and bohemians who have made their
homes alongside long-established but less conspicuous Village
families. But the artist in his garret is today mere legend. The
well-established Hollywood actor, "Madison Avenue gallery"
painter, and copywriter have replaced the struggling painter and
writer. **Eugene O'Neill** and his group at the Provincetown
Playhouse, **Maxwell Bodenheim**, **Edna St. Vincent Millay**, the
delightful, "spirited" **Dylan Thomas** at Hudson Street's White
Horse Tavern, and quiet **Joe Gould** accumulating material for
his "oral history" at the Minetta—it was such as these who once

Jefferson Market Library

made the Village's reputation international. Their forerunners were writers of the 19th century who took up residence here, attracted by modest rents, the leisurely pace and the delightful streets and houses. They included **Poe** and **Melville**, **Mark Twain**, and **Henry James**.

Though future "writers in residence" of the Village will, more frequently than not, be well-paid copywriters, they will, more than likely, seek out the same Federal and Victorian row houses and back-alleyed, converted stables that attracted the Twains and Millays almost a century ago.

The Village, though no longer bohemian, still represents the unconventional, a reputation supported by its winding streets, its tiny houses sandwiched between impersonal behemoths, and its charming shops and eateries.

[V1] Greenwich Village Historic District. Irregular boundaries: S of W. 14th St. on the N, S of W. 13th and E. 12th Sts. on the NE, W of University Place on the E, N of W. 4th St./Washington Sq. S., N of St. Luke's Place/Leroy St. bet. Hudson St. and Seventh Ave. S. on the S, E of Greenwich St. on the SW, E of Washington St. bet. Horatio and Perry Sts., S of Horatio and Gansevoort Sts. on the NW. ●

It took more than 4 years and 7 public hearings to decide upon one contiguous Historic District for the Village—at one point 18 separate districts were considered—and the enormous irregular shape of the 100-plus-block area resulted in a two-volume designation report divided into 9 sub-areas stretching from NYU's borders (the university successfully fought inclusion of much of its real estate) to the West Village's Washington Street with its adjacent, then functioning overhead freight line. And, to complicate matters further, there are two other official Historic Districts, another in this section and one in the South Village.

THE VILLAGES KEY MAP

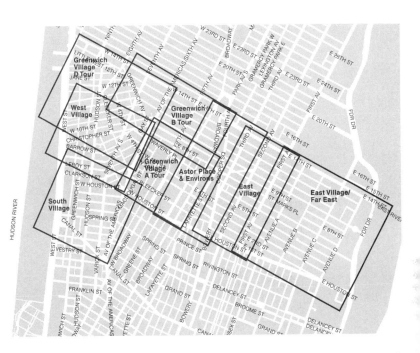

Walking Tour A: 8th Street, Washington Square, and NYU From Village Square, West 8th Street and Sixth Avenue, to West Houston Street and Sixth Avenue. **START** *at Village Square (A, B, C, D, E, F, and Q trains of the former IND Sixth and Eighth Avenue Lines to West 4th Street Station).*

Note: *Only some of the entries on this tour lie within the Greenwich Village Historic District; they are marked* ☞ *.*

Walk east along West 8th Street.
West 8th Street has seen its heyday, for the shops now are worn and the goods offered between Fifth Avenue and Sixth are more often than not glitzier, more expensive, poorer variations of what can be found elsewhere in the area.

Frederick J. Kiesler's Film Guild Playhouse (52 West 8th Street ☞) has vanished, its succession of owners having failed to value the Viennese architect-stage designer's visionary designs, though they were applauded and applied by theater architects throughout the world. But here, in 1928, Kiesler (1892-1965) made provisions for simultaneous slide projections on the side walls and created a main screen where the projection surface area could be altered in size—film projection concepts that are still considered avant-garde. Ironically, a video store proffering portable movies now fills the site. The exterior bears no trace of his hand.

Before taking a right (south) turn into MacDougal Street take a peek farther on toward Fifth Avenue, then return.

[V1a] **New York Studio School of Drawing, Painting & Sculpture**/earlier Whitney Museum of American Art/earlier Gertrude Vanderbilt Whitney House and private art gallery/originally 8, 10, 12 West 8th Street (houses), bet. MacDougal St. and Fifth Ave. Houses, 1838. Converted into House and gallery, 1931, **Auguste L. Noel** of **Noel & Miller**. Converted into Whitney Museum, 1936, **Auguste L. Noel**. ☞
    The 1930s neo-Classical entranceway remains as the single hallmark of the Whitney when it first opened at the onset of the Great Depression. The museum removed from these parts for a place next to the Museum of Modern Art garden, and then left for its current Upper East Side digs.

V1

[V2] **24, 26 West 8th Street** (houses), bet. MacDougal St. and Fifth Ave. 1838. ☞
    Town houses built (together with No. 28) as an investment by merchant **Joseph W. Alsop, Jr**. Their subsequent conversion into studios that would enjoy north light has given then distinctive—and not inharmonious—window patterns.

Now, south on MacDougal Street:

V2

[V3] **Tenth Church of Christ, Scientist**/originally factory and store. 171 MacDougal St., bet. W. 8th St. and Waverly Place. W side. 1891. **Renwick, Aspinwall & Russell**. Converted to church, 1967, **Victor Christ-Janer**. ☞
    Great corbeled brick openings in an austere façade give this a monumental scale in these narrow streets.

V3

GREENWICH VILLAGE (TOUR A)

see pages 116–126

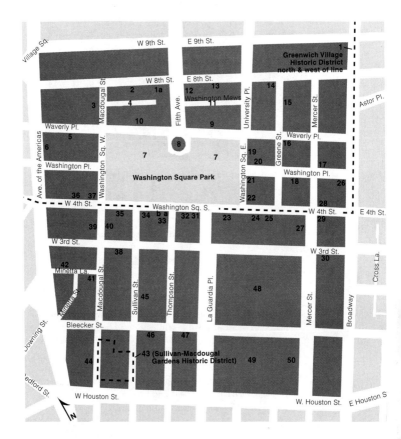

[V4] **MacDougal Alley**, off MacDougal St., bet. W. 8th St. and Washington Sq. N. E side. ♂

This charming cul-de-sac (less charming when filled with residents' cars) is jointly owned by property holders on Washington Square North and on the south side of 8th Street. The 20-story bulk of No. 2 Fifth Avenue looms over it, overwhelming its space and diminishing its small-scaled delight.

Right turn (west) into Waverly Place, and a walk around the block via a left (south) on Sixth Avenue and another left (east) into Washington Place.

[V5] **108 Waverly Place** (house), bet. Sixth Ave. and Washington Sq. W./MacDougal St. S side. 1826. Altered, 1906, **Charles C. Haight**. Garage entrance removed, 1927. ♂

In this pleasantly Classical street, this eccentric and dour granite house wears crenellations (presumably to protect the skylight against insurrection).

[V6] **Washington Court** (apartments), 360-374 Avenue of the Americas, bet. Waverly and Washington Places. E side. 1986. **James Stewart Polshek & Partners**. ♂

A brilliantly conceived, designed, detailed, and executed Post Modern apartment house (with stores on Sixth Avenue) that captures the scale, the rhythms, and something of the accretive quality of many a Village street. Yet it was built only 6 stories high in the rapidly boiling 1980s Manhattan real estate market—chalk up the low-rise character to the IND subway running under part of the plot, local hyperactive citizen watchdog groups, and a vigilant Landmarks Preservation Commission.

V6

Continue east on Washington Place into the park.

[V7] **Washington Square Park**, at the foot of Fifth Ave. Redesigned, 1971. **John J. Kassner & Co.**, engineers. **Robert Nichols**, landscape architect. Service buildings, 1971. **Edgar Tafel & Assocs.** Patchwork mosaic plaza, 1971. **Cityarts Workshop.** ⚲

[V8] **Washington Arch**, 1889-1895. **Stanford White** of McKim, Mead & White. Winged figures, **Frederick MacMonnies**. West pier, *Washington in Peace*, 1918. **A. Stirling Calder**. East pier, *Washington in War*, 1916. **Herman A. MacNeil**. ⚲

V8

Originally marshland with Minetta Brook meandering through, then a potter's field, and later the site of the hanging gallows. In the 1820s a less sadistic citizenry converted it to a public park and parade ground for the military. With this change, building quickly began on all sides of the park, the north side with its "Row," and the east, which became the site of the first NYU building in 1837.

The Memorial Arch (1895) was first erected in wood in 1889 for the centennial celebration of **George Washington**'s inauguration by **McKim, Mead & White**. It was so well liked that pianist **Jan Paderewski** gave a benefit concert to help finance construction of the permanent arch. The statue on the west pier of Washington as a civilian was sculpted by mobile maker **Alexander Calder**'s father, **Alexander Stirling Calder** (1870-1945).

In 1964 10cal and citywide groups achieved a victory in their battle to keep an underpass from being built beneath the park. They later managed to free the park entirely of vehicular traffic—Fifth Avenue buses had for years used the space around the fountain as a turnaround, idling their engines there between runs. These accomplishments were later escalated into a full-blown redesign of the park, which kept the canopy of trees and added a circular pedestrian plaza ringing the old central fountain, a fresh interpretation of the European plaza.

Despite substantial involvement of the community in the redesign, the physical changes have been the subject of great controversy. Some of this is the result of major demographic population shifts in the adjunct community—an outflow of families and an influx of outcasts.

Best seen from the park:

V9

[V9] **"The Row"**: ⚲ [V9a] **1-13 Washington Square North** (town houses), bet. University Place and Fifth Ave. 1832-1833. No. 3, new façade added, 1884, **J. E. Terhune**.

V10

Nos. 7-13, converted to apartment house, Fifth Ave. pergola added, 1939, **Scott & Prescott**. ♂

[V10] **19-26 Washington Square North** (town houses), bet. Fifth Ave. and MacDougal St. No. 20, 1829; altered, 1880, **Henry J. Hardenbergh**. Others, 1836-1839. (No. 14, the southern wing of No. 2 Fifth Avenue, 1950, Emery Roth & Sons.) ♂

According to the district's Landmarks Preservation Commission report, Nos. 1-13 are "the most important and imposing block front of early Nineteenth Century town houses in the City [*sic*]." Nos. 19-26, a Greek Revival group that includes an unusual large town house in the Federal style (No. 20), is not far behind. When built, they housed New York's most prominent merchant and banking families and, over time, other distinguished individuals. Architect **Richard Morris Hunt** lived at No. 2 between 1887 and 1895. Novelist **Henry James**, who was to immortalize the western part of the row in his novel *Washington Square*, paid many visits to his grandmother, **Elizabeth Walsh**, at No. 18, demolished in favor of 2 Fifth Avenue's low wing. In this century **John Dos Passos** wrote *Manhattan Transfer* at No. 3; others living there have been **Edward Hopper** and **Rockwell Kent**. No. 8 was once the official residence of the mayor.

Over the years community pressure and artful illusion have maintained The Row in a fairly whole condition. Those from Nos. 7 to 13, to the east of Fifth Avenue, retain the shell of their front and side façades only: Sailors' Snug Harbor gutted them for multiple-dwelling housing, and entrance to these now NYU-owned apartments is via a pergola facing Fifth Avenue. On the west side of Fifth, when the huge No. 2 Fifth Avenue apartment tower was being planned, citizens put up an outcry, and a neo-neo-Georgian wing was designed for the Washington Square frontage, conspicuously lower than the adjacent real Greek Revival row houses.

V11

Follow Fifth Avenue north for a block, past:

[V11] **Washington Mews**, from University Place to Fifth Ave., bet. E. 8th St. and Washington Sq. N. North stables remodeled, 1916. **Maynicke & Franke**. South buildings constructed, 1939. ♂

A 19th-century mews lined on its uptown side with converted stables that once served the brownstones on 8th Street and Washington Square and that now, in the case of many, serve New York University. Nos. 1-10, on the south side, were built in 1939, and almost all were stuccoed in concert, causing an unfortunate regimentation. A walk through this Belgian-block-paved

alley (private, but pedestrians are not discouraged) is the best way to sense its space:

[V12] **1 Fifth Avenue** (apartments), SE cor. E. 8th St. 1929. **Helmle, Corbett & Harrison** and **Sugarman & Berger**. ♂

A stepped-back pinnacle of cool brown brick that has been a visual landmark on lower Fifth Avenue and Washington Square ever since it was built.

V12

A turn right (east) on East 8th Street.

[V13] **4-26 East 8th Street** (converted apartments), bet. University Place and Fifth Ave. 1834-1836. Remodeled, 1916, **Harvey Wiley Corbett**. ♂

A set of stuccoed apartment buildings made picturesque by the addition of bold decorative eaves, brickwork inlaid in a stucco ground, and bits of wrought ironwork. A stage set, symbolic of the "village" of a bohemian artist but not typical of its Federal/Greek Revival architectural reality.

V13

[V14] **Iris and B. Gerald Cantor Film Center, Tisch School of the Arts**, SW cor. E. 8th and Greene Sts. 1998. **Davis Brody Bond**.

A sleek banded house for film. The super-lettering attempts some modest modernist graphic enrichment of the façade; and the sidewalk marquee provides elegant shelter for the window shopper.

Turn right (south) into Greene Street.

New York University: NYU's avaricious land-grabbing has created an empire larger than the Village holdings of Sailors' Snug Harbor, consisting of loft buildings, apartment houses, and Greek Revival rows on and around Washington Square. Once the bane of Villagers' existence, NYU's empire building was tamed in the 1970s by economic realities. **Philip Johnson** and **Richard Foster** had been commissioned to create a unified urban campus where none had existed before. Their plans called for rebuilding and refacing buildings around the east side of Washington Square with the vivid red sandstone visible in the master plan's only fruits: the Bobst Library, the Tisch Building, and the Meyer Physics Building. Happily, the rest of this grandiose scheme has been abandoned.

V14

[V15] Originally **Sailors' Snug Harbor Headquarters** (now apartments) 262 Greene St., bet. E. 8th St. and Waverly Place.

The administrative center of a compact real estate empire (within a short walk of this building) funded by **Capt. Robert Richard Randall** in 1801 to endow a home for aged seamen. The sailors' home for many years, Snug Harbor, an elegant Greek Revival landmark on Staten Island, was vacated by them in 1976 in favor of new facilities in North Carolina.

[V16] **Kimball Hall, NYU**, 246 Greene St., SE cor. Waverly Place. ca. 1890.

Gloomy brown and beige brick, patterned to simulate larger scaled stone coursing at its base.

V15

From Greene Street turn right (west) into Washington Place, and walk to Washington Square East.

The Triangle Shirtwaist Fire: *A polite bronze plaque at the northwest corner of Washington Place and Greene Street refers discreetly to "the site" of the Triangle Shirtwaist Company fire, a* *tragedy which took 146 lives, mostly those of young women, on the Saturday afternoon of March 25, 1911. The loft building on this corner, originally called the Asch Building, is the very building in which the holocaust took place; Triangle occupied the upper three floors of the 10-story building.*

[V17] **3-5 Washington Place** (lofts), NE cor. Mercer St. 1890s.

Brick and brownstone. The attached colonettes and incised tooled pier capitals are worthy enrichments.

V17

[V18] **10 Washington Place Building, NYU**/originally loft building, bet. Greene and Mercer Sts. 1891. **Richard Berger.** Façade restored, 1972.

The loss of its cornice has not seriously diminished the delicate character of this loft building's orange terra-cotta, black cast-iron, and granite façade, renovated (the original windows were removed) by NYU upon the advice of master planners Johnson and Foster.

V19

[V19] **Hemmerdinger Hall (Main Building), NYU**/earlier NYU Law School, 100 Washington Sq. E., bet. Waverly and Washington Places. 1895. **Alfred Zucker.** Remodeled, 1990s. **Polshek Partnership.**

NYU originally built this structure to accommodate a paying tenant, American Bank Note Company, on the lower 7 floors (hence the façade division at that point) and the Schools of Commerce, Law, and Pedagogy above. By the end of World War I the increase in students caused a takeover of the entire building for classes.

V20

[V20] **Grey Art Gallery, NYU Main Building**, 33 Washington Place, E of Washington Sq. E. Open to the public: Tu, Th, Fr 11-6; We 11-8:30; Sa 11-5; closed Mo. 212-998-6780.

One of NYU's bright spots: an offbeat gallery with high standards of quality. Note the grid of white-painted Doric columns on the interior, around which the exhibitions are arranged.

[V21] **Press Building, NYU**, 26 Washington Pl., SE cor. Washington Sq. E. 1890s.

Clustered brick colonettes at the 5th floor support some stone ellipses.

V21

[V22] **Paulette Goddard Hall**, 79 Washington Sq. W., NE cor. W. 4th St. 1890s.

Brick, limestone and terra cotta provide lusty pilasters, their composite capitals allowing arches to spring across the façade. Dour and delightful.

V22

▮ [V23] **Elmer Holmes Bobst Library, NYU**, 70
══ Washington Sq. S., bet. W. Broadway and Washington Sq. E. S side. 1972. **Philip Johnson** and **Richard Foster**.

Johnson in a free neo-Classicism (the "columns" are concave rather than convex). The red sandstone façade thus produced is, nevertheless, bulky and mannered. Inside, a great atrium brings light and a sense of space to its users, while the outside shades the park.

[V24] **Tisch Hall, Stern School of Business, NYU**, 40 W. 4th St., bet. Washington Sq. E. and Greene St. 1972. **Philip Johnson** and **Richard Foster**.

Another ruddy Johnsonian, this time without a meaningful inner space.

▮ [V25] **New building**, Stern School of Business, NYU, W.
══ 4th St., bet. Washington Sq. E. and Greene St. 1990s.

V23

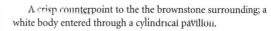

A crisp counterpoint to the the brownstone surrounding; a white body entered through a cylindrical pavilion.

For Meyer Hall and other NYU and related buildings' continue east here to Mercer Street and Broadway beyond. Resume tour at [V31].

V25

[V26] André and Bella Meyer Physics Hall, NYU, 707 Broadway, SW cor. Washington Place. 1971. **Philip Johnson** and **Richard Foster**.

More from Johnson & Co.'s brown-decades revival.

[V27] Warren Weaver Hall, NYU, 251 Mercer St., bet. W. 3rd and W. 4th Sts. W side. 1966. **Warner, Burns, Toan & Lunde**.

An early NYU attempt at an architectural identity via a new, Modern building—now dated. The Johnson-Foster master plan followed.

[V28] Brookdale Center, Hebrew Union College/Jewish Institute of Religion, 1 W. 4th St., NE cor. Mercer St. to Broadway. 1979. **Abramovitz Harris & Kingsland**.

Red brick monolith, crystalline, flat, introverted.

V27

[V29] 250 Mercer Street (lofts), SE cor. W. 4th St. 1890s.

Cast iron, brownstone, brick, and terra-cotta combine to corner West 4th and Mercer with this rich eclecticism. DoJo's downstairs looks promising.

[V30] Mercer Street Residence Hall, NYU, 240 Mercer St., SE cor. W. 3rd St. to Broadway. 1981. **Benjamin Thompson & Assocs**.

Occupying the site of the grand old Second Empire, mansard-roofed Broadway Central Hotel, which collapsed without warning in 1973, this nicely designed beige brick dorm does not live up to the rich architecture and happy interplay of scale in its neighborhood. For better vibes from the same architects, see nearby D'Agostino Hall [V38].

V29

From Bobst Library and Tisch Hall walk west along Washington Square South.

[V31] Helen and Martin Kimmel Center for University Life (student center), 566-576 LaGuardia Pl., SW cor. Washington Sq. S. 2001. **Kevin Roche John Dinkeloo & Assocs**.

The Kimmel Center stands on the site of its predecessor, the demolished Loeb, providing twice the student space in a volume that matches Bobst's bulk to the East. Crowned with a glass mansard roof, it borders on the grotesque. Harrison did it better.

[V32] Holy Trinity Chapel, Generoso Pope Catholic Center at NYU, 58 Washington Sq. S., SE cor. Thompson St. 1964. **Eggers & Higgins**.

Awkward modernism from a time when a search for form preoccupied American architects.

V32

 [V33a] Judson Memorial Baptist Church, 54-57 Washington Sq. S., SW cor. Thompson St. 1888-1893. **Stanford White** of McKim, Mead & White.

Stained glass, **John La Farge**. Marble relief, S wall of chancel (after Saint-Gaudens's plans), **Herbert Adams**.

 [V33b] Judson Hall and Tower, 51-54 Washington Sq. S., bet. Thompson and Sullivan Sts. S side. Tower, Nos. 52-54, 1895-1896, **McKim, Mead & White**. Hall, No. 51, 1877, **John G. Prague**.

An eclectic Early Christian (Roman) church and tower of yellow roman brick, limestone, and terra-cotta that once dominated Washington Square but is now dwarfed by many cacophonous neighbors. Its ornate and pompous detail, en masse, recalls

V33a

V33b

such inflated Roman churches as St. Paul's Outside-the-Walls (rebuilt at the same time after a fire, from the ground up). Look inside these walls. The 10-story campanile and adjacent former tenement are now dormitories.

[V34] **Hagop Kevorkian Center for Near Eastern Studies, NYU,** 50 Washington Sq. S., SE cor. Sullivan St. 1972. **Philip Johnson** and **Richard Foster.**

A classy but overscaled granite building matching in size the adjacent "town house." It would have been a happier neighbor to the Judson complex were it in brick.

V34

[V35] **Vanderbilt Law School, NYU,** 40 Washington Sq. S., bet. Sullivan and MacDougal Sts. 1951. **Eggers & Higgins.**

A blockful of neo-Georgian building, built much in advance of the current historicist fashions, trying to be neighborly and offering an arcaded and contained forecourt to the street.

[V36] **Washington Square Methodist Church,** 135-139 W. 4th St., bet. Washington Sq.W and 6th Ave. 1859-1860. **Gamaliel King.**

Romanesque Revival marble. See Brooklyn's Borough Hall for more of this poorly remembered architect.

V35

[V37] **37 Washington Sqare West** (apartments), NW cor. W. 4th St. 1928. **Gronenberg & Leuchtag.**

Some comely glazed terra-cotta enriches an otherwise banal façade.

[V38] **Filomen D'Agostino Residence Hall, NYU Law School,** 110 W. 3rd St., bet. Sullivan and MacDougal Sts. 1986. **Benjamin Thompson & Assocs.**

Twelve stories but detailed so as to look in scale with its smaller neighbors. Standard—not jumbo—brick, laid in Flemish bond, like the Law School; deep window reveals and weighty window frames further emphasizing the heft of the masonry walls, substantial ironwork learned from lessons of the past. A fine work.

V36

MacDougal Street: This street and vicinity between West 3rd and Bleecker was one of the most colorful and magnetic to tourists out for an evening in the Village. With the advent of the drug scene its activities took a turn to the bizarre, and many of its restaurants, coffee houses, jewelry boutiques, and folk song emporia disappeared. Some still remain or have been reincarnated.

V37

V39

[V39] **127-131 MacDougal Street** (row houses), bet. W. 3rd and W. 4th Sts. W side. 1829.

These Federal houses were built for **Aaron Burr**. The pineapple newel posts on the ironwork at No. 129 are one of the few such pairs remaining in the Village.

[V40] **130-132 MacDougal Street** (row houses), bet. W. 3rd and Bleecker Sts. E side. 1852.

Twinned entrances and an ironwork portico.

[V41] **Minetta Tavern** (restaurant), 113 MacDougal St., SW cor. Minetta Lane.

A sorry 1950s exterior masks a drinking person's museum of Greenwich Village. The walls are crammed with photographs and other mementoes of the famed characters who claimed the Minetta as a second home during the heyday of the Village. Note especially the **Joe Gould** memorabilia. Italian cooking, moderate prices.

A peek to the right (west) down Minetta Lane, and twisted, one-block Minetta Street.

[V42] **Minetta Lane Theatre**, 18 Minetta Lane, bet. MacDougal St. and Sixth Ave. N side. Converted, 1984, **Larsen-Juster**.

Converted from a deserted tin can factory is this modest 415-seat off-Broadway theater with a remarkably sophisticated façade.

[V43] **MacDougal-Sullivan Gardens Historic District**, bet. MacDougal and Sullivan Sts., W. Houston and Bleecker Sts. ca. 1923. 170-188 Sullivan St., W side. 1850. 74-96 MacDougal St., E side. 1844. Altered 1921, **Francis Y. Joannes** and **Maxwell Hyde**. 🍎

The whole-block renovation started as an idea of **William Sloane Coffin**'s (then a director of the family business, the W. & J. Sloane furniture house) to develop a pleasing residence for middle-income professionals from a slum neighborhood. He formed the Hearth and Home Corporation, which bought the block, renovated it, and by 1921, the following year, had rented nearly all the houses. Coffin's dream of a private community garden was realized around 1923; each house has its own low-walled garden that opens onto a central mall with grouped seating for adults and, at one end, a small playground. The garden is for residents only.

V43

Coffee houses:

Caffe Reggio, 119 MacDougal St., N of Minetta Lane. W side. **Café Borgia**, 185 Bleecker St., NE cor. MacDougal St. **Le Figaro**, 186 Bleecker St., SE cor. MacDougal St. **Caffe Dante**, 81 MacDougal St., S of Bleecker St. W side.

The oldest (since 1927) and most authentic is Reggio with a nickel-plated brass *macchina* spewing forth steamed espresso and various coffee, cocoa, or milk combinations. Dante's special contribution is a giant color photo mural of Florence from San Miniato. But all have pastries, hot and cold beverages, and conviviality.

[V44] **Tiro a Segno/New York Rifle Club**, 77 MacDougal St., bet. W. Houston and Bleecker Sts.

An Italian club where the shooting described is off-premises. Handsome brickwork scaled to the Gardens ensemble across the street.

[V45] Originally **Sullivan Street Industrial School**, Children's Aid Society/now Lower West Side Children's Center/Greenwich Village Neighborhood School, 209-219 Sullivan St., bet. Bleecker and W. 3rd Sts. E side. 1892. **Vaux & Radford**.

V44

A rich interplay of brick and brownstone (now simulated in stucco), solid and void, arches and angles; its renovated details have been smoothed by less skilled craftsmen than those of 1892.

East on Bleecker Street:

[V46] **The Atrium** (apartments)/originally Mills House No. 1 (men's residence), 160 Bleecker St., bet. Sullivan and Thompson Sts. S side. 1896. **Ernest Flagg**. Converted, 1976.

Reclaimed by the middle class as apartments, the structure was built originally as a hostel for poor "gentlemen" (the room rate was only 20¢ a night, but the expenses were covered by profits on the 10¢ and 25¢ meals). The building was a milestone in concept and plan: 1,500 tiny bedrooms either on the outside or overlooking the two grassed interior courts open to the sky. Eventually the courts were skylighted and paved, and the structure became a seedy hotel, The Greenwich. The courts, now neatly rebuilt with access balconies to the apartments which ring them, are the inspiration for the project's new name.

V47

[V47] **The Elbow Room**/once Bleecker Street Playhouse/originally Mori's Restaurant, 146 Bleecker St., bet. LaGuardia Pl. and Thompson St. S side. Restaurant alteration and current façade, 1920. **Raymond Hood**.

Hood, soon to gain recognition for his firm's winning entry in the Chicago Tribune Tower competition, converted a pair of old row houses to one of the Village's best-known Italian restaurants of the period, Mori's. He and his wife lived briefly in a tiny apartment over the premises. History has lost out to tawdry maintenance and economics.

V48

[V48] **Washington Square Village** (apartments), W. 3rd to Bleecker Sts., W. Broadway to Mercer St. 1956-1958. **S. J. Kessler**, architects. **Paul Lester Weiner**, consultant for design and site planning.

Superbuildings on superblocks. These crisp gargantuas are the antithesis of Village scale and charm. Spanning what were University Place and Greene Street, they come from architects' fantasies of ideal city planning that is now much discredited.

[V49] Originally **University Village**, 100 and 110 Bleecker St., and 505 LaGuardia Pl. Bleecker to W. Houston Sts., bet. Mercer St. and LaGuardia Pl. 1966. **I. M. Pei & Partners**. Central sculpture, 1970, **Pablo Picasso** (large-scale concrete translation, **Carl Nesjar**).

V49

Three pinwheel-plan towers visible for miles. What is exceptional for this high-rise housing is that the size of individual apartments can be grasped because of their articulated form. Inside, corridors are short—not the usual labyrinth—and handsomely lit and carpeted. Outside, the advances in the technology of cast-in-place concrete were remarkable to behold; the smooth surfaces and intricate curved fillets of the deeply formed concrete façade could be achieved despite the vicissitudes of on-site casting. The two Bleecker Street units (Silver Towers) are NYU owned; the other is a co-op.

Added later in the center of the project is the 36-foot-high enlargement, in concrete and stone, of **Pablo Picasso**'s small cubist sculpture *Portrait of Sylvette*. Despite sensitive craftsmanship, the work loses much in translation.

Turn right (south) into Mercer Street:

V50

[V50] **Jerome S. Coles Sports and Recreation Center, NYU**, 181 Mercer St., bet. W. Houston and Bleecker Sts. NW cor. Mercer St. 1982. **Wank Adams Slavin & Assocs.**
A bland, beige box with a running track on its roof.

The Angelika Film Center (in the Cable Building, NE cor. Mercer and Houston Sts.) is a wondrous place to savor offbeat films. At the end of a Tour, sit down in the café with pastry and coffee, and plan which movie to see, then and there.

Note: *For Bleecker Court apartments across Mercer Street, see Astor Place and Environs .*

END *of Tour A. The nearest subways are at W. Houston Street and Broadway (Broadway-Lafayette Street Station of the former IND Sixth Avenue Line, B, D, and F trains) or Bleecker and Lafayette Streets (No. 6 local of the old IRT Lexington Avenue Line local, Bleecker Street Station).*

B1

Walking Tour B: From Jefferson Market Library to East 12th Street near Broadway. START north of Village Square, at West 10th Street and Sixth Avenue (A, B, C, D, E, F and Q trains of the old IND Sixth and Eighth Avenue Lines to West 4th Street Station).

Note: Only some of the entries on this tour lie within the Greenwich Village Historic District; they are marked ☿ .

Walk east along West 10th Street.

[B1] **56 West 10th Street** (house), bet. Fifth and Sixth Aves. 1832. ☿
Among the oldest houses in this part of the Village, it has much of its original detail: pineapple newel posts (indicating welcome), with segmented ironwork in mint condition, door with fluted Ionic colonnettes and leaded lights. The cornice and dormer trim came later.

[B2] **50 West 10th Street** (originally stable), bet. Fifth and Sixth Aves. 1863-1869. ☿
The upper stories of this former stable use brick in a bold, straightforward fashion to ornament as well as to support and enclose (in contrast with the smooth nondecorative planes of brickwork elsewhere on the block). This became the residence of playwright **Edward Albee**.

B2

[B3] **40 West 10th Street** (apartments), bet. Fifth and Sixth Aves. 1890s. Altered, 1980s.
A modest house surmounted by modern penthouse terraces. Look up.

[B4] "**The English Terrace Row**" (row houses), 20-38 West 10th St., bet. Fifth and Sixth Aves. 1856-1858. ☿
The first group of row houses in the city to abandon the high "stoop," placing the entry floor only 2 or 3 steps up from the street in the English manner.

B4

Terrace does not refer to the handsome balcony that runs the length of these houses; it is the English term for a row of houses, such as are found in the Kensington and Paddington districts of London of the 1840s, 1850s, and 1860s. New Yorkers visiting England were impressed with this style and saw good reason to adopt it upon their return.

GREENWICH VILLAGE (TOUR B)

see pages 127–136

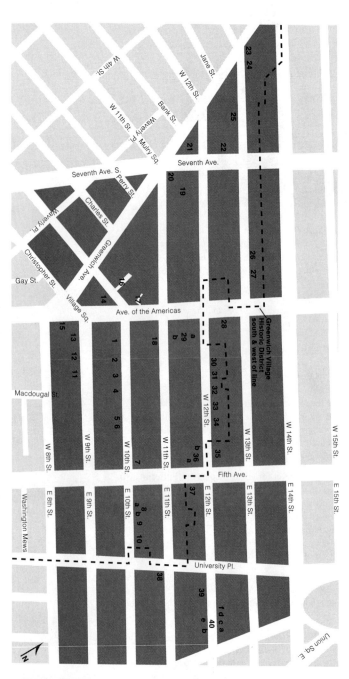

B5

Sculptor **Frederick MacMonnies** lived in No. 20 during the 1930s; painters **Louis Bouche** and **Guy Pène du Bois** lived there some years afterward.

[B5] **14, 16, and 18 West 10th Street** (town houses), bet. Fifth and Sixth Aves. 1855-1856.   ☞

Grand mansions for the small-scaled Village. No. 14 maintains the crust of its original brownstone detail. No. 18 is more serene. No. 16, in the middle, was neatly stripped.

[B6] **12 West 10th Street** (town house), bet. Fifth and Sixth Aves. 1846. Extensive renovations, 1895. **Bruce Price**.   ☞

Unique after several renovations: an important one divided it into four apartments—one for each daughter—by owner architect **Bruce Price**. One of those daughters, **Emily Post**, tells of having **President Wilson** to Thanksgiving dinner (it is rumored that he proposed to his second wife here).

B6

[B7] **Church of the Ascension** (Episcopal), 36-38 Fifth Ave., NW cor. W. 10th St. 1840-1841. **Richard Upjohn.** Interior remodeled, 1885-1889, **Stanford White of McKim, Mead & White**. Altar mural and stained glass, **John La Farge**. Altar relief, **Augustus Saint-Gaudens**. Parish House, 12 W. 11th St., bet. Fifth and Sixth Aves. 1844. Altered to present appearance, 1889, **McKim, Mead & White.**

Random brownstone ashlar in Gothic Revival dress. One of the few churches that lights up its stained glass at night, allowing evening strollers on lower Fifth Avenue to enjoy the colors. If you're wondering about the inconsistent quality of the stained glass, you're correct: not all the windows are La Farge's.

B7

[B8a] Originally Lockwood De Forest House/now **New York University, Edgar M. Bronfman Center for Jewish Student Life**, 7 E. 10th St., bet. University Place and Fifth Ave. 1887. **Van Campen Taylor**. Restored, 1994-1997. **Helpern Associates.**
[B8b] **Apartment house**, 9 E. 10th St. 1888. **Renwick, Aspinwall & Russell.**

Unique in New York is the exotic, unpainted, and intricately carved teakwood bay window that adorns No. 7. Its infectious forms influence the other East Indian details of this town house as well as those of the apartment building to the east, designed the following year. Note how the exterior teakwood here has withstood the rigors of the city's atmosphere better than the brownstone of neighboring row houses. **De Forest** (1850-1932) was an artist who worked in the Middle East and India and founded workshops in Ahmadabad to revive the art of wood-carving.

B8a

[B9] **The Lancaster** (apartments), 39-41 E. 10th St., bet. Broadway and University Place. 1887. **Renwick, Aspinwall & Russell.**

Like No. 9, above, an early apartment house from the era when those who could afford a town house still weren't in a rush to move. Beautiful terra-cotta and a fine Queen Anne entrance.

[B10] **43 East 10th Street** (lofts), bet. Broadway and University Place. 1890s.

Grand terra-cotta, brick, and cast iron complex, straddling aspects of the Classical Revival, a bit of Richardsonian Romanesque

B10

Retrace your steps to Fifth Avenue, and turn left (south) for a block and then right (west) into West 9th Street.

[B11] **The Portsmouth** (apartments), 38-44 W. 9th St., bet. Fifth and Sixth Aves. 1882. [B12] **The Hampshire** (apartments), 46-50 W. 9th St. 1883. Both by **Ralph S. Townsend.**

Lusty Victorian flats embellished with rich terra-cotta spandrels and, in the case of The Hampshire, diminished by festoons of fire escapes.

B12

[B13] **54, 56, and 58 West 9th Street** (row houses), bet. Fifth and Sixth Aves. 1853. **Reuben R. Wood**, builder.

A distinguished group: pairs of half-round arched windows set within segmental arched openings.

[B14] **Jefferson Market Branch, New York Public Library**/originally Third Judicial District (or Jefferson Market) Courthouse, 425 Sixth Ave., SW cor. W. 10th St. 1874-1877. **Vaux & Withers**. Exterior restoration, interior remodeling,

Early fire tower at Jefferson Market

1967, **Giorgio Cavaglieri**. ○ Further restoration, 1994. **Joseph Pell Lombardi**.

B14

   A mock Neuschwansteinian assemblage (after **Ludwig II** of Bavaria's castle, Neuschwanstein) of leaded glass, steeply sloping roofs, gables, pinnacles, Venetian Gothic embellishments, and an intricate tower and clock makes this one of the city's most remarkable buildings. Endangered when no use could be found for it—it had remained vacant since 1945—local residents went into action. Led by indefatigable **Margot Gayle**, they first repaired and lighted the clock and eventually persuaded city fathers to restore the entire structure as a regional branch library. Budgetary limitations meant the loss of the polychrome slate roof shingles, but the exterior did get a thorough cleaning and repair.

   Today's prominent tower served originally as a fire lookout, replacing a tall clapboard version, around which the Jefferson Market's sheds, dating from 1833, clustered. In 1877 the courthouse, and its adjoining jail along 10th Street, were completed from **Frederick Clarke Withers**'s designs. In 1883 a masonry market building designed by **Douglas Smyth** filled the remainder of the site, replacing the market's old sheds. Both jail and market were demolished in 1927 in favor of the high-rise Women's House of Detention (1931. **Sloan & Robertson**), in turn demolished in 1974.

   The trial of **Harry Thaw**, the assassin of **Stanford White**, took place in these halls.

The Jefferson Market Greening, on Greenwich Avenue between Christopher and West 10th Streets, is the official name for the fenced formal park that occupies the site of the old market and of the more recent Women's House of Detention. The greening was started (and is maintained, with help from the Vincent Astor Foundation) by members of the local community. It forms a verdant foreground to the amusing forms of the Jefferson Market Library.

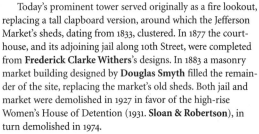

B15

   [B15] **Bigelow Building** (lofts), 412 Sixth Ave., bet. W. 8th and W. 9th Sts. E side. 1902. **John E. Nitchie**. ○
   Its ground floor still occupied by C. O. Bigelow, Chemists, Inc., this 8-story structure was built for **Clarence O. Bigelow**. Culture lag is evident here: transitional Romanesque Revival into neo-Classical, more than a decade after it had affected others. ○

Cross Sixth Avenue and continue briefly on West 10th Street where it has now joined an earlier, diagonal street grid, first to Patchin

*Place, on your right, and then retracing your steps back, and to
the left (north) onto Sixth, Milligan Place.*

[B16] **Patchin Place**, off W. 10th St., bet. Greenwich and Sixth
Aves. NW side. 1849. ♂ [B17] **Milligan Place**, Sixth Ave. bet.
W. 10th and W. 11th Sts. W side. 1848. ♂

In 1848 and 1852, respectively, Patchin and Milligan Places
were built as second-class boarding houses for the Basque wait-
ers and workers at the old Brevoort House on Fifth Avenue.
Today they are charming not for the quality of their architecture
but rather as peaceful pedestrian cul-de-sacs that contrast with
the agitated ebb and flow of Village Square crowds only a block
to the south.

B17

In the 1920s Patchin Place became famous for its writer residents. Its most renowned tenant was e. e. cummings, who lived
at No. 4. Others: **John Reed, Theodore Dreiser, Padraic Colum,
Jane Bowles,** and **Djuna Barnes.**

*Follow Sixth one block to West 11th Street, and then cross the wide
avenue (east) for a short detour to an ancient cemetery. Do an
about-face, cross Sixth again, and continue west on West 11th.*

B18

[B18] **Second Cemetery of the Spanish and Portuguese
Synagogue**, Shearith Israel, in the City of New York, 72-76 W.
11th St., bet. Fifth and Sixth Aves. 1805-1829. ♂

The original Shearith Israel cemetery is at Chatham Square.
Burials began here in 1805, in what was a much larger, square
plot extending into the present street. The commissioners' plan
had established the city's grid in 1811, but West 11th Street was
not cut through until 1830, reducing the cemetery to its present
tiny triangle. The disturbed plots were moved farther uptown to
the Third Cemetery on West 21st Street. After City law forbade
burial within Manhattan, subsequent interments have been
made in Queens. West 11th between Sixth and Seventh Avenues
is a mixed bag of ridiculous (institutional) and sublime (residential) architecture.

*Rhinelander Gardens: In 1955, P. S. 41, Manhattan—with its
garish yellow-glazed auditorium—on the south side of West 11th
Street, just west of Sixth Avenue, replaced **James Renwick, Jr.'s,**
Rhinelander Gardens. These were a one-of- a-kind group of 8
wrought-iron balconied row houses, in the manner of New
Orleans's Bourbon Street. For nostalgia's sake a bit of the wrought
iron was saved and applied to the school's rear façade—barely visible across the bleak asphalt play area from Greenwich Avenue.*

[B19] **St. Vincent's Hospital & Medical Center of New York,**
vicinity of Seventh and Greenwich Aves. ♂ [B20] **George
Link, Jr. Pavilion**, 165 W. 11th St., NE cor. Seventh Ave. 1984-
1987. **Ferrenz, Taylor, Clark & Assocs.** ♂

The old Elizabeth Bayley Seton Building, by **Schickel &
Ditmars**, was demolished in favor of this, whose lower 11th
Street wing is closer in height to its row house neighbors. The
cubistic brick architecture, however handsome in its own right,
fails to harmonize with the more intricately detailed brownstones, as its taller neighbor's did.

[B21] **Materials Handling Center, St. Vincent's Hospital &
Medical Center**, Seventh Ave. bet. Greenwich Ave. and W. 12th
St. W side. 1987. **Ferrenz, Taylor, Clark & Assocs.** ♂

This triangular site was once that of Loew's Sheridan, a vast
barn of a movie theater demolished in the 1970s. For a few years
it was a charming garden, The Village Green. The current collection of brick forms is utilitarian and inoffensive but out of place
on this site.

B20

B22

[B22] **Edward and Theresa O'Toole Medical Services Building, St. Vincent's Hospital & Medical Center**/originally National Maritime Union of America, AFL-CIo, 36 Seventh Ave., bet. W. 12th and W. 13th Sts. W side. 1964. **Albert C. Ledner & Assocs.** Altered, 1977. **Ferrenz & Taylor**. ☞

In the wake of **Frank Lloyd Wright**'s Guggenheim Museum, this huge double-dentured monument is without precedent. It suffered from the same rough concrete work as its Upper East Side cousin and so was later veneered with the small white-glazed tesserae that cover the building today. Compare with its sibling on West 17th Street.

Continue across Seventh Avenue to a gentle right onto the diagonal Greenwich Avenue (northwesterly) to West 13th Street.

Jackson Square Area: Greenwich and Eighth Avenues at W. 13th.

[B23] **IND Electrical Substation**, 253 W. 13th St., NE cor. Greenwich Ave. 1930. ☞

The City's own subway system, the Independent (independent at that time of the privately owned IRT and BMT), arrived on the scene about the time Art Deco influences did. Hence utilitarian structures such as this were ornamented in that style. They can be found all over the city.

B24

[B24] **The Great Building Crackup**/lnternational Headquarters of the First National Church of the Exquisite Panic, Inc./originally Jackson Square Branch, New York Free Circulating Library/later New York Public Library, 251 West 13th St., bet. Greenwich and Seventh Aves. N side. 1888. **Richard Morris Hunt**. Altered, 1971, **Paul Rudolph**. ☞

A benefaction of **George W. Vanderbilt**, this former library building resembles an old Dutch guildhall. Its original leaded glass windows, so important in establishing scale, were removed in a conversion to a residence and gallery. Inside the now recessed (and metal-screened) ground floor space is a large plaque worth reading—a mystical statement on the relationship of architect and client. In part, it says

THE GREAT BUILDING CRACKUP IS
AN ACTUAL COLLISION....

SINCE THIS IS AN EVENT AND NOT A
BUILDING IN ACCEPTED NOMENCLATURE,

IT POSSESSES A FLUIDITY WHICH IS
MORE EASILY UNDERSTOOD IF APPRE-
HENDED AS A METAPHOR CONCERNING
MOLECULAR PHYSICS.

IT IS NOT A RECORD OF WHAT HAS
HAPPENED BUT A CONTINUALLY
CHANGING PHENOMENON FUNCTIONING
ON A TIME SCALE WHICH IS NOT
AS RECOGNIZABLE TO HUMAN SENSE
PERCEPTION.

Proceed east on West 13th Street for two blocks.

[B25] **Lesbian and Gay Community Services Center**/formerly
Food and Maritime Trades Vocational High School/earlier
Public School 16, Manhattan, 208 W. 13th St., bet. Seventh and
Greenwich Aves. Center portion, 1844. **Thomas R. Jackson?**
Extensions, ca. 1859, ca. 1899. **C. B. J. Snyder.** Conversion to
Community Center, 1997. **Françoise Bollack.** ♂

B25

A fine example of the Italianate school buildings built by the
city in the third quarter of the 19th century.

[B26] **Portico Place** (apartments)/earlier Village
Community Church (Presbyterian)/originally 13th
Street Presbyterian Church, 143 W. 13th St., bet. Sixth and
Seventh Aves. 1847. Attributed to **Samuel Thomson**. Rebuilt
after fires, 1855, 1902. Converted, 1982. **Stephen B. Jacobs &
Assocs**. ♂

B26

Once the best Greek Revival church in the city, modeled
after the Theseum in Athens. Columns and pediment resemble
stone but are actually wood; walls are brick and stucco. The
porch is most inviting, as was the light and airy interior with its
clear glass windows. But, alas, it is no longer a church and the
entry porch is now merely a latter-day false front. Converted
into duplex apartments and flats.

*Rum, Romanism, and Rebellion: The characterization of **Grover
Cleveland**'s Democratic Party as one of rum, Romanism, and
rebellion cost Republican candidate **James G. Blaine** the presidency in 1884. The fiery speech, containing the phrase that antag-
onized the (Roman) Catholic Irish in New York City, was delivered by **Dr. Samuel D. Burchard**, long minister of what is today
Portico Place. The adjacent row house at 139 West 13th Street was
built in 1846 as the manse for Dr. Burchard when he became the
church's first rector.* ♂

[B27] **John and Mary R. Markle Memorial Residence**/
Evangeline Residence, Salvation Army, 123-131 W. 13th
St., bet. Sixth and Seventh Aves. 1929. **Voorhees, Gmelin &
Walker**. ♂

A mildly ornamented Art Deco work (check the window
grill) of great charm and understatement.

B28

[B28] **496 Sixth Avenue** (tenement), bet. W. 12th and W. 13th
Sts. E side. 1889.

Artistry for the masses in brickwork, terra-cotta, and a sheet-
metal cornice.

*At Sixth Avenue zigzag south one block, and continue east on
West 12th Street.*

[B29a] **The New School for Social Research**, 66 W. 12th
St., bet. Fifth and Sixth Aves. 1930. **Joseph Urban**. ♂
Interior (Tishman auditorium and Orozco Room), restored
1992. **Rolf Ohlhausen, Prentice & Chan, Ohlhausen**. ♂

B29a

B29b, Bridge

B29b, Auditorium

[B29b] **Jacob M. Kaplan Building, 11th Street Building, and Interior Court**, additions to the W and SW. 1958. **Mayer, Whittlesey & Glass; William J. Conklin**, associate partner in charge of design. Vera List Courtyard (renovation of courtyard and two lobbies), 1997. **Mitchell/Giurgola; Ohlhausen Dubois; Micheal Van Valkenburgh** (landscape); **Martin Puryear** (sculptor). ♂

The New School became the "university in exile" for the intelligentsia fleeing Nazi Germany in the 1930s. The original (east) building is a precocious design for New York in its restrained use of strip windows and spandrels whose brick courses set back slightly from the street as they rise. These subtleties make it appear shorter, less imposing, more in scale with the adjacent row houses on this street. The auditorium within is a dramatic example of Urban's theatrical talents and was the "model" for Radio City Music Hall; its 1992 renovation by **Rolf Ohlhausen** has restored its original glory. The school's additions to the south are linked across a rear sculpture court by an impressive glassed-in 2-story-high bridge. This has been remodeled as the Vera List Courtyard to provide accessibility for the disabled through the whole block, with new paving, planting, and sculpture.

B30

[B30] **59 West 12th Street** (apartments), bet. Fifth and Sixth Aves. 1931. **Emery Roth**. ♂

Art Deco motifs are particularly evident on the elevator and water tank penthouses atop this 14-story box.

[B31] **45 West 12th Street** (row house), bet. Fifth and Sixth Aves. 1846. ♂

Look carefully at the east side of this building for the acute angle. The side wall slants back because it originally faced the once aboveground Minetta Brook. **Frank Lloyd Wright**'s sister, **Mrs. William Pope Barney**, owned and lived in the house.

B31

[B32] **Butterfield House** (apartments), 37 W. 12th St., bet. Fifth and Sixth Aves. 1962. **Mayer, Whittlesey & Glass; William J. Conklin**, associate partner in charge of design, and **James S. Rossant**. ♂

The friendly neighborhood high rise. On residential 12th Street, this cooperative apartment rises to only 7 stories; varied windows, projected bays, and balconies break up the façade and relate it to the prevailing 19th-century residential scale of the street. A glazed courtyard passage to the north wing shares its neighbors' backyard charm. On 13th Street, though, with numerous lofts and 20th-century apartment towers, the building's flat wall rises agreeably (and economically) to 13 stories.

B32

[B33] **35 West 12th Street (house)**, bet. Fifth and Sixth Aves. 1840. Altered 1868; right half removed, 1893. ♂

Originally about 25 feet wide; the building of Nos. 31-33 consumed half of this house, leaving a curious but not unpleasing reminder.

B33

[B34] **The Ardea** (apartments), 31-33 W. 12th St., bet. Fifth and Sixth Aves. 1895, 1901. **John B. Snook & Sons.** ♂

This dark crusty façade, lyrically set off by delicate ironwork balconies, is one of many structures in the city wrongfully attributed to **McKim, Mead & White.** Buildings of great character, like this one, were designed by many distinguished firms. And **Snook** was no minor player: he designed the original 1871 Grand Central Depot. The client here was **George A. Hearn**, the department store magnate, whose dry goods emporium was once a showplace nearby on 14th Street.

B34

[B35] Originally Macmillan Company Building/now **Forbes Magazine Building**, 60-62 Fifth Ave., NW cor. W. 12th St. 1925. **Carrère & Hastings** and **Shreve & Lamb**. Galleries open to the public: Tu-Sa 10-4; closed Su & Mo. 212-206-5549.

For some four decades, **Macmillan** conducted its publishing business from this pompous limestone cube whose boring surfaces are embellished here and there with echoes of Rome's glories. Following Macmillan's relocation to an anonymous midtown tower, *Forbes* magazine assumed ownership of the stodgy pile. **Malcolm Forbes**'s various collectibles are on display in the exhibition area within.

B35

[B36a] **First Presbyterian Church**, 48 Fifth Ave., bet. W. 11th and W. 12th Sts. W side. 1846. **Joseph C. Wells**. South transept, 1893. **McKim, Mead & White**. Chancel added, 1919. ♂

[B36b] **Church House**. 1960. **Edgar Tafel**. ♂

A stately, crenellated, coursed, and dressed ashlar central tower of brownstone, set well back from Fifth Avenue, this church is identified by its bold form. Embellishing the walls of that tall prism is a Gothic Revival tracery of quatrefoils that also forms the motif for the adjacent, properly reticent, church house, built more than a century later. Note the handsome fence that rings the site—partly of cast iron and, surprisingly, partly of wood.

B36a

Boom! For years a tall wooden fence enclosed the property at 18 West 11th Street. Between 1845 and 1970 a Greek Revival row house stood here, similar to its neighbors on either side. On March 5, 1970, the street was rocked by an explosion. When the smoke cleared, little was left of the house—its cellar, it turned out, was being used by a radical group as a bomb manufactory. An attempt soon afterward, by architect **Hugh Hardy**, to build a contemporary replacement was picked to death by a combination of governmental red tape and rising construction costs. His scheme was later revived for another client (1978 **Hardy Holzman Pfeiffer Assocs.**). ♂

B36b

[B37] **Salmagundi Club**/originally Irad Hawley House, 47 Fifth Ave., bet. E. 11th and E. 12th Sts. E side. 1853. ● Exterior restoration, 1997. **Platt Byard Dovell**. Exhibitions open to the public: 1-5 daily.

The Salmagundi Club is America's oldest artists' club (founded in 1870). This private club moved to Fifth Avenue in 1917; members included **John La Farge**, **Louis C. Tiffany**, and **Stanford White**. Painting exhibitions open to the public are sometimes installed on the parlor floor, a superbly preserved interior of the period.

B37

Make a short detour south at University Place, and then resume walking east on East 12th Street.

B40a

[B38] Originally Hotel Albert/now **Albert Apartments**, University Place SE cor. E. 11th St. 1883. **Henry J. Hardenbergh**.

Dark red brick and black-painted wrought-iron trim distinguish this work of architect Hardenbergh (contemporary with his Dakota).

East 12th Street: *Between University Place and Broadway*

[B39] **Youth Aid and Property Clerk Divisions, NYC Police Department**/formerly Girls' High School/originally Public School 47, 34½ E. 12th St., S side. 1856. **Thomas R. Jackson**.

Beautifully preserved Italianate painted brownstone and painted brick from an era when most public buildings—whether school, police station, or hospital—were styled the same way. Proper but gloomy. **Lydia Wadleigh**, for whom the high school (now intermediate school) in Harlem was named, was principal here, where she fought effectively for free education for girls.

[B40a] **43 East 12th Street** (converted lofts), 1894. **Cleverdon & Putzel**. [B40b] **42 East 12th Street** (converted lofts), 1894. **Cleverdon & Putzel**. [B40c] **39 East 12th Street** (converted lofts), 1896. [B40d] **37 East 12th Street** (converted lofts), 1896. **Cleverdon & Putzel**. [B40e] **36 East 12th Street** (converted lofts), 1895. **Cleverdon & Putzel**. [B40f] **35 East 12th Street** (converted lofts), 1897. **Albert Wagner**.

A big and bold "Beaux Arts meets 1890s High-Tech" row, each multistory loft competitively outdoing the other. Look up at rich stone and brickwork. Much of the Rue Réaumur in Paris, of the same vintage, displays masonry and steel with similar integration, an effort by conservative Beaux Arts architects to enter the new mainstream.

END of Tour B. *The nearest subways are two blocks north at Union Square, along East 14th Street, between University Place and Fourth Avenue: 14th Street/Union Square Station (Nos. 4, 5, and 6 of the old IRT Lexington Avenue Line and the N and R trains of the old BMT Broadway and Canarsie Lines).*

WEST VILLAGE

Walking Tour C: The Western West Village. A ramble west of Sixth Avenue to the Hudson River. START at Village Square, Sixth and Greenwich Avenues (A, B, C, D, E, F, and Q trains of the old IND Sixth and Eighth Avenue Lines to West 4th Street Station). See Walking Tour D for the northern parts of the West Village.

Note: Only some of the entries on this tour lie within the Greenwich Village Historic District; they are marked ⚘ .

There are so many early 19th-century houses in this precinct that one is tempted to say "when you've seen one, you've seen 'em all." Not so. There are always surprises; some are squashed between 6-story lofts, others are tucked away in backyards, often they are bedecked with nostalgic but destructive wisteria vines. It is this rich texture that makes them such a valuable contribution to the Village—take away the contrasts and it would be a dull place indeed.

Walk southwesterly along Christopher Street, with a peek into little Gay Street.

[C1] **18 and 20 Christopher Street** (house), bet. Gay St. and Waverly Place. SE side. 1827. **Daniel Simonson**, builder. Alterations: storefronts. ⚘

A Federal pair with superdormers.

C1

[C2] **14 Christopher Street** (lofts), SW cor. Gay St. 1903. **Jardine, Kent & Jardine**. Altered, 1939, 1975. ⚘

This tall, simple structure contrasts beautifully with the tiny houses around the corner on Gay Street. Its back wall curves to match the bend in the side street.

[C3] **Gay Street**, bet. Christopher St. and Waverly Place. Houses, 1827-1860. ⚘

My Sister Eileen territory. A handful of little Federal houses, delightful for being so close to the street. More superdormers.

Turn left (southerly) on Waverly Place, and follow it around as it bends east.

C3

C4

C4

[C4] **Hostel for the Disabled**/formerly Northern Dispensary/originally Northern Dispensary Institute, 165 Waverly Place, on triangle with Waverly Place and Christopher St. 1831. **Henry Bayard**, carpenter; **John C. Tucker**, mason. 3rd floor added, 1854. ⚘ Restored, 1977, **H. Dickson McKenna**. Remodeled into apartments, 1997. **John Ellis & Assocs**.

An austere vernacular Georgian building with sheet metal lintels and cornice of a later period. Remarkable for having continuously operated as a public clinic since its founding in 1827. **Edgar Allan Poe** was treated here for a head cold in 1837—without charge. Closed 1989. Reopened as hostel, 1997.

C5

C6

C7

C9

The triangular **Northern Dispensary** *is the only building in New York with one side on two streets (Grove and Christopher where they join) and two sides on one street (Waverly Place, where it forks to go off in two directions).*

[C5] **88 and 90 Grove Street**, bet. W. Washington and Waverly Pls., 1827. No. 88 altered with mansard, 1860s. No. 90 remodeled, 1893. **Carrère & Hastings**.

Two personalities facing Christopher Park. Painter **Robert Blum** lived in, worked at, and commissioned the studio alteration of No. 90 in 1893. He died there in 1903. New owner **Howard Reed** can enjoy the chrysanthemums Blum painted on the dining room wall.

[C6] **Residence of the Graymore Friars**/formerly St. Joseph's Church Rectory, 138 Waverly Place, bet. Sixth Ave. and Grove St. S side. 1895. **George H. Streeton**. ○⃝

A brick and brownstone Gothic Revival outpost in this mostly Greek Revival place.

Note: The Washington Court apartments across Sixth Avenue are to be found on Walking Tour A.

Turn right (south) on Sixth Avenue, past Washington Place:

[C7] **St. Joseph's Roman Catholic Church**, 365 Sixth Ave., NW cor. Washington Place. 1833-1834. **John Doran**. ○⃝ Rebuilt after fire, 1885. **Arthur Crooks**.

This church is one of the dwindling group of Greek Revival "temples." Its recent repainting in gray and white is elegant.

[C8] **St. Joseph's Washington Place School**, 111 Washington Place, bet. Sixth Ave. and Grove St. N side. 1897. **George H. Streeton**. ○⃝

A 5-story façade embellished by ornament borrowed from Greek temples, Italian Renaissance palazzi, and Baroque country houses.

Turn sharply right (west) on W. 4th St.

[C9] **175-179 West 4th Street** (row houses), at Jones St. N side. 1833-1834. ○⃝

Three Federal houses whose parlor floors and basements gracefully house elegant shops. Look up at the exquisite dormers—No. 175 had them too until altered.

A glance down Jones Street:

[C10] **26, 28, 30 Jones Street** (row houses) bet. Bleecker and W. 4th Sts. S side. 1844. Architect unknown. ●⃝

Severely simple, late Greek Revival: 3 stories atop a low basement with low stoops.

Back to West 4th, one block to Sheridan Square:

Sheridan Square, *bounded by Washington Place and West 4th, Barrow, and Grove Streets, used to be the most unused public space in the Village, marked out with a striped asphalt triangle stanchioned with NO PARKING signs. Today that empty space is filled by a magnificent green space (only for the looking) created and maintained by neighborhood volunteers with the cooperation of the City's Department of Transportation—only too happy to show up the Parks Department when it comes to providing verdant amenities. Before this greening the Square was frequently confused with Christopher Park, around the corner where a statue of Civil War general* **Philip Sheridan** *(for whom this square is*

WEST VILLAGE (TOUR C)

see pages 137-144

named) happens, in fact, to stand. It caused havoc during emergencies when equipment rushed to the wrong place.

[C11] **Sheridan Square Triangle Association Viewing Garden**, Sheridan Sq. 1983. **Pamela Berdan**, landscape designer. **David Gurin**, planner, NYC Department of Transportation.

    If only the city had more such delights . . .

Turn left (southwest) at Barrow Street and gently left (south) at Seventh Avenue South:

[C12] **15 Barrow Street** (originally Conrad Schaper's stable), bet. W. 4th St. and Seventh Ave. S. SE side. 1896. **H. Hasenstein.** ○

    Originally a 4-story stable—note the horse's head protruding from just below the cornice.

[C13] **Greenwich House** (settlement house), 29 Barrow St., bet. W. 4th St. and Seventh Ave. S. SE side. 1917. **Delano & Aldrich.** ○

    The building, an ill-kempt Georgian Revival, is most significant for its works: social reform. In 1901, when Greenwich House was founded (by **Mary Kingsbury Simkhovitch**, daughter of an old patrician family), Jones Street, a block to the east, was home to 1,400 people—975 to the acre—then the highest density in this part of Manhattan. These were first-generation Italian, second-generation Irish, some black, some French. From Greenwich House came the Greenwich Village Improvement Society, the first neighborhood association in the city.

C12

Down Bleecker Street (and back again):

Bleecker Street adventure: *Between Seventh Avenue South and Sixth Avenue (Father Demo Square): a colorful Italo-American shopping street.*

A. Zito & Sons

Gastronomical holdouts: A. Zito & Sons (bakery), 259 Bleecker St., at Cornelia St. NE side. Loaves, long, round, sesame-seeded or not, and all crusty. Mmmm. **Faicco's** *(sausages), 260 Bleecker St. SW side. Homemade sausage since 1927. Tipico italiano.* **Rocco's Pastry Shop**, *243 Bleecker St., opp. Leroy St. NE side. Great Italian ices for a summer stroll. The Italian rum cake (with luscious frosting!) is not to be believed.*

[C14] **1 Leroy Street** (condomiums), SW cor. Bleecker St. 1999. **Stephen B. Jacobs Group**.

   A 6-story infill providing duplexes and triplexes for the super-rich to live among the exoticism of Greenwich Village. How could one resist, with Zito's for bread and Rocco's for pastry just across the street?

Resuming your walk southward on Seventh Avenue South, below Bleecker:

C15

[C15] **28 Seventh Avenue South** (retail shop/residence), bet. Leroy St./St. Luke's Place and Bedford St. W side. Building, 1921. Store redesign and residential addition, 1988, **Matthew Gotsegen**. ☞

   Serendipitous architecture for a serendipitous location, an interruption in an earlier, pre-subway grid.

Take a right (westerly) into Leroy St./St. Luke's Place.

Changing street names in midstream: St. Luke's Place assumes its name (and a sequential, rather than odd-even, house numbering system) halfway between Seventh Avenue South and Hudson Street—at the bend to be precise. The eastern portion is officially Leroy Street, a lesser thoroughfare to those who are snobbish about such things.

C16

 [C16] **5-16 St. Luke's Place**, bet. Leroy and Hudson Sts. N side. 1852-1853. ☞
   This impressive row of handsome brick and brownstone Italianate residences seems an eerie stage set in this world of converted industrial lofts visible across **James J. Walker Park**—named for the colorful mayor who lived at No. 6. Fortunately, when the street's two rows of gingko trees green they form a graceful arbor, giving form to a street only "one-sided" in winter. Between 1834 and 1898 the land occupied by what was originally called Hudson Park (**Carrère & Hastings**, 1898) was part of Trinity Parish's cemetery until that cemetery was moved up to 155th Street [see page 520]. A relic of its previous service is a large marble monument to members of Eagle Fire Engine Company No. 13, retained at the St. Luke's Place entrance. The park itself no longer resembles its initial neo-Classical design.

Turn right (northerly) on Hudson Street and right again (east) on Morton (which echoes the Leroy Street/St Luke's Place bend in the middle).

C17

[C17] **The Bespeckled Trout** ("general store"), 422 Hudson St., bet. St. Luke's Pl. and Morton St. 1993.
   Signs enrich the architecture of commerce—or vulgarize it. Here is a successful duet.

[C18] **Morton Street, from Hudson to Bedford Sts**. ☞
   If there is a typical Village block, this is it. It bends. It has a private court with its own, out-of-whack numbers (Nos. 44A, 44B). It is full of surprising changes of scale, setbacks, façade

C18, 42 Morton

treatments. No. 42 (1889) presents a bottomless caryatid of some charm. No. 66 (1852) has a bold bay; No. 59 (1828) has one of the finest Federal doorways in the Village. Old Law tenements interrupt the street, greedily consuming their property right out to the building line. In them live staunch Italian and Irish holdouts, groups that remind their more affluent neighbors of an earlier, less moneyed Village.

Take a sharp left (northwesterly) into narrow Bedford Street.

[C19] "**Narrowest house in the Village,**" 75½ Bedford St., bet. Morton and Commerce Sts. W side. 1873. ♂
    It's 9½ feet wide; originally built to span an alley to the rear court (where its main entrance is). Though narrow by any standards, it was wide enough for carriages to pass through. Unfortunately it has been defaced with a fake brick coating. This is one of several residences of **Edna St. Vincent Millay** in the Village (1923-1924).

C18

Edna St. Vincent Millay (1892-1950): This poet, closely identified with the Village in the 1920s, was given her middle name after St. Vincent's Hospital here, even though she was born in Rockland, Maine. It seems that the hospital had saved the life of a relative.

C19

[C20] **Isaacs-Hendricks House**, 77 Bedford St., SW cor. Commerce St. 1799. Alterations, 1836, 1928, 1985. ♂
    Significant for its early date; remodeling has altered, and then restored, the original Federal style. The rebuilt clapboard walls are visible to the side and rear.

Take a left (southwest) on Commerce Street to see the next pair and then circle around to the right (northeast) via Barrow Street.

[C21] **39 and 41 Commerce Street**, at Barrow St. E side. 1831 and 1832, respectively. Mansard roofs, 1873. **D. T. Atwood**. ♂
    This extraordinary one-of-a-kind pair proclaims the elegance once surrounding this and neighboring St. Luke's Place. A local legend holds that they were built by a sea captain for his two daughters—one for each because they could not live together. The records show they were actually built for a milkman, one **Peter Huyler.**

C21

Having doubled back, take a left (northerly) to resume on Bedford Street.

C23a

C24

C25

C26

C29

[C22] Originally **J. Goebel & Company**, 95 Bedford St., bet. Barrow and Grove Sts. W side. 1894. **Kurzer & Kohl.** ♂

A stable once used by a wine company, as the lettering on the façade clearly indicates; converted into apartments in 1927.

[C23a] **17 Grove Street** (house), NE cor. Bedford St. 1822. 3rd floor added, 1870. ♂ [C23b] **100 Bedford Street**, bet. Grove and Christopher Sts. 1833. ♂

William Hyde built this as his house. A sash maker who later put up a small building around the corner on Bedford Street for his workshop; his is the best preserved of the few remaining wood-frame houses in the Village. Recent coats of paint seem to hold up the façade.

[C24] **Twin Peaks**, 102 Bedford St., bet. Grove and Christopher Sts. E side. ca. 1830. Renovation, 1925, **Clifford Reed Daily.** ♂

The renovation was the work of Daily, a local resident, financed by the wealthy financier and art patron **Otto Kahn**, whose daughter lived here for some time. Daily considered the surrounding buildings "unfit for inspiring the minds of creative Villagers" and set out to give them this "island growing in a desert of mediocrity." Great fun for the kids—pure Hansel and Gretel.

[C25] **14-16 Grove Street** (row houses) bet. Bedford and Hudson Sts. S side. 1840. **Samuel Winant** and **John Degraw**, builders. ♂

A pair of vine-clad Greek Revival houses in pristine condition. Until altered in 1966, No. 14 was believed to have been the last completely untouched Greek Revival residence in the city.

[C26] **Grove Court**, viewed bet. 10 and 12 Grove St., bet. Bedford and Hudson Sts. S side. 1853-1854. Alterations. ♂

This charming, pedestrians only, cul-de-sac lined with story-book brick-fronted houses hints at the irregularity of early 19th-century property lines. Evidence of similar holdings can be glimpsed throughout the West Village. These houses were built for workingmen; the court was once known as Mixed Ale Alley.

[C27] **4-10 Grove Street** (row houses), bet. Bedford and Hudson Sts. S side. 1827-1834. **James N. Wells**, builder. ♂

An excellent row of houses—brick fronts with clapboard behinds.

Honest and humble. The Federal houses at 4-10 Grove Street represent the prevailing style of the 1820s. Americans had few architects then; instead, the local carpenters and masons copied and adapted plans and details from builders' copybooks. In translation, the detailing is less pretentious, adapting to the needs of American merchant and craftsman clients; nonetheless, there is a faint, pleasant echo of London's Bloomsbury.

[C28] **2 Grove Street** (apartments), NE cor. Hudson St. 1938. **Irving Margon.**

A modest Art Deco counterpoint to the first-class Federal architecture down the block. ♂

Cross Hudson Street for the St. Luke's church complex.

[C29] **Church of St. Luke-in-the-Fields** (Episcopal)/formerly St. Luke's Episcopal Chapel of Trinity Parish, 485 Hudson St., bet. Barrow and Christopher Sts. opp. Barrow St. W side. 1821-1822. Attributed to **Clement Clarke Moore**. **John Heath**, builder. Interior remodeling, 1875, 1886. Fire, 1981. Restoration and expansion to W and S, 1985, **Hardy Holzman Pfeiffer Assocs.** ♂

An austere country church from the time when this was "the country" to New Yorkers living on the southern tip of Manhattan.

The original church was founded independently by local residents, with some financial help from wealthy, downtown Trinity Parish. With the influx of immigrants to the area, the carriage-trade congregation moved uptown to Convent Avenue to found a St. Luke's there. After an 1886 fire this St. Luke's reopened and, from 1891-1976, was a chapel of Trinity Parish.

The additions made following the 1981 fire, which are visible from within the church property, are handsomely conceived, detailed, and executed brick masonry volumes. Emitting rich overtones of the past, they are fresh in spirit, while harmonious to the older structures.

Visit the yard and church interior, too. On leaving St. Luke's, scan the small houses along Hudson and Barrow Streets, and then proceed northward on Hudson.

C30

[C30] **473-477, 487-491 Hudson Street** (row houses), flanking St. Luke's Chapel, bet. Barrow and Christopher Sts. W side. 1825. ☿ [C31] **90-96 Barrow Street** (row houses), bet. Hudson and Greenwich Sts. N side. 1827. **James N. Wells**, builder. ☿

Only 6 houses remain of a total of 14 originally symmetrically arrayed, 7 to the north of the church and 7 to the south. Such planning was made possible because the entire tract of land was developed under a lease from the Trinity Church Corporation. The architecture is in an austere Federal mode.

Just a glance north of Christopher:

C33

[C32] **510-518 Hudson Street** (row houses), bet. Christopher and W. 10th Sts. E side. 1826. **Isaac Hatfield**, carpenter and builder. ☿

Five Federal houses of which No. 510 (except for its altered ground floor and tasteful paint job) shows the original appearance.

[C33] **248 West 10th Street** (apartments), SW cor. W. 10th St. 1988. **Norval White**, design architect.

Brick vernacular for a background building.

Turn left (southwesterly) on Christopher Street.

C34

[C34] **PATH/Port Authority Trans-Hudson Christopher Street station entrance**/originally Hudson & Manhattan Railroad station entrance, 137 Christopher St., bet. Hudson and Greenwich Sts. N side. 1912. ☿ Restored, 1985, **Port Authority of N.Y. & N.J. Architectural Design Team.**

A most wonderful restoration of a long-forgotten and sadly neglected amenity. The scene transports one—figuratively—to a London tube entrance.

C35

[C35] **The Archives** (mixed use)/originally U.S. Appraiser's Stores (warehouse)/then U.S. Federal Archives Building, 666 Greenwich St., bet. Christopher and Barrow Sts. to Washington St. W side. 1892-1899. **Willoughby J. Edbrooke. William Martin Aiken, James Knox Taylor.** ✸ Conversion, 1988. **Avinash K. Malhotra.** Street-level and lobby design, **Judith Stockman & Assocs.**, designers.

A huge, block-filling, 10-story block of smooth brick masonry in the Romanesque Revival style of **H. H. Richardson.** Great brick arches form a virile base, and arched corbel tables march across the cornice against the sky. After many false starts the structure was sold by the feds and converted to a mixed residential-commercial-retail facility, some income from which will benefit historic preservation activities via the New York Landmarks Conservancy.

C36

[C36] St. Veronica's Roman Catholic Church, 153
Christopher St., bet. Greenwich and Washington Sts. N
side. 1889-1890. **John J. Deery**.

Here are squat towers worthy of Prague's Old City.

*END of Tour C. The nearest subway stations are quite a distance
back along Seventh Avenue South or Sixth Avenue. A convenient
but unusual route to midtown is via the PATH system (uptown
to West 33rd Street and Broadway—extra fare to NYC subway
connections—via Sixth Avenue, or to Jersey City, Hoboken, or
Newark, N.J.). The PATH Christopher Street Station can be found
beneath the marquee on Christopher Street, between Greenwich
and Hudson Streets, N side.*

Walking Tour D: *A loop through the northern West Village and the West Coast. Christopher Street, Westbeth, the West Village, the West Coast, the Gansevoort Market area and back to start.*
START *at what is commonly referred to (though not with great accuracy) as Sheridan Square (Nos. 1 and 9 locals of the old IRT Seventh Avenue Line local to the Christopher Street/Sheridan Square Station).*

Note: Only some of the entries on this tour lie within the Greenwich Vi//age Historic District; they are marked ☼ .

Proceed southwesterly from Seventh Avenue South along Christopher Street.

Interesting people on Christopher Street: *Between West Street and Sheridan Square, Christopher Street is a main drag for gay New Yorkers, especially after dark. The Stonewall Inn, at No. 53, was the scene in June 1969 of a brick- and bottle-throwing rampage following a police raid on the bar. The mêlée, which sparked the gay lib movement, is commemorated in an annual parade and in a National Register of Historic Places designation for the building.*

D1

[D1] **St. John's Evangelical Lutheran Church**/formerly St. Matthew's Church (Episcopal)/originally The Eighth Presbyterian Church, 81 Christopher St., bet. Seventh Ave. S. and Bleecker St. N side. 1821-1822. Altered, 1886, **Berg & Clark**. ☼
    Eclectic! A Federal cupola over a painted brownstone and sheet metal Romanesque body. The parish house to the west, next door, is stolid brick Romanesque Revival.

[D2] **95 Christopher Street** (apartments), NW cor. Bleecker St. 1931. **H. I. Feldman**. ☼
    Using a palette of browns, this striped brick Art Deco multiple dwelling is a forceful contrast to the more typical Village scale.

D3

Take a right (north) on Bleecker Street for 3 blocks past all sorts of chic antiquaries and such, and then a right (northeasterly) onto Perry Street for a brief look.

[D3] **The Hampton** (apartments), 80-82 Perry St., bet. W. 4th and Bleecker Sts. S side. 1887. **Thom & Wilson**. ☼
    A red brick and brownstone supertenement with Moorish "keyhole" openings at the ground-floor entry and windows.

[D4] **70 Perry Street** (row house), bet. W. 4th and Bleecker Sts. S side. 1867. **Walter Jones**, builder. ☼
    The architectural gem of this block in a superb state of repair. Tooled brownstone and stately proportions give it a grand scale in the style of the French Second Empire. As a result, it seems larger than its neighbors. It isn't.

D4

*"**Dog of the Ilk**"*: *This inscription and a coat of arms embellish the gable of 43 Perry Street, a travertine curiosity altered in (1967 **Simon Zeluik**) from an 1850s stable.* ☼

Now, back on Perry southwesterly to Hudson Street, a zig to the left, a zag to the right (southwesterly) onto Charles Street.

[D5] Earlier **Sven Bernhard House**, 121 Charles St., NE cor. Greenwich St. Relocated, 1968. **William Shopsin**. ☼
    This petite white-frame mongrel has occupied at least two other sites before stopping in this unlikely spot. Its beginnings are unknown, but it wound up as a backhouse uptown on York Avenue and East 71st Street sometime in the 19th century. When it was threatened with demolition in the 1960s, the Bernhards

D5

GREENWICH VILLAGE (TOUR D)

see pages 145-151

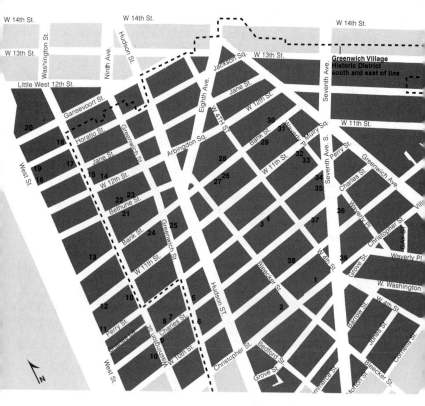

had it rolled through five miles of city streets to this West Village location. Barely visible in the summer's dense foliage.

[D6] **711 Greenwich Street** (studio), bet. Charles and W. 10th Sts. 1990s.

A radical and heavy-handed conversion in glass block and multi-panes.

[D7] **131 Charles Street** (row house), bet. Greenwich and Washington Sts. N side. **David Christie**, builder. 1834. ✒️

A Federal gem whose delicate scale contrasts—in a not unpleasant way—with the oompah details of the old police station adjacent. Note the blind oval window over the second descending doorway leading to No. 131½, a backhouse.

[D8] **Le Gendarme** (apartments)/originally 9th Precinct, NYC Police Department, 135 Charles St., bet. Greenwich and Washington Sts. N side. 1895-1897. **John Du Fais**. Converted, 1978, **Hurley & Farinella**.

A mélange of many styles, this ungainly but monumental eclecticism was the Village's police station until 1971, when operations moved to a new, bland low-rise replacement at 233 West 10th Street—today's 6th Precinct, truly a visual catastrophe. Now it serves as apartments. Revealed by the conversion: *premium vertutis honis* [sic] (loosely from **Cicero**'s *Philippics*).

D8

[D9] **The Memphis Downtown** (apartments), 140 Charles St., SE cor. Washington St. 1986. **Rothzeid, Kaiserman, Thomson & Bee**.

More appropriate to the world of the Upper East Side than to these low-rise high-density blocks. It's titled Downtown, as there is an Uptown original by other architects.

D9

D7

From Charles Street, turn right (northerly) on Washington Street

[D10] **West Village Houses** (apartments), along Washington St. bet. W. 10th and Bank Sts., W side. Also along Christopher and Morton Sts. and side streets. 1974. **Perkins & Will**.

The scene of the great war between the defenders of "Greenwich Village scale" and the Establishment, which proposed another high-rise housing project. The David in this case was critic **Jane Jacobs**, the Goliath, **Robert Moses**, then the city's urban renewal czar. A pyrrhic victory for David: the 5- and 6-story red brick products are dumpy, dull, and for their time, expensive. Scale simply isn't enough!

The Other Side of the Tracks: The old deserted New York Central Railroad freight viaduct (built in 1934) west of Washington Street for all appearances forms the western boundary of the Village. But scattered beyond this gloomy elevated structure are many 19th-century houses—some restored, others decaying—originally built for speculation or in the rush to house those fleeing the epidemics of lower Manhattan. An area to investigate if you have time.

Midblock, turn left into narrow, charming, one-block-long "cobblestoned" Charles Lane, and then right (northerly) onto West Street, Manhattan's wide Hudson front thoroughfare.

The West Coast: For years this area backing up to the West Street coastline, sandwiched between the gloomy West Side Elevated Highway and the equally gloomy New York Central elevated freight line, had no real name, except perhaps that its uptown part carried the cognomen Gansevoort Market. With the demolition of the highway and subsequent gentrification, the area has assumed the name West Coast, after an early residential conversion so named.

D11

[D11] **167 Perry Street** (apartments), wrapped around the NE cor. of West St. 1986. **William Monaghan**, 🖌 architect/developer.

A low-rise, neatly detailed complex, embracing a truck-rental yard. Please expand to fill this corner.

[D12] **River's Edge** (apartments), 366 W. 11th St., bet. West and Washington Sts. 1986. **Architects Design Studio**.

Dark red brick and unconvincingly detailed. It gets better near the top, where bay windows extend the form.

D12

D13

At Bank Street, a half-block detour to the right (easterly) will reveal the entrance and light courts of the 13-building Westbeth complex:

D14

[D13] **Westbeth** (artists' housing)/earlier Bell Labs, American Telephone & Telegraph Company, 155 Bank St., bet. Washington and West Sts. N side through to Bethune St. ca. 1861-1898. **Cyrus W. Eidlitz** and others. Converted to housing, 1969, **Richard Meier & Assocs.**

A block filler, reincarnated with major assistance from the J. M. Kaplan Fund as artists' loft housing. The exterior is a 40-year mélange of loft buildings embracing a bleak entrance court on Bank. The inner court, closer to Bethune, is a dark canyon festooned with fire-egress balconies.

Continue walking northerly on West Street, then east on 12th, to find, all by itself:

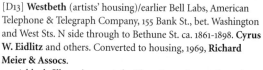

D16

 [D14] **357-359 West 12th Street** (apartments), bet. Washington and Greenwich Sts. N side. 1986.
A modernist essay in brick, articulated by columns and a lonely arch.

[D15] **Industria Superstudio**, 775 Washington St., bet. W. 12th and Jane Sts. E side. 1998. **Deborah Berke** and **Andrew Berman**.
Neat industrial exterior conceals elegance within.

[D16] **Hotel Riverview**/formerly Jane West Hotel/originally American Seamen's Friend Society Institute (shelter), 113 Jane St., NE cor. West St. 1910.
The ships, sailors, longshoremen, wicked women, and gin mills have disappeared from the Hudson's shore. But this reformers' safe haven for merchant mariners now enjoys a new life. The Jane Street Theatre is also within.

D17

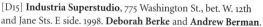

[D17] **99 Jane Street** (apartments), NW cor. Washington St. 1999. **Fox & Fowle**.
Rockrose Development creates new lofts as the supply of buildings suitable for recycling diminishes.

Turn right (easterly) on Jane Street and left (northerly) on Washington.

[D18] **The West Coast** (apartment conversion)/originally Manhattan Refrigerating Company (warehouse)/Peter J. Carey & Son (printers and publishers), 95 Horatio St., NW cor. Washington St. to Gansevoort St. 1898-1900. **George P. Chappell**. Both converted, 1984, **Rothzeid, Kaiserman & Thomson**.

The 8 once-open bays of the 2nd-story arcade of the corner structure formerly welcomed slow-moving New York Central electric switch engines shunting produce-laden reefers (refrigerator cars) to and fro.

[D19] **The West Coast** (apartments), 114 Horatio St., SE cor. West St. 1985. **Avinash K. Malhotra**.
  Eight stories of well (if sparsely) detailed brick.

Proceed north on Washington to Gansevoort Street. Note the old industrial structure across the way to the west before reversing direction proceeding easterly on Gansevoort.

Gansevoort Market Area lies roughly between Ninth Avenue and the Hudson River, from Gansevoort Street north to 14th. Busy, chaotic, earthy from before sunrise well into the day . . . empty, eerie, scary at night. From these wholesale meat markets comes the meat for many of Manhattan's restaurants and institutions. ***Herman Melville*** *(1819-1891) worked here on what was then the Gansevoort Dock as an outdoor customs inspector for 19 years. He came to this job, discouraged and unable to earn a living as a writer. It was during these years that he began* Billy Budd, *his last novel.*

[D20] **Wholesale meat market**/formerly Gansevoort pumping station, High Pressure Fire Service, NYC Fire Department/originally Gansevoort Market House, 555 West St., NE cor. Gansevoort St. 1906-1908. **Bernstein & Bernstein.** ●

D20

  Until the LaGuardia era, a neatly ordered Roman camp of 10 single-story market buildings, West Washington Market, stretched west from West Street to what was then Thirteenth Avenue and a pier for the Hudson River Night Line.
  This clumsily altered Romanesque Revival structure was originally built to serve as a market house for the informal farmers' market stand that then occupied the rest of this block. It was converted in 1908 to one of two pumping stations of Manhattan's new high-pressure water system. Before high-pressure fire trucks were introduced, this system served to increase water-main pressure to a level required to fight fires in vulnerable high-rise structures. Special fire hydrants (those large ones with 4 nozzles instead of 2) were installed in an area generally south of 23rd Street on the West Side and south of Houston on the East.

Greenmarket: With remarkable success, architect/planner Barry Benepe reintroduced the idea of urban farmers' markets for New York City in 1976. They have since proliferated in Manhattan and other boroughs. Appropriately, one has been reestablished periodically during the week along Gansevoort Street between Hudson and West.

Turn right (south) onto Greenwich Street and, after 4 blocks, at Bethune Street turn right (west) again.

D21

🏛 [D21] **19-29 Bethune Street** (row houses), bet. Greenwich and Washington Sts. S side. 1837. **Henry S. Forman** and **Alexander Douglass**, builders. ♂
[D22] **24-34 Bethune Street.** 1845. **Alexander R. Holden**, builder. N side. ♂ [D23] **36 Bethune Street.** N side. 1837. Altered, 1928.
  A block of small-scaled and handsome mongrels. Note the diminutive windows at the 3rd floor (servants' rooms), typical of early Greek Revival.

Left (south) at Washington, left (easterly) on Bank Street for a leisurely stroll on this, one of the West Village's most wonderful streets.

D24

[D24] **128 and 130 Bank Street** (row houses), bet. Greenwich and Washington Sts. S side. 1837.

Two Greek Revival houses, perfect examples in a motley row. Note the windows in the frieze.

D25

[D25] **Stephen F. Temmer House**/originally Helmut Jacoby House, 767 Greenwich St., bet. Bank and W. 11th Sts. E side. 1965. **Helmut Jacoby**, designer. **Leonard Feldman**, architect.

A Modernist single-family town house, one of fewer than a dozen in Manhattan. As crisp as a rendering but lacking passion. **Jacoby** was the star architectural renderer of the 1960s. (Renderings are realistic, usually perspective, presentation drawings.)

*Auntie Mame: Beginning in 1927, at 72 Bank Street, **Marion Tanner**, the self-described "ultimate Greenwich Village eccentric," created a haven and salon for a wide spectrum of Bohemian types. Her nephew, **Edward Everett Tanner III**—under the pen name **Patrick Dennis**—immortalized her in his best-selling novel* Auntie Mame *(1955), which became a play, then a film, and then a Broadway musical—which resulted in another film. She died nearby in 1985, aged 94, at the Village Nursing Home, 607 Hudson Street.*

D26

[D26] **68 Bank Street** (row house), bet. W. 4th and Bleecker Sts. S side. 1863. **Jacob C. Bogert**, builder.   [D27] **74 and 76 Bank Street** (row houses), 1839-1842. **Andrew Lockwood**, builder.   [D28] **55 and 57 Bank Street** (row houses), N side. 1842. **Aaron Marsh**, builder.

A charming group of houses: 68, almost a generation later than the other three, exhibits the Renaissance Revival and dour brownstone details of its time.

D29

[D29] **48 Bank Street** (town house)/originally stable, bet. Waverly Place and W. 4th St. 1910. Converted, 1969, **Claude Samton & Assocs.**

Severe brown brick and linseed-oil-brushed copper distinguish this 20th-century town house, a rarity along the Village's Federal and Victorian blocks.

[D30] **37 Bank Street** (row house), bet. Waverly Place and W. 4th St. N side. 1837.

One of the best Greek Revival houses in the Village. The block is striking—despite the curious lintel details on Nos. 16-34, and some ghastly refacing across the street.

[D31] **Ye Waverly Inn**, 16 Bank St., SW cor. Waverly Place. 1845.

Quaint, New England-style restaurant, tucked away in the basement nooks and crannies of a house dating from 1845. No lunches served on weekends (Sunday brunch only). Liquor available. Moderate prices.

Take a right (southerly) on Waverly Place.

D32

[D32] **St. John's-in-the-Village Church** (Episcopal), 216-222 W. 11th St., SW cor. Waverly Place. 1974. **Edgar Tafel.**
[D33] **Parish House**/originally South Baptist Church, 224 Waverly Place, bet. Perry and W. 11th Sts. W side. Early 1850s.

An austere red brick box disguised with a pediment and a brow of giant pseudo-Greek details. It replaced a true Greek Revival temple destroyed in a fire. A glimpse of its predecessor's style is visible in the parish house.

Bear right (south) on Seventh Avenue South

Seventh Avenue South: Before construction of the West Side IRT Subway below Times Square, around World War I, Seventh Avenue began its northward journey at Greenwich Avenue and West 11th Street. The building of the Seventh Avenue subway to connect with Varick Street and the creation of Seventh Avenue South as a surface thoroughfare made huge scars through these West Village blocks, leaving the backs and sides of many buildings crudely exposed. Isolated triangles of land once filled with dingy gas stations and parking lots are now seeing reuse as building sites. Seventh Avenue South opened for traffic in 1919.

D34

[D34] **22 Perry Street** (apartments), SW cor. Seventh Ave. S. 1987. **Architects Design Group**. ⚲

A "witch's hat" over the rounded acute-angled corner, combined with eyebrow windows in the latter-day mansard, make this a not unappealing novelty—but, because of crude detail and clumsy massing, little more.

[D35] Originally **Duane Colglazier House** (and store below), 156 Seventh Avenue S., bet. Perry and Charles Sts. W side. 1983. **Smith & Thompson**. ⚲

D35

An unabashedly personal statement that apes no Greenwich Village sentimentality, yet fits surprisingly well into the context of this odd-site-filled Seventh Avenue South corridor. A breath of fresh air. The retail space is occupied by The Pleasure Chest, a store vending sex appliances, etc.

[D36] **137 Seventh Avenue South** (infill commercial), bet. Charles and Tenth Sts. 1998. **Platt Byard Dovell**.

An unassuming constructivist infill, continuing the cosmetic surgery needed when Seventh Avenue South was slashed through this neighborhood. Stylish.

D36

[D37] **48, 50, 52-54 Charles Street** (row houses), bet. Seventh Ave. S. and W. 4th St. 1840. ⚲

Among the Village's most riotous and picturesque groupings of brick row houses. What makes them wonderful is the spirited conversion to studios, involving major changes in window size and placement. Emerson was right: a foolish consistency can be the hobgoblin of little minds!

[D38] **Chez Ma Tante** (restaurant), 189 W. 10th St., bet. W. 4th and Bleecker Sts. 1891. Radically altered, 1927. Converted, 1984, **Charles Morris Mount, Inc.**, designers. ⚲

D37

Paired French doors and refreshing graphics evoke a Gallic setting.

[D39] **59-61 Christopher Street** (apartments), NE cor. Seventh Avenue S. 1987. **Norval White** and **William Fegan** of **Levien DeLiso White Songer**. ⚲

An essay on contemporary reuse of early 19th-century architecture motifs, built on a triangular 750-square-foot site. This new, apparently neo-Federal building exaggerates history instead of simply literally resurrecting it.

END of Tour D. For the nearest subways and many places to eat, drink, and relax, continue walking south to where the tour began near Sheridan Square (IRT Seventh Avenue Line local (Nos. 1 and 9 trains) at the Christopher Street/ Sheridan Square Station).

D39

S1

S2

SOUTH VILLAGE

*Walking Tour E: The South Village. A perambulation through the less well known parts of southern Greenwich Village, ending up near Tribeca and SoHo. **START** at Sixth Avenue and Spring Street. The IND subway will take you right to the spot (IND Eighth Avenue Line local (C or E train), Spring Street Station).*

Amble south on Sixth Avenue for one block, and make almost a complete U-turn (north) onto acutely intersecting Sullivan Street. Across the way to the east:

[S1] **57 Sullivan Street** (row house), bet. Broome and Spring Sts. E side. 1817. **Frederick Youmans**, builder. Expanded upward, before 1858.

Once 2 stories with attic, the originally dormered house was increased in height to accommodate a full 3rd floor. Zealous restoration has provided pointed brick joints that are too wide for the Federal period, and dubious shutters.

[S2] **83 and 85 Sullivan Street** (row houses), bet. Broome and Spring Sts. E side. 1819. Expanded upward. ●

A pair of Federal houses, survivors from a longer row displaced by more recent construction, with cornices added later, on occasion of their upward expansion. The same brick jointing problems as No. 57.

[S3a] **James S. Rossant House**, 114 Sullivan St., bet. Spring and Prince Sts. ca. 1820. Expanded upward.
[S3b] **116 Sullivan Street** (row house). 1832. Expanded upward, 1872. ●

S3b

Another wonderful pair of row houses on an otherwise unprepossessing block. Architects of Modern high-rise housing (like Rossant) tend to spend their private lives living in low-rise structures like No. 114. The glory of No. 116 is the unique enframement of the front door within a simple round-arched masonry opening. And the brickwork should be the benchmark for those repointing, as at Nos. 57 and 83.

[S4] **203 Prince Street** (town house), bet. Sullivan and MacDougal Sts. N side. 1834. Expanded upward, 1888. ●

The almost-perfection of the restoration makes the neighbors seem shabby in contrast. Federal details (the entryway) have been inflated to Greek Revival proportions.

S4

SOUTH VILLAGE (TOUR E)

see pages 152-156

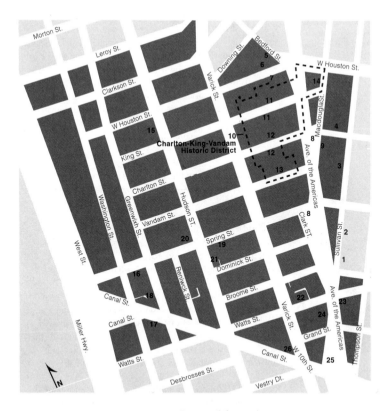

Continue north to West Houston Street, then turn left , crossing Sixth Avenue to its west side. A couple of short divertissements; then pick up the tour on the southwest corner of West Houston and Sixth:

[S5] **3 Bedford Street** (apartments), bet. W. Houston and Downing Sts. W side. 1987. **William Zeph Ginsberg**.

This red brick and cast-concrete structure is built in the bed of the ill-fated western extension of the West Houston super-street. (Since West Houston exists as a narrow street that twists to the south, the new one was to have been called Verrazano Street, as a sop to the Italian community—the bridge was yet to come.) Community opposition lasting over decades made the necessary land condemnation farther west politically untenable.

[S6] Formerly **Barney Rosset House**, 196 W. Houston St., bet. Bedford and Varick Sts. N side. Altered for Rosset, 1969, **Eugene Futterman**.

A cool, geometric façade of brown-purple vitreous-tile structural blocks (like those curved ones used in silos, but flat). One of the few Modern single-family town houses in Manhattan.

S5

[S7] **197-203 West Houston Street** (row houses), bet. Bedford and Varick Sts. S side. ca. 1820.

Four Federal houses. Note the lintels retained over a picture window intrusion on No. 201.

Return to Sixth Avenue and turn right (south) along Sixth Avenue's repaved and landscaped flank.

S6

[S8] **Avenue of the Americas Improvement,** Sixth Ave., bet. Canal and W. 4th Sts. 1975. NYC Department of Highways; **Frank Rogers,** director of urban design.

As Seventh Avenue South was cut through the West Village during World War I, the extension of Sixth Avenue below Carmine Street (opened in 1930) resulted in more urban surgery. The widenings and narrowings of the avenue's irregular swath through the South Village's already confusing grids created a speedway for cars and trucks, a battlefield for pedestrians. This sensitive municipal improvement, more than a half century later and now a quarter of a century old, places "careful consideration of pedestrian amenities on a par with the orderly flow of traffic," in the words of the Municipal Art Society, "turning a no-man's land into a community resource for sitting, playing, talking, and enjoying the city."

Across Sixth (Avenue of the Americas, if you insist), just south of Charlton/Prince Streets—the names are different on the two sides of the avenue:

S9

[S9] **Mid-rise apartment building**/earlier Quartermaster Storehouse, NYC Police Department/originally 10th Precinct Station House, 194 Sixth Ave. (originally 24 MacDougal St.) bet. Prince and Spring Sts. E side. 1893. **Nathaniel D. Bush.** Converted, 1987, **Terrance R. Williams.**

Until the City auctioned off this surplus property, the old station house was a stately—if dour—pressed brick and granite structure with great rusticated voussoirs around the arched entrance portal. Now that's about all of the original façade that remains; almost everything above the first floor is new and nowhere near the architectural quality of the original.

Richmond Hill, a country mansion built in 1767, once enjoyed magnificent views from its 100-foot-high mound near today's intersection of Charlton and Varick Streets. George Washington briefly used it as his headquarters during the Revolution, John Adams occupied it as vice-president later when the city was the nation's capital. In 1797 Aaron Burr acquired the elegant structure to lavish entertainment upon those who might further his political ambitions. It was John Jacob Astor who recognized the value of the surrounding 26 acres. He had them mapped into 25-by 100-foot lots beginning in 1817, after this and other Village hills were leveled by the Commissioners' Plan of 1811 to their present flatness, and saw the development of the row houses still extant in the Charlton-King-Vandam district. Meanwhile the mansion itself, literally knocked off its "pedestal," was moved across the street. After losing its status, it served as a theater and amusement garden and was finally demolished in 1849.

S11

By turning right (west) you have a choice of walking through any (or all) of the three east-west blocks that make up much of the Charlton-King-Vandam Historic District. Choose your route and meet at Varick and King Streets, where the tour resumes.

S11

[S10] **Charlton-King-Vandam Historic District.** 🖤
Early row houses, 1820-1829; later row houses, 1840-1849. From N to S: [S11] **1-49, 16-54 King Street.** ♂ [S12] **9-43, 20-42 Charlton Street.** [S13] **9-29 Vandam Street.** ♂ [S14] **43-51 MacDougal Street.** ♂

This Historic District, minute in size when compared with that of Greenwich Village to the north, is New York's greatest display of Federal style row houses. The two best (and best preserved) examples are Nos. 37 and 39 Charlton, whose exquisitely detailed entrances with original doors and leaded glass sidelights convey many of the style's most distinctive qualities. The later Greek Revival rows, like the ones at Nos. 20, 40, 42, 44 King

Street, almost perfectly preserved, are impressive, too. Check 29 King Street (Public School 8; **David I. Stagg**. 1886. "A lively Queen Anne").

Walk west on King Street and, after viewing No. 375 Hudson, turn left (south) on Hudson Street.

[S15] **Saatchi & Saatchi D.F.S. Compton World Headquarters**, 375 Hudson St., bet. King and W. Houston Sts. W side to Greenwich St. 1987. **Skidmore, Owings & Merrill; Lee Harris Pomeroy & Assocs; Emery Roth & Assocs**.
   The rounded corners of this wraparound, butted-glass-windowed office building conjure a mini-Starrett-Lehigh—here, however, with schematic details.

S15

Walk south on Hudson Street past industrial behemoths that once housed the city's great printing industry and which were converted for back-office use by the financial industry.

Detour: *At Spring Street, an optional detour west to see three surviving Federal row houses; or proceed south on Hudson, and take a left (east) into Watts Street for the remainder of the tour.*

S16

[S16] **Ear Inn**/originally James Brown House, 326 Spring St., bet. Greenwich and Washington Sts. S side. 1817. ◗
   Gambrel roof, dormers, and Flemish-bonded brick reveal an ill-maintained old Federal house far better known for the blacked-out lobes of the B in its neon BAR sign—making it recognizable as EAR INN, an out-of-the-way New York watering spot.

[S17] **502, 504, 506 (John Rohr House), 508 Canal Street, 480 Greenwich St**. All on NW cor. Canal and Greenwich Sts. ca. 1827.
   Federal row houses built for developer **John Rohr**, who lived in No. 516 for its first 20 years. His house remains the most intact.

S18

[S18] **486 Greenwich Street** (house), bet. Canal and Spring Sts. 1820s.
   A much altered Federal shell. Nothing remains except the pitched roof and a lamentable dormer.

End of optional detour. A swing left into Spring Street finds:

S19

[S19] **NYC Fire Department Museum**/originally Rescue Company No. 1, 278 Spring St., bet. Hudson and Varick Sts. S side. Open to the public: Tu-Sa 10-4; closed Su & Mo. 212-691-1303.
   A former specialized firehouse now filled with artifacts for fire buffs of all ages and with old equipment, photos, and other goodies.

[S20] **137 Hudson Street** (lofts), NW cor. Spring St. 1900.
   A straightforward Classical Revival loft/office building. Check out Scott Jordan's Arts & Crafts furniture on the ground floor.

S20

Continuing south on Hudson:

[S21] **284 Hudson Street** (house), bet. Dominick and Spring Sts. E side. ca. 1820.
   A Federal remnant in which some early American middle-class citizens once lived: a classic form (simple body with pitched roof and dormer windows) that now shelters a restaurant. No. 288 next door has disappeared since the previous edition of this guide.

S21

Turn left into Watts Street for a couple of blocks:

[S22] **66 Watts Street** (house), bet. Avenue of the Americas and Varick St. 1820.

Another lonely semi-survivor. Excellent above the white wainscot.

Continuing on Watts on the far side of Sixth—worth the wide crossing—to admire the bas-reliefs up close:

S23

[S23] **100 Avenue of the Americas** (lofts)/earlier 100 Sixth Avenue/originally Green Sixth Avenue Building, SE cor. Watts St. to Thompson St. 1928. **Ely Jacques Kahn.**

Three street façades are industrial window-filled Art Deco. Even the fourth, a barren lot-line wall, still lets gobs of sunlight into the building since expected high-rise neighbors to the south never materialized. Particularly note the strongly characterized bas-reliefs of artisans and workers in the 2nd-floor pilasters and other 2- and 3-dimensional masonry ornament.

[S24] **Building Services Employees International Union Headquarters**, 101 Ave. of the Americas (Sixth Ave.), bet. Watts and Grand Sts. W side. 1992. **Fox & Fowle.**

A big and loft-like schematic hulk that fails to resolve its participation in the pedestrian world at street level. Impressive but awkward.

S24

Back to the west side of Sixth and continue southward

[S25] **Juan Pablo Duarte** (statue), in Juan Pablo Duarte Sq., Sixth Ave. NW cor. Canal St. 1978.

A bearded bronze figure atop a granite plinth who vaguely resembles one of the City's colorful parks commissioners. **Duarte** (1813-1876) was founder of the Dominican Republic.

A last stop at the enormous traffic intersection of Sixth and Canal, dominated by:

[S26] **Holland Plaza Building** (lofts), 75 Varick St., NW cor. Canal St. to Watts and Hudson Sts. 1930. **Ely Jacques Kahn.**

A trapezoidal block fully covered by 16 powerful stories of industrial Art Deco, built to serve the needs of the printing trades and other downtown industries.

S26

END of Tour E. *If you are ready for more, cross the humongous Canal Street intersection and stroll through Tribeca, to the south. And to the northeast lies another fascinating area, SoHo. If you're calling it a day, the nearest subways are also here (IRT Seventh Avenue Line local (1 or 9 trains), or IND Eighth Avenue Line local or express (A, C or E train), both at their respective Canal Street Stations (no interchange available).*

ASTOR PLACE & ENVIRONS

For one brief generation in the changing fashions of New York, Lafayette Street (then Lafayette Place) was its most wealthy and elegant residential avenue. Then running only from Great Jones Street to Astor Place, it was a short, tree-lined boulevard, flanked by town houses of the **Astors, Vanderbilts,** and **Delanos.** Now the trees are gone, and only a piece of Colonnade Row (LaGrange Terrace) remains. Although in shoddy condition, its character is so strong that it still suggests the urbane qualities present up until the Civil War. Mostly developed in 1832-1833, the street was cut through Sperry's Botanic Gardens, later Vauxhall Gardens, a summer entertainment enclave where music and theatrical performances were presented in the open air. **John Lambert,** an English traveler of 1807, noted it as a "neat plantation . . . the theatrical corps of New York is chiefly engaged at Vauxhall during summer." Only 20 years after this residential development in the 1830s, the street's principal families moved away to Fifth Avenue. At the same time the Astor Library (later to become a major part of New York's Public Library) and the Cooper Union Foundation Building were built (started in 1850 and 1853, respectively), seeding the precinct with different uses: Lafayette became primarily a light manufacturing and warehousing street, with erratic or isolated physical remnants of its varied history. The Astor Library was bought by HIAS (Hebrew Immigrant Aid Society), but beginning in the late 1960s it was converted into a clutch of indoor theaters for **Joseph Papp**'s New York Shakespeare Festival.

*Astor Place Walking Tour: A walk northbound along Broadway/ Lafayette Street/Astor Place/Fourth Avenue past the Public Theater the Cooper Union, Grace Church and lesser, but still intriguing, wonders: **START** at Broadway and Houston Street (No. 6 local of the old IRT Lexington Avenue local to Bleecker Street Station or B, D, or F trains of the old IND Sixth Avenue to Broadway-Lafayette Station).*

[A1] "**Little Cary Building,**" 620 Broadway, bet. E. Houston and Bleecker Sts. E side. 1858. **John B. Snook.** ♂
    The **Daniel D. Badger Co.** constructed the vigorous Corinthian cast-iron frames, now contrasted with thoughtless, lifeless, flat, bronze-anodized aluminum windows.

A1

[A1a] **NoHo Historic District,** along Broadway, most of both sides of Lafayette Street, bet. E. Houston and 8th Sts. See map. ●♂

[A2] **Cable Building** (offices), 611 Broadway, NW cor. Houston St. 1892-1894. **McKim, Mead & White.** ♂
    The name reflects the building's original role as headquarters for, and one of the power stations of, Manhattan's not inconsiderable cable car empire. The slots between the running rails later made it possible to convert to underground electric feed around the turn of the century, enabling the subsequent trolleys that dominated such streets as Lexington Avenue. The Angelika Film Center within (Mercer Street entry. 1989. **Igor Josza** and **Don Schimenti**) offers art and offbeat film fare.

A2

[A3] Originally **The New York Mercantile Exchange,** 628 Broadway, E. Houston and Bleecker Sts. E side. 1882. **Herman J. Schwarzmann,** with **Buchman & Deisler.** ♂
    Delicate cast-iron columns and deep—very deep— window reveals, by the chief architect of Philadelphia's 1876 Centennial Exhibition. Note the name appliquéed to the 3rd- and 5th-floor span.

A3

ASTOR PLACE & ENVIRONS

see pages 157-167

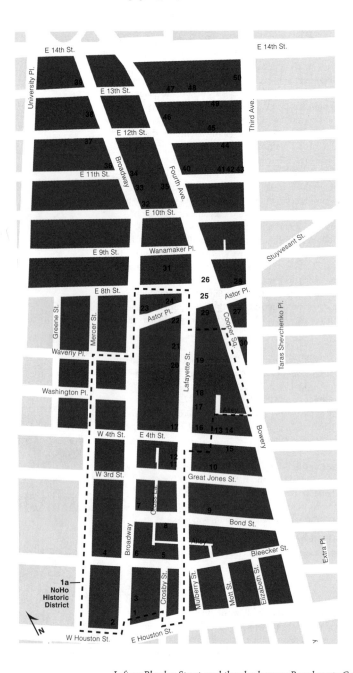

Left on Bleecker Street, and then back across Broadway to Crosby:

[A4] **Bleecker Court** (apartment complex), 77 Bleecker St., NE cor. Mercer St. to Broadway. 1981. **Avinash K. Malhotra**. 🔾

A bold joining together of older loft buildings on Bleecker Street and (burned-out) ones on Broadway with a new wing to their rear.

The Broadway Strip: *Beginning in the early 1980s, starting at Astor Place and spreading southward, leaping across Houston and linking to a similar movement coming up Broadway from Canal Street, there sprang up an impressive array of shops and restaurants (and later vibrant sidewalk flea markets) catering to the*

A5

youth culture, purveying anything from funky jewelry to recycled old clothes to Apache haircuts. The area had previously been devoted to marginal service stores addressing the needs of the textile, garment, and other humdrum wholesale and industrial tenants who occupied the upper floors of Broadway's bulky loft structures. During this period, when the street was hardly fashionable and land prices were understandably depressed, a number of sites on Broadway's west flank between West 3rd Street and Washington Place were purchased and developed by NYU and Hebrew Union College. Failing to foresee how Broadway might shift in its use, these institutions of higher learning turned their backs on Broadway and failed to provide for a potentially profitable commercial presence on their side of the street. Regrettable—but seemingly not much of a deterrent to the excitement and success of the rest of The Strip. Now high style and high prices have invaded much of the area. Dean & Deluca, emigrating from Prince Street, the Paper Shop in the Little Singer Building, with much more to come before the merchandizing frenzy abates and/or moves on.

[A5] Originally **Condict Building** (lofts)/later Bayard Building, 65 Bleecker St., bet. Broadway and Lafayette St., opp. Crosby St. N side. 1897-1899. **Louis Sullivan**, architect. **Lyndon P. Smith**, associate architect. ●′ ♂

This was a radical building in its time, a direct confrontation with the architectural establishment that had embraced American Renaissance architecture after the Columbian Exposition (Chicago World's Fair) of 1893. Sullivan, the principal philosopher and leading designer of the Chicago School (the antithesis of the American Renaissance), was the employer and teacher of Frank Lloyd Wright (who referred to him romantically as lieber Meister). The sextet of angels supporting the cornice was added at the request of his client, Silas Alden Condict. The building had little influence in New York for, as architectural historian Carl Condit wondered, "Who would expect an aesthetic experience on Bleecker Street?"

Return to Broadway.

[A6] Originally **Manhattan Savings Institution Building**/now residential lofts, 644 Broadway, NE cor. Bleecker St. 1889-1890. **Stephen D. Hatch**. Restored, 1987. ♂

A great rock-cut brownstone, terra-cotta, and brick heap (with cast-iron trim) finally recognized for its quality—and restored—after many years of neglect. Check out the cast-iron

A6

and marble floor system exposed on the underside in both the lobby and the corner store.

[A7] **670 Broadway**/originally Brooks Brothers store, NE cor. Bond St. 1873-1874. **George E. Harney.** ♂

A romantic rose brick and granite commercial structure at the 3rd of 5 sequential locations of Brooks Brothers. Eastlakian (after **Charles Eastlake**, one of the 19th century's most ornate designers).

A7

Turn right on Bond Street.

[A8] **1-5 Bond Street** (apartments)/originally Robbins & Appleton Building, SE cor. Shinbone Alley, bet. Broadway and Lafayette St. 1879-1880. **Stephen D. Hatch.** ♣ ♂

Capped by a great Second Empire mansard roof and dormers are 5 generous stories of creamy, elegant Corinthian cast iron and glass. The building was originally used for the manufacture of watch cases. Magnificent north light.

A8

[A9] **26 Bond Street** (row house), bet. Lafayette St. and the Bowery. 1830s.

Greek Revival presenting "battered majesty," according to **Christopher Gray.**

Back to Lafayette Street. Take a quick detour on Great Jones Street, and then resume your northerly walk on Lafayette.

[A10] **Engine Company No. 33**, NYC Fire Department, 44 Great Jones St., bet. the Bowery and Lafayette St. N side. 1898-1899. **Flagg & Chambers.** ♣

A10

A huge concave Beaux Arts arch, influenced by **Louis XV**'s taste and bearing a cartouche, is the substance of this wonderful Ernest Flagg façade.

[A11] **376-380 Lafayette Street** (lofts)/also known as the Schermerhorn Building, NW cor. Great Jones St. 1888-1889. **Henry J. Hardenbergh.** ♣ ♂

Designed by the architect of the Dakota and the Plaza Hotel, this free-swinging Romanesque Revival work is a rich addition to the area's architecture. From bottom (the brownstone and polished granite dwarf columns—though dimmed by paint) to

A11

top (the richly decorative cornice), it's a gem: sandstone, terra-cotta and brick. **William C. Schermerhorn** built this lusty stonework on the site of his family mansion. Look below to the Seabury Tredwell House to find a typical neighbor from Schermerhorn's time.

[A12] **382 Lafayette Street** (lofts) bet. Great Jones and E. 4th Sts. W side. 1896. **Cleverdon & Putzel.** ♂

Delicate incised ornamentation near the sky, atop an arcade.

Nearby on East 4th Street:

A12

Turn right (east) on East 4th for an interesting detour.

[A13] **Merchant's House Museum**/formerly Seabury Tredwell House/originally Joseph Brewster House, 29 E. 4th St., bet. the Bowery and Lafayette St. 1832. Restored, **Joseph Roberto** ♣ Interior ♣ Open to the public: Su-Th 11-4; closed Fr & Sa. Closed Aug. 212-777-1089.

A relic from New York's Federal past, when blocks surrounding this spot had houses of equal quality. The house and its early interior furnishings derive from Tredwell's daughter, Gertrude, who lived here for 93 years, until 1933. It has been open to the public since 1936.

A13

[A14] Originally **Samuel Tredwell Skidmore House**, 37 E. 4th St., bet. the Bowery and Lafayette St. 1845. ●'
Greek Revival. Those Ionic columns were unequaled in this vintage. Skid Row (now of buildings, not people).

[A15] **34 and 36 East 4th Street** (tenements), bet. the Bowery and Lafayette Sts. S. side. ca. 1885.
Twin structures with a joyful abundance of 3-dimensional tinplate cornice ornament and paired corbeled Corinthian columns. Handsomely restored.

Back to Lafayette.

Lafayette Street: *Between East 4th Street and Astor Place.*

A14

[A16] Originally **DeVinne Press Building**, 393-399 Lafayette St., NE cor. E. 4th St. 1885-1886. Addition, 1892. **Babb, Cook & Willard**. ●' ○'
Roman brickwork worthy of the Roman Forum's Basilica of Constantine. The waterfront of Brooklyn is graced with the poor country cousins (the Empire Stores) of this magnificent pile. Certainly this is a sample of "less is more"—especially when juxtaposed with (and compared to) No. 376-380 down the block.

[A17] **401 Lafayette Street** (lofts). E. side. ca. 1893. 400 Lafayette Street (lofts). NW cor. E. 4th St. ca. 1887-1888. **Cleverdon & Putzel**. ○'
Two different, very wonderful loft structures from the great era of Lafayette Street's expansion.

A16

A18

[A18] **411 Lafayette Street** (lofts). E side. 1891. **Alfred Zucker**. Restored, 1987. ♂

Ornate cast-iron and brick Romanesque Revival. The 3 free-standing columns—interspersed with those engaged—form a virile base.

A19

[A19] **Public Theater**, formerly HIAS Hebrew Immigrant Aid Society/originally Astor Library, 425 Lafayette St., bet. E. 4th St. and Astor Place. E side. 1853-1881. South wing, 1849-1853, **Alexander Saeltzer**. Center section, 1856-1869, **Griffith Thomas**. North wing, 1879-1881, **Thomas Stent**. Conversion into theater complex, 1967-1976, **Giorgio Cavaglieri**. ☙ ♂

A funky, generously scaled red brick and brownstone building considered by some to be the finest American example of Rundbogenstil, a German variant of Romanesque Revival. **John Jacob Astor** here contributed New York's first free library, later combined with its peers (Lenox Library, which was sited where the Frick Collection is today, and the Tilden Foundation) to form the central branch of The New York Public Library at 42nd Street. These are the theaters of the late Joseph Papp, whose outdoor Shakespeare Festival in Central Park made these its indoor habitat.

A20

[A20] Originally **Colonnade Row**/also known as LaGrange Terrace, 428-434 Lafayette St., bet. E. 4th St. and Astor Place. W side. Attributed to **Seth Geer**. 1832-1833. ☙ ♂

Four of nine houses built speculatively by **Seth Geer** in 1833. Five at the south end were demolished for the still existing Wanamaker Annex next door. An elegant urban arrangement of private structures subordinated to an imposing Corinthian colonnade (compare the Place de la Concorde in Paris). **Delanos**, **Astors**, and **Vanderbilts** lived here, until their game of social musical chairs sent them uptown.

The Astor Place Theatre presents off-Broadway at No. 434.

A22

[A21] **436 Lafayette Street** (lofts). Bet. E. 4th St. and Astor Place. W side. 1870-1871. **Edward H. Kendall**. ♂

Vigorous architecture of the 19th century's last quarter.

Along Astor Place on the left; then return.

[A22] Originally **Astor Place Building**, O. B. Potter Trust, 444 Lafayette St., SW cor. Astor Place. 1876. **Griffith Thomas**. ♂

Brick and painted cast-iron eclectic Eastlake. Its street floor now houses:

A23

[A23] **Astor Place Building**, 750 Broadway, NE cor. Astor Place (also known as 1 Astor Place). 1881. **Starkweather & Gibbs**. ♂

Intricate brickwork framed with grand terra-cotta Corinthian pilasters.

[A24] **Astor Place Hotel**/originally Mercantile Library Building/onetime District 65 Building (Distributive Workers of America), 13 Astor Place, NW cor. Lafayette St. to E. 8th St. 1890. **George E. Harney**. Remodeled as hotel, **David Chipperfield**, design architect. **William B. Tabler**, architect of record. ♂

A24

Harney's ode to Ruskin at 670 Broadway, 16 years earlier, is here replaced by establishment Harney. The new American Renaissance of the 1890s overwhelms the more picturesque recent years.

*The District 65 Building rests on the site of the Astor Place Opera House, where in May 1849 rioting between competing claques of the American actor **Edwin Forrest** and the English actor **William Macready** caused the death of 34 stalwarts. The **Seventh Regiment National Guard**, quartered in an armory then on the present site of Cooper Union's Hewitt building, quelled the passions forcibly.*

In the large open space crisscrossed by traffic and frequently the center of a sidewalk flea market:

A25

[A25] **"Alamo"** (sculpture), on traffic island, Astor Place/E. 8th St./Lafayette St./Fourth Ave. 1966, installed 1967. **Bernard "Tony" Rosenthal**, sculptor.

Installed as part of a giant but temporary citywide exhibition, "Sculpture in the Environment," *Alamo* was made permanent through a gift to the City by a private donor. A giant steel cube "en pointe," it pivots (with some difficulty) and has become a beloved fixture in these parts, much as the subway kiosk had been prior to its initial removal [see below].

[A26] **Astor Place Subway Station**, IRT Lexington Avenue Line, below Lafayette St. and Fourth Ave. at Astor Place. 1904. **Heins & La Farge**. 🌿 Restored, 1986, **Prentice & Chan, Ohlhausen**. **Milton Glaser**, artist. **Astor Place subway kiosk**. Replica, 1985, **Prentice & Chan, Ohlhausen**.

One of the city's best subway station restorations, particularly the integration of new ceramic tiles to harmonize with the original charming beaver plaques (Grueby Faience).

Best of all is architect Ohlhausen's 1985 kiosk on top, a palliative for the Transit Authority's disastrous decision to scrap all IRT kiosks. The new kiosk was cast using new wood patterns developed from **Heins & La Farge** drawings submitted to the Hecla Iron Works in Williamsburg, Brooklyn, the original fabricators. (Both **Ohlhausen** and **Glaser** are graduates of Cooper Union across the street.)

A26

The Cooper Union for the Advancement of Science and Art:

[A27] **Cooper Union Foundation Building**, E. 7th St. to Astor Place, Fourth Ave. to the Bowery, at Cooper Sq. 1853-1859. **Frederick A. Peterson**. Second-floor window alterations, 1886. **Leopold Eidlitz**. 🌿 Interior reconstructed, 1975, **John Hejduk**. Exterior restorations, 1999. **Platt Byard Dovell**. Galleries open Mo-Fr 11-7; Sa 12-5; closed Su. 212-353-4195.

A high-rise brownstone, Cooper Union is the oldest extant building framed with steel beams in America. **Peter Cooper**, its founder and a benefactor in the great Victorian paternalistic tradition (he gave presents to Cooper Union on his birthday), was partner of **Samuel F. B. Morse** in laying the first Atlantic cable and builder of the Tom Thumb steam locomotive; also an iron maker, he rolled the first steel railroad rails. Such rails were used by Cooper as beams, spanning brick bearing walls. In turn, brick

A27

floor arches jumped between rail and rail. The façade is in the Italianate brownstone tradition popular at the time with cast-iron designers, but heavier-handed, as it is in masonry except at the ground floor.

The remodeling was almost entirely internal, with simultaneous fulfillment of one of Cooper's original designs: a round elevator finally rides in his clairvoyantly round shaft. The Platt Byard Dovell exterior restoration avoids the pastiness of artificial brownstone, and delivers a new, but real, texture to the facades.

[A28] **Pasqua's Coffee Pavilion**, in the Cooper Union School of Engineering colonnade, NW cor. Third Ave. at Astor Pl. 1990s. **Smith-Miller + Hawkinson**.

The deadly space enclosed by Engineering's colonnade is translated into a lively humanistic center of urbane activity. A new "hermit crab" occupies a previously forlorn cage.

[A29] **New Hotel, Cinema and Plaza**, Astor Place, bet. Fourth Ave. and Lafayette St. 2002. **Rem Koolhaas**.
Cooper Union and Ian Schrager have plotted a prestige competition between two distinguished modernist architects to grace this parking lot with an urbane urban assemblage.

[A30] **Peter Cooper monument**, in Cooper Sq. S of E. 7th St. 1897. **Augustus Saint-Gaudens**, sculptor; **Stanford White**, architect of the base.
Cooper seated in front of his benefaction.

A30

The Bowery, once and popularly known as a skid row populated by "bums," is much more complex than that. South from Cooper Square to Canal Street the vista includes the center of commercial kitchen-equipment distribution for New York, and one of the city's principal lighting fixture sales places. Gentrification has mostly wiped out the street's "hotels" (flophouses to some), resting places of the unwanted, the alcoholic, the derelict. Panhandlers, however, still abound, particularly in the form of unwanted auto window washers, when you are inconveniently stopped at a red light.

East Village: For the area to the east, beginning at Third Avenue, including the St. Mark's Place corridor, McSorley's, and Alphabetville, see the next section, East Village.

Resume the northward walk this time along Fourth Avenue.

[A31] Originally **Wanamaker Department Store Annex**, Fourth Ave. bet. E. 8th and E. 9th Sts. to Broadway. 1904. Addition, 1907-1910. Both by **D. H. Burnham & Co**. Expanded, 1926.
The annex, in this case, was considerably larger than the main store, originally A. T. Stewart & Company (**John Kellum**,

1862) on the block to the north: almost as much space in this stolid 15-story monolith as in the 102 floors of the Empire State Building. The main store occupied a full block in Italianate cast iron, was arranged around a skylighted central court, and offered the most gracious shopping space in New York very much in the European tradition. The only Ladies Mile survivor to continue in business, it finally closed in 1954 and was consumed in a conflagration two years later.

A left on East 10th Street to Broadway, and then a right.

A32

[A32] **Grace Church (Episcopal) and Rectory**, 800 and 804 Broadway, at E. 10th St. E side. 1843-1846. **James Renwick, Jr.** Chantry, 1878-1879. **Edward T. Potter**. Front garden, 1881, **Vaux & Co.**, landscape architects. Original wood steeple replaced in marble, 1888. **James Renwick, Jr**. Chancel extension, 1903. **Heins & La Farge**. Other alterations, 1910, **William W. Renwick**. 🍎
 A magnificent Gothic Revival church, designed by an engineer who studied the copybooks of the Pugins, the great English Gothic Revival theorists and detailers. At the bend of Broadway, its tower dominates the vista from the south. One of the city's greatest treasures, together with its related buildings on Broadway and Fourth Avenue.

A33

[A33] **The Renwick** (apartments)/originally 808 Broadway (lofts), opp. E. 11th St. 1887-1888. **Renwick, Aspinwall & Russell**. Converted.
 A Gothic Revival wall forms a visual backdrop for Grace Church, built 41 years after the church's completion by Renwick's successor firm. Terra-cotta from the 4th floor up, eroding stone below. For more on fictional doings here read **Caleb Carr**'s *The Alienist*.

[A34] **810 Broadway** (lofts), E side. 1907. **Rouse & Stone**.
 Next door to The Renwick, and slightly younger, 810 is a showcase for the turn-of-the-century effort to combine a metal and glass wall and a masonry carapace.

A34

If the Grace Church complex is to your liking you may wish to retrace your steps to Fourth Avenue to see the remainder. The tour continues up Broadway.

[A35] **The Grace Church Houses:** [A35a] **The Clergy House**, 92 Fourth Ave., bet. E. 10th and E. 12th Sts. W side. 1892. **Heins & La Farge**. 🍎 [A35b] **Grace Memorial House/Huntington House**, 94-96 Fourth Ave. 1883. **James Renwick, Jr**. 🍎 [A35c] **Neighborhood House**, 98 Fourth Ave. 1907. **Renwick, Aspinwall & Tucker**. 🍎
 A trio in the Gothic Revival tradition established by the elder Renwick at Grace Church on the Broadway side of the block. Endangered in the 1970s for improvements to the school, the façades were finally saved. In this case landmark designation followed the threat of loss.

A35a

[A36] **The Cast Iron Building** (apartments)/originally James McCreery Dry Goods Store, 67 E. 11th St., NW cor. Broadway. 1868-1870. **John Kellum**. Converted and extended upward, 1971, **Stephen B. Jacobs**. [A37] **49 East 12th Street** (apartments)/formerly St. George Hotel, bet. Broadway and University Place. Converted, 1977, **Stephen B. Jacobs**.
 Two buildings converted to apartments. The old McCreery's cast-iron Corinthian columns and almost endless arches both enrich and discipline the façade—though concern for historic preservation waned at the upper stories. The old hotel is an interesting array of windows and half-round exit balconies whose reused old brick gives it the look of a slice of salami.

A36

Booksellers' Row, along Fourth Avenue and Broadway from Astor Place to Union Square: Once upon a time—and well into the 1960s—both sides of Fourth Avenue and parts of Broadway and the side streets were lined with used bookshops of all descriptions, beginning at Bible House (which occupied the site of Cooper Union's Engineering Building) and stretching almost all the way to S. Klein's on the Square (the cut-rate department store whose site is now occupied by Zeckendorf Towers). Books were displayed both within the shops and on racks along the street—a browser's delight, particularly in balmy weather. Alas, the number of shops today is reduced to a handful, dominated by giant Strand Book Store, at 828 Broadway, on the northeast corner of East 12th Street, where books are displayed on shelves that stretch on street floor and basement (and for aficionados elsewhere) for miles.

A39

[A38] **827-831 Broadway** (lofts), bet. E. 12th and E. 13th Sts. 1866.

A truly magnificent pair of Italianate business buildings fashioned in marble, patterns for the later cast-iron structures that picked up the elegant neo-Renaissance style and details imported from England.

A40

[A39] **Roosevelt Building** (lofts), 839-841 Broadway, NW cor. E. 13th St. 1893. **Stephen D. Hatch.**

Despite the mutilated ground floor, the upper parts of the sandstone and brick edifice offer a majestic expression of Romanesque Revival. Named Roosevelt after Cornelius, Teddy's grandfather, who lived on the block in midcentury, when Union Square was *the* place to reside.

Turn east on East 13th Street and south on Fourth Avenue to East 11th Street: then left:

A41

[A40] **U.S. Post Office, Cooper Station**, NE cor. Fourth Ave. and 11th St. 1930s.

Art Moderne fluted columns without capitals swoop around this neo-Classical corner.

East 11th Street between Third and Fourth Avenues
A gold mine of public buildings.

A42

[A41] **Webster Hall**/later Casa Galicia, O Noso Lar/and The Ritz (rock and roll club) 119 E. 11th St., bet. Third and Fourth Aves. N side. 1886. **Charles Rentz.**

An 1880s dance hall, turned into a 1930s ballroom, blaring 1980s music. A center of slam dancing in the mid 1980s.

[A42] Originally **St. Ann's Parochial School**/later Delehanty Institute (school), now apartments, 117 E. 11th St., bet. Third and Fourth Aves. N side. 1870.

A dignified dark red brick and terra-cotta institutional building that has seen many uses.

A43

[A43] **Loews Village VII** (cinema), 66 Third Ave., NW cor. E. 11th St. 1992. **Eli Jack Held.**

Escalate to one of 7 movies simultaneously showing in this vertical grillage. A venerable New York City Department of Public Charities building (1868-1871. **Renwick & Sands**) occupied this footprint before Loews arrived.

Left on Third Avenue and left again on East 12th Street.

[A44] **St. Ann's Shrine Armenian Catholic Cathedral**/originally 12th Street Baptist Church/later Temple Emanu-El (synagogue)/ later St. Ann's Roman Catholic Church, 120 E. 12th St., bet. Third and Fourth Aves. ca. 1847.

Ecumenism was instilled here long before it became an everyday word. It was Temple Emanu-El between 1856 and 1868.

[A45] Originally **New York Edison Company Building**/now apartments, 121 E. 12th St., bet. Third and Fourth Aves. 1896. **Buchman & Deisler**.

From before the City's 1898 consolidation, when NY Ed became Con Ed and moved north to 14th. Missing its cornice, but the Roman brickwork supports grand Romanesque Revival arches.

A46

Right on Fourth Avenue.

[A46] **Hancock Building**, 125 Fourth Ave., bet. E. 12th and E. 13th Sts. E side. 1897. **Marsh, Israels & Harder**.

Once the home of Hammacher Schlemmer, the gadget store. The apartments upstairs have an added balcony escape route around a grand Composite column. What a delight!

A48

Right on East 13th Street.

[A47] **101-107 East 13th Street**, bet. Third and Fourth Aves. 1998. Modest, sleek and smooth.

[A48] **The Genesis/Robert F. Kennedy Apartments**, 113 E. 13th St., bet. Third and Fourth Aves. 1995. **Cooper, Robertson & Partners** with **Schuman Lichtestein Claman & Efron**.

Handsome but not conspicuous, a good background building for its onetime homeless tenants.

[A49] Originally **Kearney & Van Tassel Auction Stables**, 130 E. 13th St., bet. Third and Fourth Aves. 1889. **David & John Jardine**. Annex, 128 E. 13th St. 1904. **Jardine, Kent & Jardine**.

Old horse-auction rooms—the ornament makes references. Inside, an enormous space that would hold a blimp.

A49

Look left.

[A50] **Variety Arts Theatre**/originally Variety Photoplays (movie theater), 110 Third Ave., bet. E. 13th and E. 14th Sts. W side. ca. 1900.

Some say this was the city's oldest movie house. Its marquee of both neon and incandescent lights was a cultural monument of another time and is irreplaceable. More serious theatrics are now the norm within.

END of Tour. *The nearest subways are at Union Square, at East 14th Street, between Fourth Avenue and Broadway: 14th Street/Union Square Station (IRT Lexington Avenue Line (Nos. 4, 5, and 6 trains) and BMT Broadway Line (N and R trains).*

EAST VILLAGE

The East Village is an area of vivid contrasts. Around St. Mark's-in-the-Bowery there are traces of an 18th- and 19th-century aristocracy. But elsewhere the area reveals quite a different social history.

Along St. Mark's Place, 7th, and 6th Streets is evidence of a 19th-century German community. Late in that century, population from the crowded Lower East Side was squeezed northward into the precinct generally lying between East Houston and East 14th Streets, assuming the name Lower East Side (as an extension of the already established neighborhood to the south). The area blossomed with eastern European populations, both Jewish and Gentile. To this day, favored Ukrainian and Polish dishes are still to be found in local restaurants. (On the other hand, most of the kosher delicatessens are gone.) Around First Avenue and East 11th Street the gustatorial remnants of an Italian community are evident and are being rediscovered. And McSorley's recalls the day of many other Irish saloons.

In the 1960s the area assumed the name East Village as a result of the incursion of hippies and flower children from the relatively expensive (and Establishment bohemian) Greenwich Village. The major point of entry was through the St. Mark's Place corridor, which led to Tompkins Square Park, to cheap tenement apartments, and to crash pads as far east as Alphabetville, where Manhattan's north-south avenues assume letters, rather than numbers.

This area today, between Avenues A and D, is heavily Hispanic in population and has been dubbed Loisaida (pronounced low-ees-SIDE-ah), the Puerto Rican pronunciation of Lower East Side. While heavy with poverty, there is nevertheless evidence that rubble-strewn lots, once packed with tenements, are being eyed, and even built upon, by speculators, as housing in Manhattan becomes ever more scarce.

[E1] **Bouwerie Lane Theatre**/originally Atlantic Savings Bank Building/later Bond Street Savings Bank Building, 330 Bowery, NW cor. Bond St. 1873-1874. **Henry Engelbert.** 🍎
An intricate interplay of Corinthian columns in one of the most sophisticated cast-iron buildings.

Odds and evens: Here, in these single-digit precincts of Manhattan's grid, the customary placement of odd and even house numbers is reversed. On both 1st and 2nd Streets the even numbers are on the north side; the odd numbers on the south— contrary to the pattern followed elsewhere in the grid.

E1

[E2] **New York Marble Cemetery**, interior of the block bet. E. 2nd and E. 3rd Sts., Second Ave., and the Bowery. Entrance on Second Ave. bet. E. 2nd and E. 3rd Sts., W side. 1830-now. 🍎
Not open to the public.
One of the earliest sophistications of burial practices, anticipating (and therefore preventing) a marble orchard: the interred are noted by tablets inlaid in the perimeter brick wall. [Also see E6]

E3

[E3] Originally **Public School 79**, Manhattan, 40 E. 1st St., bet. First and Second Aves. N side. ca. 1886.
Like so many of the nearby tenements whose occupants it once served (it is no longer a school) this is an ornamented red brick and terra-cotta "high-rise" walk-up. Our legs hurt.

[E4] **65 East 2nd Street** (apartments), bet. First and Second Aves. S side. ca. 1860.
Mt. Olivet's Italianate church rectory now converted to apartments. The billowing wrought-iron fire escapes echo the generous proportions of Victorian matrons.

E4

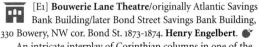

EAST VILLAGE

see pages 168-174

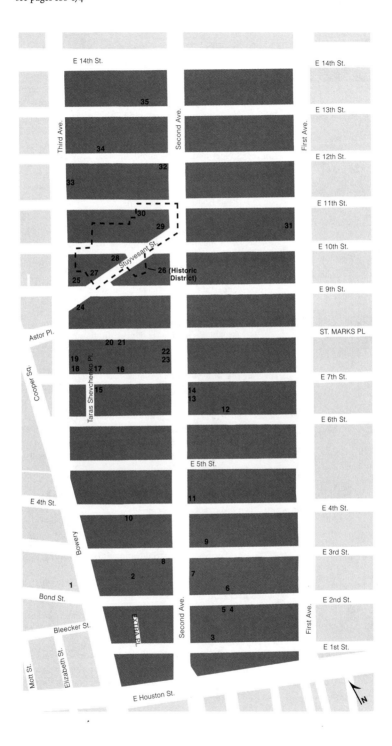

E5

E6

E7

E8

E10

[E5] **Protection of the Holy Virgin Cathedral** (Russian Orthodox Church in America)/originally Mt. Olivet Memorial Church, 59 E. 2nd St., bet. First and Second Aves. S side.

Russian Orthodox only since 1943. Mushy rock-cut limestone.

[E6] **New York City Marble Cemetery**, 52-74 E. 2nd St., bet. First and Second Aves. N side. 1832. ● Not open to the public.

President **James Monroe** was briefly interred in this, one of two remaining cemeterics in a part of town that contained many cemeteries in the 1830s and 1840s (also interred: **Mayor Isaac Varian**, shipping merchant **Preserved Fish**, financier **Moses Taylor**, book collector **James Lenox**, **James Henry Roosevelt**, founder of Roosevelt Hospital, and **Rebecca Ogilvie**, wife of **Andrew S. Norwood**: see the latter's house at 241 West 14th Street).

[E7] **Church of the Nativity** (Roman Catholic), 46 Second Ave., bet. E. 2nd and E. 3rd Sts. E side. 1970.

A modern architectural cartoon exhibiting a gross idea without detail. It replaces an elegant 1832 Greek Revival building by **Town & Davis** that was demolished in 1970.

[E8] **30-38 East 3rd Street** (row houses), SW cor. Second Ave. ca. 1830.

Five wonderful relics, particularly No. 36.

[E9] **67 East 3rd Street** (apartments), bet. First and Second Aves. 1987. **Ted Reeds Assocs**.

Clear Post-Modern evidence of gentrification in these poorer parts. (This is the Hell's Angels' block, incidentally.)

Forming the "International": Tinned-over windows and a storefront glued together with handbills and posters conceal the history of the former Labor Lyceum, at 64 East 4th Street, between the Bowery and Second Avenue. It was here on June 3, 1900, that the United Brotherhood of Cloakmakers of New York and Vicinity convened with their far-flung brethren (from Philadelphia, Baltimore, Newark, and Brownsville) to form the International Ladies' Garment Workers Union.

[E10] **Rod Rogers Dance Theater**, 62 E. 4th St., bet. The Bowery and Second Ave. 1889.

An imposing fire exit spirals down from the fourth floor loggia, amid an array of Tuscan columns and Renaissance arches.

[E11] Formerly **Industrial National Bank Building**, 72 Second Ave., NE cor. E. 4th St. ca. 1926.

Polychromed Art Deco terra-cotta detail with the original name still evident atop the south wall.

[E12] **Community Synagogue, Max D. Raiskin Center**/originally St. Mark's Lutheran Evangelical Church, 323 E. 6th St., bet. 1st and 2nd Aves. 1848.

It was the German immigrant parishioners of St. Mark's who boarded the *General Slocum* in June 1904 for that ill-fated excursion which cost over 1,000 lives, as the ship caught fire just after passing through the Hell Gate. It has been a synagogue since 1940.

Indo-Pak restaurant row: Between First and Second Avenues, the south side of East 6th Street is lined with a phalanx of restaurants serving different versions of the cuisine of the Indian subcontinent. Reading from W to E: Passage to India, Taj, Rose of India, Balaka, Bombay Dining, Ronana, Calcutta, Kismoth, Sonali, Shah Bagh (the first to take up residence), Panna, Nishan, Mitali East, AnarBagh, Ganges, Prince of India. (Some say that despite the 16 entrances there's only one kitchen.)

[E13] Formerly **Isaac T. Hopper House**, 110 Second Ave., bet. E. 6th and E. 7th Sts. E side. 1839.

A very grand Greek Revival town house. Once a home for "wayward" girls (as **Horatio Alger** would have called them).

E13

[E14] **Middle Collegiate Church** (Reform), 112-114 Second Ave., bet. E. 6th and E. 7th Sts. E side. 1892. **S. B. Reed**. Originally Middle Collegiate Church, **Church House**, 50 E. 7th St., bet. First and Second Aves. ca. 1910.

The church is rock-faced granite dressed with smooth, from the sidewalk to the very tip of the spire. All windows are by Tiffany. The old church house is neo-Romanesque.

[E15] **St. George's Ukrainian Catholic Church**, 16-20 E. 7th St., SE cor. Taras Shevchenko Place. 1977. **Apollinaire Osadca**.

A domed polychromed symbol of the parish's wealth and burgeoning membership: Atlantic City on 7th Street. It replaced the real thing—the humbler Greek Revival style St. George's Ruthenian Greek Church.

E14

[E16] **McSorley's Old Ale House**/formerly McSorley's Saloon, 15 E. 7th St., bet. Cooper Sq. and Second Ave. N side.

Opened in the early 1860s shortly after the new Cooper Union was completed, it was made famous by painter **John Sloan** and *The New Yorker* stories by **Joseph Mitchell**. Ale, brewed to their own formula, is sold in pairs of steins. The unisex toilet facilities date back to when this was a male-only retreat. The sign says 1854, but bar researcher **Richard McDermott** discovered that the site was still an empty lot in 1861.

E15

[E17] **The Surma Book and Music Company**, 11 E. 7th St., bet. Cooper Sq. and Second Ave. N side.

A fascinating Ukrainian store (books, records, decorated Easter eggs) retains the flavor of this old neighborhood's eastern European society.

[E18] **First Ukrainian Evangelical Pentecostal Church**/ formerly First Ukrainian Assembly of God/originally The Metropolitan Savings Bank, 59 Third Ave., NE cor. E. 7th St. 1867. **Carl Pfeiffer**. ●

Marble parallel to the then-current cast-iron world: such material denoted class (cast iron was used to gain elaboration inexpensively). The church use is a happy solution to the problem of preserving a grand old neighborhood friend. Not too old, however: McSorley's (wonderful) Saloon down the block is 13 years its senior.

E16

[E19] **69 Cooper Square** (apartments), on Third Ave. bet. E. 7th St. and St. Mark's Place. E side. 1985. **Kudroff Rycar Assocs**.

Bellying fire balconies and dark brick make this an acceptable infill building.

The St. Mark's Place corridor:
St. Mark's Place, although the standard width (60 feet between building lines) in theory, is actually wider, as most of the buildings are built back from their respective property lines (unusual for Manhattan). Cast-iron stairs once modulated the space, jumping from street to parlor floors as matter-of-fact pop sculpture; scarcely any remain. Basement shops now line both sides of the street, including those for dresses, jewelry, beads, buttons, and posters.

E18

[E20] **Deutsch-Amerikanische Schuetzen Gesellschaft**, 12 St. Mark's Place, bet. Second and Third Aves. S side. 1885. **William C. Frohne**.

A German marksmen's club reveled here and shot elsewhere.

[E21] Originally **Daniel LeRoy House**, 20 St. Mark's Place, bet. Second and Third Aves. S side. 1832. ●
Greek Revival swings again as the Grassroots Tavern.

E19

E22

E22

[E22] **Stuyvesant Polyclinic Hospital**/formerly Deutsches Dispensary, 137 Second Ave., bet. St. Mark's Place and E. 9th St. W side. 1883-1884. **William Schickel**. 🍎

Originally the downtown dispensary of the German Hospital, today's Lenox Hill at Park Avenue and 77th. It lost its "German" appellation as a result of rampant patriotism during World War I.

E23

[E23] **Ottendorfer Branch, New York Public Library**/originally Freie Bibliothek und Leschalle, 135 Second Ave., bet. St. Mark's Place and E. 9th St. W side. 1883-1884. **William Schickel**. 🍎 Interior 🍎

Built as a free German public library during the period of heavy German immigration to the surrounding streets. An architectural confection.

St. Mark's-in-the-Bowery and northward:

[E24] **Undergraduate Dormitory, The Cooper Union**, SE cor. Third Ave. and E. 9th St. 1990s. **Prentice & Chan, Ohlhausen**.

Rolf Ohlhausen's understated, yet powerful, contribution to the urban landscape of Cooper Union's neighborhood. See his earlier subway kiosk [A26].

[E25] **Undergraduate Dormitory, NYU**, 33 Third Ave., NE cor. E. 9th St. 1986. **Voorsanger & Mills Assocs**.

While the tower of this 16-story dorm steps back from a base matching the height of adjacent 5-story tenements, its 3 colors of brick, bold square windows, timid cornices, and lack of any small-scale detail (the windows are large and single-paned) make this look like the bully on the block. Will the curved, roofed "aerodrome" that hovers atop the tower become a beloved Third Avenue landmark?

E24

[E26] **St. Mark's Historic District**, 21-35 and 42-46 Stuyvesant St., 102 128 and 109-129 E. 10th St., 232 E. 11th St. and St. Mark's-in-the-Bowery Church.

This Historic District, subdivided and partly developed by **Governor Peter Stuyvesant**'s grandson, includes two landmarks established earlier, St. Mark's and the Stuyvesant-Fish House, as well as the "Renwick" Triangle.

E27

[E27] **Stuyvesant-Fish House**, 21 Stuyvesant St., bet. Second and Third Aves. NW side. 1803-1804.

A fat Federal house, of width unusual for its time, only 5 years younger than the body of St. Mark's down the block. The house was built by **Governor Stuyvesant**'s great-grandson as a wedding gift for his daughter, who was to marry **Nicholas Fish**—hence its hyphenated name. Overrestoration has given it a bland cast.

E28

[E28] **"Renwick" Triangle**, 114-128 E. 10th St., 23-35 Stuyvesant St., bet. Second and Third Aves. 1861. Attributed to **James Renwick, Jr.**

Buildings with differing plans but uniform façades (within, buildings vary in depth from 16 to 48 feet, in width from 16 to 32 feet) make a handsome grouping, carefully restored by new owners as 1- and 2-family houses. **Stanford White** once lived on the site of No. 118 in an earlier building (No. 110).

E29

[E29] **St. Mark's-in-the-Bowery Church** (Episcopal), Second Ave. NW cor. E. 10th St. 1799. Steeple, 1826-1828. **Ithiel Town** (Town & Thompson). Cast-iron portico, 1854. Restored, 1975-1978, **The Edelman Partnership**. Fire, 1978. Restored, 1978-1984, **The Edelman Partnership**.

This Federal body, Greek Revival steeple, and pre-Civil War portico stand on the site of a garden chapel of **Peter Stuyvesant**'s estate. The graveyard, containing Stuyvesant's vault, is now remodeled in undulating cobblestones for play purposes.

Harold Edelman not only was architect of the restoration (after a tragic fire) but also designed the new stained-glass windows.

*In 1929 **Frank Lloyd Wright** designed a cluster of three apartment towers (one at 18 stories, two at 14 stories) that presaged his later **Price Tower** in Oklahoma. Commissioned by the rector of St. Mark's-in-the-Bowery, they were to have been shoehorned into the space on either side of and behind the diminutive church—and would have totally overwhelmed it. The onset of the Great Depression scuttled the project . . . thankfully.*

E30

[E30] **Neighborhood Preservation Center**/originally Rectory, St. Mark's-in-the-Bowery Church, 232 E. 11th St., bet. Second and Third Aves. 1900. **Ernest R. Flagg.** Restoration, 1999. **Harold Edelman** of the **Edelman Partnership**.

A lesser-known work of a great architect. Note the cast-iron entrance stair. Now the home to the Historic Districts Council, the Greenwich Village Society for Historic Preservation, and the St. Mark's Historic Landmarks Fund. Drop in.

*Governor Peter (Petrus) **Stuyvesant**'s country house sat roughly at the intersection of Tenth and Stuyvesant Streets, just west of Second Avenue. The Bowery was then the Bouwerie (Dutch for "plantation") Road, bounding the southwest flank of the Stuyvesant estate (which extended north to 23rd Street, east to Avenue C, and south to 3rd Street). Stuyvesant Street was the driveway from the Bouwerie Road to the mansion, subsequently destroyed by fire in 1778.*

[E31] **171 First Avenue** (lofts), bet. E. 10th and E. 11th Sts. W side. ca. 1880.

E31

Outcast 4-story cast iron in exile from SoHo? A wonderful surprise. We could use more throughout the city to invigorate bland blocks.

[E32] Originally The Yiddish Art Theatre/later The Phoenix/later Louis N. Jaffe Art Theater/now **Village East City Cinema**, 189 Second Ave., SW cor. E. 12th St. 1925-1926. **Harrison G. Wiseman**. ☛ Interior ☛ Converted to cinema multiplex, 1991.

This part of Second Avenue was known as the Jewish Rialto, with close to 20 theaters staging performances in Yiddish in the mid 1920s when developer **Louis N. Jaffe**, a devotee of actor **Maurice Schwartz** (Mr. Second Avenue), built this theater for him. Like many a synagogue of that era searching for an architectural style, the house is a neo-Moorish adaptation. In 1932 **I. J. Singer**'s *Yoshe Kalb* ran for a record 300 performances.

E32

[E33] **Undergraduate Dormitory, NYU**, 77 Third Ave., bet. E. 11th and E. 12th Sts. 1987. **Voorsanger & Mills Assocs.**

Three connected 14-story towers astride a low base that supposedly strives to simulate the height of adjoining town houses. The heart is willing but the body doesn't follow.

Café Royal, on the SE corner of Second Avenue and East 12th Street, until it closed in 1953, was, according to the New York Times*'s **Richard F. Shepard**, "the uncontested artistic and intellectual center of the Yiddish-speaking world in America . . . an enclave where artists, actors and writers came to debate, over endless glasses of tea, the great questions of art that have gone unanswered in every civilized language." It is now a dry cleaner's.*

[E34] **201 East 12th Street** (apartments), bet. Second and Third Aves. ca. 1880. Converted, 1981, **Mullen Palandrani Grossberg**.

A beautifully detailed brick mill building (catch the decorative brick arched lintels) updated with wit for residential uses.

*Butch Cassidy of Same & Sundance Kid fame lived (1901) in a boardinghouse run by **Mrs. Catherine Taylor** at 234 East 12th Street, between Second and Third Avenues.*

E34

[A35] Formerly **Karl Bitter studio**, 249½ E. 13th St., bet. Second and Third Aves.

Bitter (1867-1915) was sculptor of the figures of Architecture, Sculpture, Painting, and Music on the Metropolitan Museum's entrance, and the figure "Pomona" atop the Plaza's Pulitzer fountain, among many well-known works. Note his (and a partner's) name carved in stone:

BITTER & MORETTI SCULPTORS

East Village/Far East: the eastern reaches of these precincts:

[E36] **The Father's Heart Ministry Center**/originally People's Home Church and Settlement (Methodist Episcopal), 545 E. 11th St., bet Avenues A and B. 1868.

E35

Italianate brick, with Gothic hooded window moldings, and an ogive arched corbel-table that may be unique. Dignified eclecticism.

[E37] **St. Nicholas Carpatho-Russian Orthodox Greek Catholic Church**/originally St. Mark's Memorial Chapel, 288 E. 10th St., SW cor. Avenue A. 1883. **James Renwick, Jr**. and **W. H. Russell**.

Gothic Revival in exuberant red brick and matching terra-cotta.

E36

[E38] **Tompkins Square Park**/originally Tompkins Square, E. 7th to E. 10th Sts., Avenue A to Avenue B. 1834.

EAST VILLAGE

see pages 174-177

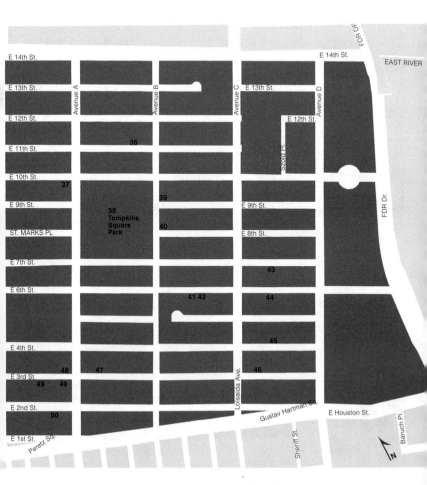

Another London (Bloomsbury) park surrounded by high-density, low-rise housing. Sixteen blessed acres in these tight and dense streets.

[E39] Originally **Christodora House** (settlement house)/now Christodora House (apartments), 1 Tompkins Sq. also known as 145 Avenue B, NE cor. E. 9th St. 1928. **Henry C. Pelton**. Conversion, 1987, **John T. Fifeld Assocs.**
   George Gershwin gave his first public recital in the original 3rd-floor concert hall. Beautifully detailed brick and stone in a transition between neo-Classical and Art Deco.

[E40] Originally **Tompkins Square Lodging House for Boys and Industrial School, Children's Aid Society** also known as Newsboys' and Bootblacks' Lodging House/later Talmud Torah Darch Moam/now apartments, 127 Avenue B, NE cor. E. 8th St. also known as 295 E. 8th St. 1887. **Vaux & Radford.**

[E41] Originally 6th Street Industrial School, Children's Aid Society/later Sloane Children's Center/now **Trinity Lower East Side Parish and Shelter** (Lutheran), 630 E. 6th St., bet. Avenues B and C. 1890. **Vaux & Radford.**
   Two of a series of industrial schools/lodging houses to which **Calvert Vaux** turned his attention and considerable talent after his Central Park-Prospect Park days were behind him. Tompkins Square's exuberant brick and terra-cotta polychromy has been muted with paint. The 6th Street School is magnificent and stately.

E39

E41

E42

E43

E44

E45

E46

[E42] Originally **Congregation Ahavath Yeshurun Shara Torah** (Love of Israel, Gates of the Torah)/now Sixth Street CommunityCenter, 638 E. 6th St., bet. Avenues B and C. 1898.

[E43] **Stone House in Lower Manhattan** (apartments)/originally Congregation Beth Hamedrash Hagodol Anshe Ungarn (Great House of Study of the People of Hungary), 242 E. 7th St., bet. Avenues C and D. 1905. Converted, 1986.

Built in the space module locally occupied by a tenement, these are each *shtiblech*, tiny synagogues; the intricate brickwork of No. 638 East 6th recalls the Moorish decorative scale of Jewish non-representational art. At No. 242 a miniature Renaissance palazzo serves the same purposes.

[E44] **Lower East Side Infill Housing II** (apartments), NYC Housing Authority, along parts of E. 4th, E. 5th, and E. 6th Sts. (and other neighboring blocks), bet. Avenues C and D. 1987. **Vitto & Oaklander**.

Three-story turnkey housing in brown brick and cast stone that helps to relieve the severe housing shortage for low-income families. Not bad.

[E45] **San Isidro y San Leandro Orthodox Catholic Church of the Hispanic Rite**/originally Russian Orthodox church, 345 E. 4th St., bet. Aves. C and D. ca. 1895.

Painted polychromy in the spirit of **John Ruskin** (except that the palette, chocolate and white, is hardly from his own).

*Loisaida, pronounced low-ees-SIDE-ah, is the term used by the predominantly Puerto Rican community for the real estate lying between Houston and 14th Streets from Avenue A eastward. The term dates from the mid 1970s, and its origin is generally credited to **Bimbo Rivas**, a local poet and playwright. In 1986, Avenue C was officially given an additional name, Loisaida Avenue. So far, its earlier name has not been changed to Avenue Si.*

[E46] **Ryan/NENA Comprehensive Health Service Center**, Northeast Neighborhood Association, 279 E. 3rd St., bet. Avenue C and Avenue D. 1976. **Edelman & Salzman**.

The façade of this multistory health center enjoys a monumentality once reserved for cathedrals. Within, the spaces (and the muted color scheme) establish a scale more appropriate to community health care.

Riis Houses Plaza, within Jacob Riis Houses:
*This was once well worth the trip. Public space, between buildings, is usually filled with either traffic or parked cars, or is grassed and fenced off from the pedestrian. Here space was made available in a construction to delight all ages: pyramids to climb on for the small, an amphitheater that accommodated all age groups, places to sit, stand, walk, talk, hop, skip, scoot, and tag. Given an asphalt street down the block from a local park, kids will most frequently pick the street to play. Planned as an alternate to streets, Riis was where the action was, in these parts. A great place. Demolished in large part due to safety standards (read avoidance of lawsuits), the wonders of Friedberg have been replaced by standardized "modular" play structures. (NYC Housing Authority, E. 6th to E. 10th Sts., Avenue D to Franklin D. Roosevelt Dr. Plaza, 1966-1998. **Pomerance & Breines**, architects. **M. Paul Friedberg**, landscape architect. Housing, 1949.)*

[E47] **Most Holy Redeemer Roman Catholic Church and Rectory**, 161-165 E. 3rd St., bet. Avenue A and Avenue B. 1870s.

A powerful, deeply modeled, limestone pile, one of the tallest structures (except for the "projects") in the community. Eclectic, of course, it might be classified as Baroque Romanesque.

E47

[E48] **Ageloff Towers** (apartments), 141 E. 3rd St., NW cor. Avenue A. 180 East 4th St. SW cor. Avenue A. 1929. **Shampan & Shampan.**

This massive apartment pair suggests that some developers may have thought the Roaring Twenties would make a silk purse even out of the Lower East Side. Needless to say, it didn't. Some charming Art Deco detail remains.

[E49] **First Houses, NYC Housing Authority**, 29-41 Avenue A, SW cor. E. 3rd St., 112-138 E. 3rd St., bet. First Ave. and Avenue A. Reconstructed into public housing, 1935, **Frederick L. Ackerman.** 🍎

The first houses built—or, rather, rebuilt, in this instance— by the City's housing authority. In a block of tenements every third was demolished, allowing the remaining pairs light and air on three sides. This, as a remodeling, and Williamsburg Houses, as new construction, are still the brightest lights in the history of this city's early public housing. Walk through the urbane cobbled and tree-filled space behind.

E48

[E50] Originally **Rectory, St. Nicholas Roman Catholic Church**/now apartments, 135 E. 2nd St., bet. First Ave. and Avenue A. 1867.

An essay in late Gothic Revival mannerism, with swell stone trim around the tiers of pointed arch windows. Note the silhouette of the demolished church on the old rectory's west wall: palimpsest.

Midtown Manhattan

M

 Colonial

 Georgian/ Federal

 Greek Revival

 Gothic Revival

 Villa

 Romanesque Revival

 Renaissance Revival

 Roman Revival

 Art Deco/ Art Moderne

 Modern/ Post-Modern

If Manhattan is the center of the city, midtown is the center of the center. Here are most of the elements one expects to find in a city core: the major railroad and bus stations, the vast majority of hotel rooms, the biggest stores, the main public library and post office. Of the four principal activities that have traditionally sustained New York, two—nationwide corporations and the garment industry—are concentrated in midtown. Another of the four, shipping—also historically centered in Midtown—has declined to a point where freight, largely in the form of container shipping, has sought available space elsewhere, in Staten Island and Brooklyn. Transatlantic passenger travel, once cause of grand experiences of arrival and departure on West Side piers, has become almost extinct, but the QE2 still stops in occasionally. Only one of Manhattan's major commercial activities—the financial center—is concentrated on another part of the island.

Social status in midtown once followed a clear-cut pattern: all the fashionable shops and living quarters ran up a central spine along Fifth and Park Avenues and Broadway. But Central Park, by driving a cleft between this spine and the Upper West Side, diverted fashionable Manhattan a bit to the east, and the purposeful development of Park Avenue in the 1920s shifted the weight a bit further, encouraging some colonies of high society to move far to the east, particularly after the demolition of that psychological barrier, the Third Avenue el, in 1956. With the construction of the United Nations Headquarters on the East River and its many ancillary and quasi-official satellites and delegations' structures, a whole new profile took shape.

MIDTOWN KEY MAP

CHELSEA

Nearly two centuries of ups and downs have left Chelsea a patchwork of town houses, tenements, factories, and housing projects. The name was originally given by **Captain Thomas Clarke** to his estate, staked out in 1750, which extended roughly from the present 19th to 28th Streets, from Eighth Avenue west to the Hudson. The modern place-name covers approximately the same area, with its eastern boundary at Seventh Avenue and its southern one at 14th Street.

Captain Clarke's grandson, **Clement Clarke Moore** (1779-1863) grew up in the family mansion near the present 23rd Street west of Ninth Avenue, dividing the estate into lots around 1830. Moore, noted in his time as a scholar of languages, is remembered now mainly for his poem "A Visit from Saint Nicholas," which sealed the unscholarly but indestructible connection between **Saint Nick** and Christmas. Moore donated one choice block for the General Theological Seminary, which is still there, and the surrounding blocks prospered as a desirable suburb. Then the Hudson River Railroad opened along Eleventh Avenue in 1851, attracting slaughterhouses, breweries, and so on, followed quickly by the shanties and tenements of workers.

In 1871 the dignity of town house blocks still unaffected by the railroad was shattered by the steam locomotives of New York's first elevated railroad, which ran up Ninth Avenue. In the 1870s a declining Chelsea was brightened by the blossoming of the city's theater district along West 23rd Street. For a decade or so, these blocks were ideally convenient to both the high society of Madison Square and the flourishing vice district along Sixth Avenue in the upper 20s and 30s. When the theater world moved uptown, artists and literati stayed on to make Chelsea New York's bohemia; early in the 20th century bohemia moved south to Greenwich Village, but the writers never quite deserted 23rd Street.

Around 1905-1915 a new art form, the motion picture, was sheltered in Chelsea, whose old lofts and theaters made economical studios until the sunshine of Hollywood lured the industry away. In the 1920s and 1930s Chelsea got a lift from some impressive new industrial buildings near the piers and some luxury apartments inland. But the greatest improvements were on the grade-level freight line, long since part of the New York Central, which ran along Eleventh Avenue (there was a Death Avenue Cowboy on horseback, carrying a red flag of warning ahead of each train); it was replaced in 1934 by an inconspicuous through-the-block elevated line just west of Tenth Avenue, now inoperative, and partly dismantled. Just prior to World War II the rattling Ninth Avenue el, the city's first above-the-streets rapid transit line, was torn down.

In the 1950s and 1960s public housing and urban renewal uprooted large chunks of slum housing, and rehabilitation of Chelsea's many fine town houses followed a slow upward trend. By the 1980s gentrification had reclaimed almost all the brick and brownstone town houses.

*For the heart of Chelsea, **START** at West 23rd Street W of Seventh Avenue. (Take the IRT Seventh Avenue Line local (Nos. 1 or 8 trains) or the IND Eighth Avenue Line (C or E train) to their respective 23rd Street Stations.)*

[H1a] **Muhlenberg Branch, New York Public Library**, 209 W. 23rd St., bet. Seventh and Eighth Aves. 1906. **Carrère & Hastings**. Renovations, 1999. **R. M. Kliment & Frances Halsband**.

A modest neo-Renaissance library overwhelmed by the powerful architecture of the Chelsea Hotel across the street.

H1

[H2] **Chelsea Hotel**/originally Chelsea Apartments, 222 W. 23rd St., bet. Seventh and Eighth Aves. 1883-1885. **Hubert, Pirsson & Co.** 🖤

Built as one of the city's first cooperative apartment houses, the Chelsea became a hotel in 1905 but has a high ratio of permanent tenants even today. The 12-story brick bearing-wall structure has been called Queen Anne or Victorian Gothic, but its style is hard to pin down. The most prominent exterior features are the delicate iron balconies (made by **J. B.** and **J. M. Cornell**) that screen the hefty brickwork. Plaques at the entrance honor writers who have lived here: **Thomas Wolfe**, **Dylan Thomas**, and **Brendan Behan**, three of a long list that runs from **Mark Twain** and **O. Henry** to **Tennessee Williams**, **Yevgeni Yevtushenko**, and **Arthur Miller**. Guests from other arts have included **Sarah Bernhardt**, **Virgil Thomson**, **John Sloan**, and **Jackson Pollock**. **Edgar Lee Masters** wrote a poem about the Chelsea, and **Andy Warhol** made it the scene of his 1966 movie *The Chelsea Girls*.

H2

*Name change: **Philip G. Hubert** (1830-1911), partner in the firm of **Hubert, Pirsson & Company**, was the son of **Charles Antoine Colomb Gengembre**, whose children adopted the surname of their mother, Hubert, since their father's was so difficult for Americans to pronounce.*

H3

[H3] **McBurney YMCA**, 215 W. 23rd St., bet. Seventh and Eighth Aves. 1914.

A stoic portico confronts the Chelsea Hotel across the street.

[H4] **240 West 23rd Street** (lofts), bet. Seventh and Eighth Aves. 1880s.

Golden rams overlook those entering the bank below. A restrained and elegant eclectic building.

[H5] **244 West 23rd Street** (lofts), bet. Seventh and Eighth Avenues. 1890s.

Romanesque Revival in brick, limestone, terra-cotta, and granite.

H5

*The Grand Opera House stood on the northwest corner of 23rd Street and Eighth Avenue until 1960, when land was cleared for the surrounding Penn Station South. Bought by the notorious financier, impresario, and bon vivant **"Jubilee" Jim Fisk** in the late 1860s, it did double service as head office of his Erie Railroad. It withstood repeated assaults by irate Erie stockholders (with steel doors reputedly 12 inches thick) and was the scene of Fisk's funeral in 1872, after he was shot by **Edward S. Stokes**, hot-blooded third party of a triangle whose apex was the famous actress **Josie Mansfield**, Fisk's onetime mistress. Fisk's demise was a preview of a similar tragedy in the assassination of **Stanford White** 34 years later.*

[H6] **Chelsea Historic District**, generally both sides of W. 20th, W. 21st and W. 22nd Sts. bet. Ninth and Tenth Aves. with irregular legs E of Ninth Ave. ● **Chelsea Historic District Extension**, includes W. 22nd St. almost to Eighth Ave. and the W half of the S side of W. 23rd St. bet. Ninth and Tenth Aves. ●

This Historic District and its extension form the kernel and hence a condensation of the best qualities of Chelsea, with architecture from all its periods: Greek and Gothic Revival, Italianate, and 1890s apartment buildings by such firms as **C. P. H. Gilbert** and **Neville & Bagge**.

[H7] **305-313 West 22nd Street** (apartments), bet. Eighth and Ninth Aves. 1873. Extended and altered upward, 1986, **Weinberg, Kirschenbaum & Tambasco**, with **Jay Almour Assocs**. ☞

Here venerable mansard roofs crested with cast iron are beautifully restored, and a modern entry tower at the west end gracefully stands in the background.

H7

[H8] **260 West 22nd Street** (apartments), bet. Seventh and Eighth Aves. Converted, 1969. **Robert Ostrow**.

This 1960s reconstructed row house was rebuilt from a shell by owner-architect Ostrow. His exterior modeling of dark brick, glass, and ribbed metal roofing reflects equally intricate interior spaces.

[H9] **Joyce Theatre**/originally Elgin (movie theater), 175 Eighth Ave., SW cor. W. 19th St. 1942. **Simon Zelnik**. Converted to dance theater, 1982, **Hardy Holzman Pfeiffer Assocs**.

A onetime neighborhood movie house, then a revival showcase, now lovingly updated to honor its Art Moderne beginnings.

H9

An excursion to South Chelsea:

[H10] **Apartments**, Eighth Ave., bet. W. 16th and W. 17th Sts., E side. 1988. **James Stewart Polshek & Partners**.

New condominium units to fill the ever-soaring demand for a niche in Greenwich Village "and vicinity." **Polshek**'s Washington Court at Sixth Avenue and Waverly Place is a more successful predecessor of this project.

H10

CHELSEA

see pages 180–188

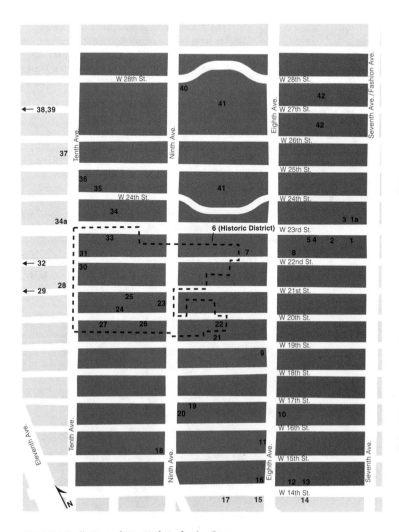

[H11] Originally **Port of New York Authority Commerce Building**/Union Inland Terminal No. 1, 111 Eighth Ave., bet. W. 15th and W. 16th Sts. to Ninth Ave. 1932. **Abbott, Merkt & Co., Lusby Simpson**, designer.

An enormous inner-city warehousing facility occupying a full city block, a whale of a structure but only a little brother to Starrett-Lehigh. Before occupying space in its World Trade Center, this was the headquarters of the Port of New York Authority (today, Port Authority of New York and New Jersey).

[H12] Originally **Andrew Norwood House**, 241 W. 14th St., bet. Seventh and Eighth Aves. 1845-1847. ✦

An Italianate brownstone with late Greek Revival detail. It, and two defaced neighbors, were the first masonry houses on the block. Next door, at 243, was the Tammany Tough Club, its basement barroom scheduled to be reopened as a public watering place.

[H13] **Iglesia Católica Guadalupe** (Roman Catholic), 229 W. 14th St., bet. Seventh and Eighth Aves.

An extraordinary brownstone conversion from row house to humble Spanish Catholic church. Its Iberian ancestry is expressed both in the language of its services and in its Spanish Colonial Baroque façade.

H12

H14

H16

[H14] **The Sequoia** (apartments), 222 W. 14th St., bet. Seventh and Eighth Aves. 1987. **Ted Reeds Assocs.**

A Post Modern apartment house displaying too many materials, but with remarkable cornices at the 7th floor.

[H15] **Off-Broadway theater**/former Manufacturers Hanover Trust Company branch/originally New York County National Bank, 75-79 Eighth Ave., SW cor. W. 14th St. 1906-1907. **DeLemos & Cordes**, succeeded by **Rudolph L. Daus.** Later addition to S. Renovations and addition, 1999. **Lee Harris** of **Hudson River Studios** and **John Reimnitz**. ●

[H16] Originally The New York Savings Bank/later Goldome Bank branch/now **Central Carpet Co.**, 81 Eighth Ave., NW cor. W. 14th St. 1897. **R. H. Robertson**. ●

A rare occurrence for this city: a pair of classically inspired sentinels guarding the western corridor of 14th Street. The two have lately given way to less mammon-inspired activities: carpets and the theater, hardly a typical case for the enlightened reuse of landmarks, but happy preservation events. The four-story addition to the old New York County National Bank mimics the spirit of **DeLemos & Cordes**'s original architecture, and within there is not only a 499-seat theater, but 11 apartments.

[H17] **The Church of St. Bernard** (Roman Catholic), 330 W. 14th St., bet. Eighth and Ninth Aves. 1875. **Patrick Charles Keely**.

Two-tone brownstone Ruskinisn Gothic Revival, with a wheel window overlooking 14th Street.

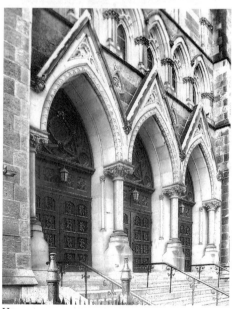

H17

[H18] **Chelsea Market**/originally Nabisco Bakery, 75 Ninth Ave., NW cor. W. 15th St. 1898. Remodeled 1990s.

Chain mail? Aggressive steel? A grand stage set for the entrance to this upscale market.

[H19] **New York Service Center, Manhattan Plaza**/originally National Maritime Union of America, Joseph Curran Annex, 346 W. 17th St., bet. Eighth and Ninth Aves. 1966.

[H20] Originally **Joseph Curran Plaza**, 100 Ninth Ave., bet. W. 16th and W. 17th Sts. Both by **Albert C. Ledner & Assocs**.

A startling white tile-faced, porthole-pierced front wall sloping 8½ degrees from vertical was the architect's way of meeting the setback requirements of the 1961 zoning resolution: the 20-foot setback required above 85 feet from the sidewalk was hereby accommodated. As novel on the exterior as the union's former

H20

main building, it was efficiently laid out inside to accommodate medical and recreational facilities for union members.

Back north to the Chelsea Historic District and its surrounds:

H21

[H21] **365 West 19th Street** (apartments), bet. Eighth and Ninth Aves. Converted, 1970, **Robert Ostrow**.
  Another special event among Chelsea's converted row houses by an architect who followed **Horace Greeley**'s (much earlier) advice: he went west.

[H22a] **St. Peter's Church** (Episcopal), 344 W. 20th St., bet. Eighth and Ninth Aves. 1836-1838. **James W. Smith**, builder, after designs by **Clement Clarke Moore**. ☞
[H22b] **Rectory**. 1832. ☞ [H22c] **Atlantic Theater**/formerly Apple Corps Theater, 336 W. 20th St. 1854-1871. ☞
  These buildings form a remarkable study in popular adaptation of styles. The rectory, which first served as the church, is austere Greek Revival, and its fine proportions give it dignity. By the time the much larger church was built, the congregation was ready to make it one of New York's earliest ventures into the Gothic Revival. Its massively buttressed fieldstone walls are articulated with spare limestone trim.

H22a

  The third building in the group, the hall east of the church, is an example of later common brick Gothic; started in 1854, it was given its strangely churchlike front in 1871. Now the Atlantic Theater lives here. The wrought-iron fence along the street is older than any of the buildings. It dates from about 1790, a hand-me-down from venerable Trinity Church, then (in the 1830s) building its 3rd incarnation.

H22c

The Kitchen, *the media center at 512 West 19th Street, began as a reuse of the old Broadway Central Hotel's food preparation area (hence its name). For years it occupied space in SoHo, but rising rents made it an expatriate to Chelsea's west edge. The place for avant-garde video, music, dance, performance, and film. And at 169 Eighth Avenue also at 19th Street, part of the Eiffel Tower's old spiral stairs gives access to the restrooms of* **Man Ray** *(restaurant).*

H24

[H23] **General Theological Seminary**, Ninth Ave., bet. W. 20th and W. 21st Sts., to Tenth Ave. Main buildings, 1883-1900. **Charles C.Haight**.
[H24] **West Building**, Nos. 5 and 6 Chelsea Sq., W. 20th St., bet. Ninth and Tenth Aves. N side. 1836.
[H25] **Chapel** on the green within. ca. 1900. ☞
  The stoutly fenced, full city block of the seminary and its garden are accessible through the building (1960. **O'Connor & Kilham**) on the Ninth Avenue front, but the major buildings can be seen from West 20th Street. The West Building, one of the city's oldest examples of Gothic Revival, was modeled after an even earlier, matching East Building (built 1827; razed 1892). Haight's surrounding dour collegiate Gothic red brick and brownstone structures are a delightful and convincing stage set for the resident Episcopalians.

H25

[H26] **The Cushman Row** (row houses), 406-418 W. 20th St.; bet. Ninth and Tenth Aves. 1840. ☞
  Built by dry goods merchant **Don Alonzo Cushman** (Don was his first name), a friend of **Clement Moore**'s who became a millionaire developing Chelsea. The fine Greek Revival detail, except for losses here and there, is intact: tiny, wreath-encircled attic windows; deeply recessed doorways with brownstone frames, handsome iron balustrades, newels, and fences. The dormers are a later addition.

H27

[H27] **446-450 West 20th Street**, bet. Ninth and Tenth Aves. 1855. ☞ **465-473 West 21st Street**, NE cor. Tenth Ave. 1853. ☞

Eight exceptional Italianate houses facing, respectively, the austere side walls (West 21st Street) and the gardens (West 20th Street) of the seminary across the streets.

H28

H28

[H28] **Church of the Guardian Angel** (Roman Catholic), 193 Tenth Ave., NW cor. W. 21st St. 1930. **John Van Pelt.**

Lush brick and limestone, Italian Romanesque.

[H29] **Paula Cooper Gallery**/former garage, 534 W. 21st St., bet. Tenth And Eleventh Aves. Remodeled 1996. **Gluckman Mayner.**

Like Dia below, it is the space within (49x49x30) that matters rather than the façade without. **Carl André** has been here, and you know he needs space.

[H30] **Clement Clarke Moore Park**, W. 22nd St. SE cor. Tenth Ave. 1968. **Coffey, Levine & Blumberg**, architects/landscape architects. ♂

A friendly, understated canopy of trees is an adjunct to this row house district.

H31

[H31] **Empire Diner**, 210 Tenth Ave., NE cor. W. 22nd St. 1943. Altered, 1976, **Carl Laanes**, designer. ♂

The reincarnation of, and ultimate homage to, the American diner. Stainless steel never looked better, set off by black and chrome furnishings.

[H32] **Dia Center for the Arts**, 548 W. 22nd St., bet. Tenth and Eleventh Aves. 1987. **Gluckman Mayner.** Open to the public. Th-Su 12-6; closed Mo-We; closed June-Aug. 212-431-9232.

A modest iudustrial exterior conceals this serious museum of the arts. Inside this shell, **Gluckman Mayner** have inserted some wonderful galleries (hermit crabs?).

H32

[H33] **428-450 West 23rd Street** (row houses), bet. Ninth and Tenth Aves. ca. 1860. ♂

A phalanx of Anglo-Italianate brownstones opposite the bulk of London Terrace. Here is a "terrace" remnant that gives a taste of what were once almost endless and uniform blocks.

[H34] **London Terrace** (apartments), W. 23rd to W. 24th Sts., Ninth to Tenth Aves. 1930. **Farrar & Watmaugh.**

This vast brick pile, in proto-Modern planar style with some Romanesque Revival details, comprises 2 rows of connected apartment buildings enclosing a blocklong private garden, invisible from the street. All in all it contains 1,670 units.

H34

[H34a] **Art Galleries and Studio**, NW cor. W. 23rd St. and Tenth Ave. 1999. **Smith & Thompson.**

Steel plates embrace a serene courtyard, serving two art galleries and the architects' studio. Modernism with a sensitivity to urbane urban space.

[H35] **437-459 West 24th Street** (row houses), bet. Ninth and Tenth Aves. 1849-1850. **Philo Beebe**, builder. ♂

A row of late Italianate brick houses unusual in their large setback from the street. No. 461 next door is an earlier Federal house. The front gardens are a refreshing pause in the streetscape.

H34a

[H36] **242-258 Tenth Avenue** (row houses), bet. W. 24th and W. 25th Sts. E side.

An Italianate commercial row provides an old New York image seemingly from an Edward Hopper painting.

[H37] Originally **H. Wolff Book Bindery**, 259-273 Tenth Ave., bet. W. 25th and W. 26th Sts. W side. ca. 1900. Addition, 1926, **Frank Parker.**

H34a

Notable for its technology—not its aesthetics: here was an early poured in-place concrete (in situ) building, an industrial monument.

H38

Famous Players in Famous Plays: Adolph Zukor, who originated this title, produced a number of old films in Chelsea. Nor was his only studio, others being **Kalem, Charles O. Bauman & Adam Kessel Films, Reliance, Majestic,** *etc. The Famous Players Studios was at 221 West 26th Street; its roster of stars contained such names as* **Mary Pickford** *and* **John Barrymore.**

[H38] **Starrett-Lehigh Building** (lofts), W. 26th to W. 27th Sts., Eleventh to Twelfth Aves. 1930-1931. **Russell G.** and **Walter M. Cory. Yasuo Matsui,** associated architect. **Purdy & Henderson,** consulting engineers. ●

About 9 miles of strip windows, with their brick-banded spandrels, streaking and swerving around this block-square, 19-story factory-warehouse structure have made it a landmark of modern architecture ever since it rose in the air rights of the former Lehigh Valley Railroad freight terminal. The office section, crowning the north facade, is, in contrast, astonishingly heavy-handed: ponderous brick and double-hung windows.

On the east side of 11th Avenue, between 27th and 28th streets stands a giant concrete high relief sculpture displaying vintage cars, while under it and within a showroom are the real things. This is the Hollywood Hype/Times Square Moderne gesture of Michael Dezer Motor Cars. Look through the glass, and walk in to find the real architecture of motoring.

Michael Dezer
Motor Cars

[H39] Originally **Central Stores, Terminal Warehouse Company,** W. 27th to W. 28th Sts., Eleventh to Twelfth Aves. 1891. **Walter Katte,** chief engineer.

Twenty-four acres of warehousing within a brick fortress composing 25 separate buildings crowned with a Tuscan arched corbel-table. The inevitable gentrification into condominium apartments might strike here next.

The Tunnel, 220 Twelfth Avenue, a mid-1980s dance club, occupies the lowest level of the Terminal Warehouse Company and milks the magic and mystery of the onetime warehouse for all it's worth. From the disco's publicity: "Opulence inside a stone fortress. Golden chambers and heavy machinery. Dungeons below ivory towers." Hype. 695-4682.

H40

[H40] **Church of the Holy Apostles** (Episcopal), 300 Ninth Ave., SE cor. W. 28th St. 1845-1848 and 1853-1854. **Minard**

Lafever. Transepts, 1858. **Richard Upjohn & Son**. Restored after 1990 fire. 🍎

This remarkably independent work fits into no stylistic slot. Called an early effort at Romanesque Revival, its brick details, bracketed eaves, and unique bronze and slate spire—completely dominating the low nave—mark it as an equally early appearance of the Italianate style, rarely seen in churches. The interior has the simple barrel-vaulted geometry of early Italian Renaissance, without the Classical details. The windows, by **William Jay Bolton**, some lost in a 1990 fire, are as unusual as the building, if less vigorous; each is composed of square panels in a colorful abstract design, with central medallions painted in a delicate monochromatic and realistic style.

H42c

[H41] **Penn Station South** (apartment complex), W. 23rd to W. 29th Sts., Eighth to Ninth Aves. 1962. **Herman Jessor**.

This 2,820-unit urban renewal development is a cooperative sponsored by the International Ladies' Garment Workers Union ("ladies" here refers to the garments), conveniently located at the southwest corner of the Garment District (which extends north to West 40th Street and east to Sixth Avenue).

[H42] **Fashion Institute of Technology**, W. 26th to W. 28th Sts., bet. Seventh and Eighth Aves. [H42a] **Administration and Technology Building**, and [H42b] **Morris W. & Fannie B. Haft Auditorium**, both on W. 27th St. N Side. 1958. [H42c] **Nagler Hall** (dormitory), W. 27th St. S side. 1962. [H42d] **Shirley Goodman Resource Center**, Seventh Ave., bet. W. 26th and W. 27th Sts. W side. 1977. [H42e] **Arts and Design Center**, Seventh Ave., bet.W. 27th and W. 28th Sts. W side. 1977.

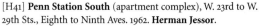

H42f

[H42f] **David Dubinsky Student Center**, Eighth Ave., bet. W. 27th and W. 28th Sts. E side. 1977. All by **DeYoung & Moscowitz**. [H42g] **New Dormitories**, W. 27th St. S side. 1988. **Henry George Greene**. [H42h] **Center for Design Innovation**, W. 27th St. 2001. **Kevin Hom + Andrew Goldman**. Galleries in Shirley Goodman Center open: Tu-Fri 12-8; Sa 10-5; closed Su & Mo. 212-760-7760.

This complex was planned as the training ground for interns for New York's garment industry. Fashions in dresses, coats, and suits change every season; so did the Institute's style of architecture over the 30 years this campus took to complete.

END of Chelsea. Nearby trains are at Seventh Avenue and 28th Street (IRT Nos. 1 and 9 trains).

L2

LADIES MILE

[L1] **Ladies Mile Historic District**, West of Park Avenue South to West of 6th Avenue; 15th to 24th streets, with wandering connections. 🍎

Sixth Avenue Emporia: The old Stern's dry goods store on West 23rd Street and other blocklong ghosts lining what is officially Avenue of the Americas recall the latter part of the 19th century, when this was the precinct termed Fashion Row. Now used again for big box shops and office space, their splendor is still quite evident, and reincarnations have slowly made these long-seedy skeletons glisten once again. In their heyday, it was quite a different avenue, with the clatter of the Sixth Avenue el bringing the middle class to this segment of what came to be a far-ranging, ready-to-wear clothing district.

[L2] Originally **Stern's Dry Goods Store**, 32-36 W. 23rd St., bet. Fifth and Sixth Aves. 1878. **Henry Fernbach**. 38-46 W. 23rd St. 1892. **William Schickel**. Altered, 1986, **Rothzeid, Kaiserman, Thompson & Bee**. ♂

A resplendent cast-iron emporium for "New York's first merchandising family." It reeks of birthday cake with vanilla icing. A new glass and iron canopy adds a note of elegant entry, but the added floors atop 32-36 are out of context.

Edith Wharton, author of such revealing New York novels as The Age of Innocence, *was born in 1862 at 14 West 23rd Street, in a 3-story brownstone altered into a store by* **H. J. Hardenbergh** *in 1882. The cast-iron columns date from yet another alteration in 1892. As a signal of the migrating social geography of her own early years, Mrs. Wharton noted that her hero,* **Newland Archer,** *in reflecting on his father-in-law to be, "knew that he already had his eye on a newly built house in East Thirty-ninth Street. The neighborhood was thought remote, and the house was built in a ghastly greenish-yellow stone that the younger architects were beginning to employ as a protest against the brownstone of which the uniform hue coated New York like a cold chocolate sauce; but the plumbing was perfect."*

L3

[L3] **61 West 23rd Street** (lofts), bet. Fifth and Sixth Aves. 1886. **John Butler Snook**. ♂

An understated cast-iron remnant of the Ladies' Mile.

LADIES MILE

see pages 189–200

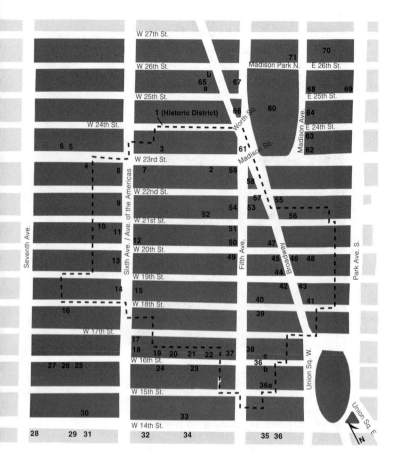

Map labels: W 27th St., W 26th St., Madison Park N., 71, 70, W 25th St., 65, b, a, 67, 68, 69, E 25th St., 1 (Historic District), 66, 60, 64, 63, E 24th St., W 24th St., North Sq., 62, 6, 5, 3, W 23rd St., 61, Madison Sq., 4, 8, 7, 2, 59, 58, 9, W 22nd St., 57, 55, 52, 54, 53, 56, Seventh Ave., 10, 11, W 21st St., 51, Sixth Ave. / Ave. of the Americas, 12, 50, 47, 45, 46, 48, 13, 49, 44, Park Ave. S., 14, 15, W 19th St., 42, 43, 16, W 18th St., 40, 41, 39, W 17th St., 17, 18, 19, 20, 21, 22, 37, 38, c, Union Sq. W., 27, 26, 25, 36, b, 24, 23, 36a, W 15th St., 30, 33, W 14th St., 28, 29, 31, 32, 34, 35, 36, Union Sq. E., N, Fifth Ave., Broadway, Madison Ave.

[L4] **The Milan** (apartments), 118-122 W. 23rd St., bet. Sixth and Seventh Aves. 1988. **Der Scutt**.

This tan brick construction, with its deeply sculpted balconies, adds a vigorous presence to this noisy street. The false gables were an early gesture to Post Modernism, but a welcome addition to the block.

[L5] **The Traffic Building** (offices), 163 W. 23rd St., bet. Sixth and Seventh Aves. 1920s.

Virtuoso brickwork by an early modernist who yearned to show that those diagonally laid were nonstructural.

[L6] **167 West 23rd Street** (commercial building), bet. Sixth and Seventh Aves. Altered, 1898, **P. F. Brogan**.

Sheet metal and cast iron make ten Ionic columns, and an elegant façade.

L4

[L7] **New Building**, 56 W. 23rd St., SE cor. Sixth Ave. 2001. **Richard Cook & Assocs**. with **Costas Kondylis & Associates**.

In the spirit of the monumental emporia that line Sixth Avenue, Cook brings us super-lofts for the super-tenants. In the works as we write.

[L8] Originally **Ehrich Brothers Emporium**, 695-709 Sixth Ave., bet. W. 22nd and W. 23rd Sts. W side. 1889. **William Schickel**.

An elegant cast-iron façade, beautifully restored.

L6

[L9] Originally Adams Dry Goods Store/now **Mattel Toys**, 675-691 Sixth Ave., bet. W. 21 St and W. 22nd Sts. W side. 1900. **DeLemos & Cordes**.

A splendid American Renaissance building, its Composite Roman columns in terra-cotta supporting a steel cornice. Note the ADG monograms among the ornament.

L9

[L10] **Third Cemetery of the Spanish-Portuguese Synagogue**, Shearith Israel, 98-110 W. 21st St., bet. Sixth and Seventh Aves. 1829-1851. ♂

A handsome private haven graced with a venerable ailanthus tree. This cemetery is the youngest of three on Manhattan Island. The others are just south of Chatham Square (Chinatown) and in Greenwich Village.

[L11] Originally **Hugh O'Neill Dry Goods Store**, 655-671 Sixth Ave., bet. W. 20th and W. 21st Sts. W side. 1875. **Mortimer C. Merritt**. ♂

The cast-iron Corinthian columned and pilastered façade, with almost full cylindrical towers, was once crowned with domes interlocked at its two corners. The name remains clearly visible in relief at the pediment.

L11

[L12] Originally **Church of the Holy Communion** (Episcopal)/ now Limelight Disco, 49 W. 20th St., NE cor. Sixth Ave. 1844-1846. Rectory, 1850. Sisters' House, 1854. All by **Richard Upjohn**. Chapel, 1879. ● ♂

More notable because Upjohn did it than because of its intrinsic architectural quality. Now a stylish disco. Churches can become lustily secular in this city when religion has vacated them.

[L13] Originally **Simpson Crawford & Simpson**/later Simpson Crawford (dry goods store), 641 Sixth Ave., bet. W. 19th and W. 20th Sts. W side. 1900. **William H. Hume & Son**. ♂

Seven stories of limestone, a sober work of architecture. The technical school at the corner thinks of itself as a 1950s sub-urb, ignoring the architecture of the "urb" of which it is a part.

L13

Witches and warlocks: The Magickal Childe, at 35 West 19th Street vends amulets, talismans, herbs, roots, and spices, ostensibly to bring protection, good luck, and/or love.

[L14] Originally **B. Altman Dry Goods Store**, 621 Sixth Ave., bet. W. 18th and W. 19th Sts. W side. 1877. **David & John Jardine**. Addition to S 1887, **William H. Hume**. Addition on W. 18th St., 1909, **Buchman & Fox**. ♂

B. Altman's (or Baltman's to some) forsook this cast-iron emporium in 1906 for its imposing stone edifice at Fifth Avenue and 34th Street.

L15

[L15] Originally **Siegel-Cooper Dry Goods Store**, 616-632 Sixth Ave., bet. W. 18th and W. 19th Sts. E side. 1895-1897. **DeLemos & Cordes**. ♂

Fifteen-and-a-half acres of space are contained in this late-comer to the area. Elaborately embellished in glazed terra-cotta, it clearly bears the stamp of the Chicago World's Fair of 1893. At one time it was a favored meeting place, the phrase "Meet you at the fountain!" referring to the jet of water graced by the figure of the Republic by **Daniel Chester French** (now reposing at California's Forest Lawn Cemetery). After a brief but turbulent retailing history, it was converted to a military hospital during World War I. Bed, Bath & Beyond give some style to the ground floor; then you can escalate to T. J. Maxx in alterations respectful of all this American Renaissance grandeur.

[L16] Originally **stables**, 126, 128, 130-132, 136, 140 W. 18th St., bet. Sixth and Seventh Aves. S side. 1864-1865. 🍎
Romanesque Revival housing for the horse-and-carriage trade north of 14th Street.

[L17] **New York Foundling Hospital**, Sixth Ave. SE cor. W. 17th St. 1988. **Perkins Geddis Eastman**.
A modestly articulated brick haven for those babies who once were ensconced in the former foundling home at Third Avenue and East 68th Street. Upper East Side real estate escalation paid for a newer and grander facility in this more economical neighborhood.

[L18] **574 Sixth Avenue** (offices)/originally Knickerbocker Jewelry Company, NE cor. W. 16th St. E side. 1903-1904. **Simeon B. Eisendrath**.
A magnificent cornice for the erstwhile Sixth Avenue Elevated riders.

L18

West 16th Street between Fifth and Sixth Avenues: a wealth of architectural styles and building types.

[L19] Originally **IRT Electrical Substation No. 41**, 27-29 W. 16th St. 1917.
A chaste tapestry of brick embellished by an intricate verdigris cornice. The New York Health and Racquet Club now enjoys some of those high ceilings.

[L20] **31 West 16th Street** (row house). Altered, 1971, **Stephen B. Jacobs**.
Syncopated rhythms mark the window placement in this redressed modernist row house.

L20

[L21] **5, 7, 9, 17, 19, 21, and 23 West 16th Street** (originally row houses). ca. 1846. 🍎
No. 17 is the Greek Revival House where **Margaret Sanger** maintained her Birth Control Clinical Research Bureau from 1930 to 1973. Its bow front (and those of its neighbors at Nos. 5-9) was a common characteristic of Boston's Greek Revival (as around Louisburg Square) but rare in New York. Nos. 19, 21, and 23 complete an ensemble with simpler detailing but matching scale; No. 23 presents magnificent ironwork.

L21

[L22] **The Center for Jewish History**, 15 and 17 W. 16th St. Remodeled with additions on 17th St. 2000. **Beyer Blinder Belle**.
Two neo-Georgian buildings, amid the landmark cluster from 5 to 23, lead to an inner and bigger world mid-block, and loft buildings on 17th Street.

[L23] **Xavier Apartments**, 30 W. 16th St. bet. Fifth and Sixth Aves. S side. 1890s
Some flamboyant limestone for those seeking apartment grandeur.

L23

[L24] **Church of St. Francis Xavier** (Roman Catholic), 40 W. 16th St. 1887. **Patrick Charles Keely**.

The monumental porch of this neo-Baroque church spills onto the sidewalk. Inside is an equally monumental Baroque space.

[L25] **Young Adults Institute**/originally New York House and School of Industry, 120 W. 16th St., bet. Sixth and Seventh Aves. 1878. **Sidney V. Stratton.** 🐦

Red brick Queen Anne eclectic, with a strong personality. The Picturesque Style was just coming into full bloom, abetted by the romantic landscapes and architecture of recently completed Central Park. This institution was founded in 1851 to teach poor women "plain and fine" sewing.

L25

[L26] **French Evangelical Church**/originally Catholic Apostolic Church/later Eglise Evangelique Française de New-York, 126 W. 16th St., bet. Sixth and Seventh Aves. ca. 1835. Current façade, 1886, **Alfred D. F. Hamlin.**

A robust example of what the Germans called Rundbogenstil. The dour dark paint almost kills it.

[L27] **136-40 West 16th Street** (apartments), bet. Fifth and Sixth Aves. 1870s.

L27

Rich brickwork and cast-iron balconies for tenement tenants.

[L28] **154-160 West 14th Street** (lofts), SE cor. Seventh Ave. 1913. **Herman Lee Meader.**

A lavish display of glazed and colored terra-cotta decoration with some flavor of the older Art Nouveau (the frieze at the 2nd floor) and yet anticipating the later Art Deco at its cornice. His Cliff Dwellers' Apartments on Riverside Drive has exotic detail of a different (Mayan?) vocabulary.

L28

🏛 [L29] **138-146 West 14th Street** (lofts), bet. Sixth and Seventh Aves. ca. 1899.

Roman Revival encrusted with elaborate terra-cotta detail; inspired by the World's Columbian Exposition of 1893. When is it Roman rather than Romanesque? In the merging of the 1893 American Renaissance with Richardsonian Romanesque.

West as well as east, 14th Street has seen better days, when the magnetism of Wanamaker's department store radiated from Broadway and East 9th Street throughout the area. Today, much of the street from Seventh Avenue to Union Square is crowded with shoppers bargaining for the cheap merchandise spilling onto the wide sidewalks from a variety of small shops. Above the bustle are the great façades from an earlier era, well worth considering and enjoying.

L29

[L30] **42nd Division Armory N.Y. National Guard**, 125 W. 14th St., bet. Sixth and Seventh Aves. 1971. N.Y.S. General Services Administration, **Charles S. Kawecki**, State Architect. 1971-1995.

A gross and overbearing modern drill hall that replaced a 19th-century fantasy fort of rich detail, soon to be replaced with new shops and housing (2001. **Costas Kondylis**).

🏛 [L31] **Salvation Army Centennial Memorial Temple and Executive Offices**, 120 W. 14th St., bet. Sixth and Seventh Aves. 1930. [L31b] **John and Mary R. Markle Memorial Residen**ce/Evangeline Residence, Salvation Army, 123-131 W. 13th St. 1929. All by **Voorhees, Gmelin & Walker.**

Art Deco on a monumental scale gives entrance to the Centennial Memorial Temple. The interior is as splashy. To the west and south (on 13th Street) are related but more subdued adjuncts.

[L32] **56 West 14th Street**/once Macy's Drygoods Store, bet. Fifth and Sixth Aves. ca. 1894.

L31

L33

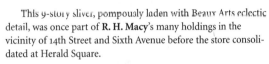

This 9-story sliver, pompously laden with Beaux Arts eclectic detail, was once part of **R. H. Macy**'s many holdings in the vicinity of 14th Street and Sixth Avenue before the store consolidated at Herald Square.

[L33] **Painting Industry Welfare Building**, 45 W. 14th St., bet. Fifth and Sixth Aves. 1960. **Mayer, Whittlesey & Glass**, **William J. Conklin**, associate partner in charge.

Bronze and glass, paper and trash.

In 1967, the *AIA Guide* said: "Hopefully, this witty and elegant refacing of a tired façade will inspire its neighbors to follow." They didn't.

L35

[L34] Originally **Ludwig Brothers Dry Goods Store**, 34-42 W. 14th St., bet. Fifth and Sixth Aves. 1878. **W. Wheeler Smith**. Enlarged, 1899, **Louis Korn**.

A subdued cast-iron building above with cheap stores below.

[L35] Originally **Le Boutillier Brothers** (dry goods), 12-16 E. 14th St. 1891. **D'Oench & Simon**.

A pioneering retailer in women's fashions. The pomp of the original façade is evident above the street-level storefront.

[L36] Originally **Baumann's Carpet Store** 22-26 E. 14th St., bet. Fifth Ave. and University Place. 1880. **David & John Jardine**.

A rich embroidery of cast iron—Composite columns, anthemia garlands, festoons, floral bas-reliefs—embraces 4 tiers of enormous double-hung windows. The economics of keeping 14th Street green (with money) has erased the results of the patternmaker's craft at street level in favor of a retail emporium.

[L36a] Originally **YWCA** (Young Women's Christian Association)/formerly Rand School, 7 E. 15th St., bet. Union Sq. W. and Fifth Ave. 1885-1887. **R. H. Robertson**. ♂

Romanesque Revival in granite, brick, and brownstone. The grand bay windows give the entrance portal a stronger stature.

L36b

[L36b] **Sidney Hillman Health Center**/originally Margaret Louisa Home, YWCA (lodging house), 16 E. 16th St., bet. Union Sq. W. and Fifth Ave. 1890. **R. H. Robertson**.

Rock-face brownstone (with some interspersed brick) in Romanesque Revival, with a charming colonnade at the top floor. A benefaction of **Mrs. Elliott F. Shepard**, **Cornelius Vanderbilt**'s eldest daughter.

L37

[L36c] **9-11 East 16th Street** (lofts), bet. Union Sq. W. and Fifth Ave. 1895-1896. **Louis Korn**. ♂

Sullivanesque limestone for the first 2 floors and then terracotta candy cane above.

[L37] Originally **Judge Building**, 110 Fifth Ave., NW cor. W. 16th St. 1888. **McKim, Mead & White**. Remodeled, 1988, **Davis, Brody & Assocs**. ♂

Early **McKim, Mead & White**: a powerful brick and granite Roman Revival monolith, now happily restored, even up to the cornice.

[L38] **91 Fifth Avenue** (lofts), bet. E. 16th and E. 17th Sts., E side. 1894. **Louis Korn**. ♂

Six busty caryatids bearing up under the weight of four Corinthian columns and two matching pilasters.

[L39] **Engine Co. NYC Fire Department**, 14 E. 18th St., bet. Broadway and Fifth Ave. 1890s. **Napoleon Lebrun**. ♂

Fussy Renaissance Revival.

L38

[L40] **America** (restaurant), 9 E. 18th St., bet. Broadway and Fifth Ave. 1985. **MGS Architects**. ♂

A grand space with a raised and skylit bar that is a stage for the restaurant-tabled audience. Here architecture is space, rather than form. Neon lances itself across the restaurant sky, a colored vibrant sculptured heaven over the pedestrian world below.

Broadway between Union and Madison Squares:
The upper class dowagers (socially, not architecturally) of
Ladies Mile congregated in this area of Broadway. Here the elite
shopped, and hence this was a precinct of the carriage trade—a
shopping strip of somewhat more elevated snobbery than that
enjoyed by Fashion Row, the great Sixth Avenue emporiums originally in the shadows of an el (but also included in the Ladies'
Mile Historic District). The latter might be termed, in contrast,
the transit trade, serving in vast department stoves great hordes of
the middle class. Here along Broadway the shined hooves of cur-
ried horses drew the glistening black enamel and leather carriages
of Society, traveling from their town houses nearby, past Lord &
Taylor, W. & J. Sloane, and their equals, from Union Square to
Madison Square. Sadly, these once participants in elegance show
their ill-cared-for forms only above the street, where "modern"
alterations have mostly defaced what were once grand doorman-
guarded entries.

[L41] **MacIntyre Building** (lofts), 874 Broadway, NE cor. E. 18th
St. 1890-1892. **R. H. Robertson.** ⟲
   Unspeakable eclectic: a murmuration of Byzantine columns,
Romanesque arches, Gothic finials and crockets—the designer
used the whole arsenal of history in one shot.

[L42] Originally Arnold Constable Dry Goods Store/now **ABC
Carpet Store**, 881-887 Broadway, SW cor. E. 19th St., through to
Fifth Ave. with a later entry and address at 115 Fifth Ave. 1868-
1869. Extended, 1873, 1877. All by **Griffith Thomas.** ⟲
   Lovers of marble walls, cast-iron façades, and mansard roofs,
rejoice! There is something here for each of you. The Broadway
façade, the oldest, is of marble. The extension to Fifth Avenue, the
youngest, is of cast iron, an economical simulation of its adjacent
parent. In between, the 2-story miraculous mansard crown rises
over the original body and the Fifth Avenue extension.

L42

[L43] **ABC Carpet**/originally W. & J. Sloane Store, 884
Broadway, SE cor. E. 19th St. 1881-1882. Expanded, 1898. All by
W. Wheeler Smith. ⟲
   Located on Broadway opposite City Hall since 1843, Sloane's
moved here (temporarily) before settling on Fifth Avenue and
45th Street. In this ornate brick and terra-cotta structure the
firm sold carpeting, oriental rugs, lace curtains, and upholstery
fabric. They later expanded to furniture.
   Now a carpeter has returned.

L44

[L44] Originally **Gorham Silver Manufacturing Company
Building**/now cooperative apartments, 889-891 Broadway, NW
cor. E. 19th St. 1883-1884. **Edward H. Kendall.** Alterations, 1912.
John H. Duncan. ● ⟲
   The skyline labors desperately to achieve a varying picturesque profile, as bits and pieces of roof interlock at random
with the brick façade. Gorham, of course, manufactured silverware. The show windows are elegant billows onto the street. The
1884 building provided two floors for Gorham surmounted by
bachelor apartments!

L45

[L45] Originally **Lord & Taylor Dry Goods Store**, 901 Broadway,
SW cor. E. 20th St. 1869-1870. **James H. Giles.** ● ⟲ Façade
restored. 1990s. **Kutnicki Bernstein.**
   An exuberant cast-iron façade, capped with a dormered
mansard roof. The corner pavilion is reminiscent of the
Renaissance architecture of Prague.

🏠 [L46] Originally **Goelet Building** (lofts), 900 Broadway,
SE cor. E. 20th St. 1886-1887. **Stanford White** of **McKim,
Mead & White.** Enlarged, 1905-1906, **Maynicke & Franke.** ⟲
   Here were bricksmiths: limestone below supports a great set of
Romanesque Revival polychromatic arches. Vandals have removed

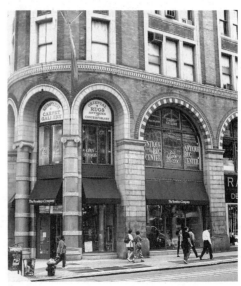

L46

the cornice and defaced the ground floor for dubious commercial enterprises. **Lewis Mumford** in *The Brown Decades* described it as "a building above fashion," but Mumford soon dismissed subsequent MM&W architecture as "learned eclecticism."

[L47] Originally **Warren Building**, 907 Broadway., NW cor. 20th St. 1890. **Stanford White** of **McKim, Mead & White**. ♂
   White trumpeted the Renaissance Revival less than five years after his lusty Romanesque Revival at Goelet, catercorner across the intersection.

[L48] **Theodore Roosevelt Birthplace National Historic Site**, 28 E. 20th St., bet. Broadway and Park Ave. S. Original building, 1848, demolished. Replicated, 1923, **Theodate Pope Riddle**. ♠ ♂
Open to the public: We-Su 9-5; closed Mo & Tu. 212-260-1616.
   After the property was recaptured by the Women's Roosevelt Memorial Association, this structure was built to reproduce the one **Roosevelt** knew (he was born here in 1858 and died elsewhere in 1919). The restoration remembered the house as of 1865, not the much altered building that was demolished in 1916.

L48

[L49] Originally **The Methodist Book Concern** (lofts), 150 Fifth Ave., SW cor. W. 20th St. 1888-1890. **Edward H. Kendall**. ♠
   Romanesque Revival in brick: the ground-floor entrance has been modernized with misunderstanding. Nevertheless, the brick on top still rests on a rock-face granite podium.

[L50] Originally **Presbyterian Building** (lofts), 154-158 Fifth Ave., NW cor. W. 20th St. 1894-1895. **James B. Baker**. ♠
   Baker created this Romanesque Revival building while a neo-Classical counterrevolution was gathering steam at the Chicago World's Fair of 1893. He hopped on board that American Renaissance express and later produced the wondrous Chamber of Commerce of the State of New York in 1901.

L49

[L51] **Merchants' Bank**/Originally Mohawk Building, 160 Fifth Ave., SW cor. W. 21st St. 1891. **R. H. Robertson**. ♂
   This Renaissance Revival pile becomes increasingly complex as it approaches its domical corner tower. Nicely cleaned and restored.

[L52] **Spero Building** (lofts), 19 W. 21st St., bet. Fifth and Sixth Aves. N side. 1907-1908. **Robert Kohn**. ♂
   Boldly scaled Art Nouveau.

L52

[L53] **The United Synagogue of America Building**/originally Scribner Building, 153 157 Fifth Avc., bct. E. 21st and E. 22nd Sts. E side. 1893-1894. **Ernest Flagg**. ●' ♂

The first headquarters built for publishers **Charles Scribner's Sons** by an architect and relative who would later build them a bookstore and headquarters uptown, a printing plant, and a family residence. This chaste façade was once enriched by a broad, semiellipsoidal cast-iron and glass canopy, in the Parisian mode.

L54

[L54] **166 Fifth Avenue** (lofts), bet. E. 21st and E. 22nd Sts. W side. 1899-1900. **Parfitt Bros**. ♂

Terra-cotta Eclectic.

[L55] **938 Broadway**/originally Brooks Brothers store (1884-1915), SE cor. E. 22nd St. 1883-1884. **Charles C. Haight**. Building remodeled, 1935, **Office of Ely Jacques Kahn**. Balance of building redesigned, 1987, **Conklin & Rossant**.

Neo-Art Moderne updates an earlier Art Moderne remodeling. The Brooks Brothers would shudder at this "trendy" styling. Along the Broadway flank is a newly relocated Just Bulbs shop where you can find those spots, floods, tubes, and other exotic bulbs (engineers call them lamps) that can enhance or romance your pad.

L55

[L56] Originally **Hotel 21**, 21 E. 21st St., bet. Broadway and Park Ave. S. 1878. **Bruce Price**. ♂

A socialite architect, Price planned the wealthy suburban private community of Tuxedo Park, N.Y., and designed many of its Shingle Style houses. His daughter, **Emily Post**, dictated social manners to the flock that wanted to join the elite. No. 21, now seedy, is an example of American Queen Anne, a picturesque composition ornamented with its original metalwork. The corbeled column supporting the bay window is a marvelous example of late Victorian structural whimsy.

L56

[L57] **Albert Building**/originally Glenham Hotel, 935 Broadway, SW cor. E. 22nd St. to Fifth Ave. 1861-1862. **Griffith Thomas**. ♂

A dignified neo-Renaissance structure despite the ravages of retail commercialism in its storefronts. Remnants of gilded wood letters that once spelled ALBERT and the projecting clock (stopped) are noteworthy mementos of past gentility.

[L58] **Flatiron Building**/originally Fuller Building, 175 Fifth Ave., E. 22nd St. to E. 23rd St., Fifth Ave. to Broadway. 1901-1903. **Daniel H. Burnham & Co**. ●' ♂ Façade restored, 1991. **Hurley & Farinella**.

The diagonal line of Broadway formed important triangular buildings here and at Times Square. **Burnham** was master of architectural ceremonies at the World's Columbian Exposition in 1893, which changed the course of civic architecture for a generation (its canons are now reappearing in Post Modern dress). In those earlier years Roman and Renaissance Revival architecture gave a face of pomp to commercial and government buildings.

Here rustications are uniformly detailed from ground to sky, in the manner of an elevatored palazzo: limestone at the bottom, giving way to brick and terra-cotta as the floors rise. The acutely chamfered corners give it an exaggerated and dramatic perspective.

L58

It is sometimes (incorrectly) thought to be the first (or at least an early sample) steel-skeletoned skyscraper; dozens of New York commercial buildings had been steel-framed in the 1890s, including the tallest at the time, the 391-foot Park Row Building.

[L59] Originally **Western Union Telegraph Building**, 186 Fifth Ave., SW cor. W. 23rd St. 1884. **Henry J. Hardenbergh**. ♂

L59

A struggling survivor from Hardenbergh's Dakota period, completed that same year. This is one of Fifth Avenue's earliest

L60

commercial buildings, from a time when the fashionable were fleeing to residences further north. Under restoration.

Madison Square and Environs:

[L60] **Madison Square Park**/earlier Madison Square/formerly part of The Parade/originally a potter's field, Fifth to Madison Aves., E. 23rd to E. 26th Sts. Opened, 1847. **Ignatz Pilat** (former assistant to **F.L.Olmsted**). Refurbished, 1999-2000. City Parks Foundation.

The city crept past this point just prior to the Civil War. Madison Avenue springs from 23rd Street on the east flank of the square, bisecting the block from Fifth to Fourth (or Park Avenue South in its 1959 renaming). The commissioners plan of 1811 had shown a Parade from Third to Seventh Avenues, 23rd to 34th Streets, a pleasant void in the surveyor's grid. The present space (6.23 acres) is all that remains of that intention, replaced in scale by Central Park (which had never been a part of the commissioners' scheme).

Statuary: **Chester Allen Arthur**, 1898. **George Bissell**. Admiral **David G. Farragut**, 1880-1881. **Augustus Saint-Gaudens**, sculptor. **Stanford White**, architect. A great and melancholy Art Nouveau memorial. **Roscoe Conkling**, 1893. **John Quincy Adams Ward**. Republican political leader. **William H. Seward**, 1876. **Randolph Rogers**. Lincoln's secretary of state. Here, owing to unsuccessful fund raising, the sculpted body is one that Rogers modeled of Lincoln (with rearranged arms and legs). With Seward's head attached, he holds one sheet of the *Emancipation Proclamation* (Lincoln held two). The **Eternal Light** flagpole is the work of **Carrère & Hastings** (1924).

The Four Squares: The laying out of Union, Gramercy, Stuyvesant, and Madison Squares in the 1830s and 1840s gave promise of urbane residential precincts for wealthy New Yorkers. All four squares were speculative developments in the spirit of London's Bloomsbury and Covent Garden (where the Dukes of Bedford had developed farmland into a grand neighborhood of Georgian architecture and garden squares).

[L61] **Sidewalk clock**, in front of 200 Fifth Ave., bet. W. 23rd and W. 24th Sts. W side. 1909. **Hecla Iron Works**. ●
A shopper's clock from the era when these blocks marked the end of Ladies Mile, an area of mercantile elegance. Its Ionic column signals the Classical allusions of those Edwardian years.

L63

[L62] **Metropolitan Life Insurance Company**, Main Building, 1 Madison Ave. in NE cor. E. 23rd St. to Park Ave. S. 1893. Altered. [L63] **Tower**, SE cor. E. 24th St. 1909. Both by **Napoleon LeBrun & Sons**. Tower altered, 1964, **Lloyd Morgan**. ●
▟ [L64] **North Building**, 11-25 Madison Ave., bet. E. 24th and E. 25th Sts. E side. 1932. **Harvey Wiley Corbett** and **D. Everett Waid**.

The tower was retained as a symbol after its adjacent base was rebuilt; stripped of its ornament, it was, for a long time, used as a warehouse for the company's records—in effect the insured world's attic: now rental offices. At the North Building, note the polygonal modeling of the upper bulk to allow it more grace—a search for form by **Harvey Wiley Corbett** in early modernist architecture—and the wondrous vaulted entrance spaces at each of the 4 corners.

The Gilded Age: Evelyn Nesbit was sixteen and a chorus girl in Floradora when a colleague in the show first brought her to lunch at Stanford White's favorite hideaway, camouflaged behind the nondescript façade of 22 West 24th Street. A few months later she returned for a champagne supper—for two. Afterward, the 48-

year-old architect showed her the tiny room with the immense green velvet couch, where mirrored walls and ceiling glimmered warmly in the glow of hidden lights. In another room a swing hung from the ceiling on red velvet ropes, green smilax trailing from its velvet seat. What dizzying fun it was, she later related in her memoirs, to swing higher and higher across the floor, her feet piercing a huge Japanese paper parasol suspended from the ceiling. In another, velvet-lined room was a four-poster bed with a mirrored canopy lit indirectly by tiny multicolored bulbs. "It's all over, kittens. Don't cry," White begged her when she awoke. "Now you belong to me."

L65a

[L65a] **Serbian Orthodox Cathedral of St. Sava**/ originally Trinity Chapel, 15 W. 25th St., bet. Fifth and Sixth Aves. 1850-1855. **Richard Upjohn.** 🍎
[L65b] **Clergy House**, 16 W. 26th St. 1866. **Richard** and **Richard M. Upjohn.** 🍎 [L65c] **Parish House**/originally Trinity Chapel School, 13 W. 25th St. 1860. **J. Wrey Mould.** 🍎 In the church: **Swope Memorial** reredos, 1892, and altar, 1897. Both by **Frederick Clarke Withers.**

L65c

This complicated midblock complex presents a somber brownstone church and clergy house joined to a playful Ruskinian Gothic polychromatic parish house to the east. An unexpected pedestrian shortcut results, from 25th to 26th Streets. A century of grime conceals the detailing and multicolor of the ensemble. **Edith Wharton**, born nearby, was married here in 1885.

A statue of **Michael Pupin** (1858-1935), a noted physicist of Serbian background, stands in the walkway. Pupin Hall at Columbia University is named for him.

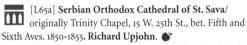

[L66] **Worth Monument**, W. 24th to W. 25th Sts., Fifth Ave. to Broadway. 1857. **James G. Batterson.**

General William J. Worth, hero of the Seminole and Mexican wars, is buried here, one of the city's few interments that is actually under the memorial monument (**General Grant** is entombed in his own mausoleum as well). Here one noted for subduing Native and Hispanic Americans rests under a Renaissance Revival obelisk. Worth Street in Lower Manhattan is named for him.

L66

[L67] Originally **Cross Chambers** (lofts), 210 Fifth Ave., bet. W. 25th and W. 26th Sts. W side. ca. 1895.

A Belle Epoque extravagance with balconies and bay windows. Look up—the riches are on high.

L68

 [L68] **Appellate Division, New York State Supreme Court**, 35 E. 25th St., NE cor. Madison Ave. 1896-1899. **James Brown Lord.** 🍎 Interior. 🍎

This small marble palace is the reincarnation of an 18th-century English country house: Corinthian columned and elaborately crowned with sculpture: *Wisdom and Force* by **Frederick Ruckstuhl** flank the portal; *Peace* by **Karl Bitter** is the central figure on the balustrade facing the Square. *Justice* (fourth from left on 25th Street) is by **Daniel Chester French**, whose seated **Lincoln** chairs the *Lincoln Memorial*.

[L69] **Provident Loan Society of New York**, 346 Park Ave. S., NW cor. E. 25th St. 1909.
　　Three stories of limestone atop a granite base: an English club dispensing credit. It followed in the footsteps of MM&W's nearby bank.

North of Madison Square:

[L70] **New York Life Insurance Company**, 51 Madison Ave., E. 26th to E. 27th St., Madison to Park Ave. S. 1928. **Cass Gilbert**.

　　Limestone Renaissance at the bottom, birthday cake at the top. Gilbert was obsessed with pyramidal hats for his buildings: compare the Woolworth Building (1913) and the Federal Courthouse at Foley Square (1936). Among Gilbert's iconic heirs, and utilizing the license of Post Moderism, **Cesar Pelli**, **Kevin Roche**, **David Childs** (of SOM), **Helmut Jahn**, and others have recently crowned many new towers all over the island.

L70

　　This site has a rich history. It was originally occupied by the Union Depot the New York terminal of the New York and Harlem Railroad. After 1871, when the first Grand Central Station opened at 42nd Street, the Depot was converted to house Gilmore's Garden and then **P. T. Barnum**'s Hippodrome; it was later refinanced and renamed (1879) Madison Square Garden. **Stanford White** then designed a lavish replacement, complete with a tower copied from the Giralda in Seville, which opened in 1892. White was shot on its roof garden in 1906 by **Harry Thaw**, whose wife, the actress **Evelyn Nesbit**, had reputedly been White's mistress before her marriage. One added irony: Madison Square Garden's quarters (two buildings later) are on the site of the demolished Pennsylvania Station, **McKim, Mead & White**'s greatest New York work.

L71

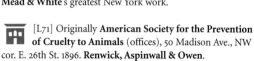 [L71] Originally **American Society for the Prevention of Cruelty to Animals** (offices), 50 Madison Ave., NW cor. E. 26th St. 1896. **Renwick, Aspinwall & Owen**.
　　A proper London club in delicately tooled limestone. Note the elaborately modeled cornice. Even stray mongrels and alley cats deserved distinguished architecture in the 1890s.

END *of Ladies Mile walking tour. The IRT Lexington Avenue line is at Park Avenue South and 23rd Street.*

UNION SQUARE TO GRAMERCY PARK

*A ramble around Union Square, followed by a saunter up Irving Place to Gramercy Park. **START** at Union Square. (Take the IRT Lexington Avenue Line (4, 5, and 6 trains), the BMT Broadway Line (N and R trains), or the 14th Street-Canarsie Line (L train) to the Union Square/14th Street Station.)*

Union Square: First named Union Place, it served as the crotch of Broadway from the southwest and the Bowery (Fourth Avenue at this point) from the southeast—its nickname then was The Forks. Before the Civil War it was a grand residential square, with an iron-fenced public park, primarily for the fashionable town house residents surrounding it, much as Gramercy Park (fenced and locked) still is today. In 1854 it blossomed as a new "uptown" the-atrical district with the opening of the Academy of Music. That venerable house was on the site of the present Con Edison Building, opposite the site of a later, namesake Academy (briefly the Palladium), now another NYU dormitory.

Union Square later became the center of the political left: here, in August 1927, protestors awaited news of the execution of **Sacco** and **Vanzetti**. May Day, the annual celebration of socialism, brought a million to this mecca where the *Daily Worker* and many other radical publications and organizations abounded.

[W1] **Union Square Park**, E. 14th to E. 17th Sts., Union Sq. W. to Union Sq. E. Laid out, 1830. Opened to public, 1839. Rebuilt, 1986. **Bronson Binger**, architect; **Hui Mei Grove**, landscape architect; **N.Y.C. Department of Parks & Recreation, Capital Projects Division. Newsstand**, Union Sq. E. opp. E. 15th St. 1986. **Kuo Ming Tsu**.

The park's raised posture is a latter-day event, allowing the subway to snake through its underworld: the original street-level park with romantically curving pathways was then totally rebuilt as a more formal public place. In those early subway times crowds gathered around their favorite debater to heckle, sup-port, or berate him or her. This was New York's Speakers' Corner; it became a sacred precinct for soapbox orators and other agitators after police excesses in repressing unemployment rallies in the 1930s.

Drug traffickers in the 1960s and 1970s controlled the scene, but the 1986 renovation removed the perimeter screens of green, making all activities within visible and returning the park to a civilized population.

The renovation, designed by the Parks Department's own staff, is the best in anyone's memory: bold replanning of the entry areas, generous stone detailing, railings in scale (for once!) with a public place (using bulbous malleable iron fittings at joints), punctuated with built-up steel and glass kiosks over the subway entrances and for the newsstand, and lighted with ornate multiglobed lamps.

The park abounds in sculpture: *Washington* (**Henry Kirke Brown**, with **J. Q. A. Ward**, sculptors; pedestal by **Richard Upjohn**), a copy of *Houdon's original horseback eulogy*, arrived in 1856. Brown also contributed *Lincoln* in 1866. In 1876 **Bartholdi**, sculptor of the *Statue of Liberty*, left *Lafayette* as a token of Franco-American relations at a point early in his unceasing campaign to raise funds for the base of *Liberty*. The flagpole base is by **Anthony de Francisi**, sculptor.

[W2] **Greenmarket**, along W. 17th St. bet. Broadway and Park Ave. S. at the N edge of Union Sq.

The ephemeral green market, an idea of architect-planner **Barry Benepe**, concerns itself with the serious architecture of cheese, tomatoes, legumes, and other edibles.

W3

[W3] Originally **Lincoln Building**, 1 Union Sq. W., NW cor. E. 14th St. 1889-1890. **R. H. Robertson**. 🌳

Romanesque Revival granite crowned with a cornice of a multitude of little windows separated by paired columns.

[W4] **Spingler Building**, 5-9 Union Sq. W., bet. W. 14th and W. 15th Sts. W side. 1890s.

Tan brick and terra-cotta clothe this modest Romanesque Revival.

[W5] **31 Union Square West**/originally Bank of the Metropolis Building, NW cor. 16th St. 1903. **Bruce Price**. 🌳

An early and unwitting sliver building, this neo-Renaissance slab now houses a restaurant in its original banking rooms, a place for Superman's lunch.

[W6] **Union Building** (condominiums)/originally Decker Building, 33 Union Sq. W., bet. 16th and 17th Sts. 1892-1893. **John Edelmann**, designer. **Alfred Zucker**, architect. Renovated for condominiums, 1990s. **Joseph Pell Lombardi & Assocs**.

Edelman was both mentor and friend of **Louis Sullivan** (and gave him his first "architectural" opportunity, in commissioning him to create the decoration for Sinai Synagogue and frescoes for Moody Tabernacle, both in Chicago). He later introduced him to **Dankmar Adler**. In 1881, the new partnership of **Adler & Sullivan** was born (Auditorium Building, Chicago. 1886. Condict Building, New York. 1897-1898). Here the incised decoration shows what Edelman, in turn, may have learned from Sullivan.

W6

[W7] Originally The Century Building/now **Barnes & Noble Bookstore**, 33 E. 17th St., bet. Park Ave. S. and Broadway to W. 18th St. 1880-1881. **William Schickel**. 🌳 Façade restoration, 1994-1995. **Li-Saltzman Architects**.

This red brick, terra-cotta, and whitestone charmer is where the popular *Century* magazine (for grown-ups) and *St. Nicholas* (for boys and girls) were published before the century turned.

[W8] **Everett Building**, 200 Park Ave. S., NW cor. 17th St. 1908. **Goldwin Starrett & Van Vleck**. 🌳

Goldwin Starrett had worked for four years in the Chicago office of **Daniel Burnham**. Careful, but bland, the Burnham touch did not rub off here.

W9

[W9] **W New York Hotel**/former Guardian Life Insurance Company/originally Germania Life Insurance Company, 201 Park Ave. S., NE cor. E. 17th St. 1910-1911. **D'Oench & Yost**. 🌳

UNION SQUARE TO GRAMERCY PARK

see pages 201–208

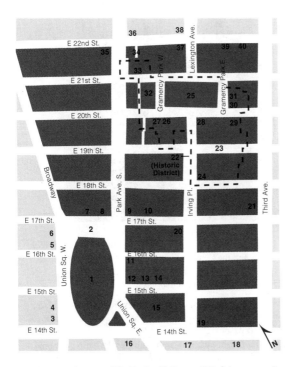

Hotel conversion, 2001. **The Rockwell Group**. [W10] **Annex**, 105 E. 17th St., bet. Park Ave. S. and Irving Place. 1961. **Skidmore, Owings & Merrill**.

The mansarded bulk of this Renaissance Revival marvel is best seen from a distance, down 17th Street or from the adjacent Union Square Park. Germania Life was a name that became an onerous millstone at the advent of World War I. The board of directors agreed to rename it, picking a name with the largest number of reusable letters that they could find. Guardian still crowns the roof against its mansard backdrop. But a rearrangement of Guardian is no help with W New York!

Next door is the sleek annex, a simple grid of aluminum and glass infilled behind with white vertical blinds. As an accessory, it is a graceful annex to the proud parent, unabashedly "modernist," an articulated annex.

[W11] **Zen Palate** (restaurant), SE cor. Union Sqs. E. and E. 16th St. 1990s.

A rich but understated medley of verdigris copper, stucco, and glass block.

[W12] **Daryl Roth Theater**/formerly American Savings Bank/originally Union Square Savings Bank, 20 Union Sq. E., NE cor. E. 15th St. 1905-1907. **Henry Bacon**. ●

A classy Corinthian colonnade is somewhat forlorn in these precincts. Bacon's best remembrance is the Lincoln Memorial. Now a space for spectacular off-Broadway theater.

W12

[W13] **105 East 15th Street** (apartments), bet. Union Sq. E. and Irving Pl. ca. 1900.

Granite shafts support terra-cotta Corinthian capitals, with gray brick and terra-cotta articulating the bayed facade above.

[W14] Century Association Building/now **Century Center for the Performing Arts**, 109-111 E. 15th St. bet. Union Sq. E. and Irving Pl. 1869. **Gambrill & Richardson**. ● Richardson Room converted to theater, 1996-1997. **Beyer Blinder Belle**.

W13

W15

H. H. Richardson in New York? But he joined Gambrill as partner and the Century as a Centurion (member: 1866-1867) after Gambrill had begun the design. Then what happened? Not too much: redbrick and a mansard roof.

[W15] **Zeckendorf Towers** (mixed use), 1 Irving Place, bet. W. 14th and W. 15th Sts. to Union Sq. E. 1987. **Davis, Brody & Assocs.**

Four finials, each with an illuminated, levitating, pyramidal yarmulke, crown a massive commercial bottom. Each finial is a separate apartment tower: a colossal project that blocks the once familiar view of Con Edison's clock tower for users of the park. But well done.

From 1921 until they were demolished in 1985 this was the site of a clutch of small 19th-century buildings that were the home of S. Klein's-on-the-Square, the original discount department store. Above them stood a Times Square-scale neon sign that advertised Klein's name to hordes of shoppers. The modest budget was served there not only with bargains but also occasional high style . . . the latter for those stalwarts with energy and sharp eyes who combed the sea of clothes racks with vigor. (Klein's closed in August 1975.)

*At the southeast corner of 15th Street and Fourth Avenue, later to be included in **Sam Klein**'s empire, stood the original Union Square Hotel. The single-tax economist **Henry George** died here on October 29, 1897. George sought simplification of the maze of taxes that were then only in their infancy. His mind would have boggled at today's Byzantium imposed by federal, state, city, and other taxes.*

W16

[W16] **Union Square South** (apartments, shops, and theaters), 14th St. bet. Fourth Avenue and Broadway. 1999. **Davis Brody Bond** and **Schuman Lichtenstein Claman & Efron**. Artwall, **Kristin Jones** and **Andrew Ginzel**.

Careful urban architecture: a mixed-use complex at a major nexus of mixed uses (within are a Virgin Megastore, a Circuit City, 14 screens of United Artists films, and 240 apartments).

Davis Brody Bond (formerly Davis Brody & Associates) have seemingly cornered the market for new construction around Union Square, much as Gruzen & Partners (once Kelly & Gruzen, now Gruzen Samton) surrounded the Civic Center with new buildings. Here DBB has contributed Zeckendorf Towers, Union Square South, and two new NYU dormitories along 14th Street. In the Civic Center the various Gruzen firms designed the Police Headquarters, the Metropolitan Correction Center, Murry Bergtraum High School, Southbridge Towers, and 100 Gold Street. The good news is that the works of both are serious urbane civic architecture.

W17

[W17] **University Hall** (N.Y.U. Dormitory), 110 E. 14th St., bet. Third and Fourth Aves. 1998. **Davis Brody Bond.**

Precast concrete echoes the limestone of Con Ed across the street. But upstairs, higher tech reigns.

[W18] **N.Y.U. Dormitory,** 126 E. 14th St., bet. Third and Fourth Aves. 2001. **Davis Brody Bond.**

Another step in making the 14th Street/Union Square area into the province of **Davis Brody Bond.** First came Zeckendorf Towers (1987), then both University Hall and the Union Square South building. Now, on the site of the old Academy of Music (more recently the **Arata Isozaki**-designed Palladium), more dormitories.

[W19] **Consolidated Edison Company Building**/originally Consolidated Gas Company Building, 4 Irving Place, NE cor. E. 14th St. 1915. **Henry J. Hardenbergh.** [C19a] **Tower,** 1926. **Warren & Wetmore.**

Hardenbergh, who gave us the Dakota, the Plaza Hotel, and the Art Students League, here delivered a very dull swan song for an establishment client—profitable no doubt, but a far cry from his earlier glories. A landmark clock tops this, Con Ed's GHQ, on the site of the original Academy of Music. The academy's namesake across the street, an aging movie palace, became The Palladium, now demolished for the NYU dormitory above.

W20

[W20] **"Washington Irving House,"** 122 E. 17th St., SW cor. Irving Place. 1845.

Irving's connection with this house is the wishful thinking of an ancient owner; this is one Washington who never slept here. In the real world, **Elsie de Wolfe** and **Elisabeth Marbury** lived here from 1894 to 1911. They maintained a salon where notables from all walks of life gathered amid Elsie's "white decor," the stylistic statement that launched her career as America's first paid (and highly paid) interior decorator. Later, as **Lady Mendl,** she gave parties with as much élan as her decor.

Where ***TIME*** *began: In an upstairs room at 141 East 17th Street in 1922* ***Briton Hadden*** *and* ***Henry Luce*** *wrote the prospectus for what was to become TIME magazine. The rent was $55 a month.*

W21

[W21] Formerly **Tuesday's Restaurant** and **Fat Tuesday's Jazz Club**/previously Joe King's Rathskeller, or The German-American/originally Scheffel Hall, 190 Third Ave., bet. E. 17th and E. 18th Sts. W side. 1894. **Weber & Drosser.**

German-American eclectic Renaissance Revival. The jazz was cool downstairs, where collegians of an earlier generation merely drank beer and made out. Later, youth of all ages could do the same—to jazz rhythms. Once upon a time the massive local immigrant German population centered its recreation here.

Gramercy Park and Environs:

[W22] **Gramercy Park Historic District,** an irregular area including the park, its west and south frontages, and part of that to the east; also much of the north side of E. 18th St., and both sides of E. 19th St. bet. Irving Place and Third Ave., including Calvary Church.

[W23] The Block Beautiful, E. 19th St. bet. Irving Place and Third Ave. Remodeled as a group, 1909, **Frederick J. Sterner**. ♂

A handsome, picturesque architectural unit, notable more for the sum than the parts. No single building is of great distinction; still, it is one of the best places in New York. Treelined, with limited traffic, it is quiet, serene, urbane.

W23

[W24] Pete's Tavern/once Portman Hotel/later Tom Healy's, 129 E. 18th St., NE cor. Irving Place. 1829.

A social landmark since 1903 in a corner tavern that has the patina of age. A shallow sidewalk café bounds two sides, and bare brick brings a vintage experience: good Italian food and burgers. One apocrypha states that **O. Henry** wrote "The Gift of the Magi" in the second booth; but it's a comforting story.

[W25] Gramercy Park, Gramercy Park E. and W., Gramercy Park N. and S., with axis on Lexington Ave. to the N, Irving Place to the S. 1831. **Samuel Ruggles**. ♂

Enlightened self-interest graced the neighborhood with this lovely park. Private and restricted to tenants occupying the original surrounding plots, it is, nevertheless, a handsome space for all strollers to enjoy. Built under the same principles employed by the Dukes of Bedford in London, it shared with Union Square this gracious urban-design approach (speculative housing at Bloomsbury and Covent Garden were made not only more delightful but also more profitable by the addition of parks and squares).

W24

Edwin Booth, brother of Lincoln's assassin **John Wilkes**, lived at 16 Gramercy Park South. His statue stands in the park, placed by sculptor **Edmond T. Quinn** in 1916.

[W26] The Players, 16 Gramercy Park S., bet. Park Ave. S. and Irving Place. S side. 1845. Remodeled, 1888-1889. **Stanford White** of **McKim, Mead & White**. ☙ ♂

Edwin Booth bought this house to found a club for those in the theater (as loosely defined). He was a star in a sense not easily conceivable today, when stars are not so rare. A super brownstone, with White's 2-story Tuscan porch bracketed by great wrought-iron lanterns.

W26

[W27] National Arts Club/originally Samuel Tilden House, 15 Gramercy Park S., bet. Park Ave. S. and Irving Place. S side. 1884. **Vaux & Radford**. ☙ ♂

Here **Calvert Vaux** (say "Vawx") of **Vaux & Radford**, once of Central Park's **Olmsted & Vaux**, reverted to a single architectural commission for **Samuel J. Tilden**, outspoken opponent of the Tweed Ring who was elected governor of New York in 1874. In 1876 Tilden ran for president against **Rutherford B. Hayes**; he won the popular vote by almost 250,000 but lost in the electoral college. Fearful of his personal security in a time of riots, Tilden had rolling steel doors built into the Gramercy Park façade (behind the windows), and a tunnel to 19th Street for a speedy exit in case the doors failed. Gothic Revival in the manner of **John Ruskin**. Brownstone and polished black granite trim. Recently restored.

W27

[W28] Formerly **Benjamin Sonnenberg House**/formerly Stuyvesant Fish House, 19 Gramercy Park S., SE cor. Irving Place. 1845. Altered. ♂

John Barrymore lived here while working on Broadway. Ben Sonnenberg was an oldtime publicist as renowned as **Ivy Lee & T. J. Ross**, or **Edward L. Bernays**, the advisor to **John D. Rockefeller** who recommended that Rockefeller give away dimes prolifically to little kids.

[W29] **The Brotherhood Synagogue**/originally Friends Meeting House, 28 Gramercy Park S., bet. Irving Place and Third Ave. S side. 1857-1869. **King & Kellum.** ● Remodeled as synagogue,

1975, **James Stewart Polshek & Partners.** ♂

An appropriately spartan brownstone box built for the Quakers and now converted to a synagogue.

[W30] **The Gramercy**/originally Gramercy Park Hotel, 34 Gramercy Park E., NE cor. E. 20th St. 1883. **George W. da Cunha.** ♂

A craggy, mysterious red brick and red terra-cotta pile whose Queen Anne forms are among the city's most spectacular. Look up to terra-cotta Indians, eagles, and geometry.

W30

[W31] **36 Gramercy Park East** (apartments), bet. E. 20th and E. 21st Sts. E side. 1908-1910. **James Riely Gordon.**

The uptown brethren of this neo-Gothic, white terra-cotta, bay-windowed apartment house have been mostly demolished to build apartments with more floors and lower ceilings. Gargoyles!

W31

[W32] **3 and 4 Gramercy Park West**, bet. E. 20th and E. 21st Sts. W side. 1846. Ironwork by **Alexander Jackson Davis**?

Notable ironwork over plain brick bodies. Davis was one of America's most versatile 19th-century architects, his other New York City work ranging from the Italianate Litchfield Villa in Prospect Park to that transported Parthenon, the Federal Hall National Memorial on Wall Street.

[W33] **Calvary Church** (Episcopal), 273 Park Ave. S., NE cor. E. 21st St. 1848. **James Renwick, Jr.** [W33b] **The Sunday School Building**, to N on Park Ave. S. 1867. **James Renwick, Jr.** ♂

Second-echelon Renwick, its wooden towers long since removed because of deterioration. The adjacent Sunday school pavilion is now rented as offices.

W33

[W34] **Protestant Welfare Agencies Building**/ originally Church Missions' House, 281 Park Ave. S., SE cor. E. 22nd St. 1894. **Robert W. Gibson** and **Edward J. N. Stent.** ● Restored, 1990s. **Kapell & Kastow.**

A glassy, articulated stone office building inspired by and equal to commercial buildings of the Flemish and Dutch Renaissance. Lovely. It provides generous light and a sleek glass wall to the street.

W34

W35

W38

W40

[W35] **Gramercy Place** (apartments)/originally New York Bank for Savings, 280 Park Ave. S., SW cor E. 22nd St. 1894. **C. L. W. Eidlitz**. Alterations to bank building and new apartment tower, 1987, **Beyer Blinder Belle**.

The shell of the old Bank for Savings presents a historical streetfronted corner entrance to an otherwise ordinary apartment tower—a link with lower Fourth Avenue history.

[W36] Originally **United Charities Building**, 287 Park Avenue S., NE cor. E. 22nd St. 1891. **R. H. Robertson** and **Rowe & Baker**.

Though ornamented, a bulky and boring work. Even Robertson could occasionally produce a bland product.

[W37] **Sage House** (apartments)/originally Russell Sage Foundation, 4 Lexington Ave., SW cor. E. 22nd St. ca. 1914. **Grosvenor Atterbury**. Tower added, ca. 1919.

Converted to apartments in 1975, this lovingly detailed Renaissance Revival rockface, rusticated sandstone building continues to bear traces of its original mission, e.g., the frieze: FOR THE IMPROVEMENT OF SOCIAL AND LIVING CONDITIONS. Among early works of the philanthropic foundation was Forest Hills Gardens.

[W38] **Mabel Dean Bacon Vocational High School**/originally Manhattan Trade School For Girls, 127-129 E. 22nd St., NW cor. Lexington Ave. 1915. **C. B. J. Snyder**.

No nonsense here: 10 stories of loft space for vocational education. The exterior, however, displays some handsome terra-cotta detailing.

[W39] **134 East 22nd Street** (apartments), bet. Lexington and Third Aves. Converted to apartments, 1975, **William B. Gleckman**.

A 7-story brown brick apartment house that yearned to be Milan in New York. The crossover balconies (for fire exits from duplex units) provide large-scaled architectural form.

[W40] **150 East 22nd Street** (carriage house), bet. Lexington and Third Aves. 1893. **S. V. Stratton**.

A Dutch gable presents its stepped brickwork to the street.

STUYVESANT SQUARE & NORTH

[S1] **Stuyvesant Square Historic District**, generally including the Square, its entire frontage on Rutherford Place, partial frontages on E. 15th and E. 17th Sts., and parts of E. 15th, E. 16th, E. 17th, and E. 18th Sts. bet. Second and Third Aves. ●

A complex area of widely mixed uses: the side streets are graced with groups of homogeneous row houses; the blocks facing the square bear religious buildings and, outside the district, hospitals. Third Avenue, to which the district barely extends, is the neighborhood shopping strip.

[S2] **Stuyvesant Square Park**/originally Stuyvesant Square, Second Ave. bet. E. 15th and E. 17th Sts., Rutherford and Nathan D. Perlman Places. 1836. Reconstructed, 1936, **N.Y.C. Department of Parks.**

This pair of parks bisected by Second Avenue brings the English tradition to what was once a strictly residential neighborhood. Squares in London are fenced green areas unlike the paved piazze, plazas, Plätze, or places of continental Europe. This duo, a gift of **Peter G. Stuyvesant**, benefited the city as well as owners of the surrounding land: the first in urban grace, the latter in future profits. Statuary: *Peter G. Stuyvesant* (1936. **Gertrude Vanderbilt Whitney**).

S3

[S3] **David B. Kriser Psychiatric Day Treatment Program**/originally Sidney Webster House, 245 E. 17th St., bet. Second and Third Aves. 1883. **Richard Morris Hunt.**

A brick and brownstone gesture to the French Renaissance.

[S4] **Hazelden New York**/formerly Salvation Army/originally St. John the Baptist House, 231-235 E. 17th St., bet. Second and Third Aves. E part, 1877, **Emlen T. Littel.** W part, 1883, **Charles C. Haight.**

Picturesque, asymmetrical Victorian Gothic. The outpost of a famous Minnesota rehab.

S4

[S5] **St. George's Church** (Episcopal), Rutherford Place, NW cor. E. 16th St., facing Stuyvesant Sq. 1846-1856. **Blesch & Eidlitz.** ●

[S6] Originally **St.George Memorial House**/now apartments, 207 E. 16th St. 1886. **Cyrus L. W. Eidlitz.**

[S7] **Chapel**, 4 Rutherford Place. 1911-1912. **Matthew Lansing Emery** and **Henry George Emery.**

[S8] **Henry Hill Pierce House**/originally Rectory, 209 E. 16th St. Early 1850s. **Leopold Eidlitz.**

S5

J. P. Morgan's church: stolid brownstone Romanesque Revival, bald and bold, cut and dressed. The adjacent chapel, outclassed by its parent, is in an overdressed Eclectic-Romanesque Revival. And around the corner on 16th Street, Pierce House, a late medieval Germanic tower, its brownstone rock faced, punctuates the streetscape.

[S9] **Friends Meeting House and Seminary**, 221 E. 15th St. NW cor. Rutherford Place, facing Stuyvesant Sq. 1860. **Charles T. Bunting.** ●

Appropriately austere Quaker architecture, a spartan image that spoke well to the era of austere modernist architecture. Here packaged in red brick, brownstone quoins, and white trim.

S9

[S10] **St. Mary's Catholic Church of the Byzantine Rite**, 246 E. 15th St., SW cor. Second Ave. 1964. **Brother Cajetan J. B. Baumann.**

A concrete and stained-glass box that glows polychromatically on the nights it is lit within.

[S11] **Old Stuyvesant High School**, 345 E. 15th St., bet. First and Second Aves. N side. ●

S10

STUYVESANT SQUARE & NORTH
see pages 209–211

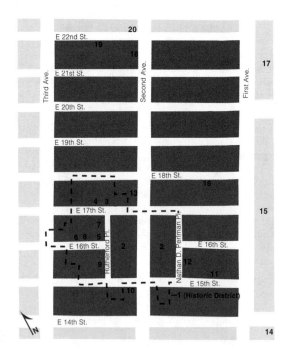

The City's prestige academic high school, its admission by examination. Most of its graduates go on to prestige colleges.

S12

[S12] Originally New York Infirmary/now **Bernstein Pavilion, Beth Israel Hospital**, Nathan D. Perlman Place, bet. E. 15th and E. 16th Sts. E side. 1950. **Skidmore, Owings & Merrill**.

Modernist architecture can become dated more rapidly than that of any other period. Here a bold 1950 "statement" seems a bore in retrospect. Alterations, of course, have dimmed its elegant detailing: clunky windows have replaced those of considerable style.

S13

[S13] **Apartments and offices**/originally Lying-In Hospital, 305 Second Ave., bet. E. 17th and E. 18th Sts. W side. 1902. **R. H. Robertson**. Converted, 1985, **Beyer Blinder Belle**.

Swaddled babies lurk in laurel wreaths in the spandrels. Otherwise this bland neo-Renaissance block is boring until the top, where a Palladian crown surmounts it all. Architects of the turn of the 20th century, concerned about the idea of a New York skyline, occasionally neglected the pedestrian, spending all their efforts—and money—against the sky.

S14

[S14] **Immaculate Conception Church** (Roman Catholic)/ originally Grace Chapel and Dispensary (Episcopal), 406-412 E. 14th St., bet. First Ave. and Avenue A. 1894-1896. **Barney & Chapman**.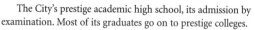

These François I-style buildings, built as an outpost of Grace Church, were purchased by the Roman Catholic archdiocese in 1943. Their picturesque forms might be found in the Loire Valley as well as those of their uptown descendant, Holy Trinity, in Yorkville.

[S15] **Stuyvesant Town** (apartment complex), E. 14th to E. 20th Sts., First Ave. to FDR Drive/Avenue C. 1947. **Irwin Clavan** and **Gilmore Clarke**.

Tax abatement allowed this Metropolitan Life Insurance Company project to supply middle-income housing to servicemen returning from World War II. The early brutality of this huge, dense (8,755 families) project is now softened by trees. Innocuous architecture, but, nevertheless, landscaping has made it a pleasant place.

S16

[S16] **326, 328, and 330 East 18th Street** (row houses), bet. First and Second Aves. 1853. 🍎

Deep front yards have caused this tiny trio to be overlooked but certainly not neglected; the charming original cast-iron work is reminiscent of New Orleans. An early development for land east of Third Avenue here leased from Cornelia Stuyvesant Ten Broeck.

[S17] **Peter Cooper Village** (apartment complex), E. 20th to E. 23rd Sts., First Ave. to FDR Drive. 1947. **Irwin Clavan** and **Gilmore Clarke**.

More space and more rent make this the rich stepbrother of Stuyvesant Town.

[S18] **Church of the Epiphany** (Roman Catholic), 373 Second Ave., bet. E. 21st and E. 22nd Sts. W side. 1967. **Belfatto & Pavarini**.

Highly styled brown brick: this is the phoenix of a 19th-century church on this site destroyed by fire. The most positive modern religious statement on Manhattan Island to date.

S20

[S19] **220 East 22nd Street** (apartments), bet. Second and Third Aves.

A conversion similar to that at 134 East 22nd.

[S20] **Gramercy House** (apartments), 235 E. 22nd St., NW cor. Second Ave. 1929-1930. **George & Edward Blum**.

An Art Deco frieze bands this early Modern apartment house in glazed terra-cotta.

S18

B2

ROSE HILL

A precinct seeking a name; 23rd to 32nd Street, Madison to Third.

[B1] **Madison Square Station, U. S. Post Office**, 149 E. 23rd St., bet. Lexington and Third Aves. 1937. **Lorimer Rich**, architect. **Louis A. Simon**, Supervising Architect of the Treasury.

A cool, stripped Classical building in polished dark red granite that was, surprisingly, in its time, the idiom of 1930s Washington, **Albert Speer**'s Berlin, or the revived memory of the mortuary temple of **Queen Hatshepsut** at Deir-eal-Bahari (1500 B.C.). Plus ça change . . .

B1

*Financier **Bernard Baruch**, City College Class of 1889, millionaire at 30 (in 1898: equal to $50,000,000 in Y2K) advised **President Woodrow Wilson** at the Versailles World War I peace conference, and subsequently counseled **Presidents Coolidge, Harding, Hoover, Roosevelt** and **Truman**. The Bernard M. Baruch School of Business and Public Administration of The City College first occupied the original 23rd Street site of the College (which had been there from its founding in 1847 to its move uptown to Hamilton Heights in 1907). In 1968 **Baruch College** was designated a senior college on its own.*

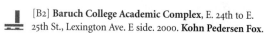

[B2] **Baruch College Academic Complex**, E. 24th to E. 25th St., Lexington Ave. E side. 2000. **Kohn Pedersen Fox**.

A megamammoth for the complex functions of an urban college; keeping up with City College's North Academic Center (which **Pedersen** designed in the offices of **John Carl Warnecke**) and **Ulrich Franzen**'s East and West Buildings for Hunter College. An ocean liner beached, its mini-city components stashed in a dizzying and magnificent interplay of vertical interlocking spaces flooded with light (a ten-story atrium).

[B3] **Newman Library and Technology Center, Baruch College**/originally Lexington Building (cable-car power station), 151 E. 25th St., bet. Lexington and Third Aves. 1895. **G.B.Waite**. Remodeled as library, 1994. **Davis Brody Bond**.

Roman brick and grand arches shelter Baruch's books in a properly monumental found shell (DBB has inserted a high-

B3
tech interior that has become the resident hermit crab). A

ROSE HILL

see pages 212–215

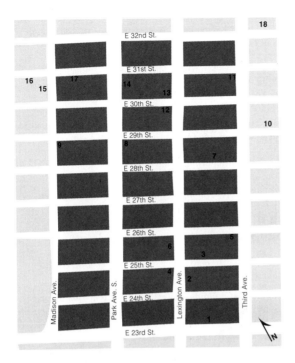

E 32nd St.

E 31st St.

E 30th St.

E 29th St.

E 28th St.

E 27th St.

E 26th St.

E 25th St.

E 24th St.

E 23rd St.

Madison Ave. S.

Park Ave. S.

Lexington Ave.

Third Ave.

N

painted sign, Fiss, Doerr & Carroll Horse Co. (carriages, wagons, & harnesses), remembered buildings next door. Lexington Avenue's cable cars were the last to be installed in the nation, running from 23rd to 105th Streets.

[B4] Originally B. W. Mayer Building (offices)/now **Friends House in Rosehill**, 130 E. 25th St. SW cor. Lexington Ave. 1915-1916. **Herman Lee Meader**. Restored, 1995-1996. **Cindy Harden & Jan Van Arnam**.

A simple terra-cotta facade by the architect of the amazing Cliff Dwellers' Apartments on Riverside Drive at West 96th Street. Now a hostel for AIDS. Coiled snakes and cattle skulls lurk about the second floor.

B4

[B5] Originally "**l Love You Kathy**" (apartments), 160 E. 26th St., SW cor. Third Ave. Altered, 1975, **Stephen B. Jacobs**.

The 26th Street façade is stuccoed sculpture, a classy solution to the architecture of fire escapes when altering an old tenement. (The building's name refers to the developer's emotional life.)

B5

[B6] Originally **69th Regiment Armory, N. Y. National Guard**, 68 Lexington Ave., bet. E. 25th and E. 26th Sts. W side. 1906. **Richard Howland Hunt** and **Joseph Howland Hunt**. 🐚

The armory of the Armory Show of 1913, the bombshell entry of cubist painting to America (**Picasso, Cézanne, Braque, Gaugin, Van Gogh, Matisse** were all there; but the show was stolen by **Marcel Duchamp**'s *Nude Descending a Staircase*; **President Roosevelt** called the show's exhibitors "a bunch of lunatics"). A brick, mansarded palace with gun bays surveying Lexington. The drill hall behind the Lexington Avenue façade shows its barrel form to the street, ribbed and buttressed with an exposed, articulated structure.

B6

B7

Presidential inauguration: *Such ceremonies normally take place in Washington. But on September 20, 1881,* **Chester A. Arthur** *was sworn in as president in the front parlor of his home at 123 Lexington Avenue, north of East 28th Street, by* **Judge John Brady** *of the New York State Supreme Court. The assassination of* **James A. Garfield** *had unexpectedly promoted Vice-President Arthur to the post.*

[B7] **St. Stephen's Church** (Roman Catholic), 149 E. 28th St., bet. Lexington and Third Aves. 1854. **James Renwick, Jr.** Extended to N, 1865, **Patrick Charles Keely**. Restored, 1949. School, ca. 1902, **Elliott Lynch**.

Brownstone Romanesque Revival and within, an airy hall. Its slender cast-iron (plaster encased) columns with elaborate foliated capitals support multiribbed vaulting. There is a mural by **Constantino Brumidi**, "decorator" of the Capitol in Washington. Unfortunately, the whole has been smoothed over in brownstone-colored stucco.

[B8] **Bowker Building** (offices), 419 Park Ave. S., SE cor. E. 29th St. 1927. **Walter Haefli** in the **Office of Ely Jacques Kahn**.

A strange multihued, almost phosphorescent, terra-cotta-clad building. Its polychromy suggests an unknown Islamic Industrial style.

B9

[B9] **Emmet Building** (offices), 89-95 Madison Ave., SE cor. E. 29th St. 1912. **J. Stewart Barney** and **Stockton B. Colt**, associated architects.

A terra-cotta neo-Renaissance confection, in the spirit of the Woolworth Building. Note particularly the canopied cavaliers and courtesans atop the first floor. Atop the top Dr. Emmet, its gynecologist-owner, maintained an apartment.

B10

[B10] **203 East 29th Street** (house), bet. Second and Third Aves. 1790? (carriage house). 1870 (house). **James Cali**, architect. **John Sanguiliano**, restoration architect.

A rare wood frame building, particularly in the Manhattan streetscape—not hidden in some out-of-the-way backyard. It seems too prim for its surrounding neighbors.

[B11] **Kips Bay Branch, New York Public Library**, 446 Third Ave., SW cor. E. 31st St. 1971. **Giorgio Cavaglieri**.

A sculptured corner-turner along Third Avenue. Just enough of a widened sidewalk to invite its users to enter.

B11

A touch of India: *The area around 28th Street, between Madison and Third Avenues, is a minibazaar of foods, fabrics, and other delicacies from the Indian subcontinent. Spice & Sweet Mahal (135 Lexington Ave., cor. E. 29th St.), for example, purveys freshly prepared snacks and desserts for sidewalk feasting, as well as the normal stock of canned and packaged foods. Diaphanous fabrics for saris are available elsewhere in this area, as well as oriental rugs.*

Old Print Shop, 150 Lexington Ave., bet. E. 29th and E. 30th Sts. W side.

Appropriately humble, like the rich wearing old clothes (or is it reverse snobbery?), a mine of maps and prints, from modest to very expensive.

[B12] **First Moravian Church**/originally Church of the Mediator (Baptist), 154 Lexington Ave., SW cor. E. 30th St. ca. 1845.

A plain brick box with gabled roof and tall, narrow, half-round arched windows. A modest gem in Lombardian Romanesque.

[B13] **Touro College, Lexington Avenue Campus**/formerly Pratt-New York Phoenix School of Design/originally New York School of Applied Design for Women, 160 Lexington Ave., NW cor. E. 30th St. 1908-1909. **Harvey Wiley Corbett**. 🍎

A great tour de force of neo-Roman design: a veritable 20th-century temple to the arts. Note the witty, single polished gray marble column (in antis) on the Lexington Avenue façade. It is said that Corbett's atelier of fledgling architects worked on the drawings.

B13

[B14] **Raymond R. Corbett Building**/originally Iron Workers Security Funds (offices), 451 Park Ave. S., bet. E. 30th and E. 31st Sts. E side. Altered, 1978. Addition, 1988, **Susana Torre** of **Wank, Adams, Slavin & Assocs.**

This "Cor-Ten" building (rusty steel meant to be rusty) expanded upward, with a new façade worthy of the union leader for whom it was renamed.

[B15] **American Academy of Dramatic Arts**/originally The Colony Club, 120 Madison Ave., bet. E. 30th and E. 31st Sts. W side. 1904-1908. **Stanford White** of **McKim, Mead & White**. 🍎 Original interiors, **Elsie de Wolfe**, designer.

B15

Georgian-Federal Revival seems appropriately not-so-fancy dress for venerably connected and socially prominent ladies. The brickwork is unusual, with the headers (short ends) facing out. Stanford White, its designer, succumbed to an assassin during its construction—and only 3 blocks away.

[B16] **22 East 31st Street** (row house), bet. Fifth and Madison Aves. 1914. **Israels & Harder.**

A very mannered Georgian Revival town house with—surprise!—7 stories.

B16

[B17] **Madison Avenue Baptist Church Parish House**, 30 E. 31st St., bet. Madison Ave. and Park Ave. S. 1906.

An offbeat gem in brick and limestone. Middle Eastern motifs decorate a Romanesque Revival body. Atop it all is a copper cornice forming an overhanging eave supported by exotic brackets.

[B18] **Milton Glaser, Inc.** (design studio)/originally Tammany Central Association Clubhouse, 207 E. 32nd St., bet. Second and Third Aves. ca. 1910.

Beaux Arts pomp and circumstance orphaned when its row house neighbors were removed for an apartment house plaza and a schoolyard. Stylish tenants have honored and been honored by its rich architecture.

B17

Baseball's beginnings: A plaque once affixed at the southeast corner of Lexington Avenue and 34th Street stated that at this site Alexander Joy Cartwright, Jr. organized the first baseball game played in America using most of the rules governing today.

B18

K2
KIPS BAY

From 23rd to 34th Streets between Second Avenue and the East River.

[K1] **East Midtown Plaza** (apartment complex), E. 23rd to E. 25th Sts., bet. First and Second Aves. 1972, 1974. All by **Davis, Brody & Assocs**.

Urbane street architecture, with the terraces of Babylon. This is an ode to brick, cut, carved, notched, and molded. The "balconies" are the essence of architectural space and form, not the common "luxury apartment" paste-ons.

K1

[K2] **Public Baths, City of New York**, E. 23rd St., NE cor. Asser Levy Place, bet. First Ave. and FDR Drive. 1904-1906. **Arnold W. Brunner** and **William Martin Aiken**. Restored, 1989-1990. Department of Parks.

Roman pomp was particularly appropriate for a public bath, a Roman building type we reproduced indiscriminately for other functions (cf. the now demolished Pennsylvania Station modeled on the Baths of Caracalla). These public baths are, in that sense, our Baths of Roosevelt (Teddy) or, on a local level, the Baths of McClellan (mayor of New York).

[K3] **United Nations International School**, 24-50 FDR Drive, opp. E. 25th St. S of Waterside. 1973. **Harrison, Abramovitz & Harris**.

A bulky, white precast-concrete block clumsily hugging the East River shore and Waterside; an illogical site for students in need of large-volume public transportation.

K4

[K4] **Waterside** (apartment complex), FDR Drive bet. E. 25th and E. 30th Sts. E side. 1974. **Davis, Brody & Assocs**.

Brown towers of a cut and carved cubism mounted on a platform tucked in a notch of the East River. Sixteen hundred units, shopping restaurants, and pedestrian plazas give a share of Manhattan's glorious waterfront back to the people. Wander about, and to the water's edge. Try not to notice the bleakness of the barren, relentlessly paved central space.

K5

[K5] **The Water Club** (restaurant), 500 E. 30th St. at the East River. 1982. **Michael O'Keeffe**, owner-designer; **Clement J. Benvenga** and **Mullen Palandrani**, architects; **M. Paul Friedberg**, landscape architect.

KIPS BAY

see pages 216–220

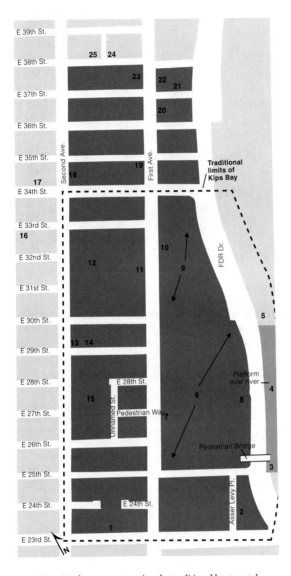

A Post Modern structure using the traditional bent-metal materials from which its wharf predecessors—alas, largely demolished—were often crafted. Popular with the "enjoy dinner with a view of Newtown Creek across the river" set. Drop in for a drink.

[K6] **Bellevue Hospital Center**, E. 25th to E. 30th Sts., First Ave. to FDR Drive. 1908-1939. **McKim, Mead & White**. [K6a] **Psychiatric Hospital**, Charles B. Meyers and Thompson, Holmes & Converse.

Its old brick hulk is now squeezed between the parking garage addition on First Avenue and a giant 22-story "wing" facing the river. The top floors and roof contain the only serious architectural embellishments: Roman brick, Corinthian columns, and pitched tile roofs. "Belle Vue" was the name of **Peter Keteltas**'s farm, which occupied this site in the 18th century.

[K7] **Bellevue Hospital Entrance Arch**, 27th St., E side of First Ave. 1995. **Lee Harris Pomeroy Assocs**.

Neo-Baroque-Romanesque-Revival? But a grand way to greet the unhappy patrons of the Hospital.

K7

[K8] **New Building, Bellevue Hospital**, E. 27th to E. 28th Sts. 1974. **Katz, Waisman, Weber, Strauss; Joseph Blumenkranz; Pomerance & Breines; Feld & Timoney**. Parking garage, 1965.

A behemoth. Each floor is 1½ acres of loft space served by 20 elevators. It's the tall beige cube you pass on the FDR Drive.

[K9] Original **Mount Sinai-N.Y.U Medical Center**, behind Skirball Institute, bet. E. 30th and E. 34th Sts. E side to FDR Drive. 1950. **Skidmore, Owings & Merrill**. Additions through 1977.

K8

A teaching hospital can attract staff and faculty of the highest stature. They are provided for here in a facility complementing Bellevue Hospital, designed in a single master plan by SOM, and constructed over more than 25 years. White glazed brick and aluminum sash.

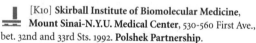

[K10] **Skirball Institute of Biomolecular Medicine, Mount Sinai-N.Y.U. Medical Center**, 530-560 First Ave., bet. 32nd and 33rd Sts. 1992. **Polshek Partnership**.

The multipurpose slab that serves as entrance to the whole medical complex. Above the vast lobby are 5 floors of biomolecular research topped by 20 floors of faculty offices and staff apartments. Behind, the various elder components of the complex unfold.

[K11] **Greenberg Hall, N.Y.U. Medical School** (housing), 545 First Ave., bet. E. 31st and E. 32nd Sts. W side. 1986. **Pomerance & Breines**.

A simple slab with elegant details. Gray brick, with subtle limestone bandings, is enhanced with vermilion window frames.

[K12] **Kips Bay Plaza** (apartment complex), E. 30th to E. 33rd Sts., First to Second Aves. S Building, 1960. N Building, 1965. **I. M. Pei & Assocs.** and **S. J. Kessler**.

K11

New York's first exposed concrete apartment houses, joined soon after by Chatham Towers (1965, **Kelly & Gruzen**) and Pei's own University Plaza (1966). No longer either fashionable or economically feasible, concrete has been replaced by stone, usually granite, in the buildings of the 1980s and 1990s.

The vast open space tries to compensate for the huge 21-story building slabs. These are stepchildren of **Le Corbusier**'s Marseilles Block, giant and beautifully detailed concrete buildings in a park. Should buildings define urban pedestrian space—streets, boulevards and plazas—or should they be free-standing objects in a park? In the 1980s and 1990s streets won the game.

K12

[K13] **Pinkerton Environmental Center, Madison Square Boys & Girls Club**, 524-528 Second Ave., NE cor. E. 29th St. 1979. **Wank, Adams & Slavin**, architects. **Zion & Breen**, landscape architects.

The club describes this as "a community garden and nature education center." Go in—it's a lovely oasis.

[K14] **Madison Square Boys and Girls Club**, 301 E. 29th St., bet. First and Second Aves. 1940. **Holden, McLaughlin & Assocs**.

A handsome, no-nonsense early Modern building in salmon brick, with a dado of shining black-glazed tile.

K14

[K15] **Phipps Plaza** (apartment complex), Second Ave. bet. E. 26th and E. 29th Sts. E side. 1976. **Frost Assocs**.

High-rise red brick that caught some styling from East Midtown Plaza to the south. Polygonal diagonal. But it fails to honor any street, as does East Midtown's glorious bow to 23rd.

[K16] **Public School 116**, Manhattan, 220 E. 33rd St., bet. Second and Third Aves. 1925. **William H. Gompert**.

Neo-Romanesque brick, terra-cotta, and limestone. Whimsical figures support arches over the "Boy's" and "Girl's" entrances.

[K17] Originally Civic Club/now **Estonian House**, 243 E. 34th St., bet. Second and Third Aves. 1899. **Thomas A. Gray**.

A lonely limestone Beaux Arts town house commissioned by philanthropist **F. Norton Goddard**.

K17

[K18] **St. Vartan Cathedral of the Armenian Orthodox Church in America**, 620 Second Ave., bet. E. 34th and E. 35th Sts. E side. 1967. **Steinmann & Cain**.

A huge (to accommodate cathedral-sized congregations) and simplified version of early Romanesque Armenian churches in Asia Minor. Note the corner crucifix dovetailings.

[K19] **Permanent Mission of the People's Republic of China to the U.N.**, 350 E. 35th St., SW cor. First Ave. 1990s.

Chinese Post Modern in two-tone polished granite. The canopy is an elegant modern version of the 19th-century Parisian marquise.

K18

[K20] **Manhattan Place** (apartments), 630 First Ave., bet. E. 36th and E. 37th St. E side. 1984. **Costas Kondylis** of **Philip Birnbaum & Assocs**. Plaza, 1984, **Thomas Balsley Assocs**., landscape architects.

A long, tall bay-windowed brick mass forcefully turned on the bias, creating a triangular plaza with fountain. Glitzy polished brass adorns the first few floors; dark anodized aluminum clads the penthouse level (as though the budget for glitz ran out).

[K21] **The Horizon** (apartments), 415 E. 37th St., bet. First Ave. and FDR Drive, to E. 38th St. 1988. **Costas Kondylis** of **Philip Birnbaum & Assocs**.

A mild but hard-edged echo of The Corinthian [K23] but even closer to the river.

[K22] Originally **Kips Bay Brewing Company**, 660 First Ave., bet. E. 37th and E. 38th Sts. E side. ca. 1895. Additions.

Its colorful posters once boasted of lager beer, ales, and porter with views of the curious mansarded cupolas that corner the roof. Brewing has disappeared here; substantial floors once meant for mash cookers and brew kettles now serve the needs of multiple business enterprises.

[K23] **The Corinthian** (apartments), 645 First Ave., bet. E. 37th and E. 38th Sts. W side. 1987. **Der Scutt**, design architect. **Michael Schimenti**, architect.

K23

A high-style fluted tower presents myriad round bay windows. This is reminiscent in detail, but not in urban posture, of the Rockefeller Apartments of Harrison & Fouilhoux, one of the city's few modern apartment buildings of distinction. Many are stylish, but the Rockefeller plan and profile are gorgeous. Here Scutt has excelled.

[K24] **Permanent Mission of Indonesia to the United Nations** (annex), 325 E. 38th St., NE cor. Queens-Midtown Tunnel access road. Complex renovated into single entity, 1998. **The Stephen Jacobs Group**.

A sober assembly of buildings for diplomatic ends.

[K25] **The Whitney** (apartments), 311 E. 38th St., bet. Second Ave. and the Queens-Midtown Tunnel access road. 1986. **Liebman Liebman Assoc**.

Smoothly syncopated balconies with alternating curved and straight edges give this yellow brick slab considerable style.

K25

MADISON SQUARE TO BRYANT PARK

Starting at the north side of Madison Square. The N and R (old BMT) trains dock at 28th Street and Broadway; the IRT (No. 6 train at 28th and Park Avenue South.

Q2

[Q1] Originally **Croisic Building** (offices), 220 Fifth Ave., NW cor. W. 26th St. 1912. **Frederick C. Browne. Rudolph H. Almiroty**, associate architect.

At the top a richly ornamented confection—watch those architectural calories. It stands on the site of another earlier Croisic apartment hotel.

[Q2] **225 Fifth Avenue** (lofts), bet. W. 26th and W. 27th Sts. E side. ca. 1900.

The new marquise (canopy in the French Belle Epoque fashion) adds to this limestone-based blockfront.

Q4

[Q3] **222 Fifth Avenue** (lofts), bet. W. 26th and W. 27th Sts. W side. ca. 1900.

Another blend of new metal and glass with a Classical limestone enframement.

An aside to Sixth Avenue:

[Q4] **Coogan Building**/originally Racket Court Club, 776 Sixth Ave., NE cor. W. 26th St. 1876. **Alfred H. Thorp.**

Dour eclectic Romanesque Revival with a cornice supported by filigreed iron brackets. **Coogan**, incidentally, is the Coogan of Coogan's Bluff, the escarpment that overlooked the New York Giants' Polo Grounds.

Q5

Back to Fifth:

[Q5] **242 Fifth Avenue** (lofts), bet. W. 27th and W. 28th Sts. W side. ca. 1892.

A triumphant pediment crowns this glassy precursor of the post-World War II curtain wall. The ground floor succumbed to "renovation." Is the building as a whole on the way to a new life?

[Q6] **Baudouine Building** (lofts), 1181 Broadway, SW cor. W. 28th St. 1896. **Alfred Zucker.**

A sliver with a temple on top. Peer upward.

Q6

[Q7] **Broadway National Bank**/originally Second National Bank/then National City Bank of New York branch, 250 Fifth Avenue, NW cor. W. 28th St. 1908. **W. S. Richardson** of **McKim, Mead & White.**

One of the few McKim, Mead & White small banking buildings (compare with the one at 55 Wall Street). No great shakes, it is in naively proportioned limestone. White, of course, had been assassinated in 1906.

[Q8] **256 Fifth Avenue** (lofts), bet. W. 28th and W. 29th Sts. W side. ca. 1892.

Terra-cotta virtuosity maximized in a neo-Venetian Gothic, somewhat Moorish phantasmagoria, mostly above the commercialized ground floor.

Q7

[Q9] **Church of the Transfiguration** (Episcopal)/"The Little Church Around the Corner" (Episcopal), 1 E. 29th St., bet. Fifth and Madison Aves. Church, Rectory, Guildhall, 1852. 1849-1850. **Unknown architect(s)**. Lich Gate, 1896. **Frederick Clarke Withers**. Lady Chapel, 1906. Mortuary Chapel, 1908. All ☙.

Its notorious nickname has stuck since 1870, when a fashionable local pastor declined to officiate at the funeral of George

Q8

MADISON SQUARE TO BRYANT PARK

see pages 221–234

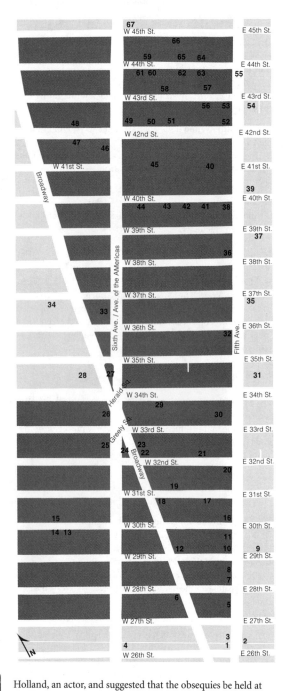

Q9

Holland, an actor, and suggested that the obsequies be held at the "little church around the corner." It has been a church for those in the theater ever since. It has a charming small scale, with a delightful garden.

[Q10] **Marble Collegiate Church** (Dutch Reformed), 1 W. 29th St., NW cor. Fifth Ave. 1851-1854. **Samuel A. Warner.**

Sharp-edged limestone Gothic Revival, contemporary with Grace and Trinity Churches. Clean planes give elegant shade and shadow to the street. Architecturally modest, Marble Collegiate is

Q12

most remembered for its former pastor, **Norman Vincent Peale**, whose many books have tried to meld popular religion with popular psychology. **Richard Nixon** attended this church in his lawyer days, between his roles as vice president and president.

Holland House: The loft building at the southwest corner of Fifth Avenue and West 30th Street [Q11] is the old and famous Holland House Hotel, spruced up in the early 1920s for use as a mercantile establishment. In its original incarnation (1891. **Harding & Gooch***) its opulent interior was adorned with marble, brocade, and lace, and the hotel was considered the peer of any in the world. Its suites were patterned on those of Lord Holland's mansion in London.*

[Q12] Originally **Gilsey House Hotel**/now apartments, 1200 Broadway, NE cor. W. 29th St. 1869-1871. **Stephen D. Hatch.** 🍎

A General Grant Second Empire eclectic extravaganza, columned and mansarded, with the vigor that only the waning years of the 19th century could muster. Cast iron (Daniel Badger Iron Works) and stone . . . but in brown? O happy the day in 1992 when the façade was restored and painted cream!

[Q13] **The S.J.M. Building** (lofts), 130 W. 30th St., bet. Sixth and Seventh Aves. 1927. **Cass Gilbert, Inc.**

Assyrian Revival. An early bronze and glass curtain wall embraced by a pair of masonry elevator towers. Figures in Mesopotanian friezes race around the walls of the building at each setback. And, over the two entrances, stylized symmetrical lions glare in polychromed terra-cotta bas-relief.

Q14

[Q14] Originally **23rd Precinct, N.Y.C. Police Department**/now Traffic Control Division, 138 W. 30th St., bet. Sixth and Seventh Aves. 1907. **R. Thomas Short.** 🍎

Battlements, merlons, embrasures, crenellations—a fortress out of place among loft buildings but serving the area by the contribution of its wit to a midtown canyon.

[Q15] **127 West 30th Street** (offices), bet. Sixth and Seventh Aves. 1920s. New canopy, 1998.

The marquise is making a comeback, and provides, as here, a vital enrichment to the pedestrian's streetscape. Don't you want to go in and look?

Q15

Q16

[Q16] **Wilbraham Building** (originally apartments), 284 Fifth Ave., NW cor. W. 30th St. 1890. **David & John Jardine**.

Brownstone and brick Belle Epoque crowned with a verdigris copper roof—one of the earliest settlers on Fifth Avenue. Here the Brown Decades that preceded the Great White City of the 1893 Chicago World's Fair were still exuding their somewhat murky medievalism, but propped up by Classical composite cast-iron columns and limestone piers.

Q17

[Q17] **Wolcott Hotel**, 4-10 W. 31st St., bet. Fifth Ave. and Broadway. 1904. **John Duncan**.

A lavish French Empire bay-windowed façade—carved, corniced, and mansard-roofed; the style conceals a white and gilt lobby that is both flamboyant and sad.

[Q18] Originally **Grand Hotel**, 1232-1238 Broadway, SE cor. W. 31st St. 1868. **Henry Engelbert**. 🍎

Two blocks from Gilsey, this renewed neighbor is simpler, but its mansarded hat gives it a strong posture on this street.

Q18

*In the 1870s and 1880s the whole section of the W. 20s and W. 30s between the respectability of Fifth Avenue and the slums of Hell's Kitchen (west of Seventh Avenue), was anointed as New York's "Tenderloin." Present Herald Square was at its center. Dance halls and cafés lined up under the el along Sixth Avenue, with bordellos on the shady side streets, all flourishing under Tammany Hall's political machine. A brief period of reform in the 1890s dimmed the gaiety of the Tenderloin, and it's lush facilities slowly faded away. Both the theater and the press (such as **James Gordon Bennett's** New York Herald) made brief stops at Herald Square in the 1890s on their way north—leaving behind one of two squares with newspaper names.*

Q20

[Q19] **Herald Square Hotel**/originally Life Building, 19 W. 31st St., bet. Fifth Ave. and Broadway. 1894. **Carrère & Hastings**.

This ornate Classical façade once enclosed the offices of the very literate humor magazine *Life* (from which the present Time-Life organization bought the name in 1936). Visible mementos include the inscriptions "wit" and "humor" and a pattern of L's back to back on handsome iron balconies. Some gross alterations mar the cornice and windows.

[Q20] **Kaskel & Kaskel Building**, 316 Fifth Ave., SW cor. W. 32nd St. 1903. **Charles L. Berg**.

A wonderful crusty old Beaux Arts building, in the process of being devoured by its crummy commercial occupants.

Q21

[Q21] **Best Western Hotel**/originally Hotel Aberdeen, 17 W. 32nd St., bet. Fifth Ave. and Broadway. 1890s.

The Parisians would call it Pompier (or Fireman Style!), after the ornate boulevard facades of the the 1890s: with neo-Baroque Composite columns support carving worthy of (but different from) churrigueresque Spanish Colonial works of the 17th century.

[Q22] **Holiday Inn**/formerly Hotel Martinique, 53 W. 32nd St. (also known as 1260-1266 Broadway), NE cor. Broadway. 1897-1900. Enlarged with annex, 1907-1911. Both by **Henry J. Hardenbergh**. ☙

An opulent French Renaissance pile, topped with several stories of mansards; the south façade is the real front. For years a notorious shelter for the homeless, now reclaimed for the middle class tourist.

 [Q23] **Wilson Building**, 1270-1280 Broadway, bet. 32nd and 33rd Sts. E side. 1911-1912. **Rouse & Goldstone**.

The arcade and cornice at the roof are an elegant crown for the rusticated body below.

[Q24] **Greeley Square**, intersection of Sixth Ave. and Broadway, bet. W. 32nd and W. 33rd Sts. Designated, 1894.

Horace Greeley, founder of the *New York Tribune*, is remembered by this triangle and a statue (1890. **Alexander Doyle**).

Q24

[Q25] **Manhattan Mall**/originally Gimbel Brothers Department Store, 1275 Broadway, bet. W. 32nd and W. 33rd Sts. opp. Greeley Sq. W side. 1908-1912. **D. H. Burnham & Co**. Converted to mall, 1987-1989. **RTKL Assocs**.

A neo-Classical box by Chicago's Burnham was hollowed out, then enveloped in glass for a Post Modern galleria for Brooklyn's A & S; after that great store's demise it has become a Stern's with continuing mall partners. High above 32nd Street, the multistory connecting bridge (look up!) is a copper-clad Art Deco sleeper (1925) by **Shreve, Lamb & Harmon**, of Empire State Building fame.

Q25

[Q26] **Herald Center**/originally Saks & Company (department store) later Saks-34th Street, 1311 Broadway, bet. W. 33rd and W. 34th Sts. 1901-1902. **Buchman & Fox**. Rebuilt, 1982-1985, **Copeland Novak, & Israel** and **Schuman Lichtenstein Claman & Efron**.

A bulbous blue whale with a demure identification sign and—a first for New York—glassed-in elevators that twinkle their way upward at the 34th Street corner.

[Q27] **Herald Square**, intersection of Sixth Ave. and Broadway bet. W. 34th and W. 35th Sts. *Minerva, the Bellringers, and Owls*, 1895. **Antonin Jean Carles**, sculptor. Plaza, 1939-1940, **Aymar Embury II**.

Namesake of the *New York Herald*, whose 2-story palazzo (1893, **McKim, Mead & White**) stood just to the north, this small triangular park is dominated by the newspaper's once crowning clock. Every hour Stuff and Guff, the bronze mannequins, pretend to strike the big bell as Minerva supervises from above. Don't confuse this square with Greeley Square to the south.

[Q28] **Macy's Department Store**, W. 34th to W. 35th Sts., Broadway to Seventh Aves. Original (Broadway) building, 1901-1902, **De Lemos & Cordes**. Successive additions to W, 1924, 1928, 1931. All by **Robert D. Kohn**.

Q28

The oldest (eastern) part of "the world's largest store" is sheathed in a dignified Palladian façade. The newer (western) parts grew increasingly Art Deco in style. At the southeast corner of the block there once was the world's busiest hot dog stand with a MACY's sign on top. It's actually a 5-story 19th-century building bought around 1900 for an outrageous $375,000 by **Robert S. Smith**, Macy's neighbor at its old location at 14th and Sixth. Smith was thought to be acting as a spoiler on behalf of the owners of Siegel-Cooper who had completed what they believed to be the world's largest store in 1896. Macy's imperiously built around the corner holdout by creating a right-angled arcade so its window shoppers could traverse the department store's perimeter without passing Smith's frontage. The arcade is gone and Macy's went on to lease the façade for a monster sign with Smith's heirs and their successors, the Rockaway Company.

The Broadway entrance and show windows have been remodeled, but the 34th Street side shows the handsome original details; note the canopy, clock, and the hefty turn-of-the-century lettering. The main floor has succumbed to a neo-Art Deco renovation. However, a quartet of older caryatids guards the 34th Street entrance (**J. Massey Rhind**).

Q29

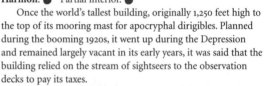 [Q29] Originally **Spear & Company** (furniture store)/now retail stores and offices, 22 W. 34th St., bet. Fifth and Sixth Aves. 1934. **DeYoung & Moscowitz**.

Now decrepit and ill-loved, it was a startling Modern work for Midtown when completed during the Great Depression. Its antecedents in the work of **Willem Dudok** in the Netherlands and in Great Britain's cinema designs of the 1930s are evident (if you take the trouble to look beneath the retail camouflage that scrambles its façade today).

Q30

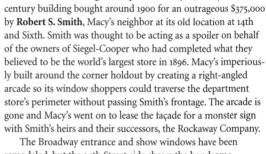 [Q30] **Empire State Building**, 350 Fifth Ave., bet. W. 33rd and W. 34th Sts. W side. 1929-1931. **Shreve, Lamb & Harmon**. 🖝 Partial interior. 🖝

Once the world's tallest building, originally 1,250 feet high to the top of its mooring mast for apocryphal dirigibles. Planned during the booming 1920s, it went up during the Depression and remained largely vacant in its early years, it was said that the building relied on the stream of sightseers to the observation decks to pay its taxes.

The monumental Fifth Avenue entrance is less interesting than the modernistic stainless steel canopies of the two side-street entrances. All of them lead to 2-story-high corridors around the elevator core (with 67 elevators in it), which is crossed here and there by stainless steel and glass-enclosed bridges.

*Empire State site: This pivotal spot has been occupied by two previous sets of landmarks. From 1857 to 1893 it was the site of two mansions belonging to the Astor family. **Mrs. William Astor**'s place, on the corner of 34th Street, was for years the undisputed center of New York social life, and the capacity of her ballroom gave the name The 400 to the city's elite. But in the early 1890s a feud developed between Mrs. Astor and her nephew, **William Waldorf Astor**, who had the house across the garden, on 33rd Street. He and his wife moved to Europe and had an 11-story hotel built on his property, naming it the Waldorf (the first **John Jacob Astor**'s native village in Germany). Within a year after it opened in 1893, Mrs. Astor wisely decided to move out of its ominous shadow (up to 65th Street and Fifth Avenue) and put a connecting hotel, the Astoria, on her property. When the 16-story structure was completed in 1897, the hyphenated hotel immediately became a social mecca. The requirement of full formal dress (tails) in the Palm Room created a sensation even then, but made it the place to be seen. Successful as it was, the old Waldorf-Astoria operated under a curious agreement that the elder Mrs. Astor could have all connections between the buildings walled up at any time on demand.*

[Q31] Originally **B. Altman & Company** (department store) 361 Fifth Ave., bet. E. 34th and E. 35th Sts. E side. 1905-1906. Extended, 1914. **Trowbridge & Livingston**. Converted to The Graduate School and University Center, CUNY (City University of New York), Fifth Ave. end and New York Public Library Science, Industry and Business Library, Madison Ave. end. 1996. **Gwathmey Siegel & Associates**.

Q31

Even after the first Waldorf-Astoria opened in 1897, Fifth Avenue from the 30s north remained solidly residential. **Benjamin Altman** made a prophetic breach by moving his department store from Sixth Avenue and 18th Street to this corner. To make the change less painful, it was designed (on its Fifth Avenue frontage) as a dignified 8-story Renaissance Revival block; the Fifth Avenue entrance shows the atmosphere Altman was trying for. Altman's set off a rush of fashionable stores to Fifth Avenue above 34th Street. Many of them made a second jump, to the 50s, leaving Altman's behind and, ironically, isolated.

[Q32] **390 Fifth Avenue**/formerly Russek's Furs/originally Gorham Building, SW cor. W. 36th St. 1906. **Stanford White** of McKim, Mead & White. Alterations. ●❜

When Altman's opened at 34th Street, Gorham's, the famous jewelers, had just completed its Italian Renaissance palace. Russek's kept the fine architecture largely intact. The lower floors have been grossly altered, but the original columns and arches are visible on the 36th Street side. Above is a superb crowning cornice.

Q32

The Garment Center: The West 30s have been the center of sewing fabrics, ruffles, and lace since entrepreneurs discovered the wealth of labor in vast pools of urban immigrants—once eastern European, now sometimes Hispanic, sometimes Asian. Fashion designers still hover around these needle-trade blocks, where the hand-sewer still vies with the machine needle. Nowadays, however, uptowners in other businesses (architects, lawyers, for example) have moved in, and condominium residences are rife. Constant threats of removal to distant pools of "more economic" labor surface, but where is this breed of economics reborn, and re-reborn again: Nueva York.

[Q33] originally Greenwich Savings Bank/now **Republic National Bank**, 1352-1362 Broadway, NW cor. W. 36th St. and Sixth Ave. 1922-1924. **York & Sawyer**. ●❜ Interior ●❜

Giant Corinthian columns march around 3 sides of this templelike bank; inside, more Corinthians define a grand elliptical rotunda with a central skylight.

Keens Chop House, 72 West 36th Street, just east of Sixth Avenue. Founded in 1878. A fixture in this area, dating back to its Tenderloin days. Known for its mutton chops (hard to find in the city's restaurants) and a display of thousands of clay pipes, each numbered and keyed to a master list, smoked by its many satisfied customers. The pipes are arrayed on the dining room's ceilings!

Q33

[Q34] **Church of the Holy Innocents** (Roman Catholic), 128 W. 37th St., bet. Seventh Ave. and Broadway. S side. 1870. **Patrick Charles Keely**.

Light sandstone and darker brownstone intermingle in this Gothic Revival church, more elegantly detailed than the prolific Keely's usual red brick models. Savor the ceiling within.

Q34

Q35

[Q35] **409 Fifth Avenue** (offices)/originally Tiffany's, SE cor. E. 37th St. 1906. **Stanford White** of **McKim, Mead & White**. Altered.

Finished within the year after the Gorham Building by the same architects, this more massive structure was modeled after the Palazzo Grimani in Venice. The 37th Street side retains the original motif of three ranks of giant paired Corinthian columns shouldering a broad cornice.

[Q36] **Lord & Taylor**, 424-434 Fifth Ave., NW cor. W. 38th St. 1914. **Starrett & Van Vleck**.

This and the old W.&J. Sloane store on the block to the south (now replaced by an office building) were the first along the Avenue to dispense with colonnades and look frankly commercial. It is pleasantly uncomplicated in the middle floors but has a grand palazzo cornice on high.

Q36

A few notions: The side streets between Fifth and Sixth Avenues in the upper 30s are full of suppliers of trimmings for garments and millinery, and their windows are a great show. Beads, rhinestones, spangles, and laces predominate on West 37th Street; milliners' flowers and feathers, on West 38th.

Q38a

[Q37] **Keppel Building**, 4 E. 39th St., bet. Fifth and Madison Aves. 1905. **George B. Post & Sons**.

The gargoyles on this small side-street building's cornice will watch you intently as you examine the sculpted heads of Whistler and Rembrandt.

[Q38a] **Republic National Bank Tower**, incorporating the former Knox Hat Building, 452 Fifth Ave. SW cor. W. 40th St. W side. 1981-1983. **Attia & Perkins**. [Q38b] Formerly **Republic National Bank Building**/originally Knox Hat Building, 452 Fifth Ave., SW cor. W. 40th St. 1902. **John H. Duncan**. 🍎

Overhead, the new digital tidal wave swells over the old Knox Building, built as an exuberant Classical showcase for **Col. Edward M. Knox**, hatter to presidents.

Q39

[Q39] **461 Fifth Avenue** (offices), NE cor. E. 40th St. 1988. **Skidmore, Owings & Merrill**.

The conservative Modernists who brought us Lever House have switched here to Post Modern (technological division), with exposed, pedimented trusswork for wind bracing decorating the building form. Atop it all is a fancy hat added to the styl-

Q40

ish ones already filling the skyline. The innovative and ultra-refined precast-concrete curtain wall, evoking memories of bent metal office cubicles (and clerks with green eyeshades), is a refreshing note.

Q40

[Q40] **The New York Public Library**, Fifth Ave. bet. W. 40th and W. 42nd Sts. W side. 1911. **Carrère & Hastings**. Lions, **E. C. Potter**, sculptor. Figures over fountains, **Frederick MacMonnies**, sculptor. ☛ Partial interior ☛ Restoration and renovations: Periodicals Reading Rooms, 1985, **Giorgio Cavaglieri** and **Davis, Brody & Assocs**. Murals, **Richard Haas**. Gottesman Exhibition Hall, 1986; Celeste Bartos Forum, 1987; and other spaces, all by **Davis, Brody & Assocs**. Rose Main Reading Room Restoration, 1998. **Lewis Davis** of **Davis Brody Bond**. Open to the public: Mo & Th-Sa 10-6; We 11-7:30; closed Su. 212-870-1630.

The apogee of Beaux Arts for New York, a white marble "temple" magnificently detailed inside and out, entered over extravagant terraces, imposing stairs, and post-flamboyant fountains, all now happily restored. Here knowledge is stored in a place worthy of aspiration—a far cry from one's local library-supermarket. The Roman Renaissance detailing is superb.

The 1980s restorations gave back public spaces claimed by librarydom's bureaucracy. Some are breathtaking; others, divorced from posters, prints, and paintings on the walls, produce a shadowless *Last Year at Marienbad* surrealism.

The 1998 renovation of the Main Reading Room is, in the words of critic **Carter Wiseman**, an event "that makes one not only proud to be a New Yorker, but an American…The oak gleams, the brass shines, and the baroque clouds of the freshly painted ceiling soar heavenward beyond the surrounding office towers."

Q41

[Q41] **The Columns** (apartments)/originally The Engineers Club, 3 W. 40th St., bet. Fifth and Sixth Aves. 1906. **Whitfield & King**.

Brick and limestone Georgian and Renaissance Revival. Giant Corinthian pilasters give this a scale appropriate to the New York Public Library opposite.

[Q42] **American Standard Building**/originally American Radiator Building, 40 W. 40th St., bet. Fifth and Sixth Aves. 1924. **Hood & Fouilhoux**. Addition, 1937, **André Fouilhoux**. Hotel conversion, 2000. **William Tabler** and **David Chipperfield**. ☛

Q42

The centerpiece in a row of Renaissance club façades is designer Hood's black brick and gold terra-cotta, Gothic-inspired tower. The first-floor façade, of bronze and polished black granite, and the black marble and mirror-clad lobby are worth a close look.

Poetic and artistic allusions include **Georgia O'Keeffe**'s *Radiator Building–Night, New York,* and in words (*Architecture* magazine. 1925): "the black…suggesting a huge coal pile, and the gold and yellow of its higher points the glow of flames of an unbanked fire." Wow!

Not to be outdone, famed renderer **Hugh Ferriss** declaimed in 1929: "It has probably provoked more arguments among lay-men on the subject of architectural values than any other struc-ture in the country."

Now a boutique hotel.

Q43

[Q43] Originally Republican Club/now **Daytop Village**, 54-56 W. 40th St., bet. Fifth and Sixth Aves. 1904. **York & Sawyer**.

Monumental Tuscan columns ennoble the grand portal of this rehabilitation center.

Q44

[Q44] **Bryant Park Studios**/originally Beaux Arts Studios, 80 W. 40th St., SE cor. Sixth Ave. 1901-1902. **Charles A. Rich**.

A Beaux Arts extravaganza. Double-height studios gather north light from across Bryant Park via double-height windows.

The land of Bryant Park and the Public Library was set aside in 1823 by the City as a potter's field. The Egyptian-style Croton Reservoir, with walls 50 feet high and 25 feet thick around a 4-acre lake, was completed on the Fifth Avenue side (site of The New York Public Library) in 1842. The locale was still at the northern fringe of the city in 1853 when New York's imitation of London's Crystal Palace opened on the park site; it burned down in 1858. The park was established in 1871 and in 1884 was named for **William Cullen Bryant**, *well-known poet and journalist; in 1899-1901 the reservoir was razed to make way for the library.*

Q45

[Q45] **Bryant Park**/originally Reservoir Square, Sixth Ave., bet. W. 40th and W. 42nd Sts. E side. 1871. Redesigned, 1934, **Lusby Simpson**. Scenic landmark ●✴ . Library stacks extended beneath park, 1989, **Davis, Brody & Assocs**. Surface reconfigured, 1989, **Hannai Olin**, landscape architects. Park restoration, 1992; Bryant Park Grill and Café, 1995. **Hardy Holzman Pfeiffer**.

Midtown's only large green space. A serene and formal gar-den redesigned (in its 1924-1989 state) through a competition among unemployed architects. Ringed by allées of trees and

Q45

filled with statues of **William Cullen Bryant** (1911. **Herbert Adams**), Phelps-Dodge copper magnate **William E. Dodge** (1885. **J. Q. A. Ward**), Goethe (1932. **Karl Fischer**), and **Jose de Andrada**, father of Brazil's independence (1954. **Jose Lima**), and formerly, a convention of drug pushers. The druggers moved out as New Yorkers regained the turf, one step behind the Hardy Holzman Pfeiffer/Hannai Olin-designed renaissance.

[Q46] **Bell Atlantic**/originally New York Telephone Company (offices), 1095 Sixth Avenue, bet. W. 41st and W. 42nd Sts. W side. 1970. **Kahn & Jacobs**.

Prominently sited, tall, and carrying a curiously modulated curtain wall that changes scale as it rises from Sixth Avenue's sidewalk. Ho-hum.

[Q47] Originally **Bush Tower** (offices), 130-132 W. 42nd St., and 133-137 W. 41st St., bet. Sixth Avenue and Broadway. 1916-1918; 1921. **Helmle & Corbett**.

Q47

This building rises 480 feet from a base only 50 by 200 feet, built by the developers of Brooklyn's vast industrial complex, Bush Terminal. Note the trompe l'oeil brickwork on its east flank. The "Terminal" is a set of immense warehouses along Brooklyn's waterfront, a staggering concept, the administration of which was operated from these eyries.

[Q48] **World's Tower Building**, 110 W. 40th St., bet. Sixth Ave. and Broadway. 1915. **Buchman & Fox**.

An elaborate and unique terra-cotta prism in the Beaux Arts mode. Sandwiched between two lower adjacent buildings, it presents 4 ornate façades; one of Edward West Browning's terra-cotta-clad developments.

[Q49] **Home Box Office Inc.** (offices)/originally Bryant Park Building, 1100 Sixth Avenue, NE cor. W. 42nd St. ca. 1912. Converted for HBO, 1985, **Kohn Pedersen Fox Assocs**.

A tedious mirrored curtain wall sitting atop a thermal granite base that attempts to tame the excesses of 42nd Street's other tawdry retail shops into a coherent whole. **Cecil B. De Mille** would have been proud of the romantic lobby. But all that square-gridded glass is a signal for the the demise of such curtain walls, originally reflecting an older, stone city and now reflecting merely other glassy neighbors.

Q49

[Q50] **W. R. Grace Building** (offices), 1114 Sixth Avenue, SE cor. W. 43rd St., also known as 41 W. 42nd St., bet. Fifth and Sixth Aves. 1974. **Skidmore, Owings & Merrill**.

A disgrace to the street. Bowing to that era's zoning requirements for setbacks produced an excuse to develop the flashy

Q50

swooping form that interrupted the street wall containing Bryant Park. The plaza behind is a bore.

[Q51] **State University College of Optometry**/formerly City University Graduate Center, CUNY/originally Aeolian Hall, 33 W. 42nd St., bet. Fifth and Sixth Aves. 1912. **Warren & Wetmore**. Redesigned, 1970, **Carl J. Petrilli & Assocs**.

What was once a concert hall and then a five-and-ten is now a bluestone-floored pedestrian arcade forming an elegant short-cut between 42nd and 43rd Streets. It also affords access to the college's spaces above and library and auditorium below, as well as a pass-through gallery for exhibitions of art and design. **George Gershwin** introduced *Rhapsody in Blue* in Aeolian Hall with **Paul Whiteman**'s orchestra in 1924.

Subway passage: Connecting the 42nd Street Station of the Sixth Avenue IND and the Fifth Avenue Station of the IRT Flushing Line is an underground passageway (1975. **N.Y.C. Transit Authority architecture staff***) that is rare for the city: It is well lighted, lined with dapper, leather-colored structural tile blocks, and enhanced by a group of bold photographic enlargements of nearby street scenes, old and new, transferred to porcelain enamel panels. Among the views are those of today's Bryant Park when it was the site of New York's Crystal Palace, the Latting Observatory tower, and the old Croton Reservoir.*

Q52

Q53

[Q52] **500 Fifth Avenue** (offices), NW cor. W. 42nd St. 1931. **Shreve, Lamb & Harmon**.

A 699-foot-high phallic pivot that once balanced a great tin can marked "500," and now simply supports an unadorned cooling tower.

[Q53] **Manufacturers Hanover Trust Company branch**/originally Manufacturers Trust Company, 510 Fifth Ave., SW cor. W. 43rd St. 1954. **Charles Evans Hughes III** and **Gordon Bunshaft** of **Skidmore, Owings & Merrill**. 🍎

This building led the banking profession out of the cellar and onto the street; a glass-sheathed supermarket of dollars. The safe in the window is a symbolic descendent of **Edgar Allan Poe**'s purloined letter.

Q55

[Q54] **Israel Discount Bank**/originally Postal Life Insurance Building, 511 Fifth Ave., SE cor. E. 43rd St. 1917. **York & Sawyer**. Remodeled, 1962, **Luss, Kaplan & Assocs., Ltd.**, designer.

Superb renovation of a Renaissance Revival bank interior. All the old fittings that could be kept have been; everything added is clearly new.

Q56

[Q55] **Sidewalk clock**, in front of 522 Fifth Ave., SW cor. W. 44th St. 1907. **Seth Thomas Company**. 🍎

As the European church signaled the hour to the town dweller, here the minutes are displayed for the more time-conscious American. The pair of harmonizing bollards are happy post-landmark-designation additions.

[Q56] **Unification Church Headquarters**/formerly Columbia University Club/originally Hotel Renaissance, 4 W. 43rd St., bet. Fifth and Sixth Aves. 1900. **Howard, Cauldwell & Morgan**, with **Bruce Price**.

A simplified Renaissance Revival palazzo, less elegant than the Century across the street—and inflated. **John Galen Howard** eventually became the architect of the University of California at Berkeley.

Q57

[Q57] **The Century Association**, 7 W. 43rd St., bet. Fifth and Sixth Aves. 1891. **Stanford White** and **Joseph Wells** of **McKim, Mead & White**. 🍎

A delicate Palladian façade for a club of artists, professionals, and intellectuals. The large window above the entrance was originally an open loggia.

[Q58] **25 West 43rd Street** (office building/longtime home of *The New Yorker* magazine, bet. Fifth and Sixth Aves. 1920s.

Several floors of this building were occupied from 1925 to 1991 by *The New Yorker* magazine; lurking about were such luminaries as **E.B. White, James Thurber, John Cheever, John Updike, Brendan Gill, A. J. Liebling, Calvin Trillin, Peter Arno,** and **Saul Steinberg.** Read the plaque. If you couldn't find them here, maybe they were at the Algonquin Round Table, across 44th Street.

[Q59] **Algonquin Hotel**/originally The Puritan Hotel, 59 W. 44th St., bet. Fifth and Sixth Aves. 1902. **Goldwin Starrett.** 🗝

The hotel/restaurant has a neo-Renaissance façade like many others, but it has long been a rendezvous for theater and literary figures. In the 1920s its Oak Room housed America's most famous luncheon club, the Round Table, around which **Franklin P. Adams, Robert Benchley, Harold Ross, Dorothy Parker,** and others sat (and ate, and talked, and drank, and drank, and drank).

Q59

1903 Algonquin prices: Sitting room, library, dining room, 3 bedrooms, 3 baths, private hall—$10.00/day. Bedroom and bath—$2.00/day.

🏛 [Q60] **Association of the Bar of the City of New York,** 37 W. 43rd St. and 42 W. 44th St., bet. Fifth and Sixth Aves. 1895. **Cyrus L. W. Eidlitz.** 🗝

A Classical limestone structure with the massive sobriety of the law. Doric, Ionic, and Corinthian orders are all there. But as an ensemble, it has the austere elegance of Greek architecture of the 5th century B.C.

Q60

[Q61] **Royalton Hotel,** 44 W. 44th St. bet. Fifth and Sixth Aves. Interiors, 1988. **Philippe Starck** and **Gruzen Samton.**

High French style brought to the public spaces and rooms of what then became a "boutique" hotel.

[Q62] **University of Pennsylvania (Penn) Club**/briefly Touro College/onetime Army & Navy Club of America/originally The Yale Club, 30 W. 44th St., bet. Fifth and Sixth Aves. 1900. **Tracy & Swartwout.**

A brick and limestone clubhouse in inflated and flamboyant neo-Georgian. George IV with elevators?

Q62

[Q63] **General Society of Mechanics and Tradesmen (Building)**/originally Berkeley Preparatory School, 20 W. 44th St., bet. Fifth and Sixth Aves. 1891. **Lamb & Rich.** Extension, 1909, **Ralph S. Townsend.** Open to the public. 🗝

A free evening technical school founded in 1820 is housed in this dour Classical structure. The interior is a surprise: a 3-story gallery-ringed drill hall housing a library and exhibits of old locks, the John H. Mossmann Collection. Savor particularly "A Very Complicated Lock."

Q63

📷 [Q64] **Harvard Club,** 27 W. 44th St., bet. Fifth and Sixth Aves. 1894. Major additions, 1905, 1915. **Charles McKim** of **McKim, Mead & White.** 🗝 Addition, 1989. **Edward Larrabee Barnes Assocs.**

Behind the modest but elegant neo-Georgian exterior are some imposing spaces; their large scale can be seen on the 45th Street rear façade. Barnes has designed an addition that enhances the facilities without competing with MM&W. It is rumored that sometimes applicants seek Harvard admission just for the future opportunity of joining here.

Q64

Q65

[Q65] **New York Yacht Club**, 37 W. 44th St., bet. Fifth and Sixth Aves. 1900. **Warren & Wetmore.** 🕊

A fanciful example of Beaux Arts design, neo-Baroque division, with windows that bear the sterns of old ships drooling pendant waves, and worked in among the columns. The America's Cup was born here.

[Q66] **Hotel Webster**/originally Webster Apartments, 38-42 W. 45th St., bet. Fifth and Sixth Aves. 1904. **Tracy & Swartwout.**

A wonderful rusticated base supports a simple brick body.

[Q67] **1166 Sixth Avenue** (offices), bet. W. 45th and W. 46th Sts. E side. 1973. **Skidmore, Owings & Merrill.**

A black Saran Wrap lemon—but only fiscally—when the bottom dropped out of the 1970s real estate boom, making it impossible to find a tenant. Finally, in 1977, it became a commercial condominium. Sleek and restrained, it is now vigorously occupied. Its midblock plaza is a very popular lunchtime picnic spot for nearby office workers.

ICP/MIDTOWN: The International Center of Photography's central business-district branch is located off the 45th St. side of 1166's plaza. A fine street-level display of photographic exhibitions that change regularly and also a source of selected books on photography. This is an adjunct of ICP's main exhibition space at 1130 Fifth Avenue. Open to the public: Tu 11-8; We-Su 11-6; closed Mo. 212-768-4682.

The closest subways *(B, D, F, and Q trains) are at 47th-50th Street/Rockefeller Center Station of the IND Sixth Avenue Line.*

MADISON SQUARE GARDEN TO THE JAVITS CENTER

In 1904 the Pennsylvania Railroad opened its tunnel under the
Hudson and cut a broad swath to its monumental 2-block-square
station (opened 1910), erasing some of the Hell's Kitchen tenements. (In the 1930s Lincoln Tunnel approaches cut down more.)
The new station quickly attracted the equally monumental
General Post Office, some major hotels, and a cluster of middle-
class department stores, which found the precinct an ideally convenient goal for their march up Sixth Avenue from 14th Street. By
the 1920s garment manufacturing had moved from the Lower East
Side into the streets surrounding these pivot points. Today's garment industry is concentrated in the West 30s and 40s between
Sixth and Eighth Avenues, with suppliers of fabrics, trimmings,
and such located to the east as far as Madison Avenue.

J1

In the 1980s the precinct was reactivated, with, most prominently, the Javits Center as its economic if not spiritual leader.

[J1] **Hotel Pennsylvania**/sometime New York Penta/onetime
Statler/originally Hotel Pennsylvania, 401 Seventh Ave., bet. W.
32nd and W. 33rd Sts. W side. 1918. **McKim, Mead & White**.

Like its neighbor to the south, the former Equitable
Building—not to be confused with its downtown namesake—
this Classical block is set back 15 feet from the building line in
response to the old Pennsylvania Station colonnade that faced it.
It was a center for the big bands of the 1930s, and **Glenn Miller**
wrote a tune called "Pennsylvania 6-5000," still the hotel's phone
number, now converted to all digits.

[J2] **Madison Square Garden Center**, W. 31st to W. 33rd St.,
Seventh to Eighth Aves. 1968. **Charles Luckman Assocs**.

Anybody who remembers the vast Roman Revival waiting
room and even vaster iron-and-glass train shed of **Charles
McKim's** (**McKim, Mead & White**) 1910 Penn Station will feel
bereaved here.

The replacement entertainment and office complex covering
two blocks includes a 20,000-seat "garden," a 1,000-seat "forum," a
500-seat cinema, a 48-lane bowling center, a 29-story office building, an exposition "rotunda," an art gallery, and the usual dining,
drinking, and shopping areas—all above the railroad station,
which was underground to begin with but had a ceiling 150 feet
high. The present "garden," the third one and closer to Madison
Square than the second, is housed in a precast concrete-clad
cylinder and roofed by a 425-foot-diameter cable structure that
only physically replaces its magnificent noble predecessor.

At one time it was to be demolished and moved two blocks
west to make room for a high-rise office tower in the form of a
fish by Los Angeles architect **Frank Gehry**. Too bad the plan fell
through.

J2

MADISON SQUARE GARDEN TO THE JAVITS CENTER

see pages 235–238

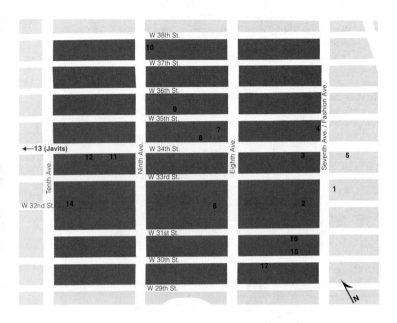

The Underground Pennsylvania Station: It was still called Penn Station, up till its reincarnation in the old General Post Office building across Eighth Avenue. From 1963 until 2000 it occupied little more than a rabbit warren under the 2-square-block Penn Plaza office building and Garden.

*On August 2, 1962 a band of architects picketed—alas, unsuccessfully—against the demolition of the **McKim, Mead & White***'s *grand Roman cum Modern glass-and-steel train shed Penn Station. Organized by AGBANY, the Action Group for Better Architecture in New York, a group of young New York architects including **Norval White, Jim Burns, Jordan Gruzen, Norman Jaffe, Diana Kirsch, Jan Rowan, Peter Samton,** and **Elliot Willensky,** among others, picketed with posters prepared by students at all of the city's architectural schools. Among the architectural notables it attracted for picketing and television interviews were **Philip Johnson, Peter Blake, Aline Saarinen, John Johansen,** and board members of the Museum of Modern Art.*

J3

[J3] **Long Island Railroad Entrance Pavilion**, W. 34th St. bet. Seventh and Eighth Aves. 1990-1994. **R. M. Kliment & Frances Halsband**, in association with TAMS.

An ethereal cage of metal and glass signals the entrance to Long Island transit. Elegant.

J4

[J4] **Nelson Tower** (offices), 450 Seventh Ave., bet. W. 34th and W. 35th Sts. W side. 1931. **H. Craig Severance**.

That slim, mysterious office tower with a rich Art Deco bas-relief at its crown, innocuous close up, is properly savored from afar.

[J5] **Old Navy** (clothing shop), 150 W. 34th St., bet. Seventh Ave. and Broadway. S side. 1999. **James McCullar & Assocs**.

An Art Deco Navy blimp hangar for the hot air of modern merchandising? Glass fiber-reinforced concrete simulates this imagery.

J6

[J6] **James A. Farley Building**/originally General Post Office, Eighth Ave. bet. W. 31st and W. 33rd Sts. W side. 1913. **McKim, Mead & White**. Annex to W, 1935. ❧ Converted to New Pennsylvania Station, 2001. **Skidmore, Owings & Merrill**; **Parsons, Brinckerhoff; Hardy Holzman Pfeiffer**.

The 2-block row of twenty 53-foot Corinthian columns, and what is probably the world's longest inscription, once faced the equally long, somewhat stubbier row of Penn Station's Doric columns.

The near future will reincarnate Pennsylvania Station within these **McKim, Mead & White** folds (but entered on the side streets), a block west from where **Charles McKim** originally planted it, and within yet another embrace of Roman splendor. The embrace will be punctuated by soaring high-tech glass, rending the Post Office's body from 31st to 33rd Streets, and providing a traveler's place of arrival again worthy of this city.

J7

[J7] Originally **New Yorker Hotel**, 481 Eighth Avenue, bet. W. 34th and W. 35th Sts. W side. 1930. **Sugarman & Berger**.

An Art Deco relic, and a popular economy-priced hotel. In its heyday it boasted 92 "telephone girls" at the 41st-floor switchboards, and a 42-chair barber shop with 20 manicurists. In 1976 it became a property of **Rev. Sun Myung Moon**'s World Unification Church.

[J8] **Manhattan Center Studios**/formerly Manhattan Center/ originally Manhattan Opera House, 311 W. 34th St., bet. Eighth and Ninth Aves. 1906. Altered.

A traditional gathering place for union-contract debate and votes. And what about the incised lettering: Ancient Accepted Scottish Rite. Masons? When were they here?

Sound films were still experimental when Warner Brothers, collaborating with Bell Laboratories, exhibited them at the Manhattan Center in 1926, when it was still known as the Manhattan Opera House. Warner created elsewhere, but here was a vast auditorium that preceded by several years Radio City, the Roxy, and other mass places of mesmerization.

[J9] **Midtown South Precinct, N.Y.C. Police Department**, 357 W. 35th St., bet. Eighth and Ninth Aves. 1970. **Frost Assocs**.

A freestanding temple to incarceration; its dark brown brick adds to the gloom of this loft-shadowed side street.

J9

For the Hungry:

[J10] **Manganaro's Grosseria**/originally Ernest Petrucci's (food shop/restaurant), 488 Ninth Ave., bet. W. 37th and W. 38th Sts. E side. 1893.

The architecture of food: pendant, stacked, glazed, bottled, canned—a symphony of color, texture, patina, and aroma. If you pass through, you will reach the Old World (self-service) restaurant. A special place.

Paddy's Market: A stretch of Ninth Avenue, between 36th and 42nd Streets, was for almost 50 years full of pushcart food venders, banished by Mayor La Guardia in the late 1930s. The market soon revived however, as indoor shops with big outdoor displays featuring fresh fruit and vegetables, Italian, Greek, Polish, Spanish, and Philippine products.

J11

[J11] **St. Michael's Church**, 424 W. 34th St., bet. Ninth and Tenth Aves. 1892. Rectory, 1906.

Romanesque Revival limestone church, the wall in rock-face ashlar, the arches and details smoothly contrasting.

[J12] **Spearin Preston & Burrows, Inc**. (offices), 446 W. 34th St. bet. Ninth and Tenth Aves. 1967. **Edelman & Salzman**.

A diminutive office block occupying a curious sliver of land left over to one side of the Lincoln Tunnel approaches.

J12

J13

J15

J17

[J13] **Jacob Javits Convention Center**, Eleventh to Twelfth Aves. bet. W. 34th and W. 37th Sts. 1986. **James Ingo Freed** of **I. M. Pei & Partners. Lewis Turner Assocs.**, associate architects.

Aspiring to be the Crystal Palace of our generation, this shiny black multifaceted set of forms conjures thoughts of geodes, those geological broken remnants that are wondrous but opaque. The ball-jointed space frames within are impressive, a complex world of filigrees against the glass-shielded sky. The first pavilion of this ilk was that of the great London exhibition of 1851, gardener **Joseph Paxton**'s fantastically inflated greenhouse, which housed **Prince Albert**'s attempts to display Britain's industrial revolution to the world. Here the events are more mundane: those of conventioneers both professional and commercial, presenting ideas or products. Paradoxically, the conventions proper are within sealed boxes (artificial controlled light for displays), and only the circulation and access occurs within the transparent shell.

At night, glowing lights give a sense of the Center's sometime transparency; by day the building might just as well be a set of opaque obsidian prisms.

[J14] Originally **Westyard Distribution Center**, Tenth Ave. bet. W. 31st and W. 33rd Sts. E side. (a/k/a 450 West 33rd Street). 1970. **Davis, Brody & Assocs.** Lobby upgrade, 1990. **Der Scutt.**

A gutsy concrete structure that spans the Penn-Central tracks below. Its penthouse once sheltered ice skating, Sky Rink, since removed to sea level at the Chelsea Piers.

[J15] **St. John the Baptist Church** (Roman Catholic), 211 W. 30th St., bet. Seventh and Eighth Aves. 1872. **Napoleon LeBrun.**
[J16] **Capuchin-Franciscan Friary**, 210 W. 31st St. 1975. **Genovese & Maddalene.**

Lost in the Fur District is this exquisite single-spired brownstone church, a Roman Catholic midtown Trinity. The interior, of white marble, radiates light. Worth a special visit. The friary is a banal new work on the opposite block front.

[J17] **Fire Patrol No. 1**, W. 30th St., bet. Seventh and Eighth Aves. 1874.

A mildly ornate eclectic "row house" for the Insurance Company funded patrols that attend major fires, protecting the goods that might potentially be damaged by smoke and, particularly, water.

J14

MURRAY HILL

The country home of **Robert Murray** once stood near where East 37th Street now crosses Park Avenue; it was here that Murray's wife is said to have entertained **General Howe** and his staff while the Revolutionary troops escaped to the northwest. In the late 19th century, social status on the fashionable hill was highest near the great mansions of Fifth Avenue, dropping off toward the east, where carriage houses gave way to tenements at el-shaded Third Avenue. When commerce moved up Fifth Avenue in the early 1900s, Murray Hill became an isolated but vigorous patch of elegance, centered about Park Avenue, where through traffic (first horsecars, then trolleys, now cars) was diverted into the old railroad tunnel from 33rd to 40th Streets. Fashionable Murray Hill has gradually shifted to the east, where carriage houses have become residences, and commerce has made slow but steady inroads on the other three sides.

Murray Hill Walking Tour: Start at Park Avenue and East 34th Street (IRT Lexington Avenue Line (No. 6 train), 33rd Street Station).

[M1] **10 Park Avenue** (apartments), NW cor. E. 34th St. 1931. **Helmle, Corbett & Harrison**.
    The massing of this apartment hotel resembles a larger-than-life crystalline outcropping of some exotic mineral. Its golden-hued brick and expansive windows (divided into tiny panes) foretell an appropriate domestic scale.

M1

[M2] **3 Park Avenue** (office building) and Norman Thomas High School, bet. E. 33rd and E. 34th Sts. E side. 1976. **Shreve, Lamb & Harmon Assocs.**, architects. *Obelisk for Peace*. **Irving Marantz**, sculptor.
    An architectural and fiscal amalgam developed by the Educational Construction Fund. The 42-story sorrel brick tower, turned diagonally to the school and street grid below, springs above its neighbors and is further accentuated at night when its top is bathed in orange light.

M2

*In memory of an armory: Though the picturesque 71st Regiment Armory (1905. **Clinton & Russell**) was demolished to build 3 Park Avenue, its bronze plaque, polished up, graces the terrace wall at East 33rd Street.*

[M3] Originally **Vanderbilt Hotel**/now offices, 4 Park Ave., bet. E. 33rd and E. 34th St. W side. 1910-1913. **Warren & Wetmore**.
    Reconstruction of the lower-floor façades robbed the building of any great street presence, but a low tile vault, cocooned over the years by acoustic ceilings, emerged: see M4 below.

M3

[M4] Originally the **Della Robbia Bar** (also known as The Crypt), 4 Park Ave. NW cor. E. 33rd St. 1910-1913. **Warren & Wetmore**. **R. Guastavino Co.** and **Rookwood Pottery Co.**, builders. 🍎
    The old Vanderbilt Hotel's vaulted crypt sheltered, until recently, what might be termed an Italian rathskeller. The Guastavino vaults are similar to those at Grand Central's Oyster Bar, but embellished by Rookwood's ornaments.

[M5] **33rd Street** (subway) Station under Park Ave. 1904. **Heins & La Farge**. 🍎
    A venerable, if not beautiful, stop on August Belmont's original IRT (Interborough Rapid Transit) line. Terra-cotta eagles remember the armory that stood above at 3 Park Avenue.

[M6] **2 Park Avenue** (offices), bet. E. 32nd and E. 33rd Sts. W side. 1927. **Ely Jacques Kahn**.
    A very neat pier-and-spandrel pattern on the walls of this

office block bursts into Art Deco angular terra-cotta decoration in primary colors at the top. Lewis Mumford wrote in 1928 that the building "...strikes the boldest and clearest note among all our recent achievements in skyscraper architecture."

[M7] **The Madison**/originally Grolier Club, 29 E. 32nd St., bet. Madison and Park Aves. 1889. **Charles W. Romeyn & Co.** ☙

Superb Richardsonian Romanesque with brownstone—smooth, rough, and carved. An unlikely specimen in a street of loft buildings.

M8

[M8] **Remsen Building**, 148-150 Madison Ave., SW cor. E. 32nd St. 1917. Altered ca. 1930, **Frank Goodwillie**.

A modest pattern of Art Moderne terra-cotta at the base, interspersed with strangely contrasting Gothicisms.

M9

[M9] **The Factory (Andy Warhol's place)**/originally New York Edison Company substation, 19 E. 32nd St., 22 E. 33rd St., bet. Fifth and Madison Aves. 158 Madison Ave., bet. E. 32nd and E. 33rd Sts. W side. Remodeled, 1983, **Proposition: Architecture**.

Here were the offices, studio space, and magazine production facilities for the late **Andy Warhol**, who has had a much greater philosophical impact on art than his Campbell's Soup can paintings suggest. As a former Con Ed electrical transformer station, its exterior is properly noted more for its former occupant than its fancy dress.

M10

The Complete Traveller (bookshop), at 199 Madison Avenue. *Travelers and tourists—and otherwise serious people—should mine this lode of guidebooks, maps, and other nuggets for those of the wandering bent. In addition to a clutch of New Yorkiana, those more brave will discover literature on Mongolia, Montparnasse, and even Montana.*

[M10] **Collectors' Club**/originally Thomas B. Clarke House, 22 E. 35th St., bet. Madison and Park Aves. 1902. **McKim, Mead & White.** ☙

A neo-Georgian town house with extravagant small-paned bay windows, reminiscent of the late 19th-century avant-garde work of the talented Briton, **Richard Norman Shaw**. The Composite-columned portal is elegant.

M11

[M11] **Community Church Entrance**, 40 E. 35th St., bet. Madison and Park Aves. 1995. **Mitchell/Giurgola**.

A modest entry for the disabled gives a new presence on the block to this understated church.

M14

MURRAY HILL

see pages 239–244

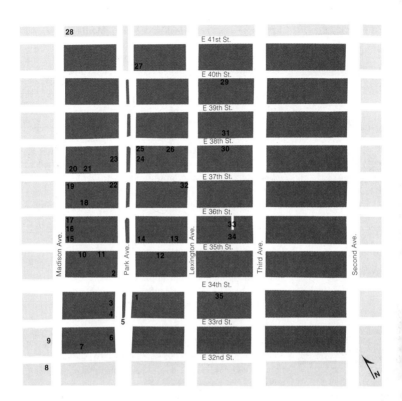

[M12] **The New Church** (Swedenborgian), 112 E. 35th St., bet. Park and Lexington Aves. 1858.

A modest Renaissance Revival complex with a garden providing spatial punctuation to the block.

[M13] **Originally James F. D. Lanier House,** 123 E. 35th St., bet. Park and Lexington Aves. 1903. **Hoppin & Koen.** ●

All intact, inside and out, this Composite-pilastered Beaux Arts town house is the tiara on a block of brownstones. Note the copper roof and dormers.

[M14] **23 Park Avenue** (apartments)/formerly Advertising Club of New York/originally J. Hampden and Cornelia Van Rensselaer Robb House, NE cor. E. 35th St. 1898. **Stanford White** of **McKim, Mead & White.** ●

Stately. An Italian Renaissance palazzo dressed in brown brick and brownstone. Above the first floor, the brownstone switches to terra-cotta.

Once a place to appropriately disguise flamboyant advertising account executives, it now merely shelters condominiums for the more than affluent. **Russel Sturgis,** a prominent critic at the time of its construction, said that it was "not a palace, but a fit dwelling house for a first-rate citizen."

M13

[M15] **Church of the Incarnation** (Episcopal), 205 Madison Ave., NE cor. E. 35th St. 1864. **Emlen T. Littel.** Enlarged, 1882. ●

[M16] **The H. Percy Silver Parish House,** 209 Madison Ave., bet. E. 35th and E. 36th Sts. E side. 1868. **Robert Mook.** Altered, ca. 1905, **Edward P. Casey** ●

Two orphans from Madison Avenue's earlier elite years: a dour Gothic church and a Renaissance Revival town house named for a rector of the adjacent church. Murals by **John La Farge,** stained glass by **Tiffany Studios.**

M15

M17

[M17] **Morgan Court** (apartments), 211 Madison Ave., bet. E. 35th and E. 36th Sts. E side. 1985. **Liebman Liebman & Assocs.**
The sliver replacing J. P. Morgan's onetime carriage house.

[M18] **Pierpont Morgan Library**, 33 E. 36th St., bet. Madison and Park Aves. 1906. **Charles McKim** of **McKim, Mead & White.** Addition at 29 E. 36th St., NE cor. Madison Ave. 1928. **Benjamin W. Morris.** 🖤 Interior 🖤 . Garden courtyard, 1990s. **Voorsanger & Mills.** Open to the public: Su 1-5; Tu-Sa 10:30-5; closed Mo. 212-685-0610.

M18

Brunelleschi would be pleased by this, his offspring. The addition, built on the site of the **J. Pierpont Morgan, Sr.** mansion after his death, modestly defers to the older part. The interior is notable not only for its exhibits of rare prints and manuscripts but also for Morgan's opulent private library, maintained just as he left it. The best place in New York to look at drawings (15th to 19th century): whitestone, brownstone, bronze, wrought iron.

The greenhouse garden court links the library and its addition to Morgan's onetime house, now reclaimed as part of this gracious complex:

M18

[M19] **Pierpont Morgan Library annex**/onetime Lutheran Church in America/originally Isaac N. Phelps House/later Anson Phelps Stokes House/onetime (1904-1943) J. P. Morgan, Jr. House, 231 Madison Ave., SE cor. E. 37th St. 1853.

A Classical block that has suffered from additions to and restoration of its brownstone. The sinuous iron balustrades on the entry stoop first-floor windows are outstanding.

The church successfully contested its official landmark designation in the courts: money is more important than history, even to Luther's heirs, who foresaw commercial development possibilities on this prime site. In spite of that threat, the house was rescued by purchase for the library—a literally antebellum house of grandeur preserved for its roles both in architectural and in social history.

M19

[M20] **Consulate General of Poland**/originally Joseph R. DeLamar House, 233 Madison Ave., NE cor. E. 37th St. 1905-1906. **C. P. H. Gilbert.** 🖤

The interiors are as opulent as the exterior, and largely intact. At one time it housed the National Democratic Club. Note the putti over the entry. **DeLamar** was a Dutch-born merchant seaman who made his fortune in mining and metallurgy.

M20

[M21] **19 and 21 East 37th Street**, bet. Madison and Park Aves. ca. 1900.

Remnant town houses. Note the Composite capitals on the porch of No. 19 (ca. 1900), the doorway and iron balustrades of No. 21 (ca. 1885).

M21

[M22]**Union League Club**, 38 E. 37th St., SW cor. Park Ave. 1931. **Morris & O'Connor**

This effete and bland neo-Georgian pile is the red brick home of a club founded by Republicans who left the Union Club in 1863, incensed by its failure to expel Confederate sympathizers.

[M23] **Scandinavia House**, 56 Park Ave., bet. E. 37th and E. 38th Sts. W side. 2000. **Polshek Partnership**.

Zinc and spruce? Those Scandinavians have led the design pack with startling and wonderful materials (remember Bonniers furnishings? And George Jensen?). Here the cool hand of Polshek brings back some of those memories.

M22

[M24] Originally Adelaide E. Douglas House/ now **Guatemalan Mission to the United Nations**, 57 Park Ave., bet. E. 37th and E. 38th Sts. E side. 1911. **Horace Trumbauer**. 🖋

More limestone Beaux Arts, now used by a Central American mission that can more lustily savor its ebullience than could its original Protestant tenant.

M24

[M25] **Church of Our Saviour** (Roman Catholic), 59 Park Ave., SE cor. E. 38th St. 1959. **Paul W. Reilly**.

Somewhat convincing neo-Romanesque archaeology. Among its inconsistencies, however, is air-conditioning equipment where, in a true Romanesque church, a carillon would be. Look up within at the neo-Baroque ceiling. Outside, the carved Gallery of Kings has all the expression of a flock of Barbie dolls.

[M26] **The Town House** (apartments), 108 E. 38th St., bet. Park and Lexington Aves. S side. 1930. **Bowden & Russell**.

An unsung Art Moderne apartment house in a reddish-black brick that sports rippling spandrels, also in brick. The cubistic composition is crowned with brilliant glazed terra-cotta panels in a broad and wondrous spectrum that can be enjoyed as a special colorful cresting from a distant skyline view.

M27

[M27] **101 Park Avenue** (offices), NE cor. E. 40th St. 1985. **Eli Attia**.

An ego event among more modest neighbors, its prismatic glass form skewed to the Manhattan grid. Here lay the Architects Building (1912, **Ewing & Chappell** and **La Farge & Morris**).

[M28] **The Library** (hotel)/originally office building, 299 Madison Ave., NE cor. E. 41st St. 1912+. **Hill & Stout**. Remodeled into hotel, 1999. **The Stephen Jacobs Group**.

An early sliver building in brick and terra-cotta (only 25 feet wide), its grand copper-clad bays give travelers a grand shot down 41st to the main façade of The Library.

M28

[M29] Originally **Jonathan W. Allen Stable**, 148 East 40th Street (carriage house), bet. Lexington and Third Aves. 1871. **Charles Hadden**, builder. 🖋

A distinguished emissary in miniature from France's Second Empire, languishing amid characterless high-rises on all sides.

[M30] **152 East 38th Street** (house), bet. Lexington and Third Aves. 1858. Remodeled, 1935. **Robertson Ward**. 🖋

A walled front garden breaks the blockfront: a happy urban design gift for this block.

M29

[M31] Originally **George S. Bowdoin Stable**, 149 East 38th Street (carriage house), bet. Lexington and Third Aves. 1902. **Ralph S. Townsend**. 🖋

A Dutch Renaissance gable displays carved heads of bulldogs and wreathed horses.

M31

M33

[M32] **130 East 37th Street** (house), SW cor. Lexington Ave.

An expatriate from Greenwich Village, crowned with a skylit studio and terrace. Here is good living with casual architecture.

[M33] **Sniffen Court Historic District**, 150-158 E. 36th St., bet. Lexington and Third Aves. 1863-1864. 🌶

Ten Romanesque Revival brick carriage houses make a mews, a tasteful oasis, and an urbane lesson for those developing dense streets. Here urban style could be replicated with whole blocks of such mews at intervals in the cityscape.

[M34] **157 and 159 East 35th Street** (carriage houses), bet. Lexington and Third Aves. ca. 1890.

Two conversions to modern use. No. 157 is restrained and successful. No. 159, the more ebullient architectural statement (note the terra-cotta garlands at the cornice), suffers from a stuffy ground-floor reconstruction.

[M35] **Armenian Evangelical Church of America**, 152 E. 34th St., bet. Lexington and Third Aves. 1840s.

A Doric temple.

END *of Murray Hill Tour: The 33rd Street IRT Local (No. 6 train at Park Avenue South) is the nearest rapid transit.*

L21

CLINTON

From Ninth Avenue westward to the Hudson, roughly opposite the Times Square theater district, lies the area known since the 1970s as Clinton, after DeWitt Clinton Park (1905) at its western edge between West 52nd and West 54th Streets. Like Cobble Hill, Carroll Gardens, and Boerum Hill in Brooklyn, Clinton is a new moniker for a community trying to live down its infamous past. From the Civil War to World War II the area south to about West 30th Street was better known as Hell's Kitchen, one of the city's most notorious precincts. Gangster rule in its early years and the abundance of slaughterhouses, freight yards, factories, and tenements (to house those whose meager livings these industries provided) established the area's physical character. It is a quality the current inhabitants wish to upgrade, and the area boasts substantial improvements toward that end. But the ubiquitous lofts, repair shops, and taxi garages and the disappearance of pier activity (as well as piers) have made this stretch unfamiliar to all except those who live, work, or play here. It remains an enigma why Clinton, so close to the heart of Manhattan's central business district, is still a relative backwater.

L2

L3

To begin: The nearest subways are not close, which helps to explain Clinton's sluggishness in being redeveloped. (Take the IND Eighth Avenue Line (A, C and E trains), the closest, to the 42nd Street Station.)

[L2] **Mercedes-Benz Showroom and Service Facility**, NE cor. Eleventh Ave. and 40th St. 1990s.
Can stylish cars breed stylish architecture to house them? Here is an isolated example of such success, sleek and glassy.

[L3] **Covenant House**/formerly Manhattan Community Rehabilitation Center, N.Y.S. Office of Drug Abuse Services, 460 W. 41st St., bet. Ninth and Tenth Aves. Conversion for N.Y.S., 1970, **Gueron, Lepp & Assocs**.
Converted for drug addicts' rehabilitation with board-framed concrete and brown brick.

L4

[L4] **St. Raphael's Croatian Catholic Church**, 41st St. bet. 10th and 11th Aves. 1890s.
Granite ashlar, limestone trim, slated and copper crested twin towers all serve this outpost of the Balkans.

[L5] **Univision**/formerly Spanish International Communications Corporation, atop the old West Side Airlines Terminal, 460 W. 42nd St., SE cor. Tenth Ave. 1986. **Hardy Holzman Pfeiffer Assocs**.

L5

CLINTON

see pages 245–251

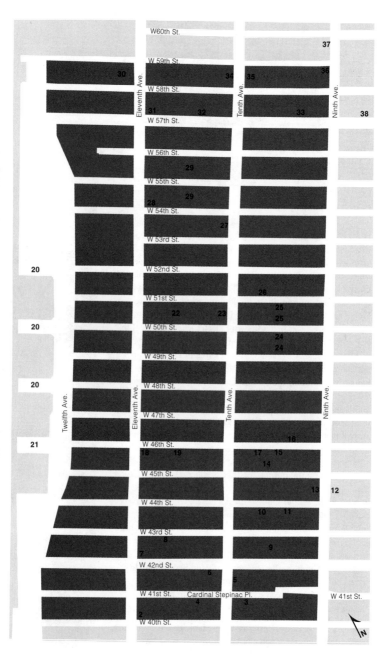

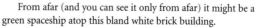

From afar (and you can see it only from afar) it might be a green spaceship atop this bland white brick building.

[L6] **Model Tenements for New York Fireproof Tenement Association**, 500-506 W. 42nd St., SW cor. Tenth Ave. and 569 Tenth Ave., bet. W. 41st and W. 42nd Sts. ca. 1900. **Ernest Flagg**.

Their fireproof qualities may have been a step forward for tenements, but having lost their ironwork embellishments, they are grim.

L7

[L7] **Riverbank West** (apartments), 555 W. 42nd St., NE cor. Eleventh Ave. 1987. **Hardy Holzman Pfeiffer Assocs**. and **Schuman, Lichtenstein, Claman & Efron**.

Polychromatic brickwork and staggered balconies make a lively if not graceful façade. The syncopated top is where most of the action is.

[L8] **Rescue Company No. 1, N.Y.C. Fire Department**, 530 W. 43rd St., bet. Tenth and Eleventh Aves. 1988. **The Stein Partnership.**

A substitute for—can you believe it?—a firehouse that burned down. Dour.

L8

[L9] **Manhattan Plaza** (apartment complex), W. 42nd to W. 43rd Sts., Ninth to Tenth Aves. 1977. **David Todd & Assocs.**

Two 45-story red brick balconied towers anchor this block-square project, built for performing artists and intended to spur redevelopment of the Clinton community. Between the towers, on the garage deck, are recreational buildings for residents of the 1,688 apartments.

L9

[L10] **Actors Studio**/originally Seventh Associate Presbyterian Church, 432 W. 44th St., bet. Ninth and Tenth Aves. 1859. 🍎 Restored 1995, **Davis Brody & Associates.**

Lee Strasberg held forth after 1955 in this simple, late Greek Revival brick church. Here was the cradle of thespians such as **Marlon Brando.**

[L11] **New Dramatists** (theater)/originally Church, 424 W. 44th St., bet. Ninth and Tenth Aves. 1880s.

A free spirited Gothic Revival fitted gracefully into a continuous row house and apartment blockfront façade. The New Dramatists enjoy another happily recycled found space.

L11

[L12] **Film Center Building**, 630 Ninth Ave., bet. W. 44th and W. 45th Sts. E side. 1928-1929. **Ely Jacques Kahn** of **Buchman & Kahn.** Lobby interior 🍎 .

Typical of 1920s Art Deco-influenced loft buildings whose designs are just skin deep. This one, however, has a gem of a polychromed elevator lobby (and an asymmetric, Moderne bronze tenants' directory).

[L13] **Film Center Café**, 635 Ninth Ave., bet. W. 44th and W. 45th Sts. W side. 1940s.

A small and stylish Art Moderne café frequented by the movie/video clan that works across the street in the Film Center.

L13

L14

L16

L17

*428 West 44th Street, the former home of actress **June Havoc**, is also the scene of mysterious tapping sounds. Perhaps its resident tapper was a friend of **Peter Stuyvesant** and afforded him temporary digs during the 1978 fire that gutted his home. Seances have been conducted to determine who the noisy ghost is. Two spirits are said to have been contacted so far.*

[L14] Playground, N.Y.C. Department of Parks & Recreation, W. 45th to W. 46th Sts., midblock bet. Ninth and Tenth Aves. Reconstructed, 1977, **Michael J. Altschuler**, architect. Outdoor mural, 1973, **Arnold Belkin, Cityarts Workshop**. Mosaics, 1974, **Philip Danzig**, with community participants.

An unusual reconstruction of the ubiquitous city playground: community-crafted mosaics on the walls, reflections and distortions from polished stainless-steel mirrors, all beneath a Mexican-inspired outdoor mural of social commentary. The train is a late but well-received arrival. Get aboard.

[L15] Clinton Court (residential group), 420 W. 46th St., bet. Ninth and Tenth Aves.

A charming backwater only partially visible through a locked gate.

[L16] St. Clement's Church (Episcopal)/formerly St. Cornelius Church/originally Faith Chapel, West Presbyterian Church, 423 W. 46th St., bet. Ninth and Tenth Aves. 1870. **Edward D. Lindsey**. Altered 1882.

Unusual and picturesque. Victorian brickwork, fish-scale slate shingles, and very pointed Gothic Revival arched windows. For years the church has also served as the home of Playhouse 46 and for many noteworthy dance and dramatic productions.

[L17] The Piano Factory (apartments)/originally **Wessell, Nickel & Gross Company**, 452-458 W. 46th St., bet. Ninth and Tenth Aves. 1888. Converted, 1980.

A New England-style mill building (complete with mill yard entered through a robust Romanesque Revival arch) squeezed onto an urban site. The factory made the innards for pianos.

[L18] Landmark Tavern, 626 Eleventh Ave., SE cor. W. 46th St.

It dates from 1868 and looks every minute of it: dark wood, dusty mirrors, floors of two-bit-sized round white tiles, and Franklin stoves for heat on cold days. There's even a paneled and stained-glass "Gentlemen's" off the bar.

[L19] Salvation Army Thrift Store/originally Acker, Merrall & Condit Company, 536 W. 46th St., bet. Tenth and Eleventh Aves. ca. 1910.

A stately warehouse of tapestry brick and expansive neo-Roman arches. But here are bargains for the practical, eccentric, or stylish.

L20

L21

[L20] N.Y.C. Passenger Ship Terminal, Port Authority of New York and New Jersey, Hudson River at W. 48th, W. 50th, and W. 52nd Sts. along Twelfth Ave. W side. 1976. Port Authority of **N.Y. & N.J. Architectural Design Team**.

When the *Liberté, Queen Mary, United States,* or *Andrea Doria* were still plying the oceans, it was said that what New York City needed to dignify transatlantic arrivals and departures was modern superliner piers. The piers were finally built; the superliners, however, were scrapped: the *Queen Elizabeth 2* (QE 2) still visits, mostly for those superaffluent who relish the luxurious ride one way—and take the Concorde back.

[L21] The Intrepid, a World War II aircraft carrier, moored at Pier 86, foot of West 46th Street (officially at the impossible-to-locate-address: 1 Intrepid Plaza).

It is both a museum where one can climb into the cockpit of a torpedo bomber (or see films of fighting in the 1940s) and giant floating architecture. (All the public spaces are heated by electricity, making the Intrepid one of Con Ed's most valued customers in cold weather.) Open to the public: Memorial Day-Labor Day 10-5 daily; Winter We-Su 10-5; closed Mo & Tu. 212-245-0072.

L22

[L22] **Park West High School,** 525 W. 50th St., bet. Tenth and Eleventh Aves. to W. 51st St. 1977. [L23] **747 Tenth Avenue** (apartment complex), SW cor. 1976. Both by **Max O. Urbahn Assocs**.

The school's West 50th Street façade presents powerful cylindrical forms, raw concrete and striated block. The West 51st Street façade, on the other hand, is disconcertingly placid. The high-rise apartment tower at the corner is banal, providing an honorable economic trick allowing the housing to pay for the school.

[L24] **High School of Graphic Communication Arts**/originally High School of Printing, 439 W. 49th and W. 50th Sts., bet. Ninth and Tenth Aves. 1959. **Kelly & Gruzen**.

One of the most vigorous International Style buildings in town, overlooked in its isolation in the west reaches of Clinton (its style has worn well). Here glass block presents a façade of style, with a sinuous articulated auditorium umbilically connected as a specially shaped form. The interior sports escalators are the first to be used in a local high school.

L24

[L25] Originally New York Telephone Company (offices) now **AT&T Company,** 425-437 W. 50th St., and 430 W. 51st St. bet. Ninth and Tenth Aves. 1930. **Voorhees, Gmelin & Walker**.

A telephone building from the era when people were still needed to complete your phone call (thus requiring windows), and the image of a company in the community was a high priority (thus justifying the willow leaf Art Deco and Art Moderne ornament).

L25

[L26] **Sacred Heart of Jesus Church** (Roman Catholic), 457 W. 51st St., bet. Ninth and Tenth Aves. 1884. **Napoleon LeBrun & Sons**. Rectory, 1881, **Arthur Crooks**.

A symmetric confection of deep red brick and matching terra-cotta frosted with light-colored stone arches, band courses, and copings: a sober, if not sturdy, Victorian Romanesque. Inside, the Romanesque (still Victorian) opts for Italian, lighter and airier colonnades, rather than the stolid masonry of France and Spain.

L26

[L27] Originally **Switching Center, New York Telephone Company**/American Telephone & Telegraph Company, 811 Tenth Ave., bet. W. 53rd and W. 54th Sts. W side. 1964. Exterior, **Kahn & Jacobs**. Interior, **Smith, Smith, Haines, Lundberg & Waehler**.

A tall windowless colossus that looks, from a distance, as though covered with glistening mattress ticking. No long distance operators here—only electronic robotry.

[L28] **Clinton Tower** (apartments), 790 Eleventh Ave., NE cor. W. 54th St., and 590 W. 55th St., SE cor. Eleventh Ave. 1975. **Hoberman & Wasserman**.

The high-rise tower and its low-rise leg on West 55th Street are clad in a combination of smooth and striated pink concrete block. They embrace a courtyard and play area that gather the noonday sun.

L29

[L29] **Harbor View Terrace, N.Y.C. Housing Authority**, W. 54th and W. 55th, and W. 55th and W. 56th Sts., bet. Tenth and Eleventh Aves. 1977. **Herbert L. Mandel**.

The Authority's best in Manhattan. The combination of cast-in-place concrete and deep-terra-cotta-colored giant brick (for walls) and bronze anodized aluminum (for balcony railings) promotes a domestic and urbane scale. The project is built over the air rights of the depressed West Side freight line.

L30

[L30] Originally Interborough Rapid Transit Company (IRT) Powerhouse/now **Consolidated Edison**, W. 58th to W. 59th Sts., bet. Eleventh and Twelfth Aves. 1904. **Stanford White** of **McKim, Mead & White**.

A brick and terra-cotta temple to power with a Stanford White exterior, that once boasted 6 tall smokestacks belching gas from enormous coal furnaces. The coal was received at an adjacent dock on the Hudson and transported to bunkers in electric conveyor belts; ashes were removed the same way. All the electricity for the original IRT subway, opened in 1904, was generated here.

L31

[L31] **BMW Manhattan Showroom**, NE cor. 11th Ave. and 57th St. 1990s.

A hi-tech glass skirt shields the Beemers with cables, clips, and struts: merchandising architecture worthy of the products on sale?

[L32] **International Flavors and Fragrances**, 521 W. 57th St., bet. Tenth and Eleventh Aves. N side. 1995. **Der Scutt**.

Squares and circles: a new façade on some old brick bulk.

[L33] **Catholic Apostolic Church**, 417 W. 57th St., bet. Ninth and Tenth Aves. 1886. **Francis H. Kimball**.

A superior work of urban architecture, three-dimensional—not merely a façade—now almost forgotten because of bulky nonentities that squeeze against but fail to conceal it. Its restrained coloring of russet brick and terra-cotta adds to its power.

L34

[L34] **John Jay College of Criminal Justice**/formerly Haaren High School/originally DeWitt Clinton High School, 899 Tenth Ave., bet. W. 58th and W. 59th Sts. 1903-1906. **C. B. J. Snyder**. Rebuilt and expanded, 1988, **Rafael Viñoly Architects**.

Flemish Renaissance Revival encrustations enliven the façades of this old high school. John Jay, the neighboring City University unit for police and ancillary criminal justice, now has a grand central building, expanded elegantly and gracefully by **Rafael Viñoly**.

[L35] **St. Luke's/Roosevelt Hospital Center**, Tenth Ave. bet. W. 58th and W. 59th Sts., E side. 1990. **Skidmore, Owings & Merrill**.

Grandiosity without grace, this 13-story cube brought the old Roosevelt block into the late 20th century: a technological set of tubes, wires, computers, and other hard assets that are encapsulated in this bland external fancy dress.

L35

[L36] **Entrance lobby, Roosevelt East**, 925 Ninth Ave./originally William J. Syms Operating Theater, Roosevelt Hospital, 400 W. 59th St., SW cor. Ninth Ave. 1890-1892. **W. Wheeler Smith**. ☛ [L36a] **Roosevelt East** (apartment houses), 925 Ninth Ave. bet. 58th and 59th Sts. 1997. **Buck/Cane** and **Schuman Lichtenstein Claman & Efron**.

Originally Roosevelt Hospital's teaching amphitheater, where spectators, on concentric, stepped seating rings oversaw the master medics at work. Now the affluent will mingle with the ghosts of surgeons past as they trundle through to their 49 stories of condos.

L36

[L37] **Church of St. Paul the Apostle** (Roman Catholic), Columbus Ave., SW cor. W. 60th St. 1876, 1885. **Jeremiah O'Rourke**. Altar and baldachino, 1887-1890. **Stanford White**. Ceiling and windows, **John La Farge**.

The largest un-cathedral in America. An unadorned fort on the outside, except for the awkward bas-relief over the entrance; a Roman basilica inside, embellished with the works of **Augustus Saint-Gaudens**, **Frederick MacMonnies**, and **John La Farge**, with the advice of **Stanford White** and **Bertram Goodhue**. All of their efforts are lost in the thick atmosphere. **O'Rourke** died before the plans were complete. Paulist **Father George Deshon**, **U.S. Grant**'s roommate at the U.S. Military Academy, took over.

[L38] Formerly **Henry Hudson Hotel**/originally Clubhouse, American Women's Association, 353 W. 57th St., bet. Eighth and Ninth Aves. 1929. **Benjamin Wistar Morris**. Remodeled, 1999. **Philippe Starck**.

A landmark on San Juan Hill, it began as a club for young women, served as bachelor officers' quarters in World War II, and once housed Channel 13. Note the bridge in the sky connecting the roof gardens of the two wings.

San Juan Hill: The rise in topography near Ninth Avenue and West 57th Street was, around 1900, a black community dubbed San Juan Hill after the heroic exploits of a black unit in the Spanish-American War. This stretch of West 57th Street between Eighth and Ninth Avenues bears a curiously European look in its architectural scale.

END of Clinton Tour: The nearest subways are along Eighth Avenue between 57th Street and Columbus Circle: the IND Sixth and Eighth Avenue Lines (A, B, C, and D trains) and the IRT Broadway-Seventh Avenue local (1 and 9 trains).

TIMES SQUARE TO COLUMBUS CIRCLE

Up to the 1890s, much of the 40s and 50s west of Seventh Avenue were written off as Hell's Kitchen, a seething mixture of factories and tenements where even the cops moved in pairs. The rich ventured in only as far west as Broadway in the upper 40s, an area of carriage shops for the horsey set called Long Acre, after a similar district in London. In 1883 the Metropolitan Opera House opened on Broadway between 39th and 40th Streets. Some said the 3,700-seat theater looked like a yellow brick brewery on the outside, but inside the city's nouveaux riches could observe each other in red and gold-encrusted splendor. They had built their very own opera house when the Old Guard denied them boxes in their Academy of Music downtown. The tide turned quickly as the moneyed classes soon flocked uptown, and three years later the Academy closed. The whole center of social gravity had now shifted from points south to the 50s on Fifth Avenue.

Then big things happened quickly. **Charles Frohman** ventured to open his Empire Theatre, directly across Broadway from the Metropolitan Opera, in 1893; **Oscar Hammerstein I** did him one better in 1895 by opening the Olympia, a blocklong palace on Broadway between 44th and 45th Streets (then a muddy stretch) with a concert hall, a music hall, a theater, and a roof garden. Soon lavish restaurants like Rector's, Shanley's, and Café de l'Opera were dispensing lobster and champagne to **Diamond Jim Brady**, **"Bet a Million" Gates**, **George M. Cohan**, and other luminaries of the theater, financial, and sporting world. When the city decided to route its first subway west from Grand Central along 42nd Street, then north on Broadway, *New York Times* publisher **Adolph Ochs** saw a chance to outdo his competitors by erecting an imposing tower at Broadway and 42nd. He got the station there officially named Times Square in April 1904.

By then the area was becoming established as the theater district, and the evening crowds and broad vistas attracted the early electric sign makers; the 1916 Zoning Resolution made specific allowances for vast signs in the area. In the 1920s, neon and movies took over. In Hollywood's heyday, movie and variety palaces preempted the valuable Broadway frontier, and legitimate theater retreated to the side streets. The signs got bigger as the crowds got bigger, and began to feature things like rooftop waterfalls and real smoke rings. As bigtime movies waned in the 1950s and 1960s, most of the palatial movie theaters were razed, and Times Square was on the verge of an office-building boom.

The banishing of sexual enterprise and the commercial renaissance of Times Square have rapidly changed its flavor: not squeaky clean, but sanitized, at least superficially. New and imposing skyscrapers have brought a daytime weekday crowd to the area. Best of all are the reconstructions of live theaters on 42nd Street.

"Long term plans include retail design and signage as implemented in accordance with '42nd Street Now!' design and use guidelines developed by the 42nd Street Development Project, Inc., **Robert A.M. Stern** and **Tibor Kalman**. These guidelines encourage eclectic tourist and entertainment uses, exuberant design, and dazzling signage on facades and rooftops." Thus spake the 42nd St. Development Project.

For Times Square: IRT Broadway-Seventh Avenue Line (Nos. 1, 2, 3, and 9 trains), Flushing Line (No. 7 train), the Shuttle from Grand Central, or the BMT Broadway Line (N and R trains) to the interconnected Times Square Station.

T1

[T1] **Parsons Center, New School University**/originally Brotherhood in Action Building, 560 Seventh Ave., NW cor. W. 40th St. 1950s. **William Lescaze**.

TIMES SQUARE TO COLUMBUS CIRCLE

see pages 252–272

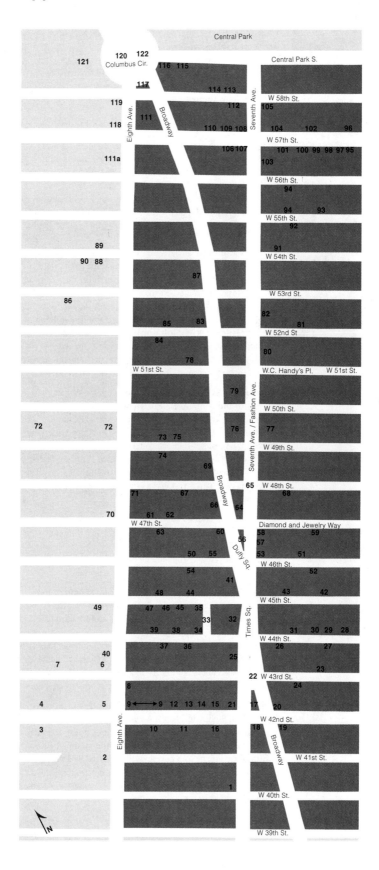

T2

Lescaze's early house [U56] is vintage Lescaze—here his later work is much less suave.

[T2] **Port Authority Bus Terminal**, W. 40th to W. 42nd Sts., bet. Eighth and Ninth Aves. 1950. Decks added, 1963. Expansion to W. 42nd St. 1980. All by **Port Authority of N.Y. & N.J. Architectural Design Team**.

Glorious Pennsylvania Station is only a memory; Grand Central Terminal basks in its glorious reconstruction. The Port Authority Bus Terminal only grows in popularity as the city's vomitory for commuters and for those reduced to using long-distance buses. The new and upgraded spaces are, happily, remarkably civilized.

T3

[T3] **Offices**/formerly GHI Building (Group Health Insurance)/originally McGraw-Hill Building, 330 W. 42nd St., bet. Eighth and Ninth Aves. 1930-1931. **Raymond Hood, Godley & Fouilhoux**. ♥

Hood designed this magnificent tower with continuous horizontal bands of blue-green terra-cotta at the time his vertically striped News Building was going up at the other end of 42nd Street.

Lewis Mumford, an early fan of modern architecture, wrote that the building was just a "stunt," and that the colors were "heavy and unbeautiful." Critic **Arthur North** (in the *American Architect*, 1932) called it a "storm center" that showed "disregard for every accepted principle of architectural designing in the most flagrant manner." Yet it was the only New York building shown in **Hitchcock** and **Johnson**'s epochal book *The International Style* in 1932. The details, however, are Art Deco/Art Moderne: the lobby an extraordinary remembrance of Carrera (opaque) glass, stainless steel, and elegant lights.

T4

[T4] **Holy Cross Church** (Roman Catholic), 333 W. 42nd St., bet. Eighth and Ninth Aves. 1870. **Henry Engelbert**. [T4a] **Holy Cross School**, 332 W. 43rd St. 1887. **Lawrence J. O'Connor**.

Claimed for the "Byzantine style" when built, the brick façade conceals the verdigris-clad octagonal drum, dome, lantern, and crucifix over the crossing. This was the parish church of Father Duffy of World War I fame [see his statue at Duffy Square]. The school, on West 43rd Street, has a rich Romanesque Revival façade of red brick and matching terra-cotta.

[T5] **American Savings Bank**/originally Franklin Savings Bank, 661 Eighth Ave., NW cor. W. 42nd St. 1974. **Poor, Swanke, Hayden & Connell**.

A modest taxpayer (ephemeral one-story building sufficient to pay taxes until future development plans unroll).

T6

[T6] **Second Stage Theater**/originally Manufacturers Hanover Bank, 681 Eighth Ave., NW cor. W. 43rd St. 1927. Converted to theater, 1999. **Rem Koolhaas** and **Richard Gluckman**.

An austere bank, with the multicolored column capitals a rich abstraction of Art Deco variations on a Classical theme. The Koolhaas/Gluckman interior is appropriately spartan (no 1920s retro flamboyance here), but the bathrooms are orange.

[T7] Originally **Charles Scribner's Sons printing plant**, 311 W. 43rd St., bet. Eighth and Ninth Aves. 1907. **Ernest Flagg**.

Flagg, architect of Scribner's headquarters, stores, and town houses, was, predictably, also architect for this straightforward industrial facility. Its iron curtain wall is marred by a thoughtless ground-floor "improvement and replacement of the gutsy, industrial steel, sash windows." See the faded SCRIBNER's on the west wall.

42nd Street, Eighth Avenue to Broadway:

[T8] **Westin New York at Times Square** (hotel), Eighth Ave., SE cor. 43rd St. 2001. **Arquitectonica**.

Extravagant form that delivers an architectural impact at a level outdoing the Times Square/42nd Street world of light bulbs and neon. Here is a bit of Florida color and Las Vegas fantasy brought to Manhattan's strict blocks.

T9

[T9] **E-Walk Complex**, NE cor. W. 42nd St. and Eighth Ave. 1999. **D'Agostino Izzo Quirk** and **Gensler Associates**. Signage, **Kupiec Koutsomitis Architects**. Within: Vegas! (restaurant), **The Cunningham Group**. 13-screen Sony theater complex, **The Rockwell Group**.

Controlled visual cacophony here hopes to outperform the traditional image of Times Square lights and action: all based on the schematic criteria developed by **Robert A.M. Stern** for a renaissance of vitality on what had become a bleak (and sex-oriented) block.

T9

[T10] **Forest City Ratner Theater & Store Complex**, including the former Harris, Liberty, and Empire Theaters, between the Candler Building and Eighth Ave., S side of 42nd St. 2000. **Beyer Blinder Belle** and **The Rockwell Group**. AMC (movie) Theaters, **Benjamin Thompson & Assocs**. [T10a] **Doubletree Hotel**, above and behind the theater and store complex. 2001. **Beyer Blinder Belle**.

The newly located Empire Theater façade (170 feet west of its birthplace) screens the lobby of a 25-screen movie house. The façades of its classmates, Harris and Liberty, punctuate the length of this all-new mega-merchandising and movie complex. Liberty leads to a merchant of athletic shoes, Just for Feet (**Lawrence M. Rosenbloom Architects**), and Harris to Madame Tussaud (she does get around; **Ohlhausen Dubois**, architects with **Architecture IMG**).

The trendy Doubletree hotel straddles wide entertainment and merchandising spaces below, astride massive trusses.

History:

Harris Theater. 226 W. 42nd St. 1914. **Thomas W. Lamb**.

Liberty Theater, 234 W. 42nd St. 1904. **Herts & Tallant**.

Empire Theater, 236 W. 42nd St. 1912. **Thomas W. Lamb**.

T10

[T11] **Candler Building** (offices), 220 W. 42nd St., bet. Seventh and Eighth Aves. 1914. **Willauer, Shape & Bready**. Renovations, 1999. **Swanke Hayden Connell**.

The nationwide success of Coca-Cola persuaded **Asa Candler**, its supersalesman, to build this gleaming white terra-cotta-clad tower off Times Square. Its skin, long begrimed, shines once more and its innards have been equally modernized. Look up, and up and away are lurking dragons. Telescope?

T11

[T12] **The New 42nd Street's Rehearsal Building**, 217 W. 42nd St., bet. Eighth and Seventh Aves. 2001. **Platt Byard Dovell**.

A glassy set of studios for actors and dancers that plugs the gap between E-Walk and a venerable and renewed theater row.

T12

[T13] **Times Square Theater**, 215 W. 42nd St., bet. Eighth and Seventh Aves. 1920. **DeRosa and Pereira**.

A grand colonnade.

[T14] **Ford Center for the Performing Arts**/originally site of Lyric and Apollo Theaters, 213 W. 42nd St., bet. Eighth and Seventh Aves. Lyric, 1903. **Victor Hugo Koehler**. Apollo, 1920. **DeRosa & Pereira**. Blended and reconstructed, 1998. **Beyer Blinder Belle**.

Behind all those signs and lightbulbs lurks a tiny but ornate façade leading to the bulky body of the theater on 43rd. Inside, reincarnations provide a massive three-dimensional collage of recycled parts, incorporating elements of the Lyric and Apollo theaters (domes, arches, vaults, boxes). (Alternately enter on 43rd to a facade of terra-cotta: snakes, rams, a deer.)

T14

T15

[T15] **New Victory Theater**/originally Republic Theater/sometime Belasco Theater/onetime Minsky's, 209-211 W. 42nd St., bet. Eighth and Seventh Aves. 1899. **Albert Westover**. Restored and remodeled, 1995. **Hardy Holzman Pfeiffer**.

T16

A glorious restoration redolent of, and with the robust flavor of, this turn-of-the-century theater's whole district (**Oscar Hammerstein I** built this one). One ascended that grand theatrical stoop to the performance as one did to a great museum. The interior is breathtaking.

[T16] **New Amsterdam Theatre**, 214 W. 42nd St., bet. Seventh and Eighth Ave. 1902-1903. **Herts & Tallant**. 🍎 Interior 🍎 Elaborately restored, 1995-1997. **Hardy Holzman Pfeiffer** and **Walt Disney Imagineering**. [T16a] **New Amsterdam Roof Theatre**/originally New Amsterdam Aerial Gardens. 1904. **Herts & Tallant**.

The sliver office tower entered on 42nd Street houses the lobby leading to the theater on 41st. Rare for New York: Art Nouveau. But what a miracle the Disney Renaissance has produced within, through **Hugh Hardy**'s extraordinary heightened restoration of **Herts & Tallant** ideas; and the ideas of artists **Robert Blum**, **George Peixotto**, and **Henry Mercer**.

Times Square: A state of mind as much as a physical location, this is the center of circulation to a much larger area of theaters and restaurants—a vast vestibule to entertainment. Gaudy signs are its nighttime architecture, their exuberant vulgarity the marquee that proclaims the theatrical wonders in the surrounding streets. Zoning and Landmarks laws have teamed up to require brilliant and pervasive signs within viewing of the central spaces created by the crossing of Seventh Avenue and Broadway.

[T17] **1 Times Square**/formerly Allied Chemical Tower/originally Times Tower, W. 42nd St. bet. Broadway and Seventh Ave., N to W. 43rd St. 1903-1905. **Cyrus L.W, Eidlitz** and **Andrew C. MacKenzie**. Reconstructed, 1966, **Smith, Smith, Haines, Lundberg & Waehler**. Warner Brothers Studio Store, 1998. **WJCA Architects**.

The *New York Times* moved into its 25-story tower with dramatic timing on December 31, 1904, marking the occasion with a fireworks display at midnight that made Times Square the place to see in the New Year ever since. The paper moved a decade later (1913) to larger quarters on West 43rd Street, but the name remained. New owners stripped off the original Italian Renaissance terra-cotta skin and replaced it with Miami Beach

T17

marble. More recent Times Square "renewal" has relegated it to a role as a supersignboard, though offices still survive within.

World's first "moving" sign: First to electrify passers-by along the Great White Way were the election returns of 1928 delivered along the Motogram, a 5-foot-high, 360-foot-long sign flasher that wrapped around the old Times Tower's 4 sides and utilized 14,800 lamps to convey its constantly changing messages. The tower has changed its face; a much revised and restored Motogram remains.

T18

[T18] **Times Square Brewery & Main Subway Entrance**, 42nd St., bet. Seventh Ave. and Broadway. S side. 1997. **Fox & Fowle**.

The temporary pavilion that activates the site of the old Crossroads Building, whose windowless tower was more the vehicle for a giant wall painting by **Richard Haas** in the 1980s than any substantial rentable space. The pavilion also provides a new entry to the Times Square subway complex.

Above, British Airways' Concorde is off to London.

[T19] **1462-1470 Broadway** (mixed use)/formerly Newsweek Building/originally Knickerbocker Hotel, SE cor. Broadway. 1901-1906 **Marvin & Davis**, architects. **Bruce Price**, consultant. Annex, 143 W. 41st St. 1907. **Trowbridge & Livingston**. Altered, 1980, **Libby, Ross & Whitehouse**. 🍎

T19

A mix of condominium uses now fills the Classical, mansard-topped shell of a hotel—originally commissioned by **Col. John Jacob Astor**—where **Enrico Caruso** and **George M. Cohan** once lived. It had a gold service for sixty and a bar so fashionable in its heyday that it was known as the 42nd Street Country Club. A mural from this bar now sets the theme for the King Cole restaurant at the St. Regis-Sheraton Hotel. There are stirrings to make it a hotel once more.

*Behemoths: On the corners of 42nd Street, Seventh Avenue, and Broadway, 4 planned giant buildings (Times Square Center) once promised to have a "sobering effect" on the neighborhood. Would they sterilize this lively urban sector, replacing its septic vitality with Sixth Avenue dullness? We had hoped that its architects (**John Burgee** with **Philip Johnson**) would yet apply some genuine architectural wit comparable to Johnson's famed verbal entertainments. They didn't. But their successors for two of the four sites have:*

T21

[T20] **Condé Nast Building**, 4 Times Sq., NE cor. Broadway. 1999. **Fox & Fowle**.

[T21] **Reuters Building**, 3 Times Sq., bet. W. 42nd and W. 43rd Sts. 2001. **Fox & Fowle**.

T20

The complicated skyscraper has replaced the skyline sky scraper to contend with the coordinated chaos of Times Square. Here two buildings compete with visual cacophony at the street, morphing into different shapes and materials as they rise, and are veneered, then crowned, with an armature of signs and finials. Each one provides a microcosm of Times Square's spirit. Condé Nast offers a further sophisticated step, providing a sedate elevation to the east. Very successful.

Fowle speaks of his "cues from Nathan's" harking back to one of SOM's earliest buildings that sat at the SE corner of Broadway and 43rd (originally Toffenetti's, lastly Nathan's of hot dog fame. 1939-1940. **Skidmore, Owings & Merrill** with **Walker & Gillette**). Built for World's Fair crowds, Toffenetti's was a sleek streamlined place of curving blue panels.

*The site of the Reuters Building had been a largely unnoticed architectural orphan, the old Rialto Building (1935. **Thomas W. Lamb** and **Rosario Candela**); the ground floor tawdry with shops. Upstairs however a swan song of Art Deco was still singing to a small group of fans.*

[T22] **U.S. Armed Forces Recruiting Station**, on an island in Times Sq. bet. Seventh Ave. and Broadway. 1999. **Parsons Brinckerhoff** and **Architecture Research Office**.

An electronic flag? For electronic warfare?

T23

[T23] **Town Hall**, 113-123 W. 43rd St., bet. Sixth Ave. and Broadway 1919-1921. **McKim, Mead & White**. 🍎 Interior 🍎.

Bland Georgian Revival on the outside shelters a large but intimate, acoustically successful concert hall within. Citizens of the world who here have spoken here include **Winston Churchill**, **Theodore Roosevelt**, **Margaret Sanger**, and **Henry James**.

T24

[T24] **Henry Miller's Theater**, 124 W. 43rd St., bet. Sixth and Seventh Aves. 1917-1918. **Allen, Ingalls & Hoffman**.

Neo-Georgian, with brick pilasters and limestone capitals. Here we were *Born Yesterday,* attended *The Cocktail Party,* and wandered *Under Milk Wood.* The Kit Kat Club was also on the premises during the run of *Cabaret.* 🍎

[T25] Originally **Paramount Theatre Building**, 1501 Broadway, bet. W. 43rd and W. 44th Sts. W side. 1926-1927. **C. W. Rapp & George L. Rapp.** 🍎

The tower, clocks, and globe (once illuminated) are sensational. In the early days there was even an observation deck. The World Wrestling Federation has opened a theme restaurant in the old theater space (the ghost of **Frank Sinatra** lurks here). **Hulk Hogan** for an appetizer?

T25

[T26] **156 West 44th Street** (offices), bet. Sixth and Seventh Aves. 1920s.

A charming neo-Gothic arch straddles a local restaurant.

[T27] Originally The Lambs Club/now **Lambs Theater and Manhattan Church of the Nazarene**, 130 W. 44th St., bet. Sixth Ave. and Broadway. 1905. **Stanford White** of **McKim, Mead & White**. Doubled westerly, 1915, **George A. Freeman**. 🍎

A neo-Federal clubhouse built for a still-lively actors' group. The group has moved elsewhere. "Floreant Agni 1874-1904." **McKim Mead & White** were all Lambs.

T27

[T28] **Belasco Theater**/originally Belasco's Stuyvesant Theater, 111 W. 44th St., bet. Sixth Ave. and Broadway. 1906-1907. **George Keister.** 🍎 Interior 🍎.

Red brick Colonial Revival; limestone pilasters support Composite capitals.

[T29] **Gerard Apartments**/onetime 1-2-3 Hotel/originally Hotel Gerard, 123 W. 44th St., bet. Sixth Ave. and Broadway. 1894. **George Keister**. 🖤

A tan brick and limestone pile—one of many that once filled Times Square's side streets—extravagantly decked out with German Renaissance gables and dormers, undulating bow windows (*beaux* bows), and the Café Un-Deux-Trois. Look up...and further up.

T29

[T30] **Hudson Theater of the Millenium Hotel**/originally Hudson Theater/once Savoy Theater, 139-141 W. 44th St., bet. Sixth and Seventh Aves. 1902-1904. **J. B. McElfatrick & Son** and **Israels & Harder**. 🖤 Interior 🖤. Restored, 1990. **Stonehill & Taylor**.

A dour survivor between two wings of the Millenium. But that's where its air rights went. Beaux Arts out, exuberant in.

[T31] **Millenium Broadway Hotel**, 143 W. 44th St., bet. Sixth Ave. and Broadway. 1990s.

A conservative limestone and granite modern façade that anchors the base of the sleek glass tower above.

T31

[T32] **Astor Plaza**, 1515 Broadway, bet. W. 44th and W. 45th Sts. W side. 1968-1970. **Kahn & Jacobs. Der Scutt**, designer.

A 50-story office tower that replaced one of Times Square's most beloved landmarks, the Astor Hotel. From afar its finial fins look like the tail of an impaled spaceship. This was the first building to exploit the special Times Square Theater District zoning bonuses that allowed developers to erect buildings of greater than normal bulk in return for constructing a new legitimate theater.

T32

[T33] **Shubert Alley**, from W. 44th St. to W. 45th St., bet. Broadway and Eighth Aves.

Now a convenience for theatergoers, this private alley was once a magnet for aspiring actors, who gathered in front of the offices of **J. J. and Lee Shubert** when plays were being cast.

Mid-Block Pedestrianism: Lengthy blocks between Sixth and Eighth Avenues offer midblock shortcuts that honor pedestrianism in this densely packed section of the city. Shubert Alley (44th-45th, bet. 7th and 8th) has been around "forever," but modern buildings often offer (sometimes a zoning-bonus requirement) air conditioned tunnels through the block. Minskoff Alley, east of Shubert, is nearby. Others include the Millenium Hotel (44th-45th, bet. 6th and 7th), the Bertelman Building (45th-46th, bet. 6th and 7th), the Marriott Hotel (45th-46th, bet. Broadway and 8th), Crowne Plaza (48th-49th, bet. Broadway and 8th), Rockefeller Center West's backsides (48th-50th Sts., W of 6th), Gershwin Alley (50th–51st, Broadway to 8th), Equitable Life (51st-52nd, 6th to 7th), and Flathotel (52nd-53rd, 6th to 7th). Look for the black and white diamond pattern and yellow arrows marking the sidewalks (thanks to the Times Square Business Improvement District).

[T34] **Sam S. Shubert Theatre**, 225 W. 44th St., bet. Broadway and Eighth Ave. at Shubert Alley. 1912-1913. **Henry B. Herts**. 🖤 Interior 🖤 [T35] **Booth Theatre**, 222 W. 45th St. 1913. **Henry B. Herts**. 🖤 Interior 🖤.

The pair of richly ornamented theaters—the large Shubert and the smaller Booth—that forms the west "wall" of Shubert Alley. The Shubert is the heart (*cum* theater and offices) of the Shubert theater empire. *A Chorus Line* showed the Empire's lasting power. And the Booth was home to *You Can't Take It with You* and *Sunday in the Park with George*.

T34

Sardi's: The restaurant at 234 West 44th Street, strategically located among theaters and at the back door to the New York Times, *has for decades been the place for actors to be seen—except during performance hours.*

[T36] **Helen Hayes Theater**/formerly Little Theater/later Anne Nichol's Little Times Hall, 240 W. 44th St., bet. Broadway and Eighth Ave. 1912. **Ingalls & Hoffman**. Interior rebuilt 1917-1920. **Herbert J. Krapp**. 🍎 Interior 🍎 .

Colonial Revival, inside and out. Producer **Winthrop Ames** sought a context for "intimate" theater.

[T37] **St. James Theater**/formerly Erlanger Theater, 246-256 W. 44th St., bet. Broadway and Eighth Ave. 1926-1927. **Warren & Wetmore**. 🍎 Interior 🍎 .

The fire escape offers a rich Moorarabic balcony to the street. Here were sung *Oklahoma!*, *Hello Dolly*, and *The King and I*.

[T38] **Broadhurst Theater**, 235-243 W. 44th St., bet. Broadway and Eighth Ave. 1917-1918. **Herbert J. Krapp**. 🍎 . Interior 🍎

[T39] **Majestic Theater**, 247 W. 44th St., bet. Broadway and Eighth Ave. 1926-1927. **Herbert J. Krapp**. 🍎 Interior 🍎 .

Two subdued, innocuous but functional playhouses. The Majestic was home to *South Pacific* and *The Phantom of the Opera*.

[T40] **Playpen** (adult videos, etc.), 693 Eighth Ave., bet. W. 43rd and W. 44th Sts. W side. ca. 1900.

It might be termed Times Square Beaux Arts: an exuberant building that might be recaptured during the uplifting of Times Square's neighborhood.

T40

[T41] **Marriott Marquis Hotel**, 1531-1549 Broadway, bet. W. 45th and W. 46th Sts. W side. 1981-1985. **John Portman, Jr**.

A spectacular lobby with glassed-in rocket ship elevators starts at the 8th floor, a superatrium here squeezed into Broadway real estate (Portman's earlier attempts in Atlanta, Chicago, and San Francisco allowed for more horizontal dimension). Inside, it is glitzy in a way developers think appropriate to Broadway.

T41   T42

[T42] **Lyceum Theatre**, 149-157 W. 45th St., bet. Sixth Ave. and Broadway. 1902-1903. **Herts & Tallant**. 🍎 Interior 🍎 .

Powerful neo-Baroque columns articulate the grandest of Beaux Arts façades. Saved from demolition in 1939, it survived to become the oldest New York theater still used for legitimate productions and the first to be landmarked. Magnificent.

T43

[T43] **Bertelsmann Building**, 1540 Broadway, between W. 45th and W. 46th Sts. Entry on 45th St. 1987-1990. **Skidmore, Owings & Merrill**.

A triumphal entry on 45th Street; a flock of requisite signs in orderly chaos facing Broadway. A mannerist layering over the sleek faceted tower "showing a bit of cleavage through those slits in the shirt."

And within, the world's largest record store: Virgin Megastore. 1990s. **BNK** (**Bibliowicz Nelligan Kriegal**) and **Irvine-Johnstone**. Official All Star Café, **The Rockwell Group**.

[T44] **Music Box Theater**, 239-247 W. 45th St., bet. Broadway and Eighth Ave. 1920. **C.Howard Crane** and **E. George Kiehler**. 📷 Interior 📷 .
Slender Federal Revival columns articulate the façade. Within some have seen *The Man Who Came to Dinner* and *Dinner at Eight*.

T44

For the Booth Theater see [T 35] above.

[T45] **Plymouth Theater**, 236 W. 45th St., Bet. Broadway and Eighth Ave. 1917-1918. **Herbert J. Krapp**. 📷 Interior 📷 .
[T46] **Royale Theater**, 242 W. 45th St. 1926-1927. **Herbert J. Krapp**. 📷 Interior 📷 . [T47] **Golden Theater**/originally Theatre Masque, 252-256 W. 45th St. 1926-1927. **Herbert J. Krapp**. 📷 Interior 📷 . [T48] **Imperial Theater**, 249 W. 45th St. 1923. **Herbert J. Krapp**. Interior only. 📷
Unassuming except for the Golden, where tall arches relieve the façade, crowned with a colonnaded gallery. **Ethel Barrymore** receiving adulation from her fans? *Tobacco Road* began here.
The Plymouth housed *The Odd Couple*, and the Royale was home to *The Night of the Iguana*. The Imperial *Gypsy*, *Cabaret*, and *Les Misérables*.

T47

[T49] **Martin Beck Theater**, 302 W. 45th St., bet. Eighth and Ninth Aves. 1923-1924. **C. Albert Lansburgh**. 📷 Interior.
Producer **Martin Beck** commissioned Lansburgh and painter **Albert Herter** to create this fantasy of Romanesque histrionics. What better place to play *Man of La Mancha*?

[T50] **Paramount Hotel**, 245 W. 46th St., bet. Broadway and Eighth Ave. Interiors remodeled, 1980s. **Phillipe Starck**.
A boutique hotel with the high style of French designer and motorcyclist **Philippe Starck**.

[T51] **Church of St. Mary the Virgin** (Episcopal); Rectory, Clergy House, Mission House, 145 W. 46th St., bet. Sixth and Seventh Aves. 1894-1895. **Napoleon Le Brun & Sons**, architects. **J. Massey Rhind**, Sculptor. 📷
A rich liturgical oasis in this precinct of Mammon, booze, and pornography—incense and liturgy here often exceed that of the Catholic Counter-Reformation. The first church in the world to be erected on a steel frame (but concealed; many before, particularly in France, were of cast- and/or wrought-iron, but there exposed).

T51

[T52] Former Public School 67. Manhattan/later High School of the Performing Arts/now **Jacqueline Kennedy Onassis High School for International Careers**, 120 W. 46th St., bet. Sixth and Seventh Aves. 1893-1894. **C. B. J. Snyder**. 📷 Restored, 1991-1993. **Jack L. Gordon**.
Brick and brownstone Romanesque Revival: a sober Protestant foil to St. Mary's quasi-Catholic façade opposite.

T52

[T53] Great women of the theater are honored in sculpture on the façade of the former **I. Miller Building** (West 46th Street, northeast corner of Seventh Avenue. 1927-1929. **Louis H. Friedland**.): **Mary Pickford** (as the title in *Little Lord Fauntleroy*), **Rosa Ponselle** (in the title role in *Norma*), **Ethel Barrymore** (as Ophelia), and **Marilyn Miller** (in the title role of the musical, *Sunny*). They are all by **A(lexander) Stirling Calder**, father of the late, famed inventor of mobiles, **Alexander Calder**. 1929. 📷

T53

[T54] **Richard Rodgers Theater**/originally Chanin's Forty-sixth Street Theater, 226 W. 46th St., bet. Broadway and Eighth Ave. 1924. **Herbert J. Krapp.** 👁 Interior 👁 .

Giant white terra-cotta Corinthian pilasters and arches suggest a style that might be termed Broadway Renaissance. Within played *Guys and Dolls.*

[T55] **Lunt-Fontanne Theater**/originally Globe Theater, 205 W. 46th St. 1909-1910. **Carrère & Hastings.** Rebuilt, 1957-1958. **Roche & Roche.** 👁

T54

A mannerist Spanish or Italian Rococo palazzo of the first order. Home to a long run of *The Sound of Music.*

Duffy Square: *The northern triangle of Times Square is dedicated to* **Father Francis P. Duffy** *(1871-1932), a national hero in World War I as "Fighting Chaplain" of New York's 69th Regiment, later a friend of actors, writers, and mayors as pastor of Holy Cross Church on West 42nd Street. His statue (1937.* **Charles Keck.***) faces the back of one representing* **George M. Cohan** *(1878-1942), another Times Square hero (1959.* **George Lober***).*

T55

[T56] **tkts**, W. 47th St., bet. Seventh Ave. and Broadway. S side. 1973-1999. **Mayers & Schiff.**

The uptown half of Duffy Square is occupied (until it's replaced) by the Times Square Theatre Center [tkts], an elegant pipe-and-canvas structure where half-price ducats are available just before showtime. Certainly eligible for landmarking in a city where such moments of joy are rare, it has deteriorated, and is to be replaced by something equally fine. Stay tuned.

[T57] **Times Square Visitors Center**/originally Embassy I Theater, 1556-1560 Broadway, bet. W. 46th and W. 47th Sts. 1925. **Thomas W. Lamb** and the **Rambusch Studio.** Interior 👁 Remodeled as visitors' center, 1998. **Ronette Riley.**

T56

Outside, McDonald's dominates. Inside, designed as a stylish (and tiny) movie house for stylish people, it became the consummate newsreel theater. The grand foyer now leads to the auditorium space Visitors Center, where booths will inform you.

[T58] **Doubletree Suites Times Square Hotel**/originally Embassy Suites Times Square Hotel, over the Palace Theater, 1564 Broadway, SE cor. W. 47th Sts. E side. Theater, 1912-1913. **Kirchoff & Rose.** Renovated, 1965-1966. **Ralph Alswang & John J. McNamara.** Interior 👁 . New superimposed and surrounding hotel, 1990-1991. **Fox & Fowle.**

Stacked signs, required by zoning, seem to support the sleek new tower above. The old building, the Carnegie Hall of vaudeville, is now enveloped by the new hotel and commercial construction. Before its immersion in this larger project the Palace had already been obliterated by signs.

T58

[T59] **United States Trust Company Headquarters**, 114 W. 47th St., bet. Sixth and Seventh Aves., S side. 1990. **Fox & Fowle.**

Octagonal in the skyline, bland granite at the base. A sober building for a conservative bank. Trust for your trust?

[T60] **Planet Hollywood Hotel**, W. 47th St. SW cor. Broadway. 2000. **Frank Williams & Associates.**

Giant projection screens bring video as an architectural element on this 54-story newcomer to Times Square.

[T61] **Biltmore Theater**, 261-265 W. 47th St., bet. Broadway and Eighth Ave. 1925-1926. **Herbert J. Krapp.** Interior only 👁 .

A simple French palace: perhaps a cut-rate Grand Trianon. *Hair* in the Trianon?

T62

[T62] **Barrymore Theater**, 243-251 W. 47th St., bet. Broadway and Eighth Ave. 1928. **Herbert J. Krapp.** 👁 Interior 👁 .

Wondrous ironmongery supports the marquee and modulates the pedestrianway. Here played *A Streetcar Named Desire*.

[T63] **Brooks Atkinson Theater**/originally Mansfield Theater, 256-262 W. 47th St., bet. Broadway and Eighth Ave. 1925-1926. **Herbert J. Krapp.** 🖋 Interior 🖋 .
Theatrical architecture here delivered a "Spanish" palazzo, Mozarabic columns, and Palladian windows.

T64

[T64] **Renaissance Hotel** (and offices), 1580 Broadway, on the island at Times Square's north end, between W. 47th and W. 48th Sts., Broadway to Seventh Ave. 1989. **Mayers & Schiff**.
Here a building is meant as much as a carriage for signs as it is a useful hotel tower. But here again it has been difficult to capture the serendipity of yore.

[T65] **49th Street BMT subway station**, below Seventh Ave. bet. W. 47th and W. 49th Sts. 1919. Renovated, 1973, **Johnson/Burgee**.
Brilliant glazed vermilion brick set the tone for this early reconstructed subway station.

T66

[T66] **Morgan Stanley Dean Witter Building**, 1585 Broadway, bet. W. 47th and W. 48th St. 1990-1995. **Gwathmey Siegel Assocs. & Emery Roth & Sons**. MSDW'S Investment/Information Center. 1998. **Brennan Beer Gorman Monk**.
A talented partnership designed its first major office building—a jump in scale difficult for all, no matter how gifted. See their addition to the Guggenheim Museum; and we await their new U.S. Delegation to the United Nations building.
The zipper stock signs have enlivened 1585's early austerity.

[T67] **Longacre Theater**, 220-228 W. 48th St. 1912-1913. **Henry B. Herts.** 🖋 Interior 🖋 .

T67

An imposing neo-Classical façade. Here we might have seen *Ain't Misbehavin'*.

[T68] **Cort Theater**, 138-146 W. 48th St., bet. Sixth and Seventh Aves. 1912-1913. **Thomas W. Lamb.** 🖋 Interior 🖋 .
Step back. The marquee masks its grand image as a Petit Trianon off Broadway.

[T69] **Crowne Plaza Hotel**, 1601 Broadway, bet. W. 48th and W. 49th Sts. W side. 1987-1989. **The Alan Lapidus Group**.
The Marriott opened the door for the return of hotels to Times Square. **Alan Lapidus**, son and sometime partner of his father, **Morris** (who created the Miami Beach hotel architecture of the 1940s and 1950s), brings a second dollop of glitz to this precinct. The bottom is in the cluttered Times Square style; the top could be from Hong Kong.

T69

[T70] **B. Smith's Restaurant**, 771 Eighth Ave., NW cor. W. 47th St. 1986. **Anderson/Schwartz**.
A supersleek Italo-new wave restaurant topped with a penthouse of corrugated steel in the fashion of California architect **Frank Gehry**. The painted stucco and simple detailing of the exterior give way to elegance inside. Gold chains brighten the terrazzo within, while bottle caps inlay the asphalt street without.

T71

▐▬ [T71] **Engine Company No. 54, Ladder Company No. 4, Battalion 9, N.Y.C. Fire Department**, 782 Eighth Ave., SE cor. W. 48th St. 1974. **Department of Public Works**.
Even the city's avenue of streetwalkers needs fire protection. This muted brown brick cubist exercise provides it. Congratulations to the D.P.W.

[T72] **Worldwide Plaza** (mixed use), Eighth to Ninth Aves., W. 49th to W. 50th Sts. Apartment towers, 1989, **Frank Williams**. Office tower, 1989, **Skidmore, Owings & Merrill**.

T72

This giant complex occupies the site of the second Madison Square Garden (1925-1966), in turn replaced by the present

T72

Garden between 31st and 33rd Streets, Seventh and Eighth
Avenues. Zoning changes have encouraged this western migration of both offices and residences, by allowing more construction here than can now be erected in East Midtown.

Heavy-handed, the office tower aspires to the serene solidity
of Rockefeller Center, but the form lacks that center's graceful
slenderness and setbacks.

T73

[T73] **St. Malachy's Roman Catholic Church**, 239-245 W. 49th
St., bet. Broadway and Eighth Ave. 1903. **Joseph H. McGuire**.

Brick and limestone neo-Gothic, best known as Broadway's
chapel for Catholic actors, where a mass could be interwoven
with their matinee and evening schedules.

[T74] **Eugene O'Neill Theater**/formerly Coronet Theater/originally
Forrest Theater, 230-238 W. 49th St. 1925-1926. **Herbert J. Krapp**.
Interior ● . Interior restoration, 1994. **Campagna & Russo**.

A delicate iron balcony suggests New Orleans. *Tobacco Road*
survived 3,182 performances here (1934-1941) after opening at
the Theater Masque.

T76

[T75] **Ambassador Theater**, 219 W. 49th St., bet. Seventh and
Eighth Aves. 1919-1921. **Herbert J. Krapp**. Interior ● .

An austere exterior with subtle brick relieving arches and
updated machicolations. *Bring In 'Da Noise, Bring in 'Da Funk*
has played here.

[T76] **Morgan Stanley Building**, 750 Seventh Avenue, bet. W.
49th and W. 50th Sts., Broadway and Seventh Ave. 1988-1990.
Kevin Roche John Dinkleloo & Assocs.

Here the heirs of **Eero Saarinen** bring high style to the
blocks north of Times Square proper. The finial finger points
accusingly at the sky. Elsewhere see their Morgan Bank
Headquarters at 60 Wall Street, the new Central Park Zoo, and
United Nations Plaza, Nos. 1, 2, and 3.

[T77] **Morgan Stanley Dean Witter Plaza**, Seventh Ave. bet. W.
49th and W. 50th Sts. E side. 2002. **Kohn Pederson Fox**.

Things to come; this will replace **Earl Carroll**'s theater.

[T78] Originally Hollywood Theater/sometime Mark Hellinger
Theater/now **Times Square Church**, 217-239 W. 51st St., bet.
Broadway and Eighth Ave. 1929-1930. **Thomas W. Lamb** and the
Rambusch Studio. ● Interior ● .

Lamb blended **Frank Lloyd Wright**, **Eliel Saarinen** outside and Hollywood Baroque within. Steamy. But the marquee demeans it all.

[T79] **Winter Garden Theater**/originally American Horse Exchange, 1634-1646 Broadway, bet. W. 50th and W. 51st Sts. 1881-1883. **David & John Jardine**. Rebuilt after fire, 1897. **A.V. Porter**. Remodeled into theater, 1910-1911. **W. Albert Swasey**. Again remodeled, 1922-1923. **Herbert J. Krapp**. New 50th Street façade, 1997. **Menz & Cook**. Interior 🌶 .

T79

A horse exchange? There was a horse ring 80 by 160, spanned by trusses, that became the volume of the future theater. *Cats* was entrenched here for years.

[T80] **Equitable Center** (offices), 787 Seventh Ave., bet. W. 51st and W. 52nd St. E side. 1986. **Edward Larrabee Barnes Assocs**.

A great atrium and through-block galleria (note the **Barry Flanagan** elephant) modulate the bulk of polished rose granite. The atrium is open to the public except on Sundays and holidays.

From afar one can see the great arch of the boardroom at the top, but up close the building skin is bland and smooth, without articulated detail, a kind of Asia Society times ten.

T80

Roy Lichtenstein's great mural dominates the lobby's central atrium space.

[T81] **Flathotel**/originally The Manhattan (apartments and offices), 131 W. 52nd St., bet. Sixth and Seventh Aves. 1987. **Rafael Viñoly Architects**.

A handsome cubistic, neo-1930s multiple-use building, where the play of glazing subdivisions (squares) is in the popular PoMo (Post-Modern) vocabulary. Precast concrete—some rough, some smooth—in differing shades of gray gives a base to the glassy construction overhead. The modeling of the upper floors is both subtle and elegant. A pedestrian allée connects with 53rd Street.

T81

[T82] **Sheraton Centre**/originally Americana Hotel, Seventh Ave. bet. W. 52nd and W. 53rd Sts. E side. 1962. **Morris Lapidus & Assocs**.

A sleek supermotel that offers characterless but efficient quarters for the traveler. For character and class go to the Plaza or St. Regis.

Here is a point to look back and savor the clocks and great metalwork globe atop the old Paramount Building to the south.

T82

[T83] **1675 Broadway** (offices and theater), NW cor. W. 52nd St. 1986-1989. **Fox & Fowle**.

A green granite slab reminiscent in its modeling of the RCA Building in Rockefeller Center. It yearns for a solidity of masonry that 1950s and 1960s Modern rejected in favor of glass (but daytime glass is visually solid, and nighttime glass a see-through negligee). Enveloped within is the old Broadway Theater (1924. **Eugene De Rosa**).

T83

Gallagher's Restaurant: 228 West 52nd Street. Slaughterhouse on Seventh Avenue, its windows a refrigerator displaying meat that is an encyclopedia of beef's possibilities. The restaurant within offers a sauce that makes the simplest sliced steak a mouth-watering proposition.

[T84] **Neil Simon Theater**/originally Alvin Theater, 250 W. 52nd St., bet. Broadway and Eighth Ave. 1926-1927. **Herbert J. Krapp**. 🌶 Interior 🌶 .

Georgian run amok. *Porgy and Bess* and *Funny Face* played here.

T85

[T85] **Virginia Theater**/once ANTA Theater/originally Guild Theater, 245 W. 52nd St., bet. Broadway and Eighth Ave. 1924-1925. **Crane & Franzheim.** 🍎
A top-of-the line Tuscan villa? Or more *Much Ado About Nothing. Mourning Becomes Electra* and *Ah, Wilderness!* played here.

Dining and dancing, Times Square style: With venerable Lindy's gone from Times Square, Jewish-American delicatessen-style food, long favored by entertainers, reaches its peak at the Stage Delicatessen, a small, crowded place at 834 Seventh Avenue between West 53rd and West 54th Streets, and the Carnegie Delicatessen, a block north at No. 854. Each has partisans who claim theirs is better. Try both and decide. Big dance halls, once common around the square, survive only in the sedate Roseland, in a former ice skating palace at 239 West 52nd Street (between Broadway and Eighth Avenue).

[T86] **St. Benedict's Church** (Roman Catholic)/formerly Church of St. Benedict, the Moor, 342 W. 53rd St., bet. Eighth and Ninth Aves. 1869. **R. C. McLane & Sons**.
This church for black Catholics was founded in 1883 at 210 Bleecker Street. In the mid 1890s the congregation moved to this Italianate building, built by an earlier Protestant Evangelical congregation, at the edge of what was then a middle-class black community.

T86

[T87] **The Ed Sullivan Theater**/originally Hammerstein's Theater, 1697-1699 Broadway, bet. W. 53rd and W. 54th Sts. 1925-1927. **Herbert J. Krapp.** 🍎
The Late Show with David Letterman is broadcast here.

[T88] **Midtown North Precinct, N.Y.C. Police Department**/originally 18th Precinct, 306 W. 54th St. 1939. **Department of Public Works**.
A serene limestone cube contrasts with the chaos of entertainment district police business flowing into and out of its doors. Note the freestanding Art Moderne lanterns of stainless steel that flank the entrances, and the moss growing under the air conditioners.

[T89] **St. George Tropoforos Hellenic Orthodox Church**/formerly New Amsterdam Building, 307 W. 54th St. 1886.
This Romanesque Revival building began as small offices and now, in sandblasted natural brick, serves as a church. The joyous ornament is still evident.

[T90] **Midtown Community Court**/originally 11th District Municipal Court, 314 W. 54th St., bet. Eighth and Ninth Aves. 1894-1896. **John H. Duncan**. 👆 Altered, 1993. **Davis Brody Bond**.

A quartet of banded Corinthian columns in terra-cotta frames the principle floor of this venerable courthouse. The Art Moderne/Classic Revival police station next door is in its own "fancy dress," but can't compete.

T90

[T91] **Rihga Royal Hotel**/originally Hotel Royal Concordia, 151 W. 54th St., bet. Sixth and Seventh Aves. N side. 1989. **Frank Williams & Assocs**.

The hotel presents a gaudy and heavy-handed base under an innocuous block of rooms above. Nevertheless, the galleria to 55th Street is a serious contribution to pedestrianism. Williams is credited with designing two of the Upper West Side's most interesting high-rise apartment buildings, the Columbia and the Park Belvedere.

T91

[T92] **154 West 55th Street**/formerly 55th Street Playhouse/originally stables and Holbein Studio, bet. Sixth and Seventh Aves. 1888. **E. Bassett Jones**.

A Romanesque Revival stable, once a movie theater, now endangered. The Rihga Hotel behind uses the ground floor as a truck delivery entrance.

T92

[T93] **City Center 55th Street Theater**/originally Mecca Temple, 135 W. 55th St., bet. Sixth and Seventh Aves. 1922-1924. **Harry P. Knowles** (d. 1923), succeeded by **Clinton & Russell**. 👆 Continuing renovations 1990s. **Bernard Rothzeid**.

Saved from destruction by **Mayor La Guardia**, this Spanish tile domed multitiered theater has served for decades as a performing arts center. The architecture is delightfully absurd, as might be expected from members of the Ancient and Accepted Order of the Mystic Shrine, its original builders.

T94

[T94] **CitySpire** (mixed use), 150 W. 56th St. through to W. 55th St., bet. Sixth and Seventh Aves. 1987. **Murphy/Jahn**.

A dull podium and a 69-story **Helmut Jahn** phallic finial are made possible by the transfer of City Center's air rights.

Like Carnegie Hall Tower and Metropolitan Tower, its neighbors across the street with equally overactive thyroids, the lower part is devoted to commercial uses and the upper, the part in the clouds, to lavish apartment living. **Stuart Eichner** (its developer) was here; for other Eichner projects see his own house by **Alfredo de Vido** on Columbia Heights in Brooklyn.

Patelson's, at 160 East 56th Street, is an emporium of sheet music, books, and oddments sought out by serious musicians from all over the world. Here each instrumentalist can find his or her score of Bach, Beethoven, or Bartok.

T95

[T95] Originally **Horn & Hardart's Automat**, 104 W. 57th St., bet. Sixth and Seventh Aves. 1938. **Ralph B. Bencker**.

One of that seductive chain of technocratic restaurants where a nickel could buy not only a cup of coffee, but a magnificent sticky bun. Drop the nickel in a slot and one could open a brass-framed glass door and "win" the sandwich or dessert behind. For a live rerun, rent *That Touch of Mink* to see the nickels and glass doors in action.

[T96] **Steinway Hall**, home of *The Economist*, 111 W. 57th St., bet. Sixth and Seventh Aves. 1925. **Warren & Wetmore**.

A sober Classical tower built by one of the many music concerns clustered around Carnegie Hall. The Ionic temple on top enriches the skyline, but has little influence at street level.

T96

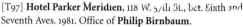

[T97] **Hotel Parker Meridien**, 118 W. 57th St., bet. Sixth and Seventh Aves. 1981. Office of **Philip Birnbaum**.

A 2-story vaulted colonnade of Tuscan columns leads to a skylit colonnaded atrium. Does the architect find this serious or a Post Modern jest? The hotel rooms, like the body of a 42nd Street theater, are on 56th Street.

T97

[T98] **130 West 57th Street** (studios), bet. Sixth and Seventh Aves. 1908. **Pollard & Steinam**. 🍎

The great tiers of bay windows here and at 140 next door are reminiscent of late high-rise Oxbridge Gothic.

[T99] **Planet Hollywood**, 140 W. 57th St., bet. Sixth and Seventh Aves. Building, 1908. **Pollard & Steinem**. 🍎 Restaurant, 1990s. **David Rockwell**.

The Planet displays its melodrama inside, not out. One of the theatrical tourist's feeding and watering troughs of 57th, along with the Hard Rock Café, the Motown Café, and the Brooklyn Diner.

T98

[T100] **Metropolitan Tower** (mixed use), 140 W. 57th St., bet. Sixth and Seventh Aves. 1987. **Schuman, Lichtenstein, Claman & Efron**.

Harry Macklowe, the developer, says that he designed this himself. If so, he can take the blame for a gross and insensitive intrusion into these blocks. Its knife-edged glass form is impressive but inappropriate. But the rock star tenants and their peers will savor its parvenu glitz.

The Russian Tea Room (150 West 57th Street) became the spacer that allowed (some) light and air to the competing Carnegie and Metropolitan towers. Now rebuilt, the Tea Room (only the façade [1873. **John G. Prague***] was saved from the original), owned and managed by* **Warner LeRoy** *(Tavern on the Green, Maxwell's Plum), and designed by* **Harman Jablin Architects** *and a cast of exotic interior designers, seats 140 on the ground floor in a décor that is said to match the 1927 original.*

Now turn around and discover (across the street) some hearty survivors from 57th Street's past:

[T101] **Carnegie Hall Tower** (mixed use), 152 W. 57th St., bet. Sixth and Seventh Aves. 1986-1990. **Cesar Pelli & Assocs**.

T101

In the venerable slot between Carnegie Hall and the Russian Tea Room ("slightly to the left of Carnegie Hall"), rises a slender tower that defers to the Renaissance Revival architecture of its parent next door. Highrise Medici?

[T102] **Row houses**, 147-153 W. 57th St., bet. Sixth and Seventh Aves. 147-151, 1886. **Douglas and John Jardine**.

No. 153's brick and limestone Renaissance Revival is cheek by jowl with two heavily made-up Queen Annes.

[T103] **Carnegie Hall**, 156 W. 57th St., SE cor. Seventh Ave. to W. 56th St. 1889-1891. **William B. Tuthill**. Office Wing, 1892-1895. **William B. Tuthill**. Studio wing, 1896-1897. **Henry J. Hardenbergh**. Richard Morris Hunt, Dankmar Adler, consultants. 🍎 Reconfigured and restored, 1986. **James Stewart Polshek & Partners**. Zankel Hall, 1990s. **Polshek Partnership**.

T102

Dour Renaissance Revival engulfed in studios and other appendices bristling above and around it. World-famous more for its acoustics than its architectural envelope, it was threatened in the early 1960s when Lincoln Center's Avery Fisher Hall rose up. Violinist Isaac Stern and others, raising a public outcry, saved it. It is now solidly booked.

T103

Lovingly restored, grander than ever, its familiar form is re-appreciated (urban architectural tastes are sometimes fickle: see the story of the Jefferson Market Courthouse).

[T104] **Columbia Artists Management**/originally Louis H. Chalif's School of Dancing, 165 W. 57th St., bet. Sixth and Seventh Aves. 1917. **George and Henry Boehm.** 🌸

Italian Mannerist with Tuscan overtones that make it a fine neighbor to Carnegie Hall across 57th. The colonnaded gallery at the top would make a magnificent apartment. **Christopher Gray** quotes **Louis Chalif** denouncing modern music as "barbarians banging on human skulls in a cannibalistic orgy." Sounds like fun.

T105

[T105] **Alwyn Court Apartments**, 180 W. 58th St., SE cor. Seventh Ave. 1907-1909. **Harde & Short.** 🌸 Restoration, 1980-1981, **Beyer Blinder Belle**; murals by **Richard Haas**.

A French Renaissance exterior, every square foot literally encrusted with terra-cotta decorations: crowns and dragons everywhere. Within the courtyard is a painted architectural façade by **Richard Haas**. Fantastic!

[T106] **Brooklyn Diner and Plaza Pergola**, W. 57th St. entry to 888 Seventh Ave. just west of 200 W. 57th below.

What sculpture provided for the elegant tower (say Noguchi at 140 Broadway), razmatazz supplies in these more theatrical precincts. Near the Hard Rock Café and Planet Hollywood, the Brooklyn Diner hopes to draw some of the more affluent members of those crowds. Affluent? Diners don't come cheap in these very pricey Manhattan reincarnations.

T106

[T107] **Office Building**/formerly Rodin Studios, 200 W. 57th St., bet. Seventh Ave. and Broadway. 1916-1917. **Cass Gilbert.** 🌸

Neo-Gothic filigree hovers over each alternate floor capping the original two-story studio spaces.

[T108] **The Osborne Apartments**, 205 W. 57th St., NW cor. Seventh Ave. 1883-1885. Enlargement of top story, 1889. **James E.Ware.** Extension to west, 1906. **Alfred S. G. Taylor.** 🌸

The muted exterior of Classical and Chicago School stonework hides magnificent interiors (including many duplex apartments), foreshadowed by the extravagant marble vestibule and lobby. In the manner of a Florentine palazzo, it is stark and dour without, lush and luxurious within.

T107

[T109] **Art Students League**/originally American Fine Arts Society, 215 W. 57th St., bet. Seventh Ave. and Broadway. 1891-1892. **Henry J. Hardenbergh**, with **W. C. Hunting & J. C. Jacobsen.** 🌸 212-247-4510. Gallery open Su 1-4:30; Mo-Fr 10-8:30; Sa 9:30-4; closed June-Aug.

A stately French Renaissance pile, originally built for an organization that included the Architectural League; now a somewhat academic art school for both amateurs and professionals, perhaps closer to the mainstream in these days of recovered realism.

T108

T109

T111

T112

T113

T114

[T110] **Hard Rock Café**, 221 W. 57th St., bet. Seventh Ave. and Broadway. 1983.

Here an impaled 1959 Cadillac still serves as its canopy, a pop insert in the context of this sober street. The lines to buy its T-shirts and other memorabilia are even longer than the lines to savor the experience firsthand.

[T111] Former **General Motors Building**, 1769-1787 Broadway, bet. 57th and 58th St., to Eighth Ave. Colonnade Building (first three floors), 1923. **W. Welles Bosworth**. Upper stories of building, 1927-1928. **Shreve & Lamb**.

After his extraordinary columnar wedding cake for AT&T on lower Broadway, Bosworth created a three-story Ionic colonnade for this site that served, shortly after, as the plinth for the 26-story General Motors building.

[T111a] Originally International Magazine Building/now **Hearst Magazine Building**, 951-969 Eighth Ave., bet. W. 56th and W. 57th Sts. W side. 1927-1928. **Joseph Urban** and **George B. Post & Sons**. 🌶

Shades of the Austrian Secession movement, this sculptured extravaganza was commissioned by the **William Randolph Hearst** publishing empire. It was a base for a skyscraper aborted due to the Depression. The foundations are still there, waiting...

[T112] **St. Thomas Choir School**, 202 W. 58th St., bet. Seventh and Eighth Aves. 1987. **Buttrick, White & Burtis**.

1930s Georgian revived. Boy sopranos here study, dwell, and sing in preparation for magnificent Bach chorales at the parent St. Thomas Church.

[T113] Originally **Helen Miller Gould stables**, 213 W. 58th St., bet. Seventh Ave. and Broadway. 1902-1903. **York & Sawyer**. 🌶

A grand mansarded brick and limestone stable bears hitching rings carved from the stone itself.

[T114] **Engine Company No. 23, N.Y.C. Fire Department**, 215 W. 58th St., bet. Seventh Ave and Broadway. 1905-1906. **Alexander H. Stevens**. 🌶

A grand fraternal twin to No. 213.

[T115] **Gainsborough Studios**, 222 Central Park South, bet. Broadway and Seventh Ave. 1908. **Charles W. Buckham**. Frieze, **Isidore Konti**. 🌶

The eponymous painter surveys the park from his second-floor perch. Two-story glazing, seeking the open park's wondrous north light, shields the real or would-be artists within. But who can afford it outside the big-name top ten?

T115

Central Park South east of No. 222 is an impressive cliff, including luxury hotels and apartments, but except for the Gainsborough Studios (above), there is little that calls for a close look. Essex House, Hampshire House, the New York Athletic Club, and the St. Moritz are all distinguished by their opulence and opulent residents. Architecturally they form a bland wall (perhaps appropriately) for the lush parkland opposite.

*The St. Moritz of 1929 was threatened with a strip tease and rebuilding by the ubiquitous **Donald Trump** as a retardataire design of, say, 1929. **Beyer Blinder Belle** might have created a class act. But a leveler head prevailed: a restoring savior appeared in the form of **Ian Schrager**, who is in the process of restoring what's there, rather than Trump's total reconstruction over the steel frame.*

 [T116] **240 Central Park South** (apartments), SE cor. Broadway. 1939-1941. **Mayer & Whittlesey.**

Two distinguished apartment towers with cubistic modeling, rise from a one-story, garden-topped podium, and give almost everyone within a good view. Note the Art Moderne zigzag storefronts on Broadway.

T117

[T117] Former **N.Y.C. Department of Cultural Affairs** (offices and gallery)/originally Gallery of Modern Art, 2 Columbus Circle, bet. Broadway and Eighth Ave. to W. 58th St. 1964-1965. **Edward Durell Stone.**

A compact white marble confection with vaguely Middle Eastern motifs, commissioned by A & P heir **Huntington Hartford** and shaped to the constricted site. It shows off well when seen from the north, on Broadway, gleaming among larger, darker structures.

T118

[T118] **1 Central Park Place** (apartments) NW cor. W. 57th St. and Eighth Ave. 1988. **Davis, Brody & Assocs.**

A very tall, very slender luxury tower by the architects who gave us the city's most distinguished publicly assisted housing. It seems sad that Manhattan's tower mania has so subverted the attitudes of developers that the firm that produced East Midtown Plaza [see E6] finally had to play the 1980s urban finial game. Nicely done, but it's not San Gimignano.

T119

[T119] **Office building**, SW cor. W. 58th St. and Eighth Ave. 1990s.

Modest modernism. At the sixth floor, columns make a slight statement. Shy developer? Shy architect?

[T120] **Columbus Circle Station**, IRT Seventh Avenue Line subway below Broadway, Eighth Ave., and Central Park W. and Central Park S. 1904. **Heins & La Farge.** 🍎 Altered.

One of the original IRT subway's architectural relics, now much degraded as a result of its joining with the IND Line.

[T121] **Columbus Center** (mixed use), Columbus Circle, W. 58th to W. 60th Sts. W side. 2001. **David Childs** of **Skidmore, Owings & Merrill**.

In a first round of fantasies, the old Coliseum would have given way to a dual set of enormous towers (**Moshe Safdie**, architect), a new colossus that threatened to throw an elongated shadow across the lawns of Central Park while exacerbating the traffic volume at this node in the Broadway corridor. Round two was initiated by the pullout of a key tenant and the winning of a lawsuit brought against the City and the Triborough Bridge and Tunnel Authority by the Municipal Art Society and allied groups, who charged double-dealing. The resultant rethinking brought a new round of proposals by myriad developers and architects. The winning scheme has a somewhat milder intensity of development and **David Childs** of **Skidmore, Owings & Merrill** at its helm.

T122

[T122] **Columbus Circle**, Broadway/Eighth Ave./Central Park W./Central Park S.

This focal point, where Broadway glances the corner of Central Park, was the obvious place for monumental treatment, but it resulted only in a few sculptures in a tangle of traffic. **Gaetano Russo**'s statue of **Columbus** (1892) is at the hub: architect **H. Van Buren Magonigle**'s *Maine Memorial* (1913) wallows in from the park corner, with a boatload of figures by sculptor **Attilio Piccirilli**. The new Columbus Center proposal may give the definition that this *rond-point* has always yearned for. Traffic has been recircled to anticipate that encircling event.

Columbus Circle's IND and IRT subways (IND A, B, C, and D trains; IRT 1 and 9 trains).

P1

GRAND CENTRAL/PARK AVENUE

Grand Central Terminal to East 57th Street:
"As a bullet seeks its target, shining rails in every part of our
great country are aimed at Grand Central Station, heart of the
nation's greatest city. Drawn by the magnetic force of the fantastic
metropolis, day and night great trains rush toward the Hudson
River, sweep down its eastern bank for 140 miles, flash briefly by
the long red row of tenement houses south of 125th Street, dive with
a roar into the 2½-mile tunnel which burrows beneath the glitter
and swank of Park Avenue and then . . . Grand Central Station!
Crossroads of a million private lives! Gigantic stage on which are
played a thousand dramas daily."

–Opening from "Grand Central Station," broadcast over the
NBC Radio Blue Network, beginning 1937.

The one-mile stretch from Grand Central Terminal to East 59th
Street—the busiest portion of Park Avenue—is a uniquely successful integration of railroad and city. The avenue itself was
built over the New York Central lines (now Amtrak and Metro-
North), and up to 50th Street the buildings along it rise on
columns sprinkled among the fan-shaped yards.

The railroad's right-of-way, down what was originally
Fourth Avenue, dates back to 1832, when the New York and
Harlem Railroad terminated at Chambers Street. The smoke
and noise of locomotives were later banned below 23rd Street,
then 42nd Street, as the socially prominent residential areas
moved north. At 42nd Street the original, cupolaed Grand
Central Depot, with a vast iron-and-glass train shed, was
opened in 1871 (**John B. Snook**, architect; **R. G. Hatfield**, shed
engineer. Remodeled, 1892, **Bradford L. Gilbert**).

In the early 1900s, when electric locomotives were introduced, the railroad took audacious steps that not only increased
the value of its property many times over but also gave the city a
three-dimensional composition that was a major achievement of
the City Beautiful era. The terminal itself was made more efficient and compact by dividing its 67 tracks between two subterranean levels, and Park Avenue north and south of the terminal
was joined in 1919 by a system of automobile viaducts wrapping
around the station.

New engineering techniques for shielding tall buildings from railroad vibrations made possible a complex of offices and hotels around the station and extending north above the yards and tracks. By the onset of the Great Depression the avenue through the 50s was lined with remarkably uniform rows of apartments and hotels, all solid blocks 12 to 16 stories high, punctuated by the divergent form of a church or club. Although some of the buildings had handsome central courtyards, their dense ground coverage must have made summer living unbearable in pre-air-conditioning times (merely luxury tenements)—but, then, people who lived here never summered in the city.

Firm as these palaces appeared, most of them lasted only a few decades. Their loss, as a result of the office building boom of the 1950s and 1960s ("convenient to Grand Central"), eliminated much of Park Avenue's air of elegance.

Park Avenue Walking Tour: From Grand Central Terminal to 60th Street. (Take a subway to the terminal itself: the IRT Lexington Avenue Line (4, 5, or 6 trains), the IRT Flushing Line (7 train), or the IRT Shuttle from Times Square.)

[P1] **Grand Central Terminal**, E. 42nd St. at Park Ave. N side. 1903-1913. **Reed & Stem** and **Warren & Wetmore**. ☕ Painted ceiling over main concourse, **Whitney Warren** with **Paul Helleu** and **Charles Basing**. Partial interior ☕. Restoration and addition of East Stair, 1998. **Beyer Blinder Belle**. Pershing Square Viaduct, 1919. ☕

The remarkably functional scheme of the terminal and its approaches is housed in an imposing Beaux Arts Classical structure. The main façade, facing south down Park Avenue, is a fine symmetrical composition of triumphal arches, filled with steel and glass, surmounted by a colossal clock and sculpture group (by **Jules Coutan**) in which Roman deities fraternize with an American eagle. The symbolism may be confusing, but the scale and composition are most imposing.

P2

The main room inside is unexpectedly spare in detail, a virtue once again articulated in its superb restoration by the current landlord, Metro-North (and its architects, **Beyer Blinder Belle**). To quote critic **Carter Wiseman**, "Led by **John Belle**...the architects redefined an aging transportation facility as a center for the city's social interaction."

P3

The simple ceiling vault, restored back to its original cerulean blue, 125 feet across, decorated with the constellations of the zodiac, is actually hung from steel trusses. (The zodiac is here seen as if viewed from the point of view of God; or, for the atheist, a mirror image.) Smaller spaces are structurally spanned by Guastavino tile vaulting left exposed, with handsome effect, in parts of the lower level, as at the Oyster Bar.

Grand Central Oyster Bar: This restaurant has been world-renowned for its shellfish stews and pan roasts. The oyster bar and its equipment are worth seeing under exposed tan tile vaulting low enough to touch.

P4

[P2] **Philip Morris Headquarters (offices) and Whitney Museum Branch**, 120 Park Ave., SW cor. E. 42nd St. (Pershing Sq.). 1982. **Ulrich Franzen & Assocs**.

A sober granite slab, somewhat schizophrenic in its elevations, housing a branch of the wondrous Whitney Museum. This oasis not only allows contemplation of art but also provides a dry and warm resting place for the harried midtown traveler: a small café lurks within.

[P3] **Cipriani's 42nd Street** (catering hall)/originally Bowery Savings Bank, 110 E. 42nd St., bet. Park and Lexington Aves. 1923. **York & Sawyer**. ☕ Interior ☕.

275

GRAND CENTRAL / PARK AVENUE

see pages 273–285

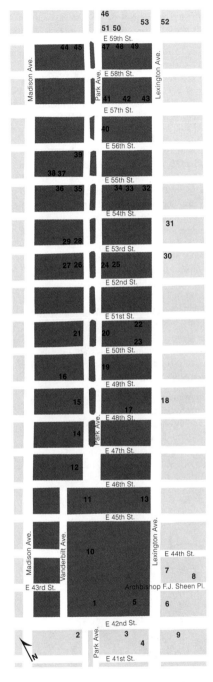

Monumental in its arched entrance, even more so in its great and richly detailed banking room. One of the great spaces of New York. But what is on the menu? Giuseppe Cipriani, together with Harry Pickering, opened Harry's Bar in Venice in 1931. Now they have expanded operations from their restaurant in the Sherry Netherland to this Romano-Byzantine basilica.

[P4] **Chanin Building** (offices), 122 E. 42nd St., SW cor. Lexington Ave. to E. 41st St. 1929. **Sloan & Robertson**. Lobby, **Jacques Delamarre**.

Surprising combinations of angular and floral decoration even Gothic buttresses—sprout on this exuberant office tower. See the lobby, especially the extraordinary convector grilles; outside, an Art Deco bas-relief by **Edward Trumbull** runs around the façades. The Chanin brothers got their start in Brooklyn and went on to develop the Times Square theater district, Central Park West, and this, among many projects. Look back on such distinguished self-improvement, Mr. Trump.

[P5] **Grand Hyatt Hotel**/originally Commodore Hotel, 125 E. 42nd St., NW cor. Lexington Ave. 1920. **Warren & Wetmore**. Rebuilt, 1980, **Gruzen & Partners** and **Der Scutt**.

A dowager hotel building reoutfitted in a somewhat rumpled reflective glass dress. Within, past the 3-D lobby, old walls lurk behind all that glitter.

P6

[P6] **Chrysler Building** (offices), 405 Lexington Ave., NE cor. E. 42nd St. 1930. **William Van Alen**. ❦ Partial interior ❦. Lobby restoration, 1978, **JCS Design Assocs.**, designers, and **Joseph Pell Lombardi**. Further renovations, 1999. **Beyer Blinder Belle**. Chrysler Building East. Reconstruction and renovations, 2000. **Philip Johnson** and **Alan Ritchie**.

The tallest building in the world for the few months before completion of the Empire State Building: 1,048 feet to the top of its spire. Stainless steel not only burnished the lancelike spire and the cowl that forms its supporting crown, but formed the gargantuan radiator cap gargoyles (look for photographer **Margaret Bourke-White**'s widely published image at work, sitting on one). And don't miss the lobby, an Art Deco confection of African marble and chrome steel. And at night that lancet crown glows in the skyline.

The annexes (Chrysler Building East, etc.) are a squalid crew, in the process of upgrade through the talents of **Philip Johnson** and **Alan Ritchie**. Beware.

[P7] **425 Lexington Avenue** (offices), bet. E. 43rd and E. 44th Sts. E side. 1988. **Murphy/Jahn**.

A flamboyant and top-heavy skyline building, that seems like an ugly dwarf next to the venerable reality of the adjacent Chrysler Building. The entranceway suggests a stage set from a terrifying 1930s movie, perhaps the portal to the lair of the Emperor Ming (Flash Gordon's nemesis).

P7

[P8] **St. Agnes Church** (Roman Catholic), 145 E. 43rd St., bet. Lexington and Third Aves. Original church. 1876. **Lawrence J. O'Connor**. Replaced after fire with a new building. 1990s.

The late building was the church of **Bishop Fulton J. Sheen**, popular television priest and converter to Roman Catholicism of such notables as **Claire Booth Luce**, author of *The Women*, wife of *Time* magazine founder **Henry Luce**, and sometime ambassador to Italy. Destroyed by fire, it has been replaced by a vaguely Jesuitical façade in cool and very crisp neo-Classical Post-Modern limestone.

P8

*Bus shelters: Patterned after Parisian bus shelters (the Gallic versions have three legs, not four, and other differences), a host of elegant brown painted steel and tempered glass pergolas began to proliferate on the city's street corners in 1975. Even the full-color advertising, which supplies light (and income to the entrepreneurs), is good-looking. Architects: **Holden, Yang, Raemsch & Terjesen**. The next step in fulfilling the promise of street furniture for the mistreated citizenry is to consummate a deal providing pay toilets à la Français at judicious intervals. Much has been promised, and nothing delivered.*

[P9] Formerly **Mobil Building**/originally Socony Mobil Building, 150 E. 42nd St. bet. Lexington and Third Aves. 1955. **Harrison & Abramovitz.**
   A 1.6 million-square-foot building sheathed with embossed stainless-steel panels. A clever bore to start off with, it is now merely the ultimate architectural tin can.

[P10] **Met Life Building**/originally Pan Am Building (office complex), 200 Park Ave. 1963. **Emery Roth & Sons**, **Pietro Belluschi**, and **Walter Gropius**. Lobby alterations, 1987, **Warren Platner.**
   This latter-day addition to the Grand Central complex was purely a speculative venture. The building aroused protest both for its enormous volume of office space—2.4 million square feet, the most in any single commercial office building at the time—and for blocking the vista up and down Park Avenue, previously punctuated but not stopped by the Helmsley (originally New York Central) Building tower. The precast-concrete curtain wall was one of the first in New York.
   Note the staid, neo-Classical Yale Club (identified in letters only one inch high) across Vanderbilt Avenue from the Pan Am at East 44th Street (1901. **Tracy & Swartwout**). It was once part of an understated neo-Renaissance group, severely compromised with the closing and recladding of the Biltmore Hotel, between 43rd and 44th.

P10

[P11] Onetime **Helmsley Building** (offices)/originally New York Central Building/later New York General Building, 230 Park Ave., bet. E. 45th and E. 46th Sts. 1929. **Warren & Wetmore.** 👁 Partial interior 👁 .
   This office tower, symbol of the then-prosperous railroad, was once visible for miles along Park Avenue. Its fanciful cupola and opulent but impeccably detailed lobby departed from the sobriety of the terminal and the surrounding buildings.
   The north façade, once a remarkably successful molding of urban space, maintained the cornice line of buildings flanking the avenue to the north, carrying it around in small curves to create an apse of grand proportions, crowned by the tower. Only a fragment of the original composition remains, in the relation of the building to 250 Park Avenue. Carved into this façade are two tall portals for automobile traffic, clearly differentiated from the central lobby entrance and the open pedestrian passages to the east and west. The renaming from Central to General required only the filling and recutting of two letters over the auto portals; Helmsley was another matter.
   The Helmsley ownership accounted for the gilding of the ornament and the spectacular nighttime illumination of the building's crown. A restoration is underway that may tone it down.

P11

[P12] Originally **Postum Building** (offices), 250 Park Ave., bet. E. 46th and E. 47th Sts. W side to Vanderbilt Ave. 1925. **Cross & Cross**, architects, **Phelps Barnum**, assoc. architect.

Saved miraculously (by its small full-block site) from being demolished and replaced by a grotesquely larger occupant, No. 250 is one of Park Avenue's few between-the-wars neo-Classical office structures that revere the idea of **Warren & Wetmore** of creating a Terminal City to surround—and enhance—their Grand Central Terminal complex.

P12

[P13] **Park Avenue Atrium** (offices), 466 Lexington Ave., bet. E. 45th and E. 46th Sts. W side. 1984. **Edward Durrell Stone Assocs**. Atrium sculpture, **Richard Lippold**.

Here one block of the original Grand Central Station complex was reincarnated and reclad. More interesting is the inner courtyard, originally open to the sky and now a glass-roofed atrium. In the manner of **John Portman**'s various hotel atriums (but here more in the spirit of a small-town Marriott), rocket ship elevators float up and down the side of this huge space.

[P14] **Chase Bank Offices**/originally Union Carbide Building (offices), 270 Park Ave., bet. E. 47th and E. 48th Sts. W side to Madison Ave. 1960. Remodeled, 1983. All by **Skidmore, Owings & Merrill**.

The 53-story sheer tower is articulated with bright stainless-steel mullions against a background of gray glass and black matte-finished steel panels. The 13-story wing to the rear (well related in scale to Madison Avenue) is linked to the tower by a narrow transparent bridge, dramatically placed at the north end of Vanderbilt Avenue. The site of the building over railroad yards made it necessary to start elevators at the second floor, reached by escalators. In charge was SOM's **Natalie DuBois**, one of Modern architecture's early prominent women.

P14

[P15] **Bankers Trust Building**, 280 Park Ave., bet. E. 48th and E. 49th Sts. W side. 1963. **Emery Roth & Sons. Henry Dreyfuss**, designer. Addition to W, 1971, **Emery Roth & Sons. Oppenheimer, Brady & Lehrecke**, associated architects.

A rare example of an industrial designer (**Dreyfuss**) playing a major role in the design of a large building, most obvious in the very neat concrete curtain wall. The effort to fit into the 1916 Zoning Resolution envelope without producing a stepped-back wedding-cake silhouette produced two rectangular masses that simply coexist.

P15

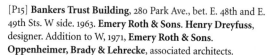

[P16] **Air China** (ticket office)/onetime Aeroflot (ticket office)/originally addo-x (showroom), 45 E. 49th St., bet. Madison and Park Aves. 1957. **Batir Design Assocs**.: **Hans Lindblom, Oskar Nitzcke**, designers.

High style for the sequential Communists who took over from the original business machine showroom.

[P17] **Hotel Inter-Continental**/originally Barclay Hotel, 111 E. 48th St., NW cor. Lexington Ave. 1927. **Cross & Cross**.

An elegant survivor of Park Avenue development in the 1920s. But for magnificent **Cross & Cross** see the Canadian Imperial Bank of Commerce on William Street.

P17

[P18] **New York Marriott East Side**/formerly Halloran House/originally Shelton Towers Hotel, 525 Lexington Ave., bet. E. 48th and E. 49th Sts. 1924. **Arthur Loomis Harmon**.

A 34-story experiment in the then-new 1916 Zoning Resolution that modeled the required setbacks for light and air into a cubistic brick composition. A powerful influence on architects and artists in the 1920s, it is embellished with a Romanesque Revival fillip here and there.

P18

[P19] **Waldorf-Astoria Hotel**, 301 Park Ave., bet. E. 49th and E. 50th Sts. E side. 1931. **Schultze & Weaver**.

When this world-famous institution moved from its original site (where the Empire State Building now stands), it chose to use a sedate version of the Art Deco style. The 625-foot Waldorf Towers, with a separate entrance on East 50th Street, has been temporary home to such notables as **President Hoover**, **General MacArthur**, the **Duke of Windsor**, **Secretary of State Henry Kissinger**, and **John F. Kennedy**.

P19

P20

[P20] **St. Bartholomew's Church** (Episcopal), Park Ave. bet. E. 50th and E. 51st Sts. E side. 1919. **Bertram G. Goodhue**. Entrances relocated from old St. Bartholomew's, Madison Ave. SW cor. E. 24th St., 1902. **Stanford White** of **McKim, Mead & White**. ● **Community House**, 109 E. 50th St., bet. Park and Lexington Aves. 1927. **Bertram G. Goodhue Assocs.** and **Mayers, Murray & Philip**. ● **Sallie Franklin Cheatham Memorial Garden**, 1971. **Hamby, Kennerly, Slomanson & Smith**, architects. **Paschall Campbell**, landscape architect.

St. Bartholomew's and the buildings behind it gave the old Park Avenue what it desperately needed: open space, color, variety of form and detail. Around its open terrace at the 50th Street corner are arrayed picturesque polychrome forms that rise to the ample dome of the church, dip, and then soar to the 570-foot pinnacles of the General Electric tower.

[P21] **320 Park Avenue, Mutual of America Offices**, bet. E. 50th and E. 51st. Sts. W side. 1950s. Reclad and restyled, 1990s.

When the latest curtain wall can be slipped over the mannequin, this is the result: a 1950s turgid wedding cake dressed for the Mardi Gras.

P21

[P22] **General Electric Building**/originally RCA Victor Building, 570 Lexington Ave., SW cor. E. 51st St. 1931. **Cross & Cross**. ●

Built to be contextual with St. Bart's, its neighbor, long before that word entered the city's development vocabulary. The Art Deco detailing at both bottom and top is both sumptuous and exuberant.

[P23] **560 Lexington Avenue** (offices), NW cor. E. 50th St. 1981. **The Eggers Group**. Brick sculpture, **Aleksandra Kasuba**.

A latter-day addition to the St. Bart's block, this reserved tower attempted consciously (with Landmarks Preservation Commission prodding) to integrate itself into the total

P22

composition. The entrance to the subway is the most serious architectural gesture.

Fire down below. What lies beneath New York's streets is often as intriguing as the buildings and monuments that adorn them—at least for Hollywood. In the 1946 fantasy Angel on My Shoulder, *set in New York,* **Claude Rains** *as the devil commuted between his world and ours via a rising sidewalk freight elevator.* **Marilyn Monroe,** *in* The Seven Year Itch, *enjoyed a world-famous burst of subway-blown air, raising* **Tom Ewell's** *eyebrows (and hopes) as her skirt billowed over an IRT subway grating. The grating is still there, in Lexington Avenue's west sidewalk, just south of 52nd Street—the buildings have changed.*

P24

[P24] **Seagram Building** (offices), 375 Park Ave., bet. E. 52nd and E. 53rd Sts. E side. 1958. **Ludwig Mies van der Rohe** with **Philip Johnson,** design architects. **Kahn & Jacobs,** associate architects. 🍎

The bronze and bronze-glass tower that reintroduced the idea of plaza to New York. **Mies van der Rohe** here brought to reality the fantasies he had proposed for Berlin in the 1920s, **Philip Johnson,** his biographer and acolyte (then, not now) designed its interiors. **Phyllis Lambert,** daughter of the Seagram board chairman, the late **Samuel Bronfman,** was the catalyst for it all, bringing architectural standards learned at Vassar.

The plaza, daring in that it was proposed at all (considering real estate values), seems, when devoid of people and active fountains, a bit of a bore. In summer, with fountains flowering and lounging lunchers, it's lively; and at Christmastime the trees and lights are like a great piling of bridal veil—a delight.

[P25] **The Four Seasons** (restaurant), 99 E. 52nd St. (in the Seagram Building), bet. Park and Lexington Aves. 1959. **Philip Johnson & Associates.** 🍎

An entrance dominated by **Picasso's** backdrop for the ballet *The Three-Cornered Hat* (1919) leads from the Seagram lobby into the restaurant (to the north) and the bar (to the south). The walnut-paneled dining room is laid out around a square pool, the other room around the square bar, over which is a quivering brass rod sculpture by **Richard Lippold.** Both rooms are impeccably designed down to the last napkin, with tableware by **L. Garth Huxtable.** At the 52nd Street entrance, planting boxes and doormen's uniforms are changed quarterly to mark the seasons.

[P25a] **The Brasserie** (restaurant), 100 E. 53rd St., bet. Park and Lexington Aves. S side. 2000. **Ricardo Scofido & Elizabeth Driller.**

A new Brasserie, replacing Philip Johnson's 1959 original, is a subterranean world of translucence, transparency and video.

P26

[P26] **Racquet and Tennis Club,** 370 Park Ave., bet. E. 52nd and E. 53rd Sts. W side. 1918. **McKim, Mead & White.** 🍎

An elegant Brunelleschian foil for the Seagram's plaza, this Florentine Renaissance palazzo is a wealthy male chauvinist's club housing squash (both lemon and racquets) and one of the few extant court tennis courts (the game of **Louis XIV**).

[P27] **Park Avenue Plaza** (offices), E. 52nd to E. 53rd St., bet. Madison and Park Aves. 1981. **Skidmore, Owings & Merrill.**

A bulky glass prism lurking behind the Racquet and Tennis Club, which sold its air rights so that the "Plaza" might enjoy a greater bulk. The Club, in turn, will in all likelihood remain unchanged forever by virtue of its landmark designation, the impossibility of replacing it with something bigger and the implacability of its members.

P27

The atrium within has a subtle waterfall and restaurant service, but feel free to sit there without ordering—mandated by the zoning concessions obtained. It is a public place and has remarkably clean public toilets!

P28

[P28] **Lever House** (offices), 390 Park Ave., bet. E. 53rd and E. 54th Sts. W side. 1952. **Gordon Bunshaft** of **Skidmore, Owings & Merrill.** ☙
This is where the glassy curtain wall began.
These prismatic forms, now small-scaled for Park Avenue, were the avant-garde of the metal and glass curtain wall, first receiving the reflections of ornate neo-Renaissance stonework from the Racquet Club to the south, and assorted classy apartments to the north and east. Glass has since been reflecting other glass almost everywhere, a phase happily almost over, now that Post Modernism (and Mature Moderism) has brought back solid form—a paradox in that there is something else to reflect again.

P29

[P29] **Banco Santander**, 45 E. 53rd St., bet. Park and Madison Aves. 1994. **Rogers, Burgun, Shahine and Deschler**.
The new kid on the block capitalizes on the open space from Lever House next door to reveal itself on two elevations as both aggressive and self-promoting.

P30

[P30] **599 Lexington Avenue** (offices), SE cor. E. 53rd St. 1987. **Edward Larrabee Barnes Assocs.**
A Barnes corner, chamfered here, overhung elsewhere (see IBM at 57th and Madison), pulls back the street façade to reveal more of Citicorp next door. The sleek gray skin also classes it as Citicorp's daughter, with a similar fabric, but with a different couturier arranging the folds.
The glassy subway kiosk is a wonderful entry to two formerly disconnected lines: the IND Lexington Avenue Station (E and F trains) and the IRT 51st Street Station (6 train), coupled as part of a zoning bonus that gave the tower more bulk.

P31a

[P31a] **Citicorp Center**, Lexington Ave. bet. E. 53rd and E. 54th Sts. E side. 1978. **Hugh Stubbins & Assocs.**, design architects. **Emery Roth & Sons**, architects. Plaza and atrium upgrading, 1997. **Gwathmey Siegel & Associates**. [P31b] **St. Peter's Church** (Lutheran). 1977. **Hugh Stubbins & Assocs. Erol Beker Chapel of the Good Shepherd. Louise Nevelson**, designer-sculptor. Interior, **Massimo Vignelli**, designer.
A tour de force as a stylish silhouette in the skyline and, for the pedestrian, a hovering cantilevered hulk under which nests St. Peter's Church. The smooth aluminum façade lacks the rich austerity of 140 Broadway (a flush, but black, predecessor by

P31b

P32

Skidmore, Owings & Merrill). The raked profile at its crest was a gesture to the idea of a sloping sun collector but now is just a vestigial form, like the Mercedes-Benz radiator ornament and logo.

P33

[P32] **Central Synagogue** (Congregation Ahawath Chesed Shaar Hashomayim), 652 Lexington Ave., SW cor. E. 55th St. 1872. **Henry Fernbach**. 💣

The oldest building in continuous use as a synagogue in New York, this one represents the rough-hewn Moorish style considered appropriate in the late 1800s. Although dour on the exterior, except for the star-studded bronze cupolas, the synagogue had an interior gaily stenciled with rich blues, earthy reds, ocher, and gilt—Moorish but distinctly American 19th-century. The 1998 fire has caused the need for substantial restorations.

Fernbach was America's first prominent Jewish architect.

[P33] **116, 120, 122, 124 East 55th Street** (former town houses), bet. Park and Lexington Aves.

A remarkable row of holdouts from the era when this block was residential. No. 116 (1928. **William Lawrence Bottomley**), bland but pleasant Neo-Georgian. No. 120, Georgian, but with some neo-Regency spunk. No. 122, Brownstone Palladian. No. 124 (1906-1910. **Albro & Lindeberg**), Banco de Chile, Collegiate Gothic.

P33

[P34] **Fifty-fifth Plaza** (offices), 110 E. 55th St., bet. Park and Lexington Aves. 1987. **The Eggers Group**.

An offbeat brick tower that looms over this once modestly scaled street of elegant town houses. Its form, narrow and tall, is difficult to reflect upon: street trees fortunately mute it all. At the base a glass pediment states baldly that we too are Post-Modern.

P36

[P35] **Chase Manhattan Bank branch**, 410 Park Ave., SW cor. E. 55th St. 1959. **Skidmore, Owings & Merrill** (bank and curtain wall). **Emery Roth & Sons** (building).

A wedding cake, common in its time, with an elegant metal and glass curtain wall, designed to fulfill the self-image of the bank on the lower two floors. The high 2nd-floor banking room is an impressive setting for an **Alexander Calder** mobile.

[P36] **Heron Tower** (offices), 70 E. 55th St., bet. Madison and Park Aves. 1987. **Kohn Pedersen Fox**.

Post Modern, 1930s division: honed gray granite with rock-face blocks punctuating the façade, a nickel-plated great grill, and spherical finials on the low streetfront block. It all brings back thoughts of a possible 1930s movie that might have been termed *Prince Kong*. Savor the lobby!

[P37] **Park Avenue Tower** (offices), 65 E. 55th St., bet. Madison and Park Aves., through to E. 56th St. 1987. **Murphy/Jahn**.

P37

Sleek and sassy, the skin below is warped in planes, then articulated with stainless-steel tori: half-round horizontal projections typical in Renaissance architecture. Although this would generally be classified as Post Modern, it has many modernist mannerisms.

[P38] **The Friar's Club**, 55 E. 55th St., bet. Madison and Park Aves. 1920s.

A bit of Neo-Renaissance frivolity with Tuscan columns below, Ionic pilasters above.

[P39] **Mercedes-Benz showroom**/originally Jaguar showroom, 430 Park Ave., SW cor. E. 56th St. 1955. **Frank Lloyd Wright**. Altered, 1982, **Taliesin Associated Architects**.

In the "master's" first New York City work, his creativity seems to have been smothered by the cramped space. More notable in that he did it (and that it's still there), rather than for what he did.

[P40] **Universal Pictures Building**, 445 Park Ave., bet. E. 56th and E. 57th Sts. E side. 1947. **Kahn & Jacobs**.

The first office building built on this once-residential portion of Park Avenue, it achieved a prismatic distinction as the first evenly stepped-back "wedding cake" form—precisely prescribed by the zoning law. Crisp.

P40

[P41] **Ritz Tower** (apartment hotel), 109 E. 57th St., NE cor. Park Ave. 1925. **Emery Roth** and **Carrère & Hastings**.

A 42-story tower, a stepped obelisk, conspicuous on the skyline. Rich details around the street-level walls now struggle with the egalitarian issues of Borders Bookstore within.

*At 111 East 57th Street (in the side flank of the Ritz Tower) stood France's greatest restaurant in America, Le Pavillon, founded by **Henri Soulé** at the New York World's Fair of 1939, then moved here to fulfill the wildest dreams of both gourmands and gourmets. After Soulé died (in 1966), the space became the home of the short lived First Women's Bank (1975. **Stockman & Manners Assocs.**, designers). Now chain store America has arrived in the form of Borders Bookstore. Go in. Pick out a ritzy book. Sit down and read it.*

P41

[P42] **The Galleria** (apartments), 119 E. 57th St., bet. Park and Lexington Aves. 1975. **David Kenneth Specter**, design architect. **Philip Birnbaum**, associated architect.

Luxury apartments stacked over offices and a club, embracing a balconied 7-story public galleria (cf. La Galleria, Milan). The skylit balconied space penetrates the block to 58th Street, affording pedestrians delight in passing through. Pretentious, but it has some grounds to be so.

P42

[P43] **135 East 57th Street** (mixed use), NW cor. Lexington Ave. 1987. **Kohn Pedersen Fox Assocs.**

New York's response to the French architecture of Spaniard **Ricardo Bofill** and his arcuated neo-Classical housing in Paris. Here the corner is king, an exedra opening to the intersection of Lexington and 57th. Within that space stands a tempietto marking what the sponsors termed the Place des Antiquaires. Silly.

P43

*An extraordinary avant-garde office building stood on the north west corner of 57th Street and Lexington Avenue from 1930 until swept away by the economics of real estate. 137 East 57th Street (1930. **Thompson & Churchill**) was framed on a structural grid set back nine feet from the building line. The perimeter walls and floors were, in turn, suspended from roof girders with tension steel hangers. Perhaps more radical than most New York skyscrapers of recent years, it went before preservation came to the top of many New Yorkers' lists.*

[P44] **500 Park Avenue Tower** (apartments), annexed to the Amro Bank Building, on E. 59th St., bet. Madison and Park Aves. 1986. **James Stewart Polshek & Partners**, design architects. **Schuman, Lichtenstein, Claman & Efron**, associated architects.

A residential condominium annexed both legally and architecturally to the elegant heirs of Pepsi-Cola. At the lower levels it matches Pepsi's sleekness. In between, deeply incised granite openings provide a strong and handsome foil.

[P45] **ABN-Amro Bank Building**/sometime Olivetti Building/originally Pepsi-Cola Building (offices), 500 Park Ave., SW cor. E. 59th St. 1960. **Gordon Bunshaft** and **Natalie DuBois** of **Skidmore, Owings & Merrill**.

An understated elegance that bowed to the scale of its Park Avenue neighbors rather than advertising itself as the newest (in its time) local Modern monument. Large bays of glass are enlivened by the seemingly random arrangements of partitions (that kiss the glass with rubber gaskets) and vertical blinds.

P45

[P46] **515 Park Avenue** (apartments), SE cor. Park Ave. and E. 60th St. E Side. 2000. **Frank Williams & Associates**.

Air rights from the Lighthouse allow a Park Avenue tower. If it had been one block to the north, it would have violated the grand ensemble of Park Avenue architecture (15+/- stories forever).

[P47] **Banque de Paris Building** (offices), 499 Park Ave., SE cor. E. 59th St. 1984. **I. M. Pei & Partners**.

This obsidian prism, blackly marking its Park Avenue corner, is so subtle externally as to be boring. Its lobby, however, presents a wondrous—and wondrously lit—tree to the passer-through (diagonally, from Park to 59th, and vice versa).

P47

[P48] **110 East 59th Street** (offices), bet. Park and Lexington Aves. 1968, **William Lescaze**.

This simple, understated, and unpretentious tower is a notch above its speculative competition. The sculpture (1973. **Tony Rosenthal**) in the south plaza (on 58th Street) is a rich, carved piece of a bronze cylinder.

[P49] **Argosy Print and Book Store**, 115 E. 59th St., bet. Park and Lexington Aves. 1966. **Kramer & Kramer**.

An elegant shop that replaces the long-gone streetstands along this block; used books, maps, and prints filled the sidewalk to the delight of browsers, as on the Left Bank of the Seine. Upstairs (by elevator) are floors devoted to old prints, painting, and specialized books.

P50

[P50] **The Lighthouse: New York Association for the Blind**, 111 E. 59th St., bet. Park and Lexington Aves. New building, 1994. **Mitchell/Giurgola**.

Rational Modern, its logic expressed clearly in its understated massing and elevations. It replaces the charming 1964 **Kahn & Jacobs** effort with a much bigger building (partially using the old steel skeleton), hence providing necessary office and residential extras.

[P51] **505 Park Avenue**/originally Aramco Building (offices), NE cor. E. 59th St. 1948. **Emery Roth & Sons**. Ground-floor façade alterations, 1987. **Der Scutt**.

A supreme stylist, Der Scutt provided a face-lift of banded glitz in black and gold.

P51

[P52] **Bloomingdale's** (department store)/originally Bloomingdale Brothers, E. 59th to E. 60th Sts. bet. Lexington and Third Aves. Main Lexington Avenue Building, 740 Lexington Ave. 1930. **Starrett & Van Vleck**.

An aggregation of Victorian and Art Deco structures, completely interlocking on the interior, houses one of America's most comprehensive and sophisticated stores.

Demolition of the Third Avenue el and the 1960s renaissance of that saloon-bespotted boulevard inspired Bloomie's to shed its bargain basement image. The castle of consumerism that emerged became, for many, and for a while, the source from which all upscale, total-lifestyle statements flow.

[P53] **750 Lexington Avenue** (offices), bet. E. 59th and E. 60th Sts. W side. 1988. **Murphy/Jahn**.

Chicago's **Helmut Jahn** has provided New York with its most exotic skyline elements since those slender finialed towers of the 1930s—from the Chrysler Building to the Canadian Imperial Bank of Commerce. The catch is that these new vast office structures have the waistline of a Dutch burgher rather than a Chanel model. Air-conditioning, virtually nonexistent in the 1930s, now allows buildings to be deep and mechanically ventilated. The Chrysler Building's air-conditioning (and light) was provided by windows.

The nearest subways are at 59th and Lexington: the IRT Lexington Avenue (59th Street Station: 4, 5, and 6 trains) or the BMT Broadway Line (Lexington Avenue Station: N and R trains).

P53

F1

THE FIFTH AVENUE SWATH

East 46th to East 60th Streets, Sixth to Madison:

This stretch of the avenue, where fashionable shops were concentrated since the 1920s, had been a solid line of mansions, churches, and clubs two decades before. Two factors sustained the elegance of Fifth Avenue as stores moved north along it: the Fifth Avenue Association (whose members had fought off billboards, bootblacks, parking lots, projecting signs—even funeral parlors), and the absence of els or subways. To provide a genteel alternative for rapid transit, the Fifth Avenue Transportation Company was established in 1885, using horse-drawn omnibuses until 1907, followed by the fondly remembered double-deck buses.

Once upon a time even the traffic lights were special: bronze standards with a neo-Grec Mercury atop, subsidized by the Fifth Avenue Association concerned with style.

One can still go to Cartier's for an occasional diamond or to the St. Regis's King Cole Restaurant for an elegant dinner dance; but much of the Fifth Avenue style has gone.

Fat—or merely avaricious—cats abound hereabouts, although the best work was done through the enlightened self-interest of old-line, hard-nosed capitalists. This precinct enjoyed the **Rockefellers, Scribner, Saks, Villard, Onassis, Heckscher,** *and others more modest, who gave some wonderful moments of class through buildings and shops to this sequence of blocks. Here look-ing up is as important as looking in; for above the luxurious, or interesting, or even sometimes tawdry shopfront, rises architecture of consequence.*

Rockefeller Center: The waves of elegant construction that rolled up Fifth Avenue never reached as far west as Sixth. Rockefeller Center was expected to trigger renewal in the 1930s, but the Sixth Avenue el, rumbling up to 53rd Street until 1938, was too grim an obstacle. It was not until an enormous new Time & Life Building went up at West 50th Street in 1959 that a Sixth Avenue building boom started, resulting in the glitzy canyon we see today. All these blocks were formerly, and almost uniformly, seas of brownstones before the glitz: middle-class dwellings that declined in elegance and opulence with each increment of their distance from Fifth Avenue. Rockefeller Center proper had erased hundreds of them, but its later annexes, and the other commercial development they inspired, were the crowning blows.

The numbering starts at Rockefeller Center, moves south along Fifth Avenue to 45th Street, then north again.

[F1] **Rockefeller Center** (office/entertainment/ retail complex) Originally W. 48th to W. 51st Sts. bet. Fifth and Sixth Aves. 1932-1940. **The Associated Architects: Reinhard & Hofmeister, Corbett, Harrison & MacMurray; Raymond Hood, Godley & Fouilhoux.** ☀ Expanded 1947-1973.

An island of architectural excellence, this is the greatest urban complex of the 20th century: an understated and urbane place that has become a classic lesson in the point and counterpoint of space, form, and circulation. Its campanile is the GE (formerly RCA) Building, a slender, stepped slab rising precipitously from Rockefeller Plaza proper, that many-leveled pedestrian space surrounding and overlooking the ice skating rink in winter, outdoor cafés in summer, all overseen by *Prometheus* (1934, **Paul Manship**). Opposite, Channel Gardens rises on a flower-boxed slope to Fifth Avenue between the low-scaled French and British Pavilions; the foliage here is changed with the seasons.

Limestone, now-grayed cast aluminum, and glass clad these towers and their low-scaled neighbors. The skin is straightforward, modern, and unencumbered by the need for stylishness— but nevertheless of great style, elegant, and perhaps the most undated Modern monument that New York enjoys.

[F1a] **1270 Sixth Avenue Building**/originally RKO Building. 1932. ☀ [F1b] **Radio City Music Hall**. 1932. **Edward Durrell Stone**, design architect; **Donald Deskey** interior design coordinator. ☀ Interior ☀ Remodeling, 1999. **Hardy Holzman Pfeiffer** and **The Rockwell Group** [F1c] **GE Building**/formerly RCA Building, 30 Rockefeller Plaza. 1933. ☀ Partial interior ☀ . [F1d] **British Empire Building**, 620 Fifth Ave. 1933. ☀

The Channel Gardens (or Promenade): The gently sloped and fountained space, which takes you from Fifth Avenue to the stairway leading into the sunken plaza, is called Channel Gardens since it is, like the English Channel, the separation between France (La Maison Française to the south) and the United Kingdom (the British Empire Building to the north).

[F1e] **La Maison Française**. 610 Fifth Ave. 1933. ☀ [F1f] **Palazzo d'Italia**. 1935. ☀ [F1g] **International Building**, 630 Fifth Ave. 1935. ☀ Partial interior ☀ . [F1h] **1 Rockefeller Plaza**/originally Time & Life Building. 1937. ☀ [F1j] **The Associated Press Building**, 45 Rockefeller Plaza. 1938. ☀ [F1k] **10 Rockefeller Plaza**/originally Eastern Airlines Building. 1939. ☀ [F1l] **Simon & Schuster Building**/originally U.S. Rubber Company Building and addition (on site of Center Theater), 1230 Sixth Ave. 1940. ☀

THE FIFTH AVENUE SWATH

see pages 286–301

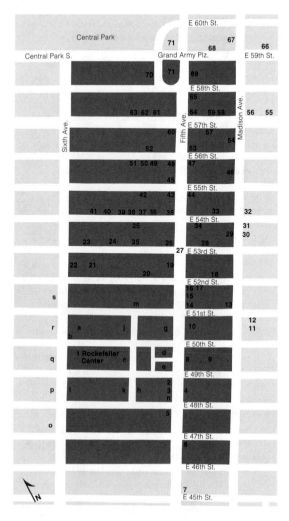

All the above, A through L, excepting the Radio City interiors, by **Associated Architects**.

Additions since the original complex (1932-1940): These assorted annexes to the Center along the Avenue of the Americas (Sixth Avenue) are of lesser stuff: posturing, bulbous boxes built in the 1960s and 1970s, grabbing onto the Rockefeller Center name, organization, and underground passages but sorry neighbors to their parent buildings. Included here are the Time & Life, the old Sperry-Rand, McGraw-Hill, Exxon, Celanese buildings and others. In concert with the Zoning Resolution of 1961, they brought barren plazas to the Avenue of the Americas: good intentions misdirected those present lifeless places, without the people who would populate an Italian piazza, windswept and dull. The midblock open-air arcades to the west of the three southernmost towers are more successful.

[F1m] **Warner Communications Building**/originally Esso Building, 15 W. 51st St., bet. Fifth and Sixth Aves. to W. 52nd St. 1947. **Carson & Lundin.** ● [F1n] **600 Fifth Avenue Building**/originally Sinclair Oil Building, NW cor. W. 48th St.

(purchased by Rockefeller Center, 1963). 1952. **Carson & Lundin**.
☛ [F1o] **Celanese Building**, 1211 Sixth Ave., bet. W. 47th and
W. 48th Sts. W side. 1973. **Harrison, Abramovitz & Harris**.
[F1p] **McGraw-Hill Building**, 1221 Sixth Ave., bet. W. 48th and
W. 49th Sts. W side. 1972. **Harrison, Abramovitz & Harris**.
[F1q] **Exxon Building**, 1251 Sixth Ave., bet. W. 49th and W. 50th
Sts. W side. 1971. **Harrison, Abramovitz & Harris**. [F1r] **Time &
Life Building**, 1271 Sixth Ave., bet. W. 50th and W. 51st Sts. W
side. 1959. **Harrison & Abramovitz**. [F1s] **Sperry Corporation
Building**/originally Sperry Rand Building, 1290 Sixth Ave., bet.
W. 51st and W. 52nd Sts. E side. 1961. **Emery Roth & Sons**.

F2

[F2] **Goelet Building**/Swiss Center (offices), 608 Fifth
Ave., SW cor. W. 49th St. 1932. **E. H. Faile & Co**. with
Victor L. F. Hafner. Lower façade altered, 1998. **Garrison Siegel**.
   Above the new base, the original crisp cubist office building
survives with a rich geometry of contrasting materials: marble,
limestone, and stainless steel.

F3

[F3] **TGI Fridays**/originally Childs Restaurant Building, 604
Fifth Ave., bet. W. 48th and W. 49 Sts. W side. 1925. **William Van
Alen**.
   A lesser work by the architect of the Chrysler Building. A
onetime church garden next door permitted the curved glass-
block corner. The brilliant blue on Fifth Avenue is a sign of
declining times.

F4

[F4] **Benetton** (women's wear)/originally Charles
Scribner's Sons (bookstore/offices), 597 Fifth Ave., bet. E.
48th and E. 49th Sts. E side. 1913. **Ernest Flagg**. ☛ Interior. ☛
Restored and remodeled for Benetton, 1996. **Phillips Janson
Group**.
   An ornate black iron and glass storefront opens to a grand,
2-story, plaster-vaulted mezzanined space: an almost-basilica.
The south side (lot-line) wall carries the original advertising.
Benetton has preserved the volume, though all those books were
part of the architecture too.

F5

[F5] **Fleet Bank**/onetime National Bank of North America/orig-
inally Black, Starr & Frost (jewelers), 592 Fifth Ave., SW cor. W.
48th St. **Carrère & Hastings**. 1912. Totally reclad, 1964, **Hausman
& Rosenberg**.
   Elongated black ports are the windows of this stark white
marble-veneered prism. The **Carrère & Hastings** neo-Classical
façade of **Black, Starr & Frost** was considered "old-fashioned"
by its owners in the early 1960s, and so it was was "modernized"
when modern was more a word for merchandising of both real
estate and goods. Think what C&H's New York Public Library
would look like after an equivalent transformation.

*Gotham Book Mart, at 41 West 47th Street, in the heart of the
city's jewelry district, is a great, though cramped and cluttered,
bookshop. Its strengths are literature, poetry, dance, and esoterica.
Its loyal customers are the literati of the city and the world.
Upstairs, in the gallery (clubhouse for the James Joyce Society),
are changing exhibitions including—in the summer—those on
postcards, its owner's passion. Go in with the spirit of the sign:*
WISE MEN FISH HERE.

[F6] **575 Fifth Avenue** (office building and arcade), SE cor. E.
47th St. 1985. **Emery Roth & Sons**.
   W & J Sloane was here, then Korvette's in the swinging sixties. Now the remnant body has been absorbed into this 40-
story granite veneered galleria *cum* offices. Go in.

F6

F7

F9

F10

[F7] **Fred F. French Building**, 551 Fifth Ave., NE cor. 45th St. 1927. **Fred F. French Co.**, **H. Douglas Ives** and **Sloan & Robertson**. 🍎 Partial interior 🍎.

The headquarters of the former designer-builder company has strange multicolored faience at the upper-floor setbacks and a well-preserved ornate lobby. From the days when even the greediest developer owed serious and intricate architectural detail and materials to the tenant and public.

[F8] **Saks Fifth Avenue** (department store), 611 Fifth Ave., bet. W. 49th and W. 50th Sts. E side. 1924. **Starrett & Van Vleck**. 🍎

A stately department store as a low-key foil to St. Patrick's to the north and the RCA Building, visible on axis through the Channel Gardens, to the west. A landmark more for its background role in counterpoint to rich neighbors; nevertheless its façade reeks of style rather than stylishness.

[F9] **Swiss Bank Tower** (offices) and Saks Fifth Avenue Expansion, 12 E. 50th St., bet. Fifth and Madison Aves. through to E. 49th St. 1989. **Lee Harris Pomeroy Assocs.** and **Abramovitz Kingsland Schiff**.

A midblock event, using the air rights of the landmark Saks store. One of the successors to a firm that shared creation of Rockefeller Center (**Abramovitz** was the latter-day partner of **Wallace Harrison**, who had been in on the Center's creation) is joined here to a newer talent, **Lee Pomeroy**.

[F10] **St. Patrick's Cathedral** (Roman Catholic), E. 50th to E. 51st Sts., bet. Fifth and Madison Aves. 1878. Towers, 1888, **James Renwick, Jr.**, **William Rodrigue**. 🍎 [F10a] **Archbishop's (Cardinal's) Residence**, 452 Madison Ave., NW cor. E. 50th St. and Rectory, 460 Madison Ave., SW cor. E. 51st St. 1880. Both by **James Renwick, Jr.** 🍎

[F10c] **Lady Chapel**, 1906. **Charles T. Mathews**. 🍎
Renwick's adaptation of French Gothic was trivialized by his use of unyielding granite and his deletion of the flying buttresses (without deleting their pinnacle counterweights). But the cathedral, with its twin 330-foot towers, is a richly carved counterfoil to Rockefeller Center, across Fifth Avenue. Go in. The Lady Chapel, added behind the altar, is in more academically correct French Gothic.

F10c

[F11a] Originally **Villard Houses**, 451-455 Madison Ave., bet. E. 50th , and E. 51st Sts. E side. 1884. Façades by **Joseph Wells**, Interiors by **Stanford White** of **McKim, Mead & White**. 🍎 Restoration, 1981, **James Rhodes**, restoration architect.
[F11b] **Helmsley Palace Hotel** (behind), 1980. **Emery Roth & Sons**.

F11a

Once there were six brownstone mansions, built as if they were a single great Renaissance palazzo: two of them—and parts of the third, fourth, and fifth—were severed from the grand Madison Avenue forecourt to create the Palace Hotel. That tall, bulky, but essentially innocuous structure can be entered grandly through the courtyard, or banally under its glitzy 50th or 51st Street canopies. The price for preservation was greater height and bulk for the hotel.

F11a

Journalist, railway promoter, and financier **Henry Villard** (born **Ferdinand Heinrich Hilgard** in Bavaria) built the surviving Madison Avenue remnants first; they were extended down the side streets immediately thereafter. After the collapse of his railroad empire, the south wing was bought by **Whitelaw** and **Elizabeth Mills Reid**, who brought **Stanford White** back to enrich the interiors. Now the hotel occupies the south wing, preserving the Gold Room as Le Cirque restaurant (**Harman Jablin**, architects. **Adam Tihany**, interior designer). The north wing is the Urban Center:

[F12] **The Urban Center**, 457 Madison Ave., SE cor. E. 51st St. entry , through the Helmsley Palace Madison Ave. forecourt. 1980. Open to the public. [F12a] **The Urban Center Bookstore**, within the Urban Center. 1980. Galleries open to the public: Mo-We, Fr, Sa 11-5; closed Th & Su. 212-935-3960.

The Municipal Art Society negotiated a lease for the Villard mansion's north wing, creating space for a cluster of concerned professional organizations in addition to itself, a venerable and sometimes feisty civic organization with a largely lay membership. The Urban Center Bookstore and the Architectural League share common exhibition and lecture facilities with the Society. The Bookstore is a matchless source of books and periodicals on architecture, planning, and urban history.

F13

[F13] Originally **Look Building**, 488 Madison Ave., NW cor. 51st Street. 1950. **Emery Roth & Sons**. Building renovated, 1997. **Hardy Holzman Pfeiffer**. Lobby renovated, 1997. **Fox & Fowle**.

Staccato setbacks and rounded corners make this one of the high-style office buildings of the 1950s. Little appreciated in the time of Lever House and the Seagram Building, such street-fronted setback architecture has made a comeback. The new "retro" lobby is onto another tack.

[F14] **Olympic Tower** (mixed use), 645 Fifth Avenue, NE cor. 51st St. 1976. **Skidmore, Owings & Merrill**. Olympic Place, from E. 51st to E. 52nd Sts. 1977. **Chermayeff, Geismar & Assocs**. with **Zion & Breen**.

F15

An elegant urban idea for multiple uses (apartments over offices over shops) in a sleek but dull skin. To the pedestrian its graces were its elegant shops, but especially the Arcade, Olympic Place, that penetrates the building midblock, from St. Patrick's to 52nd Street, with a skylit, treed, and waterfalled public space of gray granite. Its dedication to public use allowed the owner to build a bigger building than normally permitted. The waterfall is dry, the plants and furnishings tawdry. Who's minding the store?

[F15] **Versace**/onetime Olympic Airways (ticket office)/originally George W. Vanderbilt House, 647 Fifth Ave., bet. E. 51st and E. 52nd Sts. E side. 1905. **Hunt & Hunt**. Converted. 🍎

F16

[F16] **Cartier, Inc.**/originally Morton F. Plant House, 651 Fifth Ave., SE cor. E. 52nd St. 1905. **Robert W. Gibson**. Converted to shop, 1917, **William Welles Bosworth**. 🍎 Restored, 1990s. **Joseph Pell Lombardi**. [F17] **Cartier, Inc. extension**/originally N wing of Morton F. Plant House, 4 E. 52nd St., bet. Fifth and Madison Aves. **C. P. H. Gilbert**. 1905. 🍎

At one time both sides of Fifth Avenue were lined with American Renaissance mansions. These two, for Plant and a Vanderbilt, were a free interpretation of sixteenth- and seventeenth-century palazzi.

[F18] **Austrian Cultural Institute**, 11 E. 52nd St., bet. Fifth and Madison Aves. 2000. **Raimund Abraham**.

A sliver of Vienna steps back from mundane 52nd Street with a powerful presence. Abraham, a teaching theorist, here enters the hard world of New York architecture. An expressive debut.

F18

F18

[F19] **666 Fifth Avenue** (offices), bet. W. 52nd and W. 53rd Sts. W side. 1957. **Carson & Lundin**. First- and second-floor façade and lobby, 1999. **Nobutaka Ashihara Associates**.

A million square feet of office space wrapped in embossed aluminum. Note the sinuous lobby waterfall by sculptor Isamu Noguchi. The recent exterior "upgrading" is heavy-handed.

*The **21 Club**: "Jack and Charlie's place" at 21 West 52nd Street (1872. **Duggin & Crossman**) was only one of several Prohibition-era clubs on its block that became fashionable in the 1930s. But it alone remains, having become successor to Delmonico's and Sherry's as café society's dining room.*

F20

[F20] **The Museum of Television and Radio**, William S. Paley Building, 23 W. 52nd St., bet. Fifth and Sixth Aves. 1989. **John**

F21

Burgee with **Philip Johnson**. Open to the public: Tu, We, Sa, Su 12-6; Th 12-8; Fr 12-9; closed Mo. 212-621-6600.

Paley, chairman of the museum, contributed land for this new facility, to replace the one at 1 East 53rd Street (1976. **Beyer Blinder Belle**). The arched entrance is a Johnsonian variation on one of the 1789 Parisian tollgates of **Claude-Nicolas Ledoux**.

There are exhibitions and seminars; recordings of radio programs may be heard in study centers; and films and videotapes of television programs are shown in a main theater and informal videothèques.

[F21] Originally **E. F. Hutton Building** (offices), 31 W. 52nd St., bet. Fifth and Sixth Aves., through to W. 53rd St. 1987. **Kevin Roche John Dinkleloo & Assocs.** [F21b] **American Craft Museum**, 44 W. 53rd St. 1987. **Fox & Fowle**. Museum, 212-956-3535. Tu 10-8; W-Su 10-5; closed Mo.

F22

Granite neo-Assyrian polygonal columns straddle an allée through the block, punctuating a small plaza between this and the adjacent CBS Building. The thin skin of granite balloons over a steel armature. Way up there, a serrated Halloween crazy hat crowns it all, breaching the skyline.

The American Craft Museum (once located in a former row house on the site) here acquired elegant quarters enlivened by a magnificent serpentine stair.

[F22] **CBS Building** (Columbia Broadcasting System), 51 W. 52nd St., NE cor. Sixth Ave. 1965. **Eero Saarinen & Assocs.**

"Black Rock," Saarinen's only high-rise building, is a sheer, freestanding 38-story, concrete-framed tower clad in dark gray honed granite: a somber and striking understatement.

F23

One of several buildings of its time to depart from established post-and-beam framing, CBS supports its floors instead on its central core and a dense grid—in effect a bearing wall—at the exterior.

Here the lawyers and money managers sit in splendor, while creativity is rampant in lesser facilities elsewhere.

[F23] **Museum of American Folk Art**, W. 53rd. St. bet. Fifth and Sixth Aves. 2001. **Tod Williams & Billie Tsien**.

A Coming Attraction, replacing brownstones west of the Museum Tower, this new facility combines the traditional concept of folk art with "outsider art"—not little old ladies breaking into the art world, but art outside of the world of critics and museums.

[F24] **Museum Tower** (apartments), 21 W. 53rd St., bet. Fifth and Sixth Aves. 1985. **Cesar Pelli & Assocs.**

Sleek and subtly polychromatic, the Tower leaves architectural histrionics to the E. F. Hutton Building down the block. In the reconstruction of the museum complex the tower's edge will be laid bare to the Museum Garden, a slit skirt revealing a lithe leg. A compliment.

F24

[F25] **Museum of Modern Art**, 11 W. 53rd St., bet. Fifth and Sixth Aves. 1939. **Philip Goodwin** and **Edward Durrell Stone**. Additions and alterations, 1951 and 1964. **Philip Johnson**, architect. **James Fanning**, landscape architect. Further additions and alterations, 1985. **Cesar Pelli & Assocs.**, design architects. **Edward Durrell Stone Assocs.**, associate architects. New buildings and renovations, 2000-2001. **Yashio Taniguchi**. Open to the public: Su-Tu 11-6; Th & Fr 12-8:30; closed We. 212-708-9480.

F25

The history of modern art, more than its current events, is here enshrined. The 1939 building was a catechism of the International Style (a style so dubbed by MoMA's 1932 exhibition, presented by **Henry-Russell Hitchcock** and **Philip**

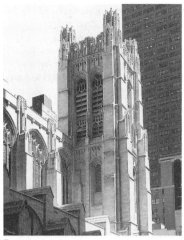

F26

Johnson): an austere streetfront of marble veneer, tile, and opaque and transparent glass, with a pleasant rooftop garden worthy of a Le Corbusier acolyte. Johnson's east wing departed radically from the original flat International Style surfaces, with deeply three-dimensional grids of painted steel standing free of the wall. His finest contribution is the 1964 garden along 54th Street, where stone, plantings, pools, and fountains have been composed into a serene and urbane oasis, one of the great urban gardens.

The guts of the museum were vastly altered and expanded (in part into Johnson's garden) by **Cesar Pelli**. The multileveled galleried and escalated interior seemed more like a shopping center of packaged aesthetics than a true museum, where the visitor could selectively inhabit the history of modern art. Happily, the Yamaguchi plans will bring back the design distinctions of the museum's various architects, complementing their work: restoring Stone's original canopy, revealing Pelli's tower, enhancing Johnson's garden.

[F26] **St. Thomas' Church and Parish House** (Episcopal), 1 W. 53rd St., NW cor. Fifth Ave. 1914. **Cram, Goodhue & Ferguson**. Reredos, **Bertram G. Goodhue**, architect; **Lee Lawrie**, sculptor. 🌶️

One of New York's finest essays in picturesque massing and detail, built on a constricted corner. Is it by the hand of Goodhue, or is it Cram's? The powerful French Gothic interior culminates in the shimmering white, richly carved reredos behind the altar. Windows by Whitefriars of London.

F28

[F27] **Fifth Avenue Station IND Subway Line**, below W. 53rd St. bet. Madison and Fifth Aves. 1933. Renovated, 1987, **Lee Harris Pomeroy Assocs.**, architects. **Pentagram Design**, graphic designers.

Here, serving the Museum of Modern Art, the American Craft Museum, the Museum of Broadcasting, and other street-level events, is a handsome redesign of this barrel-vaulted space. Graphics of local institutions adorn its walls.

F29

[F28] **Samuel Paley Plaza**, also known as Paley Park, 3 E. 53rd St., bet. Fifth and Madison Aves. 1967. **Zion & Breen**, landscape architects. **Albert Preston Moore**, consulting architect.

A parklet on the former site of the Stork Club contributed by **William S. Paley**, founder of CBS, and named for his father (1875-1963). A great oasis in good weather to refresh in the spray of the waterfall and to snack. The fall's white noise masks the cacophony of the city.

[F29] **Continental Illinois Center** (offices), 520 Madison Ave., bet. E. 53rd and E. 54th Sts. W side. 1981. **Swanke Hayden Connell**.

Polished red granite veneers bloated architectural geometry with a flared skirt below the knees and a bland body above. A holdout site occupant, Reidy's Restaurant at 22 East 54th (sporting its original front), courageously served all during construction, explaining the punctuation in the tower's north slope. Note the new sidewalk clock.

F31

[F30] **521 Madison Avenue** (mixed uses), bet. E. 53rd and E. 54th Sts. Altered, 1980s.

A supreme vulgarism that makes 527 seem the greatest of architecture. Its perpetrators don't see the joke.

[F31] **527 Madison Avenue** (offices), SE cor. E. 54th St. 1987. **Fox & Fowle**.

Pleated glass and two-toned granite modulate an otherwise simple Madison Avenue façade. Along 54th Street stretches a great glass-sheeted skylight to its entrance atrium, tilted assuredly to make Continental Illinois, across Madison, feel less out of place.

F32

[F32] **535 Madison Avenue** (offices), NE cor. 54th St. 1986. **Edward Larrabee Barnes Assocs**.

Barnes again overpowers the pedestrian as he did at IBM. Here, however, the giant cantilever is supported by a Brobdingnagian column. The bonus plaza is overwhelmed.

[F33] **Alpha Garage**, 15 W. 54th St., bet. Fifth and Madison Aves. 1965. **William Gleckman**.

The (once) white cast-in-place concrete frames that constitute its wall to the street make this garage a pleasant understated neighbor. (The original developer was in the concrete business and considered this project to be free advertising.)

F34

[F34] **Banco di Napoli**/originally William H. Moore House, 4 E. 54th St., bet. Fifth and Madison Aves. 1900. **McKim, Mead & White**. 🐾

When Fifth Avenue's flanks were lined with residential palaces, fortresses, and châteaux, side streets were littered with the runners-up. The 21st-century analogy might be as if millionaire executives, modestly enriched, ceded the Avenue to billionaires of the ilk of **Milken, Buffett, Murdoch, and Gates**.

[F35] **University Club**, 1 W. 54th St., NW cor. Fifth Ave. 1899. **Charles McKim** of **McKim, Mead & White**. 🐾

A Florentine super-palazzo beyond the Medicis' wildest dreams; only if they had had elevators to make this ten-story equivalent.

F35

F36

[F36] Originally **Philip Lehman House**, 7 W. 54th St., bet. Fifth and Sixth Aves. 1900. **John H. Duncan**.

Not only was Robert Lehman's fine private collection of paintings removed to the Metropolitan's Lehman Wing, so were this town house's interiors (although remodeled much after 1900). The oculi, perforating the crowning mansard roof, are the best part of this neo-Baroque façade.

[F37] **U.S. Trust Company**/originally James J. Goodwin House, 9-11 W. 54th St., bet. Fifth and Sixth Aves. 1898. **McKim, Mead & White**. ☛ **Haines Lundberg Waehler**, restoration architects.

Sober neo-Georgian limestone and brick from the blossoming of the Colonial Revival movement.

[F38] **William Murray Houses**, 13-15 West 54th Street, bet. Fifth and Sixth Aves. 1897. **Henry J. Hardenbergh**. ☛

Neo-Renaissance limestone outpomps the modesty of No. 11. Nelson Rockefeller maintained his private offices at No. 13 and died there on January 26, 1979.

F38

F39

[F39] **Rockefeller Apartments**, 17 W. 54th St., bet. Fifth and Sixth Aves. 1936. **Harrison & Fouilhoux**. ☛ Interior alterations, 1982, **Hobart Betts**.

Elegant cylindrical bay windows overview the Museum of Modern Art Garden—on part of a midblock strip of land acquired by the Rockefellers when their Center was assembled. The leftovers included the Donnell Library on West 53rd Street, the Museum of Modern Art, and this urbane place. This is one of the great modern apartment blocks in Manhattan. The garden within is a pleasant private oasis.

[F40] **35 West 54th Street** (row house), bet. Fifth and Sixth Aves. 1878. **James G. Lynd**. New façade, 1905, **Foster, Gade & Graham**.

Face-lifting was not uncommon in the early 20th century. To be "modern" was the goal of many a parvenu, for whom Modern came mostly as brownstone gave way to some form of Classical Revival.

[F41] **41 West 54th Street** (row house), bet. Fifth and Sixth Aves. 1878. **James G. Lynd**. New façade, 1909, **Foster, Gade & Graham**.

The second face-lift on the block by the same team veneering the work of the same original architect. Again under renovation.

[F42] **Privatbanken Building**, 20 West 55th Street, bet. Fifth and Sixth Aves. **Emery Roth & Sons** and **Hobart Betts**.

The Bank of Denmark's toehold in New York.

F43

[F43] **The Peninsula**/originally The Gotham Hotel, 2 W. 55th St., SW cor. Fifth Ave. 1905. **Hiss & Weekes**. Partly altered, 1984, **Stephen B. Jacobs & Assocs**. Altered, 1987, **Hirsch/Bender**, designers; **AiGroup Architects**, architects.

The mate of the St. Regis across the street, a little more angular but just as ornate.

[F44] **St. Regis-Sheraton Hotel**, 2 E. 55th St., SE cor. Fifth Ave. 1904. **Trowbridge & Livingston**. Addition to E, 1925.

A richly decorated Beaux Arts mass that gets better toward the top. Second only to the Plaza in number of prominent guests, the hotel is especially popular with foreign diplomats. The King Cole Restaurant is designed around the **Maxfield Parrish** mural that once graced Times Square's old Knickerbocker Hotel bar.

The brass and glass doorman's kiosk is magnificent.

F44

[F45] **Fifth Avenue Presbyterian Church**, 705 Fifth Ave., NW cor. W. 55th St. 1875. **Carl Pfeiffer**.

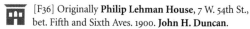

A somber brownstone neo-Gothic remnant of early days on Fifth Avenue, long before it became a boulevard of fashionable mansions.

F45

[F46] **SONY Building**/originally AT&T Headquarters, (offices), 550 Madison Ave., bet. E. 55th and E. 56th Sts. W side. 1984. **Philip Johnson/John Burgee**. Atrium and under-spaces altered into Sony Entertainment Center, 1994. **Gwathmey Siegel & Associates**.

Dubbed by the press the "Chippendale" skyscraper, this granite hulk turned the market around among developers in New York. Glass Modern was replaced with stone Post Modern, and a building's profile against the sky became a competition to create the most unique silhouette.

The atrium is smashing, its quarter-arched glass roof truly reminiscent in scale of the ancestral Milan Galleria, by **Giuseppe Mengoni**. **Gwathmey/Siegel**'s renovations have activated the ensemble (the underspace below the office tower proper was a street-level "subway station").

F46

[F47] **Corning Glass Building**, 717 Fifth Ave., SE cor. 56th St. 1959. **Harrison & Abramovitz & Abbe**. Entrance altered, 1994. **Gwathmey Siegel & Assocs**.

Mirror-smooth walls of green glass rise out of a plaza planter (once a pool), a dated modern corporate symbol. But **Gwathmey Siegel**'s vigorous new entry has brought distinction to its street-level architecture.

[F48] **Henri Bendel Building**, consolidating and expanding the sometime Rizzoli Building, 712 Fifth Ave. 1908. **Adolf S. Gottlieb**. ☛ ; and the former **Coty Building**, 714 Fifth Ave. 1909. **Woodruff Leeming**. Window glass, 1912. **René Lalique**. Both bet. W. 55th and W. 56th Sts. W side. ☛ **Rizzoli and Coty**, restored and redesigned. 1991. **Beyer Blinder Belle**. [F49] **712 Fifth Avenue** (office building), behind. 1989. **Kohn Pederson Fox Assocs**.

F48

Here two early (first growth) commercial buildings replaced town mansions of the latter 19th century. 712's giant Corinthian pilasters surmount some modesty below. 714, respendent in Lalique glass, sparkles. And **Henri Bendel** is the beneficiary.

Harry Winston, jewelers, forms the corner between the old Coty Building and the 56th Street entrance to 712 Fifth Avenue. Remodeled for Winston in the 1960s by architect Charles Luckman (with the assistance of a venerable French academic designer) it aspires to be a Hôtel de Ville: it might have been a success in a remote town in Latin America in those late 19th century Francophile years (when the clients and architects had never been to France).

[F50] **Felissimo** (store)/originally Birdsall Otis Edey House, 10 W. 56th St., bet. Fifth and Sixth Aves. 1901. **Warren & Wetmore**.

An exuberant Beaux Arts town house with a grand Palladian window over the ground floor.

F50

[F51] Originally **Harry B. Hollins House**/now Consulate of Argentina, 12-14 W. 56th St., bet. Fifth and Sixth Aves. 1901. **Stanford White** of **McKim, Mead & White**. Alterations, 1924. **J. E. R. Carpenter**. ☛

A neo-Georgian town house bearing wreathed eagles above the ground floor.

[F52] **Omo Norma Kamali** (boutique), 11 W. 56th St., bet. Fifth and Sixth Aves. 1978. **Rothzeid Kaiserman Thompson & Bee**, architects. **Peter Marino**, designer.

A framed façade. The horizontal slots suggest a fortified function, but the flags, a major element in this architecture, give golden motion to the street.

F52

F53

*Eat Street: The columnist **Earl Wilson**'s name for West 56th Street between Fifth and Sixth Avenues. It held the record for a single block, with about two dozen restaurants—from French and Italian to Japanese and Korean. Above the close ranks of canopies are some interesting old house fronts. Among the stars are some Venetian Gothic, a replication of detail from the Grand Canal's C'a d'Oro.*

[F53] **Trump Tower** (mixed use), 725 Fifth Ave., NE cor. 56th St. 1983. **Der Scutt**, design architect, with **Swanke Hayden Connell**.

Folded glass conceals a fantasyland for the affluent shopper. Within, the multilevel space houses a café with waterfalls and moving stairways to shoppers' heaven: flamboyant, exciting, and emblematic of the American Dream.

Donald Trump entered here stage left and has since delivered Trump Plaza, Trump Parc, Trump Palace, Trump Place, Trump Whatever, with casinos in Atlantic City. His aesthetics, however, are still more akin to malt liquor than to Veuve Clicquot.

F54

[F54] Originally **IBM Building** (offices and atrium), 590 Madison Ave., bet. E. 56th and E. 57th Sts. W side. 1983. **Edward Larrabee Barnes Assocs**. Gallery open to the public: Tu-Sa 11-6; closed Su & Mo. 212-745-6100.

This polished black granite monolith is a cut prism, its faceted form skewing the street. Most obvious to the pedestrian is the looming cantilevered corner at 57th and Madison. Attached at the south is its atrium, a bamboo-forested greenhouse, a restful garden where one can gain access to a snack, the Gallery, even to Nike Town and Trump Tower next door.

F55

[F55] **Four Seasons Hotel**, 57 E. 57th St., bet. Madison and Park Aves. 1990s. **I.M. Pei, Pei Cobb Freed & Partners/Frank Williams & Assocs./Associated Architects**.

A brawny insertion into this low-key block of art galleries: the Chinese "moon gate" hovers between "buttresses" surmounted by finials. Pompous.

F56

[F56] **Fuller Building** (offices), 41 E. 57th St., NE cor. Madison Ave. 1929. **Walker & Gillette**, architects. **Elie Nadelman**, sculptor. 🍎 Interior. 🍎

The Brooks Brothers of Art Deco: black, gray, and white.

[F57] **Niketown** (shoe store), 6 East 57th St., bet. Fifth and Madison Aves. S side. 1990s.

F58

Running and walking shoes (do sneakers still exist?) are sold in what appears to be (on the outside) a neo-1930s Italian railway station. Internally it's a stop on the passage between IBM's bamboo garden and Trump Tower.

F57

[F58] LVMH (Louis Vuitton, Moët Hennessy) Offices, 19 E. 57th St., bet. Fifth and Madison Aves. N side. 1999. Design architect. **Christian de Portzamparc**. Construction documents, **The Hillier Group**.

Folded planes create a sleek but aggressive glass curtain wall punctuating dour 57th Street. Its high style may soon be last year's. French Champagne does those things.

[F59] The Chanel Building, 15 E. 57th St., bet. Fifth and Madison Aves. N side. 1996. **Platt Byard Dovell**.

A sober façade in contrast to French exuberance at LVMH next door. Perfume versus champagne.

F59

Tiffany's: One of the world's oldest and most famous jewelers came to the corner of Fifth Avenue and 57th Street in 1940. The show windows in the massive polished granite façade (727 Fifth Avenue) are famous for their miniature stage-setting displays. See their original palace at 409 Fifth Avenue.

[F60] The Crown Building (offices)/formerly Genesco Building/originally Heckscher Building, 730 Fifth Ave., SW cor. W. 57th St. 1921. **Warren & Wetmore**.

One of the first office buildings erected after passage of the city's 1916 Zoning Resolution. Surprisingly, because of eclectic detailing (such as the rooster that once topped its water tank enclosure), it reveals no radical departure from the old ways. The Museum of Modern Art's first gallery opened here on the 12th floor in November 1929.

F60

[F61] 9 West 57th Street (offices), bet. Fifth and Sixth Aves. to E. 58th St. **Skidmore, Owings & Merrill**.

A black-and-white swooping form, as destructive to the street wall as its sibling overlooking Bryant Park. Wind bracing here is proudly displayed (way up there at each end) like a pair of new suspenders.

[F62] Originally **Ampico Building**/later Curtiss-Wright Building (offices/galleries), 29 W. 57th St., bet. Fifth and Sixth Aves. N side. 1923. **Cross & Cross**.

One of 57th Street's midblock office/gallery structures that represents the "old culture" of pianos and easel paintings. The ornate star on the east lot-line wall was the logo of the American Piano Company.

F61

[F63] Rizzoli Bookshop, 31 W. 57th St., bet. Fifth and Sixth Aves. N side. ca. 1905. Restored, 1986, **Hardy Holzman Pfeiffer Assocs**.

A bookshop that feels like a library in a baronial mansion, designed by the multitalented firm that restored the Carnegie mansion for use as the Cooper-Hewitt Museum.

[F64] Warner Brothers Studio Store/originally New York Trust Company Building (offices)/onetime Manufacturers Hanover Trust Company, 1 E. 57th St., NE cor. Fifth Ave. 1930. **Cross & Cross**. Store conversion, 1990s.

A heavy-handed exterior alteration (the store) to what was a classy building. Look to the top where the original neo-Classical details have been blended with elegant marble cubism.

[F65] 745 Fifth Avenue (offices)/originally Squibb Building, SE cor. E. 58th St. 1931. Office of **Ely Jacques Kahn**. Upgraded, 1988, **Hammond, Beebe & Babka**.

The longtime home of that inimitable toy store, F.A.O. Schwarz, now removed to more sumptuous quarters at General Motors. Bergdorf-Goodman Men's Store has filled the void with a characterless installation.

F64

[F66] **Delmonico Plaza** (offices), 55 E. 59th St., bet. Madison and Park Aves. 1986. **Davis, Brody & Assocs**.

Slate and granite. The ground-floor colonnade is a lusty break in the streetfront architecture, and its matte finish contrasts well with the glitter opposite.

[F67] **650 Madison Avenue** (offices)/originally C.I.T. Building, bet E. 59th and E. 60th Sts. W side. 1957. **Harrison & Abramovitz**. Reclad and tower added, 1987, **Fox & Fowle**.

The original black granite and stainless steel 8-story building has been overcome by its new tower and skin. The crowning floors are the most impressive sight, with a stainless-steel logo against the sky between incessant panels of green glass.

F67

[F68] **5 East 59th Street** (offices)/formerly Hong Kong and Shanghai Banking Corporation/onetime Playboy Club, bet. Fifth and Madison Aves. Altered, 1984, **Der Scutt**.

This modest building has passed through serial incarnations. Once the Savoy Art Galleries, it was remodeled into the Playboy Club (1962. **Oppenheimer, Brady & Lehrecke**) and, later, remodeled again (1976. **Paul K. Y. Chen**). Now sexy dining has given way to serious business.

[F69] **General Motors Building**, 767 Fifth Ave., bet. E. 58th and E. 59th Sts. to Madison Ave. 1968. **Edward Durell Stone, Emery Roth & Sons**, associated architects.

Here stood the Savoy Plaza (hotel) and a miscellany of others, none particularly distinguished. The hue and cry over the new tower was based not on building design but on the creation of a redundant plaza that weakened the definition of The Plaza—and the sacrifice of elegant shopping amenities to automobile salesmanship. An auto showroom is particularly galling at the spot in New York that most honors the pedestrian.

F69

Change is in the offing: the sunken central space is to be roofed over for a new plaza design.

[F70] **The Plaza Hotel**, 768 Fifth Ave. and 2 Central Park South, between W. 58th to W. 59th Sts. facing Grand Army Plaza. 1905-1907. **Henry J. Hardenbergh**. Addition, 1921. **Warren & Wetmore**.

A vestige of Edwardian elegance. **Hardenbergh**, its designer, graced New York with another, and equal, social and architectural monument: The Dakota (apartment house). The white glazed brick and the verdigris copper and slate mansard roof have been returned to their pristine splendor. One of the most exciting views of New York (Eloise-style) is from any room on the north side from the third to the fifth floors. From there eyes can skim the trees in a dramatic perspective of Central Park and Fifth Avenue. **Frank Lloyd Wright** was a devotee of the Plaza and used it as his New York headquarters.

F70

[F71] **The Plaza**/officially Grand Army Plaza Scenic Landmark, Fifth Ave. bet. W. 58th and W. 60th Sts. W side. Central Park, 1913-1916. **Thomas Hastings** of **Carrère & Hastings**.

Formally called Grand Army Plaza, this is The Plaza to New Yorkers; until 1973 it was New York's only public urban plaza for people. The Police Plaza is number two (chronologically). Plazas at Rockefeller Center, the World Trade Center, and World Financial Center are parts of private building complexes; but here, in the European tradition, is an outdoor room contained by buildings of varied architecture and function, an island of urbane repose. The more significant half (the area is bisected by 59th Street) to the south is centered on the Plaza Hotel on the west and the General Motors Building across Fifth Avenue.

F71

The Plaza is ornamented by varied paving and trees enclosing the Pulitzer Fountain, surmounted by Pomona, a lithe lady by **Karl Bitter** on a cascade of pools by **Carrère and Hastings**.

South are the seemingly seven separate buildings of
Bergdorf-Goodman (It was one building trying to look like a
row of seven. 1928. **Buchman & Kahn**. Façades reorganized,
1980s. **Allan Greenberg**) and the Paris Theater (1948. **Emery
Roth & Sons**, with interiors by **Warner-Leeds Assocs.**).
Looming high in the local skyline is 9 West 57th Street.

General Sherman occupies the Plaza's northern half, which
is more of a traffic turnaround than a pedestrian enclave. The
General (**William Tecumseh**) is here marching, not through
Georgia but, rather, in allegory. **Augustus Saint-Gaudens** presented this casting at the Paris Exposition of 1900, and the good
General mounted his present pedestal in 1903. Now the oldest
resident of this place, he antedates the Plaza Hotel by four years.

F66

UNITED NATIONS/TURTLE BAY

The tract known by the mid-18th century as Turtle Bay Farm extended roughly from East 40th to East 48th Streets, from Third Avenue to the East River. The little cove that gave it its name is now covered by the gardens on the northern half of the United Nations grounds. Bucolic in the early 19th century, the area was invaded around 1850 by riverfront industry, with shantytowns inland that were soon replaced by tenements. By 1880, el trains were rumbling along both Second and Third Avenues. Town houses on the Beekman tract along the river around East 50th Street remained respectable (due to deed restrictions against industry) until about 1900 and were among the first in the area to be rehabilitated. There was much ambitious building and renovation in the 1920s, but it was not until six city blocks of slaughterhouses along the river were razed in 1946 for the United Nations, and the Third Avenue el (the last one to operate in Manhattan) closed down in 1955, that Turtle Bay was ready for thorough rehabilitation.

START at Grand Central, where IRT subways abound (4, 5, 6, and 7 trains).

The world's last Automat expired at 200 East 42nd Street, in the office building at the southeast corner of Third Avenue. A cafeteria in which food was dispensed in individual portions through the doors of little glazed compartments, the Automat was born just before World War I, when technology was believed capable of solving all ills. Most of its siblings elsewhere were housed in delightful 1930s Art Deco/Art Moderne architecture, the most spectacular remnant what is now the Motown Café, 104 West 57th Street. A thousand little glass doors displayed the goodies within (baked beans, macaroni en casserole), and open to the magic of your coins. Once upon a time a nickel or two could buy almost anything in the Automat.

[U1] The Daily News Building (offices and printing plant), 220 E. 42nd St., bet. Second and Third Aves. 1930. **Howells & Hood.** ☞ Lobby. ☞ Addition SW cor. Second Ave. 1958. **Harrison & Abramovitz.**

U1

Howells and Hood abandoned the Gothic sources with which they won the Chicago Tribune tower competition in 1922, and here used a bold, striped verticality: patterned red and black brick spandrels and russet window shades alternating with white brick piers—the whole effect to minimize the appearance of windows in the prism. The 1958 addition wisely repeated the same stripes, but in different proportions, to yield wider windows. The street floor, outside and in, is ornamented in Art Deco abstractions. See the enormous revolving globe and weather instruments in the (mostly) original old lobby. The newspaper is gone, but its artifacts remain.

U2

An aside to 43rd Street:

[U2] Permanent Mission of India to the United Nations, 245 E. 43rd St., bet. Second and Third Aves. 1991. **Charles Correa. Bond Ryder & Assocs.**, associated architects.

A modest polished granite tower with a disciplined composition of large and small square openings. At the street the grand balcony is where a Bombay movie star might appear (too grand for the likes of a Gandhi). **Correa** is one of India's most noted modern architects.

U3

Back to 42nd Street:

📷 [U3] **Ford Foundation Building**, 321 E. 42nd St., bet. First and Second Aves. to E. 43rd St. 1967. **Kevin Roche John Dinkeloo & Assocs.** 🍎

People and plants share a world worthy of Kew, elegantly contained in masses of brick and stretches of glass. A truly avant-garde work that respects the street and enhances the urban fabric of the city.

U4

[U4] **United Presbyterian Church of the Covenant**, 310 E. 42nd St. bet. First and Second Aves. 1871. **J. C. Cady.** 🍎

A lonely leftover from other times, perhaps a piece of Tudor Scarsdale floated into town.

[U5] **Tudor City**, E. 40th St. to E. 43rd St., bet. First and Second Aves. 1925-1928. **Fred F. French Co., H. Douglas Ives.** 🍎

An ambitious private renewal effort that included 12 buildings (3,000 apartments and 600 hotel rooms) along its own street (Tudor City Place), hovering on abutments over First Avenue. Everything faced in, toward the private open space and away from the surrounding tenements, slaughterhouses, and generating plants. As a result, almost windowless walls now face the United Nations.

U5

[U5a] **Tudor City Historic District**, Tudor City Place and both sides of 42nd and 43rd Sts., from First Ave. halfway to Second Ave. 🍎

📷 [U6] **United Nations Headquarters**, United Nations Plaza (First Ave.), bet. E. 42nd and E. 48th Sts. E side. 1947-1953. **International Committee of Architects, Wallace K. Harrison, chairman**. Partially open to the public.
[U6a] **Library addition**, NE cor. E. 42nd St. 1963. **Harrison, Abramovitz & Harris**.

U6

John D. Rockefeller Jr.'s donation of the $8.5 million site, already assembled by real estate tyro **William Zeckendorf** for a private development, decided the location of the headquarters. The team of architects included **Le Corbusier** of France, **Oscar Niemeyer** of Brazil, **Sven Markelius** of Sweden, and representatives from ten other countries. The final massing is clearly concept from **Le Corbusier** (seconded by **Niemeyer**), but the details are largely **Harrison**'s.

The 544-foot-high slab of the Secretariat (only 72 feet thick) dominates the group, with the Library to the south, the General Assembly to the north—its form played against the Secretariat's size—and the Conference Building extending to the east over

UNITED NATIONS-TURTLE BAY

see pages 302–312

Franklin D. Roosevelt Drive, out of sight from U.N. Plaza. Every major nation has donated some work of art to the headquarters. Immediately noticeable is England's gift, a **Barbara Hepworth** sculpture standing in the pool (a gift from U.S. schoolchildren) in front of the Secretariat. Probably the most interesting are the three Council Chambers donated by three Scandinavian countries.

The city, under **Robert Moses**'s direction, made way for the U.N. by diverting First Avenue's through traffic into a tunnel under United Nations Plaza and opening up a half-block-wide landscaped park, Dag Hammarskjold Plaza, along East 47th Street—a meager space in the shadow of tall buildings, with no view at all of the U.N. Headquarters. The General Assembly lobby and gardens are open to the public, and tours of the conference spaces are available. Enter at East 46th Street.

U7

[U7] **1 and 2 United Nations Plaza** (offices/hotel), NW cor. E. 44th St. 1976 and 1983. All by **Kevin Roche John Dinkeloo & Assocs.**

Folded graph paper—elegant scaleless envelopes of aluminum and glass, one form sliced at its corner and sheltering the pedestrian at the street with an overhead glass apron. The public spaces within are some of the best in New York's modern architecture.

[U8] UNICEF (United Nations International Children's Emergency Fund) Building, 3 United Nations Plaza (E. 44th St. S side), bet. First and Second Aves. 1987. **Kevin Roche John Dinkleloo & Assocs.**

U8

Two tones of granite clad this architectural cousin of the E. F. Hutton Building. Here the columns are more restrained, and the building fits more serenely into its blockfront.

[U9] Kuwait Mission to the United Nations, 321 E. 44th St., bet. First and Second Aves. 1986. **Swanke Hayden Connell**.

A melange of Gulf States fantasies and New York State Post Modern.

[U10] Beaux Arts Apartments, 307 and 310 E. 44th St., between First and Second Aves. 1930. **Kenneth Murchison** and **Raymond Hood, Godley & Fouilhoux.**

U9

Named for the adjacent Beaux Arts Institute building, this pair of cubistic compositions in light and dark tan brick faces each other across the side street.

[U11] Permanent Mission of Egypt to the United Nations/originally Beaux Arts Institute of Design, 304 E. 44th St., between First and Second Aves. 1928. **Dennison & Hirons**.

U11

The fantasies of Beaux Arts architectural education in this country (heavily influenced by the techniques of the Ecole des Beaux-Arts in Paris) are incorporated in this structure, built when the system was already on the wane. The style is, of course, Art Deco, now reloved by the profession that despised and rejected it for so long. But how is Egypt going to cope with that monumental lettering?

[U12] United States Mission to the United Nations, 799 United Nations Plaza, SW cor. E. 45th Sts. W side. 1961. **Kelly & Gruzen** and **Kahn & Jacobs.**

U12

A precast-concrete eggcrate "sunscreen" veneers the seat of America's envoys to the UN. (Its design, of course, caters not at all to sun control—facing, as it does, east and north.) A new replacement building is due from **Gwathmey Siegel & Associates**.

On opposite sides of Second Avenue between East 44th and East 45th Streets are two classic and venerable steak restaurants providing elegant meats in simple surroundings: The Palm at No. 837 and The Palm Too at No. 840. Expensive.

[U13] Originally **Institute of International Education,** 809 United Nations Plaza, bet. E. 45th and E. 46th Sts. W side. 1964. **Harrison, Abramovitz & Harris.** Kaufmann Conference Rooms, 1965. **Alvar Aalto.**

U13

Important for an interior space—the penthouse Edgar J. Kaufmann Conference Rooms, one of only two U.S. works of the Finnish architect **Alvar Aalto**.

[U14] Anti-Defamation League/B'nai B'rith/originally Carnegie Endowment International Center (offices), 823 United Nations Plaza, NW cor. 46th St. 1953. **Harrison & Abramovitz**. Renovated for B'nai B'rith, 1991. **Der Scutt**.

A modest but dated modernist building.

[U15] Dag Hammarskjold Tower (apartments), 240 E. 47th St., SW cor. Second Ave. to E. 46th St. 1984. **Gruzen & Partners.**

U15

An understated tower with simple, faceted balconies, built of preassembled brick panels, the joints of which give a second design rhythm to the façade.

[U16] **Japan House,** 333 E. 47th St., bet. First and Second Aves. 1971. **Junzo Yoshimura** and **George Shimamoto** of **Gruzen & Partners.** Open to the public: Tu-Su 11-5; closed Mo. 212-832-1155.

Japan's public architectural emissary to the City of New York. Delicately detailed, inside and out, it stages cultural exhibitions often worth seeing. A somber black building with delicate sun grilles.

[U17] **Trump World Tower,** 845 United Nations Plaza, NW cor. First Ave. and E. 47th St., 2001. **Costas Kondylis.**

Perhaps this will be an apocryphal building. We hope so.

The tallest residential building in the world? Do we care? Does Donald care? But he does, for the extreme projects he promotes are marketing tools that bring in the maximum dollars. $1,000 a square foot? $2,000? Your mother thrown in? This is the site of the former United Engineering Center.

[U18] **United Nations Plaza** (apartments), NW cor. E. 48th St. 1990s. **Der Scutt.**

A succulent garden offers a pleasant stopping point. Skip the building.

[U19] **German House, Permanent Mission of the Federal Republic of Germany to the United Nations.** 861 First Ave., bet. E. 48th and E. 49th Sts. W side. 1990s.

The heavy-handed side of German design: picture-framed Post-Modern with gross detailing. Where was **Egon Eiermann** (architect of Germany's lovely Washington embassy) when we needed him?

U20

[U20] **860 and 870 United Nations Plaza** (apartments), bet. E. 48th and E. 49th Sts. E side. 1966. **Harrison, Abramovitz & Harris.**

Desirable for views and its ostensible social snobbery, not for its architecture.

[U21] **Beekman Tower** (apartments)/originally Panhellenic Hotel, 3 Mitchell Pl. (E. 49th St.), NE cor. First Ave. 1928. **John Mead Howells.** ●

U21

A miniature reprise of **Eliel Saarinen**'s second-prize "style-less" design in the 1922 Chicago Tribune tower competition.

Howells (with **Raymond Hood** as partner) took first prize with a free neo-Gothic entry. Originally a hotel for women members of Greek letter societies (sororities).

A walk along FDR Drive: At the east end of East 51st Street, steps lead down to a small park and a footbridge over the Franklin D. Roosevelt Drive. Cross the bridge for a back view of Beekman Place and a view of the drive disappearing at East 52nd Street under a Sutton Place South apartment house. From the walk along the river there is a good view of the waterside of Beekman Place, one of those affluent bluffs that defied industrial expansion at the commercial waterfronted edge of the city:

*Beekman Place: Along with Sutton Place and, to an extent, Gracie Square, an elegant social enclave atop a river-fronted bluff. Here, on two blocks, were once the town houses and understated apartment houses of WASPS, diplomats, movie stars, and others who savor low-key luxury. Among them is the former home of the late **Paul Rudolph**, architectural hero of the 1950s and 1960s, one time dean of the Yale School of Architecture and the controversial designer of the School's building:*

U22

[U22] **Paul Rudolph House**, 23 Beekman Place, bet. E. 50th and E. 51st Sts. E side. 1983-1987. **Paul Rudolph**.
    The egocentric effort of a very talented architect of the Modern movement. Crowning the town house is a steel-framed cage of balconies that give a strong radical presence to the local skyline.

U23

[U23] **Formerly Public School 135**, Manhattan/later United Nations School, 931 First Ave., NW cor. E. 51st St. 1892. **George W. Debevoise**. Addition, 1904. Conversion, 2000. **Conklin & Rossant**.
    Brick and brownstone Romanesque Revival multistory schoolhouse, now converting to condominiums.

U25

 [U24] **River House**, 435 E. 52nd St., E of First Ave. 1931. **Bottomley, Wagner & White**.
    A palatial 26-story cooperative apartment house with a gated, cobbled entrance court. The River Club, on its lower floors, includes squash and tennis courts, a swimming pool, and a ballroom. Prior to construction of the FDR Drive, there was even a private dock where the best yachts tied up.

[U25] **400, 414, 424, and 434 East 52nd Street** (apartments), E of First Ave. 1920s.
    Park Avenue on 52nd Street, an understated wall for the upper middle class, ornamented with handsome Art Deco details.

U26

[U26] **Recreation Center and Indoor Pool, N.Y.C. Department of Parks & Recreation**/originally 54th Street Public Bath and Gymnasium, 348 E. 54th St., bet. First and Second Aves. 1906. **Werner & Windolph**.
    A minor building with a major façade. For once the screened roof space is part of the overall design, heralded by colossal brick Classical columns.

[U27] **Le Mondrian**/originally Le Grand Palais, 254 E. 54th St. (apartments), SW cor. Second Ave. 1992. **Fox & Fowle**.
    Some class, compared to its East Side peers of the 1980s and 1990s.

U27

[U28] **St. James Tower** (apartments), 415 E. 54th St., bet. First Ave. and Sutton Place S. 1983. **Emery Roth & Sons**.
    A small public plaza is contributed for the tired nanny (or guidebook author) in return for more condominium square footage to sell.

U30

U30

[U29] **400 East 57th Street** (apartments), SE cor. First Ave. to E. 56th St. 1931. **Roger H. Bullard**, **Philip L. Goodwin**, and **Kenneth Franzheim**.

An Art Moderne apartment building in the style of Central Park West's Century and Majestic, but monotowered.

Sutton Place:

[U30] **Sutton Place town houses**, Sutton Place bet. E. 57th and E. 58th Sts. E side, Sutton Sq. (E. 58th St.), and **Riverview Terr.** (a private street bet. Sutton Sq. and E. 59th St.).

An enclave of wealth and elegance from the early 1920s, when factories and tenements largely shared the banks of the East River. The Dead End Kids were the denizens of these blocks which dead-ended into piers at the river and where summer fun included diving into that not yet fetid tidal waterway. (Construction of the East River Drive and the toiletization of the river itself ended all that.)

This group was started as an experimental enclave of private houses at a time when most of those who could afford a private house were moving to (or already living in) Park and Fifth Avenue apartments. Architects here included **Mott Schmidt** (Nos. 1, 3, 13, and 17 Sutton Place), **H. Page Cross** (No. 9), **William Lescaze** (No. 21), **Delano & Aldrich** (No. 12 Sutton Square), and **Ely Jacques Kahn** (6 Riverview Terrace). Nothing is spectacular in itself, but the whole is an intact block and a half, with riverfront private gardens that jointly provide an urbane architectural grouping. Prominent residents included **Mrs. William K. Vanderbilt** (No. 1 Sutton Place) and **Robert W. Goelet** (No. 9).

[U31] **Bridgemarket**, under the Queensboro Bridge, along E. 59th St. to E. 60th St., E of First Ave. Vaulted underbridge space, 1914. **Henry Hornbostel**. Conversion to Food Emporium and Conran's Restaurant & Housewares Store, 1999. **Hardy Holzman Pfeiffer Assocs**.

U31

Here great Guastavino tile-vaulted space is converted for use as an elegant marketplace, one of the grand found spaces formerly wasted on pedestrian storage by City agencies. Others that should be recaptured include the vast volume under the Riverside Drive viaduct in the West 150s and those beneath the Brooklyn Bridge.

The grand vaults are somewhat diminished by a restaurant mezzanine, and the view of it all by the conning-tower glass entry to the basement Conran's store.

[U32] **322 East 57th Street** (studios) bet. First and Second Aves. 1930. **Harry M. Clawson** of **Caughey & Evans**.

A simple Park Avenue façade, rusticated at the base, houses studios with dramatic 2-story windows.

U32

[U33] **311 and 313 East 58th Street** (houses), bet. Second Ave. and the Queensboro Bridge access ramp. 1856-1857. ☛

The new approaches (1930) to the bridge have partially submerged these modest onetime suburban dwellings, now squeezed by the bridge approaches and commerce looming all around.

U33

[U34] **248 East 58th Street** (shop and offices), bet. Second and Third Aves. 1980s.

A happy tour-de-force. Steel makes a structural façade into a powerful composition.

[U35] **Cinemas 1, 2 and 3**, 1001 Third Ave., bet. E. 59th and E. 60th Sts. 1962. **Abraham W. Geller & Assocs.**

Modern architecture met the movies for the first time (in New York) in 1962. A duplex that has since become a triplex, it was at first a piggyback pair. Geller and his wife, who did the interiors, produced a simple elegance with counterpoints of rich paintings and graphics. Now shopworn and somewhat degraded within.

U34

[U36] **Decoration and Design Building**, 979 Third Ave., NE cor. E. 58th St. 1965. **David & Earl Levy.**

The zigguratted New York zoning envelope capitalized into a positive architectural statement (if you look skyward). Things are pedestrian for the pedestrian at the street. There are corner windows for even the lowliest Swatch-bearers.

Here's a chance to take a rest, and continue another day. The nearest subways are at 59th Street and Lexington (IRT Nos. 4, 5, 6 trains, and the IND N and R). Or else onward to the south.

U35

[U37] **919 Third Avenue** (offices), bet. E. 55th and E. 56th Sts. E side. 1970. **Skidmore, Owings & Merrill.**

A sleek but monumental black metal and glass curtain wall that uses **P. J. Clarke**'s as its plaza "sculpture":

P. J.'s: This characteristic but truncated 19th-century relic (at 915 Third Avenue, northeast corner of East 55th Street) has always been known officially as Clarke's Bar. But to generations of collegians it has been P. J.'s, and it is partly responsible for the rash of other places called P. J. "Something." Seen by millions as the set for the 1945 movie Lost Weekend, *it has lots of real stained glass and mahogany, and one of New York's most lavish old-fashioned men's rooms. Clarke's is so economically successful that everything on the block except the first 2 of its original 4 floors was demolished for No. 919.*

U36

[U38] **909 Third Avenue** (offices), and Franklin D. Roosevelt Station, U.S. Post Office, bet. E. 54th and E. 55th Sts. E side. 1967. **Max O. Urbahn & Assocs.**

The tower's deeply coffered, cast-concrete window walls seem a honeycomb for the killer bees of Manhattan business. The podium is New York 10022's mail-handling factory. The requisite sculpture punctuates the sidewalk.

U38

[U39] **900 Third Avenue** (offices), NW cor. E. 54th St. 1983. **Cesar Pelli** and **Rafael Viñoly**, design architects. **Emery Roth & Sons**, associate architects.

Another sleek shaft with the Citicorp "bolt of cloth" for the Argentine developer **Jacobo Finkielstain**. More elegant gray and silver sleekness.

[U40] **885 Third Avenue** (offices), bet. E. 53rd and E. 54th Sts. E side. 1986. **John Burgee** with **Philip Johnson.**

A bumpy ellipse (in plan) of red-brown and pink, this acquired the sobriquet Lipstick Building because of its telescoping tiers. Columns with Turkish capitals saunter around its

U40

U39

grand ground floor. A connection to what is becoming one of
the more complex (and yet convenient) subway concourses, the
IND Lexington Avenue Station, is here provided.

U41

[U41] **312 and 314 East 53rd Street** (houses), bet. First and
Second Aves. 1866. No. 312 🍎

A pair of clapboard town houses of Second Empire inspiration with interesting corbeled entrance hoods and round-
topped dormers.

[U42] **875 Third Avenue** (offices), bet. E. 52nd and E. 53rd Sts.
1982. **Skidmore, Owings & Merrill** (Chicago office).

The ghost of a **Mies van der Rohe** grid appears in this
Windy City octopod invention that is about as much New York
as pan pizza or cherry phosphate. Poor Mies . . .

U43

[U43] **Salvation Army Building**, 221 E. 52nd St., bet. Second and
Third Aves. 1940s.

Modern for those who considered it the distillation of a
historical style, here Georgian brick translated into simple modernist forms.

[U44] **Permanent Mission of the Republic of Hungary to the
United Nations**, 227 E. 52nd St., bet. Second and Third Aves.
1990s.

The somewhat tipsy ghosts of **Palladio** and **King George IV**
combined with a developer to make this neo-18th-century
mélange. And for Hungarians?

U45

[U45] **The Enclave** (apartments), 224 E. 52nd St., bet. Second
and Third Aves. 1985. **Marvin H. Meltzer**.

A modern eccentric, in glass block and pink stucco, with
curved balconies.

U46

 [U46] **Mrs. John D. Rockefeller III Guest House**/origi-
nally Museum of Modern Art guesthouse, 242 E. 52nd St.,
bet. Second and Third Aves. 1950. **Philip Johnson & Assocs**.

Roman brick and painted steel front a house built for guests
of the **Rockefeller Brothers** (**John D., Jr., David, Nelson**, and
Winthrop), who later gave it for similar guest purposes to the
Museum of Modern Art.

[U47] **301 East 52nd Street** (apartments)/originally Kips Bay
Boys Club, bet. First and Second Aves. 1931. **Delano & Aldrich**.
Converted, 1978.

A handsome, low-key conversion. Note the segmental
arched windows and brickwork with alternating headers and
stretchers.

[U48] **Greenacre Park**, 217-221 E. 51st St., bet. Second and Third Aves. 1971. **Sasaki, Dawson, DeMay Assocs.**, landscape architects. **Goldstone, Dearborn & Hinz**, consulting architects.

A gift to the city by the daughter of **John D. Rockefeller, Jr.**, **Mrs. Jean Mauze**. An urbane place, larger and lusher than Paley Plaza (but again complete with waterfall), to rest on your rounds in the city. Food and drink available.

U47

[U49] **245 East 50th Street** (apartments), bet. Second and Third Aves. 1980. **David Kenneth Specter & Assocs**.

A modest 8-story Modern apartment house with flower-crested balconies. Look up; the bay windows look down.

[U50] **Amster Yard**, 211-215 E. 49th St., bet. Second and Third Aves. 1870. Remodeled, 1945, **Harold Sterner**. 🍎

The vagaries of early property transfers created this inner-block space. A passage with a slate floor and iron settees leads into a garden, from which the office of **James Amster Associates**, other interior designers, and a few shops could be reached. Look carefully for the mirror at the end of the garden vista. Sculptor **Isamu Noguchi** once did his work in this yard, before discovering Ravenswood (see the Noguchi Museum). In flux.

U48

[U51] **212 East 49th Street** (house), bet. Second and Third Aves. 1986. **Mitchell-Giurgola**.

An elegantly successful Post Modern town house; marble, granite, and limestone mingling in exquisite detail. The adjacent buildings to the west, with false shutters, and to the east, in a heavy-handed Modern, seem gross by comparison.

U51

[U52] **219 East 49th Street** (house), between Second and Third Aves. 1935. **Morris Sanders**.

A ground-floor office and 2 duplexes, all clearly expressed on the façade in the Modernist style of the 1930s. Dark blue glazed brick was used to fend off soot; balconies control sunlight. But a sleek modernity with a glistening façade enriched with shade and shadow was equally sought.

[U53] **Turtle Bay Gardens Historic District**, 226-246 E. 49th St., bet. Second and Third Aves. and 227-247 E. 48th St. Remodeled, 1920, **Edward C. Dean** and **William Lawrence Bottomley**. 🍎

Two rows of 10 houses each, back to back, assembled by **Mrs. Walton Martin** (**Charlotte Hunnewell Sorchan** before her marriage). A 6-foot strip was taken from the backyard of each house to form a common path and garden. Near a very old willow tree at the center of the group is a fountain copied from the Villa Medici. Low walls and planting mark off the private yards. House interiors were remodeled with living rooms opening to the yard, with lowered front doors set in pastel-painted stucco façades. Such notables as **Katharine Hepburn**, **Leopold Stokowski**, **E. B. White**, **Stephen Sondheim**, **Garson Kanin**, **Maggie Smith**, and **Tyrone Power** have lived here. White memorialized the block in his marvelous anthology *The Second Tree from the Corner*.

U53

[U54] **Sterling Plaza** (apartments), 255 E. 49th St., NW cor. Second Ave. 1985. **Schuman, Lichtenstein, Claman & Efron**, architects. **Arquitectonica**, design consultants.

The fins on top are styling added to an otherwise ordinary apartment building. Arquitectonica's normal turf is Miami, where they have created numerous resplendent and/or eccentric structures.

U54

[U55] **303-309 East 49th Street** (apartments), bet. First and Second Aves. 1984. **Architects Design Group**.

The sliver wing on Second Avenue is attached to a slab on 49th—all in smooth and striated contrasting concrete block.

U55

U56

The curved masonry balcony parapets give a strong modulation to the façade, but they are low enough, with railings atop, to allow those seated to enjoy the view.

 [U56] Originally **William Lescaze House**, 211 E. 48th St., bet. Second and Third Aves. 1934. **William Lescaze.** ☕️

A pioneering Modern town house by and for a pioneering Modern architect, protected from city atmosphere by glass block and air-conditioning. The office was at the bottom, the house above, the living room occupying the whole top floor.

U58

[U57] Onetime **Wang Building** (offices), 780 Third Ave. bet. E. 48th and E. 49th Sts. W side. 1984. **Skidmore, Owings & Merrill**.

There is an implicit indication of structure in this red granite monolith: the omitted windows draw blank diagonal lines across the façade where wind bracing lurks.

[U58] **767 Third Avenue** (offices), SE cor. E. 48th St. 1980. **Fox & Fowle**.

Brick ribbons wrap around a sinuous and stylish form. At the base is a "Japanese" Post Modern wood grillage (catercorner to the building of a Chinese computer company).

U59

[U59] **The Cosmopolitan** (apartments), 145 E. 48th St., bet. Lexington and Third Aves. 1987. **Gruzen Samton Steinglass**.

A modestly Post Modern brick building, enhanced with a curve here, a bay window there.

END of Walking Tour: *The nearest subways, at the interwoven IRT/IND stations running from 51st to 53rd Streets on Lexington Avenue are the IRT (No. 6 train) and the IND (F train).*

**LINCOLN CENTER
RIVERSIDE DRIVE/WEST END AVENUE
BROADWAY AND ENVIRONS
CENTRAL PARK WEST/THE PARK BLOCKS
WEST SIDE URBAN RENEWAL AREA
MANHATTAN VALLEY**

Colonial

Georgian/ Federal

Greek Revival

Gothic Revival

Villa

Romanesque Revival

Renaissance Revival

Roman Revival

Art Deco/ Art Moderne

Modern/ Post-Modern

In a way the Upper West Side is as much a state of mind as a place to live: a successor to Greenwich Village as a magnet for those in the vanguard of cultural or social action and also—particularly today—political action.

Early Manhattan's development was confined mostly below and to the east of Central Park; the latecomer West blossomed during a period of substantial immigration of urbane Europeans. That population, culturally crossbred with adventurous local migrants, and served by equally adventurous developers, created a mix of people and buildings with a flavor distinct from that of the East. The West once owed as much to the imported culture of Vienna, Berlin, and Budapest as to the enterprising patronage of those such as **Singer Sewing Machine heir Edward Severin Clark**. His Dakota Apartments at 72nd Street became a social outpost so remote from The 400 that it was considered the geographical equivalent—in New York City terms—of the Dakota Territory.

Whereas Greenwich Village became a Bohemian haven and a crucible for the individual painter, sculptor, writer, or poet—a place of rebellion and artistic creativity—the West Side is a nexus of group art concerts, opera, theater, and film—the cultural mecca for national as well as New York audiences. Here live a major portion of those who fill those many stages, intermingled with a locally passionate audience. Perhaps passion is a local character trait, not only of those who perform or savor performance but also of a vast group of political activists who voice their community and national concerns with a vigor unequaled elsewhere in the city.

But how did it all begin?

After the English "conquest" of New Amsterdam in 1664, **Richard Nicolls** was appointed governor by the **Duke of York** to oversee his new proprietary colony. Nicolls not only honored Dutch property owners and landlords already in place but also granted vast tracts to new patentees. The **Thousand Acre Tract**, bounded by the Hudson and (roughly) modern 50th Street, 89th Street, and Sixth Avenue, now the heart of the Upper West Side, was divided into ten lots and granted to four Dutchmen and one Englishman.

In its original verdant state the area was known as Bloomingdale, honored by its nominal association with a flower-growing region near Haarlem named Bloemendael. The Bloomingdale Road followed a serpentine Indian trail that also produced the meandering alignment of much of Broadway. As a northern extension of Lower Manhattan's principal street, it was the road to Albany, a commercial route whose scale after widening (1868-1871) allowed its ultimate potential to be planned. And so, it was briefly renamed The Boulevard until 1899, when buildings such as The Ansonia, The Belnord, The Apthorp, and The Belleclaire would begin to fulfill these plans.

It was not until public transportation had penetrated these precincts that serious development occurred. Although horsecars had reached West 84th Street by 1864, the Ninth Avenue elevated did not arrive until 1879, with stations at 72nd, 81st, 93rd, and 104th Streets (others were added later). **Clark**'s almost simultaneous construction of the Dakota (1880-1884) was an equal inspiration and stimulus. New buildings centered on these

Metropolitan Opera Building, Lincoln Center

nodes at first, with developers uncertain about the City's intentions to level and grade the streets and to evict squatters and shanty owners. But by 1886, a boom had occurred, as related grandiloquently in the *Times*:

"The West side of the city presents just now a scene of building activity such as was never before witnessed in that section, and which gives promise of the speedy disappearance of all the shanties in the neighborhood and the rapid population of this long neglected part of New York. The huge masses of rock which formerly met the eye usually crowned by a rickety shanty and a browsing goat, are being blasted out of existence. Streets are being graded, and thousands of carpenters and masons are engaged in rearing substantial buildings where a year ago nothing was to be seen but market gardens or barren rocky fields."

For the purposes of this guide we have divided the Upper West Side's 2 square miles into precincts: Lincoln Center, Riverside Drive, Central Park West, the West Side Urban Renewal Area, and Manhattan Valley. The vital center, loosely termed Broadway and Environs, embraces the powerful diagonal thoroughfare where a dual necklace of shops attempts to emulate, admittedly somewhat crassly, the boulevards of Paris. With one exception, the Urban Renewal Area, each precinct is described in an uptown sequence, moving away from the central business district. The Renewal Area, constructed sequentially from north to south, is also described in that direction.

UPPER WEST SIDE KEY MAP

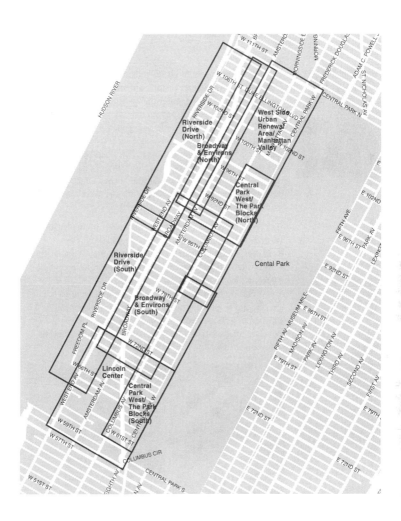

LINCOLN CENTER

The southern part of the Upper West Side developed quickly in the 1880s along Columbus Avenue, the route of the Ninth Avenue el, which intersected Lincoln Square at Broadway and 65th Street. The area was never fashionable except along Central Park. By the late 1940s the part west of Broadway was a slum, fostered by its proximity to the open New York Central railroad yards lying between West End Avenue and the river. This latter area was the subject first of low-rent subsidized apartments and then of a 12-block urban renewal project that cleared the tenements and is now the site of Lincoln Center, Lincoln Towers apartments, and Fordham University's in-town campus, as well as many other public and institutional buildings. The old railroad has proven to be a much more difficult project. The new Trump towers along Trump Place promised to be a man-made escarpment overlooking a new park down to the river. A relocated and submerged West Side Highway was part of the original plan but was eliminated for its expense: the result is an elevated highway traipsing through a park. The area described below lies between West 60th and West 70th Streets from Broadway to the Hudson River.

L1

[L1] **Trump International Hotel and Tower**/originally Gulf + Western Plaza (office building), 1 Central Park W., bet. Broadway, Columbus Circle, and W. 61st St. 1969. **Thomas E. Stanley**. Reconfigured and reclad, 1990s. **Philip Johnson** and **Alan Ritchie**.

A reincarnation in glitz for those Trumpers who seek the sleekest and latest arriviste quarters. Gulf + Western was stripped to its bones, reconfigured, and reclad as very expensive pieds-à-terre for South Americans and Europeans with wanderlust.

L2

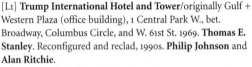 [L2] **American Bible Society Building**, 1865 Broadway, NW cor. W. 61st St. 1966. **Skidmore, Owings & Merrill**. New glass entrance, stairs, and second-floor gallery. 1998. **Fox & Fowle**.

The neatly cast-in-place concrete of this burly building is exposed: its bridge-sized beams make a giant ladder of the Broadway end. The new hi-tech steel and glass entry element relieves, at close range, some of its overweighing bulk.

[L3] **Fordham University, Lincoln Center Campus**.
[L3a] **Schools of Business, Education, Social Service** (South
Building), 113 W. 60th St., NW cor. Columbus Ave. 1962.
Voorhees, Walker, Smith, Smith & Haines. [L3b] **School of
Law** (North Building), 140 W. 62nd St., SW cor. Columbus Ave.
1969. **Slingerland & Booss**.

Part of the same urban renewal package as Lincoln Center's
performing arts spaces, these buildings fortunately skip the
travertine yet prove that, clad in limestone, their bodies are very
white and equally monotonous.

L4

[L4] **Sofia Apartments**/formerly Sofia Brothers
Warehouse)/originally Kent Automatic Parking Garage,
43 West 61st Street, NE cor. Columbus Ave. 1929-1930. **Jardine,
Hill & Murdock**. ☙ Converted to apartments, 1983-1985, **Alan
Lapidus Assocs.**, **Rothzeid Kaiserman Thompson & Bee**, and
Abraham Rothenberg.

A midblock Art Deco delight. All walls, even those on lot
lines that might have been masked by tall neighbors (such as
Lincoln Plaza Tower, for example), were embellished with some
(two-dimensional) ornament. Curiously enough, this structure
was built as an early "automatic" (meaning "elevatored") garage;
its fortresslike walls were fenestrated during conversion to
human occupancy.

L5

[L5] **The Beacon** (apartments), 30 W. 61st St., bet. Broadway and
Columbus Ave. S side. 1990s.

Serene and understated for the first few office floors, this
monolith of dark brown brick mutates into a more glassy residential mode at number six.

[L6] **Lincoln Plaza Tower** (apartments), 44 W. 62nd St.,
SE cor. Columbus Ave. 1973. **Horace Ginsbern & Assocs**.

An urbane 30-story stack of bay windows and dish-shaped
balconies caught in an embrace of cylindrical columns.

L6

Lincoln Center

[L7] **Lincoln Center for the Performing Arts**, W. 62nd to W.
66th Sts., Columbus to Amsterdam Aves. 1962-1968. **Wallace K.
Harrison**, director of board of architects (composed of the
architects of individual buildings).

This travertine acropolis of music and theater represents an
initial investment of more than $165 million of early 1960s dol-

LINCOLN CENTER

see pages 316–324

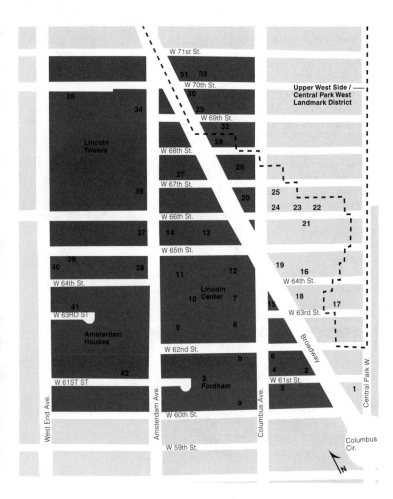

lars (nearly $1 billion in today's dollars)—mostly in private contributions—along with federal aid in acquiring the site and a State contribution to the New York State Theater. The project aroused dissent on both urbanistic and architectural grounds. The congestion caused by the location of so many large theaters in one cluster (with only meager public transportation) has been an obvious problem, left unsolved by the vast underground garage beneath the project. Making a single impressive group out of structures with such demanding interior requirements has imposed inhibitions on the individual buildings. As a result, former *New York Times* architecture critic **Ada Louise Huxtable** wrote, "Philharmonic Hall, the State Theater, and the Metropolitan Opera are lushly decorated, conservative structures that the public finds pleasing and most professionals consider a failure of nerve, imagination and talent. Fortunately," she continued, "the scale and relationship of the plazas are good, and they can be enjoyed as pedestrian open spaces."

L8

[L8] **New York State Theater**, SE cor. Lincoln Center, Columbus Ave., bet. W. 62nd and W. 63rd Sts. W side. 1964. **Philip C. Johnson** and **Richard Foster**. Reconstructed, 1982.

This 2,737-seat hall, designed mainly for ballet and musical theater, also includes a vast 4-story foyer used separately for receptions and balls. The most frankly Classical building facing the plaza, it has a ground-level lobby that suggests an understated Baroque space carved from enveloping travertine. The

L10

grand foyer above it, in contrast, is ornate with tiers of busy railings, golden chain drapery, and a velvet ceiling, all dominated by
two superb white marble sculptures, enlargements of **Elie
Nadelman** works.

[L9] **Damrosch Park**, Guggenheim Band Shell, SW cor. Lincoln
Center, W. 62nd St. NE cor. Amsterdam Ave. 1969. **Eggers &
Higgins**.

    Planned as a space for free outdoor concerts, this park sur-
rounds a flat, intricately paved center section with an edge of
verdant formal landscaping. The band shell, hugging
Amsterdam Avenue on the west, seems to derive its form from
Middle Eastern antecedents, thus adding yet another curious
dimension to the already eclectic Lincoln Center.

[L10] **Metropolitan Opera House**, W side of Lincoln Center,
bet. W. 63rd and W. 64th Sts. 1966. **Wallace K. Harrison** of
Harrison & Abramovitz. Lobby paintings facing the plaza,
Marc Chagall.

    After years of trying to remove itself from its garment center
location on Broadway between 39th and 40th Streets—negotiat-
ing at one point to occupy what eventually became the site of
Rockefeller Center's GE (once RCA) Building—the Met finally
came here, to Lincoln Center. It is the focal building of the complex and its largest hall. It is also a schmaltzy pastiche of forms,
materials (mostly travertine), and effects beginning with self-
consciously sensuous red-carpeted stairs (which wind around
themselves at the entrance) and ending with brilliant Austrian
crystal chandeliers (which hang in the tall lobby space, as they
do in the hall itself until, at the start of a performance, they
silently rise to the gold-leafed ceiling). The café at the top of the
lobby offers a dazzling view down into the entry area and out
across the plaza.

[L11] **Vivian Beaumont Theater**, NW cor. Lincoln
Center, 150 W. 65th St., SE cor. Amsterdam Ave. 1965. **Eero
Saarinen & Assocs**. [L11a] **Library and Museum of the
Performing Arts, The New York Public Library**, 111 Amsterdam
Ave. 1965, **Skidmore, Owings & Merrill**. Pool sculpture in plaza,
Reclining Figure, **Henry Moore**. Lobbies remodeled, 1997-1998.
Hardy Holzman Pfeiffer.

    An unusual collaboration of both architects and architec-
ture. The library fills the massive, travertine-clad attic story
looming over Vivian Beaumont below, forming a handsome
backdrop for the pool reflecting **Moore's** *Reclining Figure*, especially when the glassy lobby is activated with light and a theater

crowd. In the main theater—there is a smaller one below—neutral, dark interior surfaces do not compete with the colorful tiered seating or the action on the highly flexible stage. The library-museum, best entered through the link connecting it to the opera house, has typically meticulous SOM details, a fun-to-shop-in boutique specializing in performing arts books and memorabilia, and always some lively exhibits arranged by its Shelby Cullom Davis Museum. The lowest entrance from Amsterdam Avenue opens upon a small lecture hall. Under renovation.

[L12] **Avery Fisher Hall**/originally Philharmonic Hall, NE cor. Lincoln Center, Columbus Ave. SW cor. W. 65th St. 1962. **Max Abramovitz** of **Harrison & Abramovitz**. Reconstructed, 1976, **Johnson/Burgee**, architects. **Cyril Harris**, acoustical engineer. Stabile suspended from lobby ceiling, 1962, **Richard Lippold**, sculptor.

L12

The many-tiered lobby of this concert hall has a clear glass enclosure set inside an arcade defined by tall, crisply tapered travertine columns. It is the most controversial of Lincoln Center's buildings, and its hall has been rebuilt a number of times in attempts to solve its well-publicized acoustical deficiencies. The most elaborate change, in 1976, converted the hall into a classic European rectangle (and redesigned the public lobby spaces as well) to wide acclaim from both acoustical and architectural critics.

L13

[L13] **Juilliard School of Music**, 144 W. 66th St., bet. Broadway and Amsterdam Ave. 1968. **Pietro Belluschi**, with **Eduardo Catalano** and **Westermann & Miller**.

Connected to the superblock of Lincoln Center proper by a bridge over West 65th Street, this is the youngest of the Center's buildings. Monolithic in appearance, it seems to be carved from travertine. It makes the best of an irregular site caused by Broadway's diagonal slash.

Lincoln Center Mall: Late in 1966 an ill-advised plan was announced to create a landscaped mall that would link Lincoln Center's Plaza with Central Park, a long city block away. The plan called for demolishing the West Side YMCA (1930 Dwight James Baum) and the meetinghouse of the New York Society for Ethical Culture along with other structures between West 63rd and West 64th Streets—the Broadway frontage was by then an enormous parking lot. Additionally, a blocksized underground parking area was envisioned beneath the proposed greenery. The plan lost and the threatened institutions remain. From the parking lot, however, grew the ASCAP Building, a spastic work that seems unable to respect either the rectangular street grid or Broadway's diagonal. Some decades everything goes wrong.

L14

[L14] **Samuel and David Rose Building** and **Wilson Residence Hall** (mixed use), W. 65th St. NE cor. Amsterdam Ave. 1992. **Davis, Brody & Assocs**. and **Abramovitz Kingsland Schiff**.

This multiuse annex to Lincoln Center proper provides in the base an auditorium and rehearsal spaces for the Juilliard School and dormitory space and apartments in the tower. The cream and brown stonework is welcome after the sea of travertine next door.

[L15] **Dante Park**, W. 63rd to W. 64th Sts., bet. Broadway and Columbus Ave. *Dante*, 1920, **Ettore Ximenes**, sculptor.

Here a dour and grumpy Dante holds the *Commedia*, a hard act for all of Lincoln Center's halls to follow.

L14

[L16] Originally **Liberty Warehouse**, 43 W. 64th St., bet. Central Park W. and Columbus Ave. N side.

A 55-foot replica of the Statue of Liberty has crowned the storage warehouse of the same name since 1902—she lost the torch in a windstorm long ago. The ground floor has, as a result of Lincoln Center's booming attendance, seen some successful adaptive reuse as restaurants.

[L17] **West Side YMCA,** 5 West 63rd St., bet. Central Park W. and Broadway. 1930. **Dwight J. Baum**. Adjacent apartment tower (Park Laurel) on site of McBurney School, 15 W. 63rd St. 1990s. **Beyer Blinder Belle**.

A center of cultural athletics, this Y is one of two remnants from a time when young urban immigrants were merely housed in Christian or Hebrew hostels (the other is the YMHA at East 92nd Street). Here and there housing still exists (and the new apartment tower will provide 65 units for the Y on its lower floors), but the Ys are now known more for their cultural and athletic possibilities than their service as caravansaries.

L17

The West Side Y is a neo-Romanesque pile, in limestone and brick, complete with machicolations, arched corbel tables, and other medieval encrustations.

[L18] **ASCAP Building** (mixed use), 1 Lincoln Plaza, bet. W. 63rd and W. 64th Sts., E side of Broadway. also known as 20 W. 64th St. 1971. **Philip Birnbaum**.

Another behemoth from the Lincoln Center syndrome. To pay for this vast sector of 1960s urban renewal, one must seat the densest population of New York at culture's flanks. ASCAP, the noted American Society of Composers, Authors and Publishers, is housed at the base in this geographically appropriate place, but the overwhelming skewed prism has no redeeming social or architectural significance. The public arcade only allowed it to be bigger—what an urbanistic mistake!

L18

[L19] Originally **Goelet Garage,** 1926 Broadway, bet. W. 64th and W. 65th Sts. 1906-1907. **Frank M. Andrews**.

A handsome player from Broadway's past.

[L20] **Lincoln Triangle** (mixed use), 1 Lincoln Sq. (144 Columbus Ave.), bet. Columbus Ave. and Broadway, W. 66th and W. 67th Sts. 1997. **Gary Edward Handel + Assocs.**, design architect. **Schuman Lichtenstein Claman & Efron**, architects of record.

For the casual passerby this is the Barnes and Noble Building, but overhead the tower houses residents drawn to this new West Side story.

L19

American Broadcasting Company

[L21] Originally **First Battery Armory, N. Y. National Guard**/then 102nd Medical Battalion Armory/now

L20

L21

Capital Cities ABC, Inc. Studios), 56 W. 66th St., bet. Central Park W. and Columbus Ave. S side. 1901. **Horgan & Slattery**. Altered, 1978, **Kohn Pederson Fox Assocs**.

Lots of stylistic bravado here but only in the front ranks (as a sidelong glance from the east will reveal). The reserves are utilitarian and dull (never having been meant to be seen), in contrast with the elegantly attired architectural forces leading the march. The fun-filled façade might as well be one of those intricate European cardboard scale models. Nevertheless, a delight!

L23

[L22] **American Broadcasting Company** (television studios), 47 W. 66th St., bet. Central Park W. and Columbus Ave. N side. 1985. **Kohn Pedersen Fox Assocs**.

Stacked studios, each at a 2-story scale. The entry, a monochromatic Post Modern, has somewhat heavy-handed detail.

L24

[L23] **Capital Cities/ABC Incorporated headquarters**, 77 W. 66th St., bet. Central Park W. and Columbus Aves. N side. 1988. **Kohn Pedersen Fox Assocs**.

The corporate headquarters, at 23 stories, is mature Post Modern, but most important—especially to its shadowed neighbors to the north—is the arrogance of the midblock tower's height and bulk.

[L24] **ABC Building**, 147 Columbus Ave., NE cor. W. 66th St., 1990s. **Kohn Pedersen Fox**.

Post Modern meets Hi Tech, as the ABC 66th Street parade from 47 to 77 ends a decade at this corner.

[L25] **WABC Channel 7 Building**, 149-155 Columbus Ave., SE cor. W. 67th St. 1981. **Kohn Pedersen Fox Assocs**.

The TV studios are understated, handsome in their counterpoint of glass and brick, with few mannerisms.

L26

[L26] **Lincoln Square** (mixed-use apartments, offices and theaters), 101 and 111 W. 67th St. bet. Broadway and Columbus Aves. N side. 1997. **Kohn Pedersen Fox**, design architect. **Gary Edward Handel & Assocs.**, design coordinator. **Schuman Lichtenstein Claman & Efron**, architect of record.

The straw that broke some citizens' backs (or so they perceive). This intense use of apartments *cum* theaters suggested to them the penultimate congestion of the Lincoln Center neighborhood. But so has Riverside South (or Trump's venture on the river to the west) been so decried.

L27

[L27] **Abraham Goodman House/Merkin Concert Hall**, 129 W. 67th St., bet. Broadway and Amsterdam Ave. N side. 1978. **Ashok Bhavnani** of **Johansen & Bhavnani**.

A constructivist histrionic façade redolent of the magnificent Soviet architectural experiments of the early 1930s.

[L28] **The Copley** (apartments), 2000 Broadway, NE cor. W. 68th St. 1987. **Davis, Brody & Assocs**.

A sleek, smooth, modest, understated, rounded tower among the mess of Broadway. One of the few serene buildings on the old Boulevard. Excellent.

L28

[L29] **The Seminole**, 2020 Broadway (apartments), NE cor. W. 69th St. 1895-1896. **Ware & Styne-Harde**.

Granite for power; tan brick, limestone, and terra-cotta for texture. This ornamented ensemble is typical of tenements at the turn of the century, which received at least a taste of this lush treatment.

[L30] **Hotel Embassy**/originally The Ormonde, 154 W. 70th St, SE cor. Broadway. 1899-1900. **Robert Maynicke**. ♂

A soldier in the battle of Broadway, bringing substance and scale to the boulevard. This brick and limestone palazzo shares blockfront space with the former Hotel Seminole to the south,

L30

a pair of modest urban twins that match the understated streetscape of Park Avenue.

L31

[L31] **The Coronado**, 155 W. 70th St., NE cor. Broadway. 1990. **Schuman, Lichtenstein Claman & Efron**.

Understated vulgarity? That canopy, guarded by a pair of hovering chimeras: whimsy or excess? Above, simpler things happen.

[L32] **Christ and St. Stephen's Church** (Episcopal)/formerly St. Stephen's Church/originally Chapel (of the Church) of the Transfiguration, 120 W. 69th St., bet. Columbus Ave. and Broadway. S side. 1880. **William H. Day**. Altered, 1887+. ♂

Brigadoon? From the days when the West Side was still sub-urban, its lawn is now an oasis among Brobdingnagians.

L32

[L33] Originally **Pythian Temple**/now Pythian Condominium, 135 W. 70th St., bet. Columbus Ave. and Broadway. N side. 1927. **Thomas W. Lamb**. Renovated, 1986, **David Gura**. ♠

Assyrian sages guard the entry. Hollywood may have had its Grauman's Chinese, but New York has its Pythian Temple! Hidden on an anonymous side street, this opium-smoker's dream is best seen from across the street—or better still, from someone's upper-floor apartment to the south.

L33

[L34] **Lincoln Square Synagogue**, 200 Amsterdam Ave., NW cor. W. 69th St. 1970. **Hausman & Rosenberg**.

The theaters of nearby Lincoln Center set the travertine tone for the area, and this mannered, curvy, articulated synagogue picks up the cue. The travertine bank to the north actually came first, but the two together seem to be making an inadvertent comment about money changers at the temple.

[L35] **Public School 199**, Manhattan, 270 W. 70th St., bet. Amsterdam and West End Aves. S side. 1963. **Edward Durell Stone & Assocs**.

Notable mostly as an early example of an urban public school designed by a prominent architect. It was built in response to the contiguous 2,000-odd-unit Lincoln Towers megaslabs (urban renewal project).

L35

The back lot: *Exterior scenes in Hollywood productions are often filmed in studio back lots, expansive outdoor spaces in which mock-ups of the necessary scenery are concocted at considerable expense. For the filming of* West Side Story, *what better (and cheaper) substitute for Hollywood artifice than the real thing? The vacating of the Lincoln Square Urban Renewal Area in the late 1950s provided just such an opportunity for its tenements to have their day on film before they came crashing down.*

[L36] **Gladys and Roland Harriman Building, American Red Cross**, 150 Amsterdam Ave., bet. W. 66th and W. 67th Sts. W side. 1964. **Skidmore, Owings & Merrill**.

A Modern temple built with a firm but perhaps naive com-mitment to the "less is more" principle. Surveying traffic-choked Amsterdam Avenue, its low podium is hardly an acropolis.

L36

[L37] **Martin Luther King, Jr., High School**, 122 Amsterdam Ave., bet. W. 65th and W. 66th Sts. W side. 1975. **Frost Assocs.**, architects. **William Tarr**, sculptor.

A glass box of enormous size and scale sits proudly on the busy avenue. A self-weathering steel, Mayari R, was employed in both the school's carefully detailed curtain wall and in the bold-ly fashioned memorial sculpture to the slain civil rights leader that towers over the sidewalk.

[L38] **Fiorello H. LaGuardia High School**, 108 Amsterdam Ave., bet. W. 64th and W. 65th Sts. W side. 1985. **Eduardo Catalano**.

L37

L38

A strongly articulated, poured-in-place concrete building typical of the best of 1960s construction. The cost of achieving such quality in New York soon became prohibitive, and architects switched to mostly brick and metal assemblies. This exception resulted from the halt of all school construction during the City's financial crisis and completion of the original plans many years later.

[L39] **Amsterdam Houses Addition, N.Y.C. Housing Authority**, 240 W. 65th St., bet. Amsterdam and West End Aves. S side. 1974. **Oppenheimer, Brady & Lehrecke**.

A break with the dead public-housing hand of the past. Its designers' expressionistic use of angles and exposed concrete gives character (and triangular bay windows) to the project.

[L40] **Lincoln-Amsterdam House** (apartments), 110 West End Ave., bet. W. 64th and W. 65th Sts. E side. 1976. **David Todd & Assocs**.

Multistory housing is treated here almost as heroic, nonrepresentational sculpture in the round. The views across the Hudson understandably draw out the richest qualities in the design, the west façade.

[L41] **Former Phipps Houses** (apartments), 235, 239, 243, 247 W. 63rd St., E of West End Ave. (cul-de-sac). 1907. 236, 240, 244, 248 W. 64th St., bet. Amsterdam and West End Aves. 1911. Both by **Whitfield & King**.

Slum clearance efforts west of Lincoln Center left these as the only residential buildings remaining from the early 20th century: model tenement houses promoted by **Henry Phipps**'s pioneering housing society. The middle class has since arrived, marked by a greenhouse canopy and a spiffy façade cleaning.

[L42] **Alvin Ailey American Dance Theater Foundation**, 211 W. 61st St., bet. Amsterdam and West End Aves. N side. 1990s. **R. M. Kliment + Frances Halsband**.

Dancers have recaptured this industrial complex, ornamenting it with an elegant canopy.

L40

RIVERSIDE DRIVE/WEST END AVENUE

Terrain that slopes steeply west to the banks of the river, a roller coaster of north-south gradients, the water-level route of the smoke-belching New York Central and Hudson River Railroad, and the Palisades across the flowing Hudson River currents— such contrasts made the planning of "the Riverside Park and Avenue" a powerful challenge to landscape architect **Frederick Law Olmsted**. Between 1873 and 1910 Olmsted, and his associates and successors, developed a great green waterside edge for the West Side, as he and **Calvert Vaux** had earlier created "the Central Park" on the inland site. The style was in the tradition of English landscape architecture: naturalistic and picturesque. Development along Riverside Drive (and straight as an arrow West End Avenue behind it) resulted from the magnetism of this great urban design.

In the 1930s the Henry Hudson Parkway Authority, using WPA funds, added a four-lane highway (since expanded to six) to the park area and a host of recreational amenities—essentially the amalgam of asphalt and greenery we see today. This change accomplished two other important results: it covered the freight line, and it built the highway in part on landfill.

Riverside South

Stretching inland from the Hudson River shore between 59th and 72nd Streets and fostering the slums that gave rise to Lincoln Center's redevelopment plan was the former freight yard of the New York Central Railroad (and of the Hudson River Rail Road before that), a dead-flat expanse worthy of Chicago. The noisy, dusty scene included thousands of freight cars shunted day and night along scores of parallel ladder tracks, some leading to waterfront grain elevators, others to wharves projecting diagonally into the river—like half chevrons—accommodating ships and barges that helped interchange freight over the waters of the Port of New York. There was even a locomotive roundhouse and turntable. The fallow site, long abandoned by the railroad but traversed by the elevated West Side Highway viaduct, continues to separate the precinct from its nearby Hudson River shoreline. Since the railroad activities began to wind down in the 1950s, the 76-acre waterfront site had been the subject of a number of ill-fated redevelopment proposals [see Necrology] until purchased for $95 million in 1983 by **Donald J. Trump**, heir to the Brooklyn residential-development fortune accumulated by his father and grandfather. It is on these idle acres that young Trump proposed (Scene 1) to erect a 150-story tower—the world's tallest—again worthy of Chicago, as well as 7,600 units of housing and a major shopping development, using the skills of a Chicago architect, **Helmut Jahn**. Trump's dream of a relocated NBC media empire (and its attendant City subsidies) evaporated in 1987, as did Jahn. **Alexander Cooper & Assocs**. then took on the challenge (Scene 2), which included negotiating with a feisty Upper West Side community that just loves a good fight. Scene 3 unfolded with a truce worthy of **Netanyahu** and **Arafat**: Trump and his nemesis, the **Municipal Art Society**, joined hands (for how long we don't know), allowing the construction of new apartment blocks along what promised to be Riverside Drive South. Architect and planner **Paul Willen** suggested an ensemble in his proposed master plan that would combine the character of Central Park West with the new undulating avenue. Scene 4 is the reality of Trump Place (the surrogate street for Riverside Drive South), now serving the edge of this new construction from 70th Street southward.

R1

[R1] **Trump Place**, bet. W. 66th and W. 70th Sts., W of West End Ave. 1999. **Philip Johnson & Alan Ritchie** and **Costas Kondylis**.

Two from Brobdingnagia. This symbolic incarnation of Riverside Drive to the south of its 72nd Street ending has sprouted these awkward giants, from which views must be as spectacular as rents. A heavy hand here from the virtuoso Johnson; but after what happened at the Trump International Hotel, what could you hope for in a Philip and Donald act?

An aside just to the south at the end of Freedom Place:

[R2] **American Broadcasting Company Studios 23/24**, 320 W. 66th St., W of West End Ave. opp. Trump Place. 1984. **Kohn Pedersen Fox Assocs**.

A magnificent brick box, made largely opaque to serve the needs of media production, and then enlivened with ebullient brick ornamentation (reminiscent of the work of Modernist Dutch architects) to satisfy its urbanistic responsibilities. The full impact of this structure's bold silhouette is best achieved from the west: from the West Side elevated viaduct, from ships on the Hudson River, and from the heights of Jersey.

R3

Back north to 70th Street and around the corner on West End Avenue:

R4

[R3] **Hineni Heritage Center**/originally Forrest Lawther House/later Abraham Erlanger House, 232 West End Ave., bet. W. 70th and W. 71st Sts. E side. 1887. **E. L. Angell**. Altered for Erlanger, 1904, **Herts & Tallant**.

A robust Beaux Arts façade over an earlier structure at the behest of Broadway producer **Erlanger**.

The lack of a projecting stoop on West End Avenue's narrow sidewalk failed, in this unusual case, to cheat the residents of the ceremony of ascending its steps to wave a parting greeting. The alteration is stylistically reminiscent of the architects' Aguilar Branch Library.

R4

[R4] **West 71st Street Historic District**, W of West End Ave. 🍎

Thirty-three row houses in six groups, 1893-1896; and a single 1906 town house. Renaissance here at the edge of Trumpland? On the south, paint updates most of these columned, swagged, and arcuated brownstones, already struggling through Romanesque Revival toward the American Renaissance of the late 1890s. On the north, however, they got there: a Neo-Renaissance pot pourri: freestanding Corinthian columns, Baroque piers in light brick and terra-cotta.

RIVERSIDE SOUTH

see pages 325–332

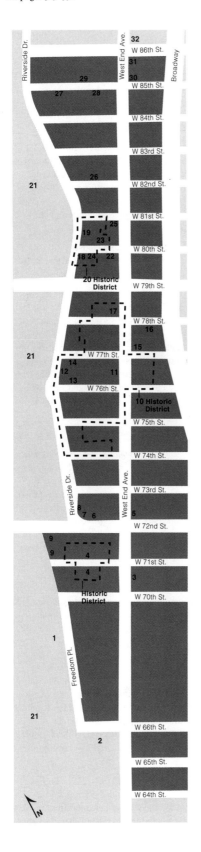

R5

[R5] Originally **Spencer Aldrich House**, 271 W. 72nd St., NE cor. West End Ave. 1897. **Gilbert A. Schellenger**. Altered.

Crass shops and signs at the street level serve only to point up the richness of what remains: the complex gabled and towered forms of the upper floors and roof. Much more interesting than Schellenger's work at No. 309.

[R6] **309 West 72nd Street**/also known as the William E. Diller House, bet. West End Ave. and Riverside Dr. N side. 1899-1901. **Gilbert A. Schellenger**. 🏠

A timid step from the Brown Decades (of Romanesque Revival, brownstone, and dark brick) into the light palette and limestone of the American Renaissance.

R7b

[R7a] Originally **John and Mary Sutphen, Jr. House**, 311 West 72nd St., bet. West End Ave. and Riverside Dr. N side. 1901-1902. **C. P. H. Gilbert**. 🏠   [R7b] Originally **Frederick and Lydia Prentiss House**, 1 Riverside Dr., NE cor. W. 72nd St. 1899-1901. **C. P. H. Gilbert**. 🏠

These come from an architect more comfortable with Renaissance copybooks.

[R8] **Philip and Maria Kleeberg House**, 3 Riverside Dr. bet. 72nd and 73rd Sts. 1896-1898. **C. P. H. Gilbert**. 🏠
A freely interpreted Dutch Renaissance town house.

[R9] **The Chatsworth** (apartments), 344 W. 72nd St., SE cor. Henry Hudson Pkwy. and 353 W. 71st St., W end of W. 71st St. 1902-1904. 🏠 **Annex**, 340 W. 72nd St. S side. 1905-1906. Both by **John E. Scharsmith**. 🏠

R9

Two of the three buildings that compose The Chatsworth face West 72nd and West 71st Streets, gracious russet-colored brick apartment blocks embellished with lavish limestone trim in the tradition of the Kenilworth and Rossleigh Court/Orwell House. The annex to the east on West 72nd is lower and all limestone.

Schwab House: A rare Gallic composition of pinnacles, spires, chimneys, and steeply sloping roofs once embellished the Drive's skyline between West 73rd and West 74th Streets. Consciously seeking to bring the joys of the French château to the banks of the Hudson, architect **Maurice Hebert** *adapted the façades of three—Blois, Chenonceaux, and Azay-le-Rideau—to the needs of* **Charles M. Schwab**, **Andrew Carnegie**'s *associate. The enormous Schwab House was not only freestanding, but it occupied, with its surrounding gardens, an entire city block (it had formerly been the New York Orphan Asylum). Schwab could afford it since he was reputed to earn, in the days before income taxes, an annual salary of $1 million. Unfortunately the mansion was not to survive New York's post-World War II building boom. Completed in 1906, it was demolished in 1948 and replaced by another Schwab House, this time a 16-story red brick human hive of a type more familiar to New Yorkers.*

R10

[R10] **West End-Collegiate Historic District** generally bet. Riverside Dr. and West End Ave., N side of W. 75th to N side of W. 78th Sts., with irregular ins and outs. 🏠

A full palette of materials and styles, bow and bay windows, copper-clad cornices and dormers—rich and wonderful. Architects include **Clinton & Russell**, **C. P. H. Gilbert**, **Lamb & Rich**, **Neville & Bagge**, and the endless and marvelous houses of **Clarence F. True**.

R11

[R11] **Row houses**, 301-305 W. 76th St., 341-357 West End Ave., W side, and 302-306 W. 77th St. 1891. **Lamb & Rich**. 🏠

A varied and witty row enlivens a whole blockfront of West End Avenue. Long may they reign! **Eberhard Faber**, the pencil king, lived at No. 341. This is what eclecticism is all about:

a studied assembly of architectural parts (from varied geography and history) and an equally conscious arrangement of contrasting buildings.

R11

Clarence F. True

*Lower Riverside Drive, as the earliest area opened to improvement, was slated to be filled with flats, according to an 1899 account by a local architect and land developer, **Clarence F. True**. It was he, he stated, who recognized the higher potential of the area by buying up all available Driveside parcels below West 84th Street and covering them "with beautiful dwellings" of his own design. Hardly typical row houses (though built speculatively and employing party walls), many of these elegant mansion-residences have survived. They are highly idiosyncratic and readily identified as being in the True style (characterized at the time as Elizabethan Renaissance): ornate roof lines, crow-stepped gables, bay, bow, and three-quarter-round oriels, and so on. Most are concentrated in these groupings:*

R12

[R12] **40-46 Riverside Drive**, bet. 76th and 77th Sts. E side. 1896-1899. **Clarence True.** ○

An eclectic ensemble that blends strong Renaissance Revival cornices with Amsterdam stepped gables.

[R13] **337 West 76th St**. and [R14] **334-338 West 77th St.**, bet. West End Ave. and Riverside Dr. 1896-1897. **Clarence True.** ○

Tan brick, bow fronts, and Baroque broken pedimented dormers.

[R15] **West End Collegiate Church and School**, West End Ave., NE cor. W. 77th St. 1891-1893. **Robert W. Gibson**. Reconstruction after sanctuary fire, 1980s. **The Hall Partnership**. Basement education center, 1990. **Peter W. Charapko.** ●

It's easy to understand the generous use of Dutch stepped gables on this church's façade, since the roots of the Reformed Church in America lie in the Netherlands. But don't draw hasty conclusions about the reintroduction of a style missing since the days of New Amsterdam. Here, along West End Avenue, McKim, Mead & White had already built such a Dutch-inspired house as early as 1885 (demolished); another one predating the church (not by M, M & W) still remains at the northwest corner of West 78th Street. And so do Clarence True's 45 and 46 Riverside Drive.

The church is in a rich palette of orange brick and terracotta, crowned with a red tile roof.

R15

R17

[R16] **The Collegiate School (annex)**, 260 W. 78th St., bet. Broadway and West End Ave. 1968. S side. **Ballard, Todd & Assocs.**

A highly disciplined façade that, because it faces north, rarely receives the sunlight necessary to show it off to best advantage.

[R17] **Row houses**, 301-307 W. 78th St. and 383-389 West End Ave. 1886. **Fredrick B. White.** ○

Powerful statements by an architect who died shortly after their completion at the untimely age of 24. The brickwork (and supporting terra-cotta) is both powerful and elegant.

R18

[R18] **74-77 Riverside Drive**, SE cor. W. 80th St., and 320-326 W. 80th St., between West End Ave. and Riverside Dr. 1898-1899. **Clarence F. True.** ○

The Dutch gable of No. 74 throws a Baroque swoop skyward.

[R19a] **81-89 Riverside Drive**, bet. 80th and 81st Sts., 307-323 W. 80th St., and 316-320 W. 81st St., bet. West End Ave. and Riverside Dr. ○

No. 89 is a dour and forbidding essay in rock-face granite.

R19

[R19b] **103-109 Riverside Drive**, 332 W. 83rd St. 1898-1899. **Clarence F. True.** 103 and 104, redesigned, 1910-1911. **Clinton & Russell.** ● 105 and 107-109, redesigned 1910-1911. **Bosworth & Holden.** ●

After a lawsuit, stoops and bow windows were removed that had encroached into the public way. No. 109 crosses a crenellated eclectic body with a Gothic Revival entry.

[R20] **Riverside Drive-West 80th Street Historic District**, Riverside Dr. to a line north-south midblock bet. Riverside Dr. and West End Ave., including the S side of W. 81st St. and both sides of W. 80th St. ●

A group of 32 row houses built between 1892 and 1899 by architects **Charles H. Israel** (308-314 W. 81st St. and 307-317 W. 80th St.) and **Clarence F. True** (319-323 W. 80th St. and 316-320 W. 81st St.). The Israel houses are crowned with surprising shades of purple/blue/red tile.

R19b

[R21] **Riverside Park and Riverside Drive Scenic Landmark**, Riverside Dr. to the Hudson River bet. W. 72nd and W. 153rd Sts. 1873-1910. Original design, **Frederick Law Olmsted.** New work, 1888. **Calvert Vaux** and **Samuel Parsons, Jr.** Completion, **Frederick Law Olmsted, Jr.** Reconstruction for Henry Hudson Parkway, 1937. **Clinton F. Loyd.** ●

To the endless relief of stifled West Siders, this green ribbon of hills and hollows, monuments, playgrounds, and sports facilities fringes some 70 blocks of winding Riverside Drive, all the while covering the abandoned rail line in a tunnel below. One of its most complex parts is the three-level structure at West 79th Street: traffic circle at the top masonry arcade and pedestrian paths surrounding a splendid, circular, single-jet fountain at the middle level; and, at the bottom, parking space for frequenters of the 79th Street Boat Basin.

R20

[R22] **411 West End Avenue** (apartments), SW cor. W. 80th St. 1936. **George F. Pelham II.**

Art Deco with touches of Corbusier-inspired ships' railings on the balconies and terraces near the top. Note how "drapes" of ornament cascade from some of the parapets (in stainless steel) and over the entrance (in cut stone).

R22

[R23] **307-317 West 80th Street** (row houses), bet. West End Ave. and Riverside Dr. N side. 1894. **Charles H. Israels.** ○

Gothickesque—neither the Gothic Revival of earlier years nor the Collegiate Gothic of the 1920s—and picturesque too. Note the stained glass over the doors and windows (except for No. 317, which has also been painted). These houses are in handsome company on both sides of the street.

R27

R26

R29

[R24] **328 West 80th Street** (row house), bet. West End Ave. and Riverside Dr. S side. 1899. **Clarence F. True.** ♂
Hyper-Georgian: some grander Renaissance detail has framed the entranceway.

[R25] **The Calhoun School Learning Center**, 433 West End Ave., SW cor. W. 81st St. 1975. **Costas Machlouzarides**.
A modern-day Cyclops must have been here and left behind his giant-sized TV. And if one picture tube (along West End Avenue) isn't enough, another (along West 81st Street) has been provided as a spare. A more unsubtle and out-of-scale response to this urban design challenge is hard to imagine. Fortunately (in the warm weather months at least), maples provide a green screen.

[R26] **309-315 and 317-325 West 82nd Street** (row houses), bet. West End Ave. and Riverside Dr. ca. 1892.
Two groups of Roman brick plus brownstone-trimmed residences, the first rich in intricately formed roofs, dormers, chimney pots, finials, and colonnettes; the second more restrained with handsome verdigris-copper cornices.

[R27] **The Red House** (apartments), 350 W. 85th St., bet. West End Ave. and Riverside Dr. S Side. 1903-1904. **Harde & Short**. ●
A romantic 6-story masterpiece, its multipaned glassiness reminiscent of the work of the English country-house architect, **Robert Smythson** in the 1590s (Wollaton Hall/Hardwick Hall)! Note the dragon and crown cartouche set up high into the brickwork. These talented architects also designed the Studio Building and the Alwyn Court Apartments.

[R28] **316-326 West 85th Street** (row houses), bet. West End Ave. and Riverside Dr. S side. 1892. **Clarence F. True**. ●
Six row houses designed as a unit. The stoop railings are only one voluptuous example of the fine stone carving everywhere abundant at the end of the nineteenth century.

[R29] **329-337 West 85th Street** (row houses), bet. West End Ave. and Riverside Dr. N side. 1890-1891. **Ralph Townsend**. ●
A face-off between Townsend on the north and True on the south. Townsend's more picturesque, True's more stolid.

[R30] **John B. and Isabella Leech House**, 520 West End Avenue/now apartments, NE cor. W. 85th St. 1892. **Clarence F. True**. ●

R32

A rock-faced brownstone and brick many-gabled former town house. A daring developer proposed to hover an apartment structure on legs above it all (1987, **William Gleckman**); the bizarre thought elicited thunderous opposition from the neighborhood.

[R31] **530 West End Avenue** (apartments), SE cor. W. 86th St. 1912. **Mulliken & Moeller.**

A representative West End Avenue example of the Renaissance palazzo adapted to high-rise living. The masonry and terra-cotta craftsmanship are in the tradition of an earlier era.

[R32] **Church of St. Paul and St. Andrew** (United Methodist)/ originally Church of St. Paul (Methodist Episcopal), 540 West End Ave., NE cor. W. 86th St. 1895-1897. **R. H. Robertson.** ●ʼ

A startling work. While other architects (including Robertson) were pursuing more or less faithful revival-styles, this is in the imaginative vein of the French neo-Classicist architects **Claude-Nicolas Ledoux** or **Etienne-Louis Boullée.** The octagonal corner tower is reminiscent of the fire tower that was once part of the Jefferson Market.

[R33] **St. Ignatius Church** (Episcopal), 552 West End Ave., SE cor. W. 87th St. 1902. **Charles C. Haight.** Shrine (inside), 1926. **Cram & Ferguson.**

One of Haight's less inspired works. Perhaps he decided that this site, adjacent to its already completed West 86th Street neighbor, demanded a piece of background architecture. Inside it's much better: a bit of London. Fortunately, these churches and remaining row houses combine to keep West End Avenue from being an apartment-house canyon.

R34

[R34] **Cathedral Preparatory Seminary** (Roman Catholic)/formerly McCaddin-McQuick Memorial, Cathedral College/originally St. Agatha's School, 555 West End Ave., SW cor. W. 87th St. 1908. **Boring & Tilton.**

Dignity personified in Collegiate Gothic red brick and limestone by the architects of Ellis Island and the Brooklyn Heights (Tennis) Casino.

[R35] **Riverside–West End Historic District**, between Riverside Drive, a north-south line midway between Broadway and West End Avenue, 87th and 94th Streets, with peninsulas north to 95th and south to 85th along Riverside Drive. ●ʼ

Clarence F. True was here, along with **Thom & Wilson, C. P. H. Gilbert,** and **Ralph Townsend.** Eclectic row houses by

RIVERSIDE NORTH

see pages 332–338

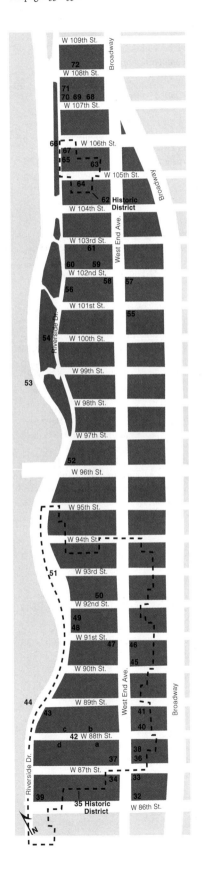

these and others abound on 88th and 89th Streets, with True dominating the blocks to the north (90th, 91st, and 92nd) between West End Avenue and Riverside Drive.

[R36] **560 West End Avenue** (town house), NE cor. W. 87th St. 1890. **Joseph H. Taft.** ♂

This house, among the many West Side projects of **W. E. D. Stokes**, once had nine similar neighbors to the north. He was developer of the Ansonia Hotel.

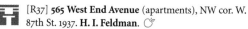 [R37] **565 West End Avenue** (apartments), NW cor. W. 87th St. 1937. **H. I. Feldman.** ♂

"The vocabulary of the neo-Renaissance expressed in Art Deco terms: brick replaces stone, corner windows substitute for quoins, dark banded brick around the base is the translation of the shadows which a rusticated plinth would have cast. And as for the pediment at the entrance, its 1930's stand-in is a small, streamlined, stainless steel cornice." – an anonymous architectural historian.

R38

[R38] **562 West End Avenue** (apartments), bet. W. 87th and W. 88th Sts. E side. 1913. **Walter Haefeli.** ♂

Well-groomed Doric columns guard this entry to middle-class apartment life. A gargantuan version of the flanking Ionic and Doric columns that marked the entries of Federal and Greek Revival houses; revived yet again, but in megastyle.

R39

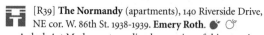 [R39] **The Normandy** (apartments), 140 Riverside Drive, NE cor. W. 86th St. 1938-1939. **Emery Roth.** ● ♂

A sleek Art Moderne streamlined cornering of this prominent 86th Street intersection. Its sensuous curves and prominent horizontal fluting at the base are notable. For earlier and more eclectic Roth, see the Beresford and the San Remo on Central Park West.

R40

[R40] **Congregation B'nai Jeshurun**, 257 W. 88th St., bet. Broadway and West End Ave. N side. 1918. **Henry B. Herts** and **Walter Schneider.** ♂ [R41] **Community Center**, 270 W. 89th St. 1928. **Henry B. Herts. Louis Allan Abramson**, associate. Restorations, 1990s. **Giorgio Cavaglieri.** ♂

The synagogue's façade is a fantasy from the waning days of an era when important Jewish houses of worship were designed in an exotic Byzantine/Romanesque mode. The community center one block north is merely a decorated multistory steel-framed box.

R42b

West 88th Street, between West End Avenue and Riverside Drive:

[R42a] **302-338 West 88th Street** (row houses), bet. West End Ave. and Riverside Dr. S side. Early 1890s. ♂

Stepped gables and Roman brick add eclectic touches to this row.

[R42b] **315-323 West 88th St.** 1896. **Theodore E. Thomson.** ♂
Bowfronted brown and white stones.

[R42c] **325-327 West 88th St.** 1894. **Thom & Wilson.** ♂
Bowfronted Roman brick.

[R42d] **329-341 West 88th St.** 1894. **Thom & Wilson.** ♂
Roman brick and colonnettes.

[R42e] **332-344 West 88th Street.** 1893-1894. **Thom & Wilson.** ♂
More Roman brick, patterned friezes, and some colonnaded bay windows.

R42d

[R43] **Yeshiva Ketana School**/originally Isaac L. Rice House "Villa Julia"/then Solomon Schinasi House, 346 W. 89th St., SE cor. Riverside Drive. 1901-1903. **Herts & Tallant.** Additions and alterations, 1908+. **C. P. H. Gilbert.** ● ♂

R43   R44

Though the Drive was once lined with freestanding mansions, only this maroon brick villa and one other survive. **Isaac L. Rice**, a successful industrial pioneer in the field of electric storage batteries, commissioned this residence and named it Villa Julia for his wife, the prescient founder of the Society for the Suppression of Unnecessary Noise. In 1907 the building was sold to **Solomon Schinasi**, a member of the well-known cigarette manufacturing firm of Schinasi Brothers. That same year, Schinasi's brother, Morris, was awaiting completion of his freestanding mansion on the Drive at West 107th Street. Curiously it is these two Schinasi mansions that survive.

[R44] **Soldiers' and Sailors' Monument**, in Riverside Park, Riverside Dr. at W. 89th St. 1897-1902. **Stoughton & Stoughton, Paul E. M. Duboy.** 🍎
    A marble monument to the Civil War dead modeled on the choragic monument of Lysicrates (335 B.C.) in Athens (a favorite question on history of architecture quizzes). Duboy was the architect of that other West Side monument, the Ansonia Hotel.

R45

[R45] **620 West End Avenue** (town house), NE cor. W. 90th St. 1899-1901. **Hugh Lamb.** ○⟋
    An eclectic amalgam of Georgian and Renaissance parts in a willful Edwardian manner. Nice brick banding at the fourth floor.

[R46] **272 West 91st Street** (townhouse), bet. West End Ave. and Broadway. S side. 1899-1901. **Hugh Lamb.** ○⟋
    Salmon brick, a Palladian window, and a quartet of Composite columns.

R47

[R47] **Greek Orthodox Cathedral Church of the Annunciation**/originally Fourth Presbyterian Church. 635 West End Ave., SW cor. W. 91st. St. 1893-1894. **Heins & La Farge.** ○⟋
    A very Anglo-American Gothic Revival church now transformed for services of a different flock. It brings a happy punctuation to the Avenue.

[R48] **190 Riverside Drive** (apartment house), NE cor. W. 91st St. 1909-1910. **Townsend, Steinle & Haskell.** ○⟋
    The rusticated limestone base and quoins frame tan brick and bay windows. At the top a grand copper cornice crowns this well-preserved relic.

R48

[R49] **194 Riverside Drive** (apartment house), bet. W. 91st and W. 92nd Sts. 1902. **Ralph S. Townsend.** ○⟋
    The deeply slotted entry creates twin forms: each with rusticated limestone and brick, square volumes intersecting cylinders.

[R50] **Montessori School**, 309 W. 92nd St., Bet. West End Ave. and Riverside Dr. N side. 1905. **Charles A. Rich.** ○⟋
    A late Georgian mansion with exaggerated lintels and early Victorian dormers.

[R51] **Joan of Arc Statue**, in Joan of Arc Park, Riverside Dr. at W. 93rd St. 1915. **Anna Vaughn Hyatt Huntington**, sculptor. **John V. Van Pelt**, architect. ○⟋

R49

R51

The **Maid of Orleans** in full armor stands in her marching steed's stirrups, looking heavenward with sword held high. The bronze equestrian sculpture sits atop a granite pedestal containing stones from Rheims Cathedral and from the old tower at Rouen in which Joan was imprisoned and tried. The 1.6-acre space straddled by the Drive is officially Joan of Arc Park.

[R52] **Cliff Dwellers' Apartments**, 243 Riverside Dr., NE cor. W. 96th St. 1914. **Herman Lee Meader**.

An odd building predating the Art Deco interest in Mayan motifs. It is known primarily for the naturalistic frieze of mountain lions, rattlesnakes, and buffalo skulls. They symbolize the life of the Arizona cliff dwellers and serve to tie these prehistoric people to Manhattan's modern cliff dwellers. All in all, an underrated façade.

R52

*Woodman, Spare That Tree: In 1837 an old elm on the property of the Stryker's Bay Mansion—which then stood on a hill northeast of the 96th Street viaduct—was to be cut down. **George Pope Morris**, journalist and poet (1802-1864), was inspired to pen the poetic exhortation which saved the tree.*

[R53] **Carrère Memorial**, Riverside Park at W. 99th St. 1916. **Thomas Hastings**.

A small granite-balustered terrace at a lower level of the park entrance contains a graffitied, barely noticeable memorial tablet to one of New York's great architects: **John Merven Carrère** (of **Carrère & Hastings**), killed in an automobile accident in 1911.

[R54] **Firemen's Memorial**, Riverside Dr. at W. 100th St. 1913. **Attilio Piccirilli**, sculptor. **H.Van Buren Magonigle**, architect.

Courage and Duty guard this large pink marble monument to SOLDIERS IN A WAR THAT NEVER ENDS. Embedded in the plaza is a bronze tablet to the firehorses who also served in that "war."

R56

[R55] **838 West End Avenue** (apartments), SE cor. W. 101st St. 1914. **George & Edward Blum**.

Intricate vinelike forms make large terra-cotta tiles into damask, thus embellishing this building and recalling a Sullivanesque approach to ornament.

[R56] **William and Clara Baumgarten House**, 294 Riverside Drive., bet. W. 101st and W. 102nd Sts. 1900-1901. **Schickel & Ditmars**. 🍎

Beaux Arts limestone mansion with a remarkable Art Nouveau window guard at the first floor. Baumgarten managed Herter Brothers, prominent interior architects of the time.

R57

[R57] **854, 856 & 858 West End Avenue**, and 254 West 102st Street House, 1892-1893. **Schneider & Herter**. 🍎

How to corner a West End Avenue complex in brownstone Queen Anne; with a guarding lion at 254.

[R58] **Ralph Samuel Townsend House**, 302 W. 102nd St., bet. West End Ave. and Riverside Dr. 1884. S side. **Ralph S. Townsend**.

Moved from the Avenue, this was originally Townsend's own home.

[R59] **303-309 West 103rd Street** (row houses), bet. West End Ave. and Riverside Dr. N side. 1895-1896. **George F. Pelham**.

Five well-groomed brownstones with syncopated bay windows.

R58

*The Gershwins and the Bogarts ; 103rd Street, 1905-1931. The Gershwins lived at No. 316 (1899. **Henri Fouchaux**) from 1925 to 1931; **Morris and Rose Gershwin** and their grown children **Ira, George, Arthur** and **Francis**. The Bogarts were at 245.*

Bogie was raised here from age 6 (1905) onward, under the eye of his surgeon father, Belmont Deforest Bogart. A histrionic change from here to Casablanca. Then again his name was Humphrey Deforest Bogart. Neither building is interesting.

R60

[R60] **Master Apartments**/formerly Master Institute of United Arts and Riverside Museum/formerly Roerich Museum, 310-312 Riverside Dr., NE cor. W. 103rd St. 1928-1929. **Harvey Wiley Corbett** of **Helmle, Corbett & Harrison** and **Sugarman & Berger**. 🍎

Built to house a school, museum, auditorium, and restaurant in a residential hotel. Artist **Nicholas Roerich**, whose museum was once located within the building, seems to have been responsible for the idea of shading the building's brickwork from a purpled base to a pale yellow top. A major Art Deco monument in brick and terra-cotta.

[R61] **312-322 West 104th Street** (row houses) bet. West End Ave. and Riverside Dr. S side. 1890s.

Six mates in brick and brownstone, many gabled against the sky; terra-cotta parapets enrich them all.

R61

[R62] **Riverside-West 105th Street Historic District**, generally along Riverside Dr. bet. W. 105th and W. 106th Sts., plus some of both sides of W. 105th St. bet. West End Ave. and Riverside Dr. 🍎

Enjoying a magnificent setting overlooking the city's great river is this enclave of English Edwardian and French Beaux Arts town houses. Executed between 1899 and 1902, they were designed by **Janes & Leo, Mowbray & Uffinger, Hoppin & Koen**, and **Robert D. Kohn**. *Of special interest are:*

R64

[R63] **301-307 West 105th Street** (row houses), bet. West End Ave. and Riverside Dr. N side. 1899-1900. **Janes & Leo**. ♂

Four houses make a brick and limestone English terrace: souped-up Georgian by some Edwardian enthusiasts.

[R64] **302-320 West 105th Street** (row houses), bet. West End Ave. and Riverside Dr. S side. 1899-1900. **Janes & Leo**. ♂

Ten houses form a Francophile terrace (it would be a *villa* or *square* in Paris). Ornate bow windows.

[R65] **New York Buddhist Church and American Buddhist Academy**, 331-332 Riverside Dr., bet. W. 105th and W. 106th Sts. No. 331, formerly Marion Davies House, 1902. **Janes & Leo**. No. 332, 1963. **Kelly & Gruzen**. ♂

R65

The heroic-size bronze statue of Shinran-Shonin (1173-1262), founder of a Buddhist sect, became a local landmark before the City designated it an official one. A church and social center occupy the two buildings.

[R66] **Statue of Franz Sigel**, Riverside Dr. at W. 106th St. 1907. **Karl Bitter**, sculptor. **W. Welles Bosworth**, architect of base.

A placid equestrian statue of a commander of the Union Army during the Civil War. In the iconography of equestrian sculpture the steed's four legs' touching terra firma means the hero died a peaceful death: in the case of Sigel (1824-1902), he resigned his military commission in 1865 and then published and edited a German-language newspaper.

R67

[R67] **River Mansion**, 337 Riverside Dr. SE cor. W. 106th St., 1900-1902. **Stewart & Smith**. ♂

A Beaux Arts brick and limestone house anchoring the corner and enjoying both river and Drive.

[R68] **305-319 West 107th Street** (row houses), bet. Broadway and Riverside Dr. N side. 1900s.

Seven beer-bellied bays in light brick and limestone protrude into the streetscape.

R68

R69

[R69] **Nicholas Roerich Museum**, 319 W. 107th St., bet. Riverside Dr. and Broadway. N side. 1898. **Clarence F. True**. 212-864-7752. Tu-Su, 2-5; closed Mo.

Permanent collection of the work of **Nicholas Roerich**, prolific artist, designer, explorer, philosopher, and collaborator of **Stravinsky** and **Diaghilev**. Architectural landmarks of his native Russia were the subjects of many of Roerich's early paintings, and he contributed to the design of 310 Riverside Drive.

[R70] **The Children's Mansion** (school)/originally Morris and Laurette Schinasi House, 351 Riverside Dr., NE cor. W. 107th St. 1907-1909. **William B. Tuthill**. 🍎

A marble freestanding château by the architect of Carnegie Hall. A Schinasi also owned the other remaining freestanding mansion on the Drive. There were once dozens of others.

[R71] **352 Riverside Drive** (town house), bet. W. 107th and W. 108th Sts. 1900s.

A grand entry portal bears a balcony for savoring Olmsted's park.

[R72] **Assumptionist Provincial House**/formerly America Press Building, 329 W. 108th St., bet. Broadway and Riverside Dr. N side. ca. 1900. **Thomas Graham**. Altered, 1902, **Horgan & Slattery**.

Two double-width row houses were joined to form an internally interlocked residence for a Roman Catholic order. Spiffy from bottom to top: ornate limestone carving, a fine cool-red brick, and verdigris copper detail. The dormers of the mansard roof have been replaced by an incongruous hat.

R70

BROADWAY AND ENVIRONS

B1

From 70th Street to Cathedral Parkway (110th Street)

Broadway's route in this area dates from 1703: the plotting of the Bloomingdale Road. Initially only 33 feet wide, the road increased in width in concert with its growing popularity. By 1871 it was 150 feet wide, its course straightened between 59th and 155th Streets, its name then The Boulevard. In 1899 it was renamed Broadway, the northern extension of the route from Bowling Green.

[B1] **The Dorilton** (apartments), 171 W. 71st St., NE cor. Broadway. 1900-1902. **Janes & Leo.** 🍎 ♂

If you are walking uptown along Broadway this robust mansarded Beaux Arts masterpiece will begin to prepare you for the even greater Ansonia two blocks north: here a cornice-copia. Look up at the frolicking freestanding amazons.

[B2] **Blessed Sacrament Church** (Roman Catholic), 150 W. 71st St., bet. Columbus Ave. and Broadway. S side. 1916-1917. **Gustave Steinback.** ♂

The façades of sanctuary and rectory are brilliantly modeled to exploit this difficult and jam-packed midblock site. Though the stonework is not heavily tooled, the vigorous interplay of volume, void, and silhouette is just enough for the shallow viewing space of a typically narrow 60-foot-wide side street. The rose window is in striking reds and blues. See Steinback's other churches.

B2

[B3] Originally **Christ Church Rectory**, 213 W. 71st. St., bet. Broadway and West End Ave. N side.

A dour tan brick, brownstone and terra-cotta remembrance of the church that used to be next door.

B3

[B4] **West End Day School**/originally The Godmothers League, 255 W. 71st St., bet. Amsterdam and West End Aves. N side. 1950. **Sylvan Bien.**

Architects had come to realize that the International Style was victor in the post-World War II battle of styles, but for some it was difficult to adjust to that new vision. This modest work reflects the struggle. A pleasant syncopation of the block.

[B5] **274, 276 West 71st Street** (row houses), bet. Amsterdam and West End Aves. S side. ca. 1890.

Shades of Philadelphia architect Frank Furness are visible in these Queen Anne mavericks.

B4

BROADWAY & ENVIRONS (SOUTH)

see pages 339–353

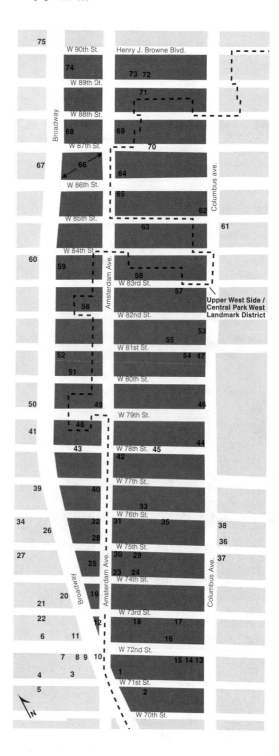

[B6] **247-249 West 72nd Street** (row houses), bet. Broadway and West End Ave. N side. 1890s.

Excellent eclecticisms: Romanesque Revival arches and gables, balustraded bow windows; all in brownstone, terra-cotta and brick.

[B7] **216-218 West 72nd Street** (row houses), bet. Broadway and West End Ave. S side. 1890s.

Cousins of 247-249 across the street, unfortunately painted. As usual the bottom tail of commerce is wagging the top dog.

B6

[B8] **206 West 72nd Street** (row house), bet. Broadway and West End Ave. S side. 1893.

The top floor gallery/conservatory serves as a grand eyrie overlooking Verdi Park and environs. A typical slice of history ravaged by the two floors of commerce below. Keep looking up.

[B9] Originally **Colonial Club**, SW cor. W. 72nd St. and Broadway. 1892. **Henry Kilburn**.

*Let them eat cake: Named for the family who settled it, the hamlet of Harsenville was one of several strung along what is now upper Broadway. Its rustic charm attracted a number of French émigrés fleeing their revolution's Reign of Terror. The statesman **Charles Maurice de Talleyrand-Perigord** sought refuge here in 1795 while heads rolled at home, and the **duc d'Orleans**—later to become **King Louis Philippe**—came here two years later. While on an extended visit, he toured much of the newborn republic from Maine to Louisiana, supplementing his meager financial resources by teaching French at the Somerindijk farmhouse, located at what is now the northwest corner of Broadway and West 75th Street. Does his ghost hover nearby, savoring the croissants, brioches, and other patisseries françaises once purveyed by Beaudesir, the site's previous occupant? Allons, enfants. . .*

[B10] **72nd Street IRT subway entrance**, Broadway and Amsterdam Ave. S of W. 72nd St. 1904. **Heins & La Farge**. 👆 Reconstruction and extension of the station, 1999-2004. **Gruzen Samton** and **Richard Dattner & Assocs**.

Cartoonist and wit **James Stevenson** termed this a "Peruvian Cathedral." See his drawings!

The traffic in and out is horrendous. Development rights for Riverside South include financing for a total reconstruction of this station complex. Included is the greening of Broadway to the north, an extended Verdi Square that caps the new subway facilities.

B10

[B11] **The Alexandria** (apartments), 201 W. 72nd St., NW cor. Broadway. 1990. **Frank Williams & Assocs**. and **Skidmore, Owings & Merrill**.

Ramses II's mummy may return to blow up this insult to ancient Egypt. It took two distinguished firms to consummate this travesty.

[B12] **Verdi Square**, Broadway, Amsterdam Ave., and W. 73rd St. 1906. *Giuseppe Verdi*, **Pasquale Civiletti**, sculptor. Scenic landmark. 👆

This small green honors the great Italian composer. At the base are life-size figures of characters from *Aida*, *Falstaff*, *Otello*, and *La Forza del Destino*. A new park will extend to the west, embracing the former northbound lanes of Broadway, and crowning the new subway station by **Gruzen Samton** and **Richard Dattner**.

B11

Gray's papaya: a local landmark long famous for its 50 cent hot dogs. Here the mustard is Dijon (Gulden's out of gallon containers). Wash it down with a glass of papaya juice, piña colada, or fresh squeezed oranges. It's all good and based on quality served in great volume.

B12

B13

B14

[B13] Originally **Park & Tilford Building** (offices), 100 W. 72nd St., SW cor. Columbus Ave. 1892-1893. **McKim, Mead & White**. ♂

An MM&W rusticated limestone and brick background building not very noticeable but a nice neighbor. The retrofitted windows are a disaster. Next door, to the west, is a humdinger:

[B14] Originally **Hotel Hargrave**, 110 W. 72nd St., bet. Columbus Ave. and Broadway. S side. 1901-1902/1905-1907. **Frederick C. Browne**. ♂

Belle Epoque bay windows give a rich modulation to this rusticated limestone and brick façade. Atop it all is a double-dormered mansard roof. All of it is redolent of Paris, except its inflated height. In Paris mansards and all would never total more than 8 floors. Here there are 12.

[B15] Originally **The Earlton** (studios), 118 W. 72nd St., bet. Columbus and Amsterdam Aves. S side. 1914-1915. **Buchman & Fox**. ♂

One of several white glazed terra-cotta studio buildings, tall and on narrow lots (the space of one former town house); these were developed by builder **Edward West Browning**, whose initials are entwined in the façade above the second floor.

Mr. Browning is remembered more for his social life than his contribution to architecture. A wealthy real estate man, he advertised in the *Herald Tribune* in 1925 to adopt a "pretty, refined fourteen-year-old." His subsequent trials and tribulations with the winner, 15-year-old **Frances ("Peaches") Heenan**, made headlines for months.

[B16] **139 West 72nd Street** (row houses), bet. Columbus and Amsterdam Aves. 1885-1887. **Thom & Wilson**. ♂

A grand pair of Gothic Revival town houses, well preserved above the commercial floors at the bottom.

B16

[B17] **126 West 73rd Street** (studios), bet. Columbus and Amsterdam Aves. 1914-1915. **Buchman & Fox**. ♂

Déjà vu? No, this is another of those slender white West Side ghosts.

[B18] **Sherman Square Studios**, 160 W. 73rd St., bet. Columbus and Amsterdam Aves. S side. 1928-1929. **Tillion & Tillion**. ♂

Apartments specially soundproofed for professional musicians, long before Lincoln Center became a neighbor. Though weathered by time, the architects' names can be found on the

B17

cornerstone to the west. Deco-Gothic brick and sandstone. The original steel casement windows have been replaced by gross aluminum double-hung units.

[B19] **Apple Bank for Savings**/originally Central Savings Bank, 2100 Broadway, NE cor. 73rd St. 1926-1928. **York & Sawyer**, architects. Decorative ironwork, **Samuel Yellin Studio.** 🍎 Interior. 🍎

The German Savings Bank in the City of New York, founded in 1859, changed its name during World War I. Board members chose the architects of the Federal Reserve Bank to create this new West Side office, a miniature Federal Reserve, and one of the area's noblest and most imposing edifices.

B19

[B20] **Ansonia Hotel**, 2109 Broadway, bet. W. 73rd and W. 74th Sts. W side. 1899-1904. **Paul E. M. Duboy.** 🍎

In the words of the Landmarks Preservation Commission, the Ansonia's effect is one of "joyous exuberance profiled against the sky." The collaboration between a demanding developer, **W. E. D. Stokes**—he was descended from **Phelps Dodge** on his paternal side and Ansonia Brass & Copper on his maternal—and an architect steeped in the forms of Parisian apartment buildings, **Paul E. M. Duboy**, seems to have had a magic result. The Ansonia is one of New York's architectural gems. Judging from the "guest list" of this apartment hotel, a galaxy of important figures thought so too: **Arturo Toscanini**, **Lily Pons**, **Florenz Ziegfeld**, **Theodore Dreiser**, **Sol Hurok**, and **Igor Stravinsky**, to name but a few.

B20

[B21] Originally **The Level Club** (of the Masonic order)/then Hotel Riverside Plaza/now condominium apartments, 253 W. 73rd St., bet. Broadway and West End Ave. N side. 1926. **Clinton & Russell.**

This neo-Romanesque/Art Deco façade retains the secret signs and symbols required by the original client, a Masonic organization.

B21

[B22] **248-272 West 73rd Street** (row houses), bet. Broadway and West End Ave. S side. 1890s.

The crowning copper-sheathed dormer and finial seems present to combat the secret signs across the street.

[B23] **161-169 West 74th Street** and 301-309 Amsterdam Avenue, NE cor. W. 74th St. 1886. **Lamb & Rich.** ♂

Early West Side row housing which, happily restored at the corner, conveys a clear sense of the area's initial development. No. 161 has been least touched by change. Brick, brownstone, and terra-cotta.

B23

[B24] **153-159 West 74th Street**, bet. Columbus and Amsterdam Aves. 1887. N side. **James Brown Lord.** ♂

More early development. No. 153 has been surgically separated from its Siamese twin—note the half remainder of its foliate cartouche. No. 159 winds up, after alteration, with two stoops: the original used as a planting bed, and a new one that makes a floral semicircle out of the original wall ornament.

B24

[B25] **Beacon Theater**, 2124 Broadway, bet. W. 74th and W. 75th Sts. E side. 1927-1929. **Walter W. Ahlschlager**. Interiors by **Rambusch Studio**. Partial interior. 🍎

Skip the exterior. It's the opulent interior, second only to that of Radio City Music Hall, that counts. Go in, even if you must attend a concert that deafens you—the interior is Greco-Deco-Empire with a Tudor palette.

[B26] **Astor Apartments**, 2141-2157 Broadway, bet. W. 75th and W. 76th Sts. W side. 1905. **Clinton & Russell**. Addition to N, 1914, **Peabody, Wilson & Brown**.

William Waldorf Astor, a major landowner in this community, ventured with this apartment complex. Bland but handsome, and the copper cornice is both potent and elegant.

B26

B27

[B27] **254 West 75th Street** (row house), bet. Broadway and West End Ave. S side. ca. 1885.

Three exuberant limestone arches make this extra special. The blocks between Broadway and West End in the 70s hold many surprises. Take a stroll and keep your eyes peeled.

[B28] **Berkley Garage**/originally The New York Cab Company (stables), 201 W. 75th St., NW cor. Amsterdam Ave. ca. 1889. **C. Abbott French**.

Three great Romanesque Revival half-round arches on 75th Street trumpeted entrance to the horses and drivers using this onetime multistory stable.

[B29] **140-142 West 75th Street** (row houses), bet. Columbus and Amsterdam Aves. S side. 1891. **George A. Bagge**.

The stoop is unique in form and decorated with bas-reliefs.

B30

[B30] **170 West 75th Street** (apartments), SE cor. Amsterdam Ave. 1888-1889. **Edward L. Angell**.

A veteran rehabilitated for the modern fray.

[B31] **Riverside Memorial Chapel** (funeral home), 331 Amsterdam Ave., SE cor. W. 76th St. 1925. **Joseph J. Furman** and **Ralph Segal**. Restored, and ground floor redesigned. 1998. **Belmont Freeman**. ♁

Designed using a limited palette of browns and dull reds; a soothing result, executed in tapestry brick, matte terra-cotta, stucco, and a gray slate roof. Gothic windows reveal the chapel proper.

[B32] **Jewish Community Center**, Samuel Priest Rose Building, Amsterdam Ave., SW cor. W. 76th St. 2001. **A.J. Diamond**.

An 8-story limestone and glass center (3 more stories below ground house a banquet room and swimming pool). Canadian architect Diamond has left distinguished work behind in and around Toronto.

B33

[B33] **153 West 76th Street** (row house), bet. Columbus and Amsterdam Aves. S side. 1885-1886. **William Baker**. ♁

Banded and piered brick and limestone; an eclectic solo.

[B34] **Hotel Churchill**, 252 W. 76th St., bet. Broadway and West End Ave. S side. 1903. **Ralph Townsend**.

Among the many Beaux Arts hotels that flock around Broadway and West End, this one is in superb condition: with bold Mannerist broken pediments over bay windows (they should be white to allow full play of shade and shadow).

B34

[B35] **West Side Institutional Synagogue**/originally St. Andrew's Methodist Episcopal Church, 120 W. 76th St., bet. Columbus and Amsterdam Aves. 1889. **Josiah Cleveland Cady**. Altered, 1958. ☾

A modernist approach translated a church (after a severe fire) into a synagogue; we recommend only the remains of the original. St. Andrew's merged with St. Paul's on West 86th and West End in 1937. Here the body has been desteepled and deroofed.

B35

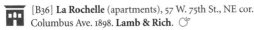

[B36] **La Rochelle** (apartments), 57 W. 75th St., NE cor. Columbus Ave. 1898. **Lamb & Rich**. ☾

Here is a grand entry portal worthy of an English Renaissance town house (but with a French name). The powerful columns are repeated in the Express shops, respectful insertion along the avenue as well. Such architectural strength is welcome: most buildings, good or bad, are mutilated along their commercial streetfronts.

B36

[B37] **The Hartford** (apartments), 60 W. 75th St., SE cor. Columbus Ave. 1890. **Frederick T. Camp**. ☾

Construction of these French flats spanned the name change from Ninth to Columbus Avenue. The pedimented stone insert at the 3rd-floor corner preserves the old name.

[B38] **The Aylsmere** (apartments), 60 W. 76th St., SE cor. Columbus Ave. 1894. **Henry Anderson**. ☾

French flats from the Brown decades of picturesque architecture but here with some growing neo-Classical influences. The verdigris bronze letters are a charming detail.

B37

[B39] **Belleclaire Hotel**, 250 W. 77th St., SW cor. Broadway. 1901-1903. **Emery Roth** of **Stein, Cohen & Roth**. ●⚲

Belle Epoque with bay windows, typical of a dozen similar exiles from the Rue Réaumur in Paris built hereabouts. Articulating its Beaux Arts body are giant Art Nouveau pilasters. While in New York to raise funds for the bolsheviks, **Maxim Gorky** and his mistress stayed here briefly in 1906. They were asked to leave when word got out that "Mme. Gorky" was not only not his wife (horrors!) but an actress (shudder!) with whom he had been living for three years.

B38

[B40] **Pyramid Garage**/originally Dakota Stables, 348-354 Amsterdam Ave., SW cor. W. 77th St. 1894. **Bradford L. Gilbert**.

A brownstone and brick "high rise," originally for horses and carriages, sullied at the ground floor by commerce and gross graphics.

[B41] **The Apthorp Apartments**, 2209 Broadway to West End Ave.,W. 78th to W. 79th Sts. 1906-1908. **Clinton & Russell**. ●⚲

Monumental and magnificent, this richly ornamented limestone Renaissance Revival building occupies an entire block. The individual entrances are reached through high vaulted tunnels and a large interior court with a fountain in its center. The best of the surviving Astor apartments in New York.

B39

[B42] **170 West 78th Street** (apartments), SE cor. Amsterdam Ave. 1890. **Higgs & Rooke**. ☾

Some Louis Sullivanesque inscribed ornament enhances a magnificent limestone Romanesque Revival arch.

[B43] **West 78th Street**, bet. Amsterdam Avenue and Broadway.

An architectural exhibit of stylistic sources—or is it a montage of Hollywood stage sets? Sturdy Romanesque Revival brownstone and brick at No. 202. Some watered-down Tudor England hangs out at No. 210. A bit of 1890s Chicago fronts No. 215. Sedate 19th-century Boston occupies No. 226. At Nos. 219-

B41

B43   B43

223 local row house talents left their own New York West Side marks.

B44

[B44] **The Evelyn** (apartments), 101 W. 78th St., NW cor. Columbus Ave. 1882-1886. **Emile Gruwe**. ○

A big, bold symphony in reds: brick with all kinds of wondrous unglazed terra-cotta flourishes.

[B45] **West 78th Street**, bet. Columbus and Amsterdam Aves. ca. 1883-1892. ○

A modern public school and other regrettable "improvements" have emasculated what was once one of the most vigorous and spirited streetscapes of the Upper West Side. The spirit was due in part to the works of **Rafael Guastavino**, who designed the idiosyncratic red and white sextet, Nos. 121-131 and Nos. 118-134 across the way (all completed in 1886). The client for these rows, **Bernard S. Levy**, allowed Guastavino, then a recent emigrant from Catalonia, to introduce his system of "cohesive construction" in No. 122, making it an entirely fireproof row house. (Levy himself lived at No. 121 between 1886 and 1904.) Look at the curious stepped balusters along the stoops in front of Nos. 157-167. Their unusual forms and shadows are a favorite among architectural photography buffs.

B45

[B46] **Park Belvedere** (apartments), 101 W. 79th St., NW cor. Columbus Ave. 1985. **Frank Williams & Assocs**. ○

A finial-fingered pencil tower that dominates the Columbus Avenue vista. Ruddy brown, it shows off some vigorous cubism at its crown.

B45

[B47] **100 West 81st Street** (apartments), SW cor. Columbus Ave. 1981. **Marvin Meltzer**. ○

A brick and stucco conversion that is schizophrenic: the body is Miami Beach, its coloring is Germanic. Shade and shadow count for little with such a dark palette.

[B48] **206-226 West 79th Street** (row houses), bet. Amsterdam Ave. and Broadway. 1894. **Thom & Wilson**. ○

A terrace of Roman brick town houses, bowed here and bayed there, based in limestone and decorated with terra-cotta. The anchoring end buildings project to meet the line of the corner apartment houses.

B47

[B49] **Hotel Lucerne**, 201 W. 79th St., NW cor. Amsterdam Ave. 1903-1904. **Harry B. Mulliken**. ○

Distinguished detailing in plum-colored brownstone and brick. The deeply modeled, banded entrance columns, adopted from the Baroque, are luscious. Now gloriously restored as a condominium—an extravagant palace for its cooperators.

[B50] **First Baptist Church**, 265 W. 79th St., NW cor. Broadway. 1894. **George Keister**.

Like the life that swirls past it on this busy corner, this church's eclectic façade is restless and polyglot. Overexuberant Italian Romanesque (Broadway division)?

B48

B49

B50

B51

B52a

Citarella

[B51] **Phoenix House**/originally West 80th Street Community Child Day Center, 223 W. 80th St., bet. Amsterdam Ave. and Broadway. 1972. **Kaminsky & Shiffer**.

The hoped-for creative plaything on the scale of side-street architecture didn't make it despite good intentions. Now abandoned, it deserves a renaissance.

[B52] **The Broadway** (apartments), 2250 Broadway, SE cor. W. 81st St. 1987. **Beyer Blinder Belle**, behind [B52a] **Staples** (office supplies)/originally RKO (Radio Keith Orpheum) 81st Street Theatre. 1914. **Thomas W. Lamb**. Converted, 1988, **Beyer Blinder Belle**.

A lush, glazed white terra-cotta, neo-Palladian theater building is the venerable frontispiece of this blank brown brick tower. Somehow what should have been architectural consonance and context here misfired.

Broadway is the quintessential New York street, providing the entire gamut of quality food shopping. Without the pretentious precincts and prices of the East Side (say upper Madison Avenue), one can find superior fruit and vegetables at Fairway (market) between 74th and 75th Streets, fresh seafood at **Citarella** *next door, and just about anything at* **Zabar's**. *Elaborate cooking is an everyday matter in this cosmopolitan neighborhood, and necessary raw, canned, pickled, smoked, or whatever materials are conveniently at hand.*

Zabar's, bet. W. 80th and W. 81st Sts. W side. A larger-than-life horn of plenty: wall-to-wall food and, on weekends, wall-to-wall people as well. What makes Zabar's remarkable is its phenomenal variety of foodstuffs from all over the world. It combines the delights of the Jewish appetizing store with charcuterie, salumeria, and Wurstgeschäft, adds an array of cheeses, coffees, and breads, and offers an extensive selection of cooking utensils and cookbooks, too.

[B53] **Endicott Apartments**/formerly Hotel Endicott, Columbus Ave. bet. W. 81st and W. 82nd Sts. W side. 1889. **Edward L. Angell**. Converted, 1984, **Stephen B. Jacobs & Assocs**. ⌕

The durability of red brick and matching terra-cotta ornament still preserves a sense of what this hotel once was—both fashionable and comfortable. Lovingly restored as a condominium; at the ground floor are elegant shops framed in understated oak.

B54

*Columbus Avenue's gentrification in the 1970s and 1980s not only brought yuppies galore to this pulsating strip, with a supporting cast of restaurants serving every eccentric taste from Buffalo chicken wings to Rocky Mountain oysters. It also created the need for the offbeat, sometimes eccentric shop, mostly of inedibles: one of the most curious and long lasting is **Maxilla & Mandible** at No. 453 selling skeletons, antlers, and carapaces of all creatures human and otherwise.*

[B54] **110 West 81st Street** (row house), bet. Columbus and Amsterdam Aves. S side. 1893. **Neville & Bagge.** ♂

Stolid brownstone mansion, rockface and smooth, with incised Sullivanesque detail. The stoop is unique.

[B55] **139-145 West 81st Street** (row houses), bet. Columbus and Amsterdam Aves. N side. Mid-1880s. ♂

Many-gabled bow-fronted triad: rockfaced limestone bears brick bows, linteled in limestone, corniced in terra-cotta.

[B56] **Holy Trinity Roman Catholic Church**, 207 W. 82nd St., bet. Amsterdam Ave. and Broadway. N side. 1900. **J. H. McGuire.** Rectory, 1928. **Thomas Dunn.** ♂

Rome and the Italian Renaissance contributed to this complex façade. The grand congregational space within is shrouded under a dome upon pendentives that bring the circle back to a square plan. Intricate brickwork contrasts with white-glazed terra-cotta. Two choragic monuments of Lysicrates once crowned it all: decapitated.

B56

[B57] **Engine Company No. 74, N.Y.C. Fire Department**, 120 W. 83rd St., bet. Columbus and Amsterdam Aves. S side. 1888. **Napoleon LeBrun & Sons.** ♂

Horses charging out of the doorway pulling a bright red and polished brass fire engine billowing clouds of water vapor? The horses and steam engine are gone, but the iron jib for hoisting hay is very much in evidence overhead. Rock-face brownstone and brick. House-scaled.

[B58] **167-173 West 83rd Street** (tenements), bet. Columbus and Amsterdam Aves. N side. 1885. **McKim, Mead & White.**

McKim, Mead & White? Italian Renaissance tenements? The noble firm builds ignoble housing for the masses? Here developer **David H. King, Jr.** believed that these floor-through apartments were the coming fashion.

B57

[B59] **The Bromley** (apartments), 225 W. 83rd St., NE cor. Broadway to W. 84th St. 1987. **Costas Kondylis** of **Philip Birnbaum & Assocs.**

A chunky filler of Broadway's belly. Post Modern green glazing and limestone give a graceful edge to West 83rd Street with Dutch stepped gables along the house-scaled entry façade.

B59

[B60] **Broadway Fashion Building** (offices), 2315 Broadway, SW cor. W. 84th St. 1931. **Sugarman & Berger**.

Long before the curtain walls of metal and glass descended upon midtown, this curtain wall of stainless steel, glass, and glazed terra-cotta came to grace Broadway. The retail signs at street level have happily improved since 1988.

B60

*Nevermore: Notwithstanding the two plaques affixed to upscale apartment buildings along West 84th Street, both claiming to be the site where **Edgar Allan Poe** put the finishing touches to "The Raven," the tenement at No. 206 just west of Amsterdam Avenue is the rightful claimant to that distinction. It was here in "the bleak December" of 1844 that Poe and his ailing wife boarded at **Patrick and Mary Brennan**'s farmhouse, which surmounted a promontory later dynamited when the site was graded. Poe would often stroll down the hill to the immense rock outcropping west of Riverside Drive near West 83rd Street that he named Mount Tom after the Brennans' young son. There he would sit alone for hours, gazing across the river. In more sociable moments he would amble up the sylvan Bloomingdale Road to the Striker's Bay Tavern, located northeast of today's Riverside Drive viaduct over 96th Street. Only one remnant survives from the "home by horror haunted": the mantel upon which Poe scratched his name, now preserved at Columbia University.*

B61

[B61] **74, 76, and 78 West 85th Street** (apartments), SE cor. Columbus Ave. 1895. **John G. Prague.** ♂

Ordinary façades with extraordinary portals; their foliate carving is ravishing, particularly that of SUDELEY at No. 76. Try to make out the letters incised over No. 74. Are they a Roman numeral? Do they spell CLIIION? Is the word CLIFTON? Or is this a rare example of a poor speller turned fine stonecutter?

[B62] **The Brockholst** (apartments), 101 W. 85th St., NW cor. Columbus Ave. 1890. **John G. Prague.** ♂

Endearingly dark and craggy rock-face stone and brick, these French flats are laced with delicate ironwork fire escapes. It announces its name in floral terra-cotta relief.

B62

[B63] **Mannes College of Music of the New School**/originally United Order of True Sisters, 150 W. 85th St., bet. Columbus and Amsterdam Aves. 1928.

A simple, austere neo-Georgian brick and limestone house for music, with a verdigris copper mansard roof and a mildly Palladian window over its portal.

[B64] **West-Park Presbyterian Church**/originally Park Presbyterian Church, 541 Amsterdam Ave., NE cor. W. 86th St. Chapel, 1884. **Leopold Eidlitz.** Sanctuary, 1890. **Henry F. Kilburn.**

Dour brownstone Romanesque Revival anchors this corner. Although overwhelmed by the grim apartment building to the north, it is one of the West Side's loveliest landmarks.

B64

[B65] **The Packard** (apartments), 176 W. 86th St., SE cor. Amsterdam Ave. 1987. **Ted Reeds Assocs.** ♂

The building is a modest attempt at style, but did the builder run out of quoins?

[B66] **Belnord Apartments**, 225 W. 86th St., Amsterdam Ave. to Broadway, W. 86th to W. 87th Sts. 1908-1909 (**H. Hobart Weekes** of) **Hiss & Weekes.** ●

Like its smaller cousin, the Apthorp, this block-square

B66

Renaissance Revival structure is an immense square doughnut. From the street it's brilliant but boring; but savor the vaulted entry tunnels and the garden court within.

B67

[B67] **The Boulevard** (apartments), 2373 Broadway, bet. W. 86th and W. 87th Sts., W side. 1988. **Voorsanger & Mills Assocs.**

Neo-Ruskinian polychromatic brickwork clads this modestly styled apartment block. Although a firm of architects associated with high design (check the entrance canopy) left its mark on the Broadway corridor, there are obvious limits on architectural possibilities. Form, as at the Montana twin towers across the street, is one of the few possibilities in street-structured Manhattan.

[B68] **The Montana** (apartments), 247 W. 87th St., NE cor. Broadway to W. 88th St. 1986. **The Gruzen Partnership**.

Named as if it were godchild of the Dakota, whose patron, Stephen Clark, bequeathed us that 72nd Street "château" in the then undeveloped territory of the Upper West Side. More than a hundred years later a new developer hopes that twin towers and a western sobriquet will give it equal cachet. Nice place to live but just a caricature of the Century or the Majestic.

B68

*Boulevard (restaurant) (1987. **Charles Morris Mount**) is a sleek, straightforward Modern restaurant within the Montana's embrace.*

B70

[B69] **Glenn Gardens** (apartments), 175 W. 87th St., NE cor. Amsterdam Ave. 1975. **Seymour Joseph**.

Two wings form this housing complex, the tall one banal, but the lower block on West 88th Street in scale with the old neighborhood.

[B70] **West 87th Street**, bet. Columbus and Amsterdam Aves. 1880s. ♂

Some fine row houses in this block: No. 145 with a fascinating regressed bay window; Nos. 135 through 141 in rockfaced brownstone, brick, with wild cornices; No. 159 has a black, weathered cornice that might almost be a Louise Nevelson sculpture.

B71

[B71] **Public School 166 Manhattan**, 140 W. 89th St., bet. Columbus and Amsterdam Aves. 1898-1899. **C. B. J. Snyder**. Upgraded, 1998. **Fox & Fowle**.

A stately, glazed terra-cotta Collegiate Gothic school by this prolific architect of schools of the 1890s. Yes, Virginia, schoolchildren do know how to walk up stairs in Manhattan. And the spaces within are much modernized.

[B72] Originally **Claremont Riding Academy**, 175 W. 89th St., bet. Columbus and Amsterdam Aves. N side. 1892. **Frank A. Rooke.** 🍎

High-rise stables housing rental horses for Central Park's bridle paths. Riding a steed from here to the park offers a special architectural experience: looking at the row house façades from a horse's back, a vantage point more usual for 19th-century viewers. It makes a difference.

In the late 1960s it was proposed that the stable be removed to make way for urban renewal, with a replacement in part of an enormous new Central Park stables and Police Facilities Complex. Park preservationists raised an outcry against tampering with the park; others pointed out that horses had always been a part of the 89th Street street scene. The preservationists prevailed, thus canceling the park project, and the forces of urban renewal ran out of money, thus extending the stables' life. Rent a horse.

[B73] **Ballet Hispanica** (dance school), 167 W. 89th St., bet. Columbus and Amsterdam Aves. N side. ca. 1890.

One of a series of carriage houses that served the grand mansions nearer and on Central Park West. Modest, but the arch is enough.

B74

 [B74] **Astor Court Apartments**, 205 W. 89th St. and 210 W. 90th St., along Broadway. E side. 1914-1916. **Charles A. Platt.**

Stolid Park Avenue style surrounds a garden court in the manner of the Apthorp and many others. But the pièce de résistance is the hovering cornice, worthy of **Michelangelo** (and perhaps copied from him?).

[B75] **The Cornwall** (apartments), 255 W. 90th St., NW cor. Broadway. 1909-1910. **Neville & Bagge.**

B75

An extraordinary cornice is the place to focus: a terra-cotta diadem, modeled and perforated as if on an Indian temple. Under it, the building's body is a normal but nice West Side limestone and brick apartment block, with a grand Corinthian piered entrance.

[B76] **263-273 West 90th Street** (row houses), bet. Broadway and West End Ave. N side. Late 1890s. ☙

A terrrace of seven houses, bowed and bayed in brick, limestone, and terra-cotta. The end units pull out to meet the line of adjacent avenue blocks.

B77

[B77] **258-270 West 91st Street** (row houses), bet. Broadway and West End Aves. S side. 1896-1897. **Alexander M. Welch.** ☙

Seven units form a terrace with bow and bay windows in yellow brick and limestone and terra-cotta on high.

The night shift: Soon after her first arrest as a madam, *Polly Adler* decided to go legit. With $6,000 in savings she and a friend opened a lingerie shop in 1922 at 2487 Broadway near West 92nd Street. Within a year the shop was out of business—and Adler was back to business as usual.

B78

[B78] **Pomander Walk** (apartment complex), 3-22 Pomander Walk, 261-267 W. 94th St. and 260-274 W. 95th St. bet. Broadway and West End Ave. 1921. **King & Campbell.** 🍎

Pomander Walk first came to New York as the name of a stage play. This charming double row of small town houses arrayed along a private pedestrian byway was modeled by developer **Thomas Healy** on the stage sets used in the New York production. What stage set would you like to inhabit?

BROADWAY & ENVIRONS (NORTH)

see pages 351–354

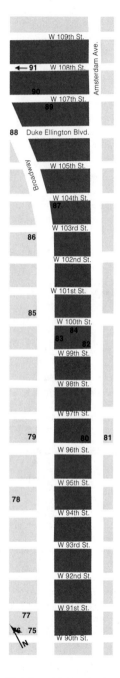

*Next door to Pomander, **Symphony Space** (**2537** Broadway, bet. W. 94th and W. 95th Sts.) is being surmounted by a new apartment house (2000. **Costas Kondylis**); the air rights will enable the theater to upgrade its facilities and rebuild the lower level sidestreet Thalia Theater (2000. **Polshek Partnership**).*

*Here **Vincent Astor** originally built a street-level produce market and underneath, and in the space that later became the Thalia Theatre, a fish market—perhaps on the theory that most mammals ride high, while the fish swim below.*

Happily, Symphony Space will be the beneficiary financially, if not aesthetically.

B79

B80

B81

B82

B84

[B79] **The Columbia** (apartments), 275 W. 96th St., NW cor. Broadway to W. 97th St. 1984. **Liebman Williams Ellis**.

Here was the site of a battle between community and commerce. Gimbel's, based at Herald Square, had an East Side beachhead at 86th St. and Lexington Avenue; an equivalent West Side outpost was to have been here. Commerce lost the battle here and, ironically, lost it on the East Side, too: another affluent apartment house now graces that site (with the very high ceilings that a department store's structure left behind).

This towering hulk is the first adventure in sophisticated modern housing on the Broadway blocks. (Central Park West's Majestic and Century were earlier housing pioneers in a different sort of West Side milieu). A bit brash, it borrows from the cubistic dreams of **Walter Gropius** in his wonderful but losing scheme for the Chicago Tribune Tower.

[B80] **Holy Name of Jesus Church** (Roman Catholic), Amsterdam Ave., NW cor. W. 96th St. 1898. **T. H. Poole**.

This uptight, ungiving Gothic Revival façade is forbidding. But enter for a more pleasing architectural experience—particularly the hammer-beamed ceiling and roof.

[B81] **CVS Pharmacy**/originally East River Savings Bank, 743 Amsterdam Ave., NE cor. W. 96th St. 1927. Expanded to N. Both by **Walker & Gillette**.

A Classical temple inscribed with exhortations to the thrifty. Note how the Ionic columns come down to the sidewalk in the Greek fashion, without pedestals. Temple to cosmetics?

[B82] **St. Michael's Church** (Episcopal), 225 W. 99th St., NW cor. Amsterdam Ave. 1891. **Robert W. Gibson**.

A somber church complex: tall double-arcaded tower, rounded apse, and a quiet garden. Inside are mosaics and Tiffany glass.

[B83] **Metro Theater**/originally Midtown Theatre, 2626 Broadway, bet. W. 99th and W. 100th Sts. E side. 1932-1933. **Boak & Paris**. 💰

Art Deco. A design more appropriate to a 1930s interior was made into a weatherproof façade through the imperviousness of glazed terra-cotta.

[B84] **Ukrainian Academy of Arts and Sciences**/originally New York Free Circulating Library, 206 W. 100th St., bet. Amsterdam Ave. and Broadway. 1898. **James Brown Lord**. 💰

Beaux Arts Ionic above, Tuscan below. Libraries were obvi-

B85

B86

B89

B90

ously intended as temples of learning in the 1890s, rather than supermarkets for checking out books.

[B85] **Metro Diner**/originally Henry Grimm Building, 2641 Broadway and 225 W. 100th St., NW cor. Broadway. 1871. Addition to W, 1900.

Amid the masonry canyons of Broadway, West End Avenue, and the side streets stands this wooden building, a holdout from the West Side's frontier days. Once a saloon, it now offers more substantial provender.

 [B86] Originally **Hotel Marseilles**/now apartments, 2689-2693 Broadway, SW cor. W. 103rd St. 1902-1905. **Harry Allan Jacobs.** ●

Another Broadway hotel springing from the renderings of the Beaux Arts; then impatiently waiting for the opening of the 103rd Street subway stop.

[B87] Formerly Horn & Hardart Automat/now **Rite Aid Drugs**, 2712 Broadway, SE cor. W. 104th St. 1930. Altered, 1928. **F.P. Platt & Brothers**.

A faint limestone and glazed terra-cotta memory is recycled as an Art Deco drugstore.

[B88] **Straus Park and Memorial Fountain**/originally Schuyler Square (1895-1907)/later Bloomingdale Square, Broadway and West End Ave., at W. 106th St. N side. 1919. **H. Augustus Lukeman**, sculptor. **Evarts Tracy**, architect.

Named Bloomingdale Square in 1907 not for the midtown department store (pure coincidence) but for the old settlement here of Bloemendael (flower valley in Dutch). The *Titanic* disaster in 1912 claimed the lives of Macy's owner **Isidor and Ida Straus** whose house, across the street at 2745 Broadway, overlooked the triangle. The park was renamed in their honor when the monument was completed two years later.

[B89] **Ivy Court** (apartments), 210, 220, and 230 West 107th St., bet. Amsterdam Ave. and Broadway. 1903. **William C. Hazlett**.

This apartment house trio imparts a town house scale and feel by use of streetfront courtyards. Two wings in limestone, three in brick, terra-cotta, and limestone. The balconies and ironwork are worthy of Paris.

[B90] **Church of the Ascension** (Roman Catholic), 221 W. 107th St., bet. Amsterdam Ave. and Broadway. 1897.

A rock-faced limestone Romanesque Revival surprise—and a pleasant one. Go inside. The adjacent rectory, nevertheless, has more guts.

[B91] **The Manhasset** (apartments), 301 W. 108th St. and 300 W. 109th St. along Broadway, W. side. First eight stories, 1899-1901. **Joseph Wolf.** Surelevated with three stories and a mansard roof, 1901-1905, **Janes & Leo.** ●

The surelevated mansard roof gives a grand if somber crown to the building once cornice at the eighth floor.

CENTRAL PARK WEST/THE PARK BLOCKS

While the Upper West Side is a place of contrasts and in constant flux, Central Park West, if not the so-called "park blocks," has generally retained its unflaggingly fashionable quality—at least up through 96th Street. The park blocks began to be converted into rooming houses following World War II, a pattern turned around somewhat by the rising desirability of brownstone living among upwardly mobile middle-class families and by the "singles" of the West Side. In the northern stretch the Urban Renewal Act helped save its row house stock on the park blocks above 86th Street; their health can often be seen to fall off the greater their distance from Central Park. **Olmsted and Vaux**'s great green space, one of the major attractions in the settlement of the West Side, still acts as an important touchstone.

This precinct begins above Columbus Circle and includes Central Park West up to 96th Street and the park block corridor up to 86th Street. North of 86th Street lies the West Side Urban Renewal Area.

C1

[C1] **Century Apartments**, 25 Central Park W., bet. W. 62nd and W. 63rd Sts. 1931. **Office of Irwin S. Chanin; Jacques Delamarre**, architectural director. ● ○

An Art Deco icon, more for the form of its crowning fins and ribbery than for decorative detail (American Art Deco concerned itself with mini-cubistic form; in Paris it was more a question of decorated surfaces). The name recalls a lavish and unprofitable Century Theater, designed by **Carrère & Hastings**, that shared this site and survived for only 21 years. Twin towers are a symbol of Central Park West, recurring at the San Remo, Majestic, and Eldorado.

C2

[C2] **New York Society for Ethical Culture Hall**, 2 W. 64th St., SW cor. Central Park W. 1909-1910. **Robert D. Kohn**, architect. **Estelle Rumbold Kohn**, sculptor. ● ○ [C3] **Ethical Culture School**, 33 Central Park W., NW cor. W. 63rd St. 1902-1904. **Carrère & Hastings** and **Robert D. Kohn**.

A clear departure from the Beaux Arts, the hall was cited in the architectural press of its time as the best Art Nouveau building designed in this century. It has since lost prestige. Not as exuberant as **Hector Guimard**'s Parisian efforts or those in Brussels by **Victor Horta**, it also fails to match the quality of **Otto Wagner**'s or **Josef Hoffmann**'s Viennese works.

C4

[C4] **The Prasada** (apartments), 50 Central Park W., SW cor. W. 65 St. 1905-1907. **Charles W. Romeyn** and **Henry R. Wynne**. ○

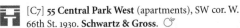

Banded limestone columns, monumental in scale, and other freely interpreted Classical ornaments embellish but do not quite animate this bulky apartment façade.

[C5] **Holy Trinity Lutheran Church**, 51 Central Park W., NW cor. W. 65th St. 1903. **Schickel & Ditmars.** ☿

Dour rock-face ecclesiastical limestone breaks Central Park West's phalanx of boxy apartment blocks. The kaleidoscopelike rose window and delicate copper verdigris flèche over the crossing are notable.

C5

[C6] **Estelle R. Newman City Center, Jewish Guild for the Blind**, 15 W. 65th St., bet. Central Park W. and Columbus Ave. 1971. **Matthew J. Warshauer.**

A horizontally striped box (dark glass and metal strip windows alternating with cream-colored precast concrete spandrels) projects from an orange salt-and-pepper glazed-brick utility core. Truly International Modern, it could, in its time, have been at home in Mexico City.

C7

[C7] **55 Central Park West** (apartments), SW cor. W. 66th St. 1930. **Schwartz & Gross.** ☿

Art Deco evolved through a carefully studied modulation of brick planes and boldly fluted ornament. If the sun seems brighter at top than at bottom, look more carefully at the brick color. It changes subtly.

[C8] **Congregation Habonim** (synagogue), 44 W. 66th St., bet. Central Park W. and Columbus Ave. 1957. **Stanley Prowler and Frank Faillance.**

A stained-glass cube set 45 degrees to itself and its neighbors along the street. Its setback permits a better understanding of the old armory next door.

For the American Broadcasting Company buildings, see Lincoln Center

Studio Street: The park block of West 67th Street is a haven for those who like studio living or living among artists: there are no fewer than six studio buildings on the block. Among them:

C10

[C9] **70 Central Park West** (apartments), SW cor. W. 67th St. 1916-1919. **Rich & Mathesius.** ☿

A bland 15-story studio building, but the 2-story industrial sash that illuminates the duplex apartments is spectacular.

C11

[C10] **Hotel des Artistes** (apartments), 1 W. 67th St., bet. Central Park W. and Columbus Ave. 1915-1918. **George Mort Pollard.** Café redecorated, 1979, **Judith Stockman & Assocs.** ☿

The fanciful façade clearly shows the balconied studios behind it. An early tenant, **Howard Chandler Christy**, painted a pinup girl (his specialty) to decorate the cozy Café des Artistes on the first floor. An all-time roster of tenants of the elaborate (and lavish) spaces would also include **Isadora Duncan**, **Norman Rockwell**, **Alexander Woollcott**, **Noel Coward**, **Fannie Hurst**, **Gordon Hyatt**, **George Dudley**, and former mayor **John V. Lindsay.**

[C11] **Central Park Studios**, 15 West 67th Street, bet. Central Park W. and Columbus Ave. 1904-1905. **B. H. Simonson** and **Pollard & Steinam.** ☿

Note the neo-Gothic portal and lobby. There may be some artists still in residence but these two-story spaces appeal to those merely affluent as well.

[C12] **67th Street Atelier Building** (apartments), 33 W. 67th St., bet. Central Park W. and Columbus Ave. 1904-1905. **B. H. Simonson** and **Pollard & Steinam.** ☿

One of the first co-op buildings built as such in New York City.

CENTRAL PARK WEST / THE PARK BLOCKS (SOUTH)

see pages 355–361

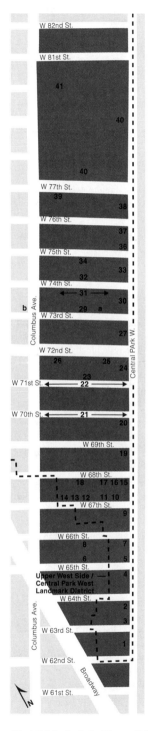

[C13] Originally **Swiss Home of the Swiss Benevolent Society**, 35 W. 67th St., bet. Central Park W. and Columbus Ave. 1904-1905. **John E. Scharsmith**. ♂

A curious eclecticism that seems a Beaux Arts interpretation of North European Renaissance.

[C14] **39-41 West 67th Street** (studios), bet. Central Park W. and Columbus Ave. 1906-1907. **Pollard & Steinam**.

C14

Four stacks of bay windows zip up the street façade of this tall narrow studio building. They are of sheet metal, not masonry—an early curtain wall. And the cornice is monumental.

Tavern on the Green: *The entrance to this chronically remodeled eating-drinking-dancing spot, built around Central Park's 1870 sheepfold, is at 67th Street and Central Park West. Expensive. (At night the trees, wrapped to their roots in minilights, suggest an invasion of the bulb people.)*

C15

[C15] **Second Church of Christ, Scientist**, 77 Central Park W., SW cor. W. 68th St. 1899-1901. **Frederick R. Comstock.** ♂

Its green domes, best seen from the edge of the park, cap a crisp neo-Classical building.

[C16] **14 West 68th Street** (apartments), bet. Central Park W. and Columbus Ave. S side. 1895. **Louis Thouvard.** ♂

A somber brownstone box whose entrance is from an adjacent green space open to the street. Imagine when the house had a view clear into Central Park.

[C17] **16-22 West 68th Street** (row houses), bet. Central Park W. and Columbus Ave. 1896. **George F. Pelham.** ♂

Roman brick, terra-cotta, and limestone bow- and bay-fronted houses.

C16

[C18] **York Preparatory School**/formerly Hebrew Union College-Jewish Institute of Religion/originally The Free Synagogue, 40 W. 68th St., bet. Central Park W. and Columbus Ave. 1923. **S. B. Eisendrath & B. Horowitz.** ♂ [C18a] **Stephen Wise Free Synagogue**, 30 W. 68th St. 1949. **Bloch & Hesse.** ♂

Somber and unobtrusive collegiate Gothic clad in Manhattan Schist ashlar (cut stone). Today's school (once college) building was the sanctuary until the new one was begotten in 1941. An important center of the Reform Judaism movement.

C18

[C19] **The Brentmore** (apartments), 88 Central Park W., SW cor. W. 69th St. 1909-1910. **Schwartz & Gross.** ♂

A prim Edwardian block, with a wonderful bracketed copper cornice.

[C20] **Congregation Shearith Israel** (synagogue), 99 Central Park W., SW cor. W. 70th St. 1896-1897. **Brunner & Tryon.** 🐾 ♂

The newest home of New York's oldest Jewish congregation, a look back to the glittering White City architecture of the 1893 Chicago World's Fair. It's a far cry from the Moorish/Middle Eastern architecture in contemporary temples elsewhere. (Or was it inspired by archaeologists' discovery of the Roman Second Temple in Jerusalem?)

C19

Shearith Israel was founded in 1655 in then New Amsterdam by Spanish and Portuguese immigrants. Three venerable Shearith Israel cemeteries that resisted the march of progress in Manhattan belong to this congregation [see index].

A connected Little Synagogue reproduces the Georgian style of the congregation's first real synagogue, built in 1730; it contains many furnishings used in that building.

[C21] **Row houses**, W. 70th St., bet. Central Park W. and Columbus Ave. Early 1890s. ♂

Bay-windowed, Nos. 9-21 intermingle yellow Roman brick with brownstone facades. No. 24 offers a grand meandering stoop. Nos. 40-58 again try for individuality within a developer's terrace.

C21

[C22] **Row houses**, W. 71st St., bet. Central park W. and Columbus Ave. Late 1880s/early 1890s. ♂

A terrific selection: No. 24 is remarkable, with its unusual

C20

stoop, cupids at its cornice, and concave shell-molded lintels over the topmost windows. Nos. 26, 28, and 30 show that handsome houses come in threes: an elegant russet color scheme (brick, stone, terra-cotta, and the cartouches) and wide doors that must certainly have encouraged the purchase of expansive furnishings. Note how the imitation cement plaster "stonework" has been tooled to disguise the removal of No. 30's stoop. On the stoops of Nos. 32-40 a gentle separation of the balusters as they reach the sidewalk subtly signals you to enter. Across the street Nos. 33-39 offer both hungry and satiated lion's-heads to decorate the doorway keystones. An architectural feast.

C22

[C23] **Hampshire Central Park Hotel**/originally Parkside Hotel/later The Bromley (studios), 31 W. 71st St., bet. Central Park W. and Columbus Ave. 1915-1917. **Robert T. Lyons**. ♂

A tall studio building faced on its narrow street frontage by white glazed terra-cotta. One of a West Side breed.

[C24] **Majestic Apartments**, 115 Central Park W., bet. W. 71st and W. 72nd Sts. 1930-1931. **Office of Irwin S. Chanin; Jacques Delamarre**, director of architecture. ● ♂

One of 5 twin-towered apartment buildings—if you include The Beresford—that make the skyline along Central Park West a unique visual treat. This streamlined building has wide banks of windows that extend around its sides. The much-copied brickwork patterns and futurist forms were designed by sculptor **René Chambellan**.

C24

[C25] **The Oliver Cromwell**, 12 W. 72nd St., bet. Central Park W. and Columbus Ave. 1927. **Emery Roth**. ♂

A monotower among the array of the twin-towered Central Park West. A pioneer, for Chanin's Majestic came later. A tempietto crowns an octagonal drum, perforated with oculi.

C25

[C26] **42 West 72nd Street** (studios), bet. Central Park W. and Columbus Ave. 1915. **Buchman & Fox**. ♂

Another lanky white studio tower by developer "**Daddy**" **Browning**.

[C27] **Dakota Apartments**, 1 W. 72nd St., NW cor. Central Park W. to W. 73rd St. 1880-1884. **Henry J. Hardenbergh**. ● ♂

The city's first luxury apartment house. Designed for Singer Sewing Machine heir **Edward S. Clark**, it dominated Central Park before the park drives were paved. A prestige address, particularly for those in the arts, since the days when this part of the city was thought to be as remote as the Dakota Territory. Note the railings with griffins and Zeuses, or are they Neptunes and sea monsters?

C27

[C28] **Central Park West-W. 73rd Street-W. 74th Street Historic District**, the whole block between W. 73rd and W. 74th Sts., Central Park W. and Columbus Ave. 🍎 Subsumed within the Upper West Side/Central Park West Historic District.

A wonderful intermixture of town houses and apartments, including:

[C29a] **15A-19 and 41-65 West 73rd Street** (row houses), bet. Central Park W. and Columbus Ave. 1882-1885. ♂ [C29b] **101 and 103 West 73rd Street** (apartments and row house), NW cor. Columbus Ave. 1879-1880. All by **Henry J. Hardenbergh**. ♂

C29b

These houses are another product of the collaboration of the client (Clark) and the architect (Hardenbergh) of the Dakota Apartments.

[C30] **The Langham** (apartments), 135 Central Park W., bet. W. 73rd and W. 74th Sts. 1904-1907. **Clinton & Russell**. ♂

A ponderous bulk until you look at the roofline, where a simple cornice has been so elaborated with ornament and ornate dormers that it sparkles with light.

[C31] **18-52 West 74th Street** (row houses), bet. Central Park W. and Columbus Ave. 1902-1904. **Percy Griffin**. ♂

A phalanx of 18 neo-Georgian row houses fills the block's south side and bears such names as Park Terrace, Riverside, and Hayden Manor. Built to compete with apartment buildings, which were growing in popularity, these 25-foot-wide, 17- to 19-room houses each boasted four or five bathrooms and an electric elevator. It is easy to understand their conversion to school and other institutional uses. The architect also designed the O-Te-Sa-Ga Hotel in Cooperstown, N.Y.

[C32] **37 West 74th Street** (town house), bet. Central Park W. and Columbus Ave. N side. 1889. **Thom & Wilson**. ♂

Sturdy Ionic pilasters frame the bow window; and below diamond rustications support it all. One of many lush neighbors, but lovingly overrestored.

C32

[C33] **San Remo Apartments**, 145-146 Central Park W., bet. W. 74th and W. 75th Sts. 1929-1930. **Emery Roth**. 🍎 ♂

Twin towers surmounted by those ubiquitous Hellenistic temples, finialed, against the sky. A base (the towers' "bustle") of chunky apartments sits below.

C33

[C34] **34, 36, & 38 West 75th Street** (row houses), bet. Central Park W. and Columbus Aves. S side. 1989-1890. **George H. Budlong**. ♂

The gabled streetfronts alternate, colonnettes supporting mock-medieval tympanums at Nos. 34 and 38, dour rusticated brownstone at No. 36.

[C35] **Central Park West-76th Street Historic District**, Central Park W. bet. W. 75th and W. 77th Sts., including W. 76th St. W to Nos. 51 and 56, and 44 W. 77th St. 🍎 Subsumed within the Upper West Side/Central Park West Historic District.

In addition to the buildings on Central Park West and West 77th Street, covered below, the Historic District encompasses a variety of row housing along West 76th Street dating from 1889 to 1900. The earliest, Nos. 27-37, is by architect **George M. Walgrove**, who used alternately smooth stone with neo-Grec incised detail, and the then newly fashionable rock-faced stonework. The most recent, Nos. 8-10, are flamboyant Upper East Side neo-Baroque town houses by **John H. Duncan**, designer of Grant's Tomb and Brooklyn's Soldiers' and Sailors' Memorial Arch. No. 34 is notable for its contrasting smooth and rockface brownstone. Works by other architects fill in both sides of the block: **Gilbert A. Schellenger**, **Schickel & Ditmars**, and **Cleverdon & Putzel**. The architecture is decorative, the designation abounding with references to garlanded brackets,

C35

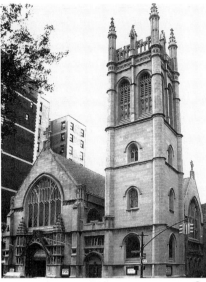

C37

Herculean heads, elegant cartouches, and spiral colonnettes.

[C36] **The Kenilworth** (apartments), 151 Central Park W., NW cor. W. 75th St. 1906-1908. **Townsend, Steinle & Haskell.** ⟳

A cubical russet-brick wedding cake topped by a grand convex mansard roof. The entry portal is the best part.

[C37] **Universalist Church of New York and Parish House/** originally Church of the Divine Paternity, Fourth Universalist Society, 4 W. 76th St., SW cor. Central Park W. 1897-1898. **William A. Potter.** ⟳

Oxford University on Central Park West: this church sports a neo-Gothic tower reminiscent of Oxford's Magdalen College.

[C38] **New-York Historical Society**, 170 Central Park W., bet. W. 76th and W. 77th Sts. Central portion, 1903-1908. **York & Sawyer.** N and S wings, 1937-1938. **Walker & Gillette.** ❦ ⟳ Restoration and improvements, 1990s. **Beyer Blinder Belle.**

C38

Reminiscent of a Parisian bibliothèque, this neo-Classical "palace" is both an important museum and a research library for American and local history. Among the library's vast holdings are the **McKim, Mead & White** files and the 432 original watercolors of **John James Audubon's** *Birds of America*.

[C39] **The Studio Building**, 44 W. 77th St., bet. Central Park W. and Columbus Ave. 1907-1909. **Harde & Short.** ⟳

Several of the adjacent apartments along West 77th Street replaced row housing when the abundant and unobstructed north light encouraged redevelopment. Though a great deal of terra-cotta was removed in 1944, the lacy tapestry of the neo-Gothic façade is still breathtaking.

C39

[C40] **American Museum of Natural History,** Manhattan Sq., Central Park W. to Columbus Ave., W. 77th to W. 81st St. General plan and first wing, 1872-1877. **Calvert Vaux** and **J. Wrey Mould.** W. 77th Street frontage, and auditorium, 1887-1901. **J. C. Cady & Co.** (later **Cady, Berg & See**). Southwest wing (Columbus Ave.), 1905-1908. **Charles Volz.** Powerhouse, 1927-1932. Southeast wing, 1912-1924. Both by **Trowbridge & Livingston.**

Theodore Roosevelt Memorial, Central Park W., 1936. **John Russell Pope**, architect. Roosevelt statue and heroic figures on attic. **James Earle Fraser**, sculptor. Animal relief, **James L. Clark**, sculptor. Library, 1990-1992. **Kevin Roche John Dinkeloo Assocs.** ❦ ⟳

C40

212-769-5100. Su-Th 10-5:45; Fr & Sa 10-8:45.

C40, Roosevelt Mem.

Conceived by **Vaux** and **Mould**, "Architects of the Department of Public Parks," to be the largest building on the continent. The museum trustees had other thoughts, and V&M's wing (the first) is now only barely visible from Columbus Avenue. The best parts of the building are Cady's Romanesque Revival efforts on West 77th Street—though Pope's pompous Central Park West façade, the Roosevelt Memorial, gets the publicity photos and therefore seems important. Exhibits range from ponderous to exhilarating. See the Hall of Minerals and Gems, 1976, and The People Center, 1973. A complex of 22 interconnected buildings.

C42

[C41] **Frederick Phineas and Sandra Priest Rose Center for Earth and Space**, including: New Hayden Planetarium, American Museum of Natural History, W. 81st St., bet. Central Park W. and Columbus Ave. S side. 2000. **Polshek Partnerhsip**. Exhibition designer, **Ralph Applebaum Associates**. ♂

An illuminated, glistening 90-foot-diameter sphere "floats" within a glass cube as if a reincarnated Boullée (alias Polshek), invigorated with hi-tech wisdom, has fulfilled one of his marvelous Revolutionary (French, that is) fantasies.

[C42] **The Beresford** (apartments), 1 and 7 W. 81st St. and 211 Central Park W., NW cor. 1928-1929. **Emery Roth**. ●' ♂

Named for the hotel it replaced, the Beresford is another of Central Park West's twin-towered luxury apartment buildings but with a plus: it has a twin-towered silhouette not only from the east but also from the south, a result of three Baroquoid projections above its roof.

C44

[C43] **Hayden House** (apartments), 11 W. 81st St., bet. Central Park W. and Columbus Ave. N side. 1906-1908. **Schickel & Ditmars**. ♂

Here cast-iron balconies modulate the façade, all topped with a mansard roof and dormer windows.

[C44a] **Congregation Rodeph Sholom** (synagogue), 7 W. 83rd St., bet. Central Park W. and Columbus Ave. N side. 1928-1930. **Charles B. Meyers**. [C44b] **Day School**, 12 W. 84th St. 1974-1977. **William Roper**. ♂

The synagogue is stolid, overblown but restrained neo-Romanesque limestone. The school, reflecting a 1970s fad of deeply recessed windows and sloped brick reveals, is a reconstruction of an earlier group of row houses.

C45

[C45] **65, 67, and 69 West 83rd Street** (row houses), and **71 West 83rd Street** (apartments), bet. Central Park W. and Columbus Ave. N side. 1884-1885. **George W. DaCunha**. ♂

These exuberant Queen Anne row houses were planned so that No. 69 carries their recessed façades out to the building line, where the group curtsies to No. 71, a restrained and exquisitely detailed apartment house.

C46

[C46] **59, 61, & 63 West 83rd Street** (town houses), bet. Central Park W. and Columbus Ave. 1890s. ♂

The rusticated and alternately smooth and rockfaced brownstone bays are a strong presence on the street.

C47

[C47] **Church of St. Matthew and St. Timothy** (Episcopal), 26 W. 84th St., bet. Central Park W. and Columbus Ave. S side. 1970. **Victor Christ-Janer**. ♂

Following a disastrous fire in 1965, this radical, cast-in-place concrete block was erected. The stark simplicity of the exterior does not prepare you for the carefully modulated circumambulatory entry and what you find within: a rich combination of white (plaster) and gray (concrete) surfaces set off by warm natural wood pews, metallic organ pipes, and a richly colored mosaic crucifix and fabric hangings. A handsome interior.

C41

[C48] **241 Central Park West** (apartments), NW cor. W. 84th St. 1930-1931. **Schwartz & Gross**. ♂

Subtly colored giant glazed terra-cotta ears of corn sprout (literally) from the brickwork of this Art Deco structure. The West 84th Street side is beautifully modeled at street level.

[C49] **247-249 Central Park West** (town houses), SW cor. 85th St. 1888. **Edward B. Angell**. ♂

Sturdy Queen Anne survivors from an earlier Central Park West assembly.

C48

[C50] **53-75 West 85th Street** (row houses), bet. Central Park W. and Columbus Ave. N side. 1886-1887. **George H. Griebel**. ♂

Serrated gables against the sky punctuate this long row of Queen Anne town houses.

[C51] **32-36 West 85th Street** (town houses), bet. Central Park W. and Columbus Ave. S side. 1897. **George F. Pelham**. ♂

Five stories of Roman brick, bay-windowed, alternately Doric columned or piered, in incised terra-cotta.

[C52] **44 and 46 West 85th Street** (town houses), bet. Central Park W. and Columbus Ave. S side. 1886-1887. **Edward L. Angell**. ♂

Exotic Gothicized bay windows, exuberant dormers, and coats of paint that exaggerate it all.

C50

[C53] **70 West 85th Street** (town house), bet. Central Park W. and Columbus Ave. S side. 1894-1895. **John G. Prague**. ♂

The incised brownstone supporting the bay window and on the stepped step walls is in the spirit of **Louis Sullivan**.

[C54] **Rossleigh Court**, 1 W. 85th St., NW cor. Central Park W. 1906-1907. **Orwell House**/formerly Hotel Peter Stuyvesant/originally Central Park View, 257 Central Park W., SW cor. W. 86th St. 1905-1906. Both by **Mulliken & Moeller**. ♂

Twin apartment buildings occupying the full Central Park West blockfront. They are of a disarming and cheery purple brick set off to advantage by limestone trim.

C52

Renewal area: *Central Park West's frontages between West 87th and 97th Streets and the park blocks in that stretch lay within the official boundaries of the old West Side Urban Renewal Area. CPW's apartment buildings (with the exception of No. 325) did not directly benefit from the designation; but many of the side-street brownstones, converted into single-room occupancy and rooming houses, did. (No. 235, slated to be demolished, was saved, upgraded, and turned into a co-op.) [For the side streets, therefore, see the*

C53

CENTRAL PARK WEST / THE PARK BLOCKS (NORTH)

see pages 363–366

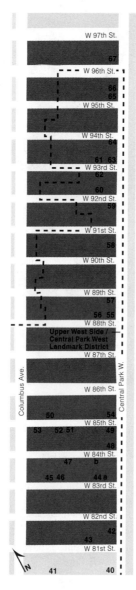

precinct called West Side Urban Renewal Area; for the continuation of CPW's buildings uptown to West 97th, see below.]

[C55] **279 Central Park West** (apartments), NW cor. W. 88th St. 1987-1990. **Costas Kondylis**. ☞

Bay windows embraced within the front plane of Central Park West, a subtle trick borrowed from the late 19th century, and a crowning ziggurat.

[C56] **The Walden School**/Andrew Goodman Building, 11-15 W. 88th St., bet. Central Park W. and Columbus Ave. N side. 1974. **Edgar Tafel**. ☞

The desire to relate the addition's façade to that of the now-demolished Progress Club, the school's Classical Revival original building, is commendable. The result, on the other hand, misses the mark. The parent building (1904. **Louis Korn**) had almost a Post Modern look, with its hefty columns supporting thin air.

C55

Moses King, author and publisher of the incomparable *King's Handbooks* and *King's Views of New York City* (and the cities of Brooklyn and Boston and even of the United States), lived in The Minnewaska, an 8-story apartment house that once stood at 2 West 88th Street. He died there on June 12, 1909.

C57

[C57] **The St. Urban** (apartments), 285 Central Park W., SW cor. W. 89th St. 1904-1905. **Robert T. Lyons.** ♂
CPW's only single-towered apartment building. Its tower is splendidly crowned by dome and cupola, gray slate shingles, and verdigris trim. And all is festooned with 16 broken-pediment dormers.

[C58] **The Eldorado** (apartments), 300 Central Park W., W. 90th to W. 91st Sts. 1929-1930. **Margon & Holder,** architect. **Emery Roth,** consultant. ♂ ♂
The northernmost of CPW's twin-towered apartment houses. Art Deco metalwork embellishes the base (subtle bronze reliefs) and the towers (Flash Gordon finials).

C58

[C59] **The Ardsley** (apartments), 320 Central Park W., SW cor. W. 92nd St. 1930-1931. **Emery Roth.** ♂
Mayan influences appear in this Art Deco apartment building, particularly in the modeling of the upper stories. At street level, closest to the eye, are precast exposed-aggregate terrazzo reliefs in subtle colors and forms. Compare this with the San Remo, completed by the same firm the previous year!

C60

[C60] **The Raleigh** (apartments), 7 W. 92nd St., bet. Central Park W. and Columbus Ave. N side. 1899-1900. **Gilbert A. Schellenger.** ♂
A magnificent tenement that modulates the street with its columnar bays, and displays mannered and luscious rustications at its lower floors.

[C61] **Columbia Grammar and Preparatory School**, 5 W. 93rd St., bet. Central Park W. and Columbus Ave. N side. 1907. **Beatty & Stone.** ♂ Remodeled, 1987. **Pasanella & Klein.**
Savor the neo-Classical frieze adorning this building below its surprisingly Classical-Moderne deep, flat cornice.

[C62] **New building, Columbia Grammar and Preparatory School**, 4 W. 93rd St., bet. Central Park W. and Columbus Ave. S side. 1986. **Pasanella + Klein.** ♂

C62

A handsome modern building, happily scaled for the block with crossed blue mullions, both lively and elegant. A welcome Modern outpost in these northern blocks.

[C63] **The Turin** (apartments), 333 Central Park W., NW cor. W. 93rd St. 1909-1910. **Albert J. Bodker**. ♂
Study the Roman medallions in the spandrels and savor the quarter-sphere marquee over the entry.

C64

[C64] **336 Central Park West** (apartments), SW cor. W. 94th St. 1928-1929. **Schwartz & Gross**. ♂
This 16-story apartment house is crowned with terra-cotta reminiscences of an Egyptian-styled cavetto cornice (Art Deco Egyptian, not the Egyptian Revival of the 1840s). The tapestry brick enriches the viewer's experience closer to eye level.

The West 95th Street park block, a diverting detour, is described below in theWest Side Urban Renewal Area.

[C65] **353 Central Park West** (apartments), NW cor. W. 95th St. 1992. **Yorgancioglu Architects & The Vilkas Group**. ♂
This subsumed Nos. 351, 352, and 353, original partners of the designated pair below. The replacement, happily, has some modeled brickwork worthy of the Central Park West landscape. Cigarette baron **Solomon Schinasi** owned the now vanished No. 351 in 1906, before buying the Rice House on Riverside Drive.

[C66] **354 and 355 Central Park West** (row houses), bet.W. 95th and W. 96th Sts. 1892-1893. **Gilbert A. Schellenger**. ● ♂
Twin early West Side speculative houses that look as though they belong on a side street, from the era when no one believed Central Park West would be anything else

C67

[C67] **First Church of Christ, Scientist**, 1 W. 96th St., NW cor. Central Park W. 1899-1903. **Carrère & Hastings**. ●
The architects of the Beaux Arts-style New York Public Library at Fifth Avenue and 42nd Street flirt here with the forms of **Nicholas Hawksmoor**'s great Baroque churches in London. Exciting.

WEST SIDE URBAN RENEWAL AREA

The blocks between West 87th and West 97th Streets, from Amsterdam Avenue to Central Park West, sheltered 40,000 residents in 1956, when this area's acute social and physical decline indicated a need for public action. In a series of moves the district, one of the nation's most densely populated, was designated the West Side Urban Renewal Area, and plans were drawn for change.

The concepts that emerged were radically different from those of earlier renewal efforts. Exploitation of the highest possible rental scales was abandoned. Clearance and rebuilding from scratch, once the only redevelopment tools, were combined with rehabilitation and renovation, particularly of the basically sound side-street brownstone row houses. Steps were taken to ensure an economic and social mix within the district by providing not only separate low-rent projects but also low-rent families within middle-income developments. Finally, the plan provided for phased development from West 97th Street south to encourage the relocation of on-site tenants. The plan as amended called for 2,500 low-income units, 5,421 middle-income units, and 151 luxury units. In addition, 485 brownstones were to be saved and renovated.

The results are most visible architecturally along Columbus Avenue, which is lined with high-rise construction. The side streets have been more subtly upgraded: behind the façades, in backyards, and with added street trees.

W1

One thing is clear. The renewal effort, though not without its critics, has done much to reverse the decline of this part of the West Side. Unlike other West Side precincts in this guide, this one proceeds from north to south to reflect the phasing of the redevelopment plan. Although the first project, Park West Village, actually predates these plans (it is within another urban renewal area, West Park), we include it first, both as a logical part of the urban renewal story and as an example of the techniques that had been abandoned. Start at West 96th Street and Amsterdam; then continue over to Columbus and proceed south.

[W1] **Park West Village** (apartment complex), 784, 788, 792 Columbus Ave., bet. W. 97th to W. 100th Sts. 1957-1958. 372, 382, 392, 400 Central Park W., 1958-1961. **S. J. Kessler & Sons.**

This large and banal housing development was built in the aftermath of the 1957 Manhattantown urban renewal scandal, with the then usual slab and balcony domino blocks and vast parking spaces. Developers had acquired six blocks of tenements at a reduced price from the City under the federal urban renewal program. Instead of developing the site, they sat tight for five years, collecting rents, neglecting repairs, and inventing ingenious schemes to exploit their unhappy tenants. Some say these disclosures marked the beginning of N.Y.C. construction czar **Robert Moses'** loss of power.

W2

West Side Urban Renewal Area

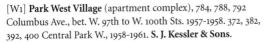

[W2] **Key West** (apartments), 750 Columbus Ave., bet. W. 96th and W. 97th Sts. W side. 1987. **Schuman, Lichtenstein, Claman & Efron.**

Bay-windowed and bold, Key West forms a happier relationship with its context than do many of the architecturally self-conscious towers of earlier urban renewal.

[W3] **New Amsterdam** (apartments), 733 Amsterdam Ave., bet. W. 95th and W. 96th Sts. E side. 1971. **Gruzen & Partners.**

Concrete balconies, private with cheek walls, exposed concrete floor slabs, and floor-to-floor window assemblies, contribute to a better-than-average effort.

W3

W5

[W4] **Congregation Ohab Zedek** (synagogue), 118 W. 95th St., bet. Columbus and Amsterdam Aves. S side. 1926. **Charles B. Meyers**.

Intricate terra-cotta ornament enriches the tall Byzantine arch that dominates the façade.

[W5] **123 and 125 West 95th St.** (row houses), bet. Columbus and Amsterdam Aves. N side.

Unique three-story brick and brownstone houses.

[W6] **Claude A. Vissani House**, 143 West 95th Street, bet. Columbus and Amsterdam Aves. N side. 1889. **James W. Cole**.

Exuberant neo-Gothicism as if done in the Renaissance fashion by a student trained at the Ecole des Beaux-Arts. It is a grand presence on this handsome block.

[W7] **West Side Manor**, 70 W. 95th St., SE cor. Columbus Ave. to W. 94th St. 1968. **Gruzen & Partners**.

A long prism perpendicular to Columbus Avenue, buff and bland.

W6

[W8] **West 95th Street**, bet. Central Park W. and Columbus Ave.

Diversely styled row houses, luxuriant trees, and lots of care make this one of the loveliest of the park blocks. A leisurely walk will reveal delightful touches: sculpted griffins and cherubs, fine lanterns, simply designed metal guards around the street-tree pits. Nos. 27 and 29 (1887. **Charles T. Mott**) display unique and glassy segmental bay windows, and No. 14 (1889. **George Holiday**, builder) bears the fluted and unfluted pilasters and arches of the American Renaissance. A rhapsodic architectural exercise in circles and arcs at the entrances, balconies, and stoops of Nos. 6 and 8 (1894. **Horace Edgar Hartwell**) is a small delight.

W7

[W9] **Jefferson Towers** (apartments), 700 Columbus Ave., bet. W. 94th and W. 95th Sts. W side. 1968. **Horace Ginsbern & Assocs**.

Alternating the arrangement of balconies—separated on odd floors and joined on even floors—creates a powerful façade rhythm—an exercise in student design more than an appropriate West Side façade.

[W10] **147 West 94th Street** (row house), bet. Columbus and Amsterdam Aves. N side. 1900s.

The ornate pressed-metal bay window and cornice give this some personal eccentricity.

W8

[W11] **125-139 and 151-159 West 93rd Street** (row houses), bet. Columbus and Amsterdam Aves. N side. ca. 1890.

Two groups of Queen Anne façades in red and gray. Curiously restrained for this style.

[W12] **Junior High School 118, Manhattan, Joan of Arc Junior High School**, 154 W. 93rd St., bet. Columbus and Amsterdam Aves. 1941. **Eric Kebbon**.

Reflecting relatively high land values, this school was built upward rather than laterally. Almost mimicking in limestone relief the high-rise character of the building is a luxuriant mythic beanstalk emerging from an urn; it "grows" between the entrance doors.

W9

[W13] **Templo Adventista del Septimo Dia**/originally The Nippon Club, 161 W. 93rd St., bet. Columbus and Amsterdam Aves. 1912. **John Van Pelt**.

The Chicago School crossbred with Florence: the brick frieze alternates with windows, simulating the metopes and triglyphs of a Greek temple (as borrowed for the Italian Renaissance). The cornice is extraordinary; it sails overhead with the assurance of **Lorenzo de' Medici**.

W11

[W14] **Columbus Park Towers** (apartments), 100 W. 94th St., SW cor. Columbus Ave. to W. 93rd St. 1967. **Ballard, Todd & Snibbe**.

WEST SIDE URBAN RENEWAL AREA

see pages 367–370

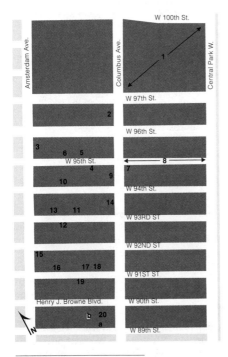

MANHATTAN VALLEY

see pages 371–372

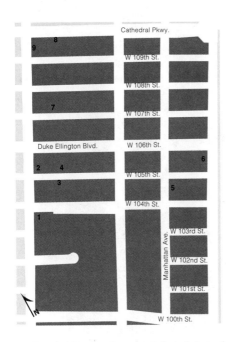

Long bold upturned concrete balcony balustrades dominate this brown brick slab.

[W15] **Central Baptist Church**, 659 Amsterdam Ave., SE cor. W. 92nd St. 1915-1916.

Collegiate Gothic, with a corner tower worthy of **Ralph Adams Cram**. Marvel at the crockets and finials.

W15

W16

W17

W18

W19

[W16] **149-163 West 91st Street** (row houses), bet. Columbus and Amsterdam Aves. 1890s.

Soulmates with Trinity School next door, some of their spaces have been co-opted by their next-door neighbor. Would you rather live in one of these venerable Romanesque brownstones or in Trinity House down the block?

[W17] **Trinity School, Main Building**, 121-147 W. 91st St., bet. Columbus and Amsterdam Aves. N side. 1893-1894. **Charles C. Haight.**

[W18] **East Building**/originally Parish House, St. Agnes Chapel (Episcopal), adjacent to and east of main building. 1888-1892. **William A. Potter.** ● Restorations, 1990s. **Buttrick, White & Burtis.**

Founded in 1709. Among the many interlocked buildings that this school occupies are the Anglo-Italianate brownstone Main Building, the wonderful Romanesque Revival remnant of an otherwise demolished Trinity Parish outpost (St. Agnes Chapel), and the podium of Trinity House.

[W19] **Play area, Stephen Wise Towers**, N.Y.C. Housing Authority, W. 90th to W. 91st Sts., midblock bet. Columbus and Amsterdam Aves. Play area only. **Richard G. Stein & Assocs.**, architects. **Constantino Nivola**, sculptor.

A modern horse fair for West Side cowchildren is the feature of this play area, subsidized by the J. M. Kaplan Fund to enliven otherwise pedestrian public housing. It has seen some heavy use but, alas, there is no ASPCA to protect concrete horses.

[W20] **600 Columbus Avenue** (apartments), bet. W. 89th and W. 90th Sts. W side. 1987. [W20a] **103-105 West 89th Street** ("town houses"), bet. Columbus and Amsterdam Aves. 1987. [W20b] **Community Garden**, bet. W. 89th and W. 90th St. behind 600 Columbus Ave. 1988. All by **Hoberman & Wasserman**, architects. **The Schnadelbach Partnership**, landscape architect.

The greenhouses along Columbus Avenue make a graceful transition from the setback slab and the streetfront stores below. The "town houses" are a pleasant bow to the tradition of the sidestreeted West Side. But whereas most of the West Side was originally composed of single-family houses, these were built to be apartment units from the start.

W20a

MANHATTAN VALLEY

A new event in Manhattan's usually predictable gridiron plan occurs at West 100th Street. It is here, between Central Park West and Columbus Avenue, that a new north-south thoroughfare is born: Manhattan Avenue, which strikes out northward across Cathedral Parkway into Harlem. As it moves north, the topography it covers begins to drop (as does the economic level of the community), and this descent of the terrain has given rise to the area's unofficial name: Manhattan Valley. We define it in this guide as bordered by West 100th Street and Cathedral Parkway (West 110th Street) and by Central Park West and Amsterdam Avenue.

M1

M2

[M1] **American Youth Hostels**/originally Association for the Relief of Respectable Aged Indigent Females, 891 Amsterdam Ave., bet. W. 103rd and W. 104th Sts. E side. 1881-1883. **Richard Morris Hunt**. Addition, **Charles A. Rich**. 1907-1908 🖤 Converted to hostel, 1990. **Larsen Associates**.

Vacated by the Association in 1975, this institutional landmark, once open only to women who had not "lived as servants," is now an international youth hostel. Its red brick forms and its busy, dormered and gabled roof lines are a visual asset to the neighborhood.

 [M2] **West End Presbyterian Church**, 325 Amsterdam Ave., NE cor. 1 W. 105th St. 1891. **Henry Kilburn**.

Restrained Romanesque Revival—in the subdued north Italian mode, much in contrast to **H. H. Richardson**'s lusty works. The tall, delicately striped, brick corner tower anchors this intersection from afar. The pressed terra-cotta ornament reads as incised stone, delicate in its intricate detail.

[M3] **Public School 145, Manhattan, The Bloomingdale School**, 150 W. 105th St., bet. Columbus and Amsterdam Aves. S side. 1961. **Unger & Unger**.

Bright vermilion columns, with a concrete entrance canopy reminiscent of angels' wings, highlight this school's façade.

[M4] **St. Gerasimos Greek Orthodox Church**, 155 W. 105th St., bet. Columbus and Amsterdam Aves. N side. 1951. **Kokkins & Lyons**.

M4

A historicist design that "foresaw the future": a Post-Modernist might have been pleased to accomplish this exaggerated façade.

[M5] **Manhattan Valley Town Houses**, Manhattan Ave. bet. W. 104th and W. 105th Sts. E side. 1986. **Rosenblum/Harb**.

M5

A reductionist row that pales in comparison to the richly detailed 1888 houses across Manhattan Avenue.

[M6] Originally **New York Cancer Hospital**/later Towers Nursing Home/now apartments, 2 W. 106th St., SW cor. Central Park W. 1884-1886. Additions, 1889-1890. **Charles C. Haight.** ● Remodeled and adjacent residential tower added, 2001. **RTKB Architects**, **Perkins Eastman Architects**, and **Victor Caliandro**.

M6

This castellated emigré from the Loire Valley has charmed the Upper West Side for more than a century. The first American hospital devoted exclusively to cancer patients, it later served as a nursing home and may yet be party to the condominiums that so many have promised on this site for so long.

[M7] **171-173 West 107th Street** (apartment house)/originally Edison Company substation, bet. Columbus and Amsterdam Aves. N side. ca. 1916. Remodeled with added tower, 1990s.

Even dynamos were once housed in utilitarian structures of architectural interest. Cleaned up, and en-towered, it forms classy apartments and the entrance to the towered superposed annex.

M7

[M8] **Cathedral Parkway Houses** (apartments), 125 W. 109th St., bet. Columbus and Amsterdam Aves. to Cathedral Pkwy. N side. 1975. **Davis Brody & Assocs.** and **Roger Glasgow**.

Two enormous zigzag towers occupy opposite corners of this hilly midblock site; between them a private, terraced, open space leaps from level to level, street to street. The towers, cousins to **Davis, Brody**'s Waterside, Yorkville, and Ruppert, and Riverpark in the Bronx, are here more self-consciously articulated in plan and massing to minimize their impact upon the adjacent smaller-scale community. The site was formerly occupied by Woman's Hospital.

[M9] **West 110th Street substation, Con Edison**, 464 W. 110th St. SE cor. Amsterdam Ave. to W. 109th St. 1964. **Con Edison architectural staff.**

M8

Albert Speer might have liked this forbidding mausoleum, which takes far too much for granite. But perhaps that's an insult to Speer.

Colonial

Georgian/ Federal

Greek Revival

Gothic Revival

Villa

S6, Bethesda Fountain

Romanesque Revival

Central Park Scenic Landmark, Fifth Avenue to Central Park West, 59th Street to 110th Street. 1858-1876. With many later modifications. **Frederick Law Olmsted** and **Calvert Vaux.**

Renaissance Revival

This great work of art, the granddaddy of America's naturally landscaped parks, was named a **National Historic Landmark** in 1965. Better still, for the sake of its eternal preservation, it is now a "scenic landmark," so designated by the New York City Landmarks Preservation Commission. This latter designation, happily, has teeth (whereas the national one is largely honorific and hopeful). Many believe that this park, Prospect Park, and the Brooklyn Bridge are the three greatest creations in New York City.

Roman Revival

But who made this 840-acre (larger than Monaco) masterpiece possible in the center of New York City? One of the first was the poet and newspaper editor **William Cullen Bryant,** who in 1844 called for a large, public pleasure ground (at that time Washington Square was considered uptown). After landscape architect **Andrew Jackson Downing** appealed for a park, the idea caught on, and both mayoralty contestants made it a promise in the 1850 campaign. The winner, **Ambrose C. Kingsland,** kept his word, and the Common Council took action.

Art Deco/

Art Moderne

The site was then physically unprepossessing: "A pestilential spot where miasmic odors taint every breath of air," one report concluded. But it was available. Land was acquired (1856) for $5.5 million and surveyed by **Egbert L. Viele.** Clearing began the next year: squatters and hogs were forcibly removed, often with the aid of the police, bone-boiling works and swill mills were torn down, swamps were drained, and the omnipresent Manhattan schist was blasted.

Modern/ Post-Modern

The first Board of Park Commissioners, helped by a committee including Bryant and the writer **Washington Irving,** decided in 1857 that an open competition should determine the park's design.

Greensward, so named by contestants **Frederick Law Olmsted** and **Calvert Vaux,** won out among the 33 designs submitted. It was a simple, uncluttered plan, calling for a picturesque landscape: glade, copse, water, and rock outcroppings. Bridges (each individually designed by Vaux) separated footpaths, bridle paths, and the carriage drives—which were curved

S2

to prevent racing. The four sunken transverse roads for crosstown traffic were revolutionary.

Ten million cartloads of stone, earth, and topsoil were moved in or out of the site as Greensward construction progressed. It took nearly 20 years but, long before completion, the park became the place for rich and poor alike to promenade, to see and be seen. Today it is even more the playground for New Yorkers: for some a place to enjoy nature, for many the only "country" they have ever seen, for others a magnificently designed Garden of Eden to ease the strains of city living, and most recently a place of amateur gambling, gamboling, and beer drinking for residents of all boroughs.

Central Park is the forecourt and front garden to the residential slabs and towers of Central Park South, Central Park West, Central Park North, and Fifth Avenue (otherwise Central Park East). At the southeast corner the surrounding towers cast romantic reflections in its waters (for the postcard maker) and enjoy the Plaza's great space, a happy symbiosis for both.

Invasions: Despite continuing threats of preposterous intrusions, the original plan was closely followed until the advent of the automobile and active sports. In 1912 the gravel drives were paved with asphalt, and two new entrances were cut through on Central Park South. Permanent tennis courts were then constructed. The first paved playground, the Heckscher, appeared in 1926. By the 1950s large structures had sprung up, all partially financed by philanthropists: the Wollman Memorial Rink, the Delacorte Theater, the Children's Zoo, and the Lasker PoolRink: some worthy additions, others vulgar and ugly intruders. The establishment of the Central Park Conservancy offers an opportunity to reconstruct the park in an Olmstedian vision adapted to current needs . . . but only if the well-meaning gifts can be directed toward thoughtful goals.

CENTRAL PARK

see pages 373–379

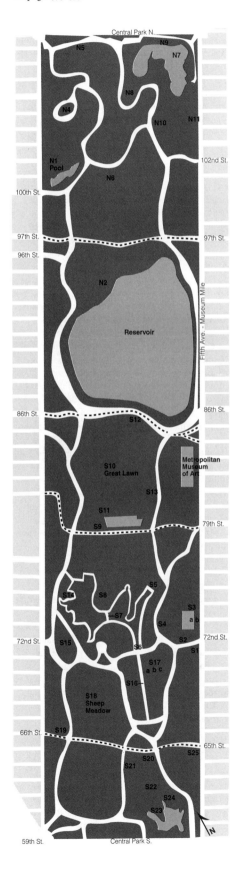

South and North:
By topography and design the park falls into two sections. The large "pastoral" south is by far the more familiar; but the once neglected north is well worth a visit for its contrasting wild picturesqueness—a worthiness best savored in groups by day (avoided totally by dusk or dark) for personal security. The following two tours are meant to serve only as an introduction to these sections.

Walking Tour A, The South: Conservatory Water (at East 72nd Street and Fifth Avenue) to Grand Army Plaza (59th Street and Fifth Avenue) or the Zoo. Arrive via 68th Street Station of the Lexington Avenue IRT subway (No. 6 train); Madison or Fifth Avenue buses.

START at Fifth Avenue and 72nd Street (this is **Inventors' Gate**, one of Vaux's 18 named gates piercing the park's wall) [S1]. Turn north, crossing the park drive, and bear left past the **Pilgrim Memorial** (1885. **John Quincy Adams Ward**, sculptor) [S2]. Note the pilgrim's spectacular bronze boots. Descend Pilgrim Hill to the **Conservatory Water** [S3a], a formal neo-Renaissance concrete basin, named for the conservatory (greenhouse) promised but unbuilt on its eastern shore. Model and toy boats, some of which are stored at the **Alice H. and Edward A. Kerbs Memorial Boathouse** (1954) [S3b], are usually sailing here (races April through October mornings). Two statues overlook this water: **Alice in Wonderland Margarita Delacorte Memorial** (**Jose de Creeft**, sculptor) and **Hans Christian Andersen** (1956. **George J. Lober**, sculptor. **Otto F. Langmann**, architect.). Neither is of any great artistic merit, but both are beloved by swarming children (storytelling at Andersen, Saturday mornings, May-September). From here look across the water to enjoy a view of Fifth Avenue through a filigree of branches and/or leaves.

S2

Continue around the western shore to the path leading west to **Trefoil Arch** [S4] (restored, 1985, **Beyer Blinder Belle**), a brownstone tunnel with a wood ceiling, and pass under the East Drive to reach the shore of **The Lake** [S5], where a gondola accompanies the flotilla of rowboats. The **72nd Street Boathouse** (1954) [S5a] is in the brick neo-Victorian style favored by one-time Parks Commissioner **Robert Moses**. Note the rowboat sculpture, from a fudgy clay, cast into bronze, in the front court (1967 **Irwin Glusker**, sculptor). The boathouse has a restaurant and a pleasant terrace overlooking The Lake. The bicycle concession to the right is jammed, particularly on those days and evenings when the park drives, closed to traffic, become the cyclist's province.

S3b

The path along the south shore reaches the **Bethesda Terrace** [S6]. (**The Ehrenkrantz Group & Eckstut**, architects; **Philip Winslow**, landscape architect.) It is the only formal architectural element of the Greensward Plan. **Jacob Wrey Mould** detailed the stonework, but Vaux was the conceptual designer. **Bethesda Fountain** (1870 **Emma Stebbins**, sculptor. **Calvert Vaux**, architect) is the centerpiece, with a bronze winged Angel of the Waters crowning vigorous chubby cherubs (Purity, Health, Peace, and Temperance). The terrace is a faded elegance of brick paving, sandstone bordered, walled, and crowned.

S6

Side trips: Northwest of The Terrace stands **Bow Bridge** [S7] (1860 **Calvert Vaux**. Restored, 1974), a cast-iron elegance spanning the Lake to the Ramble. The bosky **Ramble** [S8], where even vigilant bird watchers have been known to lose their way on the mazelike paths, contains meandering streams, exotic trees and shrubs, and small, hidden lawns. At its north the Ramble ascends to Vista Rock, topped by **Belvedere Castle** [S9], former

S9

home of the city's weather station (Restored, 1978, **James
Lamantia**). Below the Castle is Belvedere Lake, last vestige of the
old reservoir drained in 1929. The reservoir's dry bed was used by
squatters during the Depression, then filled in, becoming the
Great Lawn [S10], today's favored spot for touch football, soccer,
and softball. The **Delacorte Theater** [S11], with summer
Shakespeare, hovers over the new lake's western flank. The
Central Park Precinct, N.Y.C. Police Department [S12], on the
85th/86th Street Transverse Road, is another **Calvert Vaux** building (1871). East, behind the Metropolitan Museum of Art, rises
the **Obelisk** [S13] from the reign of Thutmose III (ca. 1450 B.C.).
A gift from the khedive of Egypt, it was erected in the park in
1881. Resting on a promontory on the west side of the Lake (near
the West 77th Street park entrance) is **The Ladies Pavilion** [S14]
(1871. **Vaux & Mould**). It was purportedly moved there from its
original location on the edge of the park at Columbus Circle,
where it had sheltered ladies awaiting streetcars, and was later
bumped for the erection of The Maine Monument. Vandalized
and ruined at the lake shore, it was reincarnated through the
efforts of the Parks Department monuments officer, **Joseph
Bresnan**, and is now a lacy cast-iron Victorian delight. To its
south, near the West 72nd Street park entrance, is the Italian
mosaic spelling out "Imagine" set in the paving of **Strawberry
Fields** [S15] (1983. **Bruce Kelly**, landscape architect), a gift from
John Lennon's widow, **Yoko Ono**, in memory of the legendary
Beatle killed in front of the Dakota, which overlooks the site.
Resume tour.

S6

The **Mall** [S16], the Park's grand promenade, lies south of the
Terrace Arcade. Pass through, noting the glazed and decorated
tile ceiling. The Mall's axis points to the Belvedere Castle, delib-
erately kept small by architect Vaux to lengthen the perspective,
but full-grown trees have obliterated the vista. Behind the intrusive limestone halfhemispherical vaulted **Naumburg Bandshell**
[S17a] is **The Pergola** [S17b]. (Rebuilt, 1987 **Laura Starr**, landscape architect.) A low, lightfiltered wood trellis, it is one of the
park's few wisteria-covered arbors. Behind it is **Rumsey
Playground** [S17c]. (Redesigned, 1986, **Philip Winslow**.) The
Mall, in recent years, has been a place for action, rather than
strolling: juggling, guitar playing, drug dealing, beer drinking,
gambling, hamburger eating, and so forth.

S13

Walter Scott

Shakespeare

On The Mall are several statues: *Fitzgreene Halleck* (1877. **J. Wilson MacDonald**), a prissy and pretentious bronze of a self-styled poet. *Walter Scott* (1872. **John Steell**). The 100th anniversary of Scott's birth is memorialized by this dour bronze, a copy of Steell's original in the Scott Memorial in Edinburgh. *Robert Burns* (1880. **John Steell**) is represented as a faraway and saccharine romantic. *Columbus* (1894. **Jeronimo Suñol**): an entranced religious maniac. *Shakespeare* (1870. **John Quincy Adams Ward**): the thoughtful bard in pantaloons.

Side trip: West of The Mall, past the park's closed Center Drive, stretches the **Sheep Meadow** [S18], a sweeping lawn where sheep could safely graze until banished in 1934 (they lived in the nearby Sheepfold, now converted to the Tavern-on-the-Green). From the north end there is a splendid view of skyscrapers. To the southwest, along Central Park West, stands the **Tavern-on-the-Green** [S19], periodically renovated for glitzy greenhouse and terrace dining. Resume tour.

Continue at the southern end of The Mall, cross the drive, and don't blame Olmsted for not providing an underground passage here: the Marble Arch, the park's most famous bridge, was removed in the 1930s. Take the southeast path along the drive, and while crossing over the 65th Street Transverse Road, notice how little the sunken drive intrudes into the park. To the right, a path leads past **The Dairy** [S20], a sturdy Gothic Revival building provided once again with a copy of its original porch (Restored, 1979, **James Lamantia** with **Weisberg Castro Assocs.**). Note Manhattan schist and sandstone neo-Gothic colonnettes. Vaux designed it.

Another side trip: Head west, to the north of the hillsite of the Kinderberg, once a large arbor. It's now replaced by the squat **Chess and Checkers House** [S21], a gift of financier **Bernard Baruch**, a red and beige brick neo-Ruskinian *cum* Moses (Robert, that is) octagonal lump. Continue west, under Playmates Arch beneath the drive to the Michael Friedsam Memorial Carousel (Building, 1951. Carousel, 1900s), another beige and red brick octagon replacing an earlier one, destroyed by fire. Resume tour.

From The Dairy, after dropping down to the left, the path passes east of the Chess and Checkers site. Skirt southeast around the **Wollman Memorial Rink** [S22] and go up the hill along the fence enclosing the **Bird Sanctuary** [S23]. **Gapstow Bridge**, crossing **The Pond** [S24], is a good place to admire the reflections of the city's towers in the water below. A few swans and many ducks are usually swimming around. Swan boats, the same as those still in Boston's Public Garden, sailed here until 1924. Leave the park by the gate across from Sherman's statue or, if you want to visit the Zoo, go via Inscope Arch under the East Drive, northeast of the Pond.

END of tour: *Nearest transit is the BMT Broadway Line (N and R trains) Fifth Avenue Station at East 60th Street or Fifth or Madison Avenue buses.*

Side trip: The Zoo [S25], off Fifth Avenue at 64th Street, is a favorite haunt of New Yorkers. It is a formal plaza once surrounded by WPA-built red brick arched buildings now totally redesigned (1988. **Kevin Roche John Dinkeloo & Assocs.**) to provide glazed arcades and more professional operation by the New York Zoological Garden staff. A constant is the centrally located and much beloved sea lion pool. The Arsenal is a participant in the Zoo plaza by default.

Walking Tour B, The North: The Pool to Conservatory Garden. (IND Eighth Avenue subway (B or C trains) to 96th Street Station.) Start at Central Park West and West 100th Street.

The Boys' Gate gives access to a path descending to **The Pool** [N1]. It is the start of the waterway that flows east to Harlem Meer and was once the course of Montayne's Rivulet, which led to the East River. Across the West Drive and to the south of the 96th Street Transverse are a group of tennis courts popular with the public but an intrusion into the Olmsted & Vaux vision. In 1987 plans were offered by the Central Park Conservancy to replace the 1930 **Tennis House** [N2] with a new structure at a higher elevation (1989. **Buttrick White & Burtis**). This area of the park is also the home of cast-iron **Bridge No. 28** [N3] (1861. **Calvert Vaux** with **E.C. Miller**), a Gothic Revival masterpiece.

Side trip: North of the Pool is the **Great Hill** [N4], where picnickers once enjoyed an unobstructed view of the Hudson and East Rivers. Perched on a cliff to the northeast is a lonely **Blockhouse** [N5], a remnant of the fortifications built during the War of 1812 when the British threatened the city. Resume tour.

At the eastern end of The Pool, the Glen Span carries the West Drive over The Ravine. On the other side flows **The Loch**, formerly an abundant body of water, now a trickle. This is very picturesque and completely cut off from the city.

Side trip: To the south, behind the slope, is the **North Meadow** [N6], scene of hotly contested baseball games: to get there, take Springbanks Arch. Resume tour.

In wet weather the Loch cascades down before disappearing under the East Drive at Huddlestone Bridge. Through the arch in front of **Harlem Meer** [N7] you can see the park's most disastrous "improvement," the **Loula D. Lasker Pool-Rink** [N8]. New Yorkers have always tried to give things—especially buildings—to their park. Few succeeded until recent generations of park administrators misguidedly began again to encourage large philanthropic bequests.

Across Harlem Meer, backing onto Central Park North, is a Central Park Conservancy project to provide quality food service and such amenities as boat rentals to an arriving upscale community at the **Charles A. Dana Discovery Center** [N9] (1993. **Buttrick, White & Burtis**).

To the right of The Loch find **Lamppost No. 0554**. (All the older lampposts, designed by **Henry Bacon** in 1907, bear a street-designating plaque; here, the first two digits indicate that this one stands at 105th Street.) A path goes sharply uphill and then turns east, crossing the East Drive below McGown's Pass, which was fortified by the British during the Revolutionary War. **The Mount** [N10], to the right, was for many years the site of a tavern; its chief ornament today is the park's mulch pile.

The path descends to **Conservatory Garden** [N11], designed by **Thomas D. Price** in 1936. The Greensward Plan called for a large arboretum of native trees and shrubs to be planted here. Instead, a conservatory was built at the turn of the century but torn down in 1934. On the east side the Vanderbilt Gate opens on Fifth Avenue (open 8 A.M.-dusk every day). Nearby is the Museum of the City of New York, where historical material about the park is on display.

N11

END of tour: Transportation: IRT Lexington Avenue subway at East 96th Street (No. 6 train), and Fifth or Madison Avenue buses.

Upper East Side

**THE GOLD COAST • METROPOLITAN MUSEUM VICINITY
CARNEGIE HILL AND BEYOND • EAST OF EDEN
HOSPITAL ROW • YORKVILLE
GRACIE SQUARE AND ENVIRONS**

 Colonial

 *Georgian/
Federal*

 *Greek
Revival*

 *Gothic
Revival*

 Villa

 *Romanesque
Revival*

 *Renaissance
Revival*

 *Roman
Revival*

 *Art Deco/
Art Moderne*

 *Modern/
Post-Modern*

The area's first development was not residential but, rather, recreational: Central Park. Toward the middle of the last century, a tremendous influx of Irish and German immigrants, dislocated by economic and political turmoil in their homeland, was straining the City's resources. Reformers were pressuring for a great public park to serve a population expected to grow even further. In the 1850s **Mayor Fernando Wood** and his Tammany Hall cronies foresaw the construction of the park as an opportunity to create enormous numbers of patronage positions among the new electorate. And the park's central site would neatly divide upper Manhattan into twin development opportunities: the rough terrain of the West Side (to be reserved for later) and the relatively flat East Side. The latter was made more accessible from downtown by cutting through Madison and Lexington Avenues as additions to the original gridiron street plan of 1811.

The first transit connections from downtown were horsecar lines along Second, Third, and Madison Avenues and steam trains (including local service) along today's Park Avenue. Not surprisingly, the first row house development, during the 1860s and until the Panic of 1873, followed these routes of opportunity. The late 1870s brought the Second and Third Avenue elevated lines from downtown—mass transit. With it came the masses, housed in an explosive development of tenements—many of which remain—in the area's eastern flank.

The elegant associations with the term Upper East Side are relatively recent. To those who could afford them, Park Avenue's steam trains provided accessibility but also brought smoke and noise, thus creating an "other side of the tracks" opportunity. Beginning in the 1890s, between Park Avenue and Central Park, a corridor formed that attracted capitalists from downtown residential enclaves, such as lower Fifth Avenue and Gramercy Park, to costly sites along Fifth Avenue—the Gold Coast—and to lesser ones along the side streets and brownstone-lined Madison Avenue. East of Park Avenue huddled a mixture of row houses, stables, and carriage houses—truly the other side of the tracks.

Most of the mansions built at the turn of the century along Fifth (except those now used largely as museums) were demolished in two waves of high-rise luxury apartment development, the first in the Roaring Twenties, the second following World War II. In response to the first building boom, Madison Avenue's brownstones were altered to provide neighborhood shops and services for an expanding number of affluent apartment dwellers. Gracie Square and parts of East End Avenue then also saw apartment development.

The post-World War II boom (to the east signaled by the 1956 demolition of the grim Third Avenue el structure) has extended—with gasps for air—to the present day. It transformed practically every Upper East Side development site into a pot of gold and turned Madison Avenue into the ultrachic shopping street for wealthy Americans—and internationals as well.

UPPER EAST SIDE KEY MAP

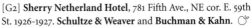

THE GOLD COAST

Borrowing a term initially used to denote Fifth Avenue along Central Park, together with its park blocks, the area included below is bounded by Fifth and and a line east of Lexington, from just above 59th Street to 78th. Much—but not all—is officially designated as the Upper East Side Historic District. The upper reaches of Fifth Avenue are covered in precincts called Metropolitan Museum Vicinity and Carnegie Hill.

[G1] **Upper East Side Historic District** 🍎
In 1981, sixteen years after the passage of the city's landmarks law, the unachievable was achieved: the establishment under Chairman **Kent L. Barwick** of a historic district that stretches along Fifth Avenue's gold coast from 59th to 78th Streets—where it abuts the Metropolitan Museum Historic District—and reaches inland in a leg that wraps up to 79th and Park. In between, its boundaries irregularly encompass properties beyond Madison and Park Avenues to the east, even crossing Lexington from 69th and 71st. Upper East Side Historic District properties in the Gold Coast area are identified:

G2

[G2] **Sherry Netherland Hotel**, 781 Fifth Ave., NE cor. E. 59th St. 1926-1927. **Schultze & Weaver** and **Buchman & Kahn**.
A tower fit for a muezzin crowns its peaked and finialed roof. The restaurant and bar along Fifth Avenue, now Cipriani's, is one of New York's greatest: venerable elegance.

G2a

[G2a] **Geoffrey Beene**/originally Diane von Furstenberg, 783 Fifth Ave. (in the Sherry-Netherland Hotel). 1984. **Michael Graves**.
A token presence from Graves. After the aborting of his scheme for expansion of the Guggenheim Museum, this remained his only work in the New York streetscape until completion of the Impala (apartments), at 75th and First Avenue.

[G3] **Sidewalk clock**, in front of 783 Fifth Ave., bet. E. 59th and E. 60th Sts. E side. 1927. **E. Howard Clock Company**. 🍎
General Sherman's timepiece as he gallops through history in The Plaza.

[G4] **The Metropolitan Club**, 1-11 E. 60th St., NE cor. Fifth Ave. 1891-1894 **Stanford White** of **McKim, Mead & White**. E wing, 1912, **Ogden Codman, Jr.** All 🍎

G4

THE GOLD COAST

see pages 382–415

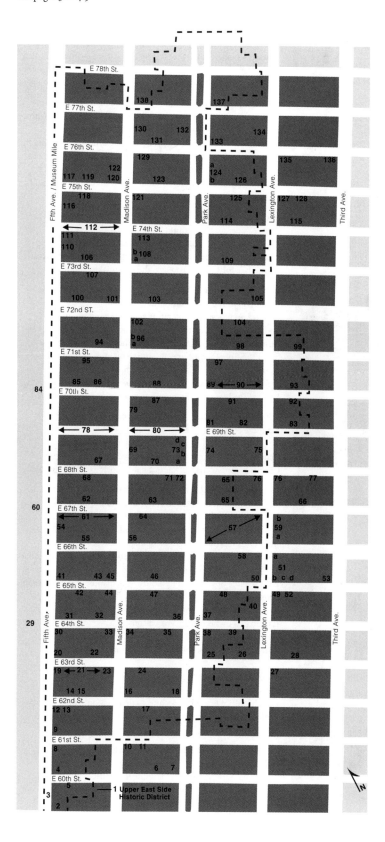

E 78th St.

138

137

E 77th St.

130   132   134

131   133

E 76th St.

129

122   123   a   135   136

117 119   120   124

E 75th St.   118   b   126

116   121   125   127 128

114

← 112 →   115

E 74th St.

111   113

110   b 108   109

106   a

E 73rd St.

107

100   101   103   105

E 72nd ST.

102   104

b 96   98   99

94   a

E 71st St.

95   97

85   86   88   89 ← 90 →   93

E 70th St.

87   91   92

79   81   82   83

84   ← 78 →   ← 80 →   E 69th St.

d

67   69   73 c   74   75

70   b

a

E 68th St.

68   71 72   65   76   76   77

62   63   65   66

60   E 67th St.

← 61 →   64   57

54   ↘

55   56   ↙

E 66th St.

58   a

41   43 45   46   50   51   53

b c d

E 65th St.

42   44   47   48   49 52   b

31   32   36   37   40

E 64th St.

30   33   34   35   38   39

20   22   25   26   28

E 63rd St.

19 ← 21 → 23   24   27

14 15   16   18

E 62nd St.

12 13   17

9   10 11

E 61st St.

8   6   7

4   6   7

E 60th St.

5   1 Upper East Side

3   Historic District

2

Fifth Ave. / Museum Mile   Madison Ave.   Park Ave.   Lexington Ave.   Third Ave.

29

N

G5

J. P. Morgan organized this club primarily for his friends who were not accepted in others. An Italian palazzo is crossed with a proper English carriage entrance and courtyard. For those able to enter, the interior is an extravaganza of space, marble coffers, and gilt: Corinthian columns, velvet ropes, and scarlet carpeting. Plans to add a 37-story residential tower (**James Stewart Polshek & Partners**) atop the east wing (now occupied by the American Academy in Rome) and its connecting link were nixed by the Landmarks Preservation Commission in 1987.

[G5] **The Harmonie Club**, 4 E. 60th St., bet. Fifth and Madison Aves. S side. 1904-1906. **Stanford White** of **McKim, Mead & White**. Altered upward and inside. 1935. **Benjamin Wistar Morris**. ♂

A high-rise Renaissance palace: giant Corinthian pilasters in terra-cotta joined by sturdy limestone Ionic columns define a rich façade over an austere limestone plinth. It is the second home of the club founded by members of the crowd chronicled in *Our Crowd*.

[G6] **The Grolier Club**, 47 E. 60th St., bet. Madison and Park Aves. N side. 1917. **Bertram G. Goodhue**. Exhibitions open Mo-Sa 10-5; closed Su. Closed Aug. 212-838-6690.

Named for the 16th-century French bibliophile **Jean Grolier**, this club is for those devoted to the bookmaking crafts.

[G7] **Christ Church** (Methodist), 520 Park Ave., NW cor. E. 60th St. 1932. **Ralph Adams Cram**.

G7

A church designed to appear aged: the random limestone and brick is intended to look like a sophisticated patch job, centuries old. Similarly, the marble and granite columns appear to be, in the Romanesque and Byzantine manner, pillage from Roman temples. Handsome, and of impeccable taste, it is an archaeological and eclectic stage set for well-to-do parishioners. Look at the mosaic ceiling, especially when lit by blue bulbs.

[G8] **Hotel Pierre**, 795 Fifth Ave., SE cor. E. 61st St. 1929-1930. **Schultze & Weaver**. ♂

G8

A tall, slender, romantic hotel-apartment house with a mansard roof tower silhouette. Founded by celebrated chef Charles Pierre, whose restaurant had been at 230 Park Avenue.

[G9] **800 Fifth Avenue** (apartments), NE cor. E. 61st St. 1978. **Ulrich Franzen & Assocs.**, design architects; **Wechsler & Schimenti**, associate architects. ♂

G9

Here, until 1977, stood the shuttered town house of **Mrs. Marcellus Hartley Dodge**, the seldom used, seemingly abandoned home of a Rockefeller kin. Its replacement is set behind a 3-story limestone-clad screen wall, responding literally to the Fifth Avenue Special Zoning District's demands, and matches in height—but not in ambience—the Knickerbocker Club to the north. On the side street a refreshing façade of brick is revealed, syncopated by tiers of curved balconies.

East 61st Street, between Madison and Park Avenues:

[G10] **667 Madison Avenue** (offices), SE cor. E. 61st St. 1987. **David Paul Helpern**.

This office tower, the architect's first in Manhattan, is a vigorous yet carefully controlled design that gracefully turns a corner within the complex rules of the Zoning Resolution.

[G11] **36 East 61st Street** (rowhouse), bet. Madison and Park Aves. 1890s.

G11

Beaux Arts grandeur in limestone and brick. The curved glass adds another notch of elegance.

East 62nd Street, between Fifth and Madison Avenues:

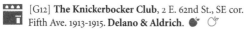

[G12] **The Knickerbocker Club,** 2 E. 62nd St., SE cor. Fifth Ave. 1913-1915. **Delano & Aldrich.** ● ♂

London Georgian more than American Federal: a revival in either instance. The renaissance of 18th-century forms in early 20th-century New York opened the door to subtle and diverse architectural options.

[G13a] **Curzon House** (apartments): Combination of 4 E. 62nd St. 1880. **Breen & Nason.** Present façade, 1898, **Clinton & Russell.** Formerly 6 E. 62nd St. 1901. **Welch, Smith & Provot.** General renovations and addition to W of former 4 E. 62nd St., 1985, **Stephen B. Jacobs & Assocs.** ♂

G12

Since 1931 old Nos. 4 and 6 had been the former York Club. In the superheated 1980s luxury housing boom, when it became clear that the Landmarks Preservation Commission would not permit the demolition of the two town houses for a high-rise replacement, they were converted to condos and expanded westward to fill the gap next to the Knickerbocker Club. The infill addition is quite respectable except for heavy-handed window framing. Particularly note the witty see-through dormers.

G13a

[G13b] **Offices and apartments**/originally Edmund L. Baylies House, 10 E. 62nd St. S side. 1906. **Hoppin, Koen & Huntington.** ♂

The floors above the parlor level decrease in height as they increase in intricacy. The French windows at the second floor offer sinuous foms overseen by guardian voussoirs.

[G14] **The Fifth Avenue Synagogue,** 5 E. 62nd St. N side. 1956. **Percival Goodman.** ♂

An urban temple. Clad in finely striated cream-colored stone, with sharply incised, cat's-eye windows filled with stained glass. In daylight they read as black cat's eyes; after dark they glow once the interior is lit.

G13b

[G15] **Residence of the Permanent Representative of Japan to the United Nations**/onetime Johnson O'Connor Research Foundation/originally. Edith & Ernesto Fabbri House, 11 E. 62nd St. N side. 1898-1900. **Haydel & Shepard.** ♂

Exuberant limestone and pale-toned brick Beaux Arts commissioned by **William H. Vanderbilt**'s eldest daughter **Margaret Louisa Vanderbilt Shepard.** Upon completion she presented it to her daughter (née **Edith Shepard**) and son-in-law, the Fabbris. In 1911 the Fabbris moved to Paris and, in 1916, back to a new house at 7 East 95th. N.B: Architect **Augustus Shepard** was Edith Fabbri's cousin.

G14

G15

East 62nd Street, between Madison and Park Avenues.

G16b

[G16a] **The Limited** (women's apparel)/originally Louis Sherry's restaurant/later assorted shops, 691 Madison Ave., NE cor. E. 62nd St. 1928. **McKim, Mead & White.** ♂ Altered into stores, 1950. Redesigned for The Limited, 1986, **Beyer Binder Belle.**

A late MM&W neo-Classical/Art Deco ho-hum candy box now metamorphosed (and gilded) with spectacular success as the flagship for the supernova Indianapolis-based national womens-wear chain. The new boxy skylight gives the building dignity and adds the bulk it needs to effectively compete—architecturally—on Madison Avenue. A magnificent renovation.

[G16b] **Revlon Corporate Offices**/originally The Studio Club, 35 E. 62nd St. N side. 1905. **George Keller.** ♂

Columns and arches in a sextet of brick, terra-cotta, and limestone, with a loggia at the summit for a breath of air on a summer's evening. The ground-floor arcade is a prominent presence to those strolling by.

G17a

[G17a] **The Links Club**, 36 E. 62nd St. S side. 1916-1917. **Cross & Cross.** ♂

Creamy travertine frames rose-red Flemish-bond brickwork, making a neo-Georgian swell-fronted façade worthy of the real thing. If God is in the details, then this warm, evocative, exquisitely realized town house confirms His existence. Compare with the Assisium School on East 63rd [G28b].

[G17b] **40 East 62nd Street** (apartments), 1910. **Albert Joseph Bodker.** ♂

An 8-floor studio building borrowing medieval forms: tier upon tier of multipaned casemented bay windows tucked with unglazed terra-cotta into the façade. The two-story glazed terra-cotta base is rich with foliage and griffins.

[G18] **The Colony Club**, 564 Park Ave., NW cor. E. 62nd St. also known as 51 E. 62nd St. 1914-1916. **Delano & Aldrich.** ♂

Female social leadership is split between the Colony and the Cosmopolitan, the former oriented more to grandes dames, the latter to activists. The Colony was founded in 1903 by the wives of Those Who Mattered. This prissy neo-Georgian town palace replaced the original on lower Madison Avenue.

G18

East 63rd Street, between Fifth and Madison Avenues:

G21a

[G19] **817 Fifth Avenue** (apartments), SE cor. E. 63rd St. 1925. **George B. Post & Sons**. ♂

[G20] **820 Fifth Avenue** (apartments), NE cor. E. 63rd St. 1916. **Starrett & Van Vleck**. ♂

High-rise palazzi of copper-corniced limestone, these are two of the great eclectic apartment houses of New York, although 817 has lost its many-paned windows to sheets of fixed thermal glass. Glass eyes upon the park without pupils or irises.

G21b

[G21a] **The New York Academy of Sciences**/originally Mr. & Mrs. William Ziegler, Jr. House, 2 E. 63rd St. 1920. **Sterner & Wolfe**. ♂ Gallery open Sept-June, Mo-Fr 10-4. 212-838-0230

A pasty palace, large but unresolved, its cornice a remnant from the architecture of earlier and lesser row houses. Commissioned by the president of Royal Baking Powder, it was later purchased by Norman Bailey Woolworth, of the 5&10 family, who gave it to the Academy. The colossal iron fence is a lesson in how something necessarily large can be detailed to be in scale with its surroundings.

G22b

[G21b] **14 East 63rd Street** (row house), 1873. **J. G. and R. B. Lynd**. ♂ [G25c] **16, 18 East 63rd Street** (row houses), 1876. **Gage Inslee**. ♂

Brownstone mansions, unlike those endless, modest middle-class rows east of Park Avenue; the Composite-columned porches of Nos. 16 and 18 are grand for their time.

[G22a] **15 East 63rd Street** (row house), 1901. **John H. Duncan**. ♂ [G22b] **17 East 63rd Street** (row house), 1901. **Welch, Smith & Provot**. ♂

A generation newer than [G21b] across the street, No. 15 was built for stockbroker **Elias Asiel**, whose daughter **Irma** became **Mrs. Lyman G. Bloomingdale**, a founder of the nearby department store. No. 17 was the home of Brooklyn brewer **Joseph Huber** between 1911 and 1945. A 1990s penthouse addition replaces the mansard roof with the swooping terrace soffit and a glass wall. *Pas mal.*

G23

[G23] **The Bank of New York**, 63rd Street Office, 706 Madison Ave., SW cor. E 63rd St. 1921-1922. **Frank Easton Newman**. ♂

A charming neo-Federal house, that boasted a garden to the south along Madison, now infilled with ATM machines. The new addition offers subtle Georgian detail: white marble window reveals, rather than merely brick returns. In London's Bedford Square these are often simulated by painting and/or stuccoing the reveal.

G24b

[G24a] **The Lowell** (apartment hotel), 28 E. 63rd St., bet. Madison and Park Aves. 1925-1926. **Henry Churchill** and **Herbert Lippman**. Entrance mosaic, **Bertram Hartman**. ♂ Renovations, 1989. **Gruzen Samton**.

Tapestry brick and steel sash are the background for a startling and stylish glazed terra-cotta Art Deco ground floor. But the canopy belongs to another building. Bronze Greek acroteria? Who's in charge?

[G24b] **Assisium School, Missionary Sisters of the Third Order of St. Francis**/originally The Hangar Club, 36 E. 63rd St., bet. Madison and Park Aves. 1929-1930. **Cross & Cross**. ♂

A bowfront bay of brick and travertine is set against the flat body, much like the same architects' Links Club on East 62nd. A neo-Georgian composition of contrasting colors and textures. Simply wonderful.

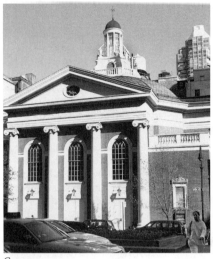

G25a

Kenneth Murchison (1872-1938), architect of such works as the railroad and ferry terminal in Hoboken (1906, extant), lived at 49 East 63rd Street between 1909 and 1926—prior to the Mediterraneanization of its façade (around 1930). In those days it still looked like No. 47, which bears the original 1884 neo-Grec brownstone front by Thom & Wilson. In the latter part of his career Murchison joined Raymond Hood, Godley & Fouilhoux, architects of the old McGraw-Hill Building and associates in the design of Rockefeller Center.

G25b

[G25a] Third Church of Christ, Scientist, 585 Park Ave., NE cor. E. 63rd St. 1923-1924. Delano & Aldrich. ☞
The lantern rises like a lighthouse over the modest dome, like a bit of Wren's London superimposed on the neo-Georgian bulk below. The unfluted Doric columns look fondly across Park Avenue toward their Colony Club Corinthian cousins a block to the south.

G26

[G25b] Originally Michael J. O'Reilly House/onetime Roy H. Frowick (Halston) House, 101 E. 63rd St., bet. Park and Lexington Aves. 1881. Cornelius O'Reilly. Altered, 1968. Paul Rudolph. ☞
A somber brown steel and dark glass grid gives an understated face to a dramatic set of domestic spaces within. Recast from a former stable-garage.

[G26] 123 East 63rd Street (townhouse), bet. Park and Lexington Aves. 1900. Trowbridge & Livingston.
The balcony for a Beaux Arts emperor: Napoleons I and III came from more austere architectural times, leaving this lush architecture for the successor waiting in the wings.

[G27] Barbizon Hotel/originally Barbizon Hotel for Women, 140 E. 63rd St., SE cor. Lexington Ave. 1927. Murgatroyd & Ogden. Lobby, restaurants, public spaces altered, 1986, Judith Stockman & Assocs., designers.
A romantic, tawny brick, neo-Gothic charmer, built originally for the young women in New York far from home, and now lovingly restored.

G28

[G28] Cyril and Barbara Rutherford Hatch House, 153 E. 63rd St., bet. Lexington and Third Aves. 1917-1919. Frederick J. Sterner. ●
A picturesque loner in well-crafted stucco by the designer of the "Block Beautiful" on 19th Street. A Spanish Baroque portal and decorative fence contrast with the austere building plane. Interesting owners: Mrs. Hatch, daughter of Mrs. William K. Vanderbilt; Broadway producer Charles B. Dillingham; ecdysiast Gypsy Rose Lee.

[G29] **The Arsenal, N.Y.C. Department of Parks & Recreation headquarters**, 821 Fifth Ave., in Central Park opp. E. 64th St. 1847-1851. **Martin E. Thompson**. Altered, 1860, **Richard Morris Hunt**. Gallery open to the public. Gallery open Mo-Fr 9-4:30; closed Sa & Su.

The "fortified" neo-Gothic retreat, in brick and "load-bearing ivy," of New York City's parks commissioners. Originally the main cache of military explosives in the state, it became City property within nine years, and then the incubator of the American Museum of Natural History. The pyramidal roofs that once topped its octagonal towers, evident in early photos, are long gone.

[G30] Originally **Edward J. Berwind House**/later Institute of Aeronautical Sciences, 2 E. 64th St., SE cor. Fifth Ave. 1893-1896. **Nathan Clark Mellen**. Dormers, 1902. **Horace Trumbauer**.

Berwind built this house for "town" and The Elms in Newport, R.I., for "country." Then the world's largest owner of coal mines, Berwind fueled the U.S. Navy throughout World War I. Note the richly modeled bronze railings that surround the "moat." After intervening institutional uses, it was pent-housed and converted to apartments in the late 1970s.

G30

[G31] **New India House**/originally Marshall Orme and Caroline Astor Wilson House, 3 E. 64th St., bet. Fifth and Madison Aves. 1900-1903. **Warren & Wetmore**. Interior altered for Government of India, 1952, **William Lescaze**.

Powerful modeled Beaux Arts limestone, but the guts are at the sky: slate and copper mansarded attic, grand dormers, and eyebrowed oculi. Mrs. Wilson was Caroline Schermerhorn Astor, daughter of *the* Mrs. Astor (Caroline Webster Schermerhorn Astor) of "400" fame. Mamma lived around the corner in a mansion on the site of today's Temple Emanu-El.

G31

G32

[G32] **Wildenstein & Company** (art gallery), 19 E. 64th St., bet. Fifth and Madison Aves. 1931-1932. **Horace Trumbauer**.

Travertine within and without: an art palace (never a house) that marked, with a ribbon, the end of Trumbauer's rich, eclectic career. Beautiful in proportion and patina. Founded in Paris in 1875, the gallery had previously been at 647 Fifth Avenue.

[G33] Originally Bank of the Manhattan Company branch/now **Chase Manhattan Bank**, 726 Madison Ave., SW cor. E. 64th St. 1932-1933. **Morrell Smith**.

A charming neo-Georgian fantasy built a hundred years

G33

after houses of this scale were built anywhere on Manhattan Island.

[G34] **The Verona** (apartments), 32 E. 64th St., SE cor. Madison Ave. 1907-1908. **William E. Mowbray**. ♂

Names were once just as important as addresses, but this high-rise palazzo deserved one from the best of Italy (check that 16th-century cornice). The lamp standards add extra panache.

G36a

[G35] **Near East Foundation**/originally Robert I. Jenks House, 54 E. 64th St., bet. Madison and Park Aves. 1907. **Flagg & Chambers**. ♂

Four stories of delicate but simpering neo-Federal detail, complete with Flemish-bond brick. Some elegant parts contribute to a bland whole.

[G36a] **57 East 64th Street** (town house), bet. Madison and Park Aves. 1905. **C. P. H. Gilbert**. ♂

From the Flemish Renaissance, with Gothic details hanging on to its finialed dormers and balustrade details. A cadaverous competitor for shade and shadow.

G36b

[G36b] **Swedish Consulate and Permanent Mission to the United Nations**/originally Jonathan Buckley House, 600 Park Ave., NW cor. E. 64th St. 1911. **James Gamble Rogers**. ♂

Neo-English Renaissance garb for an American paper manufacturer. The Swedes have lovingly restored it.

[G37] Originally **Thomas A. and Emilia Howell House**, 603 Park Ave., NE cor. E. 64th St. 1920. **Walter Lund** and **Julius F. Gayler**. ♂

Stupendous neo-Federal as though, like Popeye, it had feasted on spinach! Best from the modillioned cornice up.

G37

🏛 [G38a] **Central Presbyterian Church**/originally Park Avenue Baptist Church, 593 Park Ave., SE cor. E. 64th St. 1920-1922. **Henry C. Pelton** and **Allen & Collens**. ♂

The original Baptist congregation (previously Norfolk Street Baptist Church and later Fifth Avenue Baptist Church, where the Rockefellers worshiped) left here to build its true monument, Riverside Church, with the same architects and JDR, Jr.'s money. Collegiate Gothic (comfort for the upper middle class).

▮ [G38b] **110 East 64th Street** (town house), bet. Park and Lexington Aves. 1988. **Agrest & Gandelsonas**. ♂

Captured in conversation between a stony church and a glassy box [see next], as though at tea. This very high-style urban single house toasts its neighbors while demurely lifting its chin.

G38b

[G38c] Originally Asia House/now **Russell Sage Foundation**/Robert Sterling Clark Foundation, 112 E. 64th St., bet. Park and Lexington Aves. 1959. **Philip Johnson & Assocs.** ♂

A decorous curtain of dark glass suspended in a gossamer grid of thin, white-painted steel makes a street wall that "works" in this varied block. The sometimes disturbing opacity of the glass, mirroring the street's opposite side, disappears at night, revealing the volume of interior spaces behind the wall.

G38c

[G39] Formerly **Edward Durell Stone House**, 130 E. 64th St., bet. Park and Lexington Aves. 1878. **James E. Ware**. Front addition, 1956, **Edward Durell Stone**. ♂

Originally one of a row of four, similar in appearance to today's No. 128. In 1956 architect-owner Stone extended the façade, and hence volume, of the structure to the permissible building line. The precast terrazzo grillage echoed the design of his American Embassy in New Delhi, widely acclaimed when it was built. Stone's third wife and son stripped away this orientalism, revealing floor-to-ceiling glass, and themselves, unabashedly. The Landmarks Commission made them put it back.

G39

[G40] Originally First of August (boutique)/now **Pino Fiori**, 860 Lexington Ave., bet. E. 64th and E. 65th Sts. W side. 1978. **George Ranalli**.

A storefront of glass squares set within mini-monkey bars (as in a city playground) that crawl up an old brownstone (as ivy crawls up brick walls). Ivy is preferable.

East 65th Street, from Fifth to Madison Avenues:

G40

[G41] **Temple Emanu-El** (synagogue), 840 Fifth Ave., NE cor. E. 65th St. 1927-1929. **Robert D. Kohn**, **Charles Butler**, **Clarence Stein**, and **Mayers, Murray & Philip**, associated architects. ♂

The merging in 1927 of Emanu-El with Temple Beth-El (whose sanctuary then stood at the southeast corner of Fifth and 67th) paved the way for construction of this large, bearing-wall sanctuary on the former site of **Richard Morris Hunt**'s double mansion for Mrs. Caroline Schermerhorn Astor, *the* Mrs. Astor. North of the main space, and set back from the avenue, is the Beth-El Chapel, built in memory of the other congregation's structure (1891. **Brunner & Tryon**), which was then demolished.

G41

[G42] **Permanent Mission of Pakistan to the United Nations**/originally Mrs. William H. Bliss House, 6 and 8 E. 65th St., 1902. ♂ **Hiss & Weeks**. [G46a] **12 East 65th Street** (town house), 1909. **Walter B. Chambers**. ♂

Two Beaux Arts baubles. No. 8, unusually wide (43-foot) with a generous 2-story Parisian mansard pierced by bull's-eye dormers, is visually linked to its neighbor No. 6 by a common 2nd-floor balcony and roof cornice. No. 12, now Pakistan House, also harmonizes.

G42

[G43a] **Kosciuszko Foundation**/originally James J. Van Alen House, 15 E. 65th St. 1917. **Harry Allan Jacobs.** ♂ Gallery open Mo-Fr 9-5; but call first. 212-734-2130.

Crisp Regency limestone with an inset pink marble Palladian window. Original owner **Van Alen**, a socialite, was *the* Mrs. Astor's son-in-law. He sold the house in 1919 and moved to Europe in protest over impending Prohibition. The foundation has held it since 1945.

[G43b] **French & Company**/originally Sherman M. Fairchild House, 17 E. 65th St. 1941. **George Nelson** and **William Hamby**. New façade, 1981, **Milton Klein**. ♂

A revolutionary plan and façade in its day: 2 separate

G43a

G43b

functional elements at the front and rear of the lot, separated by an open garden court over which glass ramps sprang, linking living/dining/kitchen (front) with bedrooms (rear). The 1941 façade included a series of motor-operated wood louvers to control sunlight—Fairchild was an aircraft manufacturer. Klein's new façade is a carefully studied cubistic composition of fired (rough) and highly polished red granite veneer, set off by a polished stainless-steel ship's railing, and a lone gingko tree. A sorry fate for the Hamby/Nelson wonder.

Madison Avenue, between East 65th and East 66th Streets:

G44

[G44] Originally **Frederic H. Betts House**, 750 Madison Ave. also known as 22 E. 65th St., SW cor. Madison Ave. 1897. **Grosvenor Atterbury**. Stores added, 1915, 1936. ♔

Time has had a schizophrenic effect on this corner town house: on Madison it has become a proscenium for a succession of shops, currently Léron. On 65th the original dour Protestant character is largely retained.

[G45] **Giorgio Armani** (store), 760 Madison Ave., NW cor. E. 65th St. 1996. **Peter Marino + Assocs**. ♔

Sliced ice cream and glass. This minimal envelope is minimal without being minimalist: the details, proportions, and form all are steps below what would be achieved by John Pawson—or even the ghost of Mies.

G45

East 65th Street, between Madison and Park Avenues:

[G46a] **American Federation of the Arts**/originally Benson Bennett Sloan House, 41 E. 65th St. 1910. **Trowbridge & Livingston**. ♔ Interior remodeling, 1960, **Edward Durell Stone**.

Galleries open to the public. The Tuscan-columned loggia at the top, now glazed in, offered an eyrie for sun-sitters.

[G46b] **Albert Ellis Institute**/originally John M. Bowers House, 45 E. 65th St. 1910. **Hoppin & Koen**. ♔

A monumental quoined and corniced neo-Georgian limestone and rose-colored brick town house. The attic story in copper and slate provides an exceptional richness.

G46a

[G46c] **Sara Delano Roosevelt Memorial House, Hunter College CUNY**/originally Mrs. James (Sara Delano) Roosevelt House, 47-49 E. 65th St. 1907-1908. **Charles A. Platt**. ♥ ♔

Built as a double town house (with a single entry) by FDR's mother: she lived in No. 47 while **Franklin** and **Eleanor** lived in No. 49. It was here, in a 4th-floor bedroom, that the president-to-be convalesced from his bout with polio in 1921-1922. The structure was purchased by Hunter in 1942, and the divisions were subsequently removed.

G46d

[G46d] **55 East 65th Street** (apartments). 1892. **Thom & Wilson**. ♔

French flats of Roman brick and brownstone for wealthy pioneers in apartment living (for social implications of such life, see **Edith Wharton's** *The Age of Innocence*). The sheet-metal fire escape covers (added later) were a Bauhaus-inspired attempt to sterilize the late 19th-century vigor.

[G47] **44 East 65th Street** (town house). 1877. **John G. Prague**. Present façade, 1912. **J. M. A. Darrach**. ♔

The Tuscan-colonnaded ground level is a pleasant indention from the street. And above, brick relieving arches offer a play of arch and lintel worthy of the best Georgian.

The IRT, the city's first subway system, invariably linked to the name of its financier, August Belmont (1853-1924), was actually planned

G48

*and constructed under the supervision of engineer **William Barclay***
***Parsons**. Parsons commissioned the double-width, doublescaled neo-*
*Federal house at 121 East 65th Street from architects **Welles***
***Bosworth** and **E. E. Piderson**. It was completed in 1923.*

[G48] **114, 116 & 118 East 65th Street** (townhouses), bet.
Park and Lexington Aves. 1900. **Buchman & Deisler**. ♂
Two in limestone flank their mate in brick and limestone in
this neo-Georgian triad. Some heavy Renaissance detailing
shows how in Edwardian times architects complicated and
embellished their ancestors' simpler styles. But the same thing
happened in Alexander's Greece as well.

[G49] **The Parge House**, 132a E. 65th St., SW cor. Lexington
Ave., Altered, 1922, **Frederick J. Sterner**. Altered since.
Though compromised by the addition of a Lexington
Avenue shop, this picturesque conversion of a row house into
architect Sterner's office and apartments remains an unusual
work. Note the decorative stucco relief.

[G50] Originally **Michael and John Davis House**, 135 E. 65th St.,
NW cor. Lexington Ave., also known as 868 Lexington Ave. 1904.
Edwin Outwater. ♂
Large and ungainly, as if fearing design enrichment, this
somber brick box offers a bay window over the side street.

East 65th Street, between Lexington and Third Avenues:

[G51a] **Church of St. Vincent Ferrer** (Roman Catholic),
Lexington Ave. SE cor. E. 66th St. 1914-1918. **Bertram G.
Goodhue**. ☙ [G51b] **Priory, Dominican Fathers**/originally
Convent, 869 Lexington Ave., NE cor. E. 65th St. 1880-1881.
William Schickel. ☙ [G51c] **Holy Name Society Building**,
141 E. 65th St. 1930. **Wilfrid E. Anthony**. [G51d] **St. Vincent
Ferrer School**, 151 E. 65th St. 1948. **Elliot L. Chisling** of **Ferrenz
& Taylor**.

G51b

A fashionable parish church complex built by the
Dominican Order (and therefore not under the control of the
New York Archdiocese). The Goodhue-designed church, in
rock-face granite with limestone trim, detailing, and sculpture,
is, perhaps, too academically correct, as if restored by an acolyte
of French neo-Gothicist Viollet-le-Duc: an "improvement" on
Gothic reality. A planned 150-foot steeple was never built. Well
worth a visit within.

While the Priory is an older, quite picturesque relic, the two
newer structures along 65th Street pale in comparison to their

G52a

Lexington Avenue cousins. (The incised Old English inscription on the new school gives its date as 1954; the Buildings Department dates it 1948.)

Across 65th Street from the St. Vincent Ferrer Church complex is a picturesque set of row houses, Nos. 132-156, of varying quality but united by trees, ivy, and ironwork that peters out as it approaches Third Avenue. Among the houses are:

G52b

[G52a] **136 & 138 East 65th Street** (row houses). 1870s. Copper-clad bay windows give an understated but rich character to these brick town houses. The copper on the most notorious house (for its occupants) has (unfortunately) been painted over:

[G52b] Formerly **Richard M. Nixon House**/onetime Learned Hand House/originally Charles C. Pope House, 142 E. 65th St. 1871. **Frederick S. Barus**. Altered 1961, **Casale & Nowell**.

Between 1963 and his relocation to the White House, Richard Nixon and his family had a generous apartment at 810 Fifth Avenue. Following his resignation as president and his unsuccessful attempt to buy a co-op apartment, Nixon settled for this row house in 1979. **Federal Judge Learned Hand**, perhaps the most esteemed judge in the Federal system (but abhorred by **Franklin Roosevelt**, who denied him a place on the Supreme Court), lived here from 1906 until his death in 1961.

[G53] **The Chatham** (apartments), 181 E. 65th St., NW cor. Third Ave. 2001. **Robert A. M. Stern** and **Costas Kondylis**.

An attempt at the elegance of Park or Fifth Avenue at the base, with the inevitable tower above.

From Fifth Avenue along East 66th Street to Madison Avenue:

 [G54] **Federation of Yugoslavia Mission to the United Nations**/originally R. Livingston and Eleanor T. Beeckman House, 854 Fifth Ave., bet. E. 66th and E. 67th St. 1903-1905. **Warren & Wetmore**. 🍎 ♂

It would seem that Communists savor splendor as much as capitalists.

Two neighbors:

[G55a] **The Lotos Club**/originally Margaret Vanderbilt Shepard House/later William J. and Maria Shepard

Schiefflin House, 5 E. 66th St. 1898-1900. **Richard Howland Hunt**. ♂

Rose-colored brick and limestone Beaux Arts *Schlag*. Built for **William H. Vanderbilt**'s eldest daughter, **Margaret**, the house was presented to her daughter and son-in-law **William J. Schieffelin** of the wholesale drug firm of Schieffelin & Company. He was also president of Citizen's Union for 32 years. The Deutscher Verein took possession briefly in 1925, the Lotos in 1946.

G55b

[G55b] **Permanent Mission of the Republic of Poland to the United Nations**/originally Charles and Louise Flagg Scribner, Jr. House, 9 E. 66th St. 1909-1912. **Ernest Flagg**. ♂

An airy and masterful façade with so much glass that it presages (visually) curtain walls by a half century. Flagg also did the Scribner commercial buildings at Nos. 153-157 and 597 Fifth Avenue. (He had married into the Flagg family.)

[G55c] **Consular House, Republic of the Philippines**/ originally Harris Fahnestock House, 15 E. 66th St. 1918. **Hoppin & Koen**. ♂

The architects' chef d'oeuvre was the old Police Headquarters. This house was rumored to be one of the many shoe storehouses of former Philippine first lady **Imelda Marcos**.

G55c

[G56] **45 East 66th Street** (apartments), NE cor. Madison Ave. 1906-1908. **Harde & Short**. ● ♂

They hoped for Perpendicular Gothic. Two glassy 10-story walls of 12 over 12 double-hung windows intersect in a magnificent cylinder of even more windows, making this one of the city's grandest façades. Forgiven is the destruction of the Church of the Holy Spirit (later All Souls' Episcopal Church), on whose site this was built.

G56

East 66th Street, between Park and Lexington Avenues:

[G57] **7th Regiment Armory, N.Y. National Guard**, 640 Park Ave. (Park to Lexington Aves. bet. E. 66th and E. 67th Sts). 1877-1879. **Charles W. Clinton**. Tower removed, Park Ave. façade. ● ♂ Interiors, Park Ave. wing, **Louis Comfort Tiffany, Stanford White, Herter Brothers, Alexander Roux & Co., L. Marcotte Co.** and **Pottier & Stymus**. ● ♂

A friendly brick fortress. New York armories were composed of two distinct elements: a 3- or 4-story collection of office, meeting, and socializing spaces (Park Avenue) and a vast drill hall (Lexington). The latter, 187 × 270 feet of clear space, is sufficient for maneuvering modern military vehicles—not to mention its adequacy for tennis practice and antiques expositions. Note the regimental monument along Central Park's wall [G63].

G57

*The Armory was in large part furnished and detailed on its interior by **Louis Comfort Tiffany**, son of Charles, founder and owner of Fifth Avenue's Tiffany & Company. Louis rejected the business world for that of the applied arts. His studios eventually specialized in decorative crafts ranging from the stained glass for which he is best remembered to stone-carving, metalworking, and casting of bronze—crafts complementing the ornate Late Victorian architecture of his architect-clients. In this case some tables were turned: **Stanford White** worked under Tiffany's direction on this interior work, rather than the later, and more obvious, reversed relationship (but White was then only 24).*

[G58a] **The Cosmopolitan Club**, 122 E. 66th St., 1932. **Thomas Harlan Elett**. ♂

One of the northernmost outposts of "New Orleans" cast iron. Organized as a club for women professionals and semiprofessionals, the Cos contrasts with the Colony Club. As the Colony's architecture is prissy, the Cos's is frivolous.

[G58b] **John Hay Whitney garage**/originally Henry O. Havemeyer stable/coach house/coachman's residence, later Oliver H. Payne stable, etc., 126 E. 66th St. 1895. **W. J. Wallace** and **S. E. Gage**. ♂

A handsome brick arch, portal for 9 Whitney cars. Rarely does even consciously monumental architecture achieve such power. The archivolt is breathtaking.

G58b

[G59a] **131-135 East 66th Street** (apartments), NE cor. Lexington Ave. 1905-1906. **Charles A. Platt** of **Simonson, Pollard & Steinam**. ♠

[G59b] **130-134 East 67th Street** (apartments), SE cor. Lexington Ave. 1907. **Rossiter & Wright**. ♠

Two adjacent apartment blocks in the neo-Italian Renaissance style. Though designed by different architects of record, the driving force for both was Platt, who left one firm to join the other so that he could design a complement to his first work. (Rossiter's solo works, both in the Shingle Style and Colonial Revival, are in and around the Gunnery School in Washington, Connecticut).

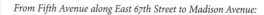

From Fifth Avenue along East 67th Street to Madison Avenue:

[G60] **7th Regiment Monument, N.Y. National Guard**, Fifth Ave. at E. 67th St. W side, fronting Central Park. 1927. **Karl Illava**, sculptor. ♠

Dynamic bronze; seething bayonets.

[G61a] **Residence of the Consul General of Japan**/originally Henri P. Wertheim House, 4 E. 67th St. 1902. **John H. Duncan**. ♂

G61a

A little brick and a lot of limestone: Beaux Arts with a slate, oculi pierced, copper crested, mansard roof.

[G61b] Formerly **Jules S. Bache House**, 10 E. 67th St. 1881. James E. Ware. Altered for Bache, 1899, **C. P. H. Gilbert**. ♂

A fashionable, but timid and pasty, neo-Classical bowed front replaced the original Queen Anne brownstone. A 1998 fire promises some restoration..

[G61c] Formerly **Jeremiah Milbank House**, 14-16 E. 67th St. (combined houses). No. 14, 1879, **Lamb & Wheeler**; altered, 1920, **Dodge & Morrison**. No. 16, 1905, **John H. Duncan**. ♂

G62a

Separate structures for Mr. Milbank linked within and harmonized without, in 1920.

[G61d] Formerly **R. Fulton Cutting House**, 22 E. 67th St. 1879. **Lamb & Wheeler**. Altered for Cutting, 1908, **Harry Allan Jacobs**. ♂

Robert Fulton Cutting (1852-1934) was known in his time as the "first citizen of New York" for his leadership of such groups as the Association for Improving the Condition of the Poor, the City and Suburban Homes Company, and the Cooper Union. He was Citizens Union's first president. A reserved limestone façade, as befits a brahmin.

G62b

[G62a] Originally **Samuel H. Valentine House**, 5 E. 67th St. 1909. **Carrère & Hastings**. ♂

A Neo-Reniaissance façade with an ornately ornamented 2-story bowed bay; and framing that bay are unfluted pilasters that bear French 16th-century bas-relief.

[G62b] **7 East 67th Street** (row house). 1882. **Thom & Wilson**. Present façade, 1900. **Clinton & Russell**. ♂

Paired Ionic columns support a porch.

G62c

[G62c] Originally **Charles C. Stillman House**, 9 E. 67th St. 1882. **Thom & Wilson**. Current façade, 1912, **Hiss & Weeks**. ♂

French Renaissance dormers and balcony enrich this otherwise austere limestone façade.

G62d

[G62d] Originally **Martin Beck House**/sometime Barbara Sears (Bobo, onetime Mrs. Winthrop) Rockefeller house, 13 E. 67th St. 1921. **Harry Allan Jacobs**. ○

Martin Beck, prominent New York theatrical figure, built the Martin Beck and Palace theaters. The Serlian arch at the 2nd floor, named after Italian architect-author **Sebastiano Serlio**, is alternately termed a Palladian window (cf. **Andrea Palladio**). Note the incised XIII. **Bobo** lived here from 1955 to 1998.

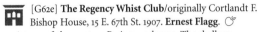 [G62e] **The Regency Whist Club**/originally Cortlandt F. Bishop House, 15 E. 67th St. 1907. **Ernest Flagg**. ○

A turn-of-the-century Paris town house. The shallow "French" balconies, in front of the French doors, for (mostly psychological) security, enliven the façade. Bishop was the first to receive a permit to drive a car in Central Park.

G62e

East 67th Street, between Madison and Park Avenues:

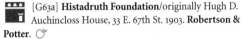 [G63a] **Histadruth Foundation**/originally Hugh D. Auchincloss House, 33 E. 67th St. 1903. **Robertson & Potter**. ○

Sober neo-Georgian brick and limestone with a cornice of Italian grandeur.

[G63b] Originally Arthur H. Scribner House/now **N.Y.S. Pharmaceutical Association**, 39 E. 67th St. 1877. **David & John Jardine**. Present façade, 1904, **Ernest Flagg**. ○

Flagg's swags enliven this limestone confection, but in relative sobriety for Scribner's town house (exuberance dominates the store on Fifth Avenue).

[G63c] Originally **James R. Sheffield House**/later (1964-1973) Gloria Vanderbilt Cooper House, 45 E. 67th St. 1913. **Walter B. Chambers**. ○

Modest, but the recessed ground floor offers a rhythm to the street that grander buildings can't match.

[G63d] **47 East 67th Street**. 1878. **J. H. Valentine**. Present façade, 1909. **William A. Bates**. ○

A neo-Georgian bowed brick façade.

[G64] **Egyptian Mission to the United Nations**/originally Elizabeth and Mary Thompson House, 36-38 E. 67th St. 1906. **Henry Bacon**. ○

A distraught shell under renovation.

East 67th Street, between Park and Lexington Avenues:

[G65] **Milan House** (apartments), 115 E. 67th St., and 116 E. 68th St. 1931. **Andrew J. Thomas**. ○

Two 11-story gems, complete with carved monsters, grotesques, and florid capitals atop colonnettes, and wonderful multipaned casements. Thomas was an important designer of enlightened apartment developments. The midblock Italian garden court between the wings, barely visible through the entry doors, is a dream.

East 67th Street, between Lexington and Third Aves:

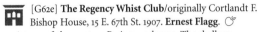 [G66a] **Kennedy Child Study Center**/originally Mt. Sinai Dispensary, 149-151 E. 67th St. 1889-1890. **Buchman & Deisler** and **Brunner & Tryon**. ●

Built as an adjunct to an earlier Mt. Sinai Hospital (1872. **Griffith Thomas**) that occupied the south side of this 67th Street block: dignified neo-Italian Renaissance styling in brick and terra-cotta that required the collaboration of two distinguished partnerships of architects.

G66b

 [G66b] **19th Precinct, N.Y.C. Police Department**/originally 25th Precinct, 153 E. 67th St. 1887. **Nathaniel D. Bush**. Altered, 1988, **The Stein Partnership**. 🍎

A Victorian palazzo: limestone and brick architecture that borrowed heavily from the Florentine Renaissance. The rusticated base supports a mannered Victorian body. A complicated 1980s restoration-reconstruction links it to:

G66c

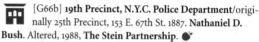 [G66c] Originally **N.Y.C. Fire Department Headquarters**/later Engine Company No. 39, Ladder Company No. 15, 157 E. 67th St. 1886. **Napoleon Le Brun & Sons**. Altered, 1988, **The Stein Partnership**. 🍎

A lusty exercise in Romanesque Revival in brownstone and brick; the herringbone decoration of the voussoirs is straight from Norman England.

G66d

[G66d] **Park East Synagogue**/Congregation Zichron Ephraim, 163 E. 67th St. 1889-1890. **Schneider & Herter**. 🍎

Inside, a Victorian preaching space, nominally made Jewish through Saracenic detail. Stripped to its essentials, it could be Civil War-period Catholic or Congregational. Outside, it is a confection that might have been conceived in a Moorish trip on LSD: a wild, vigorous extravaganza.

East 68th Street, between Fifth and Madison Avenues:

G67b

[G67a] **Republic of Indonesia Delegation to the United Nations**/originally John J. Emery House, 5 E. 68th St. 1896. **Peabody & Stearns**. ♂

A bloated mansion, impressive in size, unconvincing in character and detail.

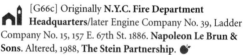 [G67b] **Doctors' Offices**/originally Mrs. George T. Bliss House, 9 E. 68th St. 1907. **Heins & La Farge**. ♂

From the spirit of **Sir John Soane**: known for his radical architecture, Soane's mansion (now a museum) at Lincoln's Inn Fields, London, is one of the great experiments in Regency architecture. Here the great Ionic columns support the sky and form a magnificent stage set.

[G67c] **The Marquand** (apartments), 11 E. 68th St., NW cor. Madison Ave. 1913. **Herbert Lucas**. ♂

The brick and bow-bay upper floors of this 11-story apartment rest atop a handsome pillow-rusticated limestone base. The structure occupies the site of 3 brownstones designed by

Richard Morris Hunt for **Henry G. Marquand** in 1880. Note the incised M at various points in the façade.

[G68a] **6 East 68th Street** (house), 1881. **John G. Prague**. 8, 10 East 68th Street (houses), 1882. **Lamb & Wheeler**. Linked and altered, 1920, **Harry Allan Jacobs**. ♂

This trio of now-interlinked mansions was owned, in varying combinations, by family members of the **Lehman Brothers** and **Kuhn, Loeb & Company** banking firms. Among them was **Otto Kahn**, who lived at No. 8 until he commissioned his grand palazzo on 91st Street. The modern surelevation is heavy-handed.

 [G68b] Originally **Henry T. Sloane House**, 18 E. 68th St. 1905. **C. P. H.Gilbert**. ♂

Don't confuse this Beaux Arts Sloane House with the one at 9 East 72nd where Sloane (1845-1937), of the W. & J. Sloane store, lived with the first Mrs. Sloane. After his divorce, he built this gem.

[G69] Originally **Dr. Christian A. Herter House**, 817-819 Madison Ave., bet. E. 68th and E. 69th Sts. E side. 1892. **Carrère & Hastings**. ♂ Storefronts added, 1922, **Carrère & Hastings**.

Severely compromised by fire escape regulations and the needs of commerce. Nevertheless, the surprise of discovering this monumental survivor above the commercial fronts offers a delicious sensation.

G69

East 68th Street, between Madison and Park Avenues:

[G70a] Originally **Mary D. Dunham House**, 35 E. 68th St. 1901. **Carrère & Hastings**. ♂

Extravagant ornament on a modest Carrère & Hastings palace.

G70c

[G70b] Originally **Ruth Hill Beard House**, 47 E. 68th St. 1907. **Adams & Warren**. ♂

Bold Italian Renaissance detail.

[G70c] **Richard Feigen & Co.**/formerly Automation House/ originally J. William and Margaretta C. Clark House, 49 E. 68th St. 1913-1914. **Trowbridge & Livingston**. 🍎 ♂

The muntined French window replacements are a happy restoration of scale: the window openings had been glazed with single sheets of fixed glass in a previous alteration.

G71a

[G71a] Formerly **John D. Crimmins House**, 40-42 E. 68th St. No. 40, 1879, **William Schickel**. No. 42, 1878, architect unknown. Joined, 1898, **Schickel & Ditmars**. ♂

Two row houses were combined to form a monumental mansarded Beaux Arts limestone complex. Crimmins was the contractor for some of the City's largest 19th-century public works.

[G71b] **Dominican Academy**/originally Michael Friedsam House, 44 E. 68th St. 1922. **Frederick G. Frost**. ♂

A bland box noted for its historical associations rather than its architecture. Businessman, philanthropist, art collector, and civic leader Friedsam succeeded Benjamin Altman as the department store's president.

G71c

[G71c] **Peter G. Peterson Center for International Studies**, 50 E. 68th Street (offices). 1999. **Bell Larson**. ♂

The entrance to a new complex that includes 50 through 56 East 68th Street, the existing buildings remodeled with substantial rear yard additions.

 [G72] **Council on Foreign Relations**/originally Harold I. Pratt House, 58 E. 68th St., SW cor. Park Ave. 1919-1921. **Delano & Aldrich**. ♂ Addition to W, 1954, **Wyeth & King**.

Harold was the youngest son of Brooklyn's 19th-century industrialist **Charles Pratt**, kerosene magnate and later major shareholder in the Standard Oil trust. Four sons built minor

G72

palaces along Brooklyn's Clinton Avenue (3 still stand) near their dad's mansion. When Harold's turn came, he was swept by changing fashions to Manhattan's Park Avenue—hence this sober limestone neo-Renaissance marvel.

The whole blockfront on the west side of Park Avenue between E. 68th and E. 69th Sts.
A whole that is much greater than the sum of its parts, although each, separated, would be distinguished in its own right. Georgian architecture's greatest contribution is not only the style of individual structures but a comprehensive attitude toward urban design. Buildings of character, quality, and refinement were integrated in a larger system of designing cities, the blithe basis of this neo-Georgian row.

G73a

[G73a] **Americas Society**/onetime U.S.S.R. Delegation to the United Nations/originally Percy and Maude H. Pyne House, 680 Park Ave., NW cor E. 68th St. 1906-1912. **Charles McKim** of **McKim, Mead & White**. 🖌 ♂ 212-249-8950. Gallery & library open Tu-Su 12-6. Closed Mo.
Client **Percy R. Pyne** (1857-1929) was a New York financier and philanthropist. It was here that **Prime Minister Khrushchev** held forth from the 2nd-floor window in 1960.

[G73b] **Spanish Institute**/originally Oliver D. and Mary Pyne Filley House, 684 Park Ave. 1925-1926. **McKim, Mead & White**. 🖌 ♂
Built by **Percy Pyne** next door for his daughter and her husband, the Filleys; on the site of Pyne's No. 680 garden.

G73d

[G73c] **Istituto Italiano di Cultura**/originally William and Francesca Crocker Sloane House, 686 Park Ave. 1916-1919. **Delano & Aldrich**. 🖌 ♂
Another Sloane (1873-1922) of the **W. & J. Sloane** clan.

[G73d] **Consulate General of Italy**/originally Henry P. and Kate T. Davison House, 690 Park Ave., SW cor. E. 69th St. 1916-1917. **Walker & Gillette**. 🖌 ♂
Henry P. Davison was a **J. P. Morgan** partner, among other things.

*Marquesa de Cuevas (a Rockefeller gone Spanish) received wide praise in 1965 for buying the endangered structures at 680 and 684 Park Avenue to save them from demolition; she then presented them (and later her own House, 52-54 East 68th Street) to her favorite charities. The Marquesa was the former **Margaret Rockefeller Strong**, married to the eighth **Marques de Piedrablanca de Guana Cuevas**.*

Hunter College
Note: Hunter College's buildings straddle the boundary of the Upper East Side Historic District. Those within the district are, like others so protected, identified: ♂ .

G74

[G74] **Hunter College, CUNY**, 695 Park Ave., bet. E. 68th and E. 69th Sts. E side. 1938-1941. **Shreve, Lamb & Harmon, Harrison & Fouilhoux**, associated architects. ♂
An interruption in the pace of Park Avenue. Hunter is not only modern and glistening with glass, it is also set back 10 feet from the lot line. A proud self-confident monument in the city's early International Modernism.

[G75] **Old Building, Hunter College, CUNY**/briefly Hunter College High School, 930 Lexington Ave., bet. E. 68th and E. 69th Sts. W side 1913. **C. B. J. Snyder**. ♂
The last gasp of **John Ruskin**'s ghost here housed quality education in an "English Gothic" shell. The prestigious Hunter High, part of the public school system, enrolled talented girls

G75

from throughout the city through a competitive examination program. Hunter High (now co-ed) later moved to the fortlike former I.S. 29 building at 94th and Park.

[G76] **South Building and East Building, Hunter College, CUNY**, E. 68th St. SW cor. and SE cor. Lexington Ave. Designed 1980, completed 1986 (delayed by City fiscal crisis). **Ulrich Franzen & Assocs.**

Resplendent, beautifully detailed Modern blocks, they are welcome additions to the cityscape. The enclosed glassy overpasses on the 3rd and 8th floors over Lexington Avenue, and the lower connection over 68th Street to old Hunter High, are unique and provide syncopation to the city's endless street vistas.

G76

[G77] **Sam and Esther Minskoff Cultural Center**, Park East Day School, 164 E. 68th St., bet. Lexington and Third Aves. 1974. **John Carl Warnecke & Assocs.**

Creamy brick articulated with granite. A throwback to the curvilinear streamlined Art Moderne architecture of the 1939-1940 World's Fair.

G78, No. 7

[G78] **East 69th Street**, Fifth to Madison Aves. Roll call:
No. 7: (1986, **Hobart Betts**) ♂ , infill: an all-court press: Neo-Georgian-Palladian-PoMo? The scale of the Tuscan columns and arch clashes with that of the windows above.
No. 9: (1917, **Grosvenor Atterbury**) ♂ , marble and brick neo-Georgian.
No. 11: American Friends of Hebrew University (1924, **Delano & Aldrich**), cool, but not calculating, limestone. ♂
No. 12: (1884; altered, 1913, **William Welles Bosworth**) ♂ , denuded and far from its Georgian antecedents.
No. 16: English-Speaking Union (1882; altered, 1930, **A. Wallace McCrea**) ♂ is in proper neo-Georgian dress for these hands-across-the-sea.

G79

[G79] Originally **Isaac and Virginia Stern House**, 835 Madison Ave., bet. E. 69th and E. 70th Sts. 1885. **William Schickel**. Storefronts added, 1921; altered 1930, and since. ♂

There's great satisfaction in discovering a weather-beaten but largely intact Queen Anne brick and limestone row house atop ubiquitous Madison Avenue storefronts.

[G80] **East 69th Street**, Madison to Park Aves.
A rich and changing block of varied architectural styles, all of human scale, and greater than the sum of its parts. Roll call:
No. 27: formerly **Lucretia Lord Strauss** (1886; altered, 1922, **York & Sawyer**). ♂ English critic **Osbert**

G80, No. 27

Lancaster might describe this as Stockbrokers' Tudor (Ford once sold Tudor cars: they had two doors).

No. 31: Consulate General of Austria/originally Augustus G. Paine, Jr. House (1918, **C P. H. Gilbert**). ☾ The windows would be too small for the Georges; the shutters are a joke.

No. 33: (1912, **Howells & Stokes**). ☾ Bland. Lightly rusticated limestone.

No. 35: (1911, **Walker & Gillette**). ☾ A monumental mansard roof with oculi.

No. 36: (ca. 1875; altered 1903, **Jardine, Kent & Jardine**; altered 1923, **Carrère & Hastings**). ☾

Lesser works by name architects:

G80, No. 42

No. 42: Jewish National Fund (1921, **C P. H. Gilbert**) ☾, for **Arthur and Alice G. Sachs**, descendants of the founders of the Goldman, Sachs Company investment banking firm. Stolid medieval.

No. 50: (1918, **Henry C. Pelton**). ☾ Both grand and bland.

[G81] **The Union Club of New York**, 701 Park Ave., NE cor. E. 69th St. also known as 101 E. 69th St. 1931-1932. **Delano & Aldrich**. ☾

New York City's oldest social club (founded in 1836) is housed in the style of the English 18th century: limestone and granite understated at street level, increasingly enriched above the piano nobile, culminating in a classical frieze (windows are triglyphs, ornate panels serve as metopes, topped with a balustraded cornice).

G81

[G82] **115 East 69th Street**, bet. Park and Lexington Aves. 1903. **Hoppin & Koen**. ☾

Modest for these creators of the old Police Headquarters.

[G83] **East 69th Street**, Lexington to Third Aves.

A roll call of idiosyncratic stables/carriage houses/garages:

No. 147: (1880. **John Correja**, present façade, 1913, **Barney & Colt**). ☾ The glassy second floor proffers multi-panes as in Perpendicular Gothic. Gutsy.

No. 149: for London subway financier **Charles T. Yerkes**/later Thomas Fortune Ryan (1896. **Frank Drischler**). ☾ A Romanesque Revival personality on the block.

No. 153: (1884. **William Schickel**). ☾ Dour brick Romanesque with terra-cotta counterpoints.

No. 159: for W. & J. Sloane's **John Sloane** (1882. **Charles W. Romeyn**). ☾ Oculi below, arched corbel-tables above.

G83, No. 147

The last three lack the character of the four above:
No. 161: for **William Bruce-Brown** (1916. **Frederick B. Loney**)
Note BB in keystone. ☿ Now the New York School of Interior
Design. Using leftovers from a Park Avenue apartment house?
No. 163: for printing-press magnate **Richard M. Hoe** (1909.
Albro & Lindeberg), now Congregation Zichron Ephraim. A
vulgar alteration at the ground floor.
No. 167: for the Museum of the American Indian's founder,
George G. Heye (1909. **Charles E. Birge**), now The Sculpture
Center. A diverse collection of 19th-century necessities.
Plodding eclectic.

G83, No. 149

[G 84] **Richard Morris Hunt Memorial**, E. 70th St. at Fifth Ave.,
W side, fronting Central Park. ☙ 1898. **Daniel Chester French**,
sculptor. **Bruce Price**, architect.
   A monument to the first American architect trained at the
Ecole des Beaux-Arts in Paris, who was also founding president
of the American Institute of Architects. Appropriately located
here opposite the site of Hunt's Lenox Library, built between
1869 and 1877. The Lenox site is now occupied by the Frick
Collection.

G84

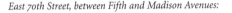

East 70th Street, between Fifth and Madison Avenues:

*The north side of this block, through to 71st Street, was developed
early in the 20th century, following the demolition of the Lenox
Library, which occupied the Fifth Avenue frontage. The library's
holdings were transferred to The New York Public Library's Astor,
Lenox & Tilden Collections at 42nd Street prior to that building's
opening in 1911.*

[G85] **Frick Collection**/originally Henry Clay and Adelaide
Childs Frick House, 1 E. 70th St., NE cor. Fifth Ave. to E. 71st St.
1913-1914. **Carrère & Hastings**. Altered as a public museum,
1931-1935, **John Russell Pope**. ☙ ☿ Addition to E, 1977, **Harry
Van Dyke**, **John Barrington Bayley**, and **G.Frederick Poehler**,
architects; **Russell Page**, landscape architect. ☙ ☿ Museum
open to the public: Tu-Sa 10-6; Su 1-6; closed Mo. 212-288-0700.
   The Collection's garden and open, balustraded stone railing
provide a welcome break in the almost endless wall of high-rises
along Fifth Avenue.
   Bland, sometimes fussy, frequently indecisive, the exterior
belies a rich interior, both in architecture and contents. The
glass-roofed courtyard, entered almost directly, is a delightful
transition from the noisy activity of the street. The soothing
sound of water from a central fountain makes this a place for
pause, utterly relaxing—not surprising in the work of Pope, who
created similar islands of light, sound, and repose at the
National Gallery in Washington.
   The eastern addition was an anachronism for 1977: not prescient Post Modernism, but conscious Historicism: a garden
court in a Beaux Arts embrace atop a world of underground
services. It precedes the Historicism of modernist Kevin Roche
at the Jewish Museum (1993) by sixteen years.

G85

G85

[G86] **East 70th Street**, Fifth to Madison Aves. Roll call:

🏛 **No. 11:** Formerly Consuelo Vanderbilt Smith House.
1909-1910. **John Duncan**. ☙ ☿
Solemn Duncan (of Grant's Tomb) limestone.

🏛 **No. 15:** Originally John Chandler and Corinne DeBébian
Moore House. 1909-1910. **Charles I. Berg**. ☙ ☿, and
No. 17: Originally Alvin W. and Angeline Krech House. 1910-1911.
Arthur C. Jackson of **Heins & La Farge**. ☙ ☿
   Interesting more for their survival as a group than for indi-
vidual merits.

G86, No. 11

No. 19: Knoedler Gallery/originally David Hennen and Alice Morris House. 1909-1910. **Thornton Chard.** 🍎 ♂

Arches spring from Tuscan columns for the stroller, but severity reigns overhead.

No. 21: Hirschl & Adler Galleries/originally Gustav and Virginia Pagenstecher House. 1918-1919. **William J. Rogers.** 🍎 ♂

Modern railings form the store's cornice.

G86, No. 19

East 70th Street, Madison to Park Aves:

[G87a] Originally Laura K. Bayer House/then Clendenin Ryan House/then **Clendenin Ryan, Jr. House**, 32 E. 70th St. 1911. **Taylor & Levi.** ♂

Stately limestone. The sequential Ryans were son and grandson of financier **Thomas Fortune Ryan**. Both Clendenin and his son committed suicide in this limestone, mansarded house, in 1939 and 1957, respectively.

[G87b] **James P. Warburg House**, 36 E. 70th St. 1885. Altered 1924, **William Lawrence Bottomley.** ♂

G87a

A double-width, eclectic, two-tone brownstone and sandstone house. James, a banker and author, is the son of **Paul M. Warburg**, whose father, **Felix M.**, conveyed the family's 92nd Street mansion to form part of the Jewish Museum.

[G87c] **40 East 70th Street (garage)**/originally Augustus G. Paine, Jr. garage. 1918. **C. P. H.Gilbert.** ♂ Surelevated, 1990s.

A heavy-handed topping to what was once a graceful garage. The twin Tuscan columns are, perhaps, the necessary structure (or its concealment), but they convert grace into stumbling Georgian.

G87c

The original charmingly designed garage was an adjunct to the town house of papermaker Paine at 31 East 69th Street [see G80].

[G87d] **Lowell Thomas Building, Explorers' Club**/originally Stephen C. Clark House, 46 E. 70th St. 1912. **Frederick J. Sterner.** ♂

An unusual, richly ornamented neo-Jacobean work commissioned by a member of the Singer Sewing Machine Clarks.

[G88a] Originally Walter N. and Carola Rothschild House/now **Twentieth Century Fund**, 41 E. 70th St. 1929. **Aymar Embury II.** ♂ Column with Objects, 1969. **Gonzalo Fonseca**, sculptor.

G87d

An austerely façaded house (now set off by a wonderful free-standing sculpture) built for the chairman of the board of Abraham & Straus department store; his wife was **Carola Warburg**, daughter of **Felix M. Warburg**.

[G88b] Originally **Walter and Florence Hope House**, 43 E. 70th St. 1928-1929 **Mott B. Schmidt**. ♂
In the warm, pocked texture of travertine.

G88b

[G88c] Originally Arthur S. and Adele Lewisohn Lehman House/now **Joseph and Estée Lauder House**, 45 E. 70th St. 1928-1929. **Aymar Embury II**. ♂
The original owner of this bland town house, a senior partner in Lehman Brothers investment bankers, was Governor Herbert H. Lehman's brother. The Lauders make cosmetics. Their house needs a serious face-lift.

G89

[G89] **The Asia Society**, 725 Park Ave., NE cor. E. 70th St. 1979-1981. **Edward Larrabee Barnes Assocs.** ♂ 212-288-6400. Gallery open Su 12-5; Tu, We, Fr, Sa 11-6; Th 11-8; closed Mo.
Open to the public. An austere, brooding, polished brown granite prism. Only when it flies colorful multistory banners above its Park Avenue entry does it extend a welcome to those who visit its fine exhibitions of Asian art. The rear façade is lively.

East 70th Street, between Park and Lexington Avenues: A block as diverse, friendly, inviting, tactile, dappled, intricate, and surprising as anyone might wish. A masterpiece of the culture rather than of narrow architectural or planning decisions.

[G90a] **The Visiting Nurse Service of New York**/originally Thomas W. and Florence Lamont House, 107 E. 70th St. 1920-1921. **Walker & Gillette**. ♂
English Gothic—or Tudor Revival, if you wish—for the taste of the country parson's son who became head of J. P. Morgan. The ashlar and cut stone, gable-roofed façade is an unexpected—and welcome—break in the rhythms of this block. Lamont, also founder of the *Saturday Review*, was associated with many philanthropies, as well as with Columbia University's Lamont-Doherty Geological observatory at Palisades, N.Y.

G90a

[G90b] Originally **I. Townsend Burden House**, 115 E. 70th St. 1922. **Patrick J. Murray**. Mansard added, 1935. ♂
A bold neo-Georgian/Italian Renaissance blend for the cousin of iron and steel magnate **James A. Burden**.

[G90c] **123 East 70th Street** (rowhouse). 1902-1903. **Trowbridge & Livingston**. ♂

G90c

G90d

G90e

G90f

G91a

G92a

G93b

The elliptical arched opening and ironwork at the third floor bring the scent of Beaux Arts Paris to the block. The glazing and French doors touch on the Art Nouveau.

[G90d] **Paul Mellon House**, 125 E. 70th St. 1965. **Mazza & Seccia**. ♂

Replacing two 1860s row houses, this is one of a limited number of row houses built in Manhattan since World War II. Anachronistic: a charming stuccoed confection of "French Provincial" that France itself never experienced.

[G90e] Originally **James and Helen Geddes House**, 129 E. 70th St. 1863. Stoop removed, 1940. ♂

The oldest survivor in the Upper East Side Historic District, speculatively built as one of five: Nos. 121-129. (The "white" stone is actually painted brownstone.)

[G90f] Formerly **Mr. & Mrs. Charles Lamed Atterbury House**, 131 E. 70th St. ca. 1871. Altered and extended, 1911, **Grosvenor Atterbury**. Store, 1940. ♂

A picturesque extravaganza fashioned from an earlier structure by Atterbury for his parents—sometimes it pays to send your son to architecture school.

[G91a] **112-114 East 70th Street** (houses), 1869. **James Santon**. ♂

Two late Italianate brownstone survivors of a matching row of 5 with English basements. No. 112 retains its original double-hung window pattern and detail; no. 114 has been "modernized," its window openings refitted (before landmarks designation) with single sheets of glass. Which do you prefer?

[G91b] Originally **Edward A. Norman House**, 124 E. 70th St. 1940-1941. **William Lescaze**. ♂

A dated Modern house that seems, on this block, to shout "look at me!" It was included in the Museum of Modern Art's Built in USA, 1932-1944 exhibition, undoubtedly because it did thumb its nose at its historicist neighbors. Lescaze's own house on East 48th Street is far more sophisticated.

East 70th Street, between Lexington and Third Avenues:

[G92a] Originally Stephen H. Brown House/now **part of New York School of Interior Design**, 154 E. 70th St. 1907. **Edward P. Casey**. ♂

This double-width Tudor Revival house was built for a family known as collectors of medieval art. Since 1932 it has served a series of private educational institutions.

[G92b] **New York School of Interior Design**/onetime Lenox School/originally Daniel G. Reid stable and groom's apartments, 170 E. 70th St. 1902. **C. P. H. Gilbert**. Converted to school, 1925, **Bradley Delehanty**. Expanded upward, 1939, 1963. ♂

The original structure is of finely worked limestone in the Renaissance Revival mode, with a rich, arched entrance.

[G93a] Originally Jules S. Bache stable/later **John D. Rockefeller garage**, 163 E. 70th St. 1902. **C. P. H. Gilbert**. ♂
[G93b] Originally Henri P. Wertheim stable/later **Stephen C. Clark garage**/now Paul Mellon garage, 165 E. 70th St. 1902. **C. P. H. Gilbert**. ♂

Supergrand carriage houses with mansard roofs, used by a series of superrich owners. No. 163 (and therefore the entire street) is compromised by the substitution for the originals of bland single-light windows.

East 71st Street, between Fifth and Madison Avenues:

The south side of this block, through to East 70th, was developed after the death (1880) of James Lenox, whose Lenox Library had occupied part of it.

[G94a] **Birch Wathen School**/originally Herbert N. Straus House, 9 E. 71st St. 1932. **Horace Trumbauer**. Roof addition, 1977. ○

Straus, of the Macy's Strauses, never occupied this mansarded house; work was stopped shortly before his death in 1933.

[G94b] Originally **Mr. & Mrs. Richard M. Hoe House**, 11 E. 71st St. 1892. **Carrère & Hastings**. ○

A town house for the owner of the printing press and saw works that once occupied a site at 504 Grand Street. The portico has seriously deteriorated.

G94c

[G94c] **13 East 71st Street** (town house). 1891-1892. **R. H. Robertson**. ○

An elegant remnant from Manhattan's Brown Decades: American Renaissance white stone, terra-cotta, and marble usurped the space of most of its ilk in Manhattan. To find a trove, travel to Brooklyn's Fort Greene, Clinton Hill, and Bedford-Stuyvesant.

[G95a] **Frick Art Reference Library**, 10 E. 71st St. 1931-1935. **John Russell Pope**. ● ○

Tall and bland, but with a grand portal, it is the verbal annex to the visual Frick. Open to researchers by appointment.

G95a

[G95b] Originally **William A. Cook House**, 14 E. 71st St. 1913. **York & Sawyer**. ○

Magnificent bronze gates set in a two-story column-embraced portal. A great overhanging cornice shelters a Guastavino-vaulted penthouse balcony. Limestone surfaces are subtly worked, as though they were tooled leather.

[G95c] **16, 18 East 71st Street** (originally houses). 1911. **John H. Duncan**. ○

Early 20th-century plain Janes which, over the years, have served as town houses, apartments, private hospitals, and private schools.

[G95d] Originally **Julius Forstmann House**/later Catholic Center for the Blind, 22 E. 71st St. 1923. **C. P. H. Gilbert**. Altered, 1942, **Robert J. Reiley**. ○

A double-width limestone house with expansive proportions that comfortably fit its broad façade: contented, self-satisfied. Forstmann was a well-known manufacturer of wool fabrics.

G98d

[G96a] **St. James Episcopal Church**, 861-863 Madison Ave., NE cor. E. 71st St. 1884. **R. H. Robertson**. Rebuilt, 1924, **Ralph Adams Cram**. Original tower, 1926, **Ralph Adams Cram**; replacement (smaller) tower, 1950, **Richard Kimball**. ○

Crisp brownstone and steel produce Modern overtones on the reworked neo-Gothic body whose intended tower (had it been built) would have been more than twice the height of the main roof peak. The stonework of Cram's more modest tower of 1926 began to crumble, and today's basketweave-ornamented replacement is a regrettable addition.

G99a

[G96b] **St. James Parish House**, 865 Madison Ave., bet. E. 71st and E. 72nd St. E side. 1937. **Grosvenor Atterbury**. ○

A late Atterbury work in the neo-Gothic, replacing a brownstone purchased by the church in 1920 and subsequently outgrown.

East of Madison Avenue:

[G97] **Viscaya (apartments)**/formerly New York Society for the Prevention of Cruelty to Children, 110 E. 71st St., bet. Park and Lexington Aves. 1917. **Hill & Stout**. Expanded upward, 1982, **Architects Design Group**. ○

A round-cornered 16-story sliver pokes through—and dramatically cantilevers over—the midsection of a dignified 5-story

G100

G98

G99

neo-Georgian town house. New Yorkers have "never seen anything like the Tower on top of the Brownstone," said the ads. True enough. Cross Park Avenue for the total effect.

[G98] Formerly **Elsie de Wolfe House**, 131 E. 71st St., bet. Park and Lexington Aves. 1867. New façade, 1910, **Ogden Codman, Jr.**, architect. **Elsie de Wolfe**, designer. ♂

The original de-stooped house. Miss de Wolfe, the original "lady decorator" (later **Lady Mendl**, the almost-original great party giver), set the pace for brownstone conversions throughout Manhattan's Upper East Side. The few remaining stoops are, in reaction, nostalgically embraced and protected.

 [G99] Formerly **Mildred Phelps Stokes Hooker House**, 173-175 E. 71st St., bet. Third and Lexington Aves. 1869. **James Fee**. Current façade, 1911, **S. E. Gage**. Altered within, 1920, 1944. ♂

A romantic neo-Gothic redesign of a pair of straightforward row houses. The owner from 1910 to 1946 was the sister of **Isaac Newton Phelps Stokes**, architect and author of the invaluable *Iconography of Manhattan Island*, who died in this house.

East 72nd Street, between Fifth and Madison Avenues:

[G100a] **Lycée Français de New York**/originally Oliver Gould and Mary Brewster Jennings House, 7 E. 72nd St. 1898-1899. **Flagg & Chambers**. ● ♂

G100a

The rich opulence of **Napoleon III**'s Paris: vermiculated and rusticated voussoirs, deep-set French windows, gracious ironwork, and that luscious copper and slate roof make this the sweetmeat of the neighborhood. This and its sibling (see below) are among the city's finest town houses.

[G100b] **Lycée Français de New York**/originally Henry T. and Jessie Sloane House/later James Stillman House, 9 E. 72nd St. 1894-1896. **Carrère & Hastings**. ● ♂

G100b

New York's French have occupied their own image, an architectural home away from home. Here colonnaded grandeur is on display in contrast to the more subtle modulation next door.

[G101] **19 East 72nd Street** (apartments), NW cor. Madison Ave. 1936-1937. **Rosario Candela** with **Mott B. Schmidt**. Entrance enframement **C. Paul Jennewein**, sculptor. ○

This timid Art Moderne apartment house replaced **Charles Tiffany**'s robust Romanesque Revival mansion (an early **McKim, Mead & White** masterpiece), later decorated and occupied by his son, **Louis Comfort Tiffany**.

[G102] **Polo/Ralph Lauren (boutique)**/onetime Olivetti Building/originally Gertrude Rhinelander Waldo House, 867 Madison Ave., SE cor. E. 72nd St. 1895-1898. **Kimball & Thompson**. Altered for shops, 1921. ● ○

G102

Every part of this building exudes personality: bay windows, a roof line bristling with dormers and chimneys. The extraordinarily ornamented neo-French Renaissance limestone palace has captured the imagination of the commercial world since 1921, when it was first occupied by an antiques firm. It has subsequently housed interior decorators, auction houses like Christie's of London, the Zabar family's East Side outpost E.A.T., and now fashion designer **Ralph Lauren**'s flagship retail outlet. **Rhinelander Waldo**, socialite, hero of the Spanish-American War, and police commissioner can be observed "in action" in the novel and movie *Ragtime*.

G103b

[G103a] **Chase Bank**/formerly Manufacturers Hanover Trust Company branch, 35 E. 72nd St., bet. Madison and Park Aves. 1931. **Cross & Cross**. ○

G104a

A bank, of all things, in the manner of the **Brothers Adam**, who worked in 18th-century London and Edinburgh. Elegant.

[G103b] **Mayer House**, 41 E. 72nd St., bet. Madison and Park Aves. 1881-1882. **Robert B. Lynd**. ○

A town house from an earlier 72nd Street, long before brick, white limestone, and marble took over.

[G104a] **176 East 72nd Street** (town house) bet. Lexington and Third Aves. 1996. **Tod Williams Billie Tsien**.

A collage of glass, steel, and limestone crowned with a north-facing skylight. Surprising on this wide street of facing monumental apartment blocks.

[E104b] **Provident Loan Society of America branch**, 180 E. 72nd St. bet. Lexington and Third Aves. ca. 1895.

An exquisitely tiny Doric temple of finance, in the shadow of:

G104b

[E104c] **Tower East** (apartments), 190 E. 72nd St., SW cor. Third Ave. to E. 71st St. 1962. **Emery Roth & Sons**.

G105

A sheer, freestanding tower: 4 apartments per floor, all with magnificent views. One of Manhattan's earliest excursions into distinctive Modern high-rise luxury housing. Built on the site of the Loew's 72nd Street movie house.

[G105] **Word of Mouth** (catering and delicacies), 1012 Lexington Ave., bet. E. 72nd and E. 73rd Sts. W side. 1979. **Alfredo De Vido Assocs.**, architect. **Roger Whitehouse**, graphic designer. Second-floor café dining, 1992. **Alfredo De Vido**.

The café upstairs has De Vido–designed furnishings reminiscent of **Charles Rennie Mackintosh**.

East 73rd Street, between Fifth and Madison Avenues:

G106a

[G106a] **5 East 73rd Street** (town house). 1901. **Buchman & Fox**. ♂

Freestanding Beaux Arts embellished by the garden next door at No. 11, and wrapped in a stole of ivy.

[G106b] Originally **Joseph and Kate Pulitzer House**/now apartments, 11 E. 73rd St. 1900-1903. **Stanford White** of **McKim, Mead & White**. Rear extension, 1904, **Foster, Gade & Graham**. Converted to apartments, 1934, **James E. Casale**. ♂

G106b

It would be happy on the Grand Canal in Venice like Palazzo Pesaro, Rezzonico, or Labia: here, paired Ionic composite columns frame a glassy body. Also note the marshmallow rustications at the ground floor columns. The Pulitzer Prize in architecture—alas, a sad omission from that set of annual awards—should be given, retroactively, to this building.

[G107] Originally **Albert Blum House**, 20 E. 73rd St. 1911. **George and Edward Blum**. ♂

The best in the row from No. 8 to No. 26 ♂ , inclusive. The other façades (1897-1923) are by such architects as **Donn Barber** (No. 8), **Harry Allan Jacobs** (Nos. 10, 12), **William A. Boring** (No. 14), **William Lawrence Bottomley** (No. 18), and **Alexander M. Welch** (Nos. 24, 26).

[G108a] **Madison Avenue Presbyterian Church**, 917 Madison Ave., NE cor. E. 73rd St. 1899-1901. **James E. Ware & Sons**. Madison Ave. entrance altered, 1960, **Adams & Woodbridge**. ♂ [G108b] **Parish House**, 921-923 Madison Ave., bet. E. 73rd and E. 74th Sts. E side. 1816-1917. **James Gamble Rogers**. ♂

The plainness of the church's walls contrasts sharply with its ornate detail, making normal neo-Gothic carving appear extravagant. The 9-story parish house is a regal neo-Renaissance neighbor with Venetian overtones.

[G109a] **105 and 107 East 73rd Street** (town houses), bet. Park and Lexington Aves. 1881-1882. **Thom & Wilson**. Present façade, 1903. ○⟋
  Offbeat Arts and Crafts in brick and multipaned glass. Refreshing.

G109a

[G109b] **The Buckley School addition**/originally Mr. and Mrs. Arthur C. Train House, 113 E. 73rd St., bet. Park and Lexington Aves. 1908. **George B. Post & Sons**. Converted, new façade added, 1962 **Brown, Lawford & Forbes**. ○⟋
  A simple, well-scaled façade for an extension through the block from 74th Street for a venerable boys' private primary school.

[G109c] Originally **Charles Dana Gibson House**, 127 E. 73rd St., bet. Park and Lexington Aves. 1903. **Stanford White** of **McKim, Mead & White**. ○⟋
  Colonial Revival in limestone and red brick for the artist who created the Gibson Girl. Under renovation.

G109c

[G110a] Formerly **Mary E. W. Terrell House**, 925 Fifth Ave., bet E. 73rd and E. 74th Sts. ○⟋ [G110b] Originally **John W. Simpson House**, 926 Fifth Ave., bet. E. 73rd and E. 74th Sts. ○⟋ Both 1899. Both by **C. P. H. Gilbert**.
  A pair of Beaux Arts 5-story town houses representative of the modest Fifth Avenue houses at the turn of the century. Of the monumental ones only those that are museums or institutions (the Frick, Stuyvesant, Vanderbilt, Carnegie, Warburg, Straight mansions) remain.

G110, a and b

[G111] **927 Fifth Avenue** (apartments), SE cor. E. 74th St. 1917. **Warren & Wetmore**. ○⟋
  A modest—in façade, not rent—neo-Italian Renaissance apartment house.

[G112] **East 74th Street**, Fifth to Madison Aves. ○⟋
  Lined with unpresuming rows of brownstones, many refaced, dating from ca. 1869-1871, when the area was seeing its earliest development. Among the best of these are 9 and 11, limestone neo-Renaissance façades with Italian tile roofs. The king of the block is No. 4 (1899, **Alexander M. Welch**), a Beaux Arts beauty for the prolific local developers, **W. W. and T. M. Hall**. Its first occupant was hatmaker Stephen L. Stetson.

G112, No.4

┃ [G113] Originally **Raymond C. and Mildred Kramer**
━━ **House**, 32 E. 74th St., bet. Madison and Park Aves. 1934-1935. **William Lescaze**. ○⟋
  A handcrafted version of the machine aesthetic common to most Bauhaus-inspired design and architecture. Its original composition of glass, glass block, and white stucco must have startled its neighbors in the 1930s.

G113

[G114] **Church of the Resurrection** (Episcopal)/originally Church of the Holy Sepulchre (Episcopal), 115 E. 74th St., bet. Park and Lexington Aves. 1869. **Renwick & Sands**. ○⟋
  A shy retiring, side-street edifice of random ashlar bluestone with a steep polychrome slate roof. An ecclesiastical sleeper.

[G115] **Saga House**, 157 E. 74th, bet. Lexington and Third Aves. 1980s.
  A modestly scaled apartment house. The shiplike railings give it a step of style over the competition.

G114

G117

From Fifth Avenue and 74th Street to 75th and Madison:

[G116] **French Consulate**/originally Charles E. Mitchell House, 934 Fifth Ave., bet. E. 74th and E. 75th Sts. 1926. **Walker & Gillette**. ♂

G116

Rusticated limestone on a timid neo-Renaissance building; a Georgian entry supports the Italianate 2nd floor (*piano nobile*).

[G117] **The Commonwealth Fund**/originally Edward S. and Mary Stillman Harkness House, 1 E. 75th St., NE cor. Fifth Ave. 1907-1909. **Hale & Rogers**. ● ♂

A classy neo-Renaissance palace guarded by an intricate wrought-iron fence. The ornate cornice sports a lush frieze under dentils and console brackets.

[G118] Formerly **Harkness House for Ballet Arts**/originally Nathaniel L. McCready House/later Thomas J. Watson, Jr. House (IBM), 4 E. 75th St., bet. Fifth and Madison Aves. 1895-1896. **Trowbridge, Colt & Livingston**. Renovated for William Hale Harkness Foundation, 1965, **Rogers, Butler & Burgun**. ♂

Standard Oil heiress **Rebekah Harkness** transformed this chaste neo-French Renaissance double house into an opulent temple of Terpsichore, as the home of her very own ballet company. Ten years and $20 million later, she changed her mind and terminated the company. Sic transit . . .

[G119] **5 and 7 East 75th Street**, bet. Fifth and Madison Aves. 1902. **Welch, Smith & Provot**. ♂

Tooled and rusticated limestone, in the Beaux Arts mode.

G119

[G120] **964 Madison Avenue** (stores and offices), NW cor. E. 75th St. also known as 21-27 E. 75th St. 1925. **George F. Pelham**. Altered, ca. 1985. ♂

White-glazed terra-cotta Corinthian pilasters provide some elegant neo-Classical dress for this modest commercial temple.

[G121] **Whitney Museum of American Art**, 945 Madison Ave., SE cor. E. 75th St. 1963-1966. **Marcel Breuer & Assocs./Hamilton Smith**. ♂ Expansion, 1995-1998. **Richard Gluckman** of **Gluckman Mayner**. Open Su & We 11-6; Th 1-8; Fri & Sa 11-6; closed Tu. 212-570-3600.

Almost as startling on the city street as the Guggenheim, it boasts its wares with a vengeance. Reinforced concrete clad in granite, moated, bridged, cantilevered in progressive steps overshadowing the mere patron, it is a forceful place and series of spaces. The cantilevered floors recall the machicolations of Carcassonne—beware of boiling oil! The Whitney, nevertheless, is at the top of the list of must-be-seen modern objects in New York.

The Gluckman additions (articulated contiguous row houses) are in appropriately low-key contrast to the wildly controversial **Michael Graves** proposal.

G121

*Whitney Museum addition: In the spirit of MOMA's residential tower, the Whitney trustees in 1978 considered building a high-tech, high-rise, 35-story mixed-use tower to the south of the Breuer building by a collaboration of British architects **Foster Associates** and **Derek Walker Associates***. This plan was canceled in favor of an expansion to the museum itself, first proposed in 1986 by **Michael Graves**. The Graves scheme, to many, buried the Breuer under a panoply of Post-Modern forms, and was, happily, discarded in favor of the more civilized Gluckman proposals.*

G122

[G122] **980 Madison Avenue** (galleries)/originally Parke-Bernet Galleries/later Sotheby, Parke-Bernet, bet. E. 75th and E. 76th Sts. W side. 1950. **Walker & Poor**, architects. **Wheeler Williams**, sculptor. Addition upward, 1987, **Weisberg Castro Assocs**. ○⟨

Parke-Bernet once understood and catered to America's cultural starvation: buy history or at least live vicariously with its remnants. Unfortunately, Parke-Bernet's "house" is an insipid box unrelated to any cultural values. The **Wheeler Williams** sculpture pinned on the façade is a dreary gatekeeper, meaningless art at the portal of "art is money." The Parke-Bernet descendants have removed elsewhere, perhaps realizing the error of their ancestors' ways.

[G123a] **Miss Hewitt's Classes**/originally Dr. Ernest Stillman House, 45 E. 75th St., bet. Madison and Park Aves. 1925. **Cross & Cross**. ○⟨

A late neo-Georgian town house. **Dr. Stillman** was an amateur fire buff (as was **Mayor La Guardia**) and had installed an alarm system that would tell him where any current fire was located. He often served, unpaid, those needing medical care.

[G123b] **57 East 75th Street** (house), bet. Madison and Park Aves. 1979. **William B. Gleckman**. ○⟨

A curious former row house, transformed into an early "sliver building," a fate happily now outlawed.

G123b

[G124a] **823 and 829 Park Avenue** (apartments), bet. E. 75th and E. 76th Sts. E side. 1911. **Pickering & Walker**. ○⟨

Floral pilasters bracket windows in gently projecting central bays in these (almost) matching midblock and corner apartment blocks. A lovely touch.

[G124b] **821 Park Avenue** (tenement and store), NE cor. E. 75th St. 1891. **Lorenz Weiher**. ○⟨

A happily preserved façade from old 4th Avenue, built before the avenue's upgrade to "Park" status (upon the depression of the railroad and its subsequent covering). When this was built trains traveled in an open cut.

G124b

[G125] **Temple Israel** (synagogue), 112 E. 75th St., bet. Park and Lexington Aves. 1966. **Schuman & Lichtenstein**. ○⟨

Overpowering and austere.

[G126] **115 East 75th Street** (garage), bet. Park and Lexington Aves. 1887-1888. **George Martin Huss**. ○⟨

Some bold arches and handsome brickwork.

[G127] **Skyline Coffee Shoppe**, 374 Lexington Ave., SE cor. E. 75th St. 1880s.

Bayed and bracketed, this was a powerful corner anchor in the days when street and avenue were continuous brownstones.

G126

G127

[G128] **168, 170, 172, 174, 176 East 75th Street** (carriage houses) bet. Lexington and Third Aves. ca. 1900.

A clinker-brick complex of stables with a very complex and picturesque roof line. A happy punctuation in the blockscape.

G128

[G129] **32 East 76th Street** (apartments), bet. Madison and Park Aves., also known as 969 Madison Ave. 1983. **Stephen B. Jacobs & Assocs**. ♂

A stylish residential high rise on an L-shaped plot that wraps around to Madison.

 [G130] **Hotel Carlyle**, 35 E. 76th St., NE cor. Madison Ave. to E. 77 St. 1929. **Bien & Prince**. ♂

One of the last gasps of the Great Boom, this became, in its latter years, New York headquarters for both **Presidents Truman and Kennedy**, who usually stayed here when visiting the city. **Ludwig Bemelmans** was unleashed with delightful success in the bar; even the ceiling was not spared his whimsical brush as airplanes and birds float overhead.

G131

[G131] **The Imperial** (apartments), 55 E. 76th St., bet. Madison and Park Aves. 1883. **F. T. Camp**. ♂

A grand and gracious high-rise brownstone, one of the earliest apartment buildings in the city (French flats, as they were the imported idea of those decadent Parisians).

G132

G135

[G132] Formerly **Leonard N. Stern House**, 870 Park Ave., bet. E. 76th and E. 77th Sts. W side. 1898. Altered, 1976, **Robert A. M. Stern** and **John S. Hagman**. ♂

An altered stable, this bow-fronted faux-limestone early-Post Modern town house is an asset to Park Avenue.

[G133] **Percy and Harold D. Uris Pavilion, Lenox Hill Hospital**, Park Ave. NE cor. E. 76th St. 1975. **Rogers, Butler, Burgun & Bradbury**.

A handsome carved-brick monolith, a stylish contrast to the same firm's banal pink metal and glass curtain wall to the north.

G133

[G134] **Lenox Hill Hospital** (original remnant), Lexington Ave., bet. E. 76th and E. 77th Sts. 1890s.

Another early neighborhood building, arched and corniced.

[G135] **St. Jean Baptiste Church** (Roman Catholic), 1067-1071 Lexington Ave., SE cor. E. 76th St. 1910-1914. **Nicholas Serracino**. ♂ Restored, 1995-1996. **Hardy Holzman Pfeiffer**.

Pomp but not pompous. Outside, various Roman parts are clustered about a nave and transepts, unfortunately with a pasty result. Inside, the neo-Baroque reigns in gold and polychromy. The congregation was originally French Canadian, and the bill was paid by Thomas Fortune Ryan, who built the streetcar lines that allowed the congregation to get here.

G136

[G136] **The Siena** (apartment house), 188 E. 76th St., SW cor. Third Ave. 1997. **Hardy Holzman Pfeiffer**.

Air rights from St. Jean Baptiste allowed this slender shaft. Punctuated at its apex by belvederes at each of its four corners in the manner of a modern day Hawksmoor.

[G137] **863 Park Avenue** (apartments), NE cor. E. 77th St. 1908. **Pollard & Steinem**. ♂

A pioneer cooperative. Architectural historian **Christopher Gray** terms it "chaste and classical." He's right.

G137

[G138] **55 East 77th Street** (townhouse), bet. Madison and Park Aves. 1902. **Charles Brendon**.

Sinuous tracery under a grand arch framed in rusticated limestone.

M2

METROPOLITAN MUSEUM VICINITY

[M1] **Metropolitan Museum Historic District**, Along the E side of Fifth Ave. from E. 78th St. to E. 86th St. running irregularly through the Fifth-Madison blocks. ☞ Buildings within the district are denoted by ♂ .

M3

[M2] **N.Y.U. Institute of Fine Arts**/originally James B. and Nanaline Duke House, 1 E. 78th St., NE cor. Fifth Ave. 1909-1912. **Horace Trumbauer**. Interior remodeled, 1958, **Robert Venturi, Cope & Lippincott.** ♥ ♂

Reputedly a push here and a pull there made the Bordeaux Château Labottière into this austere and elegant town house, originally built for the Dukes, whose resources were those of the American Tobacco Company. Now it serves New York University graciously. **Julian Francis Abele**, Trumbauer's chief designer, and an early African-American architect, was probably responsible for the design.

M4

[M3] **Cultural Services, Embassy of France**/formerly Payne and Helen Hay Whitney House, 972 Fifth Ave., and former Henry Cook House, 973 Fifth Ave., both bet. E. 78th and E. 79th Sts. Both 1902-1909. **Stanford White** of **McKim, Mead & White.** ♥ ♂

Pale neighbors to the grand Dukes adjacent; anywhere else No. 972's swell and swelling façade, with its 24 Corinthian pilasters, would be the best act in town.

[M4] **3 and 5 East 78th Street** (town house), bet. Fifth and Madison Aves. No. 3, 1897-1899. **C. P. H. Gilbert**. No. 5, 1902-1904. **C. P. H. Gilbert.** ♂

Neo-Gothic, from late northern European Gothic.

M6

[M5] **4 East 78th Street** (townhouse), bet. Fifth and Madison Aves. 1887-1889. **Edward Kilpatrick.** ♂

A great brownstone rockface elliptical arch shelters a monumental porch. Wonderful.

[M6] **N.Y.U. Institute of Fine Arts: Conservation Center**/originally Albert Morgenstern House/later Mr. & Mrs. Andrew J. Miller House, 14 E. 78th St., bet. Madison and Fifth Aves. 1887. Façade altered for the Millers, 1917, **Harry Allan Jacobs**. ♂ Altered for N.Y.U., 1983, **Michael Forstl**.

Belying the twinned Ionic columns and simple 4-story 1917 façade, the innards are reconfigured as 15 levels of conservation facilities, including a cascade of floors built atop the old roof. The added structure catches north light but is invisible from the street.

METROPOLITAN MUSEUM VICINITY

see pages 416–424

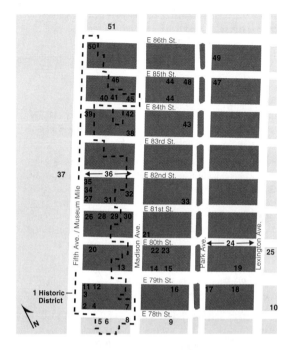

[M7] Originally **Stuyvesant and Marian Fish House**/now offices, 25 E. 78th St. NW cor. Madison Ave. 1897-1900. **Stanford White** of McKim, Mead & White. ♂

Limestone and yellow Roman brick combine for a dull façade. One of Stanford's bad days at the office.

[M8] **Philip and Beulah Robbins House**, 28 E. 78th St., SW cor. Madison Ave. 1899-1902. **McKim, Mead & White**. ♂

Comfortable Protestant Georgian, unassuming, but hardly timid.

M8

▐ [M9] **The Rabbi Joseph Lookstein Ramaz School
▬▬ Upper School**, The Morris B. and Ida Newman Educational Center, 60 E. 78th St., bet. Madison and Park Aves. 1980. **Conklin & Rossant**.

Five brownstone row houses of Finch College removed and, in their place, an Orthodox Jewish school inserted. Sleekly stylish on its arrival in 1980, dated at the Millennium. Let's pursue style, not the ephemeral stylish.

[M10] **157, 159, 161, 163-165 East 78th Street** (row houses), bet. Lexington and Third Aves. 1861. **Henry Armstrong**, builder. ●

Vernacular row houses inspired by the Italianate style, popular in the city in the 1850s and 1860s. The tall parlor windows, retained in all 5, are rare in these parts.

M9

East 79th Street, between Fifth and Madison Avenues:

▦ [M11] **Ukrainian Institute of America**/originally Isaac
▦ D. and Mary Fletcher House/then Harry F. Sinclair House/then Augustus and Ann van Horn Stuyvesant House, 2 E. 79th St., SE cor. Fifth Ave. 1897-1899. **C. P. H. Gilbert**. ♂

A French Gothic palace. The precedents are limited: few in the Middle Ages ever achieved commercial wealth. The classic comparison is the house of **Jacques Coeur** (ca. 1450) at Bourges.

M11

▞▞▞ [M12] **6 East 79th Street** (town house). 1899-1900.
▐ **Barney & Chapman**. ♂

A sensuous bowed façade converts what was designed for Anglican sobriety into an exotic Georgian Revival town house. The sturdy Doric columns at the base and the curved mansard roof add to its notability.

[M13] **Hanae Mori** (boutique)/formerly Richard Feigen Gallery, 27 E. 79th St., bet. Fifth and Madison Aves. Altered, 1969, **Hans Hollein and Baker & Blake**.
A chromium cylinder dominates this cubistic stucco entrance.

M12

[M14] **New York Society Library**/originally John S. and Catherine C. Rogers House, 53 E. 79th St., bet. Madison and Park Aves. 1916-1917. **Trowbridge & Livingston.** ☙
The library of the New York Society (rather than a library for members of society). Anyone may join for a yearly membership fee: 225,000 volumes and a quiet reading room.

[M15a] Originally **John H. and Catherine Iselin House**, 59 E. 79th St., bet. Madison and Park Aves. 1908-1909. **Foster, Gade & Graham.** ☙ [M15b] Originally **Thatcher and Frances Adams House**, 63 E. 79th St. 1902-1903. **Adams & Warren.** ☙

M14

[M15c] Originally George and Sarah Rives House/now **Consulate of Greece**, 67-69 E. 79th St. 1907-1908. **Carrère & Hastings**. Altered and expanded upward, 1962, **Pierre Zannettos.** ☙
Three different styles, each tied to Classical themes: neo-French Renaissance, neo-Georgian, neo-French Baroque, respectively.

[M16] **72-76 East 79th Street** (row and town houses)/converted to apartment tower, bet. Madison and Park Aves. Nos. 72-74, 1884. **Anson Squires.** ♂ No. 76, 1884, **James E. Ware.** ♂
M16   Conversion, 1988, **Conklin & Rossant**.
A strange tower looms over Victorian town houses: Beaux Arts Left Bank studios at the top, boredom at the waist, and a rich row of brick and brownstone at the street.

[M17] **895 Park Avenue** (apartments), SE cor. E. 79th St. 1929. **Sloan & Robertson.** ♂
Art Deco hasn't quite been embraced by these talented architects, nor has neo-Classicism been given a warm farewell. A handsome structure, nonetheless.

[M18] **Belgravia** (apartments), 124 E. 79th St., bet. Park and M17   Lexington Aves. 1987. **Gruzen Samton Steinglass**.
A suave dark red infill to the wall of tall 1920s (and post-World War II) apartments that line wide 79th.

[M19] **Hunter College School of Social Work, CUNY, Lois and Samuel Silberman Fund Building**, 127-135 E. 79th St., bet. Park and Lexington Aves. 1967. Enlarged, 1988. Both by **Wank Adams Slavin Assocs.**
The 5¢ Staten Island Ferry ride is a dim memory. But the nickel-a-year rent remains, here, thanks to the Silberman Fund, which owns the building and rents it to the school via a 20-year lease charging one dollar! After the first 20 years expansion was called for, but only in the usable space for teaching; the yearly rent—until 2007 at least—remains 5¢. The building itself sports a modest façade of vertically incised window openings in a gray terra-cotta (bottom) and white iron-spot brick (top) wall.

M19

[M20] **Franklyn and Edna Woolworth Hutton House**, and houses for her two sisters 2, 4, and 6 E. 80th St., NE cor. Fifth Ave. 1911-1916. **C.P.H.Gilbert.** ♂
F. W. Woolworth built them for his three daughters (an economical assemblage for the 5&10 cent store king). Two cool classic revivalists flank a late Gothic, Loire Valley château.

M20

M22

[M21] **45 East 80th Street** (apartments), NE cor. Madison Ave. 1987. **Liebman Liebman & Assocs.**

Twenty-seven crisp stories, with loftlike windows, faced with Italian granite and Indiana limestone. A Post Modern plinth continues Madison Avenue's 2 stories of shops and services.

[M22] **Manhattan Church of Christ**, 48 E. 80th St., bet. Madison and Park Aves. 1967. **Eggers & Higgins.**

Raw concrete from the "brutalist" years of the 1960s. **Le Corbusier** created his monastery, La Tourette, at the time of similar materials, but with a more sensitive hand and eye.

M21

[M23] **52 East 80th Street** (town house), bet. Madison and Park Aves. 1890s.

A copper-clad elliptical bay window serves as eyebrow and oriel for overlooking the street.

[M24] **East 80th Street**, Park to Lexington Aves.

Roll call on the south:

No. 116: Originally Lewis Spencer and Emily Coster Morris House. 1922-1923. **Cross & Cross.** 📷

A large, but modest, neo-Georgian residence that suffers from awkward proportions and timid windows (timid windows? Yes, dear reader, in New York they frequently lacked the impressive glassiness of the real English façade).

M24, No. 116

No. 120: Originally George and Martha Whitney House, 1929-1930 **Cross & Cross.** 📷

Cross & Cross provided better windows and a lot more self-confidence than they displayed at No. 116.

No. 124: Originally Clarence and Anne Douglass Dillon House. 1930. **Mott B. Schmidt.** 📷

Neo-Georgian again.

No. 130: Originally Vincent and Helen Astor House/now Junior League of the City of New York. 1927-1928. **Mott B. Schmidt.** 📷

Both the most subtle and most powerful of this grand grouping. Here brick Georgian gives way to travertine Regency, taut Ionic pilasters, and an elegant relieving arch in the manner of the Brothers Adam.

M24, No. 130

[M25] **Unitarian Church**, SE cor. Lexington Ave. and E. 80th Street. 1930s.

The tower's brick base is Regency in the manner of John Soane, the façade less so: the almost baroque broken pedimented entry portal takes away some of the austere power of its surrounding arch.

M25

[M26] **The Terrace, Stanhope Hotel**, 997 Fifth Ave., SE cor. E. 81st St. 1965. (Hotel, 1926, **Rosario Candela**.) ♂

A pleasurable addition to an old and elegant hotel. The sights equal those offered to café-sitters worldwide: the passing fair, the Metropolitan Museum, tottering dowagers, Jaguars, and the near jet set.

M27

[M27] **998 Fifth Avenue** (apartments), NE cor. E. 81st St. 1910-1912. **William Richardson** of McKim, Mead & White. ● ♂

A pacesetter in the design of Fifth Avenue. The understated Italian Renaissance detail rises to a rich cornice and frieze at the sky. Richardson's design grew from the work of the original partners, all dead at this point.

[M28] **14a East 81st Street** (town house), bet. Fifth and Madison Aves. 1991. **Buttrick White & Burtis.** ♂

Classical revival in limestone, a distant relative of Cheverny along the Loire? Retrofitted into the prewar landscape. Which war?

M28

[M29] **24 East 81st Street** (town house), bet. Fifth and Madison Aves. 1900-1902. **Buchman & Fox.** ♂

Rich neo-Renaissance with some late Gothic detail.

[M30] **26 East 81st Street** (apartments), SW cor. Madison Ave. 1900s.

A venerable residence from the turn of the century. The tan brick and limestone supports a glorious cornice, its frieze a continuous garland of swags.

M30

[M31] **Grenville Lindall Winthrop House**, 15 E. 81st St., bet. Fifth and Madison Aves. 1919-1921. **Julius F. Gayler.** ♂

Colonial Revival par excellence.

[M32] **La Résidence** (apartments), 1080 Madison Ave., bet. E. 81st and E. 82nd Sts. W side. 1981. **Thierry W. Despont**, designer; **Emil N. Steo**, architect.

A serene midblock high-rise addition to Madison Avenue that minimizes its tower by a setback from a carefully detailed base. Both bold and subtle, the windows are magnificent.

M32

[M33] **940 and 944 Park Avenue** (apartments), NW cor. E. 81st St. No. 940, 1926. **George & Edward Blum**. No. 944, 1929, **George F. Pelham.**

Within Park Avenue's somber urbanism, the materials, details, and textures provide an architecture of surface: here the vocabulary is Romanesque and Art Deco.

From Fifth Avenue and 82nd Street to Madison Avenue:

[M34] **1001 Fifth Avenue** (apartments), bet. E. 81st and E. 82nd Sts. 1978-1980. **Johnson/Burgee**, design architects. **Philip Birnbaum & Assocs.** associated architects. ♂

"Queen Anne front and Mary Ann behind." But here the façade, appliqué, reveals the behind as the side! The false front continues into the sky, where it is propped up for all to see.

M34

[M35] Originally **Benjamin N. and Sarah Duke House**, 1009 Fifth Ave., SE cor. E 82nd St. 1899-1901. **Welch, Smith & Provot.** ♠ ♂

It's hard to believe that this grandiose and palatial extravagance was a speculative house. Built by Upper East Side developers **W. W. and T. M. Hall**, it was quickly snapped up by a founder of the American Tobacco Company. Developers were different then.

M35

[M36] **East 82nd Street, Fifth to Madison Aves.**, on axis of the main entrance of the Metropolitan Museum. ♂

Rich façades as a group frame the Met's main entrance, as if they housed the court of the palace of art. Worth a special stroll. Roll call:

No. 2. ♂ Overblown Georgian: those console brackets got out of hand.

Nos. 3 and 5. ♂ Bowed bay and bowed front. Gargantuan dentils and florid keystones.

No. 14. ♂ The powerful bayed façade is incised with rustication and embellished with concave-surrounded arches.

Nos. 17 and 19. ♂ Look up to tan Roman brick and bowed fronts; the neo-Romanesque of the 1890s is struggling with the American Renaissance: check the cornices.

Nos. 20 and 22. ♂ Glassy eclecticisms.

M36, No. 3 & 5

[M37] **Metropolitan Museum of Art**, in Central Park facing Fifth Ave. bet. E. 80th and E. 84th Sts.

▥ **Rear façade** (now visible only within **Lehman Wing**), 1874-1880. **Calvert Vaux & J. Wrey Mould.** SW wing and façade, 1888, **Theodore Weston.**

▲ **Central Fifth Avenue façade**, 1895-1902, **Richard** ⅠⅠⅠⅠ **Morris Hunt** and **Richard Howland Hunt.**

▥ **Side wings along Fifth Ave.**, 1904-1926, **McKim, Mead & White.**

Thomas J. Watson Library, 1965, **Brown, Lawford & Forbes.**

▯ Front stairs, pools, **Lehman Wing**, and **Great Hall** reno▬ vations. 1969-1975. **Sackler Wing** for the Temple of Dendur, 1979. **American Wing**, 1980. **Michael C. Rockefeller Wing** for Primitive Art, 1981. **Dillon Galleries** for Far East Art, 1981. **André Meyer Galleries** for European Paintings, 1981. **Egyptian Wing**, 1982. **Wallace Galleries** for 20th Century Art, 1986. **Iris and B. Gerald Cantor Roof Garden**, 1987. **Tisch Galleries**, 1988. **European Sculpture and Decorative Art Wing**, 1989. All by **Kevin Roche John Dinkeloo & Assocs.** Open to the public. ♠ Partial Interior (Great Hall and Stair) ♠ Open Su & Tu-Th 9:30-5:15; Fr & Sa 9:30-8:45; closed Mo. 212-879-5500.

M36, No. 17 & 19

The neo-Renaissance design example for this elegant warehouse of art was revealed at the World's Columbian Exposition of 1893, at which the opposing Romanesque Revival style lost its position of preeminence.

Vaux's earlier Ruskinian Gothic kernel is now largely encased: the Fifth Avenue frontage filled in with a City Beautiful palace in the manner of Versailles, the behind devoured by the Lehman Wing, a flashy glass pyramid flanked by walls designed to screen what Roche and Co. considered the vulgar excesses of Vaux. It is a rich and confusing mélange—exciting, grand, controversial, often elegant, sometimes banal. The main hall is still one of the great spaces of New York, the city's only suggestion of

M37

the visionary neo-Roman spaces of the 18th-century Italian draftsman and engraver, Piranesi.

Since 1969 the museum has undergone a reconstruction and expansion, unrivaled by any museum in America (if not the world), designed by architect **Kevin Roche**. Many are offended by their impact on Central Park.

The works within are without peer. Savor them moment by moment, year by year. (Mandatory contribution—an oxymoron—on entry.)

M39

[M38] 25 East 83rd Street (apartments), NW cor. Madison Ave. 1938. **Frederick L. Ackerman** and **Ramsey & Sleeper**. Altered, 1986.

A modern monument, not in its external elegance but in its pacesetting technology: the first centrally air-conditioned apartment building in the city (note that there are no grilles penetrating the walls—air is drawn in at the roof and distributed by interior ductwork). In the 1980s the glass block "windows" thought necessary for economical cooling were removed in favor of clear glass, perhaps giving the building a new lease on life, but losing much of its prescient modernist flavor.

M40

[M39] Marymount School/originally Jonathan and Harriet Thorne House, 1028 Fifth Ave., SE cor. E. 84th St. 1901-1903. **C. P. H. Gilbert**.

Praise to the Church for preserving this handsome mansion by default. The school also occupies Nos. 1026 and 1027 (1901-1903. **Van Vleck & Goldsmith**).

[M40] 3 East 84th Street (apartments), bet. Fifth and Madison Aves. 1927-1928. **Howells & Hood**.

Cubistic modeling presages **Raymond Hood**'s later News and McGraw-Hill Buildings. The glistening spandrels seem to be fashioned of Navajo silver.

M42

[M41] **9 and 11 East 84th Street** (town houses), bet. Fifth and Madison Aves. 1902-1903. **Warren & Wetmore**.

Hood's limestone neighbors.

[M42] **1128 Madison Avenue** (stores), SW cor E. 84th St. 1986. **Rosenblum/Harb**.

A clever expansion and recladding of a dull 2-story taxpayer turns it from a pumpkin into Cinderella's coach. Through talent, not magic.

M43

[M43] **Church of St. Ignatius Loyola** (Roman Catholic), 980 Park Ave., SW cor. E. 84th St. 1895-1900. **Schickel & Ditmars**.

Vignola (mannerist Italian architect) in the American man-

M46

ner with a German accent. Limestone, superscaled, air-conditioned, grim, proper, and Park Avenue-ish. The chapel downstairs is an ethnic balancer, dedicated to **St. Laurence O'Toole**, titular saint of Yorkville's mid-1800s Irish settlers. St. Lawrence's church, the foundations of which form this basement starting in 1884, was nosed out by St. Ignatius for the final building.

[M44] **Regis High School** (Roman Catholic), 55 E. 84th St., bet. Madison and Park Aves. 1913-1917. **Maginnis & Walsh.** 🍎
Eight grand Ionic columns are the armature of this façade; the building goes through the block to 85th Street.

M44

[M45] **Row houses:** 21 East 84th Street, bet. Fifth and Madison Aves. and 1132 and 1134 Madison Ave., NW cor. E. 84th St. 1892. **John H. Duncan.** ♂
A brick and terra-cotta terrace (English grouping of jointly designed town houses), now sullied by unhappy storefronts on the avenue. But look up to the frieze.

[M46] **16 and 18 East 85th Street** (town houses), bet. Fifth and Madison Aves. 1988. **Gwathmey Siegel & Assocs.**
Brash Modernist façades of deep-set square openings (with square subdivisions) and bayed balconies. A bold, but hard, statement.

M45

[M47] **New World Foundation**/formerly Lewis Gouverneur and Nathalie Bailey Morris House, 100 E. 85th St., SE cor. Park Ave. 1913-1914. **Ernest Flagg.** 🍎
The radical English architect and urban designer Richard Norman Shaw (1831-1912) converted Georgian fantasies into such rich and complex places as this. A sprightly collision of quarter-round windows, widow's walks, and dormers flying in all directions. Among Flagg's best. For more monumental Flagg see the Little Singer Building.

[M48] **Park Avenue Christian Church** (Disciples of Christ)/originally South Reformed Church, 1010 Park Ave., SW cor. E. 85th St. 1911. **Cram, Goodhue & Ferguson.**
Native materials, here Manhattan schist, were assembled with inspiration from the Sainte-Chapelle in Paris. Such were the words of Cram, but the inspiration seems to have been effective largely for the flèche. (Sainte-Chapelle is a glass box with incidental stone supports; this is a stone box with incidental glass.)

M49

[M49] Originally **Reginald and Anna DeKoven House**, 1025 Park Ave., bet. E. 85th and E. 86th Sts. E side. 1911-1912. **John Russell Pope.** 🍎

M50

An urban adaptation of Jacobean Revival that was opportunely overlooked in the serial redevelopment of Park Avenue. DeKoven (1859-1920) was a composer of popular light opera; his "O, Promise Me" was a wedding standby for generations.

[M50] **Sabarsky Museum of German Expressionist Art**/formerly Mrs. Cornelius Vanderbilt House/originally William Starr Miller House. 1048 Fifth Ave., SE cor. E. 86th St. 1912-1914. **Carrère & Hastings.**

An elegant émigré—from the Place des Vosges without the Place; a town palace of limestone and brick (reinforced with Ionic pilasters), crowned with a slate mansard roof. Now an archive of Yiddish culture (watch for unusual exhibition subjects).

[M51] **The Town Club**/originally William and Elsie Woodward House, 9 E. 86th St., bet. Fifth and Madison Aves. 1916-1918. **Delano & Aldrich.**

An austere limestone and marble neo-Classical house with an entry that seems to lead to some building within the block and beyond.

CARNEGIE HILL AND BEYOND

Carnegie's Hill is most pronounced as you move uptown along Madison Avenue above 86th Street or downtown on Park at 96th Street, where trains bound for Grand Central dive into the 2½-mile tunnel which burrows beneath the glitter and swank of Park Avenue. The area covered here runs from 87th to 106th Streets east of Fifth, over to Lexington and environs below 96th, over to Park and environs above 96th. Remember, the Carnegie Hill Historic District is just a fraction of this area.

C1a

[C1a] **Liederkranz Club**/originally Henry and Annie Phipps House, 6 E. 87th St., bet. Fifth and Madison Aves. 1902-1904. **Grosvenor Atterbury.** ♂

The relocated sculpture in the eastern side yard (1896. **G. Moretti**, sculptor) commemorates the semicentennial of the German music society (1847-1897) that vacated its earlier quarters at 115 East 58th Street in 1949 (demolished since).

[C1b] **Phelps-Stokes Fund**/formerly Buttinger House, 10 E. 87th St., bet. Fifth and Madison Aves. 1958. **Felix Augenfeld & Jan Hird Pokorny.** ♂

Built as a house around a private library, which occupies a handsome, 2-story glass-walled place.

C1a

[C1c] **The Capitol** (apartments), 12 E. 87th St., bet. Fifth and Madison Aves. 1910-1911. **George & Edward Blum.** ♂

White brick and glazed ornamental terra-cotta sheathe this early Blum apartment block.

[C2] **Park Avenue Synagogue**, 50 E. 87th St., SE cor. Madison Ave. 1980. **James Rush Jarrett** and **Schuman Lichtenstein Claman & Efron**, associated architects.

The façade is clad in "Mankato stone, cut in a rusticated manner." Post Modern.

C2

[C3] **Solomon R. Guggenheim Museum**, Fifth Ave. bet. E. 88th and E. 89th Sts. 1956-1959. **Frank Lloyd Wright.** Aye Simon Reading Room, 1978, **Richard Meier & Assocs.** ♂ ♂ Interior ♂

Addition along E boundary facing E. 89th St. 1992. **Gwathmey Siegel & Assocs.** ♂ Open, except Th, 10-8. 212-423-3500.

The Guggenheim's central space is one of the great Modernist interiors in the world: a museum important more as architecture than for the contents it displays. To appreciate it, take the elevator (half round) to the skylighted top and meander, literally, between the structural baffles, down the helical

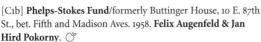

C3

C3

CARNEGIE HILL & BEYOND

see pages 425–435

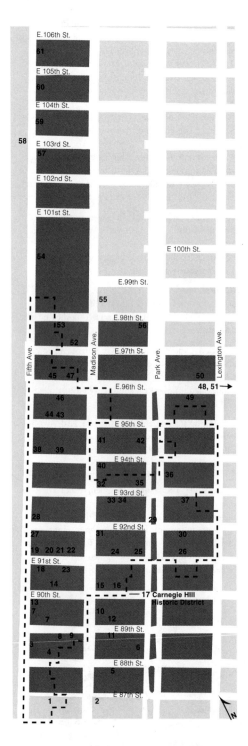

ramp. The new 89th Street addition forms a relatively neutral backdrop for Wright's spectacle, and provides much needed backup spaces for the complex.

[C4a] **5, 7 and 9 East 88th Street** (town houses), bet. Fifth and Madison Aves. 1901-1903. **Turner and Killian.**
Beaux Arts design in limestone and brick. These are Wright's

"decadent" neighbors (but he always stayed at the Plaza while working on the Guggenheim!).

[C4b] **Fulton and Mary Cutting House**, 15 E. 88th St., bet. Fifth and Madison Aves. 1919-1922. **Delano & Aldrich**. ♂

[C5] **60 East 88th Street** (apartments), bet. Madison and Park Aves. 1987. **Beyer Blinder Belle**.

A restrained midblock handshake between the traditions of the 1920s and those of the Post Modern. The French-doored balconettes are stylishly outfitted with flat metal railings.

C4a

[C6] **1082 Park Avenue** (apartments), bet. E. 88th and E. 89th Sts. W side. Altered, ca. 1927.

Tuscany in terra-cotta.

[C7] **National Academy of Design**/originally Collis P. Huntington Houses, 1083 Fifth Ave., bet. E. 89th and E. 90th Sts. **Turner & Kilian**; and 3 E. 89th St., bet. Fifth and Madison Aves. 1913-1915. **Ogden Codman, Jr.** No. 5, 1957-1959, **William and Geoffrey Platt**. ♂ Open to the public: We-Su 12-5; Fr 12-8; closed Mo & Tu. 212-369-4880.

Once a center of conservatism in the arts, it has recently become a refreshing repository for imaginative exhibitions. Founded in 1825, it includes architects, painters, and graphic designers.

C5

[C8] **St. David's School**/originally the Cutting Houses, 12, 14, and 16 E. 89th St., bet. Fifth and Madison Aves. 1919-1922. **Delano & Aldrich**. ♂

Comely Neo-Georgian town houses with elegant arched and layered façades at the ground level: designed to read as a single building.

C6

C9

C7

[C9] **Graham House** (apartments), 22 E. 89th St., SW cor. Madison Ave. 1891-1893. **Thomas Graham**. ♂

The serendipitous entry portal combines Romanesque columns with urban fantasies: a wonderful addition to the city, now entering its third century.

[C10] **45 East 89th Street**, along Madison Ave., bet. E. 89th and E. 90th Sts. E side. 1969. **Philip Birnbaum** and **Oppenheimer, Brady & Lehrecke**, associated architects.

A notch above its competition, particularly at the lower levels.

[C11] **50 East 89th Street** (apartments), bet. Madison and Park Aves., through to E. 88th St. 1974. **Emery Roth & Sons**.

A modest Modern midblock neighbor, in exposed concrete and dignified dark brick.

C11

C12

[C12] **Church of St. Thomas More** (Roman Catholic)/ originally Beloved Disciple Protestant Episcopal Church/ later East 89th Street Reformed Church, 59-63 E. 89th St., bet. Madison and Park Aves. 1870. **Hubert & Pirsson**. Chapel to the west, 1879. Rectory, 65 E. 89th St. 1880-1893.

A "country" church of Nova Scotia sandstone that has survived the percolating real estate cauldron of the Upper East Side. Over the years, its worth has been recognized by several religious denominations.

East 90th Street, between Fifth and Madison Aves:

C13

[C13] **Church of the Heavenly Rest** (Episcopal), SE cor. Fifth Ave. and E. 90th St. 1926-1929. **Hardie Philip** of **Mayers, Murray & Philip**, architects. ♂ Pulpit Madonna, **Malvina Hoffman**, sculptor. Exterior sculpture **Ulrich Ellerhausen**.

Stripped Gothic, with strong superficial massing prefiguring stylish modernism, an external dress over more conservative space within.

[C14a] Originally **George L. McAlpin House**/later Roswell and Margaret Carnegie Miller House, 9 E. 90th St. 1902-1903. **George Keister**. Connected to 2 E. 91st (Cooper-Hewitt) and altered. 1996-1997. **Polshek Partnership**. ♠ ♂

Carnegie's daughter and her family lived here, abutting her parent's garden. Now an annex to the Cooper-Hewitt Museum. Colonial Revival. But from which colony?

C14b

[C14b] Originally **William and Louise McAlpin House**/later Grafton W. and Anne Minot House, 11 E. 90th St. 1902-1903. **Barney & Chapman**. New façade and alterations, 1929. **A. Wallace McCrea**. ♠ ♂

An 18th-century façade replaced the Beaux Arts 19th-century façade by **Barney & Chapman**: 1929 vs. 1903 reverts to an earlier era! Oh, those Americans.

[C14c] Originally **Emily Trevor House**, 15 E. 90th St. 1927-1928. **Mott B. Schmidt**. ♠ ♂

Neo-Federal with Flemish-bond brick, a tepid 1920s favorite style in many of these park blocks.

C14d

[C14d] Originally **Harriet S. Clark House**, 17 E. 90th St. 1917-1919. **F. Burrall Hoffman, Jr**. ♠ ♂

This neo-Georgian house is based on a loggia, arcaded in the manner of Covent Garden or the Place des Vosges.

Sinclair Lewis and *Dorothy Thompson*, *husband and wife, lived in the undistinguished apartment block at 21 East 90th Street in the early 1930s. They maintained two sitting rooms so they could entertain guests separately.*

C15

[C15] **1261 Madison Avenue** (apartments), NE cor. E. 90th St. 1900-1901. **Buchman & Fox**. ♠ ♂

Built to house only 14 families, this gracious Beaux Arts apartment building enhances Carnegie Hill.

[C16] **57-61 East 90th Street** (row houses), bet. Madison and Park Aves. 1886-1887. **J. C. Cady & Co**. ♂

A trio, with 57 showing its original colors: brownstone alternately smooth and rockfaced. Elegant.

[C17] **Carnegie Hill Historic District**. 86th Street to 98th Street, between Madison and Fifth Avenues, with a grand peninsula eastward to Lexington Avenue, varying between 90th and 95th Streets. ♠

A landmark district continuing the spirit and embrace of the Upper East Side and Metropolitan Museum Historic Districts to the south.

C16

East 91st Street, between Fifth and Madison Avenues:

[C18] **Cooper-Hewitt Museum, National Museum of Design, Smithsonian Institution**/originally Andrew and Louise Carnegie House, 2 E. 91st St., SE cor. Fifth Ave. to E. 90th St. 1899-1903. **Babb, Cook & Willard.** ● ○ Converted to museum, 1977, **Hardy Holzman Pfeiffer Assocs.** Renovations, 1996. **Polshek Partnership.** Open to the public: Su 12-5; Tu 10-9; We-Sa 10-5; closed Mo. 212-860-6868.

C18

When Carnegie built this brick and limestone château, squatters were his neighbors. **Louise and Andrew Carnegie** lived here from 1901 until the surviving Louise's death in 1946. Its new life is as houser and exhibitor of the great collection originally assembled for the Cooper Union by the Cooper and Hewitt families—the decorative arts, from wallpaper to furniture—and as a stage for imaginative exhibitions in the decorative arts, architecture, graphics, and you-name-it.

[C19] **Duchesne Residence School faculty residence,** also known as Convent of the Sacred Heart/originally Otto and Addie Kahn House, 1 E. 91st St., NE cor. Fifth Ave. 1913-1918. **J. Armstrong Stenhouse** with **C. P. H. Gilbert.** ● ○

C19

A Leviathan house (145 feet of frontage, 6 lots wide), and an American version of an English version of an Italian Renaissance palace (cf. Palazzo della Cancelleria in Rome). It is rich but subdued, as expected in Boston or Florence.

[C20] **Duchesne Residence School**, Convent of the Sacred Heart/originally James A. and Florence Vanderbilt Sloane Burden, Jr., House, 7 E. 91st St. 1902-1905. **Warren, Wetmore & Morgan.** ● ○

C20

Built by the industrialized ironmonger from Troy, N.Y., whose commercial legacy was the American Machine and Foundry Company (AMF). A freestanding mansion with a side court.

[C21] **Consulate of the Russian Federation**/originally John Henry and Emily Vanderbilt Sloane Hammond House, 9 E. 91st St. 1902-1903. **Carrère & Hastings.** ● ○ Alterations, 1976, **William B. Gleckman.**

C21

Hammond's world was recorded in popular history when **Benny Goodman** became his son-in-law. The Soviet government appreciates style and bought it for their first New York consulate since 1942; it now houses the consulate of the Russian Federation. A palace worthy of anybody.

[C22] **Consulate of the Russian Federation**/originally John B. and Caroline Trevor House, 11 E. 91st St. 1909-1911. **Trowbridge & Livingston**. ● ○

A pale neighbor of the magnificence to the west.

[C23] **The Spence School**, 22 E. 91st St. 1929. **John Russell Pope**. Addition, 1988, **Fox & Fowle**. ○

A high-rise, watery neo-Georgian by someone who should have known better, **John Russell Pope**, whose National Gallery of Art is one of Washington's most elegant oases. The Spence addition means not to compete.

C23

[C24] **The Dalton School**, the First Program, 61 E. 91st St., bet. Madison and Park Aves. 1923-1924. **Mott B. Schmidt**. ○

Large and well scaled, a convincing neo-Georgian town house, with windows appropriately large; eaveless, with the attic roof set back behind the façade wall.

[C25] **Brick Presbyterian Church**, 1140-1144 Park Ave., NW cor. E. 91st St. 1938. **York & Sawyer; Lewis Ayres**, designer. Chapel of the Reformed Faith, 1952, **Adams & Woodbridge**. ○

C25

The safe brick and limestone American academic neo-Georgian of the 1930s.

[C26] **115-121 East 91st Street** (row houses), bet. Park and Lexington Aves. 1876-1877. **Arthur B. Jennings**. ○

Bay windows offer pregnant views across town. Simple brownstones raised to a more substantial state of architecture.

[C27] **1107 Fifth Avenue** (apartments), SE cor. E. 92nd St. 1924-1925. **Rouse & Goldstone**. ○

C26

Mrs. Marjorie Merriweather Post (Toasties) Close Hutton (later) Davies May sold her town house to a developer who provided her with a superb 54-room triplex vantage point in space. Note the elegant auto entrance on 92nd Street.

[C28] **The Jewish Museum**/originally Felix and Frieda S. Warburg House, 1109 Fifth Ave., NE cor. E. 92nd St. 1907-1909. **C. P. H. Gilbert**. Cloned addition to the north on Fifth, 1990-1993. **Kevin Roche**. ● ○ Open to the public: Su, Mo, We, Th 11-5:45; Tu 11-8; closed Fr & Sa. 212-423-3200.

This neo-Loire Valley château is a surprising envelope for a museum of Jewish art and history (the hermit crab syndrome: except here a wandering museum found a delightful carapace); but the image was so powerful that, on expansion, modernist **Kevin Roche** (from Ireland) chose to replicate precisely the existing architecture as he crept north on Fifth. AIA Guide co-author **Elliot Willensky** was a consultant to the Museum in choosing the architect who did these good works.

[C29] "**Night Presence IV**" (sculpture), on the Island in Park Ave., N of E. 92nd St. 1972. **Louise Nevelson**, sculptor. ○

This purposely rusty (self-weathering) steel construction is a feisty Modern loner in these neo-Renaissance precincts.

C30

[C30] **120 and 122 East 92nd Street** (town houses)/originally John C. and Catherine E. Rennett House and Adam C. Flanigan House, bet. Park and Lexington Aves. 120, 1871. Maybe **Albro Howell**, builder. 122, 1859. ● ○

A homely scale. Wooden houses from rural times. Even in their isolation, they had to conform to the commissioners' (grid) plan of 1811.

[C31] **1283-1293 Madison Avenue** (town houses), SE cor. E. 92nd St. 1889-1890. **James E. Ware**. ○

Vigorous pioneers from the 1880s, these Romanesque

Revivals still present their strong character over tawdry shops below.

East 93rd Street, between Madison and Park Avenues:

[C32] **1321 Madison Avenue** (row house), NE cor. E. 93rd St. 1890-1891. **James E. Ware.** 🍎 ♂

Craggy Queen Anne: mysterious and so rich in detail that the later Madison Avenue storefront insertions can almost be overlooked. Almost.

C33

[C33] Onetime **Smithers Alcoholism Center, St. Luke's-Roosevelt Hospital Center**/formerly Billy Rose House/originally William Goadby and Florence Baker Loew House, 56 E. 93rd St. 1930-1931. **Walker & Gillette.** 🍎 ♂

The last great mansion, it has the manners of **John Soane**, the avant-garde Regency architect who used classic parts with a fresh attitude toward form and space. **Florence Loew** chose the site to be near her brother, **George Baker, Jr.**

C34

[C34] **Lycée Français de New York**/formerly Permanent Mission of Romania to the United Nations/originally Virginia Graham Fair Vanderbilt House, 60 E. 93rd St. 1930-1931. **John Russell Pope.** 🍎 ♂ Altered to Lycée, 1976, **William B. Gleckman.**

Another in the flock of grand mansions dedicated to the education of a French-speaking child. Look at the voussoirs: each has the face of a different woman.

[C35a] Originally intended as **George F. Baker, Sr. House,** 67 E. 93rd St. 1931. **Delano & Aldrich.** 🍎 ♂

[C35b] Originally addition to, and courtyard for, **George F. Baker, Jr. House**, 69 E. 93rd St. 1928-1929. **Delano & Aldrich.** 🍎

[C35c] Originally Francis F. Palmer House/later George F. Baker, Jr. House/now **The Synod of Bishops of the Russian Orthodox Church Outside of Russia**, 75 E. 93rd St. 1917-1918; northern addition, 1928, both by **Delano & Aldrich.** 🍎 ♂

C35a

A beautifully fashioned urban complex in the neo-Federal style. The main building, built by Francis F. Palmer, was bought by George F. Baker, Jr. (then Chairman of the First National Bank) ten years after it was begun. Baker enlarged the house with a ballroom, garage and town house for his father, George F. Baker, Sr., the addition embracing a courtyard. An urbane gesture, much in the French manner. Unfortunately, George F. Baker, Sr. died before he could enjoy his new pied-à-terre.

[C36] **1185 Park Avenue** (apartments), bet. E. 93rd and E. 94th Sts. E side. 1928-1929. **Schwartz & Gross.** ♂

A full blockfront with a central interior court (square doughnut) in the manner of the West Side's Apthorp and Belnord. The ogee-arched pedestrian and carriage entrances are an elegant fantasy.

C36

[C37] **128 East 93rd Street** (house), bet. Park and Lexington Aves. 1866. **Edmund Waring.** ♂

A restored mansarded frame house: too much restoration (or is it reconstruction here?) can put out the flame. An entrance porch originally met the street, but basement space is precious, and the porch gave way to "progress."

[C38] **International Center of Photography**/formerly National Audubon Society/originally Willard and Dorothy Whitney Straight House, 1130 Fifth Ave., NE cor. E. 94th St. 1913-1915. **Delano & Aldrich.** Remodeled, 1974, **Robert**

C38

Simpson. ◉ ♂ Open Tu 11-8; We-Su 11-6; closed Mo.
212-860-1777.

Elegant, distilled, refined; a sharp, precise, intellectually
studied eclectic Georgian house with a homely residential scale.
The Center is a pleasant, low-keyed use of its original rooms.

C39

[C39] 5-25 East 94th Street (row houses) bet. Fifth and
Madison Aves. 1892-1894. **Cleverdon & Putzel.** ♂

A speculator's row of brownstone, whitestone, and rock-face
ashlar Romanesque Revival houses with a variety of detail for individuality. Nos. 15, 17, 21, and 25 are the most vigorous of the lot.

[C40] Carnegie Hill Tower (apartments), 40 E. 94th St., SE cor.
Madison Ave. 1983. **Edward Giannasa.**

Well tailored in pale brick. In a curious way its sliced-off
corner pays its respects to the gutsier cylindical tower of the
armory, across the street.

C41

**[C41] West façade of Squadron A Armory, 8th Regiment,
N.Y. National Guard**, Madison Ave., bet. E. 94th and E.
95th Sts. E side. 1893-1895. **John Rochester Thomas.** ◉

A fantasy of the brickmason's virtuosity: arches, corbels,
crenellations; plastic, neomedieval modeling. Now a play castle,
a backdrop for the open space of Hunter's facilities to the east.

C42

[C42] Hunter College Campus Schools/formerly Hunter
High School/originally Intermediate School 29,
Manhattan, Park Ave. bet. E. 94th and E. 95th Sts. W side. 1969.
Morris Ketchum, Jr. & Assocs. ♂

Castellated brick complementing its old machicolated neighbor, the west façade of which is preserved as a monument along
Madison Avenue. But why didn't they use the same colored
mortar?

C43

[C43] Originally Ernesto and Edith Fabbri House/now
The House of the Redeemer, 7 E. 95th St., bet. Fifth
and Madison Aves. 1914-1916. **Egisto Fabbri** and **Grosvenor
Atterbury.** ◉ ♂

A limestone palazzo with iron gates flanked by urn-support-
ing piers.

East 96th Street, between Fifth and Madison Avenues:

[C44] Lycée Français de New York/formerly Mrs.
Amory B. Carhart House, 3 E. 95th St. 1913-1916. **Horace
Trumbauer.** ◉ ♂

Another branch of this ubiquitous French school slipped into
a tranported Parisian hôtel. The carriage doors (man-door inset)
are a typical French division between the public world and the
private house and garden. Another surprise from Trumbauer's
chief draftsman, African-American Architect **Julian Abele**.

C45

[C45] Manhattan Country School/originally Ogden Codman,
Jr. House, 7 E. 96th St. 1912-1913. **Ogden Codman, Jr.** ◉ ♂

Painted limestone, a shuttered cartoon of the Renaissance.
Codman and co-author **Edith Wharton** wrote: *The Decoration
of Houses.*

[C46] Scuola New York Guglielmo Marconi/formerly The
Emerson School/originally Robert L. and Marie Livingston
House, 12 E. 96th St. 1916. **Ogden Codman, Jr.** ♂

Another Codman design for this block. Note the
garlanded swags.

[C47] Originally **Lucy Drexel Dahigren House**/later
Pierre Cartier House, 15 E. 96th St. 1915-1916. **Ogden
Codman, Jr.** ◉ ♂

A magisterial limestone town house, disciplined yet lively with French Renaissance motifs. Owner Cartier was of the originally French jewelry firm. Codman (who lived at No. 7) was something of a Francophile: he compiled an index of all known French châteaux, some 36,000!

C47

[C48] **The Monterey Public Garden**, 175 E. 96th St., NW cor. 3rd. Ave. 1994. **Weintraub & di Domenico**.

French formalism compressed into this urbane landscape. The building built it to gain zoning credits and hence more floors. The payback to the neighborhood is substantial (usually not the case with zoning bonuses).

C48

Nineteen stories or thirty-one? The higher numbers, according to the developer of the apartment tower at 108 East 96th Street, the lower according to the city's Building Department, the Board of Standards and Appeals, and a succession of state courts. The excess stories were spotted in 1986 by the president of a local community group, CIVITAS. The city's subsequent stop-work order was followed (because of a loophole) by a furious effort on the part of the developer to complete the building, working from the top of the converted dozen stories downward. The offending twelve stories were, nevertheless, demolished.

[C49] **New York Public Library**, 126 E. 96th St., bet. Park and Lexington Aves. 1900s.

A cool and sleek limestone palazzo for Carnegie Hill booklovers.

[C50] **Saint Francis de Sales** (Roman Catholic), 135 East 96th St., bet. Park and Lexington Aves. 1890s.

A triumphal façade of twin Ionic columns supporting a pediment. Rustications below make the unfluted columns and smooth wall above seem even smoother.

C50

C51

[C51] **Islamic Cultural Center** (mosque), 201 E. 96th St., NE cor. Third Ave. Mosque, 1991. **Skidmore, Owings & Merrill**. Minaret, 1991. **Swanke Hayden Connell**.

Built askew of Manhattan's grid, the mosque is oriented in the traditional fashion toward Islam's Mecca, in Saudi Arabia.

[C52] **St. Nicholas Russian Orthodox Cathedral**, 15 E. 97th St., bet. Fifth and Madison Aves. 1901-1902. **John Bergesen**. ☙

An exotic form among dour surroundings. High Victorian, Ruskinian, eclectic, polychromatic (red brick, blue and yellow

C52

tile), crosses, arches, ornations, and a bunch of delicious onion domes.

[C53] **St. Bernard's School**, 4 E. 98th St., bet. Fifth and Madison Aves. 1918. **Delano & Aldrich.** ☌

For boys, not the dogs of monks. An awkward neo-Georgian.

Mt. Sinai Medical Center:

C54a

[C54a] **Mt. Sinai Medical Center**, E. 98th to E. 102nd Sts., Fifth to Madison Aves. Original buildings, 1904, **Arnold W. Brunner.**
[C54b] **Magdalene and Charles Klingenstein Pavilion**, 1952, **Kahn & Jacobs.**

[C54c] **Annenberg Building**, 1976, **Skidmore, Owings & Merrill.**

[C54d] **Guggenheim Pavilion**, Phase 1, 1989; Phase 2, 1991. Both by **I. M. Pei, Pei Cobb Freed & Partners.**

It grew within the grid (absorbing two cross streets), rebuilding itself in the same manner as Roosevelt, Lenox Hill, and so many other hospitals; the body remained and gradually changed its appearance.

C54c

The high-rise Annenberg Building at center block, surrounded by a plaza space, is a great, rusty, cadaverous block-buster of a building, an incursive hulk that dominates the skyline of East Harlem (to its east). The Metzger Pavilion (by Brunner) faces Annenberg at midblock, a French Baroque Revival delight. But the new Guggenheim Pavilion brings elegance to the hospital patient. Built surrounding an atrium/skylit court, patients' rooms share this grand space.

Sphere (1967. **Arnaldo Pomodoro**) is a sophisticated punctuation to the plaza space.

C55

[C55] **East Building, Mt. Sinai School of Medicine**, 1425 Madison Ave., bet. 98th and 99th Sts. E side. 1997. **Davis Brody Bond.**

An austere, but richly modeled, composition providing multi-purpose research facilities.

[C56] **Jane B. Aron Residence Hall, Mt. Sinai Medical Center**, 50 E. 98th St., SW cor. Park Ave. 1984. **Davis, Brody & Assocs.**

A composition of rectangular prisms, cylinders, and subtle tapestries of golden-hued brick, interspersed with green-framed windows, inset air-conditioning grilles, and splashes of glass block. A consummate achievement.

C56

[C57] **New York Academy of Medicine**, 2 E. 103rd St., SE cor. Fifth Ave. 1926. **York & Sawyer.** Library open to the public.

Literal eclecticism—a little bit of Byzantine detail and mannerism, a pinch of Lombardian Romanesque. Monolithic and massive (windows and doors are tiny apertures).

What may be the world's largest collection of cookbooks is surprisingly housed here, the gift of **Dr. Margaret Barclay Wilson.** She (if not all physicians) believed that the enlightened, disciplined and/or enriched palate led to well-being of the mind and/or body.

C57

[C58] **Statue of Dr. J. Marion Sims, M.D., LL.D.**, Fifth Ave. along Central Park, opp. E. 103rd St. ☙

Tribute to a surgeon, philanthropist, and founder of Women's Hospital.

[C59] **Museum of the City of New York**, 1220 Fifth Ave., bet. E. 103rd and E. 104th Sts. 1928-1930. **Joseph H. Freedlander.** ☙ Renovations, 1990s. **Polshek Partnership.** We-Sa 10-5; Tu 10-2 (for groups); Su 1-5; closed Mo & Tu. 212-534-1672.

C59

The product of a competition between five invited architects, this is a bland neo-Georgian building. The contents try to make up for any architectural deficiencies: "dioramas" demonstrate the physical form and history of New York. Savor Indians, maps, Dutch and English colonists, antique toys, Rockefeller rooms, period rooms, ship models, portraits—a mishmash.

C61

Seek out the model (on the first floor) of the Castello plan (1660) of New Amsterdam, the best visualization available of that Dutch beaver-trading town.

Alexander Hamilton and **DeWitt Clinton** face Central Park from niches in the façade (**Adolph A. Weinman**, sculptor).

[C60] **El Museo del Barrio**/originally Heckscher Foundation for Children (settlement house), 1230 Fifth Ave., bet. E. 104th and E. 105th Sts. E side. Open to the public: We-Su 11-5; closed Mo & Tu. 212-831-7952.

The museum of Latin-American art, history, and culture.

[C61] **Terence Cardinal Cooke Health Care Center**/formerly Flower & Fifth Avenue Hospitals/originally The Fifth Avenue Hospital, 1240-1248 Fifth Ave., bet. E. 105th and E. 106th Sts. 1921. **York & Sawyer**.

One of York & Sawyer's lesser works; compare with their later New York Academy of Medicine, on 103rd [C57].

EAST OF EDEN

If the expanse of the Upper East Side flanking Fifth Avenue is a veritable Garden of Eden, then this precinct, lying between that ultrachic neighborhood and York Avenue's health care and research row, can be called East of Eden. It begins at Third Avenue and ranges to just short of York, from the Queensboro Bridge to East 79th Street.

E1

E2

E3

[E1] **Roosevelt Island tramway station**, Second Ave. SW cor. E. 60th St. 1976. **Prentice & Chan, Ohlhausen**.
   A spectacular exercise in transit architecture. If the aerial tramway in itself were not enough, this glassy box, perched high astride—and slightly askew of—Second Avenue, only adds to the ski-slope drama. Within the beautifully detailed industrial container is the colorful mechanism (out of **Chaplin's** *Modern Times*) that propels the cars across the East River's West Channel to the Roosevelt Island terminal. A silent, bird's-eye view of city and river, a moving observation deck. Take a trip!

[E2] **Yellowfingers** (restaurant), 1009 Third Ave., SE cor. E. 60th St. 1860s. Remodeled.
   Above some unfortunate arches on the ground floor remains the body and detail of a module of Third Avenue in the mid to late 19th century. Yellow walls and cream trim supplanted red brick, limestone, and a dark-painted sheet metal cornice.

[E3] **Evansview** (apartments)/originally Memphis Uptown, 305 E. 60th St., bet. First and Second Aves. to E. 61st St. 1987. **Abraham Rothenberg** and **Gruzen Samton Steinglass**.
   The penultimate sliver: lanky, proud, colorful, and witty. A fine addition to a jumbled area if not ultimately lost amid a sea of lesser towers.

[E4] **Day & Meyer, Murray & Young Corporation** (storage warehouse), 1166 Second Ave., bet. E. 61st and E. 62nd Sts. E side. ca. 1928.
   One of a fast disappearing urban form: a largely windowless, high-rise storage warehouse, beautifully detailed with a hint of Art Deco in brick, limestone, and terra-cotta.

[E5] **Treadwell Farm Historic District**, generally both sides of the midblocks of E. 61st and E. 62nd Sts. bet. Second and Third Aves. 1868-1876. Much altered. ●
   Two blocks of brownstone houses on the lands of **Adam Treadwell**'s farm: uniform rows of human scale sought by the affluent among surrounding commercial blocks. For another Tredwell memory—the family spelled it both with and without the *a*—this time Adam's brother: **Seabury Tredwell**'s Old

E6

EAST OF EDEN / HOSPITAL ROW

see pages 436–449

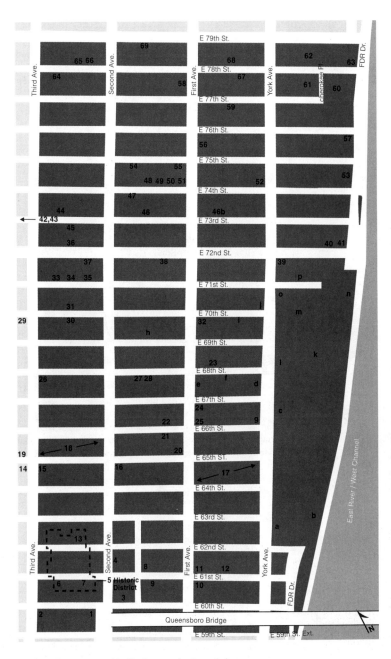

Merchant's House. In this district a stock of sturdy brownstones has been revamped and restyled with the manners of the 1920s, 1930s, and 1940s.

[E6] **206-210 E. 61st St**. 1873-1875. **Frederick S. Barus**.

A particularly tasty trio: original survivors with Roman Tuscan columns holding dentilled pediments.

[E7] **Trinity Baptist Church**/originally First Church, 250 E. 61st St., bet. Second and Third Aves. 1929. **Martin G. Hedmark**. ○⚲

Sandwiched among the brownstones of the Historic District is this early (for New York) Modern church, which echoes Swedish motifs like the Hansa gables and other elements pre-

E7

served in Stockholm's outdoor Skansen Museum. The yellow, brown, and rust brick façade is a celebration of brick—corbeled, arched, stepped, pierced, grilled—it's a mason's triumph. (In fact, it's a false front, almost twice the height of the interior space beyond.)

E8

[E8] **Our Lady of Perpetual Help Church**/Infant of Prague National Shrine (Roman Catholic) and Rectory of the Redemptorist Fathers, 321 and 323 E. 61st St., bet. First and Second Aves. 1887. [E8a] Originally Convent/now apartments, 329 E. 63rd St. ca. 1870. Converted & expanded, ca. 1977.

Once a coherent group of structures serving an immigrant working-class parish. The Romanesque Revival church is overshadowed by bridge approach and exit ramps—a sorry bit of luck.

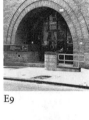

E9

[E9] **The Vertical Club**, 330 E. 61st St., bet. First and Second Aves. 1982. **Eugene Ho**, engineer.

Tier after tier of sports facilities perched above a knockoff entrance from **Frank Lloyd Wright**'s V. C. Morris Shop (San Francisco).

[E10] **400 East 61st Street** (apartments), bet. First and York Aves. 2001. **Davis Brody Bond**.

A **Sheldon Solow** project; for comparison see [E20].

[E11] **1114 First Avenue** (office building), NE cor. E. 61st St. 1980s?

A retardataire entry into the Art Moderne sweepstakes: banded brick and glass block are a far cry from the glass and metal curtain walls of the post-World War II decades.

E11

[E12] **Abigail Adams Smith Museum, Colonial Dames of America**/earlier Mt. Vernon Hotel (1826-1833)/originally William T. Robinson coach house, 421 E. 61st St., bet. First and York Aves. 1799. Open to the public: 212-838-6878. 12-4 daily.

A both real and unassuming Federal ashlar stone building. The lands of **William S. and Abigail Adams Smith**, daughter and son-in-law of **President John Adams**, were sold in 1798, due to financial setbacks, to **William T. Robinson**. Mr. Robinson built the stable for his new estate, but the memory of Abigail is a better historical fantasy than the memory of Mr. Robinson. The stable was subsequently promoted in status and served as a hotel, until converted to use as a private house.

E12

[E13] **Our Lady of Peace Roman Catholic Church**/originally Presbyterian Church of the Redeemer, 239 E. 62nd St. 1886-1887. **Samuel A. Warner**.

[E14] **The Phoenix** (apartments), 160 E. 65th St., SW cor. Third Ave. 1968. **Emery Roth & Sons**.

A sober but boring Modernist concrete grid. Some of the exuberance of the original Emery Roth at the San Remo could be used here.

E15

[E15] **200 East 65th Street** (apartments), SE cor. Third Ave. to E. 64th St. 1987. **Ulrich Franzen & Assocs**.

A stark intruder that gives little opportunity for the talents of its designer.

[E16] **The Rio** (apartments), 304 E. 65th St., SE cor. Second Ave. 1988. **Gruzen Samton Steinglass**.

Split personality: the bottom and top are in curious contrast, bristling with glass and balconies above, seeking a human scale at the street-level entry.

[E17] **City and Suburban Homes Company, First Avenue Estate** (model tenements), E. 64th to E. 65th Sts. bet. First and York Aves: 1168-1190, 1194-1200 First Ave. 1898. **James E. Ware**.

E16

403-423 E. 64th St. 1901. **James E. Ware.** 402-416 E. 65th St. 1900. **James E. Ware.** 🌑 429 E. 64th St. and 430 E. 65th St. 1915. **City and Suburban Homes Architectural Department: Philip H. Ohm**.

Experimental housing for the working classes by a do-good organization in the era before governmental intervention. The apartment groups are 6-story walk-ups similar to the ones at 79th Street: straightforward design, successful background buildings. Ware, architect of the majority of the structures, won second prize in the City and Suburban Homes Company Model Tenement Competition of 1896.

Manhattan House to Tower East:
This unnamed hillcrest runs from 66th to 72nd Streets, falling away toward the north, the south, and Second Avenue. Until 1955 its spine was the clanking steel and wood-grilled elevated trestle along Third Avenue, an economic and social wall limiting migration to its east. When the el was scrapped (reducing the convenience of rapid transit for this neighborhood), the eastern blocks blossomed with high-rise luxury.

[E18] **Manhattan House** (apartments), 200 E. 66th St., bet. Second and Third Aves. through to E. 65th St. 1950. **Skidmore, Owings & Merrill** and **Mayer & Whittlesey**.

This is the closest Manhattan offers, conceptually, to the "blocks" of **Le Corbusier**, his "machines for living" (misinterpreted by many as implying a mechanistic way of life).

E18

The subtle aesthetic decision to choose pale gray glazed brick and white-painted steel windows by itself raised this block above its coarse new neighbors (white glazed brick + aluminum sash = pasty). The balconies become the principal ornament, but unfortunately they are small and precarious for those with any trace of vertigo, and sometime in the 1980s the original windows were replaced—with regrettable aesthetic results.

The block was occupied from 1896 to 1949 by the Third Avenue Railway System car barns, where horsecars and then electric streetcars were housed in an elaborate mansarded French Second Empire "palace."

[E19] **The Chatham**, 181 E. 65th St., NW cor. Third Ave. 2000? **Robert A.M. Stern Architects**.

Limestone and brick again prevail on Third Avenue, embellished with arches and a dentil-encrusted entablature. (Can you spell entablature?) This was the site of a latter-day Dove Tavern (a block south of its original eponym at 66th Street).

*One life for my country: The Dove Tavern, a landmark for travelers on the Boston Post Road, stood at the northwest corner of what is now Third Avenue and East 66th Street, a block north of its latter-day namesake. It had been established sometime prior to 1763 and flourished for over 30 years. Commemorative plaques and statues elsewhere notwithstanding, **Captain Nathan Hale** was hanged by the British on September 22, 1776, in the Artillery Park near the tavern. Captured while reconnoitering British forces on Long Island, he was executed immediately—denied even the attendance of clergy. Though his last letters to his mother and friends were destroyed, his last words remain familiar to many.*

[E20] **265 East 66th Street** (apartments), NW cor. Second Ave. 1978. **Gruzen & Partners**.

A tall, suave, glass residential tower with 4 rounded corners—the equivalent, in architectural terms, of the gray flannel suit. A welcome subtlety is its developer's decision not to employ an ostentatious name, rare for most recent luxury apartment towers.

E22

E23

E25

[E21] **222-242 East 67th Street** (row houses), bet. Second and Third Avenues. 1984. **Attia & Perkins**.

Before choosing an architect, developer **Sheldon Solow** conducted a competition attracting entries from such world-class architects as England's **James Stirling**, **Gruzen & Partners**, and **Richard Meier**. Architect **Eli Attia** was chosen.

These 11 houses fail to capture any of the abundant spirit and charm of their linear antecedents, a boring line of richness in materials and architectural poverty. But directly opposite is a row of gems designed for horses, carriages, and grooms:

[E22] **223, 225, 227 East 67th Street** (carriage houses), bet. Second and Third Aves. ca. 1900.

Lusty recollections of the horse-and-carriage era. Their rich façades, articulated with round and elliptical arches and bull's-eye windows, shame more recent examples intended for residential purposes.

[E23] **St. Catherine of Siena Church** (Roman Catholic)/ Shrine of St. Jude Thaddeus, 411 E. 68th St., bet. First and York Aves. 1931. **Wilfred E. Anthony**.

A departure for the architect: bare red-brick neo-Gothic inside and out, revealing the influence of the English Arts and Crafts movement and **William Lethaby** (1857-1931).

[E24] **Bethany Memorial Church** (Reformed in America), 400 E. 67th St., SE cor. First Ave. 1910. **Nelson & Van Wagenen**.

A curiously fashioned church structure, much more demure (Protestant) than St. John of Nepomuk next door (Catholic).

[E25] **St. John Nepomucene Church** (Roman Catholic), 411 E. 66th St., NE cor. First Ave. 1925. **John Van Pelt**.

A wonderfully romantic paean to the Romanesque style for a Slavic (St. John of Nepomuk) congregation. Another version by the same architect, Guardian Angel, is in Chelsea.

[E26] **210 East 68th Street** (apartments), SE cor. Third Ave. 1928. **George & Edward Blum**.

An Art Deco essay with Kelly green terra-cotta embellishments.

[E27] **340 and 342 East 69th Street**, bet. First and Second Aves. 1865.

Two in a row of twelve well-preserved brownstones. Another terrace of houses that is large enough to give one a sense of the old city scale hereabouts. For a taste of what a well-meaning architect can do to disrupt the block's serenity, look at No. 310.

[E28] **First Magyar Reformed Church of the City of New York**, 346 E. 69th St., bet. First and Second Aves. 1916. **Emery Roth**.

E28

The elder Roth before his Beresford and San Remo. Here, white stucco and bright faience vernacular transported, as if by magic carpet, from Hungary to this cramped East Side site.

E29

[E29] **188 East 70th Street** (apartments), SW cor. Third Ave. 1986. **Kohn Pederson Fox Assocs**.

A Post Modern structure that hopes for a misplaced date in history (older is better—but with regard to a past that never existed!?). The superscaled allusions to classicism are perhaps a bit far-fetched, with any subtlety parboiled out, but the detail is, nevertheless, a refreshing addition to the streetscape.

[E30] **220 East 70th Street** (apartments), bet. Second and Third Aves. 1988. **Ted Reeds Assocs**.

A midblock mid-rise crafted of two tones of red brick and some modest, inoffensive Post Modern ornament. The setback at the height of neighboring row houses is an important acquiescence to the Upper East Side side street.

[E31] **Lenox Hill Station, U.S. Post Office**, 221 E. 70th St., bet. Second and Third Aves. 1935.

Once much maligned by Modernists, this W.P.A. neo-Georgian post office is now popular among Historicists (current architects seeking literal historical styles, as opposed to Post Modernists, who exaggerate and parody the styles of the past).

E32

[E32] **The Kingsley** (apartments), 400 E. 70th St., SE cor. First Ave. 1984. **Stephen B. Jacobs & Assocs**.

Rounded balconies for rhythm, but the base is less effective. Myriad towers perforating the skyline of Manhattan may eventually make the island a surrogate San Gimignano (that small Tuscan town of family house-towers for defense, and a must tourist destination). At that point the detail of the individual unit will become less important, the skyline the architectural statement. Meanwhile everyone's trying for individuality (distinction?), few are coming close.

E33

East 71st Street, between Second and Third Avenues:

[E33] **203, 207, 209, 211 East 71st Street** (town houses), Altered, 1980s. [E33b] **213 East 71st Street** (row house), ca. 1880.

Hollywood's East of Eden where the whole, rather than being the sum of the parts, as in most of the Historic Districts, is chaos. Wildly conflicting architectural statements cheek by jowl. Too bad.

No. 213 retains a largely untouched façade, a foil to its western show-offs.

[E34] **Marymount Manhattan**, 221 E. 71st St., bet. Second and Third Aves. 1940s.

High-rise neo-Georgian: a comforting image for those Catholic young women.

E35

[E35] **251 East 71st Street** (row house), bet. Second and Third Aves. Altered, ca. 1975.

Star Trek? Elliptical bubbles in aluminum frames punctuate a white stucco façade. Most serious Modernists would use this as an example of the need for extended Historic District coverage.

[E36] **235 East 72nd Street** (apartments), bet. Second and Third Aves. Altered, 1947. **Lewis J. Ordwein**. Rebuilt, 1990s.

Early Modern redesign, it became dated. Post Modern alterations have tried to steer it back into the world of high style. A wide miss.

[E37] **St. John the Martyr Catholic Church**/originally Knox Presbyterian Church, 252 E. 72nd St., bet. Second and Third Aves. ca. 1888. Rededicated, 1904.

A congregation Bohemian in origin dressed in rock-faced and smooth brownstone Romanesque Revival.

E36

E39

E41

[E38] **Le Chambord** (apartments), 350 E. 72nd St., bet. First and Second Aves. 1987. **Costas Kondylis** of **Philip Birnbaum & Assocs**.

Twenty-three stories of condos with a pudgy Post Modern plinth that replaced a much beloved Trans-Lux neighborhood movie theater. Movies are more fun.

[E39] **Sotheby's** (auction gallery)/earlier Sotheby, Parke-Bernet York Avenue Gallery/originally Eastman Kodak Company, 1334 York Ave., SE cor. E. 72nd St. to E. 71st St. ca. 1929. Converted to gallery, 1980, **Lundquist & Stonehill**. Expanded, 1999. **Kohn Pedersen Fox**. Top galleries by **Gluckman Mayner**.

An ethereal box becomes the merchandise mart for Sotheby's art auctions. Its sheer size is an indication of the speculation that infects the art world at the millennium: invest in **Picasso**, **Biedermeier**, **Bibelots**. The art market instead of the stock market reeks of culture rather than mere bucks and, perhaps, is more profitable.

[E40] **525 E. 72nd St** (apartments), E of York Ave. through to E. 73rd St., bet. York and FDR Drive. 1987. **Davis, Brody & Assocs**.

An elegant tower design occupying a back street site (73rd) but with a main-street address (72nd). The small plaza and waterfall are pleasant, but have nothing to do with the building proper.

[E41] **The "Black & Whites,"** **527, 531, 535, 541 E. 72nd St**. (tenements), at the end of 72nd St. at the E. River Drive. 1894. Remodeled as apartments, 1938. **Sacchetti & Siegel**.

Tenements, usually a pejorative for slum building (can a building be a slum, or merely its use?), here house figures and enterprises of social and intellectual prominence: among them **George Plimpton** and the *Paris Review*. What more is there to say? A lot.

Tenements, the villains, were replaced by high-rise towers in the 1930s and 1940s, on the principle that light and air bring civilized living to the underprivileged. Partially true. But today City agencies are recycling tenements for that same populace, on the principle that keeping the urban streetscape (check here with Jane Jacobs) is better in the long run. And **George Plimpton** & Company can acquire their light and air in the Hamptons.

[E42] **East 73rd Street**, between Lexington and Third Avenues. A stable block . . . of stables.

Manhattan's gridiron plan, unlike those of other cities, didn't provide back alleys for service. Therefore, in New York's horsedrawn era, certain blocks were assigned the role of service streets, addressing the needs of those four-legged beasts of burden. These smelly, noisy places were often located a distance from the properties of their well-to-do owners. Typically, the carriages were garaged in the front, the horses stabled in the rear, and grooms' quarters were above. Later, garages came, as new structures or as conversions.

Roll call of carriage houses on S side:
No. 166: Originally Henry G. Marquand's/later Joseph Pulitzer's/now **Central Gospel Chapel**, 1883-1884, **Richard Morris Hunt**. 🌶
No. 168: Originally William Baylis/later Charles Russell Lowell Putnam's, 1899, **Charles Romeyn**. 🌶 The stepped gable crowns a neo-Dutch Renaissance façade.
No. 170: Originally George C. Clausen's/later Henry T. Sloane's/later James Stillman's 1890-1891, **Frank Wennemer**. 🌶
Dour brownstone and brick.

E42, No. 168

No. 172-174: Originally James B. Layng's, 1889, **Frank Wennemer**. 🌶 Inappropriate white paint masks the sibling of No. 170: yes, there's dour brownstone and brick behind that mask.

No. 178: Originally Charles I. Hudson's, 1902. **John H. Friend.** 🖐️
A more pompous Beaux Arts effort.
No. 180: Originally Max Nathan's/later George D. Widener's
garage, 1890-1891, **William Schickel & Co.** 🖐️ Naïve
Romanesque Revival brickwork supported by a rockface granite
podium.
No. 182: Originally S. Kayton & Company (commercial stable),
1890, **Andrew Spense Mayer**. Ground floor altered, 1908,
Edward L. Middleton. Expanded upward, 1938, **James J.
Gavigan.** 🖐️ Originally a tenement for horses, now a banal
garage. Little to look at, but part of this block's history.

E42, No. 178

Roll call of carriage houses on N side:
Nos. 161 and 163: Originally Wlliam H. Tailer's, both 1896-1897;
both by **Thomas Rae**. 🖐️ Sober but lusty arches combine the
vigor of the Romanesque Revival with detail from the Colonial
Revival: note that swagged frieze.
Nos. 165, 167: Originally Henry H. Benedict's, both 1903-1904,
both **George R. Amoroux**. 🖐️ Beaux Arts whimsy at the
entries.

E42, No. 163

[E43a] **171 East 73rd Street** (row house). 1860. Vestibule and garden
wall added, 1924, **Electus Litchfield**, architect and owner. 🖐️
LaPierre, Litchfield & Partners was a distinguished architectural firm in the 1930s and 1940s.

[E43b] **175 East 73rd Street** (row house)/later blacksmith shop
on ground floor. 1860. Ground floor altered into smithy, 1896.
Restored, 1926, **Francis Livingston Pell**, architect and owner. 🖐️
Two separated "broken teeth" are all that remain of the
block's original group of 6 Italianate row houses. They reveal
the earliest stage of development, as a modest street for lower
middle-class families. The others were demolished in order to
build the adjacent carriage houses.

[E43c] Originally **J. Henry Alexandre carriage house**, 173 E.
73rd St. 1893. **Hobart C. Walker.** 🖐️
Alexandre lived at 35 East 67th Street (extant), whose façade
he had had altered (by another architect).

[E43d] Originally **Automobile Realty Company garage**,
177-179 E. 73rd St. 1906. **Charles F. Hoppe.** 🖐️
A proud, exquisitely detailed Beaux Arts container for the
newly emerging automobile. A rare surviving example of the
city's early response to the needs of the horseless carriage.

E43d

[E44] **Buckley School, The Hubball Building**, 210 E.
73rd St./209 E. 74th St., bet. Second and Third Aves. 1974.
Brown, Lawford & Forbes.
This through-block essay in 1970s concrete, red brick, and
freestanding smokestack replaced a Con Ed substation.

[E45] **220, 230, 225, 235 East 73rd Street** (apartments), bet.
Second and Third Aves. ca. 1929.
Four substantial apartment blocks, each rising 10 sheer stories on opposite sides of the street. Their detail and subtle ornament make them urban grace notes despite their large scale.

E44

[E46] **Bohemian National Hall/Národni Budova**, 321 E. 73rd
St., bet. First and Second Aves. 1895, 1897. **William C. Frohne.**
🖐️ Restoration, 1990s. **Jan Hird Pokorny**.
Lovingly cleaned after years of neglect, it brings back another
triumphal Renaissance Revival (American style, after the World's
Columbian Exposition two years earlier). Note the lion's heads.

[E46b] **Ronald McDonald House** (children's residential
facility), 407 E. 73rd St., bet. First and York Aves. 1989.
The Spector Group.
An eclectic Modernist *cum* Post Modernist façade.

E46   E48

East 74th Street, between First and Second Avenues:

[E47] **306-310 East 74th Street** (apartments). ca. 1936.

Art Moderne but unusual in its red brick livery (coarsened by poor repointing); most city buildings of that era are in orange or cream brick.

[E48] **Greek Orthodox Archdiocesan Cathedral of the Holy Trinity**/Hellenic Eastern Orthodox Church of New York, 319 E. 74th St. 1931. **Kerr Rainsford, John A. Thompson, Gerald A. Holmes**.

A little-known but much-admired neo-Romanesque red brick and limestone-trimmed edifice by the firm that later designed the vastly different neo-Gothic Hunter College Uptown (now Lehman College) in the Bronx, under the name **Thompson, Holmes & Converse**.

E50

[E49] **The Forum** (apartments), 343 E. 74th St. to E. 75th. 1986. **The Vilkas Group**.

At 25 stories, this uses air rights from the two churches that are its bookends. Tall midblock structures like this one were later made more difficult by the 59th-96th Street Upper East Side midblock downzoning, which went into effect after this heavy-handed project was on its way.

The crowning apartments, scarcely penthouses, are glazed with curtain walling on the line of the then-required setback angle.

E51

[E50] **Jan Hus (Bohemian Brethren) Presbyterian Church**, 347 E. 74th St. 1880. Church House also known as Jan Hus House, 351 E. 74th St. 1915.

Jan Hus house is better known—citywide—for the dramatic, musical, and light opera events held in its auditorium than for the parent church next door. Bohemian Gothic Revival?

[E51] **Memorial Sloane-Kettering International Center**/originally Bank, 1425 First Ave., NW cor. 74th St. 1930s. Remodeled, 1980s. **Perkins Eastman**.

Classical Revival, Regency division.

E52

[E52] **Church of the Epiphany** (Episcopal), 1393-1399 York Ave., NW cor. E. 74th St. 1939. **Wyeth & King. Eugene W. Mason**, associated architect.

The distinctive squat spire is a Scandinavian romance for Manhattan's avenuescapes. What a great silhouette!

[E53] **Consolidated Edison** (power plant)/originally Manhattan Elevated Railway/later Interborough Rapid Transit Company/later N.Y.C. Board of Transportation, 535 E. 74th St., NW cor. FDR Drive to E. 75th St. ca. 1900. **C. Wellesley Smith**.

Classicized to make it a good neighbor despite its size and smoke. Its coal was barged to the site before the FDR Drive landlocked the facility.

E54

[E54] **310 East 75th Street** (apartments), bet. First and Second Aves. ca. 1936.

Art Moderne once appropriately steel-casemented, now

demeaned with bronzed double-hung windows; golden yellow, orange, and red brick. The corner windows were not only stylish but also an exciting spatial event for the tenants. The new replacement windows are clunky in comparison.

[E55] **The Saratoga** (apartments), 330 E. 75th St., SW cor. Second Ave. 1984. **Schuman, Lichtenstein, Claman & Efron**.

The avenue tower and the sidestreet low-rise wing are neatly articulated with a V-notch. Nicely detailed, with a sidewalk clock to count the hours.

[E56] **The Impala** (apartments), First Ave., bet. E. 75th and E. 76th Sts. E side. 2001. **Michael Graves**, design architect. **RFR/Davis**, architects of record.

Not just a tower but in fact three buildings embracing a courtyard, the latter two on the 75th and 76th sidestreets. A bold façade of square windows sets into a matrix of limestone and brick. The best "name architect" attempt at a Manhattan complex in a generation.

[E57] **The Town School**, 540 E. 76th St., SW cor. FDR Drive. 1973. **Armand Bartos & Assocs**. Altered, 1978, **R. M. Kliment + Frances Halsband**.

E57

Stylish brickwork is punctuated with incised windows and a splayed entry.

[E58] **Wright Center on Aging/Burden Center for the Aging/Elderserve**, 1484-1486 First Ave., bet. 77th and 78th Sts. W side. 1999. **Suben Dougherty Partnership**.

Once there was a Woolworth's (and a sometime Rite-Aid); now senior citizens are cared for behind this new stucco, glass, and stainless-steel façade.

E59

[E59] **430 East 77th Street** (apartments), bet. First and York Aves. Converted, 1971.

A stylish conversion from tenements to luxury apartments. Brick piers, arches, and iron railings give this a rich order unmatched by the marble-framed and plastic-plant-festooned lobbies of its vulgar competitors.

[E60] **John Jay Park, Cherokee Place** (E of York Ave.) bet. E. 76th and E. 78th Sts., to FDR Drive. E side. Bath house, 1908. **Stoughton & Stoughton**.

A small neighborhood park with both a swimming pool and playground intensively used. It carries a lush parasol of trees.

[E61] Originally Shively Sanitary Tenements (apartments)/later East River Homes/now **Cherokee Apartments**, 507-515, 517-523 E. 77th St., 508-514, 516-522 E. 78th St., W side of Cherokee Place. 1909-1911. **Henry Atterbury Smith**. 🖝

The progressive environmental ideas of **Dr. Henry Shively**, intended to help cure those with tuberculosis (the second leading cause of death in the early 20th century), were translated into these model tenements with the assistance of **Mrs. William Kissam Vanderbilt**.

E61

A second glance here is well deserved. These simple buildings are rich in architectural thoughts new for their time: the triple-hung windows allow a tenant to step onto a narrow French balcony and view the river; and even without taking the step, one has a dramatic sense of space and view. The units are entered through Guastavino tile-vaulted tunnels opening into central courtyards from which, at each corner, stairs rise 5 flights. Wrought-iron seats and iron-and-glass canopies shelter the stair climber from the rain.

[E62] **City and Suburban Homes Company, York Avenue Estate** (model tenements), E. 78th to E. 79th Sts. bet. York Ave. and FDR Drive. 1194-1200 York Ave. 1901. **Harde & Short**. 503-509 E. 78th St. 1904. **Percy Griffin**.

E62

E64

Bishop Henry Codman Potter Memorial Buildings, 510-528 E. 79th St. 1912. **City and Suburban Homes Architectural Department: Philip Ohm**, chief architect.

519-539 E. 78th St. and 536 E. 79th St. 1913. **City and Suburban Homes Architectural Department: Philip Ohm**.

[E63] Originally **Junior League Hotel**/later East End Hotel for Women/now apartments, 541 E. 78th St. (once 1 East River Drive). 1910-1912. **City and Suburban Homes Architectural Department: Philip Ohm**. 🐾

Experimental housing for the working classes (and a hotel for women once operated by the Junior League). The apartment groups are 6-story walk-ups but without the charm of the neighboring Shively group on Cherokee Place. Ware, architect of the earliest group on this site, won second prize in the City and Suburban Homes Company Model Tenement Competition of 1896. **R. Thomas Short** (of **Harde & Short**) was first-prize winner in the Charity Organization Society Competition of 1900. The onetime hotel originally had balconies overlooking the East River and a windswept, wood-trellised roof garden.

*York Avenue was originally Avenue A, as the incised street names reveal at the corners of Public School 158, Manhattan, at 1458 York Avenue (between East 77th and East 78th Streets). The thoroughfare was renamed in 1928 in honor of the nation's greatest World War I hero, **Sergeant Alvin C. York**. Single-handedly he killed 25 enemy soldiers, took 132 prisoners, and silenced 35 machine guns—all in one morning's skirmish.*

East 78th Street, between Second and Third Avenues:

[E64] **208, 210, 212, 214, 216, 218 East 78th Street** (row houses). 1861-1865. **Warren and Ransom Beman, John Buckley**, builders. 🐾

A graceful terrace of brick and painted limestone town houses, each a little over 13 feet wide.

[E65] **235 East 78th Street** (row house). ca. 1870. Altered, 1964, **Bruce Campbell Graham**.

Modernized with the addition of a projecting brick wall, separating the architecture and spaces of upper and lower duplex apartments.

[E66] **237-241 East 78th Street** (row houses). ca. 1870. **255-261 East 78th Street** (row houses). ca. 1870.

Modest vernacular brick row housing.

E65

[E67] **450, 450a, 450b East 78th Street** (taxpayer), bet. First and York Aves. ca. 1855.

Shops below and residence above in this 2-story wood frame clapboard veneered structure. Manhattan miracle.

[E68] **425 East 78th Street** (apartments), bet. First and York Aves. 1880s. Altered to apartments, 1960s.

Another attempt at ganging a group of tenements with gallery-balconies that take the curse off necessary fire escapes.

E67

[E69] **Yorkville Branch, New York Public Library**, 222 E. 79th St., bet. Second and Third Aves. 1902. **James Brown Lord.** ●́ Interior redesigned, 1987, **Gwathmey Siegel & Assocs**.

A Regency neo-Renaissance "London club"—but for the masses, not the classes, with an exquisite interior redesign.

HOSPITAL ROW

The York Avenue corridor between the Queensboro Bridge and 71st Street, once the land of the tenement but now—cutting off the East River shoreline—the site for more and more facilities for health care and research. The upland area has become increasingly desirable to those seeking housing, and so the gargantuan institutions have had to build their own backup residential facilities in order to lure qualified staff and students.

E69

Rockefeller University

[Ha] **Faculty House, Rockefeller University** (apartments), 500 E. 63rd St., SE cor. York Ave. 1975. **Horace Ginsbern & Assocs**.

A stylish apartment building, from an era when few highrise apartments in the Upper East Side were actually designed.

[Hb] **Scholars Building, Rockefeller University** (apartments), 510 E. 63rd St., over FDR Drive. 1988. **Abramowitz Harris & Kingsland**.

Its architecture, closely keyed to Faculty House, is physically linked by a new pedestrian bridge, both an architectural and engineering tour de force (2000. **Wendy Evans Joseph**).

[Hc] **Rockefeller University**/originally Rockefeller Institute for Medical Research, 1270 York Ave., bet. E. 64th and E. 68th Sts. site acquired, 1901. 1903-1910. **York & Sawyer**.

A campus for research and advanced education occupies a high bluff overlooking the East River, the site once the summer estate of the Schermerhorn family of Lafayette Street. The first building opened in 1903.

Caspary Auditorium (1957. **Harrison & Abramovitz**) is the gloomy dome adjacent to York Avenue. It once sparkled with blue tile, but weather problems caused its re-roofing with what might whimsically be thought of as geodesic gutta-percha. The President's House (1958. **Harrison & Abramovitz**) is a limestone-and-glass country house tucked in a corner at the bluff's edge.

Ha

Hc

Memorial Sloane-Kettering Cancer Center

[Hd] **Memorial Sloane-Kettering Cancer Center**, 1275 York Ave. bet. E. 67th and E. 68th Sts. W side. Main Building, 444 W. 68 St. 1938. **James Gamble Rogers, Inc**. Additions.

1930s virtuoso brickwork defines the building's name in bold letters, and mini-balconies belly out on high.

[He] **Arnold and Marie Schwartz International Hall of Science for Cancer Research**/earlier James Ewing Memorial Building/originally James Ewing Memorial Hospital, N.Y.C. Department of Hospitals, First Ave. bet. E. 67th and E. 68th Sts. E side. 1950. Skidmore, Owings & Merrill.

Hd

The sensible Modernism of the 1950s, minimal and institutional. Now hospitals, in fervent competition, seek the grandiose (see, particularly, Roosevelt-St. Luke's entry on Tenth Avenue).

Hf

[Hf] **Rockefeller Research Laboratories**, 430 E. 68th St., bet. York and First Aves 1988. **Davis, Brody & Assocs**. and **Russo+Sonder**.

A sleek, banded brick and glass block shows off only at its spectacular entrance canopy.

[Hg] **Sloane House** (nurses' residence), 1233 York Ave., bet. E. 66th and E. 67th Sts. W side. 1965. **Harrison & Abramovitz**.

A dated dormitory for the medical center's valued nurses.

Hh

[Hh] **The Premier** (apartments), 333 E. 69th St., bet. First and Second Aves. 1963. **Mayer, Whittlesey & Glass**; **William J. Conklin** designer.

A simple, crisp, but forceful façade of exposed concrete and pale brick. The contained balconies are far more usable and weather-resistant than the toothy ones punctuating innumerable lesser buildings. It has happily survived the test of time.

Hi

[Hi] **Jacob S. Lasdon House, Cornell Medical College** (apartments), 420 E. 70th St., bet. First and York Aves. 1975. **Conklin & Rossant**.

Concrete and glass, elegant and crisp; a friendly, cool, and handsome neighbor.

[Hj] **Laurence G. Payson House, New York Hospital** (apartments), 435 E. 70th St., NW cor. York Ave. to E. 71st St. 1966. **Frederick G. Frost, Jr. & Assocs**.

Three staggered slabs straddle two service corridors: a dramatic freestanding form.

New York Hospital-Cornell Medical Center

[Hk] **New York Hospital-Cornell Medical Center**, York Ave. bet. E. 68th and E. 71st Sts. to FDR Drive. 1933. **Coolidge, Shepley, Bullfinch & Abbott**. Altered and expanded.

The word "massing" could have been invented to describe the original structures of this great medical complex. It has steadily expanded upland and is now growing, extending, and replacing itself on a platform over the drive (to the river's edge, in the same manner that Carl Schurz Park covers the drive in the 80s, and Rockefeller University and apartment buildings bestride it to the south).

Hk

[Hl] **William and Mildred Lasdon Biomedical Research Center**, York Ave. bet. E. 68th and E. 69th Sts. 1988. Payette Assocs., architects. **Rogers, Burgun, Shahine & Deschler, Inc.**, associated architects.

An earlier Art Deco jazz age is added to the Gothick cubism handed down from the parent hospital next door.

Hl

[Hm] **C. V. Starr Pavilion, New York Hospital**, spans E. 70th St. bet. York Ave. and FDR Drive. 1986. **Perkins & Will**.

The 1880s stained-glass seal in the lobby, by Louis Comfort Tiffany, says "Go and do likewise." It has traveled northward with the hospital: from its installation in the hospital's first building at Broadway near Duane Street, to West 15th Street off Fifth in 1877; to the nurses' quarters at 525 East 70th Street in 1932, until that structure was demolished in the 1970s; and now here, the first major hospital expansion in 50 years.

[Hn] **Hospital for Special Surgery**, 535 E. 70th St., bet. 70th and 71st Sts. **Rogers & Butler**. Operating room addition and portico, 1981. Extension over the East River Drive, 1990s. **AHSC (Architects for Health, Science and Commerce)**.

A hard-to-find adjunct to Cornell-New York enjoying river views. Almost invisible from Manhattan streets, it is a bland stacking of limestone and glass when seen from Roosevelt Island.

Hn

[Ho] **Helmsley Medical Tower** (mixed use), 1320 York Ave., bet. E. 70th and E. 71st St. E side. 1987. **Schuman, Lichtenstein, Claman & Efron**.

A smooth and very busy reinterpretation of the medical center's already smoothed neo-Gothic originals, but at the 1980s superheated scale: tall. Staff apartments and, at street level, administrative and retail space.

[Hp] **S Building, Cornell University Medical College/** originally Institute for Muscle Diseases, Muscular Dystrophy Association of America, 515 E. 71st St., bet. York Ave. and FDR Drive. 1961. **Skidmore, Owings & Merrill**.

Neat, well designed, and dull.

YORKVILLE

This northeastern quadrant of the Upper East Side is named for the village originally centered on 86th Street and Third Avenue; 86th Street later became the city's German-American *Hauptstrasse* (Main Street). In the 1930s **Fritz Kuhn** led parades of the German-American Bund until Pearl Harbor finally put an end to such antics. Other central European groups also found this area to their liking: there is still considerable evidence in church names, settlement houses, and older restaurants of the Hungarian and Czech communities. Architectural interest is scattered: because wealthy latecomers migrated only to the upper riverside near Carl Schurz Park [see the Gracie Square section], the bulk of the area's building became, until recently, housing for the lower middle class. The area is now punctuated by many new towers (some of them those damnable midblock slivers) for the nouveaux riches, and gentrification is particularly evident in the shops and restaurants along the avenues.

For the purposes of this guide Yorkville begins above 79th Street and runs to 96th, from Lexington Avenue to the East River, except for the area around East End Avenue, described in the next section, Gracie Square and Environs. Generally the entry numbers run from south to north.

Y1

Y4

[Y1] **Hungarian Baptist Church**, 225 E. 80th St., bet. Second and Third Aves. ca. 1890.

An exotic brick and terra-cotta takeoff on an Italian palazzo.

[Y2] **Lexington House** (apartments), 1190-1192 Lexington Ave., NW cor. E. 81st St. 1983. **Noah Greenberg**.

One of the early wave of sliver buildings that were later outlawed (at least in midblock locations). Others, occupying corner sites like this one, are still possible.

[Y3] **Duplex 81** (apartments), 215 E. 81st St., bet. Second and Third Aves. 1983. **William B. Gleckman**.

Sleek, and out of context; a gesture for Milan perhaps, not for Gotham.

[Y4] **420 East 81st Street** (apartments), bet. First and York Aves. ca. 1986.

Six stories of purplish brick become a friendlier neighbor than No. 215 above.

[Y5] **1220, 1222, 1224 Lexington Ave.** (originally row houses), bet. E. 82nd and E. 83rd Sts. W side. 1880.

A gray marble Italianate trio with the year 1880 carved in the central pediment. Its streetfront shops join it to its neighbors, causing most people to overlook the drama overhead. Crane your neck.

Y5

YORKVILLE

see pages 450–458

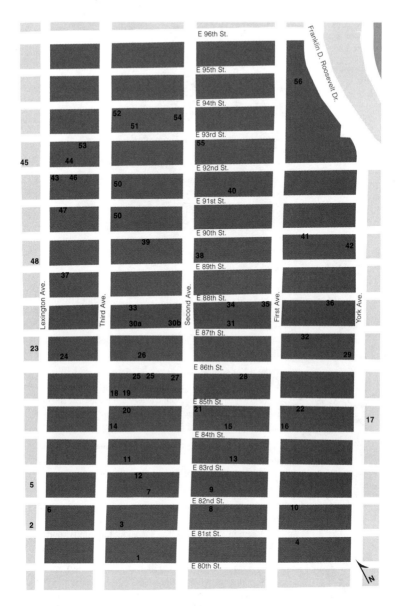

[Map of Yorkville area showing streets from E 80th St. to E 96th St., with avenues: Lexington Ave., Third Ave., Second Ave., First Ave., York Ave., and Franklin D. Roosevelt Dr. Numbered buildings throughout.]

[Y6] **J. Leon Lascoff Pharmacy**, 1209 Lexington Ave. SE cor. E. 82nd St. Building, 1870s. Pharmacy, 1899.

A neighborhood anchor and landmark that dresses its façade with some faux-Gothick shopwindows.

[Y7] **American Federation for Hungarian Education & Literature, Ltd.**, 213-215 E. 82nd St., bet. Second and Third Aves.

A pair of houses set back from the street and unified with a wrought-iron balcony. Note the plaque marking the visit of **Cardinal Mindszenty of Hungary** in 1973.

[Y8a] **306 and 306A East 82nd Street** (row house and back-house), bet. First and Second Aves. ca. 1855.

Early residents at a smaller scale.

[Y8b] **312 East 82nd Street** (tenement), bet. First and Second Aves. 1890s.

Those grand Corinthian pilasters give this simple tenement a noble façade.

Y8a

Y9

[Y9] **Old P.S. 290, 311 E. 82nd St.**, Bet. First and Second Aves. 1900s.

A baroque entrance worthy of Rome.

[Y10] **St. Stephen of Hungary Church and School** (Roman Catholic), 408 E. 82nd St., bet. First and York Aves. 1928. **Emil Szendy.**

Yellow ocher brick in timid neo-Romanesque, sporting a tile hip roof

 [Y11] **St. Elizabeth of Hungary Roman Catholic Church**, 211 E. 83rd St., bet. Second and Third Aves. 1918.

A classy, spired neo-Gothic exterior, but the treat is within: ascend the stairs to view a just heavenly groin-vaulted ceiling painted in the colors of Ravenna's mosaics.

Y12

[Y12] **222 and 224 East 83rd Street** (row house), bet. Second and Third Aves. 1850s.

A scallop shell at 222 and an extraordinary metal fence at 224 add hints of uniqueness to these early brick row houses.

[Y13] **331 East 83rd Street** (row house), bet. First and Second Aves. ca. 1880.

A gem in a time warp. Too bad about the clumsy rooftop addition.

Y14a

 [Y14a] Formerly **Mayo Ballrooms**, 1493 Third Ave., NE cor. E. 84th St. ca. 1927.

Eclectic romance in the Art Deco style, utilizing poly-chromed terra-cotta bas-relief ornament for great effect.

[Y14b] **Sidewalk clock, in front of 1501 Third Ave.**, bet. E. 84th and E. 85th Sts. E side. 1898. **E. Howard Clock Company.**

A pocket watch for Gargantua that once advertised Adoph Stern, Jeweler.

Y15a

[Y15a] **325 East 84th Street** (apartments), bet. First and Second Aves. N side. 1980s.

Each floor, or pair of floors (for the duplexes), provides a different elevation: strip, square, balcony, greenhouse; a func-tional attitude that gives some variety to a subdued façade.

[Y15b] **Zion St. Mark's Church**/earlier Zion Lutheran Church/ originally Deutsche Evangelische Kirche von Yorkville, 339 E. 84th St., bet. First and Second Aves. 1888.

A frothy reminder of the early days of German immigration to this precinct. A blessed survivor, but think how rich are the materials under all that white paint.

Y15b

[Y16] **401 East 84th Street** (apartments), NE cor. First Ave. 1980s.

The presence and rhythm of balconies close to the ground (at the third floor) give this tower a friendlier relationship with the streetscape.

Y16

[Y17] **1578-1600 York Avenue** (tenements), bet. E. 84th to E. 85th Sts. E side. ca. 1870.

An almost original blockfront of "first-class flats." Looks like a Hollywood backlot setting for Manhattan in the 1870s, but it's genuine.

[Y18] **The GAP and Equinox Health Club**/formerly Manufacturers Hanover Trust Company, Yorkville Branch (bank), 1511 Third Ave., NE cor. E. 85th St. ca. 1915. Equinox remodeling, 1996. **HLW International**.

A bank of the old school in neo-Renaissance tailored dress of stone now shelters commerce and health. The Equinox entry is an imposing hi-tech addition.

[Y19] **City Cinemas & Amsterdam Billiard Club**/originally Annex, Musical Mutual Protection Union, 227 E. 85th St., bet. Second and Third Aves. 1919. **Levitan & Fischer**. Entrance to theater at 210 East 86th St.

Y18

Colossal Classical piers support the modest entablature bearing the original building's engraved name (not surprisingly, an early musician's union). The main entrance was through a magnificent neo-Renaissance brick and terra-cotta façade on 86th Street, now demolished.

[Y20] **220-222 East 85th Street** (tenements), bet. Second and Third Aves. 1890s.

Bold and sensuous arcs and their battered bases ground these unusual tenements.

Y19

[Y21] **The America** (apartments), 300 E. 85th St., SE cor. Second Ave. 1987. **Murphy/Jahn**.

As American as apple pie, but certainly not mom's. Thirty-six stories of boring beige and gray surface decoration from the normally flashy works of Chicago architect **Helmut Jahn**.

[Y22a] **406, 408, 410 East 85th Street** (row houses), bet. First and York Aves. ca. 1865.

A charming, but dour, mansarded trio, where painted brick and lintels have taken away some of the original verve.

Y20

[Y22b] **412 East 85th Street** (dwelling), bet. First and York Aves. ca. 1855. Restored, 1998. **Alfredo De Vido**.

A rare clapboard single house, set deep in the row from a time when country houses (yes, here in the country) provided front gardens. De Vido has lovingly restored it.

[Y23] **Apartment House**/originally Gimbel's East (department store), 125 E. 86th St., and 180 East 87th Street, SW cor. Lexington Ave. **Abbott, Merkt & Co**. Converted to apartments, 1989, **Skidmore, Owings & Merrill**.

Y22b

The first ten floors were once a windowless, sheet metal-clad, anonymous box, Gimbel's East. Following the dissolution of that chain in 1986, a new use was sought. A neo-1920s style apartment block won out, crowned with a twinned setback mass that displays vaguely Art Deco serrations at the top. Lofty ceiling heights were inherited from the department store's steel frame.

The original theaters that anchored this corner before and during Gimbels remain: RKO 86th Street Twins (movie theaters).

[Y24] **Uptown Racquet Club**, 151 E. 86th St., bet. Lexington and Third Aves. 1976. **Copelin, Lee & Chen**.

A serene, stylish form in ribbed concrete block crowns a group of bustling ground-floor commercial establishments of the 86th Street corridor, who pay it no heed.

Y23

[Y25a] **222 East 86th Street** (offices)/formerly apartments, bet. Second and Third Aves. ca. 1888.

Old 86th Street abutting the 1970s Bremen House next door. Take your pick. An upgraded 222 would win, hands down.

[Y25b] **The Ventura**, 240 E. 86th Street, bet. Second and Third Aves. 1999. **Davis Brody Bond**.

A behemoth on the block, replacing the urbane four-story façades of The Mongomery. At street level, where the Karl Ehmer Wurst Haus and the Kleine Konditorei once dispensed meats and chocolates, more national chains proliferate.

Y24

[Y26a] **225 East 86th Street** (apartments), bet. Second and Third Aves. 1982. **Stephen B. Jacobs & Assocs**.

A tentative façade, unresolved: the arches read as a cardboard (single brick) thickness, the windows are ill-composed.

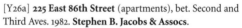 [Y26b] **The Far East** (apartments), 235 E. 86th St., bet. Second and Third Aves. 1983. **Liebman Liebman & Assocs**.

A bold and stylish statement that ignores the 86th Street context; it would be elegant freestanding in Milan but seems self-consciously slumming in these blocks.

[Y27] **The Manhattan** (apartments), 244 E. 86th St., SW cor. Second Ave. 1878-1880. **Charles W. Clinton**.

Y26b

A 6-story mild Queen Anne apartment block that was home to the family of **Senator Robert F. Wagner, Sr**. Its developers were the Rhinelander family.

[Y28] **Gristede's**/originally Grand Union (supermarket), 350 E. 86th St., bet. First and Second Aves. Altered, 1982. **Milton Glaser**, graphic designer. **Jordan Steckel**, sculptor.

Y29

The Brobdingnagian green Bartlett pear (made of colored plasticized fiberglass), once sitting on the sidewalk, announced the first of this chain grocer's empire-wide redesign. The empire has ceded this turf to Gristede's, and affixed the pear to the wall (or is it slowly crawling up from its first sidewalk stance?).

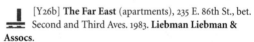 [Y29] **Channel Club Condominiums** (apartments), 455 E. 86th St., NW cor. E. 86th St. 1987. **Wechsler, Grasso & Menziuso**.

Sleek strip windows and brown glazed brick band the forty floors, a tower that manipulates the ground floor forms gracefully.

 [Y30a] **Group Residence for Young Adults**, Jewish Board of Guardians, 217 E. 87th St., bet. Second and Third Aves. 1968. **Horace Ginsbern & Assocs**.

Y30a

Bold, plastic, New Brutalist (but not brutal). Classy, personal, distinguished; monumental modernist.

Y30b

[Y30b] **247 East 87th Street** (apartments), NW cor Second Ave. to E. 88th St. 1966. **Paul & Jarmul**.

The same economics, the same materials, the same zoning and building laws as its speculative apartment house peers, here in the hands of someone who cared. The bold massing of the balconies reads as a great richness on the avenue. It was the setting for the film version of **Neil Simon's** *The Prisoner of Second Avenue* (1975).

[Y31] **339 East 87th Street** (town house), bet. First and Second Aves. 1890s.

A grand essay in brick, with limestone articulating the segmental arches: elegant.

[Y32] **St. Joseph's Catholic Church of Yorkville**, 408 E. 87th St., bet. First and York Aves. 1895. **William Schickel & Co.**

A charming basilican church with a flat neo-Romanesque limestone façade. Nevertheless, the tower ends in a quartet of vigorous Palladian openings.

Y32

[Y33a] **230 East 88th Street** (apartments), bet. Second and Third Aves. 1968. **David Todd & Assocs**.

The access to the living units is via open, grilled galleries, allowing "floor through" apartments throughout. Ah, the cross-ventilation!

Y33b

[Y33b] **232 East 88th Street** (tenement), bet. Second and Third Aves. ca. 1888.

A lusty tenement of arched and corbeled brick. Again the comparison looms: would you rather live here or in 230 next door? Lions here, sheep there?

[Y34a] **Church of the Holy Trinity** (Episcopal), St. Christopher House/Rhinelander Memorial (parish house) and Parsonage, 316-332 E. 88th St., bet. First and Second Aves. 1896-1897. Addition, 1897-1899. **Barney & Chapman**. Cloister chapel stained glass, **Robert Sowers**. All ●

Y34a

A remarkable, wonderful enclave. Using the romantic forms of the French Renaissance (**François I**) in golden brick and terra-cotta, the architects here created a touch of the Loire Valley embracing a garden oasis surmounted by one of New York's great bell towers. To come upon this verdant treasure by accident is one of the city's greatest experiences.

The entire complex was a gift of **Serena Rhinelander** as a memorial to her father and grandfather.

[Y34b] **Rhinelander Children's Center, Children's Aid Society**, 350 E. 88th St., bet. First and Second Aves. 1891. **Vaux & Radford**. Remodeled, 1958.

Once a school for crippled children, another beneficence

Y34b

Y35

Y38

Y39

Y40

Y42

(like Holy Trinity) of the Rhinelanders. Unfortunately, the brick and brownstone façade of this fine Vaux design has been muted and blurred with an expedient "brownstone" stucco coating.

[Y35] **Leighton House** (apartment tower), 360 E. 88th St., SW cor. First Ave. 1990s. **Polshek Partnership**.
Thoughtful, stylish, and articulate at ground level. The shaft above is, however, just another shaft.

[Y36a] **432 East 88th Street** (apartments), bet. First and York Aves. 1980s.
Behind all that brick bravado lurks a couple of tenement hulks, now upgraded to luxury status.

[Y36b] **434, 438 East 88th Street** (row houses), bet. First and York Aves. 1860s.
Brick and limestone town houses from a gentler streetscape.

[Y37] **146-156 East 89th Street** (row houses), bet. Lexington and Third Aves. 1886-1887. **Hubert, Pirsson & Co.** 🍎
Six spectacularly romantic Queen Anne remainders of a row of ten single-family houses; all except No. 146 are 12 feet wide, half a city lot. Originally commissioned by developer **William Rhinelander**, whose family's philanthropy can be admired at the Holy Trinity complex on East 88th.

[Y38] **1716-1722 Second Avenue** (apartments), NE cor. E. 89th St. ca. 1880.
A pair of apartment buildings with remaining detail reminiscent of one of Calvert Vaux's model tenements. The twin grand third-floor arches unite the façade.

[Y39] **Our Lady of Good Counsel Church D.O.M.** (Roman Catholic), 236 E. 90th St., bet. Second and Third Aves.
Robust, undisciplined, deeply three-dimensional: a great side-street façade of limestone and Manhattan schist, now revealed by opening up the Ruppert site across the way.

[Y40] **Our Lady of Good Counsel School** (Roman Catholic), 325 E. 91st St., bet. First and Second Aves.
The rose-colored pressed brick, limestone trim, and generous mansard overcome the regrettable loss of detail and scale contributed by this monument's original windows.

[Y41] **River East Plaza** (apartments)/formerly garage, 402 E. 90th St., bet. First and York Aves. 1983.
High upon the east, lot-line wall is a palimpsest of a former life: very powerful neo-Baroque forms. A puzzlement.

[Y42] **East River Tower** (apartments), 1725 York Ave., bet. E. 89th and E. 90th Sts. W side. 1970. **Horace Ginsbern & Assocs**.
Clever: 33 stories of alternating balconies that zig and zag between projected columns.

[Y43] **The 92nd Street Y**/also known as YM-YWHA/Young Men's and Young Women's Hebrew Association, 1395 Lexington Ave., SE cor. E. 92nd St. 1930. **Necarsulmer & Lehlbach** and **Gehron, Ross & Alley**. Expanded and altered.
A citywide center for cultural affairs, the Y's Kaufmann Auditorium holds readings from the resident Poetry Center in addition to concerts and lectures of more general interest.

[Y44] **153 East 92nd Street** (town house), bet. Lexington and Third Aves. 1890s.
An entrance portal of terra-cotta and marble worthy of a Byzantine church.

[Y45] **Adult Learning Center, The 92nd Street Y**, 125 E. 92nd St., bet. Lexington and Third Aves. N side. 2000. **Fox & Fowle**.
This brownstone-scaled civic building is to be clad in rusty-red brick with teak window frames.

Y46

[Y46] Originally **Richard Hibberd House**, 160 East 92nd Street, bet. Lexington and Third Aves. 1852-1853. Attributed to **Albro Howell**, carpenter.

A rare (in congested Manhattan) wood frame house embellished with a quartet of Corinthian-capitaled porch columns (replaced around 1930). Once the home of **Eartha Kitt**.

A block south:

[Y47] **160 East 91st Street** (apartments), bet. Lexington and Third Aves. ca. 1880.

Eight stories of softly bowed red-brick bays enhanced by strings of wrought-iron fire escapes fashioned in the curves of a violin.

[Y48] **1340-1350 Lexington Avenue** (town houses), NW cor. E. 89th St. 1880s.

Brilliant brownstone and brickwork, unfortunately painted in off-white and gray on the corner (No. 1340). A valuable urban segment of an early Upper East Side.

Jacob Ruppert's Brewery, together with Ehret's and Ringler's, occupied the multiblocks between 90th and 93rd Streets, Second and Third Avenues for the glory of the German beer hall (this is Yorkville). Thirty-four buildings accrued over three-quarters of a century. Where there were originally almost 100 breweries in New York, now there are only small breweries, established in the 1980s once the loss became painful: the larger enterprises of beermaking removed to automated stainless steel factories in places like Wichita, Kansas, Cranston, R. I., and Allentown, Pennsylvania.

Y49

[Y50] **Ruppert and Yorkville Towers** (apartment complexes), E. 90th to E. 92nd Sts. bet. Second and Third Aves. 1976. **Davis, Brody & Assocs. Ruppert Park**, E. 89th St. NW cor. Second Ave. 1979. **Balsley & Kuhl**, landscape architects.

Bulky modeled form. Notches, slots, cut corners from the vocabulary initiated by this firm at Waterside. The density is immense and overwhelming. Given that millstone, the architects have handled an unfortunate program in a sophisticated manner.

Y50

[Y51] **Arthur B. Brown and William B. Brown Gardens**, New York Foundation for Senior Citizens (housing for the elderly), 225 E. 93rd St., bet. Second and Third Aves. 1985. **Davis, Brody & Assocs**.

A low budget is outwitted here by thoughtful architectural touches: half-Tootsie Roll window sills, striped brick bands, and, best of all, open-air 2-story solariums facing southeast. Hooray!

Y51

Y53

Y55

[Y52] **Carnegie Park** (apartments), 200 E. 94th St., SE cor. Third Ave. 1983. **Davis, Brody & Assocs.**

Banded two-tone brick brings a taste of Art Moderne to this thoroughly modern complex. The embraced garden shares its urbanity with the adjacent Brown Gardens project.

[Y53] **176 East 93rd Street** (row house), bet. Lexington and Third Aves. 1973. **Gueron & Lepp.**

A brick tour de force: apartments for 3 families. Arched . . . and arch.

The Marx Brothers: While best known for their raucous Hollywood comedies, **Leonard "Chico" Marx** *(1891-1961),* **Adolph Arthur "Harpo" Marx** *(1893-1964), and* **Julius Henry "Groucho" Marx** *(1895-1977) were all Manhattan natives. Their boyhood home ("ancestral" was their term) was a 3-bedroom apartment in the row house at 179 East 93rd Street (now a gentrified and refaced tenement).*

[Y54] **Astor Terrace** (apartments/row housing), 245 E. 93rd St., NW cor. Second Ave. to E. 94th St. **Schuman, Lichtenstein, Claman & Efron.**

An avenue tower of dignified purply brick, plus a dozen midblock row houses surrounding a green central space that hoped to evoke some historic urban residential value. The blandness of these row house façades, however, is no match for the richness of their century-old predecessors.

[Y55] **The Waterford** (apartments), 300 E. 93rd St., SE cor Second Ave. 1987. **Beyer Blinder Belle** and **Vinjay Kale.**

Like the Irish crystal for which it is named, this is a particularly elegant piece of craftsmanship. The 48-story tower stands out (for now) from the surrounding urban fabric of this once not very fashionable area.

[Y56] **Stanley Isaacs Houses, N.Y.C. Housing Authority**, First Ave. bet. E. 93rd and E. 95th Sts. E side. 1966. **Frederick G. Frost, Jr. & Assocs**.

The poor sometimes have the best views—and breezes—in New York. Open-access corridors modulate the standard brick and aluminum windows of this small (coat-, not vest-pocket) housing project. The barrel-vaulted community center was intended as an architectural and social step to give place for participation in the community to project residents.

GRACIE SQUARE AND ENVIRONS

The corridor along East End Avenue's length (until 1890 called Avenue B), running from East 79th to East 92nd Streets.

[S1] **1 East End Avenue** (apartments), bet. E. 79th and E. 80th Sts. E side to FDR Drive. 1929. **Pleasants Pennington** and **Albert W. Lewis**.

A 14-story apartment building shoehorned into a narrow, trapezoidal site, 29 feet wide at the south end, 51 feet at the north, 204 feet away. Its east façade once fronted on Marie Curie Avenue, the name of the marginal street widened to create the Drive.

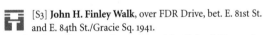 [S2] **N.Y.C. Board of Higher Education Headquarters**/ originally Welfare Island Dispensary, N.Y.C. Department of Hospitals, 535 E. 80th St., NW cor. East End Ave. 1940. **Louis E. Jallade**.

A Classical/Art Deco/Art Moderne composite that is a cousin—at least once removed—to the old Board of Transportation Building.

GRACIE SQUARE/GRACIE TERRACE/ CARL SCHURZ PARK

Robert Moses, Andre Kostelanetz, Gloria Vanderbilt, Benno Schmidt, Constantine Sidamon-Eristoff, Osborn Elliott, mayors since **Fiorello La Guardia,** and other well-connected New Yorkers have lived in these surrounds. Changes in the original low-scale and working-class demeanor were first made in the 1920s when **Vincent Astor** built the apartments at 520 and 530 East 86th Street. The zoning change of 1928 permitted residential developments along East End Avenue below 84th Street, the easternmost block of which is called Gracie Square; the corresponding block of 83rd is Gracie Terrace.

S4

Maria Bowen Chapin erected a new neo-Georgian building for her girls' school (1928. **Delano & Aldrich**) at East End Avenue and 84th. Brearley soon followed suit (1929. **Benjamin Wistar Morris**) directly on the riverfront, a site since compromised by the construction of FDR Drive—but resulting in the deck built over Finley Walk to compensate the school for the loss.

 [S3] **John H. Finley Walk**, over FDR Drive, bet. E. 81st St. and E. 84th St./Gracie Sq. 1941.

This elevated promenade was named for Finley (1863-1940), at various times editor of *Harper's Weekly*, president of City College, associate editor of the *New York Times*, and inveterate walker, shortly after his death. What makes it special are the memorable cutout identification signs that line the pathway, a collaboration between cartoonist **Edwin Marcus** and architect **Harvey Stevenson**. The walk connects with Carl Schurz Park's Esplanade.

[S4] **52-54 East End Avenue** (apartments), SW cor. E. 82nd St. 1988. **Michael Lynn Assocs**.

A 40-story corner sliver, a stratospheric spike on a 4,000-square-foot postage stamp-sized lot.

S5

[S5] **91 East End Avenue** (apartments), bet. E. 83rd St./Gracie Terrace and E. 84th St./Gracie Sq. E side.

A black stuccoed, stylish façade with a very large house number.

[S6] **525 East 85th Street** (house), bet. York and East End Aves. 1958. **Paul Mitarachi**.

Two-storied and sheathed in glass. Gardens both in front and rear allow the raised living room (via its balcony) to overview its own garden to the south.

S8

[S7] **420 East 86th Street** (apartments), bet. First and York Aves. ca. 1936.

A 6-story apartment building that looks as out of place in these parts today as it must have when built (a rare example for this neighborhood of Grand Concourse Art Moderne). Refreshing, nevertheless, particularly the polychrome brick spandrels.

[S8] **Henderson Place Historic District,** ●⌀ 549-553 E. 86th St., NW cor. East End Ave. ⌀ 6-16 Henderson Place, E side. ⌀ 140-154 East End Ave., W side. ⌀ 552-558 E. 87th St. ⌀ 1881-1882. All by Lamb & Rich.

A charming cul-de-sac provides the name for 24 (of the original 32) dwellings that survive: tiny, zesty Queen Anne row houses that transport unwary romantics to other climes and another era. Regrettably overwhelmed and vulgarized by the monster apartment to the west.

[S9] **Carl Schurz Park**/originally East River Park, E. 84th St./ Gracie Sq. to E. 90th St., bet. East End Ave. and the East River. 1876, 1891. Reconstructed, **Harvey Stevenson**, architect; **Cameron Clarke**, landscape architect.

A brilliant solution to the intersection of city, river, and highway. Suspended over FDR Drive is a sinuous expansive esplanade overlooking Hell Gate's churning waters. It is edged with a curved, user-friendly wrought-iron fence so effective that its form was appropriated for the Battery Park City Esplanade, "Imitation is the sincerest form of flattery," **Charles Caleb Colton**, 1780-1832.

Carl Schurz (1829-1906): general, minister, senator, secretary of the interior, and editor, was the most prominent German immigrant of the 19th century.

From the edge, view:

Triborough Bridge, opened 1936: an elevated viaduct on Wards and Randalls Islands connected by four overwater bridges—one between the two islands, and three to the three boroughs. The views from automobiles are handsome, particularly approaching Manhattan from Queens; even better from the same route on foot.

Hell Gate Bridge (1917. **Gustav Lindenthal**, engineer) is the reason Pennsylvania Station is a station rather than a terminal. Traffic carried under the Hudson River from the old terminal point in Jersey City can continue underground and under-river to Queens, thence over the Hell Gate and Little Hell Gate (now filled in) to the Bronx, Westchester, and Boston. The bowstring trusses (both upright and inverted) are handsome engineering.

Randalls Island became a park and headquarters of the Triborough Bridge and Tunnel Authority when the new Triborough

Bridge made it accessible—the stadium is a sometime center of European football (soccer) matches and summer concerts.

Wards Island: the Ward brothers farmed here in the 1780s. Now it's occupied by a sewage disposal plant (to the east of the Triborough's roadway), Manhattan State Hospital, and a small but lovely and very rural park connected to Manhattan by an ungainly footbridge with spectacular views.

S10

[S10] **Gracie Mansion**, official residence (since 1942) of the Mayor/onetime Museum of the City of New York/ originally Archibald Gracie House, Carl Schurz Park, East End Ave. opp. E. 88th St. 1799-1804. Attributed to **Ezra Weeks**. Expanded, 1804-1808. Restored, 1934-1936, **Aymar Embury II**. Susan Wagner Wing, added, 1965-1966, **Mott B. Schmidt**. Further restorations, 1985, **Charles A. Platt Partners** and **Robert E. Meadows**. 👆 Mansion open to public on a restricted basis.

A remote country house in its day, Gracie's has been through the mill of reconstruction and restoration. The 1966 addition permits the mayor to use the house while others think they are using it. The 1985 restoration makes it (particularly on the interior) a true executive mansion. Its country peers from the same era include the Hamilton Grange (1802), Abigail Adams Smith House (1799), Jumel Mansion (1765), and Van Cortlandt Mansion (1748).

[S11] **Gracie Square Gardens** (apartment complex), 515, 525 E. 89th St. and 520, 530 E. 90th Sts., bet. York and East End Aves. ca. 1939.

An unpretentious quartet of 6-story red brick apartment buildings with neo-Baroque entry trim, whose principal charm is their scale and lovely central garden for residents.

S12

[S12] Originally Municipal Asphalt Plant/now **Asphalt Green Sports and Arts Center**, 655 E. 90th St., NW cor. York Ave./Franklin Delano Roosevelt Drive, to E. 91st St. 1941-1944. **Kahn & Jacobs**. 👆 Altered, 1982, **Hellmuth, Obata & Kassabaum** associated architects. **Pasanella+Klein**, design architects.

Exposed concrete over a parabolic, arched steel frame that was once a single giant space containing the equipment for mixing the city's asphalt. Now divided into levels for neighborhood athletic activities. An ambitious (separate) expansion is planned.

[S13] **Asphalt Green Aquacenter**, 1750 York Ave., bet. E. 90th and E. 92nd Sts. 1993. **Richard Dattner**.

A sensuous Post Modern construction in undulating brick, glass block, and bright green sash. An honor for the neighborhood.

S13

The Heights and the Harlems

MORNINGSIDE HEIGHTS • MANHATTANVILLE
HAMILTON HEIGHTS • HARLEM • EAST HARLEM

North of Cathedral Parkway, Central Park North, and 110th Street, for the most part, lie the areas of Morningside and Hamilton Heights, Harlem, and East Harlem, the last extending southward to 97th Street east of Park Avenue. The Heights precincts are known for their college complexes—Columbia, Barnard, Teachers, the seminaries below the 125th Street valley, and CCNY above it; the Harlems are the city's best-known black and Hispanic ghettos. All four areas offer relics of the past, signs of revitalization as well as of decay, and a display of diverse life-styles that reflect their varied populations. There is much to tempt the eye . . . and the mind.

 Colonial

 Georgian/
Federal

 Greek
Revival

 Gothic
Revival

 Villa

 Romanesque
Revival

 Renaissance
Revival

 Roman
Revival

 Art Deco/
Art Moderne

 Modern/
Post-Modern

THE HEIGHTS AND THE HARLEMS KEY MAP

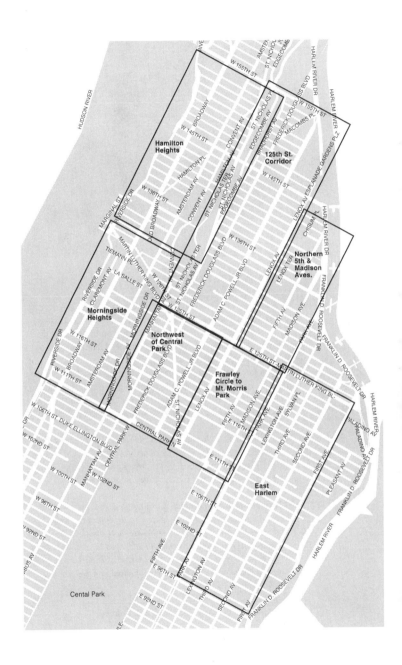

M1a
MORNINGSIDE HEIGHTS

From Cathedral Parkway north to West 125th Street, the western hilly side of Manhattan Island is Morningside Heights. Between the steep escarpment of Morningside Park on the east and the gentle slopes along the Hudson lie many of Manhattan's most impressive visual, architectural, and cultural delights. The site of a 1776 Revolutionary War skirmish, Morningside Heights became the site of the Bloomingdale Insane Asylum in 1818 and of the Leake and Watts Orphan Asylum 20 years later. The opening of Morningside Park in 1887, Riverside Drive three years later, and the simultaneous settlement here of major cultural institutions permitted the development of several magnificent groups of buildings, each in a well-designed setting. High-density housing along Riverside and Morningside Drives provided people power for the institutions and for an active community life.

M1b

Tips for touring: In general, Morningside Heights is a walker's area. Landmarks are densely spaced; students and residents populate the streets. Harlem's sights are more dispersed, so that a car is a convenience that can allow you to see much of this rich area. Nevertheless, stay out of Morningside, Jackie Robinson, and St. Nicholas Parks. They are not policed and are avoided by local residents.

St. John the Divine to Columbia's East Campus:

[M1a] **Cathedral Church of St. John the Divine** (Episcopal), Amsterdam Ave. at W. 112th St. E side. 1892-1911. **Heins & La Farge**. Work continued, 1911-1942. **Cram & Ferguson**. Assorted supporting buildings, 1909-1914. **Heins & La Farge; Cram & Ferguson; Cook & Welch; Howells & Stokes.**

[M1b] **Leake & Watts Orphan Asylum Building.** 1843. **Ithiel Town.** Cathedral open 7-5 daily. 212-316-7540.

Bishop Henry Codman Potter (1834-1908) was responsible for initiating this enormous architectural coronet to crown Morningside Heights. In 1891 he arranged to purchase the site of the Leake and Watts Orphan Asylum (whose 1843, **Ithiel Town-**

MORNINGSIDE HEIGHTS / MANHATTANVILLE

see pages 464–478

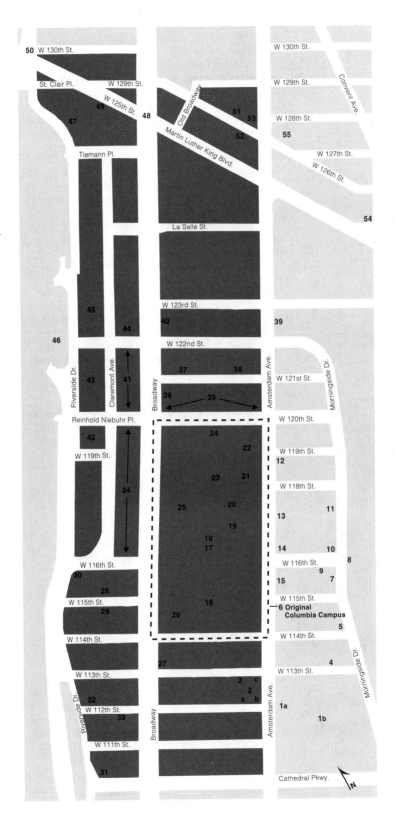

designed Greek Revival building still remains) and, after an architectural competition, commissioned **Heins & La Farge** to design the church. The apse, choir, and crossing bear their Byzantine-Romanesque influence. By 1911 the bishop and Heins had died (Potter's tomb is in the church's St. James Chapel; La Farge had been fired meanwhile), and a new architectural figure came upon the scene: **Ralph Adams Cram** of Cram & Ferguson. Cram's style was the French Gothic, though over the years other versions of Gothic (and other architects: **Henry Vaughan**, **Carrère & Hastings**) were employed, all working within Cram's grand scheme. By 1942, the year of Cram's death, only his great nave and the west front (minus its towers) were complete. There the work stopped, halted by our entry into World War II.

Completion is not imminent, but work resumed in 1979 under the surveillance of then **Bishop Paul Moore, Jr.** and **Dean James Parks Morton**, who combined the happy interests of social activism, avant-garde art and music, and a heavy and heady interest in architecture. **James Bambridge**, a British master stonemason, came to New York on the bishop's invitation to train a cadre of youths in stonecutting. The first efforts raised the south Amsterdam Avenue tower. Unfortunately, the work has been stopped and the stoneyard closed.

Finally the great lantern over the crossing will be built in accordance with Cram's original design (see the model in the Cathedral gift shop), replacing the "temporary" dome that has sheltered the worshipping flock for nearly a century. Built of Guastavino vaulting, a process developed by Spanish architect Rafael Guastavino, it required no interior support during the course of construction. Craftsmen worked from the completed vault (of three staggered laminations) as they laid the remaining swirls of tile using a special adhesive mortar. The resulting underside, handsomely patterned, is visible from within, although the plans had originally called for concealing it with mosaics.

Despite its incompleteness and mix of styles it is an impressive interior, enormous not only in plan but also in volume, its side aisles being built as high as the nave. Do visit the baptistry and ambulatory chapels radiating from the apse.

On the landscaped grounds are a number of ancillary buildings, among them the Synod House on Cathedral Parkway, whose Amsterdam Avenue portal is embellished with sculpture from Alexius to Zinzendorf.

Were St. John the Divine to be completed it would be, perhaps, the world's largest cathedral, even though it is not as large as St. Peter's in Rome. St. Peter's, large as it is, is not a cathedral. The Pope, as bishop of Rome, maintains his seat (his "cathedra") at the Church of St. John Lateran, outside the Vatican's walls. Size does not a cathedral make. Deep in the interior of the Ivory Coast a contender for size is rising.

[M2a] **Amsterdam House** (nursing home), 1060 Amsterdam Ave., NW cor. W. 112th St. 1976. **Kennerly, Slomanson & Smith.** [M2b] **Amsterdam Avenue Wing**. 1997. **Geddes Partnership.**

M2a

The original building is an elegantly designed multistory slab for the care of the elderly, its use of naturally finished wood-framed windows a masterful touch. The "wing" thickly veneering this elegance aspires to the neo-Georgian, but is a heavy-handed Disneyland crowd-pleaser. What an insult to both Amsterdam House and the Cram cathedral façade across the street.

[M2c] **Amsterdam House Adult Day Care Center**/originally 113th Street Gatehouse, New Croton Aqueduct, W. 113th St., SW cor. Amsterdam Ave. ca. 1890

M2c

Construction labor was cheap in the 1880s when the New Croton Aqueduct was built, and manufactured items, such as cast-iron pipe, were expensive. It was more economical, there-fore, to minimize the use of pipe when water pressures were low, and to use a masonry aqueduct instead. Such an aqueduct, horseshoe-shaped in cross section, ran under Convent and Amsterdam Avenues between 119th and 113th Streets until 1987, when steel pipe replacements were installed. This finely crafted stone gatehouse and its mate at 119th Street (ca. 1880s) stand above the shafts at each end of the aqueduct.

M3

[M3] **Engine Co. No. 47, New York City Fire Department,** 500 W. 113th St., SW cor. Amsterdam Ave. 1889. **Napoleon LeBrun & Sons.** ●⚲
The ubiquitous LeBrun has left many such landmarks.

[M4] **St. Luke's Hospital,** Morningside Dr., bet. W. 113th and W. 114th Sts. W side. Original building, 1896. **Ernest Flagg.**
The western pavilions have been replaced, and the hand-some baroque dome is lost, although its drum is still there; but the high mansard roofs and the profusion of Classical detail give the original buildings their dignity and charm. Still gorgeous.

M4

[M5] **Eglise de Notre Dame** (Roman Catholic), 40 Morningside Dr., NW cor. W. 114th St. Apse, Sanctuary, 1909-1910. **Daus & Otto.** Nave and façade, 1914. **Cross & Cross.** Rectory, 1913-1914. **Cross & Cross.** ●⚲
Like the nearby cathedral, this "Grotto Church of Notre Dame" is also unfinished. The interior must be lighted artificially because the oversized drum and dome, designed to bring sky-light into the church, were never built. For a sense of what com-pletion would bring, visit nearby St. Paul's Chapel at Columbia, whose drum and dome are in place. A surprising contrast to the smooth pale stone interior of the church is the rough dark con-crete replica of the grotto at Lourdes behind the altar.

M5

Columbia University:

[M6] **Columbia University campus,** W. 114th to W. 120th Sts., bet. Broadway and Amsterdam Aves. Original design and buildings, **Charles McKim** of **McKim, Mead & White.** Construction begun, 1897. Additions and changes by others.
Columbia is one of the nation's oldest, largest, and wealthi-est institutions. Prior to relocating here on the Heights, in 1897, Columbia occupied two other campuses, the first southwest of the current City Hall and later a site east of Rockefeller Center's buildings. (The university, up until 1987, owned the land under Rockefeller Center, from which it derived a substantial income.) Today's main campus occupies land bought from the Bloomingdale Insane Asylum.

M6

The earliest buildings, north of 116th Street (now a pedestri-an walkway), are situated on a high terrace, two flights of stairs above surrounding streets and separated from them by high, forbidding granite basements. The south campus, a later addi-tion south of West 116th Street, is terraced below the level of the 116th Street pedestrian way.
Arranged along Classical lines, the campus is dominated by the great, domed, limestone Low Library. The Italian Renaissance-style instructional buildings, of red brick, limestone trim, and copper-green roofs, are arranged around the periphery of the campus and are augmented by planting, tasteful paving, statues, plaques, fountains, and a variety of Classical ornament and detail. All of this, however, fails to animate the campus into either a dra-matic or picturesque composition. The old buildings, except for Low Library and St. Paul's Chapel are bland.
McKim, Mead & White's original concept of a densely built-up campus, with a central quadrangle and intimate side courts, was never followed. Only the court between Avery and Fayerweather Halls was completed, and this is now changed by

the subterranean extension of Avery Library. The abandonment of the compact plan, plus the university's explosive growth, resulted in the spread of Columbia's buildings to the remainder of Morningside Heights.

New Columbia buildings, except for **Tschumi**'s Lerner Student Center, are outside the McKim perimeter: **Polshek**'s Greene and Warren, **Gruzen Samton**'s Kraft Center, and **Gwathmey Siegel**'s East Campus Dormitory have all brought much new life to that extended campus.

M7

Columbia east of the McKim superblock:

[M7] **Cathedral Court, La Touraine, and Mont Ceris** (apartments), 44-54 Morningside Dr., bet. W. 114th and W. 116th Sts. 1904-1905. **Schwartz & Gross**.

They look comfortable from the outside, and just imagine the views. The suave handling of the recessed fire escapes makes them a rich part of the façade. Many on the Columbia faculty call these home.

M8

[M8] **Statue of Carl Schurz**, Morningside Dr. at W. 116th St. E side. 1913. **Karl Bitter**, sculptor. **Henry Bacon**, architect.

A reformer, avid conservationist, and editor of the *New York Evening Post* and the *Nation,* **Schurz** (1829-1906) has his own park too, but you can't see that from here. But this is an excellent place to view Harlem from afar. Rising from the patchwork quilt roofscape below is a tall white building to the north, the Harlem State Office Building.

To the north look down and enjoy massive buttresses supporting the Drive flanking an entry into a cavernous world.

M9

[M9] **William C. Warren Hall** (Columbia University Law Review), 410 W. 116th St., bet. Amsterdam Ave. and Morningside Dr. 1995. **Polshek Partnership**.

A sleek glass and stainless steel canopy signals the narrow entry to a much more substantial volume behind.

[M10] **President's House, Columbia University**, 60 Morningside Dr., at W. 116th St. W side. 1912. **William Kendall** of **McKim, Mead & White**.

A stern neo-Georgian palazzo, built, as is much of Columbia, of Stony Creek granite, Indiana limestone, and overburned brick. Eisenhower elected to live elsewhere.

M10

[M11] **East Campus complex** (residence hall and offices), SW cor. 118th St. and Morningside Drive. 1977-1981. **Gwathmey Siegel & Assocs**. Renovated, 1994. **Gruzen Samton**.

A sleek, gray and red tile residence slab with glass block. This is the swan song of the International Style, or is it perhaps a rooster crowing the Post Modern [PoMo] neo-International 1930s Renaissance? In any categorization, it is both elegant and handsome.

[M12] **119th Street Gatehouse**, W. 119th St., SE cor. Amsterdam Ave. ca. 1890.

M11

[M13] **Casa Italiana**, 1151-1161 Amsterdam Ave., bet. W. 116th and W. 118th Sts. E side. 1926-1927. **William Kendall** of **McKim, Mead & White**. ● Restored and east façade completed, 1996. **Buttrick, White & Burtis**, architects. **Italo Rota**, associate architect.

A Renaissance palazzo appropriate for Ivy Leaguers seeking *la cultura italiana.*

[M14a] **Law School**, 435 W. 116th St., NE cor. Amsterdam Ave. 1961. **Harrison & Abramovitz**.

[M14b] **Jerome L. Greene Hall** (street-level addition to the Law School), 435 W. 116th St., NE cor. Amsterdam Ave. 1996. **Polshek Partnership**.

M13

Law's south façade on 116th Street provided that marvelous box where a dictator might posture to harangue the multitudes. Later (1977) an enormous sculpture by **Jacques Lipchitz** moved in. Now the stylish new addition (and gracious point of entry) mutes all this with some 1990s verve.

[M15] **New Building**, Amsterdam Ave., bet. W. 115th and W. 116th St. E side. 1998. **The Hillier Group**.

Now that polychromy is back in style, the inset blue tiles add sparkle to an articulated brick and banded building.

M14b

Now to the central campus:

 [M16] **Low Memorial Library**, N of W. 116th St., bet. Amsterdam Ave. and Broadway. 1895-1897. **Charles McKim** of **McKim, Mead & White**. 👁 Interior 👁 . Exhibition space open to the public, Mo-Fr 9-5:30.

Columbia University's most noteworthy visual symbol is the monumental, domed, and colonnaded Low Library, named not for its height but for **Abiel Abbot Low**, the father of its donor. Donor **Seth Low** (1850-1916) was alternately mayor of Brooklyn, president of Columbia, and mayor of New York. Set atop three tiers of graciously proportioned steps, this dignified centerpiece for the campus is no longer the university library, its interior spaces more suited to ceremonial and administrative uses than to shelf space and reading rooms. Off the rotunda to the east is a small display of Columbiana with items of interest to those who wish to trace the university's march northward through Manhattan from its 18th-century beginnings downtown as King's College.

M15

[M17] **Alma Mater**. 1903. **Daniel Chester French**, sculptor.

Centered on the formal stair one tier below Low is Alma Mater, the once-gilded bronze statue that forms the background of nearly every university graduation ceremony. An evocative sculpture, the enthroned figure extends her hand in welcome as she looks up from the mighty tome of knowledge lying open in her lap. As a symbol, Alma Mater has understandably elicited both love (a protest in 1962 caused a newly applied gilding to be removed in favor of the more familiar green patina; now debased to statuary bronze popular with metal maintenance experts, but with the loss of the rich green matte surface so

M16

M17

M18

appropriate to the march of history) and hate (in 1968 she survived a bomb blast during that period of student unrest).

Charles Follen McKim: Despite the sometime held belief to the contrary, not all buildings produced by the architectural firm of **McKim, Mead & White** *were by its most notorious partner,* **Stanford White**. *Chief architect for the Columbia campus was* **Charles Follen McKim** *(1847-1909), commemorated in a bronze plaque set into the pavement in front of Alma Mater. The Latin inscription can be translated as "An artist's monuments look down upon us throughout the ages." Pennsylvania Station (1910-1963) was the other great McKim work in Manhattan.*

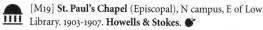

M19

[M18] **Butler Library**/originally South Hall, W. 114th St. bet. Amsterdam Ave. and Broadway. 1931-1934. **James Gamble Rogers**.

This is Columbia's principal library (named for **Nicholas Murray Butler**, Columbia's president from 1902 to 1945), its notable collections overshadowed architecturally by Low across 116th Street. The sturdy Ionic colonnade is impressive close up, but becomes diminished within the overall bland form at a distance.

[M19] **St. Paul's Chapel** (Episcopal), N campus, E of Low Library. 1903-1907. **Howells & Stokes**. 🌶

In the initial period of development of the Morningside Heights campus, general planning and design were almost entirely a **McKim, Mead & White** monopoly. One of two exceptions (the other was **Arnold W. Brunner**'s School of Mines) is this magnificent chapel, the best of all Columbia's buildings. It is a gift of **Olivia Egleston Phelps Stokes** and **Caroline Phelps Stokes**, sisters of wealthy financier and philanthropist **Anson Phelps Stokes** (1838-1913). The beautifully executed work was the design of **Howells & Stokes**, one of whose partners, **Isaac Newton Phelps Stokes** (author of *The Iconography of Manhattan Island*) was their nephew. The interior is filled with exquisite Guastavino vaulting; magnificent light pours down from above. A visit during a performance of antique works by one of Columbia's musical groups will also reveal its sonorous acoustics. Pro Ecclesia Dei.

The last surviving building of the Bloomingdale Insane Asylum, on whose site Columbia was built, is East Hall (1878), just south of St. Paul's. As part of the asylum it was called the Macy Villa. It now serves as the home of the Temple Hoyne Buell Center for the Study of American Architecture.

M20

[M20] **Avery Hall**, N campus, N of St. Paul's Chapel. 1911-1912. **McKim Mead & White**. Underground addition and courtyard to E, 1977, **Alexander Kouzmanoff & Assocs**. Exhibitions open to the public. 🌶

One of 9 similar instructional buildings, Avery Hall houses the School of Architecture and Avery Library, the nation's largest architectural library. The glazed conning towers are skylights for the undercourt addition.

[M21] **Sherman Fairchild Center for the Life Sciences**, NE campus 1977-1997. **Mitchell/Giurgola Assocs**.

A radically designed building that shields the campus from the banal façade of Seeley W. Mudd Hall. Fairchild's volume is layered with a screen wall that reveals a second skin through deeply modeled slots and openngs. The tile (a thin material) floats and picks up the color of terra-cotta pavers on Columbia's walkways (a heavy material).

M22

[M22] **Computer Science Building, NE campus**, partially under Fairchild Center for the Life Sciences, sharing

M21

terrace with Mudd Engineering and facing Amsterdam Ave. 1983.
R. M. Kliment & Frances Halsband.

An interstitial weaving of 3 buildings, a plaza, and a street,
this subtle architectural and urbanistic coup makes this campus
extension a better precinct.

[M23] **Uris Hall Extension**, N campus, N of Low Library. 1983-
1984. **Peter L. Gluck & Partners**.

Anything that could mask Uris would be a plus, and here is
a shallow (in depth, not character) and handsome Post-Modern
building to do the job.

M23

[M24] **Shapiro Center for Engineering and Physical Science
Research**, N end of Campus, abutting W. 122nd St. 1989-1992.
Hellmuth, Obata & Kassebaum.

Post Modernism with a heavy hand. Neither Historicist nor
Modernist, it fails to resolve its program gracefully.

[M25] **Earl Hall**, N Campus, W of Low Library. 1900-1902.
McKim, Mead & White.

Symmetrically modeled with Howells and Stokes's St. Paul's,
Earl looks like, but is not, a neo-Georgian house of worship.

M24

*Eats and drinks: The acclaimed watering place of Morningside
Heights is the dark, cavernous, and notorious West End Café, 2911
Broadway, between 113th and 114th, a bar which has attracted the
locals for decades and in the 1940s was where beat writers*
William Burroughs, **Jack Kerouac**, *and* **Allen Ginsberg** *hung
out.*

M25

[M26] **Alfred Lerner Hall** (student center), Columbia
University, 2920 Broadway, NE cor. W. 115th St. 1999.
Bernard Tschumi/Gruzen Samton, Associated Architects.

Tschumi said that it will be "quiet on the outside, and
dynamic on the inside," with an inner, 6-story atrium "that will
be at the cutting edge of technology with glass ramps, steel, and
translucent glass." He's right. It works elegantly, dour to
Broadway, exuberant on the inner campus.

[M27] **Broadway Residence Hall**, Columbia University, NE cor.
113th St. and Broadway. 2000. **Robert A. M. Stern**.

364 Columbia seniors fill most of the bulk over a New York
Public Library branch below. "Tawny" brick and limestone clad
this bulky pile. Stern, now the Dean of Architecture at Yale, follows a path of eclectic historicism.

M26

 [M28] **Morris A. Schapiro Hall** (dormitory), 615 W. 115th St., bet. Broadway and Riverside Dr. 1988. **Gruzen Samton Steinglass**.

An infill building in the city streetscape, outside the formal boundaries of **McKim, Mead & White**'s Renaissance university. It is a good neighbor to those next door, with architectural remembrances of the main campus in the color and texture of its brickwork.

M29

[M29] **Robert K. Kraft Center for Jewish Student Life**, W. 115th St., bet. Broadway and Riverside Dr. 1999. **Gruzen Samton**.

Jerusalem stone clads facilities for the Jewish student at Columbia.

[M30a] Originally **The Alpha Club**, 434 Riverside Dr., bet. W. 115th and W. 116th Sts. 1898. **Wood, Palmer & Hornbostel**.

An elaborate frat house in the Beaux Art mode, so stylish in its time.

M30a

[M30b] **The Colosseum** (apartments), 435 Riverside Dr., SE cor. W. 116th St. 1910. **Schwartz & Gross**.

Like a heavily embroidered tapestry, this unusual curved façade, together with its opposite-handed sibling across West 116th Street, frames the main entrance of the Columbia campus atop the hill—best seen from the Drive.

M30b

An aside to the south, west of Broadway:

[M31] **The Hendrik Hudson** (apartments), 380 Riverside Dr., bet. Cathedral Pkwy. and W. 111th St. 1907. Broadway addition/now College Residence Hotel, 601 Cathedral Pkwy., NW cor. Broadway. 1908. Both by **William L. Rouse** of **Rouse & Sloan**.

A grandiose apartment building in Tuscan villa style, pumped up to fit its Riverside Drive site. Many of its embellishments, as well as both interior and exterior elegance, have been reduced by time, economics, and the elements.

[M32] **625 West 112th Street** (apartment house), bet. Broadway and Riverside Dr. 1900s.

A luscious and civilized stack of French flats: French doors set within a recessed bay window, contained by elegant ironwork. **Mrs. Manson Mingott** (from **Edith Wharton's** *The Age of Innocence*), move over.

M31

[M33] **Bank Street College of Education**, 610 W. 112th St., bet. Broadway and Riverside Dr. 1970. **Harry Weese & Assocs.**

M32

A tall, heavy-handed, but reserved composition. This teachers' training school had its beginnings on Bank Street in Greenwich Village, hence its name.

Back to 116th Street and Broadway:

Barnard College:

[M34] **Barnard College campus**, W. 116th to W. 120th (Reinhold Niebuhr Place) Sts., bet. Broadway and Claremont Ave. [M34a] **Milbank Hall**, comprising Milbank, Brinckerhoff, and Fiske Halls, 606 W. 120th St., N end of campus. 1896-1897. **Lamb & Rich.** [M34b] **Brooks Hall** (dormitory). 1906-1907. **Charles A. Rich.**

[M34c] **Barnard Hall**, originally Students' Hall. 1916-1917. **Arnold W. Brunner.** [M34d] **Hewitt Hall** (dormitory). 1924-1925. **McKim, Mead & White.** [M34e] **Lehman Hall/Wollman Library**. 1957-1959. **O'Connor & Kilham.** [M34f] **Helen Reid Hall** (dormitory). 1957-1959. **O'Connor & Kilham.** [M34g] **Millicent Mcintosh Center**. 1966-1969. **Vincent G. Kling & Assocs.** [M34h] **Helen Goodhart Altschul Hall**. 1966-1969. **Vincent G. Kling & Assocs.**

M34c

[M34i] **Iphigene Ochs Sulzberger Hall** (dormitory). 1986-1989. **James Stewart Polshek & Partners.**

In its original **Lamb & Rich** quadrangle, crowned with **Arnold Brunner**'s 1917 Barnard Hall, Barnard obviously aped Columbia's architecture across Broadway. Later and lesser architects added Lehman, Reid, McIntosh, and Altschul, modern in their stance but without reference to the context of street or campus. Quality control has been reestablished with the construction of the new dormitory.

M34i

Barnard was established to be the undergraduate women's equivalent of Columbia in memory of **Frederick A. P. Barnard** (1809-1889), the Columbia president who had championed the cause of equal rights for women in higher education. Since Columbia itself has been coeducational since 1983, a "women's college" (with some male students) is somewhat of an anachronism within a world of unisexism.

The Lehman Library's grilled façade is the work of solar consultants **Victor and Aladar Olgyay**, Hungarian émigrés who somehow got their north arrow confused: the grillage faces slightly south of east, where there is negligible sun loading. They were, however, concerned more with architectural ideology than with its reality.

North of the Columbia Campus:

M35

[M35] **Teachers College, Columbia University**, 525 W. 120th St., bet. Amsterdam Ave. and Broadway, to 121st St. [M35a] **Main Hall**. 1892-1894. **William A. Potter**. [M35b] **Macy Hall**/originally Macy Manual Arts Building, N of Main Hall. 1893-1899. **William A. Potter**. [M35c] **Frederick Ferris Thompson Memorial Hall**, W of Main Hall. 1902-1904. **Parish & Schroeder**. [M35d] **Russell Hall**, E of Main Hall. 1922-1924. **Allen & Collens**. [M35e] **Thorndike Hall**, NW of Main Hall. 1969-1973. **Hugh Stubbins & Assocs**. [M35f] **Whittier Hall** (dormitories), Amsterdam Ave. bet. W. 120th and W. 121st Sts. W side. 1900-1919. **Bruce Price** and **M.A.Darragh**.

Tightly squeezed into a full city block, this semiautonomous branch of Columbia offers a rich range of red brick architecture largely from the turn of the 20th century. Peeking above the composition from West 121st Street—it is entered through a court from West 120th Street—is a sleek new high-rise addition, 81 years removed from the earliest building.

M36

[M36] Originally Horace Mann School/now **Horace Mann Hall, Teachers College**, Broadway bet. W. 120th and W. 121st Sts. E side. 1899-1901. **Howells & Stokes** and **Edgar H. Josselyn**.

Horace Mann School was founded in 1887 as the laboratory school for Teachers College, but those activities are now conducted in the suburban Riverdale campus. Its charming forms, however, continue to enliven the Broadway blockfront it commands, as it now serves TC in other capacities.

M37

[M37] **Corpus Christi Church** (Roman Catholic), 533 W. 121st Street, bet. Broadway and Amsterdam Aves. 1935. **Wilfred E. Anthony**.

Nothing much outside, but the interior might be that of an eccentric Wren disciple's London church. Go in.

M38

[M38] **Bancroft Hall** (apartments), Teachers College, 509 W. 121st St., bet. Amsterdam Ave. and Broadway. 1910-1911. **Emery Roth**.

Tucked away on a dark side street in the shadow of Teachers College is this ebullient eclectic warhorse of a façade: aggressive, bold, charming, mysterious. An altogether wonderful discovery, with verdigris copper-clad bay windows and a timber Italianate Tuscan roof.

M39

[M39] **Public School 36, Manhattan**, The Morningside School, 123 Morningside Dr., NE cor. Amsterdam Ave. 1967. **Frederick G. Frost, Jr. & Assocs.**, architects. **William Tarr**, sculptor.

This school is actually a group of separate buildings situated atop rock outcroppings on a site demapped from Morningside Park. Simple brick stair towers, cast concrete construction, and large rectangular windows mark the earliest arrival of the New Brutalism in upper Manhattan. The self-weathering steel sculpture is a particularly harmonious element in the overall design.

M40

[M40] **Jewish Theological Seminary**, 3080 Broadway, bet. W. 122nd and W. 123rd Sts. E side. 1928-1930. **Gehron, Ross & Alley**, architects. **David Levy**, associate architect. [M40a] **Expansion and Library**, 1980-1983. **The Gruzen Partnership**.

This clunky, oversized neo-Georgian building is the central institution of the Conservative movement in American Judaism. The corner tower, used as library stacks, houses the gateway to the inner courtyard. The Gruzen addition, a low-key brick and limestone extension, manages to be both understated and appropriate. Though hardly noticed by the passerby, it is savored by the dilettante who takes time to study its elegant detailing.

Rabbi Mordecai Kaplan (1881-1983), *founder of the Jewish Reconstructionist movement, taught at the Jewish Theological Seminary from 1909 to 1963 and established the Society for the Advancement of Judaism in 1922. He defined Judaism as a "civilization," embracing language, custom, and culture beyond the conventional limitations of religious belief.*

An early champion of equal rights for women, **Rabbi Kaplan** *is credited with having created the bat mitzvah, the rite marking a girl's arrival at the age of Jewish duty and responsibility. In 1922* **Rabbi Kaplan's daughter, Judith,** *became the first bat mitzvah.*

[M41] **Union Theological Seminary**, W. 120th (Reinhold Niebuhr Place) to W. 122nd Sts., bet. Broadway and Claremont Aves. 1906-1910. **Allen & Collens.** Altered, 1952. **Collens, Willis & Beckonert.** Burke Library renovations, 1982. **Mitchell/Giurgola.** Chapel and two towers. 🍎

A stronghold of theological modernism and social consciousness is housed in a Collegiate Gothic quadrangle of rock-face granite with limestone trim. Two handsome Perpendicular towers, an exquisite chapel, library, refectory, and dormitories recall medieval Oxbridge, or perhaps **F. Scott Fitzgerald**'s Princeton.

M41

[M42] **Interchurch Center**, 475 Riverside Dr., bet. W. 119th and W. 120th Sts. 1956-1958. **Voorhees, Walker, Smith, Smith & Haines** and **Collens, Willis & Beckonert.**

A bulky work that attempts to harmonize with—but only detracts from—lyrical Riverside Church to the north.

[M43] **Riverside Church**, 490 Riverside Dr., bet. W. 120th and W. 122nd Sts. 1926-1930. **Allen & Collens** and **Henry C. Pelton.** Parish House, 1955-1959. **Collens, Willis & Beckonert.**

The ornament of Chartres adapted to a 21-story high-rise steel-framed church. Funded by **John D. Rockefeller, Jr.**, this church enjoyed the finest in available materials, stone carving, and stained glass of its era. Its 392-foot-high tower (largely an office building disguised as a place of bells) is surmounted by the 74-bell **Laura Spelman Rockefeller Memorial Carillon**, with its 20-ton tuned bass bell. Both carillon and bell are the world's largest. Commanding an imposing site along Riverside Drive, the church was criticized upon completion for its opulence, as "a late example of bewildered eclecticism." Nevertheless, despite problems of scale that seem to make it smaller than it is (particularly when seen up close), it is easily the most prominent architectural work

M43

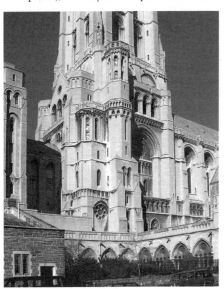

M43

M46   M46

along the Hudson from midtown to the George Washington Bridge. Within the church is the lovely Christ Chapel.

Take an elevator to the carillon and climb the open stairway past the bells to the lofty windblown observation deck.

[M44] **Manhattan School of Music**/onetime Juilliard School of Music/originally Institute of Musical Art, 120 Claremont Ave., NE cor. W. 122nd St. 1910. **Donn Barber**. Additions, 1930-1931, **Shreve, Lamb & Harmon**. [M44a] **Mitzi Newhouse Pavilion**. 1969-1970. **MacFadyen & Knowles**.

Innocuous limestone with a neat concrete and glass cafeteria.

[M45] **International House**, 500 Riverside Dr., N of Sakura Park, N of W. 122nd St. 1924. **Lindsay & Warren, Louis Jallade**, partner-in-charge.

The multistory residence for the numerous foreign (and other) students who attend the nearby centers of higher learning.

[M46] **Grant's Tomb**/General Grant National Memorial, Riverside Dr. at W. 122nd St. 1891-1897. **John H. Duncan**. Mosaic benches, 1973. **Pedro Silva, Cityarts Workshop.** Interior 🍎 Restoration, 1997. Open to the public: We-Su 9-5; closed Mo & Tu. 212-666-1640.

The contributions of 90,000 subscribers paid for this pompous sepulcher, the design chosen in an architectural competition. It is a free copy of **Mausoleus**' tomb at Halicarnassus (present-day Turkey) of 350 B.C.—one of the **Seven Wonders of the Ancient World**: hence a mausoleum. As attention-getting as this pile of granite is from Riverside Drive, here parted to create its spacious lawned site, it is a far better work inside. There, through the massive bronze doors in a great solemn white marble setting, **President Ulysses Simpson and Julia Boggs Dent Grant** rest side by side in identical polished black sarcophagi.

The sinuous mosaicked benches embracing the plaza bring shades of Gaudi and the Parque Güell—a populist huzzah for the solemn Grants.

Amiable child!

*To the memory of an amiable child: Almost lost at the edge of the monumental space commanded by **Grant's Tomb** is a tiny fenced area a bit to the north, across southbound Riverside Drive, and down a few steps. Here stands a modest stone urn "Erected to the Memory of an Amiable Child, St. Clair Pollock," a five-year-old who fell to his death from these rocks on July 15, 1797. When the property was sold, the child's uncle asked that the grave remain inviolate; and despite the bureaucratic problems involved, the request has been honored through the years. The views of the Hudson Valley are particularly beautiful from this tranquil spot.*

M47a

[M47] **560 Riverside Drive** (apartments), N of Tiemann Place. 1964. [M47a] **2 St. Clair Place** (offices), W of W. 125th St. 1969. **Brown, Guenther, Battaglia, Seckler**.

An enormous apartment complex for individuals and families connected with Columbia and its sister institutions on the Heights. Gleaming white, beveled, concrete, picture-framed windows repeat and repeat and repeat in the low office wing.

MANHATTANVILLE

Manhattanville: Along the west end of the valley that cleaves Morningside Heights (on the south) and Hamilton Heights (on the north) grew the village of Manhattanville. It straddled both sides of today's West 125th Street, which leads to the former landing of the ferry to Fort Lee. A bustling village more in the New England mill town tradition than that of New York City, the settlement supported a pigment factory, D. F. Tiemann & Company (below 125th Street), a worsted mill (on 129th Street west of Broadway), Yuengling Brewery (128th Street east of Amsterdam), as well as a grammar school, post office, and a sprinkling of churches. Manhattan College began in 1853 along Broadway at 131st Street before relocating to Riverdale. The area still retains in its structures vestiges of its 19th-century industrial beginnings.

[M48] **IRT Broadway Line viaduct**, along Broadway spanning W. 125th St. 1904. **William Barclay Parsons**, engineer. 🍎

The sweeping latticed arch and its abutments are worthy of Eiffel. The masking billboard that for many years sullied this graceful engineering is, happily, gone.

M49

[M49] **Prentis Hall** (Department of Chemical Engineering), Columbia University/originally Sheffield Farms Milk Company 632 W. 125th St., bet. Broadway and St. Clair Place. 1906. **Edgar I. Moeller.**

Milky-white glazed terra-cotta, now somewhat pock-marked and crazed, is this ex-dairy's face to the world. How appropriate (poetically, at least) that it is now a chemical engineering laboratory.

Where 125th Street turns today it once did not. The diagonal street in the valley between Morningside and Hamilton Heights was called Manhattan Street. It ran obliquely to the street grid only because the topography made the valley the natural route for a wide thoroughfare—along it ran the streetcars to the Fort Lee Ferry. In 1920, however, it was decided that Manhattan Street should be renamed West 125th Street, and the old part of the original West 125th Street, west of Morningside Avenue, was renamed LaSalle Street. Now 125th Street has vanished entirely—at least on official maps, supplanted by Martin Luther King, Jr. Boulevard. But the A train will still take you to 125th.

The city fathers also bestowed other new names: Moylan Place for West 126th Street (now eradicated by General Grant Houses), Tiemann Place (after the old color works) for 127th Street, and St. Clair Place for 129th Street. Incidentally, the oblique route of 125th follows a geological fault line similar to California's San Andreas but not nearly so active.

M50

M51

[M50] **Riverside Drive viaduct**, bet. W. 124th and W. 135th Sts. 1901. **F. Stewart Williamson**, engineer. Totally rebuilt, 1987.

From Morningside Heights to Hamilton Heights this lacy (from below) steel viaduct steps off 26 bays of filigreed steel arches across the 125th Street valley. One of the original arches was retained. The most northern one?

[M51] **St. Mary's Church-Manhattanville** (Episcopal), 521 W. 126th St., bet. Amsterdam Ave. and Old Broadway. 1909. **Carrère & Hastings** and **T. E. Blake**. Rectory. 1851. 🍎

Its name, cut into stone in Old English characters, and its archaic forms preserve the image of Manhattanville as a remote 19th-century village.

M52

[M52] **Manhattanville Neighborhood Center**/originally The Speyer School, 516 W. 126th St., bet. Amsterdam Ave. and Old Broadway. 1902. **Edgar H. Josselyn**.

Built as a demonstration school for Teachers College and as a neighborhood settlement, it is now defunct. Note the Flemish Renaissance silhouette of its parapet.

M53

[M53] **Templo Biblico**/originally Engine Company No. 37, N.Y.C. Fire Department, 503 W. 126th St., bet. Amsterdam Ave. and Old Broadway. 1881. **Napoleon LeBrun**.

Old firehouses are sturdy and readily reusable—this one is a case in point. The structure stands on a block originally devoted to a sprawling charitable institution called Sheltering Arms, today a city park and swimming pool. West on West 126th Street are other community-oriented buildings.

[M54] **St. Joseph of the Holy Family Church** (Roman Catholic), 401 W. 125th St., NW cor. Morningside Ave. 1889. **Herter Brothers**.

An unpretentious church of modest scale and detail. The north end features an interesting intersection of 4 roof gables. Note the blind oculi around the rear doors.

M54

[M55] Originally **Bernheimer & Schwartz Pilsener Brewing Company**, W end of block bounded by W. 126th and W. 128th Sts. E side of Amsterdam Ave. 1905. **Louis Oberlein**.

A phalanx of 19th-century red brick brewery buildings (a descendent of the earlier occupant of this site, Yuengling Brewery), now applied to a variety of contemporary uses.

The Met's shed

The Met's tin shed: *The grimy shed sheathed in corrugated iron occupying some two-thirds of an acre at 495 West 129th Street, east of Amsterdam Avenue, shelters all manner of bulky sets for the Metropolitan Opera House at Lincoln Center. It was built around 1895 as a storage shed for Amsterdam Avenue streetcars. The expanse of sloping roof, unusual for Manhattan, is best seen from the hill behind, along 130th Street.*

HAMILTON HEIGHTS

This precinct, west of St. Nicholas and Jackie Robinson Parks
from Manhattanville north to Trinity Cemetery, includes once-
famous Sugar Hill and the City College campuses. The area
takes its name from the country estate of Alexander Hamilton.
His home and other 19th-century houses, churches, and institutional buildings survive, but most of the apartment houses and
tenements here date from the construction of the Broadway-
Seventh Avenue IRT subway, which opened in 1904.

T2

[T1] **Riverside Drive retaining wall and viewing platforms**, W.
135th to W. 153rd Sts. 1873-1910. **Frederick Law Olmsted, Jr.**
   Smooth granite retains the Drive, crowned with a neo-
Classical balustrade (between 141st and 147th Streets). Once the
face of a seemingly fortified city, it is masked by the Henry
Hudson Parkway, the old Hudson River Railroad freight line,
and the new North River Water Pollution Control Plant. The
best view is from the plant's roof: **Riverbank State Park** (1991)
by **Richard Dattner**.

[T2] **North River Water Pollution Control Plant City of
New York**, W. 137th to W. 145th Sts. W of the Henry
Hudson Pkwy. to the Hudson River. 1986 (partial service) to
1991. **Theodore Long**, architect at **Tippetts-Abbett-McCarthy-
Stratton**. **Riverbank State Park** on top, 1991. **Richard Dattner
& Assocs.**
   Various designers have attempted to assuage the Harlem
community in return for positioning this 22-acre monster facility on their doorstep. In effect, this is the processing plant for all
sewage on the West Side from Morton Street to the Spuyten
Duyvil, the effluents of more than a million people. Park designers, in order, have included **Philip Johnson**, whose proposed
grand decorative fountains were misinterpreted as sewage-
aerating devices; **Norval White** at **Gruzen & Partners**; and
Bond-Ryder Associates. Only **Richard Dattner**'s work was
built—an activity center connected to the Riverside Drive bluff
by two umbilical bridges.

[T3] **Riverside Park** (apartments), 3333 Broadway, bet. W. 133rd and
W. 135th Sts. W side. 1976. [T3a] **Intermediate School 195,**
Manhattan, The Roberto Clemente School, 625 W. 133rd St., bet.
Broadway and Twelfth Ave. 1976. Both by **Richard Dattner &
Assocs., Henri A. LeGendre & Assocs.**, and **Max Wechsler Assocs.**
   The local leviathan: a great slab-sided half octagon that
embraces river views and the sun. A N.Y.C. Educational
Construction Fund project, this oyster has as its pearl the new
local school.

T4

HAMILTON HEIGHTS

see pages 479–487

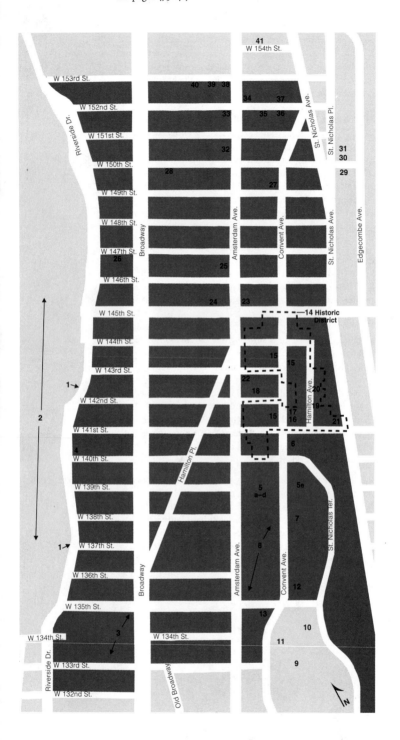

[T4] Originally Academy of the Holy Child (Roman Catholic)/then **St. Walburgas Academy**, 630 Riverside Dr., NE cor. W. 140th St. ca. 1910.

A dark forbidding building with a rock-face random ashlar raiment. Savor the tower and its terra-cotta detail.

City College:

[T5] **The City College of the City University of New York** (CUNY)/formerly City College (also known as CCNY)/originally the Free Academy, W. 138th to W. 141st Sts., St. Nicholas Terr. to Amsterdam Ave. 1902-1907. Including [T5a] **Baskerville Hall**/originally Chemistry Building; [T5b] **Compton Hall**/originally Mechanical Arts Building; [T5c] **Goethals Hall**/originally Technology Building; [T5d] **Wingate Hall**/originally Gymnasium, and [T5e] **Shepard Hall**. All but Goethals by **George B. Post**. 1903-1907. Goethals, 1930. **George B. Post & Sons**. ☛ Renovation of Shepard Hall, interior, 1982-1989. **William Hall & Assocs.**; exterior, 1993-1999. **The Stein Partnership**.

T5a

T5e

This, the second campus of what is still referred to as CCNY, is clad with the by-product of the city's transit system. Manhattan schist, excavated during construction of the IRT Broadway subway, adorns the original quadrangle, trimmed with white glazed terra-cotta. Its cathedral is Shepard Hall, a towered, skewed, Gothic bulk encrusted with terra-cotta quoins, finials, voussoirs, and other detail. Shepard's satellites to the west, across Convent Avenue, also in Gothic fancy dress, are party however to a formal neo-Renaissance plan and courtyard.

[T6] **Steinman Hall** (School of Engineering), Convent Ave. bet. St. Nicholas Terr. and W. 141st St. E side. 1962. **Lorimer & Rose**. Reclad, 1996.

Once glass-block Modern with the inescapable white glazed brick of the 1960s. (The "modernism" of that decade could not understand that an appropriate relationship might somehow have been created with Steinman next door.) Now grossly reclad in aluminum, a packaging that makes the original seem lyrical in retrospect.

T6

[T7] **Mahoney Hall** (Science and Physical Education), Convent Ave. S of 138th St. E side. 1971. **Skidmore, Owings & Merrill**.

Exposed concrete grillage on a battered rocky precast concrete base; an unfriendly place to the pedestrian. Its elevated terrace and bridge were intended to be the first link in a total campus plan that, fortunately, was aborted.

T7

[T8] **North Academic Center**, W. 135th to W. 138th Sts., bet. Convent and Amsterdam Aves. 1983. **Bill Pederson** of **John Carl Warnecke & Assocs.**

This megastructure's skewed geometry was justified by old Shepard Hall's 45 degree tilt to the city's grid. It sits on the site of Lewisohn Stadium, a winter sports field and once a summer mecca for outdoor concertgoers, where symphony orchestras held sway until the overbearing noise of planes in a landing pattern for LaGuardia Airport squelched its acoustic usefulness.

NAC crowns Hamilton Heights, the next hill from Columbia's Morningside Heights. Though perhaps an acropolis for Harlem, the Center is more likely a stranded aircraft carrier amid these small-scaled tenement and town house blocks. **Pederson**, the designer, went on to be the P of **KPF** (**Kohn Pederson Fox**), whose latest collegiate project is the new Baruch Academic Center between 24th and 25th Street and Lexington Avenue. MegaMega.

T8

[T9] **South Campus**/formerly site of Manhattanville College of the Sacred Heart, W. 130th to W. 135th Sts. bet. Convent Ave. and St. Nicholas Terr. ca. 1840-1865 [T9a] **Nursery**/onetime

T10

President's House/originally Gatehouse, Manhattanville College, Convent Ave. NE cor. W. 133rd St. 1912.

The Roman Catholic academy and convent for its teachers, the Ladies of the Sacred Heart, was established here in 1847, also giving name to adjacent Convent Avenue. In 1952 the college and the sisters moved to Westchester, and the City bought the complex for City College. Old Finley Hall has been demolished in favor of a sports complex. The newest CCNY buildings include:

[T10] **Y Building**/originally Morris Raphael Cohen Library, within the South Campus, Convent Ave. SE cor. W. 135th St. 1957. **Lorimer & Rose.**

A glass-block Modern encore (to the original Steinman, which has been rewrapped, but not by Christo). In this era of Post Modern reconsideration of all history, including the various phases of "modern" architecture, such works pique the attention of young architects. But its designation as merely Y suggests that the University Powers don't know what to do with it, and mark it for terminal leave.

[T11] **Aaron Davis Hall for the Performing Arts**, within the South Campus, Convent Ave., SE cor. W. 135th St. 1979. **Abraham W. Geller & Assocs.** and **Ezra D. Ehrenkranz & Assocs.**

An expression of complexity, this intricate building was designed to house three theaters within and to serve one—an open-air amphitheater—without. Successful within, its indecisive image adds to the incoherence of the South Campus.

T12

[T12] Originally **New York Training School for Teachers**/now A. Philip Randolph Campus High School, 443-464 W. 135th St., NE cor. Convent Ave. 1920s. 🍎

A glassy neo-Gothic complex, it served as an experimental high school for the City College School of Education.

Near the City College campuses:

[T13] **135th Street Gatehouse, New Croton Aqueduct**, W. 135th St. SW cor. Convent Ave. 1884-1890. **Frederick S. Cook.** 🍎

Rock-face brownstone and granite, it is the end of the 12-foot-diameter masonry aqueduct from High Bridge. From here the water is distributed in a network of pipery whose next stop is the 119th Street Gatehouse.

T13

[T14] **Hamilton Heights Historic District**, generally along Convent Ave. bet. W. 141st and W. 145 Sts., including parts of Hamilton Terr., W. 140th, W. 141st, W. 142nd, W. 143rd, W. 144th, and W. 145th Sts. 🍎

Until the extension of elevated rapid transit up Columbus and Eighth Avenues in 1879, this was a rural area dotted with the country houses of the affluent. Among them was **Alexander Hamilton**'s Grange on a site that is today the south side of West 143rd Street between Amsterdam and Convent Avenues.

The advent of the el brought a period of speculative expansion in the 1880s. Since Convent Avenue ended at West 145th Street (before its extension after 1900), and Hamilton Terrace formed a closed loop denying access to through traffic, this area became a protected enclave, ideally suited to high-quality residential development. That flurry of construction, dating from 1886 to 1906, resulted in the picturesque row houses that are the richness of these blocks, designed by architects **William E. Mowbray**, **Adolph Hoak**, **William Strom**, **Robert Kelly**, **George Ebert**, **Henri Fouchaux**, **John Hauser**, and the firm of **Neville & Bagge**. Punctuating the horizontality of these groups of 3- and 4-story houses are three churches marking gateways to the district: Convent Avenue Baptist, St. James Presbyterian, and St. Luke's. It was St. Luke's purchase of Hamilton's Grange that caused the Grange to be moved in 1889 to its current site, where it served as the congregation's chapel during construction of the adjacent church between 1892 and 1895.

T15

T15

The romantic appearance of the district and its varied row houses had a special appeal for professors and staff from neighboring City College who, after the campus opened in 1907, began to take up residence here. The area's popularity later waned, but brownstone revival movements of late have caused a vigorous comeback.

[T15] **280-298 Convent Avenue** (row houses), bet. W. 141st and W. 142nd Sts. W side. 1899-1902. **Henri Fouchaux. 320-336 Convent Avenue** (row houses), bet. W. 143rd and W. 144th Sts. W side. 1890-1892. **311-339 Convent Avenue** (row houses), bet. W. 142nd and W. 144th Sts. E side. 1887-1890. **Adolph Hoak.** ☞

Picturesque houses all, with a profusion of ornament and roots in a variety (and intermix) of ancient styles: Flemish, Tudor, and Romanesque. Those at the north end further enhance the streetscape by being set back behind gently raised front yards.

T16

[T16] **St. Luke's Church** (Episcopal), Convent Ave., NE cor. W. 141st St. 1892. **R. H. Robertson.** ☞

A brownstone Romanesque Revival structure, massive in scale and volume, making the most of contrasts in texture in the working of the stone surfaces. It is unfortunate that the monumental tower above the arched corner doorway, which would have completed the composition, was never finished. Note the stately arcade of half-round arches across the Convent Avenue front.

T17

[T17] **Hamilton Grange National Monument**/originally Alexander Hamilton Country House, "The Grange," 287 Convent Ave., bet. W. 141st and W. 142nd Sts. E side. 1802. **John McComb, Jr.** 🍎 ☞ Open to the public.

This, the country home of **Alexander Hamilton** for the last two years of his life, has been stored here since 1889 awaiting a suitable permanent site.

A frame house in the Federal style, now bearing the cream-colored paint of the Park Service, it stands squeezed between St. Luke's and a group of apartment buildings, a discomfiting posture for so historic a structure. The interior has not been refitted for public visitation either, beyond the bland installation of some furnishings in the parlor-floor rooms—a disappointment.

T17

T18

[T18] **Our Lady of Lourdes Church** (Roman Catholic), 467 W. 142nd St., bet. Convent and Amsterdam Aves. 1902-1904. **O'Reilly Bros.**

A bizarre reincarnation made from parts of three important buildings. The gray and white marble and bluestone façade on West 142nd Street includes elements salvaged from the Ruskinian Gothic-influenced National Academy of Design (1863-1865. **Peter B. Wight**), which stood at what is today the northwest corner of East 23rd Street and Park Avenue South. The apse of the church and parts of its east wall are built from the architectural elements of the Madison Avenue end of St. Patrick's Cathedral, removed to build the Lady Chapel that is there today. And the elaborate pedestals flanking the steps that lead up to the church are relics of department store magnate **A. T. Stewart**'s white marble mansion, (1864-1869. **John Kellum**), which embellished the northwest corner of 34th Street and Fifth Avenue until 1901.

T19

[T19] **Ivey Delph Apartments**, 19 Hamilton Terrace, bet. W. 141st and W. 143rd Sts., E side. 1951. **Vertner W. Tandy.**

Modestly scaled modernist apartments by the first African-American architect to be registered in New York State.

[T20] **23-25 Hamilton Terr.**, bet. W. 141st and W. 143rd Sts. 1900s.

Elegant town houses recycled for the millennium.

T21

[T21] **St. James Presbyterian Church and Community House**/formerly St. Nicholas Avenue Presbyterian Church, St. Nicholas Ave., NW cor. W. 141st St. 1904. **Ludlow & Valentine.**

As the century turned, the richness of Gothic Revival church architecture ebbed. The shaft, however, of St. James's stark tower makes its finialed crest much richer by contrast.

T22

[T22] **434 West 143rd Street** (tenement), SE cor. Amsterdam Ave. 1900s.

The cool, flush façade on Amsterdam, and the symbolic architrave (windows and pilasters), frieze, and overhanging cornice, make this an American Renaissance marvel for the masses.

T23

Vintage street lamp: The lazily meandering route of the old Bloomingdale Road across northern Manhattan is marked today by the diagonal of Hamilton Place. Where this street meets Amsterdam Avenue, creating the triangle of space known officially as Alexander Hamilton Square, stands an early cast-iron street lamp. It is not of the bishop's crook variety, but a more monumental version with a baronial base and two lamps rather than one. These relics can still be found infrequently throughout Manhattan. Long may they shine.

[T23] **Jackson Center of Ophthalmology**/originally Lower Washington Heights Neighborhood Family Care Center, 1727 Amsterdam Ave., NE cor. W. 145th St. 1975. **Abraham W. Geller & Assocs.**

An understated civic building; its corner plaza is the main contribution of this wide-windowed salmon brick clinic.

T24

[T24] **Hamilton Grange Branch, The New York Public Library**, 503 W. 145th St., bet. Amsterdam Ave. and Broadway. 1906. **Charles McKim** of **McKim, Mead & White.**

All the ruffles and flourishes of a Florentine palazzo transferred to a New York street. MM&W's later 115th Street Branch may be better, but this is a lush resident for this spartan block. One of myriad libraries contributed by **Andrew Carnegie**'s 1901 $5 million contribution ($100 million in 1999 dollars!).

T25

[T25] **Public School 153**, Manhattan, The Adam Clayton Powell, Jr. School, 1750 Amsterdam Ave., bet. W. 146th and W. 147th Sts. W side. 1975. **Bureau of Design, N.Y.C. Board of Education**.

Addition on a former playground along 146th St., 1990s. **David Smotrich & Partners**.

A modest school, but the new Smotrich addition is a rich and elegant complement to its parent building. It rests in the former playground, and replaces that activity on its own roof.

[T26] **Row houses**, W. 147th St., bet. Broadway and Riverside Dr. S side. ca. 1900-1905.

These houses are not extraordinary, but perched on this steep hill they make it a special street: San Francisco in New York.

[T27] **Church of the Crucifixion** (Anglican), Convent Ave., NW cor. W. 149th St. 1967. **Costas Machlouzarides**.

An airfoil roof is the hat on these curved concrete forms. One can only wish the luxuriant ivy well as it encloses this overdesigned tour de force: a kind of hallucinogenic version of Le Corbusier's Ronchamp.

T27

[T28] **City Tabernacle**, Seventh-Day Adventists' Church/originally Mt. Neboh Temple (synagogue), 564 W. 150th St., bet. Amsterdam Ave. and Broadway. 1917. **Berlinger & Moscowitz**.

From temple (Jewish) to temple (Christian) in two generations. A Spanish tile roof tops this adventure in clinker brick masonry and intricate dark brown terra-cotta. Sober but proud.

T28

[T29] **Dawn Hotel**/originally Jacob P. Baiter House, 6 St. Nicholas Place. 1886. **Richard Rosenstock**. [T29a] **8 St. Nicholas Place** (former residence), SE cor. W. 150th St. 1895. **Theodore G. Stein**.

A neglected row house (No. 6) adjoined by the ravaged one-time Shingle Style extravaganza on the corner (No. 8). The most notable of the group is across West 150th Street:

[T30] Originally James Anthony and Ruth M. Bailey House/now **M. Marshall Blake Funeral Home**, 10 St. Nicholas Place, NE cor. W. 150th St. 1886-1888. **Samuel B. Reed**. 🍎

Rock-face granite stylishly Dutch-gabled and corner-towered. Once it was a major mansion owned by circus entrepreneur Bailey, who joined with showman **Phineas T. Barnum** in 1881 to form the **Barnum & Bailey Circus**.

T30

T31

T32

T33

T34

[T31] **14 St. Nicholas Place** (house), bet. W. 150th and W. 151st Sts. E side. ca. 1890.

The ogee-coned tower caps a neighborhood survivor: reshingled in cedar, it brings back some of the essence of the Gilded Age.

[T32] Originally **Joseph Loth & Company "Fair and Square" Ribbon Factory**, 1828 Amsterdam Ave., bet. W. 150th and W. 151st Sts. W side. 1885-1886. **Hugo Kafka.** ●

In 1893, *King's Handbook of New York* praised this local version of a New England textile mill: "Good taste and a degree of public spirit were shown by the firm in so designing the outward aspect of their establishment as to avoid the prosiness of business and keep in harmony with the surroundings." Six hundred workers produced the ribbons known to seamstresses across the country in 15 widths, 200 colors, and up to 90 styles. Note the radiating wings visible from the side streets.

[T33] Originally **32nd Precinct, N.Y.C. Police Department**/African Methodist Episcopal Church Self-Help Program, 1854 Amsterdam Ave., SW cor. W. 152nd St. 1871. **Nathaniel D. Bush.** ●

A wonderful Victorian relic—long may it serve! Brick with brownstone quoins, the dignified mansard roof cresting with cast iron against the sky.

[T34] **Upper Manhattan Medical Group**, 1865 Amsterdam Ave., NE cor. W. 152nd St. 1953. **Nemeny, Geller & Yurchenko.**

Red brick within a gray-painted concrete grid: windows happen where needed rather than as part of an abstract composition. The central courtyard is an intimate sunswept delight.

[T35] **Everett Center, Dance Theatre of Harlem**, 1994. **Hardy Holzman Pfeiffer.** [T35a] **Dance Theatre of Harlem**/formerly garage, 466 W. 152nd St., bet. St. Nicholas and Amsterdam Aves. ca. 1920. Altered, 1971, **Hardy Holzman Pfeiffer Assocs.**

Through 1971: An early adaptive-reuse effort by a firm of architects who champion the ordinary both in what they begin with and what they add. Pipes, ducts, bare lighting fixtures, old walls—all get used and, miraculously, become much more in the process.

The 1994 Everett Center: polychromatic, with robust volumes serving the dance community. An outpost of sophisticated modernism (a little Post-) in this neighborhood. Goodie.

T35

[T36] **456, 458, and 460 West 152nd Street** (row houses), bet. St. Nicholas and Amsterdam Aves. ca. 1890.

A trio framed by bay-windowed projections: half-cylindrical on the west, half-hexagonal on the east. Romanesque Revival.

[T37] **Wilson Major Morris Community Center of St. John's Baptist Church**, 459 W. 152nd St., bet. St. Nicholas and Amsterdam Aves. 1970. **Ifill & Johnson**.

A modest study in beige brick, precast exposed aggregate, and glass with a particularly neat parapet treatment. Morris was founder of St. John's Church across the street at No. 448.

T37

[T38] **St. Luke A.M.E. Church** (African Methodist Episcopal)/originally Washington Heights Methodist Episcopal Church, 1872 Amsterdam Ave., SW cor. W. 153rd St.

This handsomely restored church (once painted barn-red) is one of three churches along this block of West 153rd Street opposite the stillness of Trinity Cemetery. The other two:

[T39] **Church of St. Catherine of Genoa** (Roman Catholic) and Rectory, 504-506 W. 153rd St., bet. Amsterdam Ave. and Broadway. 1890.

T38

St. Catherine's is unique and a star in this neighborhood: golden-hued brick crested with a many-stepped gable; a deep porch sheltered by a bracketed entryway.

[T40] **Russian Holy Fathers Church** (Russian Orthodox), 526 W. 153rd St. ca. 1925.

Set back some 10 feet from the adjacent housing, Holy Fathers seems reticent to reveal its lovely blue onion dome surmounted by a golden three-armed cross.

[T41] **411-423 West 154th Street** (row houses), bet. St. Nicholas and Amsterdam Aves. [T41a] **883- 887 St. Nicholas Avenue**, bet. W. 154th and W. 155th Sts. W side. ca. 1890.

T39

Survivors: these mansard-roofed row houses sit high above the street, a robust addition to the community. The magnificent elms reinforce their stance. Enjoy!

HARLEM

"... there is so much to see in Harlem."
    —Langston Hughes

To those who haven't been above 110th Street, Harlem means the black ghetto, wherever it may be. But New York is different from all other cities, and its Harlem is different from all other ghettos. This Harlem consists of a variety of contrasting little Harlems, some distinct, some overlapping. Saturday night Harlem is one place; it is a very different place on Sunday morning. There is also literary Harlem, political Harlem, religious Harlem, West Indian Harlem, black nationalist Harlem, and philanthropic Harlem.

In other cities the ghettos either radiate from the oldest and most dilapidated neighborhoods or are relegated to the wrong side of town, where they sorely lack transportation and social facilities. But Harlem became New York's black ghetto when its housing was relatively new. Here we find churches and institutions set on wide boulevards or facing well-designed parks and plazas. Three major subway lines give Harlem access to other parts of the city.

The village of Nieuw Haarlem was established by Peter Stuyvesant in 1658 in what is now East Harlem and was connected with New Amsterdam, ten miles to the south, by a road built by the Dutch West India Company's black slaves. Eight years later the British governor, **Richard Nicolls**, drew a diagonal across Manhattan, from the East River at 74th Street to the Hudson River at 129th Street, to separate New York from Harlem, which was henceforth to be known as Lancaster. Early in the 19th century **James Roosevelt** cultivated a large estate along the East River before moving to Hyde Park. A country village existed at 125th Street and First Avenue.

The opening of the New York and Harlem Railroad in 1837 marks the beginning of Harlem's development as a suburb for the well-to-do. The extension of the elevated to Harlem in 1879 was followed by the construction of tenement houses along the routes of the els and apartment houses—some on a lavish scale—along the better avenues. These were augmented by schools, clubs, theaters, and commercial buildings.

Completion of the IRT Lenox Avenue Subway in 1904 encouraged a real estate boom in Harlem, but many more apartments were built than could be rented, and entire buildings adjacent to Lenox Avenue near 135th Street remained unoccupied. Just at this time the blocks west of Herald Square, where a large part of the city's black population was living, were being redeveloped. The construction of Pennsylvania Station, Macy's department store, large hotels, offices, and loft buildings was forcing blacks to seek living space elsewhere. But in no other parts of the city were they welcome.

The black settlement in the high-prestige neighborhood of Harlem was made possible by **Philip A. Payton, Jr.** (1876-1917), a remarkable black realtor who founded the Afro-American Realty Company in 1904. Alert to both the opportunity in Harlem and the desperate housing situation in the Tenderloin, he was able to open Harlem's many vacant apartment buildings to blacks by assuming the management of individual buildings and guaranteeing premium rents to their landlords. The availability of good housing was unprecedented; the hard-pressed black community flocked to Payton's buildings, often paying exorbitant rents but, for a short while at least, enjoying good housing.

Renaming city streets: In the olden days, surnames of dignitaries became the official titles of city thoroughfares. In this fashion Sixth Avenue above Central Park became Lenox Avenue after

H1

James Lenox, philanthropist, bibliophile, and founder of what became the New York Public Library's Lenox Collection. Later, however, the style changed, to include longer names. That same Sixth Avenue below Central Park is officially Avenue of the Americas, though few use that title. And above Central Park Lenox has officially given way to **Malcolm X** *(Boulevard, not Avenue). To honor Harlem civil rights champion, provocative preacher, and flamboyant congressman* **Adam Clayton Powell, Jr.**, *Seventh Avenue north of Central Park was officially renamed and redubbed with all of Powell's names, thus creating a particularly unwieldy mouthful for addresses or directions. Similarly, Central Park West—or Eighth Avenue, if you will—is officially* **Frederick Douglass Boulevard** *as it progresses northward to the Harlem River; and 125th Street both East and West is* **Martin Luther King, Jr. Boulevard**. *The first governor of Puerto Rico is honored by* **Luis Munoz Marin Boulevard**, *as 116th Street east of Lexington is officially known.*

Since Payton's day, Harlem's troubles have been due not to the area's physical shortcomings but to the abuse and exploitation that our society visits upon its black members. The great influx of blacks during the 1920s, instead of being allowed to spread, was bottled up in this one area. The privations of the Great Depression, the inadequacy of public and private measures to deal with poverty, and the failures of urban renewal further burdened Harlem and its people.

In spite of exploitation, neglect, and the passing of time, Harlem has survived as one of New York's places of interest. Fine patrician rows of private houses and excellent churches, communal buildings, and commercial blocks—which "progress" has erased from more fashionable neighborhoods—survive in Harlem, long neglected, but now much renewed with a return of a well-to-do black middle class, and the general affluence of the late 1990s.

NORTHWEST OF CENTRAL PARK: ADAM CLAYTON POWELL BLVD TO MORNINGSIDE AVE

[H1] **Semiramis** (apartments), 137 Central Park N., bet. St. Nicholas Ave. and Adam Clayton Powell, Jr. Blvd. 1901. **Henry Anderson**. Renovated into condominiums, 1987.

Rough-cut stone and maroon brick were combined to produce a façade that lives up to its name: Semiramis was a mythical Assyrian queen known for her beauty (and to whom is

H2

H5

H6

H7

H8

H9

ascribed the building of Babylon). Unfortunately the cornice is no more.

[H2] **Towers on the Park** (apartment complex), Cathedral Pkwy. and Frederick Douglass Circle, bet. Manhattan Ave. and Frederick Douglass Blvd. N side. 1987. **Bond Ryder & James.**

Condominium apartments here anchor the northwest corner of Central Park, as do the Schomburg Towers to the northeast. Crisp but bland. They bow, however, to the circle and consciously make a corner for the park.

[H3] **Morningside Park**, bet. Cathedral Pkwy. and W. 123rd St., Manhattan and Morningside Aves. and Morningside Dr. Preliminary plan, 1873. Revised plan, 1887. Both by **Frederick Law Olmsted** and **Calvert Vaux**. Western retaining wall and bays, 1882. **J. Wrey Mould.**

This narrow strip of parkland contains the high and rocky cliff that separates Harlem, below and to the east, from Morningside Heights, above and to the west. It preserves a bit of primeval Manhattan as a dramatic foreground to the Cathedral of St. John the Divine, visible at its crest. Proposals of the mid 1960s aimed at solving both the social problems of Harlem and the space problems of institutions on the Heights by cluttering the park with buildings. Public School 36 ate away the northwest corner of the park, and a proposed Columbia University gymnasium was to have usurped two additional acres of public park. But take a walk.

[H4] **Mt. Nebo Baptist Church**, NE cor. Adam Clayton Powell Blvd. and W. 114th St. 1900s.
Neo-Georgian.

[H5] **Wadleigh School**, Junior High School 88, Manhattan, originally The Lydia F. Wadleigh High School for Girls, 215 W. 114th St., bet. Adam Clayton Powell, Jr. Blvd. and Frederick Douglass Blvd. 1901-1902. **C. B. J. Snyder.** 🖤

Built as a prestige high school for girls, Wadleigh was, in a later time, Harlem's only high school (but co-ed). The stately brick and limestone dormer windows and tower remind us (vaguely) of the Loire Valley.

[H6] **115th Street Branch, The New York Public Library**, 203 W. 115th St., bet. Adam Clayton Powell, Jr. Blvd. and Frederick Douglass Blvd. 1907-1909. **Charles F. McKim** of McKim, Mead & White. 🖤

Horizontally and radially rusticated limestone, with arched windows and a carved seal of the City, is guarded by a pair of angels, and recalls the Strozzi Palace in Florence. One of New York's handsomest branch libraries.

[H7] **Memorial Canaan Baptist Church**/originally Northminster Presbyterian Church, 141 W. 115th St., bet. Lenox (Malcolm X Blvd.) and St. Nicholas Aves. 1905.

A robust façade. Powerful circular and arched openings framed in limestone set into a field of dark red and black tapestry brickwork.

[H8] **Community Center and Charter School**, 125 W. 115th St. bet. Lenox and St. Nicholas Aves. 1998.

A trim modern brick and limestone community center, about to become a charter school as well. The entry shows off some Post-Modern style.

[H9] **First Corinthian Baptist Church**/originally Regent Theatre, 1910 Adam Clayton Powell Blvd., SW cor. W. 116th St. 1912-1913. **Thomas W. Lamb.** 🖤

Vaguely inspired by Venice's Doge's Palace and adapted to the needs of the early motion picture. **S. L. Rothafel** (1882-1936),

HARLEM NORTHWEST OF CENTRAL PARK

see pages 489–493

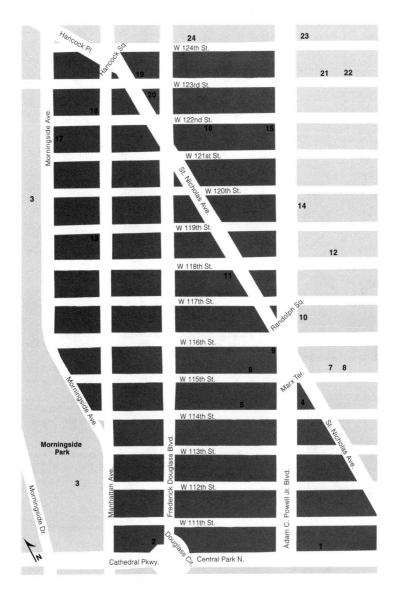

later famous as "Roxy," began his career here as a picture palace impresario, successfully steering the theater out of its initial, catastrophic management failings. It is now a flamboyant Hollywood set for religion.

[H10] **Graham Court** (apartments), 1923-1937 Adam Clayton Powell Blvd., bet. W. 116th and W. 117th Sts. E side. 1899-1901. **Clinton & Russell.** 🖋

Commissioned by **William Waldorf Astor**, this, the most luxurious apartment house in Harlem (although not open to African-Americans until 1928), contains 8 elevators. Surrounding a court, it is entered through a splendid Guastavino vaulted passageway, 2 stories high. These architects later designed the Apthorp, another courtyarded apartment.

[H11] **St. Thomas the Apostle Church** (Roman Catholic), 260 W. 118th St., SW cor. St. Nicholas Ave. 1907. **Thomas H. Poole & Co.**

H10

H11

Berserk eclecticism reminiscent of the filigrees of Milan's Cathedral or of many Flemish or Venetian fantasies. It is unnameable but wonderful.

[H12] **105-137 West 118th Street** (row houses), bet. Adam Clayton Powell and Lenox Blvds. 1890s.

A terrace of 17 houses, their bowfronts modulating this long block. A civilized place to live.

H13

[H13] **Police Athletic League Harlem Community Center**, 441 Manhattan Ave., SW cor. 119th St. 1999. **Kevin Hom + Andrew Goldman**.

Hyperactive, like many children it serves, this community sports and crafts center is literally a bright spot in the Harlem landscape.

[H14] **1971-1973 and 1975-1977 Adam Clayton Powell Boulevard** (tenements), bet. W. 119th and W. 120th Sts. E side. 1890s.

Sturdy clustered Romanesque columns flank these monumental entrances.

H16

[H15] **Washington Apartments**, 2034-2040 Adam Clayton Powell Blvd., SW cor. W. 122nd St. 1883-1884. **Mortimer C. Merritt.** ● Renovated 1992.

Queen Anne for the middle class seeking the new French flats (**Edith Wharton's** *The Age of Innocence* revealed the rude shocks stylish New Yorkers felt about apartment housing). The Victorian Baroque "pediment" gives a simple façade vigorous identity.

[H16] **236 West 122nd Street** (tenement), bet. Adam Clayton Powell and Frederick Douglass Blvds. S side. 1890s.

Those rounded corners and deep reveals make this ordinary tenement an exceptional building.

H17a

[H17a] **Church of the Master** (United Presbyterian), 86 Morningside Ave., bet. W. 121st and W. 122nd Sts. E side. 1972. **Victor Christ-Janer** and **Roger Glasgow**. [H17b] Originally **Morningside Avenue Presbyterian Church**, 360 W. 122nd St., SE cor. Morningside Ave. 1893. **William C. Haskell**.

The newer building, of vertically arranged gray concrete block resembling masonry shingling, competes unsuccessfully with the traditional orange brick church to the north.

H18

[H18] **529-533 Manhattan Avenue** (row houses), NW cor. W. 122nd St. 1890s.

A trio of stately brownstones, well-corniced, and displaying a long brick flank (the brownstone, of course, as usual in row house New York, is merely a veneer).

H21

[H19] Former **Dwyer Warehouse**/originally O'Reilly Storage Warehouse, 258-264 St. Nicholas Ave., NE cor. W. 123rd St. 1892. **Cornelius O'Reilly.**

In 1915, three storage warehouses occupied this block of St. Nicholas Avenue; today only the orange brick shell of this one, and its annex on West 124th Street, remain. Note the flush quoins in contrasting red brick; and it's verging on ruin.

[H20] **28th Precinct, N.Y.C. Police Department**, 2271 Frederick Douglass Blvd., bet. W. 122nd and W. 123rd Sts. to St. Nicholas Ave. E side. 1974. **Lehrecke & Tonetti.**

H20

Set in a triangular space left over after the chaotically arranged streets took their share, this elegantly detailed concrete 2-story police station is architecture of a level rarely achieved in modest modern civic buildings.

Between Fifth and St. Nicholas Avenues to the 125th Street Corridor:

[H21] **Greater Metropolitan Baptist Church**/originally Saint Paul's German Evangelical Lutheran Church, 147 W. 123rd St., bet. Malcolm X and Adam Clayton Powell Blvds. N side. 1897-1898. **Schneider & Herter.** 🍎

Multifinialed as if with rockets ready to pierce the heavens. Smooth and rockface Vermont marble.

H22

[H22] **Greater Metropolitan Baptist Church**, 127 W. 123rd St., bet. Malcom X and Adam Clayton Powell Blvds. N side. 1890s.

Rock faced and smooth granite girds another finialed monolith.

[H23] **Refuge Temple of the Church of Our Lord Jesus Christ**/ formerly Harlem Casino, 2081 Adam Clayton Powell, Jr. Blvd., NE cor. W. 124th St. Interior renovated, 1966, **Costas Machlouzarides**.

The Refuge Temple was founded in 1919 by the Reverend Robert C. Lawson, who criticized the lack of emotionalism in Harlem's more established churches and offered recent migrants the fire, brimstone, and personal Christianity with which they were familiar down South. The façade is retardataire Hollywood.

[H24] Originally **Pabst Concert Hall**, 243-251 W. 124th St., bet. Adam Clayton Powell Jr. Blvd. and Frederick Douglass Blvd. N side. ca. 1900.

Though the entrance to this concert hall was originally on bustling 125th Street, the fantastic vaulted roof is best seen from the rear on 124th. Note how the curve of the roof is expressed by the brick façade.

H25

FRAWLEY CIRCLE TO MOUNT MORRIS PARK

[H25] **Arthur A. Schomburg Plaza** (apartment complex), E. 110th to E. 111th Sts., bet. Fifth and Madison Aves. 1975. **Gruzen & Partners** and **Castro-Blanco, Piscioneri & Feder**.

Two vigorous 35-story octagonal prisms mark the northeast corner of Central Park—Frawley Circle. Sharing the site are an 11-story rectangle along Madison Avenue and a one-story mid-block garage podium that provides for varied outdoor activities on its inviting wood-trellised deck. A project of the N.Y.S. Urban Development Corporation.

[H26] **Public School 208, Manhattan**, The Alain L. Locke School, 21 W. 111th St., bet. Fifth and Lenox (Malcolm X Blvd.) Aves. S side. **Public School 185, Manhattan**, The John Mercer Langston School, 20 W. 112th St. N side. Both 1968. **Katz, Waisman, Weber**.

A modest pair of schools in brick and exposed aggregate trim, set back to back on the through-block site.

[H27] Originally **The Brewster** (apartments)/then The State Bank, 1400 Fifth Ave., NW cor. W. 115th St. ca. 1897.

Furnished rooms now occupy this distinguished Renaissance Revival limestone structure. It must have been an experience worthy of the Medicis to enter this banking palace.

[H28] **Helen B. Atkinson Health Center**/originally Engine Company No. 58, N.Y.C. Fire Department, 81 W. 115th St., bet. Fifth and Lenox (Malcolm X Blvd.) Aves. 1892. **Napoleon LeBrun & Sons**. Remodeled, 1998. **David W. Prendergast**.

H28

Another former firehouse, one of many designed by the architects of the Metropolitan Life tower. The renovation to a health center is both seamless and elegant.

[H29] M**alcolm Shabazz Mosque No. 7**/formerly Muhammad's Temple of Islam/originally Lenox Casino, 102 W. 116th St., SW cor. Lenox Ave. (Malcom X Blvd.) Converted to temple, 1965, **Sabbath Brown**.

An innocent translation of the forms of a Middle Eastern mosque into the vernacular materials of 20th-century shopping centers. The aluminum pumpkin-shaped dome is a parody of those found in the Middle East. Vulgar.

H29

[H30] Originally **The Avon** (apartments), 1770 Madison Ave., NW cor. E. 116th St. ca. 1896.

FRAWLEY CIRCLE TO MOUNT MORRIS PARK

see pages 494–498

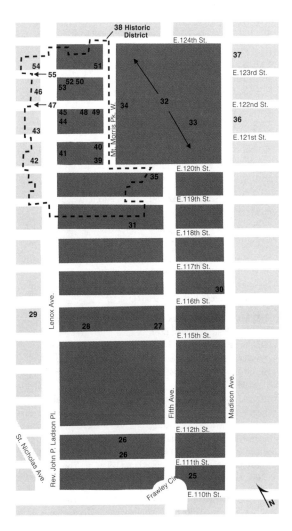

A sea of closely spaced, freely interpreted Doric columns. The upper floors are gone. Now a local church.

[H31] **Bethel Way of the Cross Church of Christ**/originally Congregation Shaari Zadek of Harlem, 25 W. 118th St., bet. Fifth and Lenox (Malcolm X Blvd.) Aves. 1900. **Michael Bernstein**.

Fanciful forms borrowed from Islamic architecture grace the façade of what, in another culture, might have been a harem. Here it beginnings were as a synagogue, later converted to church uses when demographic tides shifted. Painted, but is it a painted lady?

H31

The Mount Morris Area west to Lenox:

[H32] **Marcus Garvey Memorial Park**/formerly Mount Morris Park originally Mount Morris Square, interrupting Fifth Ave. bet. 120th and 124th Sts., Madison Ave. to Mount Morris Park W. Land purchased by the city, 1839.

Truly a mount springing out of the flat plain of central Harlem, a logical platform for the fire watchtower, which still remains. The park's unruly rocky terrain caused it to be largely left alone by park planners until the 1960s, when two major buildings were inserted. In 1973 the park was renamed in honor of black leader **Marcus Garvey** (1887-1940).

[H33] **Fire watchtower**, in park SW of Madison Ave. and E. 121st St. 1855. **Julius B. Kroehl**, engineer. 🍎

The lone survivor of many fire towers that once surveyed New York for signs of conflagration. The structure employs a post-and-lime cast-iron frame similar to that used by the early cast- and wrought-iron builder, **John Bogardus.**

[H34] **Pelham Fritz Recreation Center and Amphitheater**, N.Y.C Department of Parks & Recreation, in park, along Mt. Morris Park W opp. W. 122nd St. 1969. **Lundquist & Stonehill.**

A modest modern intrusion into the park and this historic neighborhood.

H35

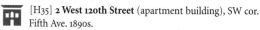 [H35] **2 West 120th Street** (apartment building), SW cor. Fifth Ave. 1890s.

A stately brick and terra-cotta supertenement, crowned with a magnificent dentiled cornice. The neo-Baroque broken pediments at the 5th floor are luscious.

[H36] **North General Hospital**, 1879 Madison Ave., bet. W. 121st and W. 122nd Sts. E side. 1980s. **AHSC Architects.**

Bland modernism, with stacked bay-windows at the center, an idea without further supporting architecture.

[H37] **Maple Plaza** (apartments), 1919 Madison Ave., bet. 123rd and 124th Sts. 1998. **AHSC Architects.**

New housing, and commendable as such, but does it have to be in the manner of lesser Queens efforts?

[H38] **Mount Morris Park Historic District**, Mt. Morris Park W. to W of Lenox Ave. (Malcom X Blvd.), bet. W. 119th and W. 124th Sts. 🍎

Stately houses along the west flank of the hilly picturesque park, others along the side streets, reflect the varied Victorian styles of the late 19th century that characterize the fabric of this small district. Interrupting the warp and woof are a sprinkling of fine churches and other institutional buildings that date from the area's urbanization as a fashionable and highly desirable community. Fortunately the area has retained its architectural character. Among the architectural firms represented in the district, in addition to those responsible for the buildings listed below, are **Thom & Wilson, James E. Ware**, and **George F. Pelham.**

H39

[H39] **1-9 Mount Morris Park West**, bet. W. 120th and W. 121st Sts. Nos. 1-5, 1893. **Gilbert A. Schellenger.** Nos. 6-10, 1891. **Edward L. Angell.** ♂

Ruins with a future? Perhaps New York deserves something equal to Tintern Abbey or Heidelberg's castle, reminding us of the ups and downs of urban life.

[H40] **11-14 Mount Morris Park West** and **1 West 121st Street.** 1887-1889. **James E. Ware.** ♂

Gabled to the park, with a corner tourelle that, unhappily, doffed its hat.

[H41] **200-218 Lenox Ave.** (Malcom X Blvd.) (row houses), bet. W. 120th and W. 121st Sts. E side. 1887-1888. **Demeuron & Smith.** ♂

A Victorian nonet with mansard roofs worthy of **Napoleon III.** Of an original ten, one tooth (No. 204) is missing. Music publisher **Carl Fischer** lived at 202 from 1894 to 1910.

[H42] **Mt. Olivet Baptist Church**/originally Temple Israel, 201 Lenox Ave. (Malcom X Blvd.), NW cor. W. 120th St. 1906-1907. **Arnold W. Brunner.** ♂

Once one of the city's most prestigious synagogues, this neo-Roman structure with a grand Ionic columned portico dates from the period when German Jewish families were taking up residence in town houses formerly occupied by families of Dutch, English, and Irish descent.

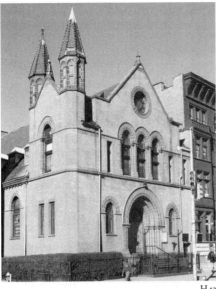

H43

H44

H47

H47

[H43] **Ebenezer Gospel Tabernacle**/onetime Congregation and Chebra Ukadisha B'nai Israel Mikalwarie/originally Lenox Avenue Unitarian Church, 225 Lenox Ave., NW cor. W. 121st St. 1889-1891. **Charles Atwood**. ♂

Romanesque Revival by Atwood, who became the design partner of Chicago's **D. H. Burnham** the year this church was completed and who executed the amazing avant-garde Reliance Building. The Unitarians were replaced by Jews in 1919, and an African-American congregation took over in 1942.

[H44] **220-228 Lenox Ave.** (Malcom X Blvd.) (row houses), bet. W. 121st and W. 122nd Sts. E side. 1888-1889. **F. Carles Merry**. ♂

No. 226 is a particular delight: raise your eyes to rockface brownstone voussoirs at the third floor; neo-Romanesque arches and columns in brownstone and terra-cotta at the fourth.

[H45] **St. Martin's Episcopal Church and Rectory**/ originally Holy Trinity Episcopal Church, 18 W. 122nd St., SE cor. Lenox Ave. (Malcom X Blvd.) 1887-1889. **William A. Potter**. ♂

Richardsonian Romanesque in granite and brownstone but not of the quality of the style's originator. The bulky tower houses one of America's finest carillons: a group of 40 bells, which places it second in size in the city to the 74 at Riverside Church.

[H46] **241 and 243-259 Lenox Avenue** (Malcolm X Blvd.), bet. W. 122nd and W. 123rd Sts. No. 241, 1883-1885. **A. B. Van Dusen**. Nos. 243-259, 1885-1886. **Charles H. Beer**. ♂

An intact blockfront of early brownstones. Imagine the whole neighborhood (both sides of the street) like this.

[H47] **103-111, 131, 133-143 West 122nd Street** (row houses), bet. Lenox Ave. (Malcolm X Blvd.) and Adam Clayton Powell, Jr. Blvd. **Nos. 103-111**, 1887-1888. **Thom & Wilson**. **No. 131**, 1890. **Julius Franke**. **Nos. 133-143**, 1885-1887. **Francis H. Kimball**. **101-111**, varied brownstones.

131, Stately gray granite Richardsonian Romanesque.

133-143, Rich Queen Anne for an English terrace. The brick and terra-cotta blend almost as a monolith (even the shingle face is in the same palette).

H48

[H48] **4-16 West 122nd Street**, bet. Lenox Ave. (Malcolm X Blvd.) and Mt. Morris Pk. W. 1888-1889. **William B. Tuthill**. ♂

The architect of Carnegie Hall here presents imposing stoops and bellying bay windows to the street.

[H49] **Mount Morris Ascension Presbyterian Church**/originally Harlem Presbyterian Church, 16-20 Mt. Morris Park W. at SW cor. W. 122nd St. 1905-1906. **Thomas H. Poole**. ♂

By the time this Eclectic church was built, the effects of the Chicago World's Fair's White City were being felt: the dome on a drum seems an alien on this Romanesque arched brownstone and ashlar body.

H49

[H50] **4-26 West 123rd Street**, bet. Mt. Morris Park W. and Lenox Ave, (Malcolm X Blvd.). 1880-1882. **Charles Baxter**. ♂

A dozen well-preserved brownstones: the whole, sometimes, is greater than the sum of the parts. And No. 4's bay window adds a touch of excellence.

[H51] **Commandment Keepers Ethiopian Hebrew Congregation**/originally John and Nancy Dwight House, 31 Mt. Morris Pk. W., or 1 W. 123rd St., NW cor. Mt. Morris Park W. 1889-1890. **Frank H. Smith**. ♂

A neo-Renaissance mansion for **John Dwight**, founder of **Arm and Hammer** brand baking soda. The body of the building is dull, the portico magnificent. Now occupied by a congregation of black Jews who believe people of African descent to be the Lost Tribes of Israel.

H50

[H52] **28-30 West 123rd Street** (houses), bet. Mt. Morris Park W. and Lenox Ave. (Malcolm X Blvd.). 1884-1885. **John E. Terhune**.

Compact Queen Anne, each 13 feet wide. ♂

[H53a] **Greater Bethel A.M.E. Church** (African Methodist Episcopal)/originally Harlem Free Library, 32 W. 123rd St., bet. Mt. Morris Park W. and Lenox Ave. (Malcom X Blvd.) 1892. **Edgar K. Bourne**. ♂

Originally built to serve as one of the city's many free libraries. In 1901 it joined the New York Public Library system, and a new branch building for the area was built in 1909 at 9-11 West 124th Street, with Carnegie funds.

H53a

[H53b] **Bethelite Community Baptist Church**/originally Harlem Club, 36 W. 123rd St., SE cor. Lenox Ave. (Malcom X Blvd.) 1888-1889. **Lamb & Rich**. ♂

When this splendid Romanesque Revival brick club opened it served the local elite. Since 1947 its sturdy brick and brownstone arches have served the local community as a church.

[H54] **Ephesus Seventh-Day Adventist Church**/formerly Second Collegiate Church/originally Reformed Low Dutch Church of Harlem, 267 Lenox Ave. (Malcom X Blvd.), NW cor. W. 123rd St. 1885-1887. **John Rochester Thomas**. Church hall at rear, 1894-1895. ♂

Stern random ashlar coursing and a lofty spire make this edifice an important Lenox Avenue landmark. The **Boys Choir of Harlem** was founded here.

[H55] **107-111 West 123rd Street** (row houses), bet. Malcolm X and Adam Clayton Powell Blvds. 1880s.

A trio of well-kept columned brownstones next door to Ephesus.

H54

NORTHERN FIFTH AND MADISON AVENUES:
125TH STREET AND ABOVE:

H56

[H56] **1944 Madison Avenue** (tenement), SW cor. W. 125th St. 1890s.

An eclectic pleasantry: brick with limestone elliptical and round voussoirs and a bay window. Tenement fun.

[H57] Originally **The Morris** (apartments and ground floor bank)/then Mount Morris Bank and Safety Deposit Vaults, 81-85 E. 125th St., NW cor. Park Ave. 1883-1884. Enlarged, 1889-1890. **Lamb & Rich.**

This formerly elegant building, once on the way to restoration, has lost its way. Look carefully—Richardsonian Romanesque arches are there!

Studio Museum in Harlem, 144 W. 125th St., bet. Lenox Ave. (Malcom X Blvd.) and Adam Clayton Powell, Jr. Blvd. New entrance and garden sculpture terrace, 1999. **Roger Marvel Architects.** *Open to the public: We-Fr 10-5; Sa & Su 1-6; closed Mo & Tu. 212-864-4500. Museum and cultural center for local and national black art.*

H59

[H58] **Metropolitan Community Methodist Church**/originally St. James Methodist Episcopal Church, 1975 Madison Ave., NE cor. E. 126th St. 1871. **Rectory**, 1981. Madison Ave. 1871.

Proper and somber Victorian brownstone clads this muted (faint buttresses, shallow arches) Gothic Revival edifice. In charming contrast is the prim, mansarded minister's house to the north, whose cast-iron cresting still remains.

[H59] **Mt. Moriah Baptist Church**/originally Mt. Morris Baptist Church, 2050 Fifth Ave., bet. E. 126th and E. 127th Sts. W side. 1888. **Henry F. Kilburn.**

Gone are the brownstone mansions, the gently pitched stoops spilling out onto the wide sidewalks, and the generous trees. What remains, among other relics of Fifth Avenue above 125th Street, is this midblock green-gray ashlar and brownstone church, morose and without the sculptural vigor of so many Harlem churches.

[H60] **Langston Hughes House**, 20 E. 127th St., bet. Park and Madison Aves. 1869. **Alexander Wilson.**

An ivied brownstone's 4th floor for Hughes. Nice house, better poet.

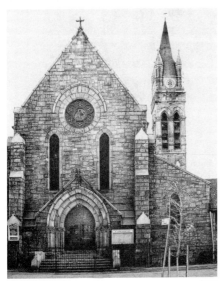

H62

NORTHERN FIFTH AND MADISON AVENUES

see pages 499–502

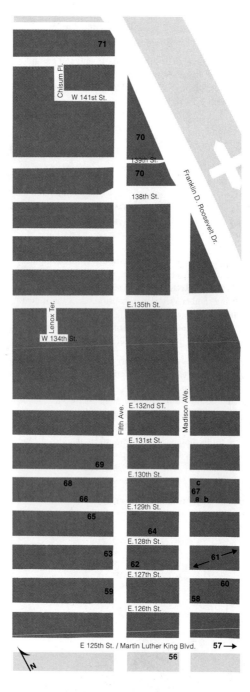

[H61] **Intermediate School 201**, Manhattan, The Arthur A. Schomburg School, 2005 Madison Ave., bet. W. 127th and W. 128th Sts. 1966. **Curtis & Davis.**

A windowless masonry doughnut raised on concrete stilts offers no glassy temptations for vandals. Despite the rich brick and concrete textures with which the architects adorned the school's exterior, and though a pleasing composition in the abstract, the public space under the building is dark, oppressive, and uninviting.

[H62] **St. Andrew's Church** (Episcopal), 2067 Fifth Ave., NE cor. E. 127th St. 1872-1873. Enlargement, 1889-1890. **Henry M. Congdon.** 🌑
A dour and rugged rock-face granite church with a tall clock tower set not at the corner of the intersection but, rather, in a more dynamic location, against the south transept along East 127th Street. The corner therefore, is available for a picturesque, south-facing side entrance.

H63a

[H63a] **2064 Fifth Avenue** (town house), bet. W. 127th and W. 128th St. W side. 1880s.
The gable is a sextet (chamber music?) of Composite pilasters with an extravagant neo-Dutch Renaissance profile. The elliptical and round arches at grade level are nice, but look up.

[H63b] **2068-2076 Fifth Avenue** (row houses), SW cor. W. 128th St. 1890s.
Brick with brownstone both rockface and rusticated, sullied by horrendous cheap aluminum windows.

H64

[H64] **17 East 128th Street** (house), bet. Fifth and Madison Aves. ca. 1864. 🌑
A Second Empire mansarded delight decked out as a Painted Lady.

[H65] **12 West 129th Street** (house), bet. Fifth and Lenox (Malcolm X Blvd.) Aves. ca. 1863. Alterations and additions, 1882-1883. **Edward Gustaveson**, builder. More work, 1886. **Asbury Baker, Tinkerer.** 1920s. Stuccoers. 🌑
A Moorish porch (1882 jigsaw work) and the nuns' protective stucco. What next?

*Wretched refuse: On the morning of March 21, 1947, police converged on 2078 Fifth Avenue at East 128th Street in Harlem, summoned by a phone tip. There was a dead body, the caller said, in the once fashionable but now decaying brownstone row house in which the strange and reclusive **Collyer** brothers—**Homer and Langley**—had been living for 38 years. Though the search was balked by barricades of refuse, Homer's emaciated body, dressed in a tattered gray bathrobe, was soon found. In a massive manhunt for Langley, police plowed through the junk-crammed mansion, while tons of debris were carted off. Buried in the mountains of garbage were five pianos, several guns, thousands of empty bottles and cans, some 1910 pinup pictures, dressmaker's dummies, and a **Model T Ford**. Finally, Langley's body—smothered by debris rigged to boobytrap burglars—was extracted. It had taken almost three weeks to find it.*

[H66] **17-25 West 129th Street** (row houses), bet. Fifth and Lenox (Malcolm X Blvd.) Aves. ca. 1885.
Tudor Gothic in red brick and red and white unglazed terra-cotta. No. 17 is the best survivor, bowing out to the street.

[H67a] **All Saints' Church** (Roman Catholic), E. 129th St. NE cor. Madison Ave. 1894. **Renwick, Aspinwall & Russell.** [H67b] **Rectory** 47 E. 129th St. 1889. **Renwick, Aspinwall & Russell.** [H67c] **School**, 52 E. 130th St. 1904. **W. W. Renwick.**
The best of Harlem's ecclesiastical groupings. The Gothic tracery and terra-cotta ribboning of the buff, honey-colored, and brown brick wall surfaces make a confection of these related buildings designed by the successor firms of **James Renwick, Jr.** Its patterned brickwork is reminiscent of Siena.

H67c

[H68] **Astor Row** (row houses), 8-62 W. 130th St., bet. Fifth and Lenox (Malcolm X Blvd.) Aves. S side. 1880-1883. **Charles Buek.** 🌑 Restoration, 1997, **Roberta Washington. Li/Saltzman**, preservation consultants.
Three-story brick, single-family row houses with wooden porches and large front and side yards. Their renaissance from

H68

H69

H70

years of neglect recoups their great understated elegance. Opposite is an almost intact terrace of brownstones.

[H69] **St. Ambrose Church** (Episcopal)/originally Church of the Puritans (Presbyterian), 15 W. 130th St., bet. Fifth and Lenox (Malcolm X Blvd.) Aves. 1875.

The original name of this rock-face granite Gothic Revival structure came as the price of its construction: a gift was proffered with the condition that the congregation (then the Second Presbyterian Church of Harlem) take on the name of Church of the Puritans, which had just sold its lease on Union Square. The gift—and name—were accepted.

And several blocks north:

[H70] **Riverbend Houses** (apartments), Fifth Ave. bet. E. 138th and E. 142nd Sts. E side. 1967. **Davis, Brody & Assocs.**

Social and aesthetic concerns meld into a single, eminently successful apartment development respectful of street lines along Fifth Avenue. Dense, compact, and of imaginatively used vernacular materials, it has 625 apartments in the sky for moderate-income families. The tall end towers consist of flats; the 8- and 10-story structures in between contain duplexes reached by outdoor passages providing tenants with semiprivate terraces overlooking the Harlem River. It was a monumental breakthrough in urban, publicly subsidized housing.

*A revolution in brick began at Riverbend Houses as a result of the skyrocketing costs of laying brick following World War II. To achieve economy and to introduce a new scale in exterior masonry units, architects **Davis, Brody & Assocs.** developed the giant brick (5½″ high × 8″ wide) first used at Riverbend.*

[H71] **369th Regiment Armory, N.Y. National Guard**, 2366 Fifth Ave., bet. W. 142nd and W. 143rd Sts. W side. Drill shed, 1921-1924. Tachau & Vought. Administration building, 1930-1933. **Van Wart & Wein.** 🖤

A superb example of the bricklayer's art. In this case the mason's efforts are in deep purpley-red and exhibit an Art Deco/Moderne style rather than an attempt to reconstruct a medieval fortress.

H70

THE 125TH STREET CORRIDOR & NORTH: LENOX TO ST. NICHOLAS AVENUES

H71

[H71a] **North General Hospital**, Paul Robeson Center/originally Koch & Company (dry goods store), 132-140 W. 125th St., bet. Lenox Ave and Adam Clayton Powell, Jr. Blvd. 1893. **William H. Hume & Son**. Altered.

The first of the old established dry goods merchants of lower Sixth Avenue to move northward. It moved too far; its success as Harlem's chief department store lasted only some 30 years. Brick, limestone, and terra-cotta Eclectic (see the Ladies Mile and area around the east side of Washington Square for a host of its peers).

[H72] **Theresa Towers** (office building)/originally Hotel Theresa, 2090 Adam Clayton Powell, Jr. Blvd., bet.W. 124th and W. 125thSts. Wside. 1912-1913. **George & Edward Blum**. Altered, 1971. ●

Long a favored meeting spot in Harlem, the Theresa attracted Cuba's **Prime Minister Fidel Castro** as his New York hotel when he visited the U.N. in 1960. Russian **Prime Minister Khrushchev** came to Harlem to visit him. It has since been converted to office use.

H73

[H73] **Apollo Theatre**/originally Hurtig & Seamon's New Burlesque Theater, 253 W. 125th St., bet. Adam Clayton Powell Jr. Blvd. and Frederick Douglass Blvd. 1913-1914. **George Keister**. ● Interior ● .

Although it dates from 1914, the Apollo did not become a Harlem high spot until 1934. That year the old Hurtig & Seamon theatre, with a white-only admissions policy, was taken over by **Leo Brecher** and **Frank Schiffman**, who renamed it the Apollo and opened its doors to the black community. Since then it has been known as the Harlem showplace for black entertainers. For years it was the attraction that drew white audiences to Harlem. **Bessie Smith**, America's "Empress of the Blues," appeared that first year, followed by other blues singers such as **Billie Holiday** and **Dinah Washington. Huddie (Leadbelly) Ledbetter** sang from its stage in the 1930s shortly after doing time for intent to murder. **Duke Ellington**'s sophisticated style and **Count Basie**'s raw-edged rhythms filled the house later. Following World War II bebop had its fling: the names of **Charlie (Bird) Parker, Dizzy Gillespie, Thelonius Monk**, and, more recently, such entertainers as **Gladys Knight** and **Aretha Franklin** have glittered on its marquee. Beginning in the 1980s it has had another cultural renaissance.

H74

[H74] **Sydenham Hospital Clinic**/originally Commonwealth Building, 215 W. 125th St., bet. Adam Clayton Powell Jr. Blvd. and Frederick Douglass Blvd. 1971. **Hausman & Rosenberg**.

Developed jointly by a local community group (black and Puerto Rican) and a suburban real estate company (white), this crisp, white concrete, precast façade is a happy addition to West 125th Street. The rear façade, on West 126th, is less pretentious but equally handsome.

H75

[H75] **Harlem State Office Building**, 163 W. 125th St., NE cor. Adam Clayton Powell, Jr. Blvd. 1973. **Ifill Johnson Hanchard**.

Built to provide a state resource and symbol within the Harlem community, this monumental work and its complementary plaza was a tangible outgrowth of 1960s racial unrest: a second cousin to Albany's Empire State Plaza edifice complex—both architecturally and politically.

[H76] **Baptist House of Prayer**/originally Methodist Third Church of Christ, 80 W. 126th St., bet. Fifth and Lenox (Malcolm X Blvd.) Aves. 1889.

H76

An offbeat Romanesque Revival complex. The colonettes, ribbed elliptical arch, and contained bay window combine for a marvelous eccentricity.

[H77] **Metropolitan Baptist Church**/originally New York Presbyterian Church, 151 W. 128th St., NE cor. Adam Clayton Powell Jr. Blvd. 1884-1885. **John Rochester Thomas**. 🍎 Auditorium, 1889-1890, **Richard R. Davis**. 🍎

Rock-faced granite, enlivened at the entrance by polished orange granite columns bearing Romanesque "Afro" capitals and, over the side chapel, by a majestic volume, the half-cone of an intersecting roof.

H77

[H78] **Salem United Methodist Church**/originally Calvary Methodist Episcopal Church, Adam Clayton Powell Jr. Blvd. NW cor. W. 129th St. 1887. Enlarged, 1890.

It once housed the city's largest Protestant church auditorium and membership, but then came Riverside Church. The grand street and avenue arches and their myriad of ancillary supporters form powerful façades, complementing the tower (note its Romanesque oriel).

H78

[H79] **Row houses**, W. 130th St. bet. Lenox Ave and Adam Clayton Powell Jr. Blvd. N and S sides. ca. 1885-1890.

Two rows of stately brownstones flanking this street, many displaying their original stoops and cast-iron balustrades, were once painted to simulate brownstone. Large trees contribute to the scene.

[H80] **Williams Christian Methodist Episcopal Church**/formerly Lafayette Theatre, 2225 Adam Clayton Powell Jr. Blvd., bet. W. 131st St. and W. 132nd St. E side. 1912. **V. Hugo Koehler**.

Ravaged by alterations but fraught with history. For three decades the Lafayette was the nation's leading black theater. The critically acclaimed production of *Darktown Follies* (1913) started the vogue of midtowners coming to Harlem for entertainment.

H79

[H81] **Lionel Hampton Houses** (apartments), 273 W. 131st St., NE cor. Frederick Douglass Blvd., 201 W. 130th St., NW cor. Frederick Douglass Blvd., [H82] **410 St. Nicholas Ave.**, bet. W. 130th and W. 131st Sts. 1974. **Bond Ryder Assocs**.

Assorted handsome modern housing on irregular sites.

[H83] **St. Aloysius' Roman Catholic Church**, 209 W. 132nd St., bet. Adam Clayton Powell Jr. Blvd. and Frederick Douglass Blvd. 1904. **W. W. Renwick**.

Deep purple brickwork and pale green glazed-brick trim harmonize with terra-cotta that resembles Belgian lace. Together

H83

THE 125TH STREET CORRIDOR & NORTH

see pages 503–512

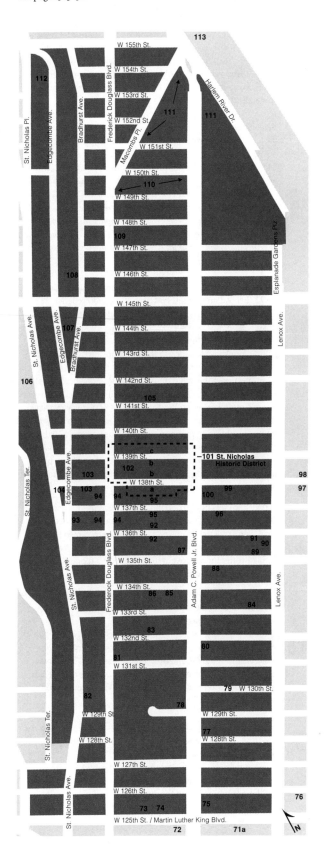

they produce an evocative and delicate façade, redolent of the exuberant Certosa at Pavia.

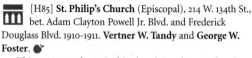 **[H84]** **Engine Company No. 59, Ladder Company, No. 30, N.Y.C. Fire Department**, 111 W. 133rd St., bet. Lenox Ave and Adam Clayton Powell Jr. Blvd. 1962. **Giorgio Cavaglieri**.

Fashionable in its time, this bright red glazed brick-plus-Miesian framed firehouse conflicts with the more enduring architectural values of its older tenement neighbors, with their richly worked, twisted steel fire-escape railings and intricate cut stone plinths.

H85

*Beale Street: Life in Harlem stimulated the curiosity of outsiders for the forbidden, particularly during the Roaring Twenties. Exploiters arranged specially trumped-up visits (for those who could pay) to see what was ballyhooed as "the primitive essence of Harlem Life." The night spots along West 133rd Street between Lenox Ave. (Malcom X Blvd.) and Adam Clayton Powell Jr. Blvd., such as Dickie Wells', Mexico's, Pod's and Jerry's, and the Nest, were in the center of such activity. A similarity to Beale Street in Memphis, made famous by black composer and blues compiler **W. C. Handy**, caused the name to be popularly applied to the street in Harlem. The Depression curtailed most of these goings-on.*

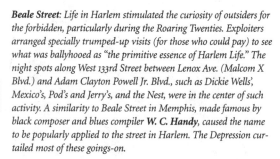 **[H85]** **St. Philip's Church** (Episcopal), 214 W. 134th St., bet. Adam Clayton Powell Jr. Blvd. and Frederick Douglass Blvd. 1910-1911. **Vertner W. Tandy** and **George W. Foster**. 🍎

This spare, northern Gothic church in salmon-colored Roman brick was founded in the notorious Five Points section of the Lower East Side in 1809. A century later it was able to sell its properties in the Tenderloin for almost $600,000. With this windfall the church purchased its present site, as well as a row of 10 apartment houses on West 135th Street previously restricted to whites. When the congregation began its move to Harlem, white tenants living in the apartment houses were evicted, and their places were made available to blacks.

The church design was a collaborative effort of two black architects; **Vertner W. Tandy** was the first black to be granted an architectural registration in New York State.

[H86] **Public School 92**, Manhattan, The Mary McCleod Bethune School, 222 W. 134th St., bet. Adam Clayton Powell Jr. Blvd. and Frederick Douglass Blvd. 1965. **Percival Goodman**.

A gentle blend: a creamy cast-in-place concrete frame infilled with Hudson River red brick create a thoughtful design but no architectural fireworks.

[H87] **2300-2306 Adam Clayton Powell, Jr. Boulevard**, NW cor. W. 135th St. 1887-1888. **Richard Davis & Son**.

Stately brick tenements.

H86

*Small's Paradise: on the southwest corner of 135th Street and Adam Clayton Powell, Jr. Boulevard. A jazz club, "The Hottest Spot in Harlem," served up to 1,500 on its opening in the 1920s and 1930s. It was revived in the 1960s as **Wilt Chamberlain's** "Big Wilt's Small's Paradise."*

[H88] **Harlem Branch, YMCA**, 180 W. 135th St., bet. Lenox Ave. (Malcom X Blvd.) and Adam Clayton Powell Jr. Blvd. 1931-1932. **James C. Mackenzie, Jr.**

A stately red-brown brick Y not to be confused with its 1919 vintage predecessor across the street. Note the pair of broken pediments molded from the same brick.

H88

[H89] Schomburg Center for Research in Black Culture, The New York Public Library, 515 Lenox Ave. (Malcom X Blvd.), bet. W. 135th and W. 136th Sts. W side. 1969-1980. **Bond Ryder Assocs.** Link, 1991. **Davis Brody Bond.**

[H90] Originally housed in the **135th Street Branch,** 103 W. 135th St., bet. Lenox Ave. (Malcom X Blvd.) and Adam Clayton Powell Jr. Blvd. 1903-1905. **Charles F. McKim** of **McKim, Mead & White.** ● Open to the public Mo-We 12-8; Th-Sa 10-6; closed Su. 212-491-2200.

H89

The 135th Street library was the unofficial headquarters of the black literary renaissance of the 1920s. **Arthur A. Schomburg** (1874-1938), a Puerto Rican black, privately undertook the task of collecting the raw materials of black American history, which were then in danger of loss through neglect by the academic community. In 1926 the Carnegie Corporation of New York purchased the collection and had it deposited here with Schomburg himself as curator. In 1972 the Schomburg Collection was formally renamed as a research center. The building is in McKim's consistent Italian Renaissance palazzo mode.

In 1978 the long-awaited Schomburg Center opened with proper facilities for storing, conserving, and disseminating the archive's treasures.

[H91] Countee Cullen Branch, The New York Public Library, 104 W. 136th St., bet. Lenox Ave. (Malcom X Blvd.) and Adam Clayton Powell, Jr. Blvd. 1942. **Louis Allen Abramson.** Restored, 1988.

This Art Moderne library, named for a poet of the Harlem Renaissance, **Countee Cullen,** was built as an extension to the original home of the Schomburg Center.

H91

*Madame C. J. Walker: Born to freed slaves shortly after the Civil War, this enterprising promoter rose from washerwoman to become reputedly the richest black woman in New York, through the development and sale of hair-straightening products. Her home and adjacent hair parlor occupied the site on which the Countee Cullen Branch Library was built. She died in 1919 in Irvington, N.Y., where she had built a house (**Vertner W. Tandy,** architect) on the main street—to the consternation of her white neighbors.*

[H92] 202-266 and 203-267 West 136th Street (row houses), bet. Adam Clayton Powell Jr. Blvd. and Frederick Douglass Blvd. Nos. 202-266, 1889-1890. **Frederick G. Butcher.** Nos. 203-267, 1891-1895. **Thomas C. Van Brunt.**

H92

Two blockfronts provide a row house flock equal to any of the Upper West Side's park blocks—except that these are in Harlem. Architect/Developer **Van Brunt** mixed sandstone in varied colors, and brick. Paint has obscured much of it.

*The Brotherhood of Sleeping Car Porters, the first African-American union, maintained headquarters at 239 West 136th from 1929 into the thirties. Its founder, **A. Philip Randolph,** waved a powerful political hand in both the **Roosevelt** and **Truman** administrations; he was catalyst for desegregation in both World War II defense industries and the military itself.*

The White Rose Mission: 262 West 136th Street. "A Christian, no-sectarian, Home for Colored Girls and Women, where they may be trained in the principles of practical self-help and right living."

[H93] 26-46 Edgecombe Avenue (row houses), bet. W. 136th and W. 137th Sts. E side, and 321 W. 136th St., bet. Edgecombe and Frederick Douglass Blvd. ca. 1885.

Victoriana set along a triangular intersection (Dorrence Brooks Square), the backdrop for which is St. Nicholas Park. Before the park's greenery was cut back to provide mediocre

H94

H96

H98

recreation space, the contrast between nature and architecture must have been vivid. No. 26 at the corner of West 136th Street is particularly noteworthy. Bay windows enliven the masonry façades.

[H94] **St. Charles Condominiums**, E and W sides of Frederick Douglass Blvd., bet. W. 136th and W. 138th Sts. 1997. **The Stephen Jacobs Group**.

120 units of affordable housing. A near miss: the architect strove, but with some more thoughtful detail and better proportioned windows this might have been in the same class as Strivers' Row.

[H95] **203-231 and 202-252 West 137th Street**, Adam Clayton Powell Jr. Blvd. and Frederick Douglass Blvd. 1897-1903. **John Hauser**.

Powerful, intact stoops guard these 41 houses.

[H96] **Mother African Methodist Episcopal Zion Church**, 140 W. 137th St., bet. Lenox Ave. (Malcom X Blvd.) and Adam Clayton Powell Jr. Blvd. 1923-1925. **George W. Foster**.

Random ashlar and terra-cotta present a great stained-glass window to the street. **George Foster** was an early African-American architect.

[H97] **Union Congregational Church**/originally Rush Memorial A.M.E. Zion Church (African Methodist Episcopal), 60 W. 138th St., bet. Fifth and Lenox (Malcolm X Blvd.) Aves. ca. 1910. [H98] **St. Mark's Roman Catholic Church**/originally Church of St. Mark the Evangelist, 65 W. 138th St. 1908.

St. Mark's has stripped its sometime paint and restored the brick and terra-cotta façade to its original crispness. Union is still clad in the dour paint they originally shared.

[H99] **Abyssinian Baptist Church**, 136-142 W. 138th St., bet. Lenox and Adam Clayton Powell Jr. Blvd. 1922-1923. **Charles W. Bolton and Son**. 🌶

A random ashlar "Princeton Gothic" church, a landmark in Harlem due to the charisma, power, and notoriety of its spellbinding preacher, **Adam Clayton Powell, Jr.** (1908-1972). Powell's reform accomplishments while a member of the House of Representatives, and his flamboyance, were known across the country. The church has established a memorial room, open to the public, containing artifacts from his life. Call before you visit.

H99

[H100] **Renaissance Theater** and **Renaissance Ballroom and Casino**, 2341-2359 Adam Clayton Powell Jr. Blvd., bet. W. 137th and W. 138th St. Theater, 1920-1921. Ballroom/casino, 1922-1923. **Harry Creighton Ingalls.**

The casino and adjacent theater once constituted a commercial community center, combining a variety of entertainments; now they're both in disrepair. The Abyssinian Development Corporation is planning a rehabilitation?

H101b

[H101] **St. Nicholas Historic District** (The King Model Houses/"Strivers' Row"), genererally W. 138th to W. 139th Sts., bet. Adam Clayton Powell Jr. Blvd. and Frederick Douglass Blvd., including
[H101a] **202-250 W. 138th St.** and **2350-2354 Adam Clayton Powell Jr. Blvd.** 1891-1893. **James Brown Lord.**
[H101b] **203-271 W. 138th St., 202-272 W. 139th St.,** and **2360-2378 Adam Clayton Powell Jr. Blvd.** 1891-1893. **Bruce Price and Clarence S. Luce.**
[H101c] **203-267 W. 139th St.** and **2380-2390 Adam Clayton Powell Jr. Blvd.** 1891-1893. **Stanford White** of **McKim, Mead & White.**

By the time **David H. King, Jr.** built these distinguished row houses and apartments, he had been widely recognized as the builder responsible for the old Times Building of 1889 on Park Row, **Stanford White**'s Madison Square Garden, and the base of the Statue of Liberty. Displaying rare vision, King commissioned the services of three architects at one time to develop this group of contiguous blocks for the well-to-do. The results are an urbane grouping reflecting the differing tastes of the architects: all with similar scale, varied but harmonious materials, and related styles—Georgian-inspired in the two southern blocks, neo-Italian Renaissance in **Stanford White**'s northern group. In addition, they share the amenity of rear alleys with entrances from the side streets. No wonder they were so prized by their original, white, occupants.

As Harlem became first a refuge for blacks and then a ghetto, the homes and apartments retained their prestige and attracted (by 1919) many ambitious as well as successful blacks in medicine, dentistry, law, and the arts (such as **W. C. Handy** [232 W 139], **Noble Sissle, Fletcher Henderson** [228 W. 139], **Eubie Blake,** and architect **Vertner Tandy** [221 W. 139]). As a result, Strivers' Row became a popular term for the district in the 1920s and 1930s.

H101c

H102

H103

H105

H106

[H102] **Victory Tabernacle Seventh Day Christian Church**/formerly Coachmen's Union League Society of New York City, 252 W. 138th St., bet. Adam Clayton Powell Jr. Blvd. and Frederick Douglass Blvd. 1895-1896. **Jardine, Kent & Jardine**.

Moorish-Venetian? Limestone frippery? It was built to sell life insurance to residents of this newly opened "suburb" of Harlem, particularly to those living in the King Model Houses.

[H103] **309-325 and 304-318 West 138th Street**. Nos. 309-325, 1889-1890. **Edwin R. Will**. Nos. 304-318, 1896. **J. Averit Webster**.

Queen Anne north, neo-Renaissance south.

[H104] **St. Mark's Methodist Church**, Edgecombe Ave. SW cor. W. 138th St. 1921-1926. **Sibley & Fetherston**.

Neo-Gothic, but heavy-handed.

[H105] **St. Charles Borromeo Church** (Roman Catholic), 211 W. 141st St., bet. Adam Clayton Powell, Jr. Blvd. and Frederick Douglass Blvd. 1888. Altered, 1973, **L. E. Tuckett & Thompson. Rectory**, 1880s.

The destruction of the nave by fire provided the opportunity for contemporary reuse by building a modern miniature sanctuary within the walls of the original. Limestone and brick neo-Gothic.

[H106] **Harlem School of the Arts**, 645 St. Nicholas Ave., N of W. 141st St. W side. 1977. **Ulrich Franzen & Assocs**.

A distinguished Harlem institution, once housed next door at St. James' Presbyterian Church Community House. Founded by the great operatic soprano in 1963, **Dorothy Maynor**, it first operated in the church proper, where **Shelby Rooks**, Maynor's husband, was rector. It now occupies its own building, nuzzled against the craggy hillside of Hamilton Terrace's backyards.

[H107] **Row houses**, Bradhurst Ave., bet. W. 143rd and W. 145th Sts. W side. ca. 1888.

Stoop removal and general lack of maintenance have hurt this inventive row of Victorian houses. Nevertheless their wit prevails.

[H108] **Jackie Robinson Play Center**/originally Colonial Play Center (swimming pool and bathhouse), in Jackie Robinson (formerly Colonial) Park, Bradhurst Ave. bet. W. 145th and W. 147th Sts. W side. 1936. **N.Y.C. Parks Department. Aymar Embury II**, consulting architect.

The most dramatic of the city's WPA-built pools. Cylindrical volumes squeeze the abutting sidewalk and alternate with an assortment of half-round arches. These spring from varied

H108

H111

Romanesque-inspired capitals to create a powerful statement in bold, red brick masonry worthy of its Roman aqueduct (hence "Romanesque") forbears. The confident design of this outdoor natatorium overcomes the shortcomings of its unskilled masons: bricks in some archways bunch up as they reach their crests, giving them almost the shape of a pointed arch. This free diversity of embellishment and unevenness in craftsmanship appropriately echoes the Romanesque style.

[H109] **PSA (Police Services Area) No. 6**, 2770 Frederick Douglass Blvd., bet. W. 147th and W. 148th Sts. E side. 1998. Design, **NYC Housing Authority**. Production, **Gruzen Samton**.
   Some smart corbels decorate the two lower floors, and the United Nations General Assembly sits on the roof. Is this the friendly police embassy to Harlem?

[H110] **Dunbar Apartments**, 2588 Adam Clayton Powell Jr. Blvd. to Frederick Douglass Blvd., bet. W. 149th and W. 150th Sts. 1926-1928. **Andrew J. Thomas.** ●
   Named for black poet **Paul Laurence Dunbar** (1872-1906), these 6 apartment buildings, grouped around a landscaped inner court, have been home to such notables as **Countee Cullen, W. E. B. DuBois, A. Philip Randolph, Bill "Bojangles" Robinson**—and **Matt Henson**, who, as part of the Peary expedition, was the first westerner to set foot upon the North Pole in 1909. Financier **John D. Rockefeller, Jr**. conceived the project as a model for solving Harlem's housing problem; under the pressures of the Depression, however, he finally foreclosed his mortgages and sold the property. It has been a rental development ever since.

[H111] **Harlem River Houses**, NYC Housing Authority, bet. W. 151st and W. 153rd Sts., Macombs Place and Harlem River Dr. 1936-1937. **Archibald Manning Brown**, chief architect in association with **Charles F. Fuller, Horace Ginsbern, Frank J. Forster, Will Rice Amon, Richard W. Buckley, John L. Wilson. Michael Rapuano**, landscape architect. **Heinz Warnecke**, assisted by **T. Barbarossa, R. Barthe, F. Steinberger**, sculptors. ●
   Riots in Harlem in 1935 precipitated the planning and design of this, the city's first federally funded, federally owned, and federally built housing project. Writing in 1938 of the 4-story apartment buildings, grouped around open landscaped courts embellished with sculpture, **Lewis Mumford** exuberantly stated that the project offers "the equipment for decent living that every modern neighborhood needs: sunlight, air, safety, play space, meeting space, and living space. The families in the Harlem Houses have higher standards of housing,

H112

measured in tangible benefits, than most of those on Park Avenue." Perhaps he was being too exuberant. Design staff architect, **John L. Wilson**, was the first African-American architect to graduate from Columbia's School of Architecture.

[H112] **409 Edgecombe Avenue Apartments**/originally Colonial Park Apartments, bet. W. 150th and W. 155th Sts. 1916-1917. **Schwartz & Gross.** 🍎

A landmark more for who lived here than what it is: in its infancy, home to **Babe Ruth**. Later, home to the elite of Black Harlem, ranging from activist and NAACP founder, **W. E. B. Dubois** to future Supreme Court Judge **Thurgood Marshall**.

Sugar Hill: The model of the sweet life in Harlem was identified, between the 1920s and 1950s, with a stretch of Edgecombe Avenue west of (and overlooking) the escarpment of Colonial Park and the Harlem Valley below. The multiple dwellings which line Edgecombe above West 145th Street as it ascends Coogan's Bluff were accommodations to which upwardly mobile blacks aspired and in which those who had achieved fame lived: **Cab Calloway, Duke Ellington, Walter White, Roy Wilkins, Thurgood Marshall, W. E. B. DuBois, Langston Hughes**. *Down by the Harlem River, the Flats below the Hill, were the old Polo Grounds, where the New York Giants once played; now a housing project.*

[H113] **Macomb's Dam Bridge and 155th Street Viaduct,** across the Harlem River bet. W. 155th St. Manhattan and Jerome Ave., The Bronx. 1890-1895. **Alfred Pancoast Boller**, consulting engineer. 🍎

A rotating truss, with supporting viaducts, that connects Harlem to the West Bronx.

E2

EAST HARLEM

East Harlem, once Italian Harlem, is today Spanish Harlem.
Unlike Central Harlem, it was never a prestigious residential district: its remaining older housing stock reveals its working-class
beginnings. For over a century it has been the home of laborer
immigrants and their families, including large German, Irish,
Jewish, and Scandinavian populations. The sizable Italian community, now virtually gone, sank its roots here prior to 1890.
Today, East Harlem is El Barrio, "the neighborhood," over-
whelmingly Puerto Rican in population, heritage, and culture,
whose first settlers came here around the time of World War I.

From the ubiquitous family-owned bodegas, or grocery
stores, found on practically every street, to El Museo del Barrio,
the sophisticated local museum on Fifth Avenue, East Harlem is
an important link to the unique traditions of a significant and
growing number of Hispanic residents.

[E1] **Baum-Rothschild Staff Pavilion**, Mt. Sinai Medical
Center, 1249 Park Ave., SE cor. E. 97th St. 1968.
Pomerance & Breines.

A snappy, slender tower with balconies that presides over the
portal of the Park Avenue tunnel into Grand Central Terminal.

[E2] **Long-Term Care Facility, Florence Nightingale
Nursing Home**, 1760 Third Ave., bet. E. 97th and E. 98th
Sts. 1974. **William N. Breger Assocs**.

A flamboyant massing of brick gives memorable form to
this nursing home. A modest program acquired some forceful
symbolism.

[E3] **Electrical substation, N.Y.C. Transit Authority**/originally
Manhattan Railway Company, 1782 Third Ave., SW cor. E. 99th
St. ca. 1902.

It was not until 1901 that electric-powered elevated trains
were first used—until then the trains were pulled by smoke-
belching miniature steam locomotives—creating the need for
substations such as this.

[E4] **MaBSTOA Bus Garage**/once Metropolitan Street Railway
Company (trolley barn), E. 99th to E. 100th Sts., Lexington to
Park Aves. ca. 1885.

In 1907 the Metropolitan Street Railway Company controlled
47 streetcar lines and 300 miles of track. That year its 3,280 cars
handled 571 million passengers—not all from this barn, thank
goodness—which limited its activities only to the Lexington

E4

EAST HARLEM

see pages 513–518

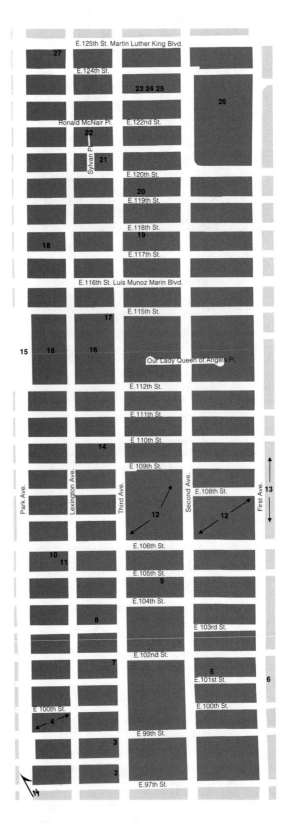

Avenue and Lenox Avenue lines. Today the brick structure, minus tracks, serves as a considerably less colorful diesel bus garage. The acronym is for Manhattan and Bronx Surface Transit Operating Authority.

[E5] **Church of the Resurrection**, East Harlem Protestant Parish, 325 E. 101st St., bet. First and Second Aves. 1965. **Victor A. Lundy**.

A cocked hat among vacant lots. Economy dictated the substitution of a built-up roof for the intended brick-paved surface, and economics has provided poor maintenance. The interior is more inviting.

[E6a] **Metro North Plaza**/Riverview Apartments, bet. E. 100th and E. 102nd Sts., First Ave. and FDR Drive. 1976. [E6b] **Public School 50**, Manhattan, The Vito Marcantonio School. 1975. Both by **Conklin & Rossant**.

E6a

Exposed cast-concrete frames with ribbed-block infill make high-rise and low-rise housing, here arranged in a chaste, symmetrical pattern. The school, approached on a ramp at the far east end of the complex, makes a dramatic statement within the discipline of the same materials.

The painted bridge: All structural steel bridges must be painted regularly to protect their vulnerable surfaces against corrosion. It is rare, however, that the colors chosen vary much from gunmetal gray or bureaucratic green. Fortunately for all of us, the idea that bridges could be painted richer, happier colors struck architects **William Conklin** *and* **James Rossant** *just as the Wards Island Pedestrian Bridge—over the East River above Metro North—was up for periodic rehueing. In 1976 the bridge came out blue-violet (towers), cadmium yellow (walkway), and vermilion (trim), making it urban sculpture of the finest sort. Spectacular! Now repainted a more sober, but less serious aesthetically, institutional green. Where was the Art Commission when we needed it?*

[E7] **23rd Precinct, N.Y.C. Police Department**, and **Engine Company No. 53, Ladder Company No. 43, 4th Division, N.Y.C. Fire Department**, 1834 Third Ave., SW cor. E. 102nd St. 1974. **Milton F. Kirchman**.

A sloping site and a combination of clients—the Police Department, the Fire Department, and the Department of Public Works, the city's coordinating agency—gave rise to this three-dimensional cubist composition.

E7

[E8a] **The Church of the Living Hope**, 161 E. 104th St., bet. Lexington and Third Aves. Altered, ca. 1969. [E8b] Originally **Engine Company No. 53, N.Y.C. Fire Department**, 179 E. 104th St. ca. 1898. [E8c] **Hope Community Hall**/originally 29th Precinct, N.Y.C. Police Department, 177 E. 104th St. 1884.

A curious trio of buildings, two of which began as the area's fire and police outposts. The somber Italianate ex-police station bears light steel-bowed fire escapes in contrast; and the steel and cast-iron Corinthian post and beams that frame the ex-fire engine entry are enlived with brilliant paint.

E8c

[E9] **Park East High School**/originally Manhattan School of Music, 230-240 E. 105th St., bet. Second and Third Aves. 1928. **Donn Barber**. Additions, **Francis L. Mayer**.

Sober and understated façades for the Manhattan School of Music. Manhattan moved to Morningside Heights in a game of musical chairs with Juilliard (School of Music); Julliard had moved to Lincoln Center.

[E10] **St. Cecilia's Church** (Roman Catholic) and **Regina Angelorum**, 112-120 E. 106th St., bet. Park and Lexington Aves. Church, 1883-1887, **Napoleon LeBrun & Sons**. ✥ Regina Angelorum, 1907. **Neville & Bagge**.

E10

E11

This ornate brick and terra-cotta façade is one of East Harlem's special treasures. Neo-Italian Romanesque, it has the exuberance that evaded Northern Europe.

[E11] **Julio de Burgos Latino Cultural Center**/originally Public School 72, Manhattan/then Public School 107, 1680 Lexington Ave., bet. E. 105th and E. 106th Sts. W side. 1878-1882. **David I. Stagg**. Addition, 1911-1913. **C. B. J. Snyder**. ☛ Converted to cultural center, 1994-1995. **Lee Borrero** and **Raymond Plumey**.

Patterned brickwork and a handsome tower give authority to this venerable onetime schoolhouse. The restoration has been as if the building had passed through the fountain of youth, a wonderful reentry into East Harlem civic life.

[E12] **Franklin Plaza Cooperative**/originally Franklin Houses, N.Y.C. Housing Authority, bet. E. 106th St. and E. 108th St., First and Third Aves. 1959. **Holden, Egan, Wilson & Corser**. Plaza and play areas altered, 1961, **Mayer & Whittlesey**.

One of the more graceful groups of residential towers of its period and patrimony in Manhattan. Corner windows, a staggered massing, and sinuous water towers add to its character.

E13

[E13] **1199 Plaza** (apartment complex), bet. E. 107th and E. 110th Sts., First Ave. and FDR Drive, plus extension to E. 111th St. along the Drive. 1975. **The Hodne/Stageberg Partners**, architects. **Herb Baldwin**, landscape architect.

32 stories of flats step down to lower wings of duplexes, housing humanely a high density of residents, 450 to the acre. The complex achieves an effective though not impolite separation between public entry and shopping space along First Avenue and the varied outdoor spaces overlooking the East River, areas that the cooperator-tenants and their guests may enjoy in comparative privacy and safety. Curiously enough, this very handsome project—make sure to see it both from First Avenue and from FDR Drive—was designed by a Minneapolis architectural firm on the basis of its winning entry (not used) in a 1963 architectural competition to develop the site. Twelve years of redesign, red tape, and construction resulted in one of the city's most impressive and most livable works of multifamily housing. Incidentally, 1199 is not an address but the name of the project's sponsors, District 1199 of the National Union of Hospital and Health Care Employees, AFL-CIO.

[E14] **Aguilar Branch, The New York Public Library**, 174 E. 110th St., bet. Lexington and Third Aves. 1898-1899. Expanded and new façade added, 1904-1905. Both by **Herts & Tallant.** ● Renovated, 1993-1996. **Gruzen Samton**.

A triumphal gateway to knowledge, 3 stories high, replaces an earlier and better one, half as wide, by the same architects. Founded in 1886 as an independent library to serve immigrant Jews (**Grace Aguilar** was an English novelist of Sephardic descent), it was brought into the New York Public Library system and expanded by a Carnegie gift. It now serves a newer, Hispanic population.

E14

[E15] "**La Marqueta**" (enclosed market), under Park Ave. railroad viaduct bet. E. 111th and E. 115th Sts.

A hothouse of small merchants. Under rumbling commuter trains is one of the most colorful, fast-moving, fragrant, and boisterous of New York's commercial pageants. A mecca for both bargain hunters and those who love to bargain. It is under new renovation.

E16

[E16] **James Weldon Johnson Houses, N.Y.C. Housing Authority**, bet. E. 112th and E. 115th Sts., Third to Park Aves. 1948. **Julian Whittlesey, Harry M. Prince**, and **Robert J. Reiley**.

Within the spectrum of public housing of the 1940s and 1950s, this is one of the best. Well-proportioned buildings of varying heights, a large plaza, small courts, and sculpture all contribute to the quality.

[E17] **Public School 57**, Manhattan, The James Weldon Johnson School, 176 E. 115th St., SW cor. Third Ave. 1964. **Ballard, Todd & Snibbe**.

An overhanging cornice, generous small-paned windows, and molded bricks make this school a warm, safe, and friendly place. The scale of this building would enhance and respect a block of row houses; but in its present setting, amid large housing projects, its attention to detail is less telling.

E17

[E18a] **St. Paul's Church** (Roman Catholic), 121 E. 117th St., bet. Park and Lexington Aves. [E18b] **Rectory**, 113 E. 117th St. Both 1908. **Neville & Bagge**.

Limestone towers punctuate a very late Romanesque Revival design.

[E19] **Assemblea de Iglesia Pentecostal de Jesucristo**/originally First German Baptist Church of Harlem, 220 E. 118th St., bet. Second and Third Aves. ca. 1895.

An ebullient façade with a wide, inviting half-round arch entrance now painted off-white and pale blue.

E18a

[E20] **Iglesia Luterana Sion**/originally St. Johannes Kirche (Lutheran), 217 E. 119th St., bet. Second and Third Aves. 1873.

An early brick church for this community, then remote from the city's center. The church began as a home for a German-speaking congregation; today it serves those who speak Spanish.

[E21] **Harlem Courthouse**, 170 E. 121st St., SE cor. Sylvan Place, bet. Lexington and Third Aves. 1891-1893. **Thom & Wilson.** ●

This bold brick and brownstone courthouse is a spectacular 1890s palace of justice, now used for far more humble functions. A rich array of forms (gables, archways, the imposing corner tower) and materials (water-struck red brick, bluestone, granite, terra-cotta, and copper) make this fine work both a Landmark and a land mark.

E20

[E22] **1-7 Sylvan Court**, E. 121st St. N of Sylvan Place, bet. Lexington and Third Aves. ca. 1885.

Seven brick town houses grouped around a pedestrian off-street walkway that suffers from a regrettable lack of care. In

E21

E23   E24

semi-ruin, the alley could regain charm equal to Greenwich
Village's Patchin Place.

[E22b] **Elmendorf Reformed Church**, 171 E. 121st St., bet. Sylvan
Place and Third Ave. ca. 1910.

A painted neo-Georgian limestone façade for the oldest congregation in Harlem, successor to the Dutch church founded
here in 1660.

[E23] **Chambers Memorial Baptist Church**/originally Carmel
Baptist Church/then Harlem Baptist Church, 219 E. 123rd St.,
bet. Second and Third Aves. 1891.

A gabled two-toned brick façade is modulated by an elegant
array of arched windows and trabeated doors.

[E24] **Police Services Area (PSA) No. 5, New York City
Police Department**, 221-235 E. 123rd St., bet. Second and
Third Aves. 1998. **Herbert Beckhard** and **Frank Richlan**.

A brick and limestone field office for what used to be the
New York City Housing Police. A nice neighbor for Chambers
Memorial next door.

[E25] **Iglesia Adventista del Septimo Dia**/originally Our
Saviour (Norwegian) Lutheran Church, 237 E. 123rd St., bet.
Second and Third Aves. ca. 1912.

A humble façade enriched by an entrance arch.

E26

[E26] **Taino Towers** (apartment complex), bet. E. 122nd
and E. 123rd Sts., Second and Third Aves. 1979. **Silverman
& Cika**.

Unlike most government-subsidized housing, this project
was neither conceived, designed, nor financed by the local housing authority; it was sponsored by a persistent coalition of local
residents, politicians, and community leaders in concert with
the project's architects. The results are an implant from Miami
Beach: crisp 35-story towers reflecting the sky in floor-to-ceiling
glass (without shading or thermal qualities later necessitated by
energy-saving requirements). A bizarre and out-of-context
neighbor.

E27

[E27] Originally Hook and Ladder Co. No. 14/now **Engine Co.
No. 36, New York City Fire Dept.**, 120 E. 125th St. 1890s. 🔥

Fire laddies and fire horses erupted from this Harlem landmark in the neighborhood's not-so-gay nineties.

WASHINGTON HEIGHTS • INWOOD

Upper Manhattan is the finger pointing northward toward the Bronx, a slender finial on the otherwise fat island. The district's southern boundary is marked by Trinity Cemetery at 155th Street, that northern ending of the 1811 commissioners plan beyond which New York "could never grow."

Indian cave dwellers once lived in Inwood Hill Park. The father of our country not only gave part of this area its name—Washington Heights—but also slept here (and headquartered) in what is now named the Morris-Jumel Mansion. This area was once a country preserve of the wealthy, and some of those estates have remained intact in a variety of forms, although the rich live elsewhere. Museums, a park, a medical center, a bus terminal, and a university now occupy such lands; and other sacred and profane institutions ornament this urban district. It is filled mainly with apartment houses, creating one of the city's most densely populated sectors; its parks, institutions, and dramatic river views make it one of the most livable. The IRT Broadway-Seventh Avenue subway, which reached Dyckman Street and Fort George Hill in 1906, was the major impetus for development of the eastern section. The IND Eighth Avenue subway arrived in 1932, encouraging still more apartment house construction.

Within Upper Manhattan, and particularly in the sector called Washington Heights, there have been a maze of ethnic subcommunities. The long-departed Irish have been replaced by blacks, Hispanics, and, surprisingly, yuppies, who are rediscovering the virtues of this enclave. Greek and Armenian populations were once large; and in the 1930s, after Hitler's accession to power, so many German-Jewish refugees settled here that the area was termed the Fourth Reich.

Colonial

Georgian/
Federal

Greek
Revival

Gothic
Revival

Villa

Romanesque
Revival

Renaissance
Revival

Roman
Revival

Art Deco/
Art Moderne

Modern/
Post-Modern

U1

U1

U2

WASHINGTON HEIGHTS

[U1] **Trinity Cemetery**, Amsterdam Ave. to Riverside Dr., W. 153rd to W. 155th Sts. Boundary walls and gates, 1876. Gatehouse and keeper's lodge, 1883. **Vaux & Radford**. Grounds, 1881. **Vaux & Co.**, landscape architects. Open to the public.

Once part of the farm of **John James Audubon**, (1785-1851), the great artist-naturalist (he is buried here), it became the rural cemetery of Wall Street's Trinity Church. Here is bucolic topography: the cemetery climbs the hill from the river to Amsterdam Avenue, affording some idea of the topography of Manhattan Island before man cut, molded, and veneered it with brick, concrete, and asphalt. Audubon's home, *Minniesland*, was near the river at 155th Street. On Christmas Eve carolers visit the grave of **Clement Clarke Moore**, author of "A Visit from Saint Nicholas."

Sadly missing today is the suspension bridge over Broadway (**Vaux, Withers & Co.**, architects, **George K. Radford**, engineer), which linked the cemetery's halves. It was demolished in 1911 to build:

[U2] **Church of the Intercession** (Episcopal)/originally Chapel of the Intercession, and **Vicarage**, 550 W. 155th St., SE cor. Broadway. 1910-1914. **Bertram Goodhue** of **Cram, Goodhue & Ferguson.**

Set in Trinity Cemetery, this was the largest chapel of Trinity Parish, now promoted to the status of independent church. Here is the dream of the Gothic Revivalist come true: a large "country" church, tower and cloister, parish house and vicarage—all mounted on a bucolic bluff overlooking the Hudson. Inside, stone piers support a wood hammer-beam roof, washed in light from glass that is seemingly from 13th-century France. Loose chairs, rather than pews, make it seem even more French. See the charming cloister at the 155th Street entry.

The memorial to the church's architect, **Bertram Grosvenor Goodhue** (**Lee Lawrie**, sculptor. 1929) gives a Protestant interpretation to the royal tombs of St. Denis: THIS TOMB IS A TOKEN OF THE AFFECTION OF HIS FRIENDS. HIS GREAT ARCHITECTURAL CREATIONS THAT BEAUTIFY THE LAND AND ENRICH CIVILIZATION ARE HIS MONUMENTS. This is perhaps the only New York memorial to an architect within one of his own works.

[U3] **Audubon Terrace Historic District**, Broadway bet. W. 155th and W. 156th Sts. W side. Master plan, 1908. **Charles Pratt Huntington.**

Three small museums, a church, and the National Institute of Arts and Letters share an awkwardly proportioned court, part of the Beaux Arts/American Renaissance of the early 20th century. As a cul-de-sac with no ground-floor activity (restaurants, shops, people, or movement), it has become an unused—and sometimes ill-used—backwater. Boring. A gift of **Archer Huntington**, Southern Pacific Railroad heir, who commissioned his cousin, **Charles P. Huntington** to do the deed.

[U3a] Originally **Museum of the American Indian, Heye Foundation**, Audubon Terr., 3745 Broadway, NW cor. W. 155th St. 1915-1922. **Charles Pratt Huntington.**

The Museum collection is relocating to new quarters on the Mall in Washington. A boutique collection remains in the old Custom House at Bowling Green.

The architecture of the building, flanked on 155th Street with a powerful Ionic colonnade, is generic museum architecture of its time, Classical and pompous. The Indians (or Native Americans as they are more properly called) had nothing to say about it. What will happen here in the future remains open—perhaps community facilities, as at Boricua College across the way.

Originally the private collection of **George Heye**, this was a comprehensive museum concerned with the prehistory of the

U3a

Western Hemisphere and with the contemporary Native American, continent-wide.

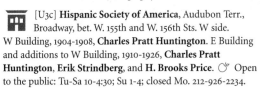 [U3b] **Boricua College**/originally American Geographical Society Audubon Terr., 3755 Broadway, SW cor. W. 156th St. 1911. **Charles Pratt Huntington**. ♂

In a world of jet travel, communications satellites, and computers, a physically central place for information storage is less than vital. The Society's map collection, the largest in the Western Hemisphere, was therefore lured to Milwaukee, where the University of Wisconsin offered better quarters and more generous financing. The building's subsequent tenant, Boricua College, is obviously more a part of this minority community than were the curators of cartography.

U3b

[U3c] **Hispanic Society of America**, Audubon Terr., Broadway, bet. W. 155th and W. 156th Sts. W side. W Building, 1904-1908, **Charles Pratt Huntington**. E Building and additions to W Building, 1910-1926, **Charles Pratt Huntington**, **Erik Strindberg**, and **H. Brooks Price**. ♂ Open to the public: Tu-Sa 10-4:30; Su 1-4; closed Mo. 212-926-2234.

A happy irony hovers over this site: the Hispanics in question were mostly those of Iberia and, sometimes, of equidistant Latin America. Another Hispanic group now surrounds this symbolic site, making it an appropriate centerpiece to a newly arrived population.

The richly appointed storehouse of Hispanic painting, sculpture, and the decorative arts confronts a pompous neo-Baroque sunken court (part of this unfortunate cul-de-sac) filled with lots of dull and academic bronze sculpture (by donor Archer Huntington's wife, **Anna Hyatt Huntington**). Would you believe **El Cid** plus a deer, a doe, a fawn, and four heroes?

[U3d] **American Numismatic Society**, Audubon Terr., Broadway, bet. W. 155th and W. 156th Sts. W side. S side of courtyard. 1907. **Charles Pratt Huntington**. ♂ Open to the public. 212-234-3130. Tu-Sa 9-4:30; Su 1-4. Closed Mo.

A museum of money and decorations: paper, coins, medals, and whatever. Here the art of commerce is expressed in the media for trading, and the honor of special events and activities is equally celebrated—a marriage of the printed franc, dollar, and yen, silver and gold coinage, with the Victoria Cross and the Congressional Medal of Honor.

[U3e] **National Institute of Arts and Letters**/American Academy of Arts and Letters, Audubon Terr. Administration Building, 633 W. 155th St. 1921-1923. **William M. Kendall** of **McKim, Mead & White**. **Auditorium and Gallery**,

UPPER MANHATTAN (SOUTH)

see pages 520–527

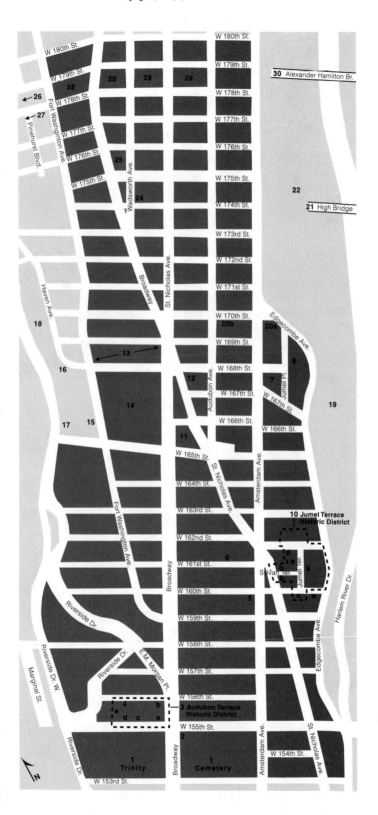

632 W. 156th St. 1928-1930. **Cass Gilbert.** ♺ Museum open to the public when exhibitions are mounted: 212-368-5900. Tu-Su 1-4; closed Mo.

An Anglo-Italian Renaissance club that houses both an institute and an academy honoring distinguished persons in literature and the fine arts. The administration building contains a permanent exhibition of the works of the American impressionist **Childe Hassam**, a library, and a museum of the manuscripts of past and present members.

Above it all the cornice is emblazed: ALL ARTS ARE ONE, ALL BRANCHES ON ONE TREE . . . HOLD HIGH THE FLAMING TORCH FROM AGE TO AGE.

U4

[U4] **Church of Our Lady of Esperanza** (Roman Catholic), 624 W. 156th St., bet. Broadway and Riverside Dr. 1912. Charles Pratt Huntington. Remodeled, 1925, **Lawrence G. White** of **McKim, Mead & White**.

The green and gold interior contains stained-glass windows, a skylight, and a lamp—all given by **King Alfonso XIII** of Spain at its opening in 1912.

U5

[U5] **The Duke Ellington School**, 500 W. 160th St., SW cor. Amsterdam Ave. 1996. **Gruzen Samton**.

A refreshing variation from the minimal boxes of the 1950s, 1960s and 1970s. Here the Duke is honored by serious architecture.

[U6] **Engine Company No. 84, Hook & Ladder No. 34, N.Y.C. Fire Department**, 515 W. 161st St., bet. Amsterdam Ave. and Broadway. N side. 1906. **Francis H. Kimball.** ✍

Beaux Arts rusticated limestone, with infilled brick à la Henri IV. Look up to an eagle, swags, and festoons.

U6

[U7] **P.S. 8, The Luis Belliard School**, 465 W. 167th St., bet. Jumel Pl. and Amsterdam Ave. N side. 1996. **Gruzen Samton**.

An exuberant set of boxes containing a tight, very European-scaled entrance courtyard. All enlivened with rampant polychromy.

U7

U8

U9

U10a

U10b

U10d

[U8] **I.S. 90 Manhattan,** Jumel Place and 168th St. 1999. **Richard Dattner & Assocs.**

A staid neighbor for P.S. 8 next door. The curved cornice (reminiscent of ancient Egyptian cavetto cornices) soberly crowns the brick body.

IRT's Hoosick: Named after the Hoosick Tunnel near North Adams, Mass., which holds the record as the longest two-track tunnel in the U.S. The tunnel, for the IRT Broadway-Seventh Avenue Line, is cut through solid rock under Broadway and St. Nicholas Avenue between W. 157th Street and Fort George.

[U9] Originally **Roger and Mary Phillipse House**/often known as the Morris-Jumel Mansion, 1765 Jumel Terr., bet. W. 160th and W. 162nd Sts. 1765. Remodeled, ca. 1810. ☞ ♂ Interior ☞. Open to the public: We-Su 10-4; closed Mo & Tu. 212-923-8008.

Built by **Roger Morris** as a summer residence for his family, it served during the Revolution as Washington's headquarters. But for most of that war the house was in British hands (as was all of Manhattan and, therefore, all of New York of that day). After the war it served as a farmhouse and tavern until 1810, when **Stephen Jumel** purchased it and partially renovated the house in the then-modern Federal style. The finest view in Manhattan is blocked by bulky apartment buildings to the south.

Tuscan-columned, Georgian-Federal style, with a façade of wood boards and quoins simulating stone, and a shingled behind. The hipped roofs to balustraded captain's walks are admirable cornices to this classic square linked to an octagon. A mile marker in the north lawn cites the distance from New York as 11 miles!

Morris's 115 surrounding acres were developed by the Jumel heirs after 1882 into 1,058 auctioned lots!

[U10] **Jumel Terrace Historic District,** around Jumel Terr. bet. W. 160th and W. 162nd Sts., Edgecombe Ave. and St. Nicholas Ave., including 50 row houses. ☞

[U10a] **10-18 Jumel Terrace** (row houses), bet. W. 160th and W. 162nd Sts. W side. 1896. **Henri Fouchaux.** ♂

Lime- and brownstone stalwarts worthy of the Upper West Side park blocks.

[U10b] **1-19, 2-20 Sylvan Terrace** (row houses), bet. Jumel Terr. and St. Nicholas Ave. 1882-1883. **Gilbert R. Robinson, Jr.** ♂

Wooden 2-story houses: savor the wooden canopies and the doors at No. 5. Here are green shutters, brown hoods, and cream clapboards: a revived memory of very old New York. The streetbed of Sylvan Terrace is the path of the Morris's original driveway.

[U10c] **West 160th Street** (row houses), bet. Edgecombe and St. Nicholas Aves. S side. **No. 418,** 1890. **Walgrove & Israels. Nos. 420-430,** 1891. **Richard R. Davis.** ♂

Brick and brownstone, with up-and-down picturesque profiles.

[U10d] **430-438 West 162nd Street** (row houses), bet. Jumel Terr. and St. Nicholas Ave. 1896. **Henry Fouchaux.**

Beautifully kept limestone bow-fronted houses.

[U10e] Originally **The Roger·Morris** (apartments), 555 Edgecombe Ave., bet. W. 159th and W. 160th Sts. 1914-1916. **Schwartz & Gross.** ☞

Count Basie, Paul Robeson, Joe Louis, and **Kenneth Clark** all passed their time here. Otherwise as innocuous as most Park Avenue apartment houses.

Columbia-Presbyterian complex:

U11

[U11] **Mary Woodard Lasker Biomedical Research Building/**
Audubon Research Park/originally Audubon Theatre and
Ballroom/then Beverly Hills Theatre/later San Juan Theatre,
Broadway at W. 165th St. E side. 1912. **Thomas W. Lamb.**
Alterations and new building, 1996. **Davis Brody Bond.**
A former theater with terra-cotta glazed polychromy
along its Broadway façade: corniced and encrusted, in counterpoint to Babies' Hospital opposite, which is detail-less, except
for its babies. In 1965, Black Muslim leader **Malcolm X** was
assassinated during a rally in the second-floor ballroom.
Movie palaces such as this once provided architectural
romance equal to the movies themselves. The 1995 addition is a
large and handsome tail that wags this ornate dog.

U12

[U12] **Russ Berrie Medical Science Pavilion,** SE cor. W.
168th St. and St. Nicholas Ave. 1997. **Davis Brody Bond.**
A clone of the vocabulary used at the Research Park down
the block. Sleek, stylish and antiseptic.

[U13] **Fort Washington Armory,** bet. W. 168th and W. 169th
Sts., Ft. Washington Ave. and Broadway. 1920s.
A monumental foil to the giant Columbia-Presbyterian
complex surrounding these streets.

U13

[U14] **Columbia-Presbyterian Medical Center,** W. 165th to W.
168th Sts., Broadway to Riverside Dr. 1928-1947. **James Gamble
Rogers.** 1947-1964, Rogers & Butler. 1964-1974. **Rogers Butler &
Burgun.**
The original complex of this vast teaching hospital, situated
on a bluff over the Hudson, is both bulky and pallid, the
streetscape a bore. Inside, however, medical wonders are performed. Perhaps one would forgive the architects and their companion clients, medical administrators, if it were a hospice for
the blind.
Later buildings, cited below, promised some respite from
this megalopolitan stance.

U15

[U15] **Milstein Pavilion/Presbyterian Hospital,** W. 165th
to W. 166th Sts., Broadway to Riverside Dr. 1989.
Skidmore, Owings & Merrill.
A handsome giant Post Modern/neo-Art Deco behemoth
overlooking the Hudson. It goes down almost as far as it goes
up, with a grand terrace looking to and stepping down to the
west, as if a prime location to stage a Busby Berkeley extravaganza. The interconnecting bridges over Fort Washington
Avenue interlace with adjacent hospital buildings and add an
appropriate visual complexity to the urban scene.

[U16a] **Julius and Armand Hammer Health Sciences Center,**
701 Fort Washington Ave., bet. W. 168th and W. 169th Sts. W
side. 1976. **Warner, Burns, Toan & Lunde.**
A somber blockbuster in self-weathering steel and rose
brick. For its soul mate, look at Mt. Sinai's Annenberg Center,
an equally bulky centerpiece of that medical complex.

U16a

[U16b] **Lawrence G. Kolb Research Building,** 722 W. 168th St.,
extended N along Haven Ave. W side. 1987. **Herbert W. Riemer.**
In stylish brown brick with sloping sills: the monolithic
image and posture of the 1970s.

[U17] **The Psychiatric Institute, New York State Office
of Mental Health,** Riverside Drive west of Milstein
Pavilion. 1998. **Peter Pran** of Ellerbe Becket.
From the computer-generated world of **Zaha Hadid** and her
acolytes. Nevertheless a serious medical building that exudes an
extraordinary aura of stylishness.

U17

Freud's library: In the Freud Memorial Room of the Neurological and Psychiatric Institutes is shelved part of Sigmund Freud's personal library.

[U18] **Bard-Haven Towers** (medical center staff housing), 100 Haven Ave., bet. W. 169th and W. 171st Sts. W side, overlooking Henry Hudson Pkwy. 1971. **Brown, Guenther, Battaglia & Galvin.**

Tall cliff-hangers (literally) that cling to the escarpment and enjoy wonderful Hudson views. The corbeled lower stories are a dramatic event to drivers who approach the George Washington Bridge.

[U19] **Highbridge Park**, W. 155th to Dyckman Sts., Edgecombe and Amsterdam Aves. to the Harlem River Dr. 1888. **Calvert Vaux** and **Samuel Parsons, Jr.** Altered.

Once the site of an amusement park, marina, and promenade, this park gains its beauty from a steep slope and rugged topography. An excellent vantage point to survey the Harlem River Valley.

U20b

[U20a] **33rd Precinct Station House**, W. 169th St., bet. Jumel Pl. and Amsterdam Ave. 2000. **Richard Dattner.**

"A curved façade recalling Castle Clinton is bisected by a playful canopied atrium, creating a 'friendly fortress' in keeping with the community policing initiatives of the NYPD". Thus saith Dattner.

[U20b] **Engine Company No. 67, N.Y.C. Fire Department**, 518 W. 170th St., bet. Amsterdam and Audubon Aves. 1901. **Flagg & Chambers.**

An uptown work by those who brought you the great firehouse on Great Jones Street and brought an economy version of its monumental façade with them.

U21

[U21] **High Bridge**/originally Aqueduct Bridge, Highbridge Park at W. 174th St. 1838-1848. **John B. Jervis.** Addition, 1860. Replacement of piers with new central span, 1923.

This is the oldest remaining bridge connecting Manhattan to the mainland, built to carry Croton water to Manhattan. Originally consisting of closely spaced masonry piers and arches, the bridge's central bays were replaced by the present cast-iron arch to accomodate the Harlem River Ship Canal. The pedestrian walk has been closed for many years.

[U22] **Highbridge Water Tower**, Highbridge Park at W. 173rd St. 1866-1872. **John B. Jervis.** Reconstructed, 1989-1990. **William Hall Partnership.**

This landmark tower, originally used to equalize pressure in the Croton Aqueduct, now simply marks the Manhattan end of High Bridge. Damaged in a fire (arson), it has been carefully restored.

U22

[U23] **Henry Hudson Parkway**, from Van Cortlandt Park to and across Henry Hudson Bridge. **Pavilion**, in Fort Washington Park on Riverside Dr. at W. 180 St. W side. 1913. **Jaros Kraus.**

Driving south into Manhattan on this Hudson-hugging parkway is one of New York's great gateway experiences. From Riverdale (the affluent West Bronx) one passes over the Henry Hudson Bridge (a dramatic object from the distance but a bore at first hand) before descending to the banks of the Hudson. Next, the Cloisters, romantically surmounting a hilltop, lonely and wondrous; through a wooded area; then under the majestic George Washington Bridge. All of a sudden the skyline of Manhattan materializes, and the rural-urban transition is complete.

U24

[U24] **Fort Washington Presbyterian Church**, 21 Wadsworth Ave., NE cor. W. 174th St. 1914. **Carrère & Hastings**.

Brick and limestone English Baroque: its Tuscan columns and pilasters, broken pediments, and console-bracketed tower bring us back to **Christopher Wren's** (& **Nicholas Hawksmoor's**) 17th-century reconstruction of London.

[U25] **United Church**/originally Loew's 175th Street Theatre, Broadway NE cor. W. 175th St. 1930. **Thomas W. Lamb**. Altered.

Cambodian neo-Classical? The Reverend Ike holds forth here in splendor reminiscent of archaic Miami Beach. This terra-cotta place was at the apogee of movie palace glamour in those long-gone days when Hollywood ruled the world and free crockery on Wednesday nights was an added fillip.

U25

[U26] **George Washington Bridge**, W. 178th St. and Fort Washington Ave. over the Hudson River to Fort Lee, N.J. 1931. **O. H. Ammann**, engineer, & **Cass Gilbert**, architect. Lower level added, 1962.

"The George Washington Bridge over the Hudson is the most beautiful bridge in the world. Made of cables and steel beams, it gleams in the sky like a reversed arch. It is blessed. It is the only seat of grace in the disordered city. It is painted an aluminum color and, between water and sky, you see nothing but the bent cord supported by two steel towers. When your car moves up the ramp the two towers rise so high that it brings you happiness; their structure is so pure, so resolute, so regular that here, finally, steel architecture seems to laugh. The car reaches an unexpectedly wide apron; the second tower is very far away; innumerable vertical cables, gleaming against the sky, are suspended from the magisterial curve which swings down and then up. The rose-colored towers of New York appear, a vision whose harshness is mitigated by distance."

—**Charles Edouard Jeanneret (Le Corbusier)**
When the Cathedrals Were White, 1947

U26

[U27] **Little Red Lighthouse**/originally Jeffries Hook Lighthouse, Fort Washington Park below the George Washington Bridge. Erected, Sandy Hook, New Jersey. 1880. Moved to present location. 1921.

Directly under the east tower of the George Washington Bridge, the lighthouse was built to steer grain barges away from the shoals of Jeffrey's Hook. When navigational lights were mounted on the bridge, it was no longer used and was put up for auction in 1951. A barrage of letters from children who had read *The Little Red Lighthouse and the Great Gray Bridge*, by **Hildegarde Hoyt Swift** and **Lynd Ward**, saved the lighthouse. The City now maintains it.

[U28] **George Washington Bridge Bus Station**, Fort Washington and Wadsworth Aves., W. 178th to W. 179th Sts. 1963. **Port of New York Authority** and **Pier Luigi Nervi**.

A concrete butterfly shelters a bus terminal at the end of the bridge, interlocking with the IND Eighth Avenue subway. The shape is excused as a form for natural ventilation for the noxious buses; it also provides the opportunity for a formal tour de force for **Dr. Nervi**, an engineer more comfortable with Italian economics, where his skills provide the cheapest, as well as the most exciting, forms.

U29

[U29] **Bridge Apartments**, bet. W. 178th and W. 179th Sts., Wadsworth and Audubon Aves. 1964. **Brown & Guenther**.

An early experiment in residential air rights over a highway, but fumes, dirt, and noise rise to the unfortunate dweller above. The buildings' curtain walls are fussy.

[U30] **Alexander Hamilton Bridge**, Highbridge Park bet. W. 178th and W. 179th Sts. over the Harlem River to the Bronx, 1964.

UPPER MANHATTAN (NORTH)

see pages 527–531

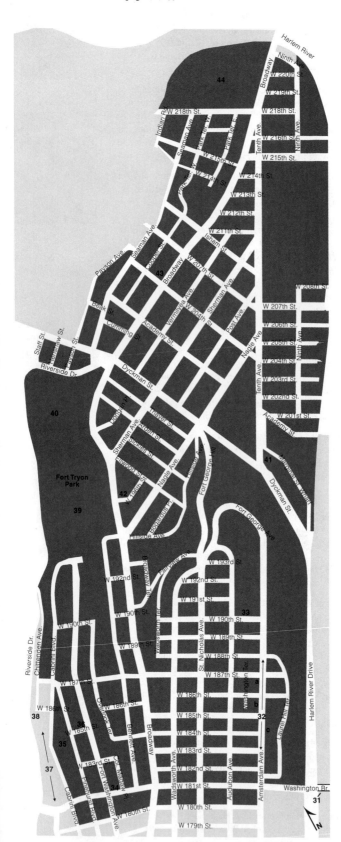

The bridge bringing the Cross-Bronx Expressway to
the George Washington Bridge approaches in Manhattan:
serviceable but dull.

[U31] **Washington Bridge**, W. 181st St. and Amsterdam Ave. over
the Harlem River to University Avenue, The Bronx. 1886-1889.
Charles C. Schneider and **Wilhelm Hildenbrand**.
Modifications, **Union Bridge Company**, **William J. McAlpine**,
Theodore Cooper, **DeLemos & Cordes**, with **Edward
H.Kendall**, Consulting Architect. Reconstruction, 1989-1993. ●

U31

A magnificent arched bridge not to be confused with the
George Washington Bridge. A great filigree of steel is enjoyed by
the Major Deegan or Harlem River driver; to those crossing on
top it's just a flat plane.

Yeshiva University area:

[U32] **Yeshiva University campus**, W. 183rd to W. 187th Sts.,
along Amsterdam Ave.

A mixed bag of architectural tricks, more a collection of separate opportunities than a whole that might have been greater
than the sum of its parts.

U32a

[U32a] **Main Building, Yeshiva University**, 2540
Amsterdam Ave., SW cor. W. 187th St. 1928. **Charles B.
Meyers Assocs.**

This is one of the great romantic structures of its time.
Domes, towers, and turrets can be seen from miles away, and the
architect's lavish use of orange stone, copper and brass, ceramic
tile, and Middle Eastern eclectic architectural detail makes a
visual treat.

[U32b] **Mendel Gottesman Library, Yeshiva University**,
2520 Amsterdam Ave., bet. W. 185th and W. 186th Sts. W
side. 1967. **Armand Bartos & Assocs.** Museum (in the library)
open to the public.

U32b

A rich composition of brick, terra-cotta, and glass highly
articulated to make the best of sun, shadow, and view: in effect,
super bay windows.

[U32c] **Science Center, Belter Graduate School of Science,
Yeshiva University**, 2495 Amsterdam Ave., at W. 184th St. E side.
1968. **Armand Bartos & Assocs.**

Bulky brick piers for a warehouse of science.

[U33] **Isabella Neimath Home and Geriatric Center**, 525
Audubon Ave., bet. W. 190th and W. 191st Sts. E side. 1965.
Joseph D. Weiss.

A home for the elderly, providing small apartments for their
special needs. The pitched and folded roof was designed ostensibly in deference to its older neighbor (the original home), which
no longer exists: it (the original home) was later replaced by an
addition to this addition. Oh, well . . .

[U34] **Fort Washington Collegiate Church**, Fort Washington
Ave. NE cor. W. 181st St. 1907.

This small country church dates from the time when
Washington Heights was suburban; brick and timber Gothic
Revival.

The highest point: *In Bennett Park, along the west side of Fort
Washington Avenue between 183rd and 185th Streets, is a rock outcropping that is the highest natural point in Manhattan, 267.75
feet above sea level. An added bonus is the outline of Revolutionary War Fort Washington, marked by stone pavers.*

U35

[U35] **Hudson View Gardens** (apartments), 116 Pinehurst Ave., bet.
W. 183rd and W. 185th Sts. W side. 1924-1925. **George F. Pelham.**

Scarsdale Tudor once encrusted with Virginia creeper, of brick with simulated half-timbering. This romantic and urbane cluster of multiple dwellings embraces private gardens and enjoys, from many parts, romantic river views.

 [U36] Hebrew Tabernacle of Washington Heights, 185th St., NW cor. Fort Washington Ave. 1930s.

From the time of Radio City Music Hall, limestone, stainless steel, and brass in the Art Moderne of the 1930s.

[U37] **Castle Village** (apartment complex), 120-200 Cabrini Blvd., bet. W. 181st and W. 186th Sts. W side. 1938-1939. **George F. Pelham II**.

U36

At Hudson View, Pelham *père* embraced his public space; at Castle Village Pelham *fils* planted himself in it. Each floor of these cruciform buildings contains 9 apartments, 8 of which have river views. The site was formerly occupied by the Charles Paterno estate; its massive retaining walls still retain the present building site.

[U38] **16 Chittenden Avenue**, at W. 186th St. (Alex Rose Place). 1920s.

The guest house of the former Paterno estate perches on a great pier that drops to the parkway's edge below. Forget the house; enjoy the pier, and be jealous of the view.

[U39] **Fort Tryon Park Scenic Landmark**, W. 192nd to Dyckman Sts., Broadway to Riverside Dr. 1930-1935. **Frederick Law Olmsted, Jr.** Planting plan, **James W. Dawson**. 🌿

A gift of the Rockefeller family to New York City, this site was, in large part, the former C. K. G. Billings estate (the triple-arched driveway from Riverside Drive was its entrance). The park is famous for its Heather Garden.

The fort's grand site still remains; a plaque states:
THE NORTHERN OUTWORK OF FORT WASHINGTON, ITS GALLANT DEFENSE AGAINST THE HESSIAN TROOPS BY THE MARYLAND AND VIRGINIA REGIMENT, 16 NOVEMBER 1776, WAS SHARED BY MARGARET CORBIN, THE FIRST AMERICAN WOMAN TO TAKE A SOLDIER'S PART IN THE WAR FOR LIBERTY.

[U40] **The Cloisters, Metropolitan Museum of Art**, Fort Tryon Park. 1934-1939. **Charles Collens** of **Allen, Collens & Willis**. Alterations to receive the Fuenta-dueña Chapel, 1961, **Brown, Lawford & Forbes**. 🌿 🌿 Open to the public: Mar-Oct: Tu-Su 9:30-5:15; closed Mo. Nov-Feb Tu-Su 9:30-4:45; closed Mo. 212-923-3700.

Named for the French and Spanish monastic cloisters imported and reassembled here in concert with a 12th-century chapter house, the Fuentadueña Chapel, and a Gothic and a Romanesque chapel. The concept and the reality are both very romantic, the siting at this river viewing crest is an overwhelming confrontation between the city and a Hudson River School painter's view of—not surprisingly—the Hudson River.

The contents are the majority of the medieval art collection of the Metropolitan Museum of Art; most impressive are the Unicorn tapestries. Concerts of medieval and Renaissance music are held here from time to time.

The tower, of course, is an office building.

De profundis: The two deepest subway stations in the city are near here (why deepest? the land merely gets higher and the tracks get—at least relatively—lower!): the IRT-Broadway Seventh Avenue station at 191st Street and Saint Nicholas Avenue (180 feet below the street, or the street is 180 feet above the subway), and the IND Eighth Avenue station at 190th Street and Fort Washington Avenue (165 feet down). In both cases elevators whisk passengers up and down: level equalizers.

U40

INWOOD

Robert A. M. Stern has proposed "The (floating) Boathouse at Swindler Cove," along Sherman Creek. If it comes to pass it will be the first serious, consciously created floating architecture in the city (as opposed to the default floating architecture of the South Street Seaport collection). Such projects can be less constrained than buildings founded on earth, so here may ride an exotic neo-Victorian pleasure craft.

U41

[U41] **P.S. 5**, 3704 Tenth Ave., NE cor. Dyckman St. 1992. **Gruzen Samton.**
Colorful and playful, a departure from many years of somber schools. It it one of the systems schools, where a kit of parts, classrooms, cafeterias, and common spaces can be reused in different assemblies and configurations.

U42

[U42] **Intermediate School 218**, The Salome Ureña de Henriquez School, 4600 Broadway, NE cor. W. 196th St. 1990s. **Richard Dattner & Associates.**
A grand exedra of banded brick, a center stairway cylinder with glass block providing a touch of 1930s nostalgia.

U43

[U43] **Dyckman House**, 4881 Broadway NW cor. W. 204th St.ca. 1785. Restoration, 1915-1916. **Alexander M. Welch.** Open to the public: Tu-Sa 11-4; closed Su & Mo. 212-304-9422.
The site is monumental, the porch lovely. Rebuilt by **William Dyckman** after the British destroyed the previous building, this is the only 18th-century farmhouse remaining in Manhattan. With its gambrel roof and brick and fieldstone lower walls, the house shows a strong Dutch influence. The interior, with random-width chestnut floors and original family furnishings, is well worth a visit.

[U44] **Columbia University Stadium, in Baker Field**, W. 218th St., NW cor. Broadway. 1986. **Richard Dattner & Associates.**
Cool concrete. A simple, graceful understated settee for Ivy League football watchers.

U44

The Other Islands

**LIBERTY ISLAND • ELLIS ISLAND
GOVERNORS ISLAND • ROOSEVELT ISLAND
WARDS ISLAND/RANDALLS ISLAND**

 Colonial

 *Georgian/
Federal*

 *Greek
Revival*

 *Gothic
Revival*

 Villa

 *Romanesque
Revival*

 *Renaissance
Revival*

 *Roman
Revival*

 *Art Deco/
Art Moderne*

*Modern/
Post-Modern*

In addition to Manhattan and Staten, which are islands unto themselves, and Long, the western part of which is occupied by the city's two largest boroughs (Queens and Brooklyn), the city is infested with yet other islands. Some are so small or low-lying that the tides keep them under water most if not all of the time. Others appear in official documents but are in fact submerged by the city's offal in numerous landfill projects. Yet others are joined, either to each other or to some "mainland," so that they are no longer truly islands. Jamaica Bay, within the jurisdiction of both Brooklyn and Queens, has bits of mucky land that fall into all of the above categories. Luckily for municipal officials already over-whelmed by less arcane issues, the National Park Service now worries about most of Jamaica Bay's islands, pols, marshes, and hassocks as part of its Gateway National Recreation Area.

Among the larger, inhabited (or once inhabited) islands within the city's waterways—in some cases not normally open to the public—are:

LIBERTY ISLAND

Known until 1956 as Bedloes Island, after Isaac Bedlow, an English merchant who owned it in the 17th century.

[O1] **Statue of Liberty** (National Monument), National Park Service, built atop Fort Wood. 1871-1886. **Frédéric Auguste Bartholdi**, sculptor, **Alexandre Gustave Eiffel**, engineer; **Richard Morris Hunt**, architect of the base. Additions to the base, 1972. Refurbished, 1986, **Thierry Despont** and **Swanke Hayden Conneil**. Open to the public. 🐾

Bartholdi's colossal sculpture *Liberty Enlightening the World* is indeed colossal: she stands 151 feet high, the tip of the flaming torch in her upraised hand rising some 395 feet above the har-bor's waters: her index finger 8 feet long, her eyes each 2½ feet wide. Journey to Liberty Island via the privately operated, regu-larly scheduled ship, and ascend the 168-step helical stair through the verdigrised sheets of 3⁄32-inch-thick copper to the observation platform in the seven-spiked crown. There—if the crowd behind allows you enough time to gaze—you will see the city's great harbor spread before you.

The New Colossus: The symbolic relationship between Liberty's welcoming form and the millions of immigrants arriving in steerage in New York harbor was not formally established until 1903. It was then that a plaque was affixed to the base bearing the lines of a poem written in 1883 by **Emma Lazarus** *as part of a fund-raising effort for the statue. Its last lines capture the cry of Liberty's silent lips:*

> *"Give me your tired, your poor,
> Your huddled masses yearning to breathe free,
> The wretched refuse of your teeming shore.
> Send these, the homeless, tempest-tost to me,
> I lift my lamp beside the golden door!"*

To the disappointment of many who climb the stair to the top, the poem is not inscribed on the tablet grasped in Liberty's left hand—that inscription reads july iv mdcclxxvi.

Long before Liberty was planned as a symbol of the centen-nial relationship between the French and American people, **Bartholdi** had conceived of a colossus of similar scale for the entrance of the Suez Canal; Liberty's progenitor would have

Liberty's torch

stood guard there as a sentry to honor that French ditch. Happily for America, the concept was quickly switched to the more gracious job of greeting the traveler and immigrant to New York harbor (but who greets their descendants at Kennedy Airport?). Bartholdi's most extravagant work (although small) is his fountain in the Place des Terreaux of Lyons; there the waterworks are in the form of water vapor spewing from the nostrils of horses arising from their fountain pool.

Not only the statue but also the lawns and walkways are open to the public, under the jurisdiction of the National Park Service.

ELLIS ISLAND

[O2] Originally U.S. Immigration Station/now **Ellis Island National Monument**, National Park Service and Ellis Island Historic District. 👌 [O2a] Main Building/now **National Museum of Immigartion**. 1897-1900. **Boring & Tilton**. Guastavino Tile Vaults, 1918. Reconstructed and restored, 1991, **Beyer Blinder Belle** and **Notter Finegold & Alexander**. Open to the public. [O2b] **Kitchen and Laundry Building**, 1898-1901. **Boring & Tilton**. [O2c] **Powerhouse**, 1900-1901. **Boring & Tilton**. [O2d] **Old Hospital**, 1901-1909. **Boring & Tilton**. [O2e] **Baggage and Dormitory Building**, 1907-1909. **James Knox Taylor**, Architect of the Treasury. [O2f] **Assorted expansions and additional buildings**, early 1900s. **James Knox Taylor**. [O2g] **New immigration building, ferry house, and recreation building**, 1934-1936. **Chester Aldrich** of **Delano & Aldrich**. Open 9:30-5 daily; last ferry (212-269-5755) at 3:30. 212-363-8340.

O2a

Successor to the old Immigrant Landing Station once housed in Castle Clinton, the Main Building, an extravagant eclectic reception structure, was created to greet (or is it process?) the hordes of, in particular, Eastern and Southern European immigrants arriving at the turn of the century: 1,285,349 entered in 1907 alone, the peak year.

Fanciful bulbous turrets bring to the heavily eastern European population arriving a remembrance of ornately detailed public buildings left behind. Restoration makes the main hall and its lesser companions a vast memorial to the principle that created America and imported all its peoples, except for the hardy but not numerous Native Americans.

Take a trip over. It can be an interstate trip, as part of the island is now in New Jersey!

GOVERNORS ISLAND

[O3] **Governors Island Historic District** 👌

Its name derives from an act of the New York legislature in 1698, which set aside the land "for the benefit and accommodation of His Majesty's governors." Since then it has also served as a sheep farm, quarantine station, racetrack, and game preserve. It is best known for its use as a fortified army base and, ultimately, a Coast Guard station. Public visitation is strictly limited, as the future is still being negotiated between the City and federal governments. If you see a notice of its opening to the public, go! It's worth waiting for.

Apocrypha: After the British evacuation of New York in 1783, Governors Island was owned by Columbia College. The first volunteers to work on the construction of Fort Jay included its students. (Columbia, then King's College, was located in Lower Manhattan at the time.) A few years later (1811), the island's major fort, Castle Williams, a more potent place, was added to guard the Battery of Manhattan.

While forts were created to protect the waterways, the island's inner land was used as a racetrack. The land was later

O3a

infilled with the houses, housing, and barracks of the U.S. Army—a curious choice: the land-based military here at sea.

In 1934 **Mayor La Guardia** proposed that Governors Island become a municipal airport. Fortunately, that idea did not succeed, for although the planes of 1934 could have landed on such a potentially short landing strip (and flying boats could use the harbor), it would be useless for modern jets.

Mayor O'Dwyer had a better idea for the island in 1945: the United Nations, where it could have been in "splendid isolation" from the commercial city.

In the end some elegant and lusty 19th-century architecture has survived these various fantasies. May the landmark status (of the original fort area) long reign to protect these lush relics for the future.

[O3a] **Fort Jay**/originally Fort Columbus (1808-1904), entrance to E of ferry landing on Andes Rd. 1806-1809. **Lt. Col. Jonathan Williams,** chief engineer, U.S. Army. Officers' Barracks within, 1834-1836. ●

The officers' dwellings set within the walls of the fort add a note of domesticity that diminishes the fearsomeness of this now dry-moated fortress, built in a pentagonal, star-shaped plan. The brownstone Federal entranceway is a felicitous effort bearing a handsome sculptural composition. It replaced an earth-bermed fortification of 1794-1796, parts of the new following the configuration of the original.

O3b

[O3b] **Castle Williams,** Andes Rd. W cor. Hay Rd., W of ferry landing. 1807-1811. **Lt. Col. Jonathan Williams,** chief engineer, U.S. Army. Converted to military prison, 1912. ●

Appearing from the harbor to be fully circular in shape (hence its onetime nickname, The Cheesebox), this 200-foot-diameter red sandstone fortification is actually chevron-shaped in plan on its inland side. Together with Castle Clinton at the Battery, it was built to crisscross the intervening waterway with cannonballs during the War of 1812. They were never used.

Williams, its designer, was **Benjamin Franklin's nephew** and the individual for whom Williamsburg, Brooklyn, was named.

[O3c] Originally The South Battery/now incorporated into **Officers' Club,** Comfort Rd. W cor. Barry Rd., SE of ferry landing. 1812.

Built to command Buttermilk Channel, the harbor's waterway between Governors Island and Brooklyn, this fort is now largely hidden by additions made to accommodate its later use as the island's officers' club.

[O3d] **Chapel of St. Cornelius the Centurion** (Episcopal), Barry Rd. W cor. Evans Rd., SE of ferry landing. 1905. **Charles C. Haight**.

Built by Trinity Parish during the period (1863-1924) when the War Department did not see fit to assign an official army chaplain to the military reservation. Inside the Gothic Revival chapel hang 87 battle flags and regimental colors from all periods of American history.

O3d

[O3e] **Post Hospital**, also known as the Blockhouse, Building 9, Barry Rd. SE of ferry landing. 1839. Hipped roof, before 1863. 🖤

Spare Greek Revival now minus its entrance steps.

[O3f] **The Admiral's House**/Originally Commanding Officer's Quarters, Building 1, Barry Rd. S of Andes Rd., SE of ferry landing. 1843. **Martin E. Thompson**. South wing, 1886. Porch, ca. 1893-1918. Rear ironwork, 1936-1937. **Charles O. Cornelius**. 🖤

This imposing brick manor house, porticoed front and rear with slender white 2-story Doric colonnades, served such illustrious generals as **Winfield Scott**, **John J. Pershing**, **Omar N. Bradley**, and **Walter Bedell Smith**.

[O3g] **The Dutch House**, Building 3, Barry Rd., S of Andes Rd., SE of ferry landing. 1845.

Built to resemble the typical house of a New Amsterdam settler but used initially as a commissary storehouse. Now officers' quarters.

[O3h] **The Governor's House**/originally a guardhouse, Building, cor. Andes and Barry Rds., SE of ferry landing. ca. 1805-1813. Roof slope altered, 1839. One-story addition and, perhaps, entrance portico, 1930s. 🖤

The island's oldest structure (updated by historians in recent years from 1708 to 1805), truly Georgian in style since its official use as residence for the British governors required textbook adherence to the style of the motherland. An unpretentious yet dignified Flemish-bonded brick manor house.

[O3i] **Brooklyn-Battery Tunnel Ventilator Building**, Triborough Bridge and Tunnel Authority, off Governors Island, SE of ferry landing. 1950.

This prominent white octagonal prism contributes little to the harbor panorama but subtracts a lot with its bulk and unfriendly scale.

Erosion and landfill: *Governors Island, called Nooten Eylandt (or Nuts Island) in the Dutch period (1625-1664), then encompassed 170 acres. But by the early 1900s the harbor's tides had washed away the southwestern portion, reducing the acreage to a mere 70. At that point the south seawall ran roughly between Castle Williams and the South Battery along today's Hay, Clayton, and Comfort Roads. The placement of material dredged from the harbor's channels together with rock excavated from subway construction subsequently extended the island to its present 173 acres.*

ROOSEVELT ISLAND

"Instant City" is what some people call Roosevelt Island but "New Town in Town" was the catch phrase preferred by the State's Urban Development Corporation. Back in 1971, UDC won the opportunity to create a high-density residential community in the center of the 2-mile-long, 600-foot-wide sliver of land in the East River then known as Welfare Island, a cordon sanitaire for the city's poor, destitute, and chronically ill. An ambitious master plan by **Philip Johnson** and **John Burgee** evoked a community for pedestrians arranged along a network

New town in town

of streets that flowed north from the island's subway stop on the 63rd Street Crosstown Line. Residents' and visitors' cars are stored in a megagarage at the foot of the small lift bridge to Long Island City, and a bus system links the garage at the north with the tramway and subway at the south.

Changes in thinking about the number of people, the height of buildings (the 8 to 10 stories in the master plan being increased to 20 along the main street), the need to coordinate construction with the demolition of existing buildings, delays in the completion of the subway link, double-digit inflation, and finally UDC's fiscal collapse all contributed to departures from the master plan. The most significant consequence was the reduction (forced by UDC's collapse) of population from the minimum "critical mass" of 18,000 needed to sustain shopping, a hotel, restaurants, and entertainment. As a result only Southtown, with 2,138 units, less than half of the number originally contemplated, was built at first. Northtown, in the space between today's residential enclave and the fire station, is only partially built.

The silent but exhilarating aerial voyage via overhead tramcar (a subway fare each way) is an appropriate way to reach Roosevelt Island. (Cars must enter via the bridge from Queens and park in the Motorgate garage.) The silent ride is echoed by the curious silence on the island, a stone's throw from Manhattan's elegant east shore. The quiet is broken only by the buzz of auto tires along FDR Drive across the channel to the west and the hum of "Big Allis," Con Edison's turbine generator, on the opposite shore. Infrequently, the eerie stillness is interrupted by the staccato beat of rotors overhead from aircraft using the 60th Street Heliport. Beyond these sounds are only the gentle noises of harbor craft and the splash of the East River waters along the seawalls that gird the island.

Walk along the length of the gently zigzagged residential spine called, naturally, Main Street, as far as Motorgate, which contains the parking garage and the community's only supermarket. On both sides of Main Street are arranged the apartment blocks, each a variation on a U-shaped plan. The open sides of the U face the river, with the highest sections making a not displeasing canyon of Main Street and the lower tiers of apartments stepping down toward the island's east and west promenades.

O4a

A walk through the community should include a saunter along the two perimeter walks, which offer entrancing views.

The Central Part:

O4a

 [O4a] **Aerial Tramway Station**, N of Queensboro Bridge. 1976. **Prentice & Chan, Ohlhausen.**

This was the main point of pedestrian arrival at Roosevelt Island until completion of the subway (which can never compete successfully with the sensuous delights of this aerial voyage). The form of this tramway station conjures up images of Switzerland, its steep ski slope roof being very different from its Manhattan mate.

O4b

[O4b] **James Blackwell Farmhouse**, Blackwell Park, E side of Main St., S of Eastwood. 1796-1804. Restored, 1973, **Giorgio Cavaglieri.** ✿ **Blackwell Park.** 1973. **Dan Kiley & Partners, landscape architects.**

This modest clapboard dwelling is the rebuilt home of the Blackwells, who owned and farmed this island, once named for the family, from the late 1660s to 1828, when it was purchased by the City. With the construction of a penitentiary the following year, the house became the residence for the first of the many island institutions' administrators.

[O4c] **Eastwood** (apartments), 510, 516, 536, 546, 556, 566, 576, and 580 Main St. E side, opp. "Big Allis," generator of Consolidated Edison. 1976. **Sert, Jackson & Assocs.**

The crisp, undulating accretion of buildings whose unifying arcades line the east side of Main Street. The occupants of its 1,000 units are low-, middle-, and moderate-income tenants. Their windows face the candy cane-striped smokestacks of Con Ed's erratic electric generator, "**Big Allis**" (for Allis Chalmers, its manufacturer), and the industrial dreariness of that part of Long Island City. (The wealthier live on the west side of Main Street.) Bright red accents on the brown ribbed-block façades, a trademark of the architects, have become the theme color for the whole development as well.

O4c

[O4d] **Rivercross** (apartments), 505, 513, and 541 Main St. W side, opp. Rockefeller University. 1975. **Johansen & Bhavnani**, architects. **Dan Kiley & Partners**, landscape architects.

Brightly painted nautical ventilating funnels announce the southernmost of the island's three luxury buildings, this one a cooperative. Like its neighbor to the north, it relies on dun-colored cement asbestos panels as cladding for much of its exterior. The material imparts a sober, urbane look from afar (good) but a thin, expressionless surface up close (bad).

[O4e] **Good Shepherd Community Ecumenical Center**/originally Chapel of the Good Shepherd (Episcopal), 543 Main St. W side. 1888-1889. **Frederick Clarke Withers**. Restored, 1975, **Giorgio Cavaglieri**. ❦ **Plaza**, 1975, **Johansen & Bhavnani**, architects. **Lawrence Halprin Assocs.**, landscape architects.

A stroke of genius to have preserved—and handsomely restored—this vigorously designed 19th-century country chapel for 21st-century use. The old bronze bell (cast in 1888 by **Mencely & Co.**, West Troy, N.Y.) has been placed on the plaza as a charming sculptural note.

O4e

[O4f] **East and West Promenades**. 1975. **Zion & Breen**, landscape architects.

Both are beautifully detailed: the west promenade, facing Manhattan, is the more complex, utilizing multilevels; the east promenade is modest, more subtle, and equally enjoyable.

[O4g] **Island House** (apartments), 551, 555, 575, and 595 Main St. W side, opp. Cornell-New York Medical Center. 1975. **Johansen & Bhavnani**, architects; **Lawrence Halprin Assocs.**, landscape architects.

More housing for the wealthier. Island House is entered, as an ocean liner, via gangplanks, brightly painted in orange and yellow. As in Rivercross to the south, there is a prominent skylight-enclosed year-round indoor pool on the river frontage.

O4i

[O4h] **Westview** (apartments), 595 and 625 Main St. W side, opp. Hospital for Special Surgery. 1976. **Sert, Jackson & Assocs.**

Dark gray-brown brick plus the idiosyncratic bright red accents mark Sert's Manhattan-facing effort for the wealthier, as contrasted with his more extensive project across Main Street for the less well-to-do, built of masonry block.

O4j

[O4i] **Manhattan Park Apartments**, Main St. W side., opp. Motorgate garage complex. 1989. **Gruzen Samton**.

The infill of this long vacant strip provides the final segments of Roosevelt Island's development. A lesser effort from excellent architects.

[O4j] **P.S./I.S. 217**, 645 Main Street, near the Motorgate garage complex. 1992. **Michael Fieldman**.

A fresh breath into the Roosevelt Island landscape. A new architect on the island gives some vigor to what was beginning to seem like a senior architectural thesis at Pratt or City College.

O4j

[O4k] **Motorgate** (garage complex), N of Roosevelt Island Bridge. 1974. **Kallmann & McKinnell**.

A parking garage with initial capacity for 1,000 cars and expansion capability for 1,500 more. The dramatic, glass-enclosed entrance structure for pedestrians is a structural tour de force.

[O4l] **AVAC Complex/Fire Station**, N of Motorgate. 1975. **Kallmann & McKinnell**.

Fire engines are housed in this terminal of the refuse collection system proven at Disney World, a giant underground vacuum collector connected to the rubbish chutes of all the new buildings.

The Southern Part:

O5a

[O5a] **Goldwater Memorial Hospital**, City of New York/originally Welfare Hospital for Chronic Diseases, S of Sports Park. 1939. **Isador Rosenfield**, senior architect, N.Y.C. Department of Hospitals; **Butler & Kohn**; **York & Sawyer**. Addition to S, 1971.

Low-rise chevron-shaped balconied wings extend from a central north-south spine, giving patients confronted with long confinements a maximum of sunlight and river views.

*The **City Hospital**/originally Island Hospital/then Charity Hospital was a grim reminder of the 19th-century's medical ministrations to the needy: built of stone quarried on the island by convicts from the adjacent penitentiary. It has since been demolished.*

[O5c] Originally **Strecker Memorial Laboratory**, in proposed Landmark Park, overlooking E channel of the East River. 1892. **Withers & Dickson**. 3rd story added, 1905, **William Flanagan**. Converted to electric substation, 1999. **Page Ayres Cowley**. �

A neo-Renaissance work that contrasts in both scale and style with its 19th-century neighbors to the north and south. In its day it was the City's most sophisticated medical research facility.

[O5d] **Smallpox Hospital**, in proposed Landmark Park, SW of Strecker Memorial Laboratory. 1854-1856. **James Renwick, Jr**. S wing, 1903-1904. **York & Sawyer**. N wing, 1904-1905, **Renwick, Aspinwall & Owen**. 🌾

Years of disuse and exposure to the elements have made this into a natural Gothick ruin. Its official landmark designation further encourages such a role in quoting architectural historian **Paul Zucker** on the qualities of ruins: "an expression of an eerie romantic mood . . . a palpable documentation of a period in the past . . . something which recalls a specific concept of architectural space and proportion." The designation suggests that the structure possesses all of these. It does.

O6a

The Northern Part:

[O6a] Originally **Octagon Tower, N.Y.C. Lunatic Asylum**/later Metropolitan Hospital, in proposed Octagon Park, N of Northtown. 1835-1839. **Alexander Jackson Davis**. Mansard roof and entry stair added, ca. 1880, **Joseph M. Dunn**. 🌾

A romantic tower that was once surmounted by a later convex mansard "dome"—now also minus the two wings that once extended from it (demolished in 1970). UDC's fiscal problems prevented its intended total restoration as a folly in the Octagon

Park (1991. **Weintraub & di Domenico**). A ruin in Westchester marble protected for, hopefully, a future reconstruction.

[O6b] **Bird S. Coler Hospital**, City of New York, N end of island. 1952. Addition to S, 1954.

An undistinguished design left over from the late 1930s. Construction was delayed by World War II and was finally begun in 1949.

[O6c] **Lighthouse**, in Lighthouse Park, N tip of island. 1872. **James Renwick, Jr.**, supervising architect, Commission of Charities and Correction. ☛ **Lighthouse Park**, 1979, **Quennell-Rothschild Assocs.**.

Built on a tiny island just off the tip of today's Roosevelt Island (and since joined to it) under the direction of the Board of Governors of the City's Commission of Charities and Correction, whose supervising architect at the time was Renwick. The lamps for this "private" lighthouse were later furnished by the U.S. Lighthouse Service. An octagonal form of rock-face Fordham gneiss—its crocketed cornice is sensuous. The park is a modest, green, ground-swelling place, with simple timber retaining walls.

*The legend of **John McCarthy**: An inscription carved on the local gray gneiss ashlar of the Lighthouse adds credence (of a sort) to the legend that a 19th-century patient at the nearby lunatic asylum was permitted to build this structure:*

THIS IS THE WORK/WAS DONE BY/JOHN MCCARTHY/WHO BUILT THE LIGHT/HOUSE FROM THE BOTTOM TO THE/TOP ALL YE WHO DO PASS BY MAY/PRAY FOR HIS SOUL WHEN HE DIES

WARDS ISLAND/RANDALLS ISLAND

Located in the vicinity of the turbulent Hell Gate at the junction of the East and Harlem Rivers, these formerly separate islands are now joined as a result of landfill operations. Randalls, the northernmost, houses the Triborough Bridge interchange as well as the administrative headquarters of the Triborough Bridge and Tunnel Authority. Entertainment and sporting events as well as the Festival of San Juan, the patron saint of Puerto Rico, are held in Downing Stadium.

Wards Island, a recreation area joined to Manhattan by a pedestrian bridge at East 103rd Street, is the site of a number of City and State facilities. Among them are:

[O7a] **Firefighters' Training Center, N.Y.C. Fire Department**/originally Firemen's Training Center, Wards Island, NE part of island opp. Astoria Park, Queens. 1975. **Hardy Holzman Pfeiffer Assocs.**

This Urban Development Corporation project, built to substitute for the old firemen's training center demolished on Roosevelt Island, is a confident work of architecture and witty, too—shades of those wonderfully exuberant Napoleon LeBrun & Sons' firehouses of the 1890s!

[O7b] **Rehabilitation Building, Manhattan Psychiatric Center, N.Y.S. Department of Mental Hygiene**/formerly Manhattan State Hospital, Wards Island, S of hospital buildings. 1970. **Caudill Rowlett Scott.**

A 2-story halfway house in the stern shadow of an earlier generation's high-rise mental hospital.

[O7c] **Manhattan Children's Treatment Center N.Y.S. Department of Mental Hygiene**, Wards Island, opp. E. 107th St. recreation pier. 1972. **Richard G. Stein & Assocs.**

Campus style low-rise residence, teaching, and treatment facilities for mentally retarded and emotionally disturbed children. Vitreous block in variegated tones of brown enrich the appearance of this handsome grouping.

Quite visible but inaccessible because of geography (the currents of the East River) are tiny bits of land such as **Belmont Island**, *south of Roosevelt opposite the United Nations; and* **Mill Rock**, *just east of 96th Street. But the richest assortment of islands, the nesting ground of thousands upon thousands of birds that migrate along the Atlantic Flyway, is the myriad group scattered in the semiaquatic wonderland of Jamaica Bay, now part of the National Park Service's Gateway National Recreation Area.*

The Bronx

THE BRONX
Borough of The Bronx/Bronx County

2

 Colonial

 Georgian/
Federal

 Greek
Revival

 Gothic
Revival

 Villa

 Romanesque
Revival

 Renaissance
Revival

 Roman
Revival

 Art Deco/
Art Moderne

 Modern/
Post-Modern

The northernmost of New York City's five boroughs, this is the only one physically joined to the North American mainland; the others are either islands by themselves or parts of another (Long Island). The only wrinkle is the borough of Manhattan, which is no longer quite the equivalent of the island of Manhattan, since the straightening of the Harlem River in 1895. This major earth-moving effort severed the community of **Marble Hill** from the northern tip of Manhattan Island and joined it instead, some fifteen years later, to the Bronx, using as fill the earth dug out of the excavations for Grand Central Terminal.

Like the County of Westchester, of which it was a part for some **200 years**, Bronx County's topography consists of hills and valleys in the west end and what was originally a marshy plain to the east. To this day are visible the rocky outcroppings and streets of steps which characterize many areas of the West Bronx. The east is, as a result of nonstop landfill and a recent population explosion in red brick housing, less identifiable as a marsh. But a drive or walk through **Pelham Bay Park** will reveal some of the borough's sylvan, preurbanized reeded landscapes along the peninsulas that extend into Long Island Sound.

In the 19th century the Bronx was covered with farms, market villages, embryo commuter towns, country estates, and a number of rambling charitable institutions. It was then a place of rural delights. In 1874 the western portion of the Bronx (designated **Western**, **Riverdale**, **Central**, and **Southern** Bronx in this guide) was annexed to the city. Bridge building and the extension of elevated rapid transit lines from Manhattan, and then a growth of population, industry, and schools followed political union. The eastern Bronx (designated as **Eastern** and **Northern** Bronx in this guide) became part of New York City in 1895.

Except for parts of **Riverdale**, the westernmost, hilliest, and least accessible part of the borough, the physical vestiges of the old villages with such names as **West Farms**, **Morrisania**, **Kingsbridge**, and **Middletown** were submerged by 20th-century development. The extension of the rapid transit lines along Jerome Avenue, Boston Road, White Plains Road, Westchester Avenue, and finally along Grand Concourse made the Bronx the next step in upward mobility for hundreds of thousands of families of average but improving means. But the post-World War II suburban exodus drained away many of their offspring. And governmental housing policy relocated many of the older generation who remained, eastward to Co-op City, a huge development of thirty-five-story apartment towers, bedding down, in aggregate, some 55,000 people.

By Y2K the Bronx had become home to a population that is predominantly nonwhite, including an inordinate number of poor. Stable communities continue to flourish with populations drawn from all racial and economic backgrounds, and much of the South, Central, and West Bronx that carried the appellation **"Fort Apache"** (with areas that had approached the appearance of a burned-out wilderness, scenes not unlike those in war-ravaged cities), is now blooming with new housing.

In contrast to visible decay in many of its communities, green leafy camouflage flourishes in the borough's larger parks and the parkways that link them. They are the result of planning by local visionaries in 1883 and executed largely in the two decades that followed. The ability of nature to rejuvenate itself (fully one-fifth of the Bronx's area—5,861 acres—is parkland, although admittedly large amounts are not yet developed) is the ascending star of the Bronx's future.

BOSTON ROAD FROM 168 ST. LOOKING EAST, BRONX, NEW YORK CITY.

Tips on touring: The Bronx, the smallest of New York's outer boroughs, is still quite large. Its southwestern quadrant, south of Fordham Road and west of the Bronx River (except for some notably healthy parts such as Belmont), is a large area that has been beset by economic and social problems. The northwest, Riverdale, is picturesque, convoluted, and very hilly. The Bronx east of the Bronx River is simply vast. All this adds up to a recommendation that touring be best done by car with enough stop-offs to stretch your legs and to permit looking with greater care—so much can be missed, even when driving at a crawl. Be prepared to roll up your windows in hot weather when approaching a fire hydrant being used to provide relief from the heat. Otherwise some playful kids will cup their hands around the spray and inundate you. It's nothing personal on their part, but it's no fun driving with a puddle in your lap. **Get a street map** before embarking. The pocket atlases of the city are large enough to read but small enough to refer to in the confines of a car. In this way you can maneuver between the Guide's district maps, and see the few entries beyond those maps' borders.

For those intrepid pedestrian wanderers a good option is a mix of **Bronx Park** (zoo and botanical garden), **Fordham University**'s Gothic-styled campus, and (except on Sundays) the nearby Italian community of **Belmont** and its wonderful European shopping street, **Arthur Avenue**. [See Central Bronx for the details.] **Mass transit** to a good starting point: Take the subway (B or D train or Jerome Avenue Line No. 4 train) to the Fordham Road Station. Then change (no additional fare if you're using a Metrocard) for Bus No. 12 eastbound to Southern Boulevard and East Fordham Road, where you will find the zoo's Rainey Gate a short walk east on the south side of the street, the garden on the north. (IRT Nos. 2 and 5 to the East 180th Street Station drop you at the south end of the zoo, very near the Boston Road Gate.)

Meanwhile, there is much to see:

THE BRONX KEY MAP

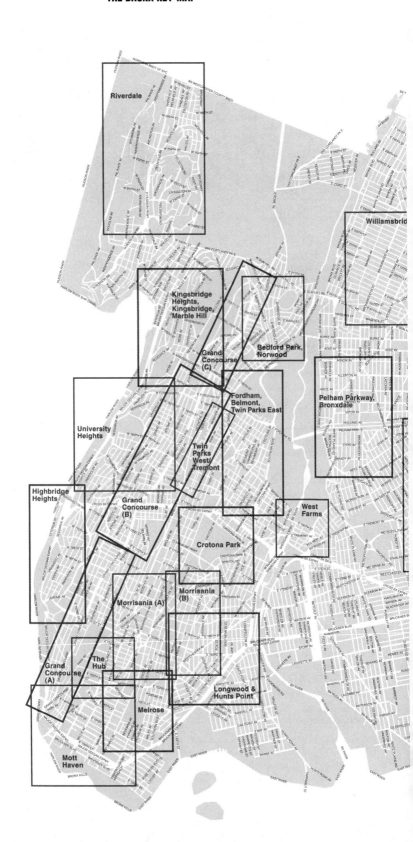

Southern Bronx

MOTT HAVEN • PORT MORRIS • MELROSE
THE HUB • MORRISANIA • CROTONA PARK
LONGWOOD • HUNTS POINT

South Bronx

Though their names persist into the present, the country villages that once existed in the South Bronx have long disappeared. Soon after the Civil War the farms that survived from colonial times began to give way to private homes and tenement rows. In more recent days these have given way to arterial highways and public housing developments. The rapid growth of other parts of the Bronx in the 20th century eclipsed the South Bronx and shifted the focus of commerce, entertainment, and government to other parts of the borough. Successive waves of immigrants and industries have passed in and out of the South Bronx, but their footprints have been hard to find. Without money, power, or prestige, the area has been unable to cultivate its ornaments. Landmarks venerated in other places were, until recently, overlooked here. Some have completely disappeared; but some survivors are happily being rediscovered.

MOTT HAVEN

[S1] Formerly **Mott Iron Works**, Third Ave. bet. Harlem River and E. 134th St., opp. Bruckner Blvd. to former Mott Haven Canal (filled in). W side. 1828-1906.

Jordan L. Mott, inventor of a coal-burning stove, established a factory west of Third Avenue, between East 134th Street and the Harlem River, in 1828. The venture prospered and grew. Some buildings of the ironworks can still be seen from the western walkway of the Third Avenue Bridge. It was Mott, who founded the village of Mott Haven, whose monogram "MH" persists in the mosaics of the 138th and 149th Street Stations of the Jerome Avenue subway.

The Broncks: The first European settlers of this area were Jonas Bronck, a Dane from Amsterdam, and his family, whose farmhouse is believed to have been located east of the Third Avenue Bridge. Though some say the borough's official name, The Bronx, owes its initial article to friends of the settlers saying "Let's pay a visit to the Broncks," the less romantic but more accurate explanation lies elsewhere. As it was common to speak of the Army of the Potomac or the valley of the Hudson, each taking its name from a river, so it was with the lands along the banks of the local river here, the Bronx River.

[S2] **Bronx Community Paper Company**, off Bruckner Boulevard next to the Triborough Bridge. 2000. **Maya Lin** and **HLW International**.

A vast project to recycle New York's paper into newsprint. The interventions of **Maya Lin** bring transparency to the project, allowing motorists to observe the flow of water and slurries, the steam from the gas boilers, etc.

Piano Town: In the last decades of the 19th century, as an emerging urban middle class was able to amass enough surplus income to seek the finer things, pianos came into demand. In the Bronx they were player pianos after the process for a "pianola" was patented in 1897. The local German immigrant population included skilled workers employed in these former piano factories, as others similarly skilled were employed across the East River at the Steinway and Sohmer factories in western Queens.

[S3] Formerly **Rupert Brewery Ice Factory**, 307-309 E. 132nd St., bet. Lincoln and Alexander Aves. N side. ca. 1899. **Julius Kastner**.

Enveloped and crowned with advertising.

S4

[S4] Originally **Haines Piano Co**. (factory)/later Kroeger Piano Co. Alexander Ave. NW cor. E. 132nd St. 1888. **Kreitler & Hebbard**.

The elliptical arches signal elegant space at the corner.

[S5] Formerly **warehouse**, 82-96 Lincoln Ave., bet. E. 132nd St. and Bruckner Blvd. E side. 1888. **C. C. Buck**.

Nice arcades; look at the 132nd Street side.

[S6] Formerly **Estey Piano Company** (factory), E. 132nd St. bet. Lincoln and Alexander Aves. N side. 1885. A. B. Ogden & Son.

Still the grande dame of the piano trade: not virgin, but all-together and proud.

S6

 [S7] **Branch, Chase Manhattan Bank**/originally North Side Board of Trade Building, 2514 Third Ave., SE cor. E. 137th St. 1912. **Albert E. Davis**.

After the Bronx became part of Greater New York, but before it became a county of its own, it was the North Side of New York County (or Manhattan). This neo-Classical white-glazed-terra-cotta structure served as headquarters of the borough's board of trade.

[S8] **2602 Third Avenue** (warehouse), NE cor. E. 140th St. ca. 1890.

Grand relieving arches, sturdy machicolations, and "decorative" iron lances elegantly stabilizing brick piers, combine to make this a superb fortress for wares in storage, and, perhaps, in need of defense.

S8

[S9] **Intermediate School 183, Bronx, The Paul Robeson School**, 339 Morris Ave., NW cor. E. 140th St. 1974. **Stein & Stein**.

A severe cast-in-place concrete structure. The later addition of mesh window grilles only intensified the building's prison-like qualities.

[S10] **Mott Haven Historic District**, generally along both sides of Alexander Ave. bet. E. 137th and E. 141st Sts.

MOTT HAVEN DISTRICT

see pages 546–551

This district, named for **Jordan Mott**, owner of the Mott Iron Works at East 134th Stret and the Harlem River, is the old Bronx at its best. Not only are there well-designed row houses and apartments—by such architects as **Carl A. Millner**, **Charles Romeyn**, and **Arthur Arctander**—but five fine institutional buildings as well, two of which, the churches, handsomely define the district at its south and north ends. No. 280 Alexander Avenue was the home of **Edward Willis**, a local land developer for whom nearby Willis Avenue is named.

The district includes:

S13

[S11] **St. Jerome's Roman Catholic Church**, 230 Alexander Ave., SE cor. E. 138th St. 1898. **Delhi & Howard.**

St. Jerome is remembered here by some vigorous late 19th-century neo-Baroque columns exuberantly breaking away from the body of the church.

[S12] **St. Jerome's School**, 222 Alexander Ave., NE cor. E. 137th St.

An earlier, sterner St. Jerome for the children of the parishioners next door.

S14

[S13] **40th Precinct, N.Y.C. Police Department,** 257 Alexander Ave., NW cor. E. 138th St. 1924. **Thomas E. O'Brien.**

A 16th-century Italian palazzo, filtered through the architectural history of 19th-century London clubs, now turns up in Mott Haven.

[S14] **Mott Haven Branch, N.Y. Public Library**, 321 E. 140th St., NW cor. Alexander Ave. 1905. **Babb, Cook & Willard.**

More neo-Renaissance (but the brick is an added American touch).

[S15] **Tercera Iglesia Bautista** (Third Spanish Baptist Church)/originally Alexander Avenue Baptist Church, 322 Alexander Ave., SE cor. E. 141st St. 1901. **Frank Ward** of **Ward & Davis**. ♂

Even the Baptists hereabouts could exult in architecture.

[S16] **261-271 Alexander Avenue** (houses), SW cor. 139th St. 1890s. ♂

S16

A somber and articulated brick terrace (in the English sense). Colonnettes support elliptical archwork. A serious architectural ensemble.

Mott Haven's other "brownstones":

[S17] **The Bertine Block Historic District** (row houses) ●, E. 136th St. bet. Willis Ave. and Brown Place: [S17a] **408-412 East 136th Street**. S side. 1877. **Rogers & Browne**. [S17b] **414-432 East 136th Street**. S side. 1891. **George Keister**. [S17c] **415-425 East 136th Street**. N side. 1892. **John Hauser**. [S17d] **434-440 East 136th Street**. S side. 1895. **Adolph Balschun, Jr.** [S17e] **8 Tenements**. 1897-1899. **Harry T. Howell**.

S17e

The Bertine Block derives its name from a grouping of ten low-stooped, tawny brick and brownstone row houses erected by developer **Edward D. Bertine** in 1891 (Nos. 414-432). The earlier houses precede Bertine's involvement and are in the less picturesque neo-Grec style. The later rows and tenements were added by Bertine in the subsequent 8 years.

[S18] **Plaza Borinquen, 3 sites**: 1) **E. 137th St. bet. Willis Ave. and Brown Place**. [S19] 2) **E. 137th St. NW cor. Brown Place**. [S20] 3) **E. 138th St. to E. 139th St., bet. Willis and Brook Aves**. 1974. **Ciardullo-Ehmann**.

Eighty-eight triplex apartments contained in groups of row houses thoughtfully planned to fill three differing scattered sites within an existing fabric of housing. The red-brown masonry, with similarly toned mortar and bright highlights in the orange and red air conditioner covers, heralded a new look for the South Bronx. Borinquen is the name given the island of Puerto Rico by its original settlers, the Taino people.

S20

Between Willis and Brook Avenues:
(Brook Avenue is one-way south.)

[S21] **Mott Haven East Historic District**, parts of East 139th and East 140th Streets, bet. Willis and Brook Aves. ●

Extant blocks encapsulating a slice of Bronx architectural life in the last quarter of the 19th century.

S23

S25

S28

S29

S32

S33

[S22] **403-445 East 139th Street** (row houses). N side. 406-450 East 140th Street (row houses). S side. 1877-1892. **William O'Gorman**. ♂

Neo-Grec, 2-story, red brick, mini-"brownstones" with powerful cast-iron railings defining the stoops.

[S23] **407 East 140th Street** (tenement). 1890s. **O'Gorman and Hornum**. ♂

The sinuous façade bows to receive the recessed line of adjacent row houses.

[S24] **409-427 East 140th Street** (row houses). N side. 1897-1900. **William Hornum**. ♂

Dutch/Flemish pediments make delightfully convoluted silhouettes against the sky.

[S25] **St. Peter's German Evangelical Lutheran Church**, 435 East 140th St. 1911. **Louis Allmendinger**. ♂

An austere and sturdy brick and limestone neo-Gothic.

[S26] **441-461 East 140th Street** (tenements). 1902-1903. **George Pelham**. ♂

[S27] **465-481 East 140th Street** (tenements). 1901-1902. **Neville & Bagge**. ♂

The Corinthian-pilastered entrance portals at No. 465 gave tenement life a certain outward grandeur.

[S28] Originally **Willis Avenue Methodist Episcopal Church**, 330 Willis Ave., NE cor. E. 141st St. 1900. **George W. Kramer**.

The glassy 141st Street façade brings a lightness to this somber building.

[S29] **404-450 East 142nd Street** (row houses). S side. 1897. **William O'Gorman**.

Again, neo-Grec returns: 24 houses maintaining another turn-of-the-century streetscape.

[S30] Originally **Congregational Church of North New York**, 415 E. 143rd St., bet. Willis and Brook Aves. N side. 1903. **Dodge & Morrison**.

Anchoring the small-scale row houses midblock is this late Romanesque Revival, creamy gray, rock-faced stone church. What a welcome relief to the humorless red brick high-rise "projects" so evident nearby!

[S31] **419-437 East 143rd Street** (row houses). N side. 1887. **H. S. Baker**. [S31a] **404-446 East 144th Street** (row houses). S side. 1887. **H. S. Baker**

And yet more neo-Grec, some lovingly restored.

[S32] **St. Ann's Church (Episcopal) and Graveyard**, 295 St. Ann's Ave., bet. E. 139th and E. 141st Sts. W side. 1840-1841. ♠

St. Ann's, erected by **Gouverneur Morris, Jr.** on his estate in memory of his mother, provides an echo from the Bronx's rural past. Mysterious hummocks in front of the edifice mark burial vaults in which early parishioners' remains are entombed. Slightly askew from the street grid (or is it rather that the street grid is slightly askew from St. Ann's?), the church faces a space that is neither street nor true oasis.

[S33] **Centro de Salud Segundo Ruiz Belvis** (neighborhood family-care center), E. 142nd St. NW cor. St. Ann's Ave. 1972. **Frost Associates**, architects; **William Tarr**, sculptor.

An important step forward: not just a needed community health center but a physical symbol of hope in the cityscape. The razor-wired chain-link fence subtracts some points from the hope column.

[S34] Originally Henry W. Boetteger Silk Finishing Factory/later **Boetteger & Heintz Silk Manufacturing Company**, 401 Brook Ave., SW cor. 144th St. 1888. **Robert Otz and George Butz**.

Were the window openings to be reopened, this factory complex would rival the old mill buildings of New England. Check the stack for its new role as microwave transmission tower.

[S35] **St. Pius V Roman Catholic Church**, 416 E. 145th St., bet. Willis and Brook Aves. 1907. **Anthony F. A. Schmidt**.

Its strong silhouette suggests a 19th-century utilities building, but in fact this substantial red brick church is an early 20th-century paean to God.

S34

PORT MORRIS

East of the Bruckner Expressway and the Bronx approaches to the Triborough Bridge and south of East 141st Street lies a peninsula of industry largely forgotten by the wheels of progress: Port Morris. It was developed as a deepwater port by the Morris family during the mid 19th century, in the hope of rivaling New York. The Hell Gate Plant of the Consolidated Edison Company is located here.

S36

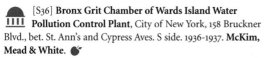 [S36] **Bronx Grit Chamber of Wards Island Water Pollution Control Plant**, City of New York, 158 Bruckner Blvd., bet. St. Ann's and Cypress Aves. S side. 1936-1937. **McKim, Mead & White.**

An exercise in the neo-Baroque: a little timid and a little late in the century for such antics.

M1

MELROSE

Dominating this community is the traditional business and entertainment center of the borough, called the Hub, the intersection of five busy streets: East 149th Street, Third, Willis, Melrose, and Westchester Avenues. Old-timers can recall the area as a bustling entertainment center, with fare ranging from silent flicks and burlesque to operatic performances, and with trolley lines converging from every direction. The Bronx stretch of the Third Avenue el, which once clattered overhead, was removed in the 1970s, but the pace on the street remains furious and chaotic, an expression of the coming together of the many Hispanic and black communities, of which Melrose and the rest of the South Bronx are today composed. If there is a word to sum up the Hub's purpose it is "buy!"

[M1] **St. Mary's Park**, St. Ann's to Jackson Aves., St. Mary's to E. 149th Sts. Reconstructed, 1936.

Named for St. Mary's Church, a wooden country church that stood on Alexander Avenue and East 142nd Street until its demolition in 1959. The crest of the hill at the north end of the park is a good place from which to survey this neighborhood. It was once known as Janes' Hill and belonged to **Adrian Janes**, whose family's famous ironworks was located nearby.

*The Capitol Dome: On the south side of Westchester Avenue between Brook and St. Ann's Avenues is the site of what was once the **Janes, Kirtland & Company Iron Works**. It was here, in one of America's largest foundries of its time, that were cast such lowly devices as iron furnaces and such elegant items of architectural ironwork as Central Park's Bow Bridge. But literally crowning partners Janes and Kirtland's many achievements was the casting and erection (using horse power) of the 8,909,200 pounds of iron that became the Capitol Dome in Washington, D.C., completed in 1863.*

West of St. Mary's Park:

M2

 [M2] **Public School 27**/also known as St. Mary's Park School/originally Public School 154, 519 St. Ann's Ave., bet. E. 147th and E. 148th Sts. W side. 1895-1897. **C. B. J. Snyder.**

Built 5 stories tall for children with good legs and good lungs. The carved limestone escutcheon over the main entrance is an effulgent work of sculpture.

East of St. Mary's Park:

M3

[M3] Former **Ward Bread Company** (bakery), 367 Southern Blvd., bet. E. 142nd St. and St. Mary's St. to Wales Ave. W side. ca. 1900.

This 6-story white, glazed terra-cotta former bakery abuts the old Port Morris Branch of the New York, New Haven & Hartford Railroad. The name is blazed in brick down the monumental stack.

[M4] Originally **Samuel Gompers Industrial High School**, 455 Southern Blvd., along Tinton Ave. bet. E. 145th and E. 146th Sts. W side, to Wales Ave. 1932. **Walter C. Martin.**

A statuesque symmetric composition in stripped neo-Romanesque/Art Deco.

M5

[M5] **St. Roch's Roman Catholic Church and Rectory**, 425 Wales Ave., bet. E. 147th and E. 149th Sts. W side. 1931. **DePace & Juster.**

Neo-Baroque, Spanish division, an exuberant style brought to Spanish America in the days of the Jesuit-led counter-

MELROSE DISTRICT
see pages 552–554

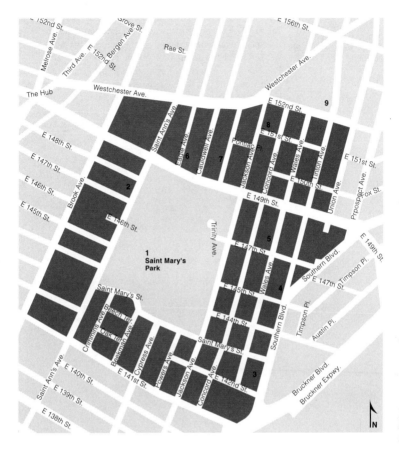

Reformation, which sought to bring back the Protestants to Catholicism with a virtuoso and theatrical architectural display. Many descendents of the Latin Americans whom the Spanish sought to convert now live in this neighborhood!

North of St. Mary's Park:

[M6] **560-584 Eagle Avenue** (2-family housing), bet. E. 149th St. and Westchester Ave. E side. ca. 1986 (Eagle Ave. one-way south).

A distinguished solution for moderately priced housing. Three-dimensional in concept, it provides real backyards for its apartment dwellers. Much of the Bronx has been infilled with two-story housing in the 1990s, most of it tacky: they did not learn the lesson this elegant example provided.

M6

[M7] **600, 610, 620 Trinity Avenue** (apartments), bet. E. 149th St. and Westchester Aves. ca. 1939.

Unusual for this area, these 6-story, cream and brown brick, Art Deco buildings reek of the West Bronx and Grand Concourse.

[M8] **Hunts Point Multi-Service Center**, 630 Jackson Ave., NE cor. E. 151st St. 1974. **Bond Ryder Assocs.**

One of a number of new institutions that grew out of the Model Cities Program in the South Bronx, this building seems a stylish foreigner with its rich, yellow-tan block and almost opaque-seeming, dark-tinted sheets of glass.

M8

M9

[M9] **St. Anselm's Church** (Roman Catholic), 673 Tinton Ave., bet. E. 152nd St. and Westchester Ave. W side. ca. 1907. **Anton Kloster**.

Bare-bones brick practically everywhere except around the entrance, where some poetically illustrated glazed tile plaques and neo-Romanesque ornament soften the bluntness of the masonry. But as the exterior is bold and forceful, the interior is soft and supple, its details a combination of Byzantine and Romanesque motifs created by brothers of the Benedictine order who came here from Germany in the 1920s. A blue-green light washes the sanctuary from a circular, stained-glass clerestory as though lighting a grotto. The walls shimmer with the brothers' ceramic tile tesserae. It is both a surprising and moving experience.

THE HUB DISTRICT
see pages 555–556

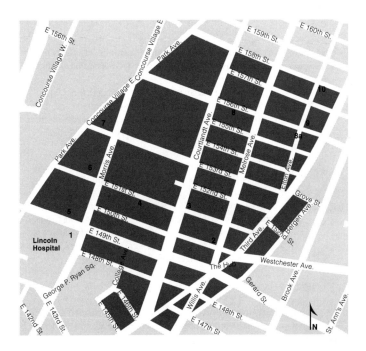

THE HUB

[H1] **Lincoln Medical & Mental Health Center**, N.Y.C. Health & Hospitals Corporation, Morris Ave. SW cor. E. 149th St. 1976. **Max O. Urbahn Assocs.** Brick bas-relief mural, **Aleksandra Kasuba.**

The brickwork of this up-to-date health care facility is just too much of a good thing. Of an indescribably strident earth color, it aggressively grabs your attention. Nevertheless, the swirled brick bas-relief on the 149th Street side is a handsome addition to the streetscape.

H1

[H2] **Immaculate Conception Church of the Blessed Virgin Mary** (Roman Catholic) 389 E. 150th St., NW cor. Melrose Ave. 1887. [H2a] **Henry Bruns. School Hall,** 378 E. 151st St., SW cor. Melrose Ave. 1901. **Anthony F. A. Schmitt.**

This austere yet richly modeled brick Romanesque Revival church boasts the highest steeple in the Bronx. It recalls the days when the Germans were the most populous ethnic group in the Bronx and their prominence in the building trades, brewing, and the manufacture of musical instruments was of central importance to the borough's prosperity. The façades of the rectory on the west, the church in the center, and the Redemptorist Fathers home on the east make a handsome composition of brick detail and arched windows. A later auditorium on the southwest corner of 151st Street and Melrose Avenue is a reserved Beaux Arts composition.

[H3] **614 Courtlandt Avenue** (apartments)/originally saloon and meeting hall, NE cor. E. 151st St. 1872. Altered, 1882, **Hewlett S. Baker.**

In a neighborhood where the tides of change are everywhere apparent, here is a miraculously intact 3-story town house complete with intricate detailing on a mansard roof. It was left here by **Jacob Ruppert**, who, not surprisingly, was promoting beer-drinking in this then Germanic neighborhood.

H3

H4

H6

H8

H8a

[H4] **Engine Company 41, N.Y.C. Fire Department**, 330 E. 150th St., bet. Courtlandt and Morris Aves. S side. 1903.

Italian Renaissance Mannerist Revival, its cornice lost to erosion in time and the spartan budget for the maintenance of New York City buildings.

[H5] **Michelangelo Apartments**, E. 149th to E. 150th Sts., bet. Morris and Park Aves. 1976. **Weiner & Gran** and **Jarmul & Brizee**.

If this project's flat, modest façade on 149th Street was meant as a foil to the more colorful, 3-dimensional one of Lincoln Medical Center across the street, it succeeds. But there must have been a better way. A project of the state Urban Development Corporation.

[H6] **Maria Lopez Plaza** (apartments), 635 Morris Ave., NW cor. E. 151st St. 1982. **John Ciardullo Assocs**.

Designed in 1975 and delayed by the City's financial crisis but well worth waiting for: white columns, half-cylindrical balconies, and thoughtful fenestration raise this housing to a level considerably above the norm. And what only the residents see—in the block-square, green interior courtyard—is brilliant housing design united with enlightened urban living.

Humble churches:

[H7] **Greater Universal Baptist Church**/originally Church of the Holy Trinity (Italian Presbyterian), 253 E. 153rd St., bet. Morris Ave. and Concourse Village E. N side. 1911.

A modest Lombardian Romanesque box (the arched corbeltable at the gable is a **Lombard** signature).

[H8] **Greater Victory Baptist Church**/originally St. Matthew's Lutheran Church 374 E. 156th St., bet. Courtlandt and Melrose Aves. S side. 1895.

The drab and dreary paint masks a handsome neo-Gothic building.

[H8a] **Plaza de los Angeles** (3-family houses), Elton Ave. bet. 155th and 157th Sts., sometimes both sides. **Larsen Shein Ginsberg & Magnusson**.

Street-fronted 3-story row housing that answers the urban problem more elegantly than the sprawl of Charlotte Gardens or the banality of endless new blocks of two-story vinylized units with their wrought-iron-gated parking bays.

[H9] Originally **Reformed Church of Melrose**, 742 Elton Ave., NE cor. E. 156th St. 1874. **Henry Piering**.

A lonely survivor among South Bronx desolation, but many a Phoenix is rising from the ashes. See the Melrose Court [S1] two blocks away.

[H10] Originally **Elton Avenue (German) Methodist Episcopal Church**, 790 Elton Ave., SE cor. E. 158th St. 1879. **John Rogers** or **H. S. Baker**.

A neighbor to the Reformed Church, just a block away. They are the architectural highlights of the new infill housing that has just arrived.

MORRISANIA

As the South Bronx was a German neighborhood in the 19th century, there was a continuing demand for lager beer. Before the advent of refrigeration, the brewing of lager (from the German liegen, to lie still) required a chilled place to age. Caves cut into hillsides made it possible to pack the beer kegs with naturally cut ice and then to seal the openings temporarily until the beer had aged. No surprise then that breweries backed up to the Eagle Avenue escarpment (it is so steep that Eagle Avenue negotiates East 161st Street over a high bridge). The caves are used today for less romantic manufacturing purposes. During Prohibition, both caves and breweries were converted into indoor mushroom farms.

Here stood the former Hupfel Brewery, St. Ann's to Eagle Aves., bet. E. 159th and E. 161st Sts. Both ca. 1875. And the former Eagle Brewery to its south.

S1

[S1] **Melrose Common**, bet. St. Ann's and Brook Aves., 156th to 159th Sts. 1994. **Marvin Meltzer**.

The best of the new Bronx. Meltzer's scheme surrounds courtyards with access stairs serving the individual units. The street façades are a bit tacky (false gables), but the inner workings are an urbane effort.

[S2] **Model Cities Housing**, Eagle to Cauldwell Aves., bet. E. 156th and E. 161st Sts. 1987. **Shelly Kroop**.

Three-story housing, an attempt to bring the scale of public housing back to people and the ground.

[S3] **Church of Sts. Peter and Paul** (Roman Catholic), 840 Brook Ave., NE cor. E. 159th St. 1932. Rectory, 833 St. Ann's Ave., bet. E. 159th St. and E. 161st St./Third Ave. W side, 1900. **Michael J. Garvin**.

Collegiate Gothic (safe, solid, expensive) in granite ashlar, looking more as though it was commissioned by an Episcopal diocese than one Roman Catholic. The rectory is a lustier reminder of the parish's earlier days.

[S4] Originally Bronx Borough Courthouse/then **Criminal Court of the City of New York**, Bronx County Branch/now occupying triangle bet. E. 161st St., Brook Ave., and Third Ave. 1905-1915. **Oscar Bluemner** and **Michael J. Garvin**. ✺

S4

MORRISANIA DISTRICT (A)

see pages 557–561

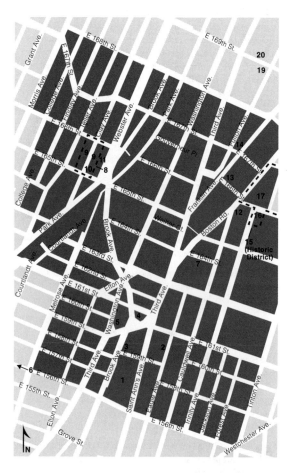

Colossal Tuscan columns mount a rusticated base: an eloquent and abandoned Beaux Arts monument. In spite of many decades of smoke, grime, neglect, and the rattling of the long-gone Third Avenue el, it remains proud, even though windows are blocked up, metalwork tarnished, and walls covered with soot. A feeble and heavy-handed replacement courthouse opened nearby in 1977. And an even newer courthouse is in the works.

S5

[S5] **42nd Precinct, N.Y.C. Police Department**/originally 36th Precinct, 3137 Third Ave. (entry on Washington Ave.), opp. E. 160th St. at George Meade Plaza. 1904. **Charles Volz.**

Once the 36th precinct, later the 46th (note the recut frieze), most recently the 42nd. This neo-Renaissance structure appears in exterior shots of *Fort Apache, The Bronx*, a 1981 movie about life in an earlier and somewhat devastated South Bronx. The real Fort Apache was actually the Simpson Street station house.

S6

[S6] **Bronx South Classic Center**, 156th St. and Morris Ave. 2000. **Agrest & Gandelsonas.**

The insitutional architecture of Melrose Houses receives an injection of sophisticated architecture. Don't miss it.

[S7] **Charlton Playground, N.Y.C. Department of Parks & Recreation**, E. 164th St. bet. Boston Rd. and Cauldwell Ave., midblock. Reconstructed, 1982, **Weintraub & di Domenico.**

A welcome anomaly in these parts of deadening municipal presence: among the surrounding "projects" and blight, a city

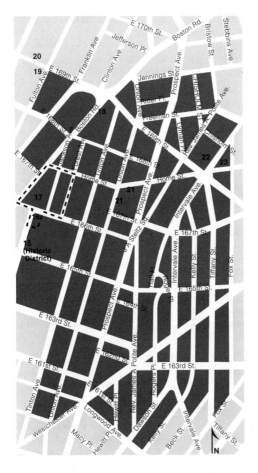

facility of great imagination and subtlety. A simple pergola perches atop a sharp rise in the topography.

[S8] **Clay Avenue Historic District**, both sides of Clay Avenue between E. 165th and E. 166th Strs.
A lovely group of classically inspired row houses on a site that had been the old Fleetwood Trotting Course until 1898. One of the richest rowhouse blocks in New York City. The apartment buildings that anchor three corners of Clay Avenue are by **Neville & Bagge** (1909-1910).

[S9] **1041-1067 Clay Avenue** (row houses), bet. E. 165th and E. 166th Sts. W side. 1902. **1040-1066 Clay Avenue** (row houses), bet. E. 165th and E. 166th Sts. E side. 1902. All by **Warren C. Dickerson.**
Both Neo-Renaissance and Eclectic, these lush rowhouses are crowned with stepped gables, bay-windowed and corniced below.

S9

[S10] Originally **Francis Keil House, 1038 Clay Avenue**, NE cor. E. 165th St. 1906. **Charles S Clark.**
In contrast to its Clay Avenue neighbors, this austere brick house, fronting on East 165th Street, seems a penitent among the flamboyant.

[S11] Former **Sheffield Farms Company (Milk) Bottling Plant**, 1051 Webster Ave., bet. E. 165th and E. 166th Sts. W side. 1914-1921. **Frank Rooke.**

S10

S12

Though milk is no longer pasteurized or bottled behind this glazed terra-cotta façade, the cows and milk bottles are still visible—in the ornament.

[S12] **1074 Cauldwell Avenue** (house). 1887. **F. T. Camp.**
[S12a] **1076 Cauldwell Avenue** (house). 1892. **Charles C. Churchill.** Both E cor. Boston Rd., S of E. 166th St.

Two gleaming, well-maintained, expansive (for this outlying area) Victorian frame houses preside over a dusty intersection that has seen better days.

S13

[S13] **Second Battery Armory**/also known as 105th Artillery Armory, N.Y. National Guard, 1122 Franklin Ave., NE cor. E. 166th St. 1906-1911. **Charles C. Haight.** Addition, 1926-1928. **Benjamin W. Levitan.**

A dark, red brick fortress with slitlike windows looks down on a steep street of stairs. Together with Hines Park and the façade of St. Augustine's Church, the armory provides the backdrop for an exciting but forgotten urban space. It is the perfect stage for a medieval melodrama or a childhood game of knights in armor.

S14

[S14] **St. Augustine's Church** (Roman Catholic), 1183 Franklin Ave., NW cor. E. 167th St. 1894. **Louis C. Giele.**
[S14a] **St. Augustine's School**, 1176 Franklin Ave., bet. E. 167th and E. 168th Sts. E side. 1904.

Renaissance and Baroque elements are combined in the somber but imposing façade of the church. The parish school across the street to the north is distinguished by glazed blue and white terra-cotta sculpture set into the tympanum of its classical pediment.

[S15] **Morris High School Historic District**, bet. Boston Rd. and Forest Ave. (incl. Jackson Ave.), bet. E. 166th St. and Home St., plus Trinity Ave. SE cor. E. 166th St. [S16] **Trinity Episcopal Church of Morrisania**, 690 E. 166th St., SE cor. Trinity Ave. 1874.

A district of row houses primarily by architect **Warren C. Dickerson**, as well as others by **John H. Lavelle**, **Harry T. Howell**, and **Hugo Auden**. The modest brick church shares its block with neighbors of the same scale. But crowning it all, however, is:

S17

[S17] **Morris High School**, 1110 Boston Rd., NE cor. E. 166th St. 1904. **C. B. J. Snyder.** Auditorium, now **Duncan Hall.**

A powerful, turreted central tower, gabled green copper roof, buff brick, and terra-cotta trim make this a superior model of Public School Gothic and a centerpiece of the neighborhood. When first begun, the school was originally to have been named Peter Cooper High School!

S18

[S18] **1266 and 1270 Boston Road** (houses), bet. E. 168th and E. 169th Sts. at McKinley Sq. E side. ca. 1890.

Somewhat more humble structures than those 3 blocks away on Cauldwell Avenue, these are in the Grant Wood/American Gothic mode, but, in the name of maintenance, much of the original detail has been shorn.

[S19] Originally **Eichler Mansion**/now **Department of Mental Health, Bronx-Lebanon Hospital Center**, Fulton Division, 1285 Fulton Ave., SW cor. E. 169th St. 1890. **De Lemos & Cordes.**

A plethora of riches: yet another residential relic of the 19th century, this time in red brick and terra-cotta. Eichler was a beer magnate—and his mansion sits on the hill—a spot that once looked west to his brewery, located at Third Avenue south of East 169th Street.

[S20] Originally **Temple Adath Israel**, 551 E. 169th St., bet. Fulton and Third Aves. N side. 1889? Altered later.

This modest edifice in banded and arched brickwork is thought by some to be the first synagogue built in the Bronx. It has since served the Puerto Rican community as a Baptist church.

S20

[S21] **Lewis S. Davidson, Sr., Houses, N.Y.C. Housing Authority**, 810 Home St., bet. Union and Prospect Aves. S side. 1150, 1152 Union Ave., bet. E. 167th and Home Sts. E side. 1221 Prospect Ave. W side. 1973. **Paul Rudolph**.

Exposed cast-in-place concrete frames with dark gray, ribbed block infill, these 8-story low-rent apartment buildings are a refreshing change from the monotonous red brick towers previously bestowed upon the city's neighborhoods by the Authority.

[S22] **Engine Company 82, Ladder Company 31, N.Y.C. Fire Department**, 1213 Intervale Ave., NW cor. E. 169th St.

This Roman brick firehouse figured prominently in the 1972 fiction bestseller about fire fighting in the South Bronx, **Dennis Smith**'s *Report from Engine Co. 82.*

S22

[S23] **Walls A.M.E. Zion Church** (African Methodist Episcopal)/ formerly Holy Trinity Lutheran Church/originally Free Magyar Reform Church, 891 Home St., NE cor. Intervale Ave. 1909. **Thompson & Frohling**.

A charmingly conceived tan and red brick church that effectively exploits a triangular peninsula opposite Engine Company 82.

S23

CROTONA PARK

P2

P1

[P1] **Junior High School 98, Bronx, The Herman Ridder Junior High School**, 1619 Boston Rd., SW cor. E. 173rd St. 1929-1931. **Walter C. Martin.** 🔔

Named for the philanthropist who was publisher of the New York *Staats-Zeitung*. On a difficult irregular site the architect has employed a handsome multifaceted tower as a focal point for the limestone-clad building. A late-blooming blend of Beaux Arts classicism and Art Deco.

[P2] **Charlotte Gardens** (houses), along the spine of Charlotte St. and Louis Nine Blvd. (formerly Wilkins Ave.) radiating out toward Crotona Park, Minford Place, and E. 170th St. **Edward J. Logue**, governmental developer.

This is the center of the notorious South Bronx, something of a geographical misnomer. **President Jimmy Carter** made Charlotte Street a rallying point when, on a personal visit in October 1977 amid the burned-out hulks of 5- and 6-story apartments, he called for reconstruction, as **Churchill** did after London's blitz. The reconstruction, these 1½-story ticky-tacky suburban dwellings, with aspiring trees, reveals another kind of destruction: that of valuable, close-in, urban land through underutilization. Silly.

[P3] **553-557 Claremont Parkway** (rowhouses), NW cor. Fulton Ave. 1990s.

One of the more sophisticated examples of infill row housing. The checkerboard tile façade and arched parapets seem elegant in contrast to the tacky projects stuffed into the 1990s Bronx streetscape.

[P4] **Crotona Park**, Fulton, Third, E. Tremont, and Arthur Aves., Crotona Park North, East, and South, and a small jog to Southern Blvd. and E. 175th St. Reconstructed, 1936.

Formerly the estate of the **Bathgate** family (for whom the nearby avenue was named—and you thought **Billy Bathgate**, **E.L. Doctorow**'s eponymous hero, was a made-up name?) Crotona Park is one of six sites for parks selected by a citizens' committee in 1883. Named for Croton, an ancient Greek city renowned as the home of many Olympic champions, the park contains a vast array of sports facilities that are in sad disarray today.

P3

CROTONA PARK DISTRICT

see pages 562-563

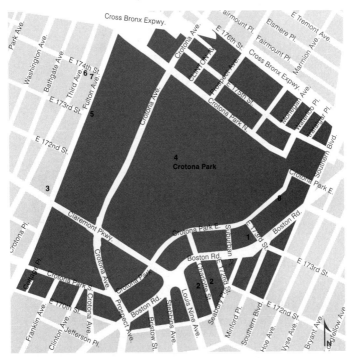

[P5] **Crotona Play Center, N.Y.C. Department of Parks & Recreation**, in Crotona Park, Fulton Ave. at E. 173th St. E side. 1936. **N.Y.C. Parks Department** and **Aymar Embury II**.

The best and, at least to the eye, the most enduring facility is the play center (actually a bathhouse and swimming pool), one of the great redbrick WPA structures of the 1930s. Its crowning clerestories give it a still avant-garde quality.

[P6] **Technical Center, Bathgate Industrial Park**, Third Ave. SE cor. E. 174th St. 1987. **Port Authority of N.Y. & N.J. Architectural Design Team**.

The most notable structure of an industrial park bounded by the Cross-Bronx Expressway, Claremont Parkway, Washington and Fulton Avenues: striped block and an arch make a humble but effective effort.

P5

[P7] **Public School 171**, SW cor. 174th St. and Fulton Ave. 1990s.

An elegantly detailed but understated and thoughtful school building. It is appropriate background architecture.

[P8] **Crotona Terrace** (apartments), 1714 Crotona Park E. bet. E. 173rd and E. 174th Sts. 1994. **Liebman Melting**.

Polychromatic neo-Art Deco. A handsome reminiscence that fits in well with its venerable Art Deco neighbors.

P8

L1

LONGWOOD

[L1] **Longwood Historic District**, parts of Macy Place, Hewitt Place, Dawson, Kelly, Beck, and E. 156th Sts., bet. Prospect Ave. and Fox St., from Leggett to Longwood Aves. 1898-1901. 🖌

Largely an enclave of intact masonry row houses, complete with stoops, wrought-iron railings, and magnificent brownstone embellishments, developed by **George B. Johnson** and designed primarily by architect **Warren C. Dickerson**.

[L2] Formerly **The Martinique Club**/sometime Longwood Club/originally Samuel B. White House, 974 E. 156th St., SE cor. Beck St. ca. 1850. ⌀

Turned at an angle to today's street grid, this ruined country house has seen a long series of adaptive reuses. Will the landmark district help its future?

L3

[L3] **United Church**/originally Montefiore Hebrew Congregation, 764 Hewitt Place, bet. 156th St. and Longwood Ave. E side. 1906. **Daumer & Co.** ⌀

This sturdy Romanesque-arched sanctuary smiles down its one-block axis, Macy Place, toward busy, noisy Prospect Avenue, one of Hunts Point's main drags. Originally a synagogue patterned after the Eastern European model, it nevertheless was crowned with twin onion domes! Today, reflecting ethnic and religious shifts in the community, a crucifix occupies the space between the domes.

L4

[L4] **Engine Company 73, N.Y.C. Fire Department**, 655 Prospect Ave., NW cor. E. 152nd St. 1900. **Horgan & Slattery**.

A mini-Beaux Arts/Baroque municipal outpost.

[L5] **711, 713, 715 Prospect Ave**. (houses), bet. E. 155th and E. 156th Sts. W side. ca. 1885.

A once wonderful trio (now somewhat bedraggled) in a marvelously eclectic block.

L6

[L6] **41st Precinct, N.Y.C. Police Department**, 1035 Longwood Ave., bet. Bruckner and Southern Blvds. N side. 1990s.

A Post-Modern collage of gathered forms.

LONGWOOD & HUNTS POINT

see pages 564-566

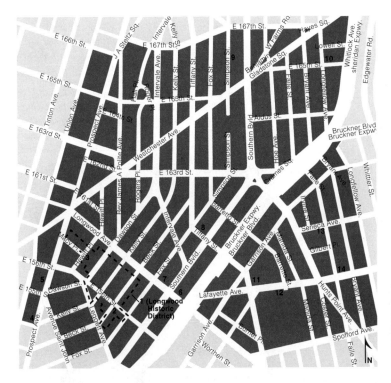

L7

L9

[L7] **Police Athletic League Bronx Community Center,** 991 Longwood Ave., bet. Southern Blvd. and Fox St. 1996. **Kevin Hom & Andrew Goldman.**

Gym/auditorium, boxing ring, fitness center, and game room: all conjoin to keep the young citizen off the street in a playful multicolored complex.

[L8] **Hunts Point Branch, N.Y. Public Library,** 877 Southern Blvd. NW cor. Tiffany St. 1928. **Carrère & Hastings.**

The architects of the public library in Manhattan here tried their hand on a modest branch with brilliant success: a knockoff of Brunelleschi's Ospedale degli Innocenti in Florence. The arcade of brick arches is memorable.

[L9] Formerly **41st Precinct, N.Y.C. Police Department/** originally 62nd Precinct/also known as The Simpson Street Station, 1086 Simpson St., bet. Westchester Ave. and E. 167th St. E side. 1914. **Hazzard, Erskine & Blagdon.** ◖ Restored, 1997. **Cabrera Barricklo Architects.**

An Italian palazzo—note those massive stone voussoirs radiating out from the entranceway—once (and, happily, briefly) standing in not-so-splendid isolation. This was the real Fort Apache. The new houses across the street now belie that bad reputation.

[L10] **Longfellow Gardens,** Longfellow Ave. bet. E. 165th St. and Lowell St. E side. 1983. **Weintraub & di Domenico.**

A bottle-columned pergola, set within a handsomely fenced space, provides visual relief and material relaxation from everyday toil.

HUNTS POINT

[L11] Originally **American Bank Note Company** (factory), Lafayette Ave. NE cor. Tiffany St. 1911. **Kirby, Petit & Green**.

The peninsular portion of the Hunts Point community is separated from the rest of the South Bronx not by a waterway but by a deep railroad cut, once the tracks of the New York, New Haven & Hartford, and by the massive elevated Bruckner Expressway. Guarding a main entry to the "peninsula" is this dark and spare Roman Revival masonry fortress, which once served to guard its own valuable contents as well. Printed within were billions of pesos, cruzeiros, colóns, sucres, and gourdes for Mexico, Brazil, Costa Rica, Ecuador, and Haiti, respectively, stock certificates, travelers' checks, and even lottery tickets.

L11

[L12] **Corpus Christi Monastery**, 1230 Lafayette Ave., at Baretto St. E side. 1890. **William Schickel**.

The best time to visit this cloistered community of Dominican nuns is on Sunday afternoon, when they sing their office. The church, with its beautiful polished mosaic floor, bare walls, and scores of candles, is then fully lighted.

[L13] **Engine Company 94, Hook & Ladder Company 48, N.Y.C. Fire Department**, 1226 Seneca Ave., SW cor. Faile St. ca. 1925.

An open-air roof gallery and colorful terra-cotta shields embellish this Renaissance Revival firehouse.

L13

[L14] **Bright Temple A.M.E. Church** (African Methodist Episcopal)/formerly Temple Beth Elohim (synagogue)/ originally **Peter A. Hoe House, "Sunnyslope,"** 812 Faile St., NE cor. Lafayette Ave. ca. 1860. Converted to synagogue, 1919. ●

This picturesque gray stone Gothic Revival mansion stands askew to today's street grid. It once shared a large estate with the now demolished "Brightside," the frame country house of **Col. Richard M. Hoe**, the famed inventor of the rotary printing press. (Peter was his younger brother.) The design was inspired by published designs of **Calvert Vaux**.

L14

TWIN PARKS WEST/TREMONT • FORDHAM
BELMONT • TWIN PARKS EAST
WEST FARMS • BRONX ZOO
NEW YORK BOTANICAL GARDEN

The Central Bronx includes the Bronx Zoo, the New York
Botanical Garden, Fordham University, and the district encompassing the Webster Avenue corridor on the west and the Bronx
River area on the east. Its south boundary is the gash of the
Cross-Bronx Expressway. Within this area can be found a great
variety of flora, fauna, land uses, housing types, and building
conditions. Institutions of world prominence are within sight of
humble and exotic neighborhood establishments. Long-forgotten
landmarks lie close to excellent new community structures that
may one day become landmarks for future generations.

TWIN PARKS WEST/TREMONT

The twin parks referred to in the urban renewal catch phrase are
Bronx and Crotona, which very roughly bracket, on the north
and south, this geographic area of the Bronx. In 1966-1967, when
renovation of existing housing stock was unfashionable and
building economics had not made arson and abandonment the
way of life in multistory communities such as this, a scattered site,
infill-housing location study was financed by the J. M. Kaplan
Fund. The results, translated into architecture by talented and
mostly young architects, form more than twenty projects scattered along the east and west flanks of a mile-square area. They
are a model of governmentally influenced urban design and
notable low- and moderate-income high-rise apartment architecture as well. Sponsors included the N.Y.C. Educational
Construction Fund (ECF), the N.Y.C. Housing Authority
(NYCHA), and—most significant and influential of all—the
N.Y.S. Urban Development Corporation (UDC). While Twin
Parks projects were on their way up, however, much of the rest of
Tremont and East Tremont went down. Since then, infill housing
has erased and replaced much of the scarred local landscape.

[C1] **1880 Valentine Avenue** (apartments), bet. Webster
Ave. and E. 178th St. E side. (Twin Parks project) 1973.
Giovanni Pasanella.
  On a seemingly unbuildable narrow triangle commanding
the undisciplined open space of a complicated street intersection and a hilly green ether once called Echo Park is this brilliant solution to a difficult problem. Stepping its way hither and
yon and up is this dark red, oversized-brick-clad UDC building
for elderly tenants.

[C2] **1985 Webster Avenue** (apartments), bet. E. 178th
and E. 180th Sts. W side. [C3] **2000 Valentine Avenue
Apartments**, bet. E. 178th and E. 180th Sts. E side. [C4] **2100
Tiebout Avenue Apartments**, NE cor. E. 180th St. (Twin Parks
project.) 1973. **Giovanni Pasanella**.
  The most controversial buildings in Twin Parks: 1) Elevators
service duplex split-level apartments by stopping every 2½
floors, thus eliminating 60% of the normal corridors and creating many very livable floor-through apartments—but at the
same time irritating the buildings' contractors, who were out for
profits, not challenges. 2) The buildings are powerful sculptural
statements, their dark red brick walls adding to their assertive-
ness. 3) A number of details were overlooked: the most glaring,
a meaningful handling of the open space between the Webster
and Valentine Avenue buildings.

 Colonial

 Georgian/ Federal

 Greek Revival

 Gothic Revival

 Villa

 Romanesque Revival

 Renaissance Revival

 Roman Revival

 Art Deco/ Art Moderne

  Modern/ Post-Modern

C1

C3

TWIN PARKS WEST / TREMONT DISTRICT

see pages 567-569

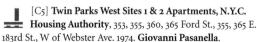

[C5] **Twin Parks West Sites 1 & 2 Apartments, N.Y.C. Housing Authority**, 353, 355, 360, 365 Ford St., 355, 365 E. 183rd St., W of Webster Ave. 1974. **Giovanni Pasanella**.

Though these low-income projects utilize the same skip-stop elevator concept as the Pasanella-designed UDC apartment buildings a few blocks to the south, they are less self-assertive. A bit more conventional.

[C6] **Patrolman Andrew F. Giannone-Webster Community Center, Police Athletic League**, 2255 Webster Ave., NW cor. Ford St. (Twin Parks project.) 1974. **Smotrich & Platt**.

With a name that is almost longer than the building, this is a refreshingly disarming small-scale community amenity built by UDC.

C6

[C7] **333 East 181st Street** (apartments), at Crane Sq., Tiebout Ave., and Folin St. E side. (Twin Parks project.) 1973. **Prentice & Chan, Ohlhausen**, architects. **R. T. Schnadelbach**, landscape architect.

Given a complex program of studio-to 5-bedroom apartments by their client (UDC) and a cliffside site that had always served as a natural line of demarcation between two neighborhoods, these architects tackled both problems head on. Elimination of an elevator corridor on every third floor and the use of duplex apartments (resulting in lyrical window patterns

C7

on the two main façades) were the responses to the problems posed by the program.

[C8] **Intermediate School 137, Bronx, The Angelo Patri School**, 2225 Webster Ave., bet. Folin St. and E. 181st St. W side. (Twin Parks project.) 1975. **The Architects Collaborative.**

Named for educational philosopher **Angelo Patri**, a hero in the nearby Italian-American community (he was principal of P. S. 45, Bronx), this exuberant concrete structure made one wonder what was ever wrong with public schools.

C8

[C9] **355, 365 East 184th Street** (apartments), bet. Marion and Webster Aves. N side. 1973. **Prentice & Chan, Ohlhausen**, architects. **R. T. Schnadelbach**, landscape architect.

Tackling another rough site, this architect/landscape architect team created a strong site plan, a sunken courtyard embraced by continuous brickwalled apartment blocks with smooth, serene window patterns.

FORDHAM, BELMONT & TWIN PARKS EAST

[F1] **Fordham University, Rose Hill Campus**, generally E of Webster Ave., N of E. Fordham Rd., S and W of Dr. Theo Kazimiroff Blvd.

[F2] **Administration Building**/central part formerly Horatio Shepheard Moat House, Rose Hill. 1836-1838. Additions, 1907. 🖋

[F3] **University Chapel**/originally St. John's Church/officially Our Lady, Mediatrix of All Graces, 1841-1845, **William Rodrigue**. Transept, chancel, crossing, and lantern added, 1928-1929. **Emile Perrot**. 🖋

[F4] **St. John's Residence Hall**, 1841-1845, **William Rodrigue**. 🖋

[F5] **Thebaud Hall**/originally Science Hall, 1886, **Eugene Kelly**.

[F6] **Keating Hall**, 1936, **Robert J. Reiley**.

[F7] Alumni House/now **Fordham University Housing office**. ca. 1840. **William Rodrigue**. 🖋

A Jesuit institution since 1846, the university began as St. John's College in 1841, founded by the **Right Reverend John Hughes** (later New York's first Catholic archbishop) and guided initially by its first president, **John McCloskey** (later America's first cardinal). Hughes commissioned his brother-in-law, **William Rodrigue**, to design a residence hall and church for the fledgling institution to accompany the already existing Rose Hill Manor House—for which this campus is named. Later Rodrigue associated with **James Renwick, Jr.**, in the design of the new St. Patrick's Cathedral, which upon completion was dedicated by then Cardinal McCloskey. (Detect a closeness here?)

Fordham derived its present name in 1905 from that of the old manor, later village, of Fordham—not the other way around, as some well-meaning community people would have you believe. The campus's physical presence, along heavily traveled East Fordham Road, is very strong. Mature trees, dense shrubs, brilliantly green lawns, and a group of harmonious gray stone Collegiate Gothic buildings (built mostly from designs by architect **Emile G. Perrot** between 1911 and 1930) offer a distinguished contrast to the tacky commercial architecture adjacent to the campus. The best of Fordham's buildings, save the early Manor House, a rough-stone country-style Greek Revival masterpiece, is the last in the Collegiate Gothic style, Keating Hall.

Two literary tales relate to the campus. It is said that the 98 acres were the setting for **James Fenimore Cooper**'s novel, *The Spy*. And it is also said that the bell in the University Church (appropriately dubbed "Old Edgar") was the inspiration for **Poe**'s poem, *The Bell* (he lived nearby).

[F8] **Fordham Plaza** (office building), 1 Fordham Plaza, E. Fordham Rd. SE cor. Third Ave. to Washington Ave. and E. 189th St. 1986. **Skidmore, Owings & Merrill**.

Fordham Plaza, long an ill-defined purgatory for pedestrians, has now been graced with some thoughtful paraphernalia for bus travel cum shops. The glitzy ziggurat on the east corner is banal at street level, bizarre from afar.

F8

BELMONT

The Bronx's Little Italy: The fork in the street grid where Crescent Avenue diverges from East 187th Street (just a few blocks southeast of Fordham University) provides a space which, straight out of the Mediterranean tradition, has fostered a great marketplace for the cohesive Italian-American community of Belmont. Along East 187th Street, past Belmont Avenue and the area's religious and social rallying point, Our Lady of Mt. Carmel Roman Catholic Church, and into busy, colorful Arthur Avenue, you will

FORDHAM, BELMONT & TWIN PARKS EAST DISTRICT
see pages 570-572

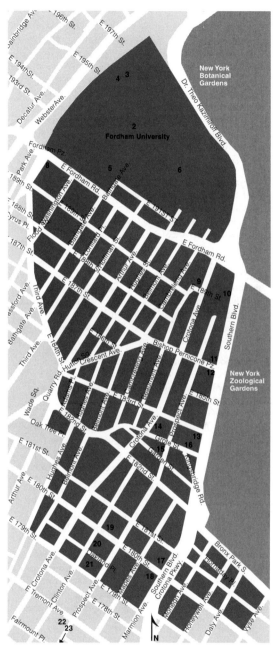

find a multitude of small retail shops resembling those which were once the mainstay of New York's streets. Long may they prosper here! Freshly baked Italian breads, salami, and olive oil. Latticini freschi, fresh fish, and clams on the half shell from a common plate served on a wooden sidewalk stand (with unlimited lemons). Drop into the European-feeling New York City Retail Market, a Fiorello La Guardia morality gesture of 1940 that removed Arthur Avenue's pushcart peddlers but, thankfully, not the street life. It's all worth an extra special good weather visit . . . every day but Sunday, of course.

F9

F10

F13

F21

F23

[F9] **2841 Crotona Avenue** (former residence), NW cor. E. 189th St. ca. 1900.

Hidden behind Keith Plaza is the shell of this old house, a stalwart stone symbol of wealth antedating Twin Parks and now partly concealed by humdrum hamburgers.

[F10] **Keith Plaza** (apartments)/**Public School 205A, Bronx** (grades 1-4), 2475 Southern Blvd., bet. E. Fordham Rd. and E. 187th St. W side. [F11] **Kelly Towers North Apartments**, 2405 Southern Blvd., NW cor. E. 187th St. [F12] **Kelly Towers South Apartments/Public School 205B, Bronx** (early childhood center), 2375 Southern Blvd., SW cor. E. 187th St. (Twin Parks projects.) 1975. **Giovanni Pasanella**.

Keith Plaza, the graceful, 30-story slab at the north end of this trio, acts as a pylon to mark an important gateway into the community, close to the point where busy East Fordham Road (U.S. 1) crosses Southern Boulevard.

[F13] **2311 Southern Boulevard**, 760 East 183rd Street (apartments), SW cor. [F14] **2260 Crotona Avenue** (apartments), bet. E. 183rd and Grote Sts. E side. [F15] **725, 735 Garden Street** (apartments), bet. Prospect and Crotona Aves. N side. (Twin Parks projects.) **Richard Meier & Assocs**. 1974. [F16] A house (Grote Street) in the existing neighborhood.

The lower two of these three dark red, oversized-brick-clad, UDC-sponsored buildings are more successful than other Twin Parks projects in admitting that the neighborhood preexisted it. The chain-link fencing added later under the buildings is, on the other hand, hard to miss . . . and regrettable.

The Grote Street house shows what was here, and what was lost in this "urban renewal" event.

[F17] **2111 Southern Boulevard** (apartments), NW cor. E. 180th St. [F18] **800, 820 East 180th Street** (apartments), SW cor. Southern Blvd. (Twin Parks projects.) 1973. **James Stewart Polshek & Assocs**.

Sponsored by UDC, these (and not Keith Plaza) were intended to be the "urban designer" gateway to Twin Parks from the east. They fail to live up to the intention despite the brash two-dimensional, black-on-tan striping of the brickwork on both the 31-story tower and its 9-story neighbor to the south.

[F19] **730 Oakland Place** (apartments). [F20] **750 East 179th Street** (apartments). [F21] **740 East 178th Street** (apartments), all bet. Prospect and Clinton Aves. All S side. (Twin Parks projects.) 1974. **Skidmore, Owings & Merrill**.

Crisp, modular, precast-concrete, 16-story rectangular prisms with crisp, modular, precast-concrete balconies. Spiffy—but what have these to do with life in the Bronx, or anywhere for that matter? Precast in sections a few miles away, the buildings were erected here as one of UDC's experimental HUD-aided Operation Breakthrough projects (experiments in prefabricated construction).

[F22] **Intermediate School 193, Bronx, The Whitney M. Young, Jr., School**, 1919 Prospect Ave., bet. E. 176th St. and E. Tremont Ave. W side. 1975. **William A. Hall & Assocs**.

A brick monolith that inserts a stable physical touchpoint into a deteriorated neighborhood.

[F23] **Department of Sanitation District 6 Garage**, E. 176th St., bet. Prospect and Marmion Aves. S side. 1990s.

A bold brick presence masking a fleet of garbage trucks. A handsome civic addition to the neighborhood.

WEST FARMS

[W1] Intermediate School 167, Bronx, The Lorraine Hansberry School, 1970 West Farms Rd., SE cor. E. Tremont Ave. 1973. **Max O. Urbahn Assocs.**

A cast-concrete structural frame and dark, rough-ribbed concrete block infill achieves their neat and dramatic geometry. Its site was once that of the Bronx Bleachery, an industry well-remembered because of its negative impact upon the purity of the adjacent Bronx River.

W1

[W2] **Circle Missions, Inc.**/former Peabody Home, 2064 Boston Rd., NE cor. E. 179th St. 1901. **E. A. Sargent**.

Across from the Lambert Houses and in the shadow of the IRT elevated lumbering overhead, this fine red brick Tudor Gothic building adds a syncopated note to the area.

[W3] Lambert Houses (apartments), Shopping Plaza, and Parking Garage, along Boston Rd. bet. Bronx Park S. and E. Tremont Ave. 1973. **Davis, Brody & Assocs.**, architects; **A. E. Bye Assocs.**, landscape architects.

These distinctive sawtooth-plan apartment, shopping, and parking structures south of Bronx Park were commissioned by Phipps Houses, a nonprofit foundation concerned with building better housing in the city. First-rate.

W3

[W4] **Old West Farms Soldiers' Cemetery**, 2103 Bryant Ave. (now a pedestrian walk), NE cor. E. 180th St. 1815 to now. 🖤

Forty veterans of four wars lie in repose amid trees and shrubs in this oasis of calm adjacent to the west edge of Lambert Houses: tombstones of soldiers from the War of 1812, the Civil War, the Spanish-American War, and World War I may be seen through the fence surrounding this ⅔-acre site.

[W5] **Beck Memorial Presbyterian Church**, 980 E. 180th St., bet. Vyse and Bryant Aves. S side. 1903.

A somber stone sentinel (capped with a terra-cotta-clad tower) overlooks the old cemetery across the street.

W5

WEST FARMS DISTRICT
see pages 573-574

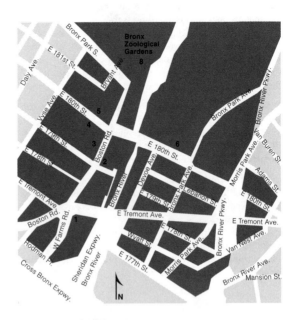

Across the Bronx River to the east:

[W6] **Fire Alarm and Telegraph Bureau, N.Y.C. Fire Department**, 1129 E. 180th St., bet. Devoe and Bronx Park Aves. N side. 1923.

A buff-brick Italian Renaissance Revival structure dedicated to housing the high tech of the 1920s. The ghost of **Brunelleschi** strikes again.

[W7] Originally New York, Westchester & Boston Railway Company Administration Building/now **entrance to E. 180th Street Station of the IRT Dyre Avenue Subway** (Nos. 2 and 5 trains), 481 Morris Park Ave., NW cor. E. 180th St. 1910-1912. **Fellheimer & Long, Allen H. Stem**, associated. 🍎

The Italian Villa style for a railroad that never made it. The N.Y., W. & B. was to have been a suburban line that would glamorously and swiftly transport commuters to the suburbs developing around White Plains and Port Chester prior to World War I; the picturesque architecture was to set the tone. It finally failed in 1937. The N.Y.C. Transit Authority still uses some of the city route.

W6

W7

BRONX ZOO

[W8] **The Wildlife Conservation Society/Bronx Zoo**/formerly New York Zoological Park, Bronx Park S of E. Fordham Rd. Founded, 1895. Opened in 1899. Original architects, **Heins & La Farge**. Open to the public. 718-367-1010. Apr-Oct: Mon-Fri, 10-5; Sat, Sun, Hol, 10-5:30. Nov-Mar: 10-4:30.

At the Bronx Zoo's opening ceremonies, visitors were officially welcomed not to one of the "small closed zoological gardens of Europe" but to "a free Park, projected upon a scale larger than has ever been a tempted before." By today's standards its 252 acres are cramped in comparison to more modern and expansive zoos in other cities. And though the zoo is "free" in the sense of rambling meadows, pastures, and dusty plains, rising costs have severely limited the times when admission is gratis.

Nevertheless, the Bronx Zoo is the largest of the city's five zoos—though privately run it occupies city parkland and receives a municipal subsidy—and is the most ambitious in both concept and execution. The area is divided into basically two parts. At the north end is Baird Court, a large space around whose grassy plots and sea lion pool are formally arrayed many of the zoo's original buildings. This part is more like a zoological garden, with indoor and outdoor caged species and a pavilion housing animal heads and horns, trophies of some of the naturalist-hunter founders. The remainder of the zoo's acreage is devoted, more or less, to a more naturalistic zoological park culminating in moated exhibitions, the African Plains, and the forest along the Bronx River displaying the wildlife of Asia. To shorten walking distances between all these places the management introduced an aerial "Skyfari" and a monorail people-mover in the Asian area.

[W8a] **Jungle World/Tropical Asia Rain Forest**, 1985. **Herbert W. Riemer**.

An exotic structure that suggests the mysteries of the fauna of Asia and then helps to remove some of them, partly through a motorized outdoor trip, labeled Bengali Express, through the Wild Asia grounds. For those old enough to remember, General Motors pioneered this kind of trip (through a city of tomorrow) at the 1939-1940 World's Fair.

[W8b] **The African Plains**, near the Boston Rd. zoo entrance. 1941. **Harrison & Fouilhoux**, architects. **Harry Sweeney**, designer.

Moats rather than bars protect the public from the lions, while other moats protect the other animals of the savannah from both lions and visitors. Full-size replicas of indigenous buildings attempt to re-create an African landscape in the Bronx. Notable as an early effort to make more natural the visual relationship between animals and visitors.

[W8c] **Carter Giraffe Building**. 1982. **Harold Buttrick & Assocs**.

Twenty-one feet high and a replacement for the original, which dated from 1908. When it opened, the *New York Times* said it looked "more like a Columbus Avenue bar than a zoo space." See for yourself. And giraffes are among nature's greatest wonders.

[W8d] **Aquatic Bird House**. 1964. **Goldstone & Dearborn**. [W8e] **The World of Darkness**. 1969. **Morris Ketchum, Jr., & Assocs**. [W8f] **The World of Birds**. 1972. **Morris Ketchum, Jr., & Assocs**.

Three works of modern architecture of the 1960s-1970s can be found in the zoo: the Aquatic Bird House; the World of Darkness, a windowless building that reverses day and night for the visitor in order to display cave-dwelling and nocturnal animals, and the World of Birds, the most effective of the three. This display of some 550 birds in 25 different habitats is a plastic, flowing composition of rounded, roughfaced concrete-block forms dramatically illuminated within by skylights. Visitors walk in rooms with birds, not on the other side of grilles separated from them . . . it makes a lot of difference.

W8f

[W8g] **Russell B. Aitken Seabird Aviary, Wildlife Conservation Society**. 1998. **FTL/Happold**.

Double-curved arches receive the almost invisible mesh drapery for this outdoor space for seabirds.

[W8h] **Paul J. Rainey Memorial Gates**. 1929-1934. **Paul Manship**, sculptor; **Charles A. Platt**, architect of gate lodges and gateposts. 🍎
[W8i] **Rockefeller Fountain**. 1910. **Heins & Lafarge**. 🍎 Both at E. Fordham Rd. entrance.

Manship's beautifully scaled Art Deco-inspired bronze gates, a gift of **Grace Rainey Rogers** (they are dedicated to her brother) open upon an earlier, handsomely detailed Italian garden. In the center of the driveway's turnaround is an early 18th-century Italian fountain picked up near Lake Como by benefactor **William Rockefeller**, **John D. Sr**.'s brother.

W8h

[W8j] **Baird Court**: [W8k] **Lion House**. 1903. [W8l] **Primate House**. 1901. [W8m] **Administration Building**. 1910. [W8n] **Main Bird House**. 1905. [W8o] **Elephant House**. 1911. **Heins & La Farge**. [W8p] **Heads and Horns Building**. 1922. **Henry D. Whitfield**. All surround Baird Court. **H. A. Caparn**, landscape architect.

The zoo's formal Baird Court was a direct outgrowth of the City Beautiful precepts of the World's Columbian Exposition of 1893. It was a controversial afterthought to what had been a desire to treat the zoo grounds as a naturalistic park. The elephant house, a classical palace with a Byzantine interior, a high dome, and terra-cotta decoration, could serve as capitol of a banana republic.

NEW YORK BOTANICAL GARDEN

[B1] **New York Botanical Garden**, Bronx Park, N of E. Fordham Rd. Site, 1895. **Calvert Vaux** and **Samuel Parsons, Jr**. Open to the public. 718-817-8500. Apr-Oct: Tues-Sun, 10-6; closed Mon. Nov-Mar: Tues-Sun, 10-4; closed Mon.

The Botanical Garden, incorporated in 1891 and patterned after the Royal Botanical Gardens at Kew, England, is one of the world's leading institutions of its kind. Its scientific facilities include a conservatory, museum, library, herbarium (a collection of dried plants), research laboratory, and a variety of groves and gardens. The selection of this site within Bronx Park, as recommended by Vaux and Parsons, enables the garden to perform a second valuable function: it contains and preserves the beautiful gorge of the Bronx River, a virgin hemlock forest, and some of the historic buildings that were here before the park was created.

B2

[B2] Originally Conservatory Range/now **Enid Annenberg Haupt Conservatory**, 1896-1902. **William R. Cobb** for **Lord & Burnham**, greenhouse manufacturers. Altered, 1938, 1953. Restored, 1978, **Edward Larrabee Barnes & Assocs.**, architects. Reconstruction, 1997. **Beyer Blinder Belle**. ☙

A great group of greenhouses in the tradition of **Decimus Burton**'s Great Palm House at Kew and **Joseph Paxton**'s Crystal Palace. In 1978, after many years of deterioration had threatened the glass fairyland and its wide-ranging plant species, restoration stemmed the decline. And in 1997 a complete reconstruction was accomplished, replacing the delicate wooden skeleton with one of aluminum. The **Lord & Burnham** image was, therefore, preserved.

[B3] **Garden Café and Terrace Room**. 1997. **Cooper Robertson & Assocs**.
A squatty neo-Georgian pavilion provides dining and catering facilities for the Garden's friends and patrons.

 [B4] **Children's Adventure Garden Discovery Center**, 1998. **Richard Dattner**, architect. **Miceli Kulik Williams**, landscape architects.
Tree-trunk columns and an eyebrow-windowed, shingle roof shelter exposed ductwork serving exhibitions, laboratories, and offices.

B5

[B5] **Museum Building**. 1902. **Robert W. Gibson**. Addition, 1973.
[B6] **Plant Studies Center**. 1999. **Polshek Partnership**.
Three contrasting works in purpose, scale, design, and age share a formal axis near the original main entrance to the garden. The Polshek Plant Studies Center is an elegant, low-key annex that is the external expression of a total renovation of the parent Museum Building to which it's attached.

B6

[B7] Old Lorillard Snuff Mill/now **Snuff Mill River Terrace Café**. ca. 1840. Restored, 1954. ●᛫
This building, together with a later gatehouse and stables, is the only improvement that remains from the extensive local landholdings of the **Lorillards**, a family whose name is still associated with the tobacco industry. Built of local fieldstone, the mill once used the adjacent waters as power to grind snuff, a tobacco product more popular in the 19th century than it is today. Fortunately the mill building, a fine example of local industrial architecture, was adapted into a public snack bar (open summer months only), and its new terrace is a lovely place to nibble to the bubbly sounds of the adjacent river.

The Bronx River Gorge: Just north of the snuff mill is an arched stone footbridge, a great spot from which to view the gorge of the Bronx River and the turbulent waters that carved it over the millennia. It is yet another surprising event in a city filled with them. The nearby hemlock forest is the last remaining part of a stand of trees that once covered much of New York City.

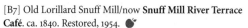

THE GRAND CONCOURSE • HIGHBRIDGE HEIGHTS
UNIVERSITY HEIGHTS • KINGSBRIDGE HEIGHTS
KINGSBRIDGE • MARBLE HILL
BEDFORD PARK • NORWOOD

The West Bronx

The West Bronx is the spot in America, second only to Miami Beach, to see the largest single array of Art Deco- and Art Moderne-inspired ornament on apartments built between 1927 and 1942. An array of housing, schools, parks, hospitals, industries, and public works of social and architectural interest are all located here.

THE GRAND CONCOURSE

The Grand Boulevard and Concourse (as it is officially named, but rarely called), one of the grand thoroughfares of New York, was designed in 1891 by **Louis Risse** as the Speedway Concourse to provide access from Manhattan to the large parks of the "annexed district" of the Bronx. The original design provided separate paths for horse-drawn vehicles, cyclists, and pedestrians, and for grade separation through underpasses at all major intersections.

[W1] **Public School 31, Bronx, The William Lloyd Garrison School**/once temporarily Theodore Roosevelt High School, 425 Grand Concourse, bet. E. 144th and E. 146th Sts. to Walton Ave. W side. 1897-1899. **C. B. J. Snyder.** ●⃕
    Known locally as The Castle on the Concourse because of its Collegiate Gothic style. A run-through for the same architect's later Morris High School.

[W2] **Hostos Community College, CUNY**, Grand Concourse bet. W. 144th and W. 149th Sts. W side. **East Academic Complex**, 1994. **Gwathmey Siegel & Assocs.** and **Sanchez & Figueroa. Allied Health Complex**, 1991. **Voorsanger & Assocs.**[W3] Originally **Security Mutual Insurance Company**, 500 Grand Concourse, SE cor. W. 149th Sts. 1965. **Horace Ginsbern & Assocs.**
    Elegant multicolored brick, a sleek bridge, and a serrated eastern façade participate in this community college jewel. The 1965 Security Mutual building adds a note of history (short, but history) to an instant step into the 1990s.

W1

[W4] **IRT subway junction**, beneath E. 149th St. and Grand Concourse. Lower level, 1904. Upper level, 1917.
    Here two subway stations have been built one below the other, separated by a mezzanine. (The trains on the upper level are marked Woodlawn Road, a nonexistent street.) The lower station, in the Parisian manner, is one large barrel vault. Despite uninspired decoration, poor lighting, and minimal maintenance, this station is one of the exciting spaces of the subway system. On the southwest corner of the intersection above is a former entrance to the station, which bears the name Mott Avenue, the thoroughfare that preceded Grand Concourse in these parts.

W2

[W5] **General Post Office**, The Bronx/originally Bronx Central Annex, U.S. Post Office Department, 558 Grand Concourse, NE cor. E. 149th St. 1935-1937. **Thomas Harlan Ellett**, architect; **Louis A. Simon**, supervising architect. ●⃕
    Chaste gray brick and white marble articulate arches with glazing deeply revealed. A timid building, it has worn well, better than many modern aggressors. There are WPA murals by **Ben Shahn** in the lobby.

W5

[W6] **Cardinal Hayes High School** (Roman Catholic), 650 Grand Concourse, SE cor. E. 153rd St. 1941. **Eggers & Higgins**.

Reticent in uninspired buff brick, the school forms a quarter circle, therefore effectively creating an inviting green forecourt. Building embellishments are modest, but in the Art Deco mode.

Franz Sigel Park: Named for a Civil War general, this craggy park, on the west side of Grand Concourse north of East 153rd Street, is the repository of graffitied concrete "park furniture" installed by overzealous governmental bureaucrats in the early 1970s in the mistaken belief that physical amenities—any amenities—will cure acute social and economic ills.

W6

A Grand Concourse Driving Tour:

Art Deco/Art Moderne and other styles:
The Roaring Twenties gave many families the needed economic lift that allowed them to move from their relatively shabby Manhattan digs to spanking new quarters in outlying places like the Bronx. The IRT Jerome Avenue elevated, running parallel to the Concourse down the hill to the west, had been finished in 1918. By the late 1920s the City was digging a trench down the center of the Grand Concourse to install the northern leg of its own Independent subway, which would open on July 1, 1933, in the depths of the Great Depression. Nevertheless, the subway did connect to Manhattan's business districts, to the Garment Center, and to the reemerging Upper West Side. The convenience was unmistakable, and developers seized the opportunity to buy potential apartment sites along the Concourse deflated in price by the economic downturn.

During the 1930s, the golden age of the Concourse, two Paris expositions were having great effect upon American style. The 1925 Exposition Internationale des Arts Décoratifs et Industriels Modernes had given birth to the ornamentalism of Art Deco; and the 1937 Exposition Internationale des Arts et des Techniques Appliqués à la Vie Moderne evoked the streamlined forms of Art Moderne, which were paralleled in the New York World's Fair of 1939-1940. The former influenced the use of decorative terra-cotta, mosaics, ironwork doors, and etched glass so rampant in the entry and lobbies of West Bronx apartments. The latter gave rise to the use of striped brick patterns, cantilevered corners, steel casement windows and particularly corner windows, and the use of highly stylized letter forms. The amalgam of these styles was concentrated along and near the Bronx's premier boulevard in dozens of 6-story apartments; these and similar works of residential architecture could be characterized as the Concourse Style. Sprinkled between the older dour apartment blocks of the 1920s are the now somewhat (often grimy, sometimes newly scrubbed) gems:

START at Grand Concourse and East 153rd Street. The tour continues north along the entire length of the Concourse with a number of divergences along the way. While on the Concourse use service road except to make left turns, permitted only from center section.

[W7] **730 Grand Concourse** (apartments), bet. E. 153rd and E. 156th Sts. E side. 1939. **Jacob M. Felson**. [W8] **740 Grand Concourse** (apartments), bet. E. 153rd and E. 156th Sts. E side. 1939. **Jacob M. Felson**. [W9] **750 Grand Concourse** (apartments), SE cor. 156th Sts. E side. 1937. **Jacob M. Felson**.

No. 750 is timid despite two colors of brick (which both Nos. 730 and 740 lack).

W9

GRAND CONCOURSE DISTRICT (A)

see pages 578-583

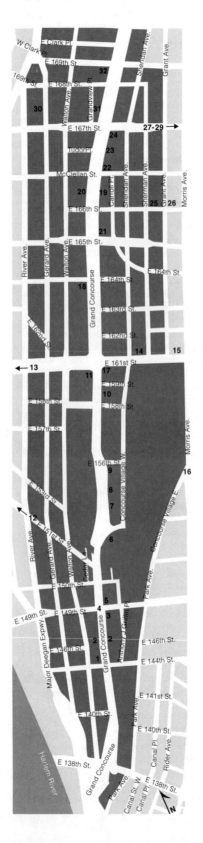

[W10] **Thomas Garden Apartments**, 840 Grand Concourse, bet. E. 158th and E. 159th Sts. E side. 1928. **Andrew J. Thomas**.

A block-square development of 5-story pre-Art Deco walk-up buildings grouped about a westernized Japanese garden in a sunken central court. All of the units are reached through the court by walking past concrete lanterns, a water course, and charming bridges. This project, named for its architect, is one of two [see Manhattan's Dunbar Apartments] designed for **John D. Rockefeller, Jr.**, who hoped to solve the problems of the slums by investing in middle-income housing.

W10

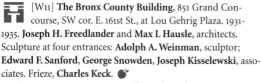

[W11] **The Bronx County Building**, 851 Grand Concourse, SW cor. E. 161st St., at Lou Gehrig Plaza. 1931-1935. **Joseph H. Freedlander** and **Max L Hausle**, architects. Sculpture at four entrances: **Adolph A. Weinman**, sculptor; **Edward F. Sanford**, **George Snowden**, **Joseph Kisselewski**, associates. Frieze, **Charles Keck**. 👌

An enormous, 10-story neo-Classical-Moderne limestone pile whose ponderous form is, luckily, relieved by sleek Moderne sculpture, both in the round and on friezes that beribbon its walls.

W12

Divergences:

[W12] **Bronx House of Detention for Men**/originally Bronx County Jail, 653 River Ave., SW cor. E. 151st St. (W of the Concourse.) 1931. **Joseph H. Freedlander**. Additions.

A curiously handsome high-rise penal institution, by the architect of the nearby Bronx County Building.

W13

[W13] **Yankee Stadium**, E. 161st St. SW cor. River Ave. (W of the Concourse.) 1923. **Osborn Engineering Co**. Rebuilt, 1976, **Praeger-Kavanagh-Waterbury**.

Built by brewery magnate **Colonel Jacob Ruppert** for the team he owned and for its most valuable player, **Babe Ruth** (the short right field helped him to set his home run record). In the early 1970s someone got the idea that the **New York Yankees** were the key to the neighborhood's, the Bronx's, and New York City's economic salvation, and so the whole stadium—as well as acres of adjacent fallow land—were rebuilt at a cost of some $100 million, a sum upon which the city will probably never stop paying interest. There are fewer columns to obstruct vision and many, many more parking spaces, but the adjacent community seems, if anything, to have increased its rate of decay.

Now owner **George Steinbrenner** has triggered a renewed hue and cry for a completely new stadium, perhaps in midtown over the tracks west of the General Post Office.

[W14] **Criminal Court/Family Court, City of New York**, 215 E. 161st St., bet. Sheridan and Sherman Aves. N side. (E of the Concourse.) 1977. **Harrison & Abramovitz**.

If architecture is expressive of the social order, then this bulky structure tells us that justice must be ponderous, rigid, and self-righteous.

W14

[W15] **New Bronx Supreme/Criminal Court Complex**, E. 161st St., bet. Sherman and Morris Aves. 2004. **Rafael Viñoly**.

Viñoly's complement to **Harrison & Ambramovitz**'s 1977 hulk next door. What a difference 27 years will make.

W17

W19

W21

W22

W26

Back to the Concourse:

[W17] **888 Grand Concourse** (apartments), SE cor. E. 161st St. 1937. **Emery Roth**.

A modest effort on an important corner by an architect whose earlier, better designs can still be found along Broadway and Central Park West.

[W18] **The Lorelei Fountain,** Joyce Kilmer Park, Grand Concourse, SW cor. E. 164th St. 1899. **Ernst Herter**, sculptor. Rebuilt and relocated, 1999.

The fountain honors the author of "Die Lorelei," **Heinrich Heine**, whose bas-relief portrait is on the south side of the base. The statue was presented to the city by a group of New Yorkers of German ancestry in 1893 after the sculptor's gift had been rejected by Dusseldorf, Heine's birthplace. The donors wanted it placed at Manhattan's Grand Army Plaza, where the Sherman statue now stands. But Heine's ethnic background—he was both a German and a Jew—together with the statue's questionable artistic merits, made that site unavailable.

[W19] **Bronx Family Court,** 1118 Grand Concourse, bet. E. 166th St. and McClellan St. 1997. **Rafael Viñoly**.

A superb Modernist building that, surprisingly, puts civic architecture in the forefront of this aging Art Deco/Art Moderne community. It flaunts high style, without being stylish.

[W20] **Andrew Freedman Home,** 1125 Grand Concourse, bet. E. 166th and McClellan Sts. 1924. **Joseph H. Freedlander** and **Harry Allan Jacobs**. Wings, 1928-1931. **David Levy**. 🍎

This subdued, gray and yellow limestone palace is French-inspired, but its setting in a garden gives it the air of a large English country house. It is a home for the aged endowed by Freedman, a leading subway contractor and owner of the baseball team that became the N.Y. Giants.

[W21] **The Bronx Museum of the Arts**/originally Young Israel Synagogue, 1040 Grand Concourse, NE cor. E. 165th St. 1961. **Simon B. Zelnik**. Expansion, 1988, **Castro-Blanco, Piscioneri & Feder**. Open to the public. 718-681-6000. Wed-Fri. 10-5; Sat-Sun, 1-6; closed Mon.

Using a vacant post-World War II synagogue building, this modest community museum has brought many intriguing displays of both art and history to the Bronx, utilizing a high level of curatorial skill. It began in the lobby of the Bronx County Building.

[W22] **1150 Grand Concourse** (apartments), NE cor. McClellan St. 1936. **Horace Ginsbern**. [W23] **1166 Grand Concourse** (apartments), bet. McClellan St. and E. 167th St. 1936. **Horace Ginsbern**. [W24] **1188 Grand Concourse** (apartments), SE cor. E. 167th St. 1937. **Jacob M. Felson**.

A full block of now-casementless apartments, No. 1188 impressive with its sawtooth patterns; No. 1150 adorned with mosaics and Moderne doors, rich with shade and shadow from its deeply revealed and canted windows.

More divergence from the Concourse: South on E. 167th Street:

[W25] **1210 Sherman Avenue** (apartments), NE cor. E. 167th St. 1937. **Charles Kreymborg**. [W26] **1212 Grant Avenue** (apartments), NE cor. E. 167th St. 1936. **Horace Ginsbern**.

Two very colorful Art Moderne survivors. Their polychrome brick makes them special.

[W27] **Daughters of Jacob Geriatric Center: Main Building/** formerly Home and Hospital of the Daughters of Jacob, 321 E. 167th St., bet. Findlay and Teller Aves. N side. 1920. **Louis Allen Abramson.** [W28] **Findlay House/Weinstein-Ratner Pavilion,** 1175 Findlay Ave. W side. 1971. **Louis Allen Abramson.** [W29] **Geriatric Center,** 1160 Teller Ave. E side. 1973. **Blumenkranz & Bernhard.**

The ungainly, tall Roman portico that rests against the entrance to the original building was supposed to give it a dignified appearance. It is that building (behind the columns), built as eight radiating-spoked wings set at the end of a generous Italian garden, that is of interest. The radiating plan was common for hospitals (and penitentiaries) always seeking more efficient centralized control.

W27

More divergence from the Concourse: This time, west.

 [W30] **Morrisania Diagnostic and Treatment Center,** 1225-1257 Gerard Ave., bet. E. 167th and E. 168th Sts. W side. (W of the Concourse.) 1973. **Armand Bartos & Assocs.**

A strongly modeled geometric interplay of square brick-veneered modules, across from the abandoned Morrisania Hospital.

[W31] **1227 Grand Concourse** (apartments), bet. E. 167th and E. 168th Sts. W side. ca. 1938.

A narrow little Art Moderne orphan with a vane of masonry at its north end, looking like a movie house sign, but of brick.

[W32] **Grand Concourse Seventh Day Adventist Temple/** originally Temple Adath Israel (synagogue), 1275 Grand Concourse, SW cor. 169th St. 1927.

W32

Predates the Concourse's Deco-Moderne heyday. Dignity here is achieved by restraint: smooth blank walls relieved by sparing use of ornamented neo-Classical columns and pilasters. The incised lettering of the original institution remains, as does the cornerstone.

[W33] Originally **Roosevelt Gardens** (apartments)/later Roosevelt Court, 1455-1499 Grand Concourse, bet. E. 171 stand E. 172nd Sts. to Wythe Place. W side. 1924. Altered, ca. 1986.

Stripped of its original Mission Style details, this once-romantic giant is now a neat but barren visual remnant of the Concourse's discovery by an emerging middle class in the 1920s. The 1980s guard station at the entrance, however, reveals its rediscovery.

 [W34] **1500 Grand Concourse** (apartments), NE cor. E. 172nd St. 1935. **Jacob M. Felson.**

The parapet limestone has been carved into folds, like velvet. Here too the original windows have been replaced since 1988. The glass block and stainless steel entry is wonderful, but in need of TLC.

[W35] **1505 Grand Concourse** (apartments), NW cor. E. 172nd St. 1930s.

W34

This galaxy of cream brick is best appreciated in its side-street series of bayed sub-façades.

[W36] **Bronx-Lebanon Hospital Center, Concourse Division/**originally Lebanon Hospital, 1650 Grand Concourse, NE cor. Mt. Eden Ave. at Chet Henderson Sq. 1942. **Charles B. Meyers.** Expanded, 1991, **Cannon/Mason Da Silva Assocs.**

Monumental, fussy, and out of context.

[W37] **1675 Grand Concourse** (apartments), SW cor. E. 174th St. (street is below the Concourse) through to Walton Ave. 1936. **Jacob M. Felson.**

W37

Poetic, graceful, inlaid designs in contrasting brick colors.

GRAND CONCOURSE DISTRICT (B)

see pages 583-588

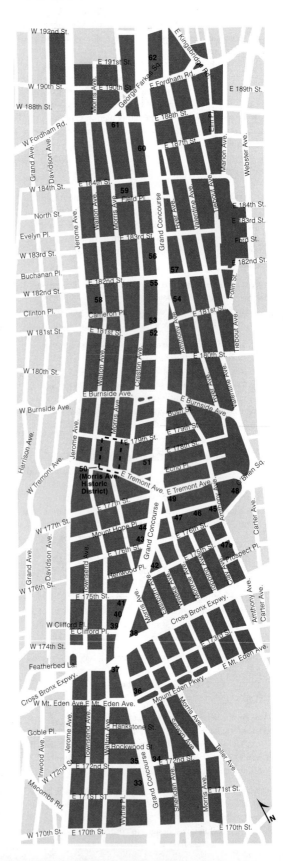

[W38] **1750 Grand Concourse** (apartments), NE cor. Cross-Bronx Expwy. (both below the Concourse). E side. 1937.
Geometric ornament, with steel casements still in place.

[W39] **Lewis Morris Apartments**, 1749 Grand Concourse, NW cor. Clifford Place. (Outdoor public stairway.) 1923. **Edward Raldiris**.
A 13-story West End Avenue high rise. Once the place to live on the Concourse.

W39

[W40] **Bell Telephone Building**, 1775 Grand Concourse, S of the SW cor. E. 175th St. ca. 1923. **McKenzie, Voorhees & Gmelin**.
A curious but bland Florentine palazzo in cream brick and limestone, expanded upward as telephones increased in number.

[W41] **1791 Grand Concourse** (apartments), SW cor. E. 175th St. 1936. **Edward W. Franklin**.
An eccentric site: the bend in the façade gave opportunity for subtle massing that enhanced the marvelous patterned brick spandrels and parapets.

W40

[W42] **Pilgrim United Church of Christ**/originally Christ Congregational Church, 1808 Grand Concourse, NE cor. E. 175th St. 1910. **Hoppin & Koen**.
A strong presence on the Concourse: neo-Georgian front and Hagia Sophia rear (don't miss that low-rise dome!).

[W43] **1835 Grand Concourse** (apartments), NW cor. E. 176th St. 1939. **H. Herbert Lillien**.
Another eccentric site.

[W44] **1855 Grand Concourse** (apartments), SW cor. Mt. Hope Place. 1936. **Thomas Dunn**.
Art Deco pilasters stand between strongly modeled bay windows. Very subtle, oblique, planar modeling.

W42

A brief divergence, downhill to the east:

[W45] Originally **Edwin and Elizabeth M. Shuttleworth House**, 1857 Anthony Ave. SW cor. Mt. Hope Place. 1896. **Neville & Bagge**. 📷
A private residence in the form of a miniature castle of rock-faced gray stone with finely carved limestone trim. Note particularly the modeling of the faces within the circular medallions near the roof. A mimosa tree and other verdant vegetation almost conceal this welcome relic in an otherwise drab area. Shuttleworth, not surprisingly, was a dealer in stone, both plain and carved.

W44

[W46] **250 Mt. Hope Place** (house), bet. Anthony and Monroe Aves. ca. 1890.
A modest neighbor of the Shuttleworths, it still proudly displays Ionic columns on its porch.

[W47] **202-204 Mt. Hope**, SE cor. Monroe Ave. 1880s.
A pair of row house survivors that completes, on this one Mt. Hope block, the range of single-family house styles hereabouts in the late 19th century.

W45

[W47a] **Casa Promesa** (AIDS-related health facility), 308 East 175th St., bet. Anthony and Clay Aves. 1995. **Rogers, Burgun, Shahine and Deschler, Inc**. and **Castro Blanco, Piscioneri & Assocs**.
A palette of Art Deco polychromy acquaints this modest modernist building firmly with the vocabulary of the Grand Concourse, 1990s division.

W48

W50

W52

W53

W57

[W48] **Tremont Towers** (apartments), 333 E. 176th St., NW cor. E. Tremont Ave., opp. Echo Park. 1937. **Jacob M. Felson**.

A grand curved façade slopes downhill from the Concourse.

Return to the Concourse:

[W49] **Mt. Hope Court** (apartments), 1882 Grand Concourse, SE cor. Monroe Ave., at E. Tremont Ave. 1914. **Otto Schwarzler**.

The Bronx's own Flatiron Building, built on a sharply acute-angled site and, for many years, the borough's tallest building, at 10 stories. Predictions that residential elevators would make the Bronx a borough of 10-story structures didn't materialize until the advent of redbrick "projects," beginning with Parkchester.

[W50] **Morris Avenue Historic District**, ♂. **1969-1999 Morris Ave.**, bet. E. Tremont Ave. and E. 179th St.W side. ● **1966-1998 Morris Ave.**, bet. E. Tremont Ave. and E. 179th St. E side. ● **60 and 108 E. 179th St.**, SW and SE cor. Morris Ave. ● 1906-1910. All by **John Hauser**.

A complete row of bowfront, 3-story row houses with wrought-iron detail, stonework, stoops, and cornices largely intact. A refreshing look back at high-quality Bronx urbanism. **August Jacob** was the developer.

[W51] **1939 Grand Concourse** (apartments), SW cor. E. 178th St. ca. 1940.

Art Moderne. One of the zigzag fronts.

[W52] **2121 Grand Concourse** (apartments), SW cor. E. 181st St. 1936. **Horace Ginsbern**.

This zig-zagger is the most stylish on the Concourse. Art Deco at its best, it needed to keep those original steel casement windows and to be delivered from those dreadful plastic store signs. Neither has happened. Note the richly molded gray cast-stone entry around the corner on East 181st.

[W53] **2155 Grand Concourse** (apartments), NW cor. E. 181st St. to Creston Ave. 1939. **H. Herbert Lillien**.

Yet another zigzag façade.

[W54] **2186 Grand Concourse** (apartments), NE cor. Anthony Ave. ca. 1939.

A mediocre cousin to the group above.

[W55] **2195 Grand Concourse** (apartments), SW cor. E. 182 St. 1938.

Neo-Classical sashaying into Art Moderne. Note the original fine ironwork on the entry doors.

[W56] **2255 Grand Concourse** (apartments), bet. E. 182nd and E. 183rd Sts. W side. 1936. **Horace Ginsbern**.

The windows are subtly bows, recessed within a flat façade. Note the three-dimensional, red-and-black granite entry surround. A tailored work.

[W57] **2230 Grand Concourse** (apartments), NE cor. E. 182nd St. (Entry on E. 182nd.) ca. 1937.

Pinstripe orange and brown brick spandrels. The banded, decorative fire escapes are an integral part of the design aesthetic.

[W58] **Engine Co. 75, Ladder Co. 33, Battalion 19**, 2175 Walton Ave., bet. 181st (or Cameron Pl.) and 182nd St. 2000. **Richard Dattner & Associates**.

A sleek new civic presence that provides a statement of progress in this aging neighborhood.

[W59] **Intermediate School 115, Bronx, The Elizabeth Browning School**/formerly Bronx High School of Science/ earlier Evander Childs, Walton, De Witt Clinton High Schools/ originally Public School 9, Bronx, E. 184th St., bet. Creston and Morris Aves. S side. 1915.

Physically, a very ordinary N.Y.C. public school, but this is where the Bronx High School of Science began in 1938 (and where its Nobel Prize-winning scientists were trained). Bronx Science is now in a custom-built structure opened in 1959 north of Lehman College.

[W60] **Loew's Paradise Theater**/now divided into Paradise Twins 1 and 2, 2417 Grand Concourse, bet. E. 184th and E. 188th Sts. W side. 1929. **John Eberson**. 🍎

Stars and clouds made the Paradise special, but its terra-cotta façade on the Concourse is still a bit of neo-Renaissance Fantasy. Inside, it was an extravaganza of ornament, ornament, and more ornament, surmounted by a deep blue ceiling over the auditorium, twinkling stars, and projected moving clouds. Considered by one connoisseur of such things the "most beautiful and elaborate" of Eberson's designs.

W60

[W61] **Creston Avenue Baptist Church**, 114 E. 188th St., bet. Creston and Morris Aves. S side. 1905.

Crushed on both sides by retail shops reaching out for customers in this competitive shopping strip, this playful, castlelike church hangs on.

[W62] **Emigrant Savings Bank**/originally Dollar Savings Bank, 2516-2530 Grand Concourse, bet. Fordham Rd. and E. 192nd St. W side. 1932-1933. **Halsey, McCormack & Helmer**. Additions: Tower, 1937-1938; 1949-1952. 🍎 Interior 🍎

This work, with a great clock, is by the deans of outer-borough bank designers. Their well-known Brooklyn's Williamsburgh Savings Bank tower and others.

W62

[W63] **Poe Cottage**, Poe Park, Grand Concourse SE cor. E. Kingsbridge Rd. ca. 1812. 🍎 Open to the public. 718-881-8900. Sat, 10-4; Sun, 1-5.

The cottage was moved to the park from its original site across Kingsbridge Road in 1913. **Edgar Allan Poe** lived here from 1846 until a few months before his death in 1849. He came here in the hope that the clear country air would aid his ailing young wife. (She died during their first winter in the small house.)

W63

[W64] **2615 Grand Concourse** (apartments), bet. E. 192nd and E. 193rd Sts. W side. 1938. **Charles Kreymborg**.

Plain-Jane Moderne.

[W65] **2665 Grand Concourse** (apartments), NW cor. Kingsbridge Rd. E. 1922. **Margon & Glaser**.
[W66] **Brockman Manor** (apartments), 2701 Grand Concourse, bet. Kingsbridge Rd. E. and E. 196th St. W side. ca. 1927. **H. I. Feldman**. [W67] **McAlpin Court** (apartments), 2825 Grand Concourse, NW cor. E. 197th St. ca. 1927. **H. I. Feldman**.

W65

These three structures are Renaissance Revival in overall style; and the latter two, at only 6 stories, are crowned with very handsome Chicago School cornices, still intact.

[W68] **Town Towers** (apartments), 2830 Grand Concourse, NE cor. E. 197th St. 1931. **Horace Ginsbern**.

Its brick piers and crenellated parapet shimmer hello as thousands drive past it. Take a peek at the spectacular lobby.

[W69] **2910 Grand Concourse** (apartments), bet. E. 198th and E. 199th Sts. E side. ca. 1940.

Beige stone models the entry; corner windows and steel casement remain. Bland.

GRAND CONCOURSE DISTRICT (C)
see pages 587-589

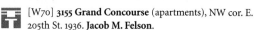   [W70] **3155 Grand Concourse** (apartments), NW cor. E. 205th St. 1936. **Jacob M. Felson**.
    A curious pergola entry and some etched glass in the lobby. Corner casement windows. Two bonuses: the vertically pin-striped spandrels and the original casement windows in much of the building.

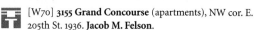   [W71] **Apartment House**, NE cor. 206th St. and St. George's Crescent. 1930s.
    The streamlined rounding of the Art Moderne gives a sensuous series of curvaceous forms to the already curving Crescent.

[W72] **Dornhage** (apartments), 2914 Jerome Ave. [W73] **Edna** (apartments), 2928 Jerome Ave. Both bet. Minerva Place and Bedford Park Blvd. E side. 1936. **William I. Hohauser**.
    Reverse the syllables of Dornhage and you have the client's name, Hagedorn. Art Deco with terrific polychromed terra-cotta.

END of Grand Concourse Driving Tour. But around the corner are:

W71

[W74] **Tracey Towers,** 20 and 40 W. Mosholu Pkwy. S., SW cor. Jerome Ave. 1974. **Paul Rudolph.**

The tallest structures in the Bronx, these two apartment buildings (one 41 stories, the other 38) offer residents phenomenal views in all directions. Similarly, the gray, ribbed-block towers are themselves visible from afar, resembling sand castles with overactive thyroids.

W72

[W75] **High Pumping Station, Jerome Reservoir,** of the former N.Y.C. Department of Water Supply, Gas & Electricity, 3205 Jerome Ave., bet. Van Cortlandt Ave. E. and W. Mosholu Pkwy. S. W side. 1901-1906. **George W. Birdsall.** 🍎

Deceptively simple, this straightforward gabled masonry form in red brick is detailed with consummate skill. The result is a superb example of industrial architecture.

HIGHBRIDGE HEIGHTS

These neighborhoods lie west of Grand Concourse and follow the University Avenue ridge and the Harlem River from Macombs Dam Park below West 161st Street northward to the vicinity of Kingsbridge Road. They contain hundreds of the familiar Bronx apartment houses, older one-family wooden homes, and a variety of institutions, public works, and landmarks, many of national fame and importance. Highbridge, the area south of the Cross-Bronx Expressway, was settled in the 1830s by Irish workers who built the Old Croton Aqueduct and High Bridge, as well as the railroad that soon appeared on the east bank of the Harlem River.

[H1] **Unused IRT Subway Tunnel**, bet. Jerome Ave. at Anderson Ave. W side, to Major Deegan Expwy. below W. 161st St. E side. 1918.

The steep ridge that forms this part of the West Bronx has barely begun before it is penetrated by this now-abandoned subway tunnel. Barely three blocks long, it was built to connect the Ninth Avenue el at the old site of the Polo Grounds baseball stadium in Manhattan with the IRT Jerome Avenue elevated line—some of the structural steel for the connecting shuttle can still be seen nearby at River Avenue and East 162nd Street. Neither tunnel portal is particularly visible; the west one can be glimpsed fleetingly from the Major Deegan Expressway. Once there were plans to use the tunnel, following its closing in 1955, for a trolley museum.

[H2] **Highbridge Woodycrest Center**/originally American Female Guardian Society and Home for the Friendless, 936 Woodycrest Ave., NE cor. Jerome Ave. 1901-1902. **William B. Tuthill.**

An eclectic limestone, terra-cotta, and brick mansion, the center sits on a commanding precipice overlooking the valley of Macombs Dam Park and Yankee Stadium.

H2

Macombs Dam Park: This park, at Jerome Avenue and West 161st Street, together with the Macombs Dam Bridge into Manhattan, recalls the nearby site of **Robert Macomb**'s *1813 dam across the Harlem River. The dam used the waterway's tidal flow to power a mill until Macomb's neighbors demolished the dam in 1838, in order to open the river to shipping. Considering the river's later success as a vital ship canal, the park and bridge should perhaps have been renamed for Macomb's prophetic neighbors.*

[H3] **Macombs Dam Bridge**/also known as Central Bridge, over the Harlem River bet. Jerome Ave., The Bronx, and W. 155th St., Manhattan. 1895. **Alfred P. Boller**, engineer. 🍎

With the replacement of the original University Heights Bridge with a larger look-alike, this stands out as the city's finest example of 19th-century swing bridges. While it may seem flimsy now, in 1895 it was one of the heaviest bridges ever built.

[H4] **Park Plaza Apartments**, 1005 Jerome Ave. bet. Anderson Ave. and E. 165th St. W side. 1929-1931. **Horace Ginsbern** and **Marvin Fine**. 🍎

One of the earliest (and best) Art Deco-inspired apartment buildings in the Bronx. Influenced both by the 1925 Exposition Internationale des Arts Décoratifs et Industriels Modernes in Paris, and motifs from Mayan architecture then fashionable. Note the elaborate polychromed terra-cotta ornament. The façade is Fine's work, the body Ginsbern's.

H4

HIGHBRIDGE HEIGHTS DISTRICT

see pages 590-592

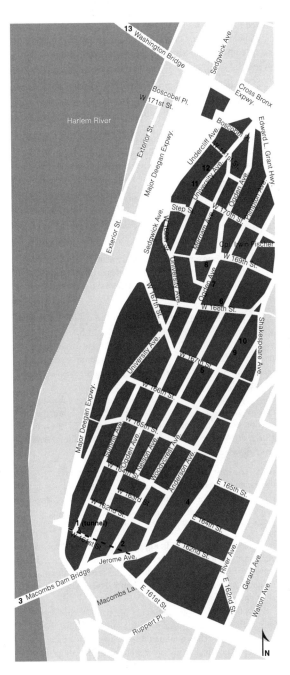

[H5] **West 167th Street housing**, bet. Nelson and Woodycrest Aves. S side. ca. 1985.

Modest modern infill housing; some of the more recent work hereabouts seems more concerned with a pseudo-historicist image.

[H6] **Noonan Plaza** (apartments), 105-145 W. 168th St., NW cor. Nelson Ave. 1931. **Horace Ginsbern**.

These 7-story apartments, arranged to form a quadrangle, are entered diagonally through a highly decorative masonry arcade that leads to a central court, the original splendors of which can only be guessed at today. Art Deco-*cum*-Mayan was

H6

H7

H11

H12

H13

the idiosyncratic style of the Ginsbern firm at the time. A major West Bronx monument.

[H7] Union Reformed Church of Highbridge, 1272 Ogden Ave. bet. W. 168th and W. 169th Sts. E side. 1889. **Alfred E. Barlow.**

A bold ashlar and browntone church contrasting magnificently with the Moderne decor of Noonan Plaza immediately adjacent.

[H8] Public School 11, Bronx/formerly Grammar School No. 91, 1257 Ogden Ave., bet. W. 168th and W. 169th Sts. W side. 1889. **George W. Debevoise.** Addition, 1905. **C. B. J. Snyder.** Addition, 1930. **Walter C. Martin.** ●

A picturesque gem. Much was lost architecturally when the late Victorian love of decoration disappeared—fortunately the best of Post-Modern architecture has brought similar detail back.

[H9] 1182 Woodycrest Avenue (house), bet. W. 167th and W. 168th Sts. E side. ca. 1875.

A surviving cream and white, painted brick, Victorian country house.

[H10] 1200 Woodycrest Avenue (apartments), bet. W. 167th and W. 168th Sts. E side. 1936. **Franklin, Bates & Heindsmann.**

Art Moderne, neglected at the street level, still holds its own upstairs.

[H11] Carmelite Monastery, 1381 University Ave., opp. W. 170th St. W side. 1940. **Maginnis & Walsh.**

When the walkway of adjacent High Bridge was open to pedestrians, the house of this cloistered community was best seen from there, from the riverside. Hugging the steep slope of the hill, which tumbles down to the Harlem River valley, this latter-day, neo-medieval building—with its tower, cells, chapel, cloister, and gardens—became visible without revealing the life of contemplation within its walls. Today only its relatively bland University Avenue façade is readily available to visitors. Serenity amid devastation.

[H12] 1411 University Avenue (house), adjacent to the Carmelite Monastery. 1850s.

A simple clapboard house from a previous era on these heights; what a wonderful aerie it would be, overlooking Manhattan and the Harlem River valley!

[H13] Washington Bridge, over the Harlem River, from University and Ogden Aves., The Bronx, to W. 181st and Amsterdam Ave., Manhattan. 1888. **C. C. Schneider,** original designer. **John McAlpine** and **William R. Hutton,** successive chief engineers. ●

Not the George Washington but just plain Washington Bridge and, in its own intricate way, a superior bridge. Two soaring sets of arches: one spanning the water, the other the river valley's flood plain. **Schneider** won the design competition, but cost overruns forced the substitution of steel latticework under the roadway. A happy compromise, particularly from the deck of a leisurely Circle Liner below.

UNIVERSITY HEIGHTS

[U1] **1660 Andrews Avenue** (NYCHA-rehabilitated apartments), bet. W. 175th and W. 176th Sts, through to University Ave. E side. ca. 1925. Altered, 1987, **Shelly Kroop** and **James McCullar**.

　Those City-added balconies add oomph to a tired stretch of street that needs them.

U1

 [U2] **South Bronx Job Corps Center**/formerly Salvation Army Training College/originally Messiah Home for Children, 1771 Andrews Ave., SW cor. W. Tremont Ave. 1908. **Charles E. Brigham.**

　Princeton may have Collegiate Gothic nailed down, but here is a neo-Jacobean complex unique to these Heights. (Brigham, and partner, **Solon S. Bemau**, designed the Christian Science Mother Church, in Boston.)

U2

Along the banks of the Harlem River: Once a decaying riverside frontage, this was the site of coal unloading docks and the Consolidated Ship Building Corporation, isolated by the tracks of the Penn Central Railroad and the Major Deegan Expressway. In the late 1960s these valuable lands were brought to public use by the combined efforts of assorted City and State agencies. The state park was renamed for Roberto Clemente, a local baseball hero killed in a plane crash; the housing was renamed, naturally, River Park Towers, to reflect its setting.

[U3] **Roberto Clemente State Park**/originally Harlem River Bronx State Park, Matthewson Rd. off W. Tremont Ave. Bridge along Harlem River. 1973. **M. Paul Friedberg & Assocs.**, landscape architects; **Dean McClure**, architect for recreation building.

　The first of a planned series of state parks in the city, this intricately designed recreation playland offers swimming, diving, gymnasium events, and a wonderful stroll along the seawall of the adjacent Harlem River. It may not have the verdancy of an upstate park, but its lively forms animate an otherwise isolated urban setting.

[U4] **River Park Towers** (apartments), 10, 20, 30, 40 Richman Plaza, off Cedar Ave. Bridge along Harlem River. 1975. **Davis, Brody & Assocs.**, architects; **M. Paul Friedberg & Assocs.**, landscape architects.

　A variation of the earlier Waterside project in Manhattan, these two intricate and tall brick apartment towers (actually two pairs of buildings joined) form a dramatic landmark from both sides of the river and to the millions of motorists who pass by them every year. To those who live in the towers (and those who visit) they are equally satisfying up close—particularly the com-

U4

bination pedestrian and vehicular plaza on which the apartment towers, parking garage, and retail stores front and from whose edges the tall shafts rise seemingly to infinity. The pedestrian plaza facing the river, however, is too large and too bleak.

[U5] **Public School 229, Bronx**/Junior High School 229, Bronx, the Roland N. Patterson School, 225 Harlem River Park Bridge, NE cor. Richman Plaza. 1977. **Caudill Rowlett Scott.**
    Built over the railroad tracks, it is unorthodox in appearance, with minimal windows and a dramatic exterior.

Old Croton Aqueduct: Completed in 1842, the Old Croton Aqueduct was the first dependable source of drinking water for the growing city. It runs a 32-mile downhill course from Croton Reservoir in Westchester County to High Bridge. In this area of the West Bronx it is particularly apparent, since much of its course is topped by a green walkway and sitting areas. Its most visible part is its southern edge along University Avenue just above West Tremont Avenue, but the green ribbon is available for public use for some fifteen blocks along a route which parallels University Avenue some 30 yards to the east. Take a stroll.

[U6] **University Heights Bridge**, over the Harlem River bet. W. Fordham Rd., The Bronx, and W. 207th St., Manhattan. 1893-1895. **William H. Burr**, consulting engineer, with **Alfred P. Boller** and George W. Birdsall. Relocated and extended, 1905-1908, **Othniel F. Nichols**, chief engineer. Widened and reconstructed, 1987-1992. 🖈
    The 1895 Tinkertoy bridge that occupied the site once spanned the Harlem River at Broadway between West 220th and 225th Streets. When the IRT Broadway Line elevated came to the Bronx in 1907, that bridge was no longer purposeful. So, rather than waste a bridge, it was floated a mile or so down the Harlem to this West 207th Street site. But in the affluent 1980s, just years after the City faced bankruptcy, a second reuse to accommodate increased traffic couldn't be justified, and so the lacy, latticework structure was demolished (but only after politically desirable landmark designation) so that a wider, stronger, modern bridge using some of the original ironwork could be erected in its place. A ghost of a landmark?

U7

Back along University Heights:

U8

[U7] **Calvary Methodist Church**, 1885 University Ave., bet. W. Tremont and W. Burnside Aves. W side. 1924.
    Rough ashlar walls contrast with refined stained-glass windows. The small but strongly composed building appears as a bastion against the changes that are sweeping the area. Built and physically endowed by a moneyed community in the 1920s, it now serves a congregation that must struggle to maintain its fine qualities.

🏠 [U8] **Gatehouse, New Croton Aqueduct**, W. Burnside Ave. SE cor. Phelan Place. ca. 1890. **Benjamin S. Church**, engineer.
    One of a series of rockface granite buildings built in the Bronx and Manhattan to service the city's second water supply system, the New Croton Aqueduct (1885-1893).

U9

▮ [U9] **Public School, P.S. 226**, NE cor. W. Burnside and Sedgwick Aves. 1990s.
    The public school as a village. The small and multiple forms create a minivillage for the lucky children who attend.

The Old N.Y.U. Uptown Campus:

[U10] **Bronx Community College, CUNY**/formerly New York University, University Heights Campus, University Ave. bet. W.

180th St. and Hall of Fame Terr., W side, to Sedgwick Ave. and vicinity. Original grounds and Ohio Field, 1892-1912. ☙ **Vaux & Co.**, landscape architects.

This was the 50-plus-acre uptown campus of New York University until 1973, when it was sold to the City as a campus for Bronx Community College. The formerly resident NYU College of Engineering was absorbed into a newly renamed Polytechnic Institute of New York in downtown Brooklyn.

Today's campus seems overpopulated by helter-skelter buildings—as opposed to one charmingly picturesque or classically formal.

U11

[U11] **The Hall of Fame for Great Americans**, entrance on Hall of Fame Terr. 1892-1912. **Stanford White** of **McKim, Mead & White**. ☙ Open to the public. 718-220-6003. 10-5, daily.

Not a hall at all but a roughly semicircular Classical arcade between whose columns are arrayed bronze busts of great Americans. They are picked by a college of more than 100 electors chosen from the fields of higher education, science, jurisprudence, and business, plus others in public life. The colonnade was conceived by N.Y.U. Chancellor MacCracken to camouflage, from Sedgwick Avenue below, the unsightly high foundation walls underpinning Stanford White's Library, Philosophy Hall, and Language Hall.

U12

[U12] **Gould Memorial Library**, 1894-1899. ☙ and interior. ☙ [U13] **Cornelius Baker Hall of Philosophy**, 1892-1912. ☙ [U14] **Hall of Languages** 1892-1895. ☙ All by **Stanford White** of **McKim, Mead & White**.

These three buildings—Gould is the domed one in the center—together with the Hall of Fame Arcade, are the pièce de résistance of this campus, all by Stanford White himself. Looked at in terms of their exquisitely detailed stone exteriors, they achieve a grand Classical Revival composition. A bit of Rome's Pantheon, coffered and columned, awaits within.

U16

[U15] **Gould Hall of Technology/Begrisch Lecture Hall**. 1964. **Marcel Breuer & Assocs.** [U16] **Colston Residence Hall and Cafeteria**. 1964. **Marcel Breuer & Assocs. Robert F. Gatje**, associate.

A modern set of sculptural essays drawn from Breuer's sketchbooks: his ideas matured over the years in abstract forms. Here was an opportunity to install them in reality.

U19

[U17] **South Hall**/formerly **Gustav H. Schwab House**. 1857. [U18] **Butler Hall**/formerly **William Henry W. T. Mali House**. ca., 1859. [U19] **MacCracken Hall**/formerly **Henry Mitchell MacCracken House**/originally **Loring Andrews House**. ca. 1880. Hall of Fame Terr. bet. Loring Place and Sedgwick Ave. N side.

Three mansions that predate the campus. Schwab was New York representative for the North German Lloyd Steamship Company. **Mali** was the Belgian consul general in New York. **MacCracken** was chancellor of N.Y.U. and founder of the Heights campus. **Loring Andrews** owned much of the land that formed the campus.

U20

[U20] **P.S. 15**, Bronx, NE cor. Hall of Fame Terr. and Loring Pl. 1998. **Ehrenkrantz & Eckstut**.

A strong brick and limestone composition with a grand stair vaguely reminiscent of **Charles Rennie Mackintosh**'s Scotland Street School, Glasgow.

[U21] **2255-2257 Loring Avenue** (houses), N of W. 183rd St. 1890s.

Copper-clad bay windows and a stepped gable both enrich these brick and limestone rowhouses.

U21

UNIVERSITY HEIGHTS DISTRICT

see pages 593-596

Beyond the old N.Y.U. Campus:

U22

[U22] **St. Nicholas of Tolentine Church** (Roman Catholic), University Ave. SW cor. Fordham Rd. 1928. **Delaney, O'Connor & Schultz.**

A conservative granite ashlar neo-Gothic church from a time when exuberance in Gothic matters had given way to solemnity. Bring back **John Ruskin**, **Viollet-le-Duc**, and their combined polychromy and structuralism.

[U23] **Fordham Hill Cooperative Apartments**/originally Fordham Hill Apartments, Sedgwick Ave. NE cor. Webb Ave. 1950. **Leonard Schultze & Assocs**.

On the former site of the Webb Academy & Home for Aged Ship Builders are these nine pristine 16-story apartment towers developed for the Equitable Life Assurance Society by an architect of the Waldorf-Astoria. Bland.

U23

*László Moholy-Nagy's widow, architectural historian **Sibyl**, and their two children moved into Fordham Hill Apartments after the death, in 1946, of the former Bauhaus instructor, photographer, and theorist. A refugee from Hitler's Germany, **Moholy-Nagy** had relocated to Chicago, where he founded the New Bauhaus and then the Institute of Design. In all the family stayed in these accommodations for about a year.*

KINGSBRIDGE HEIGHTS

K1

[K1] **Kingsbridge Veterans Hospital**/originally U.S. Veterans Hospital No. 81, 130 W. Kingsbridge Rd., bet. Webb and Sedgwick Aves. S side. New Hospital, 1979. **Max O. Urbahn Assocs, Inc**.

This commanding green hillside site affords spectacular views across the Harlem Valley of upper Manhattan and has provided for the needs of diverse occupants over the years. During the British occupation of New York it was the site of one of their forts. Later it was a private estate and served as the Catholic Orphan Asylum before becoming a veterans' hospital in the 1920s. The 1979 all aluminum-clad replacement hospital calls even more attention to itself than did its immense neo-Georgian predecessor. The Home Care Unit is a particularly handsome addition, just as the old chapel is a welcome holdover.

K3

[K2] **The Jewish Home and Hospital for the Aged**. Salzman Pavilion, 100 W. Kingsbridge Rd., bet. Webb and University Aves. S side. 1975. [K3] **Greenwall Pavilion**, 2545 University Ave., at W. 192nd St. W side. 1972. Both by **Weiss Whelan Edelbaum Webster**.

On what was once the site of the Hebrew Infant Asylum are two imposing additions to an institution for the elderly.

[K4] **2751 University Avenue** (apartments), NW cor. W. 195th St. 1936. **Edward W. Franklin**.

Art Deco in cream, orange, and brown brick, with its entry still intact.

[K5] **Rosenor Gables** (apartments), 2757 Claflin Ave., bet. W. 195th and W. 197th Sts. W side. ca. 1928.

Deeply modeled neo-Tudor. Imposing except for the post-energy crisis, brown anodized aluminum windows.

K4

[K6] **Rectory, Our Lady of Angels Roman Catholic Church**, 2860 Webb Ave., bet. W. 197th St. and Reservoir Ave. ca. 1900.

Impressive and asymmetric, this romantic country house displays a ground floor of undressed fieldstone. Catch the porte cochère millwork.

K6

North along Kingsbridge Terrace:

[K7] **2744 Kingsbridge Terrace** (house), N of W. Kingsbridge Rd. E side. 1912.

Close by the vast veterans' hospital is this tiny monument, a stucco castle with numerous gables, balconies, crenellated turrets, a weather vane, a TV antenna, and a tunnel reputedly leading from the "dungeon" to the street.

[K8] **Kingsbridge Heights Community Center**/ originally 50th Precinct, N.Y.C. Police Department, 3101 Kingsbridge Terr., SW cor. Summit Place. 1900-1902. **Horgan & Slattery**.

Referring to the political connections of this structure's successful architects, **Seth Low** in 1902 called for the "dishorganizing and unslatterifying" of municipal architecture as one of his mayoral promises. A rich Renaissance Revival-Eclectic building.

K8

[K9] **Sholom Aleichem Houses/Yiddish Cooperative Heim Geselshaft** (cooperative apartments) 3451 Giles Place, 3470 Cannon Place, 68 W. 238th St., 3605 Sedgwick Ave. Entry via Giles Place (one-way north and east) from Kingsbridge Terr. 1927. **Springsteen & Goldhammer**.

Four unembellished red-brick apartments atop a hill overlooking the Harlem River valley. Built around a meandering courtyard by a Jewish community whose common goal was the preservation of Eastern European Yiddish culture (as contrasted

K9

with the Hebrew religious culture) through membership in the Arbeiter Ring (Workmen's Circle).

The Old Jerome Park Reservoir, and its surrounding institutions:

Jerome Park Reservoir: First filled in 1905, this concrete-lined waterstorage facility holds 773 million gallons. Goulden Avenue, its eastern boundary, sits atop a combination of the Old Croton Aqueduct and a masonry dividing wall that was to separate it from another part of the reservoir planned as a second stage. The second basin, with a capacity almost twice that of the first, was excavated to the east of the present reservoir, extending to Jerome Avenue between West Kingsbridge Road north to Mosholu Parkway. Abandoned in 1912, the pit was filled in and

K10

now serves as the site for the Kingsbridge Armory, Lehman College, two subway yards, three high schools, a park, and a couple of publicly aided housing developments!

The reservoir and nearby Jerome Avenue take their name from the Jerome Park Racetrack, which occupied this site from 1876 until 1890. **Leonard W. Jerome**, **Winston Churchill**'s grandfather, was a prime mover in sponsoring the American Jockey Club, which strived (with success) to elevate horse racing in this country to the status of an aristocratic sport.

[K10] **Kingsbridge Armory**/originally Eighth Coastal Artillery Armory/later Eighth Regiment Armory, 29 W. Kingsbridge Rd., bet. Jerome and Reservoir Aves. N side. 1912-1917. **Pilcher & Tachau**. 🖌

Called the largest armory in the world, this picturesque 20th-century fortress, the Pierrefonds of The Bronx, is probably better known for peacetime activities such as indoor bicycle races than for suppressing civil insurrection. Whereas **Viollet-le-Duc**'s medieval-revival "reconstructions" (read "imaginations") at Pierrefonds were banal, the Bronx, a younger, callower place, lives well with such fantasies.

K13

[K11] **Lehman College, CUNY**/originally Hunter College Uptown, Goulden Ave. SE cor. Bedford Park Blvd. Original buildings, 1932. **Thompson, Holmes, & Converse**. [K12] **Library**

KINGSBRIDGE HEIGHTS, KINGSBRIDGE, MARBLE HILL DISTRICTS

see pages 597-599

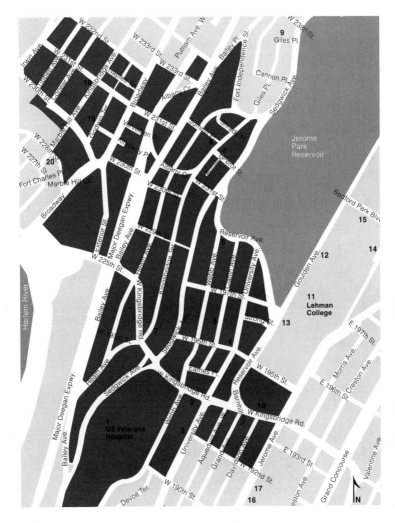

and **Shuster Hall**, 1960. **Marcel Breuer & Assocs.; Robert F. Gatje**, associate. [K13] **Carman Hall** (classrooms and cafeteria), 1970. **DeYoung & Moskowitz**. [K14] **New Library, Speech and Theater, and Auditorium Buildings**, along Paul Ave. 1980. **David Todd & Assocs.** and **Jan Hird Pokorny**.

The older buildings never had the architectural glue to unite them as a composition; the newer ones along Paul Avenue, interrupted by the City's financial crisis, are a mixed lot: **Breuer**'s entry is an unassuming block with his trademark vertical windows. **DeYoung & Moskowitz** provide some unnecessary gold and limestone histrionics. The **Todd/Pokorny** buildings are modest background modern.

[K15] **Lehman College Physical Education Facility**, along Bedford Park Blvd.West, bet. Goulden and Paul Aves. 1994. **Rafael Viñoly Architects**.

An airy crustacean (oxymoron?) that provides a north entry to the campus, and houses wondrous spaces for sport. It brings Lehman College into the 21st century. A landed space ship?

[K16] **St. James Church** (Episcopal), 2500 Jerome Ave., NE cor. E. 190th St. 1864-1865. **Henry M. Dudley** of **Dudley & Diaper. Parish House**, 1891-1892. **Henry F. Kilburn**. 🌑

K15

K18

A stone Gothic Revival church in the shadow of the IRT Jerome Avenue elevated. The greenery of the churchyard and adjacent St. James Park (1901) seems to block out some of the clatter.

[K17] **St. James Park Recreation Center**, N.Y.C. Department of Parks & Recreation, 2530 Jerome Ave., bet. E. 190th and E. 192nd Sts. E side. 1970. **Richard G. Stein & Assocs**.

The design principle of the International Style, carefully applied and with worthy effect.

KINGSBRIDGE

Kingsbridge, the flat area along Broadway below West 242nd Street, preserves the name of the earliest settlement (which grew up around the first bridge to Manhattan, built in 1693).

K19

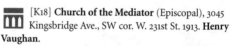 [K18] **Church of the Mediator** (Episcopal), 3045 Kingsbridge Ave., SW cor. W. 231st St. 1913. **Henry Vaughan**.

A fine, gray ashlar granite, neo-Gothic sanctuary neatly sited on a prominent corner by an architect of Washington's National Cathedral.

[K19] Originally **George H. Moller House**/formerly Residence, Brothers of the Christian Schools, 3029 Godwin Terr., bet. W. 230th and W. 231st Sts. W side. ca. 1875.

Set back from adjacent 1920s brick multiple-dwelling construction, atop a stone retaining wall, stands this mansard-roofed, stuccoed house, moved from its original site a few hundred feet west and clearly left over from another era.

K20

MARBLE HILL (MANHATTAN)

[K20] **St. Stephen's Methodist Episcopal Church**, 146 W. 228th St., SE cor. Marble Hill Ave. 1897.

A picturesque Shingle Style work with a commanding presence, it stands as a marker and a sign of welcome to Manhattan's orphaned Marble Hill community, cut off from its mother island and physically connected to the Bronx by the technologies of canal digging and earth moving.

BEDFORD PARK

[B1] **Bedford Park Presbyterian Church**, 2933 Bainbridge Ave., NW cor. Bedford Park Blvd. 1900. **R. H. Robertson**. Addition, 1929.

A granite ashlar and timber church bestows a Scarsdale tone upon this heavily trafficked street.

[B2] **52nd Precinct Station House**/originally 41st Precinct, N.Y.C. Police Department, 3016 Webster Ave., NE cor. MoCholu Pkwy. 1904-1906. **Stoughton & Stoughton**. ☛

B1

Responding to a quasi-rural setting at the turn of the century, the architects of Manhattan's Soldiers' and Sailors' Monument created a Tuscan villa for this precinct house. The tower wears a polychromed terra-cotta clock face and deeply projecting eaves—a high point in such romantic design in the city.

[B3] **Police Officer George J. Wierdann School, P.S./ M.S. 20**, Webster Ave., N of 52nd Precinct Station House. 1990s. **Ehrenkrantz & Eckstut**.

B2

Cool limestone and brick, gabled to simulate row housing, this is another attempt to bring the scale of schools to the remembered scale of children's homes.

[B4] **Bedford Park Congregational Church** (United Church of Christ), E. 201st St. NE cor. Bainbridge Ave. ca. 1890.

Tiny, but its ashlar and wood frame construction are special.

[B5] **Ursuline Academy** (Roman Catholic)/originally Mount St. Ursula Convent, 330 Bedford Park Blvd./2885 Marion Ave. ca. 1888. **Arthur Arctander**.

A venerable but bland complex, updated with paint.

B3

NORWOOD

[B6] **Mosholu Parkway**, connecting Bronx and Van Cortlandt Parks.

One of the few completed links in the network of parkways that was proposed to connect the major parks of the Bronx. At the eastern entrance to the parkway the Victory Monument serves to divide traffic.

[B7] **St. Brendan's Church** (Roman Catholic), Perry Ave. bet. E. 206th and E. 207th Sts. W side. 1966. **Belfatto & Pavarini**.

St. Brendan is the patron saint of navigators, so it should come as no surprise that this church was built to resemble the prow of a ship. Near the entrance of the upper church (there is a modest lower one), under the steeply sloping roof, the ceiling is low and the church dark, but as we move toward the altar the space and light around us grow. The steeple, part of the upswept roof, forms the prow.

B7

[B8] **Valentine-Varian House**/Museum of Bronx History/originally Isaac Valentine House, 3266 Bainbridge Ave., bet. Van Cortlandt Ave. E. and E. 208th St. E side. 1758. ☛ Open to the public. 718-881-8900. Sat, 10-4; Sun, 1-5.

A well-proportioned fieldstone farmhouse moved in the 1960s from its original location across the street on Van Cortlandt Avenue East. Today it is also the home of The Bronx County Historical Society and the site of a museum of local history.

B8

BEDFORD PARK, NORWOOD DISTRICTS
see pages 601-603

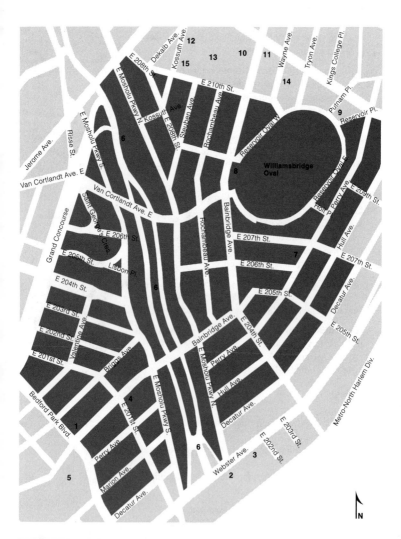

B9

Williamsbridge Oval: The embankment behind the Valentine-Varian House continues to curve around to form an oval which today encloses an elaborate city playground. *Between 1888 and 1923 the embankment formed a dam to contain the waters of the Williamsbridge Reservoir, part of the city's water supply system. After its abandonment tunnels were cut through, and play equipment and benches were introduced. Appropriately named, the surrounding streets are called Reservoir Oval East and West.*

[B9] **Mosholu Preservation Organization Headquarters**/former Keeper's House, Williamsbridge Reservoir, Reservoir Oval E. NE cor. Putnam Place. ca. 1890. **George W. Birdsall. Benjamin S. Church**, engineer.

One of the many rock-faced stone buildings built for the city's water supply system. This one, however, was meant as a residence and office rather than as a gatehouse or service facility. It has outlived the effective life of the abandoned reservoir across the street.

B11

[B10] **Montefiore Hospital and Medical Center**, E. Gun Hill Rd. bet. Kossuth and Tryon Aves. S side. Original buildings, 1913. Arnold W. Brunner.

∎ [B11] **Henry L. Moses Research Institute,**
E. Gun Hill Rd. SE cor. Bainbridge Ave. 1966.
Philip Johnson & Assocs. [B12] **Annie Lichtenhein Pavilion**
Kossuth Ave. bet. E. Gun Hill Rd. and E. 210th St. E side. 1970.
Gruzen & Partners and **Westermann/Miller Assocs.**
[B13] **Loeb Pavilion,** E of Lichtenhein Pavilion. 1966.
Kelly & Gruzen and **Helge Westermann.**

∎ [B14] **Montefiore Apartments II,** 3450 Wayne Ave., bet.
E. Gun Hill Rd. and E. 210th St. E side. 1972. **Schuman,**
Lichtenstein & Claman.

B14

Like most hospital campuses nurtured over decades and
responding to growth in population and changes in treatment
techniques, this one is chaotic in appearance. It speaks well for
administration and donors that the newer additions are exemplary in their architecture beginning with **Philip Johnson**'s 1966
work. The Montefiore Apartments II is one of the tallest in the
borough; its dark red-brown brick volume is impressive from
both near and far.

∎ [B15] **North Central Bronx Hospital,** N.Y.C. Health &
Hospitals Corporation, Kossuth Ave. NE cor. E. 210th St.
1976. **Westermann/Miller Assocs.; Carl Pancaldo; Schuman,**
Lichtenstein & Claman.

Considering the limitations of the site (space made available
from the existing Montefiore complex), this is a spectacularly
successful hospital design when viewed as public architecture.
Crisp, neat, bold forms of brick and precast concrete articulate
the street façades and present a confident and inviting appearance.

[B16] **Woodlawn Cemetery,** entrances at Jerome Ave. N of
Bainbridge Ave. E side and at E. 233rd St. SW cor. Webster Ave.
Open to the public.

A lavish array of tombstones, mausoleums, and memorials
in a richly planted setting. Many wealthy and distinguished people are buried here. Tombs and mausoleums are replicas and
small-scale reproductions of several famous European chapels
and monuments. **Jay Gould,** the **Woolworths,** and **Mayors John**
Purroy Mitchel and **Fiorello La Guardia** are among the famous
people interred at Woodlawn.

Riverdale

SPUYTEN DUYVIL • RIVERDALE • NORTH RIVERDALE
FIELDSTON • VAN CORTLANDT PARK

In this precinct, extending from Broadway west to the banks of the Hudson River, can be found lush estates and lavish mansions, low-rent subsidized housing, and block after block of very ordinary, middle-class apartments. It differs most from the rest of the Bronx, however, in that some parts—such as the private-street community of Fieldston and the slopes of the old community of Riverdale-on-Hudson—house some of the borough's most affluent and most influential people. Spuyten Duyvil is the hilly southwestern tip of this precinct, from which the graceful arch of the Henry Hudson Bridge springs to its opposite abutment in Manhattan.

SPUYTEN DUYVIL

Spuyten Duyvil, an early Dutch name for the region where the Harlem and Hudson Rivers meet, is also the name of the steeply sloped area of the Bronx that overlooks the confluence of the waters. It has been overbuilt with tall undistinguished apartments.

R1

[R1] **Edgehill Church of Spuyten Duyvil** (United Church of Christ)/originally Riverdale Presbyterian Chapel, 2550 Independence Ave., at Kappock St. S side. 1888-1889. **Francis H. Kimball.** ●
    Occupying a spit of property between two roads that set off in different directions at different grades is this exquisitely picturesque eclectic sanctuary: a base of Richardsonian Romanesque, a top of Gothic Revival, and a smattering of Tudor details.

R3

[R2] **2475 Palisade Avenue** (apartments), SW cor. Independence Ave. ca. 1930. [R3] **Villa Charlotte Bronte** (apartments), 2501 Palisade Ave., NW cor. Independence Ave. 1926. **Robert Gardner.**
    A small apartment house, 5 stories plus attic, of brick, rubblestone, and shingle designed around casement windows, and the Villa, two romantic, intricate, visually intriguing wings containing sixteen units, some partly above, some below street level. Together these habitations occupy the southwesternmost edge of the Spuyten Duyvil escarpment, one of the city's finest sites, overlooking the confluence of the Harlem and Hudson Rivers. Would that their grotesque post-WW II neighbors had been so skillfully designed.

R5

[R4] **Henry Hudson Memorial Column**, Henry Hudson Park, Kappock St. NW cor. Independence Ave. 1912. **Babb, Cook & Welch.** Column by **Walter Cook** of **Babb, Cook & Willard.** Sculpture of **Hudson**, 1938. **Karl Bitter** and **Karl Gruppe.**
    The 100-foot Doric column and base were erected on this high bluff by public subscription following the Hudson-Fulton Celebration of 1909. The 16-foot bronze of Hudson gazing out at his river from atop the column was not installed until long after.

[R5] **Spuyten Duyvil Branch, N.Y. Public Library**, 650 W. 235th St., bet. Independence and Douglas Aves. S side. 1971. **Giorgio Cavaglieri.**
    A dignified modern building in an area characterized by chaotic and unrelated development.

RIVERDALE

Riverdale, the northwest strip of this precinct, which slopes precipitously down to the Hudson's banks, was once a name reserved for the area immediately around the Riverdale station of the onetime New York Central & Hudson River Railroad at West 254th Street. Then it was called Riverdale-on-Hudson. Today, all too many high-rise apartment hulking along Henry Hudson Parkway have diminished the exclusivity of both name and community. Fortunately, however, a cadre of tenacious residents, a couple of foreign governments, and some eleemosynary institutions still preserve the mansions, the lovely landscapes, and the tranquil beauty of the older community.

A note of caution: The Riverdale area north of West 240th Street and west of Henry Hudson Parkway is an obstacle course for the unwary. Narrow, winding, hilly streets are commonplace. Without much notice they sometimes narrow first into lanes, then driveways, and then abruptly stop. Street signs are often missing or misleading. Since many of the smaller thoroughfares are not officially mapped and others are private (Fieldston's boundaries, east of the parkway, are comparatively easy to determine from the large private-street signs), maps don't help much. The condition of the streets in the area is frequently abominable, partly a result of the high cost of maintenance and partly because residents wish to discourage idle visiting. Not only do potholes abound but in some areas asphalt bumps have been added to discourage reckless driving since walking and cycling are popular. All of this has probably contributed to preserving this extra special part of New York. Contributing too are the barking dogs that remain even when the homeowners have taken their cars on an errand. Whether walking, bicycling, or driving, be careful . . . and beware.

[R6] **Delafield housing estate**/originally "Fieldston Hill," Edward C. Delafield House and estate/later Delafield Botanical Estates, Columbia University, 680 W. 246th St., SW cor. Hadley Ave. ca. 1865. House altered, 1916, **Dwight James Baum**. Converted into housing estate, 1986, **James Stewart Polshek & Partners**.

The large fieldstone home of Riverdale's old family, the **Delafields**, and their lush overgrown estate, sold by Columbia University and then converted into 33 condominium units.

R7

[R7] **Eric J. Schmertz House**, 4550 Palisade Ave., S of W. 247th St. E side. 1971. **Vincent A. Claps**.

Turned diagonally to the quiet road, this 2-story stainedwoodsheathed house is what might be termed "shaggy cubist." In comparison to its 1970s peers in modernism it shines.

[R8] Originally **William E. and Melissa Phelps Dodge House "Greyston"**/later Greyston Conference Center, Teachers College, 690 W. 247th St., SW cor. Independence Ave. 1863-1864. **James Renwick, Jr.** [R8a] **Gatehouse**, ca. 1864. S of W. 247th St.

R8a

As Riverdale became a country retreat in the 1860s, this was one of the earliest houses commissioned. The **Dodge** family was instrumental not only in the establishment of Teachers College in 1887 but also in the transfer to TC in 1961 of this large, many-gabled, many-chimneyed mansion. The gatehouse, an asymmetric composition with jerkin head roofs, is in the style of **A. J. Downing** and **Calvert Vaux**'s books on cottage design. It is once again a private house.

Riverdale's mansions and views: To call attention to every house worth mentioning in this architectural treasure chest of a community would require a tome in itself. Some of its narrow lanes (and the homes that border them) are particularly rewarding.

Sycamore Avenue above *West 252nd Street has buildings so pic-turesque that you won't believe you're in the city.* Try **Independence Avenue** *between West 248th and 254th Streets. The best view of Riverdale and the Hudson beyond is from a point just north of* **West 252nd Street**. *And visit* **Wave Hill**, *whose entrance is at* **West 249th Street**, *for a view that* **Mark Twain** *and* **Arturo Toscanini** *enjoyed.*

[R9] **"Alderbrook,"** formerly Percy Pyne House, then Elie Nadelman House, 4715 Independence Ave., S of W. 248th St. W side. ca. 1880.

An **Andrew Jackson Downing**-inspired Gothic Revival brick house full of gables and crockets, long the home and studio of sculptor **Elie Nadelman** (1882-1946). Adjacent is a group of houses snugly occupying a private community now called Alderbrook, after the estate whose lands it shares.

R10

[R10] **Riverdale Country School**, River Campus, W. 248th St./Spaulding's Lane, bet. Independence and Palisade Aves. N side. **Perkins Study Center**, 1967, **R. Marshall Christensen**. Originally **"Parkside," George H. Foster House**, ca. 1871. Originally **"Oaklawn," Henry F. Spaulding House**, ca. 1863. **Thomas S. Wall**.

The Study Center's roof is special: two concave surfaces approach one another but never quite kiss, leaving a skylight at the ridge. The older structures, particularly the northernmost, Oaklawn, are survivors from 19th-century estates, now used for school purposes.

R11

[R11] Formerly Anthony Campagna House/now **Yeshiva of Telshe Alumni School**, 640 W. 249th St., at Independence Ave. 1919-1930. **Dwight James Baum**. 🖌

Placed exquisitely at the end of a short cobblestoned drive, this stucco and tile villa comes from an aristocratic lineage, based loosely on Italian and French 19th-century models. It was commissioned, however, by a Manhattan builder who struck it rich in the Roaring Twenties.

R12

[R12] **Coachman's House, Henry F. Spaulding estate**, 4970 Independence Ave., NE cor. W. 249th St. 1879. **Charles W. Clinton**. 🖌

A Stick Style picturesque cottage, moved from the west side of Independence Avenue in 1909. Glorious.

[R13] **Wave Hill Center for Environmental Studies**, 675 W. 252nd St., SW cor. Sycamore Ave. Entrance on Independence Ave. at W. 249th St. W side. [R13a] **William Lewis Morris House, "Wave Hill,"** (northern building): center section, 1843-1844; north wing, late 19th century; armor hall, 1928, **Dwight James Baum**; south wings, after 1933; general renovation, 1975, **Stephen Lepp**. 🖌 [R13b] **"Glyndor II,"** (southern building)/now CUNY Institute of Marine and Atmospheric Sciences at City College, early 20th century. Both open to the public.
718-549-3200. May 15-Oct 15: Tues-Sun, 9-5:30; closed Mon. Oct 16-May 14, Tues-Sun, 9-4:30; closed Mon.

Early conservationist and **J. P. Morgan** partner **George Walbridge Perkins** bought this estate. The neo-Georgian Glyndor mansion, which he built soon after, bears his initials on the metal downspouts at the roof. The older Wave Hill building he rented to distinguished individuals, including **Theodore Roosevelt** and **Mark Twain**; other paying guests included **William Makepeace Thackeray, John Tyndall, T. H. Huxley,** and **Herbert Spencer**. Before Perkins's descendants presented both buildings to the city in 1960, Wave Hill was also the home of **Arturo Toscanini** and the official residence of the United Kingdom's ambassador to the United Nations. Perhaps

RIVERDALE DISTRICT

see pages 604-611

R14

Wave Hill's most intriguing tenant was **Bashford Dean**, builder of the armor hall. He was curator of arms and armor at the Metropolitan Museum of Art and also curator of reptiles and fishes at the American Museum of Natural History. Between 1906 and 1910 he held both posts simultaneously.

John F. Kennedy 1917-1963: While a youngster attending the nearby Riverdale Country School on Fieldston Road, John F. Kennedy lived in Charles Evans Hughes's former boxy stucco house on West 252nd Street at the southeast corner of Independence Avenue (officially 5040 Independence). From 1926 through 1928.

[R14] **H. L. Abrons House**, 5225 Independence Ave., NW cor. W. 252nd St. 1980. **Harold Sussman, Horace Ginsbern & Assocs**.

A complex form that, although it conflicts with the architecture of its neighbors, buffers them with dense landscaping.

R17

[R15] **Riverdale Historic District**, between Independence Avenue and the Hudson River, 252nd to 254th Streets, including all of Sycamore Avenue. 🍎

In-city sub-urbia on the slopes of the Hudson.

[R16] **5200 Sycamore Avenue**, bet. W. 252nd and W. 254th Sts. W side. 1922-1924. **Dwight James Baum**. ♂

Gambreled nostalgia.

[R17] **5249 Sycamore Avenue**, bet. W. 252nd and W. 254th Sts. 1937. **Julius Gregory**. ♂

Loose lime green neo-Federal, with an elegant clapboard and cross-barred parapet.

R18

[R18] Onetime **Nicholas deB. Katzenbach House**/onetime **Robert Colgate House**/originally William D. and Ann Cromwell House, "Stonehurst," 5225 Sycamore Ave., bet. W. 252nd and W. 254th Sts. W side. 1861. 🍎 ♂

Hidden by newer homes on Sycamore Avenue and by dense trees is another of the great stone mansions of Riverdale (such as Greyston or Wave Hill) and the Bronx (Van Cortlandt, Bartow). **Katzenbach** was U.S. Attorney General and Undersecretary of State; **Colgate**, an early entrepreneur in lead and paint.

R19

[R19] **5270 Sycamore Avenue** (barn), bet. W. 252nd and W. 254th Sts. E side. ca. 1853. ♂

[R20] **William S. Duke barn**, 5286 Sycamore Ave., SE cor. W. 254th St. ca. 1856-1858. Altered into carriage house, 1886, **Frederick Clarke Withers**. ♂

These lovely Shingle Style barns, in various stages of reuse, once served country homes to the east (atop the hill along today's Independence Avenue).

R21

[R21] **Salanter Akiba Riverdale Academy**, 655 W. 254th St., bet. Independence and Palisade Aves. N side. 1974. **Caudill Rowlett Scott Assocs**.

Given a slope and the need to conjoin the educational activities of what were once three Hebrew day schools, what better solution than a a series of classroom floors stepping downhill (with a skylit roof providing all with transfluvial views). Shades of Harvard's Gund Hall—but here a result of the topography, not whim. A harsh statement in this placid suburbia.

NORTH RIVERDALE

R23

[R22] **Ladd Road**, off Palisade Ave. bet. W. 254th St. and Sigma Place. E side.

▌ [R23] **James Strain House**, 731 Ladd Rd. E side. 1970.
═══ **Keith Kroeger Assocs**.

A group of modern houses built 1957-1970, clustered along a cul-de-sac around a private swimming pool. The site is the former estate of **Dr. William Sargent Ladd** (hence the name of the road), whose original stone gateposts guard the entrance. The Strain House provides a geometrical clarity absent in its neighbors.

[R24] **Gethsemane-on-Hudson Monastery and Cardinal Spellman Retreat House**, Passionist Fathers and Brothers, 5801 Palisade Ave., opp. Sigma Place. W side.

R25

🏠 [R25] **Riverdale Center of Religious Research**/formerly Old Residence. ca. 1895.

The old residence, a 3-story shingled Victorian country house, is delightful in its "Painted Lady" makeup (historically incorrect, but fun). The orange brick dorm, on the other hand, is a disaster. It is the new chapel, almost hidden from the road, that is a dramatic expressionistic architectural/sculptural work.

▌ [R26] **The Hebrew Home for the Aged at Riverdale**, 5901
═══ Palisade Ave., S of W. 261st St. W side. Additions:
Goldfine Pavilion. 1968. **Kelly & Gruzen. Palisade Nursing Home**. 1975. **Gruzen & Partners. Alma & Milton Gilbert Pavilion**. 1987. **Gruzen Partnership. Resnick Stolz Link Pavilion**. 1999. **Gruzen Samton. 3247 Johnson Avenue Building**. 2000. **Gruzen Samton**.

R26

This institution awakened precociously to the benefits and satisfactions of high-quality architecture for the elderly. The early work combines exposed concrete and stacked red brick and seems to express in its windows a response to the temptations of the spectacular 270° river views. A newer, 7-story all-brick north building seems carved from a monumental cube almost as sculptor **Gutzon Borglum** attacked the Black Hills of South Dakota. Even the utility building off the road shows the architect's care and talent. The more recent Resnick Stolz Link and Johnson Avenue buildings continue an architectural evolution over 32 years.

[R27.] **College of Mount Saint Vincent on Hudson**/originally Convent and Academy of Mount Saint Vincent, Riverdale Ave. and W. 263rd St. W side.

🏠 [R27a] Original College Building/now **Administration Building**, central section, 1857-1859. **Henry Engelbert**.
Additions: 1865, 1883, 1906-1908, **E. Wenz**. 1952. 🍎

🏠 [R27b] **Library**/formerly "Fonthill," Edwin Forrest House, 1848-1852. 🍎 [R27c] **Louise LeGras Hall**/originally St. Vincent's Free School, W. 261st St. opp. Netherland Ave. N side. 1875. [R27d] **Marillac Hall**/originally in part E. D. Randolph House, ca. 1855. [R27e] Originally "Fonthill" cottage 🍎 [R27f] "Fonthill" carriage house and stable/now Boyle Hall, ca. 1848-1852. 🍎

The Sisters of Charity, who operate the college, purchased this site from actor **Edwin Forrest** (his feud with **William Charles Macready** in 1849 touched off the Astor Place Riot) when their original quarters in Manhattan were to be destroyed by the construction of Central Park. Forrest's house, Fonthill, is as eccentric a building for New York as the "folly" it was patterned after was for England: **William Beckford**'s Fonthill Abbey. Though this is the best-known building on the campus, the old redbrick college itself, four stories high and oh so long, is an unfamiliar and more spectacular sight. Its 180-foot tower rises some 400 feet above the level of the Hudson. LeGras Hall was, between 1875 and 1910, the sparsely settled Riverdale's only elementary school. It is a charming building, accessible directly from adjacent West 261st Street.

R28

FIELDSTON

A community of private streets and English-inspired houses of the 1920s grouped along the streets north of Manhattan College Parkway; Fieldston Road, with its green central mall, is the quiet main thoroughfare. Among the many charms of the area is the oak tree preserved in the center of the intersection of Delafield and Iselin Avenues. If you are bicycling or driving, beware of the street paving. Potholes can be the rule.

R29d

[R28] **S. L. Victor House**, 200 W. 245th St., SW cor. Waldo Ave. 1968. **Ferdinand Gottlieb.**
A formal modernist design in now-grayed redwood siding. Slate-paved stairs ceremoniously lead to the formal entry. The street side of the house is discreet with slender windows; the rear, private, opens to the lush backyard.

[R29] **Horace Mann High School**, 231 W. 246th St., NE cor. Tibbet Ave. [R29a] **Pforzheimer Hall.** 1956. **Victor Christ-Janer.** [R29b] **Prettyman Gymnasium.** 1968. **Charles E. Hughes III** [R29c] **Gratwick Science Wing Addition and Pforzheimer Hall** renovation. 1975. **Frost Assocs.**

[R29d] **New Buildings.** 1999. **Gruzen Samton.**
Once located next to Teachers College in Manhattan, Horace Mann High School (and Horace Mann-Barnard Elementary School south of West 246th Street) now occupies this more verdant campus. The new complex by Gruzen Samton completes the campus.

[R30] Originally **C. E. Chambers House**, 4670 Waldo Ave., bet College Rd. and Livingston Ave. E side. ca. 1923. **Julius Gregory.**
A picturesque suburban house, reminiscent of the best in English country house design, by a master architect of such. Gregory did a number of similar fine houses in Fieldston.

R30

[R31] **Conservative Synagogue of Riverdale**, Congregation Adath Israel, Henry Hudson Pkwy. NE cor. W. 250th St. 1962. **Percival Goodman.**
Conservative in its religious status, not in its architectural attitudes. Strong forms in concrete and dark red brick make this synagogue an unneighborly character.

[R32] **Henry Ittleson Center for Child Research**, Jewish Board of Guardians, 5050 Iselin Ave., N of W. 250th St. E side. 1967. **Abraham W. Geller; M. A. Rubenstein**, design associate.
A handsome community of tan block pavilions capped by standing-seam metal roofs. The group, for the treatment of disturbed children, is set well back from the street (and hard to see).

R33

[R33] **Christ Church** (Episcopal), Henry Hudson Pkwy E., SE cor. W. 252nd St. 1865-1866. **Richard M. Upjohn** of **Richard Upjohn and Son.** 🖌
A small, picturesque church, of brick and local stone, with a simple pierced-wall belfry. Minimal alterations and careful maintenance have preserved this delightful edifice. The mansarded parish house is its sprightly contemporary.

A detour west across the Parkway:

R34

[R34] **Riverdale Presbyterian Church and Manse: The Duff House**, 4765 Henry Hudson Pkwy. W., at W. 249th St. W side. 1863-1864. **James Renwick, Jr.** Both 🖌
A pair of Renwick designs (much altered: check that steeple) fortunately framed from distractions on either side by heavy greenery. The Duff House is curious in that its original design called for both a mansard roof and Gothic Revival gables and dormers.

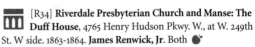

East across the Parkway and downhill to Broadway:

VAN CORTLANDT PARK

[R35] **Van Cortlandt Swimming Pool**, Van Cortlandt Park, Broadway at W. 242nd St. E side. 1970. **Heery & Heery**.
The largest of a series of system-designed, system-built pools. From a distance, it has the appearance of a high-tech Bedouin encampment.

 [R36] **Van Cortlandt Mansion Museum**/originally Frederick and Frances Jay Van Cortlandt House, Van Cortlandt Park, Broadway bet. W. 242nd and W. 246th Sts. E side. 1748-1749. ● Open to the public. 718-543-3344. Tues-Fri, 10-3; Sat-Sun, 11-4; closed Mon.
A carefully preserved fieldstone country house for a wealthy landed family. The simple exterior hides a richly decorated interior. Its farmland, to the north, now forms an enormous meadow used for a variety of sporting events, particularly cricket (enjoyed by the city's large West Indian population) and model airplane trials.

R36

*Vault Hill, overlooking the Van Cortlandt Mansion, contains the Van Cortlandt family vault. When the British occupied New York in 1776 **Augustus Van Cortlandt**, the city clerk, hid the municipal records in the vault. In 1781, **General Washington** had campfires lit here to deceive the British, while he marched to Yorktown for the battle against Cornwallis.*

On high ground, this time north of the Parkway:

[R37] **Diplomatic Residence, United Nations Mission**, Russian Federation, 355 W. 255th St., NE cor. Mosholu Ave./One Scharansky Square. 1975. **Skidmore, Owings & Merrill**.
Nineteen stories of apartments built from the top down on two cast-in-place concrete masts that form the building's cores, a process called "lift-slab construction." Each floor was fabricated on the ground and jacked up to its position in the structure along the masts.
The new address emerged in 1982 when the Bronx borough president renamed the block in honor of the then imprisoned Russian-Jewish dissident, **Anatoly Shcharansky**. The square and the dissident's name differ in spelling . . . it's The Bronx, after all.

R37

Eastern Bronx

E

**SOUNDVIEW • CLASON POINT • CASTLE HILL
UNIONPORT • VAN NEST • PARKCHESTER
WESTCHESTER SQUARE • MORRIS PARK
PELHAM PARKWAY • BRONXDALE • THROGS NECK
PELHAM BAY • COUNTRY CLUB AREA • CITY ISLAND**

 Colonial

 Georgian/ Federal

 Greek Revival

 Gothic Revival

 Villa

 Romanesque Revival

 Renaissance Revival

 Roman Revival

 Art Deco/ Art Moderne

 Modern/ Post-Modern

Until war clouds foreshadowed the start of World War II, this was a sleepy area of the Bronx. In its center was a large green space shaded by majestic trees, called the New York Catholic Protectory, an institute for destitute children. The neighborhoods around it were largely residential, with one-, two-, and four-family houses, stray apartment buildings, and all kinds of minor commercial, industrial, and institutional establishments. And many empty lots. To the north, along Pelham Parkway, and to the west, down to the Bronx River, were groups of six-story apartment buildings. To the south and east were marshland and peninsulas jutting out into the East River and the Long Island Sound: Clason Point, a resort and amusement center with a ferry to College Point, Queens; Ferry Point; and Throgs Neck. To the east were the remnants of the old Village of Westchester, called Westchester Square, hardly recognizable. And beyond lay Pelham Bay Park, the borough's largest, stretching north to the Westchester County line, and City Island, an oasis in the Sound.

Then the New York Catholic Protectory grounds were purchased by the Metropolitan Life Insurance Company, and in February 1940 the first of the 40,000 tenants who were to populate red brick, high-rise Parkchester moved in. The die was cast. Empty lots, cattail-filled swamp, even parts of Pelham Bay Park were to be decimated by the crush of a new population.

Today, the area south of Bruckner Boulevard is a phalanx of other red brick housing projects. Hospital facilities occupy the marshy lands that fed Westchester Creek, now diminished by the construction of a behemoth high school only yards from Westchester Square. Two of the peninsulas are springboards for suspension bridges to Long Island. A pleasant stretch of Pelham Bay Park along the banks of Eastchester Bay may one day become an urban ski slope, elevated by countless truckloads of smelly garbage deposited there, politely called landfill. "Progress" has come to the Eastern Bronx. Its effects are profound.

SOUNDVIEW

The community lying between the Bronx River and the parkway bearing the river's name. Cartoonist/playwright **Jules Feiffer** was raised here on Stratford Avenue when the area was predominantly Jewish (beginning with the arrival of the IRT Pelham Bay elevated in 1920). The area today is Hispanic. Don't confuse it with adjacent Clason Point, the peninsula that really does have a view of Long Island Sound. (The Sound seems to have been renamed East River by some non-tradition-bound cartographers.)

 [E1] **Public School 152**, Bronx, 1007 Evergreen Ave., NW cor. Bruckner Expwy. 1975. **Kahn & Jacobs**.
A handsomely composed earth-colored brick school structure that adds a note of gentle majesty to a physically humdrum neighborhood. It presents a particularly good appearance to users of the expressway.

Just east of Soundview:

[E2] **1341 Noble Avenue** (folk art), bet. E. 172nd and E. 174th Sts.

Semidetached brick houses are commonplace here and so, it would seem, the occupants of this particular one decided to give it some added character, adorning the exterior with the shiny detritus of our planned-to-be-obsolescent society: hubcaps, chrome-plated bumpers, etc. Don't miss a peek down the driveway.

CLASON POINT

A protuberance into either Long Island Sound or the East River, depending on your geographical alliances. It has, over the years, been labeled after its successive occupants: **Snakipins** (the native American settlement), **Cornell Point** (after **Thomas Cornell**, 1642), and finally **Clason Point** (after **Isaac Clason**). Between 1883 and 1927 it was the home of Clason Military Academy, operated by a Roman Catholic order. Before the trolley came, in 1910, public access was via boat, launch, or steamer from Long Island, Mott Haven, and Manhattan. The waters were not polluted then. The attractions were dance halls and hotels, picnic grounds and a bathing pier, restaurants, a saltwater pool, and places with names like Dietrich's, Gilligan's Pavilion and Killian's Grove, Higg's Camp Grounds, and Kane's Casino. (Kane's Casino held out until it caught fire in 1942.) Between 1923 and 1938 the City operated a popular ferry service to College Point, in Queens. Tragedy came in 1924 when a freak wind squall blew down the Clason Point Amusement Park's Ferris wheel (on the site of Shorehaven Beach Club, now endangered) killing 24. Prohibition, pollution, and competition (from filtered pools like easily accessible Starlight Park in nearby West Farms) finally doomed the resort area.

E3a

[E3] **Holy Cross Roman Catholic Church**, 600 Soundview Ave., NE cor. Taylor Ave. 1968. **Brother Cajetan J. B. Baumann, O.F.M.**

Powerful geometric brick masonry forms cry out "modern." But they cry too loud.

[E4] **Bethlehem Evangelical Lutheran Church**, 327 Bolton Ave., bet. O'Brien and Soundview Aves. W side. ca. 1915.

White aluminum clapboard-sided church with neo-Federal trim. A bit of history for this history-starved community.

E3b

Harding Park, named for President Harding, was well described by the Times *in 1981: "a folksy ramshackle village with an aura of another era. Its narrow macadam roads wander here and there, without benefit of sidewalks or street lamps, diverging off into muddy lanes and alleys. There are junked cars in driveways and wash drying on lines. Winterized bungalows of every size and shape . . . stand under tall trees." A haphazard, sewerless, but proud community that emerged from Clason Point's resort years, it abuts the waterfront south of O'Brien Avenue between White Plains Road and Leland Avenue. Still there!*

CASTLE HILL

Another peninsula projecting into the Sound/River, separated from Clason Point by an inlet called Pugsley Creek.

UNIONPORT

[E5] **Boulevard Manor** (apartments), 2001 and 2045 Story Ave., bet. Pugsley and Olmstead Aves. N side. 1974. **Gruzen & Partners**.

E5a

Among the enormous number of multistory housing developments dropped helter-skelter in the area south of Bruckner Expressway in the 1960s and 1970s, these two buildings alone deserve commendation for their architecture.

[E6] **White Plains Gardens** (apartments), 1221, 1223, 1225, 1227 White Plains Rd., bet. Gleason and Westchester Aves. W side. ca. 1929.

Enlightened middle-class housing: A privately sponsored for-profit miniproject: four 6-story elevator apartment houses wrapped around a green center court that is entered through a neo-Gothic gateway. Treed "play yards" were introduced into the empty side spaces obligated by the Multiple Dwelling Law. (The sunnier one, to the south of the buildings, was, of course, the most played in.)

VAN NEST

E6a

[E7] **Church of St. Dominic** (Roman Catholic), 1739 Unionport Rd., bet. Van Nest and Morris Park Aves. W side. 1926.

An asymmetrically placed Italian Romanesque Revival bell tower and a prominent spoked rose window brighten the narrow path of ancient Unionport Road. DOMINE • DILEXI • DECOREM • DOMUS • TUAE (Lord, I have loved the beauty of Thy house).

E6b

[E8] **1808-1814 Amethyst Street** (row houses), bet. Morris Park and Rhinelander Aves. E side. ca. 1895.

Common in Mott Haven, rare in Van Nest: brick, stone, and terra-cotta row houses, their stolid construction and form a healthy piece of history in this precinct of ephemeral materials.

PARKCHESTER

[E9] **Parkchester** (apartment development), E. Tremont Ave., Purdy St., McGraw Ave., Hugh J. Grant Circle, White Plains Rd. 1938-1942. **Board of Design: Richmond H. Shreve**, chairman; **Andrew J. Eken, George Gove, Gilmore D. Clarke, Robert W. Dowling, Irwin Clavan**, and **Henry C. Meyer, Jr.**

It was called "a city within a city" in its early days, with direct subway access to Manhattan: included were a large movie theater, over 100 stores including Macy's first branch, a bowling alley and bar/restaurant, parking garages for 3,000 cars, and 40,000 residents at a density of 250,000 people per square mile! As planning goes, however, it was an exceptionally thoughtful enterprise. Curving streets, lots of well-kept lawn, shrubbery, and trees, carefully planned pedestrian routes and recreation areas, and playful colored terra-cotta sculpture and face block— all were calculated to inspire and delight whenever visual boredom set in. Metropolitan Life Insurance Company, its sponsor, maintained it for almost 30 years until the N.Y.C.'s Human Rights Commission accused it of maintaining a white-only policy. In 1968 Parkchester was sold to real estate giant Helmsley-Spear, Inc., who proceeded to co-op it, quadrant by quadrant.

E7a

[E10] **Parkchester Branch, N.Y. Public Library**, 1985 Westchester Ave., bet. Hugh J. Grant Circle and Pugsley Ave. N side. 1985. **Richard Dattner & Assocs.**, architects. **Marcia Dalby**, sculptor.

A red brick arch with inlaid white brick crosses defines a sturdily fenced semicircular forecourt that bids welcome to those strolling under the noisy Pelham Bay elevated. Apparently, the first to have entered the fenced enclosure were oversized plasticized beasties (thanks to the city's 1% for art program).

[E11] **Starling Gardens** (apartments), 2141, 2143, 2145, 2147 Starling Ave., bet. Odell and Purdy Sts. N side. ca. 1929.

A clone of White Plains Gardens but here occupying a full blockfront. Enlightened housing for middle-class families.

WESTCHESTER SQUARE

W2

The now fractured green was the center of the old Village of Westchester, founded in 1653 and known as Oostorp under the Dutch. Between 1681 and 1759, while under British rule, the village was the seat of the County of Westchester, of which the Bronx was then part. It is now the focus of neighborhood shopping and a stop on several bus lines.

[W1] **St. Peter's Church in the Village of Westchester** (Episcopal), 2500 Westchester Ave., opp. St. Peter's Ave. E side. 1853-1855. **Leopold Eidlitz**. Clerestory addition and restoration, 1879. **Cyrus L. W. Eidlitz**. ● [W2] Originally **St. Peter's Chapel and Sunday school**/now **Foster Hall**. 1867-1868. **Leopold Eidlitz**. ●
[W3] **St. Peter's Graveyard**. 1702+ ●
A tribute to the vitality of this dour Gothic Revival composition is that it has withstood the vibration and the visual pollution of passing trains on the adjacent IRT Pelham Bay elevated structure and has survived to be dubbed an official city landmark.

W3

[W4] **Huntington Free Library and Reading Room**/ originally The Van Schaick Free Reading Room, 9 Westchester Sq., bet. Westchester and Tratman Aves. W side. 1882-1883. **Frederick Clarke Withers**. Addition to rear, 1890-1892. **William Anderson**. ●
When advised of the cost of its upkeep, local taxpayers refused to accept this gift from a fellow resident, **Peter Van Schaick**. It was only opened in 1891 (together with an extension to the rear) through the efforts (and added funding) of railroad magnate **Collis P. Huntington**, who maintained a summer residence in nearby Throgs Neck.

W4

[W5] **Owen Dolen Golden Age Center**, N.Y.C. Department of Parks & Recreation, Benson St., NW cor. Westchester Ave., Westchester Sq. ca. 1920. Altered, 1983, **John Ciardullo Assocs**.
Dramatic use of concrete and brightly painted industrial forms gives life to a preexisting senior citizens' center totally hemmed in by asphalt and traffic in this East Bronx hub.

W5

[W6] **44-53 Westchester Square** (linked row houses), bet. Ponton and Roberts Aves. E side. ca. 1912.
Look carefully and your time invested reflecting on this structure's unified glazed surfaces will be well spent: glazed brick and glazed terra-cotta wherever there are no windows or doors. A fascinating façade.

[W7] **Ferris Family Cemetery**, Commerce Ave. E of Westchester Sq., bet. Westchester Ave. and Butler Place. S side. 18th century.
As Woodlawn Cemetery is large, Ferris is small . . . but surviving, considering that its once bucolic surroundings are now a grimy industrial area. A lawnmower would help.

[W8] **Herbert H. Lehman High School**, E. Tremont Ave. at Hutchinson River Pkwy. S side. 1972. **The Eggers Partnership**, architects. **Roger Bolomey**, sculptor.
Built in response to a 1960s population explosion in the East Bronx, this school itself explodes over its site. Its gymnasium straddles the adjacent highway, its athletic facilities sit on filled-in Westchester Creek. An angular rust-brown steel sculpture boldly marks the entrance to the smooth, precast-concrete-sheathed building.

WESTCHESTER SQUARE, MORRIS PARK DISTRICTS
see pages 615-618

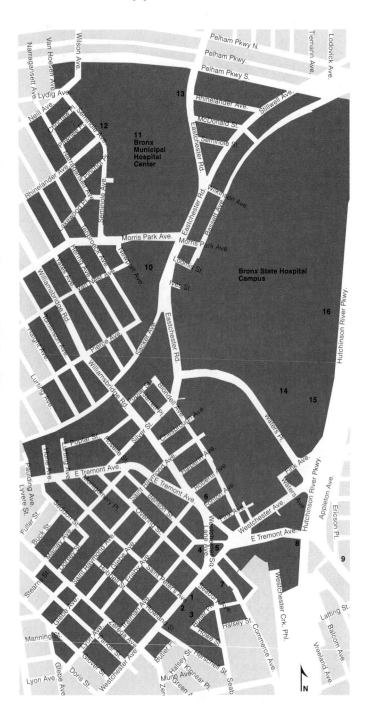

[W9] **First Presbyterian Church in Throgs Neck**, 3051 E. Tremont Ave., bet. Ericson Place and Dudley Ave. N side. ca. 1880.

Perched comfortably on a hill above a series of stone retaining walls, this red brick, limestone-trimmed church (and its graveyard to the rear) seem oblivious to the changes evident along the avenue below. Its steeple is a noteworthy marking of the land.

MORRIS PARK

Morris Park/Pelharn Pkwy/Eastchester Road hospital complex:

[W10] **Albert Einstein College of Medicine**, Yeshiva University, 1300 Morris Park Ave., SW cor. Eastchester Rd. [W10a] **Forchheimer Medical Science Building**. 1955. **Kelly & Gruzen**. [W10b] **Robbins Auditorium, Friedman Lounge, Gottesman Library**. 1958. **Kelly & Gruzen**. [W10c] **Ullman Research Center for Health Sciences**. 1963. **Kiesler & Bartos**. [W10d] Originally Bassine/now **Belfer Educational Center for Health Sciences**. 1971. **Armand Bartos & Assocs**. [W10e] **Chanin Cancer Research Center**. 1976. **Schuman, Lichtenstein, Claman & Efron**.

W9

Like Topsy (and many other college and hospital campuses), this place just grew. Most of the buildings are competent enough, but as a group they are a failure. Belfer, one of the newest, is by far the most distinguished . . . perhaps there is hope.

Across Morris Park Avenue to the north:

[W11] **Bronx Municipal Hospital Center**, N.Y.C. Health & Hospitals Corporation, Morris Park Ave. to Pelham Pkwy. S., W of Eastchester Rd. Original buildings: Abraham Jacobi Hospital and Nathan B. Van Etten Hospital. 1955. **Pomerance & Breines**. [W12] **Rose Fitzgerald Kennedy Center for Research in Mental Retardation and Human Development, Albert Einstein College of Medicine**, 1410 Pelham Pkwy. S. S side. 1970. **Pomerance & Breines**.

W10a

The same architectural firm, over a period of some 15 years, designed buildings for this hospital complex. Happily, everyone matures.

[W13] **49th Precinct, N.Y.C. Police Department**, 2121 Eastchester Rd., opp. Rhinelander Ave. W side. 1985. **Smotrich & Platt**, architects. **Ivan Chermayeff**, sculptor, **Chermayeff & Geismar Assocs**.

A geometric fantasy of a station house fronted by its own stand of—not trees—blue-painted steel bulrushes.

W12

The world's first air meets: On a 307-acre site, south of today's Pelham Parkway, between Bronxdale Avenue and Williamsbridge Road down to the former New Haven railroad right-of-way, some of the earliest public trials of powered aircraft were held in 1908 and 1909. Aviation pioneers Glenn H. Curtiss (and his partner Alexander Graham Bell) and Samuel P. Langley (of the Smithsonian) were drawn to the meets, as were as many as 20,000 spectators. The site had been, between 1889 and 1902, the Morris Park Racecourse, replacement for the earlier Jerome Park Racetrack, whose grounds in the West Bronx had been acquired to build the reservoir bearing the same name. Horse racing moved to Belmont Park in 1903; airplane meets moved too, and in 1910 a spectacular fire wiped out many of the remaining stables/hangars. Nary a trace of the course remains today save a blocked-up tunnel portal under Bronxdale Avenue, where crowded railroad coaches once deposited visitors to this onetime recreation mecca in the Bronx.

W13

Bronx State Hospital campus:

[W14] **Bronx State Hospital Rehabilitation Center, N.Y.S. Department of Mental Hygiene**, 1500 Waters Place, bet. Eastchester Rd. and Hutchinson River Pkwy. N side. 1971. **Gruzen & Partners**.

Intricate in plan, with many reentrant corners and projecting stair towers; yet the forms fall together with an effortlessness that is rare. An unassuming but fine work.

W16

[W15] **Bronx Children's Psychiatric Hospital, N.Y.S. Department of Mental Hygiene,** 1000 Waters Place, bet. Eastchester Rd. and Hutchinson River Pkwy. N side. 1969. **The Office of Max O. Urbahn.**

An attempt to lessen the oppressive institutional quality of the earliest Bronx State Hospital buildings (by the same firm) through the introduction of a domestically scaled collection of interlinked shed-roofed units.

[W16] **Bronx Developmental Center, N.Y.S. Department of Mental Hygiene,** Waters Place bet. Eastchester Rd. and Hutchinson River Pkwy. N side. 1976. **Richard Meier & Assocs.**

The advances of 20th-century technology are summed up in the forms and materials of this center for the mentally retarded. Dramatically located on a spacious and serene site along the edge of the Hutchinson River Parkway, its long, prismatic forms evoke the majesty of a rectilinear dirigible. Clad in a tightly stretched skin of natural anodized aluminum panels, it looks as if it were fabricated by an aircraft manufacturer, not by earth-bound building contractors. Windows, resembling enormous elongated portholes, add to the machine-age look, as does the proud expression of the intricate and colorful central mechanical system, which controls the building's inner environment. A consummate work of architecture, it is among the great complexes of its time.

PELHAM PARKWAY NEIGHBORHOOD

[P1] **Bronx Park Medical Pavilion**/former Bronxdale Swimming Pool Facilities, 2016 Bronxdale Ave. NE cor. Antin Place. ca. 1928.

Crowds of kids, mommas, and poppas no longer wait to plunge into the cool, chlorinated waters of this answer to the city's steamy summers. But the polychromed Art Deco terra-cotta ornament has been revived to house new socially desirable tenants.

[P2] **2009 Cruger Avenue** (apartments), ca. 1930. **2039, 2055 Cruger Avenue** (apartments), ca. 1937. All bet. Bronxdale and Brady Aves. W side. [P3] **2095, 2105 Cruger Avenue** (apartments), bet. Brady Ave. and Maran Place. W side. ca. 1938.

The West Bronx is Art Deco/Art Moderne heaven, but No. 2009 here (opposite the old Bronxdale Pool) is a strong Deco work whose vermilion glazed terra-cotta singles it out; its owners thoughtlessly removed its period metalwork after 1978. The casement windows of its Moderne neighbors up the block have been refenestrated, but the round-cornered fire escapes remain. Thank goodness!

P1

[P4] **Bronx and Pelham Parkway**, connecting Bronx Park and Pelham Bay Park.

Rarely referred to by any name other than just Pelham Parkway, this wide and luxuriant greenway has not suffered from the widenings and removal of ancient trees that other thoroughfares in the city have undergone. Prior to World War II the center lanes were closed off on Sunday mornings for bicycle racing.

[P5] **2166 and 2180 Bronx Park East** (apartments), bet. Lydig Ave. and Pelham Pkwy. S. E side. ca. 1937.

Six-story Art Moderne housing overlooking the lawns and trees of Bronx Park. The curse of the double-hung aluminum replacement sash has struck here as well.

Kosher pizza, bagels and lox, brisket and flanken: Unassuming Lydig Avenue (a block south of the Pelham Parkway Station of the IRT 241st Street-White Plains Road Lines), for about five blocks east of White Plains Road, was a busy, happy, prosperous shopping street of a vital Jewish community. The remaining Jewish merchants seem but lifeboats in a sea of the goyim. Most of the lifeboats now seem abandoned.

[P6] **Alhambra Gardens** (apartments), 750-760 Pelham Pkwy., bet. Holland and Wallace Aves. S side. 1927. **Springsteen & Goldhammer**.

PELHAM PARKWAY, BRONXDALE DISTRICTS
see pages 619-622

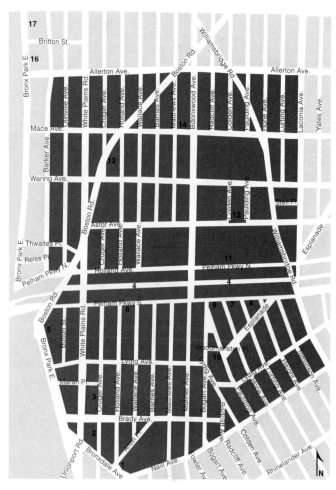

P7

P10

Unrepentantly romantic. The name Alhambra tells it all: Spanish tile, Spanish ironwork, Spanish detail all around a lush green courtyard. It's hard to accept that these are just well-planned 6-story elevator apartments.

[P7] **Morningside House** (residence for the aged), **Reception Building**, 1000 Pelham Pkwy S., bet. Lurting and Hone Aves. S side. [P8] **Administration and Medical Services Building**, bet. Lurting and Haight Aves. S side, through to Esplanade. All 1974. **Johnson Burgee**.

A rare architectural tribute to the dignity of our society's aged citizenry. An urbane pair of buildings with a carefully controlled, resortlike exterior, but without any reference to their Pelham Parkway context.

[P9] **Bronx House** (settlement house), **The Harris and Sarah Lichtman Building, and the S. H. and Helen R. Scheuer Swim Center**, 990 Pelham Pkwy. S., bet. Bogart/Paulding and Hone Aves. S side. 1970. 1973. All by **Westerman/Miller Assocs**.

Whoever thinks that "God is in the details" should look at those employed on this building. They are much too fussy and self-conscious.

[P10] **Morris Park Station, IRT Dyre Avenue Line** (No. 5 train)/originally on the former New York, Westchester & Boston Railway, The Esplanade at Paulding Ave. 1912. **Fellheimer & Long**, architects. **Allen H. Stem**, associated architect.

A Spanish Colonial Revival pavilion on axis of The
Esplanade, a diagonal thoroughfare marking the 3,940-foot-
long, cut-and-cover subway in which the defunct N.Y., W. & B.
commuter line bypassed treelined Pelham Parkway.

BRONXDALE

[P11] **New York Institute for the Education of the Blind**, 999
Pelham Pkwy. N., bet. Bronxwood Ave. and Williamsbridge Rd.
1924. **McKim, Mead & White**.

An inoffensive campus of neo-Georgian buildings for the
elementary and college-preparatory education of the blind and
visually handicapped.

P13

[P12] **Frampton Hall, New York Institute for the Education of
the Blind**, Astor Ave. NW cor. Paulding Ave. 1971. **Eggers &
Higgins**.

If blindness is not enough of a challenge, then mental retardation plus blindness is. This neatly designed facility is for the
treatment of just this combination of afflictions.

[P13] **2440 Boston Road**, N.Y.C. Housing Authority
(apartments), bet. Waring and Mace Aves. E side. 1972.
Davis Brody & Assocs.

P14

Twenty stories of housing predominantly for the elderly in
one tower, count them, two. With a bit of visual sleight of hand,
an otherwise bulky prism is made to look like two slender shafts
offset slightly from one another. And to top off this architectural
legerdemain, the tower is broader at the top (to accommodate
larger apartments) than at the bottom. The adjacent one-story
community center is a carefully contrasted foil for the tower.

[P14] **Lourdes of America**, on grounds of St. Lucy's Roman
Catholic Church, Bronxwood Ave. NW cor. Mace Ave. 1939.
Open to the public.

An amazing sight. Out of doors in a stone grotto rising high
above the adjacent sidewalks are hundreds of twinkling candles
in tiny red-glass containers, placed there by the devout who have
come to share in the many cures claimed for this replica of the
famous French shrine. (If St. Lucy's sounds strange to your ears,
think of the parish as Santa Lucia's.)

[P15] **Worker's Cooperative Colony/"The Coops"** (apartment
development), Bronx Park E. bet. Allerton and Arnow Aves. to

Barker Ave. [P16] **First House**, 2700-2774 Bronx Park E. S of Britton St. 1925-1927. **Springsteen & Goldhammer**.
[P17] **Second House**, 2846-2870 Bronx Park E. N of Britton St. 1927-1929. **Herman J. Jessor** of **Springsteen & Goldhammer**. 💣

Walk-ups built under the sponsorship of the United Workers Cooperative Association, consisting largely of unionized Eastern European Jewish garment workers, a group with strong left-wing political attachments. That may explain the use of a hammer-and-sickle motif above an entry door of First House (otherwise designed in a neo-Tudor style quite commonly found in the Bronx in the 1920s). The later Second House dispensed with both the political symbolism and the picturesque stylizing. The "Coops" (pronounced COOPS, not CO-ops) are believed to be the first cooperative housing built in the city since the successful efforts of the Finnish community in Brooklyn's Sunset Park. Since the "Coops'" advanced financing techniques were not matched by effective management, the Colony lost ownership in 1931 to the mortgage company, and thence to a private landlord in 1943. Following World War II, Jessor was architect of many large garment-union-sponsored housing developments as well as the immense Co-op City development.

THROGS NECK

Spelled with one or two g's and sometimes with an apostrophe, the name once referred to the outermost peninsula of land beyond East Tremont Avenue's end. Its name is derived from John Throckmorton, who settled here in 1643 while New York was still under Dutch rule. Until the early part of the 20th century this area was covered with estates. Today its inhabitants are modest, home-owning families.

[T1a] **St. Joseph's School for the Deaf** (Roman Catholic)/originally St. Joseph's Institute for the Improved Instruction of Deaf Mutes, 1000 Hutchinson River Pkwy., SE cor. Bruckner Blvd.
[T1b] **St. Helena's (now Commercial) High School** (Roman Catholic)/originally also St. Joseph's School for the Deaf, 55 Hutchinson River Pkwy., SW cor. Bruckner Blvd. Both ca. 1898. **Schickel & Ditmars**.

When the Hutchinson River Parkway was built in 1939 as the approach to the Bronx-Whitestone Bridge, the right-of-way cut St. Joseph's campus in two. Later, when the children of Parkchester grew in numbers to be of high school age, the parish of St. Helena's established a new secondary school, using the west half of St. Joseph's holdings. From a distance at least, these seem the epitome of 19th-century gloom, now coming back into style.

T2

[T2] **Preston High School** (Roman Catholic)/formerly "Homestead," Collis P. Huntington (summer) House/originally Frederick C. Havemeyer House, 2780 Schurz Ave., SE cor. Brinsmade Ave. ca. 1870.

It is so rare that a summer house with a recorded history survives this long that one is prepared to forgive its lack of great architectural distinction. (Huntington and family—whose wealth came from railroads—contributed a number of fine buildings in the city. Original owner Havemeyer was a sugar king.) The newer additions for high school use are unfortunate. The house became a school in 1924.

T3

[T3] **White Beach Condominiums and Marina**, 2716 Marina Dr./Schurz Ave., bet. Balcom and Huntington Aves. S side. 1985. **Mario Procida**.

White stucco, domestic resort architecture enlivened with yellow awnings and terraced with blue ships' railings. Quite appropriate in its waterfront setting between the Bronx-Whitestone and Throgs Neck bridges. Stylish order amid the ordinary.

THROGS NECK DISTRICT

see pages 622-624

[T4] **Silver Beach Gardens Corporation**, Pennyfield and Schurz Aves. to Long Island Sound. (Entrance: Chaffee Ave. at Pennyfield Ave.) [T5] Originally **Abijah Hammond House**/now **Offices, Silver Beach Gardens Corporation**, ca. 1800.

One of the three waterside communities in the Bronx where only the building is owned by the occupant, and ground rent is

T7

paid to the owner of the land. These buildings were originally summer cottages, but they now are winterized. Silver Beach Gardens' Indian Trail affords excellent views of the Sound.

The Hammond house, featuring Federal detail, was built by a wealthy trader who emigrated here after serving the Revolution in Massachusetts. Later, sugar king **Frederick C. Havemeyer**'s family occupied the house until 1914.

[T6] Fort Schuyler/now **SUNY Maritime College**, E end of Pennyfield Ave.

[T7] **Fort Schuyler.** 1833-1856. **Capt. I. L. Smith.** Conversion to Maritime College 1934-1938. Conversion of fort's dining hall (gun galleries) to the **Adm. Stephen Bleecker Luce Library, William A. Hall**, 1967. [T8a] **Vander Clute Hall** (dormitory, dining). 1963. [T8b] **Riesenberg Hall** (health and physical education). 1964. [T8c] **Marvin-Tode Hall** (science and ocean engineering). 1967. All by **Ballard Todd & Assocs.**

Don't be put off by the gate: all are welcome; stop and drive on. A tour along the perimeter road (it changes names a number of times) of this narrow neck of land will reveal views of Long Island Sound that make looking at the college's architecture difficult. Old Fort Schuyler itself is well worth a stop to visit its interior court (called St. Mary's Pentagon) and for views from its ramparts. Another 19th-century fortress (and landmark), Fort Totten, across the Sound, is more easily seen from here than from its home borough of Queens. It's hard to believe that the old fort lay abandoned between 1878 and 1934, when WPA funds enabled restoration for reuse.

Protecting our sea approaches: America's seacoast fortifications were developed in three stages. The First System was started in 1794 when it was feared that we might be drawn into the European wars that followed the French Revolution. The Second System, begun in 1807, was motivated by the potential danger from Great Britain that ended with the War of 1812. The Third System, unlike the first two (which had been responses to external threats), was initiated in a peaceful era in 1817 and continued until the time of the Civil War. Both Fort Schuyler and Fort Totten (1862-1864) were built as part of this Third System, to be able to rake with cannon fire any enemy approaching the port of New York via the Long Island Sound.

T10

[T9] **St. Frances de Chantal Church** (Roman Catholic), 190 Hollywood Ave., SE cor. Harding Ave. 1971. **Paul W. Reilly**.

It's hard to miss this church. Perhaps that's one of its faults. No faulting its stained glass, however—colorful chunks in the European style precast into concrete window panels.

T11

[T10] **Monastery of St. Clare** (Roman Catholic), 142 Hollywood Ave., bet. Schurz Ave. and Monsignor Halpin Place. N side. 1933. **Robert J. Riley**.

An eclectic blend of north European medieval crossed with virtuoso bricklaying. The entrance gable signifies a simplified Jesuitical façade. EGO • VOS • SEMPER • CUSTODIAM (Let me always watch over you).

All by itself to the northwest:

[T11] **714 Clarence Avenue** (house), bet. Randall and Philip Aves. NE side. ca. 1920.

The views over Long Island Sound make a drive along this part of Clarence Avenue unlike any other in the city. No. 714 is encrusted with mosaics applied in a vernacular style. So is the garage—even the birdhouse.

PELHAM BAY

Named for the adjacent park, this community lies west of it, contained by the Hutchinson River Parkway, Bruckner Boulevard/Expressway, and on the south by St. Raymond's (Roman Catholic) Cemetery.

P1

[P1] **Middletown Plaza** (apartments), N.Y.C. Housing Authority, 3033 Middletown Rd., bet. Hobart and Jarvis Aves. NW side. 1973. **Paul Rudolph.**

A tall, dramatic cast-concrete frame, gray, ribbed block infill, and gray window sash make this housing for the elderly Rudolph's best work in the borough and one of the Bronx's notable architectural apartment houses.

[P2] **Pelham Bay Branch, N.Y. Public Library**, 3060 Middletown Rd., SE cor. Jarvis Ave. 1976. **Alexander A. Gartner.**

A modest modern library with an inviting plaza. It shares the block with the American Indian museum's annex.

[P3] **Museum of the American Indian**, Heye Foundation Annex, Bruckner Blvd. SW cor. Middletown Rd.

This is a warehouse and research center for the museum whose public galleries are in the old Custom House at Bowling Green in Manhattan. Totem poles, Indian houses, and concrete wigwams are displayed on the lawns, but you can't go inside.

P4

[P4] **St. Theresa of the Infant Jesus** (Roman Catholic) Church, 2855 St. Theresa Ave., NW cor. Pilgrim Ave. 1970. **Anthony J. DePace.**

An exhibition pavilion? But heavily ornamented with robust stained glass and mosaic tile tesserae. The old church bell is displayed across the street, and the inscription locates the original church at Pilgrim and Morris Park Avenues. (St. Theresa Avenue is the eastern extension of Morris Park Avenue; its name was changed in 1968.)

Pelham Bay Park:

The largest of the six parks purchased as a result of the new Bronx parks program of 1883. At that time this one was outside the New York City limits. It contains two golf courses, an archery range, bridle paths, the Police Department firing range (private), and ample facilities for hiking, cycling, horseback riding, and motoring. Shell racing is held in the North Lagoon. Between 1910 and 1913 a monorail traversed the park from the New Haven Railroad line to City Island.

P6

[P5] **Pelham Bay Park World War Memorial**, Shore Rd. E of Bruckner Expwy. SE side. ca. 1925. **John J. Sheridan**, architect. **Belle Kinney**, sculptor.

One of the city's handsomest and best-maintained monuments (unlike nearby Rice Stadium).

[P6] **Bartow-Pell Mansion Museum**/originally Robert and Marie Lorillard Bartow House, Pelham Bay Park, Shore Rd. near Pelham-Split Rock Golf Course, S side. 1675. Alterations, 1836-1842. attributed to **Minard Lafever**. Restoration, 1914. **Delano & Aldrich.** 🖌 Interiors 🖌 Open to the public. 718-885-1461. Wednesday, Saturday, Sunday, 12-4; closed Mon, Tues, Thu, Fri.

Lords of the Manor of Pelham once owned this house, which was later enlarged, renovated, and remodeled in the Federal style. The mansion became the home of the International Garden Club in 1914. The Pell family plot, a magnificent formal garden, a view of Long Island Sound from the grounds, and rare and tasteful furnishings within combine to make a visit worthwhile.

P7

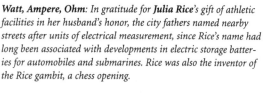 [P7] **Orchard Beach**, N.Y.C. Department of Parks & Recreation, E shore of Pelham Bay Park on Long Island Sound. 1936. N.Y.C. Parks Department, **Aymar Embury II**, architectural consultant.

A large, sandy, crescent-shaped beach reopened in 1936 after extensive remodeling by the WPA and the Department of Parks. The bathhouses are enhanced by a strong concrete colonnades, chastely decorated with blue terra-cotta tiles. A beach cafeteria rests under the spacious entry terrace. This is a good public place, monumental without being overpowering, and elegantly spartan.

[P8] **Rice Memorial Stadium**, Pelham Bay Park, NW of Middletown Rd. and Stadium Ave. 1922. **Herts & Robertson**.

This concrete stadium is unusual because of the small Greek temple atop the bleachers that frames Louis St. Lannes's heroic statue *The American Boy*. The stadium was given to the city by the widow of Isaac L. Rice as part of a complex of other athletic facilities including a 330-foot-long swimming pool, bathhouse, bleachers, and a decorative 100-foot white marble Doric column. All but the stadium are gone today. The Rices' mansion still stands along Riverside Drive at West 89th Street.

 ***Watt, Ampere, Ohm***: *In gratitude for **Julia Rice**'s gift of athletic facilities in her husband's honor, the city fathers named nearby streets after units of electrical measurement, since Rice's name had long been associated with developments in electric storage batteries for automobiles and submarines. Rice was also the inventor of the Rice gambit, a chess opening.*

COUNTRY CLUB AREA

P9

Country Club Road leads to the Westchester Country Club (named for the Bronx when it was still part of Westchester County) at the water's edge. This area has long been known for its large homes on generous sites, now the residences of affluent Italian- and Greek-Americans.

[P9] **Providence Home for Aged Women**/Generoso Pope Memorial, Sisters of St. John the Baptist (Roman Catholic), Stadium Ave. opp. Waterbury Ave. E side. ca. 1920. Additions 1936, 1957, 1967, 1979.

A comfortable place to spend one's golden years, overlooking the Sound, named for the publisher of the longtime Italian-language newspaper, *Il Progresso Italiano*, and a mover in the sand and gravel business.

CITY ISLAND

A tight little island that is part of New York City by law but has scarcely any other connections. Its first industry was the Solar Salt Works, which made salt by evaporating seawater. That was in 1830. Then came oystering and eventually yacht building. (Though this activity has declined, City Island's shipwrights have built a number of our entries in the America's Cup race including the 1967 and 1970 winner, *Intrepid*.) Filmmaking came to the island around 1900, together with D. W. Griffith, Douglas Fairbanks, and the Keystone Kops, who filmed a scene on Fordham Street. Fish and seafood fanciers are today's most important asset to the island's economy: City Island Avenue is filled with restaurants of every description. As the Hispanic population of the borough burgeons, more and more of City Island's signs seek to cultivate a Spanish-speaking clientele.

On the streets that run perpendicular to the fishbone spine of City Island Avenue are more than a handful of distinguished older houses, now engulfed by latter-day lightweights. There is space to mention only a few:

C1

[C1] **21 Tier Street** (house), W of City Island Ave. N side. ca. 1894.

A Shingle Style jewel. Compare it with its self-consciously modernized neighbor at No. 33.

[C2] **City Island Branch, New York Public Library**, City Island Ave., SE cor. Bay St. 1990s.

Soldier course brick round the corner to a light monitor for readers and a porthole to remind one of, but limit noise from, the traffic outside.

[C3] **City Island Museum**/originally Public School 17, Bronx, 190 Fordham St., E of City Island Ave. S side. 1898. **C. B. J. Snyder**. Open to the public—limited hours.

A stolid school, by the dean of New York City's early school architects, that dates from the very year of the City's consolidation. This one, properly, is a modest work befitting a remote outpost.

C4

[C4] **284 City Island Avenue** (apartments), bet. Fordham and Hawkins Sts. E side. ca. 1898.

A 19th-century high rise, at least in the context of City Island's environment: five stories tall (including its attic) but only 20 feet wide. Its gambrel roof and Palladian window add just the right zest.

[C5] T**he Boatyard Condominium**, 210 Carroll St., E of City Island Ave. Both sides. 1986. **William Milo Barnum & Assocs**.

An appropriate colony of wood-frame, modestly proportioned structures offering 70 units fronting on the Sound.

C5

Schofield Street: West of City Island Avenue.

[C6] **65 Schofield St.** (house). N side. ca. 1865.
[C7] **62 Schofield St.** (house). S side. ca. 1865.
No. 65, serene and peeling, seems a candidate for a **Hopper** painting: austere, venerable, self-confident on a shrubless lawn.

[C8] **84-86 Schofield St.** (house). S side. ca. 1875.
Only one story in height but with a grand mansard. Note the monumental porch and French doors (instead of windows) leading to it. Check No. 90 next door as well: filigreed brackets and pediment.

[C9] **95 Pell Place** (house), W of City Island Ave. N side. 1930.
An Arts and Crafts bungalow from the Sears Roebuck catalog. The masonry-piered and timber-bracketed porch brings deep shade and shadow to the street.

CITY ISLAND

see pages 627-628

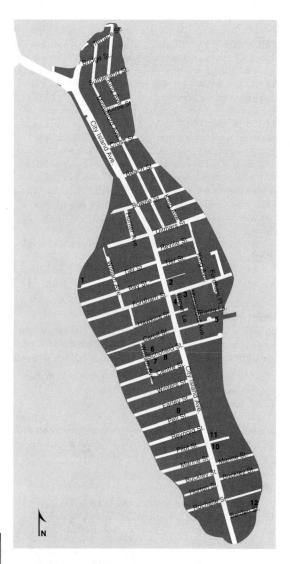

N

C10

C12

[C10] **Grace Church** (Episcopal), 104 City Island Ave., SE cor. Pilot St. 1867. [C 10a] **Rectory**, ca. 1862.

A pair of gems that befits an off-the-beaten-track seafaring community. The church is a paragon of Gothic Revival wood craftsmanship.The rectory is a modest frame structure derived from the Italian Villa Style.

[C11] **141 Pilot Street** (house), NE cor. City Island Ave. ca. 1862.

A flat-roofed Italianate delight, with lathe-turned porch posts, stepped brackets, and eyebrow windows. The flush boards hoped to simulate stuccoed masonry.

[C12] **173 Belden Street** (house), E of City Island Ave. to the water. N side. ca. 1880. 🍎 (Down a single lane, dead-end street: walk . . .)

A very well preserved picturesque cottage, rare in the city, located almost at the southernmost tip of the island.

**WILLIAMSBRIDGE • BAYCHESTER
EASTCHESTER • WAKEFIELD**

The Northern Bronx has been the site of settlement since the 17th century, and for some two months in the 18th century the nation's executive mansion was here. But most of this area's modest homes and scattered groups of apartment houses (as well as gargantuan Co-op City) date from the 20th.

WILLIAMSBRIDGE

Hillside Homes:

[N1] **Eastchester Heights**/originally Hillside Homes (apartment development), almost five city blocks, W of Boston Rd. bet. Wilson Ave. and Eastchester Rd. through to Hicks St. bet. Wilson and Fenton Aves. 1935. **Clarence S. Stein**.
  Is it high land costs or planning prejudices that seem to make it impossible to duplicate this highly successful moderate-rental housing development? Most of the buildings here are only 4 stories high, and they occupy one-third of the land. A large central playground and community center are provided for school-age children, while sandboxes and tot lots are placed away from street traffic inside 7 large sunken interior courts reached through tunnel passageways. The design builds upon Stein's earlier Sunnyside Gardens.

N1

Nineteenth-century **Williamsbridge:** *The discontinuous street pattern found in the dozen blocks northeast of the East Gun Hill Road-White Plains Road intersection marks a charmingly seren-dipitous 19th-century wood-frame residential community that is worth a brief visit. The houses reflect the 1980s adulteration of architectural integrity and detail resulting from the gullibility of naive owners swallowing the fast talk of aluminum window and siding dealers. A great loss.*

N2

[N2] **Private Chapel** (Roman Catholic), E. 215th St. bet. Holland and Barnes Ave. S side. 1905. **Frank Lisanti**.
  In contrast to the public devotions at Lourdes of America, this is a place for private meditations: a humble chapel transposed from the slopes of southern Italy. Below the bell and the ornate wrought ironwork cross is carved:

F. LISANTI
IN DEVOZIONE
DELL' IMMACOLATA
PER SE E FAMIGLIA
ERESSE
1905

N3

  (**F. Lisanti** erected [this] for himself and his family in devotion to the Blessed Virgin. 1905.)

[N3] **Regent School, Kindergarten and Primary Grades**, 719 E. 216th St., bet. White Plains Rd. and Barnes Ave. N side. ca. 1915.
  Four economically spaced Doric columns carry a substantial pediment ornamenting a sprightly (if somewhat officious-appearing) structure in this modest, lower-middle-class community.

[N4] **Crawford Memorial United Methodist Church**, 3757 White Plains Rd., bet. E. 217th and E. 218th Sts., W side. ca. 1890.
  Rock-face random ashlar, with both great arched openings and blind arches relieving the dour gneiss masses.

N4

N5

N8

N10

N12

N13

[N5] **Emmanuel Baptist Church**, 3711 White Plains Rd., bet. E. 216th and E. 217th Sts. W side. ca. 1895.

A powerful Romanesque Revival brick and terra-cotta church stands resplendent atop an earthen berm: both berm and church predate the adjacent IRT elevated structure.

[N6] Originally **St. Luke's Episcopal Church**, 661 E. 219th St., bet. Carpenter Ave. and White Plains Rd. opp. Willett Ave. N side. ca. 1885.

A country church of shingles, stucco, and half timber, engulfed by an early, urbanizing Bronx. Its space is shared, in an ecumenical marathon, by St. George's Episcopalians, St. Luke's Senior Center, the Emmanuel 7th Day Adventists, and the Restoration Church of God!

[N7] **Peter Gillings Apartments**, 737 E. 219th St., bet. White Plains Rd. and Barnes Ave. N side. ca. 1905.

The rock-faced stone façade of this early (for this neighborhood) 3-story multiple dwelling proudly proclaims its developer's name.

[N8] **St. Peter's Evangelical Lutheran Church**, 741 E. 219th St., bet. White Plains Rd. and Barnes Ave. N side. ca. 1898.

A modest Shingle Style church with intact brown-stained shingles and white trim. Ever see wood-shingled buttresses before? Quite wonderful.

[N9] **St. Valentine's** (Roman Catholic) **Church and Parish Hall**, 809 E. 220th St., bet. Barnes and Bronxwood Aves. N side. ca. 1890.

Skip the newer masonry church on East 221st Street, and gaze upon the old wood-frame hall behind—was it the original meeting place of the congregation?—before it falls to the march of progress. (The church was originally built for a Polish congregation.)

[N10] **3925 Barnes Avenue** (tenement), NW cor. E. 223rd St. ca. 1885.

A 3-story wood-frame building redolent of the late 19th century. This antique, together with the houses two blocks north, contains the seeds of the Bronx's own Old Sturbridge Village.

[N11] **777 East 225th Street** (house) and 3981 Barnes Avenue (house), NW cor. E. 225th St. ca. 1875.

A pair of diminutive, wood-shingled, gabled houses, each with a tiny front porch.

[N12] **First Presbyterian Church of Williamsbridge and Rectory**, 730 E. 225th St., bet. White Plains Rd. and Barnes Ave. S side. 1903. **John Davidson**.

A provincial shingle masterpiece. An asymetrical composition, its square belfry to one side, bearing a marvelous ogival roof atop four sets of paired pilasters. Wood-shingled eclecticism.

[N13] **47th Precinct, N.Y.C. Police Department**, 4111 Laconia Ave., bet. E. 229th and E. 230th Sts. W side. 1974. **Davis, Brody & Assocs.**

It's not unreasonable to conceive of a police station as an updated medieval castle. But when dreams become brick-and-mortar reality, problems can surface. They do here in this overly contrived design.

WILLIAMSBRIDGE DISTRICT

see pages 629-630

BAYCHESTER

[B1] **Junior High School 144,** Bronx, The Michelangelo School, 2545 Gunther Ave., SW cor. Allerton Ave. 1968. **The Office of Max O. Urbahn**.

Entirely of cast-in-place concrete, a fashionable "advanced" building system in the 1960s. It has not aged well.

[B2] **Co-op City**. Northern section: E of New England Thruway/ Baychester Ave. bet. Co-op City Blvd. and Bartow Ave. Southern section: E of Hutchinson River Pkwy. E., bet. Bartow and Boller Aves. 1968-1970. **Herman J. Jessor**, architect. **Zion & Breen**, landscape architects.

B1

Out in the middle of nowhere, on marshy land that was once the site of an ill-fated amusement park named Freedomland, a group of government officials, union representatives, and housing developers dreamed the impossible dream. Today the dream may better be described as a coma. From out of the pumped-sand fill rises a mountain range of 35-story residential towers, 35 of them, plus 236 clustered two-family houses and eight multistory parking garages. In addition, there are three shopping centers, a heating plant, a firehouse, and an educational park consisting of two public schools, two intermediate schools, and a high school. In this total non-environment, largely designed by bureaucrats with not a scintilla of wit, live some 55,000 souls, many of whom vacated sound accommodations in the West Bronx (in many cases Art Deco apartment blocks) to move here.

B3

B4

B6

Let's be thankful for the landscaping. It's the best thing at Co-op City.

EASTCHESTER

When that part of the Bronx lying east of the Bronx River was lopped off Westchester County in 1895, the dividing line ran right through the village of Eastchester. As a result, the old village green lies a stone's throw outside city limits. This community of the northeasternmost Bronx is still referred to, however, by its colonial name. It is largely a wasteland, unfortunately: automobile repair shops, fast-food operations, marginal industry, and the like. But at its edges and even within are some bright spots.

[B3] **Public School 15**, Bronx (Annex to P.S. 68, Bronx)/formerly Public School 148, Bronx/originally Village of Eastchester public school, 4010 Dyre Ave., bet. Dark and Lustre Sts. E side. 1877. **Simon Williams**. ●
  An architectural "pot of gold" at the end of the (once upon a time?) rainbow-graffitied Dyre Avenue IRT Line: a gingerbread brick-and-wood-trimmed schoolhouse that wound up on the New York City side of the boundary when Eastchester was split in two. Its cheerful forms can't help but make you smile.

WAKEFIELD

[B4] **St. Anthony's Church** (Roman Catholic), 4501 Richardson Ave., NW cor. E. 239th St. 1975. **Belfatto & Pavarini**.
  Strongly articulated brick forms topped by a tall slender pylon carrying a carefully detailed cross.

[B5] **St. Paul's Slovak Evangelical Lutheran Church**, 729 Cranford Ave., bet. White Plains Rd. and Barnes Ave. N side. 1928. Altered, 1962.
  A small but out-of-the-ordinary ashlar stone church distinguished by a trio of bronze bells embraced by the very top of its façade.

[B6] **4577 Carpenter Avenue** (house), SW cor. W. 240th St. ca. 1880.
  A house in the Eastlake Style with imbricated shingles on the Carpenter Avenue frontage and clapboard siding elsewhere. Look carefully—the mature fir trees tend to conceal detail.

Brooklyn

BROOKLYN

Borough of Brooklyn/Kings County

3

 Colonial

 Georgian/
Federal

 Greek
Revival

 Gothic
Revival

 Villa

 Romanesque
Revival

 Renaissance
Revival

 Roman
Revival

 Art Deco/
Art Moderne

 Modern/
Post-Modern

THE BROOKLYN APPROACH

"Brooklyn's situation for grandeur, beauty, and salubrity is unsurpassed probably on the whole surface of the globe: and its destiny is to be among the most famed and choice of the half dozen cities of the world . . ."
—Walt Whitman, 1861.

"New York is Babylon; Brooklyn is the truly holy City. New York is the city of office work, and hustle: Brooklyn is the region of home and happiness . . . There is no hope for New Yorkers, for they glory in their skyscraping sins; but in Brooklyn there is the wisdom of the lowly."
—Christopher Morley, 1917.

"It'd take a guy a lifetime to know Brooklyn t'roo an' t'roo. An' even den, yuh wouldn't know it all."
—Thomas Wolfe, 1935.

"Terribly funny, yes, but Brooklyn is also a sad brutal provincial lonesome human silent sprawling raucous lost passionate subtle bitter immature innocent perverse tender mysterious place, a place where Crane and Whitman found poems, a mythical dominion against whose shores the Coney Island sea laps a wintry lament."
—Truman Capote, 1946.

Legions of row houses march across the varied precincts of old and middle-aged Brooklyn (1820-1920), punctuated by apartment blocks sometimes new and viable, sometimes old and burned out, and marred with the scars of peacetime wars. In further reaches, two-, three-, and single-family houses flood the plains washed out from the glacier's last bluffs (terminal moraine), atop which old Brooklyn sits. Litter, stickball in the summer, roller skate hockey in the winter, steeples silhouetted against a sometimes smoggy sky—all edge against the imperious towers of the skyline that lies across the bay. These are the traditional caricatures of Brooklyn, valid in essence but only part of a rich civic fabric that is both urban and suburban, and that bears an extant architectural history older and richer than its more urbane fellow borough (sometime competing separate city), Manhattan.

The physical objects themselves have not undergone serious transformation; with certain notable exceptions they seem only to age and become begrimed. In large measure it is our way of seeing them that changes. Brooklyn today, even to many of its residents, is very often the image absorbed from a car on a limited-access highway: the industry of the north end, the spin along the Narrows with the Verrazano Bridge punctuating the contrast between people and nature. Motorists also remember the intricate spider web of Coney Island's Wonder Wheel, the endless stretches of swampland at Jamaica Bay, or the sinuous curves of the parkway along verdant Jackie Robinson (formerly Interboro)

Parkway (1935). The placement of our highways and the speed of our cars tend to obscure the essence of most of Brooklyn as a pedestrian-streeted residential community of variegated neighborhoods, and to mark its peripheral monuments as separate objects divorced from the borough's basic context.

Old Brooklyn today (that highland on the terminal moraine) is largely a nineteenth-century city of brownstones, town houses, and tenements, in large part intact because of enduring service as housing for the middle class. After the borough's consolidation with New York in 1898, much of the population emigrated to Manhattan. Until the end of World War II, the brownstone, whitestone, and brick row houses became—by default—the refuge of middle-class families, who banded together neighborhood by neighborhood. After their daily commute to Manhattan (New York or The City to Brooklyn natives), they retreated each night to their homes across the river. As architects succumbed to their passion for all things new and modern, Brooklyn was forgotten. The rediscovery in the late 1960s of vast stretches of brownstone Brooklyn, led by a young and sophisticated upper-income middle class marked a change in the way the borough was perceived.

Viable and venerable residential communities, seeming backwaters in the mainstream of physical change, such as Brooklyn Heights, Park Slope, the Hills (Clinton, Cobble, and Boerum), Carroll Gardens, Prospect Heights—their renaissance is now spurring the exploration of many of Brooklyn's other precincts—Williamsburg and Greenpoint, Sunset Park and Dyker Heights. Places abandoned by families in their search for a suburban Shangri-la are now being reclaimed by families who savor the architecture and life of a streetfronted, park-studded subway-served Brooklyn.

636

BROOKLYN KEY MAP

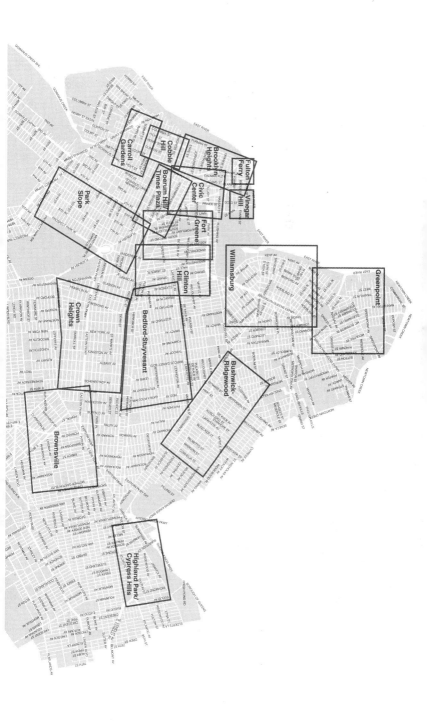

**CIVIC CENTER / DOWNTOWN BROOKLYN
BROOKLYN HEIGHTS • FULTON FERRY DISTRICT
VINEGAR HILL • COBBLE HILL • CARROLL GARDENS
GOWANUS • RED HOOK
SUNSET PARK AND ENVIRONS
BOERUM HILL / TIMES PLAZA • FORT GREENE
CLINTON HILL • NAVY YARD • PARK SLOPE
PROSPECT PARK / GRAND ARMY PLAZA
INSTITUTE PARK • BEDFORD-STUYVESANT
CROWN HEIGHTS**

Town of Brooklyn / Breukelen

Established as a town before 1658, incorporated as a city in 1834. Annexed the City of Williamsburgh and the Town of Bushwick in 1855, Town of New Lots in 1886, Towns of Flatbush, Gravesend, and New Utrecht in 1894, and Town of Flatlands in 1896. Consolidated into greater New York City in 1898.

The original Town, later City, of Brooklyn encompassed all the brownstone neighborhoods again fashionable today, mostly atop the high ground left by the last glacier, the terminal moraine. The residential precincts of Brooklyn Heights, Fort Greene, Clinton Hill, Park Slope, Bedford-Stuyvesant, Crown Heights, Cobble Hill, and Boerum Hill are all within the boundaries of the original town—as are the Brooklyn Civic Center and the shopping mall along the newly renovated Fulton Street. In addition, the once teeming waterfront facilities from the Manhattan Bridge south to the deactivated Brooklyn Army Terminal lie within the area, as do the backup residential communities of Red Hook, Gowanus, and Sunset Park. And within the old town's boundaries are half of both Prospect Park and Green-Wood Cemetery as well.

Although the extent of the old town can still be accurately charted, it is of little significance in any overall sense today when compared to the individual communities that it comprises.

CIVIC CENTER / DOWNTOWN BROOKLYN

The independent City of Brooklyn moved quickly to give form to its identity by building a city hall, which still stands as its seat of borough affairs. As the 19th century progressed, Brooklyn's population and wealth grew, and so did its civic center. With city hall as the focus, there soon emerged a variety of richly embellished governmental and commercial buildings, hotels, and shopping emporia. But to a visitor to Downtown Brooklyn during this era of expansion, the most apparent features were not its richly ornamented buildings but the spindly iron trestles that inundated many of its major streets, throwing zebra-striped shadows. For this part of Brooklyn was to be not only the city's hub of government and shopping but of transportation as well, and the elevateds crisscrossing overhead made their way down Fulton Street and Myrtle Avenue to their connections to Manhattan. It was not until after World War II that the elevated filigrees were demolished and today's Cadman Plaza Park built.

Civic Center/Downtown Brooklyn Walking Tour: From Borough Hall to the Flatbush Avenue-Fulton Street intersection, about a half-mile walk. (Subway to the Borough Hall Station of the IRT Lexington and Seventh Avenue Lines (Nos. 2, 3, 4, & 5 trains), or the BMT Court Street Station, Court Street exit (M, N, & R trains).)

The first buildings are gathered around Cadman Plaza. Walk north from Joralemon Street to Tillary Street and beyond.

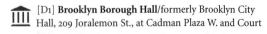 [D1] **Brooklyn Borough Hall**/formerly Brooklyn City Hall, 209 Joralemon St., at Cadman Plaza W. and Court

St. N side. 1845-1848. **Gamaliel King.** Cupola, 1898. **Vincent C. Griffith** and **Stoughton & Stoughton.** Statue of Justice installed and building restored, 1987-1989, **Conklin & Rossant.** 🕊

A Greek Revival Palace, later crowned with a Victorian cupola, it presents a bold face to Cadman Plaza, particularly monumental due to the broad, steep mass of steps rising to its entrance colonnade. First intended to be a lesser copy of New York's City Hall (1802-1811) across the river, the project went through four designs. In the elapsed time aesthetic moods changed, and the Franco-Georgian design of 1802 became the Greek Revival world of the 1830s and 1840s. According to Brooklyn's city directory, King was a grocer until 1830, then a carpenter—not unusual in an era when **Thomas Jefferson** designed the University of Virginia, and the Capitol of the United States was built according to the competition-winning design of a physician, **William Thornton.**

D1

D2

[D2] **Brooklyn Municipal Building**, 210 Joralemon St., SE cor. Court St., opposite Borough Hall. 1926. **McKenzie, Voorhees & Gmelin.**

The background building where much of the municipal bureaucracy functions, as contrasted with the foreground building, Borough Hall, the ceremonial center. A grand set of Tuscan columns presents an entrance to the subway.

[D3] **Brooklyn Law School Annex**, 250 Joralemon St., bet. Court St. and Boerum Pl. 1994. **Robert A. M. Stern.**

Post-modern in the free-wheeling neo-Renaissance sense, but blandly executed. But it is an architectural prizewinner compared to its earlier neighbor, the 1970s Law School.

D3

[D4] **Borough Hall Station**, IRT Lexington Avenue Line, below Joralemon St., E of Court St. 1908. **Samuel B. Parsons**, chief engineer. **Heins & La Farge**, architects. Redesigned and restored, 1987, **Mayers & Schiff.** 🕊

A series of richly modeled and colored faience plaques carries the abbreviation BH, and subtly colored mosaic tesserae and pink marble further humanize the straightforward engineers' works in this Contract 2 station, opened four years after completion of the original IRT Contract 1 work at Manhattan's City Hall Station. Ornate bronze dedication plaques located on the mezzanine's north wall (no fare required) explain the sequence further.

D4

[D5] **Temple Bar Building**, 44 Court St., NW cor. Joralemon St. 1901. **George L. Morse.**

Three verdigris cupolas crown this office building, Brooklyn's highest when it was built, heralding the arrival of the 20th century. Tacky at street level.

[D6] **Cadman Plaza** (officially S. Parkes Cadman Plaza), bounded by Cadman Plaza W., Court, Joralemon and Adams Sts., and the Brooklyn Bridge approaches. 1950-1960. Designed by various city and borough agencies. **Christopher Columbus** monument: statue, 1867, **Emma Stebbins**, sculptor; base and installation at this site, 1971, **A. Ottavino. Senator Robert F. Kennedy** sculpture, 1972, **Anneta Duveen**, sculptor.

Scarcely a plaza, this is an amorphous park created by demolition of several blocks east of Brooklyn Heights. A principal goal was to create a graceful setting for new Civic Center buildings that would complement Borough Hall. Almost equally important fringe benefits were the elimination of the elevated tracks that crossed the Brooklyn Bridge and crowded Fulton Street and the easing of automobile traffic through street-widening. Stebbins' statue of Columbus originally stood in Central Park. It was carved two years after she completed the Angel of the Waters and supporting cherubs for the Bethesda Fountain.

D8

[D7] **N.Y.S. Supreme Court**, 360 Adams St., S part of Cadman Plaza opposite Montague St. 1957. **Shreve, Lamb & Harmon**.

Unlike the nation's Supreme Court, New York's Supreme Court is the lowest court, where legal action first commences. **Shreve, Lamb & Harmon** are best known for the Empire State Building (1931). A handsome set of architectural nostalgia is the pair of lamps from the now-demolished Hall of Records (1905. **R. L. Daus**).

D9

[D8] **Statue of Henry Ward Beecher**, near Johnson St., S part of Cadman Plaza. 1891. **John Quincy Adams Ward**, sculptor; **Richard Morris Hunt**, architect of the base.

Mr. Beecher, the preacher and brother of **Harriet Beecher Stowe**, was relocated from his perch confronting Borough Hall to decorate the expanse of the new Cadman Plaza. The fence and lawn surrounding the sculpture are unfortunate, for Ward's strong concept should allow people to join the figures already touching the base at Beecher's feet.

[D9] **U.S. Post Office** (Downtown Brooklyn Station)/ originally General Post Office, 271-301 Cadman Plaza E, NE cor. Johnson St. 1885-1891. **Mifflin E. Bell** (original design); **William A. Freret**, successor. Remodeled, 2000. **R.M. Kliment & Frances Halsband** ☀ [9b] **U.S. Bankruptcy Court and United States Attorney's Offices**/originally North addition, Brooklyn General Post Office, 271-301 Cadman Plaza E 1930-1933. **James Wetmore**. ☀ Remodeled, 2000. **R.M. Kliment & Frances Halsband**.

The original building on the south is in an exuberant Romanesque Revival. Deep reveals and strong modeling provide a rich play of light. The taller addition is a humorless tail attempting to wag its lusty dog. The spectacular atrium may again be revealed to the general public.

[D10] **Federal Courthouse**, 275 Washington St., NE cor. Tillary St., on Cadman Plaza. 2002. **Cesar Pelli & Associates** and **HLW International**.

Another bow-bellied monster from the scrapbooks of big-time corporate architecture; 14 stories here makes 250 feet due to the height of courtroom spaces.

D12

[D11] **Brooklyn War Memorial**, N part of Cadman Plaza, opposite Orange St. 1951. **Eggers & Higgins**, architects. **Charles Keck**, sculptor.

Though its innards contain a small museum and other community facilities, its primary role is as a wall, completing the plaza's formal composition of terrace, paths, shrubs, trees, and lawn.

Return to Tillary Street and follow it east.

[D12] **New York City Technical College**, CUNY, Tillary Street, bet. Jay and Adams Sts., S side. Expanded, 1987, **Edward Durrell Stone Assocs.**

CIVIC CENTER / DOWNTOWN BROOKLYN DISTRICT
see pages 638–647

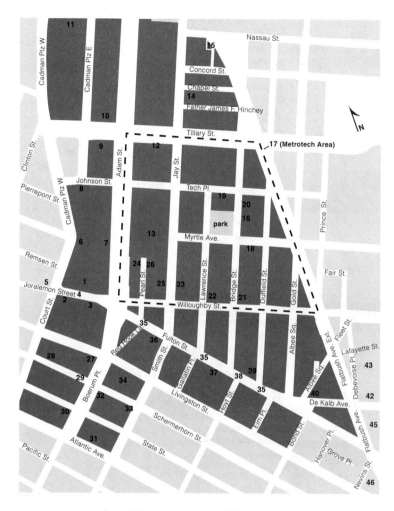

A vast new greenhouse links the two earlier buildings that separately front on Adams and Jay. The resulting plaza is a welcome urban space.

[D13] **Renaissance Plaza**, Jay Street through to Adams St., bet. Tillary and Willoughby Sts. 1999. **William B. Tabler.**

A taut skinning job, with a few bumps to busy the skyline, gives an eerie feeling of unreality to this, Brooklyn's only hotel since the demise of the St. George, the Bossert, the Standish Arms, and others. An ephemeral building, its façade seems a silk-screen of glass, panels, and mullions.

D13

[D14] **St. James Cathedral** (Roman Catholic), Jay St. bet. Cathedral Place and Chapel St. E side. 1903. **George H. Streeton.**

Neo-Georgian, with a handsome, verdigris copper-clad steeple. The first church on this site (1822) became the cathedral of Brooklyn in 1853; but in 1896, with the succession of Brooklyn's second bishop, it was officially renamed the procathedral. Pro, in this instance, means in place of, for that bishop was planning an elaborate new cathedral of his own, the giant Immaculate Conception Cathedral, which never materialized. The procathedral did not become the cathedral once again until 1972. Within there hovers a baldachino, providing a rather plain American religious space with a touch of ceremonial

D14

D15

wonder. (Cathedral means literally that church which contains the cathedra, or chair of the bishop. Size does not a cathedral make but, rather, ecclesiastical function. Therefore, there can be only one cathedral in any diocese or see.)

[D15] **Jehovah's Witnesses Dormitory**, 90 Sands St., bet. Jay and Pearl Sts. 1990s.

An ungainly mansarded tower overlooks the Manhattan Bridge.

Return to Tillary Street and turn into Bridge Street.

D16

[D16] **Polytechnic Institute, Wunsch Hall**/originally First Free Congregational Church/later Bridge Street African Wesleyan Methodist Episcopal Church, 311 Bridge St., bet. Johnson St. and Myrtle Ave. E side. 1846-1847. 🌂

A Greek Revival temple in brick with a Doric-columned porch and entablature. Chaste, apart from the later Victorian stained glass, which is exuberant even from the outside. Once a major stop on the underground railroad, it provided sanctuary for runaway slaves and those blacks fleeing the 1863 draft riots. As the Bridge Street AWME Church it was the first black congregation in Brooklyn (1854-1938).

D17, plaza sculpture

[D17] **Metrotech**, roughly bet. Flatbush Ave., Tillary, Jay, and Willoughby Sts., excepting a NW quadrant including N.Y.C. Board of Education Channel 25 and Westinghouse High School; and a SW quadrant of commercial buildings largely facing Willoughby St. 1989 Master plan, **Haines Lundberg Waehler.**

Here are 10 blocks and a billion or so dollars worth of sadly gargantuan neighbors for this firm's ancestral talent, **Ralph Walker**, whose **Voorhees, Gmelin & Walker** 1931 telephone building [D21] is a local elegance. This is an unfortunate reprise of the "urban renewal" of the 1960s, such as that which obliterated and "renewed" a vast portion of Manhattan's Upper West Side. The architecture is a mixed bag, not of tricks, but of the banal, the ordinary, and the especial (see the Dibner Library below for the latter).

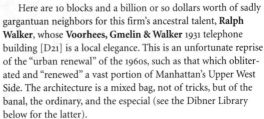

D18

[D18] **3 Metrotech Center**, on Myrtle Promenade, bet. Duffield and Bridge Sts. S Side. 1997. **Skidmore, Owings & Merrill**.

The detailing draws direct inspiration from the (D21) **Ralph Walker** Telephone Building next door.

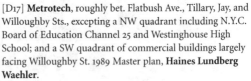

D19

[D19] **Bern Dibner Library of Science and Technology, Polytechnic University**, 5 Metrotech Center, bet. Tech Pl. and Myrtle Promenade. 1992. **Davis Brody Bond**.

An industrial elegance in precast concrete, articulated and connected with great panache. Its friendly scale dominates and humanizes the plaza.

[D20] **New York City Fire Department Headquarters**, 9 Metrotech Center, bet. Tech Pl. and Johnson St. 1997. **Swanke Hayden Connell.**

An understated background building appropriate for its tenants, and in scale with the old Bridge Street Church and Dibner Library that are its neighbors.

At Willoughby Street turn right.

D20

[D21] **New York Telephone Company**, Long Island Headquarters, 101 Willoughby St., NE cor. Bridge St. 1931. **Voorhees, Gmelin & Walker**.

Brick with a graded palette, a delicate aesthetic. Note the equally elegant Art Deco grillages over the ground-floor windows.

D23

D22

D25

[D22] Originally **New York & New Jersey Telephone Company Building**, 81 Willoughby St., NE cor. Lawrence St. 1898. **R. L. Daus**.

A grand Beaux Arts-Renaissance Revival palace, Brooklyn's first telephone headquarters. Look closely at the carved entrance surrounds: the intertwined TC (for telephone company) over the door; the free use of bells, earpieces, and ancient wall telephones that were worked into the classical Beaux Arts ornament. And hovering over it all is a grand copper-clad cornice.

Turn right at Jay Street.

[D23] Originally **City of Brooklyn Fire Headquarters**, 365-367 Jay St., bet. Willoughby St. and Myrtle Ave. E side. 1892. **Frank Freeman**.

This is a building to write home about. A powerful Romanesque Revival, brick, granite, and tile structure, it is the New York branch (with **Louis Sullivan**'s Condict Building) of the Chicago School. Freeman learned much from afar by viewing H. H. Richardson's work, as did Sullivan.

[D24] Originally **Edison Electric Illuminating Company**, Central Station for Brooklyn, 358-362 Pearl St., N of Fulton St. W side. 1891.

Another Romanesque Revival remnant. It's holding on with a bit of its old corbelled and arcuated façade.

[D25] **N.Y.C. Transit Authority Headquarters**/originally N.Y.C. Board of Transportation Building, 370 Jay St., NW cor. Willoughby St. 1950. **William E. Hauggard** & **Andrew J. Thomas**.

Home of the subway systems' managers . . . and bureaucracy. The two gracious though dingy lobbies to the subway, at north and south ends, are fringe benefits gained from a building contiguous to its subway lines. Windows here read as skin, rather than holes punctured in masonry, by the device of detailing the glass flush with its limestone surrounds. Nightly money trains once brought the take from all boroughs directly to a spur in the building's bowels.

[D26] **Brooklyn Friends School**/originally Brooklyn Law School, Pearl St. N of Fulton St., E side. ca. 1930. **Thompson, Holmes & Converse**.

D27

A curious Art Moderne building with a crowning of Romanesque Revival arches.

Follow Jay Street across Fulton—at this point its name becomes Smith—to Livingston Street.

[D27] **N.Y.C. Board of Education Headquarters**/originally Benevolent Protective Order of Elks, 110 Livingston St., SW cor. Boerum Place. 1926. **McKim, Mead & White.**

MM&W were deflated after **Stanford White**'s death, shot by a jealous husband in 1906. The partnership's other powerful talent, Charles Follen McKim, died in 1909 (Mead was the business partner). The staff thereafter produced occasional wonders, as with Manhattan's Municipal Building of 1914. But for the most part, the production, as here, was pallid.

D28

[D28] **Long Island College Hospital Therapeutic Nursery**/originally Brooklyn Public Library, 67 Schermerhorn St., bet. Boerum Place and Court St. N side. 1887. **William Tubby.** [D28a] Originally **German Evangelical Lutheran Church**, 63 Schermerhorn St., bet. Boerum Place and Court St. N side. 1888. **J. C. Cady.**

A bold pair of buildings designed at the height of Brooklyn's Romanesque Revival. The arched entry of No. 67 is a worthy but distant neighbor to that at **Frank Freeman**'s Jay Street Firehouse [D23].

[D29] **N.Y.C. Transit Authority Museum**, Schermerhorn St. NW cor. Boerum Place. Downstairs, in the former IND Court Street subway station. Open to the public. 718-330-3060. Tues.-Fri., 10-4; Sat-Sun, 11-4; closed Mon.

D31

A wonderful underground museum on an inactive spur of the subway system. Here are trains, turnstiles, and tesserae of varying vintages. Admission by a token.

[D30] Originally **St. Vincent's Home for Boys**, Boerum Place SW cor. State St. Chapel, 1927, **McGill & Hamlin.**

More interesting for who did it than what it is. **Talbot Hamlin** was professor of architectural history at Columbia, most noted for his great book, *Greek Revival Architecture in America* (1944).

D33

[D31] **Brooklyn Men's House of Detention**, 275 Atlantic Ave., bet. Smith St. and Boerum Place. N side. ca. 1950. **LaPierre, Litchfield & Partners.**

Cheerfully described as the Brooklyn Hilton, this facility holds mostly those awaiting trial who cannot post bail, as well as those considered too dangerous to roam before trial.

[D32] **Brooklyn Friends Meetinghouse**, 110 Schermerhorn St., SE cor. Boerum Place. 1857. Attributed to **Charles T. Bunting.** 🍎

Once a freestanding structure in simple Quaker brick, it is overpowered by the Central Court Building adjacent to its contiguous former school.

[D33] **Central Court Building**, 120 Schermerhorn St., SW cor. Smith St. 1932. **Collins & Collins.**

Similar in bulk to 110 Livingston Street [see D27], this Renaissance Revival hulk adds to the cityscape through its deep entrance porch, articulated by 3 great neo-Renaissance arches.

D34

[D34] **MTA (Metropolitan Transportation Authority) Building**, a block surrounded by Smith, Livingston, Schermerhorn Sts., and Boerum Place. 1989. **Murphy/Jahn.**

Low-rise jazz to come from the people who gave us 425 Lexington Avenue. The black-and-white syncopation gives some life to a drab neighborhood. But don't do another anywhere nearby.

[D35] **Fulton Street Mall**, along Fulton St. and DeKalb Ave. bet. Flatbush Ave. Ext. and Adams St. 1985. **Seelye, Stevenson, Value & Knecht**, engineers. **Pomeroy, Lebduska Assocs.**, architects.

The magnetism of the Fulton Street shopping area already fills the sidewalks with people. The mall has bestowed a blessing upon the commotion by widening the sidewalks, limiting vehicles to buses, and adding covered bus stops, kiosks, benches, and lighting.

D35

[D36] **Gage & Tollner's Restaurant**, 372 Fulton St., bet. Smith St. and Red Hook Lane. Building ca. 1875. ☙ Interior, 1892. ☙

Except for an ungainly vertical sign, building and restaurant are much as they were the day they opened: a Victorian interior of plush velvet, cut glass, mirrors, gaslight, mahogany, and bentwood chairs (although a new bar has been recently added). It would do justice to a Mississippi River steamboat. A broad menu of fish, shellfish, and crustaceans is cooked to order. Elegant architecturally, more than satisfactory gastronomically.

[D37] **Macy's**/formerly Abraham & Straus (department store), 420 Fulton St., bet. Gallatin Place and Hoyt St. Main building S side. 1929 and 1935. **Starrett & Van Vleck**. Secondary building NE cor. Gallatin Place and Livingston St. 1885. [D37a] Originally **Liebmann Brothers Building**, 446 Fulton St., SW cor. Hoyt St. 1885. **Parfitt Brothers**.

Eight interconnected buildings jointly form the great department store of Brooklyn, in a similar blockfilling manner to its Manhattan counterpart, Bloomingdale's. The main building is subdued Art Deco, but the small Romanesque Revival gem at Gallatin Place is distinguished in Roman brick, brownstone, and granite. Some of the wondrous earlier cast-iron and brownstone façades commissioned by Abraham Abraham peek over later street and storefront modernizations aside the main block.

D36

D37a

[D38] **Hoyt Street Station**, IRT Seventh Avenue Line, below Fulton St. at Hoyt St. 1908. **Samuel B. Parsons**, chief engineer. Altered. W end redesigned, 1986, **Mayers & Schiff**.

The western parts of this station's platform walls, below the A&S façade, now carry a tailored look—horizontal maroon pencil stripes but at a properly enlarged civic architecture scale—giving it a classy look it never enjoyed during its first eight decades of service.

D39

🏠 [D39] Formerly **Offerman Building**/originally Wechsler Brothers Block, 503 Fulton St., bet. Bridge and Duffield Sts. N side. 1891. **Lauritzen & Voss**.

Grossly altered. The Duffield Street façade preserves some of the Romanesque Revival detail, even at ground level, that once embellished the whole body of the building. Look up at a great incised sign. The sleazy covering of, and alteration to, the Fulton Street façade have destroyed distinguished architecture that might well have been reinforced, rather than mutilated. But still, look up.

[D40] **The Dime Savings Bank of New York**, 9 DeKalb Ave., NE cor. Fleet St., off Fulton St. 1906-1908. **Mowbray & Uffinger**. Expanded, 1931-1932. **Halsey, McCormack & Helmer**. ☙ First floor interior. ☙

A comical, columned Roman Revival palace. The interior is remarkable; plan to visit it during banking hours. Gilded, monumental Liberty-head dimes are the predominant motif. Money must have been well managed by those who could afford such grandeur.

Follow DeKalb Avenue past the Dime to the far side of Flatbush Avenue Extension.

D40

D42a

On the site of *The Gallery at Metrotech* (1980 Gruen Associates) stood the RKO Albee movie theater, one of downtown Brooklyn's last great picture palaces, demolished in 1977. It was a neo-Renaissance fantasy of columns and star-twinkling ceilings, a vast place of 2,000 seats. **Edward F. Albee**, a vaudeville impresario, was the foster father of playwright **Edward Albee**. The theater's swan song included a screening of Who's Afraid of Virginia Woolf? *based on the younger Albee's great play.*

D43

[D41] **Long Island University, Brooklyn Center**, 385 Flatbush Ave. Ext., bet. DeKalb Ave. and Willoughby St. E. side. [D41a] **Campus entry arch**, Long Island University, Flatbush Ave. Ext. N of DeKalb Ave. E side. 1985. **Park, Quennell-Rothschild** Assocs., landscape architects. Arch design, **Nicholas Quennell**.

A latter-day, brightly colored triumphal arch fashioned from structural steel sections and a steel grid. It stands in a tiny park that replaced a ragtag gas station that for years debased the L.I.U. campus entrance. A cheery welcome to both campus and to Brooklyn for the heavy traffic entering via the nearby Manhattan Bridge, but hardly competition for the real thing at Grand Army Plaza, two miles further up Flatbush Avenue [see A2].

[D42] **Arnold and Marie Schwartz Athletic Center and Tristram W. Metcalf Hall, Long Island University**/originally Brooklyn Paramount Theater and offices, NE corner Flatbush Ave. Ext. and De Kalb Ave. 1928. Altered, 1950, 1962.

Brooklyn's leading movie palace was converted in two stages to university use: the office block in 1950, the 4,400-seat auditorium in 1962. The intervening years witnessed the swan song of popcorn in these marble halls. Adjacent to the north are two distinguished new campus buildings:

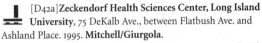 [D42a]**Zeckendorf Health Sciences Center, Long Island University**, 75 DeKalb Ave., between Flatbush Ave. and Ashland Place. 1995. **Mitchell/Giurgola**.

An austere neighbor to Metcalf Hall above, punctuated with a clock tower.

 [D43] **Humanities Building, Long Island University**/ originally Maltz Building, 1967. **Davis, Brody & Assocs**. and **Horowitz & Chun**.

D45

The structure of an existing warehouse was here reclad and extended in brick. New guts and a new envelope on an existing skeleton, with fine materials, elegant detailing, and handsome spaces, make this an extraordinary work. Developer **B. M. Maltz** created the original loft building in 1925. (The highly visible—but misleading—sign of the Pharmacy College pertains to the donor's gift elsewhere on the campus.)

[D44] **Library-Learning Center, Long Island University**, 1975. **Davis, Brody & Assocs**. and **Horowitz & Chun**.

Linked to the earlier Humanities Building by a bright red-painted, Vierendeel-trussed, glass-caged bridge, this crisp complex begins to knit together the disparate older buildings of the reworked Brooklyn Center campus.

D46

Leave the L.I.U. campus and turn left on Flatbush Avenue Extension.

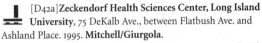 [D45] **Bell Atlantic Office Building**, 395 Flatbush Ave. Ext., bet. DeKalb Ave. and Fulton St. E side. 1976. **Skidmore, Owings & Merrill**. [D46] **Consolidated Edison Company**, Brooklyn Division, 30 Flatbush Ave., bet. Nevins and Livingston Sts. 1974. **Skidmore, Owings & Merrill**.

These two buildings are at the heart of Brooklyn's former entertainment center: where Con Ed stands stood the Brooklyn Fox, a movie and vaudeville showplace (1928-1971). Bell

Atlantic's (originally New York Telephonc's) building erased the scars of a major rebuilding of the BMT subway interchange below. Though by the same firm, the two buildings are of very differing expressions. Architecturally, at least, Con Ed has emerged the victor in this battle of the utilities.

[D47] **Pioneer Warehouse,** 153 Flatbush Ave., opp. Livingston St. 1897-1915. **J. Graham Glover**.

Neo-Baroque columns flank the faded entry to this venerable warehouse.

D47

END of Civic Center/Downtown Brooklyn Walking Tour:
The subway station here at Nevins and Flatbush offers both the IRT Lexington and Seventh Avenue service (Nos. 2, 3, 4, & 5 trains). The DeKalb Avenue Station, a block back along Flatbush Avenue Extension, provides connections to both BMT and IND subways (D, M, N, Q, and R trains).

A handsome aside to the north:

[D48] Onetime **Eskimo Pie Building**/originally Thomson Meter Company Building, 100-110 Bridge St., bet. York and Tillman Sts. 1908-1910. **Louis Jallade**.

Glazed terra-cotta swathes this lusty concrete building with lush foliage. Jallade may have seen Perret's 25bis rue Franklin in Paris, then recently completed, with an exposed concrete frame infilled with glazed tile by **Alexandre Bigot**.

D48

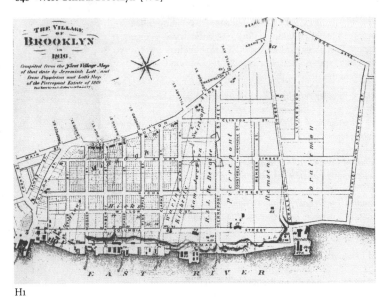

H1

BROOKLYN HEIGHTS

Colonized by well-to-do merchants and bankers from the city
across the river, Brooklyn Heights is the suburban product of a
combined land and transit speculation; in this case the transit
was the new steam-powered ferry. In 1814 Robert Fulton's invention, with financial backing from Hezekiah Pierrepont, first connected the newly renamed Fulton Streets of New York and
Brooklyn by fast boats, giving occasion to Pierrepont and others
(Middagh, Hicks, Remsen, Livingston) for profitable division
and sale of their heights "farmland." With the new ferry it was
quicker and easier to go by water from Fulton to Fulton than to
travel by omnibus on Manhattan Island. This status continued
until the New York and Harlem Railroad provided a route to the
northern "frontier": in 1832 horsecars linked the distant town of
Harlem, and in 1837 steam trains crossed the Harlem River to
Westchester. A surveyor's grid marked the Heights into 25- × 100-
foot lots as the system for parcel sales. Although other subdivisions were made by speculators, those dimensions remain the
basic module of the Heights.

That the oldest buildings (such as 155-159 Willow Street)
were built in the 1820s is not surprising. Lots did not come on
the market until 1819, and even as late as 1807 there had been
but 7 houses on the Heights, with perhaps 20 more at or near
the ferry landing at the river's edge below. By 1890 the infill was
substantially complete, and the architectural history of the
Heights primarily spans those seventy years. Occasional buildings were built much later in random locations, but the principal pre-1890 urban fabric was still intact in 1965, when the district was designated a historic district under the city's newly
enacted Landmarks Preservation Law. Vacant lots on Willow
Place afforded architects Joseph and Mary Merz a chance to
add buildings in serious modern architectural terms, but within
the scale of the surrounding environment. These, plus a few
others, have extended (with the approval of the Landmarks
Preservation Commission) a previously truncated architectural
history to the present: the others include Alfredo De Vido's
brownbrick at 222 Columbia Heights [H61], Ulrich Franzen's
building for the Jehovah's Witnesses on Columbia Heights
[H96], and a motley assortment of old and new residential
buildings on Poplar Street by Wids de la Cour, David Hirsch,
and Charles Platt [H110-112].

[H1] **Brooklyn Heights Historic District**, generally bounded on the W and N by the Brooklyn-Queens Expwy. and Cadman Plaza W., on the S by Atlantic Ave., on the E by Henry St. to Clark St., and an irregular line to Court St. and Atlantic Ave. 🖐

The first district to be designated (1965) under the Landmarks Preservation Law—a logical choice, as the Heights was the city's foremost, discrete, and substantially intact enclave of architecture.

All the listings below lie within the historic district where noted with the district symbol. ♂

H2

South Heights Walking Tour: A circuit that begins at Court and Remsen Streets (across from Borough Hall) and ends nearby at Livingston and Clinton Streets (subway to Borough Hall Station of the IRT Lexington and Seventh Avenue Lines (Nos. 2, 3, 4, & 5 trains) or Court Street Station of the BMT (N & R trains)).

[H2] Originally **The Franklin Building**, 186 Remsen St., bet. Court and Clinton Sts. S. side. ca. 1890. **Parfitt Bros**.

One of four Romanesque Revival-Queen Anne red-brick extravaganzas in the vicinity by these fraternal architects. Rock-face brownstone supports brick pilasters large and small. Sturdy granite piers articulately support the entrance archway.

H3

[H3] **McGarry Library, St. Francis College** (since 1962)/originally (1857-1895) Brooklyn Gas Light Company Headquarters/later (1895-1914) Brooklyn Union Gas Company Headquarters, 180 Remsen St., bet. Court and Clinton Sts. S side. 1857.

A miraculously saved Tuscan-columned classical temple that has seen a variety of uses. The gas company moved next door in 1914 to:

H4

[H4] **St. Francis College**/originally (1914-1962) Brooklyn Union Gas Company Headquarters, 176 Remsen St., bet. Court and Clinton Sts. S side. 1914. **Frank Freeman**.

One of 3 downtown Brooklyn buildings with classical colonnades on the upper stories. Compare it with 110 Livingston Street and the Central Court Building. The husky Tuscan columns at the entry are fluted and sport entasis, that delicate swelling of the column's profile that gave (and gives) so much visual strength to Greek temples.

H5

Ar this point you enter the Brooklyn Heights Historic District.

[H5] **Brooklyn Heights Synagogue**/formerly The Brooklyn Club, 131 Remsen St., bet. Clinton and Henry Sts. N side. ca. 1858. ♂ Converted to synagogue, 1996.

The paired Corinthian columns are a strong portal to this bland brownstone.

[H6] **Brooklyn Bar Association**/formerly Charles Condon House, 123 Remsen St., bet. Clinton and Henry Sts. N side. ca. 1875. ♂

Here are relatively jazzy chromatics of white limestone and dark red brick—an exuberant note on Remsen Street. Atop is a curved and slated mansard roof. The stonework is incised with Eastlake detail.

H6

[H7] **Our Lady of Lebanon Roman Catholic Church** (Maronite Rite)/originally Church of the Pilgrims (Congregational), 113 Remsen St., NE cor. Henry St. 1844-1846. **Richard Upjohn**. Rectory, 1869. **Leopold Eidlitz**. ♂

Certainly, Upjohn was avant-garde: this has been called the nation's earliest example of Romanesque Revival, a bold massing of ashlar stonework, a solid, carven image. The spire was removed due to deterioration and the high cost of its

H7

H9

replacement. The doors at both the west and south portals were salvaged from the ill-fated liner *Normandie*, which burned and sank at its Hudson River berth in 1942. Note the images of Norman churches and Norman-built ocean liners.

The Church of the Pilgrims moved in with Plymouth Church in 1934, and its Tiffany windows were moved to an annex, Hillis Hall, of the combined congregation.

[H8] **70 Remsen Street** (apartments), bet. Henry and Hicks Sts. S side. 1929. **H. I. Feldman.** ☺

Sturdy neo-Romanesque decorated arches over marble columns and spreading neo-Byzantine capitals give considerable style to a simple apartment block. Feldman similarly decorated the old Pierrepont Hotel.

H10

[H9] **87 Remsen Street**, bet. Henry and Hicks Sts. N side. ca. 1890. ☺

An exotic brick mansion with a melange of brownstone and terra-cotta detailing. Note the copper roof against the sky.

Turn left on Hicks Street.

[H10] **Grace Church**, 254 Hicks St., SW cor. Grace Court. 1847-1849. **Richard Upjohn.** Parish House to the west. 1931. ☺

After a radical venture completing the Church of the Pilgrims [H7], **Upjohn** went "straight," back to the more academic brownstone Gothic Revival. A bit of urban charm is the entrance court, off Hicks Street at the south side, leading to the parish house. A backwater for pedestrians, it is crowned by the umbrella of a glorious elm some 80 feet tall. Benches are available.

H12

[H11] **Grace Court**. W of Hicks St. ☺

Its delight originally derived from the juxtaposition of Grace Church and the double-deep backyards of Remsen Street's houses. In the 1960s the construction of a banal 6-story red-brick apartment building on some of those yards changed all that. The eastern half of this one-block cul-de-sac is still lovely.

[H12] **Grace Court Alley**. E of Hicks St. ☺

A real mews (for Remsen Street and Joralemon Street mansions). A walk to its end and then a turnabout will reveal many delights not visible from Hicks Street. No. 14's arched bearing wall of tooled brownstone is lusty. Many of these carriage houses still retain their iron hay cranes, some used today only for holding potted plants. Note the crisp contrasting brownstone quoins on Nos. 2 and 4. **No. 6** [H13], at the end, is a new 1994 construction by architect **Joseph Stella**: *pas mal*, but it suffers from a lack of the detail that its antecedents used to fill out their architectural vocabulary.

[H14] **263 Hicks Street**, bet. Joralemon St. and Grace Court Alley. E side. ca. 1860. Alterations ca. 1885. ☺

An Italianate brownstone up-styled in the 1880s with a new stoop, replete with Norman zigzag ornamentation, a rock-face brownstone frieze, and a dormered tile roof.

H14

[H15] **262-272 Hicks Street**, SW cor. Joralemon St. 1887. **William Tubby.** ☺

A Shingle Style terrace, designed as a group composition. The romantic corbeled brickwork, shingles, and picturesque profiles confer an identity on the various occupants. Each is different from its neighbor but part of an overall architectural composition.

H15

[H16] **Engine Company 224, N.Y.C. Fire Department**, 274 Hicks St., bet. Joralemon and State Sts. W side. 1903. **Adams & Warren.** ☺

BROOKLYN HEIGHTS DISTRICT

see pages 648–668

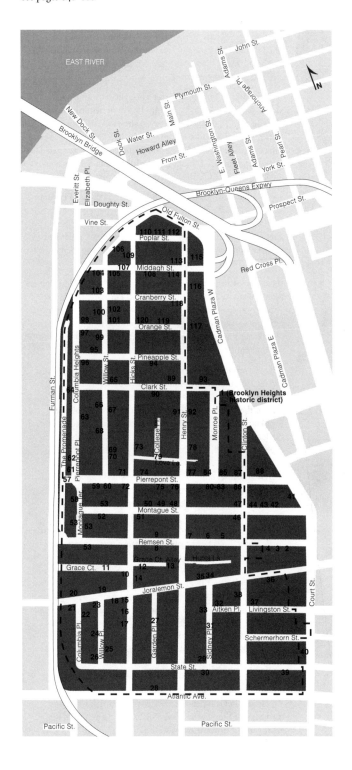

H17

H18

H20

H21

H22

A house for fire engines in scale with its house neighbors. A Renaissance Revival building, with copper-clad dormers.

[H17] **276-284 Hicks Street**, bet. Joralemon and State Sts. W side. ○

Five brick arches—two half-round, three half-ellipses—once swallowed carriages. Note the sculptured woman's head on the dormer of No. 276. More carriages resided across the street at Nos. 291 and 293.

[H18] **58 Joralemon Street**, bet. Hicks St. and Willow Place. S side. ca. 1847. Converted to present use, 1908. ○

The world's only Greek Revival subway Ventilator. It permits release of air pressure built up by IRT Lexington Avenue Line express trains rushing through the East River tunnel, deep beneath Joralemon Street. And it affords stranded passengers an emergency exit to the surface.

[H19] **29-75 Joralemon Street**, bet. Hicks and Furman Sts. N side. 1844-1848. ○

Twenty-five Greek Revival houses (several have been altered) step down Joralemon's hill. The row has a pleasant rhythm, with each pair stepping down roughly 30 inches from its neighbors.

[H20] **25 Joralemon Street**/formerly High Pressure Fire Service, Main Pumping Station, bet. Hicks and Furman Sts. N side. ○

Before superpumper fire trucks were available, this served to increase the pressure in fire mains to reach high-rise fires. Now it has joined the myriad building types converted to co-ops and condominiums.

[H21] **Riverside** (apartments), 4-30 Columbia Place, SW cor. Joralemon St. 1890. **William Field & Son**. Remodeled, 1988. **R.M. Kliment** & **Frances Halsband.** ○

On the river's side they stood, until truncated by the Brooklyn-Queens Expressway. The original contained a central garden, partially remaining between the extant units and the expressway's wall.

Alfred T. White, a prominent and paternalistic Brooklyn businessman, whose motto was "philanthropy plus 5 percent," commissioned these, as well as the Tower and Home buildings in Cobble Hill. They are the original limited-profit housing, predating the City and State's first "limited-dividend" projects (Stuyvesant Town) by 57 years. White also was a major participant in the creation of Forest Hills Gardens.

[H22] **7-13 Columbia Place**, bet. Joralemon and State Sts. E side. ○

Four charming small and modest houses, whose porches give a friendly scale to the block.

Now back a few steps to Willow Place and turn right.

[H23] **2-8 Willow Place**, bet. Joralemon and State Sts. W side. ca. 1847. ○

Gothic Revival detail decorates simple brick row houses. In the battle of the Revival styles, the basic plan and spatial arrangement of row houses were almost constant: their cornices, lintels, doorways, and portals are the variables that identify the Federal (1820s), Greek Revival (1830s), and Gothic Revival (1840s) styles. Many Federal houses were updated to the fashionable Greek Revival and, subsequently, from Greek to Gothic. The later Renaissance Revival houses had, however, both an extended plan and inflated volume.

[H24] **Willow Place Chapel**, originally a mission of the First Unitarian Church, 26 Willow Place, bet. Joralemon and State Sts. W side. 1875-1876. **Russell Sturgis**. ♂

A retired chapel now host to the Roosa School of Music, the Heights Players, and a nursery school. Ruskinian Gothic in the era of St. Ann's.

H24

[H25] **43-49 Willow Place**, ca. 1846. ♂

This recently restored Greek Revival wood colonnade joins four town houses, from an era when colonnades denoted class.

[H26] **40, 44, and 48 Willow Place**, NW cor. State St. 1965-1966. **Joseph & Mary Merz**. ♂

These 4 town houses (one is a double house) gave new life to Willow Place while respecting the scale and nature of their older neighbors. Garages occupy ground-floor space; and cement block, in a special 8-inch-square size and used with sensitivity and imagination, assumes a dignity that most thoughtless users miss by a mile. Note the compact integration of garage, rear garden terrace, and handsome wood fence on the State Street side of No. 48.

H25

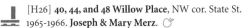
Turn left on State Street.

[H27] **Garden Place**, bet. Joralemon and State Sts. ♂

A handsome urban space, one block long, contained on four sides. Note the terra-cotta, brick, and limestone Queen Anne at No. 26, the Hansel and Gretel carriage house (No. 21), the intruders from Queens (Nos. 17, 19, 19a.), and the lush lintels at No. 34. Nos. 40 through 56 form a handsome terrace. Locals describe this as the Scarsdale of Brooklyn Heights, where the affluent nest in this cul-de-sac.

H26

[H28] **105 Atlantic Avenue** (mixed use), bet. Henry and Hicks Sts. N side. 1990s. **Stanley and Laurie Maurer**. ♂

A modest, but handsome and articulate, infill on this ragged edge of Brooklyn Heights.

H28

H29

[H29] **103-107 State Street**, NW cor. Sidney Place. ca. 1848. ♂

A trio, but only No. 107 still has the elegant cast-iron balcony that allows French doors to open to the parlor floor.

[H30] **118 State Street**, bet. Henry St. and Sidney Place. S side. Converted, 1980s, **Eli Attia**. ♂

A converted warehouse that displays a vast skylight in profile.

Turn left onto Sidney Place.

[H31] **Sidney Place**, bet. State and Joralemon Sts. ♂

A more varied and interesting version of Garden Place. Its architecture includes everything that Garden Place offers, while

H30

adding a church, St. Charles Borromeo, and such specialties as a 7-story Greek Revival house! The front gardens on the east side between Aitken Place and State Street are unusual.

[H32] **St. Charles Borromeo Church** (Roman Catholic), 21 Sidney Place, NE cor. Aitken Place. 1869. **P. C. Keely.** ○

A simplified brick Gothic Revival in maroon-painted brick. The plain interior is decorated with wood Carpenter Gothic arches and trim.

H32

[H33] **18 Sidney Place** (apartments), opposite Aitken Place. W side. ca. 1838. ○

At first glance it seems one has found the world's first 7-story Greek Revival town house (to match the world's only Greek Revival subway ventilator, around the corner). Three stories were added in the late nineteenth century to create a girls' residence.

Turn tight on Joralemon Street.

 [H34] **135 Joralemon Street**, bet. Henry and Clinton Sts. N side. ca. 1833. ○

An opposite-hand plan from 24 Middagh Street [H105]. Their similarities are concealed by a post-Civil War cast-iron porch, and the house is dwarfed by two bulky later buildings.

[H35] **129 Joralemon Street**, bet. Henry and Clinton Sts. N side. ca. 1891. **C. P. H. Gilbert.** ○

A grandly scaled outpost of the Chicago School in Roman brick is sadly squeezed between a banal apartment building and a law office with pretensions, but inappropriate scale.

Turn right on Clinton Street.

H34

[H36] **Packer Collegiate Institute**, 170 Joralemon St., bet. Court and Clinton Sts. S side. 1853-1856. **Minard Lafever.** Additions, 1884. 1886. **Napoleon Le Brun & Son.** Gym, 1957. ○

This is a parody of a British Victorian businessman's Gothick castle. The understated addition tries to remain a background neighbor. Collegiate only in the sense that it prepares students for college, not a college itself.

H35

[H37] **Annex of Packer Collegiate Institute**/originally St. Ann's Church (Episcopal), Clinton St. NE cor. Livingston St. Chapel, 1866-1867. Church, 1867-1869. **Renwick & Sands.** ○

Brownstone and terra-cotta of different colors and textures make an exuberant and unrestrained extravaganza. **Renwick** had produced more academically correct Gothic Revival churches at Manhattan's Grace and St. Patrick's—perhaps by the time of St. Ann's his confidence had mushroomed. The copybooks of the Pugins used at Grace were discarded in favor of current architectural events, particularly the "new" museum at Oxford by **Deane & Woodward**, designed and built with the eager assistance of theorist **John Ruskin**—hence "Ruskinian Gothic."

H36

St. Ann's is a monumental but comforting presence on these tight, row-housed streets, its diminutive chapel adjacent forming an articulate transition to the Packer gym to the north.

[H38] **140-142 Clinton Street**, bet. Joralemon St. and Aitken Place. W side. ca. 1855. ○

Lintels and a cornice lush with voluties and garlands, both in cast iron. The detail and profiles survived well in comparison with those carved in erodible brownstone. It looks as if its many eyebrows were surveying St. Ann's Church across the street.

H37

H38

[H39] **168-170 State Street**, bet. Clinton and Court Sts. S side. ca. 1890. ♂

Robust twin tenements with handsome bay windows from a time when architecture for the lower-income population was still architecture.

[H40] **Forest City Ratner Bookstore and Theater Building,** Court St. bet. State and Schermerhorn Sts. 2000. **Hardy Holzman Pfeiffer**. (Outside the district.)

Twelve movie theaters are stacked atop Barnes & Noble's ranks of books. Ground was broken in December 1998.

H39

Home of the Excelsiors: A plaque on the carefully groomed row house at 133 Clinton Street, southeast corner of Livingston Street, identifies this building as the onetime clubhouse of the Jolly Young Bachelors. By 1854 that social club had evolved into the Excelsiors, an amateur baseball club with the distinction of having as their pitcher **James Creighton,** *credited with having pitched the first curve ball! With the removal from Brooklyn first of the Dodgers, and then of their ball park, Ebbets Field, this brownstone remains one of the last vestiges of organized baseball in the borough.*

END of South Heights Walking Tour: To reach the Borough Hall/Court Street subway stations, return to Joralemon Street and walk one block east. If you are filled with energy, two other Brooklyn Heights walks follow. For a change of pace, respite, and refreshments, walk south to Atlantic Avenue [see Cobble Hill].

Central Heights Walking Tour: Starts and ends at Court and Montague Streets. (Subways to Borough Hall Station of the IRT Seventh Avenue and Lexington Avenue Lines (Nos. 2, 3, 4, & 5 trains), or east escalator of Court Street Station of the BMT local (M, N, & R trains).)

Montague Street: Throughout the 19th century and until the end of World War II, this was the road to the Wall Street Ferry, dipping down the bluff to its wateredge terminal. Pier 4 now occupies that site. There were companion ferries to the north, the Fulton Ferry, and to the south at Atlantic Avenue, South Ferry. The latter is remembered in name only on its Manhattan end by the terminus of the IRT Seventh Avenue local.

A stone bridge by Minard Lafever (1855) and a later passerelle called the "Penny Bridge," both located between Pierrepont Place and Montague Terrace, once carried the brow of the Heights over Montague Street's steep incline, with its appropriate cable car line.

Walk west on Montague Street.

H41

[H41] **European American Bank (EAB)**/originally Brooklyn Savings Bank, 205 Montague St., NW cor. Cadman Plaza W. 1962. **Carson, Lundin & Shaw.**

Urban renewal swallowed the Brooklyn Savings Bank's great **Frank Freeman** edifice at the northeast corner of Pierrepont and Clinton Streets, his one exercise in Roman pomp. Freeman's eclectic palette produced the neo-Renaissance Crescent Athletic Club and the great avant-garde Hotel Margaret (see Necrology).

A neat work that holds the three street lines it confronts, an important effort where Cadman Plaza Park tends to create an amorphous scene.

H42

[H41a] **Independence Savings Bank**, 195 Montague St., bet. Cadman Plaza W. and Clinton St. N side. Branch bank, 1995. **K. M. Kliment & Frances Halsband**.

A dynamic façade (and space within) sheathed in stainless steel and glass. It almost redeems the pedestrian office building into which it is plugged. Nice work.

[H42] Originally **National Title Guaranty Building**, 185 Montague St., bet. Cadman Plaza W. and Clinton St. N side. 1930. **Corbett, Harrison & MacMurray**. Entrance altered.

A bold early Art Deco building from the team that immediately after shared the design responsibility for Rockefeller Center. The bold 3-D massing remains fresh to this day.

H43

[H43] **Citibank**/originally People's Trust Company, 183 Montague St., bet. Cadman Plaza W. and Clinton St. N side. 1903. **Mowbray & Uffinger**. Pierrepont St. rear addition, 1929, **Shreve, Lamb & Harmon**.

This is a **D. W. Griffith** version of a Roman temple. The bank, unfortunately, is neither staffed nor patronized by bacchanalian revelers, so that the total effect is a little wistful, like an abandoned movie set. Built of marble, not just wire lath and plaster, it provides a sense of security to its depositors . . . and who is now around to drive the moneylenders from the temple?

The sculpture in the pediment is unconscious Pop Art, particularly when overlaid with antipigeon spikes.

H44

[H44] **Chase Bank**/formerly Manufacturers Hanover Trust Company/originally Brooklyn Trust Company, 177 Montague St., NE cor. Clinton St. 1913-1916. **York & Sawyer**. 🍎 Interior 🍎

The bottom and top of this rich Italian palace are copied from Verona's Palazzo della Gran Guardia (1610. **Domenico Curtoni**). In between, the model was stretched vertically to supply more floors for commerce. Corinthian engaged columns rest on rusticated tooled limestone.

At this point you enter the Brooklyn Heights Historic District.

[H46] Originally **Franklin Trust Company** (office building), 164 Montague St., SW cor. Clinton St. 1891. **George L. Morse**. ◷

A granite, rock-face base, sunk within a moat, bears limestone arches and, in turn, brick and terra-cotta piers, columns, and arches. All are capped with a dormered red tile roof. A gem.

H47

[H47] **St. Ann's and The Holy Trinity** (church)/ originally Holy Trinity Protestant Episcopal Church, 157 Montague St., NW cor. Clinton St. 1844-1847. **Minard Lafever**. Spire, 1866. Removed, 1905. **Patrick C. Keely**. Stained glass, **William Jay Bolton**. ◷ Restorations, 1979 to now. **Mendel Mesick Cohen Waite**.

Brownstone, unfortunately, weathers poorly. Here the New York Landmarks Conservancy has led the counterattack by citing this great neo-Gothic church as a cause célèbre. Concerts and theater of the avant-garde have aided its slow restoration, but with a citywide constituency that gives heart to serious landmark preservation and restoration.

The interior is cast and painted plaster rather than carved stone, as it might appear at first glance. Reredos by **Frank Freeman**. The whole is, unfortunately, minus its original brownstone spire.

A bust of its controversial left-wing former pastor, **John Howard Melish,** by sculptor **William Zorach,** is bracketed from the north side of the entrance vestibule.

Montague, the shopping street: Only 4 blocks long, Montague is a chameleon in that short stretch: it serves residents of the Heights at its west and denizens of the Civic Center to the east. With astronomically rising rents, the local stalwarts have slowly been squeezed out in favor of "chains" or have been ensnared in real estate owners' fantasies about the potential profits of this chic center of Brooklyn. Sadly, the successful repopulation of Brooklyn Heights by a conservative, family-oriented, young and middle-aged middle class has brought with it flocks of conspicuously affluent yuppies, both resident and influxing by day. They have created a market along the street much like that of the Upper West Side's Columbus Avenue, itself a mercantile wasteland 25 years ago and now a Gold Coast for conspicuous spending (in boutiques, not barbershops). Montague trails that landlords' nirvana, happily, but aspires to the same fantasyland.

[H48] **Montague Mews,** NW cor. Montague and Henry Sts. Remodeled, 1987, **Wronsky/Lehman.**

A simple commercial 2-story taxpayer has been Brooks Brothered: careful detail, somber colors, and neat lettering have transformed schlock disorder into the architectural equivalent of the gray flannel suit.

[H49] **The Berkeley/The Grosvenor,** 111 and 115 Montague St. bet. Henry and Hicks Sts. N side. 1885. **Parfitt Bros.**

Twin Queen Anne brownstone, terra-cotta and brick apartment houses. Unsympathetic modern ground-floor shopfronts demean the wondrous architecture above; look up! There is a 2-story Parisian-style mansard roof up there.

H49

[H50] **The Montague,** 105 Montague St., bet. Henry and Hicks Sts. N side. 1885. **Parfitt Bros.**

Another Queen Anne extravaganza. Here a brooding face peers down from its terra-cotta pediment, leaning over a console bracket.

[H51] **Hotel Bossert,** 98 Montague St., SE cor. Hicks St. 1908-1913. **Helme & Huberty.**

Now a Jehovah's Witnesses hostel, this "modern" hotel was in the fashionable center of 1920s New York social life. The Marine Roof decorated in a yachting spirit by designer Joseph Urban, offered dining, dancing, and an unequaled view of the Manhattan skyline. The home of its founder, millwork manufacturer, **Louis Bossert,** still stands.

H51

[H52] **The Arlington,** 62 Montague St., bet. Hicks St. and Montague Terr. S side. 1887. **Montrose Morris.**

And yet another apartment house. These three complexes [see H49, 50] were the modest housing of the middle class at a time when grand brownstones on adjacent Pierrepont and Remsen Streets housed single families and their servants. Shopkeepers, foremen, and others lived here next to the upper-income families of the Heights. Note the corner tower for the resident Rapunzel.

H52

H53

H55

H56

[H53a] **The Heights Casino**, 75 Montague St., bet. Hicks St. and Pierrepont Place. N side. 1905. **Boring & Tilton.**
[H53b] Casino Mansions Apartments, 200 Hicks St., NW cor. Montague St. 1910. **William A. Boring.** ○

Its founders described this indoor squash and tennis club as a "country club in the city." A handsome stepped gable dominates; the rich brickwork was later copied in the adjacent 200 Hicks Street. This apartment house stands on the former site of the Casino's outdoor tennis courts; the members required that architectural unity be retained as a condition for selling the land.

Boring also designed the major buildings of the Ellis Island immigration station.

[H54] **1-13 Montague Terrace**, bet. Remsen and Montague Sts. ca. 1886. ○ [H55] **8 Montague Terrace**, bet. Remsen and Montague Sts. S side. 1860s. ○

A complete terrace in the English sense, a set of row houses: another urbane remnant greater than the sum of its parts. Its cornice crowns the whole block, bonding it as if it were a grand single town house. **Thomas Wolfe** wrote *Of Time and the River* here in 1933-1935.

No. 8 is a particularly grand brownstone matron, broad in the beam, with sturdy Corinthian columns.

[H56] **24 Remsen Street**, bet. Montague Terrace and Hicks St. E side. ○
Roman yellow brick for a Renaissance Revival townhouse.

Take a detour to see the Manhattan skyline.

[H57] **The Esplanade**, W of Montague Terr., Pierrepont Place, and Columbia Heights, bet. Remsen and Orange Sts. 1950-1951. **Andrews, Clark & Buckley**, engineers. **Clarke & Rapuano**, landscape architects. ○

The Promenade, as it is known locally, is a fringe benefit from the construction of this section of the Brooklyn-Queens Expressway, at first proposed by **Robert Moses** to bisect the Heights along Henry Street. A cantilevered esplanade—one of the few brilliant solutions for the relationship of auto, pedestrian, and city—was projected from the crest of the Heights to overlook the harbor on a fourth level, over two levels of highway and a service road (Furman Street) for the piers below. It is simple and successful: mostly hexagonal asphalt paving block, painted steel railings, hardy shrubbery, and honey locust trees. The lesson was most recently and happily repeated at the Battery Park City Esplanade.

Return to the street and turn left on Pierrepont Place.

[H58] Originally **Alexander M. White** and **Abiel Abbot Low Houses**, 2 and 3 Pierrepont Place, bet. Pierrepont and Montague Sts. W side. 1857. **Frederick A. Peterson.** ○
The most elegant brownstones remaining in New York. They are two out of an original trio; the third (No. 1, the **Henry E. Pierrepont House. Richard Upjohn**) was demolished in 1946 in favor of a playground at the time of the esplanade-expressway construction.

Alfred Tredway White, Brooklyn philanthropist (Tower and Home and Riverside Apartments and the Botanical Garden's Japanese Garden), was born and brought up at No. 2.

Abiel Low, made a killing in the China trade, and his son, Seth, was mayor of Brooklyn, president of Columbia College, and then mayor of a consolidated New York. He lived at No. 3.

H58

A peek at Pierrepont Street and then back onto Columbia Heights

[H59] Originally **Mrs. Hattie I. James House,** 6 Pierrepont St., bet. Pierrepont Place and Willow St. S side. ca. 1890. **Parfitt Bros.** ⚲

Romanesque Revival with a strong, rock-face brownstone stair, elaborate foliate carved reliefs, and a bay window, overlooking the bay.

H59

[H60] **8-14 Pierrepont Street,** bet. Pierrepont Place and Hicks St. S side. ca. 1901. ⚲

Another terrace where the whole is greater than the sum of its parts. The bow windows form a gracious breast for these English town houses.

[H61] **222 Columbia Heights,** NW cor. Pierrepont St. 1982. **Alfredo De Vido Assocs.** ⚲

Brown, glazed modern brick, with tori (rounded moldings) to assuage its Renaissance Revival flank. The bay window and garage door spoil this hearty attempt at landmark infill.

H60

[H62] **210-220 Columbia Heights,** bet. Pierrepont and Clark Sts. W side. 1852-1860. ⚲

H61

H62

Two pairs and two singles. Altered, but the best remaining examples of group mansions in brownstone although some have been painted light colors. Note No. 210's rich Corinthian capitals and the varied neighboring mansard roofs and dormers, which create a picturesque silhouette.

[H63] **145 Columbia Heights,** bet. Pierrepont and Clark Sts. E side. ca. 1845. ⚲

Exquisite Corinthian columns on a simple brick volume.

H64

H65

H67

H68

[H64] **160 Columbia Heights** (apartments), SW cor. Clark St. 1937. **A. Rollin Caughey.**

An orange brick Art Deco/Art Moderne work with corner casement windows overlooking grand views of Manhattan.

Turn right up Clark Street.

[H65] Originally Leverich Towers Hotel/now **Jehovah's Witnesses Residence Hall**, 25 Clark St., NE cor. Willow St. 1928. **Starrett & Van Vleck.**

Comfortably affluent materials borrowed from Romanesque architectural history: brick over random ashlar stonework over granite, with lots of molded terra-cotta decoration. The 4 arched and colonnaded towers were once spotlighted nightly after sunset.

Turn right again onto Willow Street.

[H66] **Dansk Sömandskirke**, 102 Willow St., bet. Clark and Pierrepont Sts. W side.

A brownstone happily converted into the Danish Seamen's Church.

Willow Street offers a variety of buildings, all of which together form an urban allée of happy variations. Buildings of note other than those described below include No. 104, a shingled remnant, gray and white, with a Federal fanlight; No. 106, with interesting Eastlake incised lintels; Nos. 118, 120, 122, with neo-Gothic window hoods and cast-iron railings; No. 124, with a stepped neo-Amsterdam gable and weather vane; and No. 149, a vigorous tenement, bay-windowed and reclaimed.

[H67] Originally **S. E. Buchanan House, 109 Willow St.**, bet. Clark and Pierrepont Sts. E side. 1905. **Kirby, Petit & Green.**

This neo-Federal house is gross, with fat columns ill-proportioned window panes and muntins, crudely cast concrete lintels, and thick joints in the brickwork. People who embrace what they believe to be archaeology often miss the point of the styles they wish to emulate [as at H70].

[H68] **108, 110, and 112 Willow Street**, bet. Clark and Pierrepont Sts. W side. 1880. **William Halsey Wood.**

The Shingle Style in Brooklyn. Picturesque massing and profiles produce odd internal spaces and balconies for our contemporary fun. Terra-cotta reliefs, elaborate doorways, bay windows, towers, and dormers. The English architect **Richard Norman Shaw** (1831-1912) was group leader for these fantasies; in his bailiwick he produced what was strangely termed Queen Anne. This is arguably New York's finest example.

Queen Anne: A style of English architecture introduced to this country in the British pavilion at the 1876 Philadelphia Centennial Exposition, it remained popular for some twenty years. Its name is deceiving. Queen Anne of England died in 1714, a century and a half before the style was so dubbed, but it was during her 12-year reign that some of the Gothic and Renaissance elements found in this romantic style were earlier revived.

[H69] **151 Willow Street**, bet. Clark and Pierrepont Sts. E side. ca. 1870.

Allegedly a link in the underground railroad, it is aligned with an earlier town plan, set back and skewed.

[H70] **155-159 Willow Street**. bet. Clark and Pierrepont Sts. E side. ca. 1826.

Three elegant Federal houses equal to No. 24 Middagh

[H105] but in brick. The glass pavers set into No. 157's sidewalk bear an apocryphal tale that they skylit a tunnel leading to No. 151, which served the underground railroad leading slaves to northern freedom. The three houses are askew from Willow Street as they were built to the earlier geometry of Love Lane, which once extended this far west.

Take a left onto Pierrepont Street.

H70

[H71] **35 Pierrepont Street** (apartments), bet. Willow and Hicks Sts. N side. 1929. **Mortimer E. Freehof.** ○✧

The roofscape and silhouette of this apartment block have all stops pulled out. A pleasantly synthetic—or is it precocious—Post Modern bag of tricks?

[H72] Originally **George Hastings House**, now apartments, **36 Pierrepont Street**, bet. Willow and Hicks Sts. S side. 1846. **Richard Upjohn.** ○✧

A freestanding neo-Gothic house and garden. Its newly re-created Pierrepont Street stoop has recently reincarnated ogees and trefoils.

H72

[H73] **173-175 Hicks Street**, bet. Pierrepont and Clark Sts. E side. ca. 1848 ○✧

Greek Revival flutes.

[H74] Originally **Hotel Pierrepont, 55 Pierrepont St.**, bet. Hicks and Henry Sts. N side. 1928. **H. I. Feldman.** ○✧

From the days when even speculative hotels bore lion finials and griffin gargoyles. Now a neatly maintained home for the elderly. See 70 Remsen Street for more **Feldman** neo-Romanesque.

H74

[H75] **The Woodhull, 62 Pierrepont St.**, bet. Hicks and Henry Sts. S side. 1911. **George Fred Pelham.** ○✧

The dowdy ground floor belies the extravagant Belle Epoque Parisian architecture above. Had it been built in London, it would be Edwardian.

[H76] **84 Pierrepont Street**/originally **Herman Behr House**/later Palm Hotel/later Franciscan House of Studies/now a residential condominium. SW cor. Henry St. 1889. **Frank Freeman.** ○✧

After **Behr**, this mansion had a profane and then sacred existence prior to being converted in 1977 into apartments. In the Palm Hotel's declining years it was said to have housed the local madam and her lovelies. It then served as a residence for Franciscan brothers. Despite the structure's social vagaries, Freeman's design remains a distinguished monument on the Heights streetscape.

H77

[H77] **161 Henry Street** (apartments), NE cor. Pierrepont St. 1906. **Schneider & Herter.** ○✧

A peer of 62 Pierrepont. In the last 40 years, the external appearance and the view from without have been of little or no concern; interior decoration and a view from within are the requirements. For most architects the citizen of the street is eyeless. This vigorous building's strong character shows that architecture was once part of the resident's basic needs. Here it bestows identity to the occupants in the process, as do Central Park West's grand apartment houses.

H78

A short one-block detour to the left to Love Lane.

[H78] **137, 141, 143 Henry Street**, bet. Pierrepont and Clark Sts. E side. 1870s. ○✧ No. 143 restored, 1987, **Susan Podufaly**.

Three of a former quartet. Their restored painted clapboard splendor modulates the street, with bay windows and porches reinforcing the rhythm of the stoops.

[H79] **Love Lane and College Place**, both in the block bet. Henry and Hicks Sts. N of Pierrepont St. ☼

The names of these two byways are more charming than their reality, but the mystery is worth a detour. Note that Love Lane is skewed from the grid's rectilinear geometry. 28-33 College Place provide a memory of what the whole lane and place were about in the 19th century.

[H80] **104 Pierrepont Street**/originally **Thomas Clark House**, bet. Henry and Clinton Sts. S side. 1856. ☼

A brownstone row-mansion. Note the ornate console atop the majestic stoop. A magnificent bronze railing once adorned this, but parts were stolen and the present owners have yet to restore it. One of the authors of this guide lived here for 30 years.

[H81] **106 Pierrepont Street**, bet. Henry and Clinton Sts. S side. 1890s. ☼

The earlier brownstone on the block was cut without expertise, and from quarries of fragile stone. 106, on the contrary, is of harder, firmer stone, and allowed the survival of delicate detail that failed in most earlier buildings—hence the proliferation of brownstone "restoration" in these parts.

[H82] Originally **P. C. Cornell house, 108 Pierrepont Street** at Monroe Place. S side. 1840. ☼

The harried remains of a great Greek Revival double house; the only original part is the anthemion-ornamented pediment over the front door. Once two stories and basement, it was raised to three, and a post-Civil War cornice was added.

H82

[H83] **114 Pierrepont Street**/originally George Cornell House, later Alfred C. Barnes House, at Monroe Place. S side. 1840. Totally altered, 1887. Further remodeled, 1912. ☼

Once the siamese twin of No. 108, this was "modernized" in 1887 for publisher **Barnes**, a transmogrification of staggering impact. A simple brick building became a Wagnerian stage set: Romanesque Revival with some random eclectic tricks thrown in. Aside from its melodramatic architectural history, its social history includes use as a residence, as the Brooklyn Women's Club (after 1912), as a Christian Science Church, and, most recently, the fate of most if not all venerable buildings: condominiums.

H83

Monroe Place: A 700-foot-long, 80-foot-wide space, a quiet backwater on axis with the Cornell house described above. The proportions of the street and its containment at both ends are far more important than the buildings that line it; for this, like Sidney, Garden, and Willow Places, is the product of the staggered grid that fortuitously made this area so much richer than most of gridplanned Manhattan or Brooklyn. Do take a look at two houses at the north end: No. 3 (1849), with its later cast-iron planter and goldfish pond; and No. 12 (1847), where shutters have been returned to the façade.

[H84] **Appellate Division, N.Y.S. Supreme Court**, Monroe Place, NW cor. Pierrepont St. 1938. **Slee & Bryson.** ⟳

A prim and proper freestanding Classical Revival monument of the 1930s, with a pair of powerful Doric columns confronting Monroe Place.

H84

[H85] **First Unitarian Church**/properly **Church of the Saviour**, Pierrepont St. NE cor. Monroe Place. 1842-1844. **Minard Lafever.** ⟳

Lafever, a carpenter by training, was a talented and prolific architect who practiced in many styles (including Egyptian Revival for a church in Sag Harbor). He wrote a well-known and well-used copybook for builders, *The Beauties of Modern Architecture.* The cast-iron fence is guarded by 6 crenellated castelets.

[H86] **Brooklyn Historical Society**/originally Long Island Historical Society, 128 Pierrepont St., SW cor. Clinton St. 1881. **George B. Post**, architect. **Olin Levi Warner**, façade sculptures. Restorations, 1998. **Jan Hird Pokorny.** Open to the public. 718-624-0890. Tues-Sat, 12-5; closed Sun-Mon. ⟳

Post used a bright but narrow range of Italian reds at a time when earth colors were popular, from the polychromy of **Ruskin** [see H37] to the near-monochromy of Richardsonian Romanesque, such as the Jay Street Firehouse.

This is one of the city's great architectural treasures, both outside and in. There are usually small exhibits and always a great local history collection.

H85   H86

[H87] **St. Ann's School**/originally Crescent Athletic Club, 129 Pierrepont St., NW cor. Clinton St. 1906. **Frank Freeman.** ⟳

Once one of Brooklyn's most prestigious men's clubs, it boasted a swimming pool, squash courts, gym, and three grand 2-story spaces surrounded by mezzanines. After the club folded in 1940, it served as an office building until 1966, when St. Ann's Episcopal Church School bought and remodeled it.

[H88] **One Pierrepont Place** (office tower), also known as Morgan Stanley Building, Pierrepont St. bet. Clinton St. and Cadman Plaza W. N side. 1988. **Haines Lundberg Waehler.**

Brobdingnag comes to Lilliput. This behemoth not only looms over the Heights but has become an obese silhouette to much of Brooklyn. The mansarded crest gives a flashy hat to this dumpy matron.

[H88a] **Rotunda Gallery**, 33 Clinton St., bet. Pierrepont St. and Cadman Plaza W. 1991. **Smith-Miller & Hawkinson.** 718-875-4047. Tues-Fri, 12-5; Sat, 11-4; closed Sun-Mon.

"Spatial complexity is created by the juxtaposition of varied levels from which visitors can view the gallery and its exhibitions."—**Andrew Dolkart.**

END of Central Heights Walking Tour: If you are hungry, Montague Street's eateries are only a block away, as is the BMT local Court Street subway station at Montague and Clinton Streets (M, N, and R trains). The IRT is a block further east, at Court (Nos. 2, 3, 4, & 5 trains).

North Heights Walking Tour: Of the three walks through Brooklyn Heights this offers the greatest contrasts: old and very new, affluent and modest, tiny and large, domestic and institutional.

START on the southwest corner of Clark and Hicks Streets, less than a block west of the IRT Seventh Avenue Station turnstiles within the old St. George Hotel arcade (Nos. 2 and 3 trains). Walk east along Clark Street across from the old hotel, take a brief detour south into Henry Street, and then return to Clark and continue east.

[H89] Originally **St. George Hotel**, bet. Hicks and Henry Sts., Clark and Pineapple Sts. 1885. **Augustus Hatfield**. Additions, 1890-1923, **Montrose W. Morris** & others. Tower Building, 1929-1930. **Emery Roth**. ☝

The contrasts of the North Heights are properly introduced by those of the old St. George, a set of architectural accretions that occupies a full city block and that once was the city's largest hotel (with 2,632 rooms). Now divided into separate properties, the oldest buildings, opposite 52 Clark Street, are abandoned, and one has burned down; the Tower Building (111 Hicks Street) has become a towering condominium. Other segments are in various stages of development (the 60 and 70 Pineapple Street buildings are also co-ops); and the Studio Building, at the corner of Pineapple has rearrayed itself as housing for the elderly. The St. George, the Bossert, the Standish Arms, and the Towers served Brooklyn and lower Manhattan as topnotch hostelries up to World War II; the last three are now Jehovah's Witnesses residences, and the St. George Hotel holds on warily and only as the corner Weller building at 100 Hicks Street, over the subway entrance at Clark and Henry.

H89

[H90] **Clark Lane** (apartments), 52 Clark St., bet. Hicks and Henry Sts. S side. ca. 1927. **Slee & Bryson**. ☝

Eclectic architects found a style for every occasion. These, later the designers of the Appellate Courthouse [H84], chose a Romanesque arcade and Gothic gargoyles for this apartment hotel.

H90

[H91] **First Presbyterian Church**, 124 Henry St., S of Clark St. W side. 1846. **William B. Olmsted**. Memorial doorway, 1921, **James Gamble Rogers**. ☝ [H92] **German Evangelical Lutheran Zion Church**/originally Second Reformed Dutch Church. 1840. ☝

These two churches occupy sites almost opposite each other. The Presbyterian is solid, stolid, and self-satisfied. The Lutheran is spare, prim, and denuded of its northern spire. Sometimes a single thistle can be more rewarding than a bouquet of roses.

H92

The route around Cadman Towers and through Pineapple Walk takes you briefly outside the Brooklyn Heights Historic District.

[H93] **Cadman Towers**, 101 Clark St., bet. Henry St. and Cadman Plaza W. N side; 10 Clinton St., at Cadman Plaza W. W side; plus row housing along Clark St., Monroe Place, and Cadman Plaza W. 1973. **Glass & Glass** and **Conklin & Rossant**.

Urban renewal, usually a disastrous incision into the city's fabric, was tempered here by an especial concern with urban design: low-rise town house elements form façades that here bridge the scale from the towers proper to the contiguous 19th-century Heights streetscape. Tower and town houses alike are clad in handsome and well-detailed concrete and ribbed concrete-block.

H94

Turn left at Cadman Plaza West and left again into the pedestrian mall called Pineapple Walk. Continue west along Pineapple Street itself (back into the Historic District), through the dark backside of the St. George Hotel's original block, its rear mysteriously more intriguing than its bland Clark Street façade.

[H94] **60 and 70 Pineapple Street** (condominiums), bet. Hicks and Henry Sts. S side. ☞
  A renovated segment of the old St. George Hotel, cleaned of its dour gray paint down to the roseate brick. A gracious improvement of this somber street.

[H95] **13 Pineapple Street** (house), bet. Willow St. and Columbia Heights. N side. ca. 1830. ☞
  An unusually wide, gray-shingled, freestanding, white-trimmed, single house redolent of these North Heights days before the masons took over.

H95

[H96] **Jehovah's Witnesses Dormitory and Library Facility**, 119 Columbia Heights, SE cor. Pineapple St. 1970. **Ulrich Franzen & Assocs.** ☞
  An early and sensitive design under the new Landmarks Law. The three row-house façades south of this new building are integrated internally with the new structure. The stoops, with entries now closed off, are therefore no longer functional but still add to the visual enrichment of the block. Prior to the designation of the Heights as a historic district, row houses like these were wantonly destroyed by the same organization to build Nos. 124 and 107 further along the street.

H96

If you haven't savored the lower Manhattan skyline from these bluffs, cross Columbia Heights and walk to the right along the Promenade. The tour picks up one block north at:

[H97] **Jehovah's Witnesses Residence**, 107 Columbia Heights, SE cor. Orange St. 1960. **Frederick G. Frost, Jr.**, & Assoc. ☞
  One of a number of pre-Landmarks Law high-rise dormitories that proliferated in the Heights for these proselytizers of their faith. Relatively new buildings such as this, and older ones remodeled for the sect's needs, are concentrated along Columbia Heights and nearby streets. Local residents continue to fear that too much of the Heights is being gobbled up for the Witnesses' seemingly endless expansion.

[H98] **The Margaret** (apartments), 97 Columbia Heights, NE cor. Orange St. 1988. **The Ehrenkrantz Group & Eckstut.** ☞
  This new apartment house (purchased by Jehovah's Witnesses) fills the site of the great Hotel Margaret by **Frank Freeman** (1889). Under extensive renovation as condominium apartments, that magnificent structure [see Necrology] burned disastrously in 1980. The replacement has been the subject of a major legal and landmarks battle. City zoning laws, in tandem with the Historic District designation, limit the height of new construction to 50 feet. Here the owner pleaded that because his distinguished landmark building had been vastly taller, and its economics based upon that, he should be allowed to replace its bulk. A compromise allows something in between. Too orange, too green.

H98

[H99] **70 Willow Street**/originally **Adrian van Sinderen House**, bet. Orange and Pineapple Sts. W side. ca. 1839. ☞

H99

A wide Greek Revival house, originally freestanding, now cheek by jowl with Jehovah's Witnesses to the north. Former owners filled the southern gap with a set-back-from-the-street stair tower. Stage designer **Oliver Smith** rescued this from the Red Cross, to whom it had been bequeathed, restoring its multipaned windows and making other corrections.

[H100] **54 Willow Street** (apartments), bet. Orange and Cranberry Sts. W side. 1987. **Alfredo De Vido Assocs.** ○

H100

A simplistic infill of a vacant lot, here appearing neither old nor new—nor particularly noticeable. The columns are nice to have but naive.

[H101] **57 Willow Street**/originally **Robert White House**, NE cor. Orange St. ca. 1824. ○

The Orange Street wall is a lusty composition of real and blind windows, chimneys, and pitched roofs. But much of it is clothed in dense ivy in the summer, perhaps adding a subtly suggestive dress to the naked form.

H101

[H102] **47-47A Willow Street** (houses), bet. Orange and Cranberry Sts. E side. ca. 1860. ○

The apocrypha here state that there were two daughters and one site, riven to create a half for each. The internal guts are complicated by the need for tucking a stair into each 12-foot-wide unit.

[H103] **13, 15, and 19 Cranberry Street** (houses), NW cor. Willow St. ca. 1829-1834. ○

Greek Revival houses modernized, most extravagantly at No. 19. Here a mansard roof made this a fashionable grande dame when the spare classicism of the early nineteenth century gave way to elaboration. The Empire gown acquired a sturdy bodice and a bustle.

H102

[H104] **20-26 Willow Street** (houses), SW cor. Middagh St. ca. 1846. ○

No-nonsense Greek Revival, this painted brick and brownstone terrace is straightforward, austere, yet elegant. The 2-story porches at the rear look out upon the harbor, their views framed by projecting masonry walls. **Henry Ward Beecher** lived at No. 22.

[H105] **24 Middagh Street**/formerly **Eugene Boisselet House**, SE cor. Willow St.ca. 1829. ○

The queen of Brooklyn Heights houses (Nos. 2 and 3 Pierrepont Place are the twin kings): a wood-painted, gambrel-roofed Federal house with a garden cottage connected by a garden wall. Note especially the exquisite Federal doorway with its Ionic colonnettes and the quarter-round attic windows. Proportion, rhythm, materials, and color are in concert throughout.

H103

[H106] **1-9 Willow Street**, bet. Middagh and Old Fulton Sts. S side. 1990s. **Edwards Rullman and Herbert Kaufman.** A serious attempt at new row housing, with serrated façades modulating the ensemble. ○

H105

Having turned the corner into Middagh Street, continue east.

[H107] **Middagh Street**, bet. Willow and Hicks Sts. ca. 1817. ○

One of the earliest streets on the Heights, it contains most of the remaining wood houses. Aside from the glorious No. 24, they are now a motley lot: No. 28, 1829, mutilated beyond recognition; No. 30, 1824, Federal entrance and pitched roof still recognizable in spite of the tawdry asphalt shingles; No. 25, 1824, mutilated; No. 27, 1829, early Italianate here in wood shingles with painted trim; No. 29, similar to 27; Nos. 31 and 33, 1847, mutilated.

[H108] **56 Middagh Street** (house), bet. Hicks and Henry Sts. S side. 1829. Porch added, ca. 1845. ○⚲

Bold Doric columns provide both guts and style, with a rather blatant blue body behind.

H108

[H109a] Originally **Joseph Bennett House, 38 Hicks St.** ca. 1830. Restored, 1976. [H109b] Originally **Michael Vanderhoef House, 40 Hicks St.** ca. 1831. Restored, 1976. [H109c] **38A Hicks Street** (house), behind No. 38. All bet. Middagh and Poplar Sts. W side. ○⚲

An urbane trio now happily restored. The alley leading to No. 38A is effectively their common ground, a dense city's private street of identity, as are Patchin and Milligan Places in Greenwich Village.

H109a

The block between Poplar, Hicks, and Henry Streets and the Expressway (referred to by technocrats as Block 207) contains an interesting new and reconditioned residential enclave comprising a tenement, an orphan asylum, a former flophouse, and modern infillings—all under one developer's sponsorship:

[H110] **55 Poplar Street**, bet. Hicks and Henry Sts. N side. 1987. **Wids de la Cour** and **David Hirsch**. ○⚲ [H111] Originally **Brooklyn Children's Aid Society Orphanage**/now apartments, **57 Poplar St.**, bet. Hicks and Henry Sts. N side. 1883. Restored, 1987, **Wids de la Cour** and **David Hirsch**. ○⚲

Built as a home for indigent newsboys, this ornate Victorian pile was abandoned during the urban renewal craze of the 1960s—it was then being used as a machine works—before adaptive reuse tardily came to it in the late 1980s. The heavy hands that razed the blocks between Henry Street and Cadman Plaza, Poplar and Clark Streets, spared this odd gem and the candy factory [H113] to the south.

H109b

[H112] **61-75 Poplar Street**, bet. Hicks and Henry Sts. N side. 1987. **Charles A. Platt Partners**. ○⚲

A modern row recapturing some—but only some—of the appropriate scale and detail of the Heights. The remodeled units at the corner of Henry Street had been the former branch of the Bowery-in-Brooklyn, a minimal overnight bunkhouse for the homeless (restored, 1987, **Wids de la Cour** and **David Hirsch**).

H111

[H113] **Henry Street Studios**/originally Mason Au & Magenheimer Candy Company, 20 Henry St., NW cor. Middagh St. 1885. **Theobald Engelhardt**. Reconstructed, 1975. **Pomeroy, Lebduska Assocs.**, architects. **Martyn and Don Weston**, associate architects. ○⚲

A light industrial building of mill construction. Its bold brick-bearing walls, timber columns, and heavy plank flooring provide loft space for real and would-be artists. The north façade is designer **Lee Pomeroy**'s modern face where a blank wall formerly stood. Mouthwatering memories for older sweet teeth are conjured by the repainted lettering on the south façade: Peaks and Mason Mints.

H112

[H114] Former **Police Precinct Station House**, Poplar St. bet. Henry and Hicks Sts. 1920s. ○⚲

The local Florentine police palazzo, now a backup facility for more modern precinct facilities elsewhere.

[H115] **Cadman Plaza North (apartments)**, 140 Cadman Plaza W., N of Middagh St. W side. 1967. [H116] **Whitman Close (town houses)**, 33-43, 47-53, 55-69 Cadman Plaza W., S of Middagh St. W side. [H117] **Whitman Close (apartments)**, 75 Henry St., at Orange v St. E side. [H 117a] **Pineapple Walk**, Pineapple Walk bet. Henry St. and Cadman Plaza W. N. side only. 1968. All by **Morris Lapidus & Assocs.**

H114

These early, ungainly urban renewal projects attempted to heal the wound left by the excision of Cadman Plaza from the cityscape. The removal of elevated lines was a civilized advance, but it was accompanied by the demolition of blocks of sturdy Heights-scaled buildings. Token row houses (Whitman Close) and a grilled garage (Cadman Plaza North) matching the height, if not the scale, of the other side of the street, were the prosthetics. They fail, however, to define the intervening streets as urban spaces (rather than simply surfaces on which autos navigate), one of the principal qualities of the Heights. They are as inappropriate as a Greek Revival house from Willow Street would be on an acre in Scarsdale.

H117

[H118] **The Cranlyn** (apartments), 80 Cranberry St., SW cor. Henry St. 1931. **H. I. Feldman.** ♂

Art Deco on the Heights. Here the style presents glazed terra-cotta bas-relief, a bronze-plaque fantasy over the entrance, and jazzy brickwork. **Feldman** contributed two other multiple dwellings of interest to the Heights, both with Romanesque detail: 55 Pierrepont and 70 Remsen.

H118

[H119] **Plymouth Church of the Pilgrims**/originally Plymouth Church, Orange St. bet. Henry and Hicks Sts. N side. 1849-1850. **Joseph C. Wells.** [H120] **Parish House and connecting arcade**, 75 Hicks St., NE cor. Orange St. 1913-1914. **Woodruff Leeming.** ♂

Henry Ward Beecher preached here from 1847 to 1887. Excepting the porch, his church was an austere brick box of a barn on the exterior, articulated by relieving arches. (The Tuscan porch was added long after **Beecher** left.) The parish house, of an eclectic Classical Revival, happily encloses— together with its connecting arcade—a handsome garden court. Here Beecher, as seen through the eyes and hands of sculptor **Gutzon Borglum**, holds forth—or perhaps holds court. Unfortunately, in this era of vandalism, the churchyard, which could be a pleasant place of repose, is locked.

H119

In 1934 the **Congregational Church of the Pilgrims** abandoned its own church building, which is now Our Lady of Lebanon [H7], and merged with Plymouth Church, causing the combined renaming. The Pilgrims' Tiffany windows were relocated at that time to Hillis Hall, behind Plymouth.

END of North Heights Walking Tour: The nearest subways are the IRT Seventh Avenue Line in the St. George Hotel (2 and 3 trains) or, via the Whitman Close town houses at Cranberry Street, the IND Eighth Avenue Line High Street Station (A and C trains). If your legs are still nimble you may wish to visit the Fulton Ferry District, the waterfront, and the dramatic view of the Brooklyn Bridge as it leaps across the waters of the East River.

H120

FULTON FERRY DISTRICT

This flat riverfront beneath the Heights might well be termed Brooklyn Bottoms. The shore of these tidal waters, it was the natural place for a ferry landing, bringing hardy New Yorkers to the rural wilds of Long Island and exporting the produce of lush, flat Long Island farms to the city. Rowers and sailors plied this narrow link at first, a tenuous connection because of shifting tides and winds. And in 1776 it became the unhappy port of embarkation for Washington's troops fleeing Long Island under cover of darkness and fog after their defeat in the Revolution's first major battle. The first steam-powered ferry came in 1814 and, with it, an ever-increasing flow of traffic that was honored by a grand Victorian terminal in 1865. After 1883, with the opening of the new New York and Brooklyn Bridge, which still looms over this edgewater, the area was doomed as a commercial center, losing its river commuters slowly until the ferry service was discontinued in 1924. The spectacular revival of the Heights and neighboring brownstone communities has sparked the authorization of a new ferry service, a comforting alternate to the subway commute under the river.

During much of the 19th century, Fulton Street's downward curving route to the river (now renamed Cadman Plaza West or, in places, Old Fulton Street) was a bustling place, easily accessible by streetcar and elevated, lined with all manner of commercial structures, and graced by places to eat, drink, and rest one's weary bones. Some of these buildings—if not activities—remain today. Remember as you walk along Front Street that it received its name as the last thoroughfare above water. Landfill in the early 19th century pushed the bulkhead and beach further west. In retrospect, it seems strange that New York (that is, Manhattan today) was mapped to Brooklyn's high-water line, thereby assigning the water—and the islands floating within it—to Manhattan. Boaters, swimmers, divers, gulls, and garbage floating on the East River are in Manhattan.

U1a

[U1] **Fulton Ferry Historic District**, generally bounded by Water and Main Sts., the East River, Furman and Doughty Sts., and from Front St. to Water St. on a line in back of the buildings along Cadman Plaza W. (Old Fulton St.). 🕊

[U1a] Originally Long Island Safe Deposit Company, 1 Front St., N cor. Old Fulton St. 1868-1869. **William Mundell**. ♂

A cast-iron Renaissance palazzo. This monumental bank overshadowed its older neighbors in the prosperous post-Civil War era. The Brooklyn Bridge's diversion of commuting traffic after 1883 forced the bank to close its doors in 1891.

FULTON FERRY DISTRICT

see pages 669–673

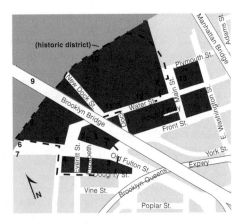

(historic district)

U2

[U2] **Pete's** (restaurant)/originally Franklin House (hotel), 1 Old Fulton St., E cor. Water St. 1835. Altered, 1850s. ☙

This simple relic of the ferry's balmy days and its neighbors recall the time before the Brooklyn Bridge, when the traffic of people and produce passed up Old Fulton Street.

U3

[U3] **Eagle Warehouse** (residential cooperative)/originally Eagle Warehouse and Storage Company of Brooklyn, 28 Old Fulton St., SE cor. Elizabeth St. 1893. **Frank Freeman.** Condominium alteration, 1980, **Bernard Rothzeid.** ☙

A stolid medieval revival warehouse, now recycled as condominiums. The machicolations (a word every cocktail party one-upman should know) are equaled only in a few remaining scattered Brooklyn armories. The bronze lettering, a lost art, articulates the grand Romanesque Revival arched entry, and the clock's glass face is the window of a spectacular studio loft. Note also the lusty ironwork at the entrance and over the streetside windows. **Freeman**, Brooklyn's greatest architect, designed two buildings tragically lost to fire [see Necrology]: the Bushwick Democratic Club and the Margaret Hotel.

U4

[U4] **8 Old Fulton Street** (apartments)/originally Brooklyn City Railroad Company Building, SE cor. Furman St. 1860-1861. Remodeled, 1975, **David Morton.** ☙

When the ferryboat was queen, horsecars would line a row of gleaming tracks inlaid in the cobbled pavement, waiting to transport commuters into the heart of Brooklyn. What more appropriate place for the headquarters of that transit combine than here, overlooking the ebb and flow of both tide and passengers?

[U5] Onetime **Fulton Ferry Museum**, National Maritime Historical Society/originally Marine Company 7, N.Y.C. Fire Department (fireboat), foot of Old Fulton St. 1926. ☙

This simple neglected structure bears a tower for the traditional drying of fire hoses, a churchlike symbol on the site of the former ferry terminal. The latter expired in 1924.

U5

[U6] **Fulton Ferry Pier**, N.Y.C. Department of Ports & International Trade & Commerce, foot of Old Fulton Street, at the East River. 1976. ☙

A sliver of river is again available to the people, in anticipation of a renewed Fulton to Fulton ferryboat. The iron railings, strangely enough, were salvaged from Park Avenue's "parks," removed to improve motorists' sight lines in 1970.

U8

[U7] **Bargemusic**, foot of Old Fulton Street, moored to the
Fulton Ferry Pier. 718-624-4061.

Here a lump of floating nonarchitecture houses wonderful
music on occasion. Call.

[U8] **River Café**, 1 Water St., foot of Old Fulton Street, secretly
sitting on piles.

A place to be in, not look at. Here the picture postcard of
lower Manhattan is displayed live. Sit at the bar and savor the
finial towers of the 1930s, the fat boxes of the 1950s, and the
constant river traffic . . . for a price. Reservations are recommended at any pseudopopular moment. River-hopping celebri-
ties can clutter the stage.

[U9] **Brooklyn Bridge**, East River bet. Adams St., Brooklyn,
and Park Row, Manhattan. 1867-1883. **John A., Washington, and
Emily Roebling**. Reconstructed, 1955. **David Steinman**, consulting engineer [see Bridges for statistics]. ●' ♂

Perhaps New York's supreme icon, this may also be its most
wondrous man-made object. The spider web of supporting and
embracing cables richly enmeshes anyone strolling across its
boardwalk, a highly recommended walk into the skyline of
Manhattan. Start at the entrance stair on Washington Street
where Cadman Plaza intersects the bridge. The current colors
are reputed to be copies of the original subtle coffee and white,
rather than the Public Works Gray that blunted lines and form
in the 1930s through 1960s. New ramps for pedestrians and
bicyclists opened in 1986, allowing (except for street crossings at
each end) movement from island to island without stairs or
steps.

[U9a] **Brooklyn Bridge Anchorage**, a museum, occupies the
underbody of the bridge off Old Fulton Street adjacent to the
elevated BQE bridge.

U9a

🏛 [U10] **Empire Fulton Ferry State Park**. [U11] **Proposed
N.Y.S. Maritime Museum**/originally Tobacco Inspection
Warehouse, 25-39 Water St., bet. New Dock and Dock Sts. N
side. ca. 1860. ♂ [U12] **Empire Stores**, 53-83 Water St., bet.
Dock and Main Sts. N side. Western 4-story group, 1869.
Eastern 5-story group, 1885. **Thomas Stone**. ♂

A clutch of post-Civil War warehouses that serviced the
freighters bearing goods to the Orient and Australia. Forgotten
by New Yorkers, they were rediscovered by photographer
Berenice Abbott in the Federal Art Project of the WPA.
Forgotten again, they were bought by Con Edison for a potential generating plant and were then considered by the City as a
relocation site for the Brooklyn meat market. Happily, all that
folly is past, and the buildings and open space may become a
symbiotic museum, shops, and park. The views of the skyline
through the Brooklyn Bridge are Hollywoodian.

U12

U13

[U13] **The Clock Tower** (apartments)/originally Gair Building No. 7, 1 Main St. ca. 1888. **William Higginson**. Converted to condominiums, 1999. **Beyer Blinder Belle**.

One of a gaggle of reinforced-concrete loft buildings erected by **Robert Gair**, a pioneering entrepreneur in the corrugated box industry. His dozen structures filled this lowland between the Brooklyn and Manhattan Bridges. They are some of the earliest concrete engineering in America. The Clock Tower's eponymous clocks surround a 3,500 square foot, 25 foot tall condominium volume.

*DUMBO (Down Under the Manhattan Bridge Overpass!): will most of the historic district plus adjacent buildings beyond its edges become another SoHo, a Brooklyn Tribeca? Here the developer **David Walentas**, having commenced conversion of the warehouses into condominiums, teases us with the proposal for a River Hotel designed by **Jean Nouvel**, cantilevering into the East River over a box of many cinemas. Nouvel is the Parisian architect who (with Architecture Studio) built the elegant, stainless steel, high-tech Arab World Institute (Institut du Monde Arabe, 1987).*

VINEGAR HILL

A lost backwater of old Brooklyn, cut off to the east by the Navy Yard, and from the west by commerce and industry.

[V1] **Vinegar Hill Historic District**, including portions of Plymouth, Hudson and Front Streets. Extant buildings, 1805-1908. 🏛

   [V2] **237-249 Front Street**, between Bridge and Gold Sts. 1840s. ♺
A Greek Revival row of 7 intact brick houses from a more prosperous time in Vinegar Hill, but now lovingly maintained.

V2

[V3] **51-59 Hudson Avenue** (house and shop), bet. Plymouth and Evans Sts. E side. ♺
A bedraggled clapboard survivor from the time before fire laws demanded non-combustible exterior materials.

[V4] Originally Benjamin Moore & Co. **Factory, 231 Front Street**. 1908. **William Tubby**. ♺
Tubby's more elegant memories can be seen at the Charles Millard Pratt House. With a bit of imagination, one could see some Chicago style in this banded brick and limestone warehouse.

V3

[V5] **Consolidated Edison Stacks**, foot of Hudson Ave.
At the foot of Vinegar Hill the gaggle of stacks for Con Ed's generating plant form a triumphal punctuation to the local skyline.

V4

VINEGAR HILL DISTRICT

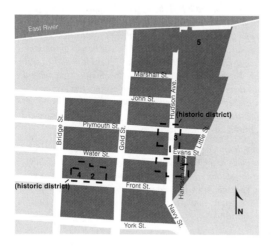

...LL

...lantic Avenue, just below fashionable Brooklyn ...es the community of Cobble Hill with vast rows of ...hed housing, many institutions, and numerous fine ..., although some of the latter have given place to condo- ...s within their Gothic Revival guts. It was overlooked by ...bane young middle class until the 1950s, when an enter- ...g real estate broker rediscovered the name Cobles hill on ...766 Ratzer map of New York and Brooklyn and updated ... spelling. As the Heights filled with a new brownstone apartment-dwelling population, and rents soared, Cobble Hill became an attractive alternate, with equivalent housing just a bit further from the bridge and skyline. Coblehill, or Ponkiesbergh, referred to the steep conical hill (since removed) near the intersection of Court Street and Atlantic Avenue. Its peak, during the Revolution, was the site of an important Continental army fortification during the Battle of Brooklyn.

C1

[C1] **E. M. Fuller Pavilion, Long Island College Hospital,** 70 Atlantic Ave., SE cor. Hicks St. 1974. **Ferrenz & Taylor.**
[C2] **Polak Pavilion, Long Island College Hospital,** Hicks St. bet. Atlantic Ave. and Amity St. 1984. **Ferrenz & Taylor.** Addition, 1988, **Ferrenz, Taylor, Clark & Assocs.**

These bulky monoliths are the heart of Long Island College's rebirth as a major medical institution. Their deeply articulated brick forms are an appropriate understatement for the position at the joint between the Brooklyn Heights and Cobble Hill Historic Districts. The hospital is a testament to the 19th-century German immigrants who lived here and established this institution to serve the community.

Atlantic Avenue: *A Near Eastern bazaar of exotic foods and gifts, cresting on the block between Court and Clinton Streets: halvah, dried fruit, nuts, pastries, dates, olives, copper and brass work, goatskin drums, and inlaid chests. And Near Eastern restaurants too, serving hummus, baba ghannouj, kibbe, stuffed squash, cabbage, and grape leaves, and wonderful yogurt delicacies. Since the 1970s Atlantic Avenue has become a milelong bazaar for antique hunters, stretching from Hicks Street to Times Plaza at the LIRR Station. For example, in the blocks between Smith Street and 3rd Avenue there are myriad dealers in 19th-century oak furniture. And each September the community stages the Atlantic Antic, a Sunday street fair that draws a million people to its shops, booths, rides, music, and general festivities.*

Under Atlantic Avenue, from the Long Island Railroad Station at Times Plaza to the East River, is a tunnel (1844) that originally linked the Station with the Ferry Terminal to Manhattan's South Ferry. The tunnel, a grim void, caused the elimination of the mall and trees that originally made this stretch an early sort of Park Avenue for Brooklyn.

C3

[C3] **Prospect Heights Pavilion, Long Island College Hospital,** 349 Henry St., NE cor. Amity St. 1963. **Beeston & Patterson.**

The earliest stroke in the hospital's renewal. Its exposed concrete frame was once considered stylish.

[C4] **Cobble Hill Historic District, Atlantic Ave. to DeGraw St., Hicks to Court Sts.,** excepting the NW corner lands of Long Island College Hospital.

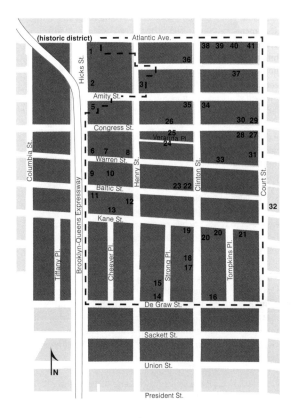

Within the district are all of the following:

[C5] **Dudley Memorial, Long Island College Hospital**, 110 Amity St., SE cor. Henry St. 1902. **William C. Hough.** ○⟋

Richly adorned and in dark red brick, this latter-day miniature Henri IV "hôtel particulier" recalls the architecture of the Place des Vosges and the Hôpital St. Louis in Paris. It is a fitting neighbor to its adjoining bourgeois row houses.

[C6] **St. Peter's, Our Lady of Pilar Church** (Roman Catholic), Hicks St. NE cor. Warren St. 1860. Patrick Charles Keely. [C7] Originally **St. Peter's Academy.** 1866. [C8] **Cobble Hill Health Center**/originally St. Peter's Hospital, 274 Henry St., bet. Congress and Warren Sts. W side. 1888-1889. **William Schickel & Co.** ○⟋

Once a full block to minister to the community's spiritual (church), educational (academy), social (home for working girls at Hicks and Congress Streets), and health (hospital) needs. The red painted brickwork held it all together. Things have changed. The church retains its sturdy, buttressed forms in brick, brownstone, and terra-cotta, crowned with a squat tower.

[C9] **Tower Buildings** (apartments), 417-435 Hicks St., 136-142 Warren St., 129-135 Baltic St., E side of Hicks St. 1878. ○⟋

[C10] **Workingmen's Cottages**, 1-25 and 2-26 Warren Place, bet. Hicks and Henry Sts., 146-154 Warren St. S side. 139-147 Baltic St. N side. 1879. ○⟋

C5

C6

C9

...me Buildings** (apartments), 439-445 Hicks St. and ... Baltic St., SE cor. Hicks St. 1876. All by **William Field** ...ed, 1986, **Maitland, Strauss & Behr**. ♂

...tion of the "sun-lighted tenements" in newly socially ...ate Victorian London inspired these 226 low-rent ...ts and 34 cottages financed by businessman **Alfred** ...**White**. White's dictum, "philanthropy plus 5%," made ...e first builder of limited-profit (and hence low-rent) ...ng in America. Innovations such as outside spiral stairs ...open balconies that serve as access corridors achieved floor-...ugh apartments with good ventilation. Common bathing facilities were originally provided in the basement. The tiny 11½-foot-wide cottages line a wondrous private pedestrian mews, Warren Place. There are no rear gardens, but twin alleys provide rear access.

C11

The Tower Buildings embrace a garden courtyard.

C12

[C12] **412-420 Henry Street** (row houses), bet. Kane and Baltic Sts. W side. 1888. **George B. Chappell**. ♂

Upon completion, these modest Renaissance Revival houses were sold to **F. A. O. Schwarz**, the toy king. Nos. 412, 414, and 416 retain their original doorways, low stoops, and some of the original ironwork.

*Winnie's Mom didn't live here: At 426 Henry Street, just south of Kane, a plaque claims that **Winston Churchill**'s mother, **Jennie Jerome**, was born in that house in 1850. Actually, she was born in 1854 in a house on Amity Street near Court. The confusion results from the fact that **Jennie**'s folks had lived with her uncle, **Addison G. Jerome**, at 292 (now renumbered 426) Henry Street prior to her birth.*

C13

[C13] **143 Kane Street** (townhouse), opp. Cheever Pl. 1997. **Joseph and Mary Merz**. ♂

A modest row house with an elegantly detailed balcony overlooking the length of Cheever Place.

[C14] **St. Francis Cabrini Chapel** (Roman Catholic)/originally Strong Place Baptist Church, DeGraw St. NW cor. Strong Place, 1851-1852. **Minard Lafever**. [C15] **Strong Place Day-Care Center**/originally Strong Place Baptist Church Chapel, 56 Strong Place. 1849. **Minard Lafever**. ♂

C14

A stolid, brownstone Gothic Revival church, charmingly pockmarked as the stucco veneer flakes off. The icing still clings to those very pointed arches of the chapel. Lafever was one of Brooklyn's greatest architects.

[C16] **South Brooklyn Seventh-Day Adventist Church**/originally Trinity German Lutheran Church, 249 DeGraw St., bet. Clinton St. and Tompkins Place. N side. 1905. **Theobald Engelhardt**. ♂

C17

A simple brick church in the second Gothic Revival. The first flowered in the 1840s, the second at the turn of the century.

[C17] Originally **Dr. Joseph E. Clark House,** 340 Clinton St., bet. DeGraw and Kane Sts. W side. ca. 1860. ♂

The widest single house in Cobble Hill, asymmetric and crowned with a slate mansard roof. Note the sinuous ironwork.

[C18] **334 Clinton Street** (house), bet. DeGraw and Kane Sts. W side. ca. 1850. Remodeled, 1888, **James W. Naughton**. ♂

A kooky mansard-roofed Queen Anne miniature, the product of **Naughton**'s remodeling of an originally simple body. Note particularly the corner tower and the lovely wrought-iron strapwork. As architect for the Brooklyn school system, **Naughton** later built the great Boys' High School.

C18

[C19] **Christ Church and Holy Family** (Episcopal), 320 Clinton St., SW cor. Kane St. 1840-1841. **Richard Upjohn**. Altar, altar railings, reredos, pulpit, lectern, chairs, 1917, **Louis Comfort Tiffany**.

English Gothic, cut ashlar brownstone by the elder of the father-and-son architects, the **Upjohns**, who lived just down the street [C22]. Four strong finials form an appropriate skyline apex in these low-rise blocks. A 1939 fire destroyed most but not all of the Tiffany windows. The red Episcopal doors give lively contrast.

C19

C20

[C20] **301-311 Clinton Street** (houses), **206-224 Kane Street** and **10-12 Tompkins Place**, 1849-1854.
Nine classy pairs of narrow Italianate houses developed by New York lawyer **Gerard W. Morris**. The street is pleasantly modulated by the rhythm of the projecting bays.

[C21] **Kane Street Synagogue**, Congregation Beth Israel Anshei Emes/formerly Trinity German Lutheran Church/originally Middle Dutch Reformed Church, 236 Kane St., SE cor. Tompkins Place. ca. 1856.
Originally a brick and brownstone Romanesque Revival, its present stuccoed exterior is bland but waterproof. The congregation is descended from a splinter group of Brooklyn's oldest synagogue, once located at State Street and Boerum Place.

C21

[C22] Originally **Richard Upjohn House, 296 Clinton St.**, NW cor. Baltic St. 1843. **Richard Upjohn & Son**. [C23] **Addition to Upjohn House**, 203 Baltic St., W of Clinton St. 1893. **Richard M. Upjohn**.

The younger **Upjohn**'s Romanesque Revival addition retains some of the elegant detail obliterated in the older corner house on its conversion to a multiple dwelling. This is interesting more for the architects who lived here than the architecture.

C22

[C24] **Verandah Place**, S of Congress St., bet. Clinton and Henry Sts. ca. 1850.
A pleasant mews, long neglected but now reclaimed as charming residences. **Thomas Wolfe**, who lived at No. 40, later described his apartment in *You Can't Go Home Again*. The bland playground is a pleasant amenity for parents and children but is out of scale with the carriage houses it confronts. Why can't street lighting in such tight and quaint surrounds be bracketed from the buildings proper, as it is in so many older European cities?

C24

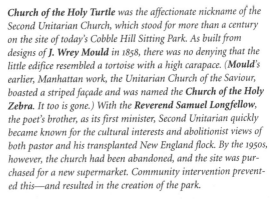

Church of the Holy Turtle was the affectionate nickname of the Second Unitarian Church, which stood for more than a century on the site of today's Cobble Hill Sitting Park. As built from designs of J. Wrey Mould in 1858, there was no denying that the little edifice resembled a tortoise with a high carapace. (Mould's earlier, Manhattan work, the Unitarian Church of the Saviour, boasted a striped façade and was named the Church of the Holy Zebra. It too is gone.) With the Reverend Samuel Longfellow, the poet's brother, as its first minister, Second Unitarian quickly became known for the cultural interests and abolitionist views of both pastor and his transplanted New England flock. By the 1950s, however, the church had been abandoned, and the site was purchased for a new supermarket. Community intervention prevented this—and resulted in the creation of the park.

C27

[C25] 166, 168, and 170 Congress Street (row houses), bet. Clinton and Henry Sts. S side. **[C26] 159, 161, and 163 Congress Street** (row houses), bet. Clinton and Henry Sts. N side. ca. 1857. ○⟲

Two triads of Anglo-Italianate row houses, each designed to read as a single unit. The southern group has segmental arched upper-floor windows; the northern group, square-headed ones.

▥ **[C27] St. Paul's, St. Peter's, Our Lady of Pilar Church**, Court St. SW cor. Congress St. 1838. **Gamaliel King**. Steeple, early 1860s. Brownstone veneer, 1888. Additions of new sanctuary and sacristy. 1906. **[C28] Rectory**, 234 Congress St., bet. Court and Clinton Sts. S side. 1936 **Henry J. McGill**. ○⟲

C29

Its tall verdigris copper-sheathed steeple is a giant finial along Court Street for blocks in both directions. It takes careful study to understand the Greek Revival form behind the later steeple. **King** was the carpenter who designed Brooklyn's City Hall, now Borough Hall.

[C29] 223 Congress Street (house), bet. Court and Clinton Sts. N side. 1851. Mansard roof, ca. 1880. ○⟲

A large stuccoed Gothic Revival house originally built as a rectory for St. Paul's opposite and the Free School for Boys. The mansard roof has been desecrated with—of all things—white aluminum clapboard.

C30

[C30] 221 Congress Street (house), bet. Court and Clinton Sts. N side. 1850s. ○⟲

An ox-bow lintel brings a touch of exoticism.

🏢 **[C31] 194-200 Court Street** (apartments), bet. Congress and Warren Sts. W side. 1898. **William B. Tubby**. ○⟲

FOSTER in the pediment names this turn-of-the-century block of tenement apartments. The storefronts are miraculously preserved in almost their original condition. Two shades of brick articulate the façade.

C32

▬ **[C32] Annex, Brooklyn Heights Montessori School**, 185 Court St., NE cor. Baltic St. 1998. **Gruzen Samton** and **De la Cour & Ferrara**.

A quiet modernist building that presents neighborly brick and windows to Baltic Street; crowned in blue seamed metal.

[C33] St. Paul's Parish School (Roman Catholic), 205 Warren St., bet. Court and Clinton Sts. 1887. ○⟲

An eclectic Victorian brick building with Corinthian-capped pilasters. Education seemed more serious in such monumental and dignified surroundings.

C34

[C34] Formerly **Ralph L. Cutter House**/originally Abraham J. S. DeGraw House, 219 Clinton St., SE cor. Amity St. 1845. Altered, 1891, **D'Oench & Simon**. ○⟲

In the early and sparsely built development of Cobble Hill, most residents could view the harbor from their parlor windows. As the blocks infilled, the view was barred, inspiring here a tower for viewing the harbor over the rooftops beyond. Still freestanding, with a grand garden, it sports a rock-face brownstone stoop with both cast and wrought ironwork.

C35

[C35] **146 Amity Street** (apartments), SW cor. Clinton St. 1986. **Saltini/Ferrara**. ♂

A modest modern infill building, trying to look as if it has always been there. Bay windows and ironwork add to the simple brown form.

*Jennie Jerome, born January 9, 1854: Cut stone veneer conceals the original body of No. 197 (once No. 8) Amity Street, where a baby girl was born to **Mr. and Mrs. Leonard Jerome**. Jennie grew up to marry **Lord Randolph Churchill** and to give birth, in turn, to a son, **Winston**. The veneer was obviously added in the hope of "modernizing" and "improving" this "old-fashioned" building, an aesthetic akin to placing iron deer, polished spheres, and assorted gnomes on one's front lawn in suburbia.*

C36

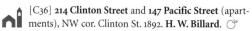 [C36] **214 Clinton Street** and **147 Pacific Street** (apartments), NW cor. Clinton St. 1892. **H. W. Billard**. ♂

Queen Anne, in rock-face brownstone and rough brick. See the face in the pediment at No. 214. The sheet-metal bay windows are ornamented with iron studs and sinuous Ionic colonnettes.

[C37] **174 Pacific Street** (apartments)/formerly Public School 78, Brooklyn, bet. Clinton and Court Sts. S side. 1889. ♂

A strong prim brick school building, looming over its row house neighbors.

C37

[C38] **191 Clinton Street** (apartments)/originally South Brooklyn Savings Bank, SE cor. Atlantic Ave. 1871. **E. L. Roberts**. Restored, 1986. ♂

A noble Eastlake commercial building in Tuckahoe marble. The bank's move to the east end of the Atlantic Avenue block in 1922 initiated years of decay. Happily, it has now been restored to a position as prominent citizen. Note the incised carvings in the lintels.

[C39] **164-168 Atlantic Avenue** (lofts), bet. Clinton and Court Sts. S side. 1859-1864. ♂

Merchant princes of the 19th century were more concerned with the quality of their architecture than those of the 20th. Note the stone quoins and bracketed roof cornices—and the horrible storefront at street level.

C38

[C40] **180 Atlantic Avenue** (lofts), bet. Clinton and Court Sts. S side. 1873. ♂

A rich and unusual—for these parts—cast-iron façade with wrought-iron railings modulating the window openings.

[C41] **Main Office, Independence Savings Bank**/formerly South Brooklyn Savings Institution, 130 Court St., SW cor. Atlantic Ave 1922. **McKenzie, Voorhees & Gmelin**. Addition, 1936, **Charles A. Holmes**. ♂

A Florentine Renaissance anchor marking the northeast corner of the Cobble Hill Historic District. A hundred eagles bear its cornice on their shoulders. The bank changed its name to unload its "Brooklyn only" image. South Brooklyn was Cobble Hill, Carroll Gardens, and Red Hook—the true south in Brooklyn's early days, before annexation of the vast southern, eastern, and northern precincts.

C39

END of Cobble Hill Historic District.

C41

CARROLL GARDENS

Historically considered part of Red Hook or South Brooklyn, the area was renamed Carroll Gardens in the blooming gentrification of the 1960s. It has always been physically distinguished from its surrounding neighbors by its unique cityscape, created by land surveyor **Richard Butts**. His 1846 map provided for a series of unusually deep blocks fronting today's 1st Place through 4th Place between Henry and Smith Streets. His plan, providing for deep front yards as well as standard backyards, was then extended eastward to Carroll, President, and Second Streets between Smith and Hoyt (Union Street is wider also, but without the gardens). Between row house façades and the narrow sidewalks are wonderful and lush front gardens, syncopated with front stoops, that gave the area its name. The sight is as urbane as any in the city. It's unfortunate that Butts' creativity has never been publicly honored.

G2

[G1] **Carroll Gardens Historic District**, generally resembling a keystone on its side, including President and Carroll Sts., bet. Smith and Hoyt Sts., and Hoyt St. bet. President and 1st Sts. 🍎

Only 2 of the 11 fine spaces of Carroll Gardens were designated as the Landmark District, an unhappy oversight. Much of the district therefore lies outside the official boundaries.

G3

[G2] **358-366 Court Street** (apartments)/formerly South Congregational Church and Chapel, NW cor. President St. Chapel, 1851. Church, 1857. 🍎

[G3] **South Congregational Church**, formerly Ladies' Parlor, to the W on President St. 1889. **F. Carles Merry**. 🍎

[G4] **Rectory**, 255 President St., bet. Court and Clinton Sts. N side. 1893. **Woodruff Leeming**. 🍎

One of several Brooklyn churches converted into condominium apartments by hook, crook, and the shrinking of the borough's Protestantism. The dour façade presents a series of stepped planes in brick, a counterpart in masonry to a theater proscenium's contoured velvet curtain. Its silhouette of verdigris-colored finials contrasts with the deep red masonry body.

G4

The still active congregation, in the former Ladies' Parlor, is housed in sturdy sophisticated terra-cotta arches, quoins, and voussoirs, with a frieze worthy of **Louis Sullivan**; the parish house next door is a brick and rockface limestone delight.

[G5] **St. Paul's Episcopal Church of Brooklyn**, 423 Clinton St., NE cor. Carroll St. 1867-1884. **Richard Upjohn & Son**.

A severe high Victorian Gothic work where light sandstone defines the Gothic openings, and serves as the architecture of a whole porch. Above is an uncompleted steeple. Judging from the corner tower, it would have been enormous had it been finished. Grim Protestants.

G5

CARROLL GARDENS DISTRICT
see pages 680-682

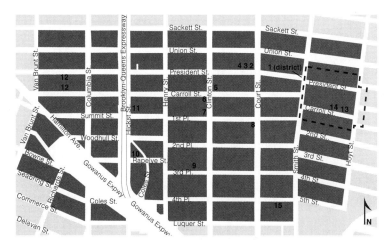

[G6] **F. G. Guido Funeral Home**/originally John Rankin House, 440 Clinton St., SW cor. Carroll St. 1840. 🌶

A grand brick Greek Revival survivor. Somber gray granite supports rosy brick and articulates sills, lintels, and capitals. Once a lone mansion amid farmland, it overlooked the Upper Bay in the same posture and prospect as the Litchfield Mansion in Prospect Park.

G6

[G7] **450 Clinton Street** (apartments)/formerly Den Norske Sjomannskirke/originally Westminster Presbyterian Church, NW cor. 1st Place. ca. 1865.

Stolid and eclectic Romanesque Revival brownstone, converted to apartments. The air-conditioning units punctuating the clerestory spaces form a bizarre frieze. Whither the Norwegian seamen?

[G8] **98 First Place**, SW cor. Court St. ca. 1860.
An brownstone bracketed Italianate corner villa.

G8

[G9] **37-39 Third Place** (houses), bet. Henry and Clinton Sts. N side. ca. 1875.

A **Charles Addams** mansarded outpost with cast-iron grillage in profile against the sky. Mansarded and magnificent.

[G10] **Institutional Services, Roman Catholic Diocese of Brooklyn**/originally Catholic Seamen's Institute, 653 Hicks St., NE cor. Rapelye St. 1943. **Henry V. Murphy**.

From the era of heavy maritime activity in this precinct. The faux Art Moderne lighthouse was intended as a moral beacon: "A challenge of the church to the barrooms of the river front."

G9

[G11] **Sacred Hearts of Jesus and Mary** and **St. Stephen's Church** (Roman Catholic)/originally St. Stephen's Church, Summit St. NE cor. Hicks St. ca. 1860. **Patrick Charles Keely**.

A lusty Gothick complex by the prolific **Keely**, who is believed to have designed 700 churches across the country. Unfortunately, he was no match for **Upjohn**.

[G12] **Columbia Terrace**, 43-57 Carroll St., N side. 250-260 Columbia St., W side. 43-87 President St., S side. 46-90 President St., N side. 1987. **Wids de la Cour** and **Hirsch & Danois**.

Understated rows infilling the blocks of this neighborhood orphaned by the slashing separation of the Brooklyn-Queens Expressway's cut. Why not cover this wound and allow the healthy neighborhood of Cobble Hill to be sutured to its western reaches?

G10

G13

G14

G15

[G13] Formerly **South Brooklyn Christian Assembly Parsonage**, 295 Carroll St., bet. Smith and Hoyt Sts. N side. 1878. ♂

A modest Victorian Gothic manse.

 [G14] **297-299 Carroll Street**, bet. Smith and Hoyt Sts. N side. 1986. ♂

Twin infill row houses that replace the old church of the South Brooklyn Christian Assembly, consumed by fire. A brave and simple modern attempt, complete with stoops and mansarded terraces.

[G15] Formerly **Calvary Baptist Church of Red Hook**/originally South Congregational Chapel, 118 4th Place, bet. Court and Smith Sts.

This robust rotund chapel is Friar Tuck to its more restrained heroic Robin Hood, the former South Congregational Church.

Optical illusions? You can tell for sure only from a land book such as E. Belcher Hyde's of 1912, for example, but it is certain that the street façades of the Carroll Gardens row houses framing Carroll and President Streets are not parallel. As a matter of fact, the difference is considerable. At the Smith Street end they are 100 feet apart, at Hoyt Street the space increases to 129 feet. The surveyor's prestidigitation is concealed, however, by the length of these blocks and their lush greenery.

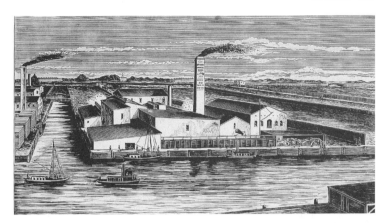

GOWANUS

A shabby, mostly dreary precinct, but occasionally one finds buildings of interest and pockets of urban charm. Among its most interesting features are the bridges and viaducts that cross the waterway bearing its name. Before 1911 the fetid Gowanus Canal was known derisively as Lavender Lake. At that time the Butler Street pumping station at its northern terminus began delivering the stale waters into New York Harbor's Buttermilk Channel, inviting freshwater to enter by hydraulic action. A new facility finally is increasing the flow (this time vice versa, drawing Buttermilk's waters into the Canal) and thus reducing stagnation. Something must be improving. Houseboats have arrived.

O1

[O1] **Butler Street Pumping Station, City of New York**, Butler St. bet. Nevins and Bond Sts. S side. New facilities, 1987.

An elegant wall screens the hardware while giving it a sophisticated interface with the street.

O2

[O2] **Wyckoff Gardens, N.Y.C. Housing Authority**, Nevins St. to Third Ave., Wyckoff to Baltic Sts. 1966. Greenberg & Ames.

Here the Housing Authority omits red brick from its palette and constructs modeled slabs with a variety of setbacks. It is a modest but welcome change in public housing, more successfully followed by those low-rise, high-density programs of the early 1970s that produced streetfronted 6- and 8-story buildings in Brownsville, East New York, and Bedford-Stuyvesant.

[O3] **St. Mark's Avenue**, bet. Third and Fourth Aves., both sides. ca. 1865.

If this street weren't so poor, it would be famous. Here are brownstones for the lower middle class, 3-story-and-basement "English" tenements marching up Park Slope like a provincial brigade.

O4

[O4] **Brooklyn Lyceum**/originally N.Y.C. Public Bath No. 7, 227-231 Fourth Ave., NE cor. President St. 1906-1910. **Raymond F. Almirall**. ☕

A magnificent glazed terra-cotta relic now the headquarters of the Brooklyn Lyceum: tours, an art gallery, special events? Really?

O5

[O5] **Carroll Street Bridge**, over the Gowanus Canal. 1888-1889. **George Ingram**, engineer-in-charge; **Robert Van Buren**, chief engineer; both of the Brooklyn Department of City Works. ☕

A retractile bridge, one that slides askew to a berth on the west side of the canal to allow waterborne traffic to pass. The oldest of four such bridges extant in the country. A gritty relic from the era when Brooklyn's public works were designed by its own municipal government.

[O6] **Vechte-Cortelyou House, in James J. Byrne Memorial Playground**, 3rd St. SW cor., Fifth Ave. Originally built, 1699. Replica, 1935.

The "Old Stone House in Gowanus," re-created by the City's Parks Department in 1935, using old sketches and what were believed to be old stones. The original house had long before fallen into total ruin. In its re-created state it serves as a playground office and comfort station.

O6

The most severe fighting in the Revolutionary War's Battle of Long Island (1776) took place here. **General Stirling**'s Continental troops fought a delaying action against **Cornwallis**' superior number of redcoats, thus permitting Washington's successful retreat.

[O7] **IND Subway high-level crossing, Smith and 9th St. Station**, over Gowanus Canal. 1933.

The land in these parts proved so uneconomical for tunnel construction that the IND subway emerges here, rising over 100 feet to meet the Canal's navigational clearance requirements. This leaves the Smith and 9th Street subway station high and dry, and embraced in a latticework of steel. A spectacular construction, it lacked an Eiffel to make it equally significant visually.

O8

[O8] **St. Agnes Church** (Roman Catholic), 417 Sackett St., NE cor. Hoyt St. 1905. **Thomas F. Houghton**.

The community's dominant structure (save for the IND crossing St. Agnes) is the local quasi-cathedral in these low rowhoused precincts. Here is dressed Manhattan schist ashlar, with limestone detailing, pushing multi-finials to the sky.

O9

*Where the **Dodgers** played: The **James J. Byrne** Memorial Playground (along the west side of Fifth Avenue south of 3rd Street) is named for the owner of the forebears of the Brooklyn Dodgers. At the time (1854) the team was playing there, the site was the first Washington Park baseball field. **Byrne** then moved them to Eastern Park, near today's Broadway Junction. Failing to attract crowds to what was then a remote location, **Charles Ebbet** persuaded the team to return to these precincts, to a new Washington Park, this time on the west side of 4th Avenue between 1st and 3rd Streets. From there the **Dodgers** moved to the more commodious stadium on Bedford Avenue named for their new owner, **Ebbets Field** (1913-1957), which Brooklynites will never forget.*

O10

[O9] **Engine Company 204, N.Y.C. Fire Department**, 299 DeGraw St., bet. Court and Smith Sts. N side. ca. 1880.

A holdover from the times when fires were fought by fire laddies stoking horsedrawn steam pumpers. This one began as Engine Company 4, Brooklyn Fire Department, as cast into the old terra-cotta shields. Brick-and-brownstone Gothic Revival, with an Italianate hat.

O11

[O10] **St. Mary's Star of the Sea Church** (Roman Catholic), 471 Court St., bet. Nelson and Luquer Sts. E side. ca. 1870. **Patrick Charles Keely**. [O11] **Girls' School**, 477 Court St., NE cor. Nelson St. [O12] **Rectory**, 467 Court St., SE cor. Luquer St.

Painted brick humility—a parish church trio for a 19th-century, immigrant, working-class parish. Compare it with other nearby Catholic churches by architect Keely. The raw, red brick body behind the painted façade has a more pleasant texture.

Don't miss taking a peek at Dennett Place, just behind St. Mary's.

Dennett Place

Dennett Place: *An atmospheric street that seems more like a stage set for **Maxwell Anderson**'s Winterset than a brick-and-mortar reality. Lying between Court and Smith Streets, it connects Luquer with Nelson Street. It is more commonly termed a mews.*

RED HOOK

Like an Edward Hopper painting, Red Hook constantly presents excerpts from his stark visions. Here are scattered residential blocks, mixed industry, and neighborhoods generally squalid. The most impressive things here are docks, warehouses, and ships. The immense Red Hook Houses of the 1930s are simply that: immense. Only 6 stories, they fail to supply the happy scale of Williamsburg Houses. Fortunately, attempts at urban quality are still in the works: Ciardullo Associates' row housing on Visitation Place was an early attempt at infilling this poorly toothed precinct. A bit of what Red Hook looked like 100 years ago can be savored on Coffey Street between Conover and Ferris Streets and on Pioneer Street between Van Brunt and Richards.

R1

R2

[R1] **71-79 Visitation Place** (row houses), bet. Van Brunt and Richards Sts. S side. **2-12 Verona Street** (row houses). N side. **9-19 Dwight Street** (row houses). E side. 1972. **John Ciardullo Assocs**.

Federally subsidized low-rent housing sponsored by the New York Urban Coalition, this was a promising example of what might be done without overbearing municipal authority. Sixty-four streetfronted units in 3-story brick and block houses. What tenants can do to personalize them is sometimes depressing. And the unfortunate chain-link fences . . .

[R2] **Louis Valentino, Jr. Park** and **Pier 39** at the end of Coffey St., W of Ferris St. 1997. **Di Domenico & Partners**.

A lance into the harbor, giving pedestrians dramatic views and allowing Red Hook residents to develop a better sense of place.

R3

[R3] Originally **Brooklyn Clay Retort & Firebrick Works**, 76-86 Van Brunt St., 99-113 Van Dyke St., 106-116 Beard St. ca. 1860.

Two sturdy granite ashlar warehouses and a manufactory with its original masonry chimney are all that remain. They are powerful relics from an era of grand industrial architecture. This great enterprise brought clay from South Amboy, N.J., to the nearby Erie Basin, where it was converted to firebrick.

Nos. 76-86 was the firebrick storehouse, Nos. 99-113 the firebrick factory, and Nos. 106-116 the boiler house, carpentry shop, and engine room.

R4

[R4] Originally **Beard & Robinson Stores**, 260 Beard St., along Erie Basin, SE cor. Van Brunt St. 1869. **Van Brunt's Stores**, 480 Van Brunt St., along Erie Basin, S of Beard St. ca. 1869.

Half-round arch openings and down-to-earth brickwork commend these and other nearby post-Civil War wharfside warehouses, the epitome of the functional tradition. Compare them with the better-known Empire Stores. A cut-stone marker modestly marks the streetside southernmost point of Beard & Robinson. Look up. With the declining need or desire for this type of warehousing, these would make magnificent waterfront residential lofts.

Erie Basin: The scythe-shaped breakwater creating this placid harbor was the brainchild of railroad contractor William Beard, who completed it in 1864. He charged ships seeking to haul American cargoes 50¢ per cubic yard for the privilege of dumping the rock carried as ballast from overseas ports—thus, a free breakwater. The longest deadend street in New York is Columbia Street, at the Erie Basin. Drive the length of the scythe and see the sea.

R5

[R5] Originally **Port of New York Grain Elevator Terminal** N.Y.S. Barge Canal System, Henry St. Basin. 1922.

Concrete silos dramatically aligned to receive grain shipments from the Midwest through the Great Lakes and the Erie Canal. The decline of grain traffic to New York Harbor led to their deactivation in 1955. The best view is from Columbia Street.

[R6] **Sol Goldman Recreation Center and Pool**, N.Y.C. Department of Parks & Recreation, Bay St. bet. Clinton and Henry Sts. N side, through to Lorraine St. 1936. N.Y.C. Parks Department, **Aymar Embury II**, consulting architect. Altered.

A WPA pool-bathhouse complex, now with added basketball and boxing. Savor the arches and massive piers.

R6

[R7] **Red Hook Community Center**, **New York City Housing Authority**, 110 W. 9th St., SW cor Clinton St. Renovation and addition, 1998. **Hanrahan + Meyers** and **Castro-Blanco, Piscioneri and Assocs**.

A 1930s social service adjunct to public housing is extended to include a skylit art gallery. The layered façade recalls **De Stijl** and **Gerrit Rietveld**.

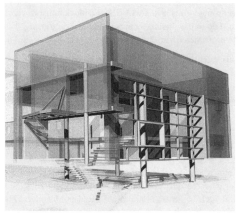

R7

SUNSET PARK AND ENVIRONS

A neighborhood named for its park, a sloping greensward facing the setting sun. Here are sweeping views of the harbor. Once almost exclusively Scandinavian, the community shelters a broad ethnic mix, with a large proportion of Hispanic population. On the flats between the elevated Gowanus Expressway (over Third Avenue, and a continuation of the Brooklyn-Queens Expressway) and the waterfront lie the Bush Terminal at the north and the old Brooklyn Army Terminal at the south. Beginning a few blocks north of Sunset Park's park is the enormous and very beautiful Victorian burying ground, Green-Wood Cemetery.

S1a

[S1] **Green-Wood Cemetery**, Fifth Ave. to Macdonald Ave. and Fort Hamilton Pkwy., 20th to 37th Sts. 1840.

[S1a] Main Entrance Gate and Gatehouse, 5th Ave. opp. 25th St. E side. 1861-1865. **Richard M. Upjohn** of **Richard Upjohn & Son.** 🖐

S1b

[S1b] **Fort Hamilton Parkway Gate and Gatehouse**, 37th St. W of Ft. Hamilton Pkwy. 1875. **Richard M. Upjohn**. Restorations, 1996. **Platt Byard Dovell**. Open to the public. Inquire at gate.

Opened in 1840, these lands were Brooklyn's first park by default long before Prospect Park was created. Here, on the highest points in Brooklyn, 478 acres of rolling landscape offered opportunities for Sunday strolling among the hills, ponds, plantings, and superb views of the harbor. Most of the more than half-million buried here (including Henry Ward Beecher, Nathaniel Currier and James Ives, Peter Cooper, Samuel F. B. Morse, "Boss" Tweed, and Lola Montez) are memorialized by extraordinary mausoleums and monuments. A veritable history of New York Victoriana is indexed by the gravestones, pyramids, obelisks, cairns, temples, and lesser markers. At the main entrance, appropriately, is an especially wondrous gatehouse, the Gothic Revival counterpart to a pair of Roman triumphal arches. Both a building and a gate, it was called the culmination of the Gothic Revival movement in New York by historian Alan Burnham. Inquire at the office to the right for permission to view the grounds.

At the Fort Hamilton parkway end, there is a guardian Second Empire brownstone country château, a happily preserved (and recently restored) remnant of the late 19th century, from the era when Fifth Avenue was lined with many of its urban cousins.

S2

[S2] **McGovern-Weir Florist**/formerly Weir & Company Greenhouse, Fifth Ave. SW cor. 25th St. G. 1895. **G.Curtis Gillespie.** 🖐

Sadly, this once-charming miniature crystal palace is sullied by inappropriate additions, alterations, and signs: once a garden showplace serving Green-Wood opposite. One apocryphal story says that it was moved to Brooklyn from the St. Louis World's Fair of 1904.

S3

[S3] **Alku Toinen** (Finnish cooperative apartments), 826 43rd St., bet. Eighth and Ninth Aves. S side. 1916.

Reputedly the first non-profit cooperative dwelling in New York City. Modest architecturally, it wears a palette of tan Scandinavian brick. Visit it more for its social history than any architectural wonders.

[S4] **Sunset Play Center, N.Y.C. Department of Parks & Recreation**, in Sunset Park at 7th Ave., bet. 41st and 44th Sts. W side. 1936. N.Y.C. Parks Department. **Aymar Embury II**, consulting architect.

Sleek round forms dominate one of several similar sports and aquatic centers built during the depression by the WPA (Red Hook and McCarren are others).

S4

[S5] **43rd Street Row Housing, bet. Seventh and Eighth Aves**. 1898-1904.

Bow-fronted yellow brick houses that are the staple of Sunset Park. Their cornices and brick-decorated belt coursing are still intact.

 [S6] **43rd Street Row Housing, bet. Fourth and Fifth Aves**. ca. 1885.

The topography gives these repetitive three-story brownstone units a chance to form strong group character.

S5

[S7] **St. Michael's Roman Catholic Church**, 4200 Fourth Ave., SW cor. 42nd St. 1905. **Raymond F. Almirall**.

Brooklyn's Sacré Coeur "beehive" sits atop a spire dominating the local skyline.

 [S8] **Sunset Park School of Music**/formerly 68th Precinct Station House and Stable/originally 18th Police Precinct House and Stable, 4302 Fourth Ave., SW cor. 43rd St. 1890-1892. **George Ingram**. ●

S7

Although nearly a ruin, its Romanesque Revival (Venetian and Norman division) is so powerful that the remnants express vigor even in their despair. We hope the musicians arrive soon, with plenty of money for this needy landmark.

[S9] **Bush Terminal**, 28th to 50th Sts., Upper Bay to 2nd Ave., (irregular) buildings 1-4, 1911. 5-13 and 19-26, various years to 1926. **William Higginson**.

Irving T. Bush opened these flats to industrial buildings in 1890. Block after block of 8-story, white-painted buildings are the reality of this mammoth industrial and warehousing enterprise, each unit of which allows a colossal 3 acres on any one floor. In the neighborhood are older brick industrial structures around First Avenue and the 40s:

S8

 [S10] Originally **National Metal Company**/now loft space, 4201-4207 First Ave., SE cor. 42nd St. ca. 1890.

A crenellated neo-Gothic tower is the local campanile. A wonderful mark in the landscape—and an enigma. But the enigma may not last if a lover cannot be found.

 [S11] **68th Precinct**, N.Y.C. Police Department, 333 65th St., bet Third and Fourth Aves. N side. 1970. **Milton F. Kirchman**.

S10

An aggressive, arbitrary, tricky, cubistic set of volumes and voids. In the loose civic commissions of the mid and late 1960s, architectural histrionics preempted any truly urbane attempts to blend into the scale and style of the neighborhood.

[S12] Originally **New York Port of Embarkation and Army Supply Base**, also known as Brooklyn Army Terminal/officially Military Ocean Terminal, Second Ave. bet. 58th and 65th Sts. W side. 1918. **Cass Gilbert**.

These utilitarian warehouses in exposed concrete are vast and appropriately devoid of extraneous ornament. The innards contain long skylit central galleries. **Gilbert**, who was not known for decorative restraint, embellished with ornament and sculpture his better-known buildings—the Woolworth Building in Manhattan and Washington's Supreme Court, among many other confections. But when military functionalism was the order of the day, he could be as austere as Gropius.

S11

[S13] Originally **N.Y.S. Arsenal**/now **Keeper's Self-Storage Warehouse**, Second Ave. bet. 63rd and 64th Sts. E side. 1925.

A grim, precast-concrete former ordnance and quartermaster facility, with limestone quoins and a battered base. Unhappily, its new owners have stripped the façade of the ivy that had once muted these bleak walls.

S13

BOERUM HILL/TIMES PLAZA

B2

Boerum Hill is another new sobriquet for a community that has revived from a neglected past, following in the gentrified footsteps of Cobble Hill and Carroll Gardens. Although the area claimed by the neighborhood association is larger, the most interesting blocks are on State, Pacific, Dean, and Bergen Streets, east of Court Street and west of 4th Avenue. The Historic District is but a small segment of it all. In the mid 19th century this was a fashionable district, as the fine row housing itself indicates. Visitors to the area included **Washington Irving**, **James Fenimore Cooper**, and **William Cullen Bryant**. **Sidney Lanier** lived briefly at 195 Dean Street. Today's residents are a racial and ethnic mix that adds special flavor to the community. Times Plaza is the eastern terminus of this area; the scale is smaller than that of the Heights or Cobble Hill. Three-story row houses and a greater share of sky give the treed blocks a softer and homier aspect, rather than the urbane character of, say, Pierrepont Street.

B3

    Charles Hoyt and his partner, **Russell Nevins**, acquired the area around their self-named streets in 1834. The oldest houses, from the mid 1840s, are in the Greek Revival style, with simple pediments and pilasters.

B4

[B1] Boerum Hill Historic District, irregular, generally lying bet. the Wyckoff St./Hoyt St. intersection on the SW, and the Pacific St./Nevins St. intersection on the NE, including sections of Pacific, Dean, and Bergen Sts. 👌
    The area chosen for designation includes some of the finest rows of housing as well as some of the precinct's architectural eccentricities, which enliven the streetscape. The row houses, single houses, and apartments listed below are among the many contained within the district's boundaries. Nevertheless, whole streets become a joint architectural ensemble and can be savored for their overall urban design, as well as in their separate parts. Buildings within the district are marked with a ⌀

B5

🏛 **[B2] Primera Iglesia Bautista**/aka First Baptist Church, Pacific St. bet. Smith and Hoyt Sts. N side. 1860s.
    Painted brick and brownstone make this a pastrymaker's version of primitive Gothic Revival.

🏛 **[B3] 358 Pacific Street**/originally a chapel, bet. Hoyt and Bond Sts. S side. 1890s. ⌀
    A retired chapel provides living and studio space to its (perhaps) resident artist?

B6

[B4] 360 Pacific Street (single house), bet. Hoyt and Bond Sts. S side. ca. 1861. ⌀
    A lone painted clapboard house, presenting a Corinthian-columned porch to the street, bereft of its eastern garden, now occupied by No. 362.

[B5] 362 Pacific Street (house), bet Hoyt and Bond Sts. S side. 1998. **John Gillis**. ⌀
    Articulated brick that smacks of **Wright** in the details but not in the whole. **Frank Lloyd Wright**, that is, who would be, at the Millennium, a 133-year-old modern architect.

[B6] 372 and 372½ Pacific Street (row houses), bet. Hoyt and Bond Sts. S side. ⌀
    A pair of small mansarded houses with double entrance doors. The slightly arched window openings are lissome.

B7

[B7] 374 Pacific Street (row house), bet. Hoyt and Bond Sts. S side. ca. 1850. ⌀
    A unique example of the Gothic Revival, unfortunately stripped of much of its detail. The district is otherwise largely homogeneous, with the earlier Greek Revival houses and later

B8

B10

B12

Renaissance Revival. Here is Lucky Pierre, always in the middle. The ornate bronze balcony fronting the parlor floor was moved from a house in Fort Greene.

[B8] **245 Dean Street** (row houses), bet. Bond and Nevins Sts. N side. 1853. **John Dougherty** and **Michael Murray**, builders. ☞

This house, one of 30 in a continuous row, remained in the ownership of one family for many generations, a typical history in this neighborhood that explains the well-maintained façades. Note the intricately built-up entrance doors.

[B9] **240 and 244 Dean Street** (row houses), bet. Bond and Nevins Sts. S side. 1858. **Wilson & Thomas**, builders. ☞

Two of four Victorian wood clapboard cottages that practiced another architectural theme than the adjacent blocks.

[B10] **87-89 Nevins Street**, bet. Atlantic Ave. and Pacific St.

Boxy bay windows glisten among their clinging vines, giving a third dimension to these sometimes flat (but for their stoops) façades.

[B11] **Hoyt Street** (group of single houses), bet. Bergen and Wyckoff Sts. E side. [B12] 157 Hoyt Street. ca. 1860. [B13] 159, 161, 163 Hoyt Street. 1871. [B14] 163½ and 165 Hoyt Street. ca. 1854. ☞

The north-south streets in this area tend to be through-traffic arteries, and therefore many houses facing them have been altered at their ground floors into retail space. This grouping is an exception. No. 157 bears an Italianate gabled roof; Nos. 159-163 are mansarded, with vestiges of cast iron against the sky. Nos. 163½ and 165 are innocuous, but their former deep-set front garden offers what might be euphemistically termed a tiny plaza.

B17

[B15] **148 Hoyt Street** (apartments), SW cor. Bergen St. 1851. **Thomas Maynard**, builder. Renovated, 1880s. ☞

Two stories of carefully stripped and repointed brick over a former tavern, once the home of the chic Boerum Hill Café. The florid and magnificent sheet-metal work dates from the 1880s alterations.

END of Boerum Hill Historic District. All the Boerum Hill buildings which follow are outside the district.

[B16] **Bishop Francis J. Mugavero Center for Geriatric Care**, Hoyt St., NE cor. Dean St, 1990s.

Five stories of geriatric care that, fortunately, fits well into the neighborhood scale. Unfortunately, the vast service and parking area toward Pacific Street spoils the streetfront composition of the neighborhood.

BOERUM HILL / TIMES PLAZA DISTRICT
see pages 689-694

B18

B20

B21

[B17] "**The State Street Houses**," 291-299 State St., bet. Smith and Hoyt Sts. N side. 290-324 State St., bet. Smith and Hoyt Sts. S side. 1847-1874. 🍎

These 23 lovingly preserved Renaissance Revival brownstones have most of the original detail. Nos. 293-297 have their original cast-iron balustrades. Nos. 295-299 retain the original portals supported by console brackets. Outside the Historic District, they are landmarked as a separate group.

[B 18] **335 State Street** (apartments), bet. Hoyt and Bond Sts., N Side. 1890s.

A grand corner-towered, brick and terra-cotta apartment house for late-in-the-century middle-class arrivals unable to afford a rowhouse.

[B19] **St. Nicholas Antiochian Orthodox Cathedral**, 355 State St., bet. Hoyt and Bond Sts. N side.

Cut ashlar schist with sandstone trim enrich this English country church. The 6 dormer windows with curved eaves at each side of the nave roof add an elfin Victorian quality.

[B20] **371 and 375 State Street**, bet. Bond and Nevins Sts. N side. 1890.

The Albemarle and the Devonshire are a pair of spruce dowagers: brick and terra-cotta monoliths over rock-face brownstone with a grand rock-face granite entrance arch. Savor the regal bas-reliefs in the separate pediments.

[B21] **Engine Company 226, N.Y.C. Fire Department**, 409 State St., bet. Bond and Nevins Sts. N side. 1889.

A simple neighborhood civic building embellished with corbeled brick and a perfect cast-iron crest against the sky. Painted a garish red.

[B22] **443-451 State Street** (tenements), bet. Nevins St. and Third Ave. N side. ca. 1895.

Six sprightly tenements, with alternating round and polygonal bow/bay-fronts and cornices. Carved brownstone enriches entries, as do the cast- and wrought-iron balustrades.

[B23] **492-496 State Street** (row houses), bet. Nevins St. and Third Ave. S side. ca. 1900.

Stoopless "English" row houses. One enters the main floor directly, rather than by walking up a stoop to the parlor floor, as in most of Brooklyn's brick and brownstone houses.

B24

B26

B27

B28

B30

B31

 [B24] **Byelorussian Autocephalic Orthodox Church**, 401 Atlantic Ave., NE cor. Bond St.

A simple Gothick brick church, articulated with buttresses and bands.

 [B25] **House of the Lord Pentecostal Church**, 415 Atlantic Ave., NE cor. Nevins St.

A picturesque late Romanesque Revival church with banded brick arches and a dour painted ocher brick body.

[B26] **Atlantic Gardens**, 525-535 Atlantic Ave., bet. Third and Fourth Aves. Late 19th century.

Developer **Ted Hilles** gathered this cluster of simple brick buildings into a cooperative entered through a central portal into the gardens behind. The Victorian storefronts are happy remnants in wood, whose bayed fronts give modulation to the street.

 [B27] **554-552 Atlantic Avenue**, bet. Third and Fourth Aves. S side.

An Arabian Nights building, fortunately now reclaimed by Arabs. Its spiral central column is a glazed candy cane, or Hollywood Bernini, with accompanying grand arches to each side.

 [B28] Originally **Brooklyn Printing Plant, New York Times**, 59-75 Third Ave., bet. Dean and Pacific Sts. E side. 1929. **Albert Kahn**.

This monumental neo-Classical limestone work hardly hints at the avant-garde industrial facilities that this architect would shortly create at the Dodge Half-Ton Truck Plant in Detroit (1938). The large windows along Third Avenue permitted the public to view the printing, collating, and folding of newspapers along a half-block-long printing press. The papers were then distributed from the through-block alley to the east.

[B29] **Bethlehem Lutheran Church**/originally Swedish Evangelical Bethelem Lutheran Church, SW cor. Third Ave. and Pacific Sts. 1894.

A very North European brick church with 2 marvelous verdigris copper-framed rose windows. It has a crisp hardness, like Saarinen père.

 [B30] **Church of the Redeemer** (Episcopal), Fourth Ave. NW cor. Pacific St. 1870. **Patrick Charles Keely**.

Presiding over the chaotic intersection, this rock-face ashlar church offers polychromatic Ruskinian voussoirs and a sturdy tower set back from Fourth Avenue on Pacific.

[B31] **Pacific Branch, Brooklyn Public Library**, 25 Fourth Ave., SE cor. Pacific St. 1904. **Raymond F. Almirall**. ●

If the Church of the Redeemer, across Fourth Avenue, is an architectural symphony, this branch library is a **Sousa** march—self-satisfied, robust, and stridently Beaux Arts. Note the cornice with torchères and swags, and the gargantuan consoles over the first floor.

Times Plaza: The 5-way intersection of 3 major routes—Atlantic, Flatbush, and Fourth Avenues—together with 2 secondary ones, Ashland Place and Hanson Place, forms Times Plaza, named for the Brooklyn Daily Times, once published nearby. It is now domi-nated by Brooklyn's tallest building, the Williamsburgh Savings Bank tower. It is at this chaotic starfish that the Long Island Railroad has its decrepit Atlantic Avenue Terminal. It is still des-tined to be crowned with new office and civic facilities. Supershopping marts have invaded the rear (eastern) portion of the old Railroad Station footprints, but the heart of the matter is still open for a vast new project. Where better could it be sited?

[B32] Originally **IRT Atlantic Avenue subway kiosk**, in the triangle formed by Flatbush, Atlantic, and Fourth Aves. 1908. **Heins & La Farge**. Under renovation.

A sorry fate overtook this anchor on the IRT subway lines. Constructed in 1908 to celebrate and advertise the new underground connection with Manhattan, it was abandoned as a working entrance and then buried within a filigree (now gone) intended to revitalize it visually and commercially. **Heins & La Farge**'s distinguished work for the subway system faintly survives on these lines, mostly in the restored mosaic works.

B33

[B33] Williamsburgh Savings Bank Tower/now the **Republic National Bank**, 1 Hanson Place, NE cor Ashland Place. 1927-1929. **Halsey, McCormack & Helmer**. 🌂 ♂ (BAM Historic District.). Interior 🌂

Inadvertently, this was New York's most exuberant phallic symbol (Manhattan's CitySpire is taking up the torch), its slender tower dominating the landscape of all Brooklyn. A crisp and clean tower, it is detailed in Romanesque-Byzantine arches, columns, and capitals. The 26th floor once included accessible outdoor viewing space, after a change of elevators. In these upper regions, all of Brooklyn's orthodontists seem to have roosted. All in all, it is 512 feet of skyline. Inside, the great basilican banking hall is called by the Landmarks Preservation Commission a "cathedral of thrift."

Records set, records broken: While the Williamsburgh Savings Bank Tower is still the tallest office building in Brooklyn, it is not the tallest structure. That honor goes to the Board of Education's lacy radio and television transmission tower for WNYE-FM and WNYE-TV atop nearby Brooklyn Technical High School, 29 Fort Greene Place (591 feet). Similarly, the Williamsburgh's illuminated clock was the largest 4-sided clock in the nation (27 feet in diameter) until the 40-foot diameter clocks on the Allen Bradley Building in Milwaukee were finished in 1962. An up-close look at the grotesquely large hands and illuminated numbers from the tower's observation deck is a worthwhile. and surrealistic experience.

[B34] **Hanson Place Central United Methodist Church**, 88 Hanson Place, NW cor. St. Felix St. 1929-1931. ♂ (BAM Historic District.).

Gothic restyled in modern dress, an exercise in massing brick and tan terra-cotta that might be termed a cubistic Art Moderne. The street level contains stores, a surprising but intelligent adjunct to ecclesiastical economics. This building replaced its predecessor, on the site from 1847 to 1927.

B34

[B35] **Baptist Temple**, 360 Schermerhorn St., SW cor. Third Ave. 1894. Rebuilt, 1917.

This Romanesque Revival fortress bears gables and a machicolated tower. The lighted cross emblazons the fundamentalist preaching within. The intersection before it, officially Temple Square, understandably acquired the nickname Brimstone Square.

B36

[B36] **N.Y.C. Board of Education Certificating Unit**/formerly Public School 15, Brooklyn/originally Brooklyn Boys' Boarding School, 475 State St., NE cor. Third Ave. ca. 1840.

A dour red-painted institutional remnant that is the far-flung outpost of the bureaucracy centered at 110 Livingston Street.

[B37] **Brooklyn Academy of Music Historic District**, bet. Lafayette Ave., Ashland, Hanson, and Fort Greene Places, plus parts of the N side of Fort Greene Place and both sides of S. Elliott Place. 🌂

The row houses of St. Felix Street are a surprising and charming foil to the bulky neo-Renaissance Academy.

B38

B39

[B38] **Brooklyn Academy of Music (BAM)**, 30 Lafayette Ave., bet. Ashland Place and St. Felix St. 1908. **Herts & Tallant**. ♂ (BAM Historic District.) 718-636-4100.

This modest building was originally crowned with a great Renaissance Revival cornice, its external architectural essential; and its loss puts the building in the role of Queen of England without a hat. A multichambered, performing arts center two generations before Lincoln Center, it now houses a symphony hall/opera house, and a multiplex movie theater. Culturally, it is where the great avant-garde experiments occur in New York, a veritable Vesuvius of talent in dance, theater, and music.

[B39] **Majestic Theater of the Brooklyn Academy of Music (BAM)**, Fulton St., NE cor. Rockwell St. 1903. Renovated, 1987. **Hardy Holzman Pfeiffer**.

This is where much of the avant-garde finds its way. The monumental (but small) arch swallows you into the grand and restored lobby, a palimpsest of real and simulated decay. Its consciously worn and reclaimed spaces are akin to old money in old clothes. **Ralph Lauren**, take note.

Fort Greene / Clinton Hill / The Navy Yard

*"To the rear of the boisterous city hall quarter was Brooklyn's other
fine residential district, the Hill. Located in the center of the city
and surrounded by diverse elements, its position was not unlike
that of the Heights; but its elegant residences were fewer in number
and their owners slightly further removed from the traditions of
genteel respectability. It abounded in churches and middle class
houses, the majority of whose owners worked in New York, but
took pride in living in Brooklyn."*
        —Harold C. Syrett, The City of Brooklyn, 1865-1898.

Fort Greene and Clinton Hill rank with Cobble Hill and
Boerum Hill as rediscovered sectors of urban delight. Clustering
around Fort Greene Park and Pratt Institute are blocks of distinguished brownstones, many mansions, and a surprisingly rich
inventory of churches and other institutions. The communities'
edges at Fulton Street, Flatbush Avenue, and along the old Navy
Yard are roughened by cheap commercial areas and by neighborhoods of urban renewal still in flux. But the body is, for the
most part, solid and handsome.

FORT GREENE

*Fort Greene Walking Tour: Start at Hanson Place and South
Portland Street, about four blocks east of either the Atlantic
Avenue Station of the IRT (2, 3, 4, and 5 trains), IND (D and Q
trains), and Long Island Railroad, or the Pacific Street Station of
the BMT (B, M, N, and R trains) (all at Times Plaza), or the
Lafayette Avenue Station of the IND (A and C trains). The walk
ends on Vanderbilt Avenue at Gates. Continue to Fulton Street
and turn left to Clinton Avenue to reach the IND subway one stop
farther away from Manhattan. Buildings surrounding Times
Plaza are covered in the Boerum Hill/Times Plaza section.*

[F1] **Hanson Place Seventh Day Adventist Church**/origi-
nally Hanson Place Baptist Church, 88 Hanson Place, SE
cor. S. Portland Ave. 1857-1860. **George Penchard.**
    A glorious Corinthian-columned portico fronts on Hanson
Place, with pilasters along the South Portland flanks. Cream
columns, trim, and pediments over a dark red body. Victorian
milk glass.

[F2] **Oxford Nursing Home**/originally Lodge No. 22,
Benevolent Protective Order of Elks, 144 S. Oxford St.,
bet. Hanson Place and Atlantic Ave. W side. 1912. **H. Van Buren
Magonigle** and **A. W. Ross**. Altered, 1955, **Wechsler & Schimenti**.
    The glorious bracketed cornice is a wide-sweeping catholic
hat on this body abused in alteration.

F1

FORT GREENE DISTRICT
see pages 695-701

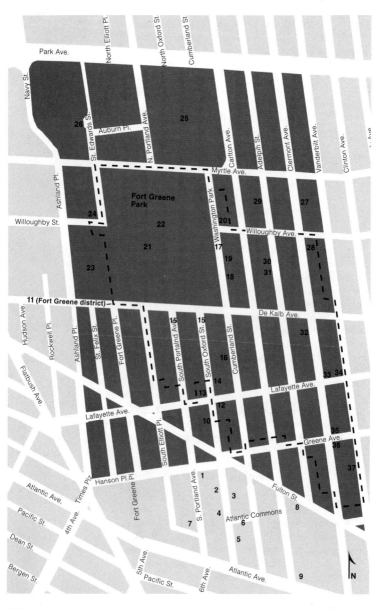

F3

[F3] **143 and 145 South Oxford Street** (row houses), bet. Hanson Place and Atlantic Ave. E side.

A handsome pair of Corinthian-columned porches, alive and loved.

[F4] **158 South Oxford Street** (single house), bet. Hanson Place and Atlantic Avenue. W side. ca. 1860.

A freestanding clapboard Italianate house with a Carpenter Gothic porch set on a unique podium for these blocks: a raised lawn.

[F5] Originally **New York & Brooklyn Casket Company**, 187 S. Oxford St., bet. Hanson Place and Atlantic Ave. E side. 1927. **Vincent B. Fox**.

A lonely limestone neo-Georgian remnant now squeezed between tennis courts and devastation.

[F6] **Atlantic Commons**, in a subdivided block between Atlantic Ave. and Hanson Pl., So. Oxford and Cumberland Sts. 1990s.

An urban historicist was here.

F6

Atlantic Avenue Urban Renewal Area

Plotted on a map, this 33-year-old urban renewal area looks faintly like a comet pointing northwest to Downtown Brooklyn and the Civic Center. Its body is the still decaying Atlantic Avenue Terminal of the Long Island Railroad's Brooklyn section. Its tail is contained within Hanson Place and Fulton Street to the north, and Atlantic Avenue to the south. It has eliminated the old Fort Greene Meat Market and has constructed new housing projects, but it has still to reconstruct the Terminal and its related commercial facilities. Once upon a time Baruch College was to have been here, in concert with a grand new terminal; but now new commercial space occupies only the eastern portion of the yards..

[F7] **170 South Portland Avenue** and **161 South Elliott Place** (apartments), bet. Hanson Place and Atlantic Ave. [F8] **455 and 475 Carlton Avenue** (apartments), bet. Fulton St. and Atlantic Ave. E side. **770 Fulton Street** (apartments), bet. Carlton Ave. and Adelphi St. S side. All buildings, 1976. **Bond Ryder Associates**.

Residential blocks sheltering a variety of apartments, expressed by the staccato placement of the windows. The spaces between the buildings are urbanely designed and arranged for playgrounds and plazas.

F7

[F9] **Atlantic Terminal Houses, N.Y.C. Housing Authority**, 487-495 Carlton Ave., NE cor. Atlantic Ave. 1976. **James Stewart Polshek & Assocs.**

These larger blocks use contrasting brick stripes to camouflage their ungainly appearance.

[F10] **98 South Oxford Street** (row house), bet. Greene and Lafayette Aves. W side. ca. 1855.

A Corinthian columned porch is a welcome variant on the street.

F10

Here we enter the Fort Greene Historic District.

[F11] **Fort Greene Historic District**, bounded by Willoughby and Vanderbilt Aves., S. Elliott Place, and an irregular line N of Fulton St., plus Fort Greene Park. ●

[F12] **Lafayette Avenue Presbyterian Church**, 85 S. Oxford St., SE cor. Lafayette Ave. 1862. **Grimshaw & Morrill.** ◎

This Romanesque Revival, cut-ashlar brownstone church, with a sturdy tower (a polygon over a square) bearing four finials, corners South Oxford and Lafayette. It is noted more, however, for its numerous Tiffany windows. The major one in the Underwood Chapel, installed in 1920, was a late work of the Tiffany firm. **Dr. Theodore L. Cuyler** a renowned preacher, was its minister—hence Cuyler Park, the triangle at Fulton Street.

F12

[F13] **The Griffin** (apartments), 101 Lafayette Ave., NW cor. S. Oxford Pl. 1920s.

Glazed polychromatic terra-cotta forms a rich arch for the main entry on South Oxford Street.

[F14] **The Roanoke**/onetime The San Carlos Hotel, 69 S. Oxford St., bet. Lafayette and DeKalb Aves. E side. ca. 1893. **Montrose W. Morris.** ◎

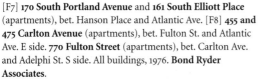

F13

F15

F16

A proud multiple dwelling, once gutted by fire. Its resurrection is the veritable Phoenix: a grand brick and rockface limestone Romanesque Revival dowager.

[F15] **South Oxford Street** and **South Portland Avenue**, bet. Lafayette and DeKalb Aves. ♂

Two handsome, tree-shaded blocks of brownstones. South Oxford's offer a range from the early 1850s to the end of the 19th century. South Portland's are mostly Italianate from the later 1860s. This district sports not only these fashionable London street names but also Adelphi, Carlton, Cumberland, and Waverly.

At the end of these blocks rises Fort Greene Park. a later stop on the tour. Turn right on DeKalb Avenue, and left at the end of the park (with an aside to F16) onto:

[F16] **252 Cumberland Avenue**, bet. Lafayette and Dekalb Aves. W side. 1870s.

Blue clapboards and a white porch give an elegant pause to these eclectic streets.

[F17] **Washington Park** (houses), that portion of Cumberland St. facing Fort Greene Park. DeKalb to Myrtle Aves. ♂

These 2 blocks of brownstones were once the equal in social stature of any in Brooklyn.

[F18] **192 and 198 Washington Park** (houses), bet. DeKalb and Willoughby Aves. E side. ca. 1880. **Marshall J. Morrill**. ♂

Italianate and Queen Anne, the former with a mansard roof that bears projecting bay windows, ending with a columned dormer at the crest.

[F19] **179-186 Washington Park** (house), bet. DeKalb and Willoughby Aves. E side. 1866. **Joseph H. Townsend**, builder. ♂

A mansarded ensemble with paired dormer windows in each slated roof. Note the stained-glass fanlight at No. 182 and the several woodframed cut-glass doors. Publisher **Alfred C. Barnes** lived at 182.

F19

[F20] **173-176 Washington Park** (houses), bet. Willoughby and DeKalb Aves. E side. ca. 1867. **Thomas B. Jackson**, builder. ♂

Lesser lights than [F19] above, they housed among others **William C. Kingsley** at No. 176 and his partner, **Albert Keeney**, next door at No. 175. **Kingsley** and **Keeney** were among Brooklyn's most affluent contractors, builders of streets and sewers, a reservoir further out on Long Island, and much of Prospect Park. In 1867, when **Kingsley** bought his house, he was

known to be the driving political force behind the Brooklyn
Bridge; he later became its largest individual stockholder.

F20

*Enter Fort Greene Park and climb the hill to the base of the giant
Doric column.*

[F21] **Fort Greene Park**/originally Washington Park, DeKalb
Ave. to Myrtle Ave., Washington Park St. to Edwards St. 1867.
Frederick Law Olmsted & Calvert Vaux. Additions, 1908,
McKim, Mead & White. Altered, 1972, **Berman, Roberts &
Scofidio.** ☞

The prospect of the harbor and Manhattan skyline from its
summit suggests that this might better have been the park
named Prospect.

F22

[F22] **Prison Ship Martyrs Monument,** center of Fort
Greene Park. 1906-1909. **Stanford White** of McKim,
Mead & White, architects. **A. A. Weinman,** sculptor. ☞
A tall Doric column, crowned with a bronze brazier, remem-
bers the 11,500 American patriots who died in the 11 British
prison ships anchored in Wallabout Bay (1776-1783). The old
Navy Yard infilled this former East River body of water.
Weinman's brazier, 148 feet above the park summit, once held
an eternal flame. The tower's stair is not open to the public.
Nearby, what was built as the world's most elegant comfort station, a square, distyle in antis Doric temple, is now the park's
visitors' center. Only open occasionally.

[F23] **The Brooklyn Hospital,** DeKalb Ave. to Willoughby St.,
from Fort Greene Park to Ashland Place. 1920. **J. M. Hewlett.**
Altered and expanded, 1967, **Rogers, Butler & Burgun.** 1985.
Rogers, Burgun, Shahine & Deschler. [F24] **Staff Residence**
(apartments), NE cor. of site, Willoughby St., SW cor. St.
Edwards St. 1976. **Walker O. Cain & Assocs.**

The residential tower plays with some cubist carving at its
crest, but the new wing springing out to DeKalb Avenue is sleek
and elegant in brown brick and glass.

[F25] **Walt Whitman Houses** and **Raymond V. Ingersoll
Houses**/originally Fort Greene Houses, N.Y.C. Housing
Authority, Myrtle to Park Aves., Carlton Ave. to Prince St. 1944.
**Rosaria Candela, André Fouilhoux, Wallace K. Harrison,
Albert Mayer, Ethan Allen Dennison, William I. Hohauser, Ely
Jacques Kahn, Charles Butler, Henry Churchill,** and **Clarence
Stein.**

Thirty-five hundred apartments (14,000 persons) on 38
acres, completed during World War II as high-priority housing
for Brooklyn's wartime industrial labor force. Within its bounds
are the Church of St. Michael and St. Edward, Cumberland
Hospital, and P.S. 67. Its architects are a roster of New York's
greatest talents in the 1930s and 1940s. Nevertheless, it is a bland
place—perhaps another case of too many cooks.

F26

[F26] **Church of St. Michael and St. Edward** (Roman Catholic)/
originally Church of St. Edward, within the bounds of Ingersoll
Houses, 108 St. Edward's St., bet. Myrtle and Park Aves. W side.
1902. **John J. Deery.** Altar, 1972, **Carol Dykman O'Connor.**
Cross, 1972, **Robert Zacharian.**

Twin conical-capped towers in the manner of a 16th-century
Loire Valley château. The interior is Pop Art plaster, with huge
sheets of pictorial stained glass (done by a **Norman Rockwell** of
the medium). The altar and cross incorporate parts of the old
Myrtle Avenue el, which once rumbled down the street next door.

*For those who remember the dappled gloom of Myrtle Avenue as
it suffocated under the el, a walk east on the wide, sunlit thoroughfare will be refreshing. Turn right at Clermont Avenue.*

F27

[F27] **181 Clermont Ave**. (apartments)/formerly 3rd Battery, New York National Guard/once Encumbrance Warehouse, N.Y.C. Department of Sanitation, bet. Myrtle and Willoughby Aves. E side. ca. 1890.

This vast carapace is in the process of conversion to, of all things, housing.

Now reenter the Historic District.

F28

 [F 28] **Eglise Baptiste d'Expression Française**/formerly Jewish Center of Fort Greene/originally Simpson Methodist Church, 209 Clermont Ave., SE cor. Willoughby Ave. 1870. ☾

The capsule history of a neighborhood's demographic change is here illustrated: first WASP, then Jewish, now Haitian. The northern Italian raiment of Lombardian Romanesque was adapted to the needs of a 19th-century Brooklyn church. Note the Star of David still ensconced above the portals.

Turn for a detour through the midblock playground to Adelphi Street

F30

[F29] **Institutional Church of God in Christ**, 164-174 Adelphi St., bet. Willoughby and Myrtle Aves. W side. 1890.

Terracotta and brick for the **Reverend C.E. Williams**.

[F30] **Church of St. Michael and St. Mark** (Anglican), 230 Adelphi St., bet Willoughby and DeKalb Aves. W side. 1888. ☾

While the "Institutional Church" above is in a sleek and sophisticated Romanesque Revival, this one is rockfaced and lusty.

[F31] **238 Adelphi Street** (house), bet. Willoughby and Dekalb Aves. W side. 1870s.

A gracious porch can make the difference for a whole block.

Return to Clermont Avenue.

F31

[F32] **292 Clermont Avenue**, bet. Dekalb and Lafayette Sts. W side. ca. 1870s.

A vigorous bay window modulates the street.

F33

[F33] **The Brooklyn Masonic Temple**, 317 Claremont Ave., NE cor. Lafayette Ave. 1906. **Lord & Hewlett** and **Pell & Corbett**. ☾

They took the word "temple" literally in 1909. Some of the vigorous polychromy that archaeologists believe was painted onto 5th century B.C. Greek temples is recalled here in fired terra-cotta.

F34

[F34] **Our Lady Queen of All Saints School, Church and Rectory** (Roman Catholic), 300 Vanderbilt Ave., NW cor. Lafayette Ave. 1910-1913. **Gustave Steinback** of **Reiley and Steinback**. ☾

George Mundelein, later cardinal at Chicago, commissioned this complex while he was pastor of this local parish. A glassy church (stained) and a glassy school (clear) suggest, on the one hand, that stained-glass glory, the Sainte Chapelle in Paris, and, on the other, the sunlit aspects of modern school buildings. Inside, the church's aisles are perhaps the world's narrowest. Outside, 24 saints stand guard over the façade. To enter the church one, in fact, tunnels through the school.

[F35] **The Chancery**/formerly Residence, Roman Catholic Bishop of Brooklyn, 367 Clermont Ave., NE cor. Greene Ave. 1887. **Patrick Charles Keely**. ☞

Dour. Hollywood would cast it as an orphan asylum in a **Charlotte Brontë** novel. The neatly dressed granite blocks and mansard roof may be austere, but they were meant to be subdued, in contrast to the proposed but never built neighboring cathedral [see below].

F35

[F36] **80 Greene Avenue** (apartments), SE cor. Clermont Ave. 1986. **Warren Gran & Assocs.** ☞

A well-scaled modern infill building, with great balconies that happily corner this intersection. The beehive-crowned Church of the Messiah stood here until it burned.

[F37] **378-434 Vanderbilt Avenue** (row houses), bet. Greene and Gates Aves. W side. ca. 1880. ☞

An almost perfectly preserved row of 29 Italianate brownstones steps down a gentle hill. At either end their march is stopped in a dignified way: Nos. 378 and 434 return to the building line, embracing a long narrow space modulated with front stoops and front gardens. Note that the balustrades are cast iron painted to look like brownstone. Industrialization rears its head.

F36

Memories of an unbuilt monument: The entire block bounded by Vanderbilt, Clermont, Lafayette, and Greene Avenues was acquired in 1860 as the site for what was to be one of the world's largest churches, the Cathedral of the Immaculate Conception. Patrick Charles Keely, one of the 19th century's most prolific architects, was chosen to execute the commission. Foundations were laid and walls rose to heights of ten to twelve feet. The Chapel of St. John, the largest of the cathedral's proposed six, was completed in 1878 and the Bishop of Brooklyn's residence, nine years later. Then funds dried up and all work stopped. The incomplete walls remained for decades, a challenging playground for imaginative neighborhood children. After Keely's death in 1896, John Francis Bentley, architect of Westminster Cathedral in London, was asked to draw new plans; but he too died, and his plans remained incomplete. The walls stood until 1931, when they and the chapel were demolished to build Bishop Loughlin Memorial High School, a tribute to the prelate who had the original dream in 1860. The only relic is the bishop's residence, now used by the brothers who teach at the high school.

F37

END of Fort Greene Walking Tour: The nearest subway is the IND, a block south and a block east, at Fulton Street and Clinton Avenue (A and C trains). If you're hungry or want a glimpse of adjacent Clinton Hill, walk north on Clinton Avenue.

CLINTON HILL

Clinton Hill Walking Tour: Starts at Clinton Avenue and Fulton Street, at the Clinton-Washington Station of the IND train (A and C trains), and ends near the same station. In between you will pass what remains of the homes on the Hill that were built by the merchant and industrial kings of Brooklyn: the Bedfords, Pfizers, Underwoods, and—most prominent of all—the Pratts. These monumental buildings present great individuality and vigorous architectural forms, with many monumental porches that make this wide avenue more plastic than typical brownstone blocks.

Walk south along Clinton Avenue. It and Washington Avenue are the wide avenues on which the most fashionable families settled.

[L1] **Church of St. Luke & St. Matthew** (Episcopal)/originally St. Luke's Episcopal Church, 520 Clinton Ave., bet. Fulton St. and Atlantic Ave. W side. 1888-1891. **John Welch.** 🍎

In the 1880s and 1890s the Episcopalians begat what seemed to be Baptist temples: eclecticism gone beserk manifested in battered greenish stone walls, Romanesque arches, and Ruskinian Gothic polychromy in three shades of brownstone. It all adds up to a great façade.

Now turn around and go north on Clinton, past Fulton Street.

L1

[L2] **487 Clinton Avenue** (apartments), bet. Gates Ave. and Fulton St. E side. 1892. **Langston & Dahlander.**

A Loire Valley château, towered, machicolated, and mated with a Richardsonian Romanesque entry.

L2

[L3] **Royal Castle Apartments**, 20-30 Gates Ave., SW cor. Clinton Ave. 1912. **Wortmann & Braun.** 🍎

An exuberant 6-story structure, intended to rise to the high style of older Clinton Avenue residences. The ornament smacks of a familiarity with the Sezession movement, the Austrian variant of Art Nouveau. The skyline gables are Viennese. Croissants?

[L4a] **Clinton Hill Historic District**, generally bet. Willoughby Ave. at the N, Vanderbilt Ave. on the W, then a line N of Fulton St., and an eastern line on Downing St. N to Gates Ave., then Grand Ave. and Cambridge Pl. N to Lafayette Ave., then W to Hall St., then N to the Willoughby Ave. start. 🍎

L4

[L4] Originally **Morgan Bogart House**, 463 Clinton Ave., bet. Gates and Greene Aves. E side. 1902. **Mercein Thomas.** ♂

Unique Renaissance Revival limestone in these parts. Note the Ionic-columned bay window, quoins, and rustications. An exile from Manhattan's Upper East Side.

[L5] **457 Clinton Avenue** (house), bet. Gates and Greene Aves. E side. ca. 1870. ♂

This crisp gray and white building shows off a porch from an earlier era than most of Clinton Avenue, with four fluted Tuscan (Roman Doric) columns and a mansard roof.

L6

[L6] **Galilee Baptist Church**/originally David Burdette House, 447 Clinton Ave., bet. Gates and Greene Aves. E side. ca. 1850. ♂

This Italianate brick villa wears sandstone quoins and two Tuscan columns at its front porch.

[L7] Originally **William H. Burger House**, 443 Clinton Ave., bet. Gates and Greene Aves. E side. 1902. **Hobart A. Walker.** ♂

An eclectic mélange, with fluted and banded Tuscan columns and a picturesque pair of gables against the mansard roof.

CLINTON HILL DISTRICT
see pages 702-710

[L8] Originally built by **Frederick A. Platt, 415 Clinton Ave.**, bet. Gates and Greene Aves. E side. ca. 1865. ♂

This General Grant box is painted brick mansarded with pink slate; the porch is borne by sturdy wood Composite columns.

[L9] Originally **Charles A. Schieren House**, 405 Clinton Ave., bet. Gates and Greene Aves. E side. 1889. **William Tubby**. ♂

A Romanesque Revival/Queen Anne monumental mansion in brick and stone.

L8

[L10] Originally **Cornelius N. Hoagland House**, 410 Clinton Ave. bet. Gates and Greene Aves. W side. 1882, **Parfitt Bros**. ♂

An eclectic Queen Anne brick, terra-cotta, and limestone mansion with picturesque dual chimneys. Note the dentils and swags.

[L11] Originally **C. Walter Nichols** and **Henry L. Batterman Houses**, 406 and 404 Clinton Ave., bet. Gates and Greene Aves. E side. 1901. **Albert Ulrich**. ♂

A Renaissance Revival pair, with a shared Tuscan-columned porch.

L11

[L12] Originally **Liebman House**, 384 Clinton Ave. bet. Greene and Lafayette Aves. W side. 1907. **Herts & Tallant**. ♂

One of the newcomers on these blocks, a product of the Colonial Revival that arrived in a backlash against Romanesque Revival and Queen Anne. A by-product of the Columbian Exposition of 1893, which had touted the Renaissance, but caused a more modest stylistic revival in houses.

[L13] Originally **John W. Shepard House**, 356 Clinton Ave., bet. Greene and Lafayette Aves. W side. 1905. **Theodore C. Visscher**. ♂

A stuccoed eccentricity, articulated with brick and limestone, with a green tile roof to suggest a return to an acceptance of context?

L12

[L14] Originally **Joseph Steele House**, 200 Lafayette St., SE cor. Vanderbilt Ave. ca. 1850. Altered. ● ♂

An extraordinary relic from the days when these precincts were farm country. Greek Revival, with elegant narrow clapboards, a bracketed cornice with eyebrow windows, and a widow's walk with a view of the harbor in those open, early days. It wears its age well, with dignity. The original Federal cottage is the eastern wing, the tail of the later Greek Revival dog.

L14

[L15] Originally **James H. Lounsberry House**, 321 Clinton Ave., bet. Lafayette and DeKalb Aves. E side. ca. 1875. **Ebenezer L. Roberts**. ♂

A super-brownstone, in the same monumental class as Nos. 2 and 3 Pierrepont Place in Brooklyn Heights.

[L16] Originally **John Arbuckle House**, 315 Clinton Ave., bet. Lafayette and DeKalb Aves. E side. 1888. **Montrose W. Morris**. ♂

Robust red brick, brownstone, and terra-cotta. Don't miss the intricately molded terra-cotta soffit below the bay window. Arbuckle was a coffee merchant who made his fortune from Yuban coffee.

L15

[L17] Originally **William Harkness House**, 300 Clinton Ave., bet. Lafayette and DeKalb Aves. W side. 1889. **Mercein Thomas**. ♂

Here are strong bay windows surmounted by a tiny Queen Anne balcony that gives stature to a child in the attic.

Take a short detour to the right along DeKalb Avenue and then resume your northern walk on Clinton.

[L18] **282-290 DeKalb Avenue** (houses), SW cor. Waverly Ave. 1890. **Montrose W. Morris**. ♂

Quintuplets unified by a pediment over the central trio and symmetrical cylindrical turrets at each end. A terrific tour de force, rare for both its design and its state of preservation.

[L19] **285-289 DeKalb Avenue**, NW cor. Waverly Ave. 1889. **Montrose W. Morris**. ♂

This time a trio, with pyramidal and conical roofs connected by an intervening mansard. Brownstone, gray stone, terra-cotta, and brick both flat and curved.

[L20] **Waverly Avenue**, bet. Gates and Myrtle Aves.

This narrow service street is sandwiched between the mansions of Clinton and Washington Avenues. Its many stables and carriage houses, remnants of service facilities for those wealthy

L18

neighbors, have been recycled as apartments, restaurants, and other independent units.

Back to Clinton Avenue.

L21

[L21] Originally **William W. Crane House, 284 Clinton Ave.**, bet DeKalb and Willoughby Sts. W side. ca. 1854. **Field & Correja.** ♂
A Newport Stick and Shingle Style house with wonderful serpentine jigsaw and carved work in its gables. The cut shingles give it a rich texture, and the varied picturesque gables provide a profile against the sky. Snazzy.

[L22] Originally **Behrend H. Huttman House, 278 Clinton Ave.**, bet. DeKalb and Willoughby Sts. ca. 1884. ♂
Bizarre columns mark a sturdy porch, with alternating smooth and rough drum segments. A neo-Baroque oddity.

[L23] **St. Joseph's College**/formerly Charles Pratt House, 232 Clinton Ave., bet. DeKalb and Willoughby Aves. W side. 1874-1875. **Ebenezer L. Roberts.** ♂
The original manor house and gardens of Pratt père: Italianate freestanding brownstone mansion. His sons across the street ventured into more daring architectural experiments.

Charles Pratt, refiner of kerosene at Greenpoint, joined his oil empire with that of John D. Rockefeller's Standard Oil Company in 1874. As legend has it, at the marriage of each of Pratt's first four sons, the couple was presented with a house opposite their father's place for a wedding present. Of these, three remain: those of Charles M., Frederic, and George. Harold, succumbing to the changing fashion stimulated by the consolidation of Brooklyn and New York, built his nuptial palace on Park Avenue at 68th Street. Fifth son, John, also chose to live (more modestly than Harold) in Manhattan.

L24

[L24] **Caroline Ladd Pratt House** (foreign students' residence of Pratt Institute)/originally Frederic B. Pratt House, 229 Clinton Ave., bet. DeKalb and Willoughby Aves. E side. 1895. **Babb, Cook & Willard.** ♂
Attached on one side and freestanding on the other, it forms a neat and handsome urban transition. The pergolaed entry supported by truncated caryatids and atlantides does the trick. The house proper is gray and white Georgian/Renaissance Revival. To the garden's rear, view another sturdy pergola borne by a dozen Tuscan fluted columns and, at the entry, a most venerable wisteria.

L25

[L25] **Residence, Bishop of Brooklyn** (Roman Catholic)/originally Charles Millard Pratt House, 241 Clinton Ave., bet. DeKalb and Willoughby Aves. E side. 1890. **William B. Tubby.** ♂
A great Richardsonian Romanesque building. The detailing in smooth, rounded forms makes this place both powerful and sensuous. Note particularly the spherical bronze lamp at the entrance and the semicircular conservatory high on the south wall.

[L26] **St. Joseph's College**/originally George DuPont Pratt House, 245 Clinton Ave. (N wing only), bet. DeKalb and Willoughby St E side. 1901. **Babb, Cook & Willard.** ♂
Red brick and limestone, quoined and corniced, this is Georgian revival (Victoria division) that reeks of Englishness—it might well be the British embassy. The additions by the college to the south are properly unprepossessing.

L26

Turn right on Willoughby Avenue.

[L27] **Clinton Hill Apartments, Section 1**, Clinton to Waverly Aves., Willoughby to Myrtle Aves. 1943. **Harrison, Fouilhoux & Abramovitz**.

World War II housing for the families of naval personnel (the old Navy Yard, now an industrial park, is a short walk away). Blue and white nautical motifs are included as ornament at the entrances, despite wartime restrictions on just about everything else. (Section 2 was completed by the same architects further south between Lafayette and Greene Avenues.)

[L28] **Pratt Institute Campus**, Willoughby Ave. to DeKalb Ave., Classon Ave. to Hall St. 1887- . Various architects.

Originally 5 blocks and the streets that served them. Urban renewal gave the Institute opportunity to make a single, campus-style superblock. As the separate buildings were built to conform to the former street pattern, and the intervening buildings were removed, the result became surreal: a kind of abstract chessboard, where the pieces sit on a blank board without a grid.

A professional school of art and design, architecture, engineering and computer information, and library sciences. **Charles Pratt** ran it as his personal philanthropic fiefdom until his death in 1891. A similar case study to that of Cooper Union, with its patron, **Peter Cooper**.

L29

[L29] **Memorial Hall, Pratt Institute**, S of Willoughby Ave. on Ryerson Walk. E side. 1926-1927. **John Mead Howells**. 🍎

Howells reversed history. Instead of grafting Byzantine capitals onto Roman columns to produce a Romanesque vocabulary, he grafted this whole building, a neo-Byzantine eclectically detailed hall, onto the adjacent Romanesque Revival Main Building.

L30

[L30] **Main Building, Pratt Institute**, S of Memorial Hall on Ryerson Walk. E side. 1885-1887. **Lamb & Rich**. Porch added, 1894. **William B. Tubby**. 🍎

A gung-ho Romanesque Revival, where sturdy, squat columns bear a porch embellished with an organically ornamented frieze. At each side, wrought-iron cradles bear spherical iron lanterns.

L31

[L31] **South Hall, Pratt Institute**. 1891. Porch, 1894. **William B. Tubby**. 🍎

Some modest Tubby in contrast to the old Charles Millard Pratt House, or his articulated library across the way.

Looking backward: To enter the Pratt Institute engine room, located on the ground floor of the East Building (originally Machine Shop Building, (1887, William Windrim), is to pass through a time warp. Inside spin a gleaming trio of late 19th-century Ames Iron Works steam engines (actually installed in 1900), whose electrical generators still supply one third of the campus buildings with 120 volt D.C. service. These and other antique artifacts form a veritable museum of industrial archaeology. On display is a name plate of the DeLavergne Refrigerating Machine Company, chandeliers from the Singer Tower's boardroom, and a "No Loafing" sign from the Ruppert Brewery complex, among other industrial memorabilia.

To your right across the campus green is the library.

L32

[L32] **Pratt Institute Library**/originally Pratt Free Library, Hall St. bet. Willoughby and DeKalb Aves. E side. 1896. **William B. Tubby**. North porch, 1936, **John Mead Howells**. Altered again, 1982, **Giorgio Cavaglieri & Warren Gran**. 🍎

Tubby's stubby: strongly articulated brick piers give a bold face to Hall Street and adjacent flanks. A free Romanesque

Revival but with a classical plan. Originally Brooklyn's first free public library, it was restricted to Pratt students in 1940. The south terrace is the roof of a mostly underground Cavaglieri and Gran addition.

L33

Walk east along the campus's long axis. At the far end is one of Pratt's newer building.

[L33] **Pratt Activity/Resource Center,** E of Steuben St. 1975. Activity center (upper part), **Daniel F. Tully Assocs.** Resource center (lower part), **Ezra D. Ehrenkrantz & Assocs.**

   Sinuously housed tennis courts in an architectural fashion outdated some time ago. These enormous hyperbolic-paraboloidal tents were, apocryphally, the response to the student unrest of the late 1960s and are now an unfortunate and bulky east-ending of this amorphous campus.

 [L34] **Children's Portico, NW cor. of the Activity/ Resource Center.** 1912.

   Here a much later appendage of the library was dismantled and relocated to the other side of Pratt Campus. It is said to be a copy of part of the King's School, Canterbury Cathedral: a Norman Revival Chevron-ornamented remnant.

L34

[L35] **Pratt Row,** 220-234 Willoughby Ave., S side. 171-185 Steuben St. E. side. 172-186 Emerson Place. W. side. 1907. **Hobart A. Walker.** 🍎

   These were preserved despite the mandates of the same federal urban renewal legislation that produced Willoughby Walk—mandates to declare a certain percentage of existing units substandard. The 27 that remain are faculty housing. Note the bay windows and alternating Dutch and triangular gables.

L35

 [L36] **Stabile Hall, Pratt Institute,** East side of Campus. 2000. **Pasanella + Klein Stolzman + Berg.**

   Three residential blocks are umbilically attached to their common services, providing a step into serious 21st-century architecture for dour Pratt.

L36

[L37] **Thrift Hall, Pratt Institute,** Ryerson Walk, NE cor. DeKalb Ave. 1916. **Shampan & Shampan.**

   The Thrift, as its classical lettering proclaims atop a neo-Georgian limestone and brick body, was built to be a bank but now houses offices behind those Corinthian pilasters. **Charles Pratt, Sr.,** initiated the idea of student savings in 1889, shortly before his death (his original building was demolished to make way for Memorial Hall). The Thrift closed as a bank in the early 1940s.

[L38] **St. James Towers**/originally University Terrace (apartments), DeKalb to Lafayette Aves., St. James Place to Classon Ave. 1963. **Kelly & Gruzen.**

   The balconies are recessed within the body of these high-rise slabs rather than projecting. Their containment on three sides not only solves a design problem but also reduces the possibilities for vertigo.

L38

L39

[L39] Originally **Graham Home for Old Ladies**, 320 Washington Ave., bet. DeKalb and Lafayette Aves. W side. 1851. **J. G. Glover**.

A simple Romanesque Revival brick building of an almost industrial scale, now painted slate gray. The inset and incised stone plaque speaks of earlier days and earlier uses.

The original patron organization was deftly titled The Brooklyn Society for the Relief of Respectable, Aged, Indigent Females, to whom paint manufacturer, **John B. Graham**, donated this building.

L41

[L40] **Underwood Park**, Lafayette Ave. bet. Washington and Waverly Aves. N side.

Mostly the site of the former **John T. Underwood** (of typewriter fame) mansion plus adjacent row houses, demolished at the direction of his widow, who saw Clinton Hill decline precipitously and did not want the grand house she shared with her husband to deteriorate in concert. Fortunately for the rest of the neighborhood, decline was checked and then reversed in the 1960s. Happy for the neighborhood, sad that we lost this one.

[L41] **Apostolic Faith Church**/originally Orthodox Friends Meeting House, 273 Lafayette Ave., NE cor. Washington Ave. 1868. Attributed to **Stephen C. Earle**.

A simple Lombardian Romanesque brick box, polychromed with vigor, in red and white paint, by its current tenants.

L42

[L42] **Emmanuel Baptist Church**, 279 Lafayette Ave., NW cor. St. James Place. 1886-1887. **Francis H. Kimball**. Chapel, 1882-1883. **Ebenezer Roberts**. School, 1925-1927.

Yellow Ohio sandstone was carved here into an approximation of a 13th-century French Gothic façade. The interior, in startling contrast, is a Scottish Presbyterian preaching space, with radial seating fanning from the pulpit and baptismal font.

L43

[L43] **Higgins Hall, Pratt Institute**/originally Adelphi Academy, St. James Place bet. Lafayette Ave. and Clifton Place. N wing, 1869. **Mundell & Teckritz**. S wing, 1887. **Charles C. Haight**. Reconstructed after fire, 1999. **Steven Holl** and **Rogers Marvel Architects**.

The brickmasons have been loose again, with piers, buttresses, round arches, segmental arches, reveals, and corbel tables. The nature of the material is exploited and exaggerated. **Henry Ward Beecher** laid the cornerstone of the north building, and **Charles Pratt** donated $160,000 for the latter. The north building is somewhat bedraggled these days, as schools of architecture (Pratt's is within) seem to be the cobbler's children; the south building is in a sturdy and well-kempt Richardsonian Romanesque.

L44

[L44] **St. James Place**, the southerly extension of Hall St.
[L45] **Clifton Place**, running E from St. James Place.
[L46] **Cambridge Place**, starting S at Greene Ave. bet. St. James Place and Grand Ave.

Three Places that are really places. Each is a showpiece of urban row-house architecture built for the Brooklyn middle class between the 1870s and 1890s. When bored by the monotony of a uniform row, architects turned to picturesque variety, giving identity of detail and silhouette to each owner, as in Nos. 202-210 St. James Place.

Nos. 179-183 St. James Place are a Romanesque Revival trio built in 1892 by **William B. Tubby**. **Nos. 127-135 Cambridge Place**, bet. Gates and Putnam Aves., are a quintet from 1894, also by **Tubby**.

If you wish a peek at Cambridge Place, turn left at Greene Avenue for a short block and then return. If not, turn right on Greene and right again at Washington Avenue, for a half-block excursion.

L47

[L47] **357-359 Washington Avenue**, bet. Greene and Lafayette Aves. E side. ca. 1860. Attributed to **Ebenezer L. Roberts**. ☿

Twin wood-clapboarded painted Victorian neighbors in pristine condition. Savor them.

[L48] Originally **Henry Offerman House, 361 Washington Ave.**, bet. Greene and Lafayette Aves. E side. 1888. ☿

Queen Anne brick body, with brownstone quoins and trim, a high mansard roof, and terra-cotta friezes. It boldly thrusts its bayed form out into the streetscape.

[L49] Originally **Van Glahn House, 367 Washington Ave.**, bet. Greene and Lafayette Aves. 1921-1922. **Dwight James Baum**. ☿

A latecomer.

[L50] **The Mohawk** (apartments)/formerly The Mohawk Hotel/originally The Mohawk (apartments), 379 Washington Ave., bet. Greene and Lafayette Sts. E side. 1904. **Neville & Bagge**. ☿

A Beaux Arts latecomer to the Hill, festooned with lime-stone quoins and monumental carved pediments. By the turn of the century, the idea of apartment living—they were termed French flats—had begun to catch on. Recently restored, it is again a distinguished residence for the middle class, after many years of seedy life as a hotel.

L48

[L51] **Clinton Hill Branch, Brooklyn Public Library**, 380 Washington Ave., bet. Lafayette and Greene Aves. W side. 1974. **Bonsignore, Brignati, Goldstein & Mazzotta**. ☿

Here a library program is in obvious conflict with the scale and character of the neighborhood. A much better solution would have been to purchase one of the grand mansions available inexpensively in the 1970s. A stunted shopping center among serious neighbors.

L52

[L52] Originally **William H. Mairr** and **Raymond Hoagland Houses**, 396 and 398 Washington Ave., bet. Greene and Lafayette Aves. W side. 1887. **Adam E. Fischer**. ☿

Bearded giants in the gables. Vermilion terra-cotta Queen Anne. And now restored as condominiums. It's about time.

[L53] **400-404 Washington Avenue** (row houses), NW cor. Greene Ave. 1885. **Mercein Thomas**. ☿

A trio of Romanesque Revival beauties, with a variegated silhouette, a corner oriel window, and entrance archways with strong character.

L53

[L54] **163-175 Greene**, NE cor. Washington Ave. 1990s. ☿

New infill housing.

[L55] **417 Washington Avenue** (house), bet. Greene and Gates Aves. E side. ca. 1860. ☿

Once upon a time there were expert carpenters (and shinglers and lathers and millworkers), and this gem is the result of such talent. Either the owner is down on his luck since last we looked in 1988, or it has been sold to the Ostrogoths. It's a mess.

L54

L55

[L56] **Brown Memorial Baptist Church**/originally Washington Avenue Baptist Church, 484 Washington Ave., SW cor. Gates Ave. 1860. **Ebenezer L. Roberts.** 🍎

A pinch of Lombardian Romanesque decorates a highly articulated square-turreted English Gothic body. The brownstone water tables (white-painted) against red brick are perhaps too harsh.

[L57] Originally **College of the Immaculate Conception**, Washington Ave. NE cor. Atlantic Ave. 1916. **Gustave Steinback**.

A neo-Gothic school building of great charm and elegance in brick and limestone.

L56

END of Clinton Hill Walking Tour: The IND stops on Fulton Street at the Clinton-Washington Station (A and C trains). Make connections with the IRT (2, 3, 4, and 5 trains) or BMT (J, M, and Z trains) at Manhattan's Broadway-Nassau/Fulton Street Station.

THE NAVY YARD

[N1] **Brooklyn Navy Yard Development Corporation/** formerly Brooklyn Navy Yard/officially The New York Naval Shipyard, Flushing Ave. to the East River, Hudson and Navy Sts. to Kent Ave.

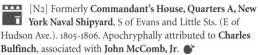

N1

Brooklyn's oldest industry, a shipyard founded here in the body of Wallabout Bay, was purchased by the Navy in 1801 and was abandoned in 1966. During World War II, 71,000 naval and civilian personnel toiled in this city within the city. Now its abandoned buildings have been put to work in a variety of free-enterprise ways.

[N2] Formerly **Commandant's House, Quarters A, New York Naval Shipyard**, S of Evans and Little Sts. (E of Hudson Ave.). 1805-1806. Apocryphally attributed to **Charles Bulfinch**, associated with **John McComb, Jr**. 🍎

Only a glimpse of the rear is possible, for the old Navy gates intervene. For most people—at least below the rank of admiral—a photograph had to suffice.

N2

[N3] **Dry Dock No. 1** of the former New York Naval Shipyard, Dock St. at the foot of 3rd St. 1840-1851. **William J. McAlpine**, engineer. **Thornton MacNess Niven**, architect and master of masonry. 🍎

Considered one of the great feats of 19th-century American engineering, this granite-walled dry dock has serviced such ships as the *Niagara*, the vessel that laid the first transatlantic cable, and the *Monitor*, the Civil War's cheesebox on a raft. The *Niagara* was conceived and financed by a consortium headed by the painter-inventor **Samuel F. B. Morse** and the entrepreneur-philanthropist **Peter Cooper**.

[N4] Originally U.S. Marine Hospital/later **U.S. Naval Hospital**, Flushing Ave., bet. Ryerson St. and Williamsburg Place. N side. 1830-1838. Wings, 1840. Alterations, 1862. **Martin E. Thompson**. 🍎

This austere Greek Revival hospice was built of Sing Sing marble quarried by those hapless prisoners. Later "classical modernists" used similar spartan lines for simplistic public buildings of the 1930s and 1940s, culminating in the pompous buildings of **Albert Speer**'s visions for **Hitler**'s Berlin or **Mussolini**'s "Third Rome." Thompson was a talented Greek Revivalist who muted his palette for such a functional program as this.

[N5] **Surgeon's House, Quarters R1, 3rd Naval District, on grounds of U.S. Naval Hospital**, opp. Ryerson St. 1863. **True W. Rollins** and **Charles Hastings**, builders. 🍎

N7

A spacious 2-story brick house crowned with a French Empire concave-profiled mansard roof. Such was the privileged residence of the Naval Hospital's chief surgeon.

[N6] **Public School 46, Brooklyn, The Edward Blum School**, 100 Clermont Ave., bet. Park and Myrtle Aves. 1958. **Katz, Waisman, Blumenkranz, Stein, Weber**.

An austere, white glazed-brick body, with a blue-banded base. The canopies, with their turned-up noses, are stylish and thus now out of style. **Edward Blum** was the son-in-law of **Abraham Abraham**, inheriting in turn the presidency of Abraham & Straus, Brooklyn's key department store.

[N7] Formerly U. S. Naval Receiving Station/later **N.Y.C. Department of Correction facility**, 136 Flushing Ave., bet. Clermont and Vanderbilt Aves. to Park Ave. 1941.

A transient facility for naval personnel arriving, leaving, and/or tarrying at the old Naval Yard. It has that Art Moderne stylishness that went with the end of the depression and the beginning of World War II. The sailors were replaced by the prison overflow of New York's drug dealers and other felons.

PARK SLOPE

A somber-hued wonderland of finials, pinnacles, pediments, towers, turrets, bay windows, stoops, and porticoes: a smorgasbord of late Victoriana and the successor to the Heights and the Hill as the bedroom of the middle class and wealthy. These three districts are together the prominent topographical precincts of old brownstone Brooklyn: the Heights sits atop a bluff over the harbor, the Hill is a major crest to the northeast, and the Slope slopes from Prospect Park down to the Gowanus Canal and the flatlands beyond.

Despite its proximity to the park, the area was slow to develop. As late as 1884 it was still characterized as "fields and pasture." **Edwin C. Litchfield**'s Italianate villa, completed in 1857, alone commanded the prospect of the harbor from its hill in present-day Prospect Park. By 1871 the first stage of the park had been constructed, yet the Slope lay quiet and tranquil, bypassed by thousands of persons making their way on the Flatbush Avenue horsecars to this newly created recreation area. By the mid 1880s, however, the potential of the Slope became apparent, and mansions began to appear on the newly laid out street grid.

The lavish homes clustered around Plaza Street and Prospect Park West eventually were christened the Gold Coast. Massive apartment buildings invaded the area after World War I, feeding upon the large, unutilized plots of land occupied by the first growth. These austere Park Avenue-like structures, concentrated at Grand Army Plaza, are in contrast to the richly imaginative brick dwellings of Carroll Street and Montgomery Place, the mansions, churches, and clubs that still remain, and the remarkably varied row houses occupying the side streets as they descend toward the Manhattan skyline to the west.

[P1] **Park Slope Historic District**, generally along the S flank of Flatbush Ave. and Plaza St., and the W flank of Prospect Park W.; W to Sixth Ave. N of Union St.; W to Seventh Ave. N of 4th St.; and W to Eighth Ave. N of 15th St.

The first draft of the Historic District originally included only the park blocks. The Slope, emerging as the latest brownstone rediscovery of the upper middle class, was soon recognized as a precinct containing a rich fabric of row housing both within and beyond those initial arbitrary boundaries. The district finally designated reaches northwesterly from the park blocks to encompass part of the richness of Sixth Avenue between Berkeley and Sterling Places. And even with the expansion, good and great architecture thrives on the Slope outside the district lines.

Park Slope Walking Tour A: *From the newsstand where Flatbush Avenue joins Grand Army Plaza (at the surface of the IRT Grand Army Plaza Station (2 and 3 trains)) south into Park Slope and return.*

Cross Plaza Street and admire:

[P2] **The Montauk Club**, 25 Eighth Avenue. NE cor. Lincoln Place. 1889-1891. **Francis H. Kimball.**

A Venetian Gothic palazzo, whose canal is the narrow lawn separating it from its cast-iron fence. Remember the Ca' d'Oro. But here in brownstone, brick, terra-cotta, and verdigris copper. It bears the name of a local tribe, which explains the 8th Avenue friezes at the 3rd and 4th stories, honoring these former local natives.

P2

Continue on Plaza Street and turn right into Berkeley Place.

[P3] Originally **George P. Tangeman House**, 276 Berkeley Place bet. Plaza St. and Eighth Ave. S side. 1891. **Lamb & Rich.**

P3

Brick, granite, and terra-cotta Romanesque Revival, paid for by Cleveland Baking Powder. Cupid caryatids hold up the shingled pediment, with bulky Ionic columns supporting a frieze of scallop shells.

[P4] **64-66 Eighth Avenue** (row houses), bet. Berkeley Place and Union St. W side. 1889. **Parfitt Brothers**. ☾

Two bold sandstone and granite residences by popular architects of that period. They bear carved foliate bas-reliefs worthy of **Louis Sullivan**.

Take a peek to the right down Union Street.

P4

 [P5] **889-905 Union Street**, bet. Seventh and Eighth Aves. N side. 1889. **Albert E. White**. ☾

More Queen Anne, a picturesque octet with eclectic medieval and classical parts. Note the brownstone friezes and bay windows.

[P6] **905-913 Union Street**, bet 7th and 8th Aves. N side. 1895. **Thomas McMahon**. ☾

A Queen Anne quintet in brick, brownstone, and shingles.

P6

[P7] **70 Eighth Avenue** (house), NW cor. Union St. 1890s. A brick pepper pot anchors this corner, scrubbed and slicked back to its Gay Nineties condition.

[P8] **869 President Street** (apartments)/originally **Stuart Woodford** House, bet. Seventh and Eighth Aves. N side. 1885. **Henry Ogden Avery**. ☾

Two bracketed oriel windows punctuate the painted brick façade, articulated by Viollet-le-Duc-inspired struts. **Woodford** was onetime ambassador to Spain.

P8

[P9] **876-878 President Street** (row houses), bet. Seventh and Eighth Aves. S side. 1889. Albert E. White. ☾

Roman brick and brownstone in a bay-windowed Queen Anne. Note the remarkably lusty rock-face brownstone stoops.

[P10] **944-946 President Street** (row houses), bet. Prospect Park W. and Eighth Ave. S side. 1886-1890. Attributed to **Charles T. Mott**. ☾

An extravagant duet in brick and brownstone, with rich wrought iron, stained glass and terra-cotta. There is a picturesque profile against the sky.

P12

[P11] **925 President Street** (row house), bet. Prospect Park W. and Eighth Ave. N side. 1870s. ☾

A magnificent and magnificently preserved row of crisp brownstones, their bayed fronts modulating this wonderful block.

[P12] **Montessori School**, 105 Eighth Avenue, bet. President and Carroll Sts. E side. 1916. **Helmle & Huberty**. ☾

A limestone Regency Revival mansion with a bowed, Corinthian-columned entry.

[P13] **18 and 19 Prospect Park West** (houses), SW cor. Carroll St. 1898. **Montrose W. Morris**. ☾

An eclectic set in limestone Renaissance Revival. Note the 2nd- and 3rd-floor Ionic pilasters and the hemispherical glass and bronze entrance canopy at No. 18.

P13

715

PARK SLOPE DISTRICT

see pages 713-722

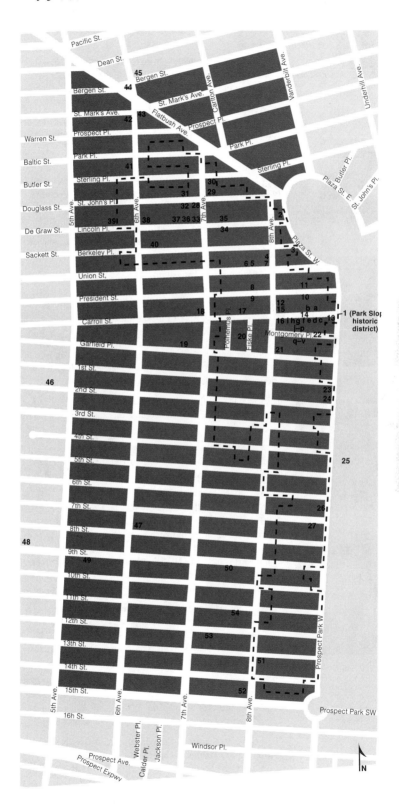

P14b

P14g

P14i

P15

P16

[P14] **Carroll Street**, bet. Prospect Park W. and Eighth Ave. 1887-1911. Various architects. ☞

The north side of this street is as calm, orderly, and disciplined as the south side is picturesque. This block of Carroll Street is visual evidence of significant changing styles:

North Side

a. **No. 863**. 1890. **Napoleon LeBrun & Sons**. ☞

Roman Brick Renaissance now buried behind the architecture of vines.

b. **Nos. 855-861. Stanley M. Holden**. ☞

A quartet of yellow Roman brick and brownstone Romanesque-Revival: stained glass, carved faces, and other decorations.

South Side

c. **Nos. 878-876**. 1911. **Chappell & Bosworth**. ☞

Park Avenue Georgian in ruddy brick and limestone-framed bay and double-hung windows.

d. **Nos. 870-872**. 1887. **William B. Tubby**. ☞

Queen Anne/Shingle Style. The recessed bay window and rockface entry voussoirs are gratifying eccentricities.

e. **No. 862**. 1889. **F. B. Langston**. ☞

Dour polychromed brick and sandstone.

f. **No. 860**. ☞

Romantic in the spirit of Philadelphia's Wilson Eyre.

g. **Nos. 858-856**. 1889. ☞

Brownstone underpinning orange Roman brick: flat, *very* flat, the arches seemingly incised from a plane. Up close the brick texture reveals them as impeccably crafted façades.

h. **No. 848**. 1905. **William B. Greenman**. ☞

A narrow bay-windowed neo-classical exile from the Upper East Side.

i. **No. 838**. 1887. **C. P. H. Gilbert**. ☞

No. 838 and its two 40-foot-wide neighbors to the east are three brownstone and brick beauties. The clustered colonnettes at No. 838 support an arch of only three voussoirs.

[P15] Originally **Thomas Adams, Jr., House**, 119 Eighth Ave., NE cor. Carroll St. 1888. **C. P. H. Gilbert**. ☞

This, and the adjacent matching house at 115 Eighth Avenue, are rock-face red sandstone and Roman brick. The Carroll Street arch is worthy of **Henry H. Richardson**, incised with naturalistic bas-reliefs, and supported by clusters of Romanesque-capped columns. These are major Romanesque Revival buildings.

[P16] **123 Eighth Avenue** (house), SE cor. Carroll St. 1894. **Montrose W. Morris**. ☞

Gray brick and terra-cotta in a free version of the Italian Renaissance, complete with pilasters, columns, and an entrance tympanum; here are ornate foliage and a gloating satyr.

[P17] **747-789 Carroll Street**, bet. Seventh and Eighth Aves. N side. 1880s. ☞

Twenty-one brownstones step up this gentle hill, from just east of Seventh Avenue to a point opposite Polhemus Place.

[P18] **Old First Reformed Church**, 126 Seventh Ave., NW cor. Carroll St. 1893. **George L. Morse**.

A bulky, somber granite and limestone neo-Gothic monolith, stolid, as if carved from a quarry.

[P19] **195 Garfield Place** (apartments), bet. Sixth and Seventh Aves. N side. Remodeled, 1986, **Saltini/Ferrara**.

A quintet of renewed Eastlake brick tenements: moated, the renovation is a respectful understatement.

[P20] **12-16 Fiske Place** (row houses), bet. Carroll St. and Garfield Place. W side. 1896. ○

A trio where bay windows are presented as an academic design exercise—a square, a semicircle, and a triangle—creating a picturesque ensemble. Back to back through the block, the same grouping occurs similarly at 11-17 Polhemus Place. The voussoirs might be studied for their lively bas reliefs, particularly at No. 14.

P20

*Turn left onto Garfield Place, and left again onto Eighth Avenue. Note, as you pass, that **James A. Farrell**, elected president of the United States Steel Corporation in 1911, lived at 249 Garfield Place during his presidential tenure.*

What shall we call it? *Naming apartment buildings to give them panache may have begun with Manhattan's Dakota. At the northwest corner of Garfield Place and 8th Avenue are four more modest works: the Serine, the Lillian, and the Belvedere. But the Gallic influence determined number four: the Ontrinue (or was that Entre Nous?).*

[P21] **Congregation Beth Elohim** (synagogue), NE cor. Eighth Ave. and Garfield Place. 1908-1910. **Simon Eisendrath & B. Horowitz**. Temple House, 1928. **Mortimer Freehof** and **David Levy**. ○

A domed Beaux Arts limestone extravaganza, its corner chamfered to receive the two resident Composite columns.

[P22] **Montgomery Place**, bet. 8th Avenue and Prospect Park W. 1888-1904. ○

One of the truly great blocks in the world of urbane row housing, built as a real estate development by **Harvey Murdock**. Seeking the picturesque, he commissioned noted architect **C. P. H. Gilbert** to create most of the scene. An Art Moderne amber brick apartment house closes the vista at 8th Avenue—an accidental and successful containment of the street's space. **Gilbert**'s works are in a powerful Romanesque Revival, with rock-face brownstone, brick, and terra-cotta strongly arched and linteled. **Dixon** contributed a fussy neoclassicism. The ensemble, however, is a symphony of materials and textures.

P21

j. **No. 11**. 1898. **C. P. H. Gilbert**. ○
Brownstone and brick Romanesque Revival with a Dutch accent (that northern European intrusion). **No. 17** is also an 1898 **Gilbert**.

P22k

k. **No. 19**. 1898. **C. P. H. Gilbert**. ○
Brick, rockface and rusticated brownstone with both semicircular and elliptical arches.

l. **No. 21**. 1892. **C. P. H. Gilbert**. ○
Brownstone and tile roofed eclecticism. Dig those vegetative friezes. **No. 25** is also an 1892 **Gilbert**.

m. **No. 35**. 1889. **Hornium Brothers**. ○

P22p

n. **Nos. 37-43**. 1891. **George B. Chappell**. ○

o. **No. 45**. 1899. **Babb, Cook & Willard**. ○

p. **No. 47**. 1890. **R. L. Daus**. ○
French Renaissance reincarnated in brownstone that would have been a shocking color in Paris.

q. **No. 16**. 1888. **C. P. H. Gilbert**. ○
Look up to a great elliptically arched balcony in two shades of brickwork. Nos. 14 and 18 are part of this trio.

r. **Nos. 30-34**. 1896. **Robert Dixon**. ○

P22q

P22v

P23

P24

P25

P26

s. **Nos. 36-46.** 1889. **C. P. H. Gilbert.** ♂
Roman brick, rock-face brownstone, and terra-cotta modillions (under the roof eaves) all embrace a shingled center.

t. **Nos. 48 & 50.** 1890. **C. P. H. Gilbert.** ♂
Fraternal twins? Same womb, different looks.

u. **No. 52.** 1890. **T. Williams.** ♂
The rockface brownstone bay window is at the scale of a tower.

v. **Nos. 54-60,** 1890. **C. P. H. Gilbert.** ♂
The delicate terra-cotta ornament is in sharp contrast to the boldly scaled detail on much of the block.

Turn right on Prospect Park West, and proceed south.

[P23] **Poly Prep Lower School**/formerly Woodward Park School/onetime Brooklyn Ethical Culture School/originally Henry Hulbert House, 49 Prospect Park W., bet. 1st and 2nd Sts. W side. 1892. **Montrose W. Morris.** ♂
A cadaverous rock-face and foliate-carved limestone Romanesque Revival. The polygonal and round corner towers compete for attention.

[P24] **Brooklyn Ethical Culture Society Meeting House**/originally William H. Childs House, 53 Prospect Park W., NW cor. 2nd St. 1901. **William B. Tubby.** ♂
A Jacobean loner in these stolid stone precincts, erected by the inventor of Bon Ami. Here cleansing powder built this monument, as opposed to baking powder at [P3].

[P25] **Brooklyn Headquarters, N.Y.C. Department of Parks and Recreation**/originally Edwin Clarke and Grace Hill Litchfield House, Grace Hill, also known as Litchfield Villa, Prospect Park W. bet. 4th and 5th Sts. E side. 1854-1857. **Alexander Jackson Davis.** ♂ Annex, 1913 **Helmle & Huberty.** Stucco restoration, 1990s. **Hirsch/Danois.** ♂
This is the villa of **Edwin C. Litchfield,** a lawyer whose fortune was made in midwestern railroad development. In the 1850s he acquired a square mile of virtually vacant land extending from 1st through 9th Streets, and from the Gowanus Canal to the projected line of 10th Avenue, just east of his completed mansion, a territory that includes a major portion of today's Park Slope.

The mansion is the best surviving example of **Davis**'s Italianate style (he also created Greek Revival temples and Gothick castles). More than 90 years of service as a public office have eroded much of its original richness: the original exterior stucco, simulating cut stone, had been stripped off, exposing common brick behind: now being restored. Note the corncob capitals on the glorious porch colonnades, an Americanization of things Roman—Corinthian or Corn-inthian? The bay window facing west contains a lush frieze of swags and goddesses.
Go in, look around, ye fellow citizen and part owner.

[P26] **108-117 Prospect Park West** (apartments), bet. 6th and 7th Sts. W side. 1896. ♂
A Roman brick terrace, pristine and proud Renaissance Revival: greater than the sum of its parts.

[P27] **580-592 Seventh Street**, bet. Prospect Park W. and Eighth Ave. S side. ♂
Dutch neo-Renaissance gables give special syncopation to this handsome block.

END of Park Slope Walking Tour A. *Walk north on Prospect Park West to the Grand Army Plaza subway station.*

Park Slope Walking Tour B: From the newsstand where Flatbush Avenue joins Grand Army Plaza (at the surface of the IRT Grand Army Plaza Station 2 and 3 trains)) to the Bergen Street Station of the same lines (2 and 3 trains). Proceed south on St. John's Place. The silhouetted spires that you see on this lovely street are those of:

P28

[P28] **Memorial Presbyterian Church**, 42-48 7th Ave., SW cor. St. John's Place. 1882-1883. **Pugin & Walter**. ○⃗
   An ashlar brownstone sculpted monolith. Tiffany glass windows embellish both church and chapel.

[P29] **Grace United Methodist Church and Parsonage**, 29-35 7th Ave., NE cor. St. John's Place. 1882-1883. Parsonage, 1887. **Parfitt Brothers**. ○⃗
   Particularly intriguing is the Moorish-Romanesque façade along St. John's Place. The parsonage is a deft transition between the church and the Ward House *cum* town houses to the north.

[P30] Formerly **Lillian Ward House**, 21 7th Ave., SE cor. Sterling Place. 1887. **Lawrence B. Valk**. ○⃗

P30

   A fanciful corner oriel worthy of the 16th-century French Renaissance guards this corner, all crowned with a slated and finialed roof. This special place (mansion to the locals) and its neighbors at Nos. 23-27 were built by **Valk** for investor **Charles Pied**, a rare and rich group to be so well preserved.

Plane crash: In the morning mist of December 16, 1960, two airliners collided over Staten Island. The pilot of one attempted an emergency landing in Prospect Park but made it only to the intersection of 7th Avenue and Sterling Place. The plane sliced the cornice off a small apartment building west of 7th Avenue (the light-colored brick marks the spot) and came to a rest with its nose on the doorstep of the old Ward Mansion. A church on Sterling Place was destroyed by the resulting fire, but miraculously the mansion was untouched.

Retrace your steps on 7th Avenue south to St. John's Place. On your right, between Sixth and Seventh Avenues are St. John's Episcopal Church at No. 139, and two robust Victorian town houses across the way at Nos. 176 and 178.

[P31] **St. John's Episcopal Church**, 139 St. John's Place, bet. Sixth and Seventh Aves. N side. Chapel, 1889. **Edward Tuckerman Potter**. Church, 1885. **John Rochester Thomas**. ○⃗
   Victorian Gothic in varied hues and tones of brownstone, another English country gardened church for Brooklyn. Cut rockface, random ashlar with, at the arched openings, alternating cream and brownstone Ruskinian voussoirs.

[P32] Originally **William M. Thallon** and **Edward Bunker Houses**, 176 and 178 St. John's Place, bet. Sixth and Seventh Aves. S side. 1888. **R. L. Daus**. ○⃗

P32

   Brownstone and brick eclectic mélange, with some flavor from the Loire Valley, some from the Black Forest. Note the caduceus in No. 178's gable: not surprisingly, both **Thallon** and **Bunker** were physicians.

[P33] **Brooklyn Conservatory of Music**/formerly Park Slope Masonic Club/originally M. Brasher House, 58 Seventh Avenue, NW cor. Lincoln Place. 1881. **S. F. Evelette**. ○⃗
   An austere brick and brownstone remnant.

[P34] **214 Lincoln Place** (house), bet. Seventh and Eighth Aves. S side. 1883. **Charles Werner**. ○⃗
   Brick and brownstone Queen Anne for **Charles Fletcher**, a gas company president.

P34

[P35] **Berkeley Carroll School**, 181 Lincoln Pl., bet. Seventh and Eighth Aves. 1992. **Fox & Fowle**. ♂
Conservative brick and limestone, gabled and bay-windowed, embraces a courtyard (with the original school building next door).

[P36] **Lincoln Plaza Hotel**/formerly F. L. Babbott House, 153 Lincoln Place, bet. Sixth and Seventh Aves. N side. 1887. **Lamb & Rich**. Enlarged, 1896. ♂
A squat tower corners this Romanesque Revival mansion.

P35

[P37] Originally **John Condon House**, 139 Lincoln Place, bet. Sixth and Seventh Aves. N side. 1881. ♂
Another Romanesque Revival, with a lion's head corbel. Condon was a cemetery florist with his greenhouse opposite the 5th Avenue gate of Green-Wood Cemetery.

[P38] **Sixth Avenue Baptist Church**, Sixth Ave. NE cor. Lincoln Place. 1880. **Lawrence B. Valk**. ♂
A small-scale brick and limestone church, de-steepled in the 1938 hurricane.

P36

[P39] **Helen Owen Carey Child Development Center**, 71 Lincoln Place, bet. Fifth and Sixth Aves. N side. 1974. **Beyer Blinder Belle**.
A strongly modeled brown brick facility, happily in scale with the neighboring townscape.

[P40] **99-109 Berkeley Place**, bet. Sixth and Seventh Avenues. N side. ♂
Three pairs of brick and rock-face brown- and limestone tenements with terra-cotta friezes and great entry arches. Here tenement is not a pejorative word.

P38

[P41] **St. Augustine's Roman Catholic Church**, 116 Sixth Ave., bet. Sterling and Park Places. W side. 1897. **Parfitt Brothers**.
Sixth Avenue is one of Park Slope's grandest streets, block after block containing rows of amazingly preserved brownstones. St. Augustine's fills a role as a rich and monumental counterpoint to such streetscape neighbors. The crusty tower, with its mottled rock-face brownstone, anchors a nave with finials and flèche, presenting an elegant angel Gabriel. Queen Victoria's best awaits you within.

P42

[P42] **182 Sixth Avenue**, SW cor. St. Mark's Place.
A magnificent commercial addition to a vernacular brown-

stone. A rare 19th-century commercial "improvement" that, in fact, enriches the street.

[P43] **Cathedral Club of Brooklyn**/originally The Carleton Club, 85 Sixth Ave., SE cor. St. Mark's Ave.

Built as an exclusive clubhouse, it was progressively the Monroe Club, the Royal Arcanum Club, and in 1907, through the efforts of a young priest, the Cathedral Club, a Roman Catholic fraternal organization. The priest went on to become **Cardinal Mundelein** of Chicago. The St. Mark's façade is continued in spirit by the adjacent Montauk (Nos. 80-82) and Lenox (Nos. 76-78) apartment buildings, bay-windowed in brick and brownstone, a handsome tiled pyramid centered atop.

P44

[P44] **Tiger Sign Company**, 245 Flatbush Ave., bet. Sixth Ave. and Bergen St.

A crisp triangular freestanding building that once housed a sign shop with apartments above: beige brick with a brownstone frieze. Here is the ultimate in streetfront architecture.

[P45] **78th Precinct, N.Y.C. Police Department**, NE cor. Bergen St. and Sixth Ave. 1925.

Another Anglo-Italianate neo-Renaissance limestone police palazzo. The cornice is super—consoled and dentiled.

END of Park Slope Walking Tour B: The Bergen Street Station of the IRT is close-by.

Miscellany: Further afield are the following entries mostly outside the Historic District, except where noted 🐾 *or* ♂ *.*

[P46] **Second Street Child Care Center**, 333 Second St., bet. Fourth and Fifth Aves. 1999. **Buttrick White & Burtis**.

Brick and limestone. Child-sized, and playgrounded. An infill building, it drops the scale to two stories. Is that because modern city children have rarely used stairs?

[P47] **Public School 39, Brooklyn, The Henry Bristow School**, 417 Sixth Ave., NE cor. 8th St. 1876-1877. **Samuel B. Leonard**, Superintendent of Buildings for the City of Brooklyn Board of Education. 🐾

A mansarded Victorian school house in painted brick and rusticated brownstone. The Second Empire (of Napoleon III) influenced the far reaches of Brooklyn only 5 years after his downfall.

P47

[P48] Originally **William B. Cronyn** House/later **Charles M. Higgins Ink Factory**, 271 Ninth St., bet. Fourth and Fifth Aves. N side to 8th St. ca. 1855. Altered, 1895, **Patrick Charles Keely**. 🐾

An extraordinary remnant of pre-brownstone Brooklyn: a freestanding French Second Empire stucco house crowned with a cupola, slate mansard roof, and cast-iron crests against the sky. India ink, that intense black fluid so misnamed (it should be Chinese ink), was made here for draftsmen, designers, artists, and calligraphers.

P48

[P49] **344 Ninth Street** (house), bet. Fifth and Sixth Aves., S side. 1890s.

A towered sandstone bay provides grandeur for this ebullient brick town house. Terra-cotta and sheet metal create the supporting details.

[P50] **466-480, 488-492, and 500-502 9th Street** (houses), bet. Seventh and Eighth Aves. 1890s.

Arches, gables, and oriels enliven these clusters of brick and limestone town houses: "town houses" because they each speak with personality, as opposed to the regimentation of "row housing."

P52

P54a

[P51] **Public School 107, Brooklyn, The John W. Kimball School**, 1301 Eighth Ave., SE cor. 13th St. 1894. **J. M. Naughton.**

A simple Romanesque Revival schoolhouse of orange-brown brick, terra-cotta, and brownstone: a stern and stately building then serving a newly mushrooming Brooklyn population (consolidation with New York was still 4 years off).

[P52] **14th Regiment Armory, N.Y. National Guard**, 1402 Eighth Ave., bet. 14th and 15th Sts. W side. 1895. **William A. Mundell.**

Picturesque massing, including battered walls, machicolations, and other heroic brick detailing, makes this a special event among the rows of brownstones. Here stands a tower where boiling oil might be poured on mythical attackers. The statue of the doughboy remembers World War I (1923, **Anton Scaaf**).

[P53] **Ansonia Court**/originally Ansonia Clock Company Factory, 420 12th St., bet. Seventh and Eighth Aves. 1881. Remodeled, 1982, **Hurley & Farinella**, architects. **Zion & Breen**, landscape architects.

Here 1,500 workers toiled in the world's largest clock factory. The brick functionalist tradition in 19th-century industrial building forms a handsome low-key envelope for apartments surrounding a central landscaped garden court.

[P54a] **Ladder Company 122, N.Y.C. Fire Department**, 532 11th St., bet. Seventh and Eighth Aves. S side. 1883. [P54b] **Engine Company 220, N.Y.C. Fire Department**, 530 11th St. 1907.

The older Italianate firehouse once was adequate for the neighborhood's needs. As the row houses filled every vacant parcel up to Prospect Park's edge, the Classical adjunct to the west was added.

PROSPECT PARK/GRAND ARMY PLAZA

[A1] **Grand Army Plaza**, within Plaza St. at the intersection of Flatbush Ave., Prospect Park W., Eastern Pkwy., and Vanderbilt Ave. 1870. **Frederick Law Olmsted** & **Calvert Vaux**. Scenic landmark. 🍎

Olmsted & Vaux designed this monumental oval traffic circle in the spirit of Paris' Etoile (now the Place Charles de Gaulle), that circular 12-spoked traffic *rond point* that bears in its central island the Arc de Triomphe, although they opposed an arch here. A masterstroke of city planning, this nexus joins their great Eastern Parkway, and their Prospect Park, with the avenues that preceded it on other geometries. This triumphal arch did not arrive for 22 years: the Soldiers' and Sailors' Memorial Arch [A2] 🍎 by **John H. Duncan**, architect of **Grant's Tomb**, was built between 1889 and 1892, commemorating Union forces that perished in the Civil War. The arch provided, as in its Parisian inspiration, an excellent armature for sculpture, planned by **Stanford White** (**McKim, Mead & White**. 1894-1901), the most spectacular of which is **Frederick MacMonnies**' huge quadriga on top (1898). Inside the arch itself is more subtle work, bas-reliefs of **Lincoln** (**Thomas Eakins**) and **Grant** (**William O'Donovan**), both installed in 1895. On the south pedestals are two bristling groups representing The Army and The Navy by **MacMonnies** (1901). A museum within the arch is open to the public.

A2

The oval island to the north of the arch is of a more homely scale, with a double ring of formally trimmed London plane trees surrounding a generous complex of stairs and terraces, and a fountain. Around the **John F. Kennedy Memorial** [A3] at the north end (1965, **Morris Ketchum**, architect, **Neil Estern**, sculptor), the scale shrinks noticeably. This little memorial, the city's only official monument to Kennedy, was originally designed as a monolithic marble cube topped by a flame on top, but it was later abandoned as an unsuitable aping of the perpetual flame at **Arlington Cemetery's Tomb of the Unknown Soldier**. This present form is a compromise, with Kennedy's bust bracketed from the side. Budget makers demeaned it all by causing the cube to be merely a box built of thin butted marble slabs. The **Bailey Fountain** (1932, **Egerton Swartwout**, architect; **Eugene Savage**, sculptor) [A4], a lush interweaving of athletic Tritons and Neptunes in verdigris bronze, is a delight when in action (unfortunately rarely in this water-conscious city).

While the arch was being embellished, a necklace of Classical ornaments, designed by **Stanford White**, was strung across the park entrances facing it (completed in 1894) [A5]. Rising out of entangling fasces, four 50-foot Doric columns are topped with exuberant eagles (by **MacMonnies**), railings, bronze urns, and lamp standards; and two 12-sided templelike

A6

gazebos. Of the whole ensemble, the gazebos, with their polished granite Tuscan columns, Guastavino vaulting, and bronze finials, show White's talents most richly.

[A6] **Main Library, Brooklyn Public Library** (Ingersoll Memorial), Grand Army Plaza at the intersection of Flatbush Ave. and Eastern Pkwy. 1941. **Alfred Morton Githens & Francis Keally**, architects; **Paul Jennewein**, sculptor of bas-reliefs; Thomas H. Jones, sculptor of the screen over the entry. ●

Streamlined Beaux Arts, or an example of how the Ecole des Beaux Arts developed the Art Moderne of the Paris Exposition of 1937. In effect it is a formal participant in the geometry of avenues radiating from the Soldiers' and Sailors' Arch; but its Moderne/Beaux Arts idiom allowed it to be stylishly modern in its costume as well as classical in its conformance to the grand plan. Inside is lots of lavish space.

PROSPECT PARK

Once past **Stanford White**'s grand entrance, one sees **Olmsted & Vaux**'s park much as they conceived it. They considered it a better work than their first collaboration, Central Park, for several reasons, none of which reflects on that earlier work. Principally, as this commission did not result from a competition, with its inevitably fixed site and program, they could change the program first given—and they did. Delay of construction due to the Civil War aided their efforts. Almost half of the land set aside for a park by the City of Brooklyn in the 1850s lay to the northeast of Flatbush Avenue, the main artery to Flatbush, which was still a town in its own right: it centered around the reservoir on

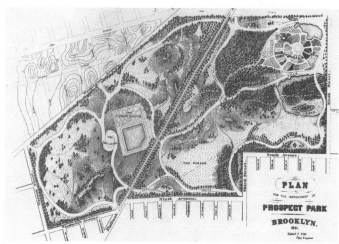

Fig. A

Prospect Hill (since filled in and used as a playground). Olmsted & Vaux rejected a scheme [Figure A] in which Flatbush Avenue completely bisected the proposed park, recommending instead that the allotted land be expanded to the south and west [Figure B]. In severing the land to the northeast, they lost the hill that gave the park its name, but they also got rid of its reservoir (a major part of Central Park to this day) and provided, by default, a tract on which related institutions (the Library, the Brooklyn Museum, and the Brooklyn Botanic Garden) could be located without consuming park space (as the Metropolitan Museum of Art does in Manhattan). Another encumbrance considerably reduced here is the roads. With a more compact shape—and without transverse cuts—Prospect Park yielded much less area to wheeled traffic.

[A7] **Prospect Park, Grand Army Plaza,** Prospect Park W., Prospect Park SW., Parkside Ave., Ocean Ave., and Flatbush Ave. Designed 1865. Constructed 1866-1873. **Frederick Law Olmsted & Calvert Vaux.** Various alterations. Scenic landmark. 🍎

A7

Prospect Park Walking Tour: Grand Army Plaza (IRT subway to Grand Army Plaza Station) to southeast entrance at Parkside and Ocean Avenues (Parkside Avenue Station).

Enter between the east (left) pair of Doric columns. Note the statue of **James Stranahan** (1891, **Frederick MacMonnies**, sculptor), whose personal 24-year crusade is largely responsible for both Prospect Park and Olmsted & Vaux's other great contributions to Brooklyn: Ocean and Eastern Parkways. Note also the pine grove along the walk; it is replicated on the opposite corner, where the symmetrical entrance composition merges with the park's picturesque layout. Like all walks entering this park, this one quickly loses visual connection with the point of entrance, through its twisting route and the modeling of the terrain's topography.

A8

Turn right at the first fork to **Endale Arch** [A8], the first structure completed (1867); a dramatic tuned transition takes you into broad daylight and a 1/2-mile vista down the Long Meadow. The arch is a bucolic vault of Ruskinian Gothic in brick and sandstone, once festooned with crockets, bosses, and finials, and lined with a wooden interior (only traces of all this remain).

Once through the arch, note the corresponding but architecturally unique **Meadow Port Arch** [A9] to the right, at the west entrance to the meadow: it is a barrel vault rather than a Gothic

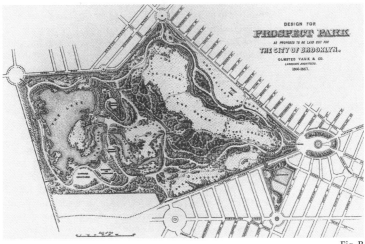

Fig. B

one. Follow the path to the left along the edge of the meadow. The recreation on the meadow itself is deftly separated but still visible from the tree-dotted hillsides along the encircling walks. The undulations of the meadow, sculpted by Olmsted, offer a sense of place, and topographical variation allows participants to perceive the mass of people present—impossible on flat ground. This same trick is the basis of St. Peter's Square in the Vatican, a series of ups and downs within a vast dish that displays to each participant the scale of the whole crowd.

About 500 feet ahead a set of steps rises to the left. Go a bit beyond for a better view of the meadow, then back, up the steps, and across the road. On the other side go left, then right at the next fork down a curving walk to the **Rose Garden** [A10] (1895, designer unknown). This space is lovely even without any apparent rosebushes these days. Turning right across the center of the circle, take the steps leading down to the **Vale of Cashmere** [A11]:

meandering free-form pools with once-upon-a-time Classical balustrades, now fallen. Deep in a hollow facing due south, the Vale once supported a lush stand of bamboo (green year-round) and multitudes of birds, some uncommon in New York.

Follow the brick path along the east side of the Vale (left as you enter) straight out along the little meadow, from which there are glimpses of the Long Meadow across the road. Continue over a modest crest and down the wooded slope to Battle Pass. The park road at this point follows roughly the alignment of the original road from Flatbush to Brooklyn, and it was at this pass that Revolutionary volunteers put up brief resistance against British troops advancing toward New York in 1776.

The Zoo [A12]: An optional and recommended detour at this point is to the Prospect Park Wildlife Conservation Center (once known as the Prospect Park Zoo), just to the south. The Center offers formal but intimate confrontations with animals, and those in need of services will find rest rooms and fast food. Its original neat semicircle of formally planned, understated brick buildings (1935, **Aymar Embury**) was decorated with bas-reliefs and murals by WPA artists, including **Hunt Diederich**, **F. G. R. Roth**, and **Emele Siebern**, representing scenes from **Rudyard Kipling**'s *Jungle Books*. The takeover by the New York Zoological Society has led to a different relationship between human and other animals, retaining the shells of the original buildings, removing most of the bars; it is an experience on paths, over a period of time, rather than a display of caged tenants. (1990s. **Goldstone & Hinz**)

A12

Of particular architectural interest is the central pavilion, an octagonal blue-tiled dome of Guastavino vaulting with 24 oculi windows. Once there were pachyderms under this pantheon—rhinoceroses, hippos, and heffalumps—but the heffalumps were removed to the Bronx Zoo when all of the City's zoos were placed under that society's aegis. To the west along the park drive is a charming sculpture of a lioness and her cubs (1899, **Victor Peter**).

At Battle Pass, cross the road and climb the stairs ahead to a plateau that was once the site of the **Dairy** [A13] (1869, **Calvert Vaux**). Turn left at the top of the stairs, and follow the brow of the plateau across the bridle path, past the red brick service building, then right to cross the high boulder bridge (very romantic rocky rock), passing over a return loop of the bridle path. From the bridge, bear right, then left up the steps, and then left again at a T-intersection along a walk that skirts the knoll on which the **John Howard Payne monument** [A13] stands (1873, **Henry Baerer**, sculptor). Climb to the crest for a sweeping view of the Long Meadow. The red brick picnic house is directly across the meadow, the more elegant **Palladian Tennis House** [A14] (1910, **Helmle & Huberty**) is to its left. Return to the walk below, and take your first left on the walk along the slope's edge. At the next T-intersection go right and then down the steps. Stop where the walk takes a sharp right for a view of the fantastic boulder bridge crossed earlier.

Continue your descent into a deep rocky glen, through which a brook gurgles happily. Turn left at the bottom, crossing a smaller boulder bridge, and follow the path along the brook. Turn right at the end of this walk, and pass through the triple [A15] **Nethermead Arches** (1870, **Calvert Vaux**), where walk, brook, and bridle path separately pass under the Central Drive. The arches are crowned with a trefoil sandstone balustrade; the bridge is supported by barrel vaults of brick, granite, and more sandstone. Continue along the brook, past some specimen trees and into the Music Grove. Here a "music pagoda," a faintly Japanese bandstand, is the site for summer concerts. Cross Music Grove and bear right on the walk that crosses Lullwater Bridge. From the bridge there is a fine view of the white terra-cotta-faced, newly restored **Boathouse** [A16] (1904, **Helmle &**

A16

Huberty). 🔊 From the other side of the bridge there is a long view down the Lullwater, meandering toward the Lake. Note that the sides of the Lullwater are hard-edged stone. At the end turn of the bridge, turn left for a closer look at the Boathouse; note particularly its elegant black iron lamp standards. The Boathouse is a pleasant terra-cotta remembrance of Palladian architecture. From the Boathouse take the path south past the Camperdown Elm, a weeping, drooping Japanese Brobdingnagian bonsai of a tree: aged, gnarled, arthritic, and eternal. Then turn left through the **Cleft Ridge Span** [A17] (1872, **Calvert Vaux**), with its two-toned incised-tile inner surface enriching this barrel vault.

Through this span is the formal **Garden Terrace** [A18] with the Oriental Pavilion (1874, **Calvert Vaux**), now happily restored after a disastrous fire. The view down this Beaux Arts-inspired garden to the Lake has suffered more than the Pavilion, for the semicircular cove at the foot of the Terrace is now filled by the Kate Wollman Skating Rink, a banal place, one of three that originally scarred this and Central Park. No matter how noble their intentions, recreational intrusions, particularly those which inflict buildings foreign to the spirit of the landscape, should be banned from the wondrous landscape art of such as Olmsted & Vaux. In this garden, on axis, is **Lincoln** (1869, **H. K. Brown**, sculptor). Follow Lincoln's gaze to the high wire fence and exposed refrigeration equipment at what was, until 1961, the edge of the lake. Lincoln seems to gesture with his right hand: "Take it away." To the left is the **Skating Shelter** [A19] (1960, **Hopf & Adler**).

Turn left around this unhappy intrusion, and then pass a World War I Memorial (1920, **A. D. Pickering**). Continuing around the edge of the lake, you will find a landing shelter. This is a 1971 reconstruction of the original (1870, **Calvert Vaux**), the sole survivor of many rustic log-braced shelters that once bordered the lake, creating a kind of mini-Adirondacks image. From here follow the path along the lake's edge; then bear left across the drive, and continue straight out of the park through the Classical porticoes, crowned with redwood trellises (1904, **McKim, Mead & White**), to the intersection of Ocean and Parkside Avenues.

For further views of the lake and a look at some of the park's finest Classical structures, don't leave the park at this point, but instead follow the walk along the park's south side, between Parkside Avenue and the drive, to the **Croquet Shelter** [A20] (1906, **McKim, Mead & White**, restored, 1967). 🔊 This Corinthian-columned pavilion of limestone, with terra-cotta capitals, frieze, and entablature, is supported within by Guastavino vaults. But there are no croquet mallets here; those Anglophile players have departed for Central Park.

INSTITUTE PARK

The green triangle contained by Eastern Parkway and Flatbush and Washington Avenues, formerly known as Institute Park after the Brooklyn Institute of Arts and Sciences (which **Olmsted & Vaux** rejected in their plan for Prospect Park), was reserved for related institutional uses. It now accommodates the Brooklyn Botanic Garden, the Brooklyn Museum, and the main branch of the Brooklyn Public Library. The garden and museum are contiguous and offer more than the expected horticultural specimens and works of art. The garden has some interesting examples of landscape architecture; and the museum houses extensive decorative craft collections, 25 period rooms, a whole Dutch Colonial house, one of the world's great Egyptian collections, and, in a garden behind, a collection of exterior architectural building parts (columns, friezes, sculptures, plaques) from demolished New York buildings.

Botanic Garden to Brooklyn Museum Walking Tour: From the BMT Prospect Park Station (D, Q and S trains) on Flatbush Avenue near Empire Boulevard (can also be reached from Grand Army Plaza Station by B41 bus) to the IRT Eastern Parkway Station (2 and 3 trains). Cross the street to the Lefferts Homestead, go back along Empire Boulevard to the Fire Department Bureau of Communications, and then enter the Botanic Gardens.

[I1] **Flatbush Turnpike Tollgate**, Empire Blvd. entrance road to Prospect Park. N side. ca. 1855.
   A wooden guardhouse moved from its old position at Flatbush Turnpike (now Flatbush Avenue) is all that remains of the days when roads were privately built and tolls were charged for their use.

[I2] **Lefferts Homestead**/originally Peter Lefferts House, Flatbush Ave. N of Empire Blvd. W side. In Prospect Park. 1777-1783. ● 718-965-6505. Mar-July, Sep-Dec, Sat-Sun, 12-4; closed Mon-Fri.
   Six slender Tuscan colonnettes support a "Dutch" eave, the edge of a gambrel roof. Painted shingle body, stained shingle roof. The English built many such copies of the basic Dutch house. Its predecessor, in 1776, was burned in the Battle of Long Island to prevent its use by the British.It was moved here in 1918 from a site on Flatbush Avenue between Midwood and Maple Streets.

I2

[I3] **Brooklyn Central Office, Bureau of Fire Communications**, N.Y.C. Fire Department, 35 Empire Blvd., bet. Flatbush and Washington Aves. N side. 1913. **Frank J. Helmle.** ●
   Brunelleschi in Brooklyn: its arcades are those of his foundling hospital in Florence.

[I4] **Brooklyn Botanic Garden**, 1000 Washington Ave., bet. Empire Blvd. and S side of Brooklyn Museum, W to Flatbush Ave. 718-622-4433.

Enter the garden through the Palladian south gate at Flatbush Avenue and Empire Boulevard. Its 50 acres are intensively planted with almost every variety of tree and bush that will survive in this climate. The most popular attraction, and one that generates traffic jams at the end of April, is the grove of Japanese cherry trees, the finest in America. For a simple tour of the garden follow the east side, consistently staying to your right. For seasonal attractions (the cherry blossoms, roses, lilacs, azaleas) not on this route, ask the guard (on a motor scooter) for directions. On the east edge of the garden, a few hundred feet from the south entrance, is a **reproduction of the garden from the Ryoanji Temple, Kyoto** [I5]. Constructed with painstaking authenticity in 1963, this replica lacks all of the atmosphere that history and a natural setting give to the original, but it offers an opportunity unique in this area to contemplate a Zen-inspired, virtually plantless landscape composition: rock islands in a sea of raked pebbles.

I3

I6

Just north of the Ryoanji are the **greenhouses**, facing a plaza with pools of specimen water lilies. The new units [I6] (1987, **Davis, Brody & Assocs.**) are hexagonal "icebergs" over sunken climatic gardens—somewhat aggressive forms that don't share the serenity of the adjacent garden. This conservatory has a tropical jungle section and a desert section, but its prize exhibit is the collection of bonsai Japanese miniature trees unequaled in the Americas. North of the conservatory is another formal terrace planted with magnolias (a dazzling display in early to mid-April) in front of the garden's **School-Laboratory-Administration Building** [I7] (1918. **McKim, Mead & White**), originally painted white but now aquatic green. Farther north is the **Japanese Garden** [I8] (1915. **Takeo Shiota**, designer), gift of philanthropist **Alfred Tredway White**. It resembles a stroll garden of the Momoyama period, but it is not copied from any one particular example. Around its small pond are examples of almost every traditional plant. This overcrowding fails to achieve the serenity of good Japanese prototypes. North of the Japanese Garden is the gate to the parking field, which leads to the Brooklyn Museum. Walk out to Washington Avenue and enter the museum via its front entrance on Eastern Parkway, now barren of its monumental staircase removed in the 1930s.

I7

[I9] **Brooklyn Museum of Art**/formerly Brooklyn Museum/originally Brooklyn Institute of Arts and Sciences, 200 Eastern Pkwy., SW cor. Washington Ave. 1893-1915. **McKim, Mead & White**. Alterations by WPA, 1935, **William Lescaze**. Addition, 1978, **Prentice & Chan, Ohlhausen**. Second Addition, 1987, **Joseph Tonetti**. ☛ Master plan competition winner, 1987, **Arata Isozaki/Polshek Partnership**, associate architects. 718-638-5000. Wed-Sun, 10-5; closed Mon-Tues.

One quarter of the grand plan envisioned for Brooklyn in the year before consolidation with New York. After the borough was incorporated in the larger metropolis, support for its museum waned. But what it lacks in sheer size, it makes up for in quality: inside is one of the world's greatest Egyptian collections.

Note the two sculptured female figures representing Manhattan and Brooklyn (1916. **Daniel Chester French**, sculptor). Although they look as if created for this location, they were placed here in 1963 when their seats at the Brooklyn end of the Manhattan Bridge were destroyed in a roadway improvement program.

The austere architecture of the lobby dates from its remodeling in the 1930s under WPA sponsorship. The lobby was moved downstairs from the "parlor floor" to the basement, and the

I9

monumental exterior stairway was removed (1934-1935). Stark functionalism replaced Classical monumentality: a sorry loss. The information desk will offer directions to the collections as well as information on concerts, lectures, and movies in the museum. Among the outstanding exhibits in architecture and interior design are the **Jan Martense Schenck House** (originally built in 1675 in the Flatlands section of Brooklyn), dismantled in 1952 and reconstructed inside the museum, and a suite of rooms from the **John D. Rockefeller Mansion**, built in 1866 at 4 West 54th Street, Manhattan, and redecorated in 1885 in the Moorish style by **Arabella Worsham**.

In the rear, adjacent to the new addition and parking lot, is the **Frieda Schiff Warburg Sculpture Garden** (1966. **Ian White**, designer). Here are pieces of **McKim, Mead & White**'s Pennsylvania Station (a column base and a capital; a figure that supported one side of a huge clock), Coney Island's Steeplechase Amusement Park (a roaring lion's head and a lamp standard), and capitals from the first-floor columns of **Louis Sullivan's Bayard** (Condict) building, still standing on Manhattan's Bleecker Street.

Curios and antiquities: Just inside the south (parking area) entrance of the museum is the Gallery Shop, once the nation's largest museum shop, with an extensive stock of handcrafted toys, jewelry, textiles, and ceramics from all over the world.

END of Botanic Garden-Brooklyn Museum Walking Tour: The IRT Eastern Parkway subway stop (2 and 3 trains) is directly in front of the museum.

[I10] **Eastern Parkway**, designated a scenic landmark between Grand Army Plaza and Ralph Ave. 1870-1874. **Frederick Law Olmsted & Calvert Vaux.** ●⚐

The first parkway in the nation, intended to bring open space into all areas of the city as part of a comprehensive park system, as yet unbuilt (and unplanned).

BEDFORD-STUYVESANT

Bedford-Stuyvesant is the amalgam of two middle-class communities of the old City of Brooklyn: Bedford, the western portion, and Stuyvesant Heights, to the east. Today's Bedford-
Stuyvesant is one of the city's two major black enclaves; the
other is its peer, Harlem. Bed-Stuy differs from its Manhattan
counterpart in its much larger percentage of home owners,
although Harlem is rapidly following its lead in gentrifying its
own blocks. The southern and western portions comprise
masonry row housing of distinguished architectural quality and
vigorous churches whose spires contribute to the area's frequently lacy skyline. The northeastern reaches have considerable
numbers of wooden tenements, containing some of the nation's
worst slums. But on the whole, Bed-Stuy has a reputation that
doesn't fit with reality: a stable community with hundreds of
blocks of well-kept town houses.

Where Bedford-Stuyvesant has distinguished architecture, it
is very good. Its façades of brownstones and brickfronts create a
magnificent townscape as good as—and sometimes better
than—many fashionable areas of Brooklyn and Manhattan.
Parts of Chauncey, Decatur, MacDonough, and Macon Streets,
and the southern end of Stuyvesant Avenue, are superb.
Hancock Street, between Nostrand and Tompkins Avenues, was
considered a showplace in its time (why not now too?). Alice
and Agate Courts, short cul-de-sacs isolated from the macro-
cosm of the street system, are particularly special places in the
seemingly endless, anonymous grid.

Bed-Stuy comprises roughly 2,000 acres and houses 400,000
people, making it among the 30 largest American cities. It
should be toured by car because the sites are dispersed.

[Y1] **Friendship Baptist Church**, 92 Herkimer St., bet. Bedford
and Nostrand Aves. S side. 1910.

A Hollywood Moorish façade crowned with sheet-metal
onion domes and a sturdy cornice over yellow patterned brickwork.

Y1

[Y2] **95 Herkimer Street** (house), bet. Bedford and
Nostrand Aves. N side. 1860s.

Opposite Friendship Baptist, this wood and clapboard house
speaks of another time in Bed-Stuy, long before the brownstones.

[Y3] **Brevoort Place**, S of Fulton St., bet. Franklin and
Bedford Aves. 1860s.

A handsome block of brownstones in excellent condition,
with their original detail mostly undamaged by the crass modernization of the city's richer areas.

Y3

Y4

Y5

Y7

Y8

Y10

Y11

[Y4] **Bethel Seventh-Day Adventist Church**/originally Church of Our Father, 457 Grand Ave., NE cor. Lefferts Place. ca. 1885.

The obtuse angle of this intersection suggested a stepped form to this architect. The brickwork is piered, arched, corbeled, and articulated, presenting pinnacles, finials, and oculi. A wonderful and vigorous brick monolith.

[Y5] **Independent United Order of Mechanics of the Western Hemisphere**/originally Lincoln Club, 67 Putnam Ave., bet. Irving Place and Classon Ave. N side. 1889. **Rudolph L. Daus.**

Elegant Republicans left this florid structure, marking the memory of these streets with a remembrance of better times. The bracketed tower is in the Wagnerian idiom popularized by the fantastic 1850s Bavarian royal castle of **Ludwig II,** Neuschwanstein.

[Y6] **Miller Memorial Church of the Nazarene**/formerly Aurora-Grata Scottish Rite Cathedral/originally East Reformed Church, 1160 Bedford Ave., NW cor. Madison St. Rebuilt, 1888.

Bedford Avenue in these blocks is nondescript, and this brick and sandstone fantasy is a welcome relief. Its history dates back to 1877, when the Aurora-Grata Lodge of Perfection, a Masonic local, bought the old East Reformed Church on this site and rebuilt it for Masonic purposes. The Masons are gone, and the church is once again a church.

[Y7] E**vening Star Baptist Church**/originally Latter Day Saints Chapel, 265 Gates Ave., NW cor. Franklin Ave. 1917. **Eric Holmgren.**

Superficially reminiscent of **Frank Lloyd Wright's Unity Temple** in Oak Park (1904), this church is a unique cubist experiment for New York. Perhaps it could be termed "homespun Schindler" after **Richard Schindler**, the Austrian-born disciple of Wright who followed this idiom in southern California.

[Y8] **118 Quincy Street** (apartments), SE cor. Franklin Ave. ca. 1890.

A modest example of the lavish apartment buildings built in this community in the last decade of the 19th century. Battered stone walls support arched and rock-linteled brick. Note the fortuitously intact frieze and cornice.

[Y9] **361 Classon Avenue** and **386-396 Lafayette Avenue**, SE cor. of Classon and Lafayette Aves. ca. 1888.

A picturesque and romantic brick and brownstone Victorian "terrace." Compare this rich massing and detail with the high-rise public housing across the street: charm and personality confronted by tombstones.

[Y10] **88th Precinct, N.Y.C. Police Department**, 300 Classon Ave., SW cor. DeKalb Ave. ca. 1890. South extension, 1924.

Mini-Romanesque Revival, it packs an arcuated castle into a tight site and at a small scale.

[Y11] **Warehouses**, 220-232 Taaffe Place, bet. Willoughby and DeKalb Aves. W side. ca. 1885.

No-nonsense Romanesque Revival with virile, vigorous brickwork and arches that bound and abound; **H. H. Richardson** would have been pleased. Some clod, however, has infilled some of these glorious voids with concrete block and sheet metal. Next door, to the south, are more sophisticated but less vigorous neo-Romanesquisms. But enjoy the ornate wrought-iron strapping for the tensile ties (stabilizing slender brick piers).

BEDFORD-STUYVESANT DISTRICT

see pages 731-739

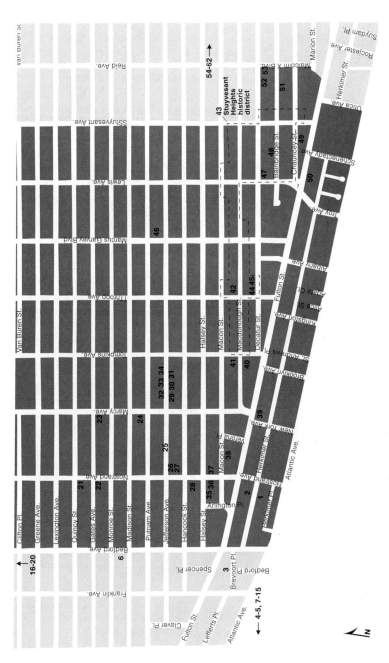

[Y12] **St. Mary's Episcopal Church**, 230 Classon Ave.,
NW cor. Willoughby Ave. 1858-1859. **Richard C.
Auchmuty** of **Renwick & Auchmuty**. 🍎

A very comfortable English Gothic country chapel in
dressed-brownstone ashlar, with a verdigris copper steeple, by a
couple of Scots. A flying Gothic arch leads to a pleasant close.

[Y13] **Convent of the Sisters of Mercy** (Roman Catholic), 273
Willoughby Ave., bet. Classon Ave. and Taaffe Place. N side. 1862.
Patrick Charles Keely.

A gloomy mansarded red brick pile.

Y12

Y16

Rope walks: Not for crossing jungle swamps or the River Kwai, but long narrow buildings created for spinning rope. In 1803 one was erected in the 2 blocks north of the Convent of the Sisters of Mercy. It was so long (1,200 feet) that a tunnel was built for it to pass beneath intersecting Park Avenue.

[Y14] Originally **St. Paul's School**, E side Taaffe Pl., bet. Willoughby and Myrtle Aves. ca. 1899.

Romanesque Revival in a ruddy palette of terra-cotta and brick. Note the basketweave brickwork surrounding the first floor arches.

Y17

[Y15] **St. Patrick's Roman Catholic Church and Rectory**, Kent Ave. NW cor. Willoughby Ave. Rectory, 285 Willoughby Ave. Academy, 918 Kent Ave. bet. Kent Ave. and Taaffe Place, N side. 1856. **Patrick Charles Keely**.

An austere Gothic Revival. Its rectory is an arch-windowed, mansarded, brick-and-brownstone cartoon from Charles Addams.

[Y16] **Wallabout Warehouse**/formerly Franklin Brewery/originally Malcolm Brewery, 394-412 Flushing Ave., bet. Franklin and Skillman Aves. S side. E section, 1869. W, section, 1890. Both by **Otto Wolf**.

A truncated pyramid crowns this pile of many-arched brickwork. Its distinctive silhouette provides a landmark to thousands of motorists passing it daily on the nearby Brooklyn-Queens Expressway.

Y18

[Y17] **St. Lucy's Roman Catholic Church**, 780 Kent Ave., bet. Flusing and Park Aves. 1921.

A **John Soane** revival? Romanesque Baroque? Tucked away in this industrial precinct stands this striking architectural personality that resurrects Regency tricks and towers.

[Y18] **Engine Company 209, Ladder Company 102, 34th Battalion, N.Y.C. Fire Department**, 850 Bedford Ave., bet. Myrtle and Park Aves. W side. 1965. **Pedersen & Tilney**.

"Modernists" first enjoyed widespread commissions for New York's public buildings in the 1960s and 1970s. Their valiant attempts (including this one) now seem to pall in light of a new understanding of and interest in architectural history and urban context. The 1869 station that this replaced, down the block between Myrtle and Willoughby Avenues, has unfortunately been demolished.

Y20b

[Y19] **CABS (Community Action for Bedford-Stuyvesant) Nursing Home & Related Health Facility**, 270 Nostrand Ave., bet. Kosciuszko and DeKalb Aves. W side. 1976. **William N. Breger & Assocs**, architects. **Leeds Assocs.**, interiors.

A stylish, elegant stacking of cubist brickwork crowned with a space-frame skylight. The atrium within is a delightful greenhouse filled with a "bamboo jungle," long antedating IBM's atrium jungle at 56th Street and Madison Avenue in Manhattan.

Y21

[Y20a] **Magnolia grandiflora**, in front of 679 Lafayette Ave., bet. Marcy and Tompkins Aves. N side., opp. Tompkins Park. 1885. 🌳
[Y20b] **677, 678, 679 Lafayette Avenue**/The Magnolia Tree Earth Center (row houses). 1880-1883. 🌳

One of two landmark trees in New York (the other is the Weeping Beech in Flushing). Here an expatriate southerner has survived many of its brownstone neighbors of the same vintage. A third wonder, the Camperdown Elm, still graces Prospect Park. The brownstones were designated landmarks to insure their continued protection of the tree from north winds.

[Y21] **John Wesley United Methodist Church**/originally Nostrand Avenue Methodist Episcopal Church, Quincy St. SW cor. Nostrand Ave. 1880.

A brick body with milky Tiffany-style stained glass is crowned with timbered gables—part of the second Gothic Revival, Shingle and Stick Style division. These were Romantic times, before a third round of Gothicism became Academic: the literalism of **Ralph Adams Cram** and the Collegiate Gothicists after 1900.

Y22

Governors: Between Marcy and Stuyvesant Avenues, streets were named for New York governors: William L. Marcy, Daniel D. Tompkins, Enos T. Throop, Joseph C. Yates, Morgan Lewis, and the Dutch director general, Peter Stuyvesant. Yates Avenue became Sumner when confusion arose between it and Gates. (The City continues to flirt with many street name changes—is nothing sacred?—so beware.)

Y23

[Y22] Onetime **IBM Systems Products Division**/formerly Empire State Warehouse/originally Long Island Storage Warehouse and Jenkins Trust Company, 390 Gates Ave., SW cor. Nostrand Ave. 1906. **Helmle, Huberty & Hudswell**.

Grand, paired Beaux Arts entry portals join the corner at this intersection. A rusticated base supports the patterned brickwork of this sturdy office-building monolith. Lost is a neo-Baroque tower that once crowned these low brownstone blocks.

[Y23] **St. George's Episcopal Church**, 800 Marcy Ave., SW cor. Gates Ave. 1887-1888. Sunday School, 1889. **Richard M. Upjohn**.

Y24

An elegantly austere Ruskinian Gothic country church in the city, in brick, brownstone, and slate. The octagonal tower is both grand and lilliputian. The architect is the son of Trinity Church's Upjohn.

[Y24] Originally **Boys' High School**, 832 Marcy Ave., bet. Putnam Ave. and Madison St. W side. 1891-1892. **James W. Naughton**. Additions, 1905-1910. **C. B. J. Snyder**.

A major Brooklyn landmark, in splendid Romanesque Revival: arched, quoined, towered, and lushly decorated in terracotta in the manner of **Louis Sullivan**.

[Y25] **Brownstone Blocks**, Jefferson Ave., bet. Nostrand and Throop Aves. 1870s.

Y28

Merely 3 blocks out of dozens in the area with staid Renaissance Revival brownstones. **F. W. Woolworth** moved to No. 209 in 1890. Changing fashion and vastly increasing wealth led him across the East River to 990 Fifth Avenue, where his later (1901) house was designed by **C. P. H. Gilbert**. Compare the similar migration of **Harold I. Pratt** from Clinton Hill to 68th Street and Park Avenue.

[Y26] **Most Worshipful Enoch Grand Lodge**/originally Reformed Episcopal Church of the Reconciliation, Jefferson Ave. SE cor. Nostrand Ave. 1890. **Heins & La Farge**.

A churchly place, its octagonal corner tower rising above milky stained glass, brick, and terra-cotta. Now a Masonic temple.

[Y27] **Clinton Apartments**, 325 Nostrand Ave., bet. Jefferson and Hancock Aves. E side. 1890s.

Roman brick and Roman arches crowned with a pressed metal garlanded cornice.

[Y28] **Renaissance Apartments**, 488 Nostrand Ave., SW cor. and 140-144 Hancock St. 1892. **Montrose W. Morris**.

Cylindrical, conically capped towers, borrowed from Loire Valley châteaux, anchor a grand apartment house that has now regained much of its former splendor both inside and out. An address restored to distinction at the heart of Bed-Stuy.

Y29

Y31

Y32

Y34

Y36

[Y29] **232 Hancock Street**, SE cor. Marcy Ave. 1886. **Montrose W. Morris**.

A mansarded extravaganza, replete with oriels, gables, and pediments—a Queen Anne wonder.

[Y30] **236-244 Hancock Street** (house), bet. Marcy and Tompkins Aves. S side. 1886. **Montrose W. Morris**.

Pompeian-red terra-cotta and brick form a rich tapestry in the manner of **George B. Post**'s Brooklyn Historical Society.

[Y31] **246-252 Hancock Street** (house), bet. Marcy and Tompkins Aves. S side. 1880s. **Montrose W. Morris**.

terra-cotta, stained glass, elliptical arches, and Byzantine columns, mansarded and pedimented against the sky. Shingle Style Richardsonian Romanesque: a "terrace," in the English sense, that is greater than the sum of its parts.

[Y32] Originally **John C. Kelley House**, 247 Hancock St., bet. Marcy and Tompkins Aves. N side. 1880s. **Montrose W. Morris**.

A formal freestanding neo-Renaissance town house (the Renaissance would have termed it a palazzo) on a triple-width site (81 feet) built for an Irish immigrant who made good. Legend claims that the brownstone was selected piece by piece to guarantee quality. The irony is that it is now crumbling and painted.

[Y33] **255-259 Hancock Street** (house), bet. Marcy and Tompkins Aves. N side. 1880s. **Montrose W. Morris**.

Round stone and elliptical brick arches bring vigorous shade and shadow to this trio.

[Y34] **273 Hancock Street** (house), bet. Marcy and Tompkins Aves. N side. 1890. **J. C. Reynolds & Son**.

Smooth and rockface browstone with a lion-faced keystone to guard the entry.

[Y35] **74 Halsey Street**, bet. Nostrand Ave. and Arlington Place. side. 1880s.

A wild Queen Anne place, with exuberant wrought-iron railings and canopy. Imagine bounding up those front steps. But please strip off that paint.

[Y36] **Alhambra Apartments**, 500-518 Nostrand Ave., bet. Macon and Halsey Sts. W side. 1889-1890. **Montrose W. Morris**. Restored, 1998. **Anderson Associates**.

Morris did better here than for Kelley, with a richer collection of terra-cotta and brick—arcaded, mansarded, chimneyed, and dormered. Once abandoned, it participates in the renaissance of middle-class housing for Bedford-Stuyvesant. New shopfront additions along Nostrand Avenue detract, however, from the grandeur overhead. **Morris** and **Frank Freeman** were Brooklyn's greatest architects.

[Y37] **N.Y.C. Board of Education Brooklyn Adult Training Center**/formerly Girls' High School/originally Central Grammar School, 475 Nostrand Ave., bet. Halsey and Macon Sts. E side. 1885-1886. Rear addition, 1891. **James W. Naughton**. Macon Street addition, 1912. **C. B. J. Snyder**.

A High Victorian painted Gothic Revival hulk.

[Y38] **64 and 68 Macon Street** (houses), bet. Nostrand and Marcy Aves. S side. 1880s.

The intervening "garden" space sets off these two classy houses, allowing No. 64's oriel window to view this urbane street and any resident Rapunzel to let down her hair. No. 68 is Romanesque Revival in brick and terra-cotta. Look for the overseeing face in the dormered roof. The second-story corner porch is an elegant incision and a counterpointing place of overview to No. 64's oriel.

[Y39] **Bedford-Stuyvesant Restoration Plaza**, 1360 Fulton St., SE cor. New York Ave. 1976. **Arthur Cotton Moore**.

Brown brick, brown glass, and a floating Victorian façade recalling this block's history give a simple face to the street but also embrace an urbane compound-plaza that is Brooklyn's answer to San Francisco's Ghirardelli Square. Stylish new and renewed buildings mix on this block, including the Billie Holliday Theater next door.

Y39

[Y40] **First African Methodist Episcopal Zion Church**/originally Tompkins Avenue Congregational Church, 480 Tompkins Ave., SW cor. MacDonough St. 1889. **George B. Chappell**.

The immense campanile that dominates the neighborhood is reminiscent of St. Mark's in Venice; brick is everywhere. Once the nation's largest Congregational congregation, it was often referred to as Dr. Meredith's church, after its well-known preacher.

Y40

[Y41] **Stuyvesant Heights Christian Church**, Tompkins Ave. NW cor. MacDonough St. 1880s.

Painted Gothic Revival. A modest form with grandly scaled windows.

[Y42] **Our Lady of Victory Roman Catholic Church**, NE cor. Throop Ave. and MacDonough St. 1891-1895. **Thomas F. Houghton**.

Dressed Manhattan schist and limestone in a late, many-pinnacled Gothic Revival.

[Y43] **Stuyvesant Heights Historic District**, an L-shaped area between Chauncey and Macon Sts., from Stuyvesant to Tompkins Aves. 1870-1920.

Y42

The wondrous row housing, particularly along Decatur, Bainbridge, and Chauncey Streets, is a cross section of Bedford-Stuyvesant vernacular architectural history. The locally designed buildings encompass attitudes from freestanding suburbia to the best of Victorian row housing and present a sampling of modest apartment units.

[Y44] **Fulton Storage Building**/originally New York and New Jersey Telephone Company (branch office), 613 Throop Ave., NE cor. Decatur St. ca. 1895.

Roman brick and Renaissance arches; the spandrels between are richly decorated in sculpted terra-cotta.

Y44

[Y45] **79-81 Decatur Street**/originally Clermont Apartments, bet. Throop and Sumner Aves. N side. 1900.

A shrunken château: here Roman brick, limestone, and pressed metal produce an Azay-le-Rideau for families of modest means.

[Y46] **13th Regiment Armory, New York National Guard**, 357 Marcus Garvey Blvd. (Sumner Ave.), bet. Jefferson and Putnam Aves. E side. 1894. **Rudolph L. Daus**. Extended, 1906, **Parfitt Brothers**.

A great granite arch gives support to twin battlemented towers: here are crenellations, machicolations, and a battered base. It is a powerful presence in this small-scale neighborhood.

Y47

[Y47] **Mt. Lebanon Baptist Church**, 230 Decatur St., SE cor. Lewis Ave. 1894. **Parfitt Brothers**.

A superb Richardsonian Romanesque building in Roman brick and brownstone. The terra-cotta shingled tower is a remembrance of a Loire Valley castle's turret.

[Y48] **113-137 Bainbridge Street** (row houses), bet. Lewis and Stuyvesant Aves. N side. ca. 1900.

The studied variegations of these 13 houses—pyramids,

Y48

arches, and cones—alternately punctuate the sky. Such a picturesque romance contrasts sharply with the normally sober regularity of mid 19th-century Renaissance Revival brownstones.

[Y49] **Fulton Park**, Chauncey to Fulton Sts. at Stuyvesant Ave.

The rumble of the subway train doesn't affect the serenity of this sliver of green space along Fulton Street. The neighborhood to the north is named after the park and, because of its well-maintained houses and stable population, is considered an important asset in the work of renewing Bedford-Stuyvesant. North of the park along Chauncey Street is a fine row of small-scale town houses with intact stoops. In the park's center is a statue of **Robert Fulton** holding his first steam ferryboat to Brooklyn, the *Nassau*. Originally placed in a niche at the Brooklyn ferry terminal, below the Brooklyn Bridge, the statue disappeared. It was later discovered and placed here in 1930 by the Society of Old Brooklyn.

Y50

City center: The geographical center of New York City lies within Bedford-Stuyvesant—to be exact, within the block bounded by Lafayette, Reid (Malcolm X Boulevard), Greene and Stuyvesant Avenues, the present site of a less than distinguished public school.

[Y50] **1660-1670 Fulton Street**, opp. Fulton Park, bet. Troy and Schenectady Aves. 1976. **Henri LeGendre**.

Medium-rise housing with a broken and cadaverous form that works happily with this predominantly low-rise neighborhood.

[Y51] **Remsen Court** (apartments), 120 Chauncey St., bet. Reid (Malcolm X Boulevard) and Stuyvesant Aves., Chauncey and Fulton Sts. 1976. **Tuckett & Thompson**.

Broken brick forms enclose private courtyards; the corner windows are stylish. Like 1660 Fulton Street, across the park, it is a New York State Urban Development Corporation project (UDC) from that heady period in the 1970s when high-quality architecture was being delivered to the outer boroughs.

[Y52] **352-356 Decatur Street** (row houses), bet. Stuyvesant Ave. and Malcolm X Blvd. 1880s.

Victorian Baroque, the cornices punctuating the streetfront with a jack-in-the-box routine.

[Y53] **366 Decatur Street** (tenement), SW cor. Malcolm X Blvd. 1890s.

Triangular (in plan) bay windows extend like prows into Decatur Street, social observation points for those staying at home.

[Y54] **417-421 Decatur Street**, bet. Malcolm X Blvd. and Patchen Ave. 1880s.

Brick and bownstone, some painted, but all coiffed with cornices that surge forward, then hang back, a horizontal version of the Victorian Baroque acrobatics seen at 352-356 Decatur above.

[Y55] **Union Baptist Church**, 461 Decatur St., bet. Patchen and Ralph Aves. 1880s.

An eclectic mélange of Renaissance forms, in exaggerated juxtapositions, that may keep your eyes nimble. Yelllow brick, limestone, terra-cotta, and sheet metal (cornices) join in this local extravaganza.

Y56

[Y56] **587-611 Decatur Street**, bet. Howard and Saratoga Aves. N side. 1891. **J. Mason Kirby**.

Pyramids and arches punctuate this picturesque group of lowscaled row houses built of assorted varieties of brick and stone.

[Y57] **Saratoga Park**, bet. Halsey and Macon Sts., Saratoga and Howard Aves.

A lovely Bloomsbury-scaled park surrounded by appropriate row houses—none distinguished, but all pleasant.

[Y58] **Modern Row Housing**, bet. Hancock St., Jefferson, Saratoga and Howard Aves. 1990s.

An attempt at row housing in scale with Bed-Stuy's history: 3 stories, corniced, and with varying arched and pitched entry lobbies.

Y58

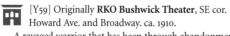

[Y59] Originally **RKO Bushwick Theater**, SE cor. Howard Ave. and Broadway. ca. 1910.

A ravaged warrior that has been through abandonment and fire; nevertheless, Egyptian goddesses crown lavish and fantastic white-glazed terra-cotta oculi that are simultaneously embraced by giant cupids. The circular pediments abound with masks, swags, and festoons.

[Y60] **Engine Co. 233, Ladder Co. 176, N.Y.C. Fire Department**, Rockaway Ave. NE cor. Chauncey St. 1985. **Eisenman/Robertson**.

Contrapuntal geometry in gray and white block tile and metal panels that might have been from the Paris Exposition of 1925. The second-floor structural expression has been crudely filled in by others, and lack of maintenance has taken a heavy toll. Firemen philistines?

[Y61] **Public School No. 73**, Brooklyn, 241 MacDougal St., NE cor. Rockaway Ave. 1888. Addition, 1895. Both by **James W. Naughton**. 🍎

Robust Romanesque Revival in brick, terra-cotta, and limestone. A gem of a façade.

Y62

[Y62] **Junior Academy**/originally Public School 26, Brooklyn, 856 Quincy St., bet. Patchen and Ralph Aves. S side. 1891. **James W. Naughton**.

Romanesque Revival brick and terra-cotta with a series of gables that give a serrated silhouette. Sturdy brick colonnettes at the second floor support rock-face lintels; their third-floor companions bear arches.

Y63

[Y63] Originally **St. John's College and Church**, Lewis Ave. bet. Hart St. and Willoughby Ave. E side. 1870. **Patrick Charles Keely**.

The church behind the college building is rough-cut brownstone ashlar, a vigorous Renaissance Revival bulk.

[Y64] **319 Broadway** (tenement), bet. Lewis and Stuyvesant Aves. 1890s.

Mildly bellying bays decorated with Gothic detail over a Romano-Gothic base. A unique tenement.

[Y65] **Antioch Baptist Church**/originally Greene Avenue Baptist Church and Church House, 828 and 826 Greene Ave., bet. Stuyvesant and Lewis Aves. Church, 1887-1892. **Lansing C. Holden** and **Paul F. Higgs**. Church House, 1891-1893. **Langston & Dahlander**. 🍎

Y65

Romananesque Revival/Queen Anne that snuggles into the midblock cityscape, providing a flock of exoticisms for its pastoral flock.

[Y66] **Ebenezer Gospel Tabernacle**, 470 Throop Ave., bet. Gates Ave. and Quincy St. W side. 1891.

A lusty and miniature Romanesque Revival gem.

Y66

CROWN HEIGHTS

The name Crown Heights is applied to the area east of Washington Avenue between Atlantic Avenue on the north, Empire Boulevard on the south, and East New York Avenue on the east. Included is the handsome portion surrounding Grant Square at Bedford Avenue and Bergen Street that was originally the center of Bedford; that community's southern boundary is now considered Atlantic Avenue.

Crown Heights, the 19th-century Crow Hill, actually includes a succession of hills south of Eastern Parkway. The old designation derisively recalls the black colony of Weeksville along the former Hunterfly Road, with extant buildings now both preserved and restored. Another old thoroughfare is Clove Road, once a 2-mile, north-south link from the village of Bedford to Flatbush, dating from 1662. Only a block of Clove Road remains, above Empire Boulevard east of Nostrand Avenue.

The community has been in transition for a generation with, in sectors, an original Jewish population first declining, then reinforced, by a reinfusion of the Orthodox. Many West Indian immigrants reside in the area, with Haitian French and British English often heard in the streets.

Frank H. Taylor wrote early in the 20th century: "In the heart of the St. Mark's section are located many beautiful mansions, products of the master hand of the architect, the artist, and the modern mechanic. These beautiful homes are seldom offered for sale. They are cherished as homes and will probably pass from one generation to another, fine demonstrations of the great confidence our wealthy men have in the stability of Brooklyn."

W2

[W1] **Crown Heights North area**, from Rogers Ave. at Grant Sq., along a line between Pacific and Dean Sts. to Albany Ave.; then along a line down to St. John's Place, and back to Grant Sq.

This was an enclave of Brooklyn wealth equal to its peers in Brooklyn Heights, Clinton Hill, and Bedford. The vagaries of social change exiled many Brooklynites to Manhattan after the consolidation of 1898, but a vast reservoir of luscious architecture was left behind. This is an obvious candidate for historic district designation, but politics may stand in its way.

[W2] **23rd Regiment Armory, New York National Guard**, 1322 Bedford Ave., bet. Atlantic Ave. and Pacific St. W side. 1891-1895. **Fowler & Hough** and **Isaac Perry**.

With its eight great round towers, one soaring over its peers, and arched entry complete with portcullis, this crenellated brick-and-brownstone "fortress" for the National Guard lacks only a moat to be out of King Arthur's realm.

W3

[W3] Formerly **Medical Society of the County of Kings**, 1313 Bedford Ave., bet. Atlantic Ave. and Pacific St. E side. 1903. **D. Everett Waid and R. M. Cranford.**

CROWN HEIGHTS DISTRICT (NORTH AREA)
see pages 740-743

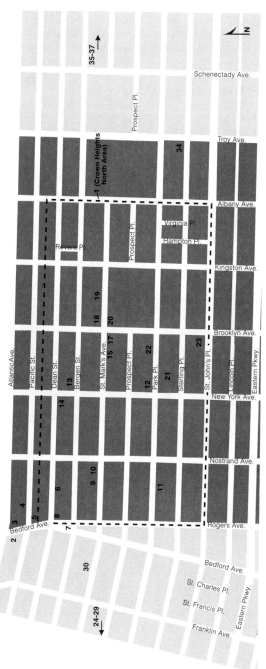

A neo-Regency play written in a Georgian vocabulary. To a future archaeologist, its tiered Tuscan and Ionic columns could seem to be a 1980s Post Modern arrangement of the 18th century.

[W4] **St. Bartholomew's Episcopal Church**, 1227 Pacific St., bet. Bedford and Nostrand Aves. N side. 1886-1890. **George P. Chappell**. 🌿

A charming and romantic place: squat and friendly, with stone and brick, and trimmed in terra-cotta. The tower is crowned with "fish scales," imbricated tiles in a sinuous profile. All in a bosky bower with a Hansel and Gretel manse.

W4

W5

W8

W9

W11

W12

W14

[W5] **Imperial Apartments**, 1198 Pacific St., SE cor. and 1327-1339 Bedford Ave. 1892. **Montrose W. Morris.**

Erected on an imperial scale, with great paired Corinthian terra-cotta columns and arches along both Pacific Street and Bedford Avenue. Advertised in their time as "elegant and well conducted" and "in the fashionable part of Bedford," the immense apartments have since been subdivided. It has many similarities with Morris's Alhambra Apartments on Nostrand Avenue.

[W6] **1164-1182 Dean Street**, bet. Bedford and Nostrand Aves. S side. 1890. **George P. Chappell**.

Ten lovingly maintained Queen Anne houses in a mélange of brick, limestone, terra-cotta, wooden shingles, and Spanish tile, with alternating stepped, peaked, and domed gables. Their new color schemes are perhaps too colorful.

[W7] **Ulysses S. Grant Statue**, Grant Sq. at Dean St. and Bedford Ave. 1896. **William Ordway Partridge**, sculptor.

A youthful Grant bestrides his charger in this amorphous square.

[W8] **Bhraggs Grant Square Senior Citizens' Center**/formerly Union League Club of Brooklyn, Bedford Ave. SE cor. Dean St. 1890. **P. J. Lauritzen**.

Once Brooklyn's most resplendent club, built to serve the social needs of Republican party stalwarts of Bedford, of which this area was considered a central part. Brownstone Richardsonian Romanesque arches support an eclectic body above; note Lincoln and Grant in the arches' spandrels and the monumental American eagle supporting the great bay window.

[W9] **671 and 673 St. Mark's Avenue**, bet. Rogers and Nostrand Aves. N side. 1888. **E. G. W. Dietrick.**

Black Forest Queen Anne: an eccentric adventure that continues the experimental vitality of St. Mark's Place, where a whole history of 19th-century experimentation will greet you. Paint stripping would reveal the brick and limestone reality masked with too much mascara.

[W10] **675 and 677 St. Mark's Avenue**, bet. Rogers and Nostrand Aves. N side. ca. 1890.

Romanesque Revival in Roman brick from the Chicago School. The flush brick arches and lintels show a subtle hand.

[W11] **MAHANAIM, Eglise Adventiste**/formerly Ancient Divine Theological Baptist Church, 814 Park Place, bet. Rogers and Nostrand Aves. S side. ca. 1890.

A neo-Flemish brick church with a stepped gable.

[W12] **919 Park Place** (apartments), NE cor. New York Ave. 1940s.

Two-tone brick and corner windows combine with the strong forms of solid parapeted balconies to create an elegant Art Moderne/Modernist apartment house.

[W13] **Union United Methodist Church**/originally New York Avenue Methodist Church, 121 New York Ave., bet. Bergen and Dean Sts. E side. 1892. **J. C. Cady & Co.**

A powerful smooth and rounded Romanesque Revival red brick and red sandstone monolith. The subtle transitions between brick and molded clay give it a special and powerful dignity.

[W14] **Hebron French-Speaking Seventh-Day Adventist Church**/originally First Church of Christ, Scientist, New York Ave. SW cor. Dean St., 1909. **Henry Ives Cobb.**

An octagonal eclectic building, torn between the Romanesque and the Classical Revival of the 1893 Chicago

World's Fair. Note the rare, flat terra-cotta shingles (as opposed
to Spanish or Roman terra-cotta tiles more commonly used).

[W15] **Marcus Garvey Nursing Home**, 810 St. Mark's Ave., bet.
New York and Brooklyn Aves. S side. 1977. **William N. Breger &
Assocs**.

A simple form of terra-cotta-colored brick, well detailed,
that replaces three major mansions, including that of Abraham
Abraham, cofounder of Abraham & Straus (A&S).

W17

*Abraham Abraham was first a partner in Wechsler and
Abraham, the forerunner of Abraham & Straus, once Brooklyn's
very own department store (the Fulton Mall main store is now a
Macy's). Among his many philanthropic accomplishments was the
founding of Brooklyn Jewish Hospital, built in 1894 as Memorial
Hospital for Women and Children. His son-in-law* **Edward Blum**
and grand-son-in-law **Robert A. M. Blum** *carried on both the
business and the philanthropic tradition. In the 1960s the latter
Blum was board chairman of both Abraham & Straus and the
Brooklyn Institute of Arts and Sciences.*

[W17] **828-836 St. Marks Avenue**, bet. New York and Brooklyn
Aves. S side. ca. 1914.

Five small fussy neo-Georgian houses. Their suburban front
yards related to the ex-mansions that were replaced by the nursing home next door.

[W18] **St. Louis Senior Citizens' Center**/originally Dean Sage
House, 839 St. Marks Ave., NE cor. Brooklyn Ave. 1869. Russell
Sturgis.

Stolid rock-face brownstone Romanesque Revival. Sturgis
was more noted as a critic and writer, and was author of the
magnificent 1902 *Dictionary of Architecture*.

[W19] **855 and 857 St. Mark's Avenue**, bet. Brooklyn and
Kingston Aves. N side. 1892. **Montrose W. Morris**.

An eclectic Romanesque Revival brick and limestone twin-
mansion, with an elegant corner tower capped by a belled cupola.

[W20] **Brooklyn Children's Museum**, Brower Park,
entrance at SE cor. of Brooklyn Ave. and St. Mark's Ave.
1976. **Hardy Holzman Pfeiffer Assocs**. 718-735-4400.
Wed-Fri, 2-5; Sat, Sun, Hol, 12-5; closed Mon-Tues.

Earth- and metalworks worthy of a missile-launching station and festooned with the architecture of movement. Highway
signs and an entrance through a transit kiosk lead into the bowels tunneled within the bermed earth mounds. The structure is
analogous to an iceberg: the pinnacle visible from outside gives
few signals of the wonders within. Have a child bring you here.

W20

*Lost mansions: The 1976 Brooklyn Children's Museum replaces
the original, organized in 1899, which occupied two Victorian
mansions on this site: the L. C. Smith (typewriter) House, an
Italianate villa of the 1890s; and the Adams House of 1867, the low
mansarded home of historian James Truslow Adams.*

W22

[W21] Originally **Brooklyn Methodist Church Home**, 920 Park
Place, bet. Brooklyn and New York Aves. S side. 1889. **Mercein
Thomas**.

It has the look of an asylum in its literal sense: a place of
refuge for the indigent. Victorian brick with appropriate
Victorian planting.

[W22] **979 Park Place** (house), bet. Brooklyn and New
York Aves. N side. 1888. **George P. Chappell**.

This could well be a prototypical model for **Vincent Scully**'s
great 1955 book *The Shingle Style*. With its projections, reces-
sions, bay windows, and porches, it is an essay in American

W23

"neo-mediaevalism," although the Middle Ages never enjoyed such middle-class grandeur.

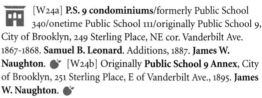 [W23] **St. Gregory's Roman Catholic Church**, 224 Brooklyn Ave., NW cor. St John's Place. 1915. **Frank J. Helmle**.

In brick, limestone, and terra-cotta, this is Roman revival, remembering early Christian churches and the very idea of a basilica. Its inspiration might well have been San Paolo Fuori le Mura in Rome.

Further afield:

W24a

[W24a] **P.S. 9 condominiums**/formerly Public School 340/onetime Public School 111/originally Public School 9, City of Brooklyn, 249 Sterling Place, NE cor. Vanderbilt Ave. 1867-1868. **Samuel B. Leonard**. Additions, 1887. **James W. Naughton**. [W24b] Originally **Public School 9 Annex**, City of Brooklyn, 251 Sterling Place, E of Vanderbilt Ave., 1895. **James W. Naughton**.

A brownstone, terra-cotta, and brick Renaissance Revival school with an infusion of some Romanesque Revival detail . . . such was the course of eclecticism in the 1890s. Grand Corinthian pilasters march around the third and fourth floors. Beautifully restored as condominiums, a dozen years ago it was almost lost.

[W25] **Police Precinct**, NE cor. Park Place and Grand St. 1890s.

Much altered, but the arch at the entry springs from the original rock-face granite.

W27

[W26] Originally **Knox Hat Factory**, 369-413 St. Marks Ave., NE cor. Grand Ave. ca. 1890.

An increasingly hatless male population spelled the doom of one of Brooklyn's once flourishing industries. The grand Manhattan headquarters of Knox are incorporated into the Republic National Bank complex across from the Public Library.

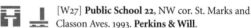 [W27] **Public School 22**, NW cor. St. Marks and Classon Aves. 1993. **Perkins & Will**.

Some classy retro-Art Moderne; the yellow brick and black steel seem reminiscent of a 1940s Word's Fair.

W28

[W28] **Nursing Home, Jewish Hospital Medical Center of Brooklyn**, Classon Ave. bet. Prospect and Park Places. 1977. **Puchall & Assocs**. and **Herbert Cohen**.

An unabashed Modernist in brown brick. Its cantilevered corners and sleek detailing bring back memories of the Bauhaus (the radical German school of architecture and the arts closed down by Hitler).

[W29] **St. Theresa** (Roman Catholic Church), NE cor. Classon and Sterling Aves. 1890s.

Central European towers with bell-like caps anchor the west end of this neighborhood church.

W29

[W30] **651-675 St. Marks Avenue** (row houses), bet. Franklin and Bedford Aves. N side. 1880s.

Simple two-story and basement, brick and limestone buildings, punctuated by a triangular and circular gables. Charming.

[W31] **49-57 Crown Street**, NW cor. Franklin Ave., near the Botanic Garden. 1976.

This slender tower is a dominant silhouette looming over the Botanic Garden.

W30

[W32] **42nd Supply and Transport Battalion, New York National Guard**/originally Troop C Armory, 1579 Bedford Ave., bet. President and Union Sts. E side. 1908. **Pilcher, Thomas & Tachau**.

The last stand of the cavalry and a mighty fortress to this day. The great arched roof, silhouetted on the outside, is a tribute to the principles of mid-Victorian train sheds, still prolific in European capitals.

[W33] **1035-1079 Carroll Street** (row houses), bet. Bedford and Rogers Aves. 1920s.

Hooded houses that might have been conceived as urban chalets.

W32

[W34] **Public School 390**, Brooklyn, The Maggie Walker School, Sterling Place, NW cor. Troy Ave. 1977. **Giorgio Cavaglieri**.

A highly articulated modern classroom building.

[W35] **Weeksville Houses**/also known as Hunterfly Road Houses, along old Hunterfly Road, 1698-1708 Bergen St., near St. Mary's Place, bet. Buffalo and Rochester Aves. Restored, 1990s. **Li-Saltzman**. ☙

Four simple wood houses occupied by **James Weeks** and friends (free black men) between 1830 and 1870. The architecture, in painted clapboard, is that of the 19th-century common man. It is the city's oldest black residential landmark.

W34

*Black history, and the architecture blacks inhabited in New York and Brooklyn, has received little attention. Bedford-Stuyvesant, for example, was an upper middle-class white enclave before migrations out and in. The preservation of the **Weeksville Houses** is a minor beginning to repair this oversight.*

[W36] **Berea Baptist Church**, Bergen St. bet. Utica and Rochester Aves. N side. 1894.

A charming, castellated neo-Romanesque place.

W36

[W37] **Intermediate School 55**, Brooklyn, The Ocean Hill Intermediate School, Bergen and Dean Sts., Hopkinson and Rockaway Aves. 1968. **Curtis & Davis**.

A grim, "fortified" place of brown brick with narrow slit windows. Its edge against the sky simulates crenellations.

[W38] **Crown Gardens** (apartments), Nostrand Ave. bet. President and Carroll Sts. E side. 1971. **Richard Kaplan**. **Stevens, Bertin, O'Connell & Harvey**, associate architects.

A modest slab shares a courtyard with 3 quadrants of stacked town houses. Here brown brick and exposed concrete present one of the neighborhood's most urbane blocks. There is a rhythmic display of balconies and stair towers in counterpoint.

W38

Another closely packed precinct with many blocks of urbane interest:

[W39] **Crown Heights South area**, generally including President and Union Sts., bet. New York and Troy Aves., and Carroll St. from New York Ave. to Albany Ave. Mostly 1910-1930.

Eleven blocks of rich row, semidetached, and freestanding houses, inhabited by black and Hasidic Jewish families, who developed a guarded relationship after initial friction. A prime area for consideration as a landmark district.

[W40] **1361-1381 Union Street** (houses), bet. New York and Brooklyn Aves. N side. 1912. **Axel Hedman**.

An eccentric neo-Renaissance row of bowed and bayed limestone fronts. They are crowned with curious geometric parapets above their modillioned cornices: triangular, semicircular, rectilinear.

[W41] **1485-1529 Union Street** (houses), bet. Kingston and Albany Aves. N side. 1909. **F. L. Hine**.

Alternating bow and bay windows modulate the streetfront. Note the friezes between the first and second floors and under the cornice.

W41

CROWN HEIGHTS DISTRICT (SOUTH AREA)

see pages 745-747

W43

[W42] **1476-1506 Union Street** (houses), bet. Kingston and Albany Aves. S side. 1909. **Harry Albertson.**

A more exuberant set than those across the street, these are alternately crowned with conical and pyramidal hats, to match their bowed and bayed windows below.

[W43] **1483-1491 President Street** (houses), bet. Kingston and Albany Aves. N side. 1913. **J. L. Brush.**

The whole façade presents a bow in these English basement (i.e., stoop-less) brownstone houses.

[W44] **1401-1425 Carroll Street** (houses), bet. Kingston and
Albany Aves. N side. 1913. **J. L. Brush**.
  Similar to Nos. 1483-1491 but with small stoops.

 [W45] **1311A-1337 Carroll Street** (houses), bet. Brooklyn
and Kingston Aves. N side. 1913. **Slee & Bryson**.
  A Federal Revival brick row with crisp white trim, strangely
crowned with eclectic slate mansard roofs. The bay windows
pleasantly modulate the street.

W45

[W46] **1294 President Street** (house), bet. New York and
Brooklyn Aves. S side. 1911. **William Debus**.
  This double house is on the imposing scale of an English
Renaissance palace.

[W47] **1281 President Street** (house), bet. New York and
Brooklyn Aves. N side. ca. 1900.
  A squat round tower with a conical tiled cupola makes this
ordinary house into something special.

W47

 [W48] **1319 President Street** (house), bet. New York and
Brooklyn Aves. N side. 1930. **H. T. Jeffrey**.
  Mock Tudor, complete with small, leaded panes, an asymmetrical composition playing the gabled bay against a pair of
decorated brick chimneys.

[W49] **1362 President Street** (house), bet. Brooklyn and
Kingston Aves. S side. 1921. **Cohn Brothers**.
  A florid and showy intruder into these mostly modest and
serene surroundings. The vocabulary comes from a smorgasbord of French Renaissance ingredients.

[W50] **1337 President Street** (house), NE cor. Brooklyn
Ave. ca. 1900.
  A neo-Georgian vocabulary clads an Italianate flat-roofed
form in this turn-of-the-century eclecticism.

W50

Colonial

*Georgian/
Federal*

*Greek
Revival*

*Gothic
Revival*

Villa

*Romanesque
Revival*

*Renaissance
Revival*

*Roman
Revival*

*Art Deco/
Art Moderne*

*Modern/
Post-Modern*

BUSHWICK-RIDGEWOOD
WILLIAMSBURG • GREENPOINT

Town of Bushwick/Boswijck-"Wooded District"
Established as a town in 1660; Town of Williamsburg separated
from in 1840; annexed to the City of Brooklyn in 1855.

This area, including the three communities of Bushwick-
Ridgewood, Williamsburg, and Greenpoint, was often referred
to as the Eastern District after the merger of 1855, to distinguish
it from the original area of the City of Brooklyn, the "Western."
In general, the term has fallen into disuse except in connection
with the names of a local high school and a freight terminal
(with some logic, as the Eastern District is now the northern tip
of Brooklyn, and South Brooklyn is, in fact, at Greater
Brooklyn's northwest corner).

Much of this part of Brooklyn is devoted to working-class
residential areas clustered between industrial concentrations
strung along the East River and Newtown Creek. It is in this
precinct that many fortunes were made in sugar, oil, rope, lumber, shipbuilding, brewing, and glue.

BUSHWICK-RIDGEWOOD

Malt and hops, barley and barrels, beer and ale. **Obermeyer** and
Liebmann, **Ernest Ochs**, **Claus Lipsius**, **Danenberg** and **Coles**.
The history of Bushwick has been the history of brewing. Beer
came to Bushwick in the middle of the 19th century when a
large German population emigrated here, some after unsuccessful uprisings in the Fatherland in 1848 and 1849, most because
of poverty and lack of opportunity.

In its early years the community was noted largely for farming, the produce being sold locally as well as ferried to
Manhattan's markets. By the 1840s **Peter Cooper** had moved his
glue factory here, since land values in Manhattan's Murray Hill
had risen so sharply that an odoriferous glue factory was no
longer of economic sense there. Cooper, always a shrewd businessman, chose this undeveloped area of Brooklyn near main
roads connecting the ferries to New York with the farms on
Long Island. His site is that of Cooper Park Houses, a low-rent
housing project. It is named after the adjacent park given to the
City of Brooklyn in 1895 by the Cooper family.

[B1] **Arion Mansions**/originally Arion Hall (catering hall), 13
Arion Place, bet. Bushwick Ave. and Broadway. E side. 1887.

Once, rich embellishment encrusted this hall, redolent of
those days when the Arion Männerchor, the Eastern District's
leading German singing society, met here. Now a dilapidated
relic searching for a new lease on life.

B1

*Bushwick Avenue once contained 20 blocks of impeccable and stol-
id mansions, freestanding (in contrast to Brooklyn Heights) town
palaces advertising the wealth and taste of local industrial magnates. Originally a gloomy set of Victorian buildings, they nevertheless revealed the spirit of their times: wealth was a burden, and
the owners' moral duty to uplift the masses was somberly fulfilled
through dour stonework. Several of the more glorious places have
burned, most tragically the Old Bushwick Democratic Club, at the
northwest corner of Bushwick Avenue and Hart Street, perhaps
the greatest single piece of architecture Bushwick ever knew (see
Necrology).*

BUSHWICK-RIDGEWOOD DISTRICT
see pages 748-751

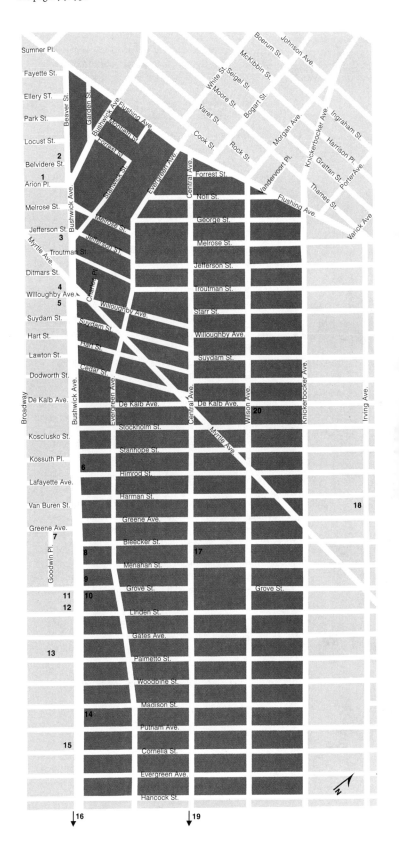

B2

[B2] Formerly **Vicelius & Ulmer's Continental Lagerbier Brewery**/later **William Ulmer Brewery**, Beaver St. bet. Locust and Belvidere Sts. SW side. 1872.

A sad and ghostly remnant of a brick brewery complex. Ulmer's mansion was on Bushwick Avenue a few blocks east.

[B3] **St. Mark's Lutheran Church and School**/originally St. Mark's Evangelical Lutheran German Church, 626 Bushwick Ave., SW cor. Jefferson St. 1892.

The verdigris-clad copper-sheathed spire dominates Bushwick Avenue for most of its length. Up close, there is glorious Victorian Gothic brick and terra-cotta trim.

B3

[B4] Originally **William Ulmer House**, 670 Bushwick Ave., SW cor. Willoughby Ave. ca. 1885.

A stolid, once solid, Romanesque Revival brick fortress, as befits a stolid, solid brewer. **Dr. Frederick A. Cook**, a later owner, was a well-known but ill-heralded Arctic explorer. He claimed to have discovered the North Pole but lost in court to the navy: Admiral **Robert E. Peary**. Now abandoned after a stint as a clinic.

[B5] Originally **Mrs. Catherine Lipsius House**, 680 Bushwick Ave., SE cor. Willoughby Ave. ca. 1886. **Theobald Engelhardt**.

A brewer's widow commissioned this strangely proportioned Italianate Revival house. Fenced in and ravaged, the porch is on the verge of collapsing. Note the windows in the frieze.

B4

[B6] **South Bushwick Reformed Church**, 855-867 Bushwick Ave., NW cor. Himrod St. 1853. **Messrs. Morgan**. Chapel and Sunday School, 1881. **J. J. Buck**. 🌿

A New England outpost in these dour streets: late Greek Revival with imposing Ionic columns. A vanishing congregation and hence religious poverty allowed paint to peel and wood to rot, scarring this elegant anachronism, with its delicate clapboard and purple and white milk glass.

The street is the namesake of the first minister, **John Himrod**.

B6

[B7] **1080 Greene Avenue** (house), NE cor. Goodwin Place.

Mustard-yellow and red trim are traces of the original polychromy on the exuberant (Goodwin Place) bay window. There are lunettes in the frieze, Tuscan columns below. It is said to have belonged to the founder of the "Bohack's" grocery chain.

[B8] Originally **John F. Hylan House**, 959 Bushwick Ave., bet. Bleeker and Menahan Sts. N side. 1885. **John E. Dwyer**.

One in a row of unpretentious brownstones (Nos. 945-965), noted principally because it was the home of "Red Mike," mayor of New York from 1918 to 1925.

B8

[B9] Originally **Gustav Doerschuck House**, 999 Bushwick Ave., NW cor. Grove St. ca. 1890.

A towered Romanesque Revival brewer's mansion, in brick and rock-face granite.

[B10] Originally **Charles Lindemann House**, 1001 Bushwick Ave., NE cor. Grove St. ca. 1890.

A Shingle Style loner, turreted, porched, dormered, and recently restored to much of its original splendor. How about the original natural materials instead of white paint?

[B11] Onetime **Arion Singing Society**/originally Louis Bossert House, 1002 Bushwick Ave., SE cor. Grove St. 1887. **Theobald Engelhardt**.

B10

A dour red-brick box crowned with a mansarded slate roof presents Gothic bracketed dormers to the street. Bossert was a successful millwork manufacturer who later built Brooklyn Heights' Bossert Hotel.

Grove Street owes its name to Boulevard Grove, a park at the intersection of that street with Bushwick Avenue. Picnics were held there as early as 1863.

[B12] **1020 Bushwick Avenue** (houses), SW cor. Linden St., and 37-53 Linden Street, bet. Bushwick Ave. and Broadway. W side ca. 1885.

Richly decorated Queen Anne brick and terra-cotta town houses. The corner house is special, enriched with a cast-iron crenellated mansard roof. These dark-red monoliths bear superb friezes: brow and waist. The wrought ironwork on the Linden Street stoops is magnificent.

B14

[B13] **Ridgewood Bushwick Community Youth Center**, Gates Ave. and Palmetto St. 2001. **Kevin Hom + Andrew Goldman**.

Things to come. This was bid in the summer of 1999. What will be there by 2000?

[B14] **Bushwick Avenue Central Methodist Episcopal Church**, 1130 Bushwick Ave., NE cor. Madison St. 1886-1912.

The octagonal Renaissance Revival tower is a local landmark, in polytonal red sandstone and gray brick.

B16

[B15] **Bethesda Baptist Church**/formerly Bushwick Avenue Congregational Church, 1160 Bushwick Ave., SW cor. Cornelia St. 1896. **Fowler & Hough**.

A powerful campanile corners this handsome brick church, but the open belfry has been bricked in, destroying its original elegance. Note the Renaissance Revival brownstone and brick parish house next door.

[B16] **1278 Bushwick Avenue** (house), bet. Halsey and Eldert Sts., N side. ca. 1880.

One of a group of simple, articulated brick row houses, corniced with a Renaissance profile in sheet metal.

B17

[B17] **St. Barbara's Roman Catholic Church**, Central Ave. NE cor. Bleeker St. 1910. **Helme & Huberty**.

Gleaming white and cream Spanish Baroque. The towers are wedding-cake icing: edible. Built to serve a parish at first German, then Italian, and now largely Hispanic. Named not only for the saint but for Barbara Eppig, whose father, brewer Leonard Eppig, was a major contributor to its construction.

[B18] **Public School 86**/also known as the Irvington School, 220 Irving Ave., bet. Harman St. and Greene Ave. 1892-1893. **James W. Naughton**. 🖊

Romanesque Revival in painted brick and rockface granite.

B18

[B19] **Engine Company 252**/originally Fire Engine Co. 52/later Engine Co. 152, 617 Central Ave. 1896-1897. **Parfitt Brothers**. 🖊

Whimsical Flemish Revival, the stepped and curling gable crowning a brick and terra-cotta façade.

[B20] **83rd Precinct, N.Y.C. Police Department**/originally 20th Precinct, Brooklyn Police Station House and Stable, 179 Wilson Ave., NE cor. DeKalb Ave. 1894-1895. **William B. Tubby**. 🖊 Restored, 1996. **Ehrenkrantz & Eckstut**.

Powerful Romanesque Revival, crenellated, machicolated, with a columned porch bearing incised Sullivanesque ornament. At its dedication the commissioner of the Brooklyn Department of Police and Excise declared it to be "commodious, architecturally ornate, and thoroughly equipped . . . the handsomest and most convenient police office in the world." The exaggeration is forgivable, for it is an architecturally distinguished station house. *Kojak* was filmed against this exterior background. Its renewal restores much of its lusty beginnings.

B20

WILLIAMSBURG

Right! Without the final "h," even though the Williamsburgh Savings Bank spells its name the old way (the "h" fell when it consolidated with the City of Brooklyn in 1855).

Though it shares its current spelling with the well-known restoration in Virginia, the resemblance ends there. This Williamsburg, formerly part of the Town of Bushwick, later a village and city in its own right, was named after Col. **Jonathan Williams**, its surveyor and grandnephew of **Benjamin Franklin**. **Richard M. Woodhull** started the community when he purchased thirteen acres of land at the foot of today's South 2nd Street, in 1802. He commissioned Williams to survey it, established a ferry to New York (Manhattan), and quickly went bankrupt (1811).

Thomas Morrell and **James Hazard** picked up where Woodhull had left off. They also established a ferry, this time to the Grand Street Market at Corlear's Hook, providing an outlet for the farmers of Bushwick to sell their produce in New York. The impetus to the area's growth, however, was the establishment of a distillery in 1819. The distillery is gone (as is the Schaefer brewery that followed it on the same site). Booze and beer helped build Williamsburg but now are only drunk here, not distilled or brewed.

The most telling impact on the community came from the opening of the Williamsburg Bridge in 1903. Overnight the community changed from a fashionable resort with hotels catering to such sportsmen as **Commodore Vanderbilt**, **Jim Fisk**, and **William C. Whitney** to an immigrant district absorbing the overflow from New York's Lower East Side. (The *New York Tribune* of the period characterized the bridge as "The Jews' Highway.") Its elegant families moved away, and its mansions and handsome brownstones from the post–Civil War era fell into disuse and then were converted to multiple dwellings.

W1

Bedford Avenue: The sequence is north, with the direction of traffic; the house numbers decrease as we proceed.

[W1] **667-677 Bedford Avenue**, bet. Heyward and Rutledge Sts. E side.

An entire blockfront of tenements magnificently encrusted with stone: rock-face and smooth, brown, tan, and gray. Architecture for the people follows here in the steps of the grander and more monumental mansions further north. Granite colonnettes with Byzantine capitals.

W2

[W2] **Beth Jacob School**/formerly Public School 71, Brooklyn/sometime United Talmudic Academy, 125 Heyward St., bet. Lee and Bedford Aves. N side. 1888-1889. **James W. Naughton.**

From **Napoléon III**'s Second Empire: a mansarded central block over brick and brownstone: an admiring follower of Lefuel and Visconti's Louvre.

W3

[W3] **Williamsburg Christian Church**, Lee Ave. SE cor. Keap St., adjoining the Brooklyn-Queens Expressway. ca. 1885.

A superarched brick outpost maintains Christianity in this now mostly Orthodox Jewish land.

Hasidic community: Along Bedford Avenue are arrayed a group of brownstones, mansions, and apartment houses such as described above: one of New York's most concentrated Hasidic (Jewish) communities. This unique settlement of the Satmarer Hasidim, recalling late medieval Jewish life in dress and customs, is a result of persecution of the Eastern European Jewish community during World War II. In 1946, Rebbe Joel Teitelbaum and

*several of his flock reached these shores and chose Williamsburg—
even then a heavily Orthodox area—as their home. At the end of
the war, the remaining survivors from Poland and Hungary
migrated to the new settlement and reestablished their lives there.
As the community grew, parts of it split off and moved to other
parts of Brooklyn and to the suburbs. Beards and uncut earlocks
identify the men; shaved but wigged heads identify the women.
Long frock coats and skullcaps are in evidence everywhere among
its male population, young and old; and in the winter, the fur-
trimmed hat, the shtreiml, is certain to make its appearance.
Evidence of its residents' heritage is everywhere apparent, from the
proliferation of Hebrew signs on the mansions to the identification
of small business establishments catering to the group.*

[W4] **Rutledge Street**, bet. Lee and Marcy Aves. N side.
One of Williamsburg's loveliest streets. This block is redolent
of Brooklyn Heights.

[W5] **17th Corps Artillery Armory**/formerly 47th
Regiment Armory/originally Union Grounds, Marcy to
Harrison Aves., Heyward to Lynch Sts. 1883.

W4

The Harrison Avenue end is a squat fort: double clerestoried, with crenellated and machicolated corner towers. The
Union Grounds were the site of early baseball games in the
1860s, between the Cincinnati Red Stockings, the Philadelphia
Athletics, the New York Mutuals, and the Brooklyn Eckfords.

[W6] **Primary School 380, Brooklyn, The John Wayne
Elementary School**, Marcy Ave. bet. Lynch and
Middleton Sts. 1977. **Richard Dattner & Assocs.**

A somber Pompeian-red brick construction, formed from
clustered polygons and happily appropriate for this dour and
solid neighborhood. The painted skirt covers graffiti, but the
upper body is the natural brick.

[W7] Formerly **Yeshiva Jesode Hatorah of Adas Yerem**,
571 Bedford Ave., bet. Keap and Rodney Sts. E side.
ca. 1890.

Rock-face brownstone and an obviously affluent client made
this a showplace. The elliptical bay window is elegant; note the
cherubs in the copper frieze, roof finials, and all the rest.

[W8] **Bais Yaskov of Adas Yereim**/formerly Hanover Club/origi-
nally Hawley Mansion, 563 Bedford Ave., SE cor. Rodney St. ca.
1875. Remodeled, 1891. **Lauritzen & Voss.**

W7

Yellow painted brick with brownstone quoins—cast iron
against the sky. But the cornice has been ripped off, and the
window detailing denuded. The other **William Cullen Bryant**
(1849-1905), publisher of the *Brooklyn Times*, was president of
the Hanover Club.

W8

W9

The Tree That Grows in Brooklyn: Williamsburg, a swampy, low-lying area, became the ideal spot for the culture of the ailanthus tree (a tree of fernlike leaves similar to those of the mimosa and locust). First imported from China about 1840, the tree was intended for use as the grazing ground of the cynthia moth's caterpillar, a great, green, purpleheaded, horned monster (¾ inch in diameter, 3 inches long) that spins a cocoon prized for its silk threads. The mills of Paterson, N.J., were to be its beneficiaries. Its grazing role proved uneconomical (the grazing still goes on, however, without cocoon collection), but the tree was believed to have another virtue for the locals: supposedly providing power to dispel the "disease-producing vapors" presumed to come from swampy lands. See Betty Smith's 1943 novel of Williamsburg life, A Tree Grows in Brooklyn.

W11

[W9] **559 Bedford Avenue** (house), NE cor. Rodney St. ca. 1890.

An imposing terra-cotta castle, now minus the conical, Spanish tile crown over its round corner tower. The bay on Bedford Avenue modulates the basic body, and an owl is perched on Rodney's pediment.

 [W10] **Yeshiva Yesoda Hatora of K'Hal Adas Yereim**/formerly Congress Club/originally Frederick Mollenhauer House, 505 Bedford Ave., NE cor. Taylor St. 1896. **Lauritzen & Voss.**

A neo-Renaissance, brick, and sandstone English clublike mansion drawn from Italian palazzo antecedents. Frederick was a son of **John Mollenhauer**, founder of the Mollenhauer Sugar Refinery (1867).

W12

[W11] Formerly the **Rebbe's House**, 500 Bedford Ave., NW cor. Clymer St.

Once the home of Grand Rabbi Josel Teitelbaum (the Rebbe), who led the bulk of the Hasidim from Europe to Williamsburg.

W14

[W12] **Epiphany Roman Catholic Church**/originally New England Congregational Church, 96 S. 9th St. bet. Bedford and Berry Aves. S side.

A Lombardian Romanesque brick church with arched corbel tables, a sturdy tower, and flaking paint.

[W13] **Light of the World Church**/originally New England Congregational Church, 179 S. 9th St., bet. Driggs and Roebling Aves. N side 1852-1853. **Thomas Little.**

A giant super-brownstone in wood, sheet metal, and stone, this Italianate church bears extraordinary console brackets. It was a remarkable architectural tack for Congregational immigrants from New England to take: theirs was for the most part the world of white clapboard and English steeples.

W15

[W14] **396 Berry Street**, NW cor. S. 8th St. ca. 1885.

This smooth terra-cotta and brick warehouse is a monolith of narrow joints and virtuoso brickwork.

[W15] **Smith Building**, NE cor. Bedford Ave. and S. 8th St. 1860s. **Grosvenor Smith.**

Cast-iron elegance, far from the Manhattan districts that honor such construction. And it would be unique, even there; the great arch led to a department store.

W16

[W16] **103 Broadway** (factory), bet. Bedford Ave. and Berry St. N side. ca. 1875.

Graceful cast iron with glassy elliptical bays now contains studio lofts. Note the console brackets that form the visual keystones, and its great Corinthian columns.

[W17] **Fruitcrest Corporation**/formerly Bedford Avenue
Theater, 109 S. 6th St., bet. Berry St. and Wythe Ave. N side. 1891.
W. W. Cole, builder.

Opened by actress Fanny Rice in a farce, *A Jolly Surprise*. Its
history as a theater was brief.

[W18] **H. Fink & Sons Building**/formerly Nassau Trust
Company, 134-136 Broadway, SW cor. Bedford Ave. 1888.
Frank J. Helmle.

Neo-Renaissance limestone and granite.

[W19] **Williamsburg Art and Historical Society**/origi-
nally Kings County Savings Bank, 135 Broadway, NE cor.
Bedford Ave. 1868. **King & Wilcox. William H. Wilcox.**

Bands of smooth and vermiculated Dorchester stone and
slender Ionic and Corinthian columns alternate to enliven the
exterior of the banking floor of this splendid Second Empire
masterpiece. Victorian at its best, even the interior is carefully
preserved, the gaslit chandeliers all present (but wired for electricity). Look at the plaited Indian hut in the entry pediment.

W18

[W20] **Williamsburgh Savings Bank**, 175 Broadway, NW
cor. Driggs Ave. 1870-1875. **George B. Post**. Additions,
1906, 1925. **Helme, Huberty & Hudswell.** Restorations,
1990s. **Platt Byard Dovell**.

The eclectic Victorian crossbreeding of Renaissance and

W20

Roman parts produced one of Brooklyn's great landmarks, particularly to those who pass by train or car over the Williamsburg Bridge. It is a sharp, hard, gray place reminiscent of the work of Brooklyn's own great architect, **Frank Freeman**, at the old, long since demolished, Brooklyn Trust Company (below the dome).

A great Williamsburg restaurant:
   Peter Luger's Steak House, 178 Broadway, bet. Driggs and Bedford Aves.
   *Alfred Hitchcock called its steak the "best in the universe." In this spartan outpost of polished oak and white aprons, far from the habitat of its elegant clientele, steak reigns supreme—all else being decoration or fodder for those who can't contend with greatness. It all began as **Charles Luger**'s Café, Billiards, and Bowling Alley in 1876. Expensive. No credit cards. No vegetarians.*

[W21] **195 Broadway**/originally Sparrow Shoe Factory Warehouse, bet. Driggs Ave. and New St. N side. 1882. **William B. Ditmars**.
   Cast-iron, with exuberant console brackets and fluted, floral-decorated Composite pilasters.

W22

[W22] **Holy Trinity Church of Ukrainian Autocephalic Orthodox Church in Exile**/formerly Williamsburg Trust Company, 117-185 S. 5th St., NW cor. New St. 1906. **Helmle & Huberty**.
   Built as a bank, this opulent terra-cotta monument is now a cathedral, the reverse of the common progression from religious to sectarian use; compare the various churches of Brooklyn Heights and Cobble Hill that are now condominiums. The architecture is the natural result of the World's Columbian Exhibition (1893), the inspiration for the American Renaissance.

W23

[W23] **Washington Plaza**, S. 4th St. to Broadway, New to Havemeyer Sts.
   Formerly the ganglion for half of Brooklyn's trolley empire, the Plaza is now a depot for nondescript buses belching forth diesel fumes between runs. Some of the old sheds and a signal tower remain, but the web of overhead copper wires is now only a memory. Furthermore, the space is cut into pieces by the elevated subway and the Brooklyn-Queens Expressway, which slice through it with abandon. The forecourt for the Ukrainian Cathedral, in the plaza's northwest corner, is formally executed and the only part of the whole deserving of the title "plaza." It contains, among disintegrating Renaissance Revival ornaments, a fine verdigris equestrian statue, **George Washington at Valley Forge** (**Henry M. Shrady**, 1906).

[W24] Formerly **Manufacturers Trust Company**/originally North Side Bank, 33-35 Grand St., bet. Kent and Wythe Aves. N side. 1889. **Theobald Engelhardt**.
   Lusty, gutsy, rock-face Romanesque, arched, cast-iron corniced, wrought iron. A super, lonely building. Don't miss it.

[W25] **American Sugar Refining Company**/formerly Havemeyer and Elder's Sugar Refining Company, 292-350 Kent Avenue, bet. S. 5th and S. 2nd Sts. W side. ca. 1890.
   Between 2nd and 3rd, and again between 4th and 5th, are bulky, bold Romanesque Revival behemoths.

[W26] **Northside Terrace** (row housing), North 3rd St., bet. Bedford and Berry Aves. 1992. **James McCullar & Associates**.
   Steel stoops for three-story brick row houses, corniced and linteled in limestone (or is it concrete?).

[W27] **Iglesia Bautista Calvario**/formerly St. Matthew's First Evangelical Lutheran Church, 197-199 N. 5th St., bet. Roebling St. and Driggs Ave. N side. 1864.
   Battered buttresses flank this brick and glass-blocked

W25

church. The shell survives; the façade has had recent TLC, stripping away the old paint.

[W28] **56-64 Havemeyer Street**/originally Convent of the Order of St. Dominic. 1889. **P. J. Berlenbach**.

A hearty Romanesque Revival institution, now revived as a condominium.

[W29] **Church of the Annunciation** (Roman Catholic), 255 N. 5th St., NE cor. Havemeyer St. 1870. **F. J. Berlenbach, Jr.**

A crisply detailed and lovingly maintained Lombardian Romanesque basilica. Its related convent across the street has been converted (see [W28]).

[W30] **Bnos Yakov of Pupa**/originally Temple Beth Elohim, 274 Keap St., bet. Marcy and Division Aves. S side. 1876.

W30

This Hebrew congregation was the first in Brooklyn, dating from 1851. Ruskinian Gothic polychromy in brick and painted brownstone, terra-cotta, stained glass, and tile. Note the lush ironwork gates.

[W31] **Iglesia Metodista Unida de Sur Tres**/originally South Third Street Methodist Church, 411 S. 3rd St., bet. Union Ave. and Hewes St. N side. 1855.

Simple Lombardian Romanesque, now painted gray.

[W32] **Iglesia Pentecostal Misionera**/originally Deutsche Evangelische St. Peterskirche, 262 Union Ave., NE cor. Scholes St. 1881.

That dour German brickwork now softened in spirit by a Hispanic congregation.

W33

[W33] Formerly **Public School 69**, Brooklyn/originally Colored School No. 3, 270 Union Ave., bet. Scholes and Stagg Sts. E side. 1879-1881. **Samuel B. Leonard.**

An Italian Romanesque miniature for a school in Williamsburg's rural days.

The Fourteen Buildings: The turn Grand Street takes at Union Avenue marks the beginning of the site of the Fourteen Buildings. The street was laid out between Union and Bushwick Avenues so that it would pass through the property of a group of men who then built for themselves a series of Greek Revival frame dwellings in 1836. Each had a dome and a colonnaded porch of fluted wood columns. The houses were arranged one per block on both sides of Grand Street, with two extras slipped in. By 1837 each of the men had suffered the consequences of that year's financial panic, and the houses changed hands. In 1850 all fourteen still remained, but by 1896 only one was left. Today there is no sign on this busy shopping street of that bygone elegance apart from the bend itself.

W34

East Williamsburg:

[W34] **Williamsburg Houses, N.Y.C. Housing Authority**, Maujer to Scholes St., Leonard St. to Bushwick Ave. 1937. Board of Design: **Richmond H. Shreve**, chief architect; with **James F. Bly**, **Matthew W. Del Gaudio**, **Arthur C. Holden**, **William Lescaze**, **Samuel Gardstein**, **Paul Trapani**, **G. Harmon Gurney**, **Harry Leslie Walker**, and **John W. Ingle, Jr.**, associate architects. Restoration and reconstruction, 1999.

The best public housing project ever built in New York but also the first and most expensive (in adjusted dollars). Its 4-story buildings embrace semiprivate spaces for both passive and active recreation. Reinforced concrete and brick infill is punctuated by pedestrian ways that connect sequential courtyards through stepped and columned portals. The apartments themselves are reached without benefit of corridors by an entry system that opens directly off the stair landings (as in Princeton Collegiate Gothic, here in serene modern dress). The new aluminum doublehung windows are a clunky alteration, replacing elegant slender-mullioned, but unhappily deteriorated, steel casements.

Stripped of its original brick, and articulated with blue tiles, the revivified Williamsburg Housing seems a fresh breath of architecture once again.

W36

[W35] **Little Zion Baptist Church**, 98 Scholes St., bet. Leonard St. and Manhattan Ave. S side. 1890s.

Articulated arches with supporting colonnettes in the Romanesque manner; then topped off with a Second Empire hat.

[W36] **174 and 178 Meserole Street**, bet. Graham and Humboldt Aves. S side. ca. 1880s.

Exuberant, painted wood tenements—No. 174 in Queen Anne, No. 178 in Renaissance Revival—two of the city's best. "Tenement" is pejorative today; in fact it describes a walk-up apartment house that covers most of its building site. Here the light in the back rooms is minimal, but the visible architecture is magnificent.

W37

[W37] **182 Graham Avenue** (tenement), SE cor. Meserole Ave. ca. 1885.

Above a sullied ground floor rises a Belle Epoque confection with a curved Second Empire mansard roof and ornate and wondrous details. It's a parody of the elegantly dressed businessperson with scruffy unshined shoes.

[W38] **New York Telephone Company Communications Center**, 55 Meserole St., NE cor. Lorimer Ave. 1975. **John Carl Warnecke & Assocs**.

Stylish and expensive ironspotted brick with gargantuan hooded windows contributing to a powerful and inhuman place for telephone equipment.

W39

[W39] **Holy Trinity Roman Catholic Church**, Montrose Ave. bet. Manhattan and Graham Aves. S side. 1882.

A huge twin-towered reprise of Manhattan's St. Patrick's Cathedral—or perhaps of the Abbaye aux Hommes in Caen.

[W40] Originally **19th Police Precinct Station House and Stable**, 43 Herbert St. and 512-518 Humboldt St. 1891-1892. **George Ingram**.

Romanesque Revival by an architect with a great sense of style. The arched entry in brick and brownstone is magnificent; the bracketed lighting elegant. Check the ironwork overhead.

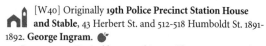

W40

[W41] **492-494 Humboldt Street** bet. Richardson and Herbert Sts. E side., and 201 Richardson Street bet. Humboldt and N. Henry Sts. N side. ca. 1850.

These were severed parts of one of several formerly great Brooklyn colonnade rows; only one still exists: on Willow Place in Brooklyn Heights. Here the decline is not one of abandonment but of cultural desecration: No. 492 has been "improved" downhill, by cladding its natural columns with fluted sheet metal, false shutters, and turgid stone wainscoting. Good intentions have succeeded here only in destroying a bit of architectural heritage.

Colonnade Rows: Only records remain of the least-known of Brooklyn's four colonnade rows, on the east end of Kent Avenue between South 8th and South 9th Streets, in Williamsburg. The last section of this ensemble was destroyed in the 1920s. Among the families who shared the extraordinary views across the river were the **Walls** *and the* **Berrys.** **Dr. Abraham Berry** *became the first mayor of the city of Williamsburgh in 1852.* **William Wall** *became the second—and last—mayor in 1854.*

W42

[W42] **St. Paul's Center**, 484 Humboldt Street, SE cor. Richardson St. ca. 1885.

Iron-spotted bricks and Romanesque Revival arches.

[W43] **Woodhull Medical and Mental Health Center**, SW cor. Broadway and Flushing Aves. 1977. **Kallman & McKinnell/Russo & Sonder**, associated architects.

W43

A space odyssey that landed at this juncture of Williamsburg, Bedford-Stuyvesant, and Bushwick, this machine for health was the most technologically and architecturally up-to-date, and the most expensive, hospital of its time. The self-weathering steel has acquired a deep purple-brown patina on this bold, cubistic place. Great human-high trusses span 69 feet, within which workers can adjust the complex piping and tubing that serve the rooms and laboratories above and below these interleaved service levels. **Kallman** and **McKinnell's** first and major monument was the competition-winning Boston City Hall. With this machine for medicine they have created a superbuilding, a somewhat scary ode to health, dedicated more to the efficiency of health economics than to the serenity of its clients. Widely reviewed in architectural literature, it has won many prizes.

[W44] **Beginning with Children School**, 11 Bartlett St., bet. Flushing and Harrison Aves. Renovations and additions, 2000. **Fox & Fowle.**

The original school, a former Pfizer industrial plant, has been remodeled and extended with a new gymnasium and classrooms.

Subway kiosks: the late-lamented cast-iron IRT subway kiosks were cast in the Hecla Iron Works on Berry Street in the northern part of Williamsburg. The recent reconstruction of one at Astor Place near Cooper Union, in Manhattan, is a wondrous revival of these great glass and metal canopies.

GREENPOINT

Greenpoint (pronounced Greenpernt in those gangster movies of the 1930s) is a quiet, ordered, and orderly community of discrete ethnic populations, with a central charming historic district all but unknown to outsiders, even those in neighboring sectors of Brooklyn.

Its modern history began with the surveying of its lands in 1832 by **Dr. Eliphalet Nott**, president of Union College, in Schenectady (America's first architecturally planned campus), and **Neziah Bliss**. Much of it was purchased for development by **Ambrose C. Kingsland**, mayor of New York (1851-1853), and **Samuel J. Tilden**, who went on to fame in politics and who is happily remembered for leaving a bequest for the establishment of a free public library in New York, an act that triggered the merger of the Astor and Lenox Libraries, and the establishment of the New York Public Library.

The area soon became a great shipbuilding center. It was here, at the Continental Iron Works at West and Calyer Streets, that **Thomas F. Rowland** built the ironclad warship *Monitor* from plans created by **John Ericsson**. The "Yankee cheesebox on a raft" was launched on January 30, 1862, and battled the Confederate *Merrimack* at Hampton Roads, Va., two months later.

By 1860 the so-called five black arts (printing, pottery, gas, glass, and iron) were firmly established in Green Point, as it was first known. In 1867, **Charles Pratt** established his kerosene refinery (Astral Oil Works)—the first successful American oil well had flowed in 1859 at Titusville, Pa. Pratt's product later gave rise to the slogan, "The holy lamps of Tibet are primed with Astral Oil." Astral Oil provided the wealth that later made possible Pratt Institute, myriad Pratt family mansions, as well as Greenpoint's Astral Apartments.

[G1] **McCarren Park Play Center**, N.Y.C. Department of Parks & Recreation, McCarren Park, Lorimer St. bet. Bayard St. and Driggs Ave. E side. ca. 1936. N.Y.C. Department of Parks. **Aymar Embury II**, consultant.

Gutted by fire in 1987, this ceremonially arched pavilion, with its imposing clerestory, announced the grand dip behind. It is one of 4 WPA-built swimming pools erected in Brooklyn during the Depression (the others are Red Hook, Sunset Park, and Betsy Head).

G1

[G2] **Russian Orthodox Cathedral of the Transfiguration of Our Lord**, 228 N. 12th St., SE cor. Driggs Ave. 1916-1921. **Louis Allmendinger**. 🖤

The Winter Palace at St. Petersburg is remembered in the yellow and beige tones of this magnificent cathedral, crowned with 5 verdigris-copper onion-domed cupolas. The real treat, however, is within: the space is small (only 250 seats), and the central cupola is supported on 4 great columns painted to simulate richly veined marble. The triple-altared eastern end is separated from the body of the church by the iconostasis, a hand-carved wooden screen on which icons were painted by the monks in the Orthodox Monastery of the Caves in Kiev. A visit should include the celebration of Divine Liturgy: architecture, incense ritual, and sound, combined in many tongues, create a deeply moving saturation of the senses.

G2

[G3] **Public School 34, Brooklyn, The Oliver H. Perry School**, Norman Ave. bet. Eckford St. and McGuinness Blvd. N side. Central block, 1867. Additions, 1870. **Samuel B. Leonard**. Wings, 1887-1888. **James W. Naughton**. 🖤

An austere mixture of Renaissance and Romanesque revivals. **Leonard** and **Naughton** were sequentially architects for Brooklyn's schools; Leonard from 1859-1879, **Naughton** following until 1898.

GREENPOINT DISTRICT

see pages 760-763

[G4] **Greenpoint Historic District**, roughly from Java to Calyer Sts., Franklin to Manhattan Aves.

A rich trove of intact churches with both row and free-standing housing. Pride of ownership here translates into buildings maintained (for the most part) in their original shape.

[G5] **Greenpoint Savings Bank**, 807 Manhattan Ave., SW cor. Calyer St. 1908. **Helmle & Huberty.**

Roman pomp under a pantheon dome, shingled delightfully in a fish-scaled pattern in slate. The Pantheon in Rome was similarly shingled but in bronze, stolen for valuable metal in medieval times. This grand Doric-columned bank is of limestone over a granite base.

[G6] **St. Elias Greek Rite Catholic Church**/formerly Reformed Dutch Church of Greenpoint, 149 Kent St., bet. Manhattan Ave. and Franklin St. N side. Church, 1869-1970. **William B. Ditmars.** Sunday school, 1879. **W. Wheeler Smith.**

G5

Bulky brick, brownstone, and whitestone, with the Victorian Gothic polychromy (note the alternating red and gray voussoirs) promoted by writer-architectural historian **John Ruskin** and hence termed Ruskinian Gothic. Note the cast-iron fence with its Gothic crests, and the octagonal Sunday school.

[G7] **Church of the Ascension** (Episcopal), 129 Kent St., bet. Manhattan Ave. and Franklin St. N side. 1865-1866. **Henry Dudley.**

Granite ashlar with brownstone trim, a double-pitched silhouette and red Episcopal doors. Its low and friendly scale is reminiscent of an English country church. Note the 3 oval oculi.

[G8] **114-124 Kent Street Houses**, bet. Manhattan Ave. and Franklin St. S side. 1867-1868.

Cast-iron lintels and sheet metal cornices enliven plain brick façades.

[G9] **130 Kent Street** (row house), bet. Manhattan Ave. and Franklin St. S side. 1859. **Neziah Bliss**, builder. ○̂

A star on this handsome street of town houses. Here a bold Corinthian-columned porch enlivens the streetscape.

[G10] Originally **Mechanics and Traders Bank**, 144 Franklin St., NE cor. Greenpoint Ave. ca. 1895. ○̂

Brooding but glorious Renaissance Revival in Pompeian red terra-cotta, brick, and rock-face brownstone, with grand pilasters crowned by fantastic Composite capitals. Savor the terra-cotta frieze among other riches adorning this lovely building.

G10

[G11] **The Astral Apartments**, 184 Franklin St., bet. Java and India Sts. E side. 1885-1886. **Lamb & Rich.** ●̂

Commissioned by **Charles Pratt** as housing for his kerosene refinery workers, by the same architects who created his Pratt Institute Main Building. This many-entried block was patterned after the Peabody Apartments in London. **Alfred Tredway White** had initiated such housing experiments in Brooklyn at Riverside in Brooklyn Heights and the Tower Home Apartments in Cobble Hill. Here we see patterned brickwork, rock-face brownstone arches and lintels, and structural steel storefronts with the rivets themselves as decoration.

G11

Milton Street: This rich block between Franklin Street and Manhattan Avenue is crowned on axis by St. Anthony's Church. It sums up the finest urban values of Greenpoint, here reaching the urbane.

[G12] **93-103 Milton Street**. N side. 1874. **James R. Sparrow**, builder. ○̂

Six brickfronted houses (Nos. 105-109 were originally three more in a set of nine) that retain their delicate archivolts over their entrance doors, curved Renaissance Revival window lintels, each façade now painted individually for identity.

[G13] **118-120 Milton Street**. S side. 1868. **Thomas C. Smith.** ○̂

This Second Empire pair has been sullied on one side by a defaced mansard roof, on the other by a bastardized cornice. Where was the Landmarks Preservation Commission when we needed it?

[G14] **119-121, 123-125 Milton Street**. N side. 1876. **Thomas C. Smith.** ○̂

The left pair survive as a single composition, the right pair have been desecrated. All four bear the ubiquitous metal canopies vended to the Brooklyn innocent.

G12

[G15] **122-124 Milton Street**. S side. 1889. **Theobald Engelhardt.** ○̂

Brick and brownstone Queen Anne. The bracketed canopies over the entrances are lusty celebrations of entry.

[G16] **128-134 Milton Street**. S side. 1909. **Philemon Tillion.** ○̂

Three cool, corniced, and bay-windowed tenements, well-kept and well loved, in brick and limestone.

[G17] **Greenpoint Reformed Church**/originally Thomas C. Smith House, 138 Milton St. S side. 1867. **Thomas C. Smith.** ○̂

G14

Italianate Greek Revival (those warring peoples could combine in style on occasion). Before 1891 this congregation resided at what is now St. Elias Church, two blocks north on Kent Street.

[G18] **140-144 Milton Street**. S side. 1909. **Philemon Tillion.** ○̂

The streetscape here is enriched by grand neo-Classical porches at street level, grand neo-Classical cornices above.

[G19] **141-149 Milton Street**. N side. 1894. **Thomas C. Smith.** ○̂

Arched and recessed loggias at the third floor enliven Milton Street's third dimension.

G15

[G20] **St. John's Evangelical Lutheran Church**, 155 Milton St. N side. 1891-1892. **Theobald Engelhardt.** ☞

In somber painted brick, this German neo-Gothic is a stolid place incised with its original name, Evangelische-Lutherische St. Johannes Kirche. Token flying buttresses and lancet windows enliven the façade.

G20

[G21] **St. Anthony of Padua Church** (Roman Catholic), 862 Manhattan Ave., at the end of Milton St. E side. 1875. **Patrick C. Keely.** ☞

Attired in red brick and white limestone, a quasi-cathedral on this religious block offers fancy dress to this dour neighborhood. Its 240-foot spire, at a bend in Manhattan Avenue, is a visual pivot not only for Milton Street and Manhattan Avenue but for all of Greenpoint.

[G22] **128-132 Noble Street Houses**, bet. Manhattan Ave. and Franklin St. S side. 1867-1868. ☞

Cast-iron lintels for this Italianate row.

[G23] **Union Baptist Church**/originally First Baptist Church of Greenpoint, 151 Noble St., bet. Manhattan Ave. and Franklin St. N side. 1863-1865. ☞

An early Romanesque Revival Baptist dissenter from the English Gothic Revivalism of the Protestant Episcopal church—a lusty architectural route for some lusty Protestant congregations.

G23

[G24] **Greenpoint Home for the Aged**, 137 Oak St., at the head of Guernsey St. N side. 1887. **Theobald Engelhardt.** ☞

An eclectic brick mansion with Italianate massing and Romanesque Revival arches.

[G25] **133-135 Oak Street** (row houses), bet. Guernsey St. and Franklin Ave. N side. 1890s.

The rockfaced lintels in juxtaposition with brick arches give this pair a special image.

G25

[G26] **Sidewalk clock**, in front of 753 Manhattan Ave. E side. ☞

One of the city's few remaining freestanding cast-iron clocks, now protected by landmark designation.

[G27] **St. Stanislaus Kostka Vincentian Fathers Church** (Roman Catholic), 607 Humboldt St., SW cor. Driggs Ave. ca. 1890.

Two complex, asymmetrical, octagonal spires of this, the largest Polish Catholic congregation in Brooklyn, dominate the local skyline. Humboldt Street and Driggs Avenue are here renamed **Lech Walesa Place** and **Pope John Paul II Plaza** with the fervency that only a monolithic local ethnic population can supply. The spires' heavy encrustation of stone ornament is in rich contrast to the painted aluminum clapboard and asbestos shingles that line the local streets like exterior wallpaper, Archie Bunker style.

[G28] **650 Humboldt Street**, bet. Driggs and Nassau Aves. E side.

An unsullied remnant of wood housing: built for a single family. It demonstrates the texture and color of the community prior to the street's recladding in artificial aluminum, genuine asbestos, and real what-have-you.

G28

[G29] **Monsignor McGolrick Park**/originally Winthrop Park, Driggs to Nassau Aves., Russell to Monitor Sts. [G 25a.] Shelter Pavilion, 1910. **Helmle & Huberty.** ❥

A park on the scale of London's Bloomsbury, with surrounding row houses too low to supply the same architectural containment. Within is a monument (**Antonio de Filippo**, sculptor) to the *Monitor* and its designer, **John Ericsson**, and the Shelter Pavilion, in 18th-century French neo-Classical style.

Colonial

 Georgian/
Federal

 Greek
Revival

 Gothic
Revival

 Villa

 Romanesque
Revival

 Renaissance
Revival

 Roman
Revival

 Art Deco/
Art Moderne

Modern/
Post-Modern

CENTRAL FLATBUSH • PROSPECT PARK SOUTH
DITMAS PARK • EAST FLATBUSH/RUGBY
WINDSOR TERRACE • PARKVILLE

Town of Flatbush/Vlackebos—"Level Forest"

Established as a town in 1652; Town of New Lots separated from
Flatlands in 1852. Annexed to the City of Brooklyn in 1894.

Until the 1880s Flatbush was a quiet place with a rural character. The introduction, in 1878, of the Brooklyn, Flatbush &
Coney Island Railroad, now the Brighton Line, encouraged the
real estate speculation and development that transformed the
farmland into a fashionable suburb by the turn of the century.
The names of these subdivisions are still used in some cases,
only dimly remembered in others: Prospect Park South (the
most affluent of those extant), Vanderveer Park, Ditmas Park,
Fiske and Manhattan Terraces, and a host of others like
Matthews Park, Slocum Park, and Yale Park.

Earlier there had been a series of abortive attempts to
impose grids of houses on the countryside, such as Parkville, the
off-axis grid surrounding Parkville Avenue (1852), and Windsor
Terrace, between Vanderbilt Street and Greenwood Avenue in
the corridor separating Green-Wood Cemetery from Prospect
Park (1862). These projects were never as successful as those in
the quiet, lightly trafficked cul-de-sacs created by the railroad's
cut on its way to Brighton Beach.

Older names, such as Midwood, a corruption of the Dutch
Midwout, are still used in areas that once constituted only a portion of that Dutch enclave.

[L1] **Prospect-Lefferts Gardens Historic District**, roughly
bounded by Flatbush Ave., Fenimore St., Rogers Ave. (with a tail
that loops almost to Nostrand Ave.), and Empire Blvd. beyond
Bedford Ave. ●

This is a neighborhood of simple, early 20th-century houses
in a variety of styles: Romanesque Revival, neo-Renaissance,
neo-Georgian, neo-Federal, and neo-Tudor. Here is a classic case
where the whole is greater than the sum of its parts, where the
ensemble—rather than individual buildings—is the landmark.
The product is best savored at the Renaissance Revival rows on
Maple and Midwood (ca. 1910. **Alex Hedman**), and the Colonial
Revival and neo-Medieval Rows on Fenimore and Midwood
Streets and Rutland Road (1920s. **Slee & Bryson**).

CENTRAL FLATBUSH

[F1] **111 Clarkson Avenue** (house), bet. Bedford and Rogers Aves.
N side. ca. 1885.

A once fairyland place that might be termed berserk eclecticism. The onion domes were redolent of **John Nash**'s Royal
Pavilion at Brighton (England, not Beach). A tragedy of neglect.

F1

F1b

 [F1a] **Erasmus Hall Museum**/originally Erasmus Hall
Academy, in the courtyard of Erasmus Hall High School,
911 Flatbush Ave., bet. Church and Snyder Aves. E side. 1786. ●
[F1b] **Erasmus Hall High School**. 1903. **C. B. J. Snyder**.

Established as a private academy by the Flatbush Reformed
Dutch Church across the street. The site was previously occupied by the first public school in Midwout (Midwood), erected
in 1658 by the New Netherlands Colony. The Academy building
is Georgian-Federal with a hipped-gambrel roof and a Palladian
window over a delicate Tuscan-columned porch.

Warning: Rule 9, Erasmus Hall Academy, 1797: "No student shall be permitted any species of gaming nor to drink any spiritous liquors nor to go into any tavern in Flat Bush without obtaining consent of a teacher."

F2

[F2] Originally **Flatbush Town Hall**, 35 Snyder Ave., bet. Flatbush and Bedford Aves. N side. 1874-1875. **John Y. Culyer.** 🍎

Flatbush did not become part of Brooklyn until 1894. This lusty Ruskinian Gothic building is happily being preserved as a community center.

[F3] **P.S. 6**, Bedford Ave., NW cor. Snyder St. 1992. **Gruzen Samton.**

A busy place, both in the sense of resident children and the architecture that encloses them (fences, piers, towers, gables). They probably like it.

F3

[F4] **Flatbush Reformed Dutch Church**, 890 Flatbush Ave., SW cor. Church Ave. 1793-1798. **Thomas Fardon.** 🍎

[F5] **Parsonage**, 2101-2103 Kenmore Terrace NE cor. E. 21st St. Moved in 1918 from 900 Flatbush Ave. 1853. Church House, 1923-1924. **Meyer & Mathieu.** 🍎

A rough, horizontally coursed-stone ashlar (Manhattan schist) church with Romanesque arched windows and doors. Crowning it all is a Georgian white-painted octagonal tower, with Tuscan colonnettes surmounted by urns. The first of three churches built according to the mandate of **Governor Peter Stuyvesant** (the others were the Flatland Dutch Reformed Church and the First Reformed Church), this is the third building to occupy the site.

Walk through the churchyard from Church Avenue, and you will pass delicately incised brownstone gravestones with elegant calligraphy. (Strangely, the limestone markers have eroded, washing off their graphics, while the brownstone survives.) Continue past the meetinghouse of the 1930s onto Kenmore Terrace. On the right is the Parsonage, a beautifully detailed late Greek Revival painted-shingled house presenting a gracious Corinthian-columned veranda, with a handsome cornice of dentils and Italianate modillions.

F6

[F6] **Albemarle-Kenmore Terraces Historic District**, includes all row houses on the two streets listed below. 🍎 [F7] **Kenmore Terrace**, E of E. 21st St., bet. Church Ave. and Albemarle Rd. South houses, 1917-1920. **Slee & Bryson.** ○

The Flatbush Reformed Church Parsonage forms one flank, and these pleasant English Arts and Crafts Revival row cottages, the other.

[F8] **Albemarle Terrace**, E of E. 21st St., bet. Church Ave. and Albemarle Rd. 1916-1917. **Slee & Bryson.** ○

Charming Georgian Revival row houses in a cul-de-sac that says dead end but that is far from dead. The simple brick architecture is enlivened by alternating bay windows, Palladian windows, entry porches, and dormers in the slate mansard roofs.

F9

[F9] **Loew's Kings Theater**, Flatbush Ave. bet. Tilden Ave. and Beverly Rd. E side. 1929. **C. W. Rapp & George L. Rapp.**

With its ornate eclectic terra-cotta façade, this is one of the last movie palaces of that vibrant era when going to the movies was as much an adventure as watching the movie on the screen.

PROSPECT PARK SOUTH

The streets between Church Avenue and Beverly Road, and between Coney Island Avenue and the open cut for the Brighton Line subway, contain as unique a community as any in the city. The entrances to most of the streets are guarded by pairs of sturdy brick piers bearing cast-concrete plaques with the letters PPS in bas-relief. The area is Prospect Park South, characterized at the time of its initial development as *rus in urbe,* or "the country in the city," a description not inappropriate even today. Here is an environment that ranks with Forest Hills Gardens and Kew Gardens in Queens as an architecturally distinguished precinct of grand freestanding turn-of-the-century single-family houses.

PPS is a monument to the vision of the realtor **Dean Alvord**. What he conceived was a garden park within the confines of the grid, abandoning the row house urbanization that had infilled most of old Brooklyn, from the Heights to Bedford-Stuyvesant, from Greenpoint to Park Slope. To these ends he installed all the utilities and paved all the streets before selling one plot of land. Trees were planted not along the curb but at the building line, giving the streets a greater sense of breadth. Alternating every 20 feet were Norway maples, for permanence, and Carolina poplars, for immediate shade. The short-lived poplars, **Alvord** and his architect, **John Petit**, reasoned, would die out as the maples reached maturity.

[F10] **Prospect Park South Historic District**, generally bet. Church Ave. and Beverly Road, and from a line E of Coney Island Ave. to the Brighton Line's subway cut. 🍎

[F11] Originally **Russell Benedict House**, 104 Buckingham Rd., bet. Church Ave. and Albemarle Rd. W side. 1902. **Carroll H. Pratt**. ♂

A stately portico with Composite columns greets the street on this painted-shingle residence. A stylish place that has seen better times.

F11

[F12] Originally **William H. McEntee House**, 115 Buckingham Rd., bet. Church Ave. and Albemarle Rd. E side. 1900. **John J. Petit**. ♂

A volumetric exercise in the Shingle Style: gambrel-roofed, incised for a porch and anchored by a corner "bell"-capped tower. The new weathered shingles suggest a New England attitude (they were originally painted).

[F13] Originally **George U. Tompers House**, 125 Buckingham Rd., bet. Church Ave. and Albemarle Rd. E side. 1911. **Brun & Hauser**. ♂

Corinthian columns and finely scaled clapboard. An Americanized Roman temple as seen through Renaissance eyes.

[F14] Originally **Frederick S. Kolle House**, 131 Buckingham Rd., bet. Church Ave. and Albemarle Rd. E side. 1902-1903. **Petit & Green**. ♂

F12

This wears Japanese fancy dress of a sophisticated sort on a stucco body. Sticks and struts, corbels and brackets, give a timber-structuralist look to what is a rather plain box underneath. Alvord's advertisement in *Country Life* described the interior as "a faithful reflection of the dainty Japanese art from which America is learning so much."

[F15] Originally **William A. Norwood House**, 143 Buckingham Rd., NE cor. Albemarle Rd. 1906. **Walter S. Cassin**. ♂

F14

A re-revival of the Italian Villa style best exemplified in Brooklyn at the Litchfield Mansion (1857) in Prospect Park.

PROSPECT PARK SOUTH DISTRICT
see pages 766-768

*Backyards: Today's 4-track Brighton Line, which abuts the rear
yards of the houses on the east side of Buckingham Road, was at
the time of the original development only a 2-track operation. In
1907 the Brooklyn Rapid Transit Company, successor to the original railroad and precursor of the later BMT, widened the cut, thus
narrowing the backyards of these houses to the nominal amount
visible today.*

[F16] Originally **Louis McDonald House**, 1519 Albemarle Rd.,
NE cor. Buckingham Rd. 1902. **John J. Petit**. ☞
  To complement the adjacent Roman temple, Italian villa,
and Japanese house here is an all-American example influenced
by the Chicago School. Note the angels in the bay windows'
panels and the corbeled caryatids.

F17

[F17] Originally **Maurice Minton House**, 1510 Albemarle
Rd., SE cor. Marlborough Rd. 1900. **John J. Petit**. ☞
  A stately mansion with a grand conservatory and stable. The
latter's huge-scale Composite columns support the roof in the
manner of many Roman buildings, such as the Temple of Vesta,
where old columns got a new hat too small for them.

[F18] Originally **J. C. Woodhull House**, 1440 Albemarle Rd., SW
cor. Marlborough Rd. 1905. **Robert Bryson** and **Carroll Pratt**. ☞
  Another Queen Anne/Colonial Revival hybrid, sullied by the
inappropriate asphalt shingles that replaced its original painted
clapboarding.

F18

[F19] Originally **Francis M. Crafts House**, 1423 Albemarle
Rd., NW cor. Marlborough Rd. **1899. John J. Petit**. ☞
  A veritable Queen Anne gem: shingled, gabled, with a bump
here and a shimmy there. It reeks of romance.

[F20] Originally **John S. Eakins House**, 1306 Albemarle Rd., bet.
Argyle and Rugby Rds. S side. 1905. **John J. Petit**. ☞
  The Shingle Style with a Colonial Revival, Tuscan-
colonnaded porch. The house has been reclad with aluminum
siding, a hideous mistake, particularly obvious on the round
corner tower.

F19

F22

[F21] **101 Rugby Road** (house), bet. Church Ave. and Albemarle Rd. 1890s.

The Shingle Style meets the Franch Renaissance, as seen through a Colonial Revival prism. Electic eclectic. Disney should take notes.

[F22] Originally **G. Gale House**, 1305 Albemarle Rd., NE cor. Argyle Rd. 1905. **H. B. Moore**. ♂

A well-preserved Classical Revival house, with eccentric second-story balconies behind the main colonnade . . . similar in a way to **Harry Truman**'s efforts at that other White House.

[F23] Originally **Herman Goetze House**, 156 Stratford Rd., bet. Hinckley and Turner Places. 1905. **George Hitchings**. ♂

Four-columned Roman temple with a Palladian-windowed bedroom in the pediment. There are elegant Corinthian columns and pilasters, narrow clapboard, and stone quoins simulated in wood.

DITMAS PARK

[D1] **Ditmas Park Historic District**, generally surrounded by Ocean, Dorchester, and Newkirk Aves., and the Brighton Line subway cut. 🍎

Another significant turn-of-the-century development in the spirit of Prospect Park South but at a more modest level. Builder Lewis Pounds and architect Arlington Isham, in particular, created a district of Bungalow Style, Colonial Revival, and neo-Tudor houses.

[D2] **East 16th Street**, Newkirk to Ditmas Aves., and a stretch N of Ditmas Ave. Nos. 511, 515, 519, 523, 549, E side., and Nos. 490, 494, 500, 510, 514, 518, 522, 550, W side. 1908-1909. A**rlington Isham**. ♂

Bungalows, in the Shingle Style, with steeply pitched roofs over front porches supported by columns frequently fat, sometimes polygonal, occasionally round. These are the brethren of myriad bungalows born in California and dotting the Midwest, which supposedly are in the Bengal style: sun-shielded and deeply sheltered from the heat. Here they are a pleasant mannerism rather than a necessity.

D2

[D3] Originally **Harry Grattan House**, 543 E. 17th St., bet. Ditmas and Newkirk Aves. E side. 1906. **Arlington D. Isham**. ♂

A special example of the blending of Queen Anne and Colonial Revival: dark stained shingles clad the volume, short Tuscan columns support brackets rather than a Classical abacus and frieze.

D3

[D4] Originally **Thomas A. Radcliffe House**, 484 E. 17th St., bet. Dorchester Rd. and Ditmas Ave. W side. 1902. **Arlington Isham**. ♂

A polygonal corner tower bears a finialed hat, and multiple gables form picturesque profiles against the sky.

[D5] Originally **Paul Ames House**, 456 E. 19th St., bet. Dorchester Rd. and Ditmas Ave. W side. 1910. **Arne Delhi**. ♂

A Spanish Mission style structure with a bracketed tile roof, intersected by a third-story pediment. An exotic composition in the exotic and eclectic spirit of a Norwegian architect practicing in Brooklyn.

[D6] Originally **Arthur Ebinger House**, 445 E. 19th St., bet. Dorchester Rd. and Ditmas Ave. E side. 1931. **Foster & Gallimore**. ♂

Slate-roofed, tapestry-brick cottage, with a multifaceted chimney at the street—the fantasy of England brought to Brooklyn suburbia.

[D7] Originally **George U. Tompers** House, 1890 Ditmas Ave., SW cor. E. 19th St. 1904. **Arlington Isham**. ♂

A stately Shingle Style/Colonial Revival mansion with steeply shingled roofs and a corner tower. The vast porch has an Italianate cornice with Tuscan columns. Seven years later Tompers purchased the Roman temple at 125 Buckingham Road.

D7

🏠 [D8] **242 Rugby Road** (house), bet. Beverly and Cortelyou Rds. W side. ca. 1890. ♂

An exceptional Shingle Style house with a polygonal onion-domed tower. The porch is incised into the building's volume. Most neighbors in these precincts present a typical columned, projecting Colonial Revival porch.

🎬 [D9] **Flatbush-Tompkins Congregational Church**, E. 18th St. SE cor. Doorchester Rd. 1910. **Allens & Collins**, with **Louis Jallade**. ♂

A Georgian body crossed with a Greek Revival Temple front, surmounted by a tower that might be left over from a

D8

DITMAS PARK DISTRICT
see pages 769-770

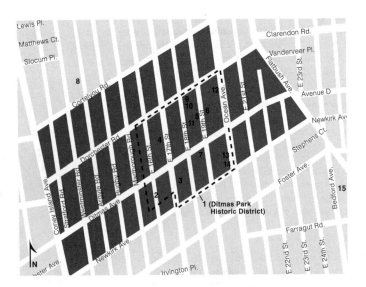

Christopher Wren reject. Mixed signals: the assemblage is bland.
Check the parish house for chutzpah.

[D10] **Flatbush-Tompkins (originally Flatbush)
Congregational Church Parish House**, 451 E. 18th St., SE cor.
Dorchester Rd. 1899. **Whitfield & King**. ○⟋

A bold polygonal dark Shingle Style parish house that, if it
were a complete form, would have 16 sides.

[D11] **499 East 18th Street** (house), bet. Dorchester Rd. and
Ditmas Ave. 1890s. ○⟋

Dour colors of the era combine with crisp architectural
forms: a Queen Anne/Shingle Style/Colonial Revival interweave.
The porch columns, however, in dark green, belie the Classic
spirit they represent.

D12

[D12] Originally **George Ramsey House**, 900 Ocean Ave.,
bet. Dorchester and Ditmas Aves. W side. 1910. **Charles G.
Ramsey**. ✦⟋

A dull Colonial Revival house complete with a timid Ionic-
columned porte-cochère.

[D13] Originally **George Van Ness House**, 1000 Ocean
Ave., bet. Ditmas and Newkirk Aves. W side. 1899. **George
Palliser**. ○⟋

Once a gracious Roman Revival mansion; the Corinthian
columns that graced its great pediment have vanished, and
crude square columns replaced them. Look at No. 1010 next
door to see what history has lost.

D13

[D14] Originally **Thomas H. Brush House**/now
Community Temple Beth Ohr, 1010 Ocean Ave., NW cor.
Newkirk Ave. 1899. **George Palliser**. ○⟋

A splendid Georgian mansion in red brick and white limestone, presenting Composite Ionic columns and pilasters to the
street. The Palladian window in the pediment is another bedroom, a trick that the Parthenon missed.

[D15] **2693 Bedford Avenue** (house), bet. Foster Ave. and
Farragut Rd. E side. ca. 1892.

The juxtaposition of deeply shadowed circular recesses and
rectangular windows in this Shingle Style house produces a feeling of a powerful volumetric interplay.

D14

EAST FLATBUSH/RUGBY

[E1] **SUNY Downstate Medical Center**.
This complex occupies an area roughly bounded by Clarkson, New York and Albany Aves., and Winthrop St., stepping down to Lenox Rd., bet. New York and Brooklyn Aves.

The various buildings listed next are within the rubric of this Center.

[E2] **Hospital and Intensive Care Unit**, 445 Lenox Rd. N side. 1966. **Max O. Urbahn**.
Concrete graph paper from a time when that meant Style. Certainly, the rigid progeny of Mies van der Rohe were honored in their austere discipline. We now seem to honor the reverse: license in architecture is bringing willful chaos, and this now inspires only boredom and yawns.

[E2a] **SUNY Health Sciences Center**, Lenox Rd., bet. New York Ave. and E. 34th St. 1990s.
A sleek and monumental megabuilding for medical students.

E2

[E3] **Dormitories**, New York Ave. bet. Lenox Rd. and Linden Blvd. E side. 1966. **Max O. Urbahn**.
Nurses' and interns' dwellings with Miami Beach styling, behind what appear to be stacked picture frames. All this seems to be part of an alien colony in these East Flatbush blocks.

[E4] **Kings County Hospital**, Clarkson Ave. bet. Brooklyn and Albany Aves. N side. 1931. **Leroy P. Ward**, architect. **S. S. Goldwater, M.D.**, consultant.
The Bellevue of Brooklyn. A high rise with bay windows, a brick body, and Spanish tile roofs, all crowned with marvelous towers and finials. This is rich architecture, reminding us that hospitals don't have to look like machines.

E2a

WINDSOR TERRACE

[W1] **Engine Company 240**, N.Y.C. Fire Department, 1309 Prospect Ave., bet. Greenwood Ave. and Ocean Pkwy. E side. 1896.
Brick, rock-face limestone, and slate: castellated Romanesque Revival with a corner oriel (its turret has gone) and an arched corbel table. **Louis Sullivan** could have been here.

W1

PARKVILLE

[K1] **Ocean Parkway**, designated a scenic landmark from Church to Seabreeze Aves. 1874-1876. **Frederick Law Olmsted** and **Calvert Vaux**. 📷
Six miles of tree-planted malls linking Prospect Park to Coney Island. An addition to the system of parkways proposed by Olmsted & Vaux when planning Eastern Parkway.

[K1a] **Parkville Congregational Church**, 18th Ave. NW cor. E. 5th St. 1895.
The stepped and shingled brackets of the gable, with its hipped-roof belfry, bring exotic detail to this lovely remnant. Note the Victorian milk glass.

K1a

[K2] **Philip Hirth Academy, Beth Jacob School**, 4419 18th Ave., bet. McDonald Ave. and Dahill Rd. S side. 1971. **William N. Breger Assocs.**
Stylish and smartly scaled red-brick cubism.

SW

BAY RIDGE/FORT HAMILTON/DYKER HEIGHTS
BOROUGH PARK • BENSONHURST/BATH BEACH

Town of New Utrecht/Nieuw Utrecht
Established as a town in 1662; annexed to the City of Brooklyn
in 1894.

 Colonial

 Georgian/
Federal

 Greek
Revival

 Gothic
Revival

 Villa

 Romanesque
Revival

 Renaissance
Revival

 Roman
Revival

 Art Deco/
Art Moderne

Modern/
Post-Modern

The old Town of New Utrecht includes the present-day
communities of Bay Ridge, Fort Hamilton, Dyker Heights,
Borough Park, Bath Beach, and much of Bensonhurst. At various times in its past, other, barely remembered communities
were identified within its boundaries—Blythebourne, Mapleton,
Lefferts Park, and Van Pelt Manor—and the area was largely
rural until the beginning of the 20th century.

BAY RIDGE/FORT HAMILTON/DYKER HEIGHTS

Some of Brooklyn's most desirable residential sites lay along the
high ground overlooking the Narrows and Gravesend Bay.
Inevitably this best of topography became the site of magnifi-
cent mansions along Shore Road and the sometimes higher
ground behind and along Eleventh Avenue in Dyker Heights.
The ornate villa of **E. W. Bliss**, of Greenpoint fame; **Neils
Poulson**'s cast-iron fantasy, by the founder of Williamsburg's
Hecla Iron Works; Fontbonne Hall, the home of **Tom L.
Johnson**, the "three-cent mayor of Cleveland"; and many oth-
ers lined the bluff overlooking the harbor. In the **Chandler
White** House the group headed by **Cyrus Field** and **Peter
Cooper** first gathered to discuss the laying of the Atlantic cable.
The Bliss mansion was once the home of **Henry Cruse
Murphy**, who, in 1865, met there with **William C. Kingsley** and
Alexander McCue to formulate the original agreement for the
construction of the Brooklyn Bridge. Except for Fontbonne
Hall, now a private school, all the mansions have been sup-
planted by endless ranks of elevator apartment buildings, form-
ing a palisade of red brick along the edge of Shore Road.

[B1] **Bay Ridge Masonic Temple**/originally New Utrecht N. Y.
Exempt Firemen's Association, 257-259 Bay Ridge Ave., bet.
Ridge Blvd. and 3rd Aves. N side. ca. 1890. Addition to west and
conversion to Masonic Temple later.
   A fine exercise in above-ground archaeology. Look carefully
at the entrance cornice and the keystones over the windows.
They bear the old volunteer fire company's seals and names
(including the now vanished community of Blythebourne) on
the east portion of the building, and the Masonic symbols (in
the stained glass, too) only in the west. The structure was once
symmetrical around its ornate entrance. Subtle changes in the
brick coloring reveal the line of the addition.

B2

*The Pier at the foot of Bay Ridge Avenue gives a promontory for
viewers of the whole bay: tankers tug at anchors surrounding, and
the distant views of the Verrazano Bridge, Staten Island, and the
lower Manhattan skyline make this a Brooklyn version of Battery
Park.*

[B2] **Madeline Court**, 68th St. bet. Ridge Blvd. and Third Ave.
ca. 1940s.
   An urban space in this in-town suburbia, brick and slate-
roofed where the whole is again serving as master of its architecturally undistinguished parts.

[B3] **Salem Evangelical Lutheran Church**, 355 Ovington St., bet.
Third and Fourth Aves. N side. ca. 1940.

Stepped gables on north German-Swedish-Dutch brick vernacular make handsome profiles against the sky.

[B4] **Bay Ridge United Methodist Church**, 7002 Fourth Ave., SW cor. Ovingston St. ca. 1895.

A green ashlar body with brownstone trim makes this a lovely cared-for local confection, with its chocolate joints oozing.

B4

[B5] **Flagg Court** (apartments), 7200 Ridge Blvd., bet. 72nd and 73rd Sts. W side. 1933-1936. **Ernest Flagg**.

Flagg Court, named for its renowned architect (Singer Buildings, Scribner Building), is a 422-unit housing development contained in 6 contiguous buildings. Among the project's avant-garde features were reversible fans below the windows (long since gone), window shades on the outside of windows (the intelligent heat shield, also gone), concrete slabs serving as finished ceilings (commonplace in current architecture), and an auditorium of vaulted concrete. Note the pendant Carpenter Gothic cornice on the 8th floor.

[B6] **131 76th Street** (house), bet. Ridge Blvd. and Colonial Rd. N side. 1865.

A grand gray neo-Georgian stuccoed mansion, with a white Composite-columned porch.

B6

[B7] **122 76th Street** (house), bet. Ridge Blvd. and Colonial Rd. S side. ca. 1900.

A Gothic Revival mansion perched (with No. 131 above) on a bluff rising 61 steps from Colonial Road; pedestrians—for once—are king here. A hexagonal tower overlooks the Upper Bay. **Dr. Elliot**, founder of the Blue Cross, and his family, dwelled here.

B7

[B8] **217 82nd Street** (house), bet. Third Ave. and Ridge Blvd. N side. ca. 1892. Perhaps **Parfitt Bros**.

An off-beat Shingle Style house, entered through a modest octagonal corner tower, from the time Bay Ridge was entering suburbia.

[B9] **Howard E. and Jessie Jones House**, 8220 Narrows Avenue, NW cor. 83rd St. 1916-1917. **J. Sarsfield Kennedy**.

A mansion disguised as a witch's hideaway. Black Forest Art Nouveau. Bumpety stone and pseudo-thatchery make this Arts and Crafts revival one of Brooklyn's greatest private fantasies.

B9

[B10] **163 and 175 81st Street** (houses), bet. Ridge Blvd. and Colonial Road. N side. ca. 1880.

Shingle Style, conical-capped, stepped gables. Note the round-cut shingles on the brick bodies. Vigorous.

[B11] **Shore Court**, bet. Colonial Rd. and Narrows Ave. S side. 1930s.

Mock Tudor paired houses embracing a cul-de-sac paved in Belgian block. Another example of European urbanism, where the ensemble is much more important than the simple architecture.

[B12] **Shore Hill Apartments** (senior citizens' residence), 9000 Shore Rd., bet. 90th and 91st Sts. E side. 1976. **Gruzen & Partners**.

A looming presence in this low-scaled neighborhood. Its tan brick anodized-windowed façade might better befit a Middle American motel.

B12

[B13] **Visitation Academy**, Visitation Nuns (Roman Catholic), 91st to 93rd Sts., Colonial Rd. to Ridge Blvd. Convent and Chapel, 1913. [B14] **Chapel**.

A fortification for virgins, with a 20-foot stone and concrete wall to protect first- through eighth-graders from sight. The attached chapel is brick Italian neo-Renaissance. Unwalled, it serves as the religious doorkeeper to the Academy.

B14

IIII [B15] Originally **James F. Farrell House**, 119 95th St., bet. Marine Ave. and Shore Rd. N side. ca. 1849.

A splendid Greek Revival wood house inundated but not drowned in an adjacent sea of red brick apartment blocks. Painted cream and white, with a Tuscan-columned porch and green shutters (they work!), it is a distinguished architectural remnant miraculously preserved among bland multiple dwellings.

B15

III [B16] **St. John's Episcopal Church**, 9818 Fort Hamilton Pkwy., NW cor. 99th St. 1890. Rectory, 1910.

A homely cottage-scaled country church in the looming shadow of the Verrazano Bridge and its ramps. Stone and shingles clad a timbered body enriched with red, white, and gold polychromy. Called the Church of the Generals, it attracted numerous military leaders from adjacent Fort Hamilton.

[B17] **Fort Hamilton Veterans' Hospital**, 800 Poly Place, bet. Seventh and Fourteenth Aves. S side. 1950. **Skidmore, Owings & Merrill**.

A sleek slab with soothing views for veterans.

B16

[B18] **Fort Hamilton Officers' Club**/originally Fort Hamilton Casemate Fort, in Fort Hamilton Reservation at Whiting Quadrangle, Shore Pkwy. E of Verrazano Bridge approaches. 1825-1831. ☛ Altered 1937-1938. Not open to the public. A granite military fort now used as an officers' club.

[B19] **Harbor Defense Museum**, in Fort Hamilton Reservation, 101st St. and Fort Hamilton Pkwy.

Closed until further notice.

▲▲▲ [B20] **Poly Prep Country Day School**/originally Brooklyn Polytechnic Preparatory School, 92nd St., bet. 7th and Dahigreen Aves. 1924.

B20

A neo-Georgian boys' school with spreading athletic fields on what is, for the city, a vast campus. It is now coeducational.

[B21a] **8302 Eleventh Avenue** (house), SW cor. 83rd St.
[B21b] **8310 Eleventh Avenue** (house), bet. 83rd and 84th Sts. W side. [B21c] **1101 84th Street** (house), NE cor. 11th Ave. All in Dyker Heights.

The mad dwarfs who built the manse at 8220 Narrows Avenue [B9] moved a mile to build these country cousins. Note, particularly, the amber conservatory.

[B22] **1265 86th Street** (house), bet. 12th and 13th Aves. N side. ca. 1885.

B21b

A handsome Shingle Style house, facing Dyker Beach golf course.

╤╤ [B23] **National Shrine of St. Bernadette** (Roman Catholic), 8201 13th Ave., bet. 82nd and 83rd Sts. E side. 1937. **Henry V. Murphy**.

A polygonal exterior, with a verdigris copper roof, houses parabolic concrete arches within. The nave is awash with colored light and features a kitsch rock-piled shrine to St. Bernadette at its east end.

BAY RIDGE DISTRICT

see pages 772-775

BOROUGH PARK

Largely built up during the 1920s with numerous one- and two-family houses and apartment buildings, this section had been rural, apart from scattered villages, at the turn of the century. Perhaps the most interesting settlement was Blythebourne, which lay southwest of the intersection of New Utrecht Avenue and 55th Street along the old Brooklyn, Bath Beach & West End Railroad, today's West End subway line. It was founded in the late 1880s by **Electus B. Litchfield**, the son of **Edwin C. Litchfield** of Prospect Park fame. A number of houses were quickly built, as well as a series of Queen Anne cottages and two churches. But before the community could take hold, a politician purchased the area north of Blythebourne and east of New Utrecht Avenue and named it Borough Park. A real estate agent at the time warned the Litchfield family to sell its holdings, explaining that the pogroms of Eastern Europe would soon cause a mass migration to the outskirts of Brooklyn, forcing land values down. **Mrs. William B. Litchfield**, who controlled the property at the time, decided not to sell. The prediction was partially fulfilled: the Borough Park section did become a heavily Jewish community, but the land values, instead of falling, rose tremendously. As a result, Blythebourne was swallowed by Borough Park and is remembered today only in the name of the local post office, Blythebourne Station. The area also embraces a second-generation Hasidic community, transposed from Williamsburg.

[B24] **Franklin Delano Roosevelt High School**, 5801 19th Ave., bet. 55th and 59th Sts. E side. 1965. **Raymond & Rado**.

A graph-paper façade in concrete brings a note of modernity to this bland and monotonous area.

BENSONHURST/BATH BEACH

This lower-middle-class residential area preserves the family name of **Charles Benson**, whose farm was subdivided into the gridiron we see today. At New Utrecht and 18th Avenues the original village of New Utrecht was settled in 1661, on a site now marked by the New Utrecht Reformed Church.

[B25] **New Utrecht Reformed Church**, 18th Ave. bet. 83rd and 84th Sts. E side. 1828. ●

A Georgian Gothic granite ashlar church, its brick-framed Gothic windows filled with Tiffany-like Victorian milk glass. An eneagled (gilt) liberty pole stands in front of the church; its predecessors date back to 1783 and have been replaced 6 times since.

B25

Liberty Poles: To harass British garrisons, or to signify their defeat, Revolutionary patriots erected flagpoles, called liberty poles, on which to raise the flag of independence. Lightning and dry rot have taken their toll on the originals, but in some communities a tradition has developed to replace them.

[B26] **New Utrecht Reformed Church Parsonage**, 83rd St. bet. 18th and 19th Aves. S side. ca. 1885.

A Shingle Style home for the pastor, with a generous Tuscan-columned porch.

[B27] **New Utrecht Reformed Church Parish House**, 1827 84th St., bet. 18th and 19th Aves. N side. 1828. 1892. **Lawrence B. Valk.** ●

Robust Romanesque Revival in a class with Frank Freeman's Jay Street Fire House.

B27

And, six long blocks to the east:

[B28] **Engine Company 253**/originally Engine Company 53, N.Y.C. Fire Department, 2425-2427 86th St., bet. 24th and 25th Aves. N side. 1895-1896. **Parfitt Brothers.** ●

The 1890's had nostalgia for forms they thought reminiscent of Dutch New Amsterdam (even though Lady Moody's English settlement at Gravesend is nearby): stepped gables and banded brick for fire engines.

Southern Brooklyn

GRAVESEND • SHEEPSHEAD BAY
MANHATTAN AND BRIGHTON BEACHES
CONEY ISLAND

 Colonial

 Georgian/ Federal

 Greek Revival

 Gothic Revival

 Villa

 Romanesque Revival

 Renaissance Revival

 Roman Revival

 Art Deco/ Art Moderne

 Modern/ Post-Modern

Town of Gravesend/'s-Gravesande

Established as a town in 1645; annexed to the City of Brooklyn in 1894.

Of the six original towns that now constitute Brooklyn, Gravesend is unique in a number of ways. First of all, it was settled by English rather than Dutch colonists. Second, its list of patentees was headed by a woman, a precocious admission of the equality of the sexes. Third, Gravesend Village was organized using a set of sophisticated town planning principles more recognized at New Haven, Philadelphia, and Savannah. Remnants of the plan survive in the neighborhood street layout.

In 1643 **Lady Deborah Moody** and her Anabaptist flock founded Gravesend after a bitter sojourn in New England, where they had encountered the same religious intolerance from which they had fled in "old" England. The free enjoyment of most religious beliefs, which characterized the New Netherlands colony, made Gravesend an obvious haven for them, an English social island in this Dutch-named place.

GRAVESEND

In the 19th century the territory of Gravesend became a great resort. No less than three racetracks were built within its bounds at various times, one northeast of Ocean and Jerome Avenues in Sheepshead Bay, another southeast of Ocean Parkway and Kings Highway, just north of the original village square. Before the development of Coney Island as a public beach and amusement area, Gravesend had fashionable hotels and piers, immense pinnacled wooden structures benefiting from the imagination and wit of Victorian elaboration. Regrettably, there is almost nothing left of its raucous spirit and lively architecture. Coney was revived after World War I following the completion of subway connections to Manhattan and the Bronx; but it has lost its popularity as a recreation area, surpassed by more attractive suburban resorts accessible by automobile on Robert Moses-built highways. The streets, the beach, and the sea remain, but there is little of the physical and social vitality that once made this the daytime resort of the modest middle class.

G1

[G1] **The Old Village of Gravesend**, Village Rd. N. to Village Rd. S., Van Siclen St. to Village Rd. E., centered on the intersection of Gravesend Neck Rd. and McDonald (formerly Gravesend) Ave.

The bounds of Lady Moody's town plan, now remembered only in its streets and the turf on the cemetery.

[G2] **Hicks-Platt House**/also known as Lady Moody House, 17 Gravesend Neck Rd., bet. McDonald Ave. and Van Siclen St. N side. 17th cent.

In the 1890s, **William E. Platt**, a real estate developer, publicized this as Lady Moody's own home, thereby becoming one of the earliest American hucksters of history. The fake stone veneer is ludicrous; bring back the clapboard! The fluted white columns are a later owner's essay into the Colonial Revival.

GRAVESEND DISTRICT
see pages 778-779

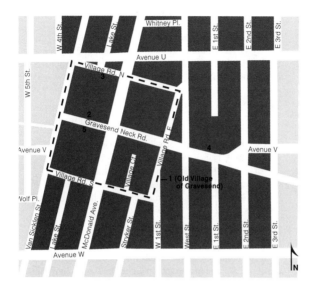

[G3] **Ryder-Van Cleef House**, 38 Village Rd. N., bet. McDonald Ave. and Van Siclen St., S side. ca. 1750.

The partial remnant of a narrow Dutch gambrel-roofed house, with later additions. Much more convincing than the Hicks-Platt collage of fake stone and dubious columns.

[G4] **Trinity Tabernacle of Gravesend**/formerly Gravesend Reform Church, 145 Gravesend Neck Rd., NW cor. E. 1st St. 1894. **J. G. Glover**.

This neo-Gothic place, built for the Reform church, replaced their original building (1655) at Neck Road and McDonald Ave. The architecture deviates considerably from the plain white wooden churches of Dutch Reform congregations.

[G5] **Old Gravesend Cemetery** and Van Sicklen Family Cemetery, Gravesend Neck Rd. bet. McDonald Ave. and Van Siclen St. S side. 1650s.

This shares history with the First Shearith Israel Graveyard as burial grounds for early religious exceptions to the main-stream Dutch Reform church. Protestant Anabaptists were interred here, whereas Sephardic Jews immigrating from Brazil were buried at Shearith Israel, starting in 1683. Lady Moody's own grave is somewhere within, but its location is lost, although many stone markers from the eighteenth century remain. The cemetery is open 4 days a year.

G3

G4

America's only Social Security office that doesn't bear the name of the neighborhood in which it's located is that on Avenue X: if traditions had been followed, it would be the Gravesend office.

SHEEPSHEAD BAY

S1

[S1] Henry and Abraham Wyckoff House/also known as Wyckoff-Bennett House, 1669 E. 22nd St., SE cor. Kings Highway. ca. 1766. Reoriented on the site. 🌶

A rural idyll: the most impressive of all the early Brooklyn houses in the Dutch style, and still in private ownership. This one is dated by a number cut into one of the wooden beams. Used as quarters by Hessian troops during the Revolutionary War, it contains this inscription scratched into a 4- by 7-inch pane:

TOEPFER CAPT OF REGT DE DITFURTH
MBACH LIEUTENANT V HESSEN HANAU ARTILERIE

[S1a] 1996 East 5th Street (house), bet. Aves. S and T. W side. 1986. **Robert A. M. Stern**.

An exquisitely detailed Post-Modern detached house in a small enclave of others that date from the 1920s. A real surprise. Brick, stucco, and a green tile roof join in a collage of neighborly materials

S1a

[S2] Elias Hubbard Ryder House, 1926 E. 28th St., bet. Aves. S and T. W side. ca. 1834. Altered, 1929. 🌶

Dutch Colonialism squeezed between neighboring middle-class funk. The funkiness is compounded by the specious shutters (non-working).

Gerritsen: A community of approximately 1,600 lilliputian bungalows on lilliputian plots, with narrow streets barely wide enough for cars to pass. It has a volunteer fire company and lots of community spirit. Centered on Gerritsen Avenue adjacent to developing Marine Park.

S2a

[S2a] Gerritsen Beach Branch Library, Gerritsen Ave., opp. a leg of Shell Bank Basin. 1997. **John Ciardullo**.

An airy space structured by a timber frame and within a carapace of brick. It stands between the sailboats of Shell Basin and Marine Park.

[S3] Good Shepherd Roman Catholic Church, Rectory, Convent, and School, Ave. S bet. Brown and Batchelder Sts. S side. School, 1932. **McGill & Hamlin**. Church, 1940. Rectory, 1950. Both by **Henry J. McGill**. Convent, 1956, **John B. O'Malley**.

McGill brought a modified California Mission Style church complex to this Marine Park section of Sheepshead Bay.

[S4] Junior High School 43, Brooklyn/The James J. Reynolds School, 1401 Emmons Ave., bet. E. 14th and E. 15th Sts. N side. 1965. **Pedersen & Tilney**.

The cast-in-place concrete has weathered remarkably well.

S3

Fishing and fish: A flotilla of fishing boats moored along Emmons Avenue from Ocean Avenue east to East 27th Street offers you the chance to catch blues, stripers, and miscellany—but you will have to rise early or go to bed late. Generations of compleat anglers have returned bearing far more fish than their extended families could eat. And at Ocean Avenue for several generations has stood a restaurant where the vast fruit of the sea is consumed:

[S5] F.W.I.L. Lundy's Restaurant/originally known as Lundy's, 1901-1929 Emmons Ave. at E. 19th St. 1934. Bloch & Hesse. Reconstructed, 1996. **Van. J. Brody**. 🌶

A big, brash, noisy place in a strangely appropriate Spanish Mission style building that served as many as 5,000 meals a day in its heyday, was closed from 1979 until its reincarnation in 1996.

S4

MANHATTAN AND BRIGHTON BEACHES

The eastern peninsula of what once was Coney Island is isolated, affluent, sometimes green, often dull. Its middle reaches harbor vast hordes of Russian Jewish immigrants; its tip houses the old World War II Naval Training Station, now infilled with the campus of Kingsborough Community College. Along the ocean sits the Brighton Beach Bath and Racquet Club, a privately owned enclave of summer fun in stylish contrast to the public sands of Coney Island proper to the west. Here developers propose six colossal towers that would complete the Brobdingnagian landscape of this onetime resort and entertainment island.

The long gone, great hotel at Brighton Beach

[M1] **Kingsborough Community College, CUNY**, main gate at the end of Oriental Blvd. bet. Sheepshead Bay and the Atlantic Ocean. Master Plan, 1968. **Katz, Waisman, Weber, Strauss**. Various buildings by **KWWS; James Stewart Polshek & Assocs.; Lundquist & Stonehill; Warner, Burns, Toan & Lunde; Gruzen Samton Steinglass**.

A sprawlingly complex complex, with some stylish modern forms particularly in profile when seen from the Belt Parkway.

CONEY ISLAND

[C1] Coney Island Hospital, 2601 Ocean Pkwy., NE cor. Shore Pkwy. 1957. **Katz, Waisman, Blumenkranz, Stein & Weber**.

A landmark to motorists arriving at the Ocean Avenue gateway to Coney Island, even though it's on the other side of the road. Now a period piece of modern architecture, it displays the articulation of its functional parts, with sunshades the major decoration permitted. It grew in the period when elimination of ornamentation was an almost holy mission, here well done by fervent acolytes of **Walter Gropius**.

[C2] William E. Grady Vocational High School, 25 Brighton 4th Rd., bet. Brighton 4th and Brighton 6th Sts. N side. 1956. **Katz, Waisman, Blumenkranz, Stein & Weber**.

Concrete is honored in the barrel vaults over the gymnasium and auditorium, but the effort is dated by its fervent modernism. Like its neighbor (by the same architects) across the parkway, it tells of that brief moment in the 1950s and 1960s when any token of architectural historicism was still rejected.

C2

[C3] New York Aquarium, The Boardwalk at NE cor. W. 8th St. **Exhibit Building**, 1955. **Harrison & Abramovitz**. **Osborn Laboratories of Marine Sciences**, 1965. **Goldstone & Dearborn**.

To be visited for the contents rather than the envelope, although both are the pressured product of the conflicting needs of museum and amusement park. The substantial things to see are the whales, penguins, octopi, and electric eels, but there are other natural and unconscious entertainments. Children, please touch—the horseshoe crabs can be fondled.

[C4] Coney Island Amusement Area, bet. W. 8th St. and W. 16th St., Surf Ave. and The Boardwalk.

Most rides are becoming vacant land, fodder for new housing. The immense spider web of the Wonder Wheel, at West 12th Street and the Boardwalk, still offers wondrous Eiffel-like engineering, startling views, and frightening routines to the Ferris-children it attracts; but Luna Park and Steeplechase Park are long gone. The rusting Parachute Jump, moved here from the 1939-1940 World's Fair, is a romance for those who wishfully hope for restoration. Roller coasters, carrousels, and Dodg'em cars remain; the Cyclone, is the most impressive remnant. The Bowery, a circus midway between the Boardwalk and Surf Avenue, provides some taste of the old charm and vulgarity of Coney's history. Don't overlook the great Greek Revival autoscooter rink between 12th and Stillwell. All this is vanishing as the middle class motors down the interstates to other pleasure grounds, bland places like "Great Adventure" and "theme parks" that invent a history that never was. Rides remain, as do games of skill, corn on the cob, slices of watermelon, and—thank God—cotton candy. The rides and buildings reveal all sorts of architectural styles and fantasia, many vernacular in origin, the work of creative local carpenters. It would be pointless to single out any special event, as "progress" is the battle cry. Look around, for there is plenty to see and enjoy.

C6

C7

[C5] Wonder Wheel, W. 12th Street and the Boardwalk. 1918-1920. **Charles Herman**, Inventor. **Eccentric Ferris Wheel Amusement Co.**, Manufacturers.

[C6] Parachute Jump, Boardwalk at W. 16th St. 1939. **James H. Strong**, inventor. **Elvyn E. Seelye & Co.**, Engineers.

[C7] Cyclone, 834 Surf Ave., near W. 10th St. 1927. **Harry C. Baker**, Inventor. **Vernon Keenan**, Engineer.

C8

[C8 Nathan's Famous (the original), Surf Ave. SW cor. Stillwell Ave. Here since 1916.

CONEY ISLAND DISTRICT

see pages 782-785

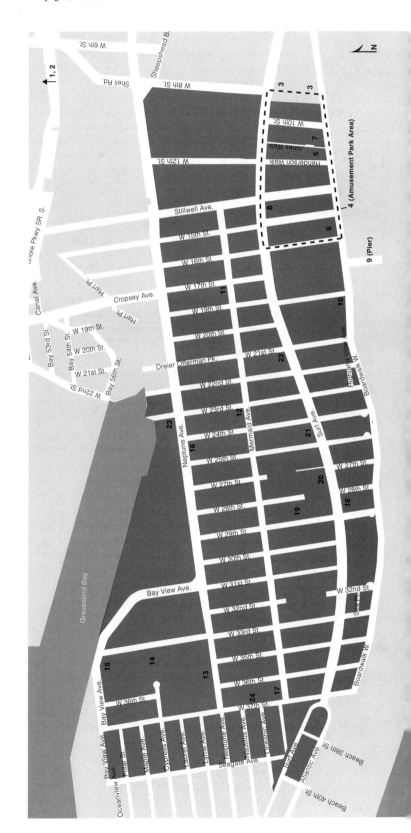

C11

C11a

After Luna and Steeplechase were erased, Nathan's Famous remains as Coney Island's most venerable institution. Once upon a time it cost a nickel on the subway to reach Coney, and a nickel bought a hot dog at Nathan's (ride and hot dog are now each 30 times a nickel). Open all year for stand-up treats, such as delicatessen sandwiches, clams on the half shell, and "shrimp boats" (shrimp cocktails in miniature plastic dinghies). We hope it lasts.

[C9] **Steeplechase Pier**, The Boardwalk at W. 17th St.
A retired monument, it is still a favored fishing dock. A walk along its 1,000 feet offers cool breezes and wonderful vantage points for summer fireworks or the setting sun. Try your hand at catching fluke, blues, flounder, or stripers. The park that went with the pier provided fantastic competition for the younger set on wooden horses that pursued tracks around a vast block, the steeples of the chase in question. The horses in question were stolen.

[C10] **Abe Stark Center, N.Y.C. Department of Parks & Recreation**, W. 19th St. at The Boardwalk. 1969. **Daniel Chait**.
A would-be Nervi created these once-stylish structural forms to house a skating rink, where precocious figure-skating stars and promising hockey teams vie for space in the midnight hours.

[C11] **Our Lady of Solace Church** (Roman Catholic), 2866 W. 17th St., NW cor. Mermaid Ave. 1925. **Robert J. Reiley**.
A plain brick neo-Romanesque church with a refreshingly austere exposed brick interior: arches, limestone columns, timbered roof. Go inside.

[C11a] **Gargiulo's Restaurant**, 2911 W. 15th St., bet. Mermaid and Surf Aves. Restaurant founded 1907; here since 1928.
A princely palace in plebeian surroundings—vast and vulgar. Elsewhere, it would be just another unimportant eatery; here it is an oasis. Expensive.

[C12] **Police Facility**, Mermaid Ave. at W. 23rd St. 1993. **Bennett Metzner Sowinski**.

*Once upon a time architects and politicians got together under the leadership of **Edward J. Logue** and the New York State Urban Development Corporation (UDC). Here power delivered to Logue by **Governor Rockefeller**, with the advice and consent of **Mayor Lindsay**, changed the rules of public housing and urban design. Coney Island was picked as one of three crucibles of experimentation (Twin Parks in the Bronx and Roosevelt Island were the others). The several projects listed below were all risk-taking experiments in urban design not attempted by the New York City Housing Authority since their late 1930s glories at Williamsburg and Harlem River Houses.*

C13

[C13] **Sea Rise I** (apartments), Neptune and Canal Aves., bet. W. 33rd and W. 37th Sts. 1976. **Hoberman & Wasserman**.
The best of the Coney Island UDC. In its successful fulfillment of a winning architectural school design, ideas from the "ivory tower" are brought down to the real world of subsidized housing. Coney Island is honored by this and its siblings.

[C14] **2730 West 33rd Street** (apartments), bet. Bayview and Neptune Aves. 1975. **Skidmore, Owings & Merrill**.
Stacked cubist balconies on a white concrete tower: professional, mechanical, orderly—and dull.

[C15] **Town houses**, Bayview Ave. SW cor. W. 33rd St. 1975. **Davis, Brody & Assocs**.

Brown brick, concrete-corniced, unassuming, understated row houses, whose broken form surrounds a garden court. Lovely.

C15

[C16] **Apartment tower and town houses**, Neptune Ave. bet. W. 24th and W. 25th Sts., S side. 1975. Tower, **Skidmore, Owings & Merrill**. Town houses, **Davis, Brody & Assocs**.

A reprise of [C10 and C11] above.

[C17] **Housing for the Elderly**, Surf Ave. bet. W. 36th and W. 37th Sts. N side. 1975. **Hoberman & Wasserman**.

The stepped terraces are remarkably empty; residents willfully cluster around the trafficked streets below, where the action is—not in their architect-assigned space. As Jane Jacobs articulated so strongly, streets are for people.

[C18] **Harry and Jeanette Weinberg Pavilion, Jewish Geriatric Center**, Surf Ave., bet. W. 28th and W. 29th Sts. S side. 1990s.

A sleek outpost of the middle class that might seem more appropriate in Miami than Coney Island.

[C19] **Sea Park East** (apartments), bet. W. 28th and W. 29th Sts. Midblock bet. Mermaid and Surf Aves. 1975. Tower, **Skidmore, Owings & Merrill**. Town houses, **Davis, Brody & Assocs**.

Another reprise.

[C20] **Sea Park East** (apartments), Surf Ave. bet. W. 27th and W. 29th Sts. N side. 1975. Hoberman & Wasserman.

Lesser versions of Sea Rise I.

[C21] **Ocean Towers** (apartments), Surf Ave. bet. W. 24th and W. 25th Sts. N side. 1975. **Prentice & Chan, Ohlhausen**.

A variety of floor plans offers the façade a mosaic of windows, rather than the stacked regularity of many apartment towers.

C18

[C22] **2920 and 2940 West 21st Street** (apartments), NW cor. Surf Ave. 1974. **James Doman & Emil Steo**.

A bland 7-story block.

[C23] **Former Fire Service Pumping Station, City of New York**, 2301 Neptune Ave., bet. W. 23rd and W. 24th Sts. N side. 1937-1938. **Irwin S. Chanin**.

This streamlined but decayed remnant recalls the Art Moderne stimulated by the Paris Exposition of 1937. The entrance of this symmetrical modern palace was once guarded by two pairs of prancing steeds, now removed to the Brooklyn Museum sculpture garden. Too bad. Coney needed to keep this piece of architectural history.

C21

[C24] **2837 West 37th Street**, bet. Neptune and Mermaid Aves. E side. ca. 1924.

Mykonos in Brooklyn, once a siamese twin, now severed. Its textured stucco and whitewashed flanks bring Mediterranean memories to this remote spit of Coney Island.

C24

Southeastern Brooklyn

SE

**MIDWOOD • FLATLANDS
CANARSIE**

Town of Flatlands/Nieuw Amersfoort

Established as a town in 1666; annexed to the City of Brooklyn in 1896.

The name Flatlands aptly describes this area. It is a billiard table, much of it still marshy; a considerable part bordering Jamaica Bay was recaptured as landfill, a no-no in present-day environmental circles. The old town included much of what is now Midwood to the north, but a good deal of the inland area is still termed Flatlands, part of which is a substantial industrial park. At its southern edges are the shorefront areas of old Floyd Bennett Field, Bergen Beach, Mill Basin, and Canarsie, tidal and aquatic edges now filled with middle-class homeowners yearning to have a powerboat at their lawn and bulkhead's edge. Boaters with sails dwell elsewhere.

MIDWOOD

[M1] **Johannes Van Nuyse House**/also known as Van Nuyse-Magaw House, 1041 E. 22nd St., bet. Aves. I and J. E side. 1800-1803.

Originally built at East 22nd Street and Avenue M, this farmhouse was moved here around 1916 and turned perpendicular to the street, to fit its new and narrow lot. The distinctive Dutch gambrel roof is therefore the end, or street, façade

M1

[M2] **Congregation Kol Israel** (synagogue), 3211 Bedford Ave., NE cor. Ave. K. Entrance on Ave. K. 1989. **Robert A. M. Stern**, architect. **Dominick Salvati & Son**, consulting architects.

A Post-Modern synagogue in banded brick successfully adapting to its semi-suburban residential setting. There is some flavor from **Frank Lloyd Wright** here.

M2

[M3] **Mesitva Yeshiva Chaim Berlin**, 1605 Coney Island Ave., bet. Aves. L and M. 1988. **Fox & Fowle**.

Polychromatic brick and granite swells out to Coney Island Avenue, the gridded windows a study hall for the resident *bachurim* (scholars).

[M4] **Joost and Elizabeth Van Nuyse House**, sometimes called the Coe House, 1128 E. 34th St., bet. Flatbush Ave. and Ave. J. W side. 1744, 1793, 1806.

A well-dressed neighbor in a tacky neighborhood, like a Harris tweed jacket among polyester leisure suits. Well maintained, it suffers from shutters and downspouts that were never part of its Dutch ancestry.

FLATLANDS

F2

[F1] Originally **Pieter Claesen Wyckoff House**, 5902 Clarendon Rd., at intersection of Ralph and Ditmas Aves. SW cor. ca. 1652, Additions, 1740 and 1820. ✎ Restored, 1982. **Oppenheimer, Brady & Vogelstein**. Open to the public. 718-629-5400. May-Nov: Thurs-Sat, 12-5; closed Sun-Wed; Dec-Apr: Thur-Fri, 12-4; closed Sat-Wed.

A lonely ancestor in a neat fenced park, marooned in these industrial precincts. A vast lawn and minimal trees surround this modest place, which remembers the New Netherlands with its handsome eaves and shingled body.

F3

[F2] **Flatlands Dutch Reformed Church**, 3931 Kings Highway, bet. Flatbush Ave. and E. 40th St. 1848. **Henry Eldert**, builder. ✎

One of three Brooklyn churches established by order of Governor Peter Stuyvesant—the others are the Flatbush Reformed Dutch and the First Reformed. Handsomely sited in a tree-filled park, this simple Georgian-Federal building stands where two earlier churches stood. The first, built in 1663, was octagonal in plan. Note the names in the adjacent cemetery: **Lott, Voorhees, Sprong, Kouwenhoven, Wyckoff.**

[F3] **Hendrick I. Lott House**, 1940 E. 36th St., bet. Fillmore Ave. and Avenue S. W side. East Wing (Johannes Lott House), 1720. Main house and west wing, 1800. ✎

Some elbowroom allows this Dutch Colonial house to remember its rural beginnings. Modest owners have provided minimal maintenance, but it needs some serious care. The small wing is Lott's grandfather's house of 1720; the main body was built by Hendrick Lott himself in 1800. The projecting Dutch eaves, more usually cantilevered, are supported by columns square on one side and round on the other.

[F4] **John and Altje Baxter House**/originally Stoothoff-Baxter-Kouwenhoven House, 1640 E. 48th St., bet. Aves. M and N. W side. Wing, ca. 1747. Main House. 1811. ✎

The form of this lonely enfenced Dutch outpost remains, but its skin has been modernized . . . to its discredit. The older, smaller tail was married and moved to join its larger, later dog. And both were reoriented to the street around 1900.

[F5] **Donwe Stoothof House**/also known as John Williamson House, 1587 E. 53rd St., bet. Aves. M and N. E side.

Another poorly altered Dutch Colonial, veneered with asphalt-impressed false brick. Nevertheless the shape is there under that dowdy fabric.

F4

F6

[F6] **Mill Basin Branch, Brooklyn Public Library,** 2385 Ralph Ave., NE cor. Ave. N. 1974. **Arthur A. Unger & Assocs.**

A serene outpost of graceful modernism in brick that is carved and curved without overkill—in contrast to the Jamaica Bay Branch below.

CANARSIE

[C1] **Bay View Houses, N.Y.C. Housing Authority** (apartments), Shore Parkway, NE cor. Rockaway Parkway, 1955. **Katz, Waisman, Blumenkranz, Stein & Weber**.

A better-than-average example of the Authority's work in those years from 1945 to 1966 when bland brick towers sprouted in enclaves all around town. Here the mere 8 stories are a blessing.

C2

[C2] **Jamaica Bay Branch, Brooklyn Public Library**, 9727 Seaview Ave., NW cor. E. 98th St. 1972. **Leibowitz, Bodouva & Assocs**.

Ribbed concrete block, slots, notches, cantilevers, and splayed sills create a histrionic little building with such a simple purpose.

C3

[C3] **Seaview Jewish Center** (synagogue), 1440 E. 99th St., bet. Seaview Ave. and Ave. N. W side. 1972. **William N. Breger Assocs**.

Carved stucco vanilla ice cream. Stylish and a world apart from the surrounding banality. Make certain to see it from the south.

[C4] **Waxman Building, Hebrew Educational Society of Brooklyn**, 9502 Seaview Ave., SE cor. E. 95th St. 1968. **Horace Ginsbern & Assocs**.

A modest building housing a society that moved, along with its community, from Brownsville to Canarsie.

C4

[C5] **Canarsie Pier, Gateway National Recreation Area**, S of Shore Pkwy. at the foot of Rockaway Pkwy.

Jutting into Jamaica Bay, this is a place to fish, rent boats, or just bask. One day, let's hope, pollution control will make it possible to gather clams and oysters once again.

Eastern Brooklyn

Colonial

*Georgian/
Federal*

*Greek
Revival*

*Gothic
Revival*

Villa

*Romanesque
Revival*

*Renaissance
Revival*

*Roman
Revival*

*Art Deco/
Art Moderne*

*Modern/
Post-Modern*

HIGHLAND PARK / CYPRESS HILLS
BROWNSVILLE • EAST NEW YORK

Town of New Lots
Separated from the Town of Flatbush in 1852; annexed to the
City of Brooklyn in 1886.

Three major neighborhoods exist within this sector.
Highland Park, also known as Cypress Hills, lies north of
Atlantic Avenue.

Brownsville occupies the roughly triangular area between
Remsen Avenue, East New York Avenue, and the tracks of the
Long Island Railroad. East New York is the remainder south to
Jamaica Bay and east to the Queens boundary, or city line, as its
residents often call it—a relic of the days when Brooklyn was a
separate city.

HIGHLAND PARK/CYPRESS HILLS

[H1] **279 and 361 Highland Boulevard** (houses), bet. Miller Ave.
and Barbey St. N side. ca. 1900.

Two gracious mansions surviving from a precinct that originally had a myriad. Many were displaced by apartment houses
seeking these spectacular views. No. 279, in gray Roman brick
and white limestone, presents a great composite Ionic-columned
porte cochère. No. 361 is now a Lithuanian cultural center, with
a banal modern auditorium attached to its side.

[H2] **101 Sunnyside Avenue** (apartment house), bet. Hendrix St.
and Miller Ave. N side. ca. 1930.

Nestled into the sharp precipice between Highland and
Sunnyside Avenues, this presents a Classical Renaissance plan to
the Sunnyside Avenue approach: a formal, symmetrical subplaza
from which to rise to the view.

*A row of town houses, on Sunnyside Avenue, between Barbey and
Miller Streets, presents a series of porches with paired Tuscan
columns and supporting bracketed shedding roofs. The group is a
powerful statement of this modest area.*

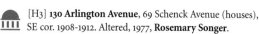

H3

H6

[H3] **130 Arlington Avenue**, 69 Schenck Avenue (houses),
SE cor. 1908-1912. Altered, 1977, **Rosemary Songer**.

Two grand Classical Revival houses of Roman brick with
great Ionic-columned porches. Wealth was once here.

[H4] Originally **James Royal House**, 18 Ashford St., SW cor.
Ridgewood Ave. 1904. **John Petit**.

A Queen Anne/Shingle Style gem, pedimented and towered,
and clad in abominable vinyl siding: note the joints in the round
tower, and the lack of strong detail at the eaves and windows. A
shame.

[H5] **68 Ashford Street** (house), bet. Ridgewood and Arlington
Aves. W side. ca. 1885.

Clapboard and fish-scale shingles, with a circle-in-the-
square hooded oriel balcony of great charm.

[H6] **St. Joseph's Anglican Church**/originally Trinity
Episcopal Church, 131 Arlington Ave., NE cor. Schenck
Ave. 1886. **Richard M. Upjohn**.

Designed by the son of Manhattan Trinity Church's Upjohn,
this is a bulky, vigorous, comforting, buttressed, brick and sandstone church with a friendly, squatting scale. It shows a
Romanesque body, with Gothic finials.

HIGHLAND PARK / CYPRESS HILLS DISTRICT
see pages 790-791

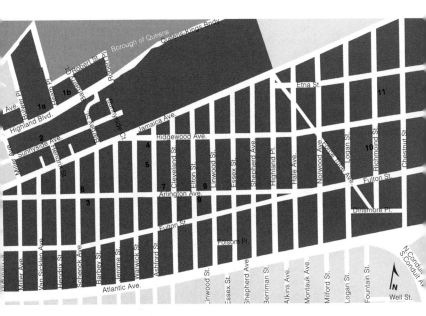

[H7] **219-225 Arlington Avenue** (row houses), bet. Ashford and Cleveland Sts. ca. 1900.

The cornices that join these tan brick, bow-fronted, row houses are as prepossessing as some of the grandest of the Italian Renaissance.

[H8] **Public School 108**, Brooklyn, 200 Linwood St., NW cor. Arlington Ave. 1895. **James W. Naughton**. 🍎

Roman brick with brownstone that is both rough and smooth. Handsome Romanesque Revival arches.

[H9] **Presbyterian Church of the Crossroads**, SE cor. Elton St. and Arlington Ave. ca. 1890.

Stolid brick Gothic Revival with a squat belfry. Terra-cotta provides fine detail more economically than carved stone; and brownstone is too porous a material to maintain such elegant profiles.

[H10] **Public School 65K**, Brooklyn, 158 Richmond St., bet. Ridgewood and Arlington Aves. W side. 1870. **Samuel Leonard**. Façade, 1889. **James W. Naughton**. 🍎

A somber painted brick outpost of education on these early frontiers of Brooklyn's urbanization.

[H11] **Andrews Methodist Church**/originally Wesleyan Methodist Episcopal Church, Richmond St. bet. Etna St. and Ridgewood Ave. E side. 1892. **George Kramer**.

Romanesque Revival/Shingle Style. A glorious rose window intersects both upper shingles and lower brick. A lovely, lonely "country" church.

H7

H9

BROWNSVILLE

Brownsville shares the bottom of the city's economic ladder with the South Bronx. It is largely Hispanic and black, with old and dilapidated housing predominating, much banal public housing, and an isolated intrusion of relatively elegant architecture by the New York State Urban Development Corporation (UDC). The neighborhood was first subdivided in 1865 by Charles S. Brown, to whom the community owes its name. In 1887 a group of real estate entrepreneurs purchased portions and began to encourage Jewish immigrants in the congested Lower East Side to move here. The arrival of the Fulton Street el in 1889 stimulated the influx, and the settlement became a great concentration of poor Eastern European Jews. The community was not free of the problems normally associated with deprived neighborhoods; some of Murder, Incorporated's most notorious leaders grew up in these streets. The completion of the New Lots branch of the IRT subway in 1922 further improved rapid transit connections to Manhattan, and the area grew mildly prosperous. Pitkin Avenue is still a major shopping street for the surrounding population, although from the 1920s through the 1940s it attracted shoppers from a much larger region—such is the fate of our assorted downtowns. The neighborhood's movie house, at Pitkin and East New York Avenues—in a brief renaissance, the Hudson Temple Cathedral—was once one of the city's great fantasy movie palaces. Following World War II, the Jewish population moved to more middle-class precincts (most lately Staten Island) and the area declined. Major renewal has been effective only in islands of activity, most notably at Rutland Plaza, Marcus Garvey Village, and the various recent row-housed blocks of the Nehemiah Plan. In between, vast scars still record the wounds sustained in peacetime wars.

B1

[B1] **Rutland Plaza**, East New York Ave. and Rutland Rd., E. 92nd to E. 94th Sts. 1976. **Donald Stull & Assocs.**
One of the best of the UDC (New York State Urban Development Corporation) incisions into the cityscape (others are at Roosevelt Island, Coney Island, and the Twin Parks section of the Bronx). Bold form and color rise over the neighboring landscape with style, but the later signs and graphics are awful.

[B2] **Public School 398**, Brooklyn, The Walter Weaver School, East New York Ave. bet. E. 93rd and E. 94th Sts. S side. 1976. **Perkins & Will**.
In an era of open classrooms, when schools were conceived as shopping centers of education, this barrel-vaulted basilica could offer partitioning (or nonpartitioning) in the most flexible manner. Terra-cotta brick, with bronze-anodized aluminum.

B3

[B3] Originally L**oew's Pitkin Theater**/later Hudson Temple Cathedral/now 3 Guys Furniture, 1501 Pitkin Ave., NW cor. Saratoga Ave. 1930. **Thomas W. Lamb**.
A landmark on this brassy shopping street. Its carefully ornate brick and terra-cotta exterior screened one of those fantasy, fairy-tale auditoriums conjured up by Lamb and his peers in the great picture palace era of the late 1920s, complete with twinkling stars and moving clouds across its ceiling-sky.

B4

[B4] Onetime **Banco de Ponce**/originally The East New York Savings Bank, Kings Highway and Rockaway Pkwy. E. side. 1962. **Lester Tichy & Assocs.**
Hollywood in Brownsville, where the romance is in the banking. Some remember Tichy's equally violent intrusion into old Pennsylvania Station with a luminous canopy that blinded you to the glorious main waiting room surrounding it.

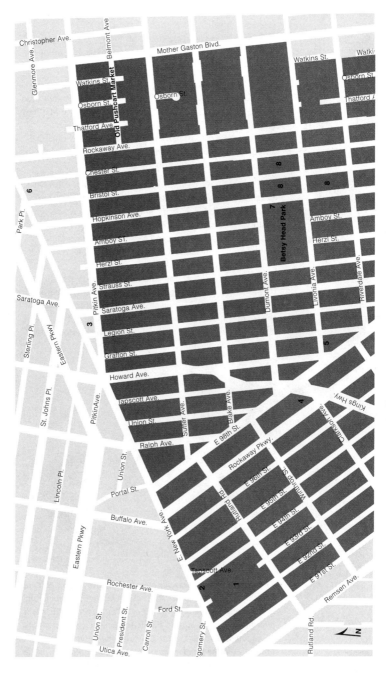

[B5] **Engine Company 238, Squad Company 4, N.Y.C. Fire Department**, 885 Howard Ave., SE cor. Livonia Ave. 1974. **Giovanni Pasanella**.

Red-brown square brick clads this simple, strong modern fire station, skylit at its rear. A modest but class act.

[B5a] Formerly **Belmont Avenue pushcart market**, Belmont Ave. bet. Rockaway and Christopher Aves.

Once one of the city's most vigorous street markets, filled with the itinerant pushcarts of Jewish merchants, Belmont still spills from storefronts onto its sidewalks, now thronged with

B7

Hispanic and black residents. The pushcarts are gone but not the merchandise, piled high on planks spread over sawhorses and milk crates.

[B6] **73rd Precinct, N.Y.C. Police Department**, 1470 East New York Ave., bet. Bristol and Chester Sts. S side. 1982. **Swanke Hayden Connell**.

A striking, serrated façade adorns this understated precinct station, an island of architectural success in this vast sea of banality.

[B7] **Betsy Head Memorial Playground Bathhouse**, N.Y.C. Department of Parks & Recreation, Strauss St. to Hopkinson Ave., Dumont to Livonia Aves. 1940. **John Matthews Hatton**.

Liberal use of glass block and a parasol roof delicately balanced on parabolic ribs distinguish the WPA bathhouse that serves an immense swimming pool.

[B8] **Marcus Garvey Village** (row housing), Dumont Ave. to a point S of Riverdale Ave., from W of Bristol St. to Chester St. and including a portion of Rockaway Ave. 1976. Prototypical design, **Theodore Liebman** of the N.Y.S. Urban Development Corporation and **Kenneth Frampton** of the Institute for Architecture and Urban Studies. Construction documents by **David Todd & Assocs.**

The UDC's pretentious experiment in low-rise, high-density housing: row houses with stoops, embracing paved and planted play and sitting areas. Austere and reminiscent of the fanatically regimented Amsterdam housing of the 1920s, it is more a scholastic architectural thesis than a prototype for urban redevelopment.

B8

*The shtetl: What Brownsville lacked in physical amenities it once made up for in the richness of its social life. Here the immigrant Jewish population recalled the life of the shtetl, their former communities in Eastern Europe. Pitkin Avenue was the street for the grand promenade, its Yiddish-speaking community addicted to thrashing out the social and political problems of the hour while shpatzeering down the avenue. At one time Hoffman's cafeteria was the area's modest but glittery version of a Delmonico's of another era and social class. Amboy Street, the turf of a youth gang immortalized in **Irving Shulman**'s The Amboy Dukes (1947), became in 1916 the home of the first birth-control clinic in America, established by **Margaret Sanger**. The Jewish population, more affluent than their grandparents, has left what they had perceived to be the asphalt jungle and emigrated en masse to suburbia. On Pitkin Avenue, Yiddish has been replaced by Spanish.*

E1

EAST NEW YORK

▥ [E1] **Grace Baptist Church**/originally Deutsche
Evangelische Lutherische St. Johannes Kirche, 223 New
Jersey Ave., bet. Liberty and Glenmore Aves. ca. 1885.
    Gothic Revival in banded brown bricks, crowned with a slated pyramidal steeple.

[E2] **Holy Trinity Russian Orthodox Church**, Pennsylvania Ave.
SE cor. Glenmore Ave. 1935.
    One great and one minor onion dome sheathed in verdigris
copper crown a salmon brick base. The porch on Glenmore
Avenue, with its fat columns and steeply pitched pediment, is an
eclectic fantasy.

E2

[E3] **East New York Neighborhood Family Care Center**, 2094
Pitkin Ave., bet. Pennsylvania and New Jersey Aves. S side. 1976.
    A decent modern building in orange-brown brick, its deeply
incised windows a popular stylistic mannerism of the 1970s. As
is usual in these unsophisticated sectors, the signs disgrace the
architecture.

E4

[E4] **HELP/Genesis Houses**, 330 Hinsdale St., bet. Blake and
Dumont Aves. 1992. **Cooper Robertson & Partners**.
    This forbidding block embraces a paved and planted court-
yard providing a gracious urban space and security for its residents (one entry point).

[E5] **Bradford Street**, bet. Sutter and Blake Aves.
    This street preserves a sense of the early urbanization of East
New York. Gaily painted, the block retains a charm that most of
Eastern Brooklyn has lost to the ravages of blockbusting, pover-
ty, and sleazy "modernizations."

E5

[E6] **New Lots Community Church**/formerly New Lots
Reformed Dutch Church, 630 New Lots Ave., SE cor. Schenck
Ave. 1823-1824. 🍎
    Built by the latter-day Dutch farmers of this area when
weekly trips to the Flatbush church became too arduous. A
painted wood-shingled body, with Gothic Revival openings.

▗ [E7] **Bethelite Institutional Baptist Church**, 446 Elton
St., bet. Belmont and Sutter Aves. 1990. **Theo. David**.
    The stepped gable and columned portal lead to a light-filled
white sanctuary; a wonderful renewal (there was a brick box to
begin with) for East New York.

E8

▗ [E8] **New Life Baptist Church**, 931 Dumont Ave., near
Elton St. 1992. **Theo. David**.
    "Simple but stunning" say *Oculus* writers **Jayne Merkel** and
Philip Nobel. And the spine, articulated on the façade by reced-
ing crosses, skylights the interior space.

▗ [E9] **Essex Terrace** (apartments), bounded by Linden
Blvd., Hegeman Ave., Linwood and Essex Sts. 1970.
Norval White.
    Crisp and well cared-for, this union-sponsored low-rise high-
density project surrounds its own central private plaza. The corner gates allow residents to admit or restrict the neighborhood at
their discretion. "Discretion" now means "permanently locked."

E9

▗ [E10] **City Line 1 Turnkey Public Housing, N.Y.C.
Housing Authority**, 460-470 Fountain Ave., and 1085-
1087 Hegeman Ave., NW cor. Fountain Ave., and 1052-1064
Hegeman Ave., and 768-774 Logan St. SW cor. Hegeman Ave.
1975. **Ciardullo-Ehmann**.
    Quasi-town houses that attempt to emulate the fussy scale of
their row house neighbors. The attempt is noble but the product

E10

is crude. Note particularly the rainwater leaders that wander aimlessly across the façades.

[E11] **Public School 306**, Brooklyn, 970 Vermont Ave., NW cor. Cozine Ave. 1966. **Pedersen & Tilney**.

An intelligent, no-nonsense, cast-in-place concrete school in an area whose flat monotony is being broken by towers sprouting everywhere. Note the stylish 1960s stair towers.

E11

[E12] **Starrett City**, bet. Flatlands Ave. and Shore Pkwy., Seaview and Louisiana Aves. 1976. **Herman Jessor**.

A surreal experience. Great building blocks, housing 5,881 apartments, are placed in the manner of a supermodel in this boondock landscape. Jessor's other giant anti-urban fantasies include Co-op City in the Bronx. The architecture of the building blocks is bland. Self-contained, the City has its own schools, churches, and synagogues and generates its own heat, light, and power.

[E13] **The Landings at Fresh Creek**, 556-630 Louisiana Ave., bet. Vandalia Ave. and Twin Pines Dr. 1995. **Herbert Mandel**.

E12

An urbane cluster of row housing embraces a courtyard. Too bad they had to fill it with cars. But in this part of Brooklyn, this is architecture of great sophistication.

▌ [E14] **Baird Special Care Pavilion, Brookdale Hospital**
▬ **Medical Center**, 1235 Linden Blvd., NW cor. Rockaway Pkwy. 1968. **Horowitz & Chun**.

Somber brown brick makes a strong, well-scaled, and serene statement in this pallid part of town. Both private physicians' offices and clinics are contained within.

E13

E4

Queens

QUEENS KEY MAP

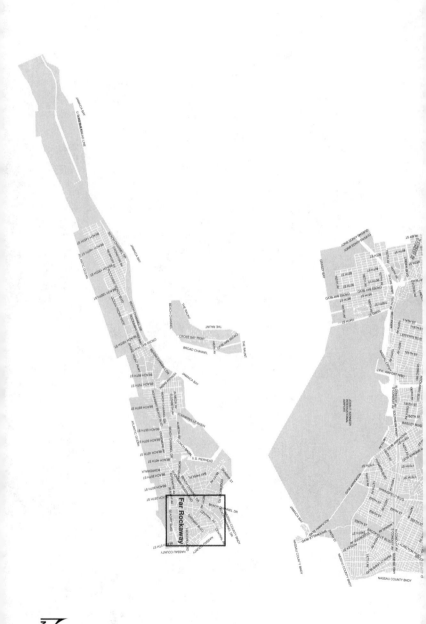

Far Rockaway

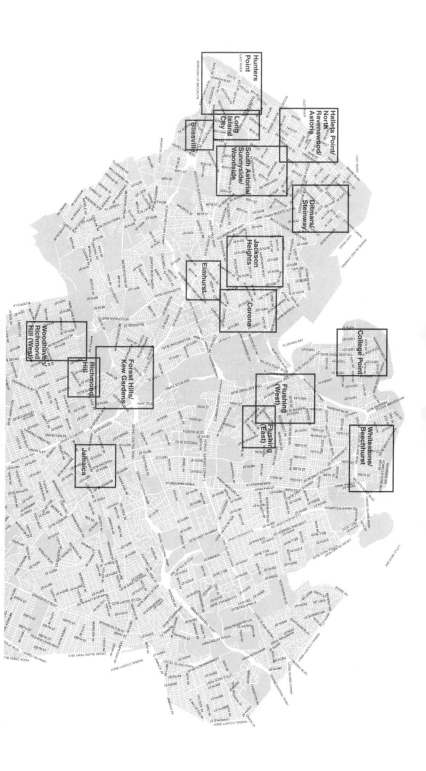

Queens

Borough of Queens/Queens County

4

 Colonial

 Georgian/ Federal

 Greek Revival

 Gothic Revival

 Villa

 Romanesque Revival

 Renaissance Revival

 Roman Revival

 Art Deco/ Art Moderne

 Modern/ Post-Modern

Queens is the home of two of the three metropolitan airports—LaGuardia and Kennedy International. Its residents are unable to forget that fact, the drone of jets and props ever reminding them as planes swoop out of the sky and into these all-weather aerodromes. Awareness of modern technology is balanced by contact with nature—postage-stamp-sized front lawns or the vastness of the Jamaica Bay Wildlife Refuge (now a part of the Gateway National Recreation Area), not to mention the borough's other parks: 16,397 acres in all. Queens is the largest borough: 114.7 square miles (126.6 including inland waters), constituting almost a third of the city's entire area, almost twice the area of Staten Island alone. In population it ranks second only to Brooklyn.

As a borough it is predominantly a bedroom community. The last great open spaces of New York were here until the late 1940s, allowing developers to meet the need for detached dwellings: suburbia within the city limits. However, a good deal of industry also thrives within its boundaries: in Long Island City and Maspeth and along the Long Island Rail Road are manufacturers of a wide variety of products.

Before Queens became a borough, it was a far larger county, encompassing its present-day area as well as that of Nassau (a new county created as a by-product of consolidation into Greater New York in 1898). The borough is named for **Catherine of Braganza, Queen of Charles II**.

The vastness of Queens and its relatively late development have encouraged the retention of the old town, village, and subdivision names for its various communities. From a strong sense of pride and identification with the outlying suburbs, residents never refer to themselves as "Queensites" but rather as living in Jamaica, or Flushing, or Forest Hills, or St. Albans. If pressed further, the response to "Where do you live?" becomes "Long Island."

HALLETS POINT • RAVENSWOOD
ASTORIA • DITMARS • STEINWAY
SOUTH ASTORIA • SUNNYSIDE
WOODSIDE • LONG ISLAND CITY
HUNTERS POINT • BLISSVILLE

Long Island City
Separated from the town of Newtown in 1870.

Between 1870 and 1898, when it was consolidated into
Greater New York, Long Island City was itself a city. It encompassed not only the area we still identify with its name but also
the adjacent communities to the north, northeast, and east.

GREATER ASTORIA

The peninsula projecting into Hell Gate's once turbulent waters
is named for the family of **William Hallet**, who received it as a
grant from **Governor Peter Stuyvesant** in 1652. From his family's early settlement and that of **Stephen Alling Halsey**, the
Father of Astoria, the village of Astoria developed. As a
Manhattan suburb its growth followed the introduction of
steam-powered ferries in 1815. By 1839 the area had been incorporated, with friends of **John Jacob Astor** winning a bitter factional fight in naming Astoria for him.

The year 1842 saw the completion of the turnpike to
Greenpoint. Soon a shipping trade was established in lumber,
particularly in exotic foreign woods. Just north of the cove on
the mount called Hallets Point, lumber and shipping magnates
built mansions, a few of which remain, though deprived of their
former splendor and spacious view-laden grounds. Nearby, at
the foot of Astoria Boulevard, the area's most significant ferry
service to Manhattan, linking easily accessible East 92nd Street,
plied the waters between 1867 and the advent of the Triborough
Bridge.

The availability of fine lumber and cheap land persuaded
piano manufacturer **William Steinway** in the early 1870s to
extend his activities from Manhattan to a company town of
some 400 acres, purchasing a superb stone house for his family
at the foot of Steinway Street. The mansion, workers' housing,
and both old and new factories all remain.

W1

HALLETS POINT

[W1] **Good Church of Deliverance**, Pentecostal, and
First Reformed Church of Astoria/originally Reformed
Dutch Church of Hallets Cove, 27-26 12th St., bet. 27th Ave. and
Astoria Blvd. W side. 1889. Steeple, 1900.

A terra-cotta, brick, and verdigris copper squat late Victorian
Goth. Bold, monolithic, homely, and magnificent.

[W2] Originally **Dr. Wayt House**, 9-29 27th Ave., NW cor. 12th
St. ca. 1845.

An austere and elegantly proportioned Italianate mansion.
The eyebrow windows are inherited from the Greek Revival.

W2

[W3] Originally **Remsen House**, 9-26 27th Ave., SW cor.
12th St. ca. 1835.

Greek Revival stuccoed house, handsomely maintained with
rural grounds, rubble garden walls, iron fence, slate sidewalk.

[W4] **House**, NE cor. 27th Ave. and 12th St. 1860s.

Some lusty Corinthian columns carry a two-story porch
from a brick body to the street. The Benner house on 14th Street
had porches far grander than this before the Vandals arrived.

[W5] **25-70, 26-04, and 26-22 12th Street** (houses), bet. Astoria Park S. and 26th Ave. 1860s.

Three Italianate survivors (with Roman Tuscan columns) that are loved by their owners, providing eccentric paint jobs.

[W6] **Astoria Branch, Queens Borough Public Library**, 14-01 Astoria Blvd., NE cor. 14th St. 1904. **Tuthill & Higgins**.

One of many branch libraries donated by **Andrew Carnegie**: in tan Roman brick with a steep hipped roof.

[W7] **St. George's Church**, SE cor. 14th St. and 27th Ave. ca. 1900??

Timber and stone join to suggest an English country church.

W8, then   W8, now

[W8] Originally **Robert Benner House**, 25-37 14th St., bet. Astoria Park S. and 26th Ave. E side. 1852.

Once proudly presenting a two-story (balconied) Doric façade, this grand Southern mansion has been raped and ravaged. Built by **James L. Stratton** and occupied by Manhattan lawyer **Robert Benner**, a fancier of flori- and arboriculture, its deep front yard harbored a magnificent copper beech tree. The tree has given way to a parking lot; the Doric and Corinthian orders and balcony, to banality.

[W9] **25-38 14th Street** (house), bet. Astoria Park S. and 26th Ave. W side. 1880s.

A survivor, unlike the disaster across the street at 25-37. But in surviving, this Shingle Style house acquiesced in fake brick (sheet asphalt siding).

W10

[W10] **25-45, 25-47 14th Place** (two-family house), bet. 26th Ave. and Astoria Park S. E side. ca. 1910.

A pair of well-designed (and maintained) houses whose common 2-story porches tie them together as a single, strong architectural composition.

Down the hill at the corner is:

W11

[W11] **14-22 Astoria Park South** (four-family house), SW cor. 14th Place. 1965. **Guy G. Rothenstein**, designer.

Lush border landscaping helps make this Modernist apartment house less obtrusive in an older area. For a number of years the designer worked for Le Corbusier.

A venture to the north across Astoria Park South:

[W12] **Astoria Park**, Shore Blvd. to 19th St., Ditmars Blvd. to Astoria Park S. [W13] **Astoria Play Center and Swimming Pool**, N.Y.C. Department of Parks & Recreation, in Astoria Park. 1936. **J. M. Hatton**.

A tilted piece of green giving picnic views of the Triborough and Hell Gate Bridges and the Manhattan skyline. Within is an expansive Art Deco/Art Moderne WPA-era pool complex and bathhouse.

W14

[W14] **Triborough Bridge**, O. H. Ammann, engineer. **Aymar Embury II**, architect. 1936.

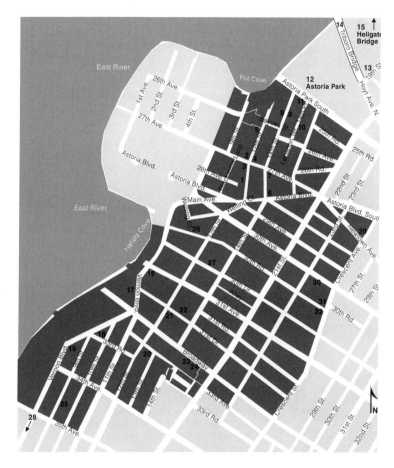

A whole highway system, trestled and bridged, of which this, the Hell Gate span, is the greatest part.

[W15] **Hell Gate Bridge**/officially the East River Arch Bridge of the New York Connecting Railroad. 1917. **Gustav Lindenthal**, engineer. **Henry Hornbostel**, architect.

The through connection for the Penn Central (now Amtrak) on its way from Washington through New York to Boston (it tunnels under both the Hudson and East Rivers, rising in Queens to pass over and through these great over- and under-slung bowstring trusses). **Hornbostel** designed the massive Classical piers, but the glory of the bridge is in the forms of **Lindenthal**'s engineering.

W15

RAVENSWOOD

W16

Ravenswood, along the East River above the Queensboro Bridge, is a low-density area with a mixture of waterside industry, like Con Ed's Big Allis, and high-rise public housing.

[W16] **Adirondack Building**/originally Sohmer Piano Company (factory), 31-01 Vernon Blvd., SE cor. 31st Ave. 1886-1887. **Berger & Baylies**. Top story and mansard added, 1910.

One of Steinway's competitors also established himself in this area in a multileveled factory. The top floors and corner Second Empire clock tower were added as business flourished. Now a loft building.

W17

[W17] **Socrates Sculpture Park**, 31-42 Vernon Blvd., bet. 31st Dr. and Broadway. W side on the bank of the East River. 1986. Open to the public. 718-956-1819. 10 am-sunset daily/free.

A fallow riverside site converted into an enormous outdoor sculpture garden through the combined efforts of the Athena Foundation, and the City's Departments of Parks & Recreation, and Cultural Affairs. On display can be found, from time to time, the lusty work of **Mark Di Suvero** (the foundation's founder), **Alice Aycock**, **Richard Serra**, and many others.

[W18] **Isamu Noguchi Garden Museum**, 32-37 Vernon Blvd., NE cor. 33rd Rd. (Entrance on 33rd Rd. bet. 9th and 10th Sts.) 1985. **Isamu Noguchi**, sculptor; **Shogi Sazao**, architect. 718-204-7088. Open to the public: April-October; Wed, Thu, Fri 10-5; Sat, Sun 11-6.

Sculptures in stone, metal, and wood grace this former **Noguchi** studio and its adjacent garden. Stage designs for **Martha Graham** and **George Balanchine**, as well as his astonishing Akari lamps, are also on display.

[W19] **Kraus Company** (administrative offices), 33-01 Vernon Blvd., bet. 33rd Rd. and 34th Ave. E side. ca. 1985.

Dark gray salt-and-pepper glazed brick and trendy circular wall-cutouts are slim architectural pickings in a neighborhood that sorely needs some fatter ones.

W20

[W20] Originally **Barkin-Levin factory** (Lassie Coats), 12-12 33rd Ave., SW cor. 13th St. 1958. **Ulrich Franzen**.

Built for an expatriate clothing manufacturer from the over-crowded garment district of Manhattan. Incomparably crisp architecture, poorly maintained, and moderately, but badly, altered.

W21

[W21] **31-41 12th Street** (house), SE cor. 31st Dr. (one-way east). ca. 1860.

Freestanding Italianate rural house inundated with brown-green composition asphalt-shingle siding that nevertheless allows the window detail, the wood trim, and the house's basic form to carry the day.

[W22] **12-15 and 12-17 31st Drive** (houses), bet. 12th (one-way north) and 14th Sts. N side. 1920s and 1870s?

Two porticos of finely crafted columns; well-proportioned columns can heal many architectural wounds.

W23

[W23] **Long Island City High School**, 14-30 Broadway, bet. 14th Place and 21st St. S side. 1995. **Gruzen Samton**.

Bulky and largely no-nonsense, the School offers a strongly articulated, polychromatic entrance bay to its teenage horde. The more playful work of **Gruzen Samton** in public schools for the younger student is here muted for the hopefully serious challenge of high schooling.

W22

W27

W28

[W24] **Community Church of Astoria**, 14-42 Broadway, bet. 14th Place and 21st St. S side. 1952. Total reconstruction, 1986, **Alfredo De Vido Assocs.**

A suave, subtle reconstruction and extension of a church serving a congregation of limited means. It's amazing what sophistication concrete block can achieve.

Lone curiosities

Lonely brownstones: At various, totally unexpected points in the largely wood-frame or brick-front Ravenswood and Astoria communities, appear late 19th-century, richly worked, 2-story sandstone-façade row houses that contrast smooth with rock-face brownstone. They are simply beautiful and always come as a surprise: [W25] **34-55 9th St.**, bet. 34th and 35th Aves. E side., [W26] **11-41 30th Rd.**, bet. Vernon Blvd. and 12th St. N side., [W27] **12-29 to 12-35 30th Drive** (one-way east), bet. 12th and 14th Sts. N side.

[W28] **Ravenswood Plant, Consolidated Edison Company of New York, Inc.**, 36th to below 40th Aves., Vernon Blvd. to East River. 1961.

Natural landmarks from all directions are these candy-striped smokestacks, two @ 450 feet, one @ 500 feet. This is the home of **Big Allis**, the enormous (and, for a time, quite cranky) electrical generator manufactured by **Allis-Chalmers**.

W29

W30

W32

ASTORIA

[W29] Our Lady of Mt. Carmel Roman Catholic Church, 23-35 Newtown Ave., NW cor. Crescent St. Narthex, 1915. Nave, 1966.

The Newtown Avenue façade is a dignified, wonderful, neo-Gothic evocation in limestone, an architectural treat for all. Mt. Carmel Institute, the parish hall, across the avenue to the southwest, is an intriguing Italian Renaissance foil.

[W30] HANAC/formerly 74th Precinct, N.Y.C. Police Department, 23-16 30th Ave., bet. 23rd and Crescent Sts. ca. 1890.

A Romanesque Revival symphony. An important architectural-cultural anchor in a neighborhood showing many conflicting tides of development. (HANAC stands for Hellenic American Neighborhood Action Committee, a social-services agency for the area's large Greek community.)

[W31] Episcopal Church of the Redeemer and Chapel, 30-30 Crescent St., NW cor. 30th Rd. 1868. Consecrated, 1879.

A dark, brooding, ashlar stone church. Instead of a spire, the bell tower supports an internally illuminated cross.

[W32] **Good Shepherd United Methodist Church**/originally First Methodist Episcopal Church of Astoria, 30-40 Crescent St., SW cor. 30th Rd. 1908.

Naïve Gothic Revival in light rockfaced granite ashlar, its stubby tower crudely crenellated.

DITMARS

Con Edison Astoria: Put into operation in 1906, and covering hundreds of acres north of 20th Avenue and west of 37th Street, the enormous Con Ed power plant is an unsung landmark of the Ditmars area of Astoria. Built by one of Con Ed's predecessors, the Consolidated Gas Company of New York, it was the world's largest cooking-gas generating plant when completed. It serves both Manhattan and the Bronx via underwater tunnels. Both natural gas and electricity are distributed from the site, which has since been considerably expanded using landfill to absorb Berrian Island.

River Crest Sanitarium: Today the multiblock site is occupied by St. John's Prep (formerly Mater Christi Roman Catholic High School), but it was once a well-known therapeutic facility (founded in 1896 on the old Wolcott estate by a local congressman, **Dr. Jonathan Joseph Kindred**) "for Mental and Nervous Diseases with Separate Buildings for Alcoholic and Drug Habituation." The grounds extend south from 21st Avenue between Crescent and 27th Streets.

D1

[D1] **Arleigh Realty Company** row housing and apartments, 21-11 to 21-77, 21-12 to 21-72 28th St., both sides. 21-12 to 21-72 29th St., W side, bet. 21st Ave. and Ditmars Blvd. ca. 1925.

Speculative midblock terraces of mansarded rowhouses work with a gentle rise in topography, offering a picturesque composition despite the repetition of the ingredients. Here, architecture enriches a locale and gives it identity, an accomplishment largely missing in postwar speculations.

[D2] **Church of the Immaculate Conception** (Roman Catholic), 29-01 Ditmars Blvd., NE cor. 29th St. 1950. **Henry V. Murphy**.

D2

Latter-day Italian neo-Romanesque. The unusual corbeled brick bell tower is a dramatic landmark, up and down Ditmars Boulevard.

[D3] **The Acropolis** (apartments)/originally Metropolitan Life Insurance Company apartments, 33rd to 35th Sts., 21st Ave. to Ditmars Blvd. (One square block.) 1924. **Andrew J. Thomas** and **D. Everett Waid**.

Innocuous outside, gracious within its courtyard.

The first Metropolitan venture into direct development of housing (later to result in Parkchester in the Bronx and Stuyvesant Town/Peter Cooper Village in Manhattan). Two muted rows of 5-story, red brick apartments (now painted off-white), defining a blocklong verdant garden.

D3

[D4] **Lawrence Family Graveyard**, 20th Rd. SE cor. 35th St. 1703. 🌶️

A memorable location in history, and the Lawrences have two such landmarked cemeteries. But don't bother to look. You can't get in or really see in.

[D5] **St. Irene Chrysovalantou (Greek Orthodox) Church**, 36-25 23rd Ave., bet. 36th and 37th Sts. N side. Altered from two former row houses, 1980.

D5

The entire north side of this block is a charming vernacular residential composition crowned by the midblock church. The real delight is within: a folk art religious extravaganza, something like walking into a box by artist **Joseph Cornell**. Plan to visit when open.

[D6] **Bohemian Park and Hall**, 29-19 24th Ave., NE cor. 29th St. 1910.

A mittel-Europa beer garden with picnic tables and lights strung on wires. A place to lift a stein, listen to music, or dance, all behind a less-than-picturesque stuccoed wall. Alas, the last of

D6

DITMARS / STEINWAY DISTRICTS

see pages 807-809

Queens's many turn-of-the-century picnic grounds. Operated by the Bohemian Citizens' Benevolent Society of Astoria.

STEINWAY

William Steinway: The individual from whom the community derives its name was a brilliant 19th-century entrepreneur. Besides being a manufacturer of pianos, Steinway was a transit magnate (today's Steinway Transit Corporation), builder of an underwater tunnel (today's Flushing Line East River crossing), and developer, together with beer baron **George Ehret**, of a working-class resort, North Beach (site of today's LaGuardia Airport).

[D7] Formerly **William Steinway House**/also known as the **Steinway Mansion**/originally Benjamin T. Pike, Jr., House, 18-33 41st St., bet. Berrian Blvd. and 19th Ave. E side. ca. 1858. 🐾

On a minimountain in a deciduous jungle inhabited by barking dogs, old cars, and trucks. **William Steinway**'s (originally optician **Benjamin Pike, Jr.**'s) dark gray granite house was a showplace in its time. (The piano factory [1872] is still at the northwest corner of 19th Avenue and 38th Street.)

D7

The mountain: *The area between 42nd and Hazen Streets, north of 19th Avenue, dominates today's view east from the Steinway Mansion. The 60-foot mountain of tailings from some long forgotten municipal project is now under the jurisdiction of the Port Authority. Given the enormity of the environmental desecration, the authority's neat little signs are ironic: NO DUMPING.*

D8

[D8] Originally **Steinway workers' housing**, 41-17 to 41-25, 40-12 to 41-20 20th (Winthrop) Ave., bet. Steinway, 41st (Albert) St. and 42nd (Theodore) Sts. Both sides. 20-11 to 20-29, 20-12 to 20-34 41st St., bet. 20th Ave. and 20th Rd. Both sides. 1877-1879.

Trim, painted Victorian brick row houses, originally rented by the Steinways to their workers. Loved. Note the carved stone nameplates on the corner houses bearing the streets' original names, those of Steinway family members.

D9

[D9] **Steinway Reformed Church**/originally Union Protestant Church, 41-01 Ditmars Blvd., NE cor. 41st St. 1891.

In 1891 neighbor **William Steinway** contributed the pipe organ to this rural Gothic Revival gem (and no doubt thereby to its change of name and denomination). The many-finialed tower and strong Shingle Style volumes read as a major monument in this neighborhood (in spite of the asbestos shingle job).

D10

[D10] **Stern's department store warehouse**/originally Steinway & Sons piano factory, 45-02 Ditmars Blvd., bet. 45th and 46th Sts. S side. 1902.

A 6-story H-plan mill (along with developments on both adjoining blocks) built by the Steinways to allow for the 1909 move from their Park (then Fourth) Avenue factory in Manhattan.

[D11] **St. Francis of Assisi Roman Catholic Church**, 45-04 21st Ave., SE cor. 45th St. 1930.

A modest neo-Tudor church..

To the east toward LaGuardia airport:

[D12] Originally **Abraham Lent House**/also known as Lent Homestead, 78-03 19th Rd., at 78th St. N side. ca. 1729.

Weathered shingled dormers and clapboard siding—a well-preserved "Dutch" farmhouse—nesting amid lush foliage that also embraces the family cemetery of the Lent and Riker families.

D12

SOUTH ASTORIA

[S1] **Sidewalk clock**, in front of 30-78 Steinway St., bet. 30th and 31st Aves. W side. 1922. 🦴

One of a group of sidewalk clocks officially designated by the Landmarks Preservation Commission. An inspired decision.

[S2] **The GAP** (store)/originally American Savings Bank, Steinway Branch, 31-02 Steinway St., SW cor. 31st Ave. 1974. **Edward Larrabee Barnes Assocs**.

Dark brown brick and sheer glass; elegance, urbanity, and chic in an older, stolid, somber, middle-class community. Mentioned because of the Barnes name, not what it is now.

Scheutzen Park: The popular 7-acre picnic park/beer garden, established in 1870 at the southeast corner of Steinway Street and Broadway contained dancing pavilions, shooting galleries, picnic tables, and groves of trees. It was the site of thousands of social events staged by members of the city's German community until it succumbed to development beginning in 1924.

S3

 [S3] **Church of the Most Precious Blood** (Roman Catholic), 32-30 37th St., bet. Broadway and 34th Ave. 1932. **McGill & Hamlin**. Stations of the cross, **D. Dunbar Beck**. St. Theresa and St. Anthony statues, **Hazel Clerc**. Stained glass, **Richard N. Spiers & Son**.

Henry J. McGill's masterpiece. Only the 37th Street façade is clad in stone, reflecting both medieval and Modernistic influences in its boxy form. The interior, however, is a celebration of superior ecclesiastical decorative arts of the 1920s and 1930s. In 1934 partner **Talbot Hamlin** retired to become Avery Librarian at Columbia University.

[S4] **Kaufman's Astoria Motion Picture and Television Center**/formerly U.S. Army Signal Corps Pictorial Center/formerly Eastern Service Studios/originally Famous Players Lasky Corporation (Paramount Pictures), irregular site along 35th Ave. bet. 34th and 38th Sts. Both sides. [S5] **Former Building No. 1**, 35-11 35th Ave., bet. 35th and 36th Sts. N side. 1919-1921. **Fleischman Construction Co.**, designer. 🦴 [S6] **Museum of the Moving Image**, 36-11 35th Ave., bet. 36th and 37th Sts. N side. Altered into museum, 1988, **Gwathmey Siegel & Assocs**. 718-784-4520. tues-Fri, 12-4; Sat, Sun, 12-6; closed Mon.

S5

One of several venerable movie studios still to be found in New York, this sprawling complex is the largest. In the silent era, **Gloria Swanson**, **Rudolph Valentino**, **W. C. Fields**, and their peers performed here. After talkies arrived, *Beau Geste, The Emperor Jones,* and the W.P.A. film *One Third of a Nation* were produced here. Its rebirth in the 1970s saw the making of *The Wiz* and other widely heralded films.

SUNNYSIDE

S7

A residential area triggered by the arrival of the IRT Flushing Line along Queens Boulevard and Roosevelt Avenue in 1917. Though surrounded by industry and cemeteries, its proximity and excellent access to Manhattan have assured its stability. Its most noted feature is Sunnyside Gardens.

[S7] **Sunnyside Gardens**, bet. 43rd and 48th Sts., Skillman and Barnett Aves. to 39th Ave., plus parts of 49th and 50th Sts. along Skillman Ave. 1924-1928. **Clarence S. Stein** and **Henry Wright**. **Frederick Ackerman**.

S7

Seventy-seven acres of barren, mosquito-infested land were transformed into a great and successful experiment in urban housing design by the City Housing Corporation, headed by **Alexander M. Bing**, a New York real estate mogul. Forced into

SOUTH ASTORIA / SUNNYSIDE / WOODSIDE DISTRICTS

see pages 810-813

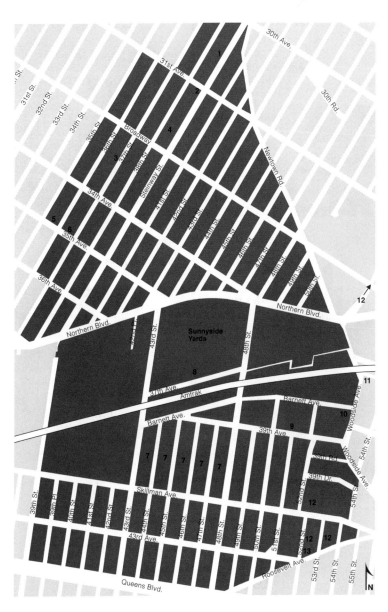

using the preordained street grid, architects **Stein** and **Wright** arranged row housing to face both the street and the interior garden spaces. Walk under umbrellas of London plane trees along the paths that penetrate each block, where the architecture is unimportant, but the urban arrangements a source of urbane delight. **Lewis Mumford** lived here from 1925 to 1936.

[S8] **New York Presbyterian Church** (Korean)/partially the former Naarden-UOP Fragrances (factory)/before that Knickerbocker Laundry Company, 43-23 37th Ave., bet. 43rd and 48th Sts. N side. 1932. **Irving M. Fenichel**. Renovations, extensions, and surelevations, 1999. **Greg Lynn**, **Michael McInturf** and **Doug Garafalo**.

They started with Knickerbocker's sleek Art Moderne concrete, seemingly molded of streamlined ice cream, a familiar monument to the hundreds of thousands of commuters who sped by on the adjacent LIRR into Manhattan. To this was

S8

S9

S10

S11

S12

added a gigantic steel-clad, computer-generated nave that billows out (a rectilinear balloon) and down the grade behind.

[S9] **Phipps Gardens** (apartments), 51-01 39th Ave. bet. 50th and 52nd Sts. N side. 1931. 52-02 to 53-20 Barnett Ave. bet. 50th and 52nd Sts. S side. 1935. **Isador Rosenfeld**, office of **Clarence S. Stein**.

A 4-, 5-, and 6-story architectural incunabulum surrounding a 2-square-block lush, green, private, center-courted world. The architecture here is clearly secondary to a sense of place. (Also, there's a second grouping behind the first.)

WOODSIDE

Just across the former Long Island City boundary.

[S10] **J. Sklar Manufacturing Company**/formerly Lathan Lithography Company, 38-04 Woodside Ave., bet. Barnett and 39th Aves. W side. 1923. **McDonnell and Pearl**.

A Tudor campus set on manicured lawns disguises this manufactory of surgical instruments. For once a factory becomes a visual amenity in the community.

[S11] Originally **New York & Queens County Railroad Company** (trolley barn)/now (what's left) gateway to shopping center, Northern Blvd. SE cor. Woodside Ave. ca. 1895. Altered, 1988.

With the electrification of the Steinway Railway Company's streetcar system, a trolley barn was built on this site, taken over in 1896 by a Philadelphia syndicate that renamed the operation NY&QCR. The structure endured a number of reuses until 1987, when much of it was demolished in favor of a shopping center. Neighborhood preservation stalwarts prevailed in a last-ditch effort to keep the wrecking ball from completing its task.

[S12] **Mathews & Company flats**, 52nd St. E side, 53rd St. both sides, 54th St. W side, bet. Skillman and Roosevelt Aves. 52-01 to 53-31 Skillman Ave., bet. 52nd and 54th Sts. N side. 1924. [S13] **Mathews Apartment Building**, 51-45 52nd St., NE cor. Roosevelt Ave. 1924.

Three-story row house apartments, and a single, corner apartment house, all of yellow Kreischerville (Staten Island) brick, by developers who helped make early 20th-century Ridgewood a special place.

And off our map to the east, along Woodside Avenue:

[S14] **St. Paul's Episcopal Church of Woodside**, 39th Ave. SW cor. 61st St. ca. 1873.

An exquisite and rare, rural, board-and-batten Gothic Revival wooden church. Let there be a miracle: save this church as a living memorial to its motto, CITY CHURCH/COUNTRY FRIENDLINESS.

[S15] **Queens Landmark Condominiums**/originally Bulova Watch factory 62-10 Woodside Ave., bet. 62nd and 63rd Sts. S side. 1926. Altered 1985, **Ralph Wuest**.

Arde Bulova's high-rise watch factory with its prominent clock tower, for decades a special event in the ho-hum Queenscape to riders on the LIRR and the Flushing Line, was externally defaced in 1985, its tower removed—and all for the sake of these crude stucco-faced condos. Then the developers had the chutzpah to name it Landmark, to help with the sales.

S15

S16

[S16] **Bulova School of Watchmaking**, 40-24 62nd St. E side. [S17] **Arde Bulova Dormitory**, 40-25 61st St., bet. Woodside and 43rd Aves. W side. 1958.

The Bulova Woodside empire remains only in this small midblock educational compound, appearing like neo-Georgian dollhouses.

LONG ISLAND CITY

L1

What is currently called Long Island City is the site of the Queensboro bridge approaches, Queens Plaza, recycled factories, and railroad yards falling into disuse.

[L1] Originally **Brewster Building**, 27-41 Queens Plaza N., bet. 27th and 28th Sts. 1910. **Stephenson & Wheeler**.

Bulky brick, surmounted by a "constructivist" clock tower, the clock long since departed. This is where **Brewster** produced his horsedrawn carriages and later assembled Rolls-Royces, shipped knocked down from England, as well as Brewster fighter planes during World War II.

[L2] Formerly **Chase Manhattan Bank Building**/originally Bank of the Manhattan Company, 29-27 41st Ave., at Queens Plaza. 1927. **Morrell Smith**.

The crenellated clock tower commands this giant tangle of elevated train viaducts.

L3

[L3] **Municipal Parking Garage**, Bridge Plaza S., 28th St., 42nd Rd., and Jackson Ave. 1976. **Rouse, Dubin & Ventura**.

They worked hard to raise a common garage to an uncommon status. Stylish smooth and ribbed concrete.

[L4] **St. Patrick's Roman Catholic Church**, 39-50 29th St. (one-way north), NW cor. 40th Ave. 1898.

Renaissance Revival, save for the neatly louvered boxes atop the unfinished twin bell towers.

L4

[L5] **LaGuardia Community College, CUNY**, Main Building/originally White Motor Company Factory, 31-10 Thomson Ave., bet. 31st St. and 31st Place. S side to 47th Ave. ca. 1920. Converted, 1977, **Stephen Lepp & Assocs**. [L6] **East Building**/originally Equitable Bag Company, 31st Place to Van Dam St. S side, to 47th Ave. 1949. Addition, 1957. Conversion, 1990, **Warner, Burns, Toan & Lunde**.

The main building is a delicious, caramel-colored marvel with vermilion window frames and a similarly painted sculpted entry gate. Its eastern neighbor tries for monumentality, but seems an awkward cousin to the parent institution.

L5

[L7] **Queens Atrium Corporate Center No. 1**/originally Adams Chewing Gum factory/onetime International Design Center (IDC), 30-30 Thomson Ave., bet. 30th Place and 31st St. S side. 1919. **Ballinger & Perot**. [L8] **Center No. 2**/originally American Eveready Building (factory), 29-10 Thomson Ave., bet. 30th St. and 30th Place. S side. 1914. [L9] **Center No. 3**/originally Loose-Wiles Sunshine Biscuit Company, Skillman Ave. bet. 29th and 30th Sts. S side. 1914. **William Higginson**. Conversion for IDC, Center Nos. 1 and 2, 1986; No. 3, 1988. Master plan, **I. M. Pei & Partners. Gwathmey Siegel & Assocs.**, architects. **Stephen Lepp Assocs.**, assoc. architects.

L7-L8

The trappings of the IDC were left behind, after this bold experiment to lure Madison Avenue to the spacious industrial boondocks failed to attract the design profession away from Manhattan.

From a Thomson Avenue vantage point, these behemoths, part of the pre-World War I Degnon Terminal and Realty Company development of this Dutch Kills area, continue to look like typical, large Long Island City factories (No. 2 was the Sunshine bakery with its famed thousand windows). From 47th Avenue, the project's south side (IDC version), another world

LONG ISLAND CITY DISTRICT

see pages 814-815

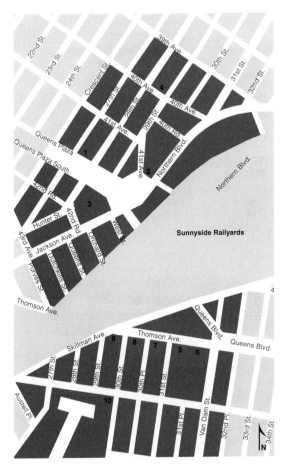

emerges, this one Post Modern. Too bad the replacement window framing is so flat—it emasculates the factories' gutsy World War I-era architecture, some of it paying late tribute to that of **Otto Wagner**. But savor the bridge across 30th Place.

[L10] **The Leaning Tower of Long Island City**, at the old Macy's/Gimbel's Warehouse, behind the sometime IDCNY. 1997. **Jeff Vandenberg**.

Nervous? Check this studied eccentricity.

L10

H1

HUNTERS POINT

Hunters Point, approaching Newtown Creek, was formerly the center of borough government and is now the focus of major development projects by Citicorp, the Port Authority, and the Queens West development.

[H1] **Citicorp office building**/former site of St. John's Hospital (Roman Catholic), 44th Dr. to 45th Ave., W of Jackson Ave. Citicorp parking garage, S of courthouse. 1989. All by **Skidmore, Owings & Merrill**.

The tower rises 48 stories, some 663 feet, the city's tallest structure outside of Manhattan. During construction, signs (cynically?) identified the owners as PERENNIALLY GREEN, INC. of 153 East 53rd Street, the address of the Citicorp Tower.

H2

[H2] **New York State Supreme Court, Long Island City Branch**/originally Long Island City Courthouse, 25-10 Court Sq., at Jackson and Thomson Aves. 1872-1876. **George Hathorne**. Rebuilt, 1904-1908. **Peter M. Coco**. ☙

Beaux Arts Baroque: limestone, brick, and three kinds of granite (smooth gray, rock-face pink, and rock-face slate gray). The present building was built upon the walls of its burned ancestor. It was in this courthouse that the famed 1927 murder trial of **Ruth Snyder** and her lover, **Henry Judd Gray**, took place and where **Willie ("the Actor") Sutton** was asked why he robbed banks. His reply: "Because that's where the money is."

H3

[H3] **Hunter's Point Historic District**, 21-09 to 21-51, 21-12 to 21-48 45th Ave., bet. 21st and 23rd Sts. Both sides. 44-70 23rd St., bet. 45th Ave. and 44th Dr. W side. Early 1870s. **Spencer B. Root, John P. Rust**, builders, and others. ☙

A street of virgin row houses, complete with original stoops and cornices. Some are faced in Westchester (or Tuckahoe) marble, a material more resistant than brownstone to weathering.

H6

[H4] **21-49 45th Rd.** (row house), [H5] **21-33, 21-35, 21-37 45th Rd.** (row houses), bet. 21st and 23rd Sts. (45th Rd. one-way east) N side. ca. 1890.

The first, a grand symphony in Romanesque Revival; the others, a melodic classical trio, 2-story brownstones of a rare sort that can sometimes be found between here and Astoria.

[H6] **P.S. 1 Contemporary Arts Center**/onetime P.S. 1 (artists' studios)/formerly Public School 1, Queens/originally Ward 1 School, 21st St. bet. 46th Rd. and 46th Ave. 1890-1900 Altered, 1976, **Shael Shapiro**. Expanded as the Arts Center, 1997. **Frederick Fisher**. 718-784-2084. Wed-Sun, Noon-6; closed Mon-Tues.

Now converted to artists' studios, galleries and supporting spaces in a continuing process of adaptive reuse for the city's artist community, this stolid Romanesque Revival building was built when **"Battle Ax" Gleason** was mayor of Long Island City. It once supported a clock tower. Now affiliated with MOMA (Museum of Modern Art), it offers the cutting edge that MOMA's historical perspective lacks.

H7

Warning!: In the country it's not unusual to find notices warning of underground telephone cable, and natural gas or oil pipelines. But it is disconcerting to find evidence of them under the concrete and asphalt of the inner city. To wit: warning disks on lampposts throughout the Hunters Point area suggest that you not cut a hole in the pavement without first calling a special telephone number. Tread lightly!

[H7] **Engine Company 258, Ladder Company 115, N.Y.C. Fire Department**, 10-40 47th Ave. (one-way west), bet. Vernon Blvd. and 11th St. S side. 1903. **Bradford L. Gilbert**.

HUNTERS POINT DISTRICT

see pages 816-820

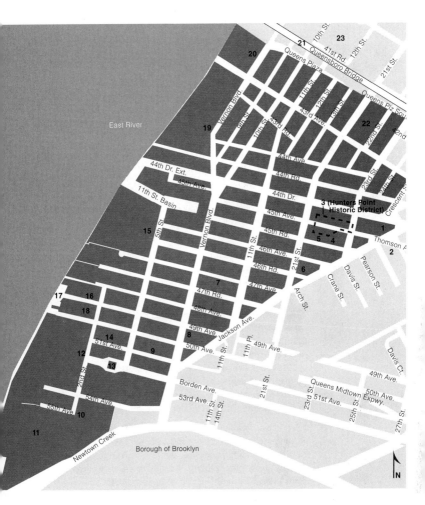

A robust multistory firehouse with stepped super-Dutch gable. Gilbert was a nationally recognized railroad architect.

[H8] **St. Mary's Roman Catholic Church**, 49-01 Vernon Blvd., SE cor. 49th Ave. 1887. **Patrick Charles Keely**.

Brick and brownstone were revealed when this local landmark was stripped of its many coats of paint. A bold neighbor for this gentrifying neighborhood.

H8

[H9] **108th Precinct, N.Y.C. Police Department**/originally 75th Precinct 5-47 50th Ave. (one-way east), bet. 5th St. and Vernon Blvd. N side. 1903. **R. Thomas Short**.

Like the nearby firehouse, this provides a bold municipal presence, here neo-Baroque (or late Mannerist) rather than the Fire House's Amsterdam revival. Particularly interesting are the extravagant bracketed torchères that frame the entrance. **Short** is better known as partner in **Harde & Short**.

*The Steinway Tunnels: The twin tubes of the Flushing Line under the East River were originally begun in 1892 by piano king **William Steinway** as a trolley car connection to Manhattan. A serious explosion, the Panic of 1893, and Steinway's death in 1896 interrupted the project until **August Belmont**, the IRT financier, revived it in 1902. The tunnel, with reversing loops at each end, became the first connection between Manhattan and Queens in 1907, though it was not put into regular use until converted to subway operation in 1915.*

[H10] **Port Distributing Corporation**, 55-01 2nd St., SE cor. 55th Ave. 1986. **David Bilow**.

Sophisticated architectural modeling, particularly in this confused industrial enclave. This is where the city's bottled beers emerge: Amstel Light, Budweiser, Michelob, Heineken . . .

[H11] Formerly **New York Daily News printing plant**, 55-02 2nd St. SW cor. 55th Ave. at Newtown Creek. 1972. **Harrison & Abramovitz**.

H10

A dated gray ghost on what for a while was called News Point. It occupies the former site, until World War II, of the National Sugar Refining Company, manufacturers of Jack Frost sugar. Slated for demolition as part of an area-wide redevelopment by the Port Authority.

[H12] **Tennisport Art Gallery**/onetime Vicino Mare Restaurant/originally Hunters Point Branch, Queens County Savings Bank, 51-02 2nd St., NW cor. Borden Ave. ca. 1895.

The coat of battleship gray paint that camouflaged a robust Romanesque Revival restaurant has been stripped, revealing brick and rock-face brownstone.

H12

[H13] **Queens Ventilating Building, Queens Midtown Tunnel**, center of Borden Ave., bet. 2nd and 5th Sts. 1939.

A Brobdingnagian utilitarian event on the bed of Borden Avenue.

[H14] Originally **Pennsylvania Railroad generating plant**/later N.Y & Queens Electric Light & Power Company, 2nd St. bet. 50th and 51st Aves. E side. 1909. **McKim, Mead & White**.

H14

This brick Renaissance Revival plant bears 4 great stacks, rampant on the Queens skyline. Note the Renaissance window guards in its granite base. Occupants include assorted manufacturing establishments and indoor tennis courts.

[H15] **Pepsi-Cola sign, Pepsi-Cola Bottling Company**, 45-00 5th St. (one-way south), bet. 46th Ave. and 46th Rd. W side. Riverfront buildings, 1910-1920. Sign, 1936, **Artkraft Sign Co.**

The upland side of this great sign (Pepsi-Cola spelled in black letters backwards?) hardly compares with the colossal neon-lighted front along the East River opposite the UN and Beekman Place. But without the building's staunch support how would Manhattan residents be able to see the sign and feel the thirst?

H15

All the blocks west of Fifth Street from 45th Road to 49th Avenue, and then west of Second Street from 50th Avenue to Newtown Creek, are part of the proposed Queens West Master Plan (a "Battery Park City" for an outer borough). The first event is Citilights, described below, a tower that brings some Manhattan style, height, and views to these shores. An outpost in a way, it abuts solid middle-class Hunter's Point districts, including the Hunters Point Historic District on 45th Avenue.

H16

[H16] **Citilights** (apartment building), 2nd St., bet. 48th and 49th Aves. E side. 1998.

A high-style apartment building that can lure needy yuppies with its magnificent views of Manhattan, easy parking, in a backwater from the sounds of roaring traffic (compare Manhattan's Third Avenue).

[H17] **Gantry State Park**, opposite Citilights bet. 48th and 49th Aves., W of Center Blvd. 1998. **Thomas Balsley Assocs.**, **Sowinski Sullivan**, and **Weintraub & di Domenico**.

The gantry cranes that served transfers of boxcars from rail barges to east-headed trains now serve as symbolic portals to

H17

this elegant new park; an accessible edge to Queens that revels in the Manhattan skyline.

[H18] **Trotwood Corporation Building** (apartments), bet. Center Blvd. and Second St., 49th and 50th Aves. E side. 2001. **Perkins Eastman**.

Things to come.

[H19] **Consolidated Edison Learning Center**, 43-82 Vernon Blvd., bet. 43rd Rd. and 44th Ave. W side. 1990s.

Some modests modern architecture supplants a wasteland of wires and poles that were here until recently.

44th Drive: This unusually wide thoroughfare leading to nowhere is the footprint for the louvered IND subway tunnel below, whose tube to East 53rd Street in Manhattan begins under your feet. Both flanks of the Drive are host to a miscellany of municipal activities, including a subway ventilator dating from 1931. The Water's Edge restaurant, at the end, is a licensee of the adjacent N.Y.C. Department of Ports, International Trade & Commerce, which just happened to have jurisdiction over the water rights.

H19

[H20] Originally **New York Architectural Terra-Cotta Company** (office), 42-10 to 42-16 Vernon Blvd., bet. Queens Plaza S. and 43rd Ave. W side. 1892. **Francis H. Kimball**. 🖊

Tudor Revival amber brick jewel with Sullivanesque terra-cotta trim. It stands proudly among the artifacts of industrial blight. Look at the chimney pots. (It's currently in mothballs, but we're worried about its future.) Terra-cotta skins ordered through this home office clad such wonders as the Ansonia and Carnegie Hall, as well as Kimball's own Montauk Club.

H20

[H21] **Queensboro Bridge**, from Queens Plaza to E. 59th-E. 60th Sts. in Manhattan. 1901-1908. **Gustav Lindenthal**, engineer. **Palmer & Hornbostel**, architects. 🖊

This ornate (note the Hornbostel finials) cantilevered bridge formed the backdrop for views from swank New York apartments in countless Hollywood films of the 1940s. Surprisingly, its completion did not lead to the migration across the river that the Williamsburg and Manhattan Bridges had caused. The last trolley car to see service in New York shuttled across the Queensboro, stopping at the (now demolished) elevator tower on Welfare (now Roosevelt) Island. The trolley and vehicular

H21

elevators were discontinued in 1955, when a bridge was completed between the island and Queens. Passenger elevator operation continued until 1975.

[H22] **Silvercup Studios** (video production studios)/originally Gordon Baking Company (commercial bakery), Queens Plaza S. to 43rd Ave., bet. 21st and 22nd Sts. ca. 1939.

The old Silvercup bakery was always reduced to a subsidiary role as pedestal for the magnificent giant neon sign advertising its product. Visible in Manhattan across the river, the refurbished sign now proclaims the bakery building's new role in media.

H22

H23

[H23] **Queensbridge Houses,** N.Y.C. Housing Authority, Vernon Blvd. to 21st St., 40th Ave. to Bridge Plaza N. 1939. **William F. R. Ballard**, chief architect. **Henry Churchill, Frederick G. Frost, Burnett C. Turner**, associate architects.

One of the best of City housing projects, in a handsome light brown brick, now minus its red window frames. Once it was the nation's largest public housing project: 3,149 units in 26 six-story buildings, occupying six superblocks. In the very center is an octagonal plaza with shops, a community center, and a small-town feeling.

BLISSVILLE

[B1] **N.Y.C. Fire Department Repair and Transportation Unit**, 48-58 35th St., NW cor. Hunters Point Ave., to 34th St. ca. 1935.

A tall radio-transmission tower and the series of exposed roof ribs identify this barrel-vaulted municipal garage where the city's fire trucks go for repairs—or to die. Once part of the city's fire college.

[B2] **St. Raphael's Roman Catholic Church**, 35-20 Greenpoint Ave., SW cor. Hunters Point Ave. 1885.

B2

A boldly modeled brick and sandstone church perched atop a hill abutting the Long Island Expressway and across from Calvary Cemetery, its steeple an orienting landmark in a widespread district.

[B3] **City View Motor Inn**/originally Public School 80, Queens, 33-17 Greenpoint Ave., bet. Gale and Bradley Aves., off Borden Ave. 1905. Altered, 1986.

This former brick and limestone elementary school, cleaned and remodeled (with characterless bronze-colored aluminum windows), shares the barren Blissville hill with St. Raphael's and Calvary's gatehouse.

B4

[B4] **Gatehouse, Old Calvary Cemetery** (Roman Catholic), Greenpoint Ave. entrance opp. Gale Ave., off Borden Ave. S side. 1892.

A romantic, vernacular, spectacular Queen Anne gem. Others of its genre have almost all been confiscated by time. (By 1916, this first part of the accretive 4-section cemetery had received 1,170,455 interments!)

[B5] **Chapel, Old Calvary Cemetery** (Roman Catholic), in the center of the cemetery (drive in). ca. 1895.

B5, Chapel

A miniature Sacré-Coeur beehive tower rises above a supporting cast of Spanish tile roofs, surrounded by huddled small Roman temple-mausoleums.

On axis with the chapel (cemetery section 3b) is the **Halloran Mausoleum**. An example of Victorian neo-Grecian: Philadelphia's **Frank Furness** and Berlin's **Karl Schinkel** could have been in partnership for this.

The Johnston Mausoleum, a small domed neo-Baroque "chapel," crowns a hill 1,000 feet away.

B5, Halloran Mausoleum

Cemetery within a cemetery: When the Roman Catholic Diocese of New York purchased the first lands for Calvary, in 1846, from the Alsop family, the deal depended upon the diocese's permitting the existing Alsop Burying Ground to remain—which it still does—241 feet from the old Penny Bridge Entrance. It contains 34 monuments dating from 1743 to 1889.

BLISSVILLE DISTRICT

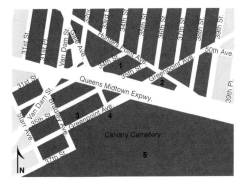

Central Queens

NORTH BEACH • JACKSON HEIGHTS • CORONA
FLUSHING MEADOWS-CORONA PARK • ELMHURST
REGO PARK • MASPETH • RIDGEWOOD
MIDDLE VILLAGE • GLENDALE
FOREST HILLS • KEW GARDENS

 Colonial

 *Georgian/
Federal*

 *Greek
Revival*

 *Gothic
Revival*

 Villa

 *Romanesque
Revival*

 *Renaissance
Revival*

 *Roman
Revival*

 *Art Deco/
Art Moderne*

*Modern/
Post-Modern*

Town of Newtown/Middleburg

Settled in 1642; chartered by the Doughty Patent of 1640.

The old Town of Newtown encompasses present-day communities that form central Queens. Its western reaches comprise endless blocks of old frame buildings, whereas the eastern and central parts have become dense apartment districts. Jackson Heights developed between the two world wars, and the trunk along Queens Boulevard in both Rego Park and Forest Hills branched out after World War II. Forest Hills was named (1901) by developer **Cord Meyer** and immortalized by Forest Hills Gardens, the magnificant town-planning/real estate scheme of the **Russell Sage Foundation**, to which Meyer had sold vast land. Rego Park is named for the developing/building Rego (Real Good) Construction Company, which pioneered building in that area.

The center of "New Towne," the outgrowth of Middleburg by 1665 and an English Puritan settlement under Dutch auspices, occupied the winding stretch of Broadway north of Queens Boulevard. Vestiges of the community remained well into the 20th century, but only a single church building still stands.

Newtown pippins, grown in the apple orchards of this area, were prized by the English, to whom they were exported for the manufacture of cider! After consolidation with New York in 1898, the name Newtown quickly fell into disuse, and the immediate community became known as Elmhurst.

NORTH BEACH

North Beach is a community no more. But prior to World War I it was Queens County's Coney Island on the Sound, as Rockaway was the borough's resort on the ocean. North Beach was an outgrowth of the working-class resort named Bowery Bay Beach, which opened in 1887 through a joint investment of piano maker **William Steinway**, beer king **George Ehret**, and patent-medicine manufacturer **Henry Cassebeer**. Bad associations with the name Bowery resulted in a renaming (1891): North Beach. Located on Queens' north shore, between 81st Street and Flushing Bay, it flourished until Prohibition. The picnic grounds and dance halls, the Ferris wheels and carrousels, and the promenades and the steamboat pier emptied of their summer crowds with the banning of alcohol. In 1930 the site became **Glenn H. Curtiss Airfield**. The City rented it in 1935 to develop what was first dubbed **North Beach Airport** and, in 1939, renamed **LaGuardia Field**.

[J1] **LaGuardia Airport**/originally North Beach Airport, N of Grand Central Pkwy. bet. 81st St. and 27th Ave. (Entries at 94th St. and 23rd Ave.)

Built for the New York World's Fair of 1939-1940 as New York's second (chronologically) municipal airport (after Floyd Bennett Field in Brooklyn). Flanking the main terminal are the old hangars of 1939 vintage (the original main building, too small for post-World War II traffic, was demolished).

[J2] **Original buildings, LaGuardia Airport**. 1939.
Delano & Aldrich.

[J2b] **Central Terminal and Control Tower**. 1965.
Harrison & Abramovitz.

The main terminal, in a great glass arc, bears a parasol roof
as a symbol of flight—no function intended for it—while the
control towers wear a stylish hyperbolic shape.

[J3] **Central Garage, LaGuardia Airport**. 1976. **Staff of
the Port of New York Authority**.

Within the main terminal's curved embrace now rests a new
garage, a once weathered steel grillage (now painted) accessible
by helical concrete ramps (the steel weathered by rusting to a
hard purple-brown patina that the Port Authority apparently
didn't like).

J2

[J4] **Marine Air Terminal, LaGuardia Airport**, entry at
82nd St. and Ditmars Blvd. 1939-1940. **Delano &
Aldrich**. 🍎 Interior. 🍎

The Marine Terminal lurks on the northwest edge of the
field. Originally built to serve flying boats of the 1930s (remember the *Yankee Clipper*?), today the Marine Terminal, a fantastic
Art Deco extravaganza, is Delta Airlines' shuttle facility.

J3

JACKSON HEIGHTS

Beginning in 1913 on what is today 82nd Street, between
Roosevelt Avenue and Northern Boulevard, a venture calling
itself the Queensboro Corporation initiated the development of
the residential community of Jackson Heights, named for **John
C. Jackson**, who laid out Northern Boulevard. Elevated transit
service along Roosevelt Avenue would not arrive until 1917, and
the lands, called "the cornfields of Queens," were still being tilled
as market gardens, with some of them serving the special needs
of the Chinatown community. At first, the Corporation's units
were rental, but after 1919 they were also marketed as cooperatives.

J4

[J10] **Jackson Heights Historic District**, mostly between
Roosevelt Avenue and 34th Avenue, 78th and 88th Streets, with
peninsulas north to Northern Boulevard and west to 76th Street.
Mostly 1914 to 1939. 🍎

J13

A vast residential community whose livability remains high to this day, even though many avenue frontages originally intended as endblock parks were developed as lesser works of architecture . . . and of habitability.

[J11] **37-46 to 37-60 83rd Street Apartments.** 1911. **Charles Peck.**
Brick and bay-windowed two-and-a-half-story row housing. The exceptional lowrise housing in this central Heights location.

[J12] **Laurel Court** (apartments) (the earliest), 33-01 to 33-21 82nd Street, SE cor. Northern Blvd. 1913-1914. **George Henry Wells.** ♂
The northern anchor and earliest entry into what was to become the Historic District. Nice to think about.

J14

[J13] **Towers Apartments**, 34th Ave. bet. 80th and 81st Sts. N side. 1923-1925. **Andrew J. Thomas.** ♂
A handsome brick apartment house morphs into Romanesque Revival towers at the sky.

[J14] **Chateau Apartments**, 34th Ave. bet. 80th and 81st Sts. S side. 1922. **Andrew J. Thomas.** ♂
Again the skyline offers history; this time in high neo-Mansart roofs. Blois in Jackson Heights?

J15

[J15] **Dunolly Gardens** (apartments), 78-11 35th Avenue, 78th to 79th Sts., bet. 34th and 35th Aves. 1939. **Andrew J. Thomas.**
Art Moderne with the very modern corner windows of the 1930s that did, in fact, expand the perceived apartment space. ♂

[J16] **Greystone** (apartments), 35-15 to 35-51, 35-16 to 35-52 80th St., bet. 35th and 37th Aves. Both sides. 1917. **George Henry Wells.** ♂
Dour gray brick and limestone, with neo-Gothic entry portals.

J17

[J17] **Fillmore Hall** (apartments), 83-10 35th Ave., bet. 83rd and 84th Sts. S side. 1936. **Joshua Tabachnik.** ♂

[J18] **Spanish Gardens** (apartments), midblock only, bet. 37th and Roosevelt Aves., 83rd to 84th Sts., 1923. **Andrew J. Thomas.** ●

[J19] **Linden Court** (apartments), midblock only, bet. 37th and Roosevelt Aves., 84th to 85th Sts., 1919-1921. **Andrew J. Thomas.** ♂

J20

[J20] **English Convertible Country Homes** (from single houses into apartments), 84th to 88th Sts. 1920s. Various architects, including **Robert Tappan.** ♂

[J21] **34-19 to 34-47 90th Street**, 34-20 to 34-48 91st Street (apartments), bet. 34th and 35th Aves. 1931. **Henry Atterbury Smith.**
Two sets of three 6-story apartments, similar in organization, but not appearance, to the same architect's Shively Sanitary Apartments on Manhattan's East 77th Street, turned diagonal to the street grid. Only the central structure of each group had an elevator; upper-floor tenants had to use roof bridges to reach adjacent buildings.

[J22] **87th to 90th Streets, 30th to 31st Avenues** (row housing), both sides. ca. 1939.
Latter-day "brownstones," in the sense that these too are embellished row houses, but in a simplified neo-Norman style.

JACKSON HEIGHTS DISTRICT

see pages 823-825

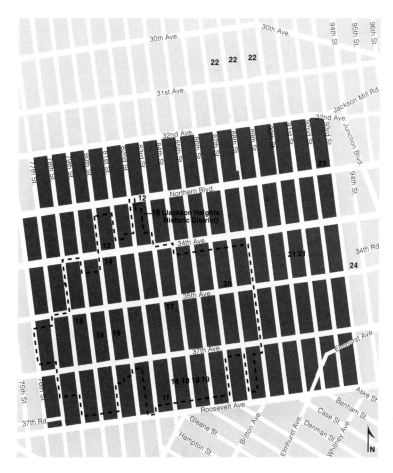

[J23] **115th Precinct, N.Y.C. Police Department**, 92-15 Northern Blvd., bet. 92nd and 93rd Sts. N side. 1985. **Gruen Assocs.**

Dark brown brick and terra-cotta make an unconvincing municipal fortress. What are they afraid of? The entrance doors recall those into a castle, but the brick arch that levitates around them gives it all away: lots of bravado but short on guts.

[J24] **Blessed Sacrament Church complex** (Roman Catholic), 35th Ave. bet. 93rd and 94th Sts. N side. Auditorium, 1933, **McGill & Hamlin.** Convent, 1937, **Henry J. McGill.** Church, 1949, **Henry J. McGill.** Additions.

The 1930s works are the best here, influenced by **Lutyens, Dudok,** and **Sir Giles Gilbert Scott.** The church was built a decade after being designed and lacks the great thirties' decorative art flourishes.

J23

C1

CORONA

A Tribute to Satchmo: An exuberant mural to **Louis Armstrong** *embellishes the otherwise ho-hum design of Intermediate School 227, which bears the trumpeter's name. (32-02 Junction Boulevard, SW corner 32nd Avenue.) Designer and team director,* **Lucinda Luvaas**, *of City Arts Workshop. 1981.*

[C1] **Langston Hughes Community Library and Cultural Center**, Queens Public Library, NE cor. 100th St. and Northern Blvd. 2000. **Davis Brody Bond**. 718-651-1100.

Frozen poetry? Here is serious architecture dedicated to a great African-American poet. Does it scan?

[C2] **P.S. 92, 99-01 34th Ave.**, bet. 99th and 100th Sts. 1993. **Gruzen Samton**.

Broken and bay-windowed forms, crowned with vaulted spaces, bring down the scale of this polychromatic brick and copper-colored metal school.

C2

[C3] **Shaw A.M.E. Zion Church** (African Methodist Episcopal)/originally Northside Hebrew Congregation, 100-05 34th Ave., bet. 100th and 101st Sts. N side. ca. 1910.

A generous pediment and 4 Ionic columns make a modest monument in the context of humility.

[C4] **Florence E. Smith Community Center**, Corona Congregational Church, 102-19 34th Ave., bet. 102nd and 103rd Sts. N side. 1981. **Medhat Abdel Salam**.

Strong, simple, necessary. The planar portico makes a dignified entry.

C3

[C5] **Louis Armstrong House Museum**/formerly Louis Armstrong House, 34-56 107th St. (one-way north), bet. 34th and 37th Aves. W side. 1910, **Robert W. Johnson**; later additions. Reconfigured for museum, 2000. **Rogers Marvel**. 🐾

Satchmo's home. As sensitive as this jazz great was to music, so, it appears, was he unconcerned with the niceties of architecture (or the neighborhood context). **Armstrong** lived here with his wife from 1943 until his death in 1971; his wife till hers, in 1983. Now elevated to museum status, it will attract hordes of dedicated followers.

C5

A trip down 104th Street:
One-way southbound.

CORONA DISTRICT
see pages 826-828

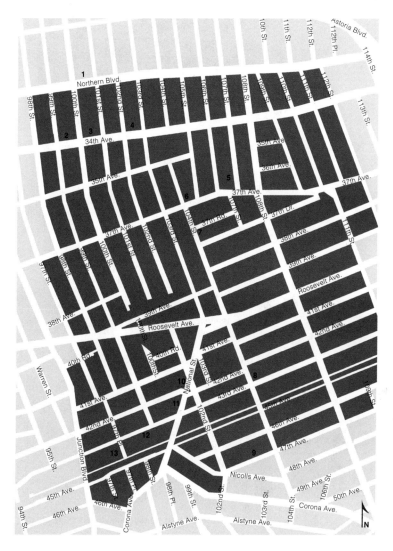

[C6] Our Lady of Sorrows Roman Catholic Church, 104-01 37th Ave., NE cor. 104th St. 1899. Convent, ca. 1895.

Originally built of red brick set in red mortar, this handsomely crafted church was once painted a cream color in the hope of sprucing it up. Now repainted in brick super-red. Regrettable. Get out the paint remover! The robust convent, adjacent, is a welcome foil.

[C7] **Emanuel Lutheran (Evangelical) Church**, 37-53 104th St., SE cor. 37th Rd. Rectory, 37-57 104th St., bet. 37th Dr. and 38th Ave. W side. ca. 1910.

Church: spartan form and austere brick. Rectory: very lovely wood frame, set back deeply from the street.

[C8] **Iglesia Metodista**/originally Corona Methodist Church, 42-15 104th St., NE cor. 43rd Ave. ca. 1905.

Whitewashed rock-face block composed as a primitive neo-Gothic tower and nave ensemble.

Along 47th Avenue:
One-way westbound.

C8

C9

[C9] Originally **Edward E. Sanford House**, 102-45 47th Ave., bet. 102nd and 104th Sts. N side. ca. 1871. 🍎🌿

A rare, largely intact survivor of the 19th-century village of Newtown, a freestanding rural house whose "fancifully carved elements . . . transform a humble, domestic structure into an architectural delight," according to the Landmarks Preservation Commission designation.

Nicholas Coppola, Sr. At the headquarters of The Corona Community Ambulance Corps, at 104-38 47th Ave., between 104th and 108th Sts., one finds a humble front yard, an often used out-door fireplace facing the street (and the community), and a large bronze marker dedicated in 1967 to the corps' founder, Mr. Coppola: A Monumental Pillar Of Compassion And Benevolence For His Fellow Men.

C11

[C10] **Union Evangelical Church of Corona**, National St. NW cor. 42nd Ave. 1873.

Another modest country church from rural years, unfortunately clad in aluminum siding (the edge and framing details become crude and out of scale).

[C11] **Masjid Alfalah** (mosque), 42-12 National St., bet. 42nd and 43rd Aves. 1990s.

A mini-minaret towers over this outpost of Islam.

C12

[C12] **Hook & Ladder Company 138/Engine Company 289, N.Y.C. Fire Department**, 97-28 43rd Ave., bet. 97th Place and 99th St. S side.

A small French Renaissance château harbors the local fire company's equipment.

[C13] Former **Tiffany & Company** (factory), 97th Place bet. 43rd and 44th Aves., N of LIRR. W side. ca. 1885.

While Tiffany Studios sold its handcrafted merchandise from a Madison Avenue address, much of the work was done in this dowdy industrial building alongside the Port Washington Branch of the LIRR.

FLUSHING MEADOWS-CORONA PARK

"This is a valley of ashes . . ." In *The Great Gatsby*, **F. Scott Fitzgerald** wrote of the Corona Dump, the landfilled marshes that once straddled the Flushing River, navigational facility to the Village of Flushing. The Dumps, worked by the old Brooklyn Ash Company, achieved park status when selected as the site for the 1939-1940 New York World's Fair, with a repeat performance in 1964-1965. Remnants of both remain in Flushing Meadows-Corona Park. A sense of the area that **Fitzgerald** captured can still be gleaned, metaphorically at least, in the junkyards east of Shea Stadium's parking lot.

[M1] **Shea Stadium**, bet. Northern Blvd. and Roosevelt Ave., Grand Central Pkwy. to 126th St. 1964. **Praeger-Kavanaugh-Waterbury**.
    The simplicity and sheer bulk of this home for the Mets dominate the flat landscape for miles. The original arbitrary exterior appliqué of pastel panels (the "wire basket in a windstorm" look) gave way the year after the team's 1986 World Series victory to the equally inspired "douse everything with Mets blue" look. Piercing!

M2

[M2] **U.S.T.A. National Tennis Center**.
[M2a]**Louis Armstrong Stadium**/originally Singer Bowl, 1964-1965 World's Fair, Roosevelt Ave. opp. Willets Point Blvd. S side. 1964. Reconstructed, 1978, **David Kenneth Specter**. Refurbished, 1997, **Rossetti & Assocs**.
[M2b] **Arthur Ashe Stadium**, 1997. **Rossetti & Assocs**.
    Two slick, snappy, substitutes for the West Side Tennis Club's beloved but undersized stadium at Forest Hills (extant)—an ever-expanding audience created by the extensive TV promotion of tennis as a big-time spectator sport. The sequential upgrades and expansion of the U.S.T.A. facilities are partially due to the enthusiastic support of former mayor **David Dinkins**.

M3

[M3] **The Unisphere**, 1964-1965 World's Fair. 1963-1964. **Peter Muller Munk, Inc.**, designer. **Gilmore D. Clarke**, landscape architect. 🍎
    A 380-ton, stainless-steel spherical grid representing the earth (together with orbiting satellites), 12 stories tall, perched on a 70-ton, 20-foot-high weathered-steel base. Weighty.

[M4] **New York Hall of Science**, Flushing Meadows-Corona Park at 111th St. opp. 48th Ave. 1964. **Harrison & Abramovitz**. Extended and remodeled, 1999. **Polshek Partnership**. Open to the public. 718-699-0005. Wed-Sun, 10-5; closed Mon-Tues.
    An undulating tapestry of stained glass set in precast concrete panels, flashy but ill-suited for museum use. It adjoins its own space park, an array of secondhand American spacecraft. The new Polshek entrance hall (with shop and canteen) improves one's experience.

[M5] **Queens Museum of Art**/originally 1939-1940 World Fair's New York City Building. 1939. Renovated, 1994. **Rafael Viñoly**. 718-592-5555. Tues-Fri, 10-5; Sat-Sun, 12-5; closed Mon.
    A sophisticated hermit crab was unleashed by Viñoly in this Art Moderne/Classical shell. The exhibits of avant-garde art may do for Queens what the radical presentations at BAM (Brooklyn Academy of Music) have done for Brooklyn. But see the panorama too.

M4

M5

A panorama of New York City: An impressive model of the whole of the city—835,000 buildings—plus streets, rivers, bridges, piers, and airports—is on view at the Queens Museum. Well worth a special visit. An elevated platform offers an airliner's view of the enormous diorama, updated regularly since it was built for the 1964-1965 World's Fair. The rest of the museum is also a treat. Open to the public.

M6

[M6] **New York State Pavilion**, 1964-1965 World's Fair, Flushing Meadows-Corona Park. 1964. **Philip Johnson** and **Richard Foster** architects. **Lev Zetlin**, structural engineer. [M6a] **Queens Theater in the Park**/originally Theaterama. **Philip Johnson** and **Richard Foster**. 1964. Reconstruction, 1993. **Alfredo De Vido**.

One of the few pavilions of 1964 that attempted to use fresh technology as a generator of form. In this case tubular perimeter columns (as well as those supporting the observation deck) were slip-formed of concrete in a continuous casting operation that proceeded vertically. The roof, originally sheathed in translucent colored plastic, is a double diaphragm of radial cables separated by vertical pencil rods to dampen flutter. It was an architectural star of the fair: a happy park building working with park space.

M6a

The reconstructed Queens Theater has brought life back to this neglected complex.

ELMHURST

[E1] **Newtown High School**, 48-01 90th St., bet. 48th and 50th Aves. to 91st St. E side. 1897. **C. B. J. Snyder**.
The tower silhouette brings memories of northern European, perhaps German, perhaps Flemish, Baroque, still bearing traces of late Gothic detail.

E1

[E2] **Korean Presbyterian Church**, Corona Ave., bet. 88th and 90th Sts. 2000.
For distinguished architecture in a Korean Presbyterian Church, see page 811. This one didn't make it.

[E3] **Reformed Dutch Church of Newtown, and Fellowship Hall**, 85-15 Broadway, SE cor. Corona Ave. Church, 1831. Hall, 1860.
Georgian-Greek Revival in white clapboard, wearing Tuscan columns. The stained glass is later: Victorian.

[E4] **St. James Parish Hall**/originally St. James Episcopal Church, Broadway SW cor. 51st Ave. 1734.
Carpenter Gothic additions updated this, the original St. James, built on land granted by the town. The steeple on the west end of this somber Colonial relic was removed at the turn of the century. A new St. James at the northeast corner of Broadway and Corona Avenue was built in 1849: now burned. Its replacement is no match for its predecessor.

E3

[E5] **James Rudel Center, LaGuardia Medical Group**, H.I.P. of Greater New York/originally Queens Boulevard Medical Building, 86-15 Queens Blvd., bet. Broadway and 55th Ave. N side. 1957. **Abraham Geller & Assocs**.
This medical building sits atop the IND subway tunnel, thus requiring heating and air-conditioning equipment normally placed in a basement to be on the roof. The splendid resulting form, a sophisticated cubist construction, bears good materials and detailing. It suffers from poor maintenance and ugly signs. A cemetery, to its east, was a welcome forelawn until some enterprising exploiter bought the space, moved the bodies, and built a gross 6-story apartment house.

[E6] **Stern's**/originally Macy's Queens, 88-01 Queens Blvd., bet. 55th and 56th Aves. N side. 1965. **Skidmore, Owings & Merrill**.
Take a difficult site, consider that a department store requires exterior walls only as enclosure, calculate the parking problem, add the SOM touch, and you get Macy's Queens (now renamed Stern's), a circular department store girded by a concentric parking garage. What could be more logical? Luckily, a recalcitrant property owner refused to part with the southwest parcel, forcing a notch to be cut into the squat cylinder of precast concrete panels; a welcome punctuation. The owner died in the early 1980s, and the intruding house was demolished in favor of a modern mediocrity.

E6

[E7] **Citibank, Elmhurst Branch**/originally First National City Bank, 87-11 Queens Blvd. (next to Macy's). 1966. **Skidmore, Owings & Merrill**.
A smaller cylinder than Macy's, by the same architects, but this time in black aluminum and glass. Apparently, circles were a brief sixties' fashion.

[E8] **Jamaica Savings Bank**, 89-01 Queens Blvd., NE cor. 56th Ave. 1968. **William Cann**.
Scarcely the Bilbao Guggenheim of Queens Boulevard, but a dynamic form concerned as much with image as with function. Too tiny for such a spirited form.

E8

[E9] **First Presbyterian Church of Elmhurst**/originally First Presbyterian Church of Newtown, Queens Blvd. SE cor. 54th

ELMHURST DISTRICT

see pages 831-832

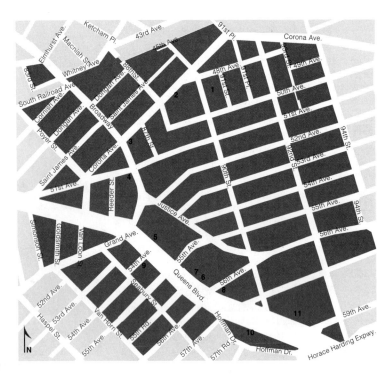

Ave. 1893. [E9a] **Manse**, 54-03 Seabury St., NE cor 54th Ave.
[E9b] **Sunday School**, 54-05 Seabury St., bet. 54th and 55th Aves.
ca. 1925.

The church, on a prominent Queens Boulevard corner, is a
sober rock-faced granite composition with an 85-foot tower and
brownstone trim. The manse behind it, however, is a domestic
delight of Shingle Style architecture, currently displaying stylish
olive-green garb.

[E10] **St. John's Queens Hospital**, Division of Catholic Medical
Center of Brooklyn & Queens, 90-02 Queens Blvd., bet 57th Ave.
and Woodhaven Blvd. S side. 1950-1963. Queens Blvd. wing, 1981.
Ferrenz & Taylor.

A clumsy Modern presence on frenetic, heavily trafficked
Queens Boulevard.

[E11] **Queens Center** (shopping mall), Queens Blvd. NE cor.
59th Ave. 1973. **Gruen Assocs.**

A sparkling 3-story space within is clad in glazed brick and
metal panels: a modernistic reprise of the 1930s. The concrete
garage behind is no-nonsense. Branches of Steinbach's (once
Ohrbach's), A & S (Brooklyn's Bloomingdale's), and Herman's
("discount" sporting goods) dominate.

E12

[E12] **Mathews Company row housing**, in the triangle
formed by the embankments of the LIRR Main Line and
the former New York Connecting Railway, N of Grand Ave.,
along Calamus and Ankener Aves., Elk Rd., and 82nd St. ca. 1930.
Louis Allmendinger.

The same yellow and brown Kreischerville brick used in vast
stretches of Ridgewood and Astoria here clads a brick Bauhaus:
these could be forms from the experimental Weissenhofsiedlung
in Stuttgart (1927): casement windows, ocean liner railings, austere cubistic form. There the work was of **Le Corbusier**, **Gropius**
and their peers. **Louis Allmendinger** didn't do so badly here
either.

REGO PARK

[R1] **AT&T, Rego Park Communications Center**, Queens Blvd. bet. 62nd Ave. and 62nd Dr. N side. 1976. **Kahn & Jacobs**.

A bold, monumental brick mass set on a battered base of slab granite. Telephone equipment in fancy dress.

[R2] **Walden Terrace** (apartment complex), 98th to 99th Sts., bet. 63rd Dr. and 64th Rd. 1948. **Leo Stillman**.

Almost 2 full blocks of 8-story apartment structures whose exposed concrete frames gave them a precocious Continental look when they were erected right after World War II. The long, narrow, midblock courtyards are a green treat.

R2

MASPETH

[M1] **Maspeth Branch, The Bank of New York**/originally Branch, Long Island Trust Company, 54-12 48th St., bet. 54th Rd. and 54th Ave. W side. ca. 1985.

A sophisticated modern banking temple in an industrial slurb.

[M2] **United Parcel Service Distribution Center**, 56th Rd. bet. 44th and 48th Sts. N side. 1967. **Francisco & Jacobus**.

Superscaled distribution by conveyor belts dictated the fingered form of this pink-mansarded complex.

[M3] **59-37 55th Street** (house), bet. Flushing and Grand Aves. E side, N of LIRR. (55th St one-way south.)

The wood-clapboard frame house, together with its railroad crossing gate, makes an unusual vignette from the past.

[M4] **St. Stanislaus Kostka Roman Catholic Church**, 57-01 61st St., SE cor. Maspeth Ave. 1913.

A neo-Romanesque structure turned diagonally to the intersection. Note the inset decorative bricks, gilded and polychromed, that subtly embellish the exterior walls.

M1

[M5] **Holy Cross Roman Catholic Church**, 61-21 56th Rd., bet. 61st and 64th Sts. N side. 1913.

The voluptuous curvilinear verdigris copper steeple makes this church extraordinary. Disney must be jealous.

[M6] **Church of the Transfiguration** (Roman Catholic). Rear, 64-10 Clinton Ave., bet. 64th St. and Remsen Place. S side. Front, 64-21 Perry Ave. E of 64th St. N side. 1962.

The Clinton Avenue façade has hints of 1930s Art Moderne ecclesiastical design; the Perry Avenue front is a kind of A-frame Modern. The prickly detail of the skylight along the continuous roof peak unites the two. The inscription MANO NAMAI MALDOS NAMAI (My house is a house of prayer) reveals this to be a Lithuanian congregation.

M6

[M7] **Replica, Lithuanian roadside shrine**, in front of 64-25 Perry St. 1981. N side. **Arthur Nelson**, designer and builder.

An exquisitely fashioned work of the master carpenter's traditional art/craft, contributed by the Knights of Lithuania, Council 110.

M7

[M8] **Maspeth United Methodist Church**/also United Methodist Korean Church of Central Queens, 66-39 58th Ave., bet. 66th St. and Brown Place. N side. 1907.

A Gothic Revival country church, now unfortunately clad in wide white bogus clapboard. The aesthetic problem is more in the detail where the boards meet, their edging and window trim, rather than in the boards themselves.

[M9] **Maspeth Town Hall, Inc.**/originally Public School 73, Queens/formerly 112th Precinct, N.Y.C. Police Department, 53-35 72nd St., bet. 53rd Rd. and Grand Ave. E side. (72nd St. one-way south.) 1897.

The people saved this one. A municipal building from the time before Queens absorbed Maspeth and its neighbors: wood frame, wood clapboard siding, with large windows so that schoolchildren would have plenty of light.

M10

RIDGEWOOD

Ridgewood was developed at and after the turn of the 20th century into a dense low-rise residential community as the growing German-immigrant population of adjacent Bushwick, in Brooklyn, enpanded. Electric streetcars came in 1894 and the Myrtle Avenue Line, in 1906 (the elevated part extended in 1915). Members of many local families worked across the county border in the numerous breweries bearing German names.

 [R1] **The Adrian and Ann Wyckoff Onderdonk House**, 18-20 Flushing Ave., bet. Cypress and Onderdonk Aves. S side. 1731. ● Open to the public. 718-456-1776. Sat, 2-4:30.

Once a burned and mutilated hulk and the only remnant of the group of "Dutch" Colonial farmhouses in this area that had withstood the onslaught of heavy industry onto their farmlands in the early part of this century. Restoration was accomplished by the Greater Ridgewood Historical Society.

R1

The Yellow Brick Houses and Mathews Model Flats:
Between 1895 and 1920 some 5,000 working-class structures were built during Ridgewood's housing boom. The earlier ones were of wood frame. But beginning around 1905 the expansion of fire limits forced brick construction on the developers, and a veritable city of 2- and 3-story yellow-brick row houses, tenements, and flats emerged.

One of the area's best-known builders was **Gustave X. Mathews** who, with his architect **Louis Allmendinger**, developed the Mathews Model Flats, considered so advanced in their planning that the City's Tenement House Department exhibited them at the 1915 Panama-Pacific Exposition, in San Francisco.

The idiosyncratic yellow brick employed by three of the area's most prolific architects, **Louis Berger & Company**, **Louis Allmendinger**, and **Charles Infanger**, was speckled (or iron-spot) brick made in the kilns of the Kreischer Brick Manufacturing Company in what was then Kreischerville (now renamed Charleston), Staten Island.

Block after golden block of these happy abodes remain, some of the best, urbanistically speaking, the setback Mathews Company rows along Bleecker and Menahan Streets, north of Cypress Avenue, across from Public School 81, Queens. Some 60 percent of the total number are recognized in what was, in 1983, the largest designation made to the National Register of Historic Places. A few special examples:

 [R2] **Stockholm Street**, between Onderdonk and Woodward Avenues. 1862-1868, 1870-1894 Stockholm Street (row houses), W side. 1867 to 1893 Stockholm Street (row houses), E side. 376, 380 Woodward Avenue (apartments), SW cor. and SE cor. Stockholm St. ca. 1905. **Louis Berger & Co**.

Ridgewood's own yellow brick road. Here, Kreischerville brick not only clads the matching rows of narrow houses, peeking from behind their white-columned piazzas, but also makes up the street bed, which rises gently to meet the green ether of Linden Hill Cemetery.

R2

[R3] **Roman Catholic Church of St. Aloysius**, and Rectory, 382 Onderdonk Ave., SE cor. Stockholm St. 1907, 1917. **Francis J. Berlenbach.**

[R4] **St. Aloysius Convent**, 1817 Stanhope St. ca. 1893. Six 5-globed cast-iron lampposts guard this neo-Renaissance church, with its 165-foot twin towers, and the adjacent stuccoed rectory. But the true gem is the convent around the corner, despite its cladding in green hexagonal composition shingles. When this parish began, the area was called Old Germania Heights.

R3

[R5] **1912-1936 Grove Street** (row apartments), bet. Woodward and Fairview Aves. E side. [R6] **11A, 15, 17 St. John's Road** (row apartments) bet. Grove and Menehan Sts. N side. 1908-1910. **Louis Berger.**

While many of Ridgewood's houses set off the yellow masonry with gray limestone trim, not all keystones bear carved human faces, as these groups do.

[R7] Formerly **J & C Platz, Inc**. (store), 65-25 Forest Ave., NW cor. Gates Ave.

Look carefully behind the roll-down security shutters: A hardware and paint store whose wooden fixtures take one back at least 75 years: oiled floors, pressed-metal ceilings, a gold leaf sign lovingly applied to the glass transom. Call a Hollywood set decorator, quick!

R5

[R8] **66-45 Forest Avenue** (row house), bet. Gates and Palmetto Sts. N side. ca. 1885.

Miraculous that this clapboard frame house has survived largely intact (meaning: it has not been entirely reclad with composition, asphalt, asbestos, aluminum, vinyl, Perma Stone, stucco, or "face" brick!) from the earliest days of Ridgewood's urbanization, before the stringent fire laws of the nearby City of Brooklyn dictated the use of masonry for densely spaced housing like this.

R8

[R9] **66-75 Forest Avenue** (originally house), NW cor. Putnam Ave. 1906. **Louis Berger & Co.**

Once the local major mansion: a Composite-columned porch fronting the Renaissance Revival body. Later it saw service as a knitting mill (!!), a common "cottage industry" in modern-day Ridgewood, but now has been rescued by a religious community.

*Movie Set: To find a location to film **Neil Simon's** Brighton Beach Memoirs (1986), Hollywood came to the NW corner of Seneca Avenue and Palmetto Street, where the Metropolitan Avenue el structure and adjacent early 1900s buildings permitted the reincarnation of Brooklyn's BMT Brighton Beach elevated of an earlier day. With the right light it was possible to read the set decorator's addition to the outside of the station mezzanine: RIDE THE OPEN AIR ELEVATED.*

R10

[R10] **St. Matthias Roman Catholic Church**, 58-25 Catalpa Ave., bet. Onderdonk and Woodward Aves. N side. 1926. [R10b, c] **Parish Hall, Rectory**, 1909. **Francis J. Berlenbach.**

Stacked Roman temples form the tower of this yellow brick and terra-cotta church. In its earlier years, the church published postcards that located it across the nearby Brooklyn border, no doubt the fulfillment of a wish by either the parish or the printer (or both).

[R11] **P.S. 88, The Seneca School Renovations and Additions**, 60-85 Catalpa Ave, bet. 60th Place and Pond Rd. Original building, 1907. Alterations and additions, 1996. **Mitchell/Giurgola.**

MIDDLE VILLAGE

M1

[M1] **Gatehouse, Mt. Olivet Cemetery**, Eliot Ave. NE cor. Mt. Olivet Crescent. ca. 1910.

The cemetery guarded by this picturesque gatehouse has not only originally interred remains but also the contents of other, discontinued burial places. For example, the remains from the vaults of the Bedford Street Methodist Episcopal Church, in Manhattan, were transferred here in November 1913; the remains from the Hallet Family Cemetery, in April and May 1905.

M2

[M2] **Fresh Pond Crematory**/originally United States Columbaria Company, 61-40 Mt. Olivet Crescent, NW cor. 62nd Ave. 1901. **Otto L. Spannhake**. South addition, 1929. Chapel, 1937.

A pompous pale brick and limestone crematory sited across from the undulating landscape of Mt. Olivet Cemetery. The neo-Gothic chapel to the north is actually a delightful (but recessive) composition, set back from the crescent as it is.

[M3] **Rentar Plaza**, Metropolitan Ave. at 65th Lane. S side. 1974. **Robert E. Levien Partners**.

M3

An aircraft carrier gone astray that parks 1,200 cars on its flight deck. Glazed brown brick, rounded stair forms. One floor is equal in area to half the Empire State Building; three floors, to an entire tower of the World Trade Center.

GLENDALE

G1

[G1] **70-12 Cypress Hills Street** (house), opp. 62nd St. W side. ca. 1860.

Compromised by time, and shorn of its detail, this Italianate frame house is nevertheless important because its strong distinctive porched form is today a rare event for this neighborhood.

[G2] **Fourth Cemetery of the Spanish-Portuguese Synagogue**, Congregation Shearith Israel, Cypress Hills St. N of Cypress Ave./Interboro Pkwy. W side. Chapel and Gate, 1885, **Vaux & Radford**. Restoration, **Harmon Goldstone**, 1962.

High atop a gentle rise, amid cemeteries representing many faiths is this small burial ground, the latest of this Central Park West congregation whose three earlier ones are landmarks. The gate and chapel here are magnificent—though largely overlooked—works of **Calvert Vaux**.

FOREST HILLS

North of Queens Boulevard:

F2

[F1] **Forest Hills South**, bet. Queens Blvd. and Grand Central Pkwy. Service Rd., 76th Rd. and 78th Ave. 1941. **Philip Birnbaum**.

Neo-Georgian architecture subsidiary to the real joy of this complex: a grand mall that presents a lush park to the pedestrian in the spring, in the space 113th Street would have passed, here claimed for people. The southern view is axial with:

[F2] **Forest Hills Tower** (offices), 118-35 Queens Blvd., NW cor. 78th Crescent. 1981. **Ulrich Franzen & Assocs**.

A prominent and exquisitely detailed 15-story office complex, by far the best large-scale architecture in these parts. Yet, too tall, too prominent, too exquisitely detailed here.

F3

[F3] **Civic Virtue** (statue), NE cor. Queens Blvd. and Union Tpke. 1922. **Frederick MacMonnies**, sculptor.

Once directly in front of City Hall in Manhattan, this Nordic male chauvinist was banished to these boondocks by popular pressure (note that the writhing women are not being stepped upon, however). **MacMonnies**, Brooklyn's great sculptor (see The Horse Tamers at Prospect Park), was in his dotage when this was carved: a sorry coda to a brilliant career.

[F4] **Queens Borough Hall**, Queens Blvd. bet. Union Tpke. and 82nd Ave. N side. 1941. **William Gehron & Andrew J. Thomas**.

A pompous neo-Classical building in red brick and limestone. Thomas was capable of much better. For that, see much of Jackson Heights.

F5

[F5] **Queens Criminal Court**, 125-01 Queens Blvd., bet. Hoover and 82nd Aves. N Side. 1996. **Ehrenkrantz & Eckstut**.

Limestone and stainless steel sweep off of the boulevard in a grand curve shielding the public corridors that serve the courtrooms proper.

[F6] **Arbor Close and Forest Close**, from the back of Queens Blvd. storefronts to Austin St., 75th Ave. to 76th Ave. side 1925-1926. **Robert Tappan**.

Picturesquely profiled row houses, clad in brick, slate, and halftimbering. The garden within offers privacy hedged at its edges. A charming, urbane place.

F6

[F7] **Forest Hills Gardens**, 71st (Continental) Ave. to Union Tpke., Long Island Railroad right-of-way to an uneven line south of Greenway South. 1913-present. **Grosvenor Atterbury**, architect. **Frederick Law Olmsted, Jr.**, landscape architect. Other architects for some individual buildings.

"Apart from its convenient location, within a quarter of an hour of the center of Manhattan Island, the Forest Hills Gardens enterprise differentiates itself . . . from other suburban development schemes most notably in that its size permits a unique layout of winding streets, open spaces and building lots and thus permits the development of an ideally attractive neighborhood, while its financial backing is such that the realization of the well studied plans is assured in advance beyond peradventure." **Alfred Tredway White** in a promotional booklet of 1911.

White, who had pioneered in housing for the working class, would not have been disappointed. This project, sponsored by the Russell Sage Foundation, has become one of Queens's most exclusive residential enclaves. It is also a splendid combination of good planning and of romantic, picturesque architecture. The old West Side Tennis Club, home to the tennis "Opens" for generations, is endangered.

F7

KEW GARDENS

A community abounding in English allusions, not the least of which is its name, designed to echo—and to derive prestige from—its London suburb namesake. Kew Gardens was developed by a Manhattan lawyer, **Albon Platt Man** (and later by his son, **Alrick Hubbell Man**), for those who, in that placid era before World War I, were already wearying of city life and desirous of finding a garden spot only a short railroad trip from Manhattan. The Mans built some 300 houses and sold them, in the prices of those years, for between $8,000 and $20,000. Kew Gardens straddles the LIRR cut south of Forest Hills and is contained by major areas of greenery, Forest Park on the northwest and Maple Grove Cemetery on the east. The heavily trafficked Union Turnpike and Queens Boulevard mark its northern boundaries and 85th Avenue and 127th Street its southerly ones.

F8

Murder in the night: Adjacent to the LIRR station on quiet Austin Street, near the location of the beloved Austin Book Store (now gone), is the site of the heavily publicized murder, in 1964, of **Catherine (Kitty) Genovese,** *who was killed as 38 neighbors ignored her screams for help.*

[F8] **Mayfair Road**, bet. Park Lane South and 116th St.
  The most notable residences are Nos. 115-19 (Italian stucco with Spanish tile roof), 115-02, 115-18, and 115-27.

[F9] **Grosvenor Lane**, bet. Park Lane S. and 116th St.
  Particularly note No. 115-01, at the Park Lane South corner, No. 115-19, and No. 115-24.

F10

Abingdon Rd:

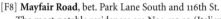 [F10] **Kew Gardens Jewish Center Anshe Sholom**, 82-52 Abingdon Rd., NW cor. 83rd Ave. 1970. **Laurence Werfel**.
  The zeal to translate religious needs into architecture here promotes an impassioned but awkward design solution: a copper-clad enclosure for the ark of the covenant slashes into a corner of the dark brick sanctuary.

[F11] **Abingdon Road**, bet. 83rd Ave. and Lefferts Blvd.
  A street of wonderful freestanding homes of the early 20th century: Nos. 83-36, comfortable and cozy with double gables; 83-42, a modest Spanish Baroque silhouette; 83-48, the Shingle Style desecrated by plastic siding and the associated ruin of corner and archway detailing; and 83-66 on the Boulevard's corner: a splendid Composite-columned portico.

F11

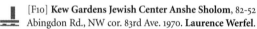 [F12] **Congregation Shaare Tova** (synagogue), 82-33 Lefferts Blvd., SE cor. Abingdon Rd. 1983. **Richard Foster**.
  A sophisticated design exercise in cubical solids and circular voids for the sanctuary of the Mashhadi community, Iranian Jews, and an extreme example of the eclectic possibilities of Abingdon Road.

F12

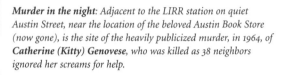 [F13] **84-40, 84-50 Abingdon Road** (houses), bet. Lefferts Blvd. and Brevoort St. S side. ca. 1910.
  Two of the finest Colonial Revival single houses in these parts. Stubby Tuscan columns articulate those wonderful porches!

[F14] **82-16, 82-18, 82-20, 82-22 Beverly Road** (residential grouping), bet. Onslow and Audley Places. W side. ca. 1925.
  Charming stucco and slate-roofed houses arranged around an intimate circular commons.

F14

FOREST HILLS / KEW GARDENS DISTRICTS
see pages 837-840

[F15] **80-55 Park Lane** (house), bet. 80th Rd. (Quentin St.) and Onslow Place. E side. ca. 1925.

Perhaps a new style that might be termed Tudor Moderne. The entrance portal seems to be a graft from the 1925 Paris Exposition des Arts Décoratifs.

[F16] **Grenfell Street**, bet. Quentin St. (80th Rd.) and Onslow Place. E side. ca. 1920.

Especially note Nos. 80-57, 80-63, 80-67, 80-83.

[F17] **119-33 to 119-43 80th Road** (houses), bet. Austin St. and Queens Blvd. ca. 1920.

A cluster of four houses with red tile roofs forming a welcome enclave on a tree-shaded street where other houses, each individually designed, are relatively bland.

[F18] **Austin Street** (house), NE cor. 80th Rd. ca. 1920.

A second floor timber balcony gives this house a powerful posture on a prominent corner.

[F19] **Kew Hall Cooperative Apartments**, 83-09 Talbot St., bet. 83rd Dr. and Lefferts Blvd. ca. 1929.

Almost a block square, this structure surrounds an inner green space so large it admits car traffic (if you belong). The replacement in the 1980s of its original wood windows has cost it much of its original character.

F15

F19

F20

F21

[F20] **84-62 Austin Street** (apartments), nr. 84th Ave. W side. 1981. **Peter Casini.**

Unusually radical façades along the LIRR Main Line in a structure built on a leftover sliver of land.

Off to one side (west on Metropolitan Avenue):

[F21] **North Forest Park Branch, Queensborough Public Library,** 98-27 Metropolitan Ave., bet. 69th Rd. and 70th Ave. N side. 1975. **Kaminsky & Shiffer.**

A modest branch library clad in a range of terra-cotta-colored, square brick. Some character to a humdrum shopping street.

[F22] **Remsen Family Cemetery,** adjoining 69-43 Trotting Course Lane, NE cor. Alderton St. (N of Metropolitan Ave. Both the Lane and Street are one-way northish.) ca. 1790 to mid 19th centuries. 💣

Typical of the small private cemeteries of Long Island, few of which remain. A handful of very old tombstones cohabits with miniature World War I concrete doughboys. The adjacent family homesteads are long gone.

COLLEGE POINT
MALBA • WHITESTONE • BEECHHURST
FLUSHING • MURRAY HILL • BROADWAY-FLUSHING
AUBURNDALE • UTOPIA • FRESH MEADOWS • BAYSIDE

Town of Flushing/Vlissingen
Settled in 1642; chartered in 1645.

The town Flushing is commonly associated with the growth of religious freedom in the New World. Founded by English settlers, it received its patent from Dutch **Governor Kieft**, who stipulated in its text that the freedom of conscience of its townspeople was to be guaranteed. Kieft's successor, **Peter Stuyvesant**, attempted to suppress the Quaker sect, a number of whose adherents had settled in Flushing. Quaker and non-Quaker residents banded together against Stuyvesant and were successful in having the patent's stipulation recognized and observed. Among these settlers was the **Bowne** family, whose house, dating from the 17th century, can still be seen. The old Quaker Meeting House of the same period also remains as a testament to this struggle for religious liberty.

Colonial

Georgian/
Federal

Greek
Revival

Gothic
Revival

Villa

Romanesque
Revival

Renaissance
Revival

Roman
Revival

Art Deco/

Art Moderne

Modern/
Post-Modern

COLLEGE POINT

This community is named for an ill-fated Episcopal divinity school founded in 1836 by the **Rev. William A. Muhlenberg** but never opened. Before religion found it, it was called Strattonsport, after **Eliphalet Stratton**, who had purchased the land in 1790 from the Lawrence family, noted early settlers. See their graveyard in Ditmars. At first, College Point was virtually an island separated from the Village of Flushing by creeks and flooded marshland and connected by a route known as College Point Causeway (now Boulevard). Landfill and recent developments have begun to change this, including the recent industrial and shopping development on the flat lands of the former Flushing Airport.

In the Civil War era the district became a lusty industrial community, only a few vestiges of which remain. It attracted large German and Swiss populations whose beer gardens and picnic groves were the focus of Sunday outings by German-born Manhattanites. Following the war the **Poppenhusen** family (Conrad was majority stockholder in the Long Island Rail Road) purchased large amounts of property and established an institute still bearing its name.

[N1] **Poppenhusen Branch, Queensborough Public Library**, 121-23 14th Ave., NW cor. College Point Blvd. 1904. **Heins & La Farge**.

One of many public library branches in the city funded by a gift from **Andrew Carnegie**. This structure is similar in style to the contemporaneous Bronx Zoo designs of its architects.

N3

[N2] **College Point Park and Parking**/originally site of Public School 27, Queens, College Point Blvd. SW cor. 14th Ave. 1988. **Richard Dattner & Assocs**.

Until the 1980s the site of a public school.

[N3] **Beech Court** (residential grouping), particularly Nos. 3 and 10 Beech Court (houses), N of 14th Ave. bet. College Point Blvd. and 121st St.

Granite entry pylons still mark this kempt and venerable oasis (behind the library) that was once the **Herman Funke** estate. Now the site of a handsome array of homes surrounding a grassy, treed, central green, including a rare Art Moderne intruder of stucco, glass block, and steel casement, at No. 10; there is a Colonial Revival survivor at No. 3.

N5

N6

N7

N10

[N4] Originally **Boker House**/then College Point Clubhouse/ now apartments, 12-29 120th St., NE cor. Boker Court (at N end of 120th St., N of 14th Ave.). 1870s.

A relic of the era when this part of College Point was a group of adjacent estates, such as **Herman Funke**'s, next door. The rich bracketed porch colonnade preserves some of the flavor of the old neighborhood.

[N5] **First Reformed Church of College Point and Sunday School**, 14th Ave. NW cor. 119th St. 1872.

Queene Anne meets Eastlake, and their style blooms. An exquisite and perfectly maintained excerpt from the most eclectic period of American architecture. Gothic and Renaissance, Colonial and Romanesque—all had a share in this enterprise.

[N6] Formerly **EDO Corporation, Governmental Systems Division**, 14th Ave. bet. 110th and 112 Sts. N side. West unit, 1983. East unit, 1985. **Steven B. Rabinoff & Assocs.**

No accident that this is at one of College Point's many waterfront edges: EDO (the acronym of its founder, **Earl Dodge Osborn**) was formed in 1922 as Edo Aircraft Corporation, producers first of seaplanes and later of metal pontoons. To accommodate its diversification, EDO commissioned this sleek metallic and blue newcomer in the "American Corporate" style.

[N7] **Poppenhusen Institute**, 114-04 14th Rd., SE cor. 114th St. 1868. **Mundell & Teckritz.**

A somber Second Empire place painted cream and chocolate brown. It sheltered one of the nation's earliest free kindergartens and provided adult education courses so that local workers could better themselves. A philanthropy of **Conrad Poppenhusen.**

[N8] **H. Flessel Restaurant**/originally Witzel's Hotel, 14-24 119th St., NW cor. 14th Rd. ca. 1890. Later additions.

Time warp. The exterior of this accretive, village hotel-restaurant complex seems totally untouched by time, save for a neon sign (clearly of the 1930s) that hangs out over the corner. Founder Witzel's other enterprise was his nearby Point View Island.

[N9] **St. Fidelis of Sigmaringen, Martyr**, Roman Catholic Church, 14-10 124th St., NW cor. 15th Ave. 1894.

Founded in 1856 for the 26 Catholic families then residing hereabouts. A sweet memorial (carved in German and later in English) for its founder, the **Reverend Joseph Huber**, stands next to the handsome octagonal baptistry. Inside, bold 1981-vintage wood sculptures hang over the altar.

[N10] Originally **H. A. Schleicher House**/later Grand View Hotel, 11-41 123rd St., on an island interrupting 13th Ave. E side. 1860.

An early showplace of College Point that predates the street grid, hence its island setting. This stretch of 13th Avenue was once called Schleicher Court, perhaps giving rise to the neighborhood rumor that the mansion was the village courthouse. Actually, Schleicher was into selling arms to the Confederate army.

[N11] **Poppenhusen Memorial**, College Point Blvd., College Place, 11th Ave. 1884.

Set in an immaculate green triangle, this modest, bronze portrait bust atop a granite stele marks the area of **Conrad Poppenhusen**'s home, a mansard-roofed structure that once commanded panoramic views from the top of this promontory.

[N12] **Hermon A. McNeil Park**/formerly College Point Shorefront Park/originally Chisholm Estate, Poppenhusen Ave. bet. 115th St./Powell's Cove Blvd. and College Place. N side.

This was to have been the site of the ill-fated St. Paul's College after which College Point is named. The founder's sister

COLLEGE POINT DISTRICT

see pages 841-844

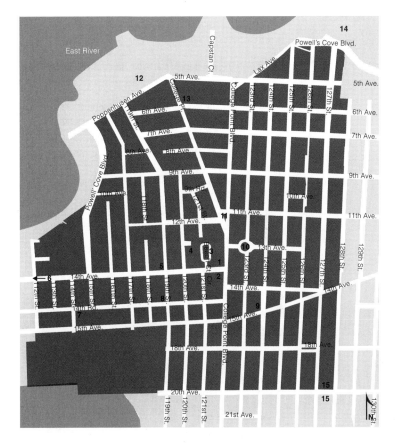

built the 1848 Chisholm mansion, which became **Mayor La Guardia**'s summer city hall. **Robert Moses** soon demolished it in favor of a park.

[N13] **5-27 College Point Boulevard** (house), NE cor. 6th Ave. [N 9b.] 122-07 6th Avenue (house), bet. College Point Blvd. and 123rd St. N side. ca. 1986.

A pair of pert 2½-story brick houses with strong silhouettes and thoughtful fenestration and detailing. A rare example, in these parts, of high-quality speculative residential design.

[N14] Originally **Tallman's Island Sewage Treatment Works, N.Y.C. Department of Public Work**s/now Tallman's Island Water Pollution Control Plant, N.Y.C. Department of Environmental Protection, Powells Cove Blvd. (extension of Lax Ave.) opp. 128th St. N side. 1939. Expanded, 1976.

A stunningly clean green oasis (despite its utilitarian purposes) studded with Art Moderne concrete and glass-block detail on the former site of a 19th-century amusement park, Joseph Witzel's Point View Island. (The view today is of the Whitestone Bridge.) Another Witzel property, his nearby hotel, is extant.

[N15] Originally **India Rubber Company**/then Hard Rubber Comb Company/then I. B. Kleinert Rubber Company/now miscellaneous industries, intersection of 127th St. and 20th Ave. 1889, 1921.

Industrial archaeology. Poppenhusen founded this complex of rubber-products manufactories in 1877. They later became

N15

N16

the home of Kleinert dress shields and earmuffs. At their tops the buildings still bear faded signs that reveal bits of their history. Look up!

College Point Industrial Park:
Along the west flank of the Whitestone Expressway (one-way south) between 14th and 20th Avenues (off our map).

[N16] **Holy Trinity Roman Catholic Church**, Whitestone Expwy. S of 14th Ave. W side. (also known as 14-51 143rd St. E side.) 1986.

Lined up along the Expressway with its more profane neighbors is this sleek modern brick church, roofed in red tile.

[N17] **GNYADA (Greater New York Automobile Dealers Association)**, 18-20 Whitestone Expwy., bet. 14th and 20th Aves. W side. 1986. **Laurence Werfel & Assocs**.

A minimalist geometric abstraction, stretched aluminum arranged in a quarter-round, pie-shape plan.

[N18] **New York Times Printing Plant**, 26-50 Whitestone Expwy., bet. 20th Ave. and Linden Place. W side. 1997. **Polshek Partnership**.

Supergraphics enhance an elegant high-tech plant for the ubiquitous New York Times. Architectural color complements the color-printed papers within (the first *New York Times* color presses).

N18

Back of the expressway, at the center of what had been the runways of the old Flushing Airport, stands a sea of new discount shopping centers and outlets: Staples, Circuit City, BJ's Club and many others are crowded along wide new 20th Avenue. Further along the expressway, beyond Linden Place, other new supermerchandising efforts are blooming: Toys R Us and its peers are building their own megabuildings. Parking is plentiful, and the giant shopping facilities that have bloomed in suburbia have finally gained a foothold in the five boroughs.

MALBA, WHITESTONE, BEECHHURST

The original community saw its major growth in the streets radiating from 14th Avenue and 150th Street. Though settled in 1645, it took the establishment of a tinware factory to convert it from a rural settlement into a thriving manufacturing center. A bit of industry survives, but the area is best known for its housing resources, such as the adjacent, formerly private, community of Malba, west of the Bronx-Whitestone Bridge; Beechhurst; and the Levitt House development, now known as Le Havre, in the shadow of the Throgs Neck Bridge: enclaves of special qualities and character.

MALBA

A small enclave, founded in 1908, of wide, sweeping, high-crowned residential streets that were private until recently. Few of the picturesque community-installed street signs remain, but the air of separateness still pervades the quiet scene.

[M1] **42 North Drive** (house), at 141st St. S side. ca. 1925.
   Among Malba's many older houses is this Italian-influenced gem, distinguished by its stately design (note the tiles inset into the stucco walls), continuing care, and commanding site, on a green berm where North and Center Drives meet. Unhappily, builder's Trophy Houses with neither sensitivity nor sense are invading these once dignified streets. Look around.

M1

[M2] **Malba Lookout**, at the end of Malba Dr. next to the Whitestone Bridge.
   A private fringe benefit for this upper-middle-class community. The view of the bridge is melodramatic.

[M3] **Kempf/Ball House**, 143-08 Malba Dr., at the East River. ca. 1937.
   Rounded, stuccoed concrete block in the Art Moderne style of the Paris Exposition of 1937, denuded of its Art Deco ornament in the past few years, and crassly marred by a glazed porch atop its north wing. A travesty.

WHITESTONE

What little industry remains occupies newer, undistinguished buildings. Churches of every description today identify the community. Its older houses have largely been compromised, with only a few exceptions.

[W1] **Martin A. Gleason Funeral Home**/formerly House, 10-25 150th St., NE cor. 11th Ave. ca. 1890.
   The crucial corner of this generous house, now seeing reuse, is a wedding cake of Ionic-columned tiered porches.

W1

[W2] **Whitestone Hebrew Center** (original sanctuary, now school), 12-41 Clintonville St., SE cor. 12th Rd. 1948. **John J. McNamara**. Addition, 1966. [W3] **Whitestone Hebrew Centre** (sanctuary), 12-25 Clintonville St., NE cor. 12th Rd. 1960.
   The earliest part, now the school, is late Art Moderne. The cantilevered corners, steel sash windows, rounded wall intersections, and bold 1930s incised lettering suggest the architecture of the Grand Concourse in the Bronx, which congregants may have then viewed as a symbol of middle-class arrival. By the time the new sanctuary had been commissioned, other concerns were evident: CENTER had become CENTRE and the quality of the architecture had deteriorated.

[W4] **Grace Episcopal Church and Sunday School**, 140-15 Clintonville St., bet. 14th Ave. and 14th Rd. E side. 1859. Gervase Wheeler. Additions, 1904, 1939, 1957.

W4

WHITESTONE, BEECHHURST DISTRICTS

see pages 845-847

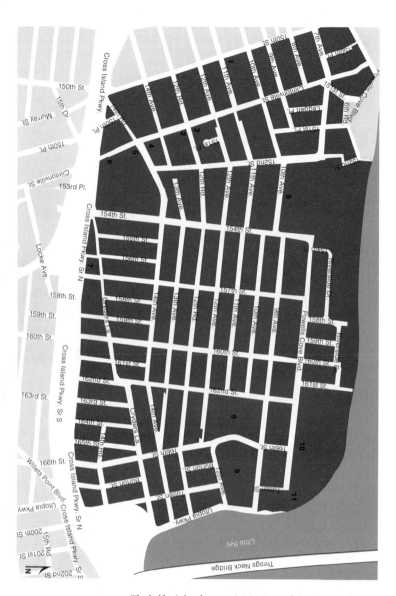

The belfry is key here, an intriguing sculpture executed in fine red brickwork, with a single bronze bell and a simple rope to toll it. Damn those electronic carillons!

[W5] **Whitestone Branch, Queensborough Public Library**, 151-10 14th Rd., SE cor. Clintonville St. 1970. **Albert Barash.** Institutional Modern.

[W6] **St. Nicholas Russian Orthodox Church of Whitestone**, 14-65 Clintonville St., bet. 14th Rd. and Cross Island Expwy. (North service road.) E side. 1969. **Sergei Padukow.**

A psychedelic fantasy blending some bizarre modern forms with the traditional onion dome of the Eastern Orthodox Church. Which would you rather have, this or the dreary institutional modern library down the hill?

W6

[W7] **156-15 Cross Island Expressway** (house), north service road (one-way west), bet. 156th and 157th Sts. N side. ca. 1860.

Finely proportioned, in the Italianate mode. Let's hope no one ever paints those blue-green-stained shingles that clad the upper story!

[W8] **The Daisy Group**/originally THC Systems, 152-15 10th Ave., bet. 152nd and 154th Sts. N side. 1978. **Wax Assocs.**

A columned Modern temple for corporate administration, built on what was once a remote freight yard of the LIRR and its predecessor, the Northside R.R., at the former Whitestone Landing.

BEECHHURST

A theatrical enclave: The 1920s saw the secluded location of Beechhurst on Long Island Sound become a favored location for Broadway theater people. Only minutes away from Manhattan via the LIRR branch whose terminal was Whitestone Landing, the area attracted actress-singer Helen Kane, Thurston the Magician, entertainer Harry Richman, and producers Joseph Schenck and Arthur Hammerstein.

W9

[W9] **Le Havre Houses** (apartments)/originally Levitt House Development, 162nd to Totten St., Powells Cove Blvd. to 12th Ave. 1958. **George G. Miller.**

Thirty 8-story beige and henna apartment buildings built by **William (Levittown) Levitt**'s brother, **Alfred**, an amateur architect, working with Miller, a pro. Actually, a very inviting housing estate, much in the style of postwar British models.

[W10] **Cryder House** (apartment tower), 166-25 Powells Cove Blvd., opp. 166th St. N side. 1963. **Hausman & Rosenberg.**

A lone apartment slab standing out dramatically—too dramatically?—from lesser construction in its vicinity. Its inhabitants enjoy great views.

W10

[W11] **Wildflower Estate Condominiums**/surrounding "Wildflower," originally Arthur Hammerstein House/later Ripples Restaurant, 168-11 Powells Cove Blvd., E of 166th St. at Cryder's Point. 1924. **Dwight James Baum.** Additions, before 1930. 🍎

The house, somewhat tarted up, is now at the center of the sprawl of new condominiums. An asymmetrically massed, deeply shadowed, intricately detailed, neo-Tudor masterpiece designed for **Arthur, Oscar Hammerstein I**'s second son. (Oscar II, the *King and I* Hammerstein, was Arthur's nephew.) Wildflower's owner was a successful Broadway producer who worked with **Gershwin, Kern, Romberg, Friml, Youmans,** and **Victor Herbert.** "A.H. Thys Hovse was bvilt in the Yere of owre Lorde MCMXXIV," read the tiles at the entrance.

FLUSHING

Until the end of World War II, Flushing was a charming Victorian community laced with some 6-story Tudor apartments constructed in the late 1920s and early 1930s. Many of its streets were lined with rambling white clapboard and shingle (Classical Revival and Shingle Style) houses dating from the last quarter of the 19th century. On its outskirts were vast reaches of undeveloped rolling land.

The construction of the Bronx-Whitestone Bridge, together with its connecting highways for the 1939-1940 New York World's Fair, set the stage for a change that was nipped in the bud by Pearl Harbor. After the war, the rush to build was on.

Two blocks of modest mansions:
Bayside Avenue, east of Parsons Boulevard, and 146th Street to 29th Avenue.

F2

[F1] **145-15 Bayside Avenue** (house), bet. Parsons Blvd. and 146th St. N side. ca. 1920.

Random granite ashlar, slate-roofed, brings a whiff of neo-Tudor to the neighborhood.

F3

[F2] **145-38 Bayside Avenue** (house), bet. Parsons Blvd. and 146th St. S side. ca. 1880.

Napoleon III's extensions to the Louvre in the 1860s triggered the Second Empire style, with exaggerated mansard roofs (named for the works of the 17th-century architect **François Mansart**). Here the mansard shows particular dominance in a two-story 1880s model.

[F3] **29-29 to 29-45 146th Street** (houses), bet. Bayside and 29th Aves. Both sides. ca. 1925.

A full, verdant, short block of 1920s Tudor, entered twixt a pair of low stone gateposts of a 19th-century estate. Check out 29-29 in particular: brick, timber, stucco, bay windows, high chimneys. Modern medieval?

[F4] **Flushing High School**, 35-01 Union St., cor. Northern Blvd. 1912-1915. **C. B. J. Snyder.** 🍎

Collegiate Gothic set on a sweeping lawn. Does grass improve the intellect?

Then, a taste of Flushing's oldest:

F5

[F5] **Bowne House**, 37-01 Bowne St., bet. 37th and 38th Aves. E side. 1661. Additions, 1680, 1696, and ca. 1830. 🍎 Open to the public. 718-359-0528. Tues, Sat, Sun, 2:30-4:30.

A simple wood house, with elegant sloping dormers, built by **John Bowne**, a Quaker. It was the first indoor meeting place of the forbidden Society of Friends; earlier they had met clandestinely in the nearby woods. Bowne was a central figure in the dispute with Governor **Peter Stuyvesant** over religious freedom. The carefully maintained interiors contain a wide variety of colonial furnishings.

[F6] **The Weeping Beech Tree, Weeping Beech Park**, 37th Ave. W of Parsons Blvd. N side. 1847. 🍎

An immense canopy of weeping branches hangs about its broad trunk, creating a natural shelter. **Samuel Parsons**, who supplied much of the plant material for Central and Prospect Parks, planted this experimental Belgian shoot in 1847. Voilà!

F7

[F7] Originally **Kingsland Homestead**/once Charles Doughty House/later William K. Murray House/now home of Queens Historical Society, 143-35 37th Ave., W of Parsons Blvd. N side. 1785. 🍎 Moved from 40-25 155th St. to

current site in 1968. Open to the public. 718-939-0647. Tues, Sat, Sun, 2:30-4:30; closed Mon, Wed, Fri.

A gambrel-roof, English-Dutch shingled house, once the home of the family for which Manhattan's Murray Hill was named.

[F8] **Bowne Street Community Church**/originally Reformed Church of Flushing, 143-11 Roosevelt Ave., NE cor. Bowne St. 1891.

Northern European brick Romanesque Revival, with a tower from Prague. The serrated brickwork at the arches and gables adds a level of elegance to the stolid volumes.

[F9] **144-85 Roosevelt Avenue** (house), bet. Parsons Blvd. and 147th St. N side. 1885.

A well-preserved but (in inner Flushing, at least) rapidly disappearing breed: a Shingle Style single house. Perfection would be still possible with some modest shingle repairs and a new coat of paint.

F8

Next, move west along Northern Boulevard from Union Street:

The New Asia: *Beginning in the 1970s Flushing became the center of an enormous and diverse Asian community comprising Chinese, Japanese, Koreans, and those from the Indian subcontinent. A visit to Union Street south of Northern Boulevard will reveal a vast array of signs in Eastern tongues.*

F10

[F10] **Flushing Armory**, 137-58 Northern Blvd., bet. Main and Union Sts. S side. 1905.

A minifort: brick over brownstone, with a battered and crenellated and machicolated tower.

[F11] Originally **Flushing Town Hall**/later Municipal Courthouse/now Flushing Council on Culture and the Arts (FCCA), 137-35 Northern Blvd., NE cor. Linden Place. 1862-1864. Maybe **William Post**. ● Renovations, including 2nd floor Great Hall. 1995-1999. **Platt Byard Dovell**.

F11

Romanesque Revival brick from the Civil War era. It served as Flushing's Town Hall until 1898, when Flushing became part of New York City. In its heydey and on its second floor its Great Hall once housed Barnum and Bailey's Circus (1897), and served as a concert hall for Swedish opera singer **Jenny Lind**. That Great Hall is now rejuvenated for modern uses. In addition to concerts, the Hall now offers a variety of events, including exhibitions, educational programs, and plays.

[F12] **Friends' Meeting House**, 137-16 Northern Blvd., bet. Main and Union Sts. S side. 1694. Additions, 1716-1719. ●

Austere and brooding, this medieval relic looks out timidly upon the never-ending stream of cars on Northern Boulevard. On its rear façade, facing the quiet graveyard, are two doors, originally separate entrances for men and women. The wood-shingled, hip-roofed structure has been used continuously since the 17th century for religious activities by the Society of Friends, except for a hiatus as a British hospital prison and stable during the Revolution.

[F13] **Latimer Gardens Community Center**, 34-30 127th St., bet. Leavitt St. and 32nd Ave. 2000. **Hanrahan-Meyers and Castro Blanco Piscioneri and Assocs.**

The sleek standing-seam-metal wrapping gives a broken profile to this elegant community facility.

F12

[F14] **Lewis H. Latimer House**, 34-41 137th St., bet. Leavitt St. and 32nd Ave. ca. 1887-1889. ●

Latimer, a noted African-American inventor, developed the long-lasting carbon filament in concert with Thomas Edison. The house was moved here to preserve it as a museum.

[F15] Formerly **RKO Keith's Flushing Theater**, Northern Blvd. opp. Main St. N side. 1927-1928. **Thomas Lamb**. Partial interior. ● Altered, 1988, **Robert Meadows**.

F14

A most obscure landmark; only the frame of the marquee is still visible. The landmarked interior was walled away.

Prince's nursery: *North of Northern Boulevard, from the site of the former RKO Keith's Theater, was a tree nursery, the first in the country, established by **William Prince** in 1737. The 8 acres had, by 1750, become the Linnaean Botanic Garden. All traces of the site are erased, but not its produce. To this day, on its streets and in its parks, Flushing displays 140 genera, consisting of 2,000 species of trees that are, in large part, the progeny of Mr. Prince.*

[F16] **Ebenezer Baptist Church**, 36-12 Prince St., bet. 36th Ave. and 36th Rd. W side. 1973. **Pedro Lopez**.

At the eastern outskirts of downtown Flushing is this ambitious, dramatically fashioned house of worship: striated concrete block and lots of amber stained glass—actually plastic—for an upwardly mobile black congregation.

F16

[F17] **St. George's Episcopal Church**, Main St. bet. 38th and 39th Aves. W side. 1854. **Wills & Dudley**.

Miraculously, this stately Gothic Revival church has withstood the commercial, cacophonous onslaught on Main Street. **Francis Lewis**, a signer of the Declaration of Independence, was a church warden in the original building, completed in 1761. Manhattan schist ashlar and brownstone; it would be more convincing without the later wood-shingled steeple.

[F18] **Flushing Regional Branch Library**, Main St., SE cor. Kissena Blvd. 1998. **Polshek Partnership**.

Sleek sinuosity, punctuated with notable notches. This is high style for a drab Main Street.

F18

[F19] **The Free Synagogue of Flushing**, 41-60 Kissena Blvd., NW cor. Sanford Ave. 1927. **Maurice Courland**.

A stately neo-Baroque presence turned diagonally to a difficult intersection of streets.

[F20] **The Windsor School**, 136-23 Sanford Ave., bet. Main St. and Kissena Blvd. N side. ca. 1845.

Greek Revival mansion (the capitals have gone back to Corinth) with a mansarded, balustraded roof.

[F21] **U.S. Post Office, Flushing**, Main St. SE cor. Sanford Ave. 1932. **Dwight James Baum** and **William W. Knowles**, architects. **James A. Wetmore**, supervising architect, U.S. Treasury Dept.

A tasteful neo-Georgian building from an era when taste was all one had to hold on to; a safe and comforting neighborhood monument.

F20

[F22] **The Waldheim Neighborhood** (East Flushing Residential Blocks), bounded by Franklin Ave., Parsons Blvd., a line bet. Cherry and 45th Aves., and Bowne St. 1875-1900.

Porches, chimneys, mansards, and gambrels; Shingle Style, Queen Anne, and eclectic miscellany. A wonderful small district that, it is said, was preserved by a "conscious preservation" action in the late 1920s after completion of the apartment house at 42-66 Phlox Place—an anticipation of the Landmarks Preservation Commission forty years later.

F21

The original Waldheim area stretched from Sanford Avenue at the north to Rose Street on the South, Kissena Boulevard on the west to Murray and 156th Streets on the east. The Wallace-Appleton

FLUSHING (EAST) DISTRICT
see pages 851-853

Company bought the 10 acres from the estate of **Allan MacDonald**; thick woods stretching across the site inspired the name Waldheim. The name disappeared for a time after 1916 (after the developer's bankruptcy, and anti-German feelings during the First World War).

Wander off Bowne St. and down Ash:

[F23] **143-10 Ash Ave.** "Moorish" in glossy (!) stucco.

[F24] **143-13 Ash Ave.** Shingle Style, well hedged.

[F25] **143-19 Ash Ave.** A neo-Georgian Buddhist temple.

F26

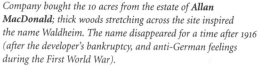 [F26] **143-32 Ash Ave.** An elegant bungalow with bumpety stone and a squat Palladian window.

[F27] **143-40 Ash Ave.** Early concrete block (1908).

[F28] **143-49 Ash Ave.** Shingle Style meets Colonial Revival.

[F29] **143-63 Ash Ave.** Awkward Classical Revival.

[F30] **143-64 Ash Ave.** Might as well be in **Frank Lloyd Wright**'s Oak Park, Ill.

F30

[F31] **Community Outreach Center, YWCA**, 42-07 Parsons Blvd., opp. Ash Ave. 1993. **Bennett Metzner Sowinski**.
   An austere stucco block houses needed social services.

Where a junior Newport "cottage" once stood, at Ash Ave., SW cor. Parsons, is one of a group of oriental temples:

 [F32] **Nichiren Shoshu Temple**, Daihozan Myosetsu-Ji, 42-32 Parsons Blvd., SW cor. Ash Ave. 1984. **Ashihara Assocs**.
   Constructed to serve the needs of a 13th-century form of Japanese Buddhism, this temple is composed of an austere stacking of rectilinear forms. It might be equally contextual on Mars.

F32

[F33] **Won Buddhist Temple**, Song Eun Building, 43-02 Burling St., SW cor. Cherry Ave. 1986. Bo Yoon & Assocs.

A Korean Buddhist temple, with stylish, but awkward, stucco forms.

[F34] **Hindu Temple Society of North America**, 45-57 Bowne St., bet. 45th and Holly Aves. E side. 1977. **Baryn Basu Assocs.** architects. Sculpture by Department of Endowments, Andhra Pradesh, India.

As one wanders through the jungles of Flushing, the houses part and reveal this exquisitely ornate Indian sculpture totally overwhelming the temple's exterior.

F34

[F35] **Martin Lande House** (apartments)/originally Kissena II Apartments, 137-47 45th Ave., off Kissena Blvd., bet. 45th and Elder Aves. N side. 1970. **Gruzen & Partners**.

Articulated, well-proportioned, and, happily, not an architectural statement in excess of its duties. The brick, glass, and sash, framed in a cast-concrete grid, are beautifully detailed.

MURRAY HILL

F35

[F36] **149-19 Elm Avenue** (house), bet. 149th and Murray Sts. N side. 1895.

A midblock wonder, sporting a half-round second-story porch. Dig those finely spaced, square wood balusters betwixt Ionic columns.

BROADWAY-FLUSHING

[F37] **St. Andrew Avalino Roman Catholic Church**, 157-01 Northern Blvd., NE cor. 157th St. 1940. **Henry V. Murphy**.

F36

A combination of neo-Romanesque and Art Deco, using materials so lovingly designed (inside and out) and finely crafted that the building itself could convert infidels to the faith. Attend a mass!

[F38] **29-12 to 29-60, 29-01 to 29-61 167th Street** (row houses) bet. 29th and 32nd Aves. Both sides. ca. 1925.

A romantic composition in brick, stone, and stucco, with slate roof tiles; served by rear central driveways and garages for the then emerging motor car.

AUBURNDALE

[F39] **189-10 to 189-30, 189-11 to 189-29 37th Avenue** (houses), bet. Utopia Blvd. and 190th St. N and S sides. ca. 1925.

Clustered Neo-Tudor housing gives style and an urbane and friendly tenor to this otherwise prosaic steet.

[F40] **Joseph Cornell** (1903-1973), shy, reticent creator of exquisite and often mysterious works of art in the form of boxes, lived in this 1920s detached wood frame house at 37-08 Utopia Parkway, between 37th and 39th Avenues.

F40

[F41] **Temple Beth Sholom**, 42-50 172nd St., NW cor. Northern Blvd. to Auburndale Lane. 1954. **Unger & Unger**. South addition, 1964. **Stanley H. Klein**.

A bold brazen wall of green slate presents subdued monumentality to the visual cacophony of Northern Boulevard.

[F42] **St. Nicholas Greek Orthodox Church Chapel and William Spyropoulos School**, 196-10 Northern Blvd., SE cor. 196th St. 1974. **Raymond & Rado**.

A spartan octagonal auditorium is crowned with a spherical dome: bold concrete and brick. The chapel is a lilliputian version of the main church, whose form is a sort of romantic "brutalism."

F42

UTOPIA

Utopia Land Company: In June 1905 the *New York Times* noted a plan to develop a 50-acre tract, to be called Utopia, for relocated residents of Manhattan's Lower East Side. The new community, a local Queens newspaper later said, would "carry out Communistic ideas." Utopia lay between today's 164th Street and Fresh Meadow Lane, from the Long Island Expressway to Jewel Avenue. But back then the north-south streets were intended to bear Lower East Side names like Houston, Stanton, Rivington, Delancey, Clinton, and Broome. The scheme failed, and the land was sold in 1911.

FRESH MEADOWS

[M1] **Fresh Meadows Housing Development**, 186th to 197th Sts., Long Island Expwy. to 73rd Ave. (irregularly). 1949. **Voorhees, Walker, Foley & Smith**; 20-story addition, 1962. **Voorhees, Walker, Smith, Smith & Haines**.

M1

This 166-acre development on the site of the old Fresh Meadows Country Club was a post–World War II project of the New York Life Insurance Company. Its (then) avant-garde site plan, including a mix of row housing, low- and high-rise apartments, regional shopping center, theater, schools, and other amenities, scores as excellent planning but dull architecture. Nevertheless, it is beautifully maintained.

M2a

[M2] **Long Island (Vanderbilt) Motor Parkway:** [M2a] **73rd Avenue overpass**, Cunningham Park W of Francis Lewis Blvd. [M2b] **Hollis Court Boulevard overpass**, N of Union Tpke. and Richland Ave. [M2c] **Springfield Boulevard overpass**, N of Kingsbury Ave. 1924-1926.

These funky reinforced-concrete overpasses date from the construction of America's first "super highway." Built by race car enthusiast **William K. Vanderbilt** especially for automobiles, the road stretched a total of 45 "dustless" miles from a toll lodge at Hillside Avenue to Lake Ronkonkoma, in Suffolk County. Cars were narrower then: the road was only 16 feet wide, making it ideal for its current reuse (in Queens, at least) as a grade-separated bikeway.

[M3] **St. John's University, Queens Campus** (Roman Catholic), Union Tpke. SW cor. Utopia Pkwy., to Grand Central Pkwy. Relocated from Brooklyn, beginning 1955. [M3a] **Frumkes Hall**, 1971. **Carson, Lundin & Thorsen**. [M3b] **Sun Yat-sen Hall**, Center of Asian Studies. 1973. **Herman C. Knebel**.

In the vast 105 acres of this campus, mighty little architecture of note exists. Sun Yat-Sen Hall, however, a faux Chinese temple and polychromed gate, adds a brilliant splash of color to an otherwise drab setting.

M4

[M4] **Queens Hospital Center, N.Y.C. Health & Hospitals Corporation**/originally Queens General Hospital, 82-68 164th St., bet. Goethals Ave. and Grand Central Pkwy. 1937. **Sullivan W. Jones, John E. Kleist, Jacob Lust**.

[M4a] **New Buildings, Queens Hospital Center**, 104th St., bet. Grand Central Pkwy. and 82nd Rd. W side. 2000. **Perkins & Will/Davis Brody Bond/Associated Architects**.

Art Deco orange brick, built long before the post–World War II building boom in Queens, now complemented with P&W/DBB's new buildings. Unfortunately, the Borough powers-that-be want to tear the 1937 building down.

[M5] Originally **Triborough Hospital for Tuberculosis** (now part of Queens Hospital Center), Parsons Blvd. NE cor. 82nd Dr. 1940. **Eggers & Higgins**.

A light, bright, softly modeled high-rise hospital turned to the sun and bedecked with south-facing tiers of balconies and solariums, designed when TB was still a scourge and sunlight was believed to be the salvation.

M5

[M5a] **107th Precinct House, N.Y.C. Police Dept.**, 71-01 Parsons Blvd., SE cor. 71st Ave. 1993. **Perkins Eastman**.

A Modernist assembly of anodized aluminum and iron-spot brick. Straightforward, but perhaps too stylish.

[M6] **Queens College, CUNY**, 65-30 Kissena Blvd., bet. Long Island Expwy. and Melbourne Ave., to Main St.

[M7] **Main Building**/originally New York Parental School. 1908.

[M8] **New Science Building**, 1987. **Davis Brody & Assocs**.

[M9] **Benjamin S. Rosenthal Library**, 1988. **Gruzen Samton Steinglass**.

[M10] **Salick Center for Molecular & Cellular Biology**. 2000. **Rafael Viñoly Architects**.

M7

When it opened in 1937, Queens College occupied 9 Spanish Mission Style tile-roofed buildings built in 1908 for use as the New York Parental School, a special school for incorrigibles and truants. The current 52 acres contain a hodgepodge of architecture ranging from a few of the original structures to the sophisticated new Science and Rosenthal Library buildings, linked by a bridge.

M9

Paul Klapper, for whom a college building and an adjacent elementary school are named, was the college's first president.

[M11] **Public School 219, Queens, The Paul Klapper School**, 144-39 Gravett Rd., E of Main St. N side. 1966. **Caudill, Rowlett & Scott**.

A domed set of open classrooms, from the era when open classrooms were guaranteed to deliver a great elementary education—and a headache for the teacher by the end of the school day.

M12

[M12] **Townsend Harris High School**, NE cor. 149th St. and Melbourne Ave. 1990s.

A heavy-handed neighbor to Queens College. There is none of the joy present in so many of the new New York City schools.

BAYSIDE

Bayside is northeast of Flushing with an attractive suburban character maintained by an abundance of detached houses and low-rise apartments. Originally settled by **William Lawrence** in 1664, it remained largely rural until linked to Manhattan by the LIRR's East River tunnels in 1910.

T1

Fort Totten: This military reservation dates from 1857, but it wasn't until 1898 that it was designated Fort Totten by President McKinley in honor of General Joseph G. Totten (1788-1864), Director of the War Department's Bureau of Seacoast Defense.

Entry from 212th Street, North of Bell Boulevard. Open to the public. Tell the guard that you want to go to the Museum, and you will be allowed to drive in. The old Officer's Club and the ruins of the Battery are musts.

[T1] **Bayside Historical Society**/originally Officers Club, The Fort at Willets Point, Fort Totten, Murray and Totten Aves. opp. Weaver Ave., Fort Totten. S side. ca. 1870. Enlarged, 1887. ☀ Restoration, 1990s. **Goldstone & Hinz**. Open to the public (obtain permission at main gate).

Castellated Gothic Revival in the spirit of **Alexander Jackson Davis** and **Andrew Jackson Downing**. Wood here simulates masonry grandeur in what began as "the castle," a casino for officers.

T2

[T2] **Fort Totten Battery and Museum**, Fort Totten. 1863-1864. William Petit Trowbridge, engineer. ☀ Open to the public (obtain permission at main gate).

A monumental, tooled granite-block fortification. Arched ways along its embrasured walls are arranged in a V-shape plan, with a bastion at its prow worthy of ancient Rome. It was built to protect, with Fort Schuyler across the strait, the east entry to New York Harbor. Park at the Museum, and enter through a 90-foot long tunnel into the battery innards. Curator **Jack Fein** will show you the way.

And much to the south of the Fort:

[B1] **Crocheron Park**, entry drive via 35th Ave. off Corbett Rd., at 216th St.

One of Queens's best-kept secrets: Mickle Pond at the southeast corner of this park, literally only a few feet from the fast-moving traffic of Cross Island Parkway. Overlooking it are:

B2

[B2] 217-17 **Corbett Road** (house), bet. 217th and 221st Sts. N side. ca. 1900.

A grand shingled "country" house magically surviving the last century, symbol of the significant architecture that once thrived hereabouts.

[B3] **217-63, 217-67, 217-71, 217-75, 217-79 Corbett Road** (houses), bet. 217th and 221st Sts. N side. 1986.

Pretentious (get a load of those two-car garages!) but mildly credible despite the aluminum siding and fussy arches.

[B4] Former **James J. Corbett House**, 221-04 Corbett Rd., SE cor. 221st St. ca. 1900.

The plaque on the boulder reveals that world's heavyweight champion, **"Gentleman Jim" Corbett** lived here between 1902 and his death in 1933. He held the title from 1892 to 1897. He evidently also had taste in architecture.

Nearby:

[B5] **All Saints Episcopal Church**, 39-30 215th St., NW cor. 40th Ave. 1962.

The shingled balloon frame gives modern form to this Gothic Revivalist church.

B5

South of the LIRR tracks:

[B6] **215-37 43rd Avenue** (apartment complex), NW cor. 216th St. 1931. **Benjamin Braunstein**.

Half-timbered, stucco and brick, slate-roofed: a meandering medieval close offers access, light, intimacy and privacy, and great charm. Meander through: there are entries to the close on both streets.

[B7] **Lawrence Family Graveyard**, 216th St. bet. 42nd Ave. and LIRR. W side. 1830. ● Not open to the public.

One of two tiny private cemeteries of the ubiquitous Queens family.

B6

[B8] **Oakland Lake, Alley Park**, Springfield Blvd. to Cloverdale Blvd., S of 46th Ave. Reconstructed, **N.Y.C. Department of Parks & Recreation Design Staff**, 1986. Open to the public.

An oasis in the Olmstedian mode: note the naturalistic joining of land and water, rarely done well in a City park. It was re-created through design.

[B9] **Queensborough Community College, CUNY**/formerly the site of Oakland Golf Course and Club, 56th Ave. NW cor. Cloverdale Blvd. to Garland and Kenilworth Drs. 1967 Master Plan: [B9a] **Library, Science, Humanities, Gymnasium, Campus Center**, 1967-1970. **Frederick Wiedersum & Assocs**. and **Holden, Egan, Wilson & Corser**. 1970-1975 Master Plan: [B9b] **Administration Building**, 1977. **Percival Goodman**. [B9c] **Medical Arts Building**, 1977. **Armand Bartos & Assocs**.

B9

Built from scratch in just 10 years on a large portion of the old Oakland Golf Course. The first round of structures is precast concrete and brick, straightforward and simple. The later 2 structures are examples of stylish form-making for its own sake. At the crest of the grand outdoor stair is the former clubhouse, now the Oakland Building, a welcome survivor.

Southern Queens

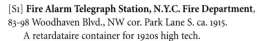

S

WOODHAVEN • RICHMOND HILL • JAMAICA HOLLIS • ST. ALBANS • SOUTH OZONE PARK

Town of Jamaica/Rustdrop
Settled in 1656; chartered in 1660.

The communities lying within the boundaries of the old Town of Jamaica contain, as a group, the widest contrasts of any section of Queens. Some, like Ozone Park, Richmond Hill, and Woodhaven, are quiet residential communities. Jamaica itself, on the other hand, is a bustling marketplace with department stores, specialty shops, and theaters. Affluence is everywhere visible in Jamaica Estates along Grand Central Parkway; poverty and squalor mark the black slums of South Jamaica; St. Albans, though, is a lovely, treelined, middle-income black community. Parts of Jamaica date from the 17th and 18th centuries; Richmond Hill, Queens Village, from the 19th.

WOODHAVEN

S1

[S1] **Fire Alarm Telegraph Station, N.Y.C. Fire Department**, 83-98 Woodhaven Blvd., NW cor. Park Lane S. ca. 1915.

A retardataire container for 1920s high tech.

[S2] **Christ Church Congregational**, 85-27 91st St. (one-way north), SE cor 85th Rd. 1914. Addition, 1928.

The imaginative carpentry at the belfry cornice (and the rooster weather vane) distinguish this grayed Italianate stucco edifice. But that neon outlined crucifix, that's another matter.

[S3] **St. Matthew's Episcopal-Anglican Church**, 1901. **R. F. Schirmer** and **J. A. Schmidt**. Parish Hall and Rectory, 85-36 96th St. (one-way southbound), bet. 85th Rd. and 86th Ave. E side.

The peaceful green compound formed by these three structures is a gift to 96th Street. The particularly lovely neo-Gothic church is built of an extremely good-looking ashlar, whose joints have been deeply raked, giving the structure great character in an otherwise softly configured neighborhood.

S2

Midblock cemetery: Immediately behind St. Matthew's is the private Wyckoff-Snediker Cemetery, accessible to the families' descendants (Elderts included) by walking around the church, and via a lane that begins at 97-01 Jamaica Avenue.

S3

[S4] Former **Lalance & Grosjean kitchenware factory**/now largely the site of Pathmark Shopping Center, Atlantic Ave. bet. 89th and 92nd Sts. to 95th Ave. 1876. Shopping center, 1986, **Niego Assocs.** [S4a] Originally **Lalance & Grosjean clock tower and factory**, Atlantic Ave. SW cor. 92nd St. 1876.

Until most of the antique, red-painted brick structures were wasted in the mid 1980s to form yet another shopping center, this intricate array of 19th-century mill buildings was a remarkable relic of the era when the Village of Woodhaven claimed a nationally known tinware and agateware manufacture. Its products graced many an American kitchen for generations, and the Lalance & Grosjean factory employed hundreds.

In the end, saving the squat clock tower atop one of the old factories became a sop to those preservation interests which sought to save more of the historic building complex from destruction.

S4a

[S5] Originally **The Wyckoff Building** (office building), 93-02 95th Ave., SE cor. 93rd St. 1889.

WOODHAVEN / RICHMOND HILL (WEST) DISTRICTS

see pages 858-860

A distinguished 19th-century commercial corner that was originally a real estate exchange and the office of the Woodhaven Bank. In this part of low-rise Queens, its four stories (plus the now missing corner egg-shaped dome) must have made it the local skyscraper when first opened.

[S6] Originally **Lalance & Grosjean workers' housing**, 85-02 to 85-20 95th Ave. and 85-01 to 85-21 97th Ave., bet. 85th and 86th Sts. Both sides. 1884.

Modest wood-frame row houses built as a paternalistic gesture to its employees by the local company. Mostly altered and in poor repair.

S5

Mae West's early career: The brassy movie queen was born in nearby Brooklyn but is said to have begun her career performing in **Louis Neir**'s Hotel, a combination tavern-hotel. The 2-story structure still exists (in remarkably original shape) at 87-48 78th Street, at the northwest corner of 88th Avenue. (The streets here are all one-way, somehow always the wrong way: 78th runs northbound below Jamaica Avenue, where Neir's is now a bar.)

RICHMOND HILL

West of Jamaica and south of Forest Park's hills lies the community of Richmond Hill. Its plan was evolved and its streets laid out by Manhattan lawyer Albon P. Man (also responsible for adjacent Kew Gardens) and his English landscape architect, Edward Richmond, from 1867 through 1872. Like Kew Gardens, Richmond Hill also owes its name to a London suburb.

Richmond Hill Driving Tour:
A meandering drive through part of Richmond Hill's finest streets ending at The Triangle.

Using a good street map or pocket atlas, begin with the former factories at the south flank of Forest Park at Park Lane South and 101st Street. Then scoot around and follow 86th Avenue (two-way) eastward as a rough spine for the trip. Take detours up and down the streets (mostly one-way) as you choose:

S7

[S7] Formerly **William Demuth & Company-S. M. Frank & Company**/now apartments, 84-10 101st St., SW cor. Park Lane. ca. 1895. Converted, 1987.

Backing up on the old LIRR Rockaway Beach Division siding, a factory where briar was turned and polished to manufacture Frank Medico smoking pipes. Built at a time when every man could afford a pipe and conversations centered on which shape burned coolest to the taste. Brickwork is embellished with stepped corbels under the cornice and basketweave on the tower (the smoking room?).

S8

[S8] **Public School 66, Queens,** The Brooklyn Hills School, 85-11 102nd St., bet. 85th Rd. and 85th Dr. E side. 1901. Additions. (102nd St. is two-way.)

Many coats of paint have muffled the terra-cotta ornament, but the Art Nouveau molded terra-cotta sign still reads loud and clear. The bell tower has lost both its bell and its pyramidal cap sometime along its journey. At the turn of the century this part of Richmond Hill took its name from the (former) great City of Brooklyn to the west, hence the school's name: Brooklyn Hills.

S9

[S9] **85-58, 85-54 104th Street** (houses), bet. 85th and 86th Aves. W side. ca. 1900. (104th St. is one-way north here.)

A pair of large gambrel-roof single houses, still bearing their original combination of large wood-shingle-and-stucco siding and diagonal wood muntins dividing the second-floor window sash.

[S10] **Trinity Methodist Church,** 107-14 86th Ave., bet. 107th and 108th Sts. S side. ca. 1910.

The church's florid neo-medieval column capitals are provincial, yet very charming.

S11

[S11] **108-03 86th Avenue** (house), NE cor. 86th Ave. and 108th St. 1890s.

Shinglework and details are largely intact in this sturdy towered and double-pedimented survivor.

RICHMOND HILL DISTRICT

see pages 860-863

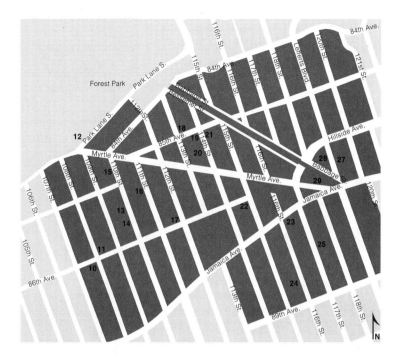

Forest Park

[S12] **Richmond Hill War Memorial**, edge of Forest Park, Park Lane S., NE cor. Memorial Drive, at Myrtle Ave. and 109th St. ca. 1925. **J. P. Pollia** sculptor.

The poignant bronze sculpture of an innocent young lad caught up in a war not of his making sits atop a granite stele with an inscription that makes use of an uncommon gender for such memorials:

ERECTED BY THE PEOPLE OF RICHMOND HILL

IN MEMORY OF HER MEN

WHO SERVED AND DIED IN THE WORLD WAR

1917-1918

Note also the small-scale but exquisitely crafted bronze flag-pole base, adjacent.

S13

[S13] **85-12 110th Street** (house), bet. 85th and 86th Aves. W side. ca. 1900. (110th St. is one-way north.)

A gambrel roof turned to the street, a broken pediment, much willful asymmetry, and fat bottle colums from the Colonial Revival. An Eclectic Shingle Style charmer.

[S14] **85-24 110th Street** (house), bet. 85th and 86th Aves. W side. ca. 1900.

The porch lathework creates airy arches within the Tuscan column and beam ensemble.

S14

[S15] **84-16 110th Street** (house), bet. Myrtle and 85th Aves. W side. ca. 1900.

Complex pyramidal geometry and an intermix of rectangular and half-round openings make a remarkable composition, marred by the new synthetic siding that doesn't provide appropriate corner or window detailing.

[S16] **85-28 111th Street** (house), bet. Myrtle and 86th Aves. W side. ca. 1900. (111th St. is two-way.)

A strong statement retaining most of its original Shingle Style livery.

S17

[S17] Church of the Holy Child Jesus (Roman Catholic), 85-80 112th St. (one-way south), NW cor. 86th Ave. 1931. **Henry V. Murphy**.

Neo-Romanesque cum Art Moderne, of orange brick and exquisitely carved limestone. Reminiscent, inside and out, of later **Bertram Goodhue** work. The bell tower is a gem.

[S18] 84-37 113th Street (house), NE cor. 85th Ave. (113th St. is one-way north) ca. 1875.

Note the shy Japanese touches at the edge of the roof beams, from a time when some architects were flirting with oriental motifs.

114th Street (two-way) between 85th and 86th Avenues; one-way south below Myrtle Avenue:

S20

[S19] 85-04 114th Street (house), SW cor. 85th Ave. ca. 1900.

Exuberance as in this house caused Victorian houses first to lose their stylishness (they tore them down for such excess in the 1950s) . . . and, more recently, to regain it. Thank God!

[S20] 85-10, 85-14, 85-20 114th Street (houses), W side. ca. 1900.

A smashing group! But if, as Mies said, God is in the details, he's withdrawn support from these. The residers and re-windowers have muted their elegance.

S21

[S21] 85-03 114th Street (house), SE cor. 85th Ave. ca. 1900.

The original porch has been partly enclosed, but above it much of the architectural interest survives.

[S22] Union Congregational Church/United Church of Christ, 86-10 115th St. (one-way north), SW cor. 86th Ave.

Built of black stone, with the mortar joints pointed in a projecting V-joint profile.

116th Street, south of Jamaica Avenue:
(One-way south.)

S23

[S23] Casa Latina/onetime Landmark Tavern Building/ originally Richmond Hill Branch, Bank of Jamaica, 116-02 Jamaica Ave., SE cor. 116th St. ca. 1900.

Gentrification has given new life to this distinctive, turn-of-the-century corner commercial building. In the mid 1980s the prescription for real estate success in this locale was "Call it a landmark." In this case, it is one (though still unofficial).

[S24] 87-72, 87-78 116th Street (houses), bet. 89th and Jamaica Aves. W side. ca. 1885.

Imagine when all the single homes on this block had basic forms like these. Some of the bones (columns) have been replaced, and a tan brick wall worthy of lesser architecture built in front of 87-78, but the old bodies are still there.

S25

[S25] P.S. 51, Early Childhood Development Center, 87-45 117th St., bet. Jamaica Ave. and 89th Ave. E side. 1994. **Gruzen Samton**.

Some new high style in the neighborhood that may give support to those repairing and restoring the neighboring 19th-century architecture. Two colors of brick, limestone, and glass block make for a children's delight.

An aside to the south:

[S26] P.S. 161, 101-23 124th St., bet. 101st and 103rd Aves. 2000. **Gruzen Samton**.

PS 161
Queens
New School

Anticipated Completion: September 2008

New York City School Construction
Building Schools for a Better Tomorrow

S26

Returning to Jamaica Avenue:

The Triangle:
Actually, many triangles are formed where Lefferts Boulevard crosses the intersection of Myrtle and Jamaica Avenues, a special event in the otherwise ho-hum local street grid. The complex streetscape is further enriched by the route of the old LIRR Montauk Division viaduct, which—using its own geometry— passes over the streets but under the old BMT Jamaica Line's elevated structure. A block west sees the northbound birth of Hillside Avenue, which swings around a quarter turn, dips beneath the LIRR viaduct, and merrily spins its way east to the Nassau County line.

The immediate area is filled with curiosities:

S27

[S27] **Richmond Hill Republican Club,** 86-15 Lefferts Blvd., bet. Hillside and Jamaica Aves. E side. 1920.
   A battered temple to the party of **President Abraham Lincoln** (archery range in basement). Richmond Hill was even more heavily Republican before the Great Depression.

[S28] **Richmond Hill Branch, Queens Borough Public Library**. 118-14 Hillside Ave., SW cor. Lefferts Blvd. 1905. **Tuthill & Higgins**.
   One of many yellow brick Carnegie gifts, this on a green triangle of its own, early on called Library Square.

S28

[S29] **Triangle Hofbrau** (restaurant)/formerly Triangle Hotel, Myrtle Ave. bet. 117th St. and Jamaica Ave. 1864.
   Once a rambling restaurant and bar with walls bedecked with old photos and arcane memorabilia. A plaque from the Native New Yorkers Historical Association claimed that this was Long Island's oldest tavern in continuous operation. In the 1890s, during the bicycle craze, it was called Wheelmen's Rest.

Frappes and sundaes: Frank Jahn's is a neo-real 1890s ice cream parlor at 117-03 Hillside Avenue (near 117th Street and Jamaica Avenue). Complete with marble countertops, leaded-glass Coca-Cola chandeliers, and wild—just wild—ice cream concoctions.

END of Richmond Hill Driving Tour.

JAMAICA

J1

[J1] **Queens Civil and Housing Court Building**, 8917 Sutphen Blvd. SE cor. 89th Ave. 1997. **Perkins Eastman**.
Monumentality within the tight cityscape, relating to surrounding buildings, rather than setting itself apart. This Civil Court is a civil citizen. A five-story atrium provides a grand spatial adventure inside.

J2

[J2] **Queens Family Court and City Agency Facility**, 151-20 Jamaica Ave. bet. 151st and 152nd Sts. 2001. **Henry H. Cobb, Pei Cobb Freed & Partners/Gruzen Samton, Associated Architects**.
A prize from the Art Commission honored this crisp courthouse before the excavators had broken ground.

[J3] **King Manor Museum**/originally Rufus King House, King Park, Jamaica Ave. bet. 150th and 153rd Sts. N side. North section, 1730; west section, 1755; east section, 1806. Additions, 1810 and ca. 1830s. 🐦 Interior 🐦 Open by appointment. 718-523-0029.
A large bland white house, more interesting for its social history than its architecture, set on a greensward that also contains a wonderful Victorian pergola once used for band concerts.

[J4] **U.S. Region II Social Security Administration Headquarters**, Jamaica Ave. SW cor. Twombly Place (Parsons Blvd.) to Archer Ave. 1987. **Gruzen Samton** and **Ehrenkrantz Ekstut**.
This big, bulky, brick, bureaucratic block proves there was big government, even during the conservative Reagan administration, whose legions built it. Mammon, here government's version, overwhelms a pair of spiritual neighbors:

[J5] **First Reformed Church of Jamaica**, 153-10 Jamaica Ave., SE cor. 153rd St. S side. 1858-1859. **Sidney J. Young**. Addition, 1902. **Tuthill & Higgins**. 🐦
Red brick Romanesque Revival arches, doorways, windows, corbel tables, with a Gothic tower. Medieval eclecticism.

J6

[J6] **Grace Episcopal Church and Graveyard**, 155-03 Jamaica Ave. bet. 153rd St. and Parsons Blvd. 1861-1862. **Dudley Field**. Chancel, 1901-1902. **Cady, Berg & See**. 🐦 Graveyard, ca. 1734.
A brownstone monolith from grass to finial. English country Gothic, appropriately, for the official church of the British Colonial government.

Along 160th Street:
Between Jamaica and 90th Avenues (one-way north).

J7

[J7] **Jamaica Business Resource Center**/originally La Casina or Casino/onetime Roxanne Swimsuits, 90-33 160th St. E side. ca. 1936. 🐦
A sophisticated mastaba of Art Deco/Moderne origins rescued by the JBRC. That sleek stainless steel is on a par with the Chrysler Building.

[J8] **Farmers Market**, 90-40 160th St., bet. Jamaica and 90th Aves. W side. 1997. **James McCullar & Associates**.
A clerestoried steel portico leads to adaptive reuse and new construction: markets for fresh food and prepared food, dining, and office space.

J8

[J9] **Parking Garage**, 90-60 160th St. W side. 1990s.
When parking garages rank with the more

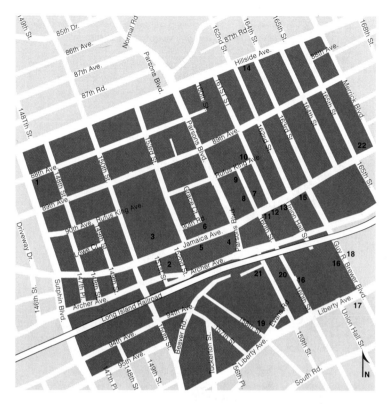

distinguished architecture in the neighborhood, something is either very right or very wrong . . .

Beyond:

[J10] **Title Guarantee Company**/formerly Suffolk Title & Guarantee Building, 90-04 161st St. NW cor. Rufus King Ave. 1929. **Dennison & Hirons**.

The decoration here is more important than the building: Art Moderne at the third-floor spandrels and the sky: blue, beige, orange, and black.

J9

[J11] Originally **Jamaica Savings Bank**, 161-02 Jamaica Ave., bet. 161st and 162nd Sts. S side. 1898. **Hough & Dewell**.

Second Empire/Beaux Arts cheek by jowl with the Renaissance Revival club below.

[J12] **Jamaica Arts Center**/originally Jamaica Register Building, 161-04 Jamaica Ave., bet. 161st and 162nd Sts. S side. 1898. **A. S. Macgregor**. ☛ 718-658-7400. Tues-Sat, 10-5; closed Sun-Mon.

In the style of an Italian Renaissance Revival London clubhouse, now happily preserved as an arts center.

J11

[J13] **Sidewalk clock**, in front of 161-02 Jamaica Ave., bet. 161st and 162nd Sts. S side. 1900. ☛

One of the city's officially designated street furniture landmarks.

The Revolution: The Battle of Long Island, in the closing days of August 1776, had its skirmishes in Jamaica as well as Brooklyn. Boulder Crest, at the terminal moraine's summit overlooking the outwash plain on which the Jamaica business district was built, held the rifle pits of the retreating Continental soldiers. A commemorative glacial boulder and plaque can be found on the lawn at the southwest corner of 150th Street and 85th Drive.

J15

[J14] **Auxiliary Services for High Schools**/formerly Hillcrest High School Annex/formerly Jamaica Vocational High School/originally Jamaica Training School, 162-10 Hillside Ave., bet. 162nd and 163rd Sts. S side.

Understated brick and brownstone.

[J15] Originally **J. Kurtz & Sons** (furniture store), 162-24 Jamaica Ave., SW cor. Guy R. Brewer Blvd. 1931. **Allmendinger & Schlendorf.** ☙

Six spectacular stories of Art Deco commercial architecture, only minimally compromised since the Kurtzes left, in 1978. Look up.

J16

South of the LIRR embankment:

[J16] **York College, CUNY**, 94-20 Guy R. Brewer Blvd., S of LIRR to Liberty Ave. W side. 1983. **The Gruzen Partnership.**

The cascade of steps at the boulevard entry leads to the neat, low, carefully controlled architecture of this campus. The Union Hall Street arched pedestrian underpass (1913) through the LIRR embankment from Archer Avenue is an intriguing way to reuse the former path of a now discontinued street.

J18

[J17] **York College Health and Physical Education Facility**, 160-02 Liberty Ave. bet. 160th St. and Guy R. Brewer Blvd. 1987. **Cain, Farrell & Bell.**

Simple and austere volumes for sports activities, with an adjacent greensward of playing fields.

[J18] **York College Auditorium and Theater**, 94-45 Guy R. Brewer Blvd. 1990s. **Polshek Partnership.**

Polychromatic brick and a great glass wall greet the audience across a great entrance lawn.

J19

[J19] **Federal Drug Administration Regional Laboratory**, 158-15 Liberty Ave., NE cor. 158th St. 2000. **Gruzen Samton.**

Black, gray, red, and white combine in a stylish ensemble. The FDA is concerned with the viability of prescription and non-presription drugs, and may yet take on the nicotine in tobacco. This elegant building may signify a presence that is more serious than ever.

[J20] Originally **St. Monica's Roman Catholic Church**, 94-20 160th St., S of LIRR. 1856-1857. **Anders Peterson,** master mason. ☙

J20

On the campus of York College, itself in monolithic brick, but demolished save for its tower; this could have become a special place for students. The tower is a haunting reminder of a different and lively neighborhood that once surrounded it.

[J21] **Prospect Cemetery**, 159th St. SW cor. Beaver Rd. 1668 onward. ☙

The first public burial ground of Jamaica. In the early years of this community the wealthy were mostly buried in church—laymen under their pews, clergymen in the chapel or beneath the pulpit. Less affluent parishioners were interred in the churchyard. The rest were buried in Prospect Cemetery.

[J22] **Tabernacle of Prayer**/originally Loew's Valencia Theater, 165-11 Jamaica Ave., bet. 165th St. and Merrick Blvd. N side. 1929. **John Eberson.** ◐
One of the city's great motion picture palaces, now a church. With the Jamaica Avenue elevated gone, the fantastic Churrigueresque (late Spanish Renaissance) decorative terracotta façade is more readily visible.

J22

America's first supermarket: It all began in June 1930 when King Kullen opened a large self-service grocery store, complete with "unlimited parking," at 171-06 Jamaica Avenue. It later became the machine shops of Thomas Edison Vocational High School.

And off to the east on Jamaica Avenue:

[J23] **Bethesda Missionary Baptist Church**/originally Jamaica First German Presbyterian Church, 179-09 Jamaica Ave., NW cor. 179th St., opp. 179th Place. 1900.
De-shingled Shingle Style, its white surfaces vivid planes where somber gray once reigned.

J23

And considerably south on Merrick Boulevard:

[J24] **Cathedral of Allen African Methodist Episcopal Church**, Merrick Blvd. SE cor. 110th Ave. 1998.
The vast church complex of the **Reverend Floyd H. Flake**, sometime congressman.

HOLLIS

[H1] **190-21 Hollis Avenue** (house), also known as 99-21 100th Avenue, bet. 191st St. and 100th Ave., opp. Farmers Blvd. N side. ca. 1875.
On a large piece of land commanding an ancient intersection: Hollis Avenue was once Old Country Road leading east into Long Island; Farmers Boulevard was the route to the farms of southeastern Queens. This large, freestanding, elaborately ornamented Italianate house is a remarkable throwback to the area's 19th-century roots.

[H2] **First United Methodist Church of Hollis**, 91-31 191st St., bet. Jamaica and Woodhull Aves. E side. ca. 1885.
A basic geometry of triangles, circles, and pyramids clad in shingles and slate. Austere and elegant.

H1

[H3] **Hollis Park development**: entrance gateposts, various locations, including 193rd St. at Jamaica Ave. N side.
The cast stone inserts on these particular brick guardians read FULTON STREET (once Jamaica Avenue's name) and HOLLIS PARK BOULEVARD. Many 1920s land speculators in the area east of Jamaica used such brick entrance posts to lend prestige to the communities they were developing, in the style of 19th-century suburban developments in Brooklyn or nearby New Jersey.

H2

ST. ALBANS

[A1] **Murdock Avenue**, bet. Linden Blvd. and LIRR. Addisleigh Park.
On either side of Murdock Avenue and on many streets nearby in greater St. Albans lies a superb suburban neighborhood, with well-kept homes and vast, immaculately manicured lawns. Here an affluent black community lives in architecture equal to Brooklyn's Prospect Park South.

A1

SOUTH OZONE PARK

O1

[O1] **St. Teresa of Avila Roman Catholic Church**, 109-71 130th St., bet. 109th and 111th Aves. W side. 1937.

Of low silhouette in the 1930s intermix of yellow brick and Art Deco/Classical styles. As the neighborhood changed from Italian at the parish's founding to black now, it is not unusual to hear spirituals being sung during collections.

[O2] **Aqueduct Racetrack**, Rockaway Blvd. to North Conduit Ave., IND Rockaway Line right-of-way to 114th St. 1894. Reconstruction, 1959. **Arthur Froehlich & Assocs**.

The Big A, as it is commonly known, is the last racetrack entirely within the city limits. As land values increase, these enormous operations sell to developers (cf. Jamaica Racetrack, now Rochdale Village). The name relates to the Ridgewood Aqueduct, Brooklyn and Queens's first large-scale water system, which still follows Conduit Avenue, the service road of Southern Parkway, in from its reservoirs on Long Island.

DOUGLASTON MANOR • DOUGLASTON • GLEN OAKS
CREEDMOOR • QUEENS VILLAGE • CAMBRIA HEIGHTS
LAURELTON • JFK AIRPORT • HOWARD BEACH

Out beyond Cross Island Parkway and Springfield Boulevard, lying along the Nassau County border or abutting the northern shores of Jamaica Bay, is the area we call Far Queens. The northern parts, such as Douglaston Manor along the east side of Little Neck Bay, are among Queens's most exclusive neighborhoods. The areas to the southeast comprise an immense—largely unknown to residents of Manhattan—group of middle-class black suburban communities. To the south of this Queens "frontier" is the megaworld of Kennedy Airport and, to its west, the large community of Howard Beach and a few smaller ones.

DOUGLASTON MANOR, DOUGLASTON, LITTLE NECK, GLEN OAKS

Douglaston Manor, Douglaston, and Little Neck lie east of the Cross Island (Belt) Parkway, New York's circumferential highway, and, as a result, many assume they are part of adjacent Nassau County. The part above Northern Boulevard certainly lends credence to this belief, since the area resembles the prosperous commuter towns on the adjacent North Shore. Originally the peninsula was all Little Neck, but in 1876 the western part was renamed Douglaston after **William B. Douglas**, who had donated the LIRR station there. It is a rocky, treed knoll with sometimes narrow, winding streets chockablock with Victorian, stucco, shingled, myriad individual houses of romance, many with splendid views of water, sunsets, and sailboats.

DOUGLASTON MANOR

[F1] **Douglaston Historic District**, including all of the peninsula north of 38th Drive and Cherry Street. 🍎

[F2] **Douglaston Club**/formerly George Douglas House/ originally Wynant Van Zandt House, 32-03 Douglaston Pkwy. (West Drive), SE cor. Beverly Rd. Before 1835, with numerous additions. ⟲
   A large, homely country house with a Tuscan-columned porch; now a tennis club.

 [F3] **Benjamin Allen House**/sometimes called the Allen-Beville House, 29 Center Dr., SW cor. Forest Rd. 1848-1850. 🍎 ⟲
   A Greek Revival snuggling up to the new Italianate style of the time. White shingles, Tuscan porch, octagonal widow's walk overlooking Little Neck Bay.

 [F4] **Cornelius Van Wyck House**, 37-04 Douglaston Pkwy. (126 West Drive), SW cor. Alston Place. 1735. Addition, mid-18th century. 🍎 ⟲
   The original "Dutch" house is barely visible, engulfed as it is by later accretions. Rent a boat to enjoy it fully.

[F5] **233-26, 233-38, 233-50 Bay Street** (houses), bet. 234th St. and Douglaston Pkwy. S side. ⟲
   A challenge: find these three Shingle Style-Victorian gems tucked away along this bosky lane. The last embraces an early gambrel-roof neighbor to its east wall.

Colonial

Georgian/
Federal

Greek
Revival

Gothic
Revival

Villa

Romanesque
Revival

Renaissance
Revival

Roman
Revival

Art Deco/

Art Moderne

Modern/
Post-Modern

F4

F5

DOUGLASTON

F6

[F6] North Hills Branch, Queensborough Public Library, 57-04 Marathon Pkwy., opp. 57th Ave. W side. 1987. **Abraham W. Geller & Assocs.**

Round and domed and bright blue and red, with a yellow canopy: a very colorful addition to the beige burbs.

[F7] Douglaston Manor Restaurant/originally North Hills Golf Course Clubhouse, 63-20 Commonwealth Blvd., opp. Marathon Pkwy. W side. ca. 1925. Additions.

A romantic Spanish-tile-plus-beige-stucco confection occupying the high ground atop a city golf course.

GLEN OAKS

[F8] North Shore Towers: Coleridge, Beaumont, Amherst (apartment towers), 269-10, 270-10, 271-10 Grand Central Pkwy., at the Nassau County line. (Entry via Grand Central Parkway's south service road, from Little Neck Pkwy.) 1975.

Ever wonder what those tall, strongly silhouetted residential towers are, just as you cross the line from Nassau County into Queens? It's too soon to be Manhattan. Hmmmm . . . Well, these are they: three of them, each 33 stories tall, a total of 1,848 units.

F9

Long Island Jewish Hospital-Hillside Medical Center:
Like most hospitals this one just started to grow and things got out of hand. But amid the physical confusion some fine architectural works stand out:

[F9] Ronald McDonald House (residential facility), 76th Ave. opp. 267th St. N side. 1986. **Lee Harris Pomeroy Assocs.**

A 2-story structure, semicircular in plan, it welcomes visitors within its curvilinear embrace. A muted, dignified, convincing design.

[F10] Helen and Irving Schneider Children's Hospital, 269-01 76th Ave., opp. 269th St. N side. 1983. **The Architects Collaborative.** **[F10b] Radich Therapy Pavilion**, 1987. **The Architects Collaborative.**

Suave in color and form without, bright and cheery in color and form within: a perfect hospital equation.

F11

[F11] Norma and Jack Parker Pavilion, Jewish Institute for Geriatric Care, 271-11 76th Ave., opp. 271st St. N side. 1972. **Katz Waisman & Blumenkranz.**

A bold, high-rise, cast-in-place concrete slab punctuated with well-detailed balconies. The composition pays homage, in a way, to Le Corbusier's Salvation Army building on the outskirts of Paris.

CREEDMOOR

Creedmoor: In 1873 the extensive lands of today's state hospital became a National Rifle Association firing range where state militia, rod-and-gun clubs, and NRA members trained and competed. Too many wild shots and too much unruly behavior caused **Governor Charles Evans Hughes** to shut the range down in 1907. It was **Conrad Poppenhusen** [see N Queens, College Point] who had sold NRA the property, a farm formerly owned by **B. Hendrickson Creed**, hence the name. Nearby Springfield and Winchester Boulevards and Musket, Pistol, Sabre, and Range Streets are all reminders of Creedmoor's earlier use.

[F12] **Queens County Farm Museum**/originally Jacob Adriance Farmhouse/also know as Creedmoor Farmhouse, 73-50 Little Neck Pkwy., bet. 73rd Rd. and 74th Ave. W side. 1772. Additions, ca. 1835 and later. ●
Open to the public.

An early farmhouse preserved by the happy accident of its location: protected by the lands of the enveloping state institution (though now officially occupying City park property).

F12

QUEENS VILLAGE

[F13] **Public School 34**, Queens, The John Harvest School, 104-12 Springfield Blvd., SW cor. Hollis Ave. ca. 1905. Addition, 1930.

Ornate limestone scrolls and other ornament elevate the old elementary school's dark brick exterior to architectural heights.

For a time beginning in 1844, the site of today's 2-acre school playground was the potter's field for poorhouse inmates of Jamaica Flushing, Newtown, Hempstead, North Hempstead, and Oyster Bay, all of which were then part of Queens County. Nassau was lopped off in 1898 as part of the deal to create a Greater New York.

[F14] **Little Sisters of the Poor Convent** (Roman Catholic), 110-39 Springfield Blvd., bet. 110th and 112th Ave. E side. Entry opp. 110th Rd. ca. 1900. Later additions. [F15] **Queen of Peace Residence**, 110-30 221st St. Entrance from 221st St. N of 112th Ave. ca. 1975.

F15

The order of the Little Sisters has quietly retrenched its urban outposts, once sprinkled on what has become prime land, in favor of this more remote location in Far Queens. Here it also operates a pompous-appearing facility for the elderly at the eastern end of its property behind a convent's high masonry walls.

CAMBRIA HEIGHTS

[F16] **Martin's Garden Center**/originally House, 119-03 Springfield Blvd., SE cor. 119th Ave. at Francis Lewis Boulevard. ca. 1860.

F16

An Italianate Villa Style wood frame mansion, complete with cupola, all seemingly dipped in whitewash and given a new existence as a garden center. Poetic?

LAURELTON

[F17] **Springfield Cemetery Chapel**, 122-01 Springfield Blvd., opp. 122nd Ave. E side. 1849.

Venerable Springfield Cemetery is contained on three sides by newer Montefiore, but the old board-and-batten chapel remains.

F17

F18

[F18] **Laurelton Estates** (row houses), 224th St. E side; 225th St. both sides; 226th St. both sides, bet 130th and 133rd Aves. Also 229th St. bet. 130th and 131st Aves. Both sides. ca. 1925.

A spectacular display of what architectural imagination, builders' skills, and a reasonable budget can do to craft the repetitive façades of row housing into a satisfying, memorable, picturesque composition. Is even this 20th-century skill forever lost to us?

JFK AIRPORT

[F19] **John F. Kennedy International Airport**/formerly Idlewild Airport/originally Anderson Field, Southern Pkwy., Rockaway Blvd., and Jamaica Bay. Entry via Van Wyck Expwy. 1942 to present.

With land claimed by fill in the swampy waters of Jamaica Bay, Kennedy's 4,900 acres are roughly equivalent in area to Manhattan Island south of 34th Street. It is so large that it's possible to run up several dollars' tariff on your taxi meter between the terminal and the airport's edge; Manhattan lies 15 miles further west. The fare will be well spent, however, for the trip will take you past every architectural cliché of the past four decades, some very handsome works, and some less distinguished hangovers from earlier periods as well.

Kennedy is best known for its Terminal City, housing the various passenger terminals, a control center, a central heating and cooling plant, and a multitude of parking places, structured and on grade. In addition the airport has many cargo complexes and service and storage facilities for the airline companies, as well as a hotel, a federal office building, and other service structures.

[F20] Originally **International Hotel**, Van Wyck Expwy. at Southern Pkwy. 1958. Additions, 1961, **William B. Tabler**.

The gateway building, by default, to this aircraft empire.

[F21] **Federal Office Building**. 1949. **Reinhard, Hofmeister & Walquist**.

Neo-frumpy, by some of the guys who helped build New York's greatest commercial wonder, Rockefeller Center.

[F22] **J.F.K. Branch, Citibank**/originally First National City Bank, along main access road. 1959. **Skidmore, Owings & Merrill**.

The stilts holding this glass box above its roadside site express just the right amount of diffidence about becoming associated with the rest of Terminal City.

[F23] **Terminal One** (Japan Airlines; Air France; Korean Air, and Lufthansa). 1998. **William Nicholas Bodouva & Assocs**.

A sexy replacement for the old Eastern Airlines: Muschamp in the *New York Times:* ". . . a trip back to an era before Kennedy became a theme park of life in modern Albania . . ." High tech and soaring spirits abound. **Napoleon III**, if resuscitated, might dub it a "parapluie de New York" (as he had described the great iron-and-glass railroad stations in Paris as the "umbrellas of Paris").

F23

F23 Garage

[F24] **Terminal Three**/originally Pan American Airways et al. 1961 with additions. **Tippetts-Abbett-McCarthy-Stratton; Ives, Turano & Gardner**, associate architects.

A tour de force produced a parasoled pavilion unfortunately marred from the beginning by gross details (i.e., the meandering drainpipes around the great piers). Now, expanded manyfold into a complex as large and confusing as the Palace of Knossos (the Minotaur's labyrinth), the parasol is but an entrance canopy to this depressing maze.

F26

[F25] **Terminal Four**/formerly International Arrivals Building, 1957. **Skidmore, Owings & Merrill**.

The principal place of Customs, and hence a string of international airlines flanked a grand, vaulted central pavilion. Once a place of sumptuous lounges and bars where one could stroll past the glass arrivals hall to see and greet incoming passengers, it is now drab and dull. On its way out in favor of a totally new replacement by the same architects. (2002. **Skidmore, Owings & Merrill**.)

[F26] **Terminal Five**/originally Trans World Airlines (TWA) Terminal. 1956-1962. **Eero Saarinen**. **Kevin Roche**, co-designer. Additions. Freestanding canopy addition, 1978, **Witthoeft & Rudolph**. 🍎

F25

Romantic voluptuary: soaring, sinuous, sensuous, surreal, and for a long time, controversial. Well worth a visit to see for yourself what all the debate was about. Unfortunately, trips through the "umbilical cord" to the original plane loading pod-lounge are forbidden to all but ticketed passengers, because of security precautions against hijackings.

[F27] **Terminal Six**/onetime TWA Terminal B/originally National Airlines Sundrome. 1972. **I. M. Pei & Partners**.

F27

A classy, classic building, the best architecture at Kennedy: rich travertine walls and floors under a great columned and corniced roof. This serene temple to transport was, in its original corporate incarnation, the "portal to Florida" for many taking the bargain flights. With National Airline's demise, TWA took over the facility.

[F28] **Terminal Seven**/originally British Airways Terminal. 1970. **Gollins Melvin Ward & Partners**.

Heavy-handed battered concrete over heavy-handed battered glass. An awkward attempt at a tour de force.

*Warnerville: Squeezed between the eastern end of Kennedy
Airport and the Nassau County town of Inwood is a waterbound
settlement, many of whose houses are built on pilings, like those of
Bangkok. Traffic along Rockaway Turnpike is rarely calm enough
to allow a leisurely notice of the entrances to this curious community split between Queens and Nassau: at East Dock Street, 1st, or
3rd Streets. Picturesque, certainly, but hardly gentrified . . . yet.*

HOWARD BEACH

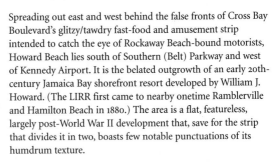

F32

Spreading out east and west behind the false fronts of Cross Bay
Boulevard's glitzy/tawdry fast-food and amusement strip
intended to catch the eye of Rockaway Beach-bound motorists,
Howard Beach lies south of Southern (Belt) Parkway and west
of Kennedy Airport. It is the belated outgrowth of an early 20th-
century Jamaica Bay shorefront resort developed by William J.
Howard. (The LIRR first came to nearby onetime Ramblerville
and Hamilton Beach in 1880.) The area is a flat, featureless,
largely post-World War II development that, save for the strip
that divides it in two, boasts few notable punctuations of its
humdrum texture.

[F32] **Rockwood Park Jewish Center**, 156-45 84th St., bet. 157th
Ave. and Shore Pkwy. E side. ca. 1972. **Hausman & Rosenberg**.
　Dignified—if trendy—forms nevertheless create a badly
needed visual punctuation in the graph-paper texture of tract
development.

F33

[F33] **St. Helen's Church** (Roman Catholic), 157th Ave. SW cor.
83rd St. 1979.
　The yellow brick of the parish's earlier, conservatively
designed buildings is here employed in a lively, asymmetrical,
self-conscious bit of ecclesiastical expressionism.

West Hamilton Beach lies at the eastern flank of Howard
Beach. Sandwiched between the banks of Hawtree Creek and
Basin, a placid inland waterway, and the speeding trains of the
Transit Authority (once LIRR) Rockaway Division right-of-way,
lies this little-known, isolated water-oriented community. Boats
are everywhere. Car access is via Lenihan's Bridge (the neighborhood name) into one north-south street (103rd according to
maps, 104th if you believe street signs); pedestrians can use the
modern 163rd Avenue bridge. For local Tom Sawyers summers
here are great—they can jump into the water whenever they feel
like it. Sitting on damp, marshy soil or on pilings are hundreds
of tiny homes along a string of threadbare lanes that dead end at
water's edge. Most are barely one car-width wide, demarked by
wooden telephone poles that sit in the gutter, rather than on
sidewalks much too narrow to accommodate them. About the
only way to determine the area's name is from reading it on the
trucks of its volunteer fire company (before Kennedy Airport
lopped off the eastern part, it was called Hamilton Beach).

FAR ROCKAWAY • BAYSWATER • ARVERNE
BROAD CHANNEL • RIIS PARK • ROCKAWAY POINT

Portion of Town of Hempstead/Hemstede
Settled and chartered in 1664.

This narrow spit of land, a barrier beach for Jamaica Bay (Floridians would term it a key), was so inaccessible prior to the coming of the railroads in 1868-1878 that it was an exclusive resort second only to Saratoga Springs. By 1900 the accessibility afforded by rail connections had driven society leaders to more remote parts of Long Island's south shore in and around the Hamptons. Neponsit and Belle Harbor retain traces of this former splendor. (The IND subway, here not sub- but on grade or elevated, replaced the LIRR as the operator of the trestled connection to Long Island and the continent.)

After the departure of high society the area became a resort for the middle class. But in much of the peninsula, this too has changed: the Hammels and Arverne, both east of the terminus of the Cross Bay Bridge, became squalid slums. Arverne never achieved the aims intended by urban renewal, its renewing momentum crushed by the cost spiral and the lack of interest by Presidents Nixon and Ford in public and publicly assisted housing. Some public and publicly assisted housing for low- and middle-income families dots the area. Unfortunately, all but Roy Reuther Houses are grim in appearance and amazingly unresponsive to their beachfront sites. The potential development of a great recreational area at Breezy Point, thanks to the successful fight waged by civic-minded citizens, holds out the greatest promise for the area. Breezy Point is a unit of the Gateway National Recreation Area.

FAR ROCKAWAY

[R1] **Sage Memorial Church**, The First Presbyterian Church of Far Rockaway, 13-24 Beach 12th St. N side. 1909. **Cram, Goodhue, & Ferguson**.

Across an immaculate Central Avenue lawn is this exquisite memory of Far Rockaway in the first decade of the 20th century: a heavy (Early English?) Gothic. (Sage the church remembers philanthropist **Russell Sage**, of Forest Hills Gardens fame.) On the lawn is a 1919 tablet to **Teddy Roosevelt** by the Village Beautiful Association.

R1

[R2] **Congregation Knesseth Israel**, 728 Empire Ave., NW cor. Sage St. 1964. **Kelly & Gruzen**.

An octagonal sanctuary: a somewhat dated local monument that has survived the modern style wars.

R2

[R3] **Roy Reuther Houses** (apartments), 711 Seagirt Ave., bet. Beach 8th and Beach 6th Sts. S side. 1971. **Gruzen & Partners**.

Middle-income housing sponsored by the United Auto Workers: a great, stepped series of monolithic slabs faces the ocean across Atlantic Beach, Nassau County's first key. Outstanding in more ways than one.

[R4] **Richard Cornell Graveyard**, center of block and bounded by Mott, Caffrey, and New Haven Aves., Gateway Blvd. (old Greenport Rd.). 18th to 19th centuries. 🍎

To see this overgrown 67 × 75-foot tombstoneless midblock site where rest the remains of an ancestor of **Ezra** (University) **Cornell**, rent a helicopter. On second thought, don't bother.

R3

[R5] **Beth El Temple** (church)/originally St. John's Episcopal Church, Mott Ave. NE cor. Scott Gadell Pl. ca. 1885.

FAR ROCKAWAY DISTRICT

see pages 807-808

Picturesque 19th-century wood chapel, up to its ears among 20th-century dissonance.

[R6] **Intermediate School 53**, Queens, The Brian Piccolo School, 1045 Nameoke St., bet. Cornaga Ave., Mott Ave., and Foam Place. 1972. **Victor Lundy**.

A many-bay-windowed volume surrounding a central courtyard. There is a grand, monumentally staired entry—the intended main entrance—now barred because of security problems. The skylight setbacks on Foam Place make great scaffolding for graffiti makers. See it from both Nameoke and from Beach 18th/Foam (one-way north).

R6

[R7] **Medical Center**/originally National Bank of Far Rockaway, 16-24 Central Ave bet. Mott Ave. and Bayport Place N side. ca. 1900. **H. Gardner Sibell**.

Renaissance Revival in white glazed terra-cotta with great Corinthian pilasters. The lattice of steel for its once prominent sign remains an element on the local skyline.

[R8] **1518 Central Avenue** (commercial structure)/originally Masonic Hall, bet. Mott Ave. and Bayport Place. N side. ca. 1890.

The ground floor is now broken up for crass commerce, but the handsome symmetrical façade reveals a more distinguished history.

R8

BAYSWATER

A peninsula on a peninsula, located on Far Rockaway's north shore, in Jamaica Bay, between Norton and Mott Basins. Take Mott Avenue west, out of the business district

R9a

[R9] **"Sunset Lodge"** (house), 1479 Point Breeze Ave., N of Mott Ave. W side. ca. 1910. [R9a] **1478 Point Breeze Avenue** (house), N of Mott Ave. E side. ca. 1910.

Two of Bayswater's venerable Shingle Style/Colonial Revival houses. Sunset Lodge is abandoned. Rescue it.

ARVERNE

R11

[R10] **Ocean Village**, Rockaway Beach Blvd. to the Boardwalk, bet Beach 56th Place and Beach 59th St. 1976. **Carl Koch & Assocs.**

Prefabricated, precast-concrete and brick slabs and towers surrounding a central courtyard at the edge of the sea: multi-family urban renewal in a sea of unrenewed weeds.

[R11] Originally **Congregation Derech Emunah** (synagogue), 199 Beach 67th St., SE cor. Rockaway Blvd. 1903. **William A. Lambert.**

A neo-Georgian nave, clad in the Shingle Style.

[R12] **Child Care Center**, 4402 Beach Channel Dr., bet. Beach 44th and Beach 45th Sts. 1999. **The Edelman Partnership.**

A sprightly addition to the Rockaways. Brick in bright colors to stimulate this dour community.

R12

[R13] **Public School 43,** bet. Beach 28th and Beach 29th, S of Seagirt Ave. 1998. **Ehrenkrantz & Eckstut.**

One of the modular schools that offered each site a Chinese menu of parts: one from Group A, two from Group B. The result is handsome, and probably as good as almost any competing system of design.

BROAD CHANNEL

R13

The community of Broad Channel occupies the southern end of Jamaica Bay's largest island, sharing it with Big Egg Marsh and, at the north, with Black Bank Marsh and Rulers Bar Hassock. Together these three constitute the Jamaica Bay Wildlife Refuge, one of **Robert Moses**'s genuine achievements and now part of the National Park Service's Gateway National Recreation Area. This is the bay's only island accessible by vehicles other than boats—it even has a subway station on the IND Line to the Rockaways. Broad Channel supports a devoted and proud, water-oriented community along narrow lanes that fan out from Cross Bay Boulevard like fishbones from a spine.

[R14] **Visitors' Center, Jamaica Bay Wildlife Refuge**, Gateway National Recreation Area, U.S. Department of the Interior,

National Park Service/originally N.Y.C. Department of Parks.
Cross Bay Blvd. one mile N of Broad Channel settlement border.
W side. 1971. **Fred L. Sommer & Assocs.** with **Elliot Willensky**.
Open to the public.

Serene, concrete and fluted concrete block, appropriately
noncompetitive with its surrounding vegetation. The individual
whose vision and incredibly hard work transformed the dunes
and marshes into an invaluable public accommodation, once
Robert Moses gave it the go-ahead, was **Herbert Johnson**, a
sainted parkie.

The wildlife refuge, most importantly a bird sanctuary
boasting both freshwater and saltwater ponds—and innumerable wild denizens changing with the seasons—is well worth a
visit. However, you must phone before coming!

RIIS PARK

R15

[R15] **Jacob Riis Park, Gateway National Recreation Area**, U.S.
Department of the Interior, National Park Service/originally
N.Y.C. Department of Parks, Beach 149th to Beach 169th Sts.,
Atlantic Ocean to Rockaway Inlet. 1937. **Frank Wallis**, designer.
Aymar Embury II, consulting architect.

A mile of sandy beach graced by simple, handsome,
WPA-era buildings. In addition to swimming, there are other
recreational possibilities, such as handball, paddle tennis, and
shuffleboard, as well as a boardwalk for strolling. In the winter
this is a haven for Polar Bear Club enthusiasts, and the 13,000-
car parking lot becomes an aerodrome for radio-controlled
model aircraft flights. Now a Gateway unit, with refreshments
available year round, as are lockers during the swimming
season (nominal charge).

ROCKAWAY POINT

[R16] **Breezy Point, Gateway National Recreation Area**, U.S.
Department of the Interior, National Park Service/originally
N.Y.C. Department of Parks. [R17] **Breezy Point Cooperative,
Inc.**, 202-30 Rockaway Point Blvd.

Appropriately named, these windswept dunes are the site of
a private, largely one-story, cooperative shorefront community—the guard at the gatehouse ensures continued privacy—
with onetime ferry access to Sheepshead Bay, Brooklyn. For
many years, its most conspicuous landmarks were the abandoned concrete frames for an ill-fated high-rise apartment
development. In 1963, owing to pressure from a group of public-
spirited citizens, City authorities courageously acquired title to
the site, adjacent to the cooperatives, for future recreational use,
and saved Breezy Point from becoming another high-rise jungle.
With the establishment of Gateway, the area—added to
Riis Park and Fort Tilden to its east—forms 3½ miles of
uninterrupted Atlantic shorefront under the managerial aegis
of the National Park Service's Smokey the Bear.

Staten Island

STATEN ISLAND
Borough of Staten Island / Richmond County

5

 Colonial

 Georgian/ Federal

 Greek Revival

 Gothic Revival

 Villa

 Romanesque Revival

 Renaissance Revival

 Roman Revival

 Art Deco/ Art Moderne

 Modern/ Post-Modern

For most tourists, Staten Island is nothing more than the terminus of a spectacular ferry ride. Few venture ashore to explore. From such thoroughfares as Bay Street or Hylan Boulevard the views are discouraging: drab brick houses, huge gasoline stations, and gaudy pizza parlors predominate. Persevere. Behind the listless dingy façades are hills as steep as San Francisco's, with breathtaking views of the New York harbor; mammoth, crumbling mansions surrounded by mimosa and rhododendron, rutted dirt roads, four-foot black snakes, and fat, wild pheasant. There are Dutch farmhouses, Greek temples, Victorian mansions beyond **Charles Addams**'s wildest fantasies, and ridges where archaeologists still find Indian artifacts.

The roughly triangular island is 13.9 miles long and 7.5 miles wide, 2½ times the size of Manhattan, and ranks third in area among the city's boroughs.

Hills and dales: One is frequently aware of being on an island: a slight salty dampness in the air, a brackish smell, a buoy braying forlornly in the distance, a feeling of isolation.

Down the backbone of the island, from St. George to Richmondtown, runs a range of hills formed by an outcropping of serpentine rock. These hills—Fort, Ward, Grymes, Emerson, Todt, and Lighthouse—are dotted with elegant mansions of the 19th and 20th centuries, many of them now occupied by private schools and charitable institutions. Todt Hill, often proclaimed the highest point on the Atlantic coast, is a dinky 409.2 feet compared with Cadillac Mountain at 1,532 on Maine's Mt. Desert Island. The views, however are justly famous.

Links to the Mainland: In the north, the steel arch of the Bayonne Bridge, opened in 1931, connects Port Richmond and Bayonne. In the northwest, the Goethals Bridge, a cantilever structure built in 1928, joins Howland Hook and Elizabeth. In the southwest is the Outerbridge Crossing—named not for its remoteness from Manhattan but for Eugenius H. Outerbridge, first chairman of the Port of N.Y. Authority. It also opened in 1928 and spans the Arthur Kill between Charleston and Perth Amboy. The Verrazano-Narrows Bridge, completed in 1964, provides a crossing to Brooklyn and is responsible for the land (and people) boom that has swelled Staten Island's population ever since.

History books notwithstanding, Staten Island was first "discovered" by the Algonquin Indians. It was first seen by a European, **Giovanni da Verrazano**, in 1524, and was named Staaten Eylandt 85 years later by **Henry Hudson** while on a voyage for the Dutch East India Company. Following a number of unsuccessful attempts, the first permanent settlement, by 19 French and Dutch colonists, was established in 1661 near the present South Beach. The island was renamed Richmond (after **King Charles II**'s illegitimate son, the **Duke of Richmond**) following the English capture of New Amsterdam in 1664.

At the beginning of the 19th century a sixteen-year-old's $100 investment in a passenger-and-produce ferry across New York harbor marked the first successful business venture of a native-born islander, **Cornelius Vanderbilt**. As a result of such improved access across New York Bay the island began, in the 1830s, to develop into a summer retreat for wealthy, if not particularly prominent, families from New York and the South, who moved into the New Brighton area. A small literary colony sprang up around the eminent eye specialist **Dr. Samuel MacKenzie Elliott**. **James Russell Lowell**, **Henry Wadsworth Longfellow**, and **Francis Parkman** came to Elliott for treat-

11961— *Board Walk at Midland Beach, STATEN ISLAND, N. Y.*

ment and stayed on the island to recuperate. Here Italy's patriot, **Giuseppe Garibaldi**, lived in exile, and **Frederick Law Olmsted** opened an experimental wheat farm. But Staten Island's connection with famous people has always been rather tenuous; more typical were gentleman farmers, shipbuilders, and oyster captains.

The rural nature of the island, however, did attract the sporting set from across the bay. Here the first lawn tennis court in America was built in 1880, and the first American canoe club founded. Lacrosse, cricket, rowing, fox hunting, fishing, bathing, and cycling engaged weekend enthusiasts. But by the beginning of the 20th century, the island's popularity had begun to wane. Fantastic schemes worthy of **Barnum and Bailey** were developed in a last-ditch attempt to lure the tourist trade. One promoter imported **Buffalo Bill's Wild West Show**, complete with sharpshooting **Annie Oakley**, "Fall of Rome" spectacles, and herds of girls and elephants.

Staten Island Ferry Ride:
We were very tired, we were very merry—
We had gone back and forth all night on the ferry.
> —Edna St. Vincent Millay

Drawbridges and rusty chains clank, engines shudder and grunt, the throaty whistle blasts, and the ferry churns out into the oily waters of New York harbor. Petulant gulls hover aloft, commuters, inured to the spectacular, settle behind newspapers, while tourists crowd to the rail. Children and even some adults become very merry.

Ferries leave frequently during daylight hours, less so on weekends. Upon boarding, move to the far end of the upper deck. From this position, Brooklyn lies to the left, and Governors Island is immediately ahead; Ellis Island, the old immigration station, and the Statue of Liberty, bound to produce a lump in the throat for even the most callous, appear in succession on the right.

The first glimpse of Staten Island is attractive. Steep, wooded hills rise behind the civic center of St. George, Greek Revival porticos appear along the waterfront, and Gothic spires and Italianate towers of schools and churches top hills on the right. On a misty or, more likely, smoggy day, the aspect is momentarily reminiscent of a small Italian town.

STATEN ISLAND KEY MAP

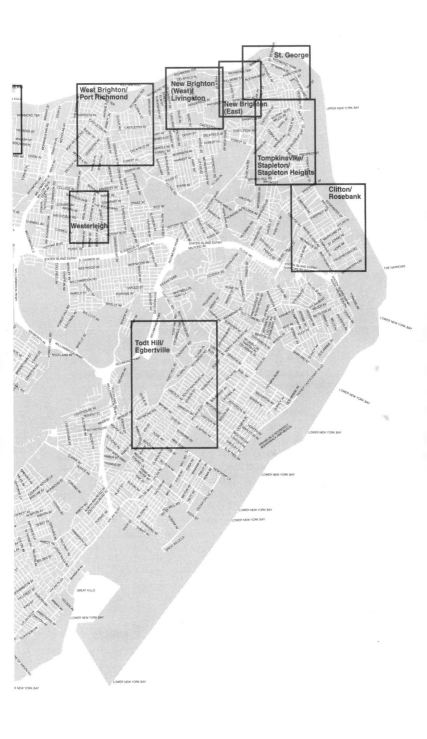

N

ST. GEORGE • NEW BRIGHTON
LIVINGSTON • WEST BRIGHTON
PORT RICHMOND • MARINERS HARBOR

N1

ST. GEORGE

[N1] **Staten Island Ferry Terminal and Entertainment. Complex.** 2001. HOK (Hellmuth Obata Kassabaum). New Staten Island Institute of Arts & Sciences. 2002. **Peter Eisenman.**

An ambitious plan to take advantage of the view of Manhattan from Staten Island's shoreline. The master plan of the complex is in the hands of **HOK**, with major elements designed by them (the ferry terminal and possibly a new stadium for Staten Island's Yankee farm team, which currently plays at the College of Staten Island). The **National Lighthouse Museum** may also be a component.

Richmond Terrace:
Between Borough Place and Hamilton Avenue.
*A grand (but incomplete) scheme of civic structures initiated by Staten Island's first borough president, **George Cromwell**.*

N2

ST. GEORGE

see pages 884–889

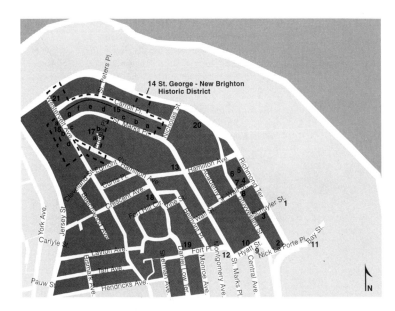

14 St. George - New Brighton
Historic District

[N2] **Staten Island Borough Hall**, Richmond Terr. NW cor. Nick La Porte Pl. 1904-1906. **Carrère & Hastings**.

With its picturesque form, this elegant brick structure, in the style of a French hôtel de ville, welcomes those arriving by ferry. And a nice greeting for architect **John Carrère** on his way home.

[N3] **Richmond County Court House**, 12-24 Richmond Terr., SW cor. Schuyler Pl. Designed, 1913. Completed, 1919. **Carrère & Hastings**.

A grand Roman Corinthian-columned portico and pediment provide pomp missing from the more people-friendly Borough Hall next door.

N3

[N4] **120th Precinct, N.Y.C. Police Department/** originally. 66th Precinct/Borough Police Headquarters, 78 Richmond Terr., NW cor. Wall St. 1922. **James Whitford, Sr.**

A bland Italian Renaissance limestone palazzo, pale in comparison with Whitford's gutsy police station in Tottenville.

[N5] **Richmond County Family Courthouse**, 100 Richmond Terr., bet. Wall St. and Hamilton Ave. W side. 1933. **Sibley & Fetherston**.

It could be an Adamesque country house, its terra-cotta façade presenting elegant Ionic columns to the visitor.

N5

[N6] **N.Y.C. Department of Health Building**, 51 Stuyvesant Pl., bet. Wall St. and Hamilton Ave. E side. ca. 1935. **Henry C. Pelton**.

Modest Municipal mid-Depression Art Deco. Doesn't hold a candle to the Ambassador Apartments, on nearby Daniel Low Terrace.

[N7] **Staten Island Museum, Staten Island Institute of Arts and Sciences**, 75 Stuyvesant Pl., NE cor. Wall St. 1918, 1927, 1999 Addition. **Robert W. Gardner**. Open to the public.

A sleepy museum, bulging from its small Georgian Revival building and waiting for the day when it will move to larger accommodations.

N6

[N8] **Shops**, SE Corner of Stuyvesant Pl. and Wall St.

Terra-cotta clads and crowns what are otherwise pedestrian shops. A little neo-Gothicism goes a long way.

[N9] **St. George Branch, N.Y. Public Library**, 10 Hyatt St., SE cor. Central Ave. 1906. Carrère & Hastings. Altered, 1987, **David Paul Helpern**. Stained glass, **David Wilson**.

A bland hulk from these usually elegant architects: one of a group of four Carnegie gifts that began to bring a semblance of culture to the rural island early in the century. The other three are smaller and with some style.

N10

[N10] **St. George Apartments**/Theater, N side of Hyatt St., opposite Central Ave.

The height and bulk of the building, along with giant eagles that top it, announced the urban aspirations of St. George.

Behind the Bay Street wall:

[N11a] Formerly **Administration Building, U.S. Coast Guard Base**, St. George/originally Office Building, U.S. Lighthouse Service, Third District Depot, 1 Bay St., S of Ferry Terminal. ca. 1865. **Alfred B. Mullett**, Supervising Architect of the Treasury. Wings, 1901. 🍎

Three mansard-roofed stories of granite and red brick, in the center of the compound, designed in the French Second Empire style by its American master, **Alfred Bult Mullett**. He was architect of that other (much larger) gem, Washington's old State, War, and Navy Department Building (now the Executive Office Building) and the old New York General Post Office in City Hall Park.

N11a

[N11b] **Tower/Bridge Base of Bay St**. 1996. **Siah Armajani**, artist. **Johansson & Walcavage**, landscape architects.

Staten Island takes a page here from the book of Battery Park City in an attempt to revitalize its waterfront: an artist's installation in the form of a symbolic bridge and lighthouse, poetry incorporated in its fence (the work of **Wallace Stevens**).

[N11c] **Plaza at The Base of Bay St**.

Bay Street descends into a pedestrian plaza at its base. At present more an abandoned movie set than a viable gathering space.

N11b

Off to St. Mark's Place:
Between Fort Place and Westervelt Avenue, north side.

[N12] **Brighton Heights Reformed Church**, 320 St. Mark's Pl., SW cor. Fort Pl. 1999.

Fire demolished the original landmark church (1866. **John Correja** ●ˇ) in 1996. The design of this less inspiring replacement has avoided any potential landmark status.

N12

[N13] **Curtis High School**, 105 Hamilton Ave, NW cor. St. Mark's Pl. 1902-1904. **C. B. J. Snyder**. Additions, 1922, 1925, 1937. Continued alterations. ●ˇ

Collegiate Gothic as applied to secondary-school education. Its lofty site and strong architectural forms add appropriately to its physical prominence as Staten Island's first municipal structure to be completed after Richmond County was absorbed into Greater New York in 1898.

N13

Hotel Castleton was opened in 1889, in the days when Brighton Heights was a well-known resort. It was a 400-room wood-frame behemoth by architect **C. P. H. Gilbert***, just across St. Mark's Place from today's* **Curtis High School***, where two large apartment towers now stand. The hotel was destroyed in 1907 in a spectacular fire, a depiction of which can be found among Borough Hall's lobby murals.*

St. Mark's Place turns softly to the west at Nicholas Street.

[N14] **Saint George/New Brighton Historic District**, Carroll Pl. and St. Marks Pl. between Nicholas Street and Westervelt Ave., with peninsulas north to Richmond Terrace. ●ˇ

N15a

[N15a] Originally **Henry H. Cammann House**, 125 St. Mark's Pl., bet. Nicholas St. and Westervelt Ave. N side. 1895. **Edward Alfred Sargent**. ♂ˇ

A squat conical-capped tower, its eyebrow windows peering outward, bellies to the street in this understated Shingle Style cottage. It was purchased in 1916 by silent film star **Mabel Normand** for use by her father, a stage carpenter.

[N15b] Originally **Vernon H. Brown House**, 119 St. Mark's Pl., bet. Nicholas St. and Westervelt Ave. N side. 1890. **Edward Alfred Sargent**. ♂ˇ

More complex than No. 125, but with less convincing volumes.

N15c

N15e

N15g

N16b

N17a

N18

[N15c] Originally **Frederick L. Rodewald House**, 103 St. Mark's Pl., bet. Nicholas St. and Westervelt Ave. N side. 1890. **Edward Alfred Sargent**. ♂

The powerful and fluid forms of the mature Shingle Style make this a monumental presence on the street. **Sargent** was not shy.

[N15d] **75 St. Mark's Place** (house), bet. Nicholas St. and Westervelt Ave. N side. ca. 1880. ♂

Muted Shingle Style with delicate Doric columns. The rear boasts three tiers of porches peering out at Manhattan across the harbor.

[N15e] **St. Peter's Roman Catholic Church**, 49 St. Mark's Pl., N side. 1900-1903. Tower, 1919. Both by **Harding & Gooch**. Rectory, 1912, **George H. Streeton**. ♂

Neo-Romanesque, with the Cardinal's Tower so named after its dedication by New York's John Cardinal Farley. (The complicated forms of the church complex are best seen from Richmond Terrace, below.)

[N15f] **17, 19 St. Mark's Place** (double house), ca. 1875. ♂
Sumptuously mansarded.

[N15g] **1, 5 St. Mark's Place** (double house), NE cor. Westervelt Ave. ca. 1860. ♂

A craggy and mysterious shingled structure properly turning the corner.

[N16a] **36-38 Westervelt Avenue** (double houses), W side. ca. 1867. ♂

More from the French Second Empire.

[N16b] **42 Westervelt Avenue** (house), W side. ca. 1860. ♂
Modest clapboard crowned with a monumental (for it) mansard.

[N16c] **65 Westervelt Avenue**, E side. 1908. **Thomas C. Perkins**. ♂

[N16d] **72-74 Westervelt Ave.**, W side. St. George Gardens Store. ♂

Before Staten Islanders discovered their cars, malls, and highways, they did more of their shopping locally. This building clad in delicately incised terra-cotta shows just how attractive the early equivalents of strip malls could be.

Phelps Place: A time warp. Three frame 19th-century houses on one flank and, on the other, a large, raw-brick low-rise apartment complex—St. George Garden Apartments, recovering from the wounds of its use as welfare housing. (It's ironic that the apartments occupy the site of the opulent Anson Phelps Stokes mansion.) In the distance, ever in view, is St. Peter's slender tower and cross.

[N17a] **7, 8 and 9, 10 Phelps Place** (double houses), W side. 1891. **Douglas Smyth**. ♂

Neo-Tudor, shingle, double-gabled house abuts the Shingle Style further within the enclave.

[N17b] **11 Phelps Place** (house), N end. ca. 1880. ♂
A modest polygonal tower anchors this understated and convincing Shingle Style cottage.

[N18] **Ambassador Apartments**, 30 Daniel Low Terrace, bet. Crescent Ave. and Fort Hill Circle. W side. 1932. **Lucian Pisciatta**.

Art Deco at its best, at least on Staten Island. The metalwork on the entrance doors, done in a peacock pattern, is exquisite.

[N19] **117 Daniel Low Terrace** (house), NE cor. Fort Pl. ca. 1885.

An eclectic essay in reds: brick with matching terra-cotta ornament. The jerkin-head gable and dormers are an exotic touch.

[N20] **202, 204, 208, 216 Richmond Terrace** (houses), bet. Stuyvesant Pl. and Nicholas St. S side. ca. 1875.

A group of currently (or formerly) mansarded frame houses in various states of repair, with their backs to the high ground and their fronts overlooking the Kill and New Jersey beyond. When built, theirs was a bucolic view. To the east are a number of stairs from the street that mark the former location of houses now vanished.

N19

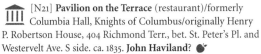

[N21] **Pavilion on the Terrace** (restaurant)/formerly Columbia Hall, Knights of Columbus/originally Henry P. Robertson House, 404 Richmond Terr., bet. St. Peter's Pl. and Westervelt Ave. S side. ca. 1835. **John Haviland?** 🖝

The last vestige of Temple Row, ten early 19th-century Greek Revival mansions built by wealthy New Yorkers and Southern planters along Richmond Terrace when the view across the Kill Van Kull was more pastoral. Sturdy Doric columns and a stately pediment recall more gracious times (for the elite) in these parts. A new and remarkable fence fronts the restaurant.

N20

N21

NEW BRIGHTON

A development begun in 1836 by **Thomas E. Davis**, a Manhattan speculator.

[B1] **St. Stanislaus Kostka Roman Catholic Church**, 109 York Ave., bet. Carlyle and Buchanan Sts. E side. 1925. **Paul R. Henkel**.

The complex forms that constitute the rear of this church are visible atop the heights overlooking Richmond Garden.

[B2] **New York State Department of Environmental Protection Drinking Water Testing Station**, NE Cor. York and Pauw Sts.

This small silver box is just another reminder of how utilities tie Staten Island to the rest of the city.

B3

*Hamilton Park: A number of suburban country dwellings of 12 to 14 rooms (nevertheless dubbed "cottages" at the time) are to be found here from the 19th-century planned community, Hamilton Park. In 1853, the same year as West Orange, N.J.'s Llewellyn Park, developer **Charles Kennedy Hamilton** began a suburban development planned along the romantic precepts of landscape gardener **Andrew Jackson Downing**. The area even then was only a half hour by steam ferry from Manhattan's tip, much the same as today. The Hamilton lands lay on the heights between today's East Buchanan, Franklin, Prospect, and York.*

B4

[B3] **119 Harvard Avenue** (house), bet. Prospect Ave. and Park Pl., opp. Nassau St. ca. 1859.

Charming brick Gothic Revival.

[B4] **32 Park Place** (house), SE cor. Harvard Ave. ca. 1864. Additions. **Carl Pfeiffer**.

Fronting on Harvard but bearing a Park Place address is this handsome brick house with a later ogee-curved mansard roof and segmental arched dormers, one of the 12 second-stage Hamilton Park cottages designed by Pfeiffer.

[B5] Originally **Pritchard House**, 66 Harvard Ave., NW cor. Park Pl. ca. 1853. **Carl Pfeiffer** 🍎

Hidden behind privet hedge, birch trees, and wisteria stands this expansive, grand, eclectic (quoins, arches, and gingerbread) stucco house. Its front entrance was placed to command the downhill view to the west—today its large backyard. This is believed to be Hamilton Park's first speculative house.

B7

[B6] **29 Harvard Avenue** (house), bet. Park Pl. and E. Buchanan St. E side. ca. 1864. **Carl Pfeiffer**.

Mansarded and urbane, another speculation of developer Hamilton.

[B7] **The Hamilton Park Cottage**, 105 Franklin Ave., bet. E. Buchanan St. and Cassidy Pl. E side. ca. 1864. **Carl Pfeiffer**. 🍎

Triple-arched, and a stolid porticoed brick house. The term "cottage" is from a state of mind that in grander circumstances referred to Newport mansions (cf., the Breakers) as cottages.

[B8] Originally **William S. Pendleton House**/later T. M. Rianhard House, 1 Pendleton Pl., SW cor. Franklin Ave. 1861. **Charles Duggin**.

The "second" Pendleton house—for the first see below. A magnificent work of freestanding residential architecture whose asphalt-composition "brick" siding does not detract enough from its distinctive Stick Style silhouette and robust forms to diminish its visual role in the community.

B8

NEW BRIGHTON (EAST)

see pages 890–892

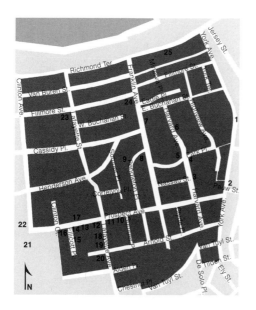

[B9] Originally **William S. Pendleton House**, 22 Pendleton Pl., bet. Franklin and Prospect Aves. N side at the curve. ca. 1855. **Charles Duggin.**

After his business ventures prospered (he was president of the local ferryboat company and dabbled in real estate), **Pendleton** forsook this wood-shingled Gothic Revival villa with crisscrossed muntin windows for the even greater confection across the street.

[B10] **172 Prospect Avenue** (house), bet. Franklin and Lafayette Aves. S side. ca. 1870.

A stately slated mansard crowns this shingled Second Empire house.

B9

[B11] **180 Prospect Avenue** (house), SE cor. Lafayette St. ca. 1885.
Neo-Tudor: simulated half-timbering infilled with stuccoed brick.

[B12] **202 Prospect Avenue** (house), SW cor. Lafayette St. ca. 1885.
Brown shingles and a gambrel roof, a sloping dormer facing north (no doubt to illuminate an artist's studio in the attic).

B12

[B13] **212 Prospect Avenue** (house), bet. Lafayette Ave. and Ellicott Pl. S side. ca. 1895.
Three sunbursts over the three multipaned windows/doors.

[B14] **232 Prospect Avenue** (house), SE cor. Ellicott Pl. ca. 1870.
Shingle Style, but unfortunately the shingles have been painted white.

Ellicott Place: Between Lafayette and Clinton Avenues. S side. Two brick gateposts and a green center island mark this one-block enclave, ever lovely in its entirety.

B14

[B15] **15 Ellicott Place** (house), S of Prospect Ave. E side. ca. 1870.
Shingle Style, enriched with ornate bargeboards and a salient bay under the gable.

[B16] **254 Prospect Avenue** (house), SW cor. Ellicott Pl. ca. 1885.
Queen Anne Revival: complex and contradictory.

[B17] **229 Prospect Avenue** (house), bet. Lafayette Ave. and Clinton Court. N side. ca. 1885.
A pale green stunner.

[B18] **270 Lafayette Avenue** (house), bet. Prospect Ave. and Arnold St. W side. ca. 1885.
Brown stained shingles, strongly chamfered corners, and a porch of turned columns with an ornate balustrade.

[B19] **280 Lafayette Avenue** (house), NW cor. Arnold St. ca. 1870.
A grand mansard crowns this Victorian clapboard house, wrapped with an elegant bracket porch.

B18

B15   B19

[B20] **176 Arnold Street** (house), SW cor. Lafayette Ave. ca. 1900.
Not much to look at, but an example of cast-in-place concrete: an early and unusual use of the material in residential construction.

[B21a] **"Woodbrook,"** Jonathan Goodhue House/now **Goodhue Children's Center Recreation Building,** 304 Prospect Ave., at Clinton Ave. S side. ca. 1845. **B. Haynard** and **James Patterson**, builders. [B21b] **William H. Wheelock Residence Facility,** Goodhue Center, 290 Prospect Ave., at Clinton Ave. S side. 1971. **Davis, Brody & Assocs.**

B21a

B23

Woodbrook presents an image of a modest Italianate palazzo with quoins simulated in wood, and a sober cornice. It shows its age, but still conveys some of the elegance it possessed when it was a villa commanding the vast acreage of the Goodhue estate. The Wheelock Building, named for a trustee of the center, is an experiment in group living for eight teenagers.

B22

[B22] **Residence, St. Peter's Boys High School**/earlier Nicholas Muller House, 200 Clinton Ave., at Prospect Ave. W side. ca. 1857.

An eclectic mansion, its double gables presented to the street, with a striking contrast of white detail against a deep red-painted brick body.

[B23] Originally **New Brighton Village Hall**, 66 Lafayette Ave., SW cor. Fillmore St. 1868-1871. **James Whitford, Sr.**

Promises of restoration (see the sign) have failed to stem the decline into ruin of this mansarded brick, former civic building. Landmark status did not solve the problem.

[B24] **Christ Church** (Episcopal), 76 Franklin Ave., SW cor. Fillmore St. 1904. **Parish Hall**, 1906.

A gray ashlar complex featuring as its off-center centerpiece a dignified neo-Gothic church that, together with the Parish Hall, forms a chaste green corner campus.

B24

[B25] **536 Richmond Terrace** (house), bet. York Ave. and Franklin Sts. S side. ca. 1875.

Another stately mansard, this one hidden atop a black ashlar retaining wall behind dense, luxuriant hedges.

[B26] **Tysen-Neville House**, also known as the Neville House, 806 Richmond Terr., bet. Clinton Ave. and Tysen St. S side. ca. 1800. Altered late 19th century.

Identified by its slender-columned 2-story veranda, it is said that the house reflects Bahamian architecture through the journeys of its retired sea captain owner, **John Neville**. Its proximity to the old Sailors' Snug Harbor, just down the Terrace, gave it a period of success as a local tavern, the Old Stone Jug. Successful, as the residents of the Harbor were not permitted through those (now-landmarked) gates with liquor!

B27

[B27] **Snug Harbor Cultural Center**/originally Sailors' Snug Harbor, 914-1000 Richmond Terr., bet. Tysen St., Snug Harbor Rd., and Kissel Ave. S side to Henderson Ave. **Building A**, 1879. **Richard Smyth.** **Building B**, 1831-1841.

B27

Minard Lafever. ☛ **Building C** (central building facing
Richmond Terr.), 1831-1833. **Minard Lafever.** Interior redecora-
tion, 1884. ☛ Interior ☛ **Building D**, 1831-1841. **Minard
Lafever.** ☛ **Building E**, 1880. **Richard Smyth.** ☛ Center (or
north) **Gatehouse**, 1873. **Richard P. Smyth.** ☛ **West
Gatehouse**, 1880. **Chapel**, 1854-1856. **James Solomon.** Interior
renovation, 1873. Additions, 1883. ☛ Interior ☛ **Iron Fence**,
1841-1845. **Frederick Diaper. Building M**, Maintenance,
renovated into **the Staten Island Children's Museum**, 1987.
**David Prendergast, Jeffrey Hannigan, James Sawyer. Keith
Goddard/Works**, graphic design. **Music hall**, 1892; restoration-
competition winner, 1987, **Rafael Vinoly.** Open to the public.

B27

Five Greek temples serenely surveying an immaculately
groomed lawn made Sailors' Snug Harbor an obvious landmark
choice back in the 1960s. A court action by the Harbor's
trustees against designation, their initial victory, and their ultimate defeat on appeal by City attorneys presaged New York
City's purchase of the buildings—and then the remainder of
the picturesque site.

B27

The Harbor was founded by **Robert Richard Randall**, who
converted his Revolutionary War privateer-father's bequest into
a fund for the support of "aged, decrepit and worn-out sailors."
For many years, the proceeds from Randall's property in
Manhattan's Greenwich Village supported the Harbor.
Following the court of appeals support of landmark designation, the Harbor's trustees moved the institution to a new site
on the North Carolina coast. This paved the way, in 1976, for
the reuse of the rich complex of Greek Revival, Victorian, and
early 20th-century edifices, and 60 acres of romantic grounds
to the south, for a new public benefit. (For those who want to
pinpoint their location the USGS has placed a benchmark on
the steps of building C.)

*Losses at Snug Harbor: A number of the Harbor's fine buildings
succumbed to the high cost of maintenance long before its landmark status was declared, explaining the public support for designation. Its most opulent structure was architect* **R. W. Gibson**'s
1892 **Randall Memorial Church**, *with a dome that echoed
London's St. Paul's but at a considerably smaller scale. (Five of its
stained-glass windows are preserved at* **Calvary Presbyterian
Church** *[1894], Castleton and Bement Avenues.) The other was
the* **Hospital**, *a neo-Classical structure cruciform in plan (like
18th-century English prisons), with four long wings extending out
from a domed central pavilion. It bit the dust in 1951.*

LIVINGSTON

[B28] **Walker Park Recreation Building**, N.Y.C. Department of
Parks & Recreation, 50 Bard Ave., SW cor. Delafield Pl. 1934.

Full-timbered with brick infill, ashlar walls, a red slate roof,
and charming casement windows, all built during the nadir of
the Great Depression.

NEW BRIGHTON (WEST) / LIVINGSTON

see pages 893–896

Walker Park: Mary Ewing Outerbridge brought lawn tennis to Staten Island from Bermuda in 1874 (vying with Nahant, Massachusetts, for the record of hosting the first sets played in this country). In 1880 the first national tennis tournament was played here, in what is now Walker Park. Ms. Outerbridge was the sister of Eugenius H. Outerbridge, for whom the Crossing is named, and the park is named for Mr. Outerbridge's good friend, Randolph St. George Walker, Jr., a casualty of World War I. Today tennis and cricket are played on the grounds.

[B29] **Dr. Samuel MacKenzie Elliott House**, 69 Delafield Pl., bet. Bard and Davis Aves. N side. ca. 1850. 🌶️

An early eye surgeon of wide repute, **Dr. Elliott**, as a result of his distinguished patients, became the focal point of a small but far-flung literary colony: **James Russell Lowell**, **Henry Wadsworth Longfellow**, and **Francis Parkman**, among others. The house itself, one of some fifteen he built in this area, is a straightforward ashlar granite box whose charm is enhanced by a serpentine vergeboard along its gabled roof. (Another Elliott-built house in granite is at 557 Bard Avenue, south of Forrest Avenue/City Boulevard, E side.) It is unclear where Elliott himself lived.

B29

[B30] Originally **Stewart Brown House**, 14-18 Livingston Court, bet. Bard and Davis Aves. S side. ca. 1860.

Bold of scale and rich of detail—note the many dormers. This fine old house squeezes Livingston Court, indicating that it predates the court. Sheathed in aluminum siding, the house has lost much of the rich detail that enriched it.

B30

B31

[B31] Originally **Cornelius Cruser House**, also known as Kreutzer-Pelton House, 1262 Richmond Terr., near Pelton Pl. S side. 1722. Additions, 1770 and 1836. ●

Typical of the area's colonial residences. First, Islanders built a one-room structure, usually of local fieldstone; rooms were later added when needed. The stone cottage on the right dates from 1722; the central clapboard section was added in 1770; the 2-story brick section on the left was built in 1836. The man who was to become England's **King William IV** in 1830 was entertained here during the Revolution.

[B32] Originally **George W. Curtis House**, 234 Bard Ave., NW cor. Henderson Ave. 1850.

Curtis (an abolitionist and Lincoln supporter) hid **Horace Greeley** here from mobs of angry Staten Islanders, who generally supported the Southern cause. Curtis High School is his namesake.

B33

[B33] **Convent, St. Vincent's Medical Center of Richmond**/originally T. F. McCurdy House/later Henry M. Taber House/later William T. Garner House/later St. Austin's School, 710 Castleton Ave., opp. Hoyt Ave. N side. ca. 1850. Rear addition, 1898, **Samuel R. Brick, Jr.** Gatehouse, Bard Ave., S of Moody Pl. E side. ca. 1850.

A huge Victorian mansion proclaims by size, if not by beauty, the prodigious wealth garnered by 19th-century businessmen (McCurdy was a wholesaler, Taber a "cotton king," Garner a cotton mill owner). **Ulysses S. Grant** considered retiring here; but his wife, visiting the house on a warm damp day, was plagued by mosquitoes that still thrive in Staten Island's marshes and swamps.

B34

St. Austin's Place: Between North St. Austin's Place and South St. Austin's Place.

B34

[B34] **Henderson Estate Company Houses**, 33 St. Austin's Pl. E side. 34 St. Austin's Pl. W side. Both, 1893. **McKim, Mead & White**.

On opposite sides of this short street a pair of dark-brown Shingle Style-meets-Colonial Revival houses, designed by the **MM & W** staff as low-budget (for them) houses.

B35

[B35] **St. Mary's Episcopal Church**, 347 Davis Ave., NE cor. Castleton Ave. 1853. **Wills & Dudley**. **Parish House**, 1910-1914. **Rectory**, 1924. Both by **Ralph Adams Cram**.

An outgrowth of a then fashionable movement called ecclesiology, the design of this small church is patterned after early 14th-century English precursors. (**Frank Wills** was the official architect of the New York Ecclesiological Society.) Cram's additions were skillfully related to the church building's unusual architecture.

WEST BRIGHTON

West Brighton: The official name of this community is West New Brighton, lying as it does to the west of New Brighton. But the "New" has been dropped by all save fuddy-duddy mapmakers and the government officials who advise them. One of the few official recognitions of the vernacular is in the foot-high lettering of the entrance sign of the West Brighton Pool.

[W1] **Edwin Markham Gardens** (public housing), Broadway to North Burgher, between Richmond Terr. and Wayne St.
   An exotic appearance: garden apartments for public housing painted in the terra-cottas and yellows of Tuscany.

Along Castleton Avenue:

[W2] **Engine Company 79, N.Y.C. Fire Department**/formerly Company 104/originally Medora Hook & Ladder Company No. 3 (volunteer), 1189 Castleton Ave., bet. Barker and Taylor Sts., opp. Roe St. N side. ca. 1885. Plaque, 1905, **Alexander Stevens, Superintendent of Buildings**.
   The City took over this eclectic 19th-century firehouse with the advent of paid firemen in 1905 (hence the plaque), but the building had long graced the community as the home of unpaid fire laddies.

W2

[W3] **Keypac Collaborative, Brooklyn Union Gas Company,** 1207 Castleton Ave., bet. Barker and Taylor Sts. N side. 1889.
   Trimmed in bluestone and sporting an Italianate cornice, this venerable commercial building is seeing renewed life.

[W4] **Our Lady of Mt. Carmel-St. Benedicta Church and Rectory** (Roman Catholic), 1265 Castleton Ave., NE cor. Bodine St. 1969. **Genovese & Maddalene**.
   A sophisticated and modern church center in contrast to the commercial strip adjacent and opposite. The dramatic skylit altar and rich modern stained glass of the interior are very effective.

W4

[W5] Originally **Captain John T. Barker House**, 9-11 Trinity Pl., bet. Taylor and Barker Sts. N side. 1851.
   An Italianate villa restored with restraint emphasizing its elegant details: bracketed roof eaves, center cupola, a porch supported by paired columns. **Barker** was a silk dyer by trade, associated with Barrett, Tileston & Company, later the New York Dyeing and Print Works, whose establishment near the foot of Broadway gave that area the name "Factoryville."

W5

[W6] **13 Dongan Street** (house), bet. Richmond Terr. and De Groot Pl. E side. ca. 1875.
   A "painted lady" in the San Francisco tradition, this time perhaps too made-up in sky blue with blush pink trim.

PORT RICHMOND

[W7] **Temple Emanu-El** (synagogue), 984 Post Ave., bet. Decker and Heberton Aves. S side. 1907. **Harry W. Pelcher**.
   Small-town Classical Revival, with a pediment, heavy columns, and a tall octagonal domed cupola. But there is strength of purpose in both the innocent pretentiousness of the street façade and the more straightforward cladding of the rest of the wood frame, with shingles once stained a deep forest green. A relic of this community's earlier days.

W7

[W8] **Along Heberton Avenue:**
   The community's prime residential thoroughfare, paralleling Port Richmond Avenue, the business street two blocks west. Among its fine older homes, reflecting the onetime affluence of this important commercial community, are:

WEST BRIGHTON / PORT RICHMOND

see pages 897–899

W8, No. 253

W8, No. 252

W8, No. 198

No. 253, Somewhat sullied by its siding and storm windows, the corner tower and gabled dormer remind us of its Shingle Style past.

No. 252, Asymmetrical and mansarded, with a wrap-around porch that surveys the streetscape.

No. 233, The central tower gives this otherwise bland building a serious posture.

No. 198, Stuccoed quoins and a Corinthian-columned portal enrich this mansarded mansion.

[W9] **Faith United Methodist Church**/originally Grace Methodist Episcopal Church, 221 Heberton Ave., NE cor. Castleton Ave. 1897. Addition, 1983. **George L. Smalle**.

An offshoot in 1867 of West Brighton's Trinity Methodist Church, this congregation's later Gothic Revival edifice, in dark brick with terra-cotta trim, sits uncomfortably beside its modest addition.

[W10] **Northfield Township District School 6**/later Public School 20 Annex/now **Parkside Senior Housing**, 160 Heberton Ave., NW cor. New St. 1891. **Addition**, Heberton Ave. SW cor. Vreeland St. 1897-1898. **James Warriner Moulton**. Converted to housing, 1993-1994. **Diffendale & Kubec**.

The original neo-Romanesque wing marks one of the island's last remaining school buildings of its genre, in which a mandatory belfry and clock made an important contribution to both the school's architecture and community life.

Across Veterans Park:

[W11] **Park Baptist Church**/originally North Baptist Church of Port Richmond, 130 Park Ave., NW cor. Vreeland St. 1843. Addition/name change, 1871.

W10

W12

[W12] **St. Philip's Baptist Church**, 77 Bennett St., bet. Heberton and Park Aves. N side. 1891. Altered, 1926, **George Conable**.

Park Baptist's congregation, overlooking the park's west edge, established a mission church in 1881 for members of the local black community. It became St. Philip's, its neo-Gothic tower fronting the north side of the park.

[W13] **Port Richmond Branch, N.Y. Public Library**, 75 Bennett St., NW cor. Heberton Ave. 1905. **Carrère & Hastings**. ●
One of **Andrew Carnegie**'s many gifts, this library, fronting on the park, was inserted into an already quite urbane island setting.

W13

All by itself:

[W14] **Catholic Youth Organization**, 120 Anderson Ave., bet. Heberton and Port Richmond Aves., opp. Park Ave. S side. 1926. **James Whitford, Sr.**
A pompous glazed terra-cotta Roman Revival temple façade, on the axis of Park Avenue.

[W15] **Staten Island Reformed Church**, 54 Port Richmond Ave., bet. old railroad viaduct and Richmond Terr., opp. Church St. W side. 1844. Sunday School, 1898, **Oscar S. Teale**.
Site of the first religious congregation on Staten Island, organized in 1663. The present Georgian Revival church replaced three earlier ones on the site. Read the various plaques outside the church and walk through the old graveyard. And visit the Sunday School interior; it's incredible.

W15

[W16] **Faber Pool, N.Y.C. Department of Parks & Recreation**, 2175 Richmond Terr., opp. Faber St. N side. 1932. **Sibley & Fetherston**. Open to the public.
A Mission Style public pool set behind a deep lawn and named for the pencil-manufacturing **Eberhard Faber** family, who once lived nearby.

[W17] **Bayonne Bridge**, Willow Brook Expwy. and Hooker Pl. to Bayonne, N.J. over Kill Van Kull. 1931. **O. H. Ammann**, engineer. **Cass Gilbert, Inc.**, consulting architects.
A graceful soaring silvery arch that rises from the water's edge and sweeps the mind away from the industrial slurbs at either anchorage.

W16

W17

MARINERS HARBOR

"Captains' Row," Richmond Terrace between Van Pelt and De Hart Aves. *(and to the east). S side:*
In the 1840s and 1850s, before the waters became fouled, wealthy oyster captains lived in a row of 2-story homes with columned 2-story porches. The houses overlooked what was then called Shore Road, along which as many as 40 to 50 oystering sloops could be found, moored in the Kill.

W19

[W18] **2868 Richmond Terrace** (house), bet. Van Pelt and De Hart Aves. S Side. ca. 1875.
    A mansarded former mansion, built decades after its neighbors to the east, with walls now sheathed with vinyl clapboard.

[W19] Originally **Stephen D. Barnes House**, 2876 Richmond Terr. bet. Van Pelt and De Hart Aves. S side. ca. 1853. ●
    A Captains' Row mansion with an eclectic combination of Italianate and Gothic Revivals, and especially unusual for the bull's-eye windows in the attic below the deep cornice.

[W20] **Staten Island Seventh-Day Adventist Church**/originally Mariners Harbor Baptist Church, 72 Union Ave., NW cor. Forest Court. 1858.
    Such fine Romanesque Revival brickwork was unusual in this early Staten Island era. This church was founded by members of Port Richmond's North (now Park) Baptist Church.

W20

MARINERS HARBOR

see pages 900–901

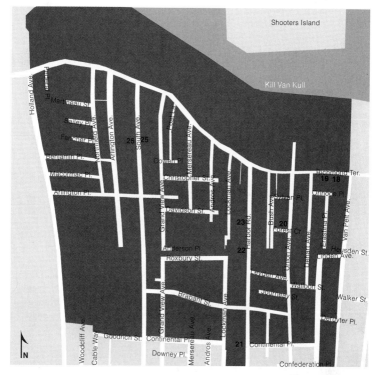

[W21] **258 Harbor Road** (house), opp. Continental Pl. W side. ca. 1845 plus addition.

Columned, battened, ribbed, picket-fenced, the dead end of Continental Place.

[W22] **Summerfield United Methodist Church**/originally Summerfield Methodist Church, 104 Harbor Rd. Parsonage, 100 Harbor Rd., both bet. Leyden Ave. and Richmond Terr. W side. 1869.

Some Classical gestures enliven this painted shingled church, with a tower that provides eclectic interest.

W22

[W23] **74 Harbor Road** (house), bet. Leyden Ave. and Richmond Terr. ca. 1845. W side.

Proof that even red, asphalt-composition, fake brick siding cannot entirely defile the character of a Greek Revival "captain's house," with its 4-columned double-height porch.

South Avenue, between Richmond Terrace and Arlington Place:

[W24] **109, 113, South Avenue** (houses). All E side.
[W25] **116 South Avenue** (house). W side. ca. 1885.

These suburban houses are outstanding examples in the area. Nos. 109 and 113 are particularly rich in Victorian detail.

W24, No. 109

W24, No. 113

Eastern Staten Island

TOMPKINSVILLE • STAPLETON • STAPLETON HEIGHTS
CLIFTON • ROSEBANK • ARROCHAR • SOUTH BEACH

This area is, to most islanders' thinking, another part of the North Shore; no one in Staten Island refers to any area as "eastern." But for the purposes of isolating the communities along the right shoulder of the island, we've grouped them under this artificial rubric.

 Colonial

TOMPKINSVILLE

 Georgian/
Federal

Established as a village around 1815 through the efforts of **Governor Daniel D. Tompkins**; hence its name. Some of its streets, Hannah and Minthorne (and Sarah and Griffin, since renamed), recall his children's names. A plaque in the park calls it **The Watering Place** where navigators before 1628 replenished their ships' supply.

 Greek
Revival

 Gothic
Revival

Between Van Pelt and De Harrt Aves.

Villa

Along or near Bay Street:

Romanesque
Revival

[E1a] **Bay Street Landing** (apartments)/originally American Dock Company, Piers 1-5, below Bay St. bet. U.S. Coast Guard Base and Victory Blvd. E side. Converted into apartments, 1982.

Renaissance
Revival

[E1b] **Harbour Pointe** (apartments), 80 Bay Street Landing. Converted into apartments, 1987, **David Kenneth Specter & Assocs**.

Roman
Revival

Alfred J. Pouch (of Terminal fame) established the American Dock Company in 1872, but the reinforced-concrete coffee and cocoa warehouses converted to residential use date from the early 20th century. The waterside redevelopment also features restaurants.

Art Deco/
Art Moderne

Modern/
Post-Modern

A trip dockside via Hannah Street:

[E2] **Joseph H. Lyons Pool**, Murray Hulbert Ave. SW cor. Victory Blvd. 1936. **N.Y.C. Department of Parks & Recreation**, **Aymar Embury II**, consultant.

Squat cylinders of economical red-brick masonry, helical concrete stairways, and Art Deco detailing identify this as one of eight city swimming pools built in the heyday of municipal construction, the Great Depression of the 1930s. Named for the commander of local V.F.W. and American Legion units.

E2

Great Depression bathhouses: Public works—and works for the public—were a great civic concern during the Great Depression. This concern, plus the availability of subsidized skilled labor, resulted in the building of great public swimming pools and even greater public bathhouses. The superior architectural design of the bathhouses (actually locker and shower facilities for pool users) makes them monuments to their period even decades later. Bronx: Crotona Park; Brooklyn: Betsy Head Park, McCarren Park, Red Hook Park, and Sunset Park; Manhattan: Colonial (now renamed) Park and Highbridge Park; Staten Island: Joseph H. Lyons Pool.

[E3a] **Richmond Chlorination Station, N.Y.C. Department of Environmental Protection**, Murray Hulbert Ave. at Hannah St. W side. 1974. N.Y.C. Board of Water Supply.

E3a

[E3b] **Tompkinsville Water Pollution Control Facility, N.Y.C. Department of Environmental Protection**,

TOMPKINSVILLE / STAPLETON / STAPLETON HEIGHTS
see pages 902–906

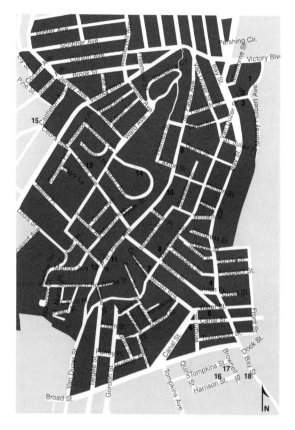

Murray Hulbert Ave. at Pier 7. W side. 1976. **Warren W. Gran & Assocs**.

The sophisticated and self-conscious control facility in Brutalist gray concrete is for society's waste products. The prim, handsomely crafted neo-Georgian chlorination station of carefully laid brick and pink granite is for another vital need: pure water.

STAPLETON

Governor Tompkins's son, **Minthorne**, and **William J. Staples** purchased land south of Tompkinsville from **Cornelius (later "Commodore") Vanderbilt**, a native of Staten Island, and established the village of Stapleton (named after Staples) in 1833. Stapleton became the home of two large breweries in the 19th century: Bechtel's, at the foot of the cliff along Van Duzer Street (opposite Broad, where evidence still exists), and the Rubsam & Hohrmann Atlantic Brewery (1870-1953), later Piel's, which finally closed in 1963 and occupied the long blockfront along Canal Street's north side.

E3b

[E4] **Paramount Theater**, 560 Bay St., bet. Prospect St. and Union Pl. ca. 1935. **C. W. Rapp & George L. Rapp**.

The Paramount presents its wondrous Art Deco false front to a messy commercial street. An adaptive reuse would give a shot in the arm to its neighbors.

[E5a] **Tappen Park**/originally Washington Park, Bay to Wright Sts., Water to Canal Sts. Park reconstructed, gazebo added, 1982. **Quennell Rothschild Assocs**. [E5b] Originally **Edgewater Village Hall**, 111 Canal St., in Tappen Park. 1889. **Paul Kühne**.

E4

E5b

Named for Edgewater, a 19th century village all but forgotten today, this fine Victorian brick civic building is an anchor for Stapleton. Sitting in Tappen Park and shaded by stately old trees, it tempers the cacophony of the many small businesses attempting on every side to invade its peaceful setting.

[E6] **Stapleton Branch, N.Y. Public Library**, 132 Canal St., SW cor. Wright St. 1907. **Carrère & Hastings**.

One of a group of four Carnegie gifts that introduced a semblance of culture to the rural island.

E8

Along Van Duzer Street:

[E7] Possibly **Richard G. and Susannah Tompkins Smith House**, 390 Van Duzer St., bet. Wright and Beach Sts. 18th & 19th centuries ● [E8] **364 Van Duzer Street House**, bet. Beach and Prospect Sts. W side. ca. 1835. **Robert Hazard**, builder. ●

Two houses in adjacent blockfronts with "Dutch kick" roofs and 2-story columned porches. No. 364 is diminutive in scale; No. 390 is positively pompous, with an elegant tetrastyle Corinthian portico. (**Mrs. Smith** was the daughter of Governor, later **Vice President Daniel Tompkins**.)

STAPLETON HEIGHTS

Along St. Paul's Avenue (one-way southbound):

[E9] **S.I. Area Office, Office of Building Services, Board of Education**/formerly Public School 15, Richmond (Daniel D. Tompkins School), 98 Grant St., SE cor. St. Paul's Ave. 1897-1898. **Edward A. Sargent.** ●

Rugged brickwork forms this eclectic complex.

E10b

[E10a] **St. Paul's Memorial Church** (Episcopal), 217-225 St. Paul's Ave. (one-way south), 1866-1870. **Edward T. Potter**. [E10b] **231 and 239 St. Paul's Avenue** (houses). ca. 1870. All bet. Clinton St. and Tarter Pl. E side. ●

A lovingly crafted English country church whose traprock walls have weathered beautifully. Nearby neighbors are two Shingle Style Victorian houses.

[E11] **387 St. Paul's Avenue** (house), bet. Cebra and Occident Aves. E side. ca. 1885.

E11   E13

An extravaganza of shingle and clapboard balloon framing; an interplay of powerful volumes bedecked with gingerbread.

[E12] **400 St. Pauls's Avenue** (house), SW cor. Occident Ave. ca. 1895.

A stucco neo-Tudor mansion that clings to the steep bank of Ward's Hill.

E12

[E13] Originally Gatehouse/altered into **James Pietsch House**, 101 Cebra Ave., bet. Ward Ave. and Rosewood Pl. N side. 1927. **James Pietsch**, builder.

Pietsch redid the existing stone gatehouse of an estate on this site. The result would intrigue **Hansel and Gretel**, as it does us. He moved from Brooklyn to Staten Island to live in the house.

[E14] Originally **Caleb T. Ward House**/later Sally and Lewis Nixon House/called Ward-Nixon Mansion/now apartments, 141 Nixon Ave. (loop), off Ward Ave. (Entrance driveway bet. Nos. 135 and 143.) 1835. **Seth Geer.** ●

Surmounting the crest of Ward's Hill and surrounded on all sides by much less distinguished 20th-century houses, this immense Greek Revival mansion once sat at the center of a 250-acre estate. It reflects the enormous wealth of its builder and the era when this and nearby areas of Staten Island were fashionable locations for the wealthy. Easier to see from a distance than from Nixon Avenue. Its panoramic views are legendary.

E14

[E15] Originally **S. R. Smith Infirmary**/later Frost Building, Outpatient Clinic, Staten Island Hospital, Castleton Ave. opp. Cebra Ave. N side. (Officially 101 Stanley Ave.) 1889. **Alfred E. Barlow**. Additions, 1890, 1891, **Bradford L. Gilbert**.

Four conical capped towers remain as a symbol of this abandoned and gutted neo-medieval fantasy. That fantasy and its commanding hilltop site contributed to its proposed conversion into gentrified condominiums. The project failed (to date), and the hulk awaits a white knight.

E15

E16

Back to Stapleton: Harrison Street and surrounds.

Between Quinn and Brownell Streets:

[E16] **53 Harrison Street**, bet. Quinn and Brownell Sts. Both sides. ca. 1875-1895. **Charles Schmeiser** and others.

Mansarded, brick, and eclectic, this was home to the brewmaster of the nearby Rubsam & Hohrmann brewery. It dominates this pleasant enclave where tightly packed individual homes of great variety and high quality stand on both sides of the street.

[E17] **First Presbyterian Church**, Brownell St. SW cor. Tompkins St. 1894.

The successor to an earlier First Presbyterian Church of Edgewater, the early name of the village. The dark masonry, large rose window, and distinctive stepped gables, reminiscent of earlier Dutch Colonial architecture, make this a special event in this backwater of Stapleton.

Back door to America: An important strategy conference brought **Winston Churchill** *to the island's shores during World War II. The prime minister secretly debarked from a British cruiser anchored off Stapleton and took the B&O Railroad directly to*

E17

Washington to confer with President Roosevelt. Thus you might say the island is the back door to America.

Back to Bay Street: South of Tappen Park.

E18

[E18] Originally **Dr. James R. and Matilde Boardman House**/later **Capt. Elvin E. Mitchell House**, 710 Bay St., bet. Broad St. and Vanderbilt Ave. W side. 1848. �

A large Italianate villa built atop the steep Bay Street slope by the resident physician of the nearby Seaman's Retreat Hospital. It was purchased in 1894 by **Capt. Mitchell** with the proceeds of an award for saving all 176 persons aboard a Cunard liner that had sunk in Long Island Sound a few years earlier.

CLIFTON

[E19] **Bayley Seton Hospital** (Roman Catholic)/ formerly U.S. Public Health Service Hospital/formerly U.S. Marine Hospital/originally Seaman's Retreat, 732-738 Bay St., NW cor. Vanderbilt Ave.

E19a

[E19a] Originally **Seaman's Retreat Main Building**, 131 Bay St. 1834-1837. **Abraham P. Maybie**, builder. Additions, 1848, 1853, and 1911-1912. � [E19b] Originally **Seaman's Retreat Physician-in-Chief's House**, 131 Bay St. 1842. **Staten Island Granite Co.**, builder. � [E19c] **Later buildings**, 1933-1936, **Kenneth M. Murchison, William H. Gompert, Tachau & Vaught**, associate architects; **J. H. de Sibou**, consultant; **James A. Wetmore, Louis A. Simon**, supervising architects, **U.S. Treasury Dept.**

Hard to spot through the trees from the exit driveway on Bay Street (but worth the effort) is the old hospital's imposing stone façade with 2-story pierced galleries and pedimented pavilions. Originally operated successively by the state and federal governments—unlike the privately run Sailors' Snug Harbor on the island's North Shore—this early marine hospital building spawned the large complex of 1930s buildings that now dominates the site. The well-known National Institutes of Health, located in Bethesda, Maryland, had their modest beginnings here in a small laboratory of this old structure. In 1981, after the Feds left, locals established the Bayley Seton, named after **Dr. Richard Bayley** of the old quarantine station and his daughter, who later became **St. Elizabeth Ann Seton**. The 1930s additions manage to use Deco detailing effectively at dramatically different scales—from the attached houses flanking the entrance to the massive central building that dominates the site.

E20

[E20] **110 to 144 Vanderbilt Avenue** (houses), bet. Talbot Pl. and Tompkins Ave. S side. 1900. **Carrère & Hastings**.

A blockfront of eight high-quality, matching, closely spaced, neo-Tudor suburban houses. The firm was responsible for other distinctive work on the island and later won the competition to design the New York Public Library's main building. The developer was **George Washington Vanderbilt**, whose enormous estate Biltmore, in Asheville, N.C., was the work of **Richard Morris Hunt** and **Frederick Law Olmsted**.

[E21] **89, 94, 112, and 120 Norwood Ave.** [E22] **241 and 242 Talbot Ave.**, S. of Norwood. All ca. 1900.

Slightly less dressy partners to the **Carrère and Hastings** row developed by **George W. Vanderbilt**.

E24

[E23] Originally Mariners' Family Asylum of the Port of New York/now **Staten Island Reception Center, New York Foundling Hospital** (Roman Catholic), 119 Tompkins Ave., bet. Vanderbilt Ave. and Hill St. E side. 1855. **J. Graham Glauber**.

Contiguous with the rear of Bayley Seton Hospital is this hostel constructed to care for the widows, wives, sisters, and

daughters of the mariners of the port under care next door at the Seaman's Retreat.

[E24] **72 Greenfield Avenue** (house), bet. Bay St. and Tompkins Ave. viaduct. S side. 19th century.
Both urban and urbane, this Renaissance Revival house is a distinguished loner in these suburban streets.

[E25] **73 Greenfield Avenue** (house), bet. Bay St. and Tompkins Ave. viaduct. N side. 19th century.
Gothic Revival with a great wraparound porch.

ROSEBANK

For much of its history a community of Italian Americans.

[E26] **Garibaldi-Meucci Memorial Museum**, 420 Tompkins Ave., SW cor. Chestnut Ave. ca. 1845. ● Open to the public. 718-442-1608. Tues-Fri, 10-5; Sat-Sun, 1-5; closed Mon.
An unlikely refuge for fiery Italian patriot **Giuseppe Garibaldi**, who lived here with his friend **Antonio Meucci** beginning in 1850. Restlessly awaiting an opportunity to return to Italy, Garibaldi made candles in a nearby factory, killing time by fishing and "shooting thrushes." The museum has letters and photographs describing Garibaldi's life and documenting Meucci's claim to invention of the telephone prior to **Alexander Graham Bell**.

Fig trees: Italians on the island love ripe figs. Consequently, many backyards are decorated with weird trees bundled up like

E25

E26

*mummies in winter, laden with clusters of ripe figs in summer
The presence of this tree is an almost foolproof clue to its owner's
nationality. The Garibaldi memorial is no exception: an Italian
caretaker lives on the second floor.*

E27

[E27] Originally **Bachman Flats**, 103-125 Chestnut Ave., bet.
Tompkins Ave. and Anderson St. N side. ca. 1865.

Workers' housing: a group of 10 brick row houses bracketed
by "pavilions" at each end.

[E28] **Church of St. Joseph** (Roman Catholic), Tompkins Ave.
bet. St. Mary's Ave. and Shaughnessy Lane. S side. 1957. **Neil J.
Convery**.

A very orange neo-Romanesque church complemented by a
sculptural freestanding bell tower with four bells.

E28

[E29] **Our Lady of Mount Carmel Society Shrine and Hall**, 36
Amity St., W of White Plains Ave. Established, 1899. (Access via
White Plains Ave. from St. Mary's Ave. Parking on Virginia Ave.
bet. Fox Hill Terr. and Fletcher St.) A plaque credits **Vito Louis
Russo** as founder and builder.

A robust outdoor year-round folk art display, fervently honoring Our Lady of Mount Carmel. The celebrations culminate
here (and at other Mt. Carmel feasts all over the city) every
summer, about the second week of July. Beat the crowds, visit
another time. It's inspiring.

E29

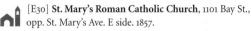 [E30] **St. Mary's Roman Catholic Church**, 1101 Bay St.,
opp. St. Mary's Ave. E side. 1857.

Tiers of round-arched triplet openings enliven the central
bell tower, which identifies this church set on a berm astride Bay
Street (once New York Avenue).

Toward the Narrows along Hylan Boulevard:

[E31] Originally **Henry and Anne McFarlane House**/briefly
New York Yacht Club/later Frederick Bredt House, 30 Hylan
Blvd., bet. Bay and Edgewater Sts., inland of Austen House. ca.
1841-1845. Additions, ca. 1860, ca. 1870s, ca. 1890s.

Now a ruin, it once enjoyed a fantastic Narrows view. While
the **New York Yacht Club**'s second home, from 1868 to 1871, its
members viewed, at the finish line (the Narrows), the first race
in challenge for the America's Cup (originally secured by the
club in 1851). What a marvelous annex it could be to the Austen
House next door (as a B & B?).

E30

[E32] **The Alice Austen House, "Clear Comfort,"** 2 Hylan
Blvd., bet Bay and Edgewater Sts., overlooking Upper New
York Bay. S side. ca. 1700-1750. North extension, porch, dormers
added, 1846, **James Renwick, Jr.**? Further changes, ca. 1852 and
1860-1878. Restored, 1985, **Beyer Blinder Belle**. Open to the
public. 718-816-4506. Thu-Sun, 12-5; closed Mon-Wed.

The original portion, built by a Dutch merchant (to take
advantage of the breathtaking view?), this house was purchased
and altered in 1844 by **John Austen**, a wealthy and cultivated
New Yorker. His granddaughter, **Alice Austen** (1866-1952), came
here at the age of two. She is remembered today for her pioneering work in photography. More than 7,000 of her glass-plate
negatives are preserved at the Staten Island Historical Society.
They depict, with consummate artistry, the world she knew
between 1880 and 1930.

The neat restoration somehow removes too many of the
qualities that time had wrought, but the restored lawn is breathtaking.

E31

E32

[E33] **St. John's Episcopal Church**, 1331 Bay St., SE cor.
New Lane. 1869-1871. **Arthur D. Gilman**.

E34a

A fine example of Victorian Gothic in rose-colored granite with handsome stained-glass windows. Unfortunately, the original steeple has been altered. The first child baptized in the original frame building of this parish was **Cornelius Vanderbilt**, born in nearby Stapleton in 1794.

[E34] **Fort Wadsworth Military Reservation**, S end of Bay St. [E34a] **Battery Weed**, originally Fort Richmond, 1845-1861. Joseph G. Totten. ☛ [E34b] **Fort Tompkins**, Hudson Road. 1858-1876. ☛ Military Museum open to the public.

The gate and guards look ominous, but visitors are welcome. Drive straight ahead; turn left beyond the bridge, follow signs to the Military Museum and the closeup view down to the land-marked Battery Weed, built at the water's edge before the Civil War. The three tiers of arched galleries make the interior of the polygonal fortress far less formidable in appearance than its severe exterior walls.

Romantic legend depicts Algonquin Indians standing here spellbound by the sight of Hudson's ship, the *Half Moon*, entering the Narrows in 1609. Since those sylvan times, Dutch, British, and Americans in times of war have stood watch here, scanning the horizon for enemy ships.

The fort was known well into the 1970s as the oldest continuously staffed military post in the United States. Parts of the site have been added to the Gateway National Recreation Area. The National Park Service has created an inviting visitors center with displays locating and describing all of the military posts guarding New York Harbor and its approaches.

And beyond the limits of our map:

ARROCHAR

[E35] **St. Joseph's Hill Academy for Girls** (Roman Catholic)/originally "Clar Manor"/later William M. McFarland estate "Arrochar," 850 Hylan Blvd., NE cor. Major Ave. ca. 1850.

E35

The Scottish name of McFarland's estate is now the name of the Arrochar community radiating from the academy. The old Italianate villa itself has been compromised over the years, and the academy's newer architecture is uninspired.

▥ [E36] **St. John's Villa Academy Convent, Sisters of St. John the Baptist** (Roman Catholic)/originally "Hawkhurst," William H. Townsend House, 57 Cleveland Pl., E of Landis Ave./Chicago Ave. intersection. S side. ca. 1846. Additions.

A brick Gothic Revival fantasy attributed to architect **James Renwick, Jr.** who had married a woman from nearby Clifton.

E36

Central Staten Island

**WESTERLEIGH • SUNNYSIDE • WILLOWBROOK
GRYMES HILL • EMERSON HILL
DONGAN HILLS/CONCORD • TODT HILL
EGBERTVILLE • NEW DORP • RICHMONDTOWN**

 Colonial

 Georgian/
Federal

 Greek
Revival

 Gothic
Revival

 Villa

 Romanesque
Revival

 Renaissance
Revival

 Roman
Revival

 Art Deco/
Art Moderne

Modern/
Post-Modern

This area of the guide stays clear of the shorefront communities of the North Shore, covered in Northern [N] and Eastern [E] Staten Island, and deals with the central belt of communities that stretches from the waters of Arthur Kill on the west to Lower New York Bay on the east. It embraces the island's chain of inland hills (Grymes, Todt, Emerson, and the Dongan Hills) and the entire Staten Island Greenbelt. That verdant carpet stretches southwesterly from the never completed interchange of the Staten Island Expressway and the unbuilt northern leg of Richmond Parkway to Richmondtown Restoration. Once the Village of Richmond, the island's county seat, Richmondtown has many charming old government structures that became the nucleus of Staten Island's own "Colonial Williamsburg."

WESTERLEIGH

[C1] **Society of St. Paul Seminary** (Roman Catholic), 2187 Victory Blvd., NW cor. Ingram Ave. 1969. **Silverman & Cika.**

Staten Island's most bizarre building: a combination of architecture and monumentally scaled sculpture. Its large size and prominent location make it visible from great distances.

*Prohibition Park, a community occupying a wooded tract of 25 acres (bounded by today's Watchogue Road and Demorest, Maine, and Wardwell Avenues) was set up in 1887 for teetotalers; lots were sold to prohibitionists throughout the country. Some streets were named for dry states—Maine, Ohio, Virginia; others for Prohibition party presidential candidates—Bidwell, Wooley, Fiske. Another resident was **Dr. Isaac Kauffman Funk**, who with his associate **Adam Willis Wagnalls** was preparing* A Standard Dictionary of the English Language *(1890). The area today is known as Westerleigh, but the original street names remain to admonish the unwary of the evils of alcoholic beverages.*

[C2] Originally **Peter Housman House**, 308 St. John Ave., NW cor. Watchogue Rd. ca. 1730-1760. 💣

Long before this area became the local focus for the national prohibition movement, this house was built in a position that is today catercorner to the street grid. **Housman** was a Loyalist during the Revolution. The tiny one-room stone unit on the

C1

WESTERLEIGH

see pages 910–911

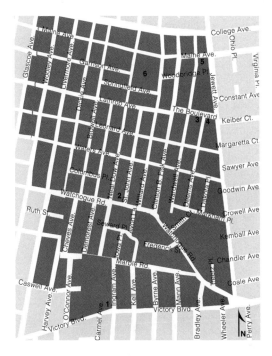

right was undoubtedly built first, with the clapboard addition following 30 years afterward.

The Boulevard: This was Prohibition Park's premier thoroughfare. Its 4,000-seat University Temple, a meeting hall similar to the Methodist facility in Ocean Grove, N. J., straddled the Fiske Avenue end with an arched entry spanning two bell towers; it burned in 1903. The Park Hotel, a large frame building, occupied the site of today's P.S. 30, between Fiske and Wardwell Avenues, on the south side. A number of the Prohibition leaders' fine 19th-century homes also remain:

C3

[C3] Originally **Frank Burt House**, 42 The Boulevard, SW cor. Deems Ave. ca. 1893. **John H. Coxhead**.

Sitting atop a one-story cobblestone plinth, this is the most substantial home remaining on The Boulevard, with its Palladian window, decorative shingles, and sunburst-pattern ornament.

[C4] Originally **Isaac K. Funk House**, 6, 8 The Boulevard, SE cor. Deems Ave. ca. 1893. **Carr, Carlin & Coxhead**.

A baronial clapboard double house whose twin projected bays on the second floor sandwich an expansive solarium.

C4

[C5] Originally the **Reverend William H. Boole House**, 682 Jewett Ave., SW cor. Maine Ave. ca. 1890.

Boole was a well-known evangelist and a cofounder of Prohibition Park. His wife, **Ella Boole**, later became a leader of the Women's Christian Temperance Union, the W.C.T.U.

[C6] **Westerleigh Park, N.Y.C. Department of Parks & Recreation**, Neal Dow to Willard Aves., bet. Maine and Springfield Aves. 1887.

Today's 2.9 acres are all that remain of Prohibition Park's original green space where band concerts and outdoor lectures were given. The bandstand in the center is an echo of the early days.

C7

Entries C7 through C19 are not on our maps, and must be found on a good map of Staten Island:

SUNNYSIDE

[C7] **Swedish Home for Aged People**/originally L. B. La Bau House, 20 Bristol Ave., bet. Cypress Ave. and Little Clove Rd. E side. ca. 1870.

The mansarded neo-Gothic home of **Commodore Cornelius Vanderbilt's** daughter **Alicia**, who married La Bau.

Clove Road:

[C8a] Originally **John King Vanderbilt House**, 1197 Clove Rd., N of Victory Blvd. E side. ca. 1836. Expanded and restored. 🌳

A charming Greek Revival frame house built by one of "Commodore" Vanderbilt's cousins. Purchased in 1955, it was later restored by **Dorothy Valentine Smith**:

[C8b] Formerly **Dorothy Valentine Smith House**/originally John Frederick Smith House, 1213 Clove Rd., N of Victory Blvd. E side. 1893-1895. Expanded and altered. 🌳

A Queen Anne late Victorian country house, the lifelong residence of one of Staten Island's most devoted chroniclers, **Dorothy Valentine Smith**.

[C9] **Julia Gardiner Tyler House**/also known as the Gardiner-Tyler House/originally Elizabeth Racey House, 27 Tyler St., bet. Clove Rd.-Broadway intersection and Burgher Ave. N side. ca. 1835. 🌳

Opposite St. Peter's Cemetery. The elegant portico of this Greek Revival faces west toward a grand view. Note the crisply fluted columns with their florid capitals (unfortunately painted black) and the chunky console brackets that connect the portico to the house proper. **President John Tyler**'s widow resided here after 1868, with her 7 stepchildren.

C9

[C10] **Staten Island Zoo, Clarence T. Barrett Park**, 614 Broadway, at Colonial Court. W side. Rear entrance from Clove Rd. S of Martling Ave. 1936. **N.Y.C. Parks Department**. Open to the public.

A small zoo, specializing in snakes, and an accompanying children's zoo (the only zoo in America exhibiting all 32 species of rattlesnakes). Snake lovers are reassured by the notice: NONE OF THESE SNAKES IS FIXED—ALL HAVE FULL POSSESSION OF FANGS.

[C11] **Scott-Edwards House**, 752 Delafield Ave., bet. Clove Rd. and Raymond Pl. S side. ca. 1730. Altered, 1840.

A formal Greek Revival colonnaded porch was added a century after its original construction as a colonial farmhouse with a so-called Dutch kick roof. The original unwhitewashed fieldstone walls are still visible on the side. The addition of dormer and vents to the graceful roof line is unfortunate.

C11

[C12] **Son-Rise Charismatic Interfaith Church**/originally Asbury Methodist Episcopal Church, 1970 Richmond Ave., bet. Rivington Ave. and Amsterdam Pl. W side. 1849. Remodeling, 1878.

The side walls of this humble church date from 1849, the arch-windowed front and tower from 1878. In the graveyard lies **Ichabod Crane**, whose name was used by his friend **Washington Irving** in the story of the headless horseman. The church itself was originally named for the circuit-riding **Reverend Francis Asbury**, the first American Methodist bishop, who made his first "circuit" on Staten Island in 1771.

C12

WILLOWBROOK

[C13a] **College of Staten Island, CUNY, Central Campus**/one-time Halloran General Hospital, U.S. Army/originally Willowbrook State School, Willowbrook Rd., SW cor. Forest Hill Rd. to Willowbrook Park. 1941. **William E. Haugaard**, N.Y. State Architect. [C13b] Originally N.Y.S. Research Institute for Mental Retardation/now **N.Y.S. Institute for Basic Research in Developmental Disabilities**, 1050 Forest Hill Rd., on Willowbrook grounds, S of Willowbrook Rd. W side. 1967. **Fordyce & Hamby**. Master plan for college, 1988, **Edward Durrell Stone Assocs**. New buildings: **Library**, 1992. **Mayers & Schiff**. **Science Labs**, 1992. **Perry Dean Rogers**. **Student Center**, 1992. **Center For The Arts**, 1993. **Edward Durrell Stone Assocs**.

Built by the State to care for retarded children, these late Art Deco facilities were taken over by the army in 1941 (and renamed for **Col. Paul Stacey Halloran**, U.S. Army Medical Corps) to care for the wounded. After 1951, the buildings were reconverted to serve their intended purpose, until court action forced their closing as places of inhumane treatment for the developmentally impaired. The later crisp but dull research institute was swept by the same revisionist tide. A 1980s proposal called for yet another conversion, this time to the central campus for the now divided activities of the College of Staten Island, the local unit of City University.

GRYMES HILL

The hill that lies north of the Clove, the "cleft," the route of the Staten Island Expressway. The main thoroughfare is Howard Avenue, which sinuously winds its way along the shoreward crest northward from Clove Road to Hero Park, at the edge of Stapleton Heights.

[C14] **Wagner College**, Howard Ave. bet. Campus Rd. and Stratford Rds. Both sides.

Founded in Rochester, N.Y., in 1883, Wagner Memorial Lutheran College moved to Staten Island in 1918 after purchasing the Cunard property 370 feet above sea level on the brow of Grymes Hill. The Cunards were a branch of the English steamship family. The college today is coeducational and nonsectarian.

C14d

If you plan to go exploring, it's best done on foot . . . put your car in a parking area.

[C14a] **Mergerle Science and Dr. Donald and Dr. Evelyn Spiro Communications Center.** 1968. **Perkins & Will.**
[C14b] **August Horrmann Library.** 1961. **Perkins & Will.**
[C14c] **Towers Dormitory.** 1964. **Sherwood, Mills & Smith.**
[C14d] **Harbor View Dormitory.** 1968. **Sherwood, Mills & Smith.** [C14e] **Student Union.** 1970. **Perkins & Will.** [C14f] **Spiro Sports Center,** 1999.

These recent additions to the Wagner campus were designed over a 30-year period by two architectural firms. The diversity of approach is apparent, but visual unity is nevertheless achieved by the acceptance of an imposed discipline of unglazed red face brick as the predominant building material. The most recent additions/modifications continue this trend.

C14g

[C14g] **Main Building, Wagner College, East Campus,** 631 Howard Ave. E side. 1930. **Smith, Conable & Powley.**

Handsome brick neo-Tudor. It reeks of higher education, as more modern works fail to do.

[C15] **Cunard Hall, Wagner College, East Campus/** originally "Bellevue," Sir Edward Cunard House, Howard Ave. E side. ca. 1851.

An Italianate mid-Victorian mansion, today used for college offices. Its name referred to the glorious view now diminished by new construction.

EMERSON HILL

C15

Emerson Hill marks the south side of the Clove, across from Grymes Hill, and is named for **Judge William Emerson,** brother of poet **Ralph Waldo Emerson,** who regularly visited him here. The narrow roads and curious homes were largely developed in the 1920s by **Cornelius G. Kolff,** a local civic leader later remembered for a ferryboat named in his honor. Nos. 3, 93, and 205 Douglas Road are among the more interesting newer houses to be found here. (Don't be surprised if practically every lane you turn onto is called Douglas Road . . . it just is that way.) Emerson Hill's quaintness results from the constricted yet rustic development patterns and a never-ending feeling of closeness with nature, but don't miss the spectacular long-distance views between the houses and the dense foliage. A memorable spot.

DONGAN HILLS/CONCORD

Before good roads were cut through to the summit of Todt Hill, and its forested slopes were opened to high-style residential development, the group of hills south of the Clove (the cleft through which the Staten Island Expressway passes between Grymes Hill and Emerson Hill) carried the omnibus name: Dongan Hills. Since the opening of the Verrazano Bridge in 1964, practically every Staten Island hillock has been separately named to meet the marketing needs of the local real estate industry. The area closer to the expressway is called Concord.

Along Richmond Road:
Between Staten Island Expressway and Four Corners Road/
Flagg Place.

C16

[C16] **St. Simon's Episcopal Church**, 1055 Richmond Rd., opp. Columbus Ave. W side. 1961. **James Whitford, Jr**.
   A simple gabled brick church enhanced by its three-bell freestanding bell tower. Called "the church on the curve" since its forebear, "the church in the clove," was destroyed for the expressway.

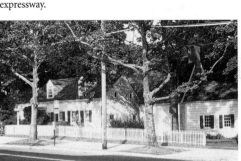

C17

[C17] **The Billiou-Stillwell-Perine House**, 1476 Richmond Rd., bet. Delaware and Cromwell Aves. SE side. ca. 1660s. Additions, ca. 1680-1830. ☀ Open to the public.
   Like the house that Jack built, this one has additions sprawling in every direction. Looking at the building from the front and reading from left to right, you see rooms dating from 1790, 1680, 1662, and 1830. The original one-room fieldstone farmhouse with steep pitched roof, built in the 1660s, is best seen from the back. Walk around the house; take a look inside and, in particular, at the magnificent open-hearth fireplace.

TODT HILL

Staten Island's most chic residential area. Its summit at 409.2 feet above sea level is the highest point along the Atlantic coastline south of Cadillac Mountain on Mt. Desert Island, Maine.

C18

Off Ocean Terrace:

[C18] **57 Butterworth Avenue** (house), N of Ocean Terr. at end. E side. ca. 1925.
   A romantic "gingerbread" house of stucco, stone, and sleek shingles.

[C19] **57 Carlton Place** (house), E of Ocean Terr. off Emerson Ave., at end. ca. 1925.
   If this place looks vaguely familiar it's because the wedding scene at the beginning of *The Godfather* was filmed here.

C21

Off and along Flagg Place:

[C20] **Richmond County Country Club**/originally "Effingham," Junius Brutus Alexander House/later Meyers House, 135 Flagg Pl. NW side. (Entrance on The Plaza, SE side.) ca. 1860. Many additions.

A much-altered Renaissance Revival house where the Island's society has played since 1897. Alexander was a wealthy Southern cotton grower who regularly voyaged north during the South's long hot summers.

C20

[C21] Originally **"Stone Court," Ernest Flagg House**, gatehouse, gate, and site/in part now St. Charles Seminary, Pious Society of St. Charles, Scalabrini Fathers (Roman Catholic), in part now "Copper Flagg Estates" [see below], 209 Flagg Pl., bet. W. Entry Rd. and Iron Mine Dr. NW side. 1898 to ca. 1917. **Ernest Flagg**. ☛ Additional landmark site and outstructures including former **South Gatehouse**, 79½ Flagg Court. NW side. Former **Water Tower**, 96 Flagg Court. SE side. Former **Stable**, 79 Flagg Court. NW side. Former **Palmhouse**, 61 Flagg Court. NE side. All part of landmark site ☛. Accessible from Coventry Rd.

C21, Water Tower

[C22] **"Copper Flagg Estates"** (residences on and adjacent to landmark site): Within the landmark site: Altered **South Gatehouse, Stable, Palmhouse**, 1987, **Robert A. M. Stern**. New residences: **15, 16, 27, 39, 51, 71 Flagg Court**. Both sides. All 1987, 1988. **Robert A. M. Stern**. Outside landmark site: New residences: **60, 61, 81 Copperflagg Lane. 255 Flagg Place**. All 1987. **Robert A. M. Stern. 15, 25 Copperleaf Terrace, 24, 36, 48, 60, 76, 88, 100 Copperflagg Lane**. All 1987, 1988. **Calvanico Assocs., Charles M. Aquavella, Di Fiore & Giacobbe, Joseph Morace**, architects; **Robert A. M. Stern**, architectural design review.

C22, 71 Flagg Court

Ernest Flagg (1857-1947) *was once one of Staten Island's largest landowners as well as a prolific and honored architect. Among his designs were the U.S. Naval Academy in Annapolis and many of New York's finest buildings, such as the Singer Tower and buildings for the Scribner publishing family. For decades Stone Court was his rural palatial residence, a grand house of unusual design which reflects Flagg's interest in, and permutations upon, the local French Huguenot colonial tradition. (Disregard the insensitive later additions to the house itself.)*

In the early 1980s the City's Landmarks Preservation Commission added the rear of the site to its earlier designation, making a total of 9½ acres, to embrace a number of the estate's outbuildings such as the fieldstone water tower, the stable, and the palm house, and a generous lawn and pool. A developer, working with architect **Robert A. M. Stern**, *altered and expanded the existing small structures (the swimming pool, for example, was filled in*

C22, 81 Copperflagg La.

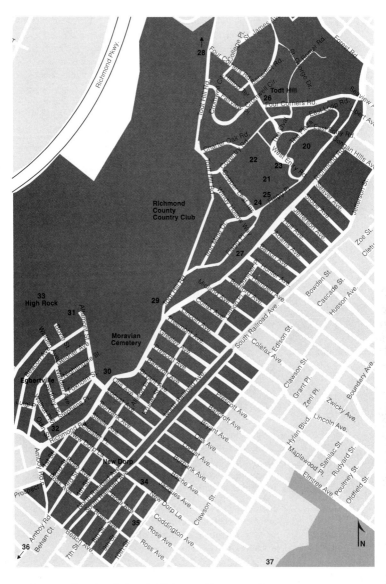

and became a formal garden), and added new residences, to encircle the lawn. The ten altered and new units on the landmark site were regulated by the commission; the thirteen planned for neighboring lands—were not. There are discernably clear differences.

Ernest Flagg's Todt Hill cottages: Flagg designed, built, and sold a number of picturesque cottages adjacent to Stone Court on lands originally owned by his Flagg Estate Company.

[C23a] **Main cottage**, 45 West Entry Rd., W of Flagg Pl. N side.
[C23b] "**Bowcot**," 95 West Entry Rd., W of Flagg Pl. N side. 1916-1918. ● [C24] "**Wallcot**," 285 Flagg Pl. NW side. 1918-1921. ● [C25] "**Hinkling Hollow**," 309 Flagg Pl. NW side. 1927. [C26] **Paul Revere Smith House**, 143 Four Corners Rd., bet. Richmond and Benedict Rds. N side. 1924.

Each house is different in plan and elevation, but all of them share in the use of local stone, serpentine, as one of their principal

C23b

C24

C27

exterior materials. That, combined with distinctive pitched roofs, a liberal use of traditional and inventive dormers, and hooded brick chimneys, gives them all a very special Flagg flavor.

[C27] Originally **The McCall's Demonstration House**, 1929 Richmond Rd., opp. and N of Hunter Ave. NW side. 1924-1925. **Ernest Flagg.** 🌰

In 1924-1925, *McCall's* magazine publicized (and sold plans at $15 each) eight house designs, ranging from four to seven rooms, responding to the needs of America's middle-class homemakers "by America's foremost architects." Flagg was one of the eight, but in his case he actually built his, on Richmond Road (a main drag even then), below his estate. Evidently an active self-promoter, he installed a sign that once read:

THIS HOUSE COST LESS THAN THE ORDINARY
FRAME HOUSE OF EQUAL SIZE

Along and off Todt Hill Road:

[C28] **St. Francis Novitiate, Franciscan Fathers** (Roman Catholic seminary), 500 Todt Hill Rd., opp. Whitwell Pl. W side. 1928.

A somber red-brick institutional structure that began as a prep school for those planning a career in the church. Set amid a flowing green lawn, its 86-foot tower surmounts one of Todt Hill's highest elevations.

C28

[C29] **New Dorp Moravian Church**, 1256 Todt Hill Rd., N of Richmond Rd. W side. 1844. **Parsonage**, ca. 1870. **Parish House**, 1913.

This "new" church is older than many of New York's "old" ones. The pretentious, gray stucco parish house in Classical Revival style was the gift of **William H. Vanderbilt**, son of Cornelius.

[C30a] **Moravian Cemetery**, Entrance, Richmond Rd. opp. Otis Ave. N side.

A large fascinating cemetery in which some of the Island's most distinguished families are interred, including, in a separate, private area, the extended Vanderbilt family. [See the Vanderbilt Mausoleum, below.] While the Vanderbilt area is not open to the public, the remainder of the cemetery's older parts offers beautiful landscapes, walks, and drives.

C29, Church

[C30b] **Old New Dorp Moravian Church**/now Church School and Cemetery Office, within Moravian Cemetery. 1763.

A good example of Dutch Colonial style, its sweeping roof extending over eaves to form a porch.

[C30c] **Vanderbilt Mausoleum**, rear of Moravian Cemetery. 1866. **Richard Morris Hunt**, architect. **Frederick Law Olmsted**, landscape architect. Not open to the public.

C29, Parish House

C30c

Seemingly carved out of the "living rock," with an ornate granite entrance and observation terrace added by **Hunt** and **Olmsted**. Buried within the 72 crypts are **"Commodore" Cornelius Vanderbilt** (who paid in advance for the tomb and was later reinterred there) and members of his family. In the remaining 14 acres of the Vanderbilt plot (there had once been 22) are others of the extended family, including the Sloans.

C31

[C31] Originally **New Dorp Light Station**/now private house, N end of Altamont Ave. Best viewed from Beacon Ave. and Boyle St. ca. 1854.

A former Coast Guard navigation beacon, it guided ships entering New York harbor. Its white clapboard tower is hardly reminiscent of the traditional lighthouse form. Now decommissioned, it sees adaptive reuse as a house.

[C32] **Gustave A. Mayer House**/originally David R. Ryers House, 2475 Richmond Rd., bet. New Dorp Lane and Odin St. NW side. (Entry at 24 St. Stephen's Pl., opp. Walnut St.) SE side. 1855-1856.

A stately villa atop the rise overlooking the New Dorp flats. In the basement Gustave, the inventor of the Nabisco wafer, compounded other savory confections.

C32

EGBERTVILLE

Along and off Rockland Avenue:
Rockland Avenue, between Richmond Road and Brielle Avenue, hugs Egbertville Ravine, the proposed route of Robert Moses's Willowbrook Expressway. The route was chosen, naturally, because it required few relocations of residents and because the costs of acquiring the site would be low. (The area between Manor Road and Brielle Avenue is part of Latourette Park and is known among devoted local naturalists as Buck's Hollow.) The fact that the ravine and forest south of Rockland Avenue in this stretch are a remarkable natural area within the larger Staten Island Greenbelt was not—at least in Moses's time—much of a concern. As the island's population continues to rise and its traffic jams increase, the question of environmental values will again pose difficult decisions.

[C33] **High Rock Park Conservation Center**, 200 Nevada Ave., at summit of hill. Open to the public.

A primarily natural rather than built environment, this hardwood forest preserve is a rarity among New York City's protected green spaces. With about 100 acres it is only a small part of the 1,000-acre Staten Island Greenbelt. There are marked, self-guiding trails, a loose strife swamp, a pond, and a visitors' center where more information is available about this nationally recognized environmental-education center.

NEW DORP

Arrayed on either side of New Dorp Lane, between both Richmond and Amboy Roads, and Hylan Boulevard, lies the community of New Dorp. It expanded easterly after the opening in 1964 of the Verrazano Bridge, all the way to the ocean (an area earlier called New Dorp Beach). Miller Field, at New Dorp Beach, was once the home of the Vanderbilts and, later, of the U.S. Army Air Corps.

[C34] **Lane Theater**, 168 New Dorp Lane, bet. 8th and 9th Sts. 1937-1938. **John Eberson**. Interior 🍎

Hidden along New Dorp Lane is a well-disguised Art Moderne movie house. The rounded corners of the sign indicate a motif repeated throughout the building's exterior (look at the façades of the corner shops on the block) as well as inside.

C34

[C35] **245 Rose Avenue** (house), SW cor. 10th St. ca. 1885.

A robust Victorian house that controls a suburban residential corner without crushing it to death. The house sports an octagonal corner cupola with an ogival roof, imbricated shingles, and a Stick Style railing on a balcony tucked beneath the jerkinhead roof.

C35

[C36] **Monsignor Farrell High School** (Roman Catholic), 2900 Amboy Rd., S cor. Tysen's Lane. 1962. **Charles Luckman Assocs**.

California Modern, stylish in its day and sophisticated (for Staten Island in the 1960s).

All by itself on the ocean:

[C37] **World War II Bunker**, on the beach at former Miller Field/now Gateway National Recreation Area, NE of the foot of New Dorp Lane. ca. 1942.

All along the beaches of the east coast during World War II the military built observation posts to spot potential invaders by sea. Simple in conception and form, they were towers of reinforced concrete gashed near the top by a narrow horizontal slot facing oceanward. When hostilities ended, the priorities for their removal were less than those that had determined their rapid construction. And so, thankfully, this remains to remind us.

C37

The following entries (C38-C56) can be found using any good map of the Island; at Richmondtown the Restoration will give you a detailed plan of the town's plan:

C38b

[C38a] **N.Y.C. Farm Colony/Seaview Hospital Historic District.** ☛ [C38b] **Seaview Hospital, N.Y.C. Health and Hospitals Corporation**, 480 Brielle Ave., bet. Manor Rd. and Rockland Ave. E and SE sides. 1914. **Raymond F. Almirall.** ♂ Open-air radial pavilions, auditorium, Group Building additions, 1917. **Edward F. Stevens** and **Renwick, Aspinwall & Tucker.** ♂ **Roman Catholic Chapel**, 1927. ♂ **Episcopal Chapel**, 1932. ♂ [C38c] Originally **The N.Y.C. Farm Colony**, Brielle Ave. bet. Walcott and Rockland Aves. W side. 1904+. **Renwick, Aspinwall & Owen**. Additional buildings, 1930-1934. **Charles B. Meyers.** ♂

The earliest buildings of Seaview, originally described as the world's largest tuberculosis hospital, are Almirall's in the Spanish Mission Style with much inset decorative tile and Spanish tile roofs. It now presents a split personality—many of the early buildings are abandoned, overgrown, and decaying, while the City continues to build new buildings in their shadows. The Farm Colony ("poorhouse" in less euphemistic language) across Brielle Road consists of many smaller structures in a range of styles in which gambrel roofs and Colonial Revival porticoes predominate. The extensive Farm Colony site was once slated for private residential redevelopment under the auspices of the City. The buildings are roofless and subsiding.

Lighthouse Hill: *West of Rockland Road (which follows the Egbertville Ravine), north of Richmond Road, and south and east of Latourette Park.*

[C39] **Eger Home** (Lutheran), 120 Meisner Ave., bet. London Rd. and Rockland Ave. S side. 1971. **Quanbeck & Heeden**.
The prismatic gray multistory masonry nursing home is too large, too noticeable, and too artificial an intrusion into the natural rhythms of the Staten Island Greenbelt. Founded in Brooklyn by **Carl Michael Eger**, this institution for aged Norwegians has owned this site since 1924.

[C40] **Nathaniel J. Wyeth, Jr., House**, 190 Meisner Ave., bet. London Court and Scheffelin Ave. S side. ca. 1850.
A lovely 2-story brick cube topped by a many-sided, many-windowed monitor. Heavily engulfed on the road side by lush landscaping, the siting offers privacy that newer homes have sacrificed to wide, showy lawns. On the far side (private) it enjoys a panorama of the approaches to New York harbor.

C40

[C41] **Jacques Marchais Center of Tibetan Art**, 338 Lighthouse Ave., W of Windsor Ave. S side. 1947. **Jacques Marchais**, designer. Open to the public. 718-987-3500. Apr-Nov: Wed-Sun, 1-5; closed Mon-Tues.
The largest privately owned collection of Tibetan art outside of Tibet. A rare treat.

C42

[C42] **"Staten Island Lighthouse"**/Ambrose Channel Range Light, Edinboro Rd. bet. Windsor and Rigby Aves. S side. 1912. **William E. Piatt?** ☛
This lighthouse, strangely distant from rocks and pounding waves, stands calmly in suburbia. The tapered octagonal structure of yellow brick, with fanciful Gothic brackets supporting its upper-level wraparound walkway, is a pleasant change from pure white cylindrical lighthouses familiar to yachtsmen. Most dramatic looking up from Lighthouse Avenue.

[C43] **"Crimson Beech"**/originally William and Catherine Cass House, 48 Manor Court, W of Lighthouse Ave. S side. 1958-1959. **Frank Lloyd Wright**.

C44

"Prefab No. 1" Design (1956) by **FLW** for **Marshall Erdman & Associates**, Madison, Wisconsin. ●

A very long, very low building (its gently pitched, bright maroon, tripped roof goes on and on) that clings precariously to the cliff edge, taking full advantage of ocean views. One of a number of prefabricated homes that were the product of Wright's late career—and certainly not of the quality of the great architect's prairie houses.

[C44] **426 Edinboro Road** (house), bet. Windsor and Rigby Aves. S side. 1987. **Steven J. Calvanico**.

A speculative Modern house, built to enjoy the spectacular views from these parts.

In LaTourette Park, accessible from Edinboro Road, Lighthouse Hill and Richmond Hill Road:

C45

[C45] Originally David LaTourette House/now **LaTourette Park Clubhouse**, LaTourette Park E of Richmond Hill Rd. ca. 1836. Altered, 1936. ●

Either in silhouette on the brow of the hill or studied more carefully up close, this (minus its 1936 WPA porch addition) is a fine masonry Greek Revival mansion. As the clubhouse for a City-owned golf course, however, its interior is a great letdown: mostly barren, dim rooms used for snack bar purposes.

C46

[C46] The (Sylvanus) Decker Farmhouse, Staten Island Historical Society, 435 Richmond Hill Rd., bet. Forest Hill Rd. and Bridgetown St. N side. ca. 1810. Porch addition, 1840. ●

A cozy clapboard Dutch-inspired white-painted (gray/white trim) farmhouse with barn-red outbuildings. A 1955 gift to the Historical Society, it will be restored, in conjunction with nearby Richmondtown, as a farmhouse of the 1830s.

RICHMONDTOWN

If you're arriving by car, the best approach is from the heights of LaTourette Park down the hairpin turns of Richmond Hill Road, from which Richmondtown Restoration appears to be a miniature village arranged under a celestial Christmas tree.

Once the county seat of Richmond County. Now the site of an ambitious project involving the restoration and reconstruction of approximately 31 buildings, and hopes for a trolley museum and operating streetcars, all under the direction of the Staten Island Historical Society.

At its founding in 1685 Richmondtown was humbly known as "Cocclestown," presumably after oyster and clam shells found in streams nearby. Here, in 1695, the Dutch erected the Voorlezer House, their first meetinghouse, used for both church services and a teaching school. Subsequently a town hall and jail were built; by 1730 the town was thriving. It had a new courthouse, one tavern, about a dozen homes, and the Church of St. Andrew. This tiny town was now the largest and most important on the island. As such, the name Cocclestown was considered inappropriate and was changed to the more staid Richmondtown. By the time of the American Revolution, when the British occupied it, Richmondtown had a blacksmith shop, a general store, a poorhouse, a tanner's shop, a Dutch Reformed Church, a gristmill, and several more private homes.

[C47] **Richmondtown Restoration, Staten Island Historical Society**, Office and public parking, 411 Clarke Ave., SE of Arthur Kill Rd. N side. Begun 1939. Restored, **Wyeth & King**, and other architects; various landscape architects. Open to the public. ●

C49

The efforts of interested members of the Society, combined with the blessings of Robert Moses, resulted in this "living historical museum" built around the physical nucleus of the county seat's remaining governmental buildings and other nearby survivors. To these have been added other endangered structures that were moved from various points on the island to this City-owned site.

[C48] **Staten Island Historical Society Museum**/formerly Richmond County Clerk's and Surrogate's Office, 302 Center St., NW cor. Court Pl. 1848. Additions up to 1918. 🍎
This charmingly scaled red brick building, once a governmental office, is today a museum. Odd bits of Americana of varying interest—china, lithographs, furniture, and toys—are on display, plus a marvelous collection of tools and the exhibit: "Made on Staten Island." To get your bearings, study the model of Richmondtown Restoration and get a map showing the buildings open to the public on the day you visit.

[C49] **Third County Court House**/now Visitor's Center, Center St. opp. S end of Court Pl. 1837. S side. 🍎
A grand Greek Revival portico succeeds in making clear that this is the architectural dean of this community.

[C50] **Stephens-Black House and General Store**, Court Pl. NE. cor. Center St. ca. 1838-1840. 🍎
Fascinating reconstruction of a 19th-century store—everything from ginger beer to quinine pills. The musty smell of soap and candles delights a modern-day shopper used to antiseptic, cellophane-wrapped goods in supermarkets. The storefront is perfectly plain: no neon signs, no billboards.

C50

[C51] **Guyon-Lake-Tysen House**, Richmond Rd. bet. Court and St. Patrick's Pl. N side. ca. 1740. Additions, ca. 1820 and ca. 1840. 🍎
One of the best examples of Dutch Colonial remaining in the metropolitan area, saved at the last minute from destruction when moved in 1962 from its original site in New Dorp. It was, of course, built almost 80 years after the Dutch ceded New Amsterdam to the Duke of York.

[C52] **Voorlezer's House**, Arthur Kill Rd. bet. Center St. and Clarke Ave. W side. ca. 1695. 🍎
An archetypical "little red schoolhouse." In Dutch communities unable to obtain a minister, a lay reader (voorlezer) was chosen by the congregation to teach school and conduct church

C51

services. It is the oldest-known elementary school building in the United States.

Other Richmondtown individual city landmarks:

C53, Basketmaker

[C53] **Basketmaker's House** (re-located from New Springville), ca. 1810-1820. ● **Bennett House** (always here), ca. 1839, addition, 1854, ● **Boehm-Frost House** (moved from Greenridge), ca. 1750, addition ca. 1840. ● **Britton Cottage** (moved from New Dorp Beach), ca. 1670, additions, ca. 1755, ca. 1765, ca. 1800. ● **Christopher House** (moved from Dongan Estate), ca. 1756. ● **Eltingville (Grocery) Store** (now print shop), ca. 1860. ● **Kruser-Finley House**, ca. 1790. **Additions**, ca. 1820 and ca. 1850-1860. ●

C53, Parsonage

▦ **Parsonage**, ca. 1855. ● **Treasure House**, ca. 1700. **Additions**, ca. 1740, ca. 1790, ca. 1860. ● **Rezeau-Van Pelt Cemetery**, one of the city's few remaining private burial grounds, 1780s to 1860s. ●

In or near Richmondtown, but not part of the Restoration:

East of Richmondtown Restoration:

C54

⌂ [C54] **St. Patrick's Roman Catholic Church**, 45 St. Patrick's Pl., bet. Center St. and Clarke Ave. E side. 1860-1862.

A brick church whose window openings carry Romanesque Revival half-round arches, but whose narrow proportions are more in keeping with Gothic Revival verticality.

C55

▤ [C55] **Reverend David Moore House**, also known as The Moore-McMillen House/formerly Rectory of St. Andrew's Episcopal Church, 3531 Richmond Rd., opposite Kensico St. W side. 1818. ●

A very good example of Federal style, with an extremely handsome doorway and neatly articulated cornice. Behind the house is a good view of the Staten Island Lighthouse.

West of Richmondtown Restoration:

C56

▦ [C56] **St. Andrew's Episcopal Church**, 4 Arthur Kill Rd., SE cor. Old Mill Rd. 1872. Attributed to **William H. Mersereau**. ●

An "English" country church in a picturesque setting complete with picturesque graveyard. Borders the marshlands of LaTourette Park.

ELTINGVILLE • GREAT KILLS • ROSSVILLE • WOODROW
CHARLESTON • RICHMOND VALLEY • TOTTENVILLE
PRINCES BAY • ANNADALE • HUGUENOT

The South Shore

The South Shore is that part of Staten Island farthest from the Verrazano Bridge and the St. George ferry, the points of interface with the rest of the city. Therefore it has naturally been the last part of the island to be developed. In the 1980s, however, the empty (i.e., occupied only by forest, marsh, clay pits, or sand dunes) lands fast began to disappear, as the rising demand to live within the five boroughs reached its zenith.

Colonial

Georgian/ Federal

Greek Revival

Gothic Revival

Villa

Romanesque Revival

Renaissance Revival

S1

ELTINGVILLE

Roman Revival

Art Deco/ Art Moderne

 [S1] **St. Alban's Episcopal Church and Rectory**, 76 St. Alban's Pl. (one-way east, formerly Old Amboy Rd.), bet. Winchester and Pacific Aves. S side. 1865, moved with enlargements, 1872. **Richard M. Upjohn**. 🍎

Modern/ Post-Modern

Board-and-batten Carpenter Gothic whose steeply pitched gables are enriched with ornate scrollwork. The entrance is not opposite the apse area but from one side—an interesting variation.

[S2] **Public School 55**, Richmond, and playground, 54 Osborne St., SE cor. Woods of Arden Rd. to Koch Blvd. School, 1965. Playground, 1967. Both by **Richard G. Stein & Assocs**.

The school, a tame New Brutalist essay, was, nevertheless, more convincing than most public schools of the 1960s. Now restored with some of the crispness of its opening years.

[S3] Originally **Poillon House**/later Frederick Law Olmsted House, 4515 Hylan Blvd., bet. Woods of Arden Rd. and Hales Ave. N side. ca. 1720. Significantly altered, 1830s. 🍎

Before he became a park designer, **Frederick Law Olmsted** lived here, running a fruit farm, planting trees, and experimenting with landscaping. When Olmsted began work on Prospect Park, he moved to Clifton, commuting daily to Brooklyn on the nearby ferry.

GREAT KILLS

[S4] Originally **Great Kills Masonic Lodge, No. 912,** 4095 Amboy Rd., NW cor Lindenwood Rd. 1928.

Colonial Revival in Greek Revival dress, with twin Corinthian columns flanked by walls in the true, 1830s Greek Revival Style (cf. Mariners Temple in Manhattan).

S4

[S5] **Gatehouse, Ocean View Memorial Park** (cemetery)/ formerly Valhalla Burial Park, Amboy Rd. opp. Hopkins Ave. ca. 1925.

A wonderfully romantic, asymmetric neo-Gothic composition in rough and dressed stone, with fine ironwork. A proper entrance to a place of repose.

[S6] **Port Regalle** (residential development), Tennyson Dr., bet. Nelson and Wiman Aves. to Great Kills Harbor. 1988. **John Ciardullo Associates**.

A "planned unit development" of clustered homes that gather around a new street, Harbour Court, at the mouth of Great Kills Harbour.

S5

ROSSVILLE

Rossville, now a veritable ghost town, was the site of the old Blazing Star Ferry to New Jersey, in service from 1757 to 1836. Stagecoaches between New York City and Philadelphia took the ferry, propelled by sail or oars, here and in Tottenville.

S7

[S7] **2286 Arthur Kill Road** (house), E of Rossville Ave. S side. ca. 1860.

A mansarded loner.

[S7a] **Sleight Family Graveyard**, also known as the Rossville Burial Ground or Blazing Star Burial Ground, Arthur Kill Rd. opp. and E of Rossville Ave. N side. 1750-1850. 🐦

Rossville was once known as **Blazing Star** and its connection to New Jersey, as the **Blazing Star Ferry**. The graveyard, one of the island's earliest extant, sits atop a concrete wall (an addition) that elevates it above the road and the dampness of the salt marshes beyond. Now overgrown.

Graveyards—industrial and others: Along Arthur Kill Road between Rossville Avenue and Zebra Place lie three waterside graveyards: two burial grounds containing the remains of the area's early European settlers, and another kind, for man-made marine castaways. The cemeteries are St. Luke's, and Sleight Family/Blazing Star [see above]. The other, at No. 2453, is Witte Marine Equipment Company. It is here, on dozens of mucky underwater acres, that rusting ships and leaky barges spend their last days prior to being liberated of their arcane spare parts for reuse on their still-operable cousins.

🏛 [S8] **Old Bermuda Inn**/originally Peter L. Cortelyou House, 2512 Arthur Kill Road, NE cor. Hervey St. ca. 1855. Additions.

This resplendent and grandly scaled Greek Revival house sits on a rise on the inboard side of the road. A 1980s front extension masks its stately 2-story wood Doric columns (six round freestanding, two square engaged).

S9

🏛 [S9] **2522 Arthur Kill Road** (house), SE cor. Hervey St. ca. 1840. Additions.

A lesser, but more visible, Greek Revival neighbor to the Bermuda Inn next door.

[S10] **St. Luke's Cemetery**/originally Woglum Family Burying Ground, Arthur Kill Rd. opp. Zebra Pl. N side. Established as St. Luke's, ca. 1847.

Another old cemetery, once the graveyard of the local Episcopal church established here in 1847, now in the shadow of the enormous (200 feet in diameter) steel cylinders built to contain liquefied natural gas (LNG). Among the family names: Guyon, Winant, Disoway. The grounds are administered by All Saints Episcopal Church in Westerleigh.

A side trip into the South Shore's forested heartland:

WOODROW

Sandy Ground: The intersection of Bloomingdale and Woodrow Roads was known on maps as Bogardus Corners—after the Bogardus family's grocery, established in 1860—or, in modern times, as Woodrow. Part of the integrated community of Woodrow (on some maps, Wood Row) was Sandy Ground, a settlement of free black oystermen who migrated in the 19th century from the shores of Chesapeake Bay, drawn by the flourishing oyster industry of nearby Princes Bay. They intermarried with local black families, and the settlement continues to this day despite the disappearance, long ago, of oystering in these waters.

[S11] **Rossville A.M.E. (African Methodist Episcopal) Zion Church Cemetery**, Crabtree Ave. 450 feet W of Bloomingdale Rd. S side. 1852+. ●
Established as the graveyard for the 1854 church on Crabtree Avenue, now gone. Its surviving gravestones help illuminate the history of Sandy Ground, a story richly told in **Joseph Mitchell**'s "Mr. Hunter's Grave," collected in his 1960 book, *The Bottom of the Harbor.*

[S12] **Woodrow United Methodist Church**/originally Woodrow Methodist Episcopal Church, 1109 Woodrow Rd., bet. Rossville and Vernon Aves. N side. 1842. Tower, 1876. ●
This starkly simple Greek Revival temple is almost—but not quite—spoiled by the awkward arcaded bell tower added atop its roof in the late 19th century, when simplicity must have gone out of favor.

S12

[S13] **Public School 25, Annex D**/once Public School 4/originally Westfield Township School No. 7, Richmond, "The Kreischer School," 4210 Arthur Kill Rd., N of Storer Ave. E side. 1896. Enlarged, 1906-1907. **C.B.J. Snyder.** ●
Cream-colored brick with orange brick quoining, trim, and "pediment," constructed from the products of the onetime brick factory for whose founder the school is named. It overlooks a tiny old cemetery and, since 1934, the fuel tanks of Port Socony, now renamed Port Mobil.

S13

[S14] **Charleston Cemetery**, Arthur Kill Rd. N of Storer Ave. W side.
Another of the tiny community cemeteries that line Arthur Kill Road atop low retaining walls. The name Storer is evident on a number of the extant markers, as it is on the nearby street sign.

S14

CHARLESTON

Charleston, formerly known as Kreischerville (Balthazar Kreischer started his brick factory in 1854), is an area rich in clay. Old clay pits can still be visited; several brickmaking firms operated here during the 19th century.

[S15a] Originally **Nicholas Killmeyer Store and House**, 4321 Arthur Kill Rd., NW cor. Winant Pl. ca. 1865.
A mansarded country store from the time when Charleston was a village in the deep rural countryside.

[S15b] **Free Magyar Reformed Church**/originally St. Peter's German Evangelical Lutheran Church, 19-25 Winant Pl., W of Arthur Kill Rd. N side. 1883. **Hugo Kafka.** ● **Parish Hall**, 1898. ● Rectory, 1926. **Royal Daggett.** ●
Kreischer originally built the church for his Lutheran brethren. Its early character peeks through despite some unfortunate modernization.

S15b

WOODROW / CHARLESTOWN
see pages 927–928

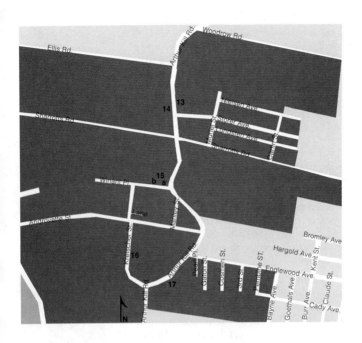

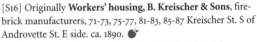

[S16] Originally **Workers' housing, B. Kreischer & Sons**, fire-brick manufacturers, 71-73, 75-77, 81-83, 85-87 Kreischer St. S of Androvette St. E side. ca. 1890. 🍎

Some remaining examples of Kreischer's industrial paternalism. Shingled façades with Kreischer brick sidewalks.

[S17] Originally **Charles C. Kreischer House**, 4500 Arthur Kill Rd., opp. Kreischer St. (bet. Englewood Ave. and Veterans Rd. W.). SE side. ca. 1888. Attributed to **Palliser & Palliser**. 🍎

This lacy Stick Style house with its delicate turret and open balcony crown an isolated high point in the surrounding flat landscape. To the northwest is the former terra-cotta and brickmaking area once called Kreischerville, after the owner's father. Originally, an identical twin house—reversed—occupied the adjacent site to the south, that of his brother, **Edward B. Kreischer**.

S16

S17

RICHMOND VALLEY

see pages 929

[S18] **Outerbridge Crossing**, connecting Richmond Pkwy., Charleston, with Perth Amboy, N.J., over Arthur Kill. 1928. **Alexander Waddell**, engineer; **York & Sawyer**, architects.

With the decision to name this ungainly cantilever truss bridge after owner Port of New York Authority's first chairman, **Eugenius Outerbridge**, it became clear this would never be called Outerbridge Bridge.

RICHMOND VALLEY

[S19a] Originally **Abraham Cole House**, 4927 Arthur Kill Road, NW cor. Richmond Valley Rd. ca. 1840, additions. [S19b] **4934 Arthur Kill Road House**, N of Richmond Valley Rd. E side. ca. 1880. [S19c] **291 Richmond Valley Road** (house), E of Arthur Kill Rd. N side. ca. 1870.

A trio of houses that dignifies a corner of remote Staten Island with stylistic idiosyncrasies decades apart, yet in harmony with one another.

S19a

TOTTENVILLE

The community at Staten Island's southernmost tip, across the mouth of Arthur Kill from Perth Amboy, N.J. Ferry service was available from the last stop of the SIRT (train) until October 1963.

S20

[S20] **5403 Arthur Kill Road** (house), NW cor. Tyrell St. ca. 1855.

An embellished 2-story cube. The flat roof and bracketed cornices of Italianate architecture join with Tuscan columns to form a delightful cross-cultural blend.

[S21] **5414 Arthur Kill Road** (house), bet. Tyrell and Main Sts. S side. ca. 1870.

A bracketed and dormered mansard roof is balanced by an intricately scrolled porch.

S21

TOTTENVILLE

see pages 929-931

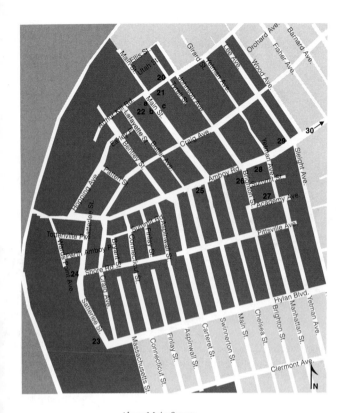

Along Main Street:
One-way south.

[S22a] **104 Main Street** (house), opp. Arthur Kill Rd. W side. ca.

The miles of twisting, turning, ever-surprising Arthur Kill Road end at this sprightly Carpenter Gothic cottage. (Actually Arthur Kill Road jogs a bit north here, but it seems to end.) It makes the trip worthwhile!

[S22b] **123rd Precinct, N.Y.C. Police Department**/originally 70th Precinct, 116 Main St., bet. Arthur Kill Rd. and Craig Ave. W side. 1924. **James Whitford, Sr.**

Italian Renaissance Revival, somewhat out of context with the small-scale village it inhabits, but elegantly conceived.

[S22c] **127 Main Street** (house), bet. Arthur Kill Rd. and Craig Ave. E side. 1890s.

A collection of ebullient Shingle Style volumes is enriched with turned columns, crossed lath, sprockets, and other décor of machined woodworking so popular in the late 19th century. Wonderful!

S22a

Conference House area at the southern tip of Hylan Boulevard:

[S23] **The Conference House**, also known as Bentley Manor/originally Captain Christopher Billopp House, Conference House Park, Satterlee St. W side. ca. 1675. ● Open to the public. 718-984-2086. March-Dec: Wed-Sun, 1-4; closed Mon-Tues.

A fieldstone manor house built by British naval captain **Christopher Billopp**, the gentleman mistakenly credited for Staten Island's inclusion in New York State. (Myth had it that he

S22b

S23

sailed around the island in less than the stipulated 24 hours, thereby winning the island from New Jersey.) The house was the site of a Revolutionary War conference (hence the name) during which the British representatives offered "clemency and full pardon to all repentent rebels" should they lay down their arms. **Benjamin Franklin**, **John Adams**, and **Edward Rutledge**, representing the unrepentant rebels, politely demurred . . . and the war continued.

[S24] Originally **Captain Henry Hogg Biddle House**, 70 Satterlee St., opp. Shore Rd. W side. ca. 1840. 🍎 (Satterlee is one-way north.)

A clapboard captain's house (like the ones on Captains' Row, in Mariners Harbor) but with a pair of matching tetrastyle 2-story porticoes, one facing Perth Amboy across the narrow Arthur Kill, the other facing inland.

S24

Easterly, on and off Amboy Road:

[S25] **St. Paul's Methodist Episcopal Church**, 7558 Amboy Rd., bet. Main and Swinnerton Sts. S side. 1883.

The stolid Romanesque Revival gabled brick sanctuary contrasts with and is enhanced by spare but frothy window framing and roof trim.

[S26] **24 Brighton Street** (house and former stable), bet. Amboy Rd. and Pittsfield Ave. opp. Summit St. W side. ca. 1880.

A country house now surrounded by the later town.

S25

[S27] **Tottenville Branch, N.Y. Public Library**, 7430 Amboy Rd., bet. Brighton St. and Yetman Ave. S side. 1903-1904. **Carrère & Hastings.** 🍎 Renovation, 1994. **Stephen D. Weinstein/John Ellis & Assocs.**

One of four (and of three similar) Carnegie libraries for Staten Island, with knowledge announced by Tuscan columns and served by gracious new access for the disabled.

[S28] Originally Westfield Township District School No. 5/now wing of **Public School 1 Richmond**, Yetman St. NW cor. Academy St. 1878. Enlarged, 1896-1897. **Pierce & Brun.** 🍎

Some vernacular brickwork topped with an Italianate cornice and broken pediment.

S27

[S29] Formerly **Dr. Henry Litvak House and Office**, 7379 Amboy Rd., NW cor. Lee Ave. ca. 1895. Altered to present form, 1941, **Eugene G. Megnin.**

White stucco and glass-block, perhaps inspired by Le Corbusier, but more a matter of exterior styling, as in the work of Corbu's contemporary, stage designer Mallet-Stevens. It is particularly startling to discover among (and out of context with) its Tottenville neighbors.

S28

S29

[S30] **Bethel Methodist Episcopal Church**, 7033 Amboy Rd., NE cor. Bethel Ave. 1886.

A bold brick and terra-cotta façade.

S30

Along Hylan Boulevard:

Mount Loretto:

[S31] **Church of St. Joachim and St. Anne** (Roman Catholic), Mt. Loretto Home for Children, Hylan Blvd. bet. Sharrott and Richard Aves. N side. 1891. **Benjamin E. Lowe**. New nave, 1976.

A disastrous fire in 1973 destroyed the church except for its main façade. In an imaginative architectural solution, the towered Gothic Revival front was preserved, and a simple A-frame nave was built against it. Economy, simplicity, harmony.

S31

PRINCES BAY

Spelled variously Princes Bay, Prince's Bay, Prince Bay, Princess Bay.

Once a prosperous fishing and oystering village. Oysters from here were so famous that fashionable restaurants in New York and London carried "Prince's Bays" on their menus. An area of run-down shacks with tar paper flapping, paint peeling, and curious developers seeking opportunities for profit.

[S32] Originally **John H. Ellsworth House**, 90 Bayview Ave., 400 feet S of SIRT. E side. ca. 1879.

An delightful clapboard oysterman's house overlooking the Lemon Creek salt meadow.

S32

[S33] Originally **Abraham J. Wood House**, 5910 Amboy Rd., bet. Bayview Ave. and Seguine Ave. S side. ca. 1840.

Unpretentious Greek Revival domestic architecture for a Princes Bay oysterman.

[S34] Originally **Joseph H. Seguine House**, 440 Seguine Ave., bet. Wilbur St. and Hank Pl. Set back on W side. 1837. Altered.

A modest version of a Southern plantation, with Greek Revival columns supporting a second story verandah.

S33

[S35] **The Manee-Seguine Homestead**/originally Abraham Manee House/later Henry Seguine House/ later Homestead Hotel/later Purdy's Hotel, 509 Seguine Ave., NE cor. Purdy Pl. ca. 1690 to ca. 1820.

The early home of two families of French Huguenot descent who derived their income from harvesting the local oyster beds and farming the surrounding acres. The original house is the eastern part, built in two stages, of rubblestone walls. The additions to the west and north are of wood frame. **Henry Seguine**'s oldest son, **Joseph**, built the larger house across Seguine Avenue. In 1874 the Manee-Seguine structure was purchased by **Stephen Purdy** for use as a hotel.

ANNADALE/HUGUENOT

S34

[S36] **Reformed Church of Huguenot Park**/originally Memorial Church of the Huguenots, 5475 Amboy Rd., NW cor. Huguenot Ave. Library, 1903-1905. Church, 1923-1924. **Ernest Flagg**. Assembly Hall, 1954-1955. **James Whitford, Jr.**

A refreshing church design for its time (and place) by one of America's most original architects. Built of native serpentinite, a stone quarried on the architect's estate in the Todt Hill section of the island, the church was dedicated as the national monument of the Huguenot-Walloon Tercentenary celebration in 1924. The library is the small framed structure of vaguely Classical style on the corner of the property up Amboy road. (Now the headquarters of an environmental preservation group.)

S35

*Annadale-Huguenot: The community of Annadale owes its name to the train station which honored **Anna S. Seguine**, of the nearby (Princes Bay) Seguine family; **Joseph** was the railroad's president. "Huguenot" honors the early European settlers who had come here fleeing persecution. The two areas will perhaps be forever linked because of a City urban renewal proposal bearing their hyphenated names. It outlined a disciplined plan for growth for the large tract that was 70% undeveloped, sewerless, and largely City-owned. It tried to preclude the development of yet more thoughtless, uneconomical, and destructive tract housing. After the 1965-1975 freeze on new home construction (during which the Annadale-Huguenot Urban Renewal Plan was scuttled anyway), the City's Health Department ruled on minimum lot sizes for septic tanks, and new construction began. While the seemingly endless, loathsome tracts of Heartland Village [q.v.] were ultimately avoided, Annadale-Huguenot is still hardly a city planner's dream.*

INDEX

The names of those involved in creating the works indexed appear in capital letters; unless otherwise identified, they are architects.

Boldface page numbers indicate photographs of the cited building(s), and when they are the only number cited, the entry is on the same page; roman type alone indicates entries without photos; if a roman number and a boldface are both given, the descriptive entry is on the roman numbered page.

D

G

K

U

ILLUSTRATION CREDITS

All photographs, except those listed below, and excepting those for Staten Island are by Norval White. Staten Island photos are by James Sexton, except as noted NW for Norval White.

The first number is the page number, followed by the entry number or kind of image. EW = Elliot Willensky. AC = from the authors' collections. INPS = from the *Iconography of Manhattan Island*, by I.N. Phelps Stokes. ctsy = courtesy of. Images cited are photographs except as otherwise indicated.

4 map, INPS; 30, 34, drawings, INPS; 47, B3, rendering ctsy Gary Edward Handel; 49, tempietto & robots, ctsy Alexander Gorlin; 52, B43, rendering ctsy Gruzen Samton; 69, drawing, City Hall, INPS; 70, drawing, Bklyn Bridge, AC; 89, E23, EW; 106, H37, drawing, AC; 130, B5, AC; 134, B29b, ctsy Rolf Ohlhausen; 137, C4, drawing, AC; 148, D13, ctsy Richard Meier; 156, S24, rendering, ctsy Fox & Fowle; 164, drawing, AC; 181, H1A, ctsy R.M.Kliment + Frances Halsband; 212, B2, rendering ctsy, Kohn Pedersen Fox; 255, T12, rendering ctsy Platt Byard Dovell; 258, T21, rendering, ctsy Fox & Fowle; 262, T58, rendering ctsy Fox & Fowle; 274, aerial view csty Rockefeller Center Inc.; 292, model photo, ctsy, Austrian Cultural Institute; 293, F23, rendering ctsy Tod Williams & Billie Tsien; 308, D31, rendering ctsy Hardy Holzman Pfeiffer; 363, C41, rendering ctsy The Polshek Partnership; 457, Y45, model photo ctsy Fox & Fowle; 470, M22, ctsy R.M.Kliment + Frances Halsband; 472, M26, ctsy Tschumi/Gruzen Samton; 472, M29, rendering ctsy Gruzen Samton; 473, M34, ctsy The Polshek Partnership; 532, O1, drawing, AC; 533, O2a, Margaret Latimer; 535, ctsy Johansen & Bhavnani; 537, O4h, Norman McGrath, ctsy Johansen * Bhavnani; 543, postcard, AC; 556, H8a, rendering, ctsy Ginsberg & Magnusson; 610, R29d model photo, ctsy Gruzen Samton; 634, 635, drawings, AC; 646, D42, ctsy Mitchell/Giurgola; 648, map, AC; 659, H61, ctsy Alfredo de Vido; 662, H82, AC; 663, H85+H86, drawings, AC; 674, C1, ctsy Long Island College Hospital; 683, drawing, AC; 686, R7, ctsy Hanrahan + Meyers; 707, L36, ctsy Pasanella + Klein Stolzman + Berg; 711, N2, ctsy United States Navy; 724, 725, maps, AC; 731, drawing, AC; 740, W2, drawing, AC; 757, W25, drawing, AC; 781, drawing, AC; 796, E13, courtesy Herbert Mandel; 802, W8, left image, EW; 836, M3, ctsy Skyviews Survey, Inc.; 864, J2, model photo ctsy Pei Cobb Freed; 873, F 24, Exra Stoller ctsy TWA; 881, postcard, AC; 884, N1, rendering ctsy Hellmuth Obata & Kassabaum; 884, postcard, AC; **all Staten Island photos except as listed below by James Sexton**; 891, B9, NW; 802, B15,B21a, NW; 893, B23, postcard, AC; 893, B27, NW; 896, B24, NW; 897, W7, NW; 899, W10, NW; 900, W17, NW; 904, E11, NW; 909, E34a, NW; 914, C14d, Manuel V. Rubio ctsy Wagner College; 918, C30c, EW; 925, S3, Mina Hamilton; 927 S17b, NW; 930, S 24b, NW; 931, S27c, NW.

Heritage Trails at-a-Glance

Established in 1995 as a non-for-profit cultural and educational institution, Heritage Trails promotes the history, architecture, sites and attractions of Downtown New York. The TrailsMap and 40 site markers, coupled with activities such as guided tours and special events, make Downtown's history easily accessible and eminently entertaining. For more information about Heritage Trails, call (212) 466-3600.

Walk through History on the Heritage Trails

Heritage Trails New York is the street-smart way to see all of Downtown

Self-Guided Tours

Red, Green, Blue, Orange Heritage Trails and the new Art Trail. 40 informative Site Markers that tell the stories of Downtown. FREE TrailsMaps-available at locations shown on the map.

Guided Walking Tours

The World of Finance—a 2-hour walking tour of Wall Street and New York City's financial district, including a visit <u>inside</u> the New York Stock Exchange. Start at the Museum of American Financial History, 28 Broadway, every Friday at 10 a.m. rain or shine, year-round. $15 for adults, $10 for seniors, students with ID and children under 12. **No reservations are required for individuals**. For more information or to book a group tour, call (212) 908-4110.

Destination Downtown: New York Old and New. FREE 1-1/2 hour walking tour sponsored by the Downtown Alliance and Heritage Trails, 12 noon, every Thursday, year-round, rain or shine. Meet at U.S. Customs House/Smithsonian's National Museum of the American Indian (G15 on the Green Trail). For information call: (212) 606-4064.

To find out about other individual and group tours on the Heritage Trails, call Big Onion Walking Tours (212) 439-1090.